股份有限公司

Group Co., Ltd.

Approved by the Ministry of Foreign Trade and Economic Cooperation, China Jin Mao Group Co., Ltd . (CJM), the former name of which was the China Shanghai Foreign Trade Centre Co., Ltd. (CSFTC), was established on the 10th February 1993. The CJM is a shareholding enterprise co-invested by 14 world-renowned corporations such as the China National Chemicals Import & Export Corp., the China National Cereals, Oils and Foodstuffs Import & Export Corp., the China National Metals and Minerals Import & Export Corp. and so forth.

Enterprise's name: China Jin Mao Group Co., Ltd.

Legal representative: Wang Bao Chen(Vice-Director & President)

Registered capital: RMB2.635 billion

Enterprise's form: Shareholding company

Operation Period: Permanent

Scope of business:

- Developing and operating real estate along with property management, including operation and management of the 88-storey Jing Mao Tower;
- Dealing with,or acting as an agent for import and export business;
- Developing high-technology products and dealing with technology import and export business,and trade by barter and/or entrepot;
- Dealing with domestic trade,wholesale and retail;
- Organizing large fairs and exhibitions at home and abroad and dealing with or acting as an agent for advertising business;
- Developing and engaging in services in transportation, storage, information and consultation and cultural entertainment.

The Jin Mao Tower, the highest of its kind in China, which is developed and being operated by the CJM,is situated at the hub of Lujiazui Financial and Trading Zone in Pudong. With a total of 88 storeys and towering to a height of 420.5 meters, it is composed of the main tower, the podium and the basement, where levels 3-50 are used for offices, levels 53-87 for the world's highest super-deluxe hotel-the Grand Hyatt Shanghai, the level 88 for the observation deck, the 6-level podium for the multi-functional promise and the 3-level basement for parking lot. The Jin Mao Tower is recognized as an intelligent and high-class building combined with office, seminar/exhibition, hotel,tourism and shopping. It is conceived in anticipation of the 21st Century, designed in view of developing knowledge economy and created in preparation for involving in economic globalization.

Depending on the Jin Mao Tower, the CJM is considering service trade as its core business and internationalized operation and management as its development strategy. Its aim will cover five "first classes" as follows: First-class quality; First-class operation; First-class management; First-class benefit; and First-class talent.

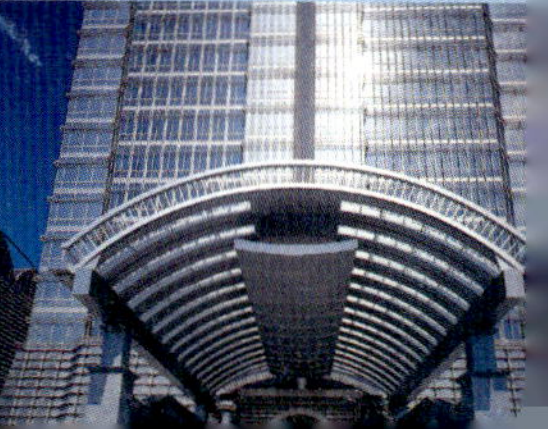

1999/2000

中国对外经济贸易年鉴

中国对外经济贸易年鉴编辑委员会

中国对外经济贸易出版社

京工商广临字 99099 号

图书在版编目(CIP)数据
中国对外经济贸易年鉴:1999～2000 年版/中国对外经济贸易年鉴编委会编. －北京:中国对外经济贸易出版社,1999
ISBN 7－80004－778－4

I.中… II.中… III.对外贸易－中国－1999～2000－年鉴 IV.F752－54

中国版本图书馆 CIP 数据核字 (99)第 43650 号

责任编辑　钟边武
版式设计　张瑞文
责任校对　王素珍

中国对外经济贸易年鉴 1999 / 2000
中国对外经济贸易年鉴编辑委员会
中国对外经济贸易出版社　出版发行
北京安定门外大街东后巷 28 号　邮政编码:100710
新华书店北京发行所　发行
兵器工业出版社印刷厂　印刷
787×1092 毫米　16 开本　56.25 印张　76 插页　1690 千字
1999 年 10 月第 1 版　1999 年 10 月第 1 次印刷
印数:5000
ISBN 7－80004－778－4
Z.81
定价:260.00 元

1998年1月27日国家主席江泽民在北京钓鱼台国宾馆会见世界知识产权总干事卡末勒·伊德里斯博士。

1998 年 6 月 26 日国务院总理朱镕基在北京中南海会见美国财政部长鲁宾。

1998年10月29日国务院副总理李岚清和欧洲联盟委员会主席雅克·桑特（前左二）出席中国与欧盟民航与通信领域的工业合作谅解备忘录签字仪式。

1999年2月19日国务委员吴仪在北京考察中外合资企业的市场供应情况。

中华人民

哈萨克斯坦
吉尔吉斯斯坦
塔吉克斯坦
阿富汗
巴基斯坦
印度
尼泊尔
不丹
孟加拉国
缅甸
老挝
泰国
蒙古
新疆维吾尔自治区
西藏自治区
青海
甘肃
四川
云南
内蒙古
塔里木盆地
准噶尔盆地
昆仑山
天山
喜马拉雅山
冈底斯山
唐古拉山
祁连山
阿尔泰山
孟加拉湾
图例
首都
省级行政中心
地级市行政中心
县级行政中心
村镇（外国一般城镇同）
外国首都或首府
国界
未定国界
省、自治区、直辖市界
特别行政区界
地区界、军事分界线
双轨铁路
单轨铁路（外国铁路同）
高速公路、公路
航海线
常年河
时令河
运河
渠道
常年湖
时令湖
水库
蓄洪区
井或泉
干河床
沼泽
沙漠
珊瑚礁
山峰
长城
山口、关隘
本图上中国国界线系按照我社1989年出版的1:400万《中华人民共和国地形图》绘制

和国地图

世　界

西半球
北冰洋
大西洋
印度洋
南极洲
中华人民共和国
俄罗斯
蒙古
哈萨克斯坦
阿尔及利亚
利比亚
埃及
尼日尔
乍得
苏丹
马里
沙特阿拉伯
伊朗
印度
澳大利亚
马达加斯加
埃塞俄比亚
毛德皇后地
恩德比地
玛丽皇后地
威尔克斯
图例
首都和首府
居民点
洲界
国界
未定国界
地区界
军事分界线
铁路、公路
运河
航海线
海岸线
河流、瀑布
湖泊
季节河
季节湖
冰架
山峰
地磁极
图中代号:
①阿塞拜疆
②圣基茨和尼维斯
③荷属安的列斯
本图上中国国界线系按照我社1989年出版的1:400万《中华人民共和国地形图》绘制。
巴勒斯坦地区内的地区界系1947年11月联合国安理会决议所规定的"犹太国"(以色列)疆域。

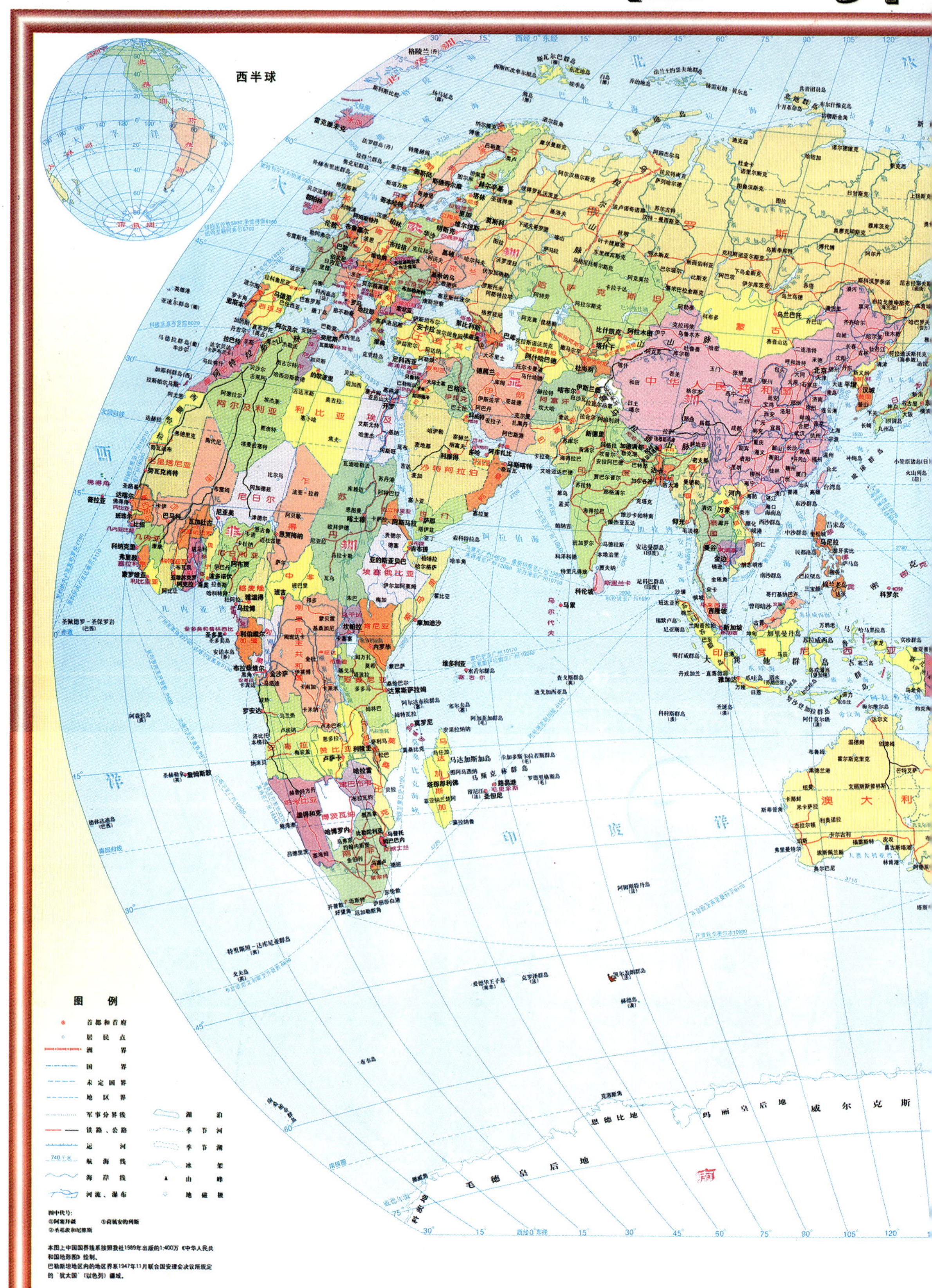

东半球

格陵兰(丹)
巴芬湾
巴芬岛
伊丽莎白女王群岛
哈德孙湾
拉布拉多海
加拿大
北美洲
美国
阿拉斯加
白令海
阿留申群岛
渥太华
华盛顿
纽约
芝加哥
旧金山
洛杉矶
墨西哥
墨西哥城
墨西哥湾
哈瓦那
古巴
加勒比海
夏威夷
檀香山
太平洋
大西洋
波利尼西亚
密克罗尼西亚
美拉尼西亚
基里巴斯
图瓦卢
斐济
苏瓦
汤加
努库阿洛法
萨摩亚
阿皮亚
瓦努阿图
维拉港
新喀里多尼亚
努美阿
新西兰
惠灵顿
北岛
南岛
法属波利尼西亚
帕皮提
危地马拉
伯利兹
贝尔莫潘
洪都拉斯
特古西加尔巴
圣萨尔瓦多
尼加拉瓜
马那瓜
哥斯达黎加
圣何塞
巴拿马
巴拿马城
哥伦比亚
圣菲波哥大
委内瑞拉
加拉加斯
圭亚那
乔治敦
苏里南
帕拉马里博
法属圭亚那
卡宴
厄瓜多尔
基多
加拉帕戈斯群岛
秘鲁
利马
玻利维亚
拉巴斯
苏克雷
巴西
巴西利亚
里约热内卢
圣保罗
巴拉圭
亚松森
乌拉圭
蒙得维的亚
阿根廷
布宜诺斯艾利斯
智利
圣地亚哥
火地岛
合恩角
马尔维纳斯群岛
南乔治亚岛
南美洲
南极洲
玛丽伯德地
埃尔斯沃思地
别林斯高晋海
罗斯海
南极圈
赤道
北回归线
南回归线

同中国签有经济贸易和投资保护协议的国家和地区简表

"●"表示同我国签有贸易协定或议定书及经济合作协定的国家和组织

"▲"表示同我国签有双边投资保护协定的国家和地区

亚洲			
蒙古	● ▲	塔吉克斯坦	●
朝鲜	●	乌兹别克斯坦	● ▲
韩国	● ▲	土库曼斯坦	● ▲
日本	● ▲	格鲁吉亚	● ▲
越南	● ▲	阿塞拜疆	● ▲
老挝	● ▲	亚美尼亚	● ▲
柬埔寨	● ▲	巴基斯坦	● ▲
缅甸	●	伊朗	●
泰国	● ▲	科威特	▲
马来西亚	● ▲	沙特阿拉伯	▲
新加坡	▲	巴林	▲
菲律宾	● ▲	卡塔尔	▲
印度尼西亚	● ▲	阿拉伯联合酋长国	▲
尼泊尔	●	阿曼	▲
孟加拉国	● ▲	也门	▲
印度	●	叙利亚	▲
斯里兰卡	● ▲	塞浦路斯	●
哈萨克斯坦	● ▲	土耳其	● ▲
吉尔吉斯斯坦	● ▲	以色列	▲

欧洲			
冰岛	● ▲	瑞士	● ▲
丹麦	● ▲	荷兰	● ▲
挪威	● ▲	比利时	● ▲
瑞典	● ▲	卢森堡	● ▲
芬兰	● ▲	英国	● ▲
爱沙尼亚	● ▲	爱尔兰	●
拉脱维亚	●	法国	● ▲
立陶宛	● ▲	西班牙	● ▲
俄罗斯	●	葡萄牙	● ▲
白俄罗斯	● ▲	意大利	● ▲
乌克兰	● ▲	马耳他	●
摩尔多瓦	● ▲	南斯拉夫联盟	● ▲
波兰	● ▲	斯洛文尼亚	● ▲
捷克	●	克罗地亚	● ▲
斯洛伐克	●	马其顿	▲
匈牙利	● ▲	罗马尼亚	● ▲
德国	●	保加利亚	● ▲
奥地利	● ▲	阿尔巴尼亚	● ▲
列支敦士登	瑞士托管	希腊	● ▲

非洲			
埃及	● ▲	吉布提	●
利比亚	●	肯尼亚	●
突尼斯	●	坦桑尼亚	●
阿尔及利亚	● ▲	卢旺达	●
摩洛哥	● ▲	布隆迪	●
毛利塔里亚	●	刚果	● ▲
马里	● ▲	加蓬	● ▲
佛得角	● ▲	安哥拉	●
几内亚	●	赞比亚	● ▲
科特迪瓦	●	莫桑比克	●
加纳	● ▲	毛里求斯	▲
多哥	●	津巴布韦	● ▲
贝宁	●	博茨瓦纳	●
尼日尔	●	纳米比亚	●
尼日利亚	● ▲	南非	● ▲
喀麦隆	● ▲	厄立特里亚	●
赤道几内亚	●	塞拉利昂	●
中非	●	索马里	●
埃塞俄比亚	● ▲	马达加斯加	●

大洋洲			
澳大利亚	● ▲	密克罗尼西亚联邦	●
新西兰	● ▲	萨摩亚	●
巴布亚新几内亚	● ▲	库克群岛	●
瓦努阿图	●	斐济	●
基里巴斯	●		

北美洲			
美国	●	古巴	▲
墨西哥	●	牙买加	▲
特立尼达和多巴哥	●		

南美洲			
哥伦比亚	●	巴西	●
委内瑞拉	●	玻利维亚	● ▲
苏里南	●	智利	● ▲
厄瓜多尔	● ▲	阿根廷	● ▲
秘鲁	● ▲	乌拉圭	● ▲

中国国际技术智力合作公司

CHINA INTERNATIONAL INTELLECTECH CORPORATION

公司领导　左起：副总经理王旭东、总经理陈伟力、副总经理彭小梅
PRESIDENTS OF CIIC　left: Vice President Wang Xu Dong
middle: President Chen Wei Li
right: Vice President Peng Xiao Mei

中国国际技术智力合作公司(简称中智公司)成立于1987年，直属中华人民共和国国务院，是以技术智力密集型服务贸易为特色的大型国有独资企业。公司主要经营外企服务、国际劳务合作、进出口贸易、工程承包、咨询代理、教育培训、航空客货运销售代理等业务，外经贸业务已拓展到76个国家和地区。

公司总部设在北京，在境内外设立分支机构19家，实行境内外联网经营。1994年起中智公司主要经济指标连续五年在全国900余家外经企业中名列前茅，1998年经国家财政部综合经济效益评价居第四位。

China International Intellectech Corp. (CIIC), incorporated in 1987 and directly under the State Council, is a large state-owned enterprise featuring intellectech-oriented services. The company is headquartered in Beijing with 19 branch offices in China and abroad. It operates as a united business network.

CIIC's business scope includes: services to foreign enterprises, international technical personal cooperation, import and export trade, international engineering contracts, consulting, training and express mail services.The company's international business and clients have expanded to include 76 countries and regions.

In 1999, CIIC was ranked among the top position of China's 900 foreign trade companies for the fifth consecutive year. In terms of comprehensive economic performance, the Ministry of Finance ranked CIIC fourth in 1998.

公司所在地
ADDRESS OF CIIC

Address: 25th Floor, West Wing Han Wei Plaza, 7th Guang Hua Road, Beijing China 100004
Telephone: (8610)65613920
Fax: (8610)65613900/10
Website: http: // www.ciic.com.cn
E-mail Address: ciic@ciic.com.cn

地　　址：中国北京朝阳区光华路7号汉威大厦西区25层(100004)
电话总机：(8610)65613920
传　　真：(8610)65613900/10
互联网址：http://www.ciic.com.cn
电子邮件：ciic@ciic.com.cn

序

对外贸易经济合作部部长
《中国对外经济贸易年鉴》编委会主任委员 石廣生

《中国对外经济贸易年鉴》1999/2000年版与广大的海内外读者见面了。多年来，《年鉴》较为详尽地刊载了我国对外贸易、吸收外资、对外工程承包与劳务合作、对外援助、对外投资、多双边经贸关系等方面的文献、专论、法规、统计数字以及发展概况，内容全面、系统，是一部难得的反映我国外经贸改革与发展成就，宣传我国外经贸方针、政策，提供我国外经贸发展基本情况的大型工具书。《年鉴》的出版发行，一直得到广大读者的一致欢迎和好评，也受到社会各界人士的大力支持。在此，我代表外经贸部和《年鉴》编委会，向关心、支持我国外经贸事业发展和《年鉴》编辑出版发行的海内外各界朋友表示诚挚的谢意。

1998年，我国对外经济贸易顶住了亚洲金融危机带来的巨大压力，战胜了国内特大洪涝灾害的不利影响，经受了国内外空前困难的考验，取得了来之不易的成绩。

进出口贸易总额略降，出口贸易低速增长。据海关统计，1998年，我国进出口总值为3239.3亿美元，比上年下降0.4%，其中出口1837.6亿美元，增长0.5%；进口1401.7亿美元，下降1.5%。我国在世界贸易排名为第十一位，其中出口排名世界第九位，进口排名世界第十一位。1998年进出口贸易的主要特点是：出口增幅总体上逐月回落，但全年出口仍保持了低速增长；进口平稳减缓，全年进口略低于上年，既反映了国内进口需求不旺，也反映出亚洲金融危机的负面影响逐步加深；市场多元化取得显著成绩，我国对亚洲以外其他地区出口保持了较快增长，部分抵消了亚洲金融危机的影响；进出口商品结构进一步优化，资本、技术密集型产品增加，机电产品继续保持我国第一大出口商品类别。

1998年全国新批合同外资金额521.3亿美元，扭转了1996年、1997年连续两年大幅下降的局面，实现了恢复性增长，增长2.2%；实际利用外资455.8亿美元，增长0.67%。1998年来自欧美和部分自由港地区的对华投资增长较快，外商投资产业结构进一步优化，平均单项利用外资金额有所提高，中西部地区吸收外资的增幅明显高于东部地区。

对外承包工程和劳务合作取得较大成绩。1998年新签对外工程承包、劳务合作和设计咨询合同金额117.7亿美元，增长3.7%；完成营业额101.3亿美元，增长20.9%，首次突破百亿美元大关。援外方式改革和援外工作继续稳步推进，全年同16个国家签订了18笔优惠贷款框架协议，总金额18.6亿美元。

外经贸管理体制改革取得积极进展。进一步放开了进出口经营权，放宽了省市外贸企业在上海浦东新区设立子公司的审批条件，放宽了主动配额管理范围，提高了配额使用效率，特别是将被动配额可分量的15%直接分配给自营出口纺织工业企业，支持了纺织行业解困。

多双边关系继续发展。我国加入WTO谈判取得重要进展，我国还积极参加亚太经合组织活动，坚持推进亚太地区贸易投资自由化和亚太地区经济技术合作“两个轮子一起转”。我国与发达国家经贸往来频繁，与周边国家和亚非拉等广大发展中国家经贸关系不断加强。祖国内地与香港的经贸关系，随着香港的回归更加密切；与澳门的经贸关系平稳发展，为澳门的顺利回归创造了条件；祖国大陆与台湾的经贸关系继续发展，有利于早日实现两岸“三通”，完成祖国和平统一大业。

今年是新中国成立五十周年。五十年来，在党和政府的坚强领导下，我国对外经济贸易事业经过不断开拓进取，克服了来自国外的重重困难，取得了举世瞩目的成就，为新中国国民经济的恢复和发展做出了重要贡献。特别是党的十一届三中全会以来，在邓小平理论的指引下，经济体制改革不断深化，对外开放水平不断提高，我国外经贸发展迅速，成为国民经济的重要组成部分。世纪之交，世界科技进步日新月异，经济全球化明显加快，知识经济初露端倪，我国外经贸要充分发挥对国民经济的促进作用，就必须以较高的速度，在更高层次和水平上取得更大发展，这就需要社会各界人士包括《年鉴》广大读者的关心和支持。

为了更好地为广大《年鉴》读者服务，《年鉴》编委会决定从今年起将《年鉴》编辑部改设在对外贸易经济合作研究院，《年鉴》1999/2000版继续以中英文分册出版，其中所载有关内容均由外经贸部和有关部门及地方外经贸主管部门的负责人、专家、学者拟定或提供。我衷心希望《年鉴》能继续得到各界朋友、各有关方面的积极支持和通力合作，更好地发挥提供信息、沟通情况、增进了解的桥梁作用。

1999年6月

编　辑　说　明

一、《中国对外经济贸易年鉴》（以下简称《年鉴》）由中华人民共和国对外贸易经济合作部《年鉴》编辑委员会编纂，编委会主任由对外贸易经济合作部部长石广生同志担任。

二、本《年鉴》创刊于1984年，每年出版一期，每期用中文、英文两种文字分册出版，本期为第16期。

三、本《年鉴》是中国对外经济贸易领域仅有的一部专业性年鉴，内容全面、系统，资料翔实，数据准确，是海内外经济、贸易、工商、金融等各界人士了解、研究中国贸易、投资和对外经济合作的指南，是具有指导性的资料参考书和工具书。

四、本《年鉴》保持连续性和完整性，但上期刊登过的内容，下期不再重复。读者欲了解1997年或以前的中国对外经济贸易情况，请参阅前15期《年鉴》。

五、本期《年鉴》共设9个栏目，即："文献"、"专文"、"法规"、"地方经贸"、"国别（地区）经贸"、"统计"、"大事记"、"机构"、"附录"。全面、系统地记述了1998年中国对外经济贸易的发展成就和基本概况。

（一）"文献"栏目。精选党和国家领导人关于中国经济形势、改革开放方针政策的论述等重要文件3篇；收录对外贸易经济合作部有关领导关于中国对外经济贸易政策和情况的文章或发言6篇。

（二）"专文"栏目。约请对外贸易经济合作部部分职能司负责人和财政部、海关总署、国家进出口商品检验局、国家旅游局等部门有关负责人撰写我国对外经济贸易有关情况的文章，共14篇。

（三）"法规"栏目。收录1998年我国公布的涉外经济贸易法律、条例、规定、办法等，共50篇。

（四）"地方经贸"栏目。刊载包括台湾省在内的全国各省、自治区、直辖市、计划单列市、沿海开放城市、经济特区、香港特别行政区以及澳门地区等1998年对外经济贸易基本情况和统计数字，共57篇。

（五）"国别（地区）经贸"栏目。刊载13篇介绍我国同有关国家和地区双边经济贸易关系的文章。

（六）"统计"栏目。包括对外贸易、利用外资和对外经济合作3个部分。

（七）"大事记"栏目。主要记载1998年全国外经贸工作中的重大事件。

（八）"机构"栏目。刊登中国驻外经济商务机构通信录。

（九）“附录”栏目。分为两部分，第一部分刊有中国国民经济基本情况统计和中国对外经济贸易方面的大量信息资料；第二部分刊有有关世界黄金储备、外汇储备、进出口贸易、引进外资、经济援助和经济合作方面的统计数字，以及1998年中国进出口额最大企业和世界最大企业等排序表。

六、“地方经贸”等栏目里的有关数字，由于统计口径、方法不一致，有些与“统计”栏目中的数字不完全一致，以“统计”栏目中的数字为准。

七、各省、自治区、直辖市的排列顺序，按照国务院行政区划统一规定的先后排列，计划单列市、沿海开放城市和经济特区等均排在其所属的省、自治区后面。

八、本《年鉴》自创刊以来，承蒙各部门、各地方、各公司和作者、译（审）者的积极支持协助，受到国内外广大读者的欢迎和鼓励，在此谨表示衷心谢意，并祈望继续给予关心和支持。对《年鉴》存在的不足之处，诚请提出批评和改进意见，以使本《年鉴》日臻完善。来信请寄：北京市安定门外东后巷28号外经贸部《年鉴》编辑部，电话：010－64246856。

《中国对外经济贸易年鉴》编辑部

1999年7月于北京

《中国对外经济贸易年鉴》编辑委员会

《中国对外经济贸易年鉴》编辑人员

《中国对外经济贸易年鉴》特约撰稿人名单

邓丽阳　对外贸易经济合作部亚洲司
朱国志　对外贸易经济合作部西亚非洲司
江　辉　对外贸易经济合作部欧洲司
俞建华　对外贸易经济合作部欧洲司
凌　激　对外贸易经济合作部欧洲司
许明德　对外贸易经济合作部美洲大洋洲司
李家鹏　对外贸易经济合作部美洲大洋洲司
张新宇　对外贸易经济合作部美洲大洋洲司
杨石翟　对外贸易经济合作部美洲大洋洲司
姜海英　对外贸易经济合作部美洲大洋洲司
刘晓辉　对外贸易经济合作部台港澳司
邢玉芬　对外贸易经济合作部条约法律司
于培伟　对外贸易经济合作部办公厅
储士家　对外贸易经济合作部办公厅
李晋琳　对外贸易经济合作部办公厅
付　强　对外贸易经济合作部国际贸易经济合作研究院
刘雪琴　对外贸易经济合作部国际贸易经济合作研究院
邢厚媛　对外贸易经济合作部国际贸易经济合作研究院
薛　宏　对外贸易经济合作部国际贸易经济合作研究院
石宝祥　国家出入境检验检疫局
赖永添　财政部
高　云　海关总署
李小维　国家统计局
黄洪博　国家外汇管理局
高顺礼　国家旅游局
张学群　北京市对外经济贸易委员会
穆　群　天津市对外经济贸易委员会
王密科　河北省对外贸易经济合作厅
吕美荣　秦皇岛市对外贸易经济合作局
刘付云　山西省对外贸易经济合作厅
李春生　内蒙古自治区对外贸易经济合作厅
王　迪　辽宁省对外贸易经济合作厅
徐　森　辽宁省对外贸易经济合作厅
许克非　沈阳市对外经济贸易委员会
姜中科　大连市对外经济贸易委员会
王海涛　吉林省对外贸易经济合作厅
孟繁军　长春市对外贸易经济合作局
朱丽华　黑龙江省对外贸易经济合作厅
张国照　哈尔滨市对外贸易经济合作局
乐淑君　上海市对外经济贸易委员会
宋义军　江苏省对外经济贸易委员会
黄建新　南京市对外经济贸易委员会
王百奇　连云港市对外经济贸易委员会
成昌宏　南通市对外经济贸易委员会
陈志成　浙江省对外贸易经济合作厅
沈洁玉　宁波市对外贸易经济合作局
汪丐罗　温州市对外贸易经济合作局
王凤鸣　安徽省对外经济贸易委员会
吴文华　福建省对外经济贸易委员会
黄寿荣　厦门市贸易发展委员会
朱光华　福州市对外经济贸易委员会
杨宝根　江西省对外贸易经济合作厅
蔡玉祥　山东省对外经济贸易委员会
郭　林　青岛市对外经济贸易委员会
姜英松　烟台市对外经济贸易委员会
卢凤英　河南省对外贸易经济合作厅
曹文铸　湖北省对外经济贸易委员会
韩　菁　武汉市对外经济贸易委员会
张永青　湖南省对外经济贸易委员会
周树德　广东省对外经济贸易委员会
曹卫红　广州市对外经济贸易委员会
蒋海玲　深圳市贸易发展局
邝沛林　珠海市对外经济贸易委员会
邱长奕　汕头市对外经济贸易委员会
孙海峰　湛江市对外经济贸易委员会
李亦之　广西壮族自治区对外贸易经济合作厅
蒋维明　北海市对外贸易经济合作局
杨照耀　海南省商贸经济合作厅
何德麟　重庆市对外贸易经济委员会
孙跃华　四川省对外贸易经济合作委员会
陈小兵　成都市对外贸易经济合作委员会
曾　韵　贵州省对外贸易经济合作厅
刘可杰　云南省对外贸易经济合作厅
冯林国　西藏自治区对外贸易经济合作厅
王哲军　陕西省对外贸易经济合作厅
苏福祥　西安市对外经济贸易委员会
黄智杰　甘肃省对外贸易经济合作厅
公　保　青海省对外贸易经济合作厅
刘进国　宁夏回族自治区对外贸易经济合作厅
关　群　新疆维吾尔自治区对外贸易经济合作厅

中国粮油食品进出口(集团)有限公司

CHINA NATIONAL CEREALS,OILS & FOODSTUFFS IMP. & EXP.CORP.

中国粮油食品进出口(集团)有限公司(简称中粮公司,英文简称COFCO)1952年在北京成立，经过四十多年的艰苦奋斗，中粮公司已由单一的贸易公司，发展成为集贸易、实业、金融、信息、服务和科研为一体的国有大型企业集团，并初步形成了实业化、国际化、集团化，综合化协调发展的战略布局，47年来，中粮公司进出口额累计达到1350亿美元，粮食贸易量累计4.5亿吨；1994-1998年，中粮公司连续5年被美国《财富》杂志评为世界企业500强。1996年，按净资产在“中国的脊梁”国有企业500强中居第63位，名列外经贸行业前茅。1998年列中国进出口额500强企业第3位和出口额200强企业第1位，截止1998年底，海内外资产总额近47.7亿美元。

中粮公司已于1998年底改制为国有独资企业，下一步发展目标是：从现在起到2005年，把公司的实业化、国际化、集团化和综合化建设不断推向新的阶段，使公司的经济实力、竞争能力、管理水平跻身于全国外经贸行业的前列，成为在国内外具有较强经济实力和竞争能力的大型企业集团。

China National Cereals, Oils & Foodstuffs Import & Export Corporation("COFCO") was founded in 1952. Thanks to the pioneering and diligent work of its people over the past 47 years,COFCO has expanded from a simple trading company to a multinational conglomerate engaged in trade, industry, finance, scientific research, information and other services, and achieved initial success in industrialization, globalization, conglomeration and diversification. Up to now, COFCO has realized an accumulated import and export volume of USD135 billion, and a total trade volume of grains of 450 million tons. From 1994 to 1998, COFCO ranked among the world top 500 companies In the U.S magazine "Fortune" for five consecutive years. In 1996, it ranked the 63_{rd} among China's 500 "backbone" state owned enterprises in terms of net assets. In 1998,COFCO ranked the third among China's top 500 import and export enterprises, and the first among China's top 200 export enterprises.The domestic and overseas assets of the corporation totaled USD4.77 billion by the end of 1998.

In 1998, COFCO transformed from a state-run enterprise into a state-owned enterprise. From now on to the year of 2005, COFCO will continuously devote to its industrialization, globalization, conglomeration and diversification, enhance its economic strength, competitiveness and managing level, build itself to be a leading import and export company in China, and a powerful multinational conglomerate around the world.

地址：北京建国门内大街8号中粮广场A座　　邮编：100005

Add: Towera, COFCO PLAZA, No.8, Jian Guo Men Nei Ave., Beijing 100005,China

电话 (Tel): (010)65268888　　传真 (Fax): (010)65278612

中国五金矿产进出口总公司

China National Metals and Minerals Import and Export Corporation

中国五矿集团是以中国五金矿产进出口总公司(简称中国五矿总公司)为核心企业，以国际贸易为主业的综合经营的大型企业集团，1998年末总资产达180亿元人民币；1998年总营业额达31.87亿美元，其中出口额8.32亿美元，比1997年增长18.86%。集团整体经济效益基本达到了预期目标，实现了国有资产保值增值任务，继续位居中国500家最大外贸企业的前列。

中国五矿总公司成立于1950年，长期以来从事以钢铁、有色金属、非金属建材、矿产品、金属制品等商品为主的进出口业务，49年来累计进出口贸易额达1200亿美元，形成了广泛的营销网络和经营优势，积累了丰富的国际贸易经验，在国内外享有良好的声誉。

中国五矿总公司的集团化建设始于80年代初，在国家经济体制和外贸体制改革的引导和推动下，实施了国际化、实业化和以国际贸易为主、多种经营并举的发展战略，广泛参与市场竞争，促使公司由过去国家进出口计划的执行者，迅速转变发展成为市场平等竞争的主体和新型外贸企业集团。1992年，中国五矿集团成为中国政府重点促进发展的国家首批57家企业集团之一。如今，中国五矿集团所属各二级公司按照行业和商品的划分实行专业化经营，致力于发展以国际贸易为主，包括金融、运输、房地产及物业、工业、工程承包与劳务等支柱产业，各项业务优势互补、效益互增、风险分散，形成了结构合理的企业综合经营格局。1998年，五矿集团与世界第二大保险公司法国AXA集团合资成立上海金盛人寿保险公司，标志着多元化发展达到了新的水平。

为加快企业发展的步伐，中国五矿总公司于1996、1997、1998连续三年在美国成功发行每年2亿美元的商业票据，拓展了在国际资本市场直接融资的渠道；1997年5月，又以6家主力二级公司为基础组建了五矿发展股份有限公司，发行7500万A股并在上海证券交易所成功上市。1998年，五矿发展入选上证30指数样本股。1999年，又以其优良的业绩被评为“沪市50强”。通过对外发行商业票据和国内上市，集团进入直接融资市场，开始从单一商品经营走向了资产资本经营，进一步增强了企业实力和发展后劲。

目前，中国五矿集团在世界22个国家和地区拥有44家海外公司和机构，在国内13个省区拥有98家全资或合资企业。海外企业经过近几年的整固，资产质量有了明显提高，其中中国五矿香港控股公司被香港中银认为在港中资企业资产质量前五名。

展望未来，中国五矿集团将继续以推动经济发展、促进社会进步为己任，不断进取、追求卓越。在为建设国际一流跨国集团而不懈努力的过程中，将一如既往奉行“平等互利、共同发展”的精神，以优质高效的服务，积极与海内外客商开展广泛的经济贸易合作，携手共进，迎接21世纪。

Centered on China National Metals & Minerals Import & Export Corporation ("China Minmetals" for short), China Minmetals Group is a giant multi-business enterprise group focusing on international trade. Its total assets by the end of 1998 amounted to RMB 18 billion yuan. The total turnover of 1998 reached USD 3.187 billion, among which the export volume was USD 832 million, an increase of 18.86% compared with that of 1997. The overall economic profits of China Minmetals Group basically reached the expected target, achieving the goal to maintain and increase the value of state owned assets and it continues to rank at the top of China's 500 biggest foreign trade enterprises.

Established in 1950, China Nation Metals & Minerals Import & Export Corporation has long been specialized in the import & export of such commodities as iron and steel, nonferrous metals, non-metallic construction materials and minerals. The accumulated volume of import and export over the past 49 years has totaled USD 120 billion. With extensive marketing networks and rich experience accumulated over the years in international trade, it enjoys great prestige both at home and abroad.

The conglomeration of China National Metals & Minerals Import & Export Corporation was initiated back in the early 1980's. Propelled by the nation's restructuring of its economy and foreign trade system, the corporation has since adopted the development strategy of internationalization, industrialization as well as business diversification centered on international trade. As an equal and independent competitor, on the market solely responsible for its own profit and loss, it has accomplished its shift from implementing state import and export plans to competing actively and equally on the market as a new foreign trade conglomerate. In 1992, China Minmetals Group became one of China's first 57 conglomerates that have been granted top priority in the central government's strategic development program. At present, all the subsidiaries of China Minmetals Group are engaged in specialized operation in terms of business sector and commodity. With international trade as the leading line of business, it is also devoted to developing such pillar businesses as finance, transportation, property development and management, industrial production as well as engineering contracting and labor service. This has resulted in a well-structured corporate operational framework in which various business lines increase their profits by creating synergies among themselves and spread up their risks through diversification. In 1998, along with AXA Group of France, the second largest insurance company in the world, China Minmetals Group established a joint venture named AXA-Minmetals Assurance Company in Shanghai, symbolizing the diversified development reached a new level.

In order to accelerate the growth of the corporation,China National Metals & Minerals Import & Export Corporation expended its direct financing channels on the international capital market by successfully issuing USD 200 million worth of commercial papers annually in the United States in the year of 1996,1997 and 1998.In May 1997,Minmetals Development Co.Ltd.was established on the basis of six of its major subsidiaries and managed to get listed on the Shanghai Securities Exchange with the issuance of 75 million A shares.In 1998,Minmetals Development Co.has made its way into the 30 sample stocks that form the basis for the Shanghai Composite Index.In 1999,with excellent business achievements,it entered "SSE 50 (Shanghai Securities Exchange 50)".By issuing commercial papers abroad and getting listed at home,the group entered direct financing market,which marked the conglomerate's move from mere commodity marketing to capital operation and has thereby increased its overall strength and potential for growth.

At present,China Minmetals Group has 44 overseas subsidiaries and other kinds of organizations in 22 countries and regions around the world as well as 98 solely funded or jointly funded domestic enterprises in 13 provinces and autonomous regions.Through recent years of restructuring and upgrading,the asset quality of Minmetals' overseas subsidiaries has been obviously improved. China Bank Hong Kong Branch regarded China Minmetals H.K.(Holdings) Ltd. as ranking top five with regard to asset quality among Chinese enterprises in Hong Kong.

Committed to boosting economic growth and promoting social progress,China Minmetals has made unstinted effort to turn itself into a top worldclass transnational conglomerate. Adnering to the principle of "equality,mutual benefit and mutual development" and with its commitment to providing premium products and efficient services, China Minmetals Group is now taking the initiative to establish and develop business relations with both its domestic and overseas clients.As close partners in a great variety of economic and trade co-operations,China Minmetals Group and its clients are working together to usher in the twenty-first century,and the new millenium.

地址：北京市朝阳区安慧里四区十五号楼

邮编： 100101

电传： 22190 MIMET CN　**电话：** 64916666(总机)

传真： 64917031　**电挂：北京** 6655(国内)

Add: Bldg 15, BLock 4 Anhuili, Chaoyang District, Beijing, China 100101

TELEX: 22241 MIMET CN

(TEL) : 64916666(SWITCHBOARD) (FAX): 64917031

Cable: 6655(domestic); MINMETALS BEIJING (international)

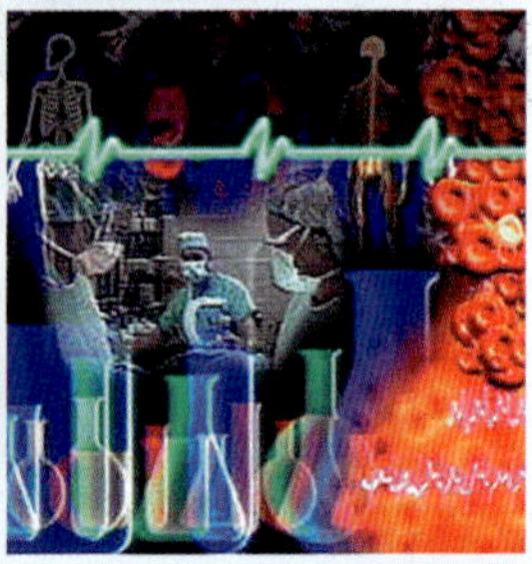

康佳集团股份有限公司

KONKA GROUP CO.,LTD.

康佳集团是国有控股上市公司，也是国家300家及广东省、深圳市重点扶持发展的大企业集团，以彩电为主导产业，年彩电生产能力已达700万台，“KONKA”商标已被国家工商局认定为中国驰名商标。公司以创造世界名牌为目标，国内零售市场占有率已跃居前茅，是深圳市首家营业额超百亿的工业企业，在美国硅谷设有技术开发中心，并在印度、墨西哥组建了控股生产企业。产品远销澳大利亚、印尼、俄罗斯、南美、北美及中东等60多个国家和地区。康佳彩电在沙特和香港地区的市场占有率超过20%，在澳大利亚达10%，均名列当地前茅。

“KONKA”集团总部雄姿

Headoffice of the KONKA Group Co.,Ltd

KONKA GROUP CO., LTD is a state-owned listed enterprise and one of the 300 enterprises which would be greatly supported by the state government, Guang Dong province and the municipality. With annual production capacity of color television 7 million units, the Group focuses its mind on color TV manufacturing. Its brand "KONKA" was appraised as a Chinese top brand by the National Bureau of Industry and Commerce while the goal for the Group is to make it an international top brand. The Group is the first enterprise in ShenZhen which achieved a turnover exceeds 10 billion RMB and occupies the first place in the national retail market. The Group built a R & D center in Silicon Valley, USA, and production facilities in India and Mexico and its products are exported to over 60 countries and regions including Australia, Indonesia, Russia, South America, North America and Middle East. The KONKA brand color TV occupies more than 20% of the market share in Saudi Arab and Hongkong and 10% in Australia,which makes it among the best-selling TV in the local market.

美国数字电视联盟(ATSC)主席向“KONKA”颁发会员单位证书

Chairman of the Advanced Television Standard Committee(ATSC) releasing certificate of membership to KONKA

澳大利亚居民节日排队购买“KONKA”彩电

Residents of Australia queuing for KONKA brand color TV in holidays

地址：中国深圳特区华侨城　Add: OVerseas ChineseTown, Shen Zhen Special Economic Zone, P.R.China.

电话 (Tel): (0755)6608866　传真 (Fax): (0755) 6600082　6602621　邮编 (Postcode): 518053

网址：http: // www.konka.com.cn

天津日电电子通信工业有限公司

Tianjin NEC Electronics & Communications Industry Co.,Ltd.

天津日电电子通信工业有限公司(简称天津日电公司)成立于1992年1月1日，是中日双方在高科技领域的一家合资企业。旨在引进NEC公司先进的电子信息技术，从事NEAX61系列局用程控交换机的制造、销售、安装工程及维护。生产能力从开始的年产交换机30万线发展到目前的年产300万线。目前，在中国电信网上运行的NEAX61设备已有1200万线，占全国公众通信网交换机容量11%，是国内现行局用交换机的重要制式之一，作为“八五”国家重点项目、国家程控交换机骨干企业，在“全国高科技百强企业”和“全国电子工业系统综合效益百强企业”中占有重要位置。

天津日电公司把“为实现中国通信现代化作出贡献，为全人类的沟通作出贡献”作为企业信念，把中国自强自产精神和NEC公司“C&C”理念相结合，紧跟科学技术进步和信息化时代的新近步伐，在竞争中求发展，其产品不仅适应大容量、高速度、高效率、多功能信息交换业务的迫切要求，并能满足未来通信技术宽带化、综合化、智能化发展需要。

Tianjin NEC Electronics & Communications Industry Co., Ltd, the abbreviated name Tianjin NEC Company,is a joint venture of China and Japan in high technology field, and was founded in January Ist 1999. For the purpose of importing advanced electronic & information technology of NEC Company, the company is engaged in manufacturing, selling,installing and maintaining NEAX61 series digital switching system. The production capacity of the Company is increased from beginning 300,000 lines per year to now 3,000,000 lines per year. At present,12,000,000 lines of NEAX61 installations are working in communication web of China, occupying 11% capacity of digital switching system.And the NEAX61 installation has been one of the important equipments in office exchange.Being national important item in "85 project" and the core enterprise in national digital switching system manufacturers,Tianjin NEC Company takes an important place both in hundreds of major high technology enterprises,and hundreds of high comprehensive benefit enterprises of electronic industry.

The faith of the Company is "Contribution for achieving modernization of communication of China ,and contribution for linking up of whole people around the world".Combining "C&C" belief with admiration of independence and self-improving in China, the Company is developing through competition, and keeping in step with development of science and advanced information technology.The products of the company not only meet the urgent demand of large capacity, high speed,high efficency, and more function in telecommunication field,but also satisfy the request of the development of comprehensive and intellect communication technology.

地址：天津市南开区红旗路216号
邮编：300190
电话：(022)27361887　27361878
传真：27361848　27361883　27361887

Add: No. 216, Hongqi Road,Nankai District, Tianjing, China　Postcode: 300190
Tel: (022)27361887　27361878
Fax: 27361848　27361883　27361887

对外贸易经济合作部国际贸易经济合作研究院

国际贸易经济合作研究院是对外贸易经济合作部直属的集研究、信息、新闻、出版和咨询服务为一体的综合性多功能社会科学研究机构。1948年8月创建于香港，新中国成立后迁至北京。研究院由原外经贸部国际贸易研究所、国际经济合作研究所等单位合并而成。在50余年的历史中，为中国对外经贸事业的发展，特别是在外经贸理论与政策研究、咨询和信息服务等方面，发挥了重要的作用，在国内外享有较高声誉。

业务范围

- ◆从事世界经济、国际贸易、国际经济合作、金融货币、商品市场、利用外资、引进技术、多(双)边援助、世界和地区经济贸易组织机构以及中国对外经贸战略、政策和实务等问题的调查研究
- ◆对经贸信息和情报进行搜集、加工、整理并提供服务
- ◆承担国内外机构委托的有关经贸咨询和市场调查业务
- ◆编辑、出版、发行对外经济贸易及国际经济合作专业图书、报刊、杂志、翻译有关书刊资料
- ◆培养和培训专业技术人员
- ◆举办国际贸易及经济技术合作等方面的学术交流活动

对外贸易经济合作部国际贸易经济研究院 电话：(010)64245741
地址：北京安定门外东后巷28号 (010)64216661-1601/1201
邮编：100710 传真：(010)64212175

浙江中大集团股份有限公司
ZHEJIANG ZHONGDA GROUP CO., LTD.

浙江中大集团股份有限公司是浙江省外贸行业的骨干企业，于1992年由国有企业改制为股份制企业，并于1996年6月经中国证监会批准，成为国家外经贸部推荐的上市公司。

公司自改制以来，遵循"一业为主，多种经营，全方位开拓发展"的经营方针。外贸主营业务下设六家专业公司，三家出口货源工厂和一家国际货运公司。多种经营业务迅速发展，公司控股的房地产开发公司是目前浙江省房地产行业极有影响力的公司之一。对外投资的金融、公路、信息产业等项目已有较稳定的回报和发展前景。1998年公司出口实绩3.2亿美元，实际利润1.3亿元，净资产已达8.3亿元。经《中国证券报》等单位评选，公司被评为99年中国极具发展潜力的50家上市公司之一。

中大股份将高举改革锐取的大旗，继续保持稳定健康发展的思路，做好商品经营和资本经营两大文章，成为能延续百年的现代化大企业。

Zhejiang Zhongda Group Co., Ltd., a key foreign trade enterprise in Zhejiang Province, was reformed from a state-owned company to a stock-share enterprise in 1992, and was recommended by the Ministry of Foreign Trade and Economic Co-operation of PRC. and authorized to be a public listed share enterprise in June, 1996.

Since the reform, the enterprise has followed the management strategy of "one key business, multimanagement and all-round development", six companies for mainly dealing foreign trade, three factories for producing export goods and one international transportation company were set up. The multimanagement has been developed rapidly, the Real Estate Development Company, which is share holding by the enterprise, is becoming one of the greatest influence real estate companies in Zhejiang Province. The investments in finance, highway and information industry have gainde steady development and repay. The total foreign trade value topped USD 320 million with reality profit of RMB130 million and the net capital reached to RMB 830 million in 1998. The enterprise was evaluated one of the 50 best enterprises with development potentiality in China in 1999 by "China Stock" and some other authorities.

公司名称：浙江中大集团股份有限公司
地　　址：杭州市莫干山路110号
董 事 长：陈继达
总 经 理：马金龙
邮政编码：310005
电　　话：0571-8833088（总机转）、8833898
传　　真：0571-8839922

Name of Company: Zhejiang Zhongda Group Co., Ltd.
Add: No. 110. Moganshan Road. Hangzhou, Zhejiang, China.
Chairman of the Board & Legal person: Mr. Chen jida
General manager: Mr. Ma jinlong
P.code: 310005
Tel: 0571-8833088, 8833898
Fax: 0571-8839922

一汽—大众汽车有限公司

FAW-Volkswagen Automotive Company, Ltd.

一汽—大众汽车有限公司是由中国第一汽车集团公司和德国大众汽车股份公司及奥迪汽车股份公司合资经营的大型轿车生产企业。公司于1991年2月8日正式成立，1996年12月全面建成投产。公司整个项目总投资111.3亿元人民币，注册资本为37.12亿元人民币，其中一汽占60%的股份，大众占30%的股份，奥迪占10%的股份。公司位于长春西南部，占地面积116万平方米。公司第一期工程的设计能力为年产15万辆整车、27万台发动机、18万台变速箱，同时，实现部分整车、总成及零部件的出口。达产后的员工总数为5700人。

1991年，国家对外经济贸易部确认一汽—大众为"先进技术企业"；1995年，国家统计局授予一汽—大众为"中国汽车制造名优企业"。

FAW – Volkswagen Automotive Company, Ltd. s a Joint Venture set up by the First Automobile Works of China and Volkswagen AG of Germany and is a car manufacturer on a large sale.The Company was estabished on February 8,1991, completed and launched into production in December, 1996.The total investment for this project is 11.13 billion RMB and the registered capital is 3.712 billion RMB,with 60% of the share from FAW, 30% from Volkswagen AG and 10% from Audi AG. The Company is located in the south-west of Changchun City, covering an area of 1.16 million square meters.The production capacity for the first phase of the project will be 150,000 cars, 270,000 engines and 180,000 transmissions per year.At the same time, FBU cars, assemblies and parts and components will be exported. It is planned that the total headcount of the employees will be 5700 when the Company reaches its full capacity.

In 1991, FAW-Volkswagen was named as "Enterprise with Advanced Technology" by the Ministry of Foreign Economy and Trade. In 1995, the Company won the award of "Well-Known and Superior Quality Enterprise in China's Automobile Industry" given by the National Statistics Bureau.

法人代表：林敢为　　总经理：陆林奎

地址：吉林省长春市东风大街　　邮编：130011

电话：0431-5990151　　传真：0431-5990130

应运而生的郑州日产汽车

ZNC Emerging as the Times Require

结实耐用的标准型货车
Strong and durable standard trucks

适合各种路面的多功能厢式车
Sport & Utility Wagon suit for all kinds of roads

城乡间方便实用的短途运输小货车
Lorry for Short-distance transportation between city and countryside

富有力量和高级感的时尚皮卡
Full of strength feeling and advanced times-style Pickup

郑州东风轻型载货汽车
Zhengzhou DongFeng truck

小旋风厢式汽车
Pathfinder SUV

ZN1020 普及型皮卡
ZN1020 economical Pickup

郑州日产 D22 皮卡
Zhengzhou NISSAN D22 Pickup

面对正在进入的汽车时代，我们无不感受到汽车带来的好处：

大量迅速地搬运物品，输送旅客，人们能在更大范围内安心工作、休闲，探索未知的世界

—郑州日产汽车也正是基于这种人类需求应运而生。

郑州日产开发、引进生产的多款优质的汽车，在提高人们工作、生活质量的同时，也提高了郑州日产向未来挑战的信心和实力。

与发展中的社会同步发展，是郑州日产的目标。您的所需，我们的所有。请继续关注、支持为您而生的郑州日产汽车。

Facing the approaching Automobile times, no one doesn't feel the convenience of automobile: transporting large quantities of commodities quickly, carrying passengers, making people work and play leisurely at much larger scope and explore the unknown world.

— It is as the times require that ZhengZhou Nissan Automobile CO., LTD. (ZNC) emerges.

Many styles of automobiles, developed and imported by ZNC, increase not only the qualities of work and life, but also the self-confidence and strength that ZNC challenges the future.

The target of ZNC is developing with the development of the society. What you require is what we have .

Please continue watching and supporting ZNC emerging for you.

郑州日产汽车
The Pioneer Of Pickup

郑州日产汽车有限公司
ZHENGZHOU NISSAN AUTOMOBILE CO.,LTD.

地址：郑州市陇海东路 62 号　电话：(0371) 6345367 6326500　传真：(0371) 6321108　欢迎访问：WWW.zhengzhounissan.com.cn　E-mail：zznissan@public2.zz.ha.cn

Add: No.62 of East Longhai Road, Zhengzhou　Tel: (0371) 6345367 6326500　Fax: (0371) 6321108　Net add: WWW.zhengzhounissan.com.cn　E-mail:zznissan@public2.zz.ha.cn

青岛啤酒股份有限公司

Tsingtao Brewery Company Limited

Tsingtao Brewery Company Limited is the earliest bee manufacturer in China,can trace its root back to 1903 wher its predecessor, Tsingtao Brewery Factory,was firs established. Being a world-famed brand, Tsingtao beer is wel received by people for its crystal clarity,snow-white fine foams with prolonged adhesion to the glass and its refeshing ,mellov taste.It has been awarded the China National Gold Medals seven times and the championship prizes three times in the international wine appraisals held in the Unite States. Tsingtac beer has been exported since 1954 and presently it is availabl in over 40 countries and regions. The annual production fc the year 1998 reached 557,000 tons,while the export volum was almost 30,000 tons. Now the company's import and expor business is handled by Tsingtao Brewery Imp.& Exp.Co., Ltd Friends who are interested in establishing busines relationship with our company may feel to contact us.

青岛啤酒股份有限公司前身为国有青岛啤酒厂，始建于1903年，是中国历史悠久的啤酒生产厂。青岛啤酒素以酒体澄澈清亮，香醇爽口，泡沫洁白细腻，挂杯持久享誉世界，广受世界各地消费者的欢迎，7次荣获国家金奖，3次在美国国际评酒会上获得冠军。青岛啤酒自1954年出口以来，现已畅销40多个国家和地区。1998年，公司全年啤酒产量已达到55.7万吨，出口量近3万吨。

目前，公司的各种进出口业务由青岛啤酒进出口有限公司具体负责。欢迎对青岛啤酒外销及原材辅料供应有兴趣的朋友们随时与我们联系。

产品规格：

1）330毫升×24瓶/箱，330毫升×4×6瓶/箱 1008箱/20’柜
2）355毫升×24瓶/箱，355毫升×4×6瓶/箱 1040箱/20’柜
3）640毫升×24瓶/箱 570箱/20’柜
4）500毫升×12瓶/箱 1750箱/20’柜
5）330毫升×12罐/箱 2200箱/20’柜

Specifications of Tsingtao Beer:

1) 330CC × 24BTLS/CARTON, 330CC × 4 × 6BTLS/CARTON 1008CARTONS/20 CONTAINER
2) 355CC × 24BTLS/CARTON, 355CC × 4 × 6BTLS/CARTON 1040CARTONS/20 CONTAINER
3) 640CC × 24BTLS/CARTON 570 CARTONS/20’ CONTAINER
4) 500CC × 12BTLS/CARTON 1750 CARTONS/20’CONTAINER
5) 330CC × 24CANS/CARTON 2200 CARTONS/20’CONTAINER

公司地址：青岛市香港中路五四广场
青啤大厦16楼
电　　话：(0532)5712437　5715165
传　　真：(0532)5714533
电子信箱：sale@tsingtaobeer. com. cn
联 系 人：汪治国先生　　初良镜先生

Add: 16/F, Tsingtao Beer Tower, May 4th Square, Hong Kong Road Central, Qingdao, China.
Tel: (0532)5712437　5715165
Fax: (0532)5714533
Contact person:
Mr. Wang Zhiguo　Mr. Chu Liangjing
E-mail: sale@tsingtaobeer. com. cn

深圳开发科技股份有限公司

SHENZHEN KAIFA TECHNOLOGY CO., LTD.

深圳开发科技股份有限公司创立于1985年7月，致力于中国计算机和高科技电子、通讯产品的开发制造。1993年进行股份制改造，1994年初公司“A”股股票正式上市，以其优异的业绩成为中国高科技企业一颗璀灿的明珠。

经过十多年的艰苦创业，深科技建立了良好的组织管理体系和技术网络，在香港地区、新加坡、美国、中国建立了开发科技的姐妹公司形成了集生产、供销、信息、研究开发、产品试验和售后服务于一体的世界性大企业战略框架。多年来公司被评为“全国外商投资双优企业”、“AAA级信得过企业”、“计算机行业利税状元”等。

公司董事局制定的发展方针是：以生产为基础，以高科技为主导，以国际市场为主要销售方向，争取三、五年内把“开发”建成一个国际化的集团公司。

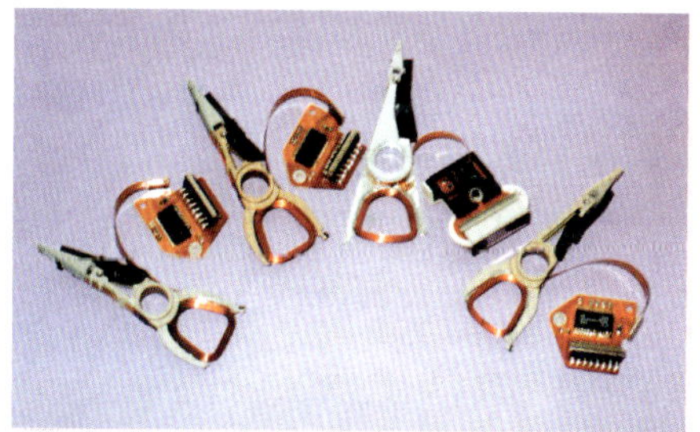

Founded In July 1985, SHENZHEN KAIFA TECHNOLOGY CO., LTD. mainly manufactures computers and hi-tech electronic and communication products. In 1993, Kaifa was famed as stock company. At the beginning of 1994, Kaifa was publicly listed in Shenzhen Stock Exchange. With its outstanding achievements, Kaifa becomes a shining pearl in the hi-tech enterprises of China.

After more than 10 years development, Kaifa has set up well organized management system and technology network with branches in Hongkong, Singapore and USA. Compiling of production, purchasing, inflammation, research and development, product experiment and client services in one body,the international enterprise service structure of Kaifa is famed. In the past years, Kaifa has been rewarded various certificates, such as"Grade AAA Credible Enterprise, "most profitable in computer enterprises".

Kaifa's developing strategy (made by th board of directors)is: on the basis of industry,depending on hi-tech, sales oriented to world market, Kaifa will become an internationalized group.

地址：中国深圳市福田区彩田路7006号
电话：(86-755)3216063
传真：(86-755)3325539
邮编：518035

Add: Kaifa Complex,Caitian Rd.,FutianDist,Shenzhen,P.R.C.
Tel: (86-755) 3216063
Fax: (86-755) 3325539
Post code: 518035

中国电子进出口总公司

China National Electronics Import & Export Corporation

中国电子进出口总公司——中国电子行业最大的进出口企业，是以电子技术及产品进出口为主兼营其它的综合型外贸公司，主要经办电子技术、设备、元器件及产品的进出口和政府间的协议贸易，以及承包国际工程、劳务出口、合作生产、合资经营、三来一补业务，承办国外电子厂商在华设立维修服务中心及销售代理、零配件寄售、软件开发以及金融租赁、储运包装、展览广告、提供市场信息和对外贸易法律咨询等。公司成立以来，坚持为我国电子工业和国民经济发展服务；坚持改革，坚持贸工结合、贸技结合、进出结合；坚持以进出口业务为主，开展多种经营、全面发展；坚持两个文明一起抓，加强经营管理，公司业务不断发展，规模不断扩大，从1980年至1998年，公司进出口总额达203.26亿美元，其中进口95.7亿美元，出口107.56亿美元，为我国电子工业的技术改造和生产能力、产品质量、经济效益的提高，为我国电子产品走向世界做出了重要贡献。1992年以来，公司进出口总额在全国500家最大进出口企业中位居前十名，出口连年过10亿美元，同世界上130个国家和地区建立了贸易关系。出口商品600多种。1987年以来，公司多次被评为经贸行业的先进单位，机电产品出口先进企业，首都文明单位，中央国家机关文明单位标兵，中国对外经贸行业先进单位，中国对外经贸行业质量效益型企业。

经过多年的发展，公司已发展成为一个具有46个子公司、100多个独资、合资、控股、渗股企业、20多个驻外点的综合型大型外贸企业。

目前，公司正在按《公司法》和建立现代化企业制度的要求，对公司进行改造。进行公司资产和管理重组，建立激励机制，使公司在国内外市场竞争中更具活力。

公司的精神是：团结、开拓、求实、奉献；服务、信誉、效益、效率。

公司的发展目标是：以国际贸易为龙头，以实业为基础，以科技为先导，以金融为依托，以国际、国内两个市场为目标，实行流通、生产、科研、金融、服务相结合。把公司发展成为综合化、实业化、国际化、国内一流、国际一流的集团公司。

China National Electronics Import and Export Corp.(CEIEC) is the largest electronics importer and exporter in China. As a comprehensive foreign trade company, CEIEC is mainly engaged with elecrtonic technology, products and other services. The main business scope includes: undertaking the import and export of electronic technology,equipment, components and parts; government agreement trade, contracting international engineering projects, labor service, co-production, joint ventureoperation, processing with supplied materials, samples and blueprints, compensation trade, setting up maintenance and post-sale service centers by foreign electronics mamufacturers, sales agent, consignment sale of spare parts; software development and financial leasing,packing and transportation, exhibition and advertising, market information and legal consultancy service in the field of foreign trade,etc.

since the establishment, CEIEC has been adhering to the principle of serving the development of the national electronics industry and national economy; It persists in the reform and the combination of trade and industry, trade and technology development, import and export; It operates with foreign trade as its main business while diversifying business line for all around developments; By strengthening the operation and management and placing equal emphasis on material Progress and ethical and cultural progress, CEIEC has made great progress in business. The trade volume from 1980 to 1998 totaled USD20.326 billions, of which export reaches USD9.57 billions and imports USD10.756 billion.All these achievements contributed a lot to the technical update and the improvement of productive capability,product quality and economic performance, as well as the promotion of China's electronics into the world market. Since 1992, CEIEC has been ranked among the top ten within the 500 largest Chinese importers and exporters with an annual export volume of USD1 billbion for consecutively several years. At present, it has established trade relations with more than 130 countries and regions in the world and export over 600 Varities of commodities. Since 1987,CEIEC has,on many occasions, been honored as the "National Advanced Unit in Economics and Trade", "Advanced Unit in Electro-Mechanical Products Export","Beijing Model Unit of Civilization", "Pacesetter among Government Departments","National Excellent Foreign Trading Corporation","National Advanced Trading Corporation with High Quality and Good Efficiency".

Through years of development,CEIEC has grown into a large corporation of 46 subsidiaries throughout the country,more than 100 solely funded,equity participation and holding companies,joint ventures,as well as over 20 subsidiaries and offices abroad.

CEIEC is now carrying out a self-transformation according to the Corporation Law and the modem enterprise system.Through reorganization of its assets and management,CEIEC will perfect its motivation mechanism and make itself more competitive in both domesic and overseas markets.

The motto of CEIEC is:Unity,Pioneering,Reality,Devotion,Service,Reputation,Efficiency and Benefit.

The goal of CEIEC is:to implement combination of circulation,production,R & D,financing and servicing by means of taking international trade as its mainstay,industry as its fondation and science and technology as its guiding force,relying on financing.Aiming at international and domestic markets,it will exert its efforts to turn CEIEC into a first class internationalized,diversified,industrialized enterprise group company both both at home and aborad.

公司法人代表、总裁：钱本源
副总裁：齐述华、冯学昌、张志杰
地址：北京市复兴路甲23号电子大楼 邮编：100036
电话：68219550 68219532 传真：68212352
电子信箱：ceiec@ceiec.com.cn
网址：http://www.ceiec.com.cn http://www.ceiec.com

President & CEo: Qian Benyuan
Vice Presidents: Qi Shuhua,Feng Xuechang,Zhang Zhijie
Add: Electronics Building, A23,Fuxing Road, Beijing 100036
Tel: (86 10)68219550,68219532 Fax:68212352
E-mail: ceiec@ceiec.com,cn
http://www.ceiec.com.cn http://www.ceiec.com

走向国际电信工程市场的 CESEC

中国电子系统工程总公司 (CESEC)

CESEC, Stepping to International Telecommunication Engineering Market

中国电子系统工程总公司(CESEC)，于一九七五年经国务院批准成立，是隶属于信息产业部的国家大型企业，具有国内外工程承包权，进出口权和劳务输出权，是建设部授予的具有一级施工总承包和电子系统工程专项甲级设计资质单位。公司在北京、上海、天津、南京、深圳等一些大中城市设立了分、子公司，现有员工四千余人，其中高中级技术人员一千余人。二十多年来，公司在电子系统工程、民用建筑、机电安装等领域，业务不断发展壮大。

公司主要业务是承包国内外各类电子系统工程，其中包括各类通信系统工程；广播、电视、电声系统工程；计算机应用，工业过程控制及安全防范工程；智能化大厦，楼宇弱电工程；通信设备的开发、研制、生产；通信领域的国外工程，国内外工程项目的设备、材料进出口业务，劳务输出；工业和民用建筑机电设备安装及其它业务。

近年来，公司与沙特阿拉伯中东电信公司签订了TEP6—SRS项目和TEP6—OSP项目施工合同，开拓了中东电信工程市场，为实现公司立足国内、面向世界的可持续发展的战略目标，奠定了坚实的基础。

China Electronic Systems Engineering Corp (CESEC) was founded in 1975 with the approval of the State Council.As a big-scale state-owned enterprise owned by the Ministry of Information Industry, CESEC owns Overseas Project-contract right, Commodity Import & Export right and Labor Service Exportright. Approved by the Ministry of Construction, CESEC is First-class General-contract Enterprise and Grade-A Electronic-system-engineering-design Enterpise.Its headquarters is in Beijing and has set up many sub-companies and branches in many big cities such as Shanghai, Tianjin, Nanjing and Shenzhen. Now, CESEC has more than 4,000 staffs,including over 1000 professional technical ones.During the past 20 years, CESEC has been active in the field of electronic systems engineering project,civil construction project, mechanical-electrical installation project, etc. and got stronger and stronger.

The main major of CESEC is to contract all kinds of electronic systems engineering project in civil and aboard,including telecommunication systems engineering project; broadcasting/ video/audio systems engineering project; computer application,industrial process automatic-control and security / fire-proof project; PDS / Weak-electric project; developing, researching and producing telecommunication equipment; aboard telecommunication project; importing and exporting equipment and materials concerned with works in civil and aboard; labor service export; mechanical-electrical equipment installation for industrial / civil building and so on.

Moreover, during the past two years,we signed two contracts of TEP6-SRS and TEP6-OSP with Middle East Telecom Co. which deploited telecommunication market for CESEC in Middle East and will establish stable base for the CESEC's strategy aims of continuous development not only in civil,but also aboard.

公司地址：北京市丰台区小屯路8号
总 经 理：张丰年
电　　话：010-68689619　68680628
传　　真：010-68687516　邮编：100039

Add: No 8,Xiaotun Road, Fengtai District,Beijing, P. R. China
General Manager: Mr. Zhang Fengnian
Tel: 0086-10-68689619, 68680628
Fax: 0086-10-68687516　　Post Code:100039

赛特集团

SCITECH GRUOP

董事长：杨壮生

赛特集团对众多海内外人士来说，是一个熟悉的名字。

赛特集团崛起于20世纪90年代初，在短短数年中，已迅速发展成为一个以旅游服务业为中心，以商业管理、物业管理为基础，跨行业、跨地区、多元化、国际化发展的现代化企业集团。

赛特集团位于中国北京商务外交机构和著名企业云集的黄金地段——建国门外大街。以中外合资的赛特集团有限公司为核心企业，拥有赛特大厦、赛特饭店、赛特购物中心、赛特广场、赛特俱乐部等五座高档次现代化建筑，集办公、酒店、购物、会议、餐饮、健身、娱乐等诸多功能于一体，向中外宾客提供高品质、个性化和全方位的服务。

赛特集团不同凡响之处在于其超前的经营理念、创新的营销意识、独特的企业文化和卓著的经营业绩。在专注于高档写字楼、商务酒店和购物中心的经营并获巨大成功的同时，赛特集团开创了向国际市场接轨并适合中国特色的全新输出商业和物业管理模式，以丰富的管理经验、雄厚的人力资源和企业文化优势，不断扩大输出管理的成果和规模。多元化发展方针的实施，更使赛特集团在国内外拥有10余家成员公司，业务涉及国际贸易、旅游、高科技开发、网络服务、广告、汽车租赁、文化艺术等多领域，均有不凡的建树。

奉行"团结、实干、高效"企业精神的赛特集团，以引导高品位时尚，服务美好生活为已任，愿同各界人士携手共进，开创未来。

SCTTECH GROUP, a familiar name to many people in China and abroad,was founded in the early nineties of the 20th Century and has rapidly developed into a trans-regional, multi-industrial modern enterprise with its focus on tourism services and its roots in shopping center and commercial property management.

SCITECH GROUP is sitnated in the prime location of Beijing, China. JianGuoMenWai Avenue, where many well-known companies and diplomatic agencies have established their Beijing offices. It is a joint venture enterprise called SCITECH GROUP COMPANY LTD. which comptises of five high level modern entities SCITECH TOWER, SCITECH HOTEL, SCTTECH PLAZA, SCITECH PLACE and SCITECH CLUB, providing various high-quality services of office space, conference rooms, hotel accommodations, catering services, fitness and entertainment facilities as well as shopping areas.

The uniqeness of SCTTECH GROUP is its advanced management concept, innovative marketing philosophy, unique company identity, and remarkable achievements in operation.SCITECH GROUP has achieved great success in its management of high-grade office buildings, business hotel, and shopping centers. At the same time, it has also crcated new patterns for shopping centers and property management designed for modern Chinese lifestyle that also align to international market practice. with rich experience of management, abundant human resources and supemrior enterprise culture, SCITECH GROUP is continually expanding through the transference of the management experience. In the implementation of the policy for multi-industrial development. the Group has established more than 10 member companies, domestic and international, in the fields of international trade, tourism, high-tech development, internet service, advertisement, car rental entertainment and more.

Under the corporate motto of "Teanwork, Action, Efficiency", SCITECH GROUP'S mission is to be the leading Provider of services for a high quality lifestyle Through cooperation With various circles of society, we will create a brighter future.

地址 (Add)：北京市朝阳区建国门外大街22号 (100004)
22 Jianguomen wui Avnue,Beijing P.R.China
电话 (Tel)：65122288
传真 (Fax)：65123679

中化江苏进出口公司

Sinochem Jiangsu

总经理：房林
General Manager: Fang Lin

中化江苏进出口公司是中国化工进出口总公司在京外的直属子公司之一，主要经营有机／无机化工原料、医药原料、农药原料、染料、颜料、涂料、各种化工中间体、橡塑制品、石油化工产品等的进出口。公司年进出口规模2亿美元以上。1997年和1998年出口额分别达到21606万美元和21653万美元。在1997年中国出口额100强外贸(工贸)公司排名中名列第62位，在1998年中国出口额200强企业中排名中名列第87位。1999年6月，公司建立的ISO9002质量体系通过了在英国认证服务机构(UKAS)注册的SGS雅斯利国际认证有限公司的审核认证，并获得了在该认证公司注册的ISO9002注册证书（证书号Q16438)。

SINOCHEM JIANGSU import and export corporation is one of the subsidiaries directly under SINOCHEM head office in Beijing. It mainly handles import and export business of organic & inorganic chemicals,pharmaceuticals, pesticides, dyestuffs, pigments, coatings, all kinds of chemical intermediates, rubber & plastic products, petro chemicls and etc. An annual turnover of the corporation is over USD 200 million, with the export volumes of USD 216.00 million and USD 216.53 millions in 1997 and 1998 respectively.The corporation was ranked as the 62nd place in the top 100 foreign trade (industrialtrade) companies of China in export volumes in 1997, and the 87th place in the top 200 enterprises of China in export volumes in 1998. In June, 1999, the quality management system ISO9002 set up by the corporation was certified by SGS Yarsley International Certification Services Limited (SGS-ICS) wich is accredited by United kingdom Accreditation Service (UKAS). The corporation has been granted with ISO9002 Certificate of Registration issued by SGS-ICS.

公司办公楼 Office building of SINOCHEN Jiangsu

法人代表：房林
地址：江苏省南京市中华路50号江苏国际经贸大厦
电话：025-2258718, 2254368
传真：025-2257789, 2252114, 4407789
电子信箱：jschem@public1.ptt.js.cn
网址：http: //www.sinochemjiangsu.com

Address: Jiangsu International Business Mansion, 50 Zhonghua Road, Nanjing, P.R. of China
Tel: +86-25-2258718, 2254368
Fax: +86-25-2257789, 2252114, 4407789
E-mail: jschem@public1 .ptt. js.cn
Web site: http: //www. sinochemjiangsu. com

浙江省土产畜产进出口公司

ZHEJIANG NATIVE PRODUCE & ANIMAL BY-PRODUCTS I/E CORP.

浙江省土产畜产进出口公司成立于1975年2月，经过二十多年的发展，已成为中国外经贸系统大型企业之一，拥有员工270人，下设三个子公司，18个业务部、6个职能管理部门、3个直属工厂、2个自有仓库、3个海外分支机构。经营品种达20个门类、200余种，远销世界80多个国家和地区。90年代起，实施了“安全、规模、效益”经营方针后，企业获得了长足的发展，到1998年实现进出口31444万美元，其中出口29509万美元，进出口额列全国进出口企业500强第57位；出口额列全国200强出口企业第36位，并连续两年人均年创汇达百万美元，列全国外贸之前茅。

本公司注册资金为7418万人民币，1998年国有资产增长率达10.49%，资金可靠，实力雄厚，与世界五大洲2000家客商建立了稳定的贸易关系，并始终坚持“质量第一，信誉至上，服务优良，互惠互利”的宗旨，竭诚欢迎世界各地的商界朋友来华以各种贸易方式与我洽谈生意，我方将根据客户需求不断开发新的经营项目和品种。

Zhejiang Native Produce & Animal By-Products Imp. & Exp. Cor was established in Feb.1975.Through over twenty years developmen it has become one of the large-scale enterprises in China's foreig economic and trade circle.It employs 270 staff members, consists of subsidiary companies and possesses 18 business depts, management (functional) depts, 3 affiliated factories, 2 wholly owne warehouses, 3 overseas branch offices.The corp.deals with 2 categories, more than 200 varieties of products, selling well over 8 countries and regions in the world. Since the 1990s, the corp. ha achieved great development through carring out the managemen principle: "Safety、Large scale、Efficienty". In 1998, its import and expo volume amounted to USD314.44 millions, ranking 57th among the to 500 import and export enterprises in China; the export volume reache USD295.09 millions, ranking 36th among the top 200 export enterprise in China. The annual foreign exchange earning has reached USD million per capita for two consecutive years,ranking first in China foreign trade circle.

Registered capital of the corp. is RMB74.18 millions.The growt rate of state-owned assets increased by 10.49% in 1998. With goc credibility and sound financial capabilities,the corp. enjoys hig reputation at home and abroad, and has established steady trad relations with 2000 customers in the world.Adhering to the principle "quality first, reputation first, excellent service, mutual benefit", w cordially welcome business friends from all parts of the world to our corp, for business negotiation through various trade methods. We will also devote to the development and improvement of new products or items in accordance with customer's requirements.

公司总经理：龚荣祥先生

GENERAL MANAGER: MR.GONG RONGXIANG

地址：中国杭州中山北路308号　　邮编：310003

ADD: 308 NORTH ZHONGSHAN ROAD, HANGZHOU, CHINA 310003

电话：0086-571-5773808/5773705

传真：0086-571-5773780/5773706

E-mail: znac@mail.hz.zj.cn

http://www.zjnac.com

中国铁道建筑总公司

CHINA RAILWAY CONSTRUCTION CORPORATION

中国铁道建筑总公司是经国家批准具有一级工程总承包资质和拥有对外经营权的特大型企业，下辖铁道部第十一至二十工程局、石家庄铁道学院、铁道建筑研究设计院、工厂局、物资局等30多个单位。现有职工15万人，拥有机械设备2万多台／套，运输车辆8000余辆。

公司主要承担国内外铁路、公路、桥梁、隧道与地下工程、水利、电力、机场、港口、矿山、市政、工业与民用建筑等工程的设计、施工、设备安装、工程监理和技术咨询；物资采购和水泥、大型钢结构件、预应力混凝土桥梁、轨枕生产；铁路施工机械，养路机械制造等多种经营。

自1995年以来，中国铁道建筑总公司连续3年入选世界225家国际承包商和全球承包商排行榜。

新加坡房建工程
House Building Works in Singapore

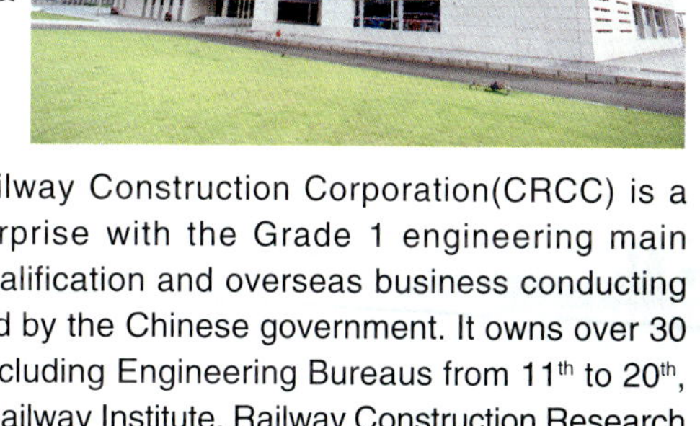

澳门法院大楼
Supreme Courthouse in Macao

澳门松山隧道
Songshan Tunnel in Macao

新加坡乌鲁班丹污水处理厂工程
Ulu Pandan Waste Water Plant Works in Singapore

China Railway Construction Corporation(CRCC) is a gigantic enterprise with the Grade 1 engineering main contracting qualification and overseas business conducting license granted by the Chinese government. It owns over 30 subsidiaries including Engineering Bureaus from 11th to 20th, Shijiazhuang Railway Institute, Railway Construction Research & Design Institute, Factory Bureau, Material Bureau, etc.. It has over 150,000 employees, and possesses more than 20,000 units of plant & equipment and over 8,000 transport vehicles.

CRCC mainly undertakes the design, construction, equipment installation, engineering supervision and technical consultation for international and domestic railways, highways, bridges, tunnels & underground engineering, water conservancies, electric powers, airports, harbors, mines, municipal works, industrial & civil buildings, etc.. It also operates the business such as procurement of material, production of cement, heavy steel structures, prestressed concrete beams & sleepers, and manufacture of railway constructing & maintaining machines.

Over the past 3 years since 1995, CRCC has been on the list of The Top 225 International Contractors and The Top 225 Global Contractors.

地址：北京市复兴路40号
邮编：100855
电话：86-10-63227114
传真：86-10-68217382
电子信箱：crccod@public.gb.com.cn

Add: No. 40, Fu Xing Road, Beijing 100855, China
Tel: 86-10-63227114
Fax: 86-10-68217382
E-mail: crccod@public.gb.com.cn

江苏省轻工业品进出口集团股份有限公司

JIANGSU LIGHT INDUSTRIAL PRODUCTS IMPORT & EXPORT(GROUP) CORPORATION

董事长兼总经理：杨元福

江苏省轻工业品进出口集团股份有限公司创建于1974年1月，主要经营以轻工业品为主的各类商品和技术进出口业务，开展“三来一补”、进料加工、对销贸易和转口贸易等。集团公司总资产近10亿元人民币，98年进出口总额2.4亿美元，被评为：全国质量效益型先进企业、国家外经贸部重点联系的31家专业外贸公司之一、中国对外经贸优秀企业和中国进出口额500强企业的前百强，并于今年4月通过ISO9002国际认证。

集团公司，以“求实创新”为经营宗旨，全面运行ISO9002质量体系，力求服务最优、客户满意，目前公司已基本形成以进出口贸易为龙头，包含实业、海外企业、房地产业、国际货代、宾馆旅游业等在内的综合化经营格局，正朝着综合商社模式的知识型外贸企业发展。

Founded in January 1974, Jiangsu Light Industrial Products Import & Export (Group) Corporation mainly deals with the import and export business of various kinds of products and technologies with the light industrial products playing the leading role. Its business scope also includes processing materials sent in from abroad and compensation trade, counter trade and entrepot trade.The total assets of the Corporation are nearly RMB￥1 billion . In 1998, its import and export volume reached USD $240 million. It has been honoured as "A National Advanced Enterprise in Quality and Profit-netting" and one of the 31 specialized foreign trade companies by the Ministry of Foreign Trade and Economic Co-operation. It was awarded the title "A National Excellent Foreign Trade Enterprise" and has ranked among the Top 100 of the 500 biggest import and export enterprises in China. In April 1999, it has successfully established the ISO9002 quality authentication system.

The Corporation adheres to the principle of "novelty and reality" and runs under the ISO9002 quality system. It aims at excellent service and making customers satisfied. At present, the Corporation has formed a comprehensive management system including industry, overseas enterprises, real estate, international forwarding agent, hotels and tourism with import and export business playing the leading role. It is now developing in the direction of a knowledge-based foreign trade enterprise with a mode of comprehensive international firm.

地址 (ADD): 南京市建邺路100号 邮编 (P.C.): 210004

100 JIANYE ROAD, NANJING, CHINA

电话 (TEL): 86-25-4464466, 4468888

传真 (FAX): 86-25-4208398, 4209520

电传 (TELEX): 34105 INDNK CN

CABLE: INDUSTRY NANJING

电子信箱 (Email): jsl@public1.ptt.cn

网址 (URL): //www.jst.group.com

二十五年奋斗结硕果而今迈步从头越

98年11月20日，江苏省轻工业进出口集团股份有限公司乔迁，搬进了属于自己的30层智能化办公大楼。

集团公司办公楼外景

中国飞跃

FEIYUE

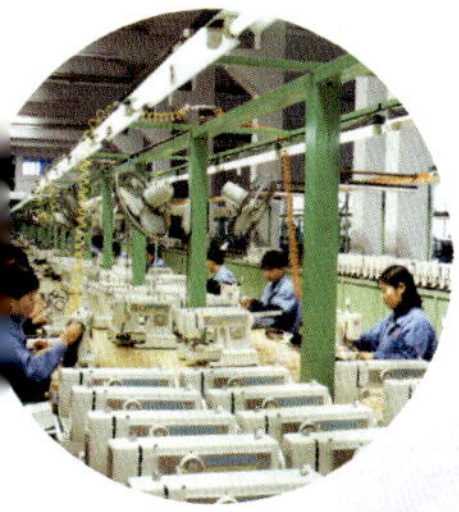

公司的“飞跃”，“YAMATA”商标在国际上有一定的影响。
"FEIYUE" "YAMATA" Brands have a good reputation.

飞跃集团辖6个生产区和飞跃缝纫机研究所、飞跃精工制作分公司，是中国目前最大的缝纫机生产基地和出口基地。拥有强劲的新产品研制开发能力和当今世界先进的自动化生产加工设备。

近年来，飞跃集团形成了高速和超高速包缝机、平缝机、绷缝机、家用多功能缝纫机、三自动平缝机、特种机等22大系列70多个品种的生产能力。其中机电一体化的家用多功能缝纫机、超高速包缝机和三自动平缝机，已具有国际水平并居国内领先地位。

飞跃集团完全按照ISO9000质量体系进行生产和管理。近年，又有多种产品通过了CE和GS认证。

Feiyue Group includes 6 manufacturing factories, a R&D institute, and a machine assembling center. In recent years, Feiyue has developed 22 series and more than 70 types of high speed and supper high speed overlock sewing machines, lockstitch sewing machines, flatlock sewing machines, multi-function domestic sewing machines, semi-auto lockstitch and other special types of sewing machines to fulfill the domestic and industrial needs. Feiyue's multi-function domestic sewing machine, super high speed overlock sewing machine and semi-auto lockstitch machine are regarded as the industry's leading technology.

All Feiyue's product lines are managed and operated strictly under the ISO9000 Quality Control System. Most of the products have passed the CE and GS approvals.

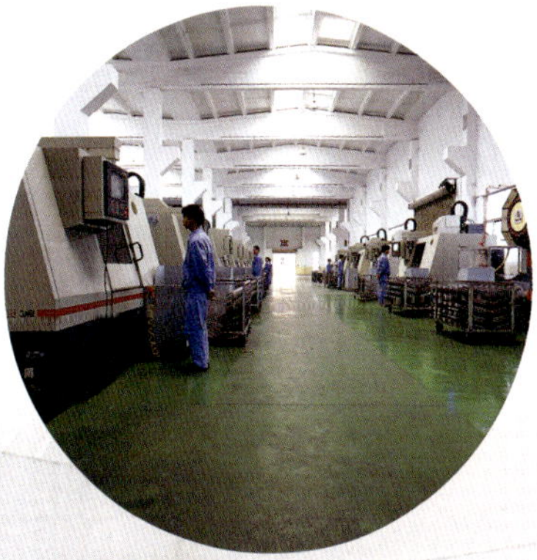

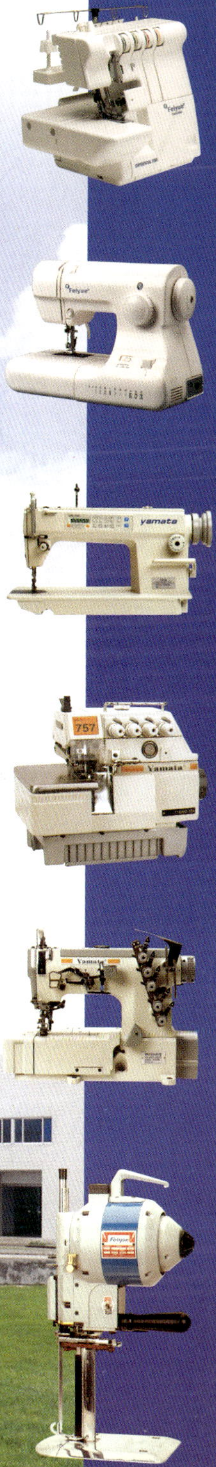

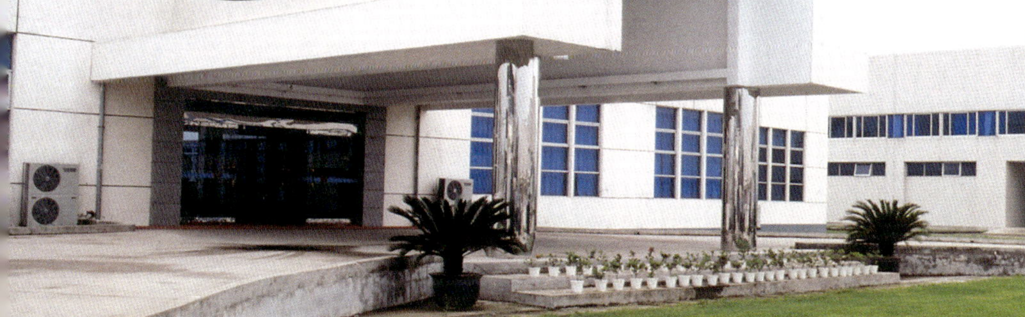

中国飞跃缝纫机集团公司
CHINA FEIYUE SEWING MACHINERY GROUP CORPORATION

地址：中国浙江省台州市椒江机场中路　Add: Middle Airport Rd.Taizhou City.Zhejiang Province. PRC.
电话 Tel: 0086-576-8155811 / 8155801 / 8155802 / 8155809　传真 Fax: 0086-576-8155800 / 8155815 / 8155813
电报 Cable: 7211 Taizhou Jiaojiang　E-mail: info@feiyue.com　http: //www.feiyue.com　邮编 Post Code: 318010

珠海國際貿易展覽（集團）有限公司

Zhuhai International Trade & Exhibition (Group) Ltd.

珠海国际贸易展览（集团）有限公司是国家外经贸部核准，并经广东省工商局注册，享有全国进出口报关权、各种专项产品的业务经营权和技术进出口权，具有举办国内外各类展览会经营权的多元化、综合性集团企业。公司主要开拓以欧美等地为主的远洋出口业务，高新技术推广和出口产品基地的建设，经营代理制报关业务、旅游、酒店及酒店管理、物业租赁管理及各种投资业务。

公司拥有珠海国际贸易展览中心、石景山旅游中心、商业广场以及香港、上海、杭州等境内外企业十多家。公司总资产超过10亿元人民币。

Zhuhai International Trade & Exhibition (Group) Ltd. is a comprehensive group enterprise, approved by the Ministry of Foreign Trade and Economic Cooperation of the People' s Republic of China, and registered in the Industrial & Commerce Administration Bureau of Guangdong Province, having the nationwide right to declare customs in import & export, engaging business in all kinds of special products and the import and export of technology, holding various exhibitions from home and abroad. The company mainly develops the export business overseas, spreads the new and high technology, constructs the bases of export products, acts as agency in customs declaration, undertakes tourism, hotel management, property renting and all sorts of investments.

The company owns Zhuhai International Trade & Exhibition Centre, Paradise Hill Hotel, Commerce Plaza and more than ten enterprises in HongKong, Shanghai, Hangzhou and abroad. The total investment is over 1000 million Renminbi yuanº.

公司以诚为本，信守合同，竭诚与社会各界共创美好未来。

We will abide by the contract with sincerity, and create the prosperous future with all circles of society.

法人代表：韦仰方
地址：广东省珠海市吉大景山路一号
电话：0756-3332656
传真：0756-3333440
邮编：519015

Legal Person: Wei Yangfang
Address: No. 1, Jingshan Road, Jida District, Zhuhai City, Guangdong Province
Tel:0756-3332656 Fax: 0756-3333440
Post code: 519015

目　　录

文　　献

第一部分

第二部分

专　　文

目录

法　　规

综　　合

对外贸易

利用外资

对外经济合作

目录

海关、税收

金融、外汇

检验、检疫

港口、运输

地 方 经 贸

国 别（地 区）经 贸

统　　计

对外贸易

利用外资

对外经济合作

大　事　记

目录

机　　构

附　　录

第一部分

第二部分

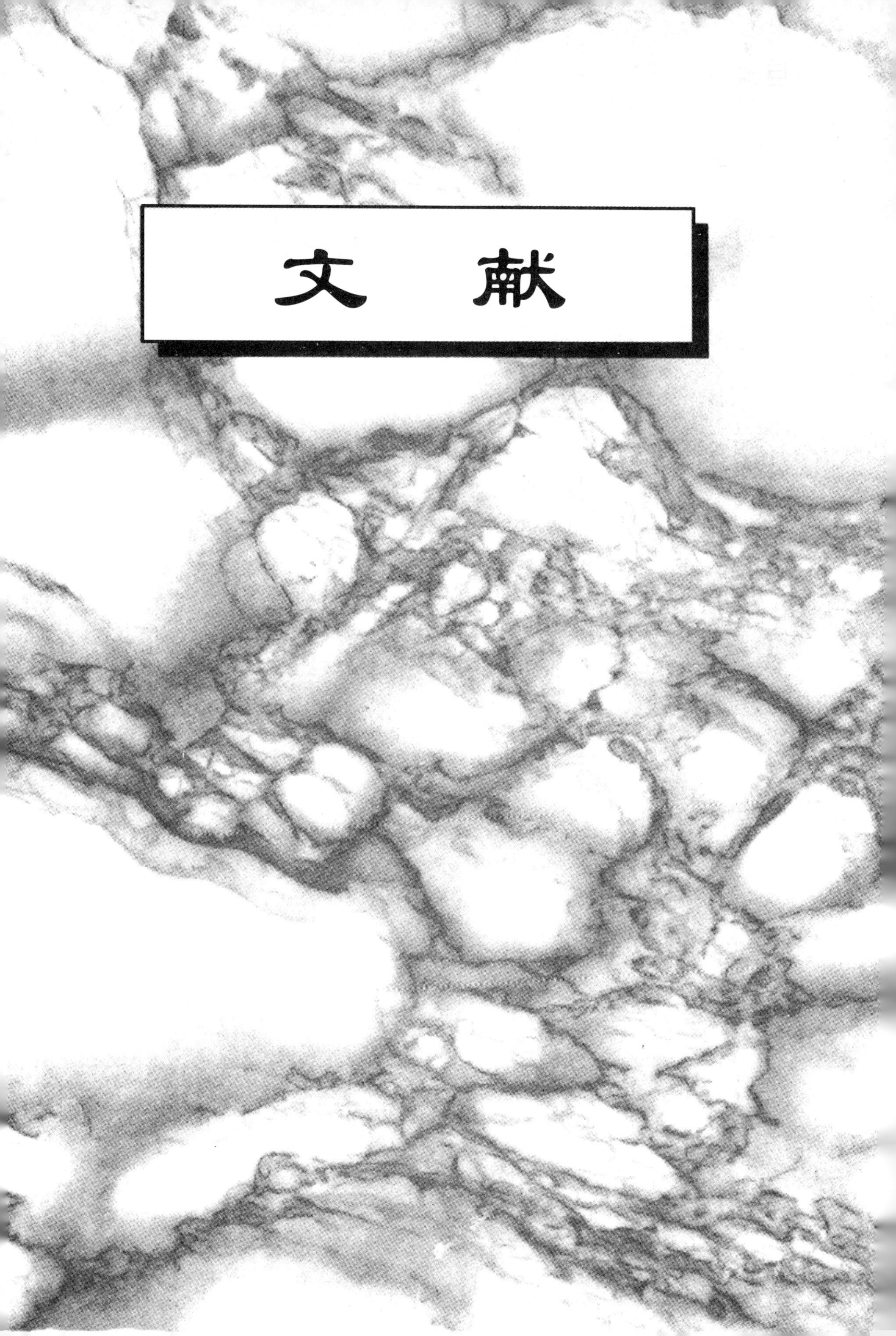

文献

第一部分

国家主席江泽民在亚太经合组织第六次领导人非正式会议上的讲话（节录）

1998 年 11 月 18 日　马来西亚　吉隆坡

在去年温哥华会议上，亚洲一些国家发生的金融危机引起亚太经合组织成员的广泛关注。时隔一年，危机的影响仍在加深，不仅给亚洲一此国家和地区造成严重的经济困难，而且波及整个世界经济。

这场金融危机是在经济全球化趋势加速发展的国际背景下发生的，给世人提供了重要的启示。

经济全球化趋势是当今世界经济和科技发展的产物，给世界各国带来发展的机遇，同时也带来严峻的挑战和风险，向各国特别是发展中国家提出了如何维护自己经济安全的新课题。

经济全球化趋势要求各国积极参与国际经济合作，但各国在扩大开放时应根据本国的具体条件，循序渐进，注重提高防范和抵御风险的能力。

经济全球化趋势使各国经济的相互依存、相互影响日益加深。一旦某些国家和地区发生经济危机，不仅发展中国家会深受其害，发达国家也难以置身其外。全球化的经济需要全球性的合作。国际社会的所有成员应本着责任与风险共担的精神，共同维护世界经济的稳定发展。

经济全球化趋势是在不公正、不合理的国际经济旧秩序没有根本改变的情况下发生和发展的，因而势必继续加大穷国与富国的发展差距。根本的出路在于努力推动建立公正合理的国际经济新秩序，以有利于各国共同发展。

当前，国际社会普遍关心如何尽快克服这场金融危机的影响，防止世界经济衰退。为了促进国际金融稳定发展和推动建立国际金融新秩序，我愿提出三点主张：

一、加强国际合作，制止危机蔓延，为受这场危机冲击的国家和地区恢复经济增长创造有利的外部环境。发达国家应采取负责任的态度，通过财政、货币政策，刺激经济增长，扩大内需，增加进口，不搞贸易保护主义。同时增加对受危机冲击国家的资金援助，并为减轻他们债务负担作出适当安排，帮助他们稳定金融，恢复经济。这既有利于这些国家渡过难关，也符合发达国家的自身利益。

二、改革和完善国际金融体制，确保国际金融市场安全有序运行。对国际金融具有影响的大国有责任采取有效措施，加强对国际金融资本流动的监管，遏制国际游资的过度投机，提高对金融风险的预测、防范和救助能力。应遵循平等互利原则，在国际社会广泛参与的基础上，通过发达国家和发展中国家的对话与协商，探讨建立符合各方利益的国际金融新秩序。我赞同由亚太经合组织财长会议对国际金融体制改革的有关问题进行研究并提出建议。

三、尊重有关国家和地区为克服这场危机自主作出的选择。发生金融危机和受其影响的国家和地区，经济发展水平和历史传统不同，危机引发的原因和造成的影响也不同。他们克服危机和恢复经济，没有也不可能有固定的模式和统一的药方，应支持他们根据自己的实际采取相应的措施。国际社会和国际组织应尊重有关国家的自主权，在平等协商的基础上，帮助他们尽快走出困境。发展中国家特别是发生金融危机和受其影响的国家与地区，应根据各自的情况对经济结构和经济政策进行必要调整，妥善处理经济发展中存在的突出问题，充分利用内部外部的有利条件增加经济发展活力。

这场金融危机给中国经济的发展也造成了不利影响和很大压力。中国政府采取了高度负责的态度。中国在国际货币基金组织安排的框架内，并通过双边渠道，向有关国家提供了援助。中国从保持经济持续增长和维护国际经济发展的大局出发，作出人民币不贬值的决策。为此，中国是付出了很大代价的。我们还战胜了今年夏天发生的特大洪涝灾害。我们正在深化改革、采取积极的财政政策，增加基础设施建设投入，扩大国内需求，努力实现今年经济社会发展的目标。

亚太经合组织作为本地区最重要的国际经济组织，要顺应新的形势，坚持通过经济合作缩小差距、实现共同繁荣的宗旨，及时调整合作重点，更好地满足占多数的发展中成员的需求。当前，坚持以尊重差别、自主自愿、协商一致为主要内容的“亚太经合组织方式”，比以往任何时候都更加重要。亚太经合组织应坚持通过这种方式为促进本地区的稳定和繁荣作出自己的贡献。

促进成员之间的经济技术合作，是亚太经合组织的一项重要任务，也是促进共同发展的基本途径。当今世界，科技进步日新月异，知识经济正在兴起，只有加大发展高新技术的力度，加快经济结构调整，才能促进各成员的经济长期稳定发展。我们高兴地看到，在东道主马来西亚的主持下，亚太经合组织今年制定了《走向 21 世纪的科技产业合作议程》和《技能开发行动计划》。这是各成员进一步加强经济技术合作的重大步骤。为表示对实施这两个文件的重视和支持，中国政府专门拨款 1000 万美元，设立“中国亚太经合组织科技产业合作基金”，用于资助中国同其他成员在科技产业等领域的合作，并提出了一系列合作项目的建议。为促进企业参与亚太经合组织活动，中国还成立了“亚太经合组织中国企业联席会议”。

促进贸易投资自由化，是亚太经合组织的另一项重要任务。在全体成员的共同努力下，这方面已取得积极的进展，还将继续前进。在当前形势下，应注重既积极又稳妥的方针，在自主自愿、灵活务实的基础上，允许各成员以适合自己情况的速度和方式，按照两个时间表，为实现贸易投资自由化的目标进行努力。

亚太地区一些国家和地区目前遇到的困难是暂时的。我认为，亚太地区的经济活力和发展潜力是巨大的。只要大家共同努力，加强合作，克服困难，亚太地区经济社会发展的前景是广阔的光明的！。

政府工作报告（节录）

国务院总理朱镕基1999年3月5日在第九届全国人民代表大会第二次会议上的报告

各位代表：

现在，我代表国务院，向大会作政府工作报告，请予审议，并请全国政协各位委员提出意见。

一、1998年工作回顾和1999年工作的总体要求

过去一年，面对复杂严峻的国内外经济环境，全国各族人民团结奋斗，克服重重困难，取得了改革开放和社会主义现代化建设的巨大成就。年初确定的改革和发展的各项目标基本实现。

国民经济保持较快增长。国内生产总值比上年增长7.8%，虽然略低于8%的预定目标，但这是在抵御亚洲金融危机的冲击和战胜国内特大洪涝灾害的情况下取得的，来之不易。为了应对亚洲金融危机的影响，我们年初就采取了增加投资、扩大内需的对策。但是亚洲金融危机发展的广度、深度和对我国的影响程度，比预料的更为严重。由于外贸出口增长速度大幅度回落和国内需求对经济拉动的力度不够，上半年经济增长速度出现减缓趋势。针对这种情况，中央果断决定实施积极的财政政策，经全国人大常委会批准调整预算后，国务院增发1000亿元财政债券，重点用于增加基础设施建设投资。下半年国有单位固定资产投资增长显著加快，全年增长19.5%，全社会固定资产投资增长14.1%。投资的较大幅度增加，对拉动经济增长发挥了明显作用。

去年长江、嫩江和松花江流域发生历史罕见的洪涝灾害，直接经济损失2000多亿元，许多工矿企业停产，长江部分航段中断航运1个多月，对生产建设和内外贸易造成很大影响。在党和政府的坚强领导下，广大军民团结奋战，特别是人民军队发挥了不可替代的关键作用，取得了抗洪斗争的伟大胜利，把灾害损失减到了最低限度。灾后恢复生产和重建家园的工作进展顺利。大灾之年，农业仍然获得了好收成。抗洪抢险斗争中焕发出来的伟大抗洪精神，成为推进我们事业发展的强大动力。

在周边许多国家货币大幅度贬值的情况下，我们权衡利弊，坚持人民币不贬值。同时，实行鼓励出口和吸引外资等多种政策，深入开展严厉打击走私和骗汇、逃汇、套汇的斗争，避免了对外贸易和利用外资出现大的波动，外汇储备有所增加。实践证明，保持人民币不贬值是完全正确的，这不仅有利于我国经济的稳定和发展，也对亚洲乃至世界金融和经济的稳定作出了积极贡献。

在经济发展的同时，改革继续推进。国有企业改革进一步深化。纺织、煤炭、石油和石

化、冶金等行业以及国防工业的调整和改组，取得新的进展。国务院向部分国有重点企业派出稽察特派员的试点工作，取得初步成效。国有企业下岗职工基本生活保障和再就业工作普遍加强，大多数下岗职工进入了再就业服务中心，并且领到了基本生活费，全年共有600多万下岗职工实现了再就业。企业离退休人员的养老金基本做到了按时足额发放。粮食流通体制改革稳步推进，国有粮食收储企业基本停止了新的亏损。金融体制改革和防范金融风险等工作迈出重要步伐。国务院机构改革进展顺利，实现了预定目标。国务院组成部门从40个减少到29个，部门内设机构精简1/4，移交给企业、社会中介机构和地方的职能200多项，人员编制总数减少一半，机关建设和工作作风出现了新的气象。中央关于军队、武警部队和政法机关不再从事经商活动，中央党政机关与所办经济实体和管理的直属企业脱钩的决策得到落实。中国人民解放军的建设和改革取得新成绩，裁军50万人的工作进展顺利。城镇住房制度改革、城镇职工医疗保险制度改革的方案正在实施。大多数城市建立了居民最低生活保障制度。各项改革的推进，对建立社会主义市场经济体制、促进经济和社会发展，发挥了积极作用。

科技教育和各项社会事业继续发展。国务院成立了国家科技教育领导小组，加强对科技教育工作的指导，中央财政较多地增加了对科教的投入。科技创新体系的建设取得新进展，关键性技术的攻关研究取得一批新成果，多项国家重大科学工程开始建设实施，基础研究得到加强。各级各类教育进一步发展。高等教育体制改革和结构调整的步伐加快。全国基本普及九年义务教育和基本扫除青壮年文盲的工作达到了年度目标，中等职业教育有了进一步发展。治理和保护环境工作的力度加大。重点地区生态工程建设和长江、黄河上游天然林保护工程全面展开。治理淮河、太湖污染初见成效。社会主义精神文明建设和民主法制建设得到加强。文学艺术、新闻出版、广播影视、社会科学、计划生育、卫生、体育等各项社会事业，取得新的成绩。各级政府依法行政的水平有所提高。农村基层民主建设加强。社会治安综合治理收到积极成效，维护了社会稳定。廉政建设和反腐败斗争取得新进展。

城乡人民生活水平继续提高。农村居民人均纯收入，考虑价格下降因素，比上年实际增长4.3%，城镇居民人均可支配收入实际增长5.8%。市场商品供应充足。经济适用住房的建设和销售有较大幅度增长。城市基础设施、环保设施建设加强。城乡人民的生活条件进一步改善。

过去的一年，我们能够取得这样大的成绩，主要是由于以江泽民同志为核心的党中央的坚强领导，及时果断地作出了一系列正确决策；二十年改革开放和经济发展，为战胜巨大困难创造了物质基础和体制条件；各地区、各部门认真贯彻中央的方针政策，全国各族人民齐心协力，奋发进取，发挥了高度的主动性和创造性。在此，我代表国务院，向奋斗在全国各条战线上的广大工人、农民、知识分子、干部、人民解放军、武警部队官兵和公安干警以及各界人士、表示崇高的敬意！向关心与支持祖国建设和统一的香港特别行政区同胞与澳门、台湾同胞和海外侨胞，表示衷心的感谢！

在肯定成绩的同时，我们清醒地看到，前进中还存在不少困难和问题。主要是：市场需求不旺，启动难度较大；多年重复建设造成大多数工业行业生产能力过剩，经济结构矛盾更加突出，经济运行质量和效益不高；部分国有企业经营困难加剧，多年积累的金融风险不容忽视；财经纪律松弛，经济秩序比较混乱；乱收费、乱集资、乱摊派、乱罚款屡禁不止，一些地方农民和企业不堪重负；部分群众生活仍然比较困难，社会就业压力较大，生态环境恶化的问题相当突出；某些消极腐败现象还比较严重，有些地方的社会治安状况不好。我们对这些问题十分重视，正在采取措施，逐步加以解决。

各位代表！1999年，我们将庆祝新中国成立五十周年，迎接澳门回归祖国，做好各项工作的意义十分重大。今年政府工作总的要求是：高举邓小平理论伟大旗帜，深入贯彻落实党的十五大和十五届三中全会精神，继续推进改革开放，大力实施科教兴国战略和可持续发展战略，把扩大国内需求作为促进经济增长的主要措施，稳定和加强农业，深化国有企业改革，调整经济结构，努力开拓城乡市场，千方百计扩大出口，防范和化解金融风险，整顿经济秩序，保持国民经济持续快速健康发展，切实加强民主法制建设和精神文明建设，促进社会全面进步，进一步处理好改革、发展、稳定的关系，确保社会政治稳定，以改革开放和社会主义现代化建设的优异成绩迎接新中国成立五十周年。

当前，世界金融市场和经济走势不确定的因素增加，国际竞争日益激烈，扩大出口的难度加大，国内也存在不少矛盾和隐忧。对此，我们必须保持清醒头脑，作好克服更大困难的准备。同时应该看到，有利条件也很多：去年以来采取的扩大内需等政策措施的效应正在进一步发挥，国内市场还有很大潜力；物资储备和外汇储备比较充裕；我们逐步积累了在新的形势下正确进行宏观调控和促进经济增长的经验和办法；我国政治、社会稳定，经济持续发展，改革逐步深化，为扩大对外开放提供了好的环境。我们要统一思想、坚定信心，抓住机遇、知难而进，团结一致、艰苦奋斗，争取把今年各个方面的工作做得更好。

二、继续扩大内需和实施积极的财政政策

综合分析国内外的有利条件和制约因素，今年的经济增长预期为7%左右。在优化结构、提高质量和效益的基础上，实现7%左右的增长速度并不容易，但是预计经过努力还是可以达到的。这个增长速度是指导性的，是就全国来说的，各地情况不同，有的增长速度可能高一点，有的也可能低一点。

实现今年经济较快增长，必须首先立足于扩大国内需求，继续实施积极的财政政策。去年的实践证明，这是在需求不旺的情况下拉动经济发展的有效举措。今年我们面临的外部经济环境仍然十分严峻，国内消费需求一时也难以有较大的增长。因此，继续由财政向商业银行发行长期国债，主要用于加强基础设施建设，同时采取多种办法，拓宽融资渠道，鼓励和引导集体、个体和社会其他方面增加投资，进一步扩大投资需求，势在必行。随着经济发展和税收的增加，财政债务可以得到偿还，财政赤字也可以逐步缩小。

在通常情况下，靠扩大财政赤字搞建设，势必会引发通货膨胀，这在我国历史上有过多次深刻的教训。但是，在当前的特定条件下，发生这种危险的可能性不大。现在银行储蓄存款比较多，通过财政债券将一部分储蓄转化为对基础设施的投资，不会过量发行货币；粮食等主要农产品、工业消费品和生产资料供应充裕，物价比较稳定，适度扩大财政赤字和国债规模，如果运用得当，不会引发通货膨胀。去年财政增发1000亿元国债加强基础设施建设，

银行也相应增加了贷款，但全年货币发行还比年初计划少了近500亿元；社会商品零售价格和消费价格的总水平都比上年下降。今年中央财政预算赤字1503亿元，比去年增加了，但发债规模并没有扩大。现在财政赤字和累计国债余额占当年国内生产总值的比重，还低于国际公认的警戒线，是可以承受的。

当然，靠扩大财政赤字搞建设也不是没有风险，问题在于能不能用好这笔钱。如果一哄而起，乱铺摊子，大搞重复建设和劣质工程，那就会给财政背上沉重包袱，迟早要引发严重的通货膨胀。党中央、国务院对这个问题非常重视，去年就明确提出，利用财政债券搞建设，一定要确保资金的合理投向，集中力量搞好农林水利、交通通信、城市公用设施和环境保护、城乡电网改造、粮食仓库等基础设施建设，并且优先安排在建项目。要注意向中西部地区倾斜，推动中西部地区经济发展。现有企业的技术改造要促进经济结构的调整，主要由银行信贷安排，财政债券也应给予必要支持，但决不能是单纯扩大生产能力，继续搞重复建设，而必须是符合市场需求、能够增加品种、提高质量和效益的项目。基础设施是我国的薄弱环节，总体上不存在重复建设问题，加强基础设施建设，不仅可以拉动当前经济增长，还可以增强经济发展的后劲。

进行基础设施建设，首先要全面规划，合理布局，选好项目，认真论证，决不能草率上马。上述这些领域的项目，有些可以通过收费偿还投资；有些虽然没有直接经济效益，但是社会效益显著，有利于整个经济发展，从而增强国家财政的综合偿还能力。其次，必须确保工程建设质量。最近暴露出来一些工程的严重质量事故，给国家造成重大损失，必须引起高度重视。不久前，国务院专门召开了全国性会议，部署加强工程质量管理的工作。工程建设是百年大计，必须坚持质量第一。要认真贯彻《建筑法》。所有项目都要严格执行建设程序，加强可行性研究，按规定的权限进行审批，精心勘察设计和施工，认真做好竣工验收工作；必须改革、整顿和规范建设市场，积极推行项目法人责任制、招标投标制、工程监理制和合同管理制，严禁层层转包和违法分包；要层层落实领导责任制，综合运用经济、法律、行政和舆论监督等手段严把工程质量关，对事故责任者和有关领导人必须严肃查处，直至追究刑事责任。第三，要严禁挤占、挪用财政债券资金，绝不允许把资金拿去弥补经常性开支或搞其他建设，甚至搞楼堂馆所。对重大项目要进行专项审计和跟踪审计。加大执法力度，依法严厉惩治建设领域的各种腐败行为。

实施积极的财政政策，决不是可以敞开口子花钱，而必须珍惜人民的血汗钱。要强化预算管理，努力增收节支。继续加强税收征管，堵塞漏洞，清缴欠税，做到依法治税、应收尽收。大力提倡艰苦奋斗、勤俭建国，反对铺张浪费，坚决压缩一切不必要的行政开支，保证重点支出。严格财经纪律，规范和加强预算外资金管理。要进一步完善财税体制改革，重点是全面清理和规范收费，逐步实行“费改税”。这是一项理顺分配关系、增强宏观调控能力和加强党风政风建设的重大举措，今年要以交通和车辆收费改革为突破口，积累经验，再逐步推开。

这里需要特别指出，实施积极的财政政策是特定条件下采取的特定政策。从中、长期来说，仍然要坚持财政收支基本平衡的原则，实行适度从紧的财政政策，严格控制并逐步缩小财政赤字。

在扩大投资需求的同时，要采取有力措施引导和扩大消费需求，形成投资和消费对经济增长的双重拉动。要通过多种渠道增加城乡居民特别是低收入群众的收入；加快发展消费信贷，推进城镇住房制度改革，支持居民购买住房和大件耐用消费品；积极引导居民增加文化、娱乐、体育健身和旅游等消费，拓宽服务性消费领域。活跃市场流通，大力开拓国内市场特别是农村市场，要从各地农村的实际出发，生产和供应适销对路商品，以满足广大农村居民生产和生活的需要。

三、促进农业和农村经济全面发展（略）

四、大力推进国有企业改革

中央前年提出，用三年左右的时间，通过改革、改组、改造和加强管理，使大多数国有大中型亏损企业摆脱困境，大多数国有大中型骨干企业初步建立现代企业制度。今年是实现这个目标的关键一年。国有企业改革的思路和方针政策已经明确。一批企业在市场竞争中发展壮大，一些企业已经或正在走出困境，在实践中积累了许多成功的经验。只要各方面共同努力，扎实工作，中央提出的国有企业改革和发展的目标就能够实现，对此我们充满信心。现在最重要的是，进一步统一思想，坚定不移地贯彻执行中央确定的方针政策。今年政府要突出抓好以下几项工作。

第一，制止重复建设，加快行业调整和改组的步伐。今年，除少数属于提高技术水平、产品升级又有市场的项目之外，各级政府要停止审批工业建设项目，银行也要停止向这类建设项目贷款。要继续压缩纺织、煤炭、冶金、石化、建材、机电、轻工等行业过剩的生产能力，坚决淘汰那些技术落后、浪费资源、产品质量低劣和污染严重的小企业；同时，要按照打破垄断、鼓励竞争的原则，通过联合、兼并、改组，形成技术水平高、有竞争能力的企业集团。这样坚持几年，就可以逐步形成优胜劣汰的机制，为企业发展创造良好的宏观环境和市场条件。

第二，继续做好国有企业下岗职工基本生活保障和再就业工作。这是深化企业改革的重要任务，也是保持社会稳定的重要措施。抓好这项工作，关键是要落实资金。坚持实行企业、社会、财政各负担三分之一的办法。企业、社会筹集不足的部分，财政要给予保证。中央企业由中央财政负担，地方企业由地方财政负担。今年各地财政一定要调整预算支出结构，优先、足额安排这项资金，财政确有困难的省、自治区，中央财政通过转移支付给以一定支持。特别要加强多种形式的职业培训，拓宽就业门路，引导职工转变择业观念，争取尽可能多的下岗职工实现再就业。下岗职工再就业以后，要与原企业解除劳动关系。三年以后还没有再就业的下岗职工，也要与原企业解除劳动关系，转到社会保险机构领取失业保险金；享受失业保险两年后仍未就业的，转到民政部门领取城镇居民最低生活费。这“三条保障线”，是目前条件下有中国特色社会保障制度的重要组成部分。

要完善养老保险制度，确保企业离退休人员养老保险金的按时足额发放，并尽快补发拖欠的养老金。要按照国际通行的做法，扩大养老保险覆盖面，国有企业、城镇集体企业、私营企业、外商投资企业都要参加养老保险。要努力提高收缴率。完善养老金省级统筹制度，加强养老金管理。

第三，推进政企分开，健全监管制度，整顿和加强企业领导班子。国务院各部门已经解除了与所属企业的行政隶属关系，不再直接管理企业，今年地方政府也要按照同样原则进行改革。同时，必须加强国家对企业的监管，保护所有者权益和国有资产安全。今年要继续做好向国有重点企业派出稽察特派员的工作。搞好国有企业，关键要加强企业领导班子建设。要坚持德才兼备原则，选拔政治素质高、经营管理能力强、公正廉洁的优秀人才担任企业领导。全心全意依靠工人阶级，发挥职工的民主监督作用，坚持职代会评议企业领导人的制度。加强对企业领导班子的考核，达不到标准的，限期整顿；对因经营管理不善而严重亏损的企业一把手，一年黄牌警告，两年予以撤换；对贪污受贿、腐败堕落者，依法惩办，决不手软；对企业效益好、社会贡献大的，要给予奖励。

搞好国有企业，还必须十分重视企业内部的改革和管理。要按照社会主义市场经济的要求，以市场为中心转换经营机制，实行科学决策制度，推行现代管理科学，严格内部劳动纪律，重点加强质量管理和财务、成本管理，建立全国统一的会计制度和现代企业管理制度。同时，要不拘一格，延揽人才，加强技术开发，努力开拓市场，全面提高企业的活力和竞争能力。

继续采取多种形式放开搞活国有小企业。不能把出售作为国有小企业改革的主要形式，需要出售的要按照国家规范的办法进行，坚决制止名卖实送、半卖半送和逃废银行债务及国家税款、规避安置职工的错误做法。要从信贷、技术、信息和培训等方面，扶持有市场前景的中小企业特别是科技型企业发展。

在推进国有企业改革的同时，大力发展多种形式的城乡集体经济，不断巩固公有制的主体地位。要采取积极的政策措施，鼓励、支持和引导个体经济、私营经济等非公有制经济的健康发展，充分发挥它们对满足居民多样化需要、增加就业、促进国民经济发展的重要作用。

五、认真做好金融工作，防范和化解金融风险

我国金融运行平稳，金融改革取得重要进展。在亚洲金融危机影响加深和世界金融市场动荡、我国经济生活中深层矛盾逐渐显现的情况下，进一步做好金融工作，对于改革、发展和稳定的全局，具有十分重要的意义。

要实行稳健的货币政策，适当增加货币供应量，把握好金融调控力度，保持人民币币值稳定。银行既要坚持商业信贷原则，保证贷款质量，防范金融风险；又要努力改进金融服务，拓宽服务领域，运用信贷杠杆，促进扩大内需和增加出口，积极支持经济增长。

深入贯彻落实1997年中央召开的全国金融工作会议的精神和部署，继续做好深化金融改革、整顿金融秩序、防范金融风险的工作。一是认真完善银行、证券、保险和信托业分业经营和管理的体制，实行金融监管责任制，切实加强对各类金融机构的监管。二是加快国有商业银行的改革，落实银行经营自主权，推进按经济区划和业务量设置分支机构的工作，撤

并机构，精简人员，强化内部控制。推行贷款质量五级分类办法，逐步建立金融资产管理公司，负责处理银行原有的不良信贷资产，对银行新增贷款质量实行严格的责任制。三是办好政策性银行，贯彻国家产业政策，提高资金使用效益。四是依法规范和维护金融秩序。清理、整顿非银行金融机构和地方性金融机构，化解金融机构的风险，保持金融稳定。促进其他商业银行和城乡信用社在改革中稳步发展。认真贯彻《证券法》，规范和发展证券市场。整顿和规范保险市场，促进保险业健康发展。严肃查处金融机构各种违规违纪行为，依法严惩金融犯罪活动。

六、千方百计扩大出口和有效利用外资

要继续贯彻对外开放的基本国策，努力开拓国际市场，力争对外贸易和利用外资有所增长。这对于实现今年经济的持续增长，保持国际收支平衡和人民币汇率稳定，至关重要。

千方百计扩大出口。积极实施以质取胜和市场多元化战略，综合运用出口信贷、退税等各种国际通行的政策手段，促进出口，增加收汇。以扩大机电产品、高附加值产品和优质名牌产品的出口为重点，调整出口结构，开拓新的市场。下大力气抓好一般贸易，完善和加强对加工贸易的管理。进一步扩大生产企业自营出口，调动企业增加出口的积极性。要从资金、技术、人才培训等方面，支持和鼓励有条件的企业到境外有市场潜力的地区发展加工贸易，带动国内商品出口。改进对外贸出口企业考核的内容和方法。外贸企业要知难而进，深化改革，改善管理，提高经济效益和竞争能力。增加必要的进口，改善贸易平衡，把进口与国内产业调整和升级、技术引进结合起来。要发展国际旅游，增加非贸易收汇。

充分发挥我国社会政治稳定、宏观经济形势良好的优势，尽可能多地吸引外资，特别是吸引著名跨国公司的投资，提高利用外资的质量。合理引导外资投向，优化利用外资的结构和地区布局。进一步改善外商投资环境，有步骤地放宽外商投资领域，依法健全对外商投资企业的管理。加强外债的全口径管理，控制规模，优化结构，加强监测预警，提高外债的偿还能力。继续办好经济特区和上海浦东新区。

继续保持人民币汇率稳定。加强外汇收支管理，保持国际收支平衡和外汇储备稳定。严格结售汇制度、禁止非法外汇交易，严厉打击各种骗汇、逃汇、套汇行为。强化缉私力量，深入持久地开展打击走私斗争。

（以下略）

以十五大精神为指针 认清形势　克服困难　增强责任感 全面完成各项外经贸任务

国务院国务委员　吴　仪

1998年2月8日

一、1997年对外经济贸易在我国国民经济中的作用进一步增强

1997年是极不平凡的一年。我国顺利实现了对香港恢复行使主权，标志着"一国两制"构想取得巨大成功；党的十五大胜利召开，对我国现代化建设的跨世纪发展做了规划；国民经济步入高增长、低通胀的发展轨道，形势很好。1997年也是外经贸工作取得较大成绩的一年，外经贸各项工作都完成得很好。

进出口贸易有了进一步发展。据海关统计，1997年全国外贸进出口总额3250.6亿美元，比上年增长12.1%，其中出口1827亿美元，增长20.9%；进口1423.6亿美元，增长2.5%。我国首次位居世界贸易排位的第十位。1997年对外贸易的主要特点是：出口快速增长，增长幅度连续12个月超过20%，进口回升平缓；一般贸易与加工贸易同步发展，一般贸易进出口额为1170亿美元，增长14.5%，占进出口总额的36%，加工贸易进出口额1698.1亿美元，增长15.8%，占进出口总额的52.2%；国有企业进出口增长速度超过外商投资企业，并继续居主导地位。国有企业进出口额为1636.6亿美元，增长12.7%，占进出口总额的50.4%，外商投资企业进出口额为1526.2亿美元，增长11.3%，占进出口总额的46.9%；初级产品进口增长迅速，出口商品结构进一步优化，工业制成品占出口总额的比重由上年的85.5%提高到86.9%；全国各地外贸出口蓬勃发展，增长幅度超过20%的省市区有16个，出口额居前10位的省市是广东、上海、江苏、山东、福建、浙江、北京、辽宁、天津、河北，这十个省市合计出口1621.9亿美元，占全国出口总额的88.8%；全年贸易顺差为403.4亿美元，国家外汇储备年底达到1399亿美元，国际支付能力和抗风险能力显著增强。

实际吸收外商直接投资保持增长。1997年全国新批外商投资企业21028家，合同外资金额518亿美元，分别比上年下降14.37%和29.36%；实际利用外资金额452.6亿美元，增长8.47%。截至1997年底，全国累计批准外商投资企业30.48万多家，合同外资金额5211.64亿美元，实际利用外资金额2218.71亿美元。1997年外商投资有几个特点：实际利用外资金额创历史最高记录，而合同金额下降幅度较大；外商独资企业首次在数量上超过中外合资企业数；新批外商投资企业中，中西部地区所占比重略有增加；香港仍是内地吸引外资最主要的来源地；外商投资企业进出口首次出现贸易结汇大于资本结汇。在争取外国政府

贷款和选择承贷项目、回收贷款等方面也取得了明显效果。

援外方式改革与援外工作稳步推进，援助效果较好。1997年，我国与14个国家签订了14笔政府贴息优惠贷款框架协议。截至1997年底，我国已同31个国家签订了38笔政府贴息优惠贷款框架协议。我部向中国进出口银行推荐项目50多个，其中23个项目已开始支款启动。援外改革取得实质性进展，无偿援助、援外合资合作及成套项目建设进展顺利，效果较好。我国对外援助的国家累计达114个，已建成援助项目1531个。援外工作有力地配合了外交工作和市场多元化战略的实施。

对外经济合作取得较大成绩。1997年，全国新签对外承包工程和劳务合作合同金额113.6亿美元，比上年增长10.5%；完成营业额83.8亿美元，增长8.9%。对外经济合作的规模和档次有所提高，大项目和总承包项目增多，设计咨询业务发展迅速。

实施市场多元化战略取得新的进展。1997年，在对亚洲、欧洲及北美洲等传统市场的出口继续保持较大增长的同时，对拉美、非洲及大洋洲的出口增长更快，增幅分别达47.7%、24.9%和22.1%。1997年开始，我们在非洲的埃及、科特迪瓦、马里、几内亚、喀麦隆、加蓬、坦桑尼亚、赞比亚、莫桑比克、尼日利亚设立投资开发贸易中心，目前已有8个开业运行，为企业在非洲开展贸易与投资提供一条龙服务。近期还将在印度、南美、俄罗斯设立投资开发贸易中心。这些中心的设立，将为企业开拓国际市场提供良好的服务。

外经贸体制改革有了重要进展。在企业改革方面，1997年，我们按照中央的部署，加大了国有外经贸企业改革的力度。一是遵照中央经济工作会议关于"要对企业领导班子进行考核，加强领导班子建设"的要求，全国各级外经贸主管机关对所属企业普遍进行了综合考核。我部在完成了对部直属企业领导班子的综合考核后，部党组将十五位不称职的总公司正副总经理降职或免职，突破了总公司总经理层领导干部能上不能下的陈规，实现了企业的司局级领导干部能上能下。二是加大企业兼合并力度，推动国有外经贸企业走规模经营的道路。各地在这方面都制订了规划和方案，采取切实措施予以推动，比如上海的工贸一体化大集团战略已初见成效，江苏、山东等地在这方面也做了积极探索。我部通过资产重组，实现了中技、中机、中仪和海经四个部直属总公司"强强联合"，组建中国通用技术（集团）控股有限责任公司，并准备用三年左右的时间，在实行一套全新机制的基础上，把这个控股公司建成跨行业、跨地区、跨所有制的、多元资产构成的大型股份制跨国企业集团。这套全新的机制集中体现在两个"两权分离"上，即所有权与经营权分离、决策权与执行权分离。三是按照"三改一加强"的方针，各地积极推进当地外经贸企业内部职工持股的试点工作和企业内部机制转换，使国有外经贸企业适应市场竞争的能力进一步增强。四是加强了对全行业国有企业改革的指导，修订与完整企业改革方面的政策与法规，组织和指导企业到邯钢实地学习改革与加强企业内部管理的经验，在山东诸城召开全国地县外贸企业改革与发展现场会，推动全行业的企业改革。

在外经贸宏观管理体制改革方面：完善出口配额分配管理办法，打破分配上的"终身制"，对出口企业使用配额的情况在动态核查的基础上，按出口实绩进行"奖高减低"的调整，提高了配额的使用率和出口效益。配合纺织行业解困，制定了相应的措施。进一步扩大实行出口配额有偿招标的商品范围，制定与完善了出口商品配额招标的有关政策规定，使招标工作进一步规范。深化对进出口经营权审批制的改革，逐步放宽审批标准，进一步调动各类企业参与外经贸活动的积极性。一是进一步放宽了国有生产企业和科研院所自营进出口的审批标准；二是将赋予商业物资企业进出口经营权的工作由试点阶段转入正常审批；三是颁布实施《经济特区生产企业自营进出口权自动登记暂行办法》，将经济特区内的生产企业通过依法登记自动获得进出口权的试点工作在五个经济特区全面展开；四是中外合资经营对外贸易的试点工作正式开始进行，首批4家中外合资外贸公司已经获得国家批准，并已开始经营外贸业务。目前，全国共有各类外经贸企业16万多家，其中外贸企业5300家、自营进出口生产企业7800家、科研院所295家、外经企业686家、外商投资企业14.5万多家。

多双边经贸关系继续发展。双边关系方面：1997年，中美经贸关系有重大进展。江主席成功地对美国进行了访问，与克林顿总统就中美两国建立面向21世纪的建设性战略伙伴关系达成共识，大大推动了两国关系的发展，也为发展两国经贸关系创造了条件。中日经贸关系发展较为顺利，双边贸易继续保持增长，日本企业对华投资、中日政府间资金合作情况良好。中欧经贸关系取得新的进展，欧盟将取消把我国作为“非市场经济国家”的认定。中俄确定了面向21世纪的战略协作伙伴关系，建立了一系列促进两国关系全面发展的机制，特别是两国总理定期会晤机制。我国与周边国家的经贸关系稳定发展。祖国内地与香港的经贸关系，在保证香港顺利回归和保持香港繁荣稳定方面发挥了重要作用。祖国大陆与台湾的经贸交流初步形成相互促进、互补互利的局面，促进了海峡两岸经济的共同发展。我国与东盟就建立面向21世纪的睦邻互信伙伴关系达成一致，与广大发展中国家特别是与非洲、南美的经贸合作也有较大发展。

多边关系方面：1997年，我国在加入世贸组织议定书的谈判上取得一定进展，已就外贸经营权、非歧视条款和司法审议条款与谈判各方达成一致。我国与新西兰就我国加入WTO的双边谈判率先结束，并与日本达成了货物贸易协议。与匈牙利、捷克、斯洛伐克、土耳其、新加坡等国家签署了双边市场准入协议。同时，我国还积极参与了亚太经合组织的贸易与投资自由化进程，大力推动成员间的经济技术合作；积极参与了亚欧会议的各项活动。

1997年对外经济贸易在我国现代化建设中的作用进一步增强，成为国民经济增长的重要动力。据国家统计局计算，仅我国外贸出口对国民经济增长的拉动幅度近两个百分点。外经贸工作之所以有如此大的进步，我们认为主要取决于以下几个方面的因素：

第一，中央政府实施的宏观政策使得我国经济成功地实现了“软着陆”，国民经济保持了高增长、低通胀的良好发展势头。良好的国内经济环境为出口企业降低成本、调整商品结构、提高经济效益、扩大出口规模提供了有利条件。

第二，与外贸出口密切相关的政策环境有所改善，对出口增长起到了非常重要的作用。一是企业资金紧张状况得到了明显改善，特别是1996年中央财政支付出口退税款828亿元，基本上解决了前几年严重困扰我国外贸出口发展的出口欠退税问题；中央银行连续两次调低货款利率，对外贸企业降低出口成本产生了显著效果。二是尽管人民币升值压力较大，但中央银行努力保持人民币汇率基本稳定，为扩大外贸出口创造了十分重要的外部条件。

第三，从中央和国务院领导到各部门、各级地方政府都高度重视外经贸工作，将对外经济贸易特别是外贸出口作为经济发展新的增长点来抓，不少地方政府采取返还企业所得税、建立外贸周转金、调整出口商品结构、鼓励企业兼并等各种措施，加大支持力度。

第四，国有外经贸企业加大改革力度，积极转变经营观念，进一步挖掘内部潜力，切实加强管理，适应市场经济体制和国内外市场变化的能力日渐增强，大多数外经贸企业已树立了以经济效益为中心、以市场为导向的经营指导思想。

第五，对外“大经贸”的格局进一步发展。各项外经贸工作和各种外经贸合作形式有机结合，贸、工、农、技、商、银等各部门密切配合，各类外经贸企业共同努力，有力地保证了外经贸事业的发展。1997 年有进出口经营权的生产企业出口 175.6 亿美元，比 1996 年增长 33.2%，占全国出口总值的 9.6%；外商投资企业出口 749 亿美元，增长 21.7%，占全国出口总值的 41%。

第六，外交工作活跃，我国的国际地位进一步提高，多双边经贸工作结合取得很大进展，为我国对外经济贸易的发展创造了良好的国际环境。

第七，1997 年世界经济及国际贸易发展势头较好，西方国家经济以较高速度增长，国际市场需求相对旺盛，为我国扩大外贸出口提供了重要的市场条件。

二、全面认识我国对外经济贸易工作所面临的形势

根据党的十五大精神和中央经济工作会议的要求，1998 年全国经济工作的总方针是“稳中求进”，外经贸工作也要贯彻这一方针。1998 年我国国内生产总值的增长幅度确定为 8%或更高一点，外贸进出口的宏观调控目标确定为 3450 亿美元，这是国务院根据国民经济与社会跨世纪发展规划的要求提出的；同时，要在利用外资、开展对外承包工程与劳务合作、发展各种形式的经济技术合作、扩大对外投资、改革援外工作等方面也有相应的发展。我们感到责任重大、任务艰巨，因为通过综合分析国内外形势，可以看到，1998 年我国对外经贸工作面临的形势是相当严峻的。

就一般而言，近几年相类似的困难因素从国际环境看主要有：我国尚未加入世贸组织，不能享受该组织多边协定的权利，使我国在国际竞争中处于明显不利地位；随着外贸出口的快速发展，我国在双边贸易中顺差增加，与贸易伙伴发生贸易摩擦的可能性增大；国际上贸易保护主义不时滋生，国外对我出口商品实施反倾销及其他各种限制增多；国际经济问题政治化的倾向继续存在，我国的对外经贸工作将不可避免地受到国外各种非经济因素的干扰，等等。从国内环境看，主要有：国有外经贸企业规模普遍偏小，一些企业的经营机制尚不能完全适应市场经济的要求，应变能力较差；出口商品结构不够优化，出口商品仍以劳动密集型产品为主，价值含量低，竞争力不强；退税单证繁多、手续繁琐，不利于退税机关和企业操作，影响了退税政策效应的发挥；外经贸经营秩序比较混乱；现行进口管理体制与社会主义市场经济体制的要求不相适应，未能形成进出口相互促进、协调发展的局面；外商对华直接投资的合同外资金额连续几年下降，影响今年我国利用外资的规模和发展速度；我国的利用外资政策和投资环境尚有一些不尽人意的地方。

我们讲 1998 年面临的形势相当严峻，主要是亚洲金融危机的影响。对这场危机对我国外经贸工作产生的不利影响，我们决不能低估。这场金融危机已经从亚洲波及到欧洲和拉

美，它波及的面还有多广、危害的程度还有多深、持续的时间还有多长，现在还很难做出结论，即使就目前的程度而言，对我国的外贸出口、吸引外商投资、开展对外承包工程与劳务合作等都会产生重大的不利影响。最近，我部了解到一些情况，亚洲金融危机对我国出口的影响已开始显现，很值得重视：1. 出口增长明显回落。据海关统计，1997 年第四季度，我国对东盟出口增幅逐月下降，由 9 月的 33.1%降至 12 月的 1.52%，对日本、韩国出口呈负增长，分别由 9 月的 2.24%和 39.07%降至 12 月的 －9.96%和 －6.47%，我国对上述地区出口总额比 9 月份减少 5.3 亿美元。同时，对北美、欧盟的出口增幅也分别由 25.47%和 29.34%下降至 4.35%和 4.37%，总额减少了 3.56 亿美元。2. 出口成交下降。1998 年以来，外贸公司普遍反映来自东南亚、韩国的订单大幅度减少。3. 部分已谈好的合同不签约。4. 出口竞争力减弱。如上海宝钢向韩国出口钢材，韩元汇率从 800 韩元兑 1 美元降至 1800 韩元兑 1 美元时，原 320 美元/吨的镍铬钢卷在韩国市场上只售 160 美元/吨，使宝钢的产品无法进入韩国市场。5. 由于有的商品出口受阻，已对国内生产产生不利影响。如东南亚是国际上水泥的主销市场之一，也是我国水泥的主要出口市场。由于金融危机影响，国际市场的水泥价格已下跌 20%以上，相形之下，我国出口水泥失去价格竞争力，原有的市场份额受到极大威胁。

就对我国外经贸整体工作而言，亚洲金融危机可能带来如下一些不利影响：

出口方面主要有：1. 受这次金融危机危害最大的东盟、韩国和日本都是我国重要的贸易伙伴。1997 年我国商品对这些国家和地区出口 529.7 亿美元，占当年我国出口总额的 29%；其中对日本出口 318.2 亿美元，对东盟出口 120.3 亿美元，对韩国出口 91.2 亿美元，分别占当年我国出口总额的 17.4%、6.6%、5%。金融危机使得这些国家和地区的经济增长速度放慢、国际收支能力下降、进口需求减少，我国对这些国家和地区的出口将直接受到影响。2. 我国与东南亚国家出口商品结构接近，都以劳动密集型产品为主，主要出口市场也都集中在美、欧、日、香港等国家和地区。这场金融危机已导致东南亚及我国周边一些国家和地区的货币纷纷贬值，造成人民币相对升值，削弱了我国出口商品的竞争能力，增加了我们扩大出口的难度。

利用外资方面主要有：1. 港台、日、韩和东南亚地区是我国吸收外商直接投资的主要来源地。金融危机使得这些国家和地区的投资者实力下降，影响其对我国内地的投资。2. 从长期看，金融危机会使东南亚国家在吸收外资方面制定更为优惠的政策，从而与我国形成更加激烈的竞争。

对外工程承包与劳务合作方面主要是：东南亚地区与韩国占我国对外工程承包与劳务合作业务量的 65%。金融危机发生后，这些国家取消了上百亿美元的工程承包计划项目。我国企业在该地区承揽的承包工程项目有的合同被取消，在建工程由于当地货币贬值而效益大大降低，有的已难以进行下去。

由此可见，金融危机对我国外经贸的影响是方方面面的，但同时也可能带来某些机遇。在这次金融风波中，我国所受的影响相对较小，宏观经济保持稳定，而金融危机使得亚洲地区的投资风险加大，欧美一些跨国公司可能看好我国投资环境的比较优势，将投资转向我国；金融危机使得东南亚和东亚国家市场萎缩、购买力下降，可能使欧美对我国市场的依赖程度加大；东南亚国家有可能进一步扩大开放市场，我们可以藉此寻找经贸合作的机会，同时东南亚国家由于资金困难，不得不削减从西方进口高档产品转而寻找低价代用品，这就为我国产品出口提供了机遇；金融危机使得东南亚国家货币贬值、资产价格下跌，给我们介入东南亚的资源开发创造机会，也可能给我国企业开拓当地市场带来机会等。

做好1998年的外经贸工作也存在不少有利条件。从国内看主要有：党的十五大将邓小平理论确立为党的指导思想，对我国经济与社会的跨世纪发展做了规划，并确定了一系列改革与发展的方略；中央经济工作会议对今年的经济工作制定了正确的方针和措施；我国经济实现“软着陆”以来，保持了高增长、低通胀的良好发展势头，工农业生产持续发展，为各类外贸企业扩大出口提供了重要的经济条件和物质基础；从中央到各级地方政府高度重视对外经济贸易工作，都在采取各种措施给予支持；外经贸企业适应市场经济体制和国内外市场变化的能力日渐增强；我国现代化建设蓬勃发展，市场机会巨大，对外商有很大的吸引力。从国际环境看，1998年的国际政治格局将继续向多极化方向发展，国际局势继续趋向缓和，和平的国际环境和稳定友好的周边环境有可能得以保持；世界经济增长速度虽放缓，但仍会保持一定幅度的增长；世界经济一体化不断发展，有利于国际间经贸合作的开展；世界产业结构加速调整，发达国家和新兴工业国家的传统产业加快向发展中国家转移，国际资本向经济发展较快、社会保持稳定的发展中国家和地区的投入增加。

全面认识我们所面临的形势，是为了更好地去面对困难，充分利用有利条件，千方百计去战胜困难。所有从事对外经济贸易工作的同志都应认识到，我们正处在一个十分特殊的时期。这个时期的特殊任务就是要应对亚洲金融危机所带来的挑战。对这场挑战我们应对得好不好，不仅关系到我国外经贸事业的发展，而且关系到我国经济能否保持持续快速健康发展。

对外经济贸易工作在国民经济中发挥着越来越重要的作用。我国的外贸出口总值目前大体相当于国内生产总值的20%，整个对外经贸工作对拉动经济增长、增加就业、保持国际收支平衡，都具有重要作用。我们所从事的这项事业既是十分光荣的，我们肩上的担子也是很重的。在目前这个时期，我们尤其要发扬爱国主义精神，以保持国民经济持续快速健康发展为己任，奋发图强，自力更生，艰苦奋斗，埋头苦干，不当伸手派，不等不靠不要，挖掘企业内部潜力，适时地抓住机遇，大胆地迎接挑战，千方百计使今年的对外经济贸易继续保持增长。我相信，经过1998年的奋战和考验，我国的外经贸企业一定会变得更加成熟，一定会在市场经济的大潮中不断发展、壮大。

三、调动一切积极因素，克服困难，千方百计把今年的外贸出口搞上去，全面完成各项外经贸任务

在1998年外经贸工作面临严重困难的形势下，我们以什么样的态度面对困难、迎接挑战？部党组提出，今年外经贸工作的指导思想是：以邓小平理论和党的十五大精神为指针，以改革为动力，认清形势，发扬爱国主义精神，增强责任感，调动一切积极因素，努力克服困难，全面完成外经贸工作任务。根据这个指导思想，我们要努力抓好以下工作：

（一）大力发展外贸出口，适当增加进口，努力保持外贸进出口的稳定增长

在讲求经济效益的前提下扩大出口，是我们发展出口的基本原则。1998 年要在处理好规模与效益关系的基础上，大力发展外贸出口，保持出口的稳定增长，同时适当增加进口，逐步减少贸易顺差。

要采取切实有效的政策措施，积极开拓国际市场，大力发展外贸出口。第一，各类外经贸企业要大力挖掘内部潜力，千方百计降低成本，压缩库存，加快资金周转，提高资金利用率，努力增强自身的竞争能力。第二，加快优化出口商品结构。制定鼓励政策，在保持一般商品出口增长的同时，积极鼓励和发展一批技术含量高、附加值高的商品出口。要从商品选择、技术分析、政策制定的角度加以研究。第三，采取多种形式，努力扩大出口。一般商品贸易是外贸出口的主要形式，同时也要利用好加工贸易这种形式。在我国目前的发展阶段，这种形式在解决社会就业、发挥我国劳动力多和劳动成本相对低的优势、促进出口方面具有重要作用。还要根据地域条件开展边贸和易货对销贸易。第四，制定一系列见效快的鼓励出口的措施，加强银贸结合、税贸结合，完善出口退税制度，简化退税手续，加快退税进度。鼓励所有的外经贸企业扩大出口，特别要抓好大型外贸企业和大型自营进出口工业企业的出口工作。第五，把对外援助、对外经济技术合作、对外投资与外贸出口有机结合起来，促进出口。第六，继续保持和深度开发美、日、欧盟等传统市场，同时大力开拓新市场。美、日、欧盟的经济规模都很大，市场容量也很大，尽管我国与它们的双边贸易均已达到相当的规模，但仍有很大潜力可挖，只要增长一个百分点，绝对量就相当可观。要深入搞好市场调研，深度开发这些市场，同时发扬艰苦奋斗精神，大力开拓非洲、拉美、独联体等市场。

这里，我还要特别强调一下，面对亚洲金融危机，各类出口企业要十分注意收汇风险的问题。这场金融危机使得很多国家和地区的银行呆帐严重、国际信誉降低，导致其他地区的银行不再向其委托结算业务，拒绝保兑其所开的信用证。我国企业向这些地区出口一定要慎重操作，采取更为稳妥的交易与结算方式，避免损失。

在努力扩大出口的同时，还要结合国内产业结构、出口商品的结构调整和国内技术进步，采取有效措施适当增加进口。各地要注意，适当扩大进口，不等于盲目进口。在增加进口的同时，要坚决打击假进口、真逃汇的行为。

（二）全面贯彻全国外资工作会议精神，积极合理有效地利用外资

党中央、国务院对利用外资工作十分重视，专门成立了由李岚清副总理兼任组长的国务院利用外资工作领导小组。在 1997 年 12 月召开的全国外资工作会议上，中央领导同志都充分肯定了利用外资对国民经济发展的积极作用，并对今后外资工作提出了更高的要求。全国外资工作会议对今后利用外资工作做了全面部署，提出了明确的工作思路和政策取向。全面利用外资工作领导小组办公室和各有关部门要抓紧工作，把政策取向逐条具体化为可以操作的政策措施，抓住机遇，加快行动，抓紧实施，努力扭转外商直接投资合同额连续几年滑坡的局面，保持和扩大吸收外商投资的规模。

首先要办好现有的外商投资企业。克服“重办轻管”的做法，依法保护外商投资企业的权益，同时也要坚持联合年检制度，监督外商投资企业依法经营，并保护中方投资者和员工的合法权益。

进一步改善投资环境。在继续完善基础设施等“硬环境”的同时，注重改善投资的“软环境”。把治理“三乱”（乱收费、乱摊派、乱罚款）作为当前一项重要工作来抓。涉外管理和服务的政策与制度要公开、透明、让外商中心有数。同时维护好社会治安环境，严打严禁黄、赌、毒。

结合我国发展战略，调整利用外资的结构。加大吸引欧美跨国公司来华投资的力度。积极引导外资投向高新技术产业、基础产业和基础设施建设，鼓励外商兴办产品出口型项目和参与农业的产业化经营，严禁上污染环境、破坏生态平衡的项目。鼓励外商投资更多地进入中西部地区，促进中西部地区的开发开放。

有步骤地推进服务业的对外开放。搞好内贸、外贸、旅游等服务业的对外开放试点，抓紧研究扩大建筑业和会计、法律等服务领域的对外开放，审慎、稳妥地从事金融业的对外开放。

做好利用外国政府贷款的工作。进一步完善借、用、还机制，加大清欠力度，落实偿债措施。在贷款的使用上要体现行业和地区倾斜政策，支持中西部的开发开放。

（三）继续深化外经贸管理体制改革

1. 加快审批企业的对外经营权。为了支持国有大型生产企业的改革和发展，我们准备在原有对5个经济特区生产企业自营进出口试行自动登记制的基础上，扩大自动登记的试行范围，首先扩大到国家重点联系的1000家国有大型企业中的生产企业，以进一步取得这方面的经验。同时，根据十五大精神，抓紧研究和进行混合所有制企业经营外经贸业务的试点。随着改革的深化，相当一些小型国有外经贸企业在放开搞活的过程中所有制性质会发生变化，对这些企业的对外经营权的转移要制定明确的政策。

2. 在出口配额与许可证管理改革方面，要有突破性进展。虽然我们对部分出口商品配额的分配采取了招标的方式，但仍不适应市场经济的新形势，必须继续进行改革。出口配额与许可证管理要适应社会主义市场经济发展的要求。只要有利于扩大出口、对国家经济发展又没有大影响的商品、大部分都应放开经营。经营秩序的问题，通过加强行政执法和发挥中介机构的作用来解决。今年要遵照国务院关于以纺织行业为解困重点的部署，为纺织行业实现解困目标排扰解难。

3. 加大进口管理体制改革力度。进一步放宽进口，减少进口配额、许可证管理的范围，简化审批手续，实行进出口结合。今后国家对进口的调控应主要通过市场导向、关税和技术标准等手段来实现。

4. 强化中介机构的作用，特别要加大进出口商会的改革力度，发挥商会协调与服务的功能。现有商会的设置及其工作方式还不能完全适应市场经济的需要，必须进行改革。要在研究和借鉴其他国家商会成功做法的基础上，根据我国的实际情况制定改革方案，逐步稳妥地实施。

5. 加强对原产地证签发工作的管理。针对原产地证的签发工作比较混乱，随意发证、降低标准发证的情况时有发生的问题，组织有关商会对发证情况进行全面调查，摸清情况，参照国际通行做法，制定改进措施。

（四）加快国有外经贸企业改革步伐

加快国有企业改革，是党的十五大和中央经济工作会议确定的今年经济工作的重点，也是我国社会主义市场经济体制能否成功建立的关键环节。搞好国有外经贸企业改革，关键是抓好“三改一加强”方针的落实。

第一，要“抓大放小”。在全国范围选择一批具有相当经营规模的大中型国有外经贸企业，利用现有政策对它们实施重点支持、重点改革，打一场改革的攻坚战，力争用三年左右的时间，使这些企业达到十五大报告中所要求的“初步建立现代企业制度”经营状况明显改善”的目标，使它们充分发挥在我国对外经济贸易中的主导作用。特别是国有大中型国际经济技术合作企业，不能再靠政府扶持过日子，不能再当“皮包公司”，要坚持实业化的方向，增强实力。同时，按十五大精神，对小型国有外经贸企业采取改组、联合、兼并、租赁、承包经营和股份合作制、出售等形式，加快放开搞活。

第二，充分利用好国家关于国有大中型企业的兼并政策，通过联合与兼并，加快培育外经贸行业的“旗舰”和“航空母舰”，增强国际竞争能力。企业兼合并要有利于外经贸业务的发展，要坚持贸、工、农、技相结合。

第三，继续抓好外经贸企业股份制试点工作。推动国有外经贸企业实行内部职工持股，完善相关政策，争取在今年取得新的进展；积极支持国有外经贸企业组织优质资产上市，广泛吸收社会资金，以较少的国有资产调动和控制较多的社会资本；引导已上市的公司通过资本经营进行扩张、壮大实力。

第四，加强国有外经贸企业的内部管理。重点是加强财务管理，核心是资金管理。通过盘活、挖潜，加速资金周转，使有效的资金发挥最大的效益。强化投资管理，严格做好投入前的可行性分析，坚持集体审批制度，避免投资决策失误。厉行节约，反对铺张浪费，反对大手大脚，减掉一切不必要的开支，提倡过紧日子。1996 年我们曾提出“三挖潜、四清理”，1998 年我们在此基础上强调“双降”，就是降低成本、降低费用，目的是在金融危机影响的条件下，进一步增强我国出口商品的竞争能力。

第五，进一步整顿海外企业。海外企业从 1979 年开始发展，资产规模越来越大。海外企业搞不好，不仅会造成国有资产流失，从最近有的国家发生金融危机的情况看，还会给国民经济埋下隐患。国务院领导同志对此已有多次批示，加强海外企业管理迫在眉睫。外经贸部今年准备召开会议进行专题研究和部署。各地不要等，要“从我做起，从现在做起”，管好本地的海外企业，各派出单位更要管好自己的海外企业。

（五）进一步深化援外方式改革，大力开展对外承包工程与劳务合作

1995 年以来，按照国务院《关于援外工作改革的批复》精神，我们对援外工作进行了改革和调整，大力推行政府贴息优惠贷款的援助方式和开展我国企业与受援国企业进行合资合作。经过三年多的工作，新的援外方式逐步为受援国所接受，援外改革取得了可喜的进展。1998 年要大力抓好政府贴息优惠贷款框架协议项下已确定项目的落实，并切实保证援外工程及设备、物资的质量，同时认真总结经验，针对工作中遇到的困难和问题，采取措施深化和加快援外方式改革。

援外采取何种具体方式，要根据受援国的具体情况确定。对援外项目招标工作也要进行改革，招标和选择企业不仅面向国际经济技术合作公司，也要面向有实力、有经验的大中型生产企业、建筑单位和科研院所。

对外承包工程与劳务合作要在受到金融危机影响的情况下，认真总结经验教训，采取切实措施规避汇率风险，下大决心加强管理、整顿秩序，在维护和巩固老市场的同时，努力开拓新市场。不仅开拓发展中国家市场，也要下功夫开拓发达国家市场，在这方面我们是有相对优势的。

当今世界，经济全球化加速发展。货物、资金、技术、劳务等各种经济要素的流动相互融合、相互渗透。在这种情况下，开拓任何一个市场，在具体运作方式上都不能“单打一”，需要树立对外“大经贸”的观念，从战略的高度出发，把对外援助和对外投资、工程承包、劳务合作等各种经贸合作方式有机结合起来，形成相互带动、相互促进的局面。

（六）发展对外投资，努力开拓国际市场和利用国外资源

进行社会主义现代化建设，必须充分利用国内、国际两个市场和两种资源。对外经济贸易工作主要是通过开拓国际市场和开发、利用国外资源来为国内现代化建设服务。发展对外投资，是开拓国际市场、开发国外资源的重要措施。我们要认真落实江总书记在十五大报告中提出的“鼓励能够发挥我国比较优势的对外投资”，做好对外投资的工作。

国家有必要制定一些鼓励措施，推动有条件的企业发展对外投资。结合国内产业结构调整，积极引导和推动我国具有比较优势的加工工业向境外转移，在当地开展有资源、又有市场需求的商品的生产、加工与装配，并进入当地的销售系统，开拓在该国乃至周边国家的市场，开辟新的经济增长点。

鼓励有条件的国内企业（包括中外合资企业）到国外开发和利用国外的石油、天然气、木材和其他重要资源，有的可以在当地进行初加工或深加工，带动我国的设备和劳务出口，并开展第三国贸易。对外投资还必须有统一的规划。在国家的统筹安排下，协调划分好投资开发区域，避免一哄而上、自相竞争。要鼓励有经济实力、有专业技术力量的企业到境外投资办厂；在充分论证、确有把握的基础上投资，避免投资的盲目性；发挥驻外使馆经济商务参赞处的作用，做好我国企业在驻在国投资的指导与协调工作。

（七）抓住有利时机，进一步发展多双边经贸关系，创造良好的国际环境

在1998年面临严重困难的情况下，加强多双边经贸工作，创造更好的外部环境和更大的空间，对我国外经贸事业的持续发展具有至关重要的意义。

按照中央确定的方针，积极推进加入WTO的谈判进程，争取尽早加入WTO，享受我国应有的权益；采取主动行动，积极参与亚太经合组织贸易与投资自由化进程，大力推进成员间的经济技术合作，争取发挥我国在其中的主导作用。

做好以美国、欧盟、日本为重点的发达国家的工作，处理好与他们的贸易摩擦，避免矛盾升温。抓住我国与这些国家的双边关系全面发展的有利时机，积极从这些国家引进先进技术与设备，逐步减少我方贸易顺差，同时以进带出，努力扩大对这些国家的出口。

大力发展同亚非拉广大发展中国家的双边关系，特别是做好开拓非洲和拉美市场、开发和利用非洲和拉美资源的工作。做好对台港澳地区的经贸工作，及时研究和处理好在新形势下出现的新问题，保持香港的繁荣稳定，保证澳门顺利回归，促进海峡两岸的经济交往。

（八）加强法制建设，加大执法力度

以《对外贸易法》为基础，继续完善和实施涉外经济贸易的法律法规。抓紧制订货物进口管理条例、对外承包工程和劳务合作管理条例和技术进口、技术出口管理条例等，适时修订现行利用外资的几个基本法律和出口配额管理办法等，进一步完善外经贸法律体系。

抓紧实施《反倾销法》，推动《反垄断法》尽快出台，为内外资企业开展平等竞争创造良好条件。

做好保护知识产权的工作，既保障国外技术转让者的利益，也保障我们依法取得国外先进适用技术的权利。

认真实施《外经贸系统“三五”普法规划》，增强广大干部职工的法制观念和法律意识，推动外经贸领域的法治化进程。

（九）加快“金关工程”建设，普及网络知识，尽快提高外经贸工作的信息化程度

目前，全国“金关工程”进展顺利，中国国际电子商务网已经开始运营，并初步建立了进出口统计、配额出口许可证管理、结售汇等系统，使外经贸管理的电子化程度有所提高。国际电子商务网的建立与运营，标志着我国对外经济贸易向信息化方向迈出了重要的一步。

1998年要按照“强化宣传、加快应用、完善网络、协调发展”的原则，重点抓好普及应用工作。各级外经贸管理机关要充分利用这个网络，加快实现政府管理与服务工作的标准化、科学化。各类进出口企业要积极入网，利用现代化手段，及时了解政府的政策和市场信息，接受宏观指导。各地要树立大局意识，齐心协力搞好这张网，不要再搞另外的网。要把这个网络逐步建成一个信息网、管理网、服务网，逐步提高对外经济贸易的无纸化程度，降低交易成本，提高工作效率。

（十）深入学习，更新知识，努力提高政治思想水平和驾驭现代化建设的能力

随着社会主义市场经济体制的建立，政府部门对经济运行的管理正在从直接控制型向间接控制型转变，各级外经贸主管部门的职能也在向宏观管理和宏观指导转变，这就要求我们必须提高宏观管理的水平和驾驭全局的能力。提高宏观管理水平和驾驭全局的能力，需要以较高的理论水平为基础。只有掌握了理论，才能站得高、看得远。因此，加强学习，是形势发展对各级外经贸土管部门和每一个下部提出的要求。

毛主席、邓小平等老一辈无产阶级革命家一贯重视学习，提倡实事求是，理论联系实际。江总书记强调要“讲学习、讲政治、讲正气”，号召我们要学习、学习、再学习。在改革开放飞速发展的情况下，不加强学习，“以己昏昏，使人昭昭”是不行的。为努力提高政治思想水平和驾驭现代化建设的能力，外经贸部党组已做出决定，把1998年确定为外经贸部机关的学习年。在此，我们也希望各级外经贸主管部门和各类外经贸企业组织广大干部职工加强学习，掀起一个“讲学习、讲政治、讲正气”的热潮。

加强学习，最重要的是学好十五大文件。党的十五大是我们党在世纪之交召开的一次具有划时代意义的重要会议。江总书记在会上的报告高举邓小平理论的伟大旗帜，对我国社会主义初级阶段的特征和党在社会主义初级阶段的基本路线与基本纲领做了深刻的阐述，明确了一系列带有突破性的重大理论问题。可以预见，我国的经济体制以及社会各个方面将随之而发生广泛而深刻的变化。我们只有深刻领会、准确把握十五大精神，用十五大精神指导我们的工作，用邓小平理论武装广大干部职工特别是各级领导干部的头脑，才能在改革的实践中出思路，在发展的进程中找到动力，做好新形势下的外经贸工作。

1998年任务重、困难大，企业改革将在改制、改组、改造和下岗分流、减员增效方面迈出更大的步伐，各级政府机构改革也要实行带职交流、定向培训、充实重点、调整结构，这会触及很多干部和职工的切身利益。在这种情况下，要发挥党组织的战斗堡垒作用，加强思想政治工作，引导大家以改革的精神和积极的态度支持改革，顾全大局，服从国家和企业整体利益的需要。同时，各级外经贸主管部门和企业也要对下岗分流作出精心的安排，做到“无情下岗、有情操作”，保证改革顺利进行。在机构改革的新形势下，要加大反腐败的力度。对可能出现的走后门送礼跑官要官、以隐蔽的手段转移和私吞国有资产等现象，要提高警惕，严加惩戒。

1998年是“九五”计划的第三年。做好1998年的外经贸工作，对于巩固前两年的经济与社会发展成果，保证“九五”计划目标顺利实现，对于贯彻党的十五大精神，把建设有中国特色社会主义事业全面推向21世纪，具有非常重要的意义。让我们在以江泽民同志为核心的党中央的领导下，以十五大精神为指针，按照中央经济工作会议的部署，增强历史使命感和工作责任感，开拓进取，为全面完成1998年各项外经贸工作任务而努力奋斗！

（本文系1998年2月8日对外贸易经济合作部吴仪部长〈现任国务院国务委员〉在全国对外经济贸易工作会议上的报告）

对外开放20年

对外贸易经济合作部部长　石广生

1978年召开的党的十一届三中全会，是我国社会主义发展历程的伟大转折点，从此，我国社会主义现代化建设进入了改革开放的新时期。改革开放20年来，我国经济与社会发生了巨大变化，综合国力大大增强，人民生活大大改善，国际地位大大提高，成就举世瞩目。20年的实践告诉我们，坚定不移地实行对外开放，是加快我国现代化进程的强国之路，是我国的一项长期基本国策。

一、我国对外经济贸易的发展进程和状况

对外经济贸易是我国对外开放的重要内容。70年代以来，世界科技、经济全球化趋势日益明显，新的形势使得任何国家要发展经济，都必须实行对外开放，积极参与并利用国际分工，建立国际间长期稳定的经济关系，大力发展同外国的经济技术交流。具体地讲，就是开展进出口贸易、利用外资和对外投资、国际经济技术合作和对外援助等各项对外经济贸易活动，最大限度地参与货物、资本、技术、劳务、信息等经济资源在国际间的流动，以有效地利用国际市场和国外资源，促进本国经济发展。

（一）1978年以前我国的对外经济贸易

我国政府和人民一贯主张在平等互利的基础上积极发展同世界各国的贸易和经济技术合作。早在新中国成立之初，以毛主席为首的第一代中央领导集体就代表中国人民表达了愿意同世界各国开展贸易往来和经济技术合作的良好愿望。毛主席提出：中国人民愿意同世界各国人民实行友好合作，恢复和发展国际间的通商事业，以利发展生产和繁荣经济。但由于历史条件的局限，1978年以前我国的对外经济贸易基本上仅包括对外贸易和对外援助。

1. 对外贸易的发展历程

新中国的对外贸易，是在解放区已经开展的对外贸易的基础上，经过摧毁帝国主义在华特权和没收官僚资本，并对民族资本外贸行业进行社会主义改造而逐步建立起来的。

50年代，由于西方资本主义国家对我国采取敌视、封锁政策，我国对外贸易的主要国际市场是原苏联和东欧社会主义国家。当时，我国根据恢复和发展国民经济的需要，本着“积极协作、平等互利、实事求是”的方针，积极开展对苏联、东欧国家和其他友好国家的贸易和经济合作，不断突破西方国家的封锁、禁运，对医治我国战争创伤、恢复和发展国民经济起到了积极作用。如当时我国通过贸易和使用苏联政府贷款从苏联和东欧国家引进156

项重点建设项目的成套设备和技术，建设了一批钢铁、电力、煤炭、石油、机械、化工、建材等骨干企业，为我国的工业化打下了初步基础。那时，我国同社会主义国家的贸易额占全国对外贸易总额的比重，1951 年为 52.9%，1952 年至 50 年代末，都在 70%以上；其中对苏联的贸易额约占全国对外贸易总额的 50%。

50 年代期间，我国还为逐步发展同亚非民族独立国家的贸易关系，发展祖国内地同港澳地区的贸易和努力开拓对西方国家的民间及政府贸易，进行了卓有成效的努力。我国同亚非国家贸易关系的发展，增进了亚非国家同中国的友谊，促进了亚非国家民族经济的发展；我国保证对港澳地区的供应，积极扩大对港澳出口及经港澳转口贸易，开辟了反封锁、打破禁运的新战线；我国继 1950 年同瑞典、丹麦、瑞士、芬兰建立外交和贸易关系后，又利用各种机会和途径，争取和团结其他西方国家工商界及开明人士，以民促官，推动了我国同日本、西欧等西方国家的民间贸易以至官方贸易。

1960 年，随着中苏关系的变化，我国对苏联和东欧国家的贸易急剧下降，新中国的对外贸易迎来了第一次较大的曲折。在这一形势下，我国对外贸易的主要对象开始转向资本主义国家和地区。我国在坚持内地对港澳地区长期稳定供应，积极发展同亚非拉民族独立国家贸易关系的同时，进一步打开对西方国家贸易的渠道。经过努力，我国同日本和西欧的贸易取得了突破性进展。中日贸易由 50 年代的民间贸易转入 60 年代的友好贸易和备忘录贸易；1963 年，我国同日本签订了第一个采用延期付款方式进口维尼纶成套设备合同，打开了西方国家从技术上封锁中国的缺口。1964 年，我国与法国建交，中法两国政府间贸易关系迅速发展，带动西欧掀起了开展对华贸易的热潮。到 1965 年，我国对西方国家贸易额点全国对外贸易总额的比重由 1957 年的 17.9%上升到 52.8%。

1966 年，“文化大革命”开始，打乱了我国社会主义建设的进程，我国对外贸易遭到严重的干扰和破坏，遭遇了建国后的第二次曲折。我国对外贸易自 1967 年起连续 3 年出现停滞和下降。在周总理和邓小平等老一辈无产阶级革命家的关心与直接领导下，经过艰苦努力，我国对外贸易从 1970 年开始逐渐好转。

70 年代前期，国际环境发生了有利于我国的变化。1971 年联合国恢复我国的合法席位，1972 年美国总统尼克松访华，中美发表《联合公报》，并在正式建交前先恢复了贸易关系。之后，我国对外关系取得了重大进展，西方国家纷纷同我国建立外交关系或使外交关系升格。中日邦交实现了正常化，中国与欧共体建立正式关系，我国对外贸易的国际环境明显改善，对外贸易额迅速增长。

然而，我国对外贸易的全面恢复和持续、快速发展，还是 1976 年粉碎“四人帮”、结束十年动乱之后。

从新中国成立到 1978 年，我国对外贸易是在几经曲折中向前发展的，并为国民经济的恢复和发展做出了重要贡献。1950 年，我国对外贸易总额 11.35 亿美元，其中出口 5.52 亿美元，进口 5.83 亿美元。到 1978 年，我国对外贸易总额发展到 206.38 亿美元，其中出口 97.45 亿美元，进口 108.93 亿美元。建国初期，我国出口商品的 80%以上是初级产品，反映了中国当时的经济结构和生产水平。“一五”计划后，我国工业迅速发展，出口商品结构发生较大变化，但直到 70 年代，初级产品出口占我国出口总额的比重仍在 50%以上。我国对外贸易的经营和管理也由建国初期的国家统制对外贸易政策，到 1957 年后适应国民经济转入计划经济，形成了国营外贸公司集中统一经营，国家对外贸公司实行指令性计划管理和统收统支、统负盈亏，管理和经营一体化的高度集中的对外贸易体制。对外贸易被看作社会主义扩大再生产的补充手段，局限于互通有无、调剂余缺。

2．对外援助的发展历程

新中国成立后，中国政府一直把对外提供经济技术援助作为履行国际主义义务的重要内容。中国政府和人民历来都认为援助和支持从来都是相互的。中国人民不会忘记，在中国革命和建设的道路上世界各国人民给予的支持和帮助。中国同广大第三世界国家历史上有着相似的遭遇，又面临着维护世界和平、发展本国经济的共同任务。中国有责任、有义务支持被压迫民族和第三世界国家争取和维护民族独立、发展民族经济。

我国的对外援 助是与我国对外关系的发展和国内经济状况密切相关的。大体说来，1978 年以前我国的对外援助可分为三个阶段：1950 年至 1963 年为初始阶段，1964 年至 1970 年为发展阶段，1971 年至 1978 年为急剧增长阶段。援助的内容是向受援国提供贷款或无偿援助。那时，我国提供的贷款一般都是无息贷款。对外援助的方式包括成套项目援助、技术援助、物资援助及现汇援助等。

在初始阶段，尽管我国百业待业，但根据当时的国际局势，我国仍竭尽全力支援朝鲜和越南抗击外来侵略，帮助它们恢复和发展经济；其后，还向其他经济不发达的社会主义国家提供了援助。1955 年万隆会议之后，随着对外关系的发展，我国对外援助的范围逐步扩大到亚洲、非洲一些民族主义国家。

1964 年初，周恩来总理在访问亚非十四国时，亲自主持制定了我国对外援助的指导原则——被称为国际经济合作领域“独树一帜”的中国援外八项原则，我国对外援助进入了新的发展阶段。在这一阶段，我国同更多的亚非民族主义国家建立了经济合作关系，援助非洲国家的第一批项目迅速建成，对越南的抗美救国斗争给予了全力支援，对朝鲜、阿尔巴尼亚等社会主义国家继续提供援助，受援国由初始阶段的 20 个增加到 31 个，援助金额增大，成套项目援助有了较大发展。

1971 年联合国恢复我国的合法席位后，要求我国提供援助的国家迅速增多，对外援助的规模急剧扩大。针对这种情况，我国对援外的规模和结构等进行了调整。

从新中国成立到 1978 年底，我国共向 66 个国家提供了援助，帮助其中 38 个国家建成 880 个成套项目。在八项原则指导下，我国对外援助创立了国际经济关系中真诚合作的典范，博得了受援国政府和人民的广泛赞扬和高度评价。此间，我国援建的坦赞铁路被誉为“解放之路”、“南南合作之路”，在非洲乃至全世界产生了广泛影响，增进了我国与第三世界国家的了解和信任；我国援外专家和医疗队以良好的精神风貌和突出的工作成绩成为联系中国人民与第三世界国家人民友谊的纽带，得到了第三世界国家人民的高度赞扬。

（二）1978 年以来我国对外经济贸易的发展

1978 年党的十一届三中全会确立了以经济建设为中心，实行改革开放，发展国民经济，加快社会主义现代化建设的路线，并明确提出：“在自力更生的基础上积极发展同世界各国平等互利的经济合作，努力采用世界先进技术和先进设备”。随后，我国又提出社会主义现代化建设要利用两种资源——国内资源和国外资源；要打开两个市场——国内市场和国际市场；要学会两套本领——组织国内建设的本领和发展对外经济关系的本领。这是我国经济战略思想的重大转变，也为对外经济贸易的发展奠定了思想理论基础。

1. 我国对外开放新格局的初步形成

我国对外开放是从沿海开始，逐步向内地推进的。

1979 年 7 月，党中央、国务院决定对广东、福建两省的对外经济活动实行特殊政策和优惠措施。1980 年 5 月，决定在深圳、珠海、汕头、厦门设置经济特区。1984 年 5 月，开放大连、秦皇岛、天津、烟台、青岛、连云港、南通、上海、宁波、温洲、福州、广州、湛江、北海 14 个沿海港口城市。1985 年 2 月，决定分两步开放长江三角洲、珠江三角洲、闽南厦漳泉三角地区和辽东半岛、胶东半岛。1988 年，设立海南省，建立海南经济特区。1990 年，决定开发和开放上海的浦东。1991 年，开放满洲里、丹东、绥芬河、珲春四个北部口岸。1992 年 8 月，决定以上海浦东为龙头，开放重庆、岳阳、武汉、九江、芜湖 5 个沿江城市，同时，开放哈尔滨、长春、呼和浩特、石家庄 4 个边境、沿海地区省会城市及太原、合肥、南昌、郑州、长沙、成都、贵阳、西安、兰州、西宁、银川等 11 个内陆省会城市。在随后的几年，又陆续开放了一大批符合条件的内陆市县。至此，我国全方位的对外开放的格局初步形成。

随着对外开放的不断发展，我国对外经济贸易开始向内容丰富、形式多样、各种对外经济交往互相融合、互相促进的新格局发展，向广度和深度推进。对外贸易总额迅速增加，市场不断扩大，经营方式日趋灵活多样；利用外资、对外承包工程与劳务合作、对外多边经济合作、对外投资等从无到有、从小到大不断发展。1987 年，党中央又提出并实施沿海地区经济发展战略，大力发展外向型经济，要求沿海地区积极参加国际交换和竞争，扩大产品出口，大力发展“三资企业”，并加强沿海和内地的横向经济联系，以带动整个国民经济发展。同时，对外经济贸易体制改革也逐步走向深入。我国对外经济贸易进入了欣欣向荣的大发展时期。

2. 我国对外贸易体制的改革与发展

我国原有的高度集中的对外贸易体制是与传统的计划经济体制相适应的，虽然在历史上曾发挥过重要作用，但随着国内和国际形势的变化，特别是党的十一届三中全会决定实行改革开放和党的十四大提出建立社会主义市场经济体制以来，原有外贸体制的垄断经营、大锅饭、财政补贴的弊端日益显现，成为我国外贸发展的障碍。

从 1978 年至今，我国外贸体制改革大体经历了四个阶段：1979 年至 1987 年的探索阶段，1988 年至 1990 年的整体推进阶段，1991 年至 1993 年的攻坚阶段，1994 年至现在的继续深化阶段。

在探索阶段，外贸体制改革主要采取了如下措施：一是改革高度集中的经营体制，包括增设对外贸易口岸，下放外贸经营权；二是改革单一的指令性计划管理体制，实行指令性计划、指导性计划和市场调节相结合；三是完善外贸管理，重新实行进出口许可证制度，建立外贸经营权审批制度；四是探索促进工贸（技贸、农贸）结合的途径；五是采取鼓励出口的政策，实行外贸减亏增盈分成制度和地区差别的外汇分成制度，对出口商品实行退税等，并在外经贸管理上，实行中央统一领导、统一政策、统一规划，中央和省两级管理。

这一阶段的改革对调动各方面积极性，推动外贸发展，取得了一定成效。但是，由于外贸体制改革是一项十分复杂的系统工程，它与整个国民经济体制的改革有着密切的联系，外贸体制中的统负盈亏、政企不分等主要问题仍未解决，改革只能是阶段性的进展。

在整体推进阶段，外贸体制改革主要是在全行业实行承包经营责任制。其内容是：核定各地方和有关外贸总公司的出口收汇、上缴外汇和经济效益指标，三年不变；完成承包指标内的外汇按留成比例分成；超亏自负，减亏增盈留成。同时，在全国建立若干外汇调剂市场，企业自有外汇可随时进入市场，自由调剂；各专业外贸进出口总公司与大部分省市外贸专业分公司脱钩，地方的分公司下放到地方管理；外贸的宏观调控体系开始形成，国家逐步运用价格、汇率、利率、退税、出口信贷等经济手段调控对外贸易；在轻工、工艺、服装行业进行自负盈亏的改革试点。

实行外贸承包经营责任制，调动了地方、部门和企业扩大出口的积极性，对于改善企业内部经营机制，提高经济效益，促进对外贸易特别是出口贸易的发展，起到了重要作用。但由于受整个经济体制改革阶段性的制约，外贸承包经营责任制只能是一种过渡和探索的形式。

在攻坚阶段，外贸体制改革主要是取消对外贸出口的财政补贴，从建立自负盈亏机制入手，使外贸逐步走上统一政策、平等竞争、自主经营、自负盈亏、工贸结合、推行代理制的轨道。这次改革的特点是：取消出口补贴，按照国际通行作法由外贸企业自负盈亏；实行以大类商品区分的全国统一的外汇留成比例办法，为企业平等竞争创造条件；外贸体制改革与调整汇率和关税配套进行，外贸的宏观调控体系进一步完善；重视发挥市场调节的作用，行政管理部门不得用行政手段干预外汇资金的横向流通；增加企业支配使用的外汇，为外国商品进入中国市场提供更多的机会；鼓励出口的政策和外贸管理措施保持了相对的稳定性和连续性。

这次改革使对外贸易体制开始适应国际贸易规范，有利于广泛地参与国际经济合作和交流。但是，按照建立社会主义市场经济体制和适应国际贸易规范的要求，我国外贸体制依然存在诸多不相适应的方面。

在继续深化阶段，外贸体制改革按照党的十四大确定的统一政策、放开经营、平等竞争、自负盈亏、工贸结合、推行代理制的方向继续深化：建立与完善外贸宏观调控体系，实行单一的、有管理的浮动汇率制；强化外经贸企业自负盈亏机制，取消各类外汇留成，同时实行银行结售汇制。进一步调整与完善出口退税政策和有利于出口发展的信贷政策，建立进出口银行，设立出口商品发展基金和风险基金。取消国有外贸企业普遍实行的承包制，代之以赋税制，按照现代企业制度改造国有外经贸企业，积极推行股份制试点，推动企业开展一业为主、多种经营，走实业化、集团化、国际化、多元化的路子。进一步降低进口关税，同时取消部分进口商品的减免税。加快赋予有条件的生产企业、商业物资企业和科研院所等外贸经营权，对经济特区内生产企业的外贸自营权进行依法自动登记试点。充实与强化商会、协会等中介组织的职能，健全与完善外经贸协调服务体系。实行人民币在经常项目下的可自由兑换。在金融和商业零售、外贸等服务性行业进行利用外资试点。

20年的改革，我国外贸体制发生了根本变化。一是行政性直接干预大大弱化，外贸宏观管理逐步走上以经济、法律手段调控为主的轨道。二是外经贸经营主体多元化格局已经形成，自负盈亏的经营机制不断得到加强和完善，国有外经贸企业从计划经济体制下国家计划的执行者转变为社会主义市场经济条件下自主经营、自负盈亏、自我约束、自我发展的经营者。三是外贸政策的统一性和透明度进一步增强，涉外法规日益健全。四是外贸中介服务体系开始形成。五是外贸经营的领域和渠道进一步拓宽，总体效益和竞争能力大大提高。

3．我国利用外资的迅速发展

从1979年颁布《中华人民共和国中外合资经营企业法》、1980年批准第一批三家外商投资企业以来，我国利用外资经过1979年至1986年的起步阶段、1987年至1991年的持续发展阶段和1992年以来的高速发展阶段，逐渐成为我国对外经济贸易的重要内容之一。

在起步阶段，我国先后对经济特区、沿海开放城市和沿海经济开放区内吸收外资，举办“三资企业”实行一些特殊政策，采取措施扩大地方外商投资的审批权限，并逐步完善立法，初步改善了我国的投资环境，发挥了各地利用外资的积极性，吸收外资的规模不断增加。这一阶段，我国吸收的外商投资主要来自港澳地区，以劳动密集型的加工项目和宾馆、服务设施等第三产业项目居多，并主要集中在广东、福建和其他沿海省市。

在持续发展阶段，由于1986年10月国务院颁布的《关于鼓励外商投资的规定》，对外商投资举办产品出口企业和先进技术企业给予更为优惠的待遇，改善了外商投资企业的生产经营条件。同时，随着我国对外开 放的不断扩大，吸收外资的环境得到进一步改善，外商投 资发展较快。这一阶段，我国吸收外商投资的结构有较大改善，生产性项目及产品出口企业大幅增加，宾馆、旅游服务项目的比重大大降低，外商投资的区域和行业有所扩大，台湾厂商的投资开始进入，并迅速增加。

在高速发展阶段，随着我国全方位对外开放格局的初步形成，我国的投资环境得到更大改善，吸收外资在广度和深度上都有了新的大发展。1995年6月，国务院批准发布《指导外商投资方向暂行规定》和《外商投资产业指导目录》；1998年，党中央又针对新的形势提出了进一步扩大对外开放、提高利用外资水平的若干意见。外商投资的规模和领域进一步扩大，外资的来源国家和地区持续增加，越来越多的西方国家大跨国公司进入我国，资金、技术密集的大型项目和基础设施项目增加较多，平均单项外商投资规模不断提高，在沿海地区外商投资迅速增长的同时，中西部地区吸收外资有了较快发展。

此外，我国利用外国政府和国际金融机构的贷款，以及国际证券投资等在20年中也获得很大发展。

4．我国对外援助在调整与改革中不断发展

党的十一届三中全会以后，在改革开放的总方针指引下，我国的对外援助工作根据形势的发展进行了合理的调整与改革，继续向更多的第三世界国家提供力所能及的援助，方式更为灵活，援建的项目更加实用。

从1979年至1990年，我国对援外方式进行了一些探索性的改革与调整：通过统筹安排，扩大了援助面，使受援国由1978年底的66个增加到1990年的93个；将我国援助同联合国多边援助、受援国自筹部分资金、国际金融组织或第三国援助等相结合，在投入较少援款的情况下推动互利经贸业务，促进援外与互利合作相结合；因地制宜地对不同项目采取技术合作、管理合作、代管经营，租凭经营、合资经营等方式，改善和提高援助效益；进行援外管理体制的初步改革，在援外项目实施阶段，由试行投资包干逐步试行承包责任制。

从1991年至1994年，围绕着主要帮助受援国发展当地有需要又有资源的中小型项目，并与发展多双边互利合作的经贸关系相结合，促进受援国和我国共同发展，主要做了以下工作；调整援外结构，成套项目占60%，重点建设生产性项目、适当援建人员培训和社会公益性项目，也援建受援国有特殊需要、规模适当的个别社会公共建筑；大力推动我国企业与受援国企业合资、合作经营生产性援助项目；设立多种形式援助专项资金；增加形式多样、灵活、及时的小额赠送；将一部分援外资金与联合国发展机构的资金相结合，开展发展中国家间的技术合作；进一步调整、改革援外项目的管理体制。

1995年以来，我国对援外工作进行了全面改革。根据国务院关于改革援外工作的批复精神，为使有限的援外资金发挥更大的效益，我国在继续遵循援外八项原则的基础上，对外援助主要采用以下方式：一是积极推行政府贴息优惠贷款。由我国政府向受援国提供具有援助性质的优惠贷款，国家用援外经费贴息，以扩大对外援助的规模，提高援外资金的使用效益，推动双方企业的投资合作，带动我国设备、材料和技术出口；二是积极推动援外项目合资合作。以利于政府援外资金与企业资金相结合，扩大资金来源和项目规模，巩固项目成果，提高援助效益。

5．我国对外经济合作迅速发展

我国的对外经济合作事业开始于70年代末，是改革开放带来的新生事物，经过20年的不断努力，迅速发展为我国对外经济贸易的重要组成部分。20年来，我国对外经济合作大体经历了1978年至1982年的起步阶段、1983年至1989年的逐步发展阶段和1990年以来的稳步发展这三个阶段。

在起步阶段，我国共批准了29家企业从事对外工程承包和劳务合作业务，我国的对外承包劳务队伍第一次走向国际舞台，主要市场集中在西亚、北非。经过创业之初的艰难开拓，我国的对外经济合作取得了初步发展，4年中共与45个国家和地区签订了承包劳务合同755项，总金额11.96亿美元。

在逐步发展阶段，我国的对外经济合作业务在国际承包劳务市场萎缩、条件苛刻的困难条件下，经过奋力开拓，取得了持续发展。在此期间，我国的对外经济合作队伍不断壮大，1990年底达到113家，初步形成了一支活跃在国际承包劳务市场上的骨干队伍；业务量不断增加，8年间共签订承包劳务合同138．64亿美元，在国际承包劳务市场上占有了一席之地；市场逐步扩大；为90年代对外经济合作的发展奠定了坚实的基础。

在稳步发展阶段，我国对外经济合作迎来了健康、稳定、快速发展的新时期。经营对外经济合作业务的企业由流通领域的窗口型公司为主逐步转向生产领域的实体公司为主，企业的经营水平不断提高，在外承揽的业务规模不断扩大，档次不断提高，市场多元化战略初见成效，取得了良好经济效益和社会效益。1997年，我国新签对外承包劳务合同金额已达113.6亿美元，完成营业额83.8亿美元。

另外，我国的对外投资也在20年中取得显著成就，逐渐发展成为我国对外经济贸易的重要组成部分。

二、20年来我国对外经济贸易发展的巨大成就、作用和基本经验

对外开放20年来，我国对外经济贸易随着生产力的发展不断壮大，对外经济贸易活动的深度和广度不断拓展，质量和水平不断提高，在国民经济和社会发展中的地位和作用不断增强，促进了我国经济通过对外经济贸易的渠道，日益融入世界经济体系、加入到经济全球化的时代潮流之中，并取得了进一步发展的宝贵经验。

（一）20年来我国对外经济贸易发展的巨大成就

对外开放20年来，在党中央、国务院的正确领导下，我国对外经济贸易各项业务都取得了巨大成就。

对外贸易发展迅速。1978年，我国进出口贸易总值仅有206亿美元，1997年则达到3250.6亿美元，19年增长了15倍多。其中，1992年确立社会主义市场经济体制目标以来的6年是我国对外贸易发展最快的时期。1992－1997年间，我国对外贸易总值达14938亿美元，比从新中国成立到1991年的总和还要多，年均增速15.7%，这个速度不仅高于同期我国国民经济的增长速度，而且比世界贸易的年均增长速度高出近8个百分点。对外贸易对国民经济增长的拉动作用显著增强，在世界贸易中的地位也大大提高，位次排列由1978年的第32位跃升为1992年的第11位，并在连续保持5年后，1997年又跃升至第10位。截至1997年底，我国外汇储备1399亿美元，在世界居第二位。

出口商品结构明显优化。1997年，工业制成品出口占出口总额的比重由1978年的45.2%上升到86.9%，实现了由主要出口初级产品向主要出口制成品的历史性转变。技术含量和附加值较高的机电产品出口迅速增长，1997年当年机电产品出口额达到593.2亿美元，占当年出口总额的比重达32.5%，连续三年超过纺织品，成为我国最大的出口商品类别。

贸易伙伴遍及世界各地，对外贸易的国际市场走向全球。目前，我国的贸易伙伴由1978年的几十个发展到227个国家和地区，与传统市场的经济贸易关系稳步推进，与新开拓市场的经济贸易关系不断增强。

利用外资成就显著。利用外资是邓小平理论的重要组成部分，是我国对外开放基本国策的重要内容，是建设有中国特色社会主义经济的伟大实践之一。经过20年的发展，利用外资已成为我国国民经济乃至社会生活中不可分割的重要组成部分。特别是1992年以来，我国吸纳外资的领域不断扩大，规模不断增加，水平不断提高，成就举世瞩目。截至1997年底，我国累计批准外商投资企业30.48万家，合同外资金额5211.61亿美元，实际利用外商直接投资金额2218.71亿美元。目前，外商投资企业已开业14.5万家，就业人数1750多万人。我国利用外国政府和国际金融机构的贷款、证券投资等其他形式的外资也达到一定规模，累计达1400多亿美元。从1993年到1997年，我国连续5年成为利用外资最多的发展中国家，在全球仅次于美国，列第二位。

在利用外资规模不断扩大的同时，我国利用外资的环境也不断改善，各项涉外法规日益

健全，利用外资的质量有所提高、结构有所改善；资金和技术密集型项目明显增加，国家鼓励投资类项目增加较多，限制类项目减少，基础产业和基础设施项目成为外商投资的热点；中西部地区对外商的吸引力增强；世界知名大跨国公司来华投资增多，大项目继续增加，平均单项外商投资规模不断提高。

对外工程承包和劳务合作快速发展。由改革开放之初仅几家企业从事这项业务发展为一支由近700家企业组成的门类比较齐全、具有较强国际竞争力的队伍，业务范围向技术性较强的领域不断扩展，项目越做越大，经济效益和社会效益明显提高。在1997年美国《工程新闻杂志》(ENR）评选出来的世界最大225家国际承包商中，有27家中国企业；业务范围遍及世界五大洲的180多个国家和地区。截至1997年底，我国累计签订对外经济合作合同额716.93亿美元，完成营业额482.37亿美元，外派劳务超过154万人次。

援外工作在改革中稳步推进。从1995年实行援外方式改革到1997年底，援外方式改革取得了实质性进展，已同31个国家签订了38笔政府贴息优惠贷款框架协议，新的援外方式得到越来越多受援国的理解和拥护。截至1997年年底，我国对外援助的国家累计达114个，援建成套项目1531个。

对外投资保持快速发展势头。我国对外投资虽起步较晚，但近年来呈现出逐步发展势头，在开拓国际市场、开发展外资源，充分利用国际国内两个市场、两种资源为我国现代化建设服务方面做出了贡献。

多双边经贸合作成就瞩目，我国主张在平等互利基础上通过和平协商解决经济贸易争端，使得我国加入世界贸易组织的谈判取得了较大进展；我国积极参与亚太经合组织会议和亚欧会议，推进亚太地区贸易与投资自由化和亚太、亚欧地区经济技术合作，江泽民主席先后四次出席亚太经合组织经济领导人非正式会议，李鹏总理和朱镕基总理先后出席亚欧会议，并发表重要讲话，体现了我国坚持改革开放、重视同世界各国和地区发展经济贸易关系的基本立场，得到了亚太、亚欧地区乃至全世界的普遍关注和赞赏；我国与美、日、欧等主要经济贸易伙伴及其他国家和地区的双边关系也不断加强，赢得了发展国民经济、加快现代化进程的良好国际环境。

（二）20年来对外经济贸易在国民经济和社会发展中的作用不断增强

对外开放20年来，我国对外经济贸易突破了过去互通有无、调剂余缺的局限，由社会主义扩大再生产的补充手段发展为国民经济的重要组成部分，在国民经济和社会发展中的地位显著提高，作用不断增强。

1．对外经济贸易的迅速发展，提高了我国的综合国力

衡量一国的综合国力，需要从政治、经济、军事、科技水平等多方面进行综合判定。从经济角度分析，主要看该国的国民生产总值（GNP)、主要产品的产量、同世界经济的交换量和国际收支能力等方面的指标。而这些指标的变化，与该国的对外经济贸易状况都有着直接的关系。比如一国对外经济贸易的规模大小和质量高低，不仅直接关系着该国同世界经济的交换量和国际收支能力，而且直接影响着GNP的规模和主要产品的产量。因此，发展对外经济贸易与提高综合国力密切相关。改革开放以来，我国对外经济贸易的规模成倍扩大，与世界经济的交换量也成倍增加，有力地促进了我国综合国力的提高。1978年以来的20年

间，我国国民经济以年均11%的速度增长，而同期我国进出口贸易总额以年均15.6%的速度增长。1978年，我国的进出口总额仅206亿美元，占国民生产总值的8.8%；1997年，我国进出口总额达到3251亿美元，占国内生产总值的36.4%。吸引外资作为对外经济贸易的重要内容，20年来，有效地弥补了我国建设资金的不足，引进了先进的技术、设备与管理经验，促进了我国经济的市场化进程，对综合国力的提高也发挥了积极的推动作用。

2. 对外经济贸易的迅速发展，加快了我国开放型经济的形成

改革开放以前，我国国民经济长期处于封闭、半封闭状态。随着对外开放政策的实施，我国对外经济贸易迅速发展，在国民经济中的比重越来越大，使得我国国民经济摆脱了封闭、半封闭状态，逐步转向开放型经济。目前，我国的对外开放地域从经济特区、沿海开放城市，扩大到沿边、沿江地区和省会城市等内陆地区；开放领域从一般加工工业向基础产业、基础设施和高新技术产业扩展，向金融、保险、外贸、旅游、通信、商业零售、法律咨询和会计等服务行业延伸。同时，我国多次对进口关税税率进行大幅度下调，进口关税平均水平已从1992年的43.2%降至目前的17%。到2000年，我国的进口关税平均水平将进一步下降到15%左右。开放型经济的初步形成，为21世纪我国经济的持续发展打下了坚实基础。

3. 对外经济贸易的迅速发展，促进了我国国民经济的持续稳定增长。

现代市场经济理论认为，对外经济贸易对国民经济发展具有“助推器”的作用。有的经济学家还提出了对外经济贸易是国民经济发展的“引擎”的观点。我国经济的发展，充分证明了这一理论和观点的实践性。据国家统计局分析，1997年我国仅外贸出口对国民经济增长的拉动就约为2个百分点。对外经济贸易的扩大，不仅带动了国内生产，使国内众多产品通过出口在国际市场实现了价值，获得了比较利益，而且引进了国内经济建设需要的资金、技术、原材料和管理经验，创造了更多的就业机会，增加了国家税收和外汇收入，带动了相关产业的发展，从而在外延和内涵两个方面促进了国民经济的持续稳定增长。

4. 对外经济贸易的迅速发展，促进了我国国民经济结构的调整与优化，增强了我国经济的国际竞争能力

目前，我国经济发展已进入由规模扩张为主向质量效益为主转变的时期。调整和优化国民经济结构，包括产业结构、产品结构、企业组织结构等，成为中国经济发展最迫切的任务。面对科技、经济的全球化趋势，我国国民经济结构的调整和优化，不仅要立足于本国经济实际，而且要依托国际经济和国际市场，使调整和优化的方向符合国际分工发展的客观要求，以保持经济结构在国际上的相对先进性。我国对外经济贸易作为连接国内经济和国际经济的桥梁与纽带，对国民经济结构调整发挥了积极、能动的导向作用。对外经济贸易的迅速发展，及时获取国际商品市场发展变化的最新信息，为我国商品结构的调整起导向作用，进而促进我国产业结构的调整和优化。同时，还通过引进国外资金、技术和设备，为国内产品升级换代和产业结构升级提供保证，增强我国产品和产业的国际竞争力，促进国民经济的市场化和经济结构的合理化。

5. 对外经济贸易的迅速发展，推动了我国在国际经济交换中价值最大化的实现，提高了国民经济的效益。

随着我国对外经济贸易从侧重商品的互通有无和调剂余缺逐步向参与国际分工、发挥比较优势、优化资源配置的方向转变，从侧重商品使用价值的交换向实现商品价值最大化的方向转变，我国已经开始把确保经济效益作为发展对外经济贸易的一项基本前提，从而使得我国在国际经济交换中不仅能实现或在一定程度上超过国内市场的平均价值，而且还可以实现或在一定程度上超过国际市场的平均价值，达到了提高国民经济效益的目的。

6．对外经济贸易的迅速发展，有利于促进世界和平与发展

和平与发展是当今世界的主题。冷战结束后，国与国之间的关系是以经济关系为主展开的，和平共处、共同发展成为国家关系的重要特征。改革开放20年来，我国对外经济贸易的迅速发展，不仅极大地促进了我国经济的发展，而且增进了同世界各国政治、经济和文化的交流与合作，这本身就是对世界和平与发展的贡献。同时，我国对外经济贸易的迅速发展，密切了同世界各国的经济关系，逐渐在经济上形成“你中有我，我中有你”的相互交融的局面，从而有利于创造国际和平环境，为我国现代化建设赢得进一步发展的良好机遇。

（三）20年来我国对外经济贸易发展的基本经验

总结对外开放20年来我国对外经济贸易的发展实践，可以得出以下基本经验：

1．对外开放为对外经济贸易的发展提供了根本动力

党中央在总结历史经验和研究当代世界经济特点的基础上，把对外开放作为长期的基本国策，这是我国经济发展战略指导思想的重大转变。在对外开放政策指引下，我国对外经济贸易明确树立了参与国际分工与交换，充分利用国际国内两个市场、两种资源为社会主义现代化建设服务的指导思想。随着我国全方位、多层次、宽领域的对外开放格局的形成，全国人民的对外开放意识大大增强，国内市场和国际市场的联系更加密切，从而为对外经济贸易的发展提供了前所未有的良好环境和客观条件。20年的实践证明，没有对外开放，我国对外经济贸易就没有今天这样的成就。与此同时，我国对外经济贸易的迅速发展也加快了我国对外开放的进程，从深度和广度两个方面促进了我国对外开放新格局的形成。

2．国民经济的持续稳定发展为对外经济贸易的发展提供了坚实的基础和物资保障

改革开放以来的20年，我国国民经济迅速发展，综合国力不断增强。1997年，我国经济总量在世界排名第七，经济增长率连续5年居世界首位。我国已经告别了短缺经济，初步形成了主要生产资料和消费品的买方市场；国民经济的市场化、货币化程度进一步提高，市场配置资源的基础性作用不断增强；特别是1996年实现“软着陆”以来，我国国民经济继续保持高增长、低通胀的良好态势，素质和效益不断提高。国民经济的持续健康发展为外经贸提高竞争能力、优化结构、提高效益和扩大规模创造了有利的国内条件，从而为对外经济贸易的发展提供了坚实的基础和物资保障。与此同时，我国对外经济贸易的迅速发展，也有力地推动了国民经济增长、促进了国民经济素质与效益的提高。

3．社会主义市场经济的发展为对外经济贸易的发展注入了生机和活力

随着我国改革开放的不断发展，1992年召开的党的十四大明确提出，建立社会主义市场经济体制是我国改革开放的总体目标。经过近年来的快速发展，我国经济体制发生了根本变化，市场在资源配置中的基础性作用不断加强，社会主义市场经济体制的框架初步形成。实践证明，用社会主义市场经济体制取代高度集中的计划经济体制，有效地促进了我国生产

力的发展，为我国国民经济增添了全新的内容。在当今世界，国际市场的经济也就是国际范围的市场经济。因此，我国实行社会主义市场经济，有利于国内市场与国际市场的接轨，有利于我国经济更好地参与国际经济，实现国内经济与国际经济的互接互补，使我国经济真正成为世界经济中富有活力的组成部分，从而为对外经济贸易的发展注入了生机和活力。与此同时，我国对外经济贸易的迅速发展，也加快了我国经济融入世界经济的进程，大大促进我国社会主义市场经济的进一步发展。

4．社会主义初级阶段是对外经济贸易改革与发展的出发点和基本依据

江泽民总书记在党的十五大报告中，从历史和现实、理论和实践的结合上对我国现在处于并将长期处于社会主义初级阶段这一最大国情进行了深刻论述。他指出，我们讲一切从实际出发，最大的实际就是中国现在处于并将长期处于社会主义初级阶段。因此，我们提出对外经济贸易的各项任务和政策，都必须从我国这一实际国情出发，以“三个有利于”为判断是非取舍的标准。我国对外经济贸易的发展实践证明，凡是符合社会主义初级阶段这一国情的方针和政策，就能够推动对外经济贸易的改革与发展。因此，社会主义初级阶段是我国对外经济贸易改革与发展的出发点和基本依据。

5．中国国际地位的不断提高为对外经济贸易的发展提供了广阔的空间

冷战结束以来，和平共处、共同发展成为国家关系的重要特征。我国一贯奉行独立自主的和平外交政策，坚持在平等互利、和平共处五项原则的基础上积极发展同世界各国的友好合作关系，赢得了国际社会的普遍赞赏和尊重。改革开放20年来，我国政治稳定，经济发展，社会进步，综合国力不断增强，国际地位进一步提高，多双边关系取得很大进展，极大地促进了我国对外经济贸易的发展，为我国对外经济贸易提供了广阔的空间。与此同时，我国对外经济贸易的迅速发展，加深了我国与世界各国的经济联系，增进了我国同世界各国的相互了解和友谊，我国经济实力的增强，又大大提高了我国的国际地位。

6．外经贸队伍素质的不断提高是对外经济贸易发展的重要条件

我国对外经济贸易取得的巨大成就，是与长期以来在党的领导下加强外经贸队伍建设、提高外经贸队伍的整体素质密不可分的。古今中外的历史一再证明，任何一项事业的兴衰成败，关键在人。外经贸工作常常处在复杂的国际环境中，我国外经贸工作人员本着对国家、对人民高度负责的、精神，时时处处维护国家利益，体现了良好的政治素质；在外经贸业务不断拓展和国际市场风云变幻中，我国外经贸工作人员刻苦钻研，艰苦奋斗，体现了良好的业务素质。正是由于我国拥有一支较高素质的外经贸队伍，才保障了我国对外经济贸易的持续发展。

三、我国对外经济贸易的发展前景和努力方向

按照党中央、国务院的战略部署，在本世纪的最后几年，我国经济每年要增长8%以上，通货膨胀率控制在5%以下；在下世纪前10年，建立起比较完善的社会主义市场经济体制，实现国民经济增长方式由粗放型向集约型转变，并使中国经济仍保持7%的年均增长速度；再经过三四十年的努力，到下世纪中叶，全面实现我国的现代化，建成富强、民主、

文明的社会主义国家。根据这一规划，我国的对外经济贸易必须相应地有更大的发展：到2000年，我国当年的进出口总额要达到4000亿美元，利用外资等其他各项外经贸业务也要获得较大发展；到2010年，我国进出口总额要适应国民经济的发展比2000年再翻一番。正如江泽民总书记在党的十五大报告中指出的：对外开放是一项长期的基本国策。面对经济、科技全球化趋势，我们要以更加积极的姿态走向世界，完善全方位、多层次、宽领域的对外开放格局，发展开放型经济，增强国际竞争力，促进经济结构优化和国民经济素质提高。

由于我国尚处于社会主义初级阶段，实行对外开放也只有20年时间，受社会生产力发展水平和自身发展历程的局限，我国的对外经济贸易总体上还处于较低水平，与一些发达国家相比尚有一定差距。目前，我国是世界贸易大国，但还不是世界贸易强国。

我国的对外贸易总额在世界贸易总额中的比重依然很小，1997年仅为3%；对外经济贸易的增长方式尚未实现由粗放型向集约型的根本性转变，总体上效益不高，竞争力不强；出口商品结构、国际市场结构、利用外资结构尚需进一步优化；外经贸体制改革尚未完成，国有外经贸企业改革任务仍很艰巨；外经贸法制建设不够完善，执法监督机制不强；尚未加入世界贸易组织，参与国际经济的程度相对较低。

我国对外经济贸易目前的发展水平，与我国现代化建设的要求尚有一定差距，与我国的大国地位和在国际经济中应该发挥的作用也不相称，因此，今后我们要在以江泽民同志为核心的中央领导集体和新一届中央政府的领导下，加倍努力，勤奋工作，坚定地扩大对外开放，努力提高对外开放水平，不断发展对外经济贸易。特别是在面对亚洲金融危机的情况下，更要激发爱国心，增强责任感，以促进国民经济持续稳定增长和素质、效益的提高为己任，寻找和捕捉危机可能带来的机遇，大力发展对外经济贸易。

（一）加快实现外经贸领域的两个根本性转变

党的十四届五中全会提出，到2010年，我国国民经济的发展要实现经济体制和经济增长方式两个根本性转变。根据这一要求，我国对外经济贸易一方面要加快建立适应社会主义市场经济体制要求、符合国际经济通行规则的新型外经贸体制；另一方面，要加快转变外经贸增长方式，使对外经济贸易的增长从主要依靠数量增长和规模扩张的粗放型向主要依靠质量、效益和信誉的集约型转变。为此，首先要转变观念，尽快从长期计划经济体制下形成的以追求数量增长和规模扩张为主的思维模式中解脱出来，坚持以经济效益为中心，正确处理规模与效益的关系，在讲求经济效益、质量、信誉的前提下，发展各项外经贸业务。其次要加快外经贸企业改革，切实抓紧、抓好“三改一加强”，推动外经贸企业按照现代企业制度的要求，尽快建立起适应社会主义市场经济体制要求的内部运行机制，并推动外经贸企业的联合兼并，发展规模经济。第三要发展外经贸的集约化经营，加快外经贸经营方式的转变，大力推行外经贸代理制；提高外经贸的经营层次和经营水平，在保持商品经营优势的同时，积极稳妥地推行资本经营。第四要积极贯彻“科技兴贸”战略，努力提高外经贸的科技含量和附加值，提高我国外经贸的国际竞争能力。

（二）扩大对外经济贸易的规模，提高对外经济贸易的效益

事物的发展有两个重要标志：一个是量的增加，另一个是质的提高。因此，要推动对外经济贸易的进一步发展，必须一方面努力扩大规模，另一方面努力提高效益。而在事物的发展过程中，特别是在社会经济活动中，规模和效益不是孤立的，两者既相联系又相区别：保持或达到一定的规模是取得效益的前提；反过来，保持或达到一定效益的规模扩大才有实际意义。为了保障21世纪我国对外经济贸易的发展，必须坚持在讲求经济效益的前提下发展各项外经贸业务，推动进出口贸易稳定增长，努力保持和扩大吸收外商投资的规模，优化外商投资结构，并以此为重心，带动各项外经贸工作的发展。

（三）继续深化外经贸体制和援外方式改革

我国对外经济贸易的改革与发展是紧密联系的。要继续深化外经贸的各项改革，加强外经贸宏观调控，完善汇率机制，调整关税结构，探索科学的退税机制，规范涉外税收、信贷扶持措施，搞好外经贸运行的监测、预测和调控；加快赋予各类企业的对外经营权，扩大工业企业自营进出口自动登记的试行范围，抓紧研究和进行混合所有制企业经营外经贸业务的试点；改革进出口配额与许可证管理体制，扩大出口商品配额招标的范围并逐步放开经营；强化外经贸中介机构的作用，完善外经贸中介服务体系；大胆利用一切反映社会化生产规律的经营方式和组织形式，按市场经济规律，深化国有外经贸企业改革，实行联合兼并和股份制改造，推动规模经营，提高企业的整体素质和竞争力；继续改革援外方式，保证援外工程及设备、物资的质量。

（四）继续实施以质取胜战略，大力优化进出口商品结构，特别是出口商品结构

大力优化进出口商品结构、特别是出口商品结构，是实现外经贸增长方式转变、保持外经贸事业持续发展的关键所在。当前，人类已进入知识经济时代，科学技术的日新月异，迅速地改变着社会生产方式和人们的生活方式，更新着人们的思想观念。在新的形势下，要进一步贯彻以质取胜战略，依靠科技进步和科学管理，着眼于国际市场的现实需要和未来发展，发挥自身优势，不断提高进出口商品的质量，优化出口商品结构，扶持和培育名牌产品，大力发展机电产品特别是成套设备出口，提高出口商品的科技含量和附加值，增强我国对外经济贸易的发展后劲。

（五）继续实施市场多元化战略，大力开拓国际市场

我国的市场、劳动力素质、资源、科技、加工能力等在国际上具有相对优势，今后要进一步发挥这些优势，加大开拓国际市场的力度，发展和深度拓展传统市场，大力开发非洲、拉美、东欧和独联体等市场，加大开拓新市场的力度。加速实现市场多元化，包括进出口市场多元化、吸收外资多元化和对外经济合作多元化，为我国对外经济贸易的持续、稳定发展创造条件。积极发展对外投资，鼓励能够发挥我国比较优势的对外投资，努力开拓国际市场和利用国外资源，并以此带动我国的设备和劳务出口，培育外经贸新的增长点。

（六）进一步发展多双边经贸关系，创造良好的国际环境

在坚持权利与义务平衡和发展中国家地位的基本原则下，积极推进我国加入世界贸易组织（WTO）的谈判进程，争取尽早加入WTO，享受我国应有的权益；积极参与亚太经合组织和亚欧会议，推进亚太经合组织贸易与投资自由化进程，加强亚太和亚欧地区的经济技术合作，发挥我国在其中的重要作用。密切我国与联合国开发计划署、儿童基金、人口基金等经济机构的合作。做好对美、欧、日等发达国家的工作，妥善处理好与他们的贸易摩擦。抓住我国与这些发达国家双边关系全面发展的有利时机，积极从这些国家引进先进技术与设备，逐步减少我方贸易顺差。大力发展同亚非拉广大发展中国家的双边关系，为发展我国的对外经济贸易开辟更为广阔的国际空间。做好对台港澳地区的经贸工作，及时研究和处理好在新形势下出现的新问题，保持香港的繁荣稳定，保证澳门顺利回归，促进海峡两岸的经济交往。

（七）加强外经贸法制建设，创建公开、公平、公正的国内竞争环境

加强法制建设，加大执法力度，以《对外贸易法》为基础，继续完善和实施涉外经济贸易的法律法规，推动外经贸领域的法治化进程。抓紧制订货物进口管理条例、对外承包工程和劳务合作管理条例和技术进口、技术出口管制条例，适时修订现行利用外资的基本法律和出口配额管理办法，进一步完善外经贸法律体系。抓紧实施《反倾销法》，推动《反垄断法》尽快出台，为内外资企业开展平等竞争创造良好条件。做好保护知识产权工作，既保障国外技术转让者的利益，也保障我们依法取得国外先进适用技术的权利。

（八）提高外经贸队伍的整体素质，培养和造就面向21世纪的外经贸人才

重视培养和造就面向21世纪的外向型人才，以邓小平理论为指导，按照党中央、国务院的要求，有目的、有计划地加大外经贸工作人员的教育和培训，全面提高外经贸工作人员的政治素质、业务素质、道德素质和身体素质，增强发展意识、开放意识、竞争意识和法律意识，为促进我国对外经济贸易的进一步发展创造条件。

继续深化外经贸体制改革 推动私营生产企业外向化发展

对外贸易经济合作部副部长　孙振宇

1998 年 12 月 23 日

各位代表、同志们：

首先，我代表外经贸部祝贺这次私营企业外向化发展高层研讨会的召开，并向参加研讨会的各位代表表示欢迎！

关于深化对外经贸体制改革问题，江总书记早就有过论述。他在十五大报告中指出："深化对外经济贸易体制改革，完善代理制，扩大企业外贸经营权，形成平等竞争的政策环境。积极参与区域经济合作和全球多边贸易体系。"江总书记还指出，努力扩大商品和服务的对外贸易，优化进出口结构。坚持以质取胜和市场多元化战略，积极开拓国际市场。私营企业经过 20 多年的巨大发展之后，已成为我国社会主义市场经济的重要组成部分，理应在贯彻和落实十五大报告的这一精神中作出自己的贡献。今天，中华全国工商业联合会和中国对外贸易经济合作企业协会联合举办的这次私营企业外向化发展高层研讨会，其目的就是要与各私营企业代表共同研讨如何尽快贯彻十五大报告的这一精神，在深化外经贸体制改革中推动私营生产企业外向化发展，使私营生产企业为我国外经贸事业的发展做出贡献。

下面，我着重讲三个问题。

一、我国对外经贸体制改革二十年的简要回顾

1978 年改革开放以后，我国开始逐步改革外贸经营体制，主要措施有以下几点：

（一）生产企业外贸经营权自动登记扩大试点，并通过试点逐步过渡到完全的登记备案制。为了稳步实行外贸经营从审批制向登记制过渡，在去年对 5 个经济特区的生产企业外贸经营权实行自动登记试点的基础上，今年扩大了试点范围，首先做好对国家重点联系的 1000 家国有大型企业外贸经营权实行登记备案制的试点工作；进而通过试点，逐步取消对生产企业自营进出口的审批制度，取而代之以登记备案制，实现我国的对外承诺，即在加入世界贸易组织后 3 年内实现进出口经营权依法登记制。

（二）加快审批和赋予其他国有大中型生产企业的对外经营权，逐步放宽地县有实力的外经贸企业申报对外经营权的条件，并赋予一大批企业边境贸易经营权。同时，对边境贸易继续放宽优惠政策。

（三）建立进出口企业经营权资格证书年审制度。外经贸部决定从 1999 年起建立进出口企业资格证书年审制度，规定凡经外经贸部或其授权审批机关批准或备案登记的各类进出口企业必须参加每年的年审。

（四）赋予私营生产企业和科研院所自营进出口权。1998 年 10 月 1 日外经贸部发布《关于赋予私营生产企业和科研院所进出口经营权的暂行规定》，从 1999 年 1 月 1 日起，符

合规定的私营生产企业和科研院所可从事进出口贸易，并享受与公有制自营进出口生产企业和科研院所同等待遇。

中国外贸经营权曾是中国外贸经营体制的核心和基础之一。从 50 年代中期到改革开放以前，中国实行由国家统制外贸，国营外贸专业总公司高度集中垄断的经营体制。当时中国只有十几家外贸专业总公司，包括总公司在各地的分支机构，总数约为 100 多家。当时的外贸政策是以自力更生为主，以出定进，进出平衡，调剂余缺，外贸体制与国内高度集中的计划经济相适应。外贸经营体制的主要特点是高度集中，政企不分，统负盈亏。这种以高度集中为主要特征的外贸经营体制是在我国产品经济和单一计划经济基础上，面对帝国主义的经济封锁，对外贸易只能以社会主义国家为主的环境下建立的。在当时的历史条件下，这种外贸经营体制对打破西方国家的封锁禁运，集中全国财力，恢复和发展国民经济发挥过重大积极作用。

对外开放 20 年来，我国对外经济贸易随着生产力的发展不断壮大，对外经济贸易活动的深度和广度不断扩展，截至 1998 年 11 月底，具有对外经营权的国内各类外经贸企业已达 18 万多家，其中外贸流通公司 9000 多家，自营进出口生产企业和科研院所 1 万家，边贸企业 3000 多家，外经企业 800 多家。再加上已开业的 16 万家三资企业，目前已形成多层次、多渠道的外贸经营格局，外贸经营主体的多元化不仅体现在外贸企业数量的增加，而且具体反映在外经贸企业不仅包括原有的外贸专业公司，还进一步扩展到各类工贸公司、生产企业、科研院所、大专院校、商业批发和零售企业、粮食和物资企业、农民合作经济组织（供销社）、建筑公司、劳务公司、专业工程公司和设计院，以及三资企业，几乎覆盖了我国国民经济的所有部门。

二、非公有制经济是我国市场经济的重要组成部分

党的十五大报告指出，“公有制为主体、多种所有制经济共同发展，是我国社会主义初级阶段的一项基本经济制度”，“非公有制经济是我国社会主义市场经济的重要组成部分”。这些论述对个体、私营等非公有制经济的性质、地位和作用作出了新的评价，是我们的政策依据，它将贯穿整个社会主义初级阶段，我们应当继续鼓励、引导个体、私营等非公有制经济，使之健康发展。

在改革开放的这 20 年中，私营企业迅速发展壮大。据有关部门统计，1997 年，全国私营企业新登记 26.6192 万家，在 20 年中，年增长率 17.2%，总数达 96.07 万家。从业人员 1349.26 万人，比上年增长 15.21%。其中，私营企业出口创汇的 5659 家，比上年增长 28.8%；出口创汇折合人民币 111.91 亿元，比上年增长 12.22%。1997 年全国个体工商户、私营企业共向国家缴纳税金 540 亿元，比上年增长 20%，占全国工商税收的 7%。自 1988 年以来的十年间，个体、私营经济税收年平均增长速度为 36%，已成为财政收入的重要来源之一。在某些省份和地区，经营灵活、效益显著的私营企业已成为新的增长点，同时，这些企业在充分利用社会资源、增加社会财富和增加国家税收，以及支持进出口贸易等各方面都起到重大作用，相当一部分私营企业正在向规模化、集团化发展，走向跨省、跨行业，甚至跨国经营之列，它们为我国的社会主义市场经济的建立和完善作出了巨大贡献。

近20年改革实践证明，个体、私营等非公有制经济对满足人们日益增长的多样化的需要，增加就业，促进国民经济的发展有重要作用。因此，发展非公有制经济是符合“三个有利于”的标准的。目前，我国的私营企业还在以高速增长，同时企业规模不断扩大，外向型企业增多，这些都让我们看到了私营企业发展的光辉前景。

私营企业近年来的迅速发展，也让我们看到它本身的一些独特的优势。例如，私营企业机制灵活、产权明晰、与市场贴近，企业文化既有艰苦奋斗、诚实守信的传统美德，又有积极竞争、敢为人先的时代精神，这些都更有利于运用市场规律来约束、完善和发展自我。广大私营企业领导者在认识到私营企业的这些优势以后，将会更好得发挥这些优势，在市场经济发展过程中，私营企业要抓住机遇，积极竞争。这种竞争不仅仅指国内竞争，还包括国际竞争，要放眼世界，走出国门，参与到世界市场的竞争中，只有走外向化的道路，才能提高我们的竞争能力，才能在市场竞争的惊涛骇浪中立于不败之地。在私营企业外向化发展的过程中，外经贸部将根据国家的有关方针政策，给予私营企业以积极的支持。

三、积极争取自营进出口权，为我国外贸事业做贡献

1998年10月1日，外经贸部发布了《关于赋予私营生产企业和科研院所自营进出口权的暂行规定》，并将于1999年1月1日起实行。这一规定的颁布和实施，标志着我国在深化外贸体制改革的进程中又迈出了可喜的一步。

当前，全球经济一体化已成为世界经济不可扭转的发展趋势，判断各国经济水平的高低，外贸进出口额也已成为一项重要的衡量指标。我国发展外贸，历来以国有外贸公司为主，但近年以来，这种固有的外贸体制已经越来越不能满足我国日益发展对外贸易的需要，有一些外贸公司由于历史的包袱，和经营机制的束缚，难以发展，甚至陷入困境。鉴于这些情况，为促进我国外贸事业的更快发展，根据国务院的批准，赋予符合条件的私营生产企业自营进出口权，这对私营生产企业来说应该是一个前所未有的机遇。私营生产企业通过申请获得自营进出口权有利于更快、更及时地获得海内外经贸信息；由于省去代理商这一环节，企业可直接面对有关机构及海外客户，有利于减少沟通传递上的失误，还降低了产品成本，有利于增加企业效益和出口竞争力。私营生产企业应该抓住这个机遇，积极开拓国外市场，增强企业自身的实力，以体现非公有制经济在社会主义市场经济中的重大作用。

今年我国对外经贸发展遇到了空前的困难，特别是亚洲金融危机对我国出口的负面影响更加明显。另外，再加上今年夏季的特大洪灾，对一些企业的生产造成损失，我国外贸出口的形势不容乐观。

但是，在目前严峻的外经贸形势下，我国外贸出口在人民币币值保持稳定的条件下，仍保持了一定幅度的增长，1月－11月，全国进出口总额2865亿美元。其中，出口1639亿美元，增长0.2%；进口1226亿美元，下降0.6%，进出口顺差413亿美元，增长2.3%。取得这样的成绩是与党中央、国务院的正确决策是分不开的。这再次证明了，我国改革开放以来综合国力不断增强，国民经济的抗风险能力和对外经贸的应变能力的增强。这对我国的经济建设也是一次难得的考验。

经过20年的实践证明，我国的经济发展，不仅要靠国有企业的努力，同时更与广大私

营生产企业的努力是分不开的。广大私营生产企业在参与国际竞争中虽然比国有企业具有一定优势，但是也应看到，在一些方面，我们的企业与发达国家的企业相比还有较大差距，为了适应外向化需要，为从事进出口贸易做好充分准备，在些提出以下几点建议：

（一）明确目的，端正思想。企业家应认识到，获得自营进出口权不是目的，把产品、企业打出去，面对国际市场，国际竞争，为发展我国外贸事业做贡献才是真正的目的。因此，企业领导必须端正指导思想，脚踏实地，一步一个脚印地做好工作。

（二）注意培育和发展企业的著名品牌、名优产品。我们要注意研究国际市场的需求，坚决贯彻“以质取胜”和“市场多元化”二大发展战略。要强化质量意识，提高出口商品质量，坚持走质量效益型的发展道路。要不断优化产品结构，提高产品科技含量和技术附加值，特别要注意大力发展各类机电产品、深加工产品，不断提高企业竞争能力。

（三）注意信息收集工作。搞出口贸易、项目投资切忌盲目性，注意广泛收集国内外信息，以适应知识经济时代的需要。

（四）注意人才的培养。市场竞争主要是人才的竞争，外经贸工作不仅是面对国内外两个市场的经济工作，同时又是外事工作，必须培养思想素质、政治素质、文化素质、业务素质都比较高的业务骨干队伍。

（五）遵纪守法，维护正常的外贸经营秩序。要立足于国际市场上的竞争，对外经贸工作政策性比较强，我们从事外经贸工作的企业要增强法制观念，认真学习，自觉执行国家早已颁布的《对外贸易法》、《商检法》、《海关法》等一系列法律法规和行政规章。一定要从国家的根本利益出发，坚决制止、纠正抬价抢购、低价竞销的不正当的行为，坚决反对走私，反对逃汇、套汇、骗税等不法行为。在市场竞争中，要守合同、讲信誉，不断提高企业的声誉，这样才能树立起良好的企业形象，才能在竞争中立于不败之地。

（六）不断强化企业内部管理。外经贸业务环节多，涉及到方方面面，容易在运作过程中出现漏洞，暴露出薄弱环节。企业一定要练好内功，建立现代企业制度，完善企业经营机制，把企业建成现代化的外向型私营企业，为我国的外贸事业做更大的贡献。

关于经济全球化问题的几点思考

对外贸易经济合作部首席谈判代表　龙永图

去年7月始于泰国的金融危机迅速波及东南亚各国，继而冲击韩国和日本，引起全球震荡，使人们更深刻地意识到各国经济间那种日益相互关连、相互渗透、相互影响、相互依存的关系。经济全球化确实已经成为一个不能回避的现实，一个不以人们意志为转移的大趋势。我们只有从经济全球化这个大背景下，才能认识东南亚金融危机产生的深刻原因，从而对今后如何做好我们的经济工作提出符合实际的政策建议。

经济全球化的主要特点

一般认为、经济全球化是一种新的国际关系体制，它包括生产、企融和科技三个方面的全球化。三者之间，生产发展决定金融和科技的发展，同时金融和科技的发展又对生产发展产生巨大的反作用。因此，经济全球化的主要特点是生产的全球化，而企业作为经济增长和生产发展的原动力，在制造就业机会，发展新兴科技、积累物质财富方面都发挥着关键作用，成为了以生产全球化为主要特点的经济全球化的主导力量。这样，谈论经济全球化就不能不从这个现代经济的“细胞”谈起。

近年来，企业运营的一个趋势是世界上越来越多的公司企业走出国界，实行跨国经营，从而形成了一大批跨国公司，这些跨国公司在全球范围内组织生产和流通活动，成为经济全球化的动力和主体力量。根锯联合国《97年投资报告》的最新统计，目前全世界已有4．4万个跨国公司母公司和28万个在国外的子公司和附属企业，形成了一个庞大的全球生产和销售体系。这些跨国公司控制了全世界1/3的生产总值，掌握了全世界70%的对外直接投资，2/3的世界贸易，70%以上的专利和其他技术转让。这几个数字后面，特别引人注意的是，由于跨国公司通过直接投资，在全球范围内组织生产和销售，国际经济关系中投资的重要性和发展速度，已经大大超过了贸易。

从发展速度来看，国际直接投资从1983年至1995年，每年平均增长17.2%，大约是国际贸易年增长率的一倍。从重要性来说，举美国的例子，美国在1994年的出口只有2350亿美元，而美国海外投资的总销售额该年已高达一万亿美元。这是一个重要的变化，因为贸易的全球化是早已有的现象，而通过国际投资形成的生产和销售全球化的结合，就使经济的全球化形成一个新的趋势。

怎样来认识经济全球化呢？从实质上来看，经济的全球化，是一场以发达国家为主导，跨国公司为主要动力的世界范围内的产业结构调整。这一次产业调整，不但反应到一些产业的整体转移，而且更重要的是影响同一产业的一部分生产环节的转移。过去，产业结构的调整大多是在一个国家内部进行的，在一国内部进行产业结构调整的代价比起通过经济全球化进程进行的产业结构调整更高，经历的时间更长。所以，西方国家，特别是在投资和贸易比较开放的国家，比如美国和英国，由于在全球范围内实行了产业结构调整，正在经历着从工业经济向“知识经济”的过渡，从而给经济带来了强劲的发展势头。

这次世界范围内的产业结构调整，大体上采取两种形式，一是发达国家之间，通过跨国公司之间的相互交叉投资，企业兼并，在更大的经济规模基础上配置资源，开拓市场，更新技术，从而实现了发达国家间的技术和资金密集型产业的升级。这一过程主要开始于80年代，那时所有的外国投资的95%都是从发达国家流出，然后又由它们吸收整个75%的投资。交叉投资和兼并的结果，形成了许多诸如电讯、汽车等国际化程度很高的产业，形成了你中有我，我中有你的局面。二是发达国家把劳动和资源密集型的产业向发展中国家转移，特别是把这些产业，包括高技术产业中的劳动密集型生产环节向发展中国家转移。这一转移始于80年代，90年代愈演愈烈，促使了90年代以来发展中国家在全球吸引外资总量的比例从80年代的25%逐步上升，1992年达32%，1996年达到37%。

认识全球化的这一实质很重要，只有从全球产业结构调整的大背景下来考虑我们参与经济全球化进程的总体战略，才能使我国对外开放工作与国内经济工作紧密联系，从而使我国经济的发展在以全球产业结构调整为主要特点的经济全球化进程中趋利避害，争取最大利益，防范和减轻经济全球化可能产生的风险和弊端。

经济全球化产生的原因

经济全球化产生的原因是多方面的。冷战的结束，使经济因素在整个国际关系中占有越来越重要的地位．实现资源在更大范围内的有效配置，成为国际经济与合作的战略目标。同时，各国都在实行以市场经济为导向的改革，国际经济组织大力推动贸易投资自由化，促进了资金、技术、人员在全球范围更加自由、更加大规模的流动。这些无疑都是形成经济全球化的重要原因。但是，经济全球化产生的最重要的原因应该是当代科学技术日新月异的发展，可以说技术的进步是经济全球化的物质基础。美国未来学家约翰·奈斯比特在他的著作《全球杂谈》(Global Paradox) 中描述经济全球化的背景时指出，跨国界的计算机网络和信息高速公路的建立，使电视、电话、计算机连为一体，将整个世界变成了地球村。

在促使经济全球化形成的技术进步中，首先是制造业技术，特别是增长最快的电子机械和信息技术的发展。由于技术更新的加快．使产品的零部件和生产阶段具有越来越明显的可分性，使得同一种产品（比如汽车和大型电信设备）可以同时分布在十几个、几十个国家生产，使每个国家发挥其技术、劳动力成本等方面的优势，使最终产品成为万国牌的，“国际性产品”，产生明显的技术和成本竞争的优势。即使是在全球处于垄断地位的波音公司，其飞机零部件也来自十几个国家和地区，这些大型企业由于国际化生产而带有明显的全球化特点。著名的ABB公司总部设在瑞士，总裁是瑞士人，工作语言是英语，财务报表以美元为单位，生产销售遍及全世界。这个公司的总裁说过，“ABB公司四海为家，是许多个国家的公司在世界范 围内协作的联盟。”

当然，跨国公司要把生产过程分布到全球各地，最重要的条件是要提高通讯和运输的效率，并降低其成本，这样才能实现生产和服务的国际化进程。

从1930年到1990年，空运的成本已从平均每英里68美分降到1 1美分，纽约与伦敦的三分钟的电话费从244美元降到3美元，估计到2010年，这种费用可以降到3美分，使跨大西洋的通讯费几乎降到零。由于信息技术的发展、使快速、经济地在全球范围内传递大量信息数据成为可能，这样跨国公司的生产者和经理们，才可以把生产的各个阶段广泛分布在世界各地，通过信息传递，把这些生产统一组织起来而不至于形成管理的失控，从而使管理科学来了一次飞跃。此外，由于信息技术的发展，使管理者可以在瞬息之间了解世界各地的市场情况，并进行必要的计算，找出针对各地市场进行最有效的配置资源的赢利机会。

正是由于新兴技术和信息技术的发展，形成了全球化的趋势，所以大力发展高新技术，特别是信息技术，成为我们参加世界经济全球化的前提条件。

几 点 思 考

1．抓住经济全球化产业结构大调整的机遇，结合中国的国情，使外资更好地为经济服务

什么是中国的基本国情呢？第一，我们还是一个发展中国家、人口多，底子薄，地区发展不平衡，经济发展水平总的来看还不高。因此，我们要充分利用发达国家通过全球化进程进行产业结构调整的机会，把发达国家技术先进的劳动密集型产业转移到中国。我们要打破劳动密集型产业就一定是技术落后产业的旧观念，同时也要打破发展高新技术产业就不能利用我们低劳动力成本优势的旧观念。随着适用技术，如微电子技术、信息技术、生物技术和新材料技术在越来越多的产业里的快速应用，劳动密集型产业的技术含量也大大提高，同时，我们还要看到，在资金技术密集型的产业中，包括高新技术产业中也有劳动密集型的生产环节，我们要充分发挥我国人口多，劳动力成本相对较低的优势，大力发展技术含量高的劳动密集型产业，以及高技术产业中的劳动密集型生产环节，这不仅可以壮大我国的国力、而且可以解决十分重要的就业 问题。特别是由于我国地域辽阔、经济水平的地区差异较大，我们将在比较长的时间内保持我国劳动力成本低的优势。经济和发展组织（OECD）一份研究报告说，中国至少在今后 30 年内可以为外国投资者提供一个劳动力成本较低的投资市场。这一优势是韩国、马来百亚、菲律宾，更不要说是新加坡这样的国家可以比拟的。

第二，中国又是一个大国，我们必须有一个门类比较齐全的产业结构，特别是在世界上最新的产业部门中我们应占有一席之地。通过经济全球化的进程，许多发达国家已经实现了技术和资金密集型产业的升级。我们要通过吸引外资，特别是与资金技术力量雄厚的大的跨国公司合作，在发展劳动密集型产业的同时，建立我们自己的技术和资金密集型产业。要做到这一点、关起门来引进是不可能做到的。过去，在生产技术提高和产品升级换代的速度都相对较慢的时候，发展中国家，特别是国内市场较大的国家，可以通过引进先进技术，在国家政策的保护下进行国产化、建立自己的工业体系，赶上世界的先进水平。但是，在科学技术日新月异的时代、特别在电子、通讯、计算机、生物制品、精密仪器这些新的技术产业中，关起门来搞引进，等我们花几年时间自己搞出产品，技术早已落后，更不要说成本、市场等问题了。因此，我们必须在开放的环境中来发展这些产业，捷径就是利用外资，与有资金技术的大的跨国公司合作，成为跨国公司的国外生产基地，成为他们整个国际生产线中的一个环节和国际销售网络的一部分。这样，把他们的经济利益与他们在我国建立的合资企业的效益联系起来，他们才有动力不断地提供最新的技术，最新 的管理方式，我们的新技术

产业才能跟上全球技术更新发展的潮流，不断地保持技术的先进性，并在这一过程中壮大我们自己的专业技术和管理人才队伍，从而建立和发展我们的新技术产业。

总之，由于发达国家为了摆脱经济困境，实行自己的产业升级，发起了以跨国公司为主体的向外投资，寻求出路的整体战略，为我们大规模吸引外资提供了条件，创造了机遇，这是日本、韩国在60年代和70年代所不可能得到的机会。由于我国的国情，我们又可以同时充分利用发达国家在经济全球化进程中正在进行的两种形式的产业结构调整。大规模利用外资的工作，外部条件是具备的。主要由于有大的国内市场，国际资本的海外投资，一直看好我国，我国连续4年成为仅次于美国的全球第二大直接投资东道国，这实际上是国际经济社会对我国政治稳定、宏观经济健康的肯定。我们要利用经济全球化带来的机遇、从产业结构调整这个新的角度出发，把利用外资与国内经济结构调整紧密联系起来，以此提高利用外资的质量和效益。

2．从全球化的新视野出发，优化出口商品结构，全面参与国际贸易

信息时代所带来的新的生产方式和跨国公司在全球范围内布署生产和销售，已大大改变了传统国际贸易的分工模式，一个国家出于效率和成本的考虑，已不再一味地追求完整地占领一个产业，而是根据自身的综合实力和比较优势，尽力抢占一个产业的高技术和高附加值生产环节，同时把劳动密集和低附加值的生产环节留给其他国家，从而形成了新的国际贸易分工体系。由于全球化带来的这一新的贸易格局，那种以出口什么产品来决定出口结构优劣的传统观念已经过时。我们要从这个全新的视野，看待出口商品结构的“优化”，不要片面地认为在出口产品中制成品的比率高了，农副产品的比率下降了，出口结构就“优化”了。现在世界农产品的出口大国主要是发达国家，就从反面说明了这一点。目前，我国制成品在出口商品中的比重已达87%，但粗加工比重很大，出口制成品中进口零部件，特别是技术含量高的关键零部件仍占很大比例。因此，出口结构的优化不完全在于出口什么产品，关键看出口产品的技术含量和国际竞争力，看出口产品所包含的零部件中，特别是技术含量高的零部件中有多少是自己生产的，因为这才真正反映了对外贸易的效益，反映了外贸对于国民经济增长的贡献程度。当然，由于我国仍是一个发展中国家，解决就业问题十分重要，发展经济效益较低的加工贸易仍必须长期坚持，但大的方向应是增加一般贸易的比重。

从经济全球化带来的全新的国际生产分工出发，从观念上走出传统有关于优化出口结构的误区，不仅对于发展对外贸易，而全对于整个国民经济的发展都有重要意义。我们不能为了优化出口结构，而笼统在提出发展外向型的制造业和高新技术产业，这样有可能使各地一窗蜂地大搞某种出口制成品的项目，从而造成重复建设。许多地方为了在较短时间增加制成品的出口，可能不顾条件地上大项目，结果使一个工厂仅仅成为经济效益很低的产品组装车间。我们应从全球化带来的新的生产分工体系出发，鼓励各地根据自己的情况，有的占领一个产品生产环节的高附加值、高技术环节，有的从事附加值相对低的生产环节，然后通过各种不同的机制互相联合起来，或是与国外的跨国公司联合起来，成为全国甚至全球生产和销售系统的一部分，这样才有可能保证较高的生产效益和稳定的出口市场。我们的外贸企业应该在各个生产环节的分工和联系过程中，在生产与国际销售的联系过程中发挥独特作用。

近20年的改革开放、特别是全球化带来的新的贸易格局和贸易方式，也应该改变我国

外贸“进出口”的传统观念，而代之以“国际贸易”的新观念。传统的“生产什么出口什么，需要什么进口什么”的事应该主要留给有外贸权的工矿企业去做，专业外贸进出口公司应改为国际贸易公司，成为国际化生产和销售的组织者，建立自己的国际市场网络。在加工贸易中，专业贸易公司应该承担类似“外商”的角色，在“进料”和“来料”的过程中，在销售出口产品中，发挥更大的作用，使我国的加工贸易逐步走出只拿一点工本费的初级阶段，从而大大地提高加工贸易的经济效益。我们的专业贸易公司应逐步走向世界，大搞国与国之间的转口贸易，而不仅仅局限于中国与其他国家的进出口，从而成为名副其实的国际贸易公司。这样，我们的专业贸易公司才大有用武之地，而不致于因为外贸权的全面放开而惶惶不可终日。也只有这样，我们才能真正成为世界的贸易大国，改变我们的贸易额仍低于主要从事转口贸易的欧洲一些小国以及香港的这种被动局面。

3. 在贸易投资方面与跨国公司建立长期合作关系

经济全球化的主要推动力是跨国公司，特别是大的跨国公司。在美国，1995 年最大的 50 家跨国公司的对外投资占了美国对外投资的 63%，英国占了 71%、德国占了 51%，最高为澳大利亚，50 家最大公司占了其整个国家对外投资的 96%。从量上看是如此，从掌握的技术、市场网络来看，更是如此。特别值得注意的是，在发展中国家处于劣势的先进技术产业中，例如生产电信通讯产品、计算机、半导体产品、汽车、生物制品、光学仪器等行业中，全球化趋势发展更快、大的跨国公司通过全球化生产和销售，使这些产业的国际化和全球化程度大大提高、可以说不参加跨国公司在这些产业的全球性生产和市场网络，就很难加入这些产业发展的世界主流。因此，我们要顺应全球化的潮流，与跨国公司建立长期合作的战略伙伴关系。今后搞好利用外资工作的一个重点应该是吸收大的跨国公司的投资，抓好这个重点，我们就能从利用外资的数量上和质量上有一个大提高。在贸易上，我国外贸企业应跻身于跨国公司内部和跨国公司之间的贸易，这两项相加已占到世界贸易总量的 2/3，这里也有一个进入世界贸易主流的问题。应该说，我们和跨国公司建立战略伙伴关系的条件是具备的。跨国公司，特别是大的跨国公司在 80 年代以来，很大程度上调整了自己的经营战略，主要一个变化就是当地化，技术开发、人才开发和经营管理的当地化。上面讲到的 ABB 公司、总部只有 100 来人，而在全世界 160 个国家和地区建立的附属机构和企业雇用了 20 多万人。跨国公司的这种“当地化”经营战略对我们是有利的，经过几十年的努力，特别是改革开放以来，我们已经有了一定的工业基础，有了一批素质较高的人才，我们已有可能在相对平等的基础上与跨国公司合作，加之我们有市场的优势，可以用我们的一部分国内市场，吸引大的跨国公司来华投资建厂，同时换取进入跨国公司国际销售网络的机会，换取跨国公司转让技术的承诺。今后如果我们能够建立一批可以同大型跨国公司竞争的国内大企业，我们就可以在更有利的环境和条件下，搞好与外国跨国公司的合作。在以跨国经营为主要特点的经济全球化时代，中国作为一个大国，应该有一批跨国经营的公司和管理人才。

当然，开展大规模的跨国经营困难很大，最大的困难是没有具有国际经验的管理和其他专业人才。这方面，我们也需要同国外跨国公司合作，一是欢迎外国跨国公司，特别是大的跨国公司来华建立生产和销售基地，要是母公司能来则更好，我们可以同这些跨国公司联合，对外进行投资；二是在国外收购和兼并一些中小型跨国公司，以它们的技术、管理、市场渠道加上我们的资金，实行跨国经营，三是建立我们自己的跨国公司，先雇用外国人进行管理，然后逐步培养起我们自己的管理队伍。

4. 积极参与多边和区域经济和贸易合作

如果说企业是经济全球化的重要动力，那么各国政府、特别是国际组织则在这个进程中起了推动和规范的作用。在经济全球化的进程中，企业，特别是跨国企业的生产经营活动已经从国家的范围走向了全球的范围，这样就有一个在更广泛的范围内制定和实施规范全球经济贸易活动规则的必要性和紧迫性。这些多边国际组织、特别是制定和监督实施国际经贸规则的组织的重要性加大了，这明显地表现在世贸组织的工作中。为了推动经济全球化，使贸易、资金、人员、技术、金融的流动更加自由、更加规范，近年来各国际组织和区域经济组织大力倡导贸易投资自由化，也就是在全球范国内降低关税、减少非关税措施和改善投资环境、从而促进了资金、货物、技术、金融、人员在国与国之间的自由流动，表现为各国政府顺应经济全球化的浪潮，以政府行为推动经济全球化的特点。

根据世界贸易组织的资料，由于执行乌拉圭回合协议，发展中国家的平均关税水平在2000年将降到10%－12%，发达国家将降到3%～5%，配额和许可证管理的最后一个堡垒——纺织品的数量限制也将在2005年消失。最近世贸组织的《信息技术协议》，要求在2000年将270多种信息技术产品、零部件的进口关税降为零，就是适应新技术产业在全球布点的形势，为促进零部件在国与国之间的自由流动而达成的协议。这一协议将大大促进21世纪最重要的产业——信息技术产业的国际化生产。

关于区域集团化问题，50年代就有，但到了80年代加快了步伐，再到90年代已经形成了一个大气候。根据世贸组织的统计，目前世界上各种类型和层次的区域经济贸易集团和组织已达100多个，几乎所有国家和地区都不同程度的参与其中。其中，欧盟、北美自由贸易区和亚太经合组织发展最快，影响最大，而且最具活力。区域集团化的本质就是在一个地区率先实现贸易投资自由化，然后以此推动全球的贸易投资自由化，所以我们已经发现亚太经合组织在贸易投资自由化的很多领域已经走在世贸组织前面。

为了适应经济全球化带来的新的国际经济环境，我们应该积极参与全球和区域经济合作，特别是要争取参加新的国际贸易和投资规则的制定，在多边和区域组织推动贸易投资自由化的进程中，注意维护发展中国家的利益，为建立一个在权利和义务平衡基础上的公平合理的国际经贸新秩序而努力。

5. 发展壮大自己，迎接经济全球化的挑战

在我们看到经济全球化可能带来的机遇，并敢于抓住这个机遇，使中国进入世界经济主流的同时，我们也要看到它带来的巨大挑战。如果我们不能正视这个挑战，全球化可能给我们带来风险。在许多国家，特别是一些发展中国家，这些风险都已经造成了实际的影响，一些国家的产业特别是金融遭受冲击造成了经济不稳定，一些国家政府控制经济的能力下降，一些国家经济结构调整过快而带来大量失业等，一些小国更面临着被全球化发展“边际化”的趋势。所有这些都不得不引起我们的极大关注。

但是在谈论经济全球化所带来的机遇和风险、利和弊时，我们不能把二者割裂开来，象开中药方一样分两类列出机遇有哪些，风险有哪些，利有哪些，弊有哪些，实际上它们是一

个矛盾的两个方面，或者形象地说是一个铜板的两个方面，它们是同时存在一个矛盾体中的。我们的工作就是要把机遇和利变成矛盾的主要方面，从而使矛盾在总体上向对我们有利的方面发展。为了使我们在经济全球化中趋利避害，关键是要壮大我们的经济实力。首先是营造一个能应付风险的国内环境。构成这种环境的重要因素包括良好的宏观经济政策，符合国际规范的健全的经济法规体制，能配合经济发展进度的相应的基础设施，特别是“软设施”，即高效率的教育和科技事业。应该说，在以上几个方面，我们近年来都取得了举世瞩目的成就，使我们的经济力量不断发展，从而在这次巨大的亚洲金融危机中站稳了脚跟。但是，应该看到，我们仍有许多工作要做，特别是在建立和实施健全的经济法规体制上。

现在看来，全球化对我们的最大挑战之一在于我们能否建立一套相互配合、一致连贯的政策法规体系。一般来说，政府可以依赖如下几种政策：外国直接投资政策、贸易政策、与国内经济活动有关的政策、竞争政策等配套使用、规范经济活动的行为，以确保对外开放工作对我发展国民经济有利。这一点应该看成是对外开放中的一个共性问题。从各行各业来看，我们应该不怕开放，怕就怕没有一整套系统的、行之有效的法律法规，没有一支素质优良，清廉公正的执法队伍来进行管理。

在这一方面，更具有挑战性的还是在对外投资政策与贸易政策、国内有关经济管理政策方面的协调。如前所说，随着国际投资的重要性比国际贸易越来越大，一个国家的贸易政策要很好地为外资政策服务。比如关税问题，以后恐怕要更多地与怎样更好地促进吸引外资的工作联系起来。最近我们决定参加《信息技术协议》，把《协议》涉及的通讯、半导体、计算机等270多种信息技术产品的关税大部分在2000年降到零，主要就是为了能使我们成为国际跨国公司信息技术产品全球生产基地的一部分，从而同时进入国际销售网络。看起来，降税以后可能会减少关税收入，但建立了新兴产业，今后可以收取更多的国内税，应该说是利大于弊。此外，还要针对吸引外资方面存在的垄断市场、逃避税收、违约违法等问题，充分利用符合国际惯例的国内政策措施保护我们的利益，通过制定反倾销、反补贴、反垄断等法律，规范市场竞争机制，限制外资的不正当经营行为。总之，只要有一整套行之有效的法规、政策体系，我们就可以更加放心大胆地发展对外贸易，更大规模地吸引外资，加快我国加入经济全球化的步伐。经济全球化是大势所趋，我们只要能够壮大自己，就一定能在这一进程中趋利避害，在开放的大环境中，使中国成为21世纪的经济大国。

从封闭走向全方位、多层次、宽领域的对外开放

对外贸易经济合作部党组成员、中纪委驻部纪检组长　刘向东

在邓小平同志的倡导下，党的十一届三中全会作出了对外开放的重大决策，开辟了我国对外开放的新纪元，为我国经济和社会发展注入了新的活力。20 年来的实践证明，解放思想，实事求是，搞好对外开放，对于把我国建设成为富强、民主、文明的社会主义现代化国家意义重大，影响深远。

一

20 年前，在我国历史发展的转折时期，邓小平同志以其非凡的政治敏锐和判断力，精辟地总结了我国发展的历史经验教训以及世界各国发展的经验，分析了和平与发展成为时代主题，我们争取长时间和平环境进行国内建设的必要性和可能性；准确及时地把握时代发展的脉搏和契机，提出了当今世界是开放的世界，任何国家的发展都离不开世界这个时代的趋势，果断地提出实行对外开放的重大决策。他指出，对外开放是面向全世界的开放，既对西方发达国家开放，也对苏联、东欧国家开放，对广大第三世界发展中国家开放。邓小平同志预见到对外开放可能遇到的风险和阻力，鼓励大家大胆实践，要坚决；对外开放是坚定不移的，但在开放过程中要小心谨慎；要采取两手政策，一手抓改革开放，一手抓严厉打击经济犯罪，包括抓思想政治工作。针对国内外有些人的担心和疑虑，邓小平同志反复阐明，对外开放不会导致资本主义，伤害不了我们；开放得还不够，要继续开放，更加开放；对外开放是长期政策，不会改变，要变的话，只能变得更加开放。20 年来，邓小平同志对外开放思想已形成较完整的体系，成为邓小平理论重要组成部分。

邓小平同志身体力行，亲自领导我国对外开放的实践。党的十一届三中全会结束不久，我国就试办了深圳、珠海、汕头、厦门四个经济特区。随后又开放 14 个沿海港口城市。相继将珠江三角洲、长江三角洲、闽南厦漳泉三角地区辟为沿海经济开放区；开放辽东半岛、山东半岛；举办海南经济特区；开发和开放上海浦东新区、沿长江流域的一些城市以及陆地边境城市和内地省会城市等；在一些开放城市的适宜地区设立保税区。1992 年春，邓小平同志到南方巡视，再次鼓励大家："改革开放胆子要大一些，敢于试验，不能像小脚女人一样。认准了的，就大胆地试，大胆地闯。深圳的重要经验就是敢闯。"

20 年来，我国实现了对外开放的历史性飞跃，为全世界所瞩目。目前，我国形成了由沿海到内地、由一般加工业到服务业的全方位、多层次、宽领域的对外开放格局，国民经济由封闭和半封闭状态走向开放型经济。外经贸管理体制改革朝着"统一政策、放开经营、平等竞争、自负盈亏、工贸结合、推行代理制"的方向不断深化。对外开放口岸由原来的少数几个增加到今天的海陆空一类口岸 240 多个，关税平均总水平由 40% 以上降低到 17%，非关税措施也大幅度减少，人民币实现了贸易经常项目下的可兑换。对外经济贸易合作破除许

多旧的思想框框束缚，开辟了利用外资、对外承包工程和劳务合作、技术出口、对外投资、接受援助等新领域；对外贸易渠道拓宽，方式更加灵活；援外方式不断改进，正向互利合作发展；技术贸易实现引进和输出的双向发展，整个对外经济贸易形成了商品、资金、技术、劳务紧密结合，相互促进的局面，外经贸经营主体多元化，正由经营许可制向自主登记制转变，初步形成了覆盖全社会、各物质生产部门共同参与的空前活跃的大经贸格局。目前，我国已同世界上 220 多个国家和地区有贸易关系，150 多个国家和地区有资金合作，130 多个国家和地区开展承包工程和劳务合作，对 90 多个国家提供经济技术援助，同绝大多数国际经济组织特别是联合国发展系统发展了广泛的合作关系，参与了许多区域性经济组织及单项商品国际组织的合作，形成了双边、多边经贸关系相互促进、共同发展的生动局面。我国在对外经贸合作中，重合同、守信用，坚持以质取胜，国际信誉和合作水平大为提高。对外开放使我国经济发展的回旋余地扩大，避免了以往的大起大落，1979 年—1997 年，年均保持了 9% 以上的持续、快速、健康发展。对外贸易进出口额由 1978 年的 206 亿美元增加到 1997 年的 3250 亿美元，年均增长 15.6%，远远高于同期世界贸易增长速度，在世界贸易中位次由 1978 年的第 32 位上升到 1997 年的第 10 位。国家外汇储备由几亿美元增加到 1400 亿美元。利用外资从无到有，实际投入资金累计达到 3483 亿美元，兴办外商投资项目的 30 多万个，年直接投资额仅次于美国，居世界第二位，列发展中国家第一位。对外承包工程和劳务合作异军突起，累计签订合同额 710 亿美元，完成营业额 470 亿美元，成为国际承包市场一支生力军。

对外开放，特别是对外经济贸易的大发展，在国民经济发展中发挥了不可替代的重要作用。

第一，扩大了资源的有效配置范围，拓宽了经济发展的回旋余地。随着生产技术的发展，对资源的需求更为广泛，各国必须通过国际间的交换，利用国内外两种资源和两个市场，互通有无，取长补短。我国人均资源占有量少，资源储量很不平衡，有的资源探明储量很少，不能满足经济发展的需要；有的由于资金技术等问题不能解决，难以充分供应。这些都需要通过对外经济贸易活动来解决。我国出口已占当年国民生产总值的 20% 以上，利用外资 1997 年上升到占社会固定资产总投资的 14.9%，成为支持国民经济发展的重要因素。

第二，发挥比较优势，促进经济结构和产业结构的调整，提高国民经济运行的整体效益。我国发展起步晚，底子薄，基础设施和技术比较落后，资金严重不足。我们利用优势条件吸引外来投资，引进先进适用技术，加快了我国的水利、能源、交通、通讯等基础设施建设，加快了企业的技术改造；促进了机械、电子、石化、汽车和建筑业等支柱产业的发展。

第三，吸取人类创造的文明成果，在较高的起点上发展，形成后发优势。按照我国现代化建设三步走的战略，我们要用 100 年时间，达到西方发达国家用了三百多年的时间达到的经济发展水平。这就要求我们通过国际经济技术交流和合作，吸取和借鉴人类共同创造的一切文明成果，特别是先进技术和管理经验，在更高的起点上开发、创新、赶上世界经济技术的发展水平。我国航天、造船、石化、家电、汽车以及纺织、轻工等行业的发展就是有力证明。

第四，提高了我国的国际地位，有利于维护国家的安全。对外经济贸易是国家经济实力的综合反映，是联系各国间经济的纽带。我国经济实力和与各国、各地区的利益关系是通过对外经济贸易体现出来的。对外经济贸易的发展使别的国家、地区对我国依赖加大，又使我国的实力明显反映出来，其他国家对我采取不友好措施，首先要考虑对自身的损害；在冷战结束，各国转向以综合国力竞争为主的今天，经济合作关系日益成为巩固外交关系的重要因素；对外经济贸易发展有利于我国加强同世界各国的了解和友好关系，创造建设社会主义现代化的良好外部环境，制约别国对我采取敌视损害行动，有利于国家的安全。

第五，推动了祖国和平统一进程。内地和香港、澳门间的经济贸易发展，为香港、澳门的平稳过渡，主权顺利回归创造了条件。台湾与祖国大陆之间经济贸易合作的发展，加深了台胞对祖国大陆的了解，也使越来越多的人认识到台湾经济发展离不开祖国大陆；我国同世界各国经贸关系的发展，实施市场多元化战略，也有利于遏制台湾当局的“弹性外交”，都有利于促进祖国的和平统一。

二

20年来，我国之所以从封闭走向全方位、多层次、宽领域的对外开放，最根本的一条就是始终遵循邓小平同志一贯倡导和强调的要解放思想，实事求是的思想路线，正确认识了世界发展的趋势，科学借鉴别国现代化建设的经验服务于我国现代化建设的实践，冲破了一系列障碍，从实际出发创造性地开展了工作，正确地处理了对外开放过程中出现的新情况、新问题。

扩大对外开放、吸收外商直接投资，会不会冲击“民族工业”和“民族经济”发展，动摇社会主义经济基础？对此，邓小平同志在1991年视察上海时就指出：“开放不坚决不行，现在还有好多障碍阻挡着我们。说‘三资’企业不是民族经济，害怕它的发展，这不好嘛。发展经济，不开放是很难搞起来的，世界各国的经济发展都要搞开放，西方国家在资金和技术上就是互相融合、交流的。”（〈邓小平文选〉第3卷第367页）从历史上看，保护民族工业是在中国处于半封建、半殖民地，统治者腐败无能，西方列强依仗不平等条约取得特权，不断扩大外资在华的势力，控制中国的经济命脉的历史条件下，一些爱国志士和民众提出来的，反映了要求国家独立、自主、富强的进步潮流。如果延用历史上“民族工业”的概念，现时我国的“民族工业”包括国有工业、集体所有制工业和私营工业，还应包括台港澳地区以及海外华侨在国内投资办的企业。虽然我国对台港澳地区实行“一国两制”，在经济贸易合作方面比照对外经济贸易处理，但毕竟都是中华民族，是中国领土不可分割的部分。海外侨胞是中国的公民，他们来国内投资，是国民资金的回归。而在我国利用外资的统计中，台港澳同胞在内地的投资占68%，如果再加上海外华侨和华人，应在70%以上。如把这些都排除在“民族工业”之外，显然是不合情理的。建设有中国特色的社会主义，实现现代化目标，必须发展最广泛的爱国统一战线。这就要求我们高举爱国主义旗帜，团结一切可以团结的力量，调动一切积极因素，化消极因素为积极因素，为推进社会主义现代化建设和改革开放服务，为促进“一国两制”、和平统一祖国、振兴中华服务。

我们是以公有制为主体的社会主义国家，利用外资是否影响了社会主义公有制的主体地位？1997年外商投资企业内销产值仅占全国的0.5%。改革开放以来，利用外资在国民经济发展中发挥了多种作用。弥补了建设资金不足，建设起一批急需发展的项目，开辟了新的财税来源，1997年来源于外商投资企业为主的涉外税收993亿元（不包括关税和土地使用费)，比上年增长29.9%，占全国工商税的13.16%，是增长最快的税源之一。引进了先进技术和管理经验，推动了相关工业的技术进步，缩小了与国际先进水平的差距，填补了一些技术空白，使一大批产品更新换代，培养了一大批现代管理人才。促进了进出口贸易发展，改善了国际收支平衡。1997年外商投资企业进出口值占全国进出口总值的46.9%，其中出口占41%，其出口的机电产口占全国同类产品出口的57.8%。1987年以来，外商投资企业外汇平衡连年有余，1997年外汇调剂中心净调出和银行结汇顺差165.86亿美元，其中贸易项下销售汇顺差81.62亿美元。增加了劳动就业岗位，已开业的“三资”企业共容纳劳动力1750万人。实践证明，吸收外商直接投资，对现有企业进行嫁接改造，有利于壮大公有制的实力，保持公有制的主体地位，不是限制外商投资，而应是如何利用外资使其发展壮大。

强调扩大对外开放、发展对外经济贸易，绝不能忽视自力更生。历史已经作出结论，中国只能走社会主义道路，不能走资本主义道路；中国要发展，必须从本国国情出发，走自己的路，把立足点牢牢地放在主要依靠自己力量的基础上。只有增强自力更生的能力，才能在国际上获得较高的信誉，吸引更多的合作者；才能更好地消化吸收外国的投资、先进技术与管理经验，取得更好的经济和社会效益，加快本国经济发展。对属于国家经济命脉的产业应当主要依靠自己的力量来发展，将主动权牢牢掌握在自己手里。在下大力气加快引进技术的消化、创新的同时，应主要靠自己的力量超前开发对经济发展具有重要战略意义的技术。这样，我们在对外开放中才能掌握自己的命运，才能通过扩大对外经济技术交流和合作，促进我国的现代化建设。

注意培养造就有理想、有道德、懂业务的涉外经济人才。对外开放政策要靠人去执行。国际竞争归根到底是人才的竞争。在重视专业技术教育、提高技术和管理水平的同时，通过各种途径和方式，坚持不懈地对全民进行爱国主义、社会主义、自力更生、艰苦奋斗和理想、信念、道德的教育，发扬中华民族的光荣传统和为国家富强献身的精神。历史的经验表明，如果任凭妄自菲薄、崇洋媚外、拜金主义和享乐思想滋长，将会产生不可低估的腐蚀作用，涣散我们的斗志。随着我国经济的发展，人民的物质生活将会逐步改善，但不能一味地强调物质待遇和物质享受，不可高估物质刺激的作用。我们共产党人激发人们建设社会主义的积极性，靠的主要是精神的力量，靠正确的理想和信念。我们要培养起一代又一代忠实于社会主义事业的有理想、有道德、有文化、有纪律的人才，只有这样，才能永远立于不败之地。

三

开放20年，弹指一挥间。在对外开放的道路上，我们已迈出了成功的一步，但还有相当长的路要走；我们虽已取得了巨大成就和丰富经验，但依然面临种种困难。在新世纪即将来到的时候，我们要高举邓小平理论的伟大旗帜，勇敢面对严峻的挑战，不失时机，抓住前所未有的有利条件和大好机遇。当前，世界政治、经济继续向多极化格局发展，和平与发展仍然是当今世界的两大主题，客观上为我国发展经济提供了相对稳定的国际环境。世界商品贸易，服务贸易仍将以较高的速度增长，国际金融市场容量将进一步扩大，高新技术进一步发展和广泛应用，为我国扩大商品和服务贸易、引进先进技术和资金提供更多的机会。世界经济全球化和地区经济集团化趋势加强，世界经济结构正在进行新的调整，以关税与贸易总协定为代表的一系列规范国际贸易、国际技术扩散的框架性协议得以签订，许多跨国性的金融集团和投资集团正在膨胀。

但是，我们扩大对外开放也面临不少困难。如世界经济区域集团化步伐加快，贸易保护主义加剧，加大了我国商品进入这些市场的难度，国际经济关系政治化倾向日趋严重。一些西方国家不断制造麻烦，妄图遏制我国发展，东亚金融危机引起国际经济的动荡，对我造成的影响不可忽视，我国技术比较落后，产品结构改变较慢，在国际分工和世界经济结构发生深刻变化的情况下，不利于在国际市场上的竞争。

江泽民同志在党的十五大报告中强调："能否抓住机遇历来是关系革命和建设兴衰成败的大问题"。他号召："现在全党一定要高度自觉，牢牢抓住世纪之交的历史机遇，迈出新的步伐。"我们要针对形势的特点，采取适当的政策措施，抓住机遇，趋利避害，扩大对外开放，使国民经济更好地发展。

第一，建立规范成熟的对外开放体系。根据国家产业结构调整导向和优先发展基础工业、基础设施的战略部署，充分发挥中西部地区的资源和劳动力优势，通过扩大对外开放，引进外来资金、技术和人才，加快中西部地区资源的开发和基础设施建设；继续推动沿海地区对外开放向纵深方向发展，提高沿海地区对外开放的水平和层次；积极创造条件扩大对外开放的领域，使对外开放进一步向广度发展。根据参与多边贸易体制和亚太区域经济合作的要求，逐步实现货物、服务、资金、技术的合理、双向自由流动，适当开展对外直接投资，全面提高其他各项对外经济技术合作与交流的水平。统一规范全国对外开放政策，除经济特区实行国际上通行的自由贸易区政策外，全国其他地区都要实行统一的开放政策；不同经济成分的企业要在统一政策下平等竞争。建立符合国际规范的对外经济贸易宏观调控体系。按照进出结合、统一管理、放开经营、关税调节、总量控制的基本原则，统一对外承担多双边义务，增强外经贸管理的统一性和透明度，建立有利于形成总体竞争优势的组织管理形式；在宏观管理方式上，形成以汇率、关税、税收、信贷等手段为主的促进国际收支和进出口平衡机制；统一关税政策，逐步将关税总水平降低到与我国经济发展水平和对外开放形势相适应的水平，并减少非关税措施；健全法制，依法经营管理。

第二，深化外经贸企业改革，实现增长方式的根本转变。对外经济贸易在国民经济现代化建设中的地位日益重要，深化企业改革，转变增长方式更为迫切。我国长期处于外汇短缺的状况，增加创汇是主要矛盾，受经济技术水平和经营水平的局限，一直以出口商品数量的增加来增加创汇，而对提高单位商品创汇率和人民币的盈亏重视不够。现在，我国外经济贸易的规模已经不小，现代化建设对外汇的需要更加迫切，国际市场的竞争日趋激烈，我国的基本国情又是人口多、人均资源少，必须提高商品技术含量和附加值，以较少的资源消耗，创造更多的外汇。即使采取"两头在外"的发展战略，也要以较高的效益为条件。而且现在面临着人民币汇率升值，成本提高，经营环境趋紧的严重困难。所以，必须通过改革，使外贸发展转向以效益为中心的集约化发展轨道。

第三，抓住时机，积极、合理、有效地利用外资。要正确引导外资投向，优化投资结构，把利用外资和国内产业结构调整有机结合起来，鼓励外资投向国家优先发展的领域，严格执行外资导向政策，加大产业倾斜政策的力度。正确实施以市场换技术的政策，对国家鼓励的、投资额较大的技术密集型项目和高新技术项目，让出部分国内市场。沿海举办的出口加工项目要向高技术、高附加值发展。根据实际情况与条件，有步骤地通过试点，逐步对外资扩大开放金融、商业、外贸、旅游、运输等服务产业。根据我国利用外资的总方针，参照国际惯例，在保持政策连续性和稳定性的条件下，逐步给外商投资企业以国民待遇。

第四，坚持不懈地贯彻实施以质取胜和市场多元化战略。质量反映一个民族的素质，关系着我国的对外形象和信誉；开拓市场和提高经济效益，冲破贸易保护主义，也都需要有好的商品和优质的服务，质量的标准是国际标准，要积极推广国际质量标准认证；要加快调整和改善进出口商品结构、吸收外商投资结构、对外承包工程和劳务合作结构、提高技术含量和附加值；要强化品牌意识，每个企业要有自己的品牌，创国际名牌，争取创出一批在国际上叫得响的名牌，带动我国出口商品和工程质量、信誉的普遍提高。

实施市场多元化战略，有利于在动荡多变的国际形势下减少风险；有利于冲破贸易保护主义和区域经济集团排他性措施，扩大市场；有利于发展中国家的团结和合作，以及抵制台湾当局的“弹性外交”，促进祖国统一。所以，我们要加大市场多元化的开拓力度，要下功夫深度开拓欧美等发达国家市场，下大力气开拓我国商品占有率很低的非洲、拉美、独联体、东欧、中东、南亚以及南太平洋国家等市场，确保经济贸易合作的稳步发展。

坚持双边、多边和区域合作并重的原则，继续巩固和发展多双边经贸关系。积极参与多边贸易体系活动符合我国长远利益，符合我国改革开放的需要。要争取在权利和义务平衡的原则下，尽快加入世界贸易组织（WTO)。世界贸易组织建立了一整套有关自由贸易制度的法律规则和条文，各缔约方都要遵守，因此，它也是我国处理与贸易伙伴双边关系的准则。随着我国对外贸易和经济合作规模的扩大，加入世界贸易组织更为紧迫。现在，我们要同某些发达国家乘机提高要价作斗争，也需要国内统一认识，加强协调配合，形成合力。

（文章选自《求是》杂志 1998 年第 22 期）

对外开放是我国一项长期基本国策

对外贸易经济合作部副部长　孙广相

1998 年 11 月 5 日

实行全方位对外开放是中国近、现代史无前例的伟大创举，它使中国经济社会发展逐步融入世界经济发展的主流，推动我国发生了重大而深刻的变化。

增强国民经济实力，提高了我国的综合国力

对外开放促使我国从原来的封闭、半封闭型经济开始逐步向开放型经济转变，利用“两个市场、两种资源”的水平有了很大提高，促进了生产要素在国际范围内的优化配置，实现了国内外的优势互补，增强了国民经济的实力。1979 年至 1997 年，我国对外贸易进出口额年均增速达 14.3%，高于全球 8 个百分点；占全球贸易总额的比重由 1978 年的 0.78%上升到 1997 年的 3.3%。对外贸易的高速增长成为我国经济发展的重要推动力量。我国国内生产总值由 1978 年的 3624 亿元上升到 1997 年的 74772 亿元，年均增长速度达到 9.81%，成为世界上经济增长速度最快的国家之一，总体经济实力明显增强。

促进了产业结构和劳动力布局结构调整，提高了经济发展质量，增强了我国经济的国际竞争能力。通过对外开放，我国原有的“重工业过重，轻工业过轻”的不合理产业结构得到一定改善，部分支柱产业和其他产业在竞争机制的作用下获得迅速发展，填补了国内市场空白，满足了经济发展需要。1979 年至 1997 年，在我国协议利用外资额中，农业项目占 1.57%，工业项目占 58.52%，第三产业占 39.91%。1983 年实际利用外资额占全社会固定资产投资总额比重仅 1.26%，1997 年这一比例上升到 14.79%。与此同时，对外开放还促进了生产要素在全国范围内的优化配置，通过劳动力由西部向东部流动、农村向城市流动，创造了大量就业机会，从事加工贸易就业人员约 3000 万人，三资企业从业人员达 1750 万人，在相当程度上缓解了我国经济和社会生活中最突出的矛盾之一。

通过不断扩大对外开放，我国对外贸易始终保持了快速、健康的发展势头，连续多年以两位数的速度增长，在全球贸易中的地位不断上升，即使在今年面临亚洲金融危机巨大影响的严峻形势下，1 至 9 月出口贸易仍比去年同期增长 3.9%。对外开放的扩大和对外经济贸易的迅猛发展，使得我国经济实力和综合国力大为增强，人民生活水平不断提高，在全球经济中的地位得到较大提升，国民经济抗风险能力显著增强。

对外开放加快了香港、澳门、台湾与祖国大陆融合的速度，为最终实现和平统一创造了有利条件。目前香港转口贸易的 70%是民内地直接相关的。香港赴内地实际投资也达到 851.9 亿美元，成为内地吸引外来投资的首要来源地。台湾与祖国大陆经济联系日益紧密，贸易和投资业务发展迅速。台湾已成为祖国大陆的第五大贸易伙伴和第二大进口市场，祖国大陆成为台湾的第二大出口市场。台湾赴大陆实际投资 142 亿美元，居祖国大陆吸引境外投

资的第二位。

对外开放面临的问题及矛盾

20 年来，我国的对外开放取得很大成绩，但也面临一些问题和矛盾，对进一步扩大对外开放形成了制约。这些问题和矛盾主要表现在：

1. 人们的思想观念和思维方式不适应社会主义市场经济体制和对外开放的要求。当前经济全球化趋势持续发展，世界科技进步一日千里，知识创新速度大大加快，综合国力竞争日益激烈，这一切，既为我国跨世纪发展提供了良好机遇，也给我国提出了严峻挑战。我们要按照江总书记指示精神，继续深入学习和领会邓小平理论，进一步解放思想、转变观念。

2. 经济体制和企业经营机制不适应对外开放的需要。在经济体制转轨过程中，现行的经济体制和企业经营机制很不适应对外开放的需要，增加了对外开放的成本和阻力。

3. 政府宏观管理和指导方式不适应对外开放的要求。目前政府宏观管理和指导方式虽然逐步有所改变，但直接行政干预手段仍频繁使用，各项政策不配套，降低了资源配置效率和对外开放的效果。

4. 基础设施和产业结构落后不适应对外开放的需要。改革开放后，我国基础设施和产业结构虽然得到一定改善，但中西部基础设施相对落后和产业结构中的深层次矛盾仍然存在，成为进一步扩大对外开放的制约因素。特别是主导产业国际竞争力较弱，扩大对外开放与保护国内产业安全、维护国家经济安全成为我们面临的新的矛盾。

5. 国际因素的制约。由于我国尚未加入世贸组织，对外开放不仅取决于我们的主观愿望和努力，也受到国际经济环境的制约。

“解放思想实事求是”——对外开放的基本经验及启示

改革开放 20 年的伟大实践，积累了大量成功的经验和作法，是建设有中国特色社会主义理论和实践的一笔宝贵财富，对于指导我国进一步扩大对外开放具有重大而深远的指导意义。

解放思想、实事求是是对外开放的前提。我国对外开放政策从提出到每一次大的开放举措出台，都是在党的实事求是思想路线指导下解放思想、转变观念的结果。特别需要指出的是，从我国对外开放政策的提出到对外开放过程中每个关键时刻，邓小平同志都发挥了重大历史作用。他在总结古今中外历史经验教训的基础上明确提出将对外开放作为我国的一项基本国策；以后在举办经济特区、海南开发开放、浦东开发开放、推进全方位开放和 1992 年利用外资政策的完善等重大开放举措上，小平同志都发挥了关键作用。实践证明，解放思想、实事求是不仅是对外开放的前提，也是我国对外开放不断前进的重要保证。

“开放也是改革”

扩大对外开放不仅有力促进了国民经济的持续快速健康发展，也为我国加快市场化改革提供了重要动力和借鉴，对外开放在推动现代化建设和建设社会主义市场经济过程中发挥了重大历史作用，正如邓小平同志指出的，开放也是改革；同时，国内市场化改革的深化和经济的发展也为扩大对外开放创造了条件，为对外开放的逐步扩大打下了坚实的基础。今后，我们必须根据“三步走”战略的部署，不失时机地扩大对外开放程度，提高对外开放水平，为改革和经济建设创造更好的条件。

邓小平同志历来强调，改革开放要敢闯、敢试，必须抓住机遇大胆开放；对外开放要与自力更生相结合，要通过对外开放更好地利用国外资源、技术、资金和市场，要体现小平同志“两手抓”的指导思想，在对外开放的同时搞活国内经济，增强国有企业竞争力。在明确对外开放的方向的同时，我们一定要注意把握好对外开放的时机和力度。在这次亚洲金融危机中，我国经济能够保持基本稳定，是与我们在资本市场的稳步开放分不开的。

全方位对外开放利于确保国家经济安全

20年来，我国对外开放地域从经济特区、沿海开放城市，扩大到沿边、沿江地区和省会城市等内陆地区；开放领域从一般加工工业向基础产业、基础设施和高新技术产业扩展，向金融、保险、外贸、旅游、通信、商业零售、法律咨询和会计等服务行业延伸。开放型经济已初步形成，为21世纪我国经济的持续发展打下了坚实基础。我国还积极参与多边贸易体系活动和亚太区域经济合作，努力扩大与世界各国（地区）的双边经贸关系，实施市场多元化战略，高度重视扩大与亚非拉发展中国家（地区）和前苏联东欧国家的经贸合作。在一个相互依赖的世界经济体系中，提高对外开放的广度和深度，提高参与国际分工和交换的水平和层次，有利于增强我国抵御国际上各种风险的能力，增强经济发展的回旋空间和自我调整能力，从总体上有利于确保国家经济安全。

按国际经济通行规则办事

我国要参与国际竞争与合作，就必须参照国际经济通行规则，不断深化经济体制和外贸体制的改革，并为企业按国际惯例经营创造条件。我国对外开放的一条重要经验就是，适应国际经济通行规则的要求，不断改革外经贸体制及其他方面的体制，为我国经济与国际经济互接互补创造条件。

不断提高对外开放质量和水平

党中央、国务院历来重视提高对外开放的质量和水平，党的十四届五中全会和十五大又特别强调了提高对外开放水平的重要战略意义。要根据实行两个根本性转变的要求，针对对外开放现有的差距和尚存的问题，在扩大对外开放程度的同时，着力提高对外开放的质量和水平，重点是提高利用外资的质量、档次和对外贸易的经济效益，转变外贸增长方式，使之在现代化建设中发挥更大的作用。

对外开放仅仅20年，我国经济和社会发展就发生了重要而深刻的变化。我们有理由相信，只要我们继续坚持对外开放的基本国策，我国一定能够逐步实现邓小平提出的“三步走”战略目标，使我国的综合国力和人民生活水平再上新台阶。

选自《国际商报》改革开放二十年征文

大力实施“科技兴贸”战略 推动我国外经贸事业持续发展

对外贸易经济合作部副部长　张　祥

1998年2月4日

一、实施“科技兴贸”战略对我国外经贸发展的重大意义

1.“科技兴贸”战略的提出

90年代以来，适应外经贸发展内外部环境的变化，我们先后提出了“市场多元化”、“以质取胜”和“大经贸”三大战略，对于指导外经贸发展与改革发挥了十分重要的作用。随着全球知识经济的到来，面对发达国家高科技的巨大优势，我国外经贸特别是出口发展面临的外部环境发生了重大变化，我国外贸发展进入一个调整和转型期。为此，石广生部长代表我部党组提出了要在继续实施三大战略的同时，大力实施“科技兴贸”战略的要求。这是我们实现外经贸跨世纪可持续发展的一个新战略。

2.“科技兴贸”战略是科教兴国战略在外经贸领域的具体体现

去年，新一届政府组成后，就把积极贯彻党的十五大提出的“科教兴国”战略作为本届政府的最大任务，把科技和教育提到了前所未有的高度。从去年我国外经贸工作的实践看，我国高新技术产品和机电产品出口在世界经济和贸易量增速放慢的情况下，保持了稳定、快速的增长。这充分说明，高新科技不仅对国民经济发展具有重大的推动作用，而且对外经贸发展也具有巨大的促进作用。高新技术产品出口已经成为外贸出口的新的增长点，具有很大的发展潜力。因此，我部把落实“科技兴贸”战略作为今年外经贸工作的重点之一，并成立了科技兴贸领导小组，由我任组长。此外，外经贸部还积极同科技部和信息产业部加强协作，建立联合工作机制，共同努力抓好“科技兴贸”战略的贯彻实施。

3.“科技兴贸”战略是我国由贸易大国走向贸易强国的必由之路

众所周知，当今世界各国经济实力的竞争，归根结底是科学技术的竞争。在国际市场竞争中，科学技术正日益成为最重要的决定性因素之一。从去年我国的外贸工作实践来看，虽然我国外贸出口总体上受到了世界经济贸易增速放缓的影响，但是高新技术产品和技术含量较高的机电产品出口都仍然保持了稳定、快速的增长。这充分说明，依靠科学技术，实施“科技兴贸”，提高我国商品的竞争力，是我们适应国际市场竞争的必然要求。我国在世界贸易中的排名由改革开放初期的第32位，变为1998年我国出口位居世界第九位，可以说，中国已经成为世界贸易大国。但是，中国还不是一个世界贸易强国，特别是从出口商品构成来看，中国出口商品虽然实现了由主要是初级产品向主要是工业制成品的飞跃，但是，科技含量和附加值高的商品在出口中的比重还不高，经济效益也不高。因此，中国要由贸易大国向

贸易强国迈进，就必须加大实施“科技兴贸”战略的力度。

4.“科技兴贸”是适应国际经济贸易发展规律的必然要求

知识经济兴起信息技术革命加快全球产业结构升级，高新技术产业蓬勃兴起。目前OECD国家高新技术产业产值占制造业产值的比重平均已近30%，2002年将达到40%，而我国台湾地区目前此比值已达37.5%；世界制成品出口中高新技术产品接近20%，2002年将达到25%，OECD国家平均已接近40%，其中美国达到49.6%，日本56%，我国台湾地区目前为48%，新加坡为70%。

而我国1998年高新技术产品出口在我国工业制成品出口额中仅占7%，和世界先进国家水平有着很大差距。国际经济贸易发展新趋势昭示着我们，顺应世界科技经济发展的新潮流，加速调整我国产业结构，大力发展高新技术产业，扩大高新技术产品出口，提高传统出口商品的技术含量，根本改变我国对外贸易产品结构，是时代的要求。只有这样，我们才能跟上时代发展的步伐，不断提高我国出口产品的国际竞争力，在国际经济和贸易中占据我们应有的一席之地。

世界一些国家的经验也充分说明了顺应世界发展潮流，抢占科技制高点，积极调整产业结构和进出口商品结构，对于增强一国国际竞争优势的重要意义。

20世纪80年代，美国由于传统制造业的国际竞争力遭到削弱，因此从里根政府开始，根据世界科技经济未来发展趋势，果断地实行经济结构调整，推动以信息技术为代表的高技术产业迅速发展。结果从1990年～1998年，美国经济连续9年保持增长态势。这主要得益于美国经济在政府主导下迅速实现了产业结构调整，以信息技术为代表的高技术产业支撑了美国的经济，使其在国际高新技术产品的竞争中保持领先地位。

台湾和新加坡作为新兴工业化国家和地区，积极顺应世界科技经济发展新潮流，大力扶持和发展高新技术产业，促进高新技术产品出口，取得了显著的成就。在东亚其他国家经济受金融危机影响都是负增长的时候，1998年台湾经济增长4.8%，新加坡经济增长1.5%。

印度根据世界经济科技发展新动向，选择软件这项高科技产业作为突破口，采取各种措施促进国内软件业的发展，不仅软件出口迅速增长，成为世界上仅居美国之后的第二大软件出口国，1998年，印度软件出口达24.5亿美元，在世界高科技领域占据一席之地，而且也促进了国内经济的发展。

以色列以高科技兴国，努力发展国际尖端技术。由于其在电信、医疗设备、环保技术、电脑软件、生物技术和化工、农业等领域处于世界领先地位，近几年以色列一直保持年均10%以上的出口增长率，高新技术产品占出口总量的70%。

爱尔兰由于政府制定了发展高科技的国策，高度重视教育，大力发展高科技和重点软件产品，已成为世界软件出口大国。仅有350万人口的爱尔兰已一个农业国家快速发展为高科技贸易国家。1997年人均出口1万埃镑（1埃镑相当于11元多人民币），是美国的5倍，日本的3倍。爱尔兰经济以每年8%速度增长，而欧盟国家仅为2%，在欧洲各国中一枝独秀。

二、实施科技兴贸战略的主要内容

1. 大力推动高新技术产品出口

目前，我国高科技产品在出口总额中的比重很低，与我国的国际地位和世界贸易大国地位还不相适应。而高新技术产品出口前途无量，是具有很大潜力的外贸出口新的增长点。因此，外经贸部将会同国家科技部等有关部门，加紧研究扶持鼓励措施，加快科技成果商品化，推动高科技产品出口，不断优化出口商品结构。外经贸部还将会同有关部门采取有效措施，加强祖国内地与香港的科技合作，充分发挥内地的科技优势和香港的市场优势，加快推动我国科技产品特别是高科技含量、高附加值的产品走向国际市场。1999 年，还将会同有关部门和地区积极筹备、在深圳举行的首次全国高新技术成果交易会，促进高新技术产品出口。经过一个时期的努力，我国高新技术产品出口将迎头赶上，缩小与发达国家的差距。

2. 利用高新技术改造传统出口产业

我国工业经过几十年的发展，已经形成门类齐全、成龙配套的工业体系，这就为我们运用高技术改造传统出口产业提供了一个良好的基础。只要我们积极推动在高起点上采用高技术，尤其是微电子技术、新材料技术和自动化技术改造我国的传统出口产业，就可迅速提高我国传统出口产品档次、水平，提高生产效率，降低生产成本，增强竞争力。在这方面我国最大的工业城市——上海市做得较早，成绩也较好。例如：上海机床公司将微电子技术和计算机技术用于机床工业，生产数控机床，出口产品档次和竞争力大大提高。又如上海微型轴承厂因在机械加工、热处理、内外自动分选、性能测试等多个环节实现了规模性一体化，大大提高了出口产品的质量，满足了供货期限和多品种适应能力的要求。

目前我国多数传统出口产业在采用高技术方面刚刚起步，在当今知识经济即将到来、高技术发展日新月异的环境下，我国传统出口产业可有机会选择利用世界最新的高技术成果，因此我国传统出口产业改造、传统出口产品提高科技含量、提高附加值潜力巨大，大有可为。

3. 积极落实促进高新技术产品出口的“五定”方案

“五定”方案就是以国际市场为导向，在中国具有优势的高新技术领域选择一批有市场竞争能力、附加值高、对开辟和拓展我国出口市场有较大作用的高新技术产品，通过定产品、定企业、定市场、定目标、定时间“五个确定”，创造有利的出口条件，力争在短期内形成一定的出口规模。目前，我们已经确定把信息、生物医药、新材料、消费类电子和家电等五个领域作为促进出口的重点突破行业，并成立了相应的五个工作小组进一步研究在这五个领域中选定具体出口商品、确定主要生产企业、选定出口市场、确定出口目标、规定时间进度等有关事宜。最近，各地的外经贸和科技主管部门正在这一原则的指导下，按照因地制宜的原则，根据本地实际情况，逐步做好这项工作的具体落实。

4. 制定鼓励和扶持发展高新技术产业、扩大高新技术产品出口的政策措施

发展高新技术产业和扩大高新技术产品出口，需要有一个稳定、良好的政策环境。外经贸部会同科技部等有关部门，正加紧研究有关推动高新技术产品出口的指导性意见和各种扶持鼓励措施。例如对高新技术产品出口实行全额出口退税，利用出口信贷和出口信用保险支持扩大高新技术产品出口；选择少数具备严格封闭监管条件的高新技术产业开发区建立规范化的出口加工区，为其商品、人员、资金等进出境创造便捷高效的运作环境，在更高程度上参与全球高新技术产业合作与竞争；加强对高新技术产品出口企业的金融支持，建立实行市场化运作的国家高新技术产品出口发展基金，支持出口规模大、前景好的高新技术产品及企业进行技术改造、产品开发、市场开拓和跨国经营，允许较为成熟的高新技术产品出口企业在国内外证券市场上优先上市和直接融资；对经过国家有关部门认定的高新技术产品生产企业自营进出口权实行登记备案制；为高新技术产品出口企业提供市场开拓支持等。以加快科技成果向商品转化，推动高科技产品的出口。

5. 搞好信息服务工作，促进国际经贸交流

我们正在研究组建专门的高新技术产品出口信息网，通过我驻外使馆经商处、科技处广泛搜集国外市场需求情况及有关国家促进高新技术产品出口的政策措施，做好高新技术产品全球市场状况及我国产品主要竞争对手的专题调查研究，及时为各方面提供最新的市场信息，为企业和科研院所牵线搭桥。

此外积极组织我国高新技术企业参加国际著名的博览会、展览会，开拓视野、激发灵感、结识客户、寻求机会、在国内开办国际高新技术交易市场、举办各类高新技术产品展览会、交易会。从今年起，每年秋季，国家将在深圳举办国际性高新技术成果交易会，为我国高新技术产品开拓国际市场提供一个展示自己的舞台。北京高新技术产品国际周也是这些经贸交流活动中重要的一项，外经贸部十分重视这项活动，我们将采取更多的必要措施支持科技周，使之更好地为我国的科技进步和产业发展服务。

三、创办充满活力的高新技术工业园区

高科技工业园是指一批大学、科研机构和企业在一定地域相对集中，以开发高新技术及其产业为目标，促进科技、经济同步发展的科研、生产以及贸易有机结合的基地。世界各国通过建立高新技术工业园区，孵化大批高新技术成果，促进高新技术的成熟，开在充分参与国际分工的条件下高起点地发展高新技术产业，增强国际竞争力，扩大出口。

美国硅谷是世界上第一个科技工业园，依托斯坦福大学、加州大学伯克利分校、圣何塞大学等，以其作为“人才源”、“信息源”，辐射区内的高新技术公司，从而带动和促进高新技术产业化。硅谷研究开发出许多先进的微电子技术，它生产的半导体元件占国际市场的四分之一，一些国际著名品牌商品，如苹果计算机、SUN微机系统等都是从这里走向世界。

为适应台湾经济转型升级的需要，发展高新技术产业，进一步提高科技水平和国际竞争力，摆脱内外部各种不利因素对经济进一步发展的制约，台湾当局仿照美国“硅谷”的做法，于1980年设立新竹科学工业园。经过近20年的发展，新竹科学工业园取得了很大的成功，形成六大高新技术支柱产业。1997年园区营业额达4002亿元，比上年增长25.6%，预计1999年可达4500亿新台币。高新技术产品出口取得重大突破，1997年出口90亿美元，1998年上半年出口额为1241亿新台币，全年出口超过100亿美元。

这些成功经验为我们发展自己的科技工业园区提供了有益的借鉴。

我国于1985年开始建立高新技术产业开发区，目前已有53个国家级高新技术开发区，区内社会化支撑服务体系不断完善，是我国高新技术产业发展和高新技术产品出口的重要基地。1998年，高新技术开发区内高新技术企业已达16097家，产值4339亿元，比1997年增长39%；出口额达85.3亿美元，比1997年增长32%，占全国高新技术产品出口总额的

74.8%。电子信息、新能源、光机电一体化、新材料成为支撑新技术产业开发区高技术产品出口的四大支柱。

为了进一步促进高新技术产业开发区的发展，建议采取以下措施：

第一，选择一批有条件的国家级高新技术产业开发区，培育和建立国家高新技术产品出口基地。充分发挥园区高新技术产业集中、信息快、机制活、人才多等有利条件，扩大高新技术产品出口，加快园区的国际化进程。

第二，试办高新技术产品出口加工区。选择3-4家有条件的国家高新技术产业开展区，在其中划出一定区域，建立高新技术产品出口加工区，实施国际上规范的出口加工区管理办法，最大限度地方便区内企业的各种国际交流，有利于促进高新技术产业的发展。

第三，办好中关村科技园区。中关村位于我国第一个高新技术产业开展区——北京新技术产业开发试验区中，聚集了包括北京大学、清华大学在内的30多所高校，包括中科院在内的130多个科研机构，高级知识分子5万多人，智力密集程度世界罕见，现有高新技术企业4546家，形成以电子产业为主体，包括光电一体化、新材料和新能源及环境科学、新药物及生物技术四大支柱产业，但是中关村目前与世界一流水平的高科技园区相比还有很大差距，我们要通过制定各种鼓励措施，建立适宜的环境，加速中关村的发展，使其尽快成为国际一流的高科技园区，带动我国高新技术产业的振兴，在推动高新技术产品出口方面发挥更大的示范和先导作用。

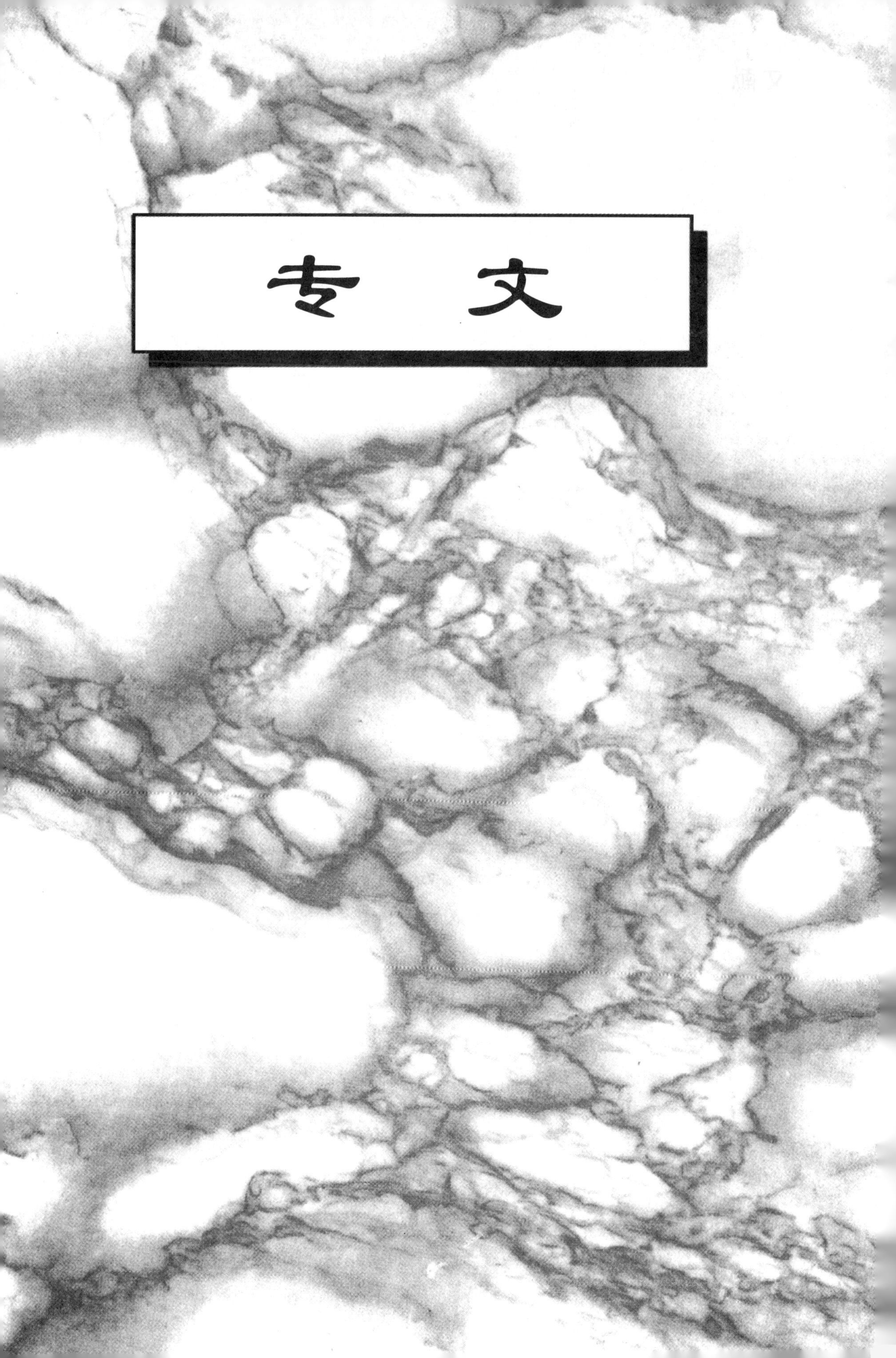

专　文

加强引导、做好服务，支持私营企业扩大出口

对外贸易经济合作部外经贸政策和发展司副司长　鲁建华

为了促进私营经济的发展，为私营企业参与国际竞争创造必要条件，截至到1999年6月，外经贸部先后赋予希望集团有限公司、广东爱多电器有限公司等142家私营生产企业自营进出口权。这标志着，作为我国社会主义市场经济重要组成部分的非公有经济已开始进入外贸领域，其积极意义不仅在于国家取消了对私营经济在外贸领域的准入限制，为各类所有制企业创造了公平竞争的环境，更重要的是为私营经济开辟了更广阔的发展空间，使私营企业有条件通过参与国际竞争，加速自身的发展壮大，同时也为国家的外贸发展做出应有的贡献。

一、赋予私营生产企业和科研院所自营进出口权政策出台的背景

我国当代私营经济是在转型开放的历史条件下，随着经济体制转轨和社会转型孕育、产生和发展起来的。由于其具有以市场为基础配置社会资源、产权关系清晰、机制灵活的特点，因而成为改革开放20年来国民经济发展最快、效益最好的一种经济成分，在国民经济中的地位和作用日益增强。根据国家工商局统计，到目前为止，全国登记的私营企业投资者已达200多万人，私营企业户数达130万家，注册资金达7000亿元。另据调查，1997年，私营企业从业人员达1349万人，产值3923亿元，消费品零售额1855亿元。1989－1997年，私营企业户数、从业人员、注册资金、产值、消费品零售额平均增长分别为：34.3%、30.1%、67.2%、58.8%、64.9%，私营经济快速发展已成为我国改革开放以来最引人注目的社会经济现象。

在私营经济快速发展的同时，私营企业通过开展出口生产，为出口提供资源、委托外贸代理等形式，参与外贸活动日益增多，不仅为我国外贸的快速发展做出贡献，自身的国际竞争力也得到提高。要求直接参与国际竞争的呼声也日益强烈。在这种情况下，外经贸部认真贯彻党的十五大的有关精神，就私营经济从事外贸问题组织了专题调研，并在深入调研的基础上，经国务院批准，以石广生部长签发1998年外经贸部1号部令的形式，发布了《关于赋予私营生产企业和科研院所自营进出口权的暂行规定》，为依法规范审批私营生产企业申请进出口权提供了依据。

二、已获自营进出口权私营生产企业的基本情况

截至到1999年6月，经外经贸部批准，已有142家私营生产企业获得自营进出口权。首批获权的私营生产企业注册资本总额达13.6亿元人民币，平均每家企业注册资本为6800万元人民币，年销售收入总值为129.8亿元人民币，平均每家6.49亿元人民币；第二批获得自营进出口权的41家私营生产企业注册资本总额达15亿多元人民币，平均注册资本达3600万元，1997年年销售收入48亿多元人民币，平均销售额为1.2亿元，均是我国私营企业中经营规模较大和经营业绩较为突出的。这61家私营生产企业分布在全国20多个省、市、自治区，主要集中在四川、广东、福建、上海、北京，涉及机电、建材、轻工、食品、饮料、医药、工艺、金属冶炼、纺织服装、信息产业、生物工程等多种行业。

三、加强政策引导，鼓励私营企业扩大出口

受亚洲金融危机影响，今年我国外贸发展面临前所未有的严峻形势。千方百计扩大出口，力争一定程度增长，增加贸易收汇，是今年我国外经贸工作的首要任务。私营进出口生产企业应与其他各类进出口企业一道，开拓进取、奋力拼搏，共同为我国外贸事业的发展、出口创汇的扩大多做贡献。虽然，私营生产企业开展进出口工作刚刚起步，要在我国外贸发展中发挥更大作用还需要有个过程，但是应该看到，私营生产企业开展进出口业务自身具有很多优势，机制灵活，比较适合参与国际竞争；

掌握商品生产基础环节，扩大出口有资金保障；直接面对国际市场，能减少交易成本，也能对国际市场的要求作出快速反应。我相信，只要私营生产企业对出口工作高度重视，措施得力，私营生产企业扩大出口一定能有一个好的开端。

为了支持和鼓励私营生产企业扩大出口，国家在外贸政策方面赋予私营生产企业与公有制企业同等待遇。外经贸部也将加强对私营进出口生产企业的政策引导与服务，包括举办私营生产企业外贸政策与实务培训班，对私营企业有关管理人员业务人员进行培训，跟踪调研私营企业进出口工作开展的情况，帮助解决其开展进出口业务中遇到的问题，等等。同时我们也希望私营进出口企业在开展进出口业务时，要注意以下问题：

第一，认真学习外经贸政策，主要途径是订阅《对外贸易经济合作部文告》；

第二，通过网络获取政策和业务信息。外经贸部“中国电子商务中心”主办的《中国国际电子商务网》（http：//www.ec.com），具有国家政策发布、外经贸咨询、国际市场信息查询、企业网上交易服务等功能，该中心还在因特网上开通了《中国商品交易市场》、《中国技术出口交易会》网页。私营企业可上网发布自己的产品和技术信息，查询贸易机会和信息，随着国家“金关”工程的逐步实施，企业还可通过网络办理配额许可证的申领、进出口货物报关、出口退税等手续；

第三，重视外贸人才的引进和培养，建立规范的组织机构和完善的制度；

第四，参加相关的进出口商会，有选择地参加国内的出口商品交易会、国际著名的博览会、专业展览会，建立客户渠道，获取国际市场信息。

总之，赋予私营生产企业自营进出口权，体现了我国以公有制为主体，多种经济成分共同发展的政策导向。这对维护和促进非公有制经济的健康发展，为各类企业创造公平竞争的环境，鼓励企业扩大出口创汇，同时推动我国对外贸易经营和管理体制向国际贸易规范靠拢均有积极意义。私营生产企业应珍惜国家给予的发展机遇，在加快发展的同时，为国家的出口创汇多作贡献。

继续完善外贸管理体制　为扩大出口服务

对外贸易经济合作部对外贸易管理司司长　刘国胜

1998 年是我国对外贸易形势非常严峻的一年，我们在继续完善外贸管理体制的同时，千方百计抓出口，取得了一定成效。

一、进一步完善外贸管理体制

（一）加大出口商品管理体制改革力度

大幅度减少出口配额与许可证管理的范围。1998 年取消了 29 种商品的出口许可证（或放行证）管理。制订了 1999 年《出口许可证管理商品分级发证目录》。该目录，对出口许可证管理的商品范围进行了重大调整，从原 115 种减少为 59 种，减少后的许可证商品出口金额占出口总值的 8%，将一些不该管、管不了的商品由市场来调节，为企业扩大出口创造宽松的政策环境。

完善配额管理办法。制订了《出口商品配额编报下达和组织实施暂行办法》和《供港鲜活冷冻商品管理暂行办法》。

修改完善《出口商品配额招标办法》及其《实施细则》。新办法改变了评标规则，为企业提供了平等竞争的政策环境；简化了招标方式，由原来的 4 种方式减为 2 种即公开招标和协议招标。

改革出口商品经营体制。取消了两纱两布和茶叶出口的统一联合经营；取消了两纱两布部分海外总代理；改进了供港澳鲜活冷冻商品的经营管理。这些措施调动了出口企业的积极性。

（二）纺织品配额分配制度改革取得突破性进展

一是扩大招标范围，由原来的7个类别增加到21个，这些品种都是使用率高、供求矛盾大的紧俏类别。二是对非紧俏类别，实行总量控制、自主申领的分配方式。即有经营能力的各类进出口企业都可以凭出口合同等有关单据直接向签证机关申领配额许可证。从1998年下半年开始，对99个类别实行这种方式的管理，并根据市场情况进行调整。三是对既不实行招标又不实行总量控制、自主申领签证类别的配额，由以往将配额直接分配到拥有基数配额的企业，改为以切块形式下达到各地外经贸主管部门，由各地外经贸主管部门根据外经贸部制订的《纺织品被动配额管理办法》和当地实际情况进行二次分配。这样大大地调动了各地的积极性，减少了微观管理事务。四是大力支持纺织生产企业，外经贸部按纺织品被动配额可分量的一定比例直接安排给国家纺织工业局推荐的自营出口生产企业，1998年为配额总量的16%，1999年增加到20%。五是配额分配向名牌产品出口企业倾斜，鼓励高附加值国产名牌产品出口，如从输美、输欧羊绒衫类配额中切出一块配额，安排给内蒙古鄂尔多斯集团、鹿王集团和宁夏圣雪绒集团。

（三）完善加工贸易管理，促进加工贸易健康发展

加强了对加工贸易的研究，制订了明确的工作思路，引导加工贸易健康发展。根据我部与有关部委联合印发的《关于加强和完善加工贸易管理的通知》要求，拟定了《加工贸易审批管理办法》。

（四）探索进口体制改革，做好进口管理工作

加强进口经营管理。做好实行核定公司经营管理商品的管理工作。取消了对木材进口核定公司经营管理的限制；对原已核准的进口核定经营企业进行清理。

（五）研究制订了《进出口商品管理体制改革总体方案》

该《方案》明确了进出口商品管理体制改革的原则和总体目标，提出了进出口商品宏观管理思路，制订了具体实施方案。还制订了《进出口商品配额执行情况核查反馈办法》，明确通过电子网络对进出口商品配额的执行情况进行反馈和监控，实行动态管理。

（六）加快外贸管理现代化步伐

一是“配额许可证管理系统”建设取得进展。加快了“金关工程”四个子系统之一的“配额许可证管理系统”的组织建设工作。进出口许可证联网核查系统于9月开始试运行；出口配额管理系统的程序编制工作已基本完成。

二是建立电子招标系统，实施电子招标并取得圆满成功。电子招标是1998年招标工作的重大举措。招标委员会成功地组织了1999年度纺织品被动配额电子招标工作。电子招标大大加快了贸易管理现代化的步伐，减轻了企业负担，提高了招标的工作效率。

二、全力以赴抓出口

一是抓大商品出口。对二十多种大商品建立了大宗出口商品的资料库，定期跟踪分析，研究并落实若干扩大出口的具体措施。会同有关部门协调解决某些商品出口中出现的问题。整顿锑、抽纱、维C出口经营秩序，扩大出口规模，提高出口效益。及时收集、汇总各地对加工贸易进口商品配额的需求和使用情况，适时追加加工贸易进口配额，促进了加工贸易稳步发展。

二是抓出口配额的动态管理。严格按照规则化分配的要求，实事求是地追加配额。对羊绒、棉漂布等27种招标商品，及时调整为有偿使用，鼓励有能力的企业扩大出口。

三是抓大市场。制订了对有关国家出口焦碳和出口糠醇有关规定。对香港市场出现的“禽流感”事件、违禁药物事件等及时采取措施，最大限度地减少了损失。积极应诉美国对我蜂蜜、定尺碳素钢板、蘑菇罐头等的反倾销立案调查，与美方达成了中止协议。

三、加大对外谈判和交涉的力度

签署了中国－欧盟第六个双边纺织品协议。该协议在出口配额数量上获得了一定程度的增长。签署了中国－土耳其第二个双边纺织品协议。与加拿大续签了为期三年的纺织品协议，增加了冬装类别配额。

与日本达成1998年度中日捻丝和绸缎贸易协议。还与日本就生姜、大蒜、蔺草、棉府绸等商品出口分别进行了多次磋商，维护了上述商品对日本的正常出口。

与巴西、阿根廷等国进行多次交涉，要求他们尽快取消对我纺织品的进口限制。

四、充分发挥进出口商会作用

加强了对进出口商会工作的管理、指导。下发了《关于改进出口商品协调价格管理的通知》、《关于重申进出口商品协调价格报部备案的通知》和《关于建立进出口商会（协会）会议备案制度的通知》，探讨了商会管理体制改革问题。

更多更好地吸收外商投资，为国民经济持续稳定增长作出贡献

对外贸易经济合作部外国投资管理司司长　汪师嘉

1998年，面对国际金融市场持续动荡、跨国直接投资增长趋缓以及国内特大洪涝灾害的严峻挑战，在党中央、国务院的正确领导下，在全国外资战线广大干部、职工的辛勤努力下，我国吸收外商投资工作取得了来之不易的较好成绩，实现了合同外资金额、实际使用外资金额和外商投资企业出口三项指标同步增长，为国民经济持续稳定增长作出了贡献。

一、1998年我国吸收外商直接投资保持了稳定增长，实际使用外资创历史最高水平

1998年全国共批准设立外商投资企业19799家，比1997年下降5.72%；新批合同外资金额521.02亿美元，同比增长2.15%，扭转了1994年、1996年、1997年三年大幅度下滑的局面，实现了恢复性增长；实际使用外资金额454.63亿美元，同比增长0.46%，创历史最高水平，但增幅降至历年最低点。截至1998年底，全国累计批准设立外商投资企业324620家，合同外资金额5724.95亿美元，实际使用外资金额2671.09亿美元。

（一）外商投资来源国别/地区结构

1998年欧盟、美国和部分自由港对华投资持续增长，来自亚洲国家和地区的投资下降。欧盟、美国和部分自由港对华投资合同外资金额比1997年分别增长39.79%、25.84%和29.21%，实际投资金额分别增长了3.06%、20.79%和100.74%；来自亚洲十国/地区（香港、澳门、台湾省、日本、菲律宾、泰国、马来西亚、新加坡、印度尼西亚和韩国）的合同外资金额和实际投入金额同比分别下降13.4%和9.27%，在总量中所占的比重分别减少了9.74和7.46个百分点。1998年对华投资前十位的国家和地区依次为（按实际投入外资金额计，下同）：香港、维尔京群岛、美国、新加坡、日本、台湾、韩国、英国、德国、荷兰。

截至1998年底，对华投资前十位的国家和地区依次为：香港、日本、美国、台湾、新加坡、韩国、维尔京群岛、英国、德国、澳门。

（二）外商投资产业结构

1998年外商投资产业结构进一步改善。在新批合同外资金额中，工业企业所占比重为64.58%，比1997年所占比重（61.64%）上升了2.94个百分点；农业占2.31%，同比提高0.22个百分点；房地产业占7.84%，同比下降4.36个百分点；其他服务业占5.78%，增长0.55个百分点。全年新批外商投资企业单项平均吸收外资金额为263.15万美元，比1997年增加了20.29万美元，增长了8.35%。由于加强了对外商投资产业的引导，外商投资低水平重复建设得到一定的遏制。

（三）外商投资方式结构

在1998年新批准的外商投资企业中，中外合资、合作企业10110家，合同外资金额289.42亿美元，实际使用外资金额280.67亿美元，分别占总量的51.03%、55.55%和61.74%；新批外资企业（外商独资）数、合同外资金额、实际使用外资金额占总量的比重为48.86%、41.75%和36.23%，所占比重分别上升了3.14、7.13和0.46个百分点。

截至1998年底，在累计批准的外商投资企业、合同外资金额和实际使用外资金额中，中外合资、合作企业所占比重分别为73.16%、68.02%和69.35%，仍然是我国吸收外商投资的主要方式。

（四）外商投资地区分布结构

1998年中西部地区新批合同外资金额68.02亿美元，比1997年增长2.90%，高于东部地区0.7个百分点；实际使用外资金额57.94亿美元，同比下降8.64%，与东部地区增长1.94%相比低10.58个百分点。在全国新批合同外资金额和实际使用外资金额中，东部地区所占比重为86.94%和87.26%，中西部地区新批合同外资金额在总量的比重略有增长，实际使用外资在总量中的比重略有下降。

截至1998年底，在累计批准的合同外资金额和实际使用外资金额中，东部地区所占比重分别为88.35%和87.83%。

二、外商投资有力地促进了国民经济持续稳定增长

在截至1998年底累计批准设立的324620家外商投资企业中，目前仍在运营的企业约25万家（已终/中止或停止运营的企业近7万家），直接就业人员逾1800万人，占非农业劳动人口的11%左右。1998年新批准设立的外商投资企业在未来1年～2年内至少可吸纳100万人～150万人就业。

（一）外商投资企业工业产值大幅增长

1998年已开业投产的外商投资工业企业工业产值14162.50亿元（年销售额500万元以上企业），比1997年增长17.40%，占全国工业总产值（58195.23亿元）的24%，高出全国工业总产值增幅（10.7%）6.7个百分点。在1998年全国工业总产值增量中，外商投资企业工业产值增量占37.3%。

同期，外商投资工业企业工业产值现价为15532亿元，其中工业内销值（以工业产值现价计，下同）约为8836.50亿元，占全国工业内销值的16.10%。

同期，外商投资工业企业完成工业增加值3835亿元，占全国完成工业增加值（20046亿元）的19.13%，同比增长12.7%，高于全国增幅（8.8%）3.4个百分点。

（二）实际使用外资金额占全社会固定资产投资总额的比重

1998年全国实际使用外资金额454.63亿美元（约合3759.79亿元），占全社会固定资产投资总额的13.11%，比上年的14.79%下降了1.68个百分点。

（三）外商投资企业税收迅速增加

1998年全国涉外税收收入达1230亿元（外商投资企业税收占涉外税收的98%以上），比上年增长25.94%，占全国工商税收（8551.74亿元）的14.38%。其增幅比全国工商税收增长幅度（13.3%）高12.64个百分点，所占比重较1997年增加1.22个百分点。1998年全国涉外税收净增加237亿元，占全国工商税收净增加额（1003.7亿元）的24%，外商投资企业税收仍是全国增长最快的税源之一。

（四）外商投资企业进出口继续增长

1998年外商投资企业进出口总值1576.79亿美元，同比增长3.3%，占全国进出口总值的48.68%。其中：出口809.62亿美元，同比增长8%，占全国出口总值的比重为44.06%；进口767.17亿美元，十几年来首次出现负增长，下降1.3%，占全国进口总值的比重为54.73%，投资项下进口的设备、物品144.97亿美元，同比下降19.1%，占外商投资企业进口总值的18.90%。

同期，外商投资企业加工贸易进出口占其进出口总值的74.48%，其中：加工贸易出口额为691.81亿美元，占其出口总值的85.45%（进料加工出口占加工贸易出口的89.56%）；加工贸易进口额为482.57亿美元，占其进口总值的62.9%。

外商投资企业出口商品结构进一步优化，全年出口机电产品401.18亿美元，同比增长16.9%，高于全国机电产品出口增幅近4个百分点，占外商投资企业出口额的49.55%，占全国机电产品出口总值的60.29%。

出口自产产品逾千万美元的外商投资企业1279家，比1997年增加98家。其中出口逾5000万美元的大型出口企业120家，出口近10亿美元的特大型出口企业3家。1279家企业的出口额占外商投资企业出口总额的52.65%。

（五）外商投资企业银行结售汇继续保持顺差

1998年外商投资企业银行结售汇顺差值16.24亿美元（全国银行结售汇逆差18.72亿美元），占全国外汇储备净增长额的32.04%。其中，贸易结售汇顺差值7.44亿美元，非贸易结售汇顺差值

11.29亿美元，资本结售汇逆差值2.49亿美元。从1998年9月起外商投资企业扭转了自2月份起连续7个月结售汇逆差状况，后四个月结售汇顺差值30.29亿美元。

（六）外商投资企业外汇平衡进一步改善

1998年外商投资企业外汇总体平衡有余。贸易顺差42.45亿美元，扣除投资项下进口的设备、物品（144.97亿美元），外商投资企业进出口净顺差值187.42亿美元，比1997年增加36.42亿美元，增长24%。1998年我国实际吸收外资455亿美元，外商投资企业资本支出62.49亿美元（偿还外汇贷款本息57.57亿美元，利润汇出4.11亿美元，其他支出0.81亿美元），资本顺差392.51亿美元。外商投资企业资本支出占全国资本支出的28.38%。

（七）外商投资企业人民币贷款增加，外汇贷款减少

1998年外商投资企业人民币贷款增加，外汇贷款减少。截至1998年底，全国金融机构对外商投资企业人民币贷款余额2487.52亿元，与年初相比增长31.71%，净增598.90亿元。外商投资企业贷款余额中，绝大部分为短期贷款。

截至1998年底，外商投资企业人民币贷款余额占非国有经济贷款余额（36186.98亿元）的6.90%，占全国金融机构全部贷款余额（86159.48亿元）的2.9%，从外商投资企业工业增加值(3835亿元）占全国工业增加值（20046亿元）19.13%分析，今后金融机构对外商投资企业的贷款将有所扩大。

截至1998年底，全国金融机构对外商投资企业外汇贷款余额130.07亿美元，比年初（144.33亿美元）下降9.88%，净减少14.26亿美元。其中：外商投资企业短期外汇贷款余额99.07亿美元，占外汇贷款额的76.2%，比年初（107.90亿美元）下降8.18%，净减少8.83亿美元；中长期外汇贷款余额31亿美元，占外汇贷款余额的23.8%，比年初（36.43亿美元）下降14.91%，净减少5.43亿美元。

（八）外商投资企业外债增幅回落，外债结构改善

截至1998年底，外商投资企业外债余额452.4亿美元，与1997年底外债余额相比，增长21.1%，比1997年增幅（50.3%）回落29.2个百分点。外商投资企业外债余额占全国外债余额（1460.4亿美元）的31%，比年初所占比重高出2.5个百分点。1998年当年外商投资企业外债余额净增加值78.8亿美元，占全国外债净增加值（150.8亿美元）的52.3%。

外商投资企业外债期限结构有所改善。截至1998年底，外商投资企业中长期外债余额344.8亿美元，同比增长26.1%，占外商投资企业外债余额76.2%，比1997年所占比重（73.2%）增加了3个百分点。1998年当年外商投资企业中长期外债余额净增加值71.4亿美元，占其外债余额净增加值的90.6%。截至1998年底，外商投资企业短期外债余额107.6亿美元，同比增长7.4%，净增加7.4亿美元，占外商投资企业外债余额23.8%，与1997年所占比重（26.8%）相比，下降了3个百分点。

三、我国吸收外商投资面临的形势和今后的发展趋势

利用外资为改革开放和社会主义现代化建设服务，是邓小平理论的重要组成部分，是对外开放基本国策的重要内容，是建设有中国特色社会主义经济的伟大实践之一。党的十一届三中全会以来，在邓小平理论的指引下，我国利用外资迅速发展，规模不断扩大，水平逐步提高，取得了举世瞩目的伟大成就，有力地促进了国民经济持续快速健康发展。20年来对外开放的实践证明，利用外资有利于发展社会主义社会的生产力，有利于增强社会主义国家的综合国力，有利于提高人民的生活水平。依法设立的外商投资企业作为中国企业的一部分，是混合所有制经济和非公有制经济的形式之一。这种所有制经济是社会主义市场经济的重要组成部分。

在世纪之交的重要历史时期，随着改革开放的进一步深入和市场经济体制的不断完善，利用外资面临着新的形势。知识经济的到来、全球经济一体化趋势的日益加强以及科技进步的迅猛发展深刻地改变了世界经济和社会生活的面貌，加速了各国经济结构调整和产业升级的步伐。21世纪将是一个更加充满挑战和机遇的时代。一方面，国际间跨国投资出现了一些新的动向和新的特点，跨国购并已成为全球直接投资的最主要形式，跨国公司购并是跨国间直接投资增长的主要驱动力，特别是亚洲金融危机以来，跨国投资在拉动经济增长中的作用受

到各国的普遍重视，跨国公司已成为全球资源配置的重要力量，各个国家争夺国际投资的竞争越来越激烈。另一方面，随着我国宏观调控的成功、经济"软着陆"的实现，为继续保持经济持续稳定增长，中央采取了增加投资、扩大内需、实施积极财政政策的新举措，我国经济体制和经济增长方式正在发生着深刻的变化，这就给对外开放、利用外资工作提出了更高的要求，使我国吸收外商投资工作面临着扩大领域、改善结构、提高质量和水平的新课题。

面对新的形势，1998 年 4 月，党中央、国务院对利用外资工作作出了全面部署，提出了进一步扩大对外开、提高利用外资水平的若干要求。今后进一步利用外资总的指导思想是：坚持以邓小平理论为指导，认真贯彻党的十五大精神，围绕推进经济体制和经济增长方式两个根本转变，提高国民经济素质和效益，增强综合国力和国际竞争力，进一步发展和完善全方位、多层次、宽领域的对外开放，充分利用国内国外两个市场、两种资源，更多更好地利用外资，促进国民经济持续快速健康发展和社会全面进步。必须长期坚持积极合理有效地利用外资的指导方针。

根据上述指导思想和方针，进一步做好利用外资工作的基本要求是：适应经济持续增长的需要，保持利用外资的一定规模，使吸收外商直接投资继续处于发展中国家的前列。引导外资投向，调整引进外资结构，为提高国民经济素质和效益服务。坚持以市场换技术的方针，加大引进高新技术产业和先进适用技术的力度，推动产业升级。促进解决经济和社会发展的突出矛盾，创造更多的就业机会，弥补资源不足。坚持国际收支基本平衡，保持必要的外汇储备。正确处理扩大对外开放与独立自主、自力更生的关系，维护国家经济安全。

为落实上述指导思想、指导方针和基本要求，今后将继续把吸收外商直接投资作为利用外资的重点，并采取如下措施：

（一）进一步优化外商投资的产业结构。重点鼓励外资投向农业、高新技术产业、基础工业、基础设施、环保产业和出口创汇型产业。积极引导外资投向传统产业和老工业基地的技术改造。继续发展符合产业政策的劳动密集型项目。对国家鼓励和支持的外商投资项目进口的设备及技术，免征关税和进口环节增值税。

（二）继续扩大外商投资领域。进一步开放竞争性产业。有区别、有重点地吸收外资开发利用矿产资源。有步骤地推进服务贸易的对外开放。

（三）努力完善外商投资的地区布局。在继续支持东部地区积极发展资金、技术密集型产业和出口型产业的同时，采取切实措施积极引导和鼓励外资投向中西部地区。中西部地区选择确定的优势产业和项目，经国家批准后，享受鼓励类外商投资项目政策。适当放宽限制类和限定外商股权比例项目的设立条件和市场开放程度。国家优先安排一批农业、水利、交通、能源、原材料和环保项目在中西部地区吸引外资。到中西部地区再投资的外商投资比例超过 25% 的项目，视同外商投资企业，享受相应待遇。国家允许开展试点的开放领域和试点项目，原则上在东中西部地区同时进行。

（四）多渠道多方式吸收外商投资。实施利用外资多元化战略。在继续吸收港澳台地区和东南亚国家的投资同时，加大吸收北美、日本、欧盟等发达国家和地区投资的力度。继续进行多种方式吸收外商投资的试点。积极发展加工贸易和补偿贸易。鼓励国有大中型企业采取多种方式利用外资进行资产重组。允许国有小型企业和集体企业对外合资、合作、出售，允许私营企业吸收外资发展经济。利用现代电子信息技术，改进招商引资方式。

（五）大胆引进和积极引导跨国公司投资。继续实行以市场换技术的方针，进一步开放国内市场。有重点地推动国有大型企业开展与跨国公司的合作，促进新兴产业、支柱产业的发展，建立研究开发中心，增强技术消化和创新能力，带动相关企业和产业共同发展。

（六）认真办好现有外商投资企业。充分发挥现行利用外资法律和政策的作用，促进现有外商投资企业健康发展。积极帮助企业解决生产经营中遇到的困难，给予外商投资企业必要的信贷支持，解决好合资企业增资扩股中中方股权比重下降的问题。

（七）在进一步改善投资硬环境的同时，着力改善投资软环境。坚决制止对外商投资企业一切形式的乱检查、乱收费、乱摊派、乱罚款。切实保障外商投资企业经营管理自主权，维护投资各方的合法权益不受侵犯，依法保护劳动者的正当权益。提高各级政府办事效率，减少管理层次。加快建设统一开放、竞争有序的市场环境。逐步对外商投资企业实行国民待遇。依法加强对外商投资企业的监督管理，完善联合年检工作。

1999年我们将全面深入贯彻党的十五大精神，继续将贯彻落实中央关于进一步扩大对外开放、提高利用外资水平的若干要求作为全年的中心任务，坚持积极合理有效地利用外资的方针，进一步完善和稳定利用外资政策，千方百计、更多更好地吸引外资，在保持吸收外商投资相当规模的同时，注重提高吸收外商投资的质量、水平和效益，促进国民经济持续快速健康发展。

实施积极的财政政策　促进对外贸易平衡发展

财政部经贸司副司长　严伟华

1998年，我国遭到了百年不遇的洪涝灾害，同时面临始至1997年7月爆发的亚洲金融危机的巨大冲击。为了克服自然灾害的消极影响，化解亚洲金融危机给我国经济发展带来的矛盾，财政部门实施了一系列积极的财政政策，有效地启动经济，促进对外贸易实现平稳发展。

一、正确分析形势，强化财务管理

随着亚洲金融危机对我国经济影响的逐步加深，我国外贸出口面临前所未有的困难和挑战，外贸出口形势也日益受到人们的关注。为此，财政部注意收集有关资料，分析出口动态，随时反映外贸财务管理中的新情况、新问题，定期通报全国外贸财务信息。机构改革后，及时召开全国外贸及境外投资财务管理工作会议，总结地方外贸及境外投资财务管理工作，剖析外贸经济形势及发展态势，以及境外投资财务管理的现状，研究了如何发挥财政职能，运用财政政策调控外贸扩大出口，提高外贸企业经济效益，进一步加强境外投资的财务管理，控制国有资产流失等方面的问题。在调查研究的基础上，下发了《关于做好1998年地方外贸财务管理工作的指导意见》，为落实工作计划，指导地方财政在新形势下开展外贸财务管理，尤其是如何扩大出口，防止外贸企业增加新的亏损挂帐，提出了政策性措施和意见。

二、调整进出口税收政策，增强发展对外贸易的信心

进出口税收政策是国家财政调节对外贸易发展的有效手段。在关税方面，按照1997年调整方案，我国关税算术平均税率已降低到17%，加权平均税率为13.3%，使我国经济向国际化迈进了一大步，对于促进对外贸易、提高对外开放水平，具有积极意义。在进口设备税收方面，国务院决定，从1998年1月1日起，对国家鼓励和支持发展的外商投资和国内投资项目进口设备，在规定范围内免征关税和进口环节增值税；对1997年12月31日以前批准的老项目进口设备，继续实行减免税优惠。这项政策有效地增强国内、国外投资者对我国经济发展的信心，削弱亚洲金融危机的消极影响，对于鼓励引进国外先进技术和设备，促进产业结构调整和企业技术进步，发挥了积极作用。在边境贸易税收方面，为了有利于加强同周边地区的经济联系，进一步繁荣我国边境地区经济，国务院决定，将于1998年到期的边境贸易进口减半征税优惠政策延长至2000年。

在刺激进口需求的同时，国家相继出台了一系列调整出口退税政策的措施，以便减轻外贸企业的间接税负，支持外贸出口。一是提高部分出口货物的退税率，包括：从1998年1月1日起，纺织品、纺织原料及制品的出口退税率由9%提高到11%，以出顶进的钢材出口退税率由9%提高到17%；从1998年1月1日至2000年12月31日，纺织机械的出口退税率提高到17%；从1998年6月1日起，煤炭、钢材、水泥及船舶的适用出口退税率分别提高到9%、11%、11%和14%；从1998年7月1日起，将通信设备等七类机电产品、自行车等五类轻工产品的出口退税率从9%提高到11%。二是恢

复部分产品的出口退税，主要是在1997年10月1日起恢复新闻纸出口退税的基础上，1998年8月1日起，恢复食糖出口退税，退税率为9%等。三是改进出口退税管理办法，主要是从1998年7月1日起，对出口企业按照近年出口退税情况分为A、B、C、D四类，分别实行不同的出口退税管理办法，有效地简化了出口退税手续，加快了退税进度，减少了骗税漏洞。

三、启动中央外贸发展基金，改善对外贸易的条件

建立外贸发展基金，并尽快发挥其在外贸发展中的调控作用，是贯彻实施《中华人民共和国对外贸易法》的具体要求。1998年针对我国外贸出口增幅下滑的严峻形势，财政部与有关部门积极配合，管好用好中央外贸发展基金。一是根据国务院确定的原则，有重点地扶持在国际市场上受欢迎的出口产品的生产，增加花色品种，提高产品质量。二是支持外贸实施多元化市场战略，根据国务院领导关于发展与非洲经贸关系的指示精神，财政部参与研究利用中央外贸发展基金在尼日利亚、坦桑尼亚、肯尼亚设立贸易中心以及在埃及建立经济开发区、在莫斯科开办商城等问题，为外贸企业开拓市场创造条件。三是调控茧丝绸行业的发展。财政部利用中央外贸发展基金建立茧丝绸发展风险基金，用于茧丝绸农业科技投入，促进茧丝绸产业结构的调整。四是推进“金关工程”的建设。为了适应进入信息社会的形势，尽快实现无纸贸易，提高外经贸商务效率，财政部从中央外贸发展基金拨付专款，用于支持外经贸商务网的建设。

四、利用出口信用保险手段，支持机电产品的出口

出口信用保险是国际通行的支持机电产品扩大出口的政策手段，国家以财政作后盾，通过提供信用保险，转移外贸企业向发展中国家或地区出口的收汇风险以及银行向企业提供中长期出口信贷的收款风险，从而达到扩大机电产品，特别是成套设备出口的目的。我国实行出口信用保险，既要有利于扩大机电产品的出口，又要控制出口风险，兼顾国家财政的承受能力。1998年，财政部通过审核批准出口信用保险项目，支持了上百亿美元的机电产品出口，对于稳步开拓多元化市场，扩大我国成套设备的出口，并带动劳务的输出，发挥了积极的作用。

五、落实外贸企业改革措施，促进现代企业制度的建立

为了有效实行“政企分开”，解除长期实行计划经济体制形成的政府部门与国有企业的行政隶属关系，推进现代企业制度的建立，根据中共中央、国务院关于党政机关与所属国有企业脱钩的决定，财政部门配合有关部门研究审定了具体的国有企业脱钩方案，制定了有关脱钩企业国有资产、财务关系移交的实施办法，把党政机关与所属国有企业脱钩的工作纳入有章可循的轨道，为把国有企业改革成为“自主经营、自负盈亏、自我约束、自我发展”的独立法人奠定基础。

在国有企业与行政主管部门脱钩的同时，财政部结合职能转变的需要，总结1997年试行部分国有企业年度会计报表由注册会计师审计的经验，决定从1998年开始，除部分特殊行业企业以外，全面推行国有企业年度会计报表由注册会计师审计，并制定暂行办法。财政部下发了《关于做好1998年度外贸企业财务报告编报审计工作的通知》，对外贸企业年度财务报告编报的要求以及注册会计师审计的重要内容作出了部署，对注册会计师审计国有企业年度会计报表过程中出现的问题，随时予以协调解决。这项制度的建立，有效地发挥会计师事务所等中介机构的作用，促进国有企业建立健全守法、科学、有效的内部管理机制。

1998年我国技术进出口综述

对外贸易经济合作部科技发展和技术进出口司司长　许复兴

1998年我国技术进出口保持了良好的发展态势。据我部业务统计，1998年我国共对外签订技术进出口合同8754项，合同总金额为230.62亿美元，合同金额与去年同期相比增长了7.55%，占全国外贸进出口总额的7.21%。其中，技术引进合同6254项，合同总金额163.75亿美元，同比增长2.84%，占全国外贸进口总额的11.68%；技术出口合同2500项，合同总金额66.87亿美元，同比增长21.12%，高出全国外贸出口增幅20.62个百分点，占全国外贸出口总额的3.64%。虽然我国的技术出口占全国外贸出口总额的比重很小，但从整个外贸的发展趋势看，技术出口的潜力巨大，前景广阔，对整个外贸增长及国民经济发展的拉动作用也将逐步加大。

1998年我国技术进出口的主要特点是：

一、技术引进

（一）从投资方向来看，技术引进与设备进口主要涉及领域为能源、交通、通讯、电子、化工等，符合国家的产业政策。这些技术与设备的引进对我国的经济结构调整、基础设施建设及国有大中型企业的技术改造等起到了重要作用。

（二）从技术引进国别来看，共涉及33个国家和地区，主要引进的国别仍然集中在美国、俄罗斯、日本、德国、意大利等发达国家。

（三）合同总金额中技术费所占的比例大大增加，为40.13亿美元，比去年同期上升69.40%，占当年技术引进总金额的25%。这主要是因为我国实施“科教兴国”战略以来，国家调整产业结构，积极鼓励企业引进高新技术，提高技术水平，降低生产成本，生产适销对路的高技术含量、高附加值的产品打入国际市场的政策获得了成效。

（四）从引进的项目来看，高起点的尖端技术所占比例有所增加，所涉及的行业主要有核电、移动通讯、卫星地面站、复合材料、计算机软件等。

二、技术出口

（一）技术和成套设备出口稳步增长。合同额22.61亿美元，同比增长9%。1000万美元以上项目有35项，金额共计14.5亿美元。东南亚地区依然是我成套设备出口的主要市场，占我成套设备出口市场份额的32.5%，主要国家是缅甸、泰国。其次为西亚、非洲、欧洲，所占份额分别为15.2%、12%、11.9%。

（二）大型设备出口降幅明显，合同额18.83亿美元，同比下降8%。主要原因是由于国际船舶市场受到日本和韩国的低价格竞争，以及东南亚市场受金融危机影响需求萎缩。欧洲、西亚是主要市场，分别占到我大型设备出口市场份额的52.9%和14.4%。

（三）高技术产品出口增势迅猛，合同额23.48亿美元（不包括外资企业的出口），同比增长92%。高技术产品出口已占技术出口总额的35.1%。随着《中国高技术产品出口目录》的颁布和国际市场对高新技术产品需求趋旺，高技术产品出口成为我技术出口新的增长点。

目前我高技术产品出口以电子信息、光机电一体化、材料、生物技术和医药类产品为主，其中电子信息类产品签约额为17.56亿美元，占整个高技术产品出口额的74.8%。从出口市场看，香港是我高技术产品出口最大的市场，占我高技术产品出口市场份额的46.15%。其次为东亚、北美、欧洲，所占比例分别为17.8%、10.2%、9.24%，主要国家是日本、美国、韩国、德国。

（四）出口市场结构进一步调整。在我技术出口的主要市场中，东南亚所占份额为14%，欧洲为22%，港澳地区为19%，西亚10%，北美为8%。技术出口市场逐步从东南亚市场向欧洲、西亚、美国转移并保持了一定的出口规模和水平，从而增强了抵御风险的能力，在一定程度上避免了由于市场变化对技术出口的不利影响，这也表明了“优化出口商品结构战略”及“市场多元化战略”

已初见成效。

（五）在以技术无形资产作为投资、建立海外企业方面，技术出口取得新进展。主要是我家电企业以技术做股本投入在国外合资办厂、进行散件组装等，如安徽荣事达洗衣机有限公司向墨西哥出口洗衣机生产技术，合同额为134万美元；海尔向印度、伊朗出口洗衣机生产技术，合同额分别为111.4万美元、149.4万美元。

（六）全国各省市高度重视技术贸易，特别是加大技术出口力度，出口增势良好。有十一个省市技术出口额超过一亿美元，广东、辽宁、上海、江苏、山东继续居于全国前列。深圳市在高技术产品出口方面优势明显，占全国高技术产品出口的35%。

（七）贸工技的结合，提高了技术出口的整体水平和竞争能力。科研院所成为技术出口的一支新生力量，凭借自身的科技实力出口，具有很大的发展潜力。

尽管去年我国受到亚洲金融危机和洪水灾害的严重影响，我国的技术贸易仍然保持了良好的发展态势，我们主要采取了以下措施：

一、技术引进

（一）加强协调，完善联合监督。

（二）加强对外工业技术合作。

（三）积极促进技术引进，不断提高引进技术的质量，改善技术引进的结构。

（四）积极研究改进和完善技术引进宏观管理体制，进一步加强技术引进的宏观调控，规范技术引进行为，保证国家技术引进产业政策的全面实施。

（五）重点项目重点指导、跟踪管理。

（六）及时研究新情况，解决新问题，开拓新业务。

二、技术出口

（一）想方设法、千方百计，宣传科技兴贸，拟定鼓励措施，积极促进技术出口发展。

（二）采取多种形式，努力开拓市场，促进技术出口。

（三）及时跟踪、协调大项目，促进企业出口成交。

（四）健全法制，深化改革，完善管理，加强服务，为扩大技术出口创造有利环境。

（五）加强调研基础工作，积极收集国外项目信息，指导企业开拓国际市场。

1998年我国国外经济合作业务稳步增长，再创佳绩

对外贸易经济合作部国外经济合作司司长　陈健

一、1998年国外经济合作业务发展的基本情况

1998年亚洲金融危机的影响不断深入和扩大，国际承包劳务市场随之发生很大变化，我国的国外经济合作面临严峻的外部环境。在党中央和国务院的正确领导和统一部署下，外经战线的全体干部职工齐心协力，克服困难，发扬伟大的抗洪精神，在工作中认真贯彻大经贸、以质取胜和市场多元化战略，保证了我国国外经济合作业务的顺利开展和稳步增长，取得了比较好的成绩：

1998年我国国外经济合作业务营业额首次突破100亿美元，达到101.34亿美元，比上年增长20.9%，其中：承包工程77.69亿美元，劳务合作22.76亿美元，设计咨询0.89亿美元；新签合同额117.73亿美元，同比增长3.7%，其中：承包工程92.43亿美元，劳务合作23.90亿美元，设计咨询1.4亿美元；12月末在外劳务人数35.2万人，在外人数比上年增加18，362人。

二、1998年国外经济合作业务的主要特点

（一）营业额大幅增长，合同额增幅下降。由于前两年合同额增长较快，1998年的营业额保持了较高的增长速度，增幅为20.9%，大大超过1997年的8.9%。但由于受亚洲金融危机的影响，1998年新签合同额增幅逐月下降，由第一季度10.2%，减至第三季度的4.2%，全年为3.7%。

（二）市场开拓取得较好成效。1998年在东亚、东南亚市场的业务较上年增长0.51%，远低于1997的15.4%。其中在香港、马来西亚、韩国、新加坡、菲律宾等市场的业务下降较大，但在老挝、缅甸、孟加拉、柬埔寨、尼泊尔、沙特、也门等国家的业务有了较快增长，使在亚州市场的业务整体上比上年增长了1.8%。在非洲新签合同额20.2亿美元，增长16.5%，苏丹、尼日利亚成为我国重要的承包劳务市场。对欧洲、北美市场新签合同额增长均为14.6%，其中，对德国、英国、瑞典、美国的业务增长较快。

（三）承揽的大型工程项目技术含量增加，带动国产设备材料出口显著增长。1998年新签合同额在1000万美元以上的项目146个，比上年增加13个，其中5000万美元以上的项目23个，超过1亿美元的项目10个，这些项目大多为总承包或技术含量较高的项目。据我部统计，1998年全年对外承包工程带动国产设备材料出口7.59亿美元（通过普通贸易方式出口的未统计在内），同比增长52.5%。1998年对外承包劳务企业进出口总额13.56亿美元，比去年同期增长27%。

（四）大企业的骨干作用明显。截至1998年底，全国具有对外经济合作经营权的企业达955家。据统计，其中位居前50名的企业的合同额约占合同总额的65.1%；专业性实体企业的合同额约占合同总额的70%。1998年新签的大项目大多是专业公司承揽的，充分显示了其发展优势和潜力。

三、我国国外经济合作的发展前景及1999年的工作举措

据有关方面的统计，1998年的全球建设投资达到3.2万亿美元，预计1999年将达到3.35－3.4万亿美元，跨国流动的劳动力总量超过3000万人。目前，我国这项业务在国际市场上的占有率还很低，发展的余地和空间很大。随着改革开放的深入、国力的增强、科技水平的提高，我国进入国际承包劳务市场的综合比较优势也逐渐增强，发展的潜力很大。

根据全国外经贸会议关于“大力发展对外承包工程与劳务合作”的精神，1999年外经贸部将对我国对外承包工程和劳务合作管理体制进行改革，逐步建立起既符合我国社会主义市场经济体制又适应国际规范和国际通行做法的对外承包工程与劳务合作管理体制；加大国际承包劳务市场开拓力度，加快实现市场多元化；继续贯彻以质取胜战略，不断提高项目的技术含量、质量和档次；加强整顿和规范经营秩序，保证和促进我国的国外经济合作业务健康、持续、快速发展。主要举措如下：

（一）优化经营主体结构。按照发展“大经贸”的要求，加快外经权审批工作的改革，放宽对外经营资格的审批标准和范围，实行大企业战略，重点引导、推动有实力的国有大企业参与国际市场的竞争，鼓励各类企业公平竞争，优势互补，形成多层次、多渠道对外的经营格局。

（二）建立市场开发机制。政府部门要从转变职能入手，由具体项目的审批转向市场调研，制订市场政策和发展战略，建立市场信息及开发体系，通过政府和非政府渠道及各种形式的营销活动，运用行政推动或经济调节手段，指导并支持企业有序开拓市场。

（三）逐步建立宏观调控体系。按照政府机构改革的要求，转变管理职能和方式，在制订政策、方针和发展战略、规划的同时，逐步建立起符合市场经济内在规律的包括国家法律、行政法规和部门规章多层次、科学完善的法律体系，建立起包括行政、财政金融、人员、海关、技术、主动国别市场监管等方面内容的监管机制，建立起企业间的协调机制和自律机制。

（四）研究适时进行外派劳务管理体制改革。按照国际通行做法，改革现行外派劳务的经营方式和管理体制，积极稳妥地推行外派劳务中介制；研究设立外派劳务企业保证金制度，通过经济手段规范企业的经营活动，保障外派劳务人员的合法权益。改革外派劳务人员培训制度，使外派劳务人员的培训向社会化方向发展，逐步将外派劳务人员出国前适应性培训改为适应性培训和技能培训并举。简化劳务人员出国手续，减少中间环节，为企业的

经营和劳务人员进入国际市场营造宽松的环节。

1998年中国对外援助

对外贸易经济合作部对外援助司司长　李国庆

1998年，我国对外援助工作继续深化改革，加快落实优惠贷款项目，援外方式改革取得重大进展。加强对无息贷款和无偿援助项目的规范化管理，援外项目的投资、进度和质量得到有效控制。

一、援外方式改革取得重大进展

援外方式改革重点是推行优惠贷款援助方式，经过3年多的努力，1998年取得重大进展。

全年，我国同16个国家签订了优惠贷款框架协议18笔，累计同43个国家签订优惠贷款协议56笔。中国进出口银行签订项目借贷协议16个，累计签订42个项目借贷协议。大部分优惠贷款项目进展顺利。我国企业使用援外合资合作项目基金累计在32个国家实施项目49个。

推行优惠贷款援助方式3年多来，呈现如下几个方面的特点：一是接受优惠贷款援助方式的国家逐渐增多，1995年只有11个，1998年末达到43个，非洲、亚洲、拉丁美洲和南太地区岛国都有国家接受这种新的援助方式。二是我国企业的主动性、积极性高。1995年探讨优惠贷款项目的企业只有8家，1998年末已达70多家。这些企业中，实体性生产企业越来越多。三是优惠贷款项目多样化。有资源开发项目，工业生产项目和机电产品带料加工项目，基础设施项目，社会福利性项目，提供国产成套设备和机电产品等项目。四是促进了我国企业与受援国企业间的直接合作，企业承担援外项目的同时，迅速进入发展中国家市场，受到这些国家政府和企业的欢迎。

1998年，我们在深入推行优惠贷款援助方式方面主要做了如下几项工作：

1. 做好对内对外宣传解释工作。对内，我部在北京、并派人赴青岛、西安等地与外经贸委及其组织的当地企业座谈，宣传解释优惠贷款援助方式，推动优秀企业到发展中国家探讨落实项目。对外，我部举办第二届中国援外方式改革国际研讨会，向拉美、加勒比及南太地区来华官员介绍我国现行援外方式并同他们座谈；在外经贸部和外交部举办的中国、非洲经济官员研修班上，向来华官员介绍我国现行援外方式，并同他们座谈。

2. 采取措施加快落实优惠贷款项目。我部积极推动企业探讨落实项目，并加快对企业申报项目的审核工作，全年向中国进出口银行推荐项目29个。我部于5月份召开了落实优惠贷款项目座谈会，与有关部门探讨落实优惠贷款项目。

3. 研究解决推行优惠贷款援助方式遇到的困难和问题。这些问题包括贷款条件、贷款发放方式等。

4. 做好优惠贷款和援外合资合作项目的宏观调控工作。为避免企业探讨项目的盲目性，规范项目管理，我部发出通知，要求企业赴受援国探讨考察项目，必须报经批准后，方可进行考察，以便加强宏观调控。

二、援外项目管理得到加强，各项援外工作进展顺利

1998年，中国同83个国家新签援款协议，在28个国家新承担43个成套项目，主要有巴基斯坦精密机械技术中心、莫桑比克外交部办公楼、厄立特里亚奥罗特医院、桑给巴尔莱市场、马里布古尼中学、圣卢西亚体育场等；在18个国家承担25个技术合作项目。新开工项目36个，如尼泊尔游泳池、佛得角国家图书馆、萨摩亚小学校等，这些项目都为受援国急需；竣工项目23个，如贝宁政府办公楼、柬埔寨农业中学、莱索托国际会议中心、秘鲁主窑水泥厂等。援外项目的投资、进度和质量得到有效控制，进展情况良好。

我国还向53个国家和国际组织提供101批一般物资，主要包括朝鲜10万吨粮食、2.8万吨大豆、2万吨尿素、8万吨原油及药品和零配件，莱索托64台微机，阿尔及利来残疾人用品，喀麦隆教学文体用品，贝宁发电机组和墨西哥救灾物资等等，我提供的物资均为受援国急需。

同时，我还向亚、非、拉美及东欧地区的67个国家提供了多边援助，举办了22个技术培训班，专业涉及农业、环保、肉类加工、小水电、陶器等。

为进一步加强援外项目的管理，保证援外工程的质量，在援外项目管理方面引入和贯彻ISO9000质量管理和质量保证体系。全年贯标试点工作取得了一定的进展。同时，还举办援外项目主要负责人培训班。承担援外项目的技术组组长、总工程师、总会计师、设计代表和项目国内负责人学习援外方针、政策，目的是加强项目管理，分工协作搞好援外项目。

1998年，援外项目的管理得到加强，上述竣工移交的23个成套项目，经内部验收，全部评为优良工程，优良率达到100%。援外项目的质量、进度和投资得到了有效控制。

1998年海峡两岸经贸关系

对外贸易经济合作部台港澳司司长　王晖

1998年是极其不平凡的一年，外有弥漫全球的金融危机浓雾的包围，内有百年不遇特大洪水的肆虐；台湾当局继续实行“戒急用忍”的大陆经贸政策，并重启“南向政策”，这些都给两岸经贸发展造成极其不利的影响。但在祖国大陆积极推动和两岸工商界共同努力下，两岸经贸仍然继续向前发展。

对台出口一枝独秀

1998年5月，中共中央召开了对台工作会议，会议期间江泽民总书记和钱其琛副总理发表了重要讲话。在中央“和平统一、一国两制”对台工作总方针的指引下，结合对台经贸实际，我们继续主动采取了许多切实有效措施，积极推动两岸贸易的发展。

为了消除亚洲金融危机对我外贸的不利影响，根据外经贸中心任务和对台经贸方针政策，我部、各级政府和企业加大了推动对台出口工作力度。例如，继续大力支持厦门于4月8日—12日成功举办了第二届对台出口商品交易会，这是专门针对台湾市场和台商举办的商品交易会，交易会成交金额达1.46亿美元。5月，外经贸部发出通知，放开对台贸易进口经营权，各类进出口企业均可在其经营范围内开展对台进口业务。12月，外经贸部宣布开放台湾企业单独在大陆举办商品展览会，这是我们推动两岸直接通商的又一新举措。

1998年对台进出口总额205亿美元，比1997年增长3.3%，由于我采取积极的措施努力扩大对台出口，对台出口在我主要贸易伙伴中一枝独秀，对台出口38.7亿美元，增长13.9%，其中机电产品、钢材等对台出口增长显著，自台进口166.3亿美元，增长1.1%。对台贸易三项指标均好于祖国大陆整体水平，对台出口增幅是我总体外贸出口增幅的27.8倍。台湾是我第五大贸易伙伴和第二大进口市场，大陆是台湾第二大出口市场。截至1998年底，两岸贸易额累计1369.1亿美元，其中，祖国大陆对台出口220.5亿美元，自台进口1148.6亿美元。

保护台商投资合法权益掀起高潮

祖国大陆特别注重保护台商投资的合法权益。1998年我们继续进行《中华人民共和国台湾同胞投资保护法实施细则》的起草工作，并进一步征求台湾工商团体、有关党派的意见。征求意见的过程成为宣传祖国大陆保护台商合法权益的过程，增强了各级政府部门的法律意识，增加了台商对祖国大陆政策法规的认同感，体现了祖国大陆保护台商合法权益的诚意。《实施细则》已四易其稿，有关部门正抓紧做好必要的工作，争取使《实施细则》尽早颁布实施。

1998年，司法部、国台办、外经贸部在全国范围内联合开展了《中华人民共和国台湾同胞投资保护法》系列宣传活动，并于11月份在昆山召开贯彻《台湾同胞投资保护法》的高层研讨会，两岸工商界、新闻界及大陆官员共100多人与会，引起很大的反响。通过这次宣传活动，增强了广大干部群众保护台胞投资合法权益的法制观念，为台胞在祖国大陆投资营造了一个良好的法制氛围。

台商投资领域拓宽，层次提高，规模扩大

1998年我各级政府和部门重视对台经贸工作，积极采取措施切实协助解决台商在经营中遇到的困难，使合同台资金额实现高水平恢复性增长。1998年新批台资企业2937家，比1997年下降2.55%，合同台资金额31.07亿美元，增长10.38%，实际利用台资30.45亿美元，下降7.43%。截至1998年底，累计批准台资项目41422个，协议台资金额412.79亿美元，实际利用台资214.2亿美元。台资居我吸收境外直接投资第四位。祖国大陆仍然是台商岛外投资的首选地区。不少大企业受祖国大陆经济发展前景吸引并基于自身生存与发展的需要，突破台湾当局“戒急用忍”政策的诸多限制，依然加快投资祖国大陆的步伐，筹措巨额资金，设立大型生产基地，为企业发展创立新的根基。过去的一年，台商投资祖国大陆除继续注重制造业等传统投资领域外，逐步向其它领域和行业发展，体现出如下的特点：

1. 两岸农业领域的产业合作在深化。1997年外经贸部、国务院台办和农业部联合批准在漳州、福州设立“海峡两岸农业合作试验区”以后，1998年闽台经济合作有进一步的发展。祖国大陆农民劳动力价格低，土地价格低，物种资源、气候资源，土地多样性资源丰富，而且人口众多，使包括台资企业在内的农业企业有2/3的经营收入处于持平或盈利状态，大大高于外商投资企业的平均水平。琼台农业合作发展也很快。

2. 零售业也是1998年台商投资祖国大陆的热点之一。目前台湾100多家大企业中已有40多家在祖国大陆设立了100多个流通网点。

3. 台商开始步入金融领域。1998年6月台湾当局决定开放证券业在祖国大陆设办事处后，台湾证券业者纷纷展开行动，到年底已有10多家证券公司在北京、上海、深圳等地设立办事处及咨询公司。台商对航天航空领域的合作也表现出浓厚的兴趣。台湾5家航太公司首次参加在珠海举行的航空航天展，并表现了进一步合作的意向。

4. 大企业投资增加。从90年代初起，投资主体由中小企业主导发展为大企业主导。台湾大企业1998年在祖国大陆投资逐渐增多，台商投资规模大型化的趋势更加明显。

5. 台资更多涌入香港，港台合作进一步加强。香港回归后，港台关系成为两岸关系的特殊组成部分，港台经贸关系成为两岸经贸关系的特殊组成部分。根据“一国两制”、“港人治港”、高度自治的大政方针，中央政府支持和鼓励香港特别行政区在一个中国原则基础上与台湾地区继续保持和发展经济、文化、科技等领域的民间交流与合作，加强两地同胞的交往，鼓励和欢迎台胞和台湾各类资本到香港从事投资、贸易和其他工商活动，这对促进两地经济繁荣、促进两岸关系的进一步发展，具有极其重要的积极意义。因此，香港以其独特的区位条件和作为国际金融、贸易、航运、信息中心的重要地位，继续为沟通海峡两岸同胞的往来、促进两岸经济交流与合作发挥了桥梁和中介作用。香港继续成为台资走向祖国大陆的重要桥梁，也是台资走向世界市场的重要通道。目前在港正式运作的台资公司已逾3000家，大部分是台湾的中小企业以及一些大企业的分公司，行业分布广泛，近年来在地产、航运、金融服务行业等都有较大的发展。1998年香港受亚洲金融风暴的影响，外围和内部环境均出现一些不利因素，台资却逆势而上，仅经台湾当局批准的投入香港的资金就比上年增长13%。

6、台商投资祖国大陆效益明显。台商投资祖国大陆促进了海峡两岸经济的共同发展，许多台湾企业通过投资祖国大陆自身得到不断的发展与壮大，并取得了相当可观的效益。1998年这一情形尤为显著。在外经贸部公布的1997/1998年度最大的500家外商投资企业名单中，冠捷电子（福建）有限公司排名第45位，天津新宝天洋家电有限公司、辽宁大成农牧实业有限公司、上海太平洋百货有限公司等多家台资企业也榜上有名。1989年开始在祖国大陆投资的台湾顶新国际集团，旗下天津顶益、广州顶益、杭州顶益三家企业上榜。顶新国际集团所生产的“康师傅”系列食品，现在仅方便面项目，年产量就高达154亿包，占有了祖国大陆方便面市场的42%。顶新集团从名不见经传的企业通过在大陆投资成为顶尖的大企业并回岛内收购味全集团。多家台湾机电业的上市公司，其大陆厂的投资收益超过台湾母公司。

两岸科技合作与交流迈出新步伐

1998年2月，祖国大陆200多人组成代表团赴台参加APEC技术市场博览会；4月，联想集团赴台寻求两岸科技产业合作商机；7月，海峡两岸在台共同举办“两岸科技成果交流研讨会”，祖国大陆90多位代表带去246项科研技术成果与台湾同行进行交流，达成了多项合作意向；随后在北京举办的“京台科技成果商品化研讨交易会”，达成68个合作协议或意向，总金额2.3亿美元。1998年两岸这一连串的科技交往与合作引人注目，在两岸科技与工商界引起热烈反响。1998年台湾高科技产业加速外移，据台湾“资策会”调查，信息产业的产能已有1/3转往大陆生产。1998年岛内资讯业在祖国大陆的产值已达98亿美元，比1997年增长28%。

对台劳务合作稳步发展

1998年派出对台近海渔工和远洋船员31761人次，合同金额为1.14亿美元，营业金额为1.10亿美元，分别比上年增长7.0%、3.1%和13.9%。截至1998年底，我累计派出对台近海渔工和远洋船员189042人次，合同金额为7.17亿美元，营业金额为4.13亿美元。

前景展望

展望未来，海峡两岸经贸合作将继续向前发展。台湾当局的“戒急用忍”政策只会增加两岸经贸交流的成本，根本阻挡不了两岸经贸合作向前发展的趋势。因为两岸经贸交流符合民心，两岸经贸交流互利互惠，有百利而无一害。由于台湾是典型的岛型经济，在亚洲金融危机中很难独善其身，金融危机的的滞后影响不断显现出来，自1998年下半年起，大中企业纷纷发生巨额跳票等财务问题，外贸受到严重影响。而祖国大陆在金融危机中经济继续持续、快速、健康发展。台湾如果不以祖国大陆为经济腹地，失去这一大市场将失去许多发展机会。“戒急用忍”政策人为地隔断台湾上、中、下游产业的联系，已在祖国大陆投资的台资企业不能就近获得原料，企业竞争和发展受到制约；岛内上游产业也将失去市场。“戒急用忍”政策试图减轻台湾对祖国大陆经济依赖，最终将严重影响台湾经济的发展，严重损害台湾人民的利益。台湾当局重启“南向政策”也只会使台商损失惨重。两岸只有加强经济合作，才能共同抵御各种经济风险。希望台湾当局从中华民族的整体利益出发，尽快消除人为的政治障碍，全面开放直接“三通”，放弃僵化的“戒急用忍”政策，使两岸经贸交流向“直接、双向”的方向发展，扩大合作的领域、地域和范围，以利于中华民族经济的全面振兴。我们将遵循江泽民主席关于“不以政治分歧去影响、干扰两岸经济合作”的主张，一如既往采取一切有利措施继续推动两岸经贸交流。经过两岸人民的共同努力，两岸经贸交流一定会继续向前发展。

积极开展多边和区域经贸活动
为改革开放创造良好的国际环境

对外贸易经济合作部国际经贸关系司副司长　易小准

1998年对中国来说是极不平凡的一年。经济全球化浪潮方兴未艾，亚洲金融危机横扫亚洲许多国家，冲击了俄罗斯经济，波及到拉美，对中国经济构成极大的威胁。回首1998年，可以清楚地看到，经济全球化给各国，特别是发展中国家带来了迅速发展的历史机遇，同时也对他们构成了风险与挑战。在参与经济全球化进程中，发展中国家必须从本国的实际出发，选择适合自己的发展道路，积极参与多边和区域经济贸易活动，注意防范和化解各种风险，维护自身经济安全和金融安全，循序渐进，扎扎实实地发展壮大自己。

1998年，中国在积极参与多边和区域经贸活动方面作出了更为积极的努力，取得了长足的进展。

1998年，中国继续推进加入WTO的多、双边谈判，与一些WTO成员有货物贸易、服务贸易以及加入议定书等方面进行了密集的双边磋商。取得了重要进展。中国加入WTO工作组分别于1998年4月和7月召开了第七次和第八次会议。目前，在与中国正式举行双边市场准入谈判的35个国家中，已有下列10个国家与中国结束了双边市场准入谈判：捷克、匈牙利、印度尼西亚、日本（货物贸易）、韩国、新西兰、巴基斯坦、新加坡、斯洛伐克和土耳其。

参加多边贸易体制是中国经济改革的自身需要，是对外开放政策的一个组成部分。中国自1986年申请恢复关贸总协定缔约国地位到现在谈判加入WTO，前后已历时13年。中国对加入WTO的立场和态度从来没有改变。

这十几年来，中国始终致力于改善投资和贸易环境，向国际规范靠拢，采取了一系列促进贸易自由化的措施，大幅度降低进口关税和逐步取消非关税措施。这些努力在促进了本国经济体制改革的同时，客观上也为WTO成员创造了巨大的商业机会。目前，中国进口产品的平均关税水平已从1992年的43%降到目前的不到17%，中国承诺在2005年将工业品平均关税降至10%；在非关税措施方面，中国已经把1992年实行配额许可证管理的1247个税号的产品，减少到目前的不到400个税号，并承诺在加入WTO后逐步取消非关税措施。服务贸易领域的开放也取得积极进展，中国已承诺今后就电信、金融、法律、会计、专业服务等领域实行有步骤的开放。

作为世界第十大贸易国和第二大外国直接投资的东道国，中国已成为世界经济贸易的重要组成部分，并愿以负责任的态度参加多边贸易体制，为之作出贡献。中国这种讲信义、负责任的态度在亚洲金融危机中得到了充分证明。目前，大多数WTO成员都认识到，加入WTO既是中国的需要，也是WTO的需要。没有中国的全面参与，WTO将是不完整的，缺乏代表性和普遍性的。各方均希望中国在1999年底WTO新一轮多边贸易谈判开始之前加入WTO。

然而，也有个别WTO成员出于政治和经济上的考虑，在谈判中漫天要价，致使谈判久拖不决。中国是一个讲原则的国家，绝不会牺牲自己的根本利益来换取加入WTO。中国在谈判中始终坚持权利和义务平衡的原则，只能承担作为一个发展中国家与其国力相适应的义务和条件。

在积极参与多边贸易体制活动的同时，我们还积极参与了亚太、亚欧等区域经济贸易合作活动，努力为我国的经济发展、扩大出口和吸引外资工作创造一个稳定有利的外部环境。

亚太经合组织（APEC）作为亚太地区最具影响力和实质内容的区域经济合作组织，不仅对本地区经济发展和贸易体制自由化与便利化进程有着重要影响，对全球经济合作和多边贸易体系也有一定的推动作用。1998年是APEC的转折年，APEC从一个比较松散的区域经济论坛开始转变为一个具有明确的贸易投资自由化目标和具体行动方案的区域经济合作组织。

1998年，中国与其它成员一道，继续积极地参与了APEC关于贸易投资自由化问题的磋商，并在自主自愿的基础上进一步改进了贸易投资自由化的单边行动计划。中国新提交的改进的单边行动计划，内容包括关税、非关税措施、服务、投资等15个具体领域，在降低关税、减少非关税壁垒、扩大服务贸易市场准入、改善投资环境等方面采取了实质性措施。

中国积极参加了亚欧会议（ASEM）的活动，全面参与了《贸易便利化行动计划》和《投资促进行动计划》的制定与实施，并与亚欧会议成员国一起在标准、动植物检疫、投资促进方面开展了一系列具体的合作活动，这些活动对促进亚欧间贸易和投资的双向流动产生了积极的影响。1998年4月，第二届亚欧首脑会议在伦敦举行。朱镕基总理代表中国政府出席此会，并提出了加强亚欧合作应以经贸合作为重点等一系列原则和主张。中国将继续积极参与亚欧会议框架下的亚欧合作，为建立面向21世纪更加稳定的亚欧、中欧关系做出贡献。

1998年，中国继续与曼谷协定成员就加入该协定问题进行了一系列双边谈判。目前，中国与斯里兰卡已签署双边备忘录。与印度和孟加拉的谈判已接近尾声，只有少量技术问题有待澄清。韩国政府提出了有关结束中韩双边谈判的积极建议。各方都希望中国能够尽快加入曼谷协定。

中国继续积极参与联合国贸发会议、国际贸易中心、商品共同基金和一些国际商品组织的活动和讨论，议题涉及贸易效率、电子商务、普惠制、投资和竞争政策、内陆和过境国的运输安排等。通过参加这些活动，中国表明了立场和主张，维护了自身及广大发展中国家的权益。与此同时，中国也及时了解到大量的信息，增加了中国产品的出口机会和吸收外资的能力，为对外开放和经贸体制改革起到了有益的咨询作用。

中国还进一步加强了与经济合作与发展组织(OECD) 的对话合作关系。

多年来，中国一直利用国际组织和外国政府对华提供的无偿援助，与这些组织和国家在经贸、技术交流，引进技术设备，培养人才等领域开展了积极的合作。1998 年，中国接受联合国儿童基金、人口基金以及澳大利亚、加拿大、欧盟、德国、日本、荷兰及新西兰等国家的无偿援助项目金额总额约合 2.2 亿美元，共安排项目 100 多个。这些项目涉及教育、环保、扶贫、农业、妇幼福利保健、小额贷款发展经济以及社会保障体系等各个方面，更大程度地向中西部地区倾斜。同时，通过参与联合国机构制定有关经济和社会协调发展政策，积累了宝贵的经验。此外，为配合国内经济体制改革，中国还开展了大量的人员培训、专题研究、模式试验、经验交流等活动，收到了良好的效果。1998 年中国发生了百年不遇的特大洪水。为克服洪灾，中国积极动员国际社会向灾区提供援助，共争取到了 6330 万美元的国际多双边援助，促进灾后重建。这些无偿多双边援助促进了中国，特别是中西部边远地区的社会进步和经济发展。

中国对外经济贸易法制的新发展

对外贸易经济合作部条约法律司司长　张玉卿

1998 年，在“依法治国、建设社会主义法制国家”基本方略的指引下，外经贸法制建设紧紧围绕对外经济贸易事业发展这个中心，适应改革开放和建设社会主义市场经济体制的需要，在立法、执法、执法监督、普法等多个方面又有了新的发展，对于巩固外经贸体制的改革成果，促进外经贸事业的发展起到了重要的作用。

一、加强外经贸立法，使外经贸工作有法可依

立法是法制工作的前提和基础，1998 年围绕建立和完善对外经贸法律体系的目标，在对外贸易、利用外资、国际经济合作、技术贸易等方面的立法都有了新的进展，并积极参与了国家的立法工作：

(一) 外贸立法：

1998 年外贸立法的一个重要进展是有关外贸代理的问题在国家法律中作了规定。基于我国特定国情而产生的对外贸易代理制在外贸发展过程中起到了巨大的作用，但同时在实践中也产生了一些问题，主要是作为代理人的外贸公司承担的权利义务极不平衡。这个问题在现有的法律规定中很难解决，长期以来一直困扰着外贸公司。这次我们抓住制定《合同法》这一契机，积极参与该法的起草工作，在广泛征求有关单位意见的基础上多次向全国人大法工委提出了我们的意见，最终在新颁布的《合同法》“委托合同”一章中增加了与解决外贸代理问题有关的规定。这些规定既立足于我国国情，同时又积极参考其它国家的作法和《联合国国际货物销售代理公约》的规定，从而从法律上解决了外贸代理中存在的问题。

为配合国务院关于严厉打击逃、套汇行为的通知，制定了一系列相关的法规和规章，如《规范进出口代理业务的若干规定》、《外经贸企业收汇考核办法》和《对违规、走私企业给予警告、暂停或撤销对外贸易、国际货运代理经营许可行政处罚的暂行规定》等，这些规定在很大程度上遏制了企业的逃、套汇违法行为，有助于保障经济的健康发展。《对外贸易法》1994 年颁布实行后，制定外贸法的配套法规就成为一项紧迫工作。根据立法计划，1998 年起草制订了《货物进口条例》和《进出口商会条例》，均已上报国务院。为了使我国的反倾销反

补贴条例更加完善、透明，更加符合国际惯例，目前正在积极起草有关实施《中华人民共和国反倾销反补贴条例》的规定。

（二）外资方面

改革开放以来，我们吸引了大量的外资，这对于促进我国国民经济的发展起到了重要的作用。但是吸引外资工作中很多内容需要进行规范，一些新的利用外资的领域、行业和方式也需要用法律法规来加以规范。按照中共十五大精神及党中央6号文件的要求，1998年积极进行了利用外资基本法律的修订、完善工作。《台湾同胞投资保护法实施细则》（草案）的起草工作也基本结束，有望于1999年由国务院批准颁布实施；1998年还发布了《关于解决外商投资企业董事不出席董事会会议问题的指导意见》、《中外合资旅行社试点暂行办法》等一批行政法规和规章。

（三）在国际经济合作和技术贸易方面，为了促进和规范对外工程承包与劳务合作的发展，正在积极起草《中华人民共和国对外工程承包与劳务合作条例》。为配合科技兴贸的发展战略，规范技术贸易行为，正在加强技术贸易立法，1998年已公布《核两用品及相关技术出口管制条例》，同时，正在拟定《中华人民共和国技术进出口条例》、《限制出口技术管理办法》等。

（四）此外，向国家各有关立法机关起草的法律、法规提出立法意见也是立法工作的重要组成部分。1998年，我们对全国人大、国务院及有关部门的法律、法规提供了立法意见，如《中华人民共和国合同法》、《中华人民共和国土地管理法》、《证券法》、《行政复议法》等。

二、加强双边、多边国际谈判，维护我国的权益

（一）知识产权谈判

1998年1月和6月，中美双方举行了两次知识产权磋商，磋商涉及中美知识产权协议的执行问题，中国打击CD盗版的问题，版权法修改的问题，特别是政府机构使用非法计算机软件的问题。我们还积极参与了亚太经合组织举行的两次知识产权专家组会议，就成员之间的知识产权合作问题进行探讨。中欧知识产权合作也在继续进行。此外，还协助处理了9起有关知识产权的案件。

（二）投资保护协定方面

1998年经谈判我国与也门、埃塞俄比亚、佛得角、巴巴多斯等国家签署了双边投资保护协定，并与加拿大、巴林、墨西哥、波黑、芬兰等国家就签署及修改双边投资保护协定进行了谈判；还对有关外国投资者向多边投资担保机构的投保申请进行了审查。

三、反倾销调查与应诉

（一）国内反倾销调查

反倾销调查政策性、涉外性很强且有严格的时限，根据国际反倾销调查的形势，随着关税与非关税壁垒的日益减少，反倾销手段会越来越得到世界各国政府的充分利用和强化。自1997年12月10日我国首例新闻纸反倾销调查案正式公告立案，对原产于加拿大、韩国和美国的进口新闻纸开始反倾销调查。1998年7月9日，外经贸部公布外经贸部和国家经贸委对此案的初步裁定，认为原产于上述三国的进口新闻纸存在倾销，国内相关产业存在实质损害，并且国内相关产业的实质损害与进口产品倾销之间存在因果关系。根据初裁结果，决定自1998年7月10日起，进口经营者在进口原产于上述三国的新闻纸时，必须向中华人民共和国海关提供与初步裁定确定的倾销幅度相适应的现金保证金。初裁以后，各利害关系方向有关调查当局提交了补充材料，外经贸部和国家经贸委也分别赴国外生产企业和国内申请企业进行了实地核查。经过进一步调查分析，外经贸部和国家经贸委分别做出肯定性的最终裁定。经国务院关税税则委员会批准，外经贸部于1999年6月3日发布公告，决定对原产于加拿大、韩国和美国的进口新闻纸征收反倾销税，反倾销税税率与最终裁定确定的倾销幅度相同。这标志着历时一年多的我国首例反倾销调查顺利结案。

此外，1998年12月8日正式接受了武汉钢铁公司的对来自俄罗斯的硅钢进行反倾销调查的申请书，并于1999年3月12日正式立案，硅钢反倾销调查是我国的第二例反倾销调查案。

（二）国外反倾销应诉和复审工作

在1998年面临严峻的亚洲金融危机和繁重的出口任务的情况下，反倾销应诉和复审是一项事关我国外贸发展的重要工作。1998年国外共对华立案进行反倾销调查19起，产品涉及到我五矿化工、轻纺、机电、土畜和医保各类产品，涉案金额超过1亿美元。此外，1997年所立的部分旧案在1998年仍需花费大量时间和精力继续应诉。为此，我们作了大量的工作：政府交涉取得很大进展；在具体案

件的交涉工作中我们也取得了显著的成绩，如在韩国糠醇案、欧盟棉坯布案、墨西哥对华反倾销案、印度对华焦炭反倾销案都取得了不同程度的胜利；参与和指导商会和有关企业的反倾销应诉工作，培训人员，提高政府部门、商会和企业的应诉水平；利用反倾销案件交涉费用聘用律师等。

四、制订贸易示范合同

为进一步推动我国对外贸易的发展，改进和完善中外企业间的贸易合同，自九十年代初以来，分别与日本、韩国、德国、澳大利亚和新西兰进行了双边贸易示范合同的谈判与编制工作。到目前为止，已制订完成了《中日货物买卖合同条款集》、《中韩货物买卖示范条款集》和《中澳新羊毛买卖标准合同》；另外，《中日设备与技术示范合同》和《中德技术转让示范合同》正在谈判当中。这些示范合同以中外双方国家现行的法律、法规及国际条约、协定为基础，采纳现行的国际贸易惯例，照顾双方贸易的特殊性，体现平等互利、公平合理的原则，从而促进了双边贸易的发展。

五、大力开展普法工作，提高干部职工的法律意识和法制观念

1998年5月份在北京召开了外经贸系统“三五”普法中期工作会议，总结了前半段的工作，部署了下一阶段的任务。1998年分别在北京和乌鲁木齐分别举办了中德经济法合作项目“合同法”培训班，在福建举办了“外经贸企业股份制改造”培训班，收到了很好的效果。12月份在北京举办中德法律合作项目第一期两个月的法律培训班，并出版了专用教材。年底在加拿大举办一期境外法律培训班，对外经贸系统法律工作人员进行定向培训，提高法律专业人员素质。

六、严格依法行政，加强执法监督

（一）加强合同和章程审查工作，协助企业解决法律纠纷

外贸方面，为重大外贸案件的解决提供法律意见也是一项重要工作。1998年对大量的经贸纠纷案件提供了咨询意见，如中化尹坚诈骗外汇案、海经公司广州分公司与湖南株洲石油公司经济纠纷案、中化雷蒙公司金融期货交易纠纷案、上海五矿公司被香港国恩公司诈骗案金融案等，以事实为依据、以法律为准绳，对上述案件进行了妥善处理。外资方面，参与重大利用外资项目的审查批准工作，并就利用外资新方式及新问题，如投资性公司、股份有限公司、合并、分立、海外投资问题提出法律意见。对于外商投资企业出现的重大，有代表性的纠纷及问题，积极参与协调解决，维护了法律的严肃性，也体现了行政部门的公正，使得大部分问题得以顺利友好解决，如黄河铝业，武汉长江大桥、河南春都等纠纷的解决。此外还积极向企业提供法律、法规的咨询服务，宣讲我国利用外资的法律、法规。

（二）行政复议工作

随着我国行政立法的完善及行政复议制度的建立，1998年我部受理多起行政复议申请。年初顺利审结了海南某公司起诉北京外经贸委案，这是我部审理的第一起行政复议案。9月份又审结了澳大利亚某公司诉上海市外资委的行政复议案。此外，还处理了上海两家合资企业诉外经贸部以及某中国国营专业公司诉北京市外经贸委行政复议案。同时，还具体指导了地方外经贸委的行政复议工作，并根据行政复议工作的需要，下发了《若干行政案件情况介绍》、《深圳贤成大厦案给我们的几点启示》等，以推动外经贸系统的依法行政。行政复议工作防止和纠正了违法或不当的具体行政行为，保护了公民、法人和其它组织的合法权益，同时也维护了行政机关依法行政的权威。

（三）外贸法执法检查

为检验外贸法实施四周年来的成果及各地的执法情况，我们继续对《外贸法》执法情况进行了检查。在检查过程中，认真听取当地单位的汇报，展开细致调查，得到大量第一手的珍贵资料，并对受查地区工作做了指导，并形成报告，注意总结、推广先进执法经验。

七、外经贸领域立法趋势展望

今后，我国外经贸立法的发展趋势将表现为以下几个方面：

1．为配合政府实现转变职能的需要，围绕《对外贸易法》将制定一系列新的配套法规和规章，因此，从形式上看，我国外经贸立法的系统性将有所加强，外经贸立法体系将进一步完善；从内容上看，将进一步体现政府转变职能的要求，贯彻审批从宽、管理从严的指导思想，例如对外贸易和国际经济合作领域的经营权审批标准将进一步放宽，而对经营者经营活动的监督管理将进一步加强。

2．各项立法将进一步贯彻与国际惯例接轨的指导思想，对照世界贸易组织的规则体系，我国将着

手进行“废、改、立”的工作。所谓“废、改、立”，即经过对照审查，废除现行法律法规中与世界贸易组织协议相违背的规定，修改现行法律法规中与国际规范不符的规定，同时依照国际公约和条约授权性规范，制定我国国内法中的相应规范，从而使我国享有根据国际规范应有的权益。另外，在修改和制定国内法律方面，如正在进行的我国利用外资法律的修改，应注意保持与我国承担义务的国际规范和广泛适用的国际惯例相符。

3. 为完成和实现1999年外经贸“千方百计扩大出口、千方百计利用外资”的任务，将根据改革发展的形势以及党中央和国务院的指示，在现有的法律框架下，将通过法规和部门规章的形式制定和颁布若干能够促进出口和引资工作的具体措施。

精简机构，转变职能，面向新世纪

对外贸易经济合作部人事教育劳动司司长　魏建国

1998年，在中央、国务院和部党组的正确领导下，我部紧紧围绕江泽民总书记在党的十五大提出的关于推进国家行政机关机构改革的任务，按照九届全国人大一次会议审议通过的《国务院机构改革方案》中确定的机构改革的总目标、总原则和总要求，认真做好部机关机构改革的各项工作，在组织实施过程中不动摇，不变调，不走样，顺利完成了我部机关机构改革的各项任务。机构改革后，我部机关行政编制（含原国务院机电办公室）精简到457人，比原来减少了402人，减幅达46.8%；司局级机构减少2个，处室机构减少了37个；司局级职数减少了7人，处级职数减少了86人。我部机构改革工作取得了新的较大的成果。

一、进一步解放思想，转变观念，切实转变行政管理职能

我们认为，职能转变是机构改革的关键，解决不好，就难于克服多头管理、政出多门的弊端，难以实现精简的任务和提高机关工作效率。转变职能的关键是解决思想，转变观念，严格按照这次政府机构改革的总目标和基本原则，切实在转变职能上下功夫。中央、国务院提出，这次机构改革总目标是，适应经济发展和社会全面进步的要求，建立办事高效、运转协调、行为规范的行政管理体系，完善国家公务员制度，建设高素质的专业化的国家行政干部队伍，提高为人民服务的水平。基本原则有四条：一是按照发展社会主义市场经济的要求，转变政府职能，实现政企分开；二是按照统一、效能的原则，调整政府组织结构，实行精兵简政；三是按照权责一致的原则，调整政府部门的职责权限，明确划分部门之间的职能分工；四是按照依法治国、依法行政的要求，加强行政体系的法制建设。因此，我部机构改革决不是单纯地裁并几个司局，精减几个人员，而是外经贸行政职能管理体制的一场深刻革命，是上层建筑领域适应经济的一场深刻革命。改革开放以来的外经贸事业飞速发展的实践也证明，要建立社会主义市场经济体制，保证我国外经贸事业的不断发展，外经贸行政管理部门必须切实转变职能，实现微观管理、事务性管理到宏观调控、社会管理和公共服务方面来。因此，我们要求机关公务员进一步解放思想，转变观念，提高改革的自觉性和坚定性。只有牢牢把握这一点，机构改革才会取得实质性的进展，机构和人员也能减得下来，否则改革就无法进行。转变观念还在于我部广大机关干部首先是各级领导干部必须以党和人民的利益为重，从改革的大局出发，树立局部利益服从整体利益的全局观念，克服狭隘的部门利益的驱动，正确处理机构改革中遇到的问题。应该下放和调整的职能，要坚决下放和调整；应该履行和保留的职能，也就应该坚决保留下来。这次机构改革，国务院批准的我部“三定”方案确定了我部机关的职能，其中划入的职能有3项，划出的职能有11项，转变的职能有7项。总的来讲，具体的微观事务性减少了，宏观调控的职能大大增强。

二、按照社会主义市场经济和外经贸战略发展的总要求，做好我部机关职能配置、内设机构和人员定编工作

职能配置、内设机构和人员定编是我部机关机构改革的中心工作。在部党组的部署下，我们积极

采取有力措施，紧紧围绕这一中心工作展开机构“三定”的各项工作任务。一是抽调专人成立了机构改革工作小组，参与了外经贸部职能配置即划出职能、划入职能和调整职能的研究和确定工作；二是逐一核对机关人员变动情况，准确统计出部机关现有人员情况，更新了人员信息数据库，统计、整理了部机关人员概况、增减情况和干部队伍情况分析等资料。据此，对我部19个司（厅）和机关党委的职责进行了研究，对部分单位的职责做了调整。并对19个司（厅）和机关党委领导职数、内设机构、人员编制进行了逐一核定；三是依据中办和国办的有关文件精神，结合我部实际情况，经过反复研究修改，制定下发了《外经贸部机关人员定编定岗实施办法》和《外经贸部机关人员分流安排和培训的实施办法》。并制定了配套的实施细则，为做好我部“三定”工作提供了政策依据和制度保障，保证了我部机关人员定岗和分流培训工作得以有条不紊地进行；四是认真做好部机关人员的思想动员工作，提高认识，统一思想，为顺利实施我部“三定”方案奠定了良好的思想基础。

三、严格按照“工作需要，群众参与，综合考评，组织决定”的原则，本着优化人员结构的要求，做好部机关人员定岗工作

人员定岗是这次机构改革的重点，为做好这一工作，我们提出了总的指导思想：坚持干部“四化”方针，注重德才兼备，加强定向培训，开发人才资源，发挥个人专长，调整和加强部机关公务员队伍和驻外干部队伍，提高机关工作效率。建设一支精干、廉洁、高素质的专业化公务员队伍，以适应建立社会主义市场体制和发展外经贸事业的需要。具体地说，就是要做到“四个结合”：一是与优化机关干部队伍的专业、年龄结构结合起来；二是与改革干部人事制度结合起来，强化竞争激励机制，做到公务员队伍的能进能出，能上能下；三是与加强机关作风建设结合起来，切实转变机关工作作风，改进工作方法和态度，提高工作效率，促进勤政廉政；四是与加强制度建设结合起来，要建立完善各项规章制度，规范行政行为，提高依法行政的水平。在具体实施过程中，我们严格按中央和国务院确定的“工作需要，群众参与，综合考评，组织决定”的原则进行。各司局按照部机关“三定”方案的要求，根据本司局的职能和人员编制及领导职数，合理地设置处（室）和职位，明确职责任务及任职资格条件。定岗人员的基本条件按照《党政领导干部选拔任用工作暂行条例》和《国家公务员暂行条例》的有关规定严格把关，注意人员的优化配备。人员定岗工作按干部管理权限分级负责；部党组确定司局级干部人选，各司局提出处级干部人选，主任科员以干部由各司局按双向选择的办法确定。在具体实施过程中，要确保人员定岗工作的透明度，力求公平公正。为此，我们组织了部机关全体处级干部民主测评所有现职正、副司长，并在部机关范围内民主推荐可担任司级领导人选；组织各司局全体干部民主测评本司局正、副处长，并在本司局范围内民主推荐处级干部人选。从而为部党组研究决定司级领导班子成员人选和各司局决定处级班子人选提供了重要依据。在这次机构改革中，我们共任免正、副司长85人，其中，提拔正司长6人；副司长11人；免职17人；平调51人。其任处长123人，办理副处长备案162人。领导干部队伍也进一步年轻化，部机关司局级干部的平均年龄由机构改革前的49.7岁下降到48.1岁，下降了1.6岁；处级领导干部的平均年龄由机构改革前的40.09岁下降到38.16岁，下降了1.93岁。在定岗过程中，强化了竞争机制，领导干部在能上能下、轮岗交流方面取得了明显进展。

四、严格按照“带职分流，定向培训，加强企业，优化结构”的原则，切实做好人员分流工作

人员分流工作是历次机构改革的难点，是改革能否成功的重要保证。这次改革，我部机关行政编制总数要减少近一半，是历次机构改革减编最多的，三年内部机关需分流人员达402人，人员分流任务相当艰巨。做好人员分流，关键必须处理好“留”与“分”的关系，不能随随便便的“留”谁和“分”谁，更不能甩“包袱”。而是根据岗位、专业和干部的工作能力等实际需要，科学组合和调整。“留”在机关的，并不意味全是能力强，学历高的；“分”出去的，也并不意味着就是能力差，学历低的。对分流人员，中央和国务院提出了“带职分流，定向培训，加强企业，优化结构”分流办法。结合我部实际，我们对分流人员采取以下安排途径：一是外派到驻外经商机构工作；二是选派有专业特长和管理经验的人员充实到部直属企业、事业单位及商会、协会、学会；三是鼓励和支持分流人员自行联系工作，调动到其它单位工作或自谋职业；四是安排分

流人员带职学习，参加各种形式的职业、岗位和学历等方面的学习和培训；五是严格干部退休制度；六是对不称职的或因其他原因不能坚持正常工作，以及不适宜在机关安排工作的公务员，予以辞退。对符合提前退休条件的办理提前退休手续。为做好这项工作，我们还成立了专门负责分流人员管理工作的临时机构，在部党组的直接领导下，本着“温暖如家，负责到底，尽量做到人人满意”的原则，切实做好人员分流工作。同时各级领导也大力协助，积极做好大家的思想政治工作，从而保证了人员分流工作的顺利进行。由于各级领导的高度重视，认真负责，我部分流工作进行平稳，分流人员中，参加各种学习培训的有125人，待派出国的有117人，到部属企事业单位的有36人，提前离岗的有31人，自谋职业的有14人，调往其他机关的有13人，待安排的有42人。按照中央和国务院的要求，我们将于2000年底之前完成人员分流的任务。

我部这次机构改革，调整和优化了干部队伍结构，岗位设置更趋科学，人员配置更加合理。初步实现了干部年轻化和知识化的目标。在这次深度和广度都较大的变革中，每个人都受到了强烈的冲击、震撼和考验，竞争意识和危机感增强了，激发了大家学习理论和业务的热潮，以提高自身素质，适应时代的发展和时代的要求。我部机构改革取得了圆满成功，这归功于部党组的高度重视，贯彻党中央国务院的总体部署态度坚决，工作扎实，组织工作周密，实施办法有效；也归功于全体机关干部以高度的政治责任感，自觉的态度。下一步，我们要按照依法治国、依法行政的要求，加强行政管理的制度化和规范化，用经济手段和法律手段进行行政和行业管理，这既是社会主义市场经济的客观要求，也是保证外经贸事业持续稳定发展的重要保证。我们相信只要我们坚持以邓小平理论为指导，同心同德，扎实工作，就一定能完成我部机构改革的任务，把我部行政管理工作和人事工作提高到一个新的水平，以新的姿态迈向新世纪，为外经贸事业的发展作出我们应有的贡献。

依法行政，为国把关，全面推进现代海关制度建设

海关总署办公厅副主任　黄胜强

一、打击走私成绩显著

1998年，全国打击走私工作会议以后，全国海关认真贯彻落实党中央、国务院关于打击走私的重大决策，雷厉风行，严防猛打，开展了声势浩大的反走私斗争。先后组织了珠江、西江水域，北部湾、北仑河水域和中蒙、中朝边境的缉私联合行动。积极开展海上缉私，加强海上缉私巡逻，加强珠江水道进出境中途监管，加强对来往港澳小型船舶走私活动的打击力度。严厉打击货运渠道走私，开展了打击“两车”（汽车、摩托车）、“两油”（成品油、食用油）、“两料”（化工原料、纺织原料）和移动通讯设备等重点商品的专项斗争，加强对重点商品的前期布控、现场查验和后续稽查。全年，全国海关共查获走私案件8381起，案值154亿元。其中查获偷逃税款5万元以上案件1805起，案值136.9亿元。严厉查处一批案值巨大、情节严重、影响恶劣的重大走私案件，依法移送公安机关走私嫌疑案件908起和走私罪嫌疑人837人。全年上缴罚没收入36.8亿元，比上年增长10.8%。查获的主要走私物品有：汽车3887辆、成品油31.8万吨、食用油15.37万吨、化工原料11.23万吨、化纤5.4万吨、香烟4.9万箱、钢材16.51万吨、移动通讯设备39.4亿元、计算机4.32万台。还查获走私海洛因等各类毒品642公斤，精神药物86万片，罂粟壳（籽）15.6吨、易制毒化学品32.7吨，反动、淫秽、盗版、散发性宗教宣传品和音像制品1281万件，各类枪支28支、弹药19321发，文物5326件。积极运用科技防伪和计算机手段，查获“三假”走私案件297起，案值21.22亿元，查获假单证4353份，假印章79枚。认真做好缉私警察机构的筹备组建工作，研究建立“联合缉私、统一处理、综合治理”缉私新体制。海关总署走私犯罪侦查局的组建工作已经就绪，首批直属海关走私犯罪侦查分局的筹备工作也基本完成，1999年初将陆续挂牌。在反

走私斗争中，各地海关按照“海上抓、岸边堵、口岸查、市场管、处罚严”的方针，紧紧依靠各级地方党政，加强与有关执法、司法等部门的密切协作，积极推进反走私综合治理工作。进一步完善MOU工作，完善与银行、外汇管理、外经贸、税务等部门的计算机联网，积极配合有关部门严厉打击骗汇、骗税、逃证等经济犯罪活动。1998年鉴别发现伪造报关单3万份，其中涉及骗汇金额193.5亿美元，查获骗取出口退税案20起，涉及可能骗取退税额1.83亿元。通过海关与各地、各部门的合力打击，形成了反走私的高压态势，目前大规模的走私活动得到初步遏制，一批走私犯罪分子受到严惩，一些重点行业经营状况好转，反走私斗争取得了明显效果。

二、关税征管工作取得突破

1998年，全国海关认真贯彻落实国家扩大内需政策和增加国家财力的要求，克服亚洲金融危机影响加深、外贸进出口总体下降等不利因素，识大体、顾大局，发扬抗洪精神，树立全国海关一盘棋思想，依法治税，严格征管，加强综合治税，把税收征管工作放在突出位置上抓紧抓好。积极采取有效措施，加大审单、审价、查验、归类、化验等环节的执法力度，认真严格执行税收政策，强化加工贸易管理，有效实施稽查手段，积极推广使用关税征管的计算机系统，向管理要税，提高税收征管质量，努力实现国家税收应收尽收。1998年全国海关共征收关税和进口环节税918亿元，扣除各种政策性退税，净缴中央财政879亿元，比1997年增长6.58%，比年初计划超收99亿元，为增加国家财力作出了重大贡献。其中，关税入库322.82亿元，进口环节税入库553.43亿元。通过审价补税21.99亿元，化验及归类补税3.62亿元。

三、进出境监管工作取得进展

1998年，海关进一步强化物流监控，提高查验率，加强对进出境运输工具、货物和物品的实际监管。先后恢复和建立大铲、三门、桂山、湾仔4个中途监管站，有效地加强了对来往港澳小型船舶的监管。加强科技手段在监管工作中应用，在一些重点监管现场安装了电子地磅、集装箱检查设备。全年海关共监管进出境货物4.44亿吨，其中进口货物2.37亿吨，出口货物2.07亿吨。监管进出境运输工具1587万辆（艘），监管进出境集装箱1504万箱次。深化行邮监管制度改革，方便旅客合法进出，全年监管进出境人员1.57亿人次，邮件9225万件。进一步规范和加强加工贸易管理，严格合同审批和单耗管理，加大中期核查和下厂核销力度，进一步规范加工贸易异地加工和深加工结转管理。加强与外经贸、银行、税务等部门的联系配合，完善加工贸易银行保证金台帐制度。加强对保税区和保税仓库的管理，清理整顿了一批保税仓库。全国海关1998年登记备案加工贸易合同37万份，核销到期合同37.57万份，批准内销补税74.33亿元。查获偷逃税款5万元以上加工贸易走私案件726起，案值45.9亿元。知识产权海关保护工作进展良好，全年查处进出口侵权案件金额达636.22万美元。

四、海关稽查工作取得突出成绩

1998年，全国海关加大稽查力度，深入企业开展稽查，全年稽查企业15063家。全国海关先后对进口移动通讯设备、显像管、食用油、成品油、硅铁、白（铜）板纸、不锈钢、香蕉、橡胶等近20种重点商品及一些保税仓库组织开展了专项稽查。查获违规案件1173起，案值44.9亿元。查获并移交调查部门涉嫌走私案件243起，案值16.7亿元，稽查补税26.41亿元。特别是对进口移动通讯设备的专项稽查，查获一些地区邮电部门存在利用包税方式进行走私及偷漏税问题，补征税款和收取税款抵押金达31亿余元。海关稽查工作的有效开展，有力地配合了全国反走私联合行动和专项斗争，较好地发挥了海关稽查作为完善海关监管体系和打击走私第二道防线的作用。

五、海关总署机构改革顺利完成

1998年，根据党中央、国务院的决定，海关总署的机构、职能和人员编制作了重大调整。将外经贸部的原国家进出口商品检验局、农业部的原进出口动植物检疫局、卫生部的原进出境卫生检疫局合并，成立国家出入境检验检疫局，由海关总署管理；撤销国家口岸办公室，将其口岸规划、审理等职能交由海关总署承担；撤销全国打击走私领导小组，其职能交由海关总署承担，由海关总署统一负责打击走私工作；将原由对外贸易经济合作部负责的出口商品原产地规则协调管理职能，交由海关总署承担；将原由国务院关税税则委员会负责的有关立法调研工作、税法起草工作和税法执行过程中的一般性解释工作，交由海关总署承担；海关总署建立走私犯罪侦查局，受海关总署与公安部双重领导、以海关总署领导为主，组建海关缉私警察队伍，由海关和公安双重垂直领导、以海关领导为主，实行“联合缉私，统一处理，综合治理”的反走私斗争新体制；海关总署升格为正部级机构。按照党中央、国务院决定，遵循精简、统一、效能的原则，并充分吸收了现代海关制度及通关作业改革、口岸体制改革、缉私体制改革等改革成果，海关总署完成了机构改革和“三定”工作，对总署机构设置及职责分工作了较大调整，内设12个司局和5个直属事业单位，精简和分流了大批行政人员。海关的职能作用得到极大加强，工作效率得到较大提高。

六、通关作业改革初见成效

1998年是实施现代海关制度建设两步走战略的第一年。通关作业改革作为现代海关制度建设的中心环节和突破口正式启动。全国各海关积极参与通关作业改革试点方案的研究与完善。从1998年4月1日起在天津、青岛、上海、深圳4个海关开始首批试点。10月1日起，又在北京、大连、南京、杭州、福州、广州等6个海关进行了第二批试点。试点海关进行了重新划分总署、直属海关和隶属海关三级事权，重新设计通关作业流程，重新设置职能机构并转变职能管理方式等改革。海关系统开发和应用了现代海关业务管理信息化系统、国家口岸专网以及全国报关单核查系统等计算机管理系统。从试点情况看，新的作业模式和流程运作良好，已显示其优越性和生命力。海关执法更加规范，实际监控有所增强，海关监管整体效能和通关速度进一步提高。特别是在提高海关执法规范化水平、强化垂直领导和加强廉政建设等方面效果明显，为推进现代海关制度建设奠定了坚实的基础。

七、支持外贸出口取得成效

1998年，面对亚洲金融危机的影响，全国海关坚决贯彻党中央、国务院关于应对亚洲金融危机的一系列决策，实施了应对亚洲金融危机支持外经贸发展的10项措施。海关部署与外经贸部建立了支持扩大出口、打击走私的合作机制。加强与有关商会及出口企业的协作，积极扶持出口招标商品、国家支柱产业产品和高新技术产品的出口。努力提高通关效率，加强出口货物验放，缩短企业退税周期。认真落实进口设备税收优惠政策，严格减免税审批管理，全年免税594.52亿元。第一时间向国务院和外经贸部传送出口统计快报，每月提前3天向外经贸部提供电子数据，充分发挥海关统计为国家外经贸决策服务的职能。

1999年是建国50周年和迎接澳门回归的具有特殊意义的一年，也是海关改革和建设的关键一年，全国海关将认真贯彻“依法行政，为国把关”的方针，常备不懈，严防猛打，深入持久地开展反走私斗争，全面强化实际监管，严格依法治税；坚持以改革促发展，积极推进现代海关制度建设；坚持“从严治关”的方针，以开展“三讲”教育和清除执法腐败为重点，狠抓队伍建设，全面完成海关各项任务。

1998年我国出入境检验检疫工作步入新阶段

国家出入境检验检疫局办公室主任　魏传忠

1998年是我国出入境检验检疫事业发展史上重要的一年。经国务院批准，由原国家进出口商品检验局、卫生部卫生检疫局和农业部动植物检疫局合并组建了国家出入境检验检疫局。这标志着我国出入境检验检疫事业进入了一个新的历史发展时期。一年来，在党中央、国务院的正确领导下，出入境检验检疫系统的广大干部职工以邓小平理论为指导，深入贯彻落实十五大精神，坚持既把关又服务的方针，严格执法、热情服务，为我国外经贸事业的发展和对外开放战略目标的顺利实现做出了应有贡献。

一、严把进出口商品质量关，较好地维护了国家经济利益和对外经贸信誉

1998年，全国出入境检验检疫机构共检验进出口商品251.76万批，比上年增长8.8%，检验货值为1057.88亿美元，比上年减少2.4%。在此过程中，堵住不合格出口商品1.0万批，占出口商品检验批次的0.5%，维护了对外经贸信誉；查出不合格进口商品1.8万批，货值达16.8亿美元，经及时出具商检证书供有关单位对外索赔，挽回了大量经济损失。在严格审核的基础上，各地出入境检验检

疫机构共签发普惠制产地证书185万份，一般产地证书41.5万份，签证金额分别为406亿美元和132.7亿美元，较好地满足了对外贸易需要。检验中，全系统还重点加强了对以下几类进出口商品的质量把关工作，取得了良好成效。一是援外物品。通过加强检验管理，认真落实检验标准，使援外物品质量得到了较好保证。二是出口棉花。经及时与外经贸部和有关出口企业协调，统一检验力度，使国储棉出口存在的问题得到了妥善解决。三是进口旧机电产品。经与有关部门密切配合，严格进口旧机电产品备案登记和检验，遏制了旧机电产品随意进口的势头，起到了保护我国环境和生产安全的作用。四是进口废物。通过狠抓进口废物装运前检验规定的落实，进一步防止了“洋垃圾”向我国转移。

二、出入境动植物检疫管理工作得到进一步加强，有效保护了我国农林牧业生产安全，并在促进我农副产品出口方面取得好成果

1998年，国家出入境检验检疫部门广泛搜集了世界各国近两年发生的主要动植物疫病资料，建立了国外动植物疫情信息库，为进境动植物检疫审批提供了科学依据。根据比利时发生疯牛病、澳大利亚发生新城疫、俄罗斯发生牛瘟、泰国发生口蹄疫、美国发生地中海实蝇等疫情，及时发布了有关进口动植物的禁令，防止了这些动植物疫病传入我国。为促进我农副产品出口，国家出入境检验检疫局与有关国家检疫部门进行了多次接触，通过采取相应措施，使我国牛肉再次打入以色列市场，并扩大了对俄罗斯的肉类出口。与此同时，对加拿大、美国的鸭梨出口和对美国、日本的荔枝出口，也有显著增加。各地出入境检验检疫机构还顺利完成了对日本出口大米的检验检疫任务。在处理出入境动植物检疫重大问题和突发事件方面，成效也很明显。一是针对1997年到1998年初香港发生的禽流感事件，全系统及时开展了禽流感疫情普查监测工作，并加强了供港家禽检疫和饲养场的注册登记工作，从而使病源不在内地的问题得到了澄清，迅速恢复了家禽的对港供应。二是针对供港猪盐酸克伦特罗残留问题，全系统及时加强了对供港猪场、饲料场的检验检疫，严格禁止含有违禁药品的饲料、猪肉输港，取得了良好效果。三是就我国出口货物木质包装检疫问题，国家出入境检验检疫局一方面与美国、英国、加拿大等国有关主管部门进行了深入交涉，另一方面，认真组织各地出入境检验检疫机构和有关出口企业采取相应措施，从而使问题得到了妥善解决，保证了有关出口贸易的顺利进行。

三、认真开展卫生检疫工作，较好地防止了传染病传入传出我国

1998年，全国出入境检验检疫机构不断加强对出入境人员、交通工具和口岸从业人员的疫病监测工作，尤其是针对东南亚登革热爆发流行、中朝边界发生传染性腹泻、中蒙边界和中哈边界发生鼠传染病等情况，采取有力措施，加大了对周边地区流行病监测和出入境人员检疫的力度。一年间共对57.7万人进行了疾病监测体检，查出各种疾病人数4.9万人。其中，艾滋病及艾滋病毒感染者80例，霍乱2例，性传染疾病1014例，疟疾42例，结核730例，登革热14例，肝炎4875例，澳抗阳性5202例，其他疾病29603例。对各种病例均按规定采取了相应措施。针对部分口岸急性传染病较严重的情况，各地出入境检验检疫机构普遍开展了鼠间鼠疫监测及灭鼠工作，并制定了处理登革热、鼠疫、霍乱、O157、克里米亚刚果热等疫情的应急方案。为了保护我医疗安全，国家出入境检验检疫局还重新制定了进口血浆等特殊医疗物品的卫生管理规程，进一步提高了全系统对进口卫生物品实施检疫的效能。

四、加强外商投资财产鉴定工作，有力地维护了有关各方的合法权益

1998年，各地出入境检验检疫机构认真坚持了公正、准确的鉴定原则，共鉴定外商投资财产1万多批，价值27.5亿美元。其中，鉴定结果为升值的1800多批，累计升值额达1.1亿美元，从而有效抑制了部分外商在投资中的逃漏关税行为；鉴定结果为降值的1900多批，累计降值额达2.1亿美元，从而较好地维护了中方合资者的合法权益。在此过程中，为贯彻国家有关鼓励引进外资的政策，全国出入境检验检疫机构还统一实行了投资额增大，鉴定收费比率相应降低的办法，主动将收费标准降低6%－7%，同时大力改进服务措施，简化了手续，提高了效率，受到了有关各方的欢迎。

五、继续扩大认证认可范围，进一步促进了有关进出口生产企业提高质量管理水平

1998年，全国出入境检验检疫机构共颁发ISO9000证书693份，并进一步开展了ISO14000认证业务；受理了30多个国家500多个工厂的进口商品安全质量申请，核发许可证书1789份，发放安全标志1500余万枚，并对215个已获证国外企业进行了跟踪调查。继续加强对出口食品生产企业的卫生注册管理，推行HACCP（危险与关键点控制）制度的力度进一步加大。为了确保我出口机电产品质量和维护UL认证生产厂家的合法权益，各地出入境检验检疫机构还对102家涉嫌假冒美国UL标志的企业进行了调查，对其中假冒情节严重的进行了严厉处罚，也收到了较好效果。

六、检验检疫标准与规章建设取得新成绩，为“三检”职责和业务的深度融合奠定了良好基础

1998年，国家出入境检验检疫局圆满完成了国务院《关于研究解决出口农副产品中农药、兽药残留问题会议纪要》下达的任务，制订和发布农兽残检验行业标准276个。在规章建设方面，共清理原有规章和规范性文件518件，确定继续使用的有237件，需修改的210件，应予废止的71件。在此基础上，调整了《进出口商品检验种类表》、《进出境动植物检疫商品与HS目录对照表》和《进口卫生监督检验食品与HS目录对照表》，拟订了出入境检验检疫报检规定、出入境检验检疫流程管理规定草案，制订了出入境检验检疫单证、印章调整方案，并对制订新的出入境检验检疫收费标准、收费管理办法等问题进行了调研，提出了调整意见。这些工作成果，对于出入境检验检疫事业的健康发展，都将产生积极的促进作用。

七、深入开展国际交流与合作，为对外经贸工作的顺利进行提供了便利

1998年，国家出入境检验检疫局积极与国际有关组织和外国政府有关部门进行交流与合作，进一步密切了相互间的合作关系。与有关国家签订了《中华人民共和国政府和巴西联邦共和国政府为保证进出口商品质量对两国政府间经济合作协议的补充协定》、《关于从乌拉圭进口羊肉的检疫和卫生条件议定书》。与英国标准协会、德国VDE、TUV等检验机构的合作也有了进一步扩大。经过努力，中国国家进出口企业认证机构认可委员会（CNAB）还于1998年11月与太平洋认可合作组织（PAC）签署了多边承认协议，成为PAC/MLA正式成员。另外，国家出入境检验检疫局不通过成功举办APEC食品标签法规与标准国际研讨会、第四届中国国际旅行卫生保健学术大会等国际会议，加深了与各国检验检疫界的相互了解和友谊。这对于促进我对外经贸关系的顺利发展也具有重要意义。

1998年的中国旅游业再创好成绩

国家旅游局局长　何光暐

1998年，我国旅游业经受了亚洲金融危机和历史罕见的洪涝灾害的影响，仍然保持了良好的发展势头。

一、1998年旅游业发展概况

1. 入境旅游接待：1998年全国入境人数接待6347.84万人次，增长10.23%。其中，外国人710.77万人次，下降4.31%；港澳同胞5407.53万人次，增长12.79%；台湾同胞217.46万人次，增长2.69%；华侨12.07万人次，增长21.92%。来华过夜旅游者人数达2507.29万人次，比上年增长5.5%。

2. 旅游外汇收入：全国旅游外汇收入126.02亿美元，比上年同期增长4.37%。其中，过夜旅游者在华花费112.46亿美元，占全国外汇收入的89.24%；一日游游客在华花费为13.56亿美元，占10.76%。按不同客源地划分的旅游者花费情况：外国旅游者花费45.99亿美元，比上年同期下降8.72%，占总花费的36.49%；华侨旅游者的花费为0.93亿美元，增长9.45%，占总花费的0.47%；港澳地区旅游者在内地花费57.14亿美元，增长18.37%，占总花费的45.34%；台湾旅游者在内地花费21.95亿美元，增长3.4%，占总花费的17.42%。

3. 主要客源市场：来华旅游外国人与上年相比，美洲和大洋洲旅客保持增长，其他各洲旅客均有不同程度地下降。在我国的十五个主要客源国中，澳大利亚有较大幅度的增长，俄罗斯、韩国、印度尼西亚、马来西亚和泰国有较大幅度下降，日本、新加坡和菲律宾来华人数略有下降。具体情况是：日本157.21万人次，增长-0.61%；俄罗斯69.20万人次，增长-14.95%；美国67.73万人次，增长9.87%；韩国63.28万人次，增长-18.99%；蒙古36.48万人次，增长6.38%；新加坡31.64万人次，增长-0.12%；马来西亚30.01万人次，增长-16.94%；菲律宾25.65万人次，增长-7.29%；英国24.29万人次，增长6.57%；加拿大19.60万人次，增长12.56%；德国19.19万人次，增长3.88%；澳大利亚18.64万人次，增长18.87%；泰国14.43万人次，增长-14.35%；法国13.80万人次，增长5.15%；印尼10.46万人次，增长-29%。

4. 国内旅游：1998年出游总人数6.94亿人次，比上年增加5040万人次，增长7.8%；人均花费344.5元，比上年增加16.3元，增长4.97%；旅游收入2391.18亿元人民币，比上年增加278.48亿元，增长13.2%。

5. 出境旅游：1998年我国公民出境总人数为842.56万人次，比上年增长3.06%。其中，因公出境人数523.53万人次，同比下降8.73%，占出境总人数的62.14%；因私出境人数319.02万人次，同比上升30.77%，占出境总人数的37.86%。我国公民出境前往人数最多的10个目的地（第一站）依次是：香港、澳门、泰国、日本、俄罗斯、美国、韩国、新加坡、朝鲜、澳大利亚。

6. 旅游总收入：1998年我国国际旅游和国内旅游总收入3438.64亿元人民币，比上年增长10.5%。

二、1998年主要工作成绩

1. 入境旅游整体保持增长。全行业针对金融危机对入境旅游市场的突发性、连锁性影响，确定了“抓重点市场，促新兴市场”的指导思想，以’98华夏城乡旅游、’99昆明世博会等为主题促销，积极寻找工作突破点，通过加大对外促销投入和促销频率，改进促销方法和技术手段，加强与主要客源国和国际旅游组织的交往，进一步扩大了中国旅游业的国际影响和竞争力，在入境旅游市场异常严峻的形势下，仍保持了整体入境旅游接待10%以上的增长，外国人入境仅有4.31%的下降，将金融危机的影响减小到了最低限度，这在涉外行业和服务贸易行业中是为数不多的。

2. 国内旅游保持了持续发展的势头。在1998年夏季特大洪涝灾害的不利影响下，国内旅游仍提高了占旅游总收入的比重1.8个百分点，为我国旅游总收入整体保持10%以上的增长做出了重要贡献。主要特点：一是宣传促销凭借多种形式，形成较大的声势、密集度和覆盖面，在居民生活中产生了明显的消费导向。二是国内旅游发展中的政府主导型作用更加突出，一些省市明确提出把发展国内旅游作为活跃市场、扩大内需、繁荣经济的载体，推出了一系列配套措施，刺激扩大了国内旅游消费。三是景点开发进一步加快，各地不断推出的一批观光、度假、休闲、科考、探险、体育、健身、生态旅游、专项旅游产品和新的景点景区，成为促进国内旅游市场繁荣的重要因素，基本改变了国内旅游产品单一的局面。四是旅游交通更为便利快捷，国内包机、旅游专列、城际快车、旅游专线车、观光巴士、“一日游”车辆等有较快发展。

3. 创建产生了首批54个“中国优秀旅游城市”。自1995年国家旅游局倡导创建中国优秀旅游城市以来，有75个城市积极响应，其中54个城市经过省级初审、通过了国家旅游局验收，荣获“中国优秀旅游城市”的称号。这是改革开放以来旅游业发展历程中的一件大事，不仅改善了有关城市旅游业的发展环境和旅游环境，加快了旅游城市向国际化、现代化方向发展的步伐，也促进了与旅游相关行业的发展和精神文明建设，也为旅游业的跨世纪腾飞积蓄了后劲。

4. 行业管理有了新的开拓。1998年各地认真贯彻实施了《漂流旅游安全管理暂行办法》、《旅游统计管理办法》等行业法规和大批地方管理法规；查处了一批侵犯旅游者权益的案件，严肃处理了一批违规经营者，加强了对出国旅游的管理和规范；各级旅游质监所的效能进一步发挥，旅游市场执法与质量监督得到加强；旅游标准化工作进一步推进；旅游规划工作有所加强。

5. 进一步扩大了旅游行业对外开放。为适应国家扩大服务贸易开放的需要，提高旅行社企业素质，国务院批准了《中外合资旅行社试点暂行办法》，允许具有一定资质条件的中外旅行社进行合资试点，经营范围限于入境旅游和国内旅游。我国旅行社市场的进一步开放，不仅有利于增加新的客源渠道，引进海外旅行社经营管理的经验，也将给我国旅行社市场引入新的竞争机制。与此同时，我国还增辟韩国、日本为中国公民自费出国旅游目的地，扩大了内地居民赴香港、澳门旅游的渠道，使我国出国（境）旅游市场进一步拓宽。

6. 旅游管理体制改革取得新的进展。国家旅游局通过新一轮的机构改革，机构和人员精简了40%，新增了制定并组织实施各类旅游景区景点的设施标准和服务标准的职能，明确了指导优秀旅游城市创建工作的职能。如期完成了与经济实体脱钩的工作，完成了对部分旅游行业协会的整改工作。一些省市也积极进行了旅游管理体制的改革探索，不同程度地强化了职能、扩大了行业管理的范围。这些改革对于进一步理顺社会主义市场经济下的旅游行政管理体制，对于提高我国旅游行业的规划、管理、协调和服务水平具有积极意义。

7. 各地旅游业的政策支持体系进一步健全。各级政府对旅游业更加重视和支持，越来越多地体现在建立健全综合政策扶持体系上。一是加快出台扶持旅游业发展的政策措施。1998年又有四川、重庆、吉林、河南、湖南、山西等省份和一大批城市作出了加快旅游业发展的决定，目前出台这类文件的省市达到60%以上，较普遍地实现了地方政府对发展旅游业的鼓励和扶持。二是积极推进旅游业的法制建设，又有广西、陕西、新疆、哈尔滨等省市出台了旅游管理条例，黑龙江等省发布了旅游管理规章，全国70%以上的省份和旅游城市开始形成依法治旅的格局，使旅游部门管理旅游市场、参与建设项目审批、旅游行政执法等职能进一步得到落实和强化。三是旅游工作的研究决策已普遍列入各级党委和政府的工作议程。有的省市连续几年由省市政府主持召开旅游工作会议，很多省市“一把手”亲自解决旅游业发展的重点和难点问题。四是财政、计划、统计、民航、工商、公安、侨办、台办、技术监督、环保等各部门对旅游工作更加重视、支持和配合，各新闻单位也主动支持旅游工作，在许多方面形成了支持旅游业发展的大好局面。

8. 成功地举办了上海国际旅游交易会。这次交易会是亚太地区规模最大、档次较高的国际旅游交易会，38个国家和地区的1300多个旅游机构和企业、3000多海外旅游界人士和国内1万多业内人士参加交易会，中国旅游界首次以买家和卖家的双重身份参加，全国31个省、自治区、直辖市和香港特别行政区的旅游同行们同时登台亮相，不仅展示了中国旅游的整体形象，而且其本身就是对中国旅游业克服金融危机的信心、魄力和能力的最好宣传。

三、1998年的主要工作体会

1. 1998年我国旅游业之所以能够抵御金融危机的风险，根本取决于改革开放20年来的总体成就。我国旅游业得改革开放之利，借改革开放之力，走改革开放之路，当改革开放先导，充满了生机和活力，这是旅游业抵御金融危机影响的根本保证。改革开放20年来，我国旅游业从小到大，从弱到强，逐步形成了较大规模的产业体系，在国际地位、国内协调、产业发展等各个方面已有相应的基础；我国旅游产品丰富、结构趋于合理，开始适应市场多元化的消费需求，市场互补的能力和优势正在增强；在主要客源市场都已有一定的促销基础，即使一些客源国遇到一些突发性问题，在总体客源市场上仍具有相当的吸引力和竞争力；我国的国内旅游业迅猛发展，与国际旅游业在产品及消费上的同一性逐步增强，即使国际旅游遇到了较大的困难，旅游经济主体仍能保持稳定。

2. 对旅游产业发展形势的认识和把握，必须深入研究、未雨绸缪、随机应变。1998年初，国家旅游局为贯彻党的十五大精神，分析了旅游业跨世纪发展的主要趋势和任务，对全行业起到了预警和导向性的作用；针对旅游市场状况而提出的五个需要重点突破的方面——对公众促销、联手专业促销、现代化促销手段、客源市场格局、促销经费渠道，成为各级旅游部门、各地旅游企业的指导原则和努力方向。正是由于对旅游市场形势的准确判断和超前把握，各地主动调整市场策略，狠抓国内旅游，形成了入境旅游、国内旅游、出境旅游互补互促的发展格局，增强了在大风大浪中驾驭市场的能力。

3. 旅游业的大发展必须找到与地方经济社会发展和“两个文明”建设非常合拍、紧密结合的切入点。实践证明，最近三年开展的创建中国优秀旅游城市的活动，就是这样的切入点。继续抓好这个切入点，大产业、大市场、大旅游的体系才能深化发展，政府主导型战略才能落到实处，各有关方面发展旅游业的积极性才能真正调动和凝聚起来，形成强大的合力。

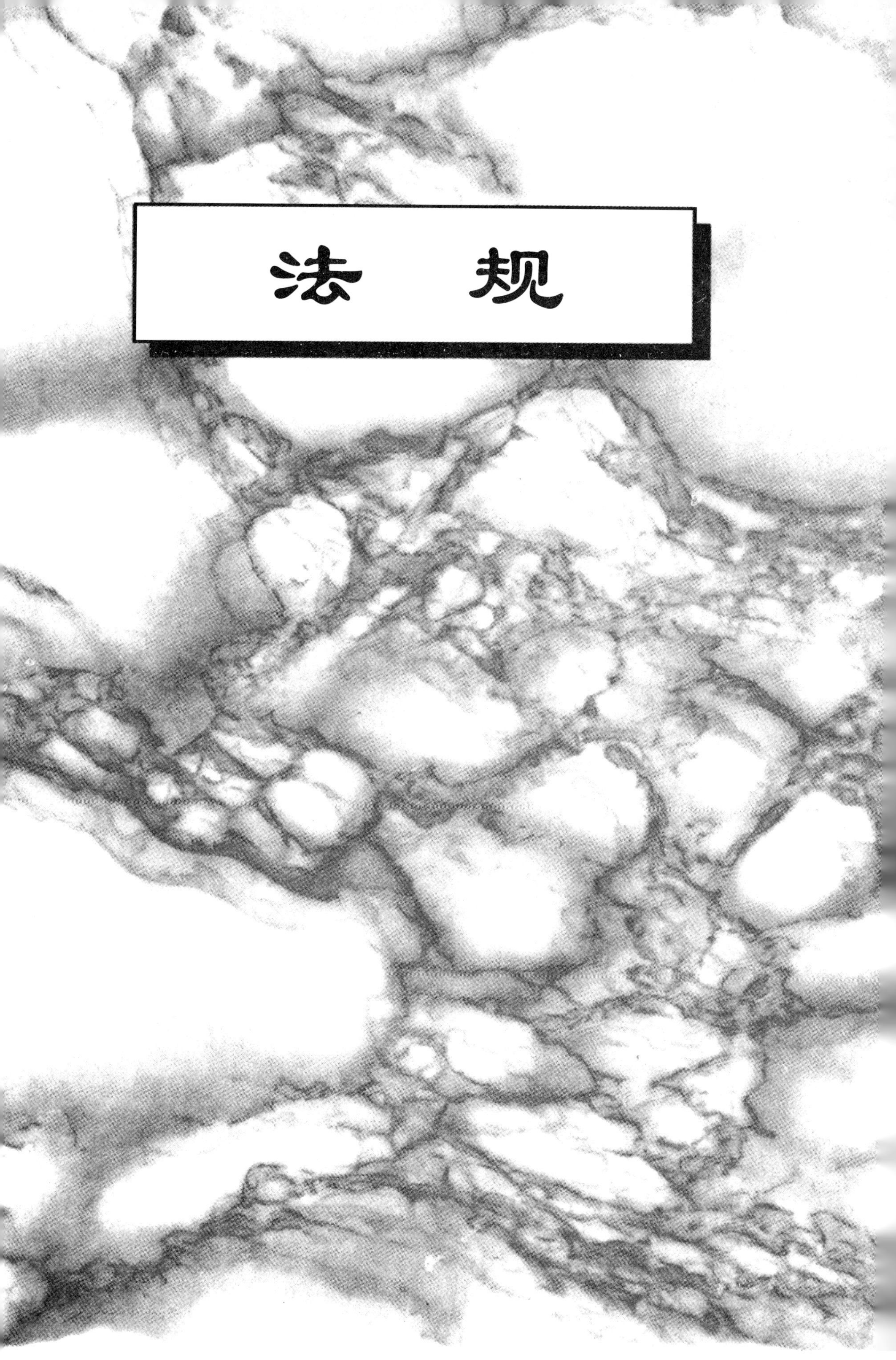

法 规

国务院办公厅关于印发对外贸易经济合作部职能配置内设机构和人员编制规定的通知

国办发〔1998〕122号
1998年8月14日

对外贸易经济合作部职能配置、内设机构和人员编制规定

根据第九届全国人民代表大会第一次会议批准的国务院机构改革方案和《国务院关于机构设置的通知》(国发〔1998〕5号),设置对外贸易经济合作部。对外贸易经济合作部是主管对外贸易与经济合作的国务院组成部门。

一、职能调整

(一)划出的职能

1. 将外贸货运协调的职能,交给国家经济贸易委员会承担。

2. 将管理外国政府贷款的职能,分别交给财政部和中国进出口银行承担。其中,外国政府贷款的对外谈判与磋商职能交给财政部承担,外国政府贷款的转贷业务交给中国进出口银行承担。

3. 将管理出口货物原产地的职能,交给海关总署承担。

4. 将审批地方外经贸企业内部职工持股的职能,交给地方人民政府承担。

5. 将审批境外(未建交国家和香港特别行政区及澳门、台湾除外)承包工程、劳务合作、设计咨询项目的职能,分别交给国务院有关部门和地方人民政府承担。

6. 将外派劳务人员许可证的年度审核职能,分别交给国务院有关部门和地方人民政府承担。

7. 按商品管理权限,将审批外商投资企业进出口许可证的职能,逐步交给地方人民政府承担。

8. 将协调进出口商品价格、市场、客户(少数关系国计民生和特定商品除外)的职能,交给进出口商会承担。

9. 将海外承包工程投标的协调职能,交给对外承包工程商会承担。

10. 将组织大型招商会、洽谈会的职能,逐步交给有关社会中介组织承担。

11. 将部机关和在京直属单位、驻外机构的行政后勤、基建等事务,交给机关服务中心(对外称对外贸易经济合作部行政事务管理局)承担。

(二)划入的职能

1. 原关税和贸易总协定谈判委员会、全国外资工作领导小组、国务院对非洲经济贸易技术合作协调小组的工作和国家机电产品进出口办公室及其进出口招标管理工作。

2. 原国家计划委员会制定对外贸易、经济合作和外商投资政策、管理一般进出口指标和配额的职能。

3. 原国家进出口商品检验局制定、调整并公布《实施检验的进出口商品种类表》的职能。此表的制定、调整由对外贸易经济合作部委托国家出入境检验检疫局负责,对外贸易经济合作部负责或委托国家出入境检验检疫局发布。

(三)转变的职能

1. 部机关与直属各企业要通过多种方式逐步脱钩,由国务院派出稽察特派员进行稽察监督。

2. 取消编制下达一般性商品进出口计划,对外承包工程和劳务合作年度计划,外贸货物运输的年度、月度计划和车皮计划,直属企业进出口财务

计划，直属单位基建物资计划等职能。

3．逐步实行生产企业自营进出口经营权登记备案制。

4．将在敏感国家与地区的承包工程、劳务合作、设计咨询项目的审批制逐步改为登记备案制。

5．凡能实行招标的出口商品配额均实行招标。

6．取消管理全国外经贸各项外汇收支的职能。

7．逐步撤销对外贸易经济合作部派驻地方的特派员办事处。

二、主要职责

根据以上职能调整，对外贸易经济合作部的主要职责是：

（一）拟定和贯彻实施对外贸易、经济合作和外商投资的具体政策、改革方案；拟定外经贸和外商投资法律法规草案，制定和执行有关实施细则、管理规章；负责外经贸法规、规章之间及其与国家条约、协定之间的衔接；指导国有外经贸企业的改革。

（二）拟定和执行外贸进出口中长期规划和发展战略；分析国际经贸形势和我国进出口状况，提出总量平衡、结构调整等项宏观调控建议；拟定和执行进出口商品配额招标政策；研究和推广各种新贸易方式（含电子商务）；负责进出口配额计划的编报、下达和组织实施，制定和管理进出口商品目录，负责配额、许可证的确定和发放；依法负责我国对外反倾销、反补贴以及保障措施中的有关事务，指导、协调外国对我国出口商品的反倾销应诉；管理出口商品商标注册登记后的有关事务；指导出口广告宣传。

（三）拟定和执行对外技术贸易的政策、管理规章以及鼓励技术和成套设备出口的政策；管理技术引进、设备进口和国际招标，管理国家限制出口的技术和引进技术的出口与再出口；拟定和执行国家出口管制政策，颁发与防扩散相关的出口许可证。

（四）分析、研究全国外商投资情况，定期向国务院报送有关动态；宏观指导全国外商投资工作；拟定和执行外商投资的管理规章，参与制定外商投资的发展战略和中长期规划；汇总、发布《外商投资产业指导目录》；核准国家规定的限额以上、限制投资和涉及配额、许可证管理的外商投资企业的设立；核准大型外商投资项目的合同、章程及其变更；监督检查外商投资企业执行有关法律法规和合同、章程的情况；指导和管理全国招商引资、投资促进及外商投资企业的进出口。

（五）归口管理我国的对外援助；拟定和执行对外援助的政策、规章、制度和援助方案，签署有关协议；编制和组织实施年度援助计划；监督检查对外援助项目的实施情况；管理援外经费、专项优惠贷款、专项基金等；推行援外方式改革。

（六）负责全国国外经济合作工作；拟定和执行国外经济合作的政策、规章，指导和监督对外承包工程、劳务合作、设计咨询等项业务的管理。

（七）拟定和执行国别（地区）外经贸政策；组织双边混合（联合）委员会会议，同外国政府进行经贸谈判并签署有关文件；处理国别（地区）经贸关系中的重要事务；管理同未建交国家的经贸活动；指导我驻外使（领）馆经商参处（室）的业务，联系外国驻华官方商务机构。

（八）拟定和执行多边经贸政策；代表我国政府参加国际经济贸易组织的活动；负责多边对外经贸谈判、国际服务贸易谈判和国际经贸条约、协定的谈判与签署，协调国务院有关部门在谈判过程中的立场和意见；负责知识产权对外谈判；掌握国际经贸条约和协定的国内实施情况；管理多、双边对华无偿援助及赠款；管理联合国发展业务系统和有关国际组织对华经济技术合作事务；指导我国驻联合国及有关国际组织的经贸代表机构的业务。

（九）拟定和执行对香港特别行政区及澳门、台湾的经贸政策、贸易中长期规划、管理规章；与香港特别行政区及澳门有关经贸主管机构和台湾受权的民间组织进行经贸谈判并签署有关文件。

（十）制定各类企业外经贸经营权和国际货运代理企业的资格标准，承担法律法规规定的资格审定；制定境外发展、投资的管理办法和具体政策；核准国内企业在境外投资开办企业（金融企业除外）并实施监督管理；管理外国、香港特别行政区及澳门、台湾常驻商业代表机构的核准业务；指导与监督境内各种外经贸交易会、展览会、展销会、洽谈会和招商活动等，拟定和执行赴境外举办上述活动的管理办法。

（十一）参与外经贸方面宏观调控政策的研究并提出有关建议；负责中央外贸发展基金项目的选定和风险基金管理；监管直属境内外企事业单位的国有资产；指导和管理外经贸财务会计工作，负责外经贸统计及其信息发布，提供信息咨询服务；负责外经贸的标准化、信息化工作。

（十二）负责我驻外经商参处（室）和有关国际组织代表机构的队伍建设、人员选派和管理；指导进出口商会和有关协会、学会的工作。

（十三）承办国务院交办的其他事项。

三、内设机构

根据上述职责，对外贸易经济合作部设 19 个职能司（厅）：

（一）办公厅

处理部机关日常政务，办理领导交办事项；负责重要会议的组织和会议决定事项的督办；负责公文管理、秘书事务、办公自动化、重要文件的起草、新闻发布和宣传、政务信息、机要、保密、保卫、档案、通信、文印、信访等事务。

（二）人事教育劳动司

负责部机关国家公务员及直属单位的机构编制、队伍建设、专业技术职务、部管干部、劳动工资的管理；指导外经贸行业的劳动工资工作；负责驻外、驻香港特别行政区及澳门等机构的人员选派和管理；管理部属高等院校，实施国际商务专业资格制度，负责有关专业培训工作。

（三）外经贸政策和发展司

调查研究外经贸发展中的重大问题，提出促进外经贸发展的建议；拟定外经贸中长期规划；拟定各项外经贸政策、发展战略和体制改革方案；研究和推广各种新贸易方式（含电子商务）；制定各类企业外经贸经营权的资格标准，承担法律法规规定的资格审定；拟定境外发展、投资的管理办法和具体政策；核准国内企业在境外投资开办企业（金融企业除外）并实施监督管理；监督境内各种外经贸交易会、展览会等，拟定赴境外举办上述活动的管理办法；管理外国、香港特别行政区及澳门常驻商业代表机构等的核准业务；指导出口广告宣传。

（四）计划财务司

编报外经贸中长期规划；分析国际经贸形势和我国进出口状况，提出总量平衡、结构调整等项宏观调控建议；参与拟定关税、外汇及有关税收、信贷、价格、保险等政策；负责全国外经贸宏观运行状况的监测、分析；管理中央各项外经贸业务资金、专项基金、援外经费、外事经费、基建投资等；指导国有外经贸企业改革；负责境内外直属企事业单位的国有资产监管和清产核资；指导和管理外经贸财务会计工作，负责外经贸统计工作及其信息发布工作；负责部机关和在京直属单位、驻外机构的财务及固定资产管理；负责外经贸系统的内部审计工作。

（五）亚洲司

（六）西亚非洲司

（七）欧洲司

（八）美大司

以上 4 个地区司的主要职责是：拟定和执行国别（地区）外经贸政策；组织双边混合（联合）委员会会议，同外国政府进行双边经贸谈判并签署有关文件；处理双边经贸关系中的重要事务；提出对主管国家（地区）的援助意见；管理赴境外举办展销会、洽谈会和招商活动；管理同未建交国家的经贸活动；指导我驻主管国家使（领）馆经商参处（室）的业务，联系外国驻华官方商务机构。

（九）台港澳司

拟定和执行对香港特别行政区及澳门、台湾的经贸政策、参与编制对香港特别行政区及澳门、台湾贸易中长期规划；参与制定利用台资的政策和管理规章，协调台商投资项目；宏观管理和指导对台贸易，编制对台贸易年度计划，组织对台大宗商品的进出口；组织与香港特别行政区及澳门有关经贸主管机构和台湾受权的民间组织的经贸谈判并签署有关文件；核准和管理大陆企业赴香港特别行政区及澳门、台湾和台商在大陆举办的经贸交易会、展销会、洽谈会、广告业务以及赴香港特别行政区及澳门经贸团组等其他经贸活动；管理台商在大陆设立常驻机构的核准工作。

（十）国际经贸关系司

组织多边对外经贸谈判（包括与各国际经济贸易组织的谈判）、国际服务贸易对外谈判和国际经贸条约、协定的谈判等，拟定谈判方案，协调国务院有关部门在谈判过程中的立场和意见；负责多边国际经贸组织事务和区域性国际组织的经贸事务；掌握国际经贸条约和协定的国内实施情况；提出调整我国外经贸体制和重大外经贸政策的建议；拟定和执行我国参与联合国发展业务系统的多边经贸和技术合作的政策，组织参加有关国际会议；管理多边和双边对华无偿援助及赠款，编制我国使用无偿援助的中长期规划和年度执行方案，监督检查受援项目的执行情况；指导我国常驻联合国及有关国际组织代表机构的经贸业务，联系国际组织驻华机构的经贸业务。

（十一）对外贸易管理司

编报全国进出口商品配额（包括各种贸易方式）年度计划并下达组织实施，管理进出口许可证，拟定和执行进出口商品配额招标政策、加工贸易政策；负责易制毒化学品的进出口管理，制定和管理进出口商品目录；管理出口商品商标注册登记后的有关事务；联系进出口商会。

（十二）机电产品进出口司

拟定和执行机电产品进出口的政策、管理规章、中长期发展规划和年度指导性计划；分析机电产品进出口情况，编发有关资料；管理和调整机电产品进口目录，编报和执行机电产品配额的年度进口方案；制定进口机电产品招标规则和管理办法并组织实施；参与有关关税税则、税目和税率的研究拟定；参加有关国际谈判。

（十三）外国投资管理司

分析、研究全国外商投资的情况，定期向国务院报送有关动态；拟定和执行外商投资的政策、管理规章，参与制定外商投资的发展战略和中长期规划；汇总、发布《外商投资产业指导目录》；编报下达和组织执行外商投资企业进出口配额年度计划；宏观指导和管理全国外商投资项目合同、章程的核准工作；核准国家规定的限额以上、限制投资和涉及配额、许可证管理的外商投资企业的设立；核准大型外商投资项目的合同、章程、核准合同、章程的变更；监督外商投资企业执行有关法律法规和合同情况并协调解决发生的问题；指导和管理全国招商引资和投资促进工作；负责外资统计工作；联系外商投资企业协会。

（十四）对外援助司

拟定和执行对外援助的政策、规章和方案；编制对外援助计划并组织实施；负责对外援助谈判并签署、执行有关协议；负责由政府间处理的援助事务；确定对外援助的具体内容，组织实施并监督检查项目的实施情况；负责对外援助资金的具体使用和管理；推进援外方式改革。

（十五）国外经济合作司

拟定和执行对外经济合作的政策、规章；指导海外市场开发、规范经营秩序；处理有关重大事件；负责国际经济合作基金的使用；对赴敏感国家（地区）的承包工程、劳务合作、设计咨询项目进行登记备案；负责有关的业务培训；联系中国对外工程承包商会和中国国际工程咨询协会。

（十六）科技发展和技术进出口司

拟定和执行对外技术贸易的政策、管理规章以及鼓励技术和成套设备出口政策；拟定高技术产品出口目录和国家禁止、限制进出口技术目录；管理技术和大型、成套设备及高技术产品的出口，管理技术引进、设备进口和国际招标；拟定和执行国家出口管制政策，颁发与防扩散出口相关的出口许可证；组织多边和双边工业技术合作；负责外经贸科技发展、技术进步和信息化、标准化等项事务。

（十七）外贸货运司

管理国际货运代理，拟定和执行国际货运代理行业的政策、法规、规章，制定国际货运代理企业的资格标准，负责有关的资格审定；负责供应香港特别行政区和澳门鲜活冷冻商品“三趟快车”运输的组织协调；参与政府间及国际多边运输协定的谈判；指导外经贸仓储行业管理；联系国际货运代理协会和货主协会等社会中介组织。

（十八）条约法律司

拟定外经贸法律法规草案，起草有关文件和规章；负责国际经贸公约的拟定以及多边和双边经贸条约、协定等谈判文件的审核；参与重大经贸协议、合同、章程和重大争议案的研究与协调；负责外经贸法规、规章之间及其与国际条约、协定之间的衔接；负责多边和双边知识产权对外谈判；依法承办我国对外反倾销、反补贴及保障措施中的有关事务，指导、协调外国对我国出口商品的反倾销应诉；负责行政复议和行政诉讼，负责组织对外经贸法律交流和国内外有关法律培训。

（十九）交际司

制定礼宾工作规章制度；管理部机关的外事礼宾和重大外事活动；负责部分国家领导人和部领导的外事活动和出访活动的联系与安排，接待部邀请的外国副部长级以上代表团；指导外经贸系统的外事礼宾工作；负责办理部机关及直属单位人员的出访事宜。

机关党委。负责机关和在京部属单位以及部属国外企业和部属单位派驻国外机构的党群工作。

四、人员编制

对外贸易经济合作部机关行政编制为457名。其中：部长1名，副部长5名（含副部长级首席谈判代表1名），司局级领导职数67名（含部长助理3名和机关党委专职副书记）。

离退休干部工作机构、后勤服务机构及编制，按有关规定另行核定。

五、其他事项

（一）关于管理外商投资的职能。对外贸易经济合作部管理外商投资的职能，待投融资体制改革方案确定后，再作相应调整。

（二）关于利用外资政策的发布问题。国家发展计划委员会、国家经济贸易委员会、对外贸易经济合作部在各自的职责范围内研究拟定外商投资的有关政策，经国务院批准后，由对外贸易经济合作部对外发布。

（三）关于境外承包工程等审批与管理问题。国务院有关部门和地方人民政府负责具体审批和管理境外（未建交国家和香港特别行政区及澳门、台湾除外）承包工程、劳务合作、设计咨询项目，对外贸易经济合作部负责宏观管理和监督。

（四）关于进出口配额发放有关问题。关系国计民生和大宗、重点工业品、原材料的进出口配额由对外贸易经济合作部根据国家经济贸易委员会制定的进出口计划发放，并向国家经济贸易委员会备案。

对外贸易经济合作部
关于印发我部各司（厅）职责的通知

1998年8月27日外经贸办发第637号

办公厅职责

一、拟定部的年度工作安排和有关工作制度，督促检查各个时期中心工作的贯彻执行情况。处理部机关日常政务，协助部领导了解和掌握部的全面工作情况。

二、办理党中央、国务院领导的批示、上级机关的交办事项及全国人大建议、议案和全国政协提案。

三、拟定并协调部机关各单位职责的分工。

四、负责部党组会议、部长办公会议的有关工作，督办会议议决事项；负责部政务值班。

五、负责部党组、部领导的秘书工作和部级老干部的秘书服务工作。

六、归口管理我部各类会议；组织承办重要的全国性综合会议。

七、组织起草重要的综合性文件。

八、负责公文管理及部发重要文件的核稿。

九、负责外经贸系统政务信息工作；归口管理部机关和直属企事业单位的内部刊物及公开发行的刊物；统一编发文告及部工作简报、新闻公报、年鉴、文件汇编。

十、主管外经贸宣传和新闻发布；接待和安排国内外记者和外国新闻团组的采访。

十一、负责我部文电的收发、批分、管理和部印章、部党组印章的使用和管理。

十二、管理部机关档案，指导部属各单位、驻外使（领）馆经商参处（室）和外经贸系统的档案工作。

十三、负责部机关、部属企事业单位、驻外使（领）馆经商参处（室）的保密工作，指导外经贸系统的保密工作。

十四、会同有关单位规划和组织部机关办公自动化。

十五、联系部驻各地特派员办事处。

十六、负责办理部长接待日有关事宜，处理人民来信和接待来访。

人事教育劳动司（简称人事司）职责

一、负责本部公务员制度的实施和公务员的录用：调配、职务升降、考核、奖罚、辞职、辞退、离退等管理工作。

二、负责部属单位的干部队伍建设和司、局级领导班子及处级、后备领导干部的管理，办理部领导的各项兼职。

三、负责本部援藏、定点扶贫、地方挂职、驻各地特派员办事处干部的选派和管理。

四、负责部驻外使（领）馆经商参处（室）、代表处、联合国机构人员及国际职员和部属贸易中心、驻港澳机构的人员选派（其中主要领导干部的选派，商地区司或有关单位）和管理，宏观管理部属单位海外企业和临时出国人员工作；制定我驻外使（领）馆经商参处（室）工勤人员轮换选派计划并负责人员的审批、派遣和管理工作。

五、负责本部行政、事业单位和全国性外经贸社团人员的编制、机构设置和领导职务设置及职数限额的管理。

六、负责本部机关人员的业务培训，归口管理部属单位在职干部的培训，管理部属单位出国（境）培训工作，宏观指导外经贸行业职工的培训工作；负责部属高等院校和职工子弟学校的教育行政管理。

七、负责部属单位高级专业技术职务任职资格的评审，并对中、初级专业技术职务的评聘进行宏观管理，负责管理全国国际商务专业资格制度的实施。

八、负责部机关人员的工资管理及福利工作，管理部属企事业单位、社团的劳动工资并监督其内部工资、奖金的分配，宏观指导外经贸行业的劳动工资管理和安全生产工作。

九、负责部机关、直属企事业单位及社团的社会保障统筹工作。

十、负责外经贸系统荣誉称号评比表彰的管理工作。

十一、负责部属单位的安全保卫；负责部安全委员会、部国家公安小组和部社会治安综合治理委员会的有关工作；协助公安机关侦破、查处各类刑事案件和责任事故。

外经贸政策和发展司（简称发展司）职责

一、研究国际、国内经济和贸易的发展趋势，提出我国对外经贸的发展战略和重大政策。参与拟定外经贸中长期发展规划。

二、综合研究和组织实施外经贸体制改革；指导各地外经贸体制改革工作。

三、研究世界经济贸易、区域一体化、集团化和我国的相关对策；研究和组织实施市场多元化的方针、战略和政策措施。

四、研究和组织实施外经贸企业改革，具体实施部属企业改革，指导全国外经贸企业改革。

五、拟定提高出口商品质量的政策措施，推动“以质取胜”战略的贯彻落实；参与管理《实施检验的进出口商品种类表》。

六、研究和提出促进对外经贸活动的措施并组织实施；宏观指导和管理境内对外经济技术贸易展览会、洽谈会、出口商品交易会及各地方小交会，会同地区司管理赴境外举办展销会、洽谈会、招商活动等（涉及利用外商投资的会签外资司）；会同地区司审批部属企事业单位组织的跨地区、跨部门、跨行业的出国经贸团组。

七、研究和推广各种新的国际贸易方式、电子商务；指导和管理对销贸易（易货、转口等）业务；拟定全国性边境贸易政策、汇总有关情况，协调有关问题；参与拟定加工贸易政策。

八、会同有关单位研究海外发展、投资的战略、方针，拟定管理办法和政策；核准国内企业在境外投资开办企业（金融企业除外）并实施监督管理。

九、制定各类企业外经贸经营权的资格标准，负责全国各类企业（包括企业集团）外经贸经营权的资格审定工作；管理外国、香港特别行政区及澳门常驻商业代表机构的核准业务。

十、联系中国对外贸易中心（集团）；会同有关单位宏观指导部属驻国外贸易中心、分拨中心；配合有关地区司宏观指导在境外设立的中国投资开发贸易促进中心。

十一、指导出口广告宣传。

十二、联系企业管理协会和老干部政策咨询组。

计划财务司（简称计财司）职责

一、根据国家制订的发展规划和年度计划，编报外经贸中长期规划和年度进出口总值计划并组织实施。

二、分析国际经贸形势和我国进出口状况，提出总量平衡、结构调整等项宏观调控建议；参与拟订关税、外汇及有关的税收、信贷、价格、保险等政策并提出建议。

三、负责全国外经贸宏观运行状况的监测、分析；拟定和执行贸易平衡的宏观政策和措施。

四、负责进出口业务统计，汇总和统一对外发布各项外经贸（含机电产品进出口、外商投资、对外援助、国外经济合作、技术贸易）统计资料；研究和拟定外经贸统计制度改革方案并组织实施。

五、指导和管理外经贸财务会计工作。拟定外经贸财会制度并监督执行；指导外经贸行业的财会业务；参与管理外经贸行业出口退税；预测全国进出口贸易的成本、盈亏、资金需求，掌握分析执行情况。

六、审批并汇总编报部属企业的进出口财务计划和会计决算；管理我部系统所属海外企业的财会工作。

七、管理国际经济合作基金、联合国多边援助资金，检查分析使用效益；负责管理对外援助资金，汇总、监督、报批预决算。

八、汇编、审批部属单位非贸易外汇的预决算；管理我部总的外事经费；管理部属单位的预算外资金。

九、编报、管理、审批部属单位的基建投资计划和财务决算。

十、管理扶持出口生产、简易建筑、轻纺、中央外贸发展、风险等各项外经贸业务资金。

十一、负责援藏、定点扶贫及对口支援三峡库区移民工作。

十二、监管部属境内外企事业单位的国有资产。负责部属企事业单位的清产核资，监督部属企业国有资产的保值增值。

十三、指导外经贸行业和负责部属企业兼并破产和股份制工作。

十四、负责指导部属企事业单位住房制度改革。

十五、负责对部直属企事业单位的内部审计工作；指导全国外经贸系统内部审计工作。

亚洲司职责

一、拟定和执行对主管国家（地区）的经贸政策。

二、负责主管国家（地区）经济贸易的综合调研，掌握双边的全面经贸情况，监测、分析双边经贸运行态势；协调部内外关于双边经贸关系的立场，处理双边经贸关系中的重要事务，推动双边经贸发展；参与拟定有关的政策措施。

三、组织政府间的经贸谈判和双边混合（联合）委员会；同外国政府进行经贸谈判并签署有关文件。

四、负责对主管国家（地区）市场多元化战略的贯彻实施；参与管理赴主管国家（地区）举办展销会、洽谈会、招商活动和部属企事业单位组织的跨地区、跨部门、跨行业的经贸团组；参与监督海外企业的设立与管理；就对主管国家（地区）的援助工作参与提出意见；参与拟订同主管地区周边国家的边境贸易政策。

五、管理同未建交国家的经贸活动；就核准在未建交或敏感国家（地区）的承包工程、劳务合作、设计咨询项目参与提出意见。

六、参与主管地区的区域性外经贸活动，拟订有关协议。

七、指导我驻主管国家使（领）馆经商参处（室）的业务，联系相应国家驻华官方商务机构。

亚洲司主管国家和地区

日本、泰国、菲律宾、马来西亚、新加坡、印度尼西亚、汶莱、缅甸、印度、尼泊尔、斯里兰卡、巴基斯坦、孟加拉、阿富汗、伊朗、土耳其、塞浦路斯、马尔代夫、不丹、锡金、韩国、越南、老挝、柬埔寨、朝鲜、蒙古。

西亚非洲司职责

一、拟定和执行对主管国家（地区）的经贸政策。

二、负责主管国家（地区）经济贸易的综合调研，掌握双边的全面经贸情况，监测、分析双边经贸运行态势；协调部内外关于双边经贸关系的立场、处理双边经贸关系中的重要事务，推动双边经济贸易发展；参与拟定有关的政策措施。

三、组织政府间的经贸谈判和双边混合（联合）委员会；同外国政府进行经贸谈判并签署有关文件。

四、负责对主管国家（地区）市场多元化战略的贯彻实施；参与管理赴主管国家（地区）举办展销会、洽谈会、招商活动和部属企事业单位组织的跨地区、跨部门、跨行业的经贸团组；参与监督海外企业的设立与管理；参与指导部属驻主管国家（地区）贸易中心、分拨中心的工作；宏观指导驻主管国家（地区）的中国投资开发贸易促进中心的工作；就对主管国家（地区）的援助工作参与提出意见。

五、管理同未建交国家的经贸活动；就核准在未建交或敏感国家（地区）的承包工程、劳务合作、设计咨询项目参与提出意见。

六、参与主管地区的区域性外经贸活动，拟定有关协议。

七、指导我驻主管国家使（领）馆经商参处（室）的业务，联系相应国家驻华官方商务机构。

八、具体承担原国务院对非洲经济贸易技术合作协调小组的工作。

西亚非洲司主管国家和地区

埃及、利比亚、苏丹、摩洛哥、突尼斯、阿尔及利亚、伊拉克、约旦、叙利亚、以色列、黎巴嫩、科威特、沙特阿拉伯、巴林、卡塔尔、阿拉伯联合酋长国、阿曼、也门、巴勒斯坦、加那利群岛、梅利利亚、休达、西撒哈拉、喀麦隆、刚果（布）、刚果（金）、加蓬、中非、马里、毛里塔尼亚、塞内加尔、多哥、贝宁、乍得、布基纳法索、尼日尔、几内亚、科特迪瓦、尼日利亚、加纳、冈比亚、塞拉利昂、利比里亚、赤道几内亚、圣多美和普林西比、几内亚比绍、佛得角、津巴布韦、毛里求斯、纳米比亚、博茨瓦纳、索马里、南非、马拉维、斯威士兰、莱索托、圣赫勒拿岛、坦桑尼亚、赞比亚、肯尼亚、埃塞俄比亚、厄立特里亚、乌干达、马达加斯加、吉布提、莫桑比克、安哥拉、卢旺达、布隆迪、留尼旺、科摩罗、塞舌尔。

欧洲司职责

一、拟定和执行对主管国家（地区）的经贸政策。

二、负责主管国家（地区）经济贸易的综合调研，掌握双边的全面经贸情况，监督、分析双边经贸运行态势；协调部内外关于双边经贸关系的立场；处理双边经贸关系中的重要事务，推动双边经济贸易发展；参与拟定有关的政策措施。

三、组织政府间的经贸谈判和双边混合（联合）委员会；同外国政府进行经贸谈判并签署有关文件。

四、负责对主管国家（地区）市场多元化战略的贯彻实施；参与管理赴主管国家（地区）举办展销会、洽谈会、招商活动和部属企事业单位组织的跨地区、跨部门、跨行业的经贸团组；参与监督海外企业的设立与管理；参与指导部属驻主管国家（地区）贸易中心、分拨中心的工作；就对主管国家（地区）的援助工作参与提出意见；宏观指导同原苏联、东欧国家的易货贸易，参与拟订同主管地区周边国家的边境贸易政策。

五、管理同未建交国家的经贸活动；就核准在未建交或敏感国家（地区）的承包工程、劳务合作、设计咨询项目参与提出意见。

六、参与主管地区的区域性外经贸活动，拟定有关协议。

七、指导我驻主管国家使（领）馆经商参处（室）的业务，联系相应国家驻华管方商务机构。

欧洲司主管国家和地区

俄罗斯联邦、白俄罗斯、乌克兰、哈萨克斯坦、乌兹别克斯坦、塔吉克斯坦、吉尔吉斯斯坦、土库曼斯坦、格鲁吉亚、亚美尼亚、阿塞拜疆、摩尔多瓦、爱沙尼亚、拉脱维亚、立陶宛、罗马尼亚、南斯拉夫、斯洛文尼亚、克罗地亚、保加利亚、波黑、马其顿、匈牙利、波兰、捷克、斯洛伐克、阿尔巴尼亚、欧洲联盟、比利时、卢森堡、英国、法国、希腊、西班牙、葡萄牙、爱尔兰、马耳他、德国、瑞士、奥地利、丹麦、意大利、挪威、荷兰、芬兰、瑞士、冰岛、摩纳哥、安道尔、列支敦士登、圣马利诺、梵帝冈、法罗群岛、直布罗陀。

美大司职责

一、拟定和执行对主管国家（地区）的经贸政策。

二、负责主管国家（地区）经济贸易的综合调研，掌握双边的全面经贸情况，监测、分析双边经贸运行态势；协调部内外关于双边经贸关系的立场、处理双边经贸关系中的重要事务，推动双边经济贸易发展；参与拟定有关的政策措施。

三、组织政府间的经贸谈判和双边混合（联合）委员会；同外国政府进行经贸谈判并签署有关文件。

四、负责对主管国家（地区）市场多元化战略的贯彻实施；参与管理赴主管国家（地区）举办展销会、洽谈会、招商活动和部属企事业单位组织的跨地区、跨部门、跨行业的经贸团组；参与监督海外企业的设立与管理；参与指导部属驻主管国家（地区）贸易中心、分拨中心的工作；就对主管国家（地区）的援助工作参与提出意见。

五、管理同未建交国家的经贸活动；就核准在未建交或敏感国家（地区）的承包工程、劳务合作、设计咨询项目参与提出意见。

六、参与主管地区的区域性外经贸活动，拟定有关协议。

七、指导我驻主管国家使（领）馆经商参处（室）的业务，联系相应国家驻华官方商务机构。

美大司主管国家和地区

美国、加拿大、澳大利亚、新西兰、斐济、巴布亚新几内亚、瓦努阿图、萨摩亚、基里巴斯、密克罗尼西亚、马绍尔群岛、瑙鲁、汤加、图瓦卢、所罗门群岛、库克群岛、纽埃、关岛、美属萨摩亚、贝劳、北马里亚纳、法属波利尼西亚、新喀里多尼亚、瓦利斯和富图纳、托克劳、皮特开恩、托里斯海峡群岛、伊里安查亚、墨西哥、古巴、哥伦比亚、委内瑞拉、圭亚那、苏里南、牙买加、特立尼达和多巴哥、巴巴多斯、安提瓜和巴布达、巴西、厄瓜多尔、秘鲁、玻利维亚、智利、阿根廷、乌拉圭、危地马拉、洪都拉斯、萨尔瓦多、哥斯达黎加、巴拿马、海地、多米尼亚、圣文森特和格林纳丁斯、圣卢西亚、多米尼克、巴哈马联邦、圣克里斯托弗、巴拉圭、尼加拉瓜、格林纳达、伯利兹、阿鲁巴、开曼群岛、库腊索、法属圭亚那、瓜德罗普、马提尼克、蒙特塞拉特、波多黎各、圣马丁岛、特克斯和凯科斯、圣其茨 、英属维尔京、百慕大、塞班、美属维尔京、安圭拉、荷属安的列斯、约翰斯顿岛、中维岛、威克岛、豪兰岛和贝克岛、诺克福岛、美属波多黎各。

台港澳司职责

一、负责对台港澳经济贸易的综合调研，全面掌握对台港澳地区的经贸情况和信息，根据“一国两制”总方针和形势需要，研究和提出对台港澳地区的经贸发展战略和建议。

二、拟定对香港特别行政区及澳门、台湾的经贸政策、有关管理办法，规章制度并负责组织实施；宏观指导对香港特别行政区及澳门、台湾经贸工作。

三、参与编制对香港特别行政区及澳门、台湾贸易的中长期规划；编制对台进出口贸易的年度计划，经贸管司总量平衡后监督执行。

四、组织与香港特别行政区及澳门有关经贸主管机构和台湾受权的民间组织的经贸谈判并签署有关文件。

五、参与制定利用台资的政策和管理规章，协调台商投资项目；宏观管理和指导对台贸易，编制对台贸易的年度计划，组织对台大宗商品的进出口；参与对港澳鲜活商品配额和年度运输计划的安排意见。

六、核准和管理台商来大陆和大陆企业赴台举办经贸展销会、洽谈会、广告业务和赴香港特别行政区及澳门、台湾经贸团组等其他经贸活动，核准和管理赴香港特别行政区及澳门的经贸交易会、展销会；管理台商在大陆设立常设机构的核准工作。

七、指导我部驻港澳贸易处和企业管理处（“窗口公司”）的业务，负责联系香港华润、康贸和澳门南光三公司的工作。

八、参与研究拟订对香港特别行政区及澳门、台湾的工程承包和劳务合作的政策法规。

九、负责协调赴台参加有关国际会议的政策和协调有关国际经济组织、国际会议中的涉台问题。

国际经贸关系司（简称国际司）职责

一、根据国务院的授权，负责多边对外经贸谈判（包括与各国际经济贸易组织的谈判）、国际服务贸易谈判和国际经贸条约、协定的谈判与签署，拟定谈判方案，协调国务院有关部门在谈判过程中的立场和意见。

二、代表我国政府参加国际经济贸易组织的活动。

三、负责我国参加的区域性国际组织（如亚太经合组织、亚欧会议等）的经济贸易事务并组织对内协调工作。

四、拟定和执行多边经贸政策，掌握国际经贸条约和协定的国内实施情况。进行与谈判相关的政策研究，并根据对外承诺就我国外经贸体制改革和重大外经贸政策的调整提出建议，提供咨询。

五、管理多边、双边对华无偿援助和全部赠款（如英国政府赠款）。

六、管理联合国发展业务系统和有关国际组织对华经济技术合作事务，组织参加有关国际会议。

七、根据我国接受援助的政策，会同有关国际组织和外国政府编制我国使用无偿援助的中长期规划和年度执行计划。

八、协调各地区、各部门接受无偿援助和赠款的管理工作，监督检查项目的执行情况。

九、指导我国常驻有关国际组织代表机构的业务，联系国际组织驻华机构的经贸业务。

十、具体承担原关税和贸易总协定谈判委员会的工作

对外贸易管理司（简称贸管司）职责

一、根据国内外市场形势，研究和拟定进出口商品发展的战略规划并组织实施；研究和拟定管理进出口商品的政策并组织实施。

二、参与编制全国进出口商品中长期规划。

三、编报全国进出口商品配额（包括各种贸易方式）年度计划并下达组织实施；根据国家确定的进出口计划，下达关系国计民生和大宗、重点工业品、原材料的进出口配额。

四、负责确定和管理进出口商品配额。研究和拟定进出口商品配额管理制度改革方案并组织实施；负责确定和调整进出口许可证管理的商品品种，拟定有关进出口商品许可证管理制度和管理进出口商品许可证的印制和发放；研究和拟定有关进出口商品许可证制度的改革方案并组织实施。

五、会同有关单位拟定和执行进出口商品配额招标政策。

六、负责出口商品被动配额和设限商品的对外谈判，出口商品主动、被动配额的宏观管理和分配，监督配额的使用；负责对纺织品配额许可证书的印制和管理的指导、监督和协调工作。

七、制定和管理进出口商品目录，会同有关单位管理《实施检验的进出口商品种类表》。

八、会同有关单位拟定加工贸易（含来、进料加工 贸易、外商投资企业加工 贸易）政策并组织实施。

九、负责进出口商品经营的协调管理；负责易制毒化学品的进出口管理工作。

十、管理出口商品商标注册登记后的有关事务和普惠制工作。

十一、负责小额贸易经营权的审批。

十二、联系进出口商会工作。

机电产品进出口司（简称机电司）职责

一、研究和拟定机电产品进出口的发展战略、方针、政策并组织实施。

二、拟定和执行机电产品进出口管理的政策和法规、规章。

三、拟定和 执行机电产品进出口中长期发展规划、年度指导性计划。

四、推动机电产品出口生产体系建设和出口生产企业的技术改造。

五、指导协调和管理大型和成套设备出口项目，组织协调开拓国际机电产品市场和建立正常进出口秩序。

六、管理和调整机电产品进出口目录；参与管理《实施检验的进出口商品种类表》。

七、核准和管理进口机电仪产品售后维修站。

八、参与制定进出口商品配额招标政策。编报和执行机电产品配额的年度进口方案。

九、协调、管理和监督全国进出口机电产品的招标工作。制定进出口机电产品招标规则和管理办法并组织实施。负责利用国外贷款项目的国际评标工作，承担国家评标委员会的日常工作。

十、负责对全国机电产品进出口情况进行监控，并进行汇总、统计及分析工作，编发有关资料。

十一、负责组织选定中央外贸发展基金中的机电产品出口发展基金项目。

十二、参与机电产品进口关税税则、税目、税率的制订，参与有关国际谈判。

外国投资管理司（简称外资司）职责

一、指导、管理和协调全国外商投资工作。分析、研究全国外商投资情况，定期向国务院报送有关动态，协调各部门的意见，向国务院提出研究外商投资重大问题的建议。

二、拟定和执行外商投资的各项方针政策、法规、规章、协调制订及实施中的重大问题，监督检查各部门、各地区和企业的执行情况，配合条法司拟定利用外资的法律草案。

三、对外发布各部门拟定的经国务院批准的利用外资政策；汇总、发布《外商投资产业指导目录》。

四、参与制定外商投资的发展战略及中长期规划。

五、负责宏观指导和管理全国外商投资项目的核准及管理工作，核准国家规定的限额以上外商（包括台港澳商）投资企业、补偿贸易项目、限制利用外商投资的项目、BOT 项目、设立外商投资股份公司、投资性公司、分公司和法规规定由外经贸部核准的项目及上述企业合同、章程的变更：核准涉及国家实行配额、许可证管理进出口商品（含台港澳地区）的外商投资企业立项申请。

六、监督检查外商投资企业执行有关法律法规和合同、章程的情况并协调解决发生的问题；牵头并协调国务院七部委对外商投资企业联合年检工作。

七、研究和拟定投资促进战略，指导和管理全国招商引资和投资促进工作。

八、指导和管理外商投资企业的进出口；编报外商投资企业涉及国家实行配额许可证管理的进出口商品的年度计划，经有关司总量平衡后下达并组织实施，监督计划执行情况，协调计划执行中的问题；参与拟定加工贸易、进出口商品配额招标政策。

九、负责外商投资统计工作，并定期作出综合统计分析。

十、负责联系经济特区、保税区等地区利用外商投资方面的业务；负责中国—新加坡两国政府苏州工业园区联合协调理事会的中方组织、联络和协调工作。

十一、联系中国外商投资企业协会。

十二、具体承担原全国外资工作领导小组的工作。

对外援助司（简称援外司）职责

一、管理我国的对外援助；拟定和执行对外援助政策、规章和方案。

二、编制对外援助计划并组织实施。

三、会同地区司研究和拟定国别援助政策和援助方案，负责政府间援助谈判，商签政府间的援助协议并组织实施。负责办理由政府间处理的对外援助事务。

四、编制对外援助项目和一般物资援助资金的预决算，具体管理其资金的使用，检查分析使用效益。

五、确定对外援助的项目、一般物资和现汇援助，组织实施并监督、检查实施情况。

六、研究和推行对外援助方式改革。

国外经济合作司（简称合作司）职责

一、负责全国国外经济合作工作；归口管理全国对外承包工程、劳务合作、设计、咨询、监理业务。

二、拟定和执行国外经济合作的发展战略、方针、政策和管理规章。

三、参与编制全国对外承包工程、劳务合作的中长期规划；编制年度指导计划。

四、研究国际承包劳务和涉及咨询的市场情况，指导海外市场开发、规范经营秩序；指导协调和管理非工业项目的成套设备出口；处理有关重大事件。

五、参与双边和多边对外谈判，组织实施有关协议。

六、负责国际经济合作基金的使用。

七、会同地区司核准在未建交或敏感国家（地区）的相关项目；负责宏观管理和监督国务院有关部门和地方人民政府具体审批和管理境外（未建交国家和香港特别行政区及澳门、台湾除外）承包工程、劳务合作、设计咨询项目。

八、归口负责外经企业外派人员和经营管理人员的管理和培训。

九、负责国际经济合作公司扩大经营范围的推荐工作。

十、联系中国对外工程承包商会和中国国际工程咨询协会。

科技发展和技术进出口司（简称科技司）职责

一、拟定和执行对外技术贸易的战略、方针、政策、管理规章以及鼓励技术出口政策；参与编制国家技术进出口项目的长远规划和年度计划，并组织国家技术引进计划项目的下达和实施。

二、拟定和执行国家出口管制政策，管理涉及国内、外出口管制的有关事务。出具外国对华出口所需最终用户证明并监督其执行情况；负责出口管制商品和技术的出口审批，颁发与防扩散相关的出口许可证。

三、管理技术和高技术产品的出口；指导协调和管理以技术出口为主所带动的成套设备出口项目。管理国家限制出口的技术和引进技术的出口与再出口；拟定高技术产品出口目录和国家禁止、限制进出口技术目录。

四、管理技术引进和国际招标。

五、负责外经贸生产企业科技发展、技术进步、技术改造；管理科研周转金和技术改造贷款，审批科研项目及科研成果的评定和奖励。

六、研究和推进技贸结合战略实施；负责外经贸科技发展、技术进步等项事务。组织指导外经贸系统的科技研究，推动外经贸生产企业的技术进步和技术改造。

七、组织协调技术出口市场的开拓；统一归口组织协调双边、多边工业技术合作。

八、负责外经贸标准化、信息化工作；参与管理《实施检验的进出口商品种类表》。

九、负责技术进出口的统计工作，并定期作出综合统计分析。

外贸货运司（简称贸运司）职责

一、管理国际货运代理，拟定和执行国际货运代理行业的政策、法规、规章、制定国际货运 代理企业资格标准，负责有关的资格审定。

二、负责供应香港特别行政区和澳门鲜活冷冻商品“三趟快车”运输的组织协调。

三、参与政府间及国际多边运输协定的谈判。

四、负责掌握外贸运输动态，就外经贸运输等有关问题与有关部门进行协调。

五、指导外经贸仓储行业管理。

六、联系国际货运代理协会和货主协会等社会中介组织。

七、负责外贸运输人员业务培训和国际交流工作。

条约法律司（简称条法司）职责

一、统一管理本部条约法律工作；研究境内外经济贸易法律。

二、制订并组织实施外经贸立法规划和计划。

三、拟定外经贸（含进出口商品检验）法律、法规草案，组织或参与拟定外经贸法规性文件和规章。

四、负责国际经贸公约的制定以及多边和双边条约、协定等谈判文件的审核。

五、负责外经贸法规、规章之间及其与国际条约、协定之间的协调与衔接。

六、参与重大经贸协议、合同、章程和重大争议案的研究与协调。

七、依法承办我国对外反倾销、反补贴及保障措施中的有关事务，指导、协调外国对我国出口商品的反倾销应诉。

八、负责多边和双边知识产权对外谈判。

九、负责外经贸系统行政复议和行政诉讼。

十、负责国际法律组织有关事务，组织对外经贸法律交流和国内外有关法律培训。

交际司职责

一、制定礼宾工作规章制度。

二、负责协调、联系和安排部领导的正式外事活动及出访计划；综合平衡部邀请的外国副部长级以上代表团来访计划并负责接待；负责协调、联系和安排国家领导人会见我部及直属单位接待的重要外宾。负责国家领导人率领的政府经贸代表团的出访安排。

三、管理部机关的外事礼宾和重大外事活动；指导外经贸系统的外事礼宾工作。

四、负责党和国家领导人会见我部邀请的外国代表团组的翻译工作和部领导的外事翻译工作。

五、负责本部及部直属单位的出国团组护照签证的管理和申办工作。

六、负责办理部机关及直属单位人员的出访事宜。

部直属机关党委工作职责

一、负责部机关、特派员办事处、在京部属单位以及部属国外企业和部属单位派驻国外机构的党群工作。

二、组织党员认真学习、宣传和坚决执行党和国家的方针、政策、保证党的各项方针、政策在我部的贯彻执行。

三、从严治党，抓好党组织的自身建设，保持党组织的先进性。

四、认真做好基层党组织的建设，充分发挥党员的先锋模范作用，积极支持和协助行政领导保证完成部门的各项工作任务。

五、对党员，特别是党员领导干部实施有效的监督。

六、配合行政领导做好职工的思想政治工作。

七、协助部党组管理机关和所属单位党群组织和群众组织的干部；配合干部人事部门对行政领导干部进行考核和民主评议并对其任免、调动和奖惩提出意见和建议。

八、配合行政领导做好统战工作。

九、领导本部机关和直属单位工会、共青团、妇委会等群众组织。

十、承担部党组及上级党组织交办的事项。

对 外 贸 易

关于加强旧机电产品进口管理的通知

国经贸机〔1997〕877 号

各省、自治区、直辖市及计划单列市经贸委（经委、计经委）、外经贸委（厅、局）、外经贸部驻各地特派员办事处、配额许可证事务局、广东海关分署、各直属海关、各直属商检局，国务院各部门：

近几年来，旧机电产品进口量越来越多，一些产品如旧的液压挖掘机、船用柴油机、医用 X 射线断层检查仪（CT）、医用 X 光诊断仪等的进口，不仅污染环境，严重危及人身和生产安全，也扰乱了正常市场秩序。为了有效地保护环境，保障人民健康和生产安全，提高社会效益，现就加强旧机电产品进口管理问题通知如下：

一、自 1998 年 1 月 1 日起，除因特殊需要经国家机电产品进出口办公室批准外，不论何种外汇来源、贸易方式和进口渠道，一律不准进口旧的机电产品。

二、未经批准，各有外贸经营权的单位不得对外签订进口旧机电产品的合同或有约束力的协议。

外汇管理部门和银行凭国家机电产品进出口办公室出具的进口旧机电产品的《配额产品证明》或《机电产品进口证明》、《机电产品进口登记表》售、付汇联办理售、付汇业务。

三、凡进口旧的机电产品，海关按产品管理方式，分别凭国家机电产品进出口办公室、外经贸部签发并注明为旧品的《配额产品证明》、《机电产品进口证明》、《机电产品进口登记表》和《进口许可证》以及商检机构出具的《旧机电产品进口备案书》一并验放。违者由海关按有关规定予以处理。

四、商检机构负责对所有经国家批准进口的旧机电产品实施商品检验（旧船舶由中国船级社实施检验）。

对符合国家安全和环保强制性标准及合同所规定检验标准的旧机电产品，商检机构签发《进口商品检验情况通知单》。对不符合的，按照商检有关规定处理。

五、严禁使用新机电产品的进口证件报关进口旧机电产品。一经发现，由海关予以没收。

进口的旧机电产品，以不低于该产品新品价值的 60% 为基础，计征关税及其它税费。

六、本通知下达前已由地方或部门批准进口而未到货者，限 1998 年 3 月 31 日前报国家机电产品进出口办公室复核，并换发相应进口证件。

国家经贸委
对外贸易经济合作部
海关总署
国家进出口商品检验局
1997 年 12 月 22 日

对外贸易经济合作部　海关总署
关于加工贸易进口设备有关问题的通知

〔1998〕外经贸政发第383号

1998年7月1日

各省、自治区、直辖市及计划单列市外经贸委（厅、局），深圳市经发局，海关广东分署，各直属海关，各外贸中心，各部委直属公司：

根据《国务院关于调整出口设备税收政策的通知》（国发〔1997〕37号）规定，对“加工贸易外商提供的不作价进口设备”，“除《外商投资项目不予免税的进口商品目录》所列商品外，免征关税和进口环节增值税”。“加工贸易单位进口外商提供的不作价设备，凭批准的加工贸易合同到其主管海关办理进口免税手续。海关根据这些手续并对照不予免税的商品目录进行审核”。为贯彻落实以上加工贸易进口设备税收调整政策，现就有关问题通知如下：

一、加工贸易外商提供的不作价进口设备，指与加工贸易经营单位开展加工贸易（包括来料加工、进料加工及外商投资企业从事的加工贸易，下同）的外商，以免费即不需经营单位付汇进口、也不需用加工费或差价偿还方式，向经营单位提供的加工生产所需设备。

二、免税进口和使用外商提供的工作价设备必须符合下列条件之一：

（一）设有独立专门从事加工贸易（即不从事内销产品加工生产）的工厂或车间，并且不作价设备仅限在该工厂或车间使用。

（二）对未设有独立专门从事加工贸易的工厂或车间、以现有加工生产能力为基础开展加工贸易的项目，使用不作价设备的加工生产企业，在加工贸易合同（协议）期限内，其每年加工产品必须是70%以上属出口产品。

三、经营单位进口不作价设备，须在加工贸易合同（协议）中列明进口不作价设备的条款（即列明外商以免费方式提供，不需加工贸易经营单位付汇进口、也不需用加工费或差价偿还设备款），并附《加工贸易不作价设备申请备案清单》。

四、外经贸主管部门按加工贸易分级审批管理权限和有关规定，在审批加工贸易合同（协议）时，对照《外商投资项目不予免税的进口商品目录》一并办理审批进口不作价设备。外经贸主管部门审批进口不作价设备，须审查以下内容：

（一）是否具备免税进口和使用不作价设备的条件。

（二）加工贸易合同（协议）中的进口不作价设备条款是否符合规定。

五、加工贸易合同（协议）备案地主管海关负责审核办理不作价设备免税手续。

（一）经营单位凭批准的加工贸易合同（协议）和《加工贸易不作价设备申请备案清单》到其主管海关办理进口免税手续。

（二）主管海关根据外经贸主管部门批准的加工贸易合同（协议）和《加工贸易不作价设备申请备案清单》及其他有关单证，对照《外商投资项目不予免税的进口商品目录》，经审核后，由主管海关予以备案并核发《登记手册》（加贴防伪标签）。

（三）经营单位凭《登记手册》向口岸海关办理报关手续，口岸海关凭《登记手册》验放。

六、对临时进口（期限在半年以内）加工贸易生产所需不作价设备（限模具、单台设备），海关按暂时进口货物办理，逾期补征税款。

七、上述免税不作价设备自进口之日起至退运出口并按海关规定解除监管止，属海关监管货物。监管期限为5年，在监管期限内，不得擅自在境内销售、串换、转让、抵押或移作他用。

免税不作价设备在监管期间，加工贸易经营单位要在每年的一月份分别向外经贸主管部门和主管海关书面报告免税不作价设备使用情况，海关要定期核查。

加工贸易经营单位因故终止或解除加工贸易合

同，经原外经贸审批部门批准后，由主管海关核准，方可将免税不作价设备退运出境，或按设备使用年限折旧后的价值，缴纳关税和进口环节增值税。

八、加工贸易免税不作价设备退运出境，或补缴关税和进口环节增值税，或超过海关监管年限的，经营单位应及时办理解除监管手续，向海关提交解除监管的书面申请、设备《登记手册》及其他有关单证，海关核准后，解除监管并发给其解除监管证明。

九、进口不作价设备如属《外商投资项目不予免税的进口商品》所列商品，主管海关按国家有关规定照章征收关税和进口环节增值税。

十、凡违反本通知第二、三、七条规定，以及假借加工贸易不作价设备名义骗取免税、偷逃税款的，外经贸主管部门停止审批其新的加工贸易合同(协议)，海关将全额补征关税和进口环节增值税，并根据《中华人民共和国海关法》、《中华人民共和国海关法行政处罚实施细则》和其他有关法律、法规的规定严肃处理。对触犯法律的，移交司法机关依法追究其刑事责任。

十一、由海关监管的不作价设备，如涉及进口配额、特定或登记的产品，免予办理配额、许可证、登记或进口证明。在监管期内（即5年），如提前解除监管并且不将设备退运出境，应按有关规定补证。

十二、各级外经贸主管部门、各主管海关要加强配合，工作中既要简化环节、精简程序，又要严格审批、加强监管，把国务院此项重大调整政策尽快落到实处，收到实效。

十三、对1998年1月1日以前已经进口的、由海关计税并凭保函登记放行的不作价设备，办理办法另行通知。

各单位在执行中有何问题，请及时与外经贸部和海关总署联系。

附件：如文

附件一

加工贸易不作价设备申请备案清单（略）

附件二

加工贸易分级审批管理权限和有关规定的主要文件目录

一、《关于印发〈关于加工贸易进口料件试行银行保证金台账制度期间外经贸部审批管理实施细则〉的通知》(〔1995〕外经贸政发第791号)

二、《关于对外商投资企业开展加工贸易实行银行保证金台账进行审核有关问题的通知》(〔1996〕外经贸资发第508号)

三、《关于印发〈来料加工装配项目分类指导目录〉及有关问题的通知》(〔1998〕外经贸政发第193号)

四、《海关总署关于贯彻国务院关于调整进口设备税收政策的通知的紧急通知》(署税〔1997〕1062号)

五、《关于统一使用加工贸易业务（合同）批准证的通知》(〔1998〕外经贸政发第21号)

注：今后如有新的规定，按新规定办理。

中华人民共和国对外贸易经济合作部　令

1998 年　第 1 号

《关于赋予私营生产企业和科研院所自营进出口权的暂行规定》已于 1998 年 9 月 2 日经国务院批准，现予发布，自 1999 年 1 月 1 日起施行。

部　长：石广生

1998 年 10 月 1 日

关于赋予私营生产企业和科研院所自营进出口权的暂行规定

1998 年 9 月 2 日国务院批准

（1998 年 10 月 1 日对外贸易经济合作部发布）

第一条　为深化外贸体制改革，保持和引导非公有制经济健康发展，积极推动私营生产企业或科研院所参与国际竞争，根据《中华人民共和国对外贸易法》，制定本规定。

第二条　本规定所指的私营生产企业和科研院所系指依法登记注册、资本属于私人所有或私人资本控股的生产性企业或科研机构（包括独资企业、合伙企业、有限责任公司和股份有限公司）。

第三条　申请资格

一、同时具备下列条件的私营生产企业可申请自营进出口权：

（一）已经在生产企业所在地工商行政管理机关依法登记注册、领取了营业执照，注册资本和净资产均在 850 万元人民币以上；

（二）连续两年年销售收入、出口供货额分别在 5000 万元人民币和 100 万美元（机电产品生产企业年销售收入、出口供货额分别在 3000 万元人民币和 50 万美元）以上；

（三）具有自营进出口业务所必需的专业人员。

二、同时具备下列条件的私营科研院所（包括高新技术企业）可申请自营进出口权：

（一）已经在科研院所所在地工商行政管理机关登记注册、领取了营业执照，注册资本和净资产均在 850 万元人民币以上；

（二）科研院所年销售收入在 300 万元人民币以上，经过省级以上科技主管部门认定的高新技术企业年销售收入在 3000 万元人民币（开发型高新技术企业年销售收入在 1000 万元人民币）以上；

（三）具有自营进出口业务所必需的专业人员。

第四条　申报材料

一、私营生产企业或科研院所申请自营进出口权的报告；

二、企业或院所章程；

三、企业法人营业执照（正本复印件）

四、工商行政管理机关出具的连续两年企业年检合格证明和资产情况证明；

五、申请的自营进出口商品目录；

六、代理出口的外贸企业出具的出口供货证明材料；

七、县级以上税务部门出具的纳税证明；

八、高新技术企业需出具科技主管部门颁发的《高新技术企业证书》。

第五条　申报和审批程序

私营生产企业或科研院所向注册所在地外经贸

主管部门提出书面申请，经省、自治区、直辖市及计划单列市外经贸主管部门审查后报对外贸易经济合作部（以下简称外经贸部）审批。

第六条 经批准取得自营进出口权的私营生产企业或科研院所，凭批准文件到海关、出入境检验、外汇、工商、税务等部门办理有关手续，向省、自治区、直辖市及计划单列市外经贸主管部门申领《进出口企业资格证书》后开展自营进出口业务。取得自营进出口权的私营生产企业或科研院所分立、合并、变更自营进出口商品目录，须报外经贸部批准；变更企业名称须经工商行政管理机关办理名称预先核准，报外经贸部办理相应批准手续；注销的须报外经贸部备案。

第七条 权利和义务

经批准取得自营进出口权的私营生产企业和科研院所享有的权利和应承担的义务如下：

一、可以直接从事自营进出口业务。

二、在批准的进出口业务范围内，可以经营本企业或院所自产产品的出口业务，经营本企业或院所生产、科研所需的机械设备、零配件、原辅材料的进口业务。

三、可以申请加入进出口商会、参加国家和地方外经贸主管部门组织的有关对外经济贸易活动，并得到国家对外贸易方针和政策的指导。

四、在从事自营进出口贸易活动中，可以享受与公有制自营进出口生产企业或科研院所相同的待遇。

五、遵守国家有关对外贸易的方针政策和法律、法规。

六、接受外经贸主管部门和进出口商会的监督、管理和协调。

七、积极出口创汇。

第八条 各级外经贸主管部门对取得自营进出口权的私营生产企业或科研院所开展进出口业务，要积极支持，加强指导，做好服务和规范化管理工作。

第九条 取得自营进出口权的私营生产企业或科研院所如违反国家有关政策规定，将视具体情况给予通报批评、警告或撤销自营进出口权的处罚。

第十条 本规定由外经贸部负责解释。

第十一条 本规定自 1999 年 1 月 1 日起施行。

对外贸易经济合作部　海关总署　国家外汇管理局
关于印发《规范进出口代理业务的若干规定》的通知

〔1998〕外经贸政发第 725 号

1998 年 10 月 6 日

各省、自治区、直辖市、计划单列市及哈尔滨、长春、沈阳、南京、杭州、济南、武汉、广州、西安、成都外经贸厅（委、局），各地方、各部委机电产品进出口办公室；广东分署，各直属海关，国家外汇管理局各省、自治区、直辖市分局，深圳分局；各部委直属公司，各贸易中心：

为进一步规范进出口代理业务，打击和防范各种走私违规、骗汇、逃套汇和骗税行为，坚决杜绝“四自三不见”（自带客户、自带货源、自带汇票、自行报关和不见进口产品、不见供货货主、不见外商）的进口代理方式，对外贸易经济合作部、海关总署、国家外汇管理局联合制定了《规范进出口代理业务的若干规定》（以下简称《规定》），现印发你们，请遵照执行。

请各外经贸主管部门即将《规定》转发至各从事进出口业务的企业，各企业必须严格按《规定》从事进出口代理业务。

附件：《规范进出口代理业务的若干规定》

附 件

规范进出口代理业务的若干规定

第一条 为进一步规范进出口代理业务，打击和防范各种走私违规、骗汇、逃套汇和骗税行为，防止出卖或变相出卖进出口经营权和许可证，特制定本规定。

第二条 本规定适用于外贸企业（指各类经批准具有进出口经营权的企业，以下均同）以自己名义从事的进出口代理业务。

第三条 从事进出口代理业务的外贸企业，必须经对外贸易经济合作部或其授权的地方外经贸主管部门批准具有进出口代理经营范围。

对国家实行核定公司经营的进口商品和国家组织统一联合经营的出口商品，无该项商品进口或出口经营权的外贸企业不得以任何方式从事代理业务。

自营进出口生产企业和科研院所、外商投资企业（经批准允许从事进出口代理业务的投资性公司和合资外贸公司除外）等均不得以任何方式从事进出口代理业务。

第四条 代理人要加强对代理合同、进出口合同和各种单证的审核、管理，建立健全合同、单证的登记、备案、保存制度和代理进口购汇、付汇内部审批制度，并对所办单证的真实性负责。

第五条 从事进出口代理业务，代理人必须与委托人签订书面代理合同，并由代理人根据代理合同与外商签订进出口合同。

代理合同和进出口合同的条款内容，必须符合国家法律、法规规定。

第六条 代理人要加强对外商资信情况（如注册情况、经营能力、信誉等）进行调查。

对由委托人联系的外商，资信调查费用由委托人承担，代理人可以预收。对经调查资信不良的外商，代理人有权停止代理业务。

第七条 代理人必须按照本规定认真履行其职责。进出口代理业务的合同、有关单证的以下项目（栏目），均必须为代理人：

（一）进出口合同：对外签约人；

（二）进出口许可证：进口商或出口商；

（三）进口证明或登记表：对外签订合同单位；

（四）海关报关单：经营单位；

（五）结汇、购付汇及核销单证：进口单位或出口单位。

第八条 对国家实行进出口许可证管理的商品，一律由代理人负责按规定办理许可证，不得交由委托人（包括配额持有单位）或其他第三方代办。

对国家实行进口证明、进口登记管理的产品，由委托人或由代理人（凭委托人的委托书）按规定办理进口证明、登记表。

第九条 海关报关和纳税手续，由代理人或由代理人委托经海关批准注册的专业报关单位（凭代理人的委托书）按规定办理，不得交由委托人或其他第三方代办。

对违反上述规定办理报关的，海关不予受理。对构成走私和违规的，海关根据报关企业管理办法，给予暂停或取消其报关权。

第十条 海关查验货物时，代理人应到场，或通知委托人到场，接受海关查验。

第十一条 代理人、委托人的外汇收支活动必须按有关外汇管理规定办理。

进口代理业务，一律由代理人负责对外付汇，不得由委托人对外付汇。进口货款由委托人及时向代理人支付。

出口代理业务，一律由代理人负责收汇。委托人为经批准允许保留现汇的企业，代理人凭有关外汇管理法规规定的有效凭证和商业单据将原币划转给委托人；委托人为不允许保留现汇的企业，代理人结汇后将货款按有关规定支付给委托人。

第十二条 代理人要全过程参与和跟踪进出口代理业务和合同执行。

对在执行进出口合同中所出现的问题，代理人应及时与委托人联系。涉及对外索赔、理赔，代理人和委托人应按合同约定，积极处理。

在对外索赔过程中，如委托人拒绝预付索赔所需费用（指应由委托人承担的），代理人可以自行承担费用和风险，索赔所得归代理人所有。

第十三条 违反本规定从事进出口代理业务，各外经贸主管部门、外汇管理部门不予办理审批、发证、售付汇及其他有关手续。

第十四条 对违反本规定从事进出口代理业务构成走私、违反海关监管规定、逃套汇和骗税、出卖或变相出卖进出口经营权、许可证的，由海关、外汇管理机关、外经贸主管部门分别依据有关法律、法规给予处罚。构成犯罪的，依法追究其刑事责任。

第十五条 本规定自1998年12月1日起施行。

对外贸易经济合作部
关于对国家确定的1000家重点企业实行
进出口经营权登记备案制的通知

〔1998〕外经贸政发第829号

1998年11月4日

国务院各部委、各直属机构、办事机构、直属事业单位，各省、自治区、直辖市及计划单列市外经贸委（厅、局）：

外贸经营权由审批制向依法登记制过渡是我国外贸经营体制改革的一项重要内容。经国务院批准，从1997年开始，对五个经济特区内的生产企业自营进出口权已试行登记制，效果良好。根据中共中央关于“积极推进大中型生产企业实行自营出口”的指示精神，经国务院办公厅批准，对国家确定的1000家重点企业实行进出口经营权登记备案制。现就有关事项通知如下：

一、凡属国家确定的1000家重点企业（以下简称千家企业）均可根据本通知的规定申请登记（国家重点联系企业进出口经营权登记证书的格式详见附件）。

二、千家企业中的国务院各部门所属企业，直接向外经贸部申请登记。

三、千家企业中的地方所属企业，直接向所在省、自治区、直辖市及计划单列市外经贸主管部门申请登记。

四、千家企业申请登记须提交下列文件：

（一）企业的书面申请（包括国家重点联系企业进出口经营权登记证书的有关内容）；

（二）企业法人营业执照（复印件）；

（三）申请的进出口商品目录；

（四）如申请企业为生产性集团公司，需提供集团批准文件、成员企业名单。

五、外经贸部及各省、自治区、直辖市及计划单列市外经贸主管部门须在15个工作日内对千家企业的进出口经营权予以登记，并颁发《国家重点联系企业进出口经营权登记证书》。企业凭该证书到海关、出入境检验检疫、外汇、工商、税务等管理部门办理有关手续后，向外经贸部或所在省、自治区、直辖市及计划单列市外经贸主管部门申领《中华人民共和国进出口企业资格证书》，即可开展进出口业务。

六、千家企业的进出口经营范围：

（一）非生产性企业的进出口经营范围，按照外贸公司的进出口经营范围核定，即：

1. 自营和代理除国家组织统一联合经营的出口商品和国家实行核定公司经营的进口商品以外的其他商品和技术的进出口业务（不另附进出口商品目录）；

2. 经营进料加工和“三来一补”业务；

3. 经营对销贸易和转口贸易。

（二）生产性企业的进出口经营范围，按照自营进出口生产企业的进出口经营范围核定，即：

1. 经营本企业和成员企业自产产品的出口业务（经营国家组织统一联合经营的出口商品需专案上报审批）。

2. 经营本企业和成员企业生产所需的机械设备、零配件、原辅材料的进口业务（经营国家实行核定公司经营的进口商品需专案上报审批）；

3. 加工贸易和补偿贸易业务。

（三）千家企业的进出口经营范围由外经贸部或省、自治区、直辖市及计划单列市外经贸主管部门核准。

七、千家企业经营进出口业务，必须遵守国家的外经贸政策和有关法律、法规，接受当地外经贸主管部门的指导和监督，并服从有关进出口商会的协调。

八、各地外经贸主管部门须及时将登记情况报外经贸部备案。

特此通知。

附件：国家重点联系企业进出口经营权登记证书（略）

对外贸易经济合作部　海关总署关于进一步发展边境贸易的补充规定的通知

〔1998〕外经贸政发第844号

1998年11月19日

内蒙古自治区、辽宁省、吉林省、黑龙江省、广西壮族自治区、云南省、西藏自治区、甘肃省、新疆维吾尔自治区、新疆生产建设兵团外经贸委（厅、局），海南省商业贸易厅，哈尔滨、长春、大连、乌鲁木齐、呼和浩特、满洲里、南宁、海口、昆明、拉萨、兰州海关：

为贯彻党的十五大精神，进一步促进我国边境地区经济发展，扩大出口，增强民族团结，繁荣、稳定边疆，巩固和发展我国同毗邻国家的睦邻友好关系，经国务院批准，在《国务院关于边境贸易有关问题的通知》（国发〔1996〕2号）的基础上，就进一步发展边境贸易作如下补充规定：

一、边民通过互市贸易进口的商品（仅限生活用品），每人每日价值在人民币3000元以下的，免征进口关税和进口环节增值税；超过人民币3000元的，对超出部分按法定税率照章征税。

二、边境小额贸易企业通过指定边境口岸进口原产于毗邻国家的商品，除烟、酒、化妆品以及国家规定必须照章征税的其他商品外，在2000年底前，继续实行进口关税和进口环节增值税按法定税率减半征收的政策。

三、边境地区对外经济技术合作项下换回物资的进口，在2000年底前，继续执行边境小额贸易的进口税收政策。

四、边境小额贸易企业出口本地自产的粮食等国家重点管理的商品（目录见附件），对外贸易经济合作部（以下简称外经贸部）每年根据上年度边境小额贸易出口情况、生产情况及供求关系等因素，专项给边境省、自治区下达一定数量的出口配额，并授权边境省、自治区外经贸主管部门发放出口许可证；其他有特殊规定的商品，如实行全国统一招标、监控化学品及易制毒化学品等的出口，仍按现行规定办理；出口国家实行配额和许可证管理的其他商品，一律免领配额和许可证。

五、边境小额贸易企业进口原产于毗邻国家的属国家实行进口配额和限量登记管理的商品（除汽车及关键件外），外经贸部每年从年度进口计划总量中切块下达进口配额或限量登记额度，并授权边境省、自治区外经贸主管部门签发进口许可证和进口商品登记证。

六、边境省、自治区在外经贸部已核准的边境小额贸易企业中，根据外经贸部核定的总量和统一制定的条件及企业的经营能力，自行审批经营国家重点管理的出口商品的边境小额贸易企业，以及经营国家实行核定公司经营的进口商品的边境小额贸易企业，企业名单需报外经贸部备案。

七、边境小额贸易企业均享有对外经济技术合作经营权，开展与毗邻国家边境地区的承包工程和劳务合作业务；边境地区对外经济技术合作企业均享有边境小额贸易权。

八、边境小额贸易企业开展与毗邻国家边境地区经济技术合作项目换回的原产于毗邻国家的物资（除汽车及关键件外）可随项目进境，不受经营分工的限制。如换回物资属进口配额和限量登记管理的商品，须在承包工程和劳务合作项目立项前报外经贸部审批，各边境省、自治区外经贸主管部门凭外经贸部下达的外经项下的进口配额和限量登记额度及有关规定，签发进口许可证和进口商品登记证，海关凭进口许可证或进口商品登记证验放。

九、边境地区的地级市（州、盟）政府或外经贸主管部门可在本地区主办以边境贸易和经济技术合作为主要内容的交易会或洽谈会，由所在省、自治区外经贸主管部门审批，并报外经贸部备案。边境地区的地级市（州、盟）政府或外经贸主管部门可组织本地区企业赴毗邻国家举办招商办展活动，按现行程序报外经贸部批准。

边境省、自治区在执行上述规定的同时，要加大对边贸管理的力度，严厉打击各种走私和偷逃税行为。对犯有走私和偷逃税行为的企业，外经贸部和海关总署依据有关法律、法规予以惩处。

海南省对越小额贸易进出口商品及税收等项政策，参照本补充规定办理，但不得超过本补充规定。

本补充规定未涉及的内容，仍按国发〔1996〕2号文件及相关的规定执行。

本通知自1999年1月1日起执行，由外经贸部和海关总署负责解释。

附件：国家重点管理的出口商品名单

附　件

国家重点管理的出口商品名单（11种）

大米、玉米、煤炭、原油、成品油、钨（钨砂、仲钨酸铵、三氧化钨、钨酸）、锑（锑锭、氧化锑）、锌（锌锭、锌矿砂）、锡（锡锭、焊锡及锡砂）、锯材、蚕丝类（含厂丝）。

对外贸易经济合作部　海关总署关于发布《对违规、走私企业给予警告、暂停或撤销对外贸易、国际货运代理经营许可行政处罚的暂行规定》的通知

〔1998〕外经贸政发第929号

1998年12月1日

国务院各部委、各直属机构，各省、自治区、直辖市及计划单列市外经贸委（厅、局），广东海关分署，各直属海关：

为贯彻落实全国打击走私工作会议精神，对外贸易经济合作部和海关总署联合制定了《对违规、走私企业给予警告、暂停或撤销对外贸易、国际货运代理经营许可行政处罚的暂行规定》，现予发布，请遵照执行。

特此通知。

附件：《对违规、走私企业给予警告、暂停或撤销对外贸易、国际货运代理经营许可行政处罚的暂行规定》

附　件

对违规、走私企业给予警告、暂停或撤销对外贸易、国际货运代理经营许可行政处罚的暂行规定

第一条　为严厉打击走私犯罪活动，根据《中华人民共和国行政处罚法》、《中华人民共和国对外贸易法》及有关法律、法规，特制定本规定。

第二条　本《规定》所指违规、走私企业，系指依据《中华人民共和国海关法》和有关法规，经海关认定，已构成违反海关监管规定行为或走私行为的各类外经贸企业（包括外贸公司、自营进出口生产企业和科研院所、有进出口权的商业物资企业、对外承包劳务企业、加工贸易企业、边贸企业、旅游小额贸易企业、国际货运代理企业等）。

第三条　对违规、走私企业给予警告、暂停或撤销对外贸易、国际货运代理经营许可的行政处罚的基本前提是：违规、走私行为事实成立，已由海关给予行政处罚，且该行政处罚已经生效；或构成走私罪，法院已作出判决。对外贸易经济合作部或其授权的省级外经贸主管部门在接到海关或法院书面通知后，有权对违规、走私企业作出警告、暂停或撤销对外贸易、国际货运代理经营许可的行政处罚。

第四条　对外贸易经济合作部或其授权的省级外经贸主管部门在海关依法给予行政处罚的基础上，可对性质恶劣、情节严重的违规，走私企业给予以下行政处罚：

（一）对在一年内出现两次违规行为，或走私偷逃应缴税款5万元人民币以上、不满50万元人民币的企业，给予警告处罚并予以通报。

（二）对在两年内出现三次违规行为，或走私偷逃应缴税款50万元人民币以上、不满100万元人民币的企业，暂停其6个月单项商品或单项业务的对外贸易经营许可或国际货运代理经营许可。

（三）对在两年内出现两次走私行为，或走私偷逃应缴税款100万元人民币以上，不满300万元人民币的企业，暂停其6个月对外贸易、国际货运代理经营许可。

（四）对走私偷逃应缴税款300万元人民币以上（多次走私应合并计算）的企业，撤销其对外贸易、国际货运代理经营许可。

（五）对走私国家禁止进出口物品的企业，撤销其对外贸易、国际货运代理经营许可。

（六）对伪造、变造对外贸易经济合作部文件或进出口许可证的企业，撤销其对外贸易、国际货运代理经营许可。

（七）对构成走私罪、司法机关已对其主管人员和直接责任人员依法追究刑事责任的企业，撤销其对外贸易、国际货运代理经营许可。

第五条　对能自查自纠的企业，或在案件查处中能主动配合海关、积极挽回或避免国家损失的企业，对外贸易经济合作部经商海关总署后，可减轻或免予本规定设定的行政处罚。

第六条　对外贸易经济合作部或其授权的省级外经贸主管部门在对违规、走私企业作出本《规定》第四条所列行政处罚之前，应告知企业，企业有要求举行听证的权利；企业要求听证的，对外贸易经济合作部或其授权的省级外经贸主管部门应组织听证。听证结束后，对外贸易经济合作部或其授权的省级外经贸主管部门依据有关法律、法规及听证情况，最终决定是否给予行政处罚或减轻行政处罚。

第七条　对外贸易经济合作部或其授权的省级外经贸主管部门作出行政处罚决定后，应于7日内将处罚决定书送达企业；无法直接送达的，公告送达。

第八条　企业对行政处罚决定不服的，可以依照《行政复议条例》向对外贸易经济合作部行政

复议委员会提起行政复议，或依照《中华人民共和国行政诉讼法》提起行政诉讼。

第九条 本《规定》适用于外商投资企业。对外贸易经济合作部可比照本《规定》第四条，对违规、走私外商投资企业分别给予警告、通知海关暂停或停止其办理进出口业务的行政处罚，并通知外方母公司。

第十条 本《规定》由对外贸易经济合作部负责解释。

第十一条 本《规定》自发布之日起施行。

对外贸易经济合作部 国家经济贸易委员会
关于赋予生产企业“两纱两布”自营
出口权有关事项的通知

〔1998〕外经贸政发第236号

1998年3月19日

各省、自治区、直辖市及计划单列市外经贸委（厅、局）、经贸委（经委 计经委）：

为了深化外贸体制改革、扩大纺织品出口、缓解纺织行业面临的困难，根据国务院领导的指示精神，将赋予纺织企业“两纱两布”自营出口权的工作由试点阶段转入正常审批，现将有关事项通知如下：

一、申报及审批标准

（一）凡列入国家重点联系的1000户企业名单的“两纱两布”生产企业，只要提出申请，即赋予其“两纱两布”自营出口权。

（二）对其他符合下列条件之一的纺织生产企业可以申请“两纱两布”自营出口权：

1. 连续两年“两纱两布”出口供货额平均超过500万美元的国有大型纺织企业。

2. 连续两年“两纱两布”出口供货额平均超过1000万美元的国有中型纺织企业。

3. 对少数民族地区（主要是新疆）可考虑适当放宽标准。

二、申报及审批程序

（一）凡列入国家重点联系的1000户企业名单的“两纱两布”生产企业，可直接通过地方外经贸主管部门向外经贸部申报。申报材料应包括：国家经贸委和中国人民银行联合下发的国家重点联系的1000家国有企业名单；外经贸部批准企业经营进出口业务的批复文件；企业法人营业执照（以上均为复印件）。

（二）1000家国家重点联系企业以外的“两纱两布”生产企业由各省、自治区、直辖市及计划单列市经贸委、外经贸委（厅、局）向国家经贸委、外经贸部申报。申报材料包括：企业经营“两纱两布”出口业务的申请报告；企业行政主管部门意见；外经贸部批准企业经营进出口业务的批复文件复印件；企业法人营业执照复印件；国有大中型企业的批准文件或证书复印件等。

国家经贸委收到各地方、部门申报文件后，对企业进行审查，将符合条件的企业的审查意见送外经贸部，由外经贸部予以审核批复。

特此通知。

对外贸易经济合作部关于印发《来料加工装配项目分类指导目标》及有关问题的通知

〔1998〕外经贸政发第193号

1998年4月24日

各省、自治区、直辖市、计划单列市及哈尔滨、长春、沈阳、南京、武汉、广州、西安、成都市外经贸委（厅、局），深圳市经发局，海关广东分署，各直属海关，各外贸中心，各部委直属公司：

为使来料加工装配（以下统称来料加工）业务持续健康发展，规范来料加工管理，经商海关总署，我部制订了《来料加工装配项目分类指导目录》（以下简称《目录》），现印发你们，请遵照执行，并就有关问题通知如下：

一、《目录》是指导审批管理来料加工业务的依据。目录分为允许、限制和禁止三类。其中限制类分为限制类甲和限制类乙。限制类主要是进口料件或返还制成品属于敏感的配额许可证商品、易造成污染、国际市场有限并易冲击一般贸易出口的来料加工。

限制类和禁止类来料加工列入《目录》。允许类来料加工不在《目录》中具体列名。

二、限制类甲来料加工，须经对外贸易经济合作部（以下简称外经贸部）批准，由省、自治区、直辖市及计划单列市外经贸主管部门（以下统称省级外经贸主管部门）凭外经贸部批准文件（批准内容包括：经营单位、加工生产企业、加工规模等）进行审批管理（包括审批项目协议和加工贸易合同，下同）。

（一）地方经营单位开展限制类甲来料加工，由经营单位所在地省级外经贸主管部门审核后报外经贸部批准。

（二）部委直属公司及其子公司开展限制类甲来料加工，由总公司征求加工生产企业所在地省级外经贸主管部门意见后报外经贸部批准。

（三）外商投资企业开展限制类甲来料加工，不需报外经贸部批准，由省级外经贸主管部门负责审批管理。

三、限制类乙、允许类来料加工，由经营单位所在地省级外经贸主管部门负责审批管理。

部委直属公司及其子公司开展限制类乙和允许类来料加工，由其注册所在地省级外经贸主管部门负责审批管理。

限制类乙来料加工的审批权限不得不放。

四、开展来料加工业务较多的地方（县），经所在地省级外经贸主管部门同意，地市（县）外经贸主管部门可审批本地市（县）经营单位开展的允许类来料加工。

五、各级外经贸主管部门要严格按照有关规定和要求，对来料加工进行审批管理。

本《目录》自1998年6月1日起执行，凡过去规定与本《目录》有抵触的，以本《目录》为准。本《目录》由外经贸部负责解释。

附件：如文

附　件

来料加工装配项目分类指导目录

《来料加工装配项目分类指导目录》分为允许、限制和禁止三类。其中限制类分为限制类甲和限制类乙。允许类不具体列名。分类项目所涉及的商品，以海关商品品目（即4位码）或商品编号（即8位码）及其对应的商品名称为准。

一、禁止开展来料加工的项目

（一）进口料件属下列商品之一的：

1. 我国禁止进口商品（包括旧服装、含淫秽内容的废旧书刊、含有害物、放射性的工业垃圾等）

2. 废旧汽车、摩托车及其主要部件

（二）返还制成品属下列商品之一的：

1. 易制毒化学品、军民通用化学品

2. 我国加入国际公约并对外作出出口数量承诺的商品

3. 麝香

05100030　麝香

4. 天然牛黄

05100010　天然牛黄

（三）其他国家明令禁止开展来料加工的项目

二、限制类来料加工项目

Ⅰ　限制类甲

（一）进口料件属下列商品的来料加工项目：

1. 食糖（仅指用于加工后复出口白糖、绵白糖的原糖）。

17011100　甘蔗原糖，未加香料或着色剂

17011200　甜菜原糖，未加香料或着色剂

2. 氧化铝

28182000　氧化铝，但人造钢玉除外

3. 棉花（仅指用于加工复出口两纱两布的项目）

5201　未梳的棉花

5202　废棉（包括废棉纱线及回收纤维）

5203　已梳的棉花

（二）返还制成品属下列商品的来料加工项目：

1. 蘑菇罐头

20031011　小白蘑菇（洋蘑菇）罐头

2. 钨及钨制品

26110000　钨矿砂及其精矿

26209010　主要含钨矿灰及残渣

28259011　钨酸

28259012　三氧化钨

28259019　未列名钨的氧化物及氢氧化物

28418010　仲钨酸铵

28418020　钨酸钠

28418030　钨酸钙

28418040　偏钨酸铵

28499020　碳化钨

81011000　钨粉

81010100　未锻轧钨，包括简单烧结而成条、杆；废碎料

3. 稀土

25309020　稀土金属矿

26122000　钍矿砂及其精矿

28053010　未相互混合或相互熔合的稀土金属、及钇

2846　稀土金属、钇、及其混合物的无机或有机化合物

85051110　稀土永磁体

4. 维生素C

29362700　未混合的维生素C及其衍生物

5. 包装物料纸制品（指新成立加工贸易企业的项目）

4804　成卷或成张的未经涂布的牛皮纸及纸板，但不包括品目4802或4803的货品

4805　成卷或成张的其他未经涂布的纸及纸板，加工程度不超过本章注释2所列范围

4807　成卷或成张的复合纸及纸板（用粘合剂粘合各层纸或纸板制成），未经表面涂布或未浸渍，

	不论内层是否有加强材料
4808	成卷或成张的瓦楞纸及纸板（不论是否与平面纸胶合）、皱纹纸及纸板、压纹纸及纸板、穿孔纸及纸板，但品目 4803 的纸除外
4810	成卷或成张的单面或双面涂布高岭土或其他无机物资（不论是否加粘合剂）的纸及纸板，未涂布其他涂料，不论是否染面、饰面或印花
4811	成卷或成张的经涂布、浸渍、覆盖、染面、饰面或印花的纸、纸板、纤维素絮纸及纤维素纤维网纸，但品目 4803、4809 或 4810 的货品除外
4822	纸浆、纸或纸板（不论是否穿孔或硬化）制的筒管、卷轴、纡子及类似品

6. 坯绸及蚕丝

5001	适于缫丝的蚕茧
5002	生丝（未加捻）
5003	废丝（包括不适于缫丝的蚕茧，废纱及回收纤维）；
5004	丝纱线（绢纺纱线除外），非供零售用
5005	绢纺纱线，非供零售用
50071010	未漂白（包括未精练及精练的）或漂白抽丝机织物
50072011	未漂白（包括未精练及精练的）或漂白桑蚕丝机织物，含丝 85%及以上
50072021	未漂白（包括未精练及精练的）或漂白柞蚕丝机织物，含丝 85%及以上
50072031	未漂白（包括未精练及精练的）或漂白绢丝机织物，含丝 85%及以上

7. 两纱两布（棉纱、棉涤纶纱、棉坯布、棉涤纶坯布）

5204	棉制缝纫线，不论是否供零售用
5205	棉纱线（缝纫线除外），按重量计含棉量在 85%及以上，非供零售用
5206	棉纱线（缝纫线除外），按重量计含棉量在 85%以下，非供零售用
5207	棉纱线（缝纫线除外，供零售用
52081100	含棉 85%及以上未漂白平纹机织物，每平方米重量不超过 100 克
52081200	含棉 85%及以上未漂白平纹机织物，每平方米重量超过 100 克，但不超过 200 克
52081300	含棉 85%及以上未漂白三线或四线斜纹机织物，包括双面斜纹机织物，每平方米重量不超过 200 克
52081900	其他含棉 85%及以上未漂白机织物，每平方米重量不超过 200 克
51091100	含棉 85%及以上未漂白平纹机织物，每平方米重量超过 200 克
52091200	含棉 85%及以上未漂白三线或四线斜纹机织物，包括双面斜纹机织物，每平方米重量超过 200 克
52091900	其他含棉 85%及以上未漂白机织物，每平方米重量超过 200 克
52101100	含棉 85%以下主要或仅与化学纤维混纺的未漂白平纹机织物，每平方米重量不超过 200 克
52101200	含棉 85%以下主要或仅与化学纤维混纺的未漂白三线或四线斜纹机织物，包括双面斜纹机织物，每平方米重量不超过 200 克
52101900	含棉 85%以下主要或仅与化学纤维混纺的未漂白其他机织物，每平方米重量不超过 200 克
52111100	含棉 85%以下主要或仅与化学纤维混纺的未漂白平纹机织物，

每平方米重量超过200克

52111200 含棉85%以下主要或仅与化学纤维混纺的未漂白三线或四线斜纹机织物，包括双面斜纹机织物，每平方米重量超过200克

52111900 其他含棉85%以下主要或仅与化学纤维混纺的未漂白机织物，每平方米重量超过200克

55131110 含聚酯短纤85%以下主要或仅与棉混纺的未漂白平纹机织物，每平方米重量不超过170克

55131210 含聚酯短纤85%以下主要或仅与棉混纺的未漂白三线或四线斜纹机织机，包括双面斜纹机织物，每平方米重量不超过170克

55131310 其他含聚酯短纤85%以下主要或仅与棉混纺的未漂白机织物，每平方米重量不超过170克

55141110 含聚酯短纤85%以下主要或仅与棉混纺的未漂白平纹机织物，每平方米重量超过170克

55141210 含聚酯短纤85%以下主要或仅与棉混纺的未漂白三线或四线斜纹机织物，包括双面斜纹机织物，每平方米重量超过170克

55141310 其他含聚酯短纤85%以上主要或仅与棉混纺的未漂白机织物，每平方米重量超过170克

8. 白金

71101100 未锻造铂，铂粉

71101910 铂板、片

9. 硅铁及硅锰铁合金

72022100 硅铁，按重量计含硅量在55%以上

72022900 硅铁，按重量计含硅量在55%及以下

72023000 硅锰铁

10. 铜及铜基合金

7402 未精炼铜，电解精炼用的铜阳极

7403 未锻轧的精炼铜及铜合金

11. 镍及镍基合金

7502 未锻轧镍

12. 铝及铝基合金

7601 未锻轧铝

13. 铅及铅基合金

7801 未锻轧铅

14. 锌及锌基合金

7901 未锻轧锌

15. 锡（包括：锡锭、焊锡、锡基合金）

8001 未锻轧锡

16. 锑（包括：锑锭、锑基合金、氧化锑）

8110 锑及其制品，包括废碎料

17. 返还港澳的冷冻商品（包括：整只或分割冻猪肉、冻鸡、冻鸭）

02031900 冻整头及半头猪肉

02032190 其他冻整头及半头猪肉

02032200 冻带骨猪前腿、猪后腿及其肉块

02032900 其他冻猪肉

02064100 冻猪肝

02064900 其他冻猪杂碎

02071200 整只鸡，冻的

02071400 鸡块及杂碎，冻的

02073310 整只冻鸭

02073610 冻的鸭块及杂碎

Ⅱ限制类乙

（一）进口料件（不包括价值比例在10%以内的辅料）属下列商品的来料加工项目：

1. 粮食

1001 小麦及混合麦

1005 玉米

1006 稻谷、大米

2. 食糖（不包括用于加工复出口砂糖、绵白糖的原糖）

17019910 砂糖

17019920 绵白糖

3. 植物油

1507 豆油及其分离品，不论是否精制，但未经化学改性

1508 花生油及其分离品，不论是否精制，但未经化学改性

1511 棕榈油及其分离品，不论是否

	精制，但未经化学改性
1512	葵花油、红花油或棉子油及其分离品，不论是否精制，但未经化学改性
1514	菜子油或芥子油及其分离品，不论是否精制，但未经化学改性
15152100	初榨的玉米油
15155000	芝麻油及其分离品

4. 原油及成品油

27090000	石油原油及从沥青矿物提取的原油
27100011	车用汽油及航空汽油
27100012	汽油型喷气燃料
27100013	石脑油
27100021	煤油
27100031	轻柴油
27100032	重柴油
27100040	其他燃料油

5. 聚酯切片

39076010	聚对苯二甲酸乙二酯切片

6. 天然橡胶

40011000	天然橡胶乳，不论是否予硫化
40012100	烟胶片
40012200	技术分类天然橡胶（TSNR）
40012900	其他形状的天然橡胶

7. 木材

4403	原木，不论是否去皮、去边材或粗锯成方

8. 胶合板

4412	胶合板、单板饰面及类似的多层板

9. 羊毛

5101	未梳的羊毛
51031010	羊毛落毛
51051000	粗梳羊毛
51052100	精梳羊毛片毛
51052900	羊毛条及其他精梳羊毛

10. 棉花（不包括用于加工复出口两纱两布的项目）

52010000	未梳的棉花
52030000	已梳的棉花

11. 涤纶纤维

54022000	聚酯高强力纱
54023310	聚酯弹力线
54023390	其他聚酯变形纱线
54024200	部分定向聚酯纱线，未加捻或捻度每米不超过 50 转
54024300	其他聚酯纱线，未加捻或捻度每米不超过 50 转
54025200	聚酯纱线，捻度每米超过 50 转
54026200	聚酯多股纱线或缆线
54041000	截面尺寸不超过 1 毫米，细度在 67 分特及以上的合成纤维单丝
55012000	聚酯长丝丝束
55032000	聚酯短纤，未梳或未经其他纺前加工
55062000	聚酯短纤，已梳或经其他纺前加工
55092100	含聚酯短纤 85% 及以上的单纱
55092200	含聚酯短纤 85% 及以上的多股纱线或缆线
55095100	含聚酯短纤 85% 及以下主要或仅与人造纤维短纤混纺的纱线
55095200	含聚酯短纤 85% 以下主要或仅与羊毛或动物细毛混纺的纱线
55095300	含聚酯短纤 85% 以下主要或仅与棉混纺的纱线
55095900	含聚酯短纤 85% 以下与其他纤维混纺的纱线

12. 腈纶纤维

54023990	其他合成纤维长丝变形纱线
54024990	其他合成纤维长丝单纱，未加捻或捻度每米不超过 50 转
54025990	其他合成纤维长丝单纱，捻度每米超过 50 转
54026990	未列名合成纤维长丝多股纱线或缆线
55013000	聚丙烯腈或变性聚丙烯腈长丝丝束
55033000	聚丙烯腈或变性聚丙烯腈短纤，未梳或未经其他纺前加工
55063000	聚丙烯腈或变性聚丙烯腈短纤，已梳或未经其他纺前加工
55093100	含聚丙烯腈或变性聚丙烯腈短

纤85%及以上的单纱

55093200　含聚丙烯腈或变性聚丙烯腈短纤85%及以上的多股纱线或缆线

55096100　含聚丙烯腈或变性聚丙烯腈短纤85%以下主要或仅与羊毛、动物细毛混纺的纱线

55096200　含聚丙烯腈或变性聚丙烯腈短纤85%以下主要或仅与棉混纺的纱线

55096900　含聚丙烯腈或变性聚丙烯腈短纤85%以下，与其他纤维混纺的纱线

13. 钢材

7206　铁及非合金钢，锭或其他初级形状（品目72.03的铁除外）

7207　铁及非合金钢的半制成品

7208　宽度在600毫米及以上的铁或非合金钢平板轧材，经热轧，但未经包覆、镀层或涂层

7209　宽度在600毫米及以上的铁或非合金钢平板轧材，经冷轧，但未经包覆、镀层或涂层

7210　宽度在600毫米及以上的铁或非合金钢平板轧材，经包覆、镀层或涂层

7211　宽度小于600毫米的铁或非合金钢平板轧材，但未经包覆、镀层或涂层

7212　宽度小于600毫米的铁或非合金钢平板轧材，经包覆、镀层或涂层

7213　不规则盘卷的铁或非合金钢的热轧条、杆

7214　铁或非合金钢的其他条、杆，除锻造、热轧、热拉拔或热挤压外未经进一步加工，包括轧制后扭曲的

7215　铁及非合金钢的其他条、杆

7216　铁或非合金钢的角材、型材及异型材

7304　无缝钢铁管及空心异型材（铸铁的除外）

7305　其他圆形截面钢铁管（例如，焊、铆及用类似方法接合的管），外经超过4064毫米

7306　其他钢铁管及空心异型材（例如，辊缝、焊、铆及类似方法接合的）

14. 废铜、废铝、废钢、废纸、废塑料等以国家环境保护局、对外贸易经济合作部、海关总署、国家工商局、国家商检局联合下发的《关于颁布〈废物进口环境保护管理暂行规定〉的通知》（环控〔1996〕204号）和《关于增补国家限制进口的可用作原料的废物目录的通知》（环控〔1996〕802号）文件所列的海关商品编号和商品名称为准）

（二）返还制成品属下列商品的来料加工项目：

1. 中药材（包括：鲜蜂王浆、人参、甘草制品、当归、枸杞、黄芪、虫草、半夏、党参）

04100020　鲜蜂王浆

04100030　鲜蜂王浆粉

12112010　西洋参

12112020　野山参（西洋参除外）

12112091　鲜人参

12112099　其他人参

12119011　当归

12119013　党参

12119016　冬虫夏草

12119019　半夏

12119023　黄芪

12119031　枸杞

13021200　甘草液汁及浸膏

2. 芦笋罐头

20056010　芦笋罐头

3. 棉漂布及棉涤纶漂布

5208　棉机织物，按重量计含棉量在85%及以上，每平方米重量不超过200克（但不包括商品编号为52081100、52081200、52081300、52081900的商品）

5209　棉机织物，按重量计含棉量在85%及以上，每平方米重量超过200克（但不包括商品编号为52091100、52091200、52091900的商品）

5210　棉机织物，按重量计含棉量在

85%以下，主要或仅与化学纤维混纺，每平方米重量不超过200克（但不包括商品编号为52101100、52101200、52101900的商品）

5211　棉机织物，按重量计含棉量在85%以下，主要或仅与化学纤维混纺，每平方米重量超过200克（但不包括商品编号为52111100、52111200、52111900的商品）

5513　合成纤维短纤纺制的机织物，按重量计合成纤维短纤含量在85%以下，主要或仅与棉混纺，每平方米重量不超过170克（但不包括商品编码为55131110、55131210、55131310的商品）

5514　合成纤维短纤纺制的机织物，按重量计合成纤维短纤含量在85%以下主要或仅与棉混纺，每平方米重量超过170克（但不包括商品编码为55141110、55141210、55141310的商品）

4. 苎麻（包括：苎麻纱、精干麻、苎麻条球、苎麻坏布）

53089011　按重量计苎麻含量在85%及以上的未漂白或漂白的纱线

53089013　按重量计苎麻含量在85%以下的未漂白或漂白的纱线

53059911　经加工、但未纺制的苎麻

53099912　苎麻的短纤及废麻

53110012　按重量计苎麻含量在85%及以上未漂白机织物

53110014　按重量计苎麻含量在85%以下的未漂白机织物

5. 抽纱

5804　网眼薄纱及其他网眼织物，但不包括机织物、针织物或钩编织物；成卷、成条或成小块图案的花边，但品目60.02的织物除外

5810　成匹、成条或成小块图案的刺绣品

5811　经绗缝或其他方法用一层或几层纺织材料与胎料组合制成的被褥状纺织品，但名目5810的刺绣品除外

6213　手帕

三、允许类来料加工项目

除禁止类和限制类以外的来料加工项目，均属允许类来料加工项目。

说明：

1. 易制毒化学品、军民通用化学品、我国加入国际公约并对外作出承诺的商品，其具体目录以外经贸部等有关部门公布的为准。

2. 本目录所列进口料件和返还制成品，其4位码为海关商品品目、8位码为海关商品编号、商品名称为协调制度商品名称。

3. 对只列品目的商品，包括该品目中所有商品编号及其对应的商品。

对外贸易经济合作部
国家发展计划委员会 国家经济贸易委员会
关于赋予试点企业集团进出口经营权和
对外承包劳务经营权有关事项的通知

〔1998〕外经贸政发第348号
1998年4月30日

国务院各部委、各直属机构，各省、自治区、直辖市、计划单列市外经贸委（厅、局）、经贸委（经委、计经委）：

为深化大型企业集团试点工作，根据《国务院批转国家计委、国家经贸委、国家体改委关于深化大型企业集团试点工作意见的通知》（国发〔1997〕15号）要求，现就赋予试点企业集团进出口经营权和对外工程承包、对外劳务合作经营权有关事项通知如下：

一、赋予国家试点企业集团进出口经营权

（一）试点企业集团母公司属于生产性企业的集团

1. 母公司可赋予进出口经营权，经营本集团自产产品出口和本集团所需设备物资进口；还可经营与本企业集团产品相关或同类商品的进出口业务。

2. 按现行规定，符合条件的集团子公司和其他成员企业，可单独申请进出口经营权。

3. 试点企业集团经批准可成立一家具有独立法人资格的进出口公司，承担企业集团的进出口业务。

（二）试点企业集团母公司属于商业、物资和外贸等流通性企业的集团

1. 母公司可赋予进出口经营权，经营除国家组织统一联合经营的出口商品和国家实行核定公司经营的进口商品以外的其他商品和技术的进出口业务，不再成立集团的进出口公司。

2. 符合条件的集团子公司和其他成员企业，可视其经营性质，单独申请进出口经营权。

（三）试点企业集团母公司属于其他非生产性企业的集团

1. 母公司可视其行业特点赋予相应的进出口经营权。

2. 符合条件的集团子公司和其他成员企业，可视其经营性质，单独申请进出口经营权。

3. 经批准，可成立一家具有独立法人资格的进出口公司，经营本集团的进出口业务。

二、赋予国家试点企业集团对外工程承包和劳务合作经营权

（一）母公司经批准可赋予对外工程承包和劳务合作经营权，经营本集团有关行业的对外工程承包和劳务合作业务。

（二）企业集团的子公司和其他成员企业，凡具备建设部颁发的一级工程资质证书的，可单独申请本行业对外承包劳务经营权；具备设计、生产包括组织生产、出口大型成套设备能力的，经批准可赋予与出口自产设备相关的对外工程承包权和设计、安装调试、操作等技术人员及售后服务人员的外派劳务权。

三、申报及审批程序

1. 试点企业集团母公司申请进出口经营权和对外承包劳务经营权，凡属计划单列的试点企业集团可根据国发〔1997〕15号文，直接向外经贸部申报。非计划单列试点企业集团可通过上级主管部门或所在省、自治区、直辖市及计划单列市外经贸部门向外经贸部申报。企业申报时，同时抄送所在省、市经贸委。

2. 国家试点企业集团子公司和其他成员企业申报及审批进出口经营权，仍按国务院国发〔1992〕30号、国发〔1993〕76号及相关文件办理。

3. 提出申请的试点企业集团需上级企业的申请

材料（包括企业集团的介绍）、法人营业执照（复印件）、公司章程、进出口商品目录等。

对外贸易经济合作部
国家发展计划委员会　海关总署
关于地方政府部门统一使用海关进出口统计数据有关问题的通知

〔1998〕外经贸计财发第927号

1998年12月9日

各省、自治区、直辖市及计划单列市计（经）委、外经贸委（厅、局），广东海关分署，各直属海关：

根据国务院领导同志的指示精神，为统一口径，便于比较、避免混乱、有利工作，现决定统一使用海关统计数据反映进出口情况。现将《各直属海关向地方政府部门提供海关统计数据的办法》印发给你们，请遵照执行，并就有关事项通知如下：

一、各地区在制定政策、研究问题、指导工作时，涉及进出口业务的，要以海关进出口统计数据为依据。

二、对外公布、使用实际出口和进口到货数据，要以海关统计数据为准，并标明数据来源。

三、要以海关统计数据口径制定本地区进出口调控目标，考核进出口完成情况。

四、要妥善处理海关统计和外经贸业务统计的关系。海关统计是我国官方的进出口统计，各地方外经贸主管部门要认真抓好海关统计资料的开发和利用工作，充分挖掘海关统计信息资源为外经贸业务管理服务；外经贸业务统计中实际进出口数据主要服务于内部管理，弥补海关统计之不足，原则上不得对外公布。

五、各海关要进一步做好统计工作，提高统计数据质量，按照《各直属海关向地方政府部门提供海关统计数据的办法》按时向地方政府部门通报本地区进出口统计数据，并做好统计信息咨询服务工作。

六、各海关向地方政府部门提供海关统计数据后，外经贸部向各地方外经贸主管部门反馈海关统计数据的渠道与范围维持不变。

七、请各海关与各地方外经贸主管部门按上述精神于今年年底之前，协商提供统计数据工作的具体运作事宜，建立联系配合制度。有关此项工作的进展情况及存在的问题，请于1999年3月15日前分别报外经贸部（计划财务司）和海关总署（综合统计司）。

特此通知。

附件：各直属海关向地方政府部门提供统计数据的办法

附　件

各直属海关向地方政府部门提供海关统计数据的办法

海关统计作为我国官方的进出口统计，已在国家宏观经济管理中广泛应用。为了进一步发挥海关统计的作用，加强国家对进出口贸易的管理，现就各直属海关向地方政府部门提供有关数据的办法规定如下：

一、提供统计数据的时间

各海关应于每月12日（法定节日顺延）将总署反馈的上月初步数据向地方政府部门通报。此项工作从提供1999年1月份的数据开始。

二、提供统计数据的范围

（一）各省、自治区、直辖市及计划单列市（大连、青岛、宁波、厦门、深圳）进出口总值；

（二）进出口商品贸易方式总值；

（三）国别（地区）进出口总值；

（四）主要商品进出口量值（进出口主要商品按1997年海关总署规定的口径及目录，由各直属海关与地方外经贸主管部门根据本地实际情况商定）；

（五）进出口贸易方式企业性质总值；

（六）运输方式进出口总值。

三、提供的数据如超出上述第二项所列范围，需要海关再做加工的，可予收费。收费应按《海关总署关于执行〈海关统计资料及统计数据开发费收费标准〉的通知》（署财〔1996〕602号）规定办理。

四、各海关提供统计信息咨询服务时应注意的事项

（一）不提供涉及保密范围的进出口商品统计资料；

（二）原则上不提供具体经营单位的进出口商品量值。如确因管理需要，可以提供，但应说明该项资料不得公开使用；

（三）各地方的统计数据按经营单位所在地范围加工、整理。

五、地方政府部门使用海关统计数据时应注意的事项

（一）地方政府部门不得利用海关统计资料从事商业咨询活动。海关统计咨询业务由海关总署及各直属海关或海关总署授权的咨询服务机构负责。

（二）若发现海关提供数据有误或有疑问之处，地方政府部门应及时与当地海关联系，由海关负责核查，确实有误的，应予更正。

六、各省、自治区、直辖市及计划单列市政府部门所需数据原则上由所在地直属海关提供。负责对下列地区政府部门提供数据的海关是：

广东省——广州海关

辽宁省——大连海关

山东省——青岛海关

七、各直属海关的统计部门具体负责提供数据的工作。海关总署综合统计司归口管理对外提供贸易统计数据的咨询工作。

对外贸易经济合作部
关于委托省级外经贸主管部门负责审批
外经贸有限责任公司内部职工持股
试点工作有关问题的通知

〔1998〕外经贸计财发第221号

1998年3月27日

各省、自治区、直辖市及计划单列市外经贸委（厅、局）：

自1994年开展外经贸企业内部职工持股试点工作以来，这一工作取得了较大进展和明显成效。为了进一步加快外经贸企业以内部职工持股改制为重点的公司制改制步伐，实现外经贸企业三年转制和解困目标，同时也为了简化审批手续，根据李岚清副总理关于持股试点工作“应纳入十五大有关企业改革的方针和有关具体规定实施”的要求，我部决定，委托省级外经贸主管部门负责审批外经贸有限

责任公司内部职工持股试点工作。现将有关问题通知如下：

一、受托审批外经贸有限责任公司内部职工持股试点工作的省级外经贸主管部门需具备以下条件：

（一）下属企业中至少有两家以上企业（含两家）已经参加了外经贸部内部职工持股试点，并已获外经贸部原则批复或已完成改制；

（二）已经成立股改领导小组，有专门的机构和专职人员负责内部职工持股试点，专职人员中至少有一人参加过外经贸部举办的内部职工持股试点培训并获合格证书；

凡不具备以上条件的，不得擅自审批。

二、省级外经贸主管部门在受托审批外经贸有限责任公司内部职工持股试点的过程中，必须统一政策、严格按照《外经贸股份有限公司和有限责任公司内部职工持股试点暂行办法》（〔1997〕外经贸计财发第188号）及其配套文件进行。要充分发挥中介机构作用，特别是律师的主协调作用。

三、实行受托审批后，试点企业可以凭省级外经贸主管部门的批复到相应的工商行政管理部门办理名称预先核准及公司设立登记或变更登记手续。

四、实行受托审批后，试点企业可以凭省级外经贸主管部门的批复到相应的民政部门办理设立内部职工持股会的有关登记手续。

五、受托审批的省级外经贸主管部门，应将改制企业根据《外经贸企业设立内部职工持股的股份有限公司和有限责任公司申报文件目录（试行）》（〔1997〕外经贸计财字第466号）要求制作的申请设立公司的全套申报材料报外经贸部备案。

六、外经贸部对受托审批的省级外经贸主管部门实行稽查监督制度，凡不具备条件擅自审批或违规操作的，一律取消受托审批权。

七、本通知自发布之日起实行。

对外贸易经济合作部
关于调整部分出口商品配额
管理办法的通知

〔1998〕外经贸管发第487号

1998年7月6日

各省、自治区、直辖市及计划单列市外经贸委（厅、局），外经贸部驻各地特派员办事处，配额许可证事务局，各进出口商会，外资协会，广东海关分署，各直属海关：

为加快出口商品管理体制改革，促进我国外贸出口发展，经商海关总署，我部决定对实行出口配额许可证管理商品种类及统一联合经营商品种类再次进行调整。现将调整内容通知如下：

一、取消废钢、四环素、烧碱、纯碱、肝素纳、鸡肉（供港澳配额除外）出口配额管理，实行一般许可证管理，发证机关凭出口企业的出口合同发证，原发证机关不变；

二、取消松茸、铝及铝基合金、镍及镍基合金的一般许可证管理；

三、取消茶叶出口统一联合经营，具体管理办法另行通知；

四、为支持企业扩大配额招标商品出口，对人参、羊绒、无毛绒、兔毛、棉漂布、棉涤纶漂布、苎麻纱、苎麻坯布、苎麻条／球、精干麻、鲜蜂王浆（粉）、单缸柴油机、皮制劳保手套、芝麻、红小豆、甘草制品、木杆铅笔、电风扇、黑白电视机、自行车（输美除外）等商品，凡具有投标资格的企业，均可按照《关于印发〈出口商品配额有偿招标办法实施细则〉的通知》（〔1996〕外经贸管发第302号）规定的程序，向招标办公室按中标平均价交纳费用后领取配额，配额当年有效。外商投资企业全年累计领取配额数量（含中标数量）不得超过外经贸部核准的出口规模。

本通知自1998年7月10日起执行。

附件：取消出口许可证管理商品目录

附 件

取消出口许可证管理商品目录

序号	出口许可证	协 调 制 度 目 录	
	商品名称	商品编号	商品名称
1	松茸	07095110 07108010 07119032	鲜或冷藏的松茸 冷冻松茸 盐渍松茸，不适于直接食用的
2	镍及镍基合金	75022000 75021000	未锻轧的镍合金 未锻轧的非合金镍
3	铝及铝基合金	76011000 76012000	未锻轧的非合金铝 未锻轧的铝合金

对外贸易经济合作部关于印发《1999年出口许可证管理商品分级发证目录》及有关问题的通知

〔1998〕外经贸管发第975号

1998年12月28日

各省、自治区、直辖市及计划单列市外经贸委（厅、局），外经贸部驻各地特派员办事处，配额许可证事务局，各进出口商会：

为积极推进出口商品管理体制的改革，千方百计扩大出口，完成1999年外贸出口任务，经商海关总署，我部对实行出口许可证管理的商品种类和发证机关作了较大的调整。现将《1999年出口许可证管理商品分级发证目录》（见附件）印发给你们，请遵照执行，并就有关问题通知如下：

一、经调整，实行出口许可证管理的商品为58种，按实际操作分解为73种（396个商品编码），其中，配额许可证事务局（简称“事务局”）发证商品为17种，特办发证商品为40种，省级发证机关发证商品为16种。

二、凡实行配额招标管理的出口商品（具体目录另行通知），除对设限国家纺织品被动配额招标商品以外，无论何种贸易方式（包括来料加工），均实行全球配额管理，各授权发证机关凭《申领配额招标商品出口许可证证明书》签发出口许可证。

有关被动配额商品管理仍按现行规定执行。

三、棉坯布的发证机关调整为：

（一）事务局负责办理各部委直属总公司的出口许可证。

（二）各省级发证机关负责办理本地区各类外贸企业的出口许可证。

四、对美国出口蜂蜜，企业按规定申领出口许可证后，到事务局办理“配额证书”，海关凭“双证”验放。

五、松香渣列入松香管理范围，各发证机关按松香管理办法签发出口许可证。

六、对部分定向出口商品实行对个别国家（地区）的配额许可证管理：

（ ）对日本和港澳出口硅锰铁合金；对日本出口棉坯布、磷片石墨、桐木及板材。

（二）对韩国出口糠醇。

（三）对美国出口定尺碳素钢板。

七、对部分商品实行全球许可证下的个别地区配额许可证管理：

（一）对港澳出口活牛、活大猪、活中猪、活乳猪、活鸡、牛肉、猪肉、乳猪肉、鸡肉、大闸蟹；

（二）对奥门出口活鸭、活鹅、活乳鸽、鸭肉。

八、为维护正常的经营秩序，对部分出口商品实行指定发证机关发证和指定出口口岸管理。各类外贸企业出口这类商品，均须到指定的发证机关申领出口许可证，并在指定的口岸报关出口；授权发证机关须按指定的口岸签发出口许可证。

（一）锑品（包括锑砂、氧化锑、锑及其制品）：由黄埔、北海、天津口岸出运。

（二）轻（重）烧镁：由大连特办发证，西藏出口由成都特办发证；指定大连、营口、鲅鱼圈、大东港、中山、青岛、天津、长春、满洲里为出口口岸，有关商检证明亦由指定出口口岸商检局办理。

（三）羊绒、无毛绒：一律由天津特办发证，西藏出口羊绒、无毛绒不再由成都特办发证；

（四）活牛、活大猪、活中猪、活乳猪、活鸡、活鸭、活鹅、活乳鸽、猪肉、牛肉、乳猪肉、鸡肉、鸭肉；陆运由广州、深圳特办发证，其他运输方式由各特办发证；

（五）栗子：对日本出口板栗，山东省和青岛市由青岛特办签发，其他省市由天津特办发证；对其他国家（地区）出口其他栗子由各特办发证。

对东南亚出口栗子，北京市、天津市、河北省、山东省、山西省、大连市、青岛市在本省（市）或就近口岸报关；其他省、市、自治区在上述省市各口岸以外的其他口岸报关。

（六）乌龙茶：福建省由福州特办发证，其他省市由广州特办发证；

（七）苇及苇制品：山东省和青岛市由青岛特办发证，其他省市由天津特办发证；

（八）大闸蟹：江苏、安徽、江西、湖北外经贸委签发本省的出口许可证，其他省市由上海市外经贸委签发；

九、为便于实施进出口许可证联网核销，对不实行“一批一证”管理的商品，发证机关在签发进出口许可证时在许可证“备注”栏内填注“非一批一证”。

十、进料加工复出口“铜及铜基合金”，发证机关按对外贸易经济合作部《关于“铜及铜基合金”发证问题的通知》（〔1995〕外经贸管制函字第134号）文件的规定办理。

十一、根据国务院关于边境贸易有关问题的通知精神，边境小额贸易进出口企业凡出口国家实行配额和许可证管理的出口商品（实行全国统一招标、监控化学品及易制毒化学品和国家重点管理的出口商品〔大米、玉米、煤炭、原油、成品油、钨砂、仲钨酸铵、三氧化钨、钨酸、锑锭、氧化锑、锌锭、锌矿砂、锡锭、焊锡、锡砂、锯材、蚕丝类及厂丝〕除外），一律免领许可证。边境小额贸易进出口企业出口全国统一招标的商品和监控化学品及易制毒化学品，仍按现行规定，向外经贸部授权的发证机关申领许可证。边境小额贸易进出口企业出口国家重点管理的出口商品，外经贸部授权边境省、自治区外经贸主管部门根据外经贸部下达的边境小额贸易出口配额签发出口许可证。

十二、禁止出口商品（包括麝香、天然牛黄、铜及铜基合金、白金），任何企业不得经营出口。特殊情况需要出口的，须报外经贸部个案处理，海关凭外经贸部的批件或外经贸部签发的出口许可证验放。

十三、各发证机关要严格执行外经贸部关于许可证联网核销上报发证数据的规定，每日将所有发证数据传输至外经贸部EDI中心。

本通知自1999年1月1日起执行，由外经贸部负责解释。外经贸部《关于印发“出口许可证管理商品分级发证目录”及有关问题的通知》（〔1997〕外经贸管发第736号）同时废止。

附件：出口许可证管理商品分级发证目录

附　件

出口许可证管理商品分级发证目录

（共73种）

配额许可证事务局核发出口许可证商品（共17种）

出口许可证		协调制度目录		
序号	商品大类名称	商品编号	商品名称	单位
1	玉米	10051000	种用玉米	公斤
		10059000	其他玉米	公斤
		11042300	经其他加工的玉米(含玉米碎)	公斤
2	黄大豆	12010010	种用大豆	公斤
		12010091	黄大豆,不论是否破碎	公斤
3	钨砂	26110000	钨矿砂及其精矿	公斤
		26209010	其他含有钨的矿灰及残渣	公斤
4	锑砂	26171010	生锑	公斤
		26171090	其他锑矿砂及其精矿	公斤
	锑砂:黄埔、北海、天津为指定出口口岸			
5	仲钨酸铵	28418010	仲钨酸铵	公斤
		28418040	偏钨酸铵	公斤
6	钨制品	28259012	三氧化钨	公斤
		28259019.01	蓝色氧化钨	公斤
		28259011	钨酸	公斤
		28418020	钨酸钠	公斤
		28418030	钨酸钙	公斤
		28499020	碳化钨	公斤
		81011000	钨粉末	公斤
		81019100	未锻轧钨,包括简单烧结而成条、杆;废碎料	公斤
7	煤炭	27011100	无烟煤	公斤
		27011210	炼焦煤	公斤
		27011290	其他烟煤	公斤
		27011900	其他煤	公斤
		27021000	褐煤,不论是否粉化,但未制成型	公斤
8	原油	27090000	石油原油及从沥青矿物提取的原油	公斤
9	成品油	27100011	车用汽油及航空汽油	公斤
		27100012	汽油型喷气燃料	公斤
		27100013	石脑油	公斤

续表

出口许可证		协调制度目录		
序号	商品大类名称	商品编号	商品名称	单位
		27100019	其他轻油	公斤
		27100021	煤油	公斤
		27100029	其他中油	公斤
		27100031	轻柴油	公斤
		27100032	重柴油	公斤
		27100052	润滑油脂	公斤
		27100059	其他重油(不包括白油)	公斤
		27111100	液化天然气	公斤
10	氧化锑	28258000	锑的氧化物	公斤
	氧化锑:黄埔、北海、天津为指定出口口岸			
11	重水	28451000	重水(氧化氘)	公斤
12	监控化学品			
	可作为化学武器的化学品	29211930	HN1:N,N-二(2-氯乙基)乙胺	公斤
		29211940	HN2:N,N-二(2-氯乙基)甲胺	公斤
		29211950	HN3:三(2-氯乙基)胺	公斤
		29309090.01	2-氯乙基氯甲基硫醚	公斤
		29309090.02	芥子气:二(2-氯乙基)硫醚	公斤
		29309090.03	二(2-氯乙硫基)甲烷	公斤
		29309090.04	倍半芥气:1,2-二(2-氯乙硫基)乙烷	公斤
		29309090.05	1,3-二(2-氯乙硫基)正丙烷	公斤
		29309090.06	1,4-二(2-氯乙硫基)正丁烷	公斤
		29309090.07	1,5-二(2-氯乙硫基)正戊烷	公斤
		29309090.08	二(2-氯乙硫基甲基)醚	公斤
		29309090.09	氧芥气:二(2-氯乙硫基乙基)醚	公斤
			路易氏剂	
		29309090.94	烷基(甲基、乙基、正丙基或异丙基)硫代膦酸烷基(氢或少于或等于10个原子的碳链,包括环烷基)-S-2-二烷(甲、乙、正丙或异丙)氨基乙酯及相应烷基化盐或质子化盐 例如:VX:甲基硫代膦酸乙基-S-2-二异丙氨基乙酯	公斤
			硫芥气	
		29310000.91	路易氏剂1:2-氯乙烯基二氯胂	公斤
		29310000.92	路易氏剂2:二(2-氯乙烯基)氯胂	公斤
		29310000.93	路易氏剂3:三(2-氯乙烯基)胂	公斤
		29310000.94	烷基(甲基、乙基、正丙基或异丙基)氟膦酸烷(少于或等于10个碳原子的碳链,包括环烷)酯 例如:沙林:甲基氟膦酸异丙酯	公斤

续表

出口许可证		协调制度目录		
序号	商品大类名称	商品编号	商品名称	单位
			梭曼:甲基氟膦酸频那酯	
		29310000.95	二烷(甲、乙、正丙或异丙)氨基氰膦酸烷(少于或等于10个碳链,包括环烷)酯 例如:塔崩:二甲氨基氰膦酸乙酯	公斤
		29310000.96	烷基(甲基、乙基、正丙基或异丙其)膦酰二氟 例如:DF:甲基膦酰二氟	公斤
		29310000.97	烷基(甲基、乙基、正丙基或异丙基)亚膦酸烷基(氢或少于或等于10个碳原子的碳链,包括环烷基)-2-二烷(甲、乙、正丙或异丙)氨基乙酯及相应烷基化盐或质子化盐 例如:QL:甲基亚膦酸乙基-2-二异丙氨基乙酯	公斤
		29310000.98	氯沙林:甲基氯膦酸异丙酯 氯梭曼:甲基氯膦酸频那酯	公斤
		30029010	石房蛤毒素	公斤
		30029020	蓖麻毒素	公斤
	化学武器关键前体	28121044	三氯化砷	公斤
		29033010	PFIB:1,1,3,3,3,-五氟-2-三氟甲基-1-丙烯(又名:全氟异丁烯;八氟异丁烯)	公斤
		29051910	频哪基醇:3,3-二甲基丁-2-醇	公斤
		29181910	2,2-二苯基-2-羟基乙酸;二苯羟乙酸;二苯乙醇酸	公斤
		29211960	二烷(甲、乙、正内或异内)氨基乙基-2-氯及相应质子化盐	公斤
		29221929	二烷(甲、乙、正丙或异丙)氨基乙-2-醇及相应质子化盐 例外:二甲氨基乙醇及相应质子化盐 二乙氨基乙醇及相应质子化盐	公斤
		29299020	二烷(甲、乙、正丙或异丙)氨基膦酰二卤	公斤
		29299030	二烷(甲、乙、正丙或异丙)氨基膦酸二烷(甲、乙、正丙或异丙)酯	公斤
		29309090.91	胺吸膦:硫代磷酸二乙基-S-2-二乙氨基乙酯及相应烷基化盐或质子化盐	公斤
		29309090.92	烷基(甲、乙、正丙或异丙)氨基乙-2-硫醇及相应质子化盐	公斤
		29309090.93	硫二甘醇:二(2-羟乙基)硫醚;硫代双乙醇	公斤
		29309090.95	含有一个磷原子并有一个甲基、乙基或(正或异)丙基原子团与该磷原子结合的化学品,不包括含有更多碳原子的情形,但第一	公斤

续表

出口许可证		协调制度目录		
序号	商品大类名称	商品编号	商品名称	单位
			类名录所列者除外。 例如:甲基膦酰二氯;甲基膦酸二甲酯 例外:地虫磷:二硫代乙基膦酸-S-苯基乙酯	
		29333910	BZ:二苯乙醇酸-3-奎宁环酯	公斤
		29333920	奎宁环-3-醇	公斤
	化学武器原料	28111910	氰化氢	公斤
		28121020	磷酰氯:三氯氧磷;氧氯化磷	公斤
		28121010	亚硫酰氯:氯化亚砜;氧氯化硫	公斤
		28121030	光气:碳酰二氯	公斤
		28121041	一氯化硫	公斤
		28121042	二氯化硫	公斤
		28121043	三氯化磷	公斤
		28121045	五氯化磷	公斤
		28139000.01	五硫化二磷	公斤
		28371110	氰化钠	公斤
		28371910	氰化钾	公斤
		28510020	氯化氰	公斤
		29049030	氯化苦:三氯硝基甲烷	公斤
		29141900.01	频哪酮	公斤
		29181990.01	二苯乙醇酸甲酯	公斤
		29209011	亚磷酸三甲酯	公斤
		29209012	亚磷酸三乙酯	公斤
		29209013	亚磷酸二甲酯	公斤
		29209014	亚磷酸二乙酯	公斤
		29211100.01	二甲胺	公斤
		29211100.02	二甲胺盐酸盐	公斤
		29221310	三乙醇胺	公斤
		29221320.91	三乙醇胺盐酸盐	公斤
		29221930	乙基二乙醇胺	公斤
		29221940	甲基二乙醇胺	公斤
		29333990.91	3-羟基-1-甲基哌啶	公斤
		29333990.92	3-奎宁环酮	公斤
13	易制毒化学品	28061000	氯化氢(盐酸)	公斤
		28070000	硫酸	公斤
		28416100	高锰酸钾	公斤
		29023000	甲苯	公斤
		29091100	乙醚	公斤

续表

出口许可证		协　调　制　度　目　录		
序号	商品大类名称	商品编号	商　品　名　称	单位
		29141100	丙酮	公斤
		29141200	丁酮(甲基乙基(甲)酮)	公斤
		29143100	苯丙酮(苯基丙-2-丙酮)	公斤
		29152400	乙酸酐(醋酸酐)	公斤
		29163400.01	苯乙酸	公斤
		29224310	邻氨基苯甲酸	公斤
		29242990.91	N-乙酰邻氨基苯酸	公斤
		29329100	4-丙烯基-1,2-亚甲二氧基苯(异黄樟脑)	公斤
		29329400	4-烯丙基-1,2-亚甲二氧基苯(黄樟脑)	公斤
		29329990.01	3,4-亚甲基二氧苯基-2-丙酮	公斤
		29333210	哌啶(六氢吡啶)	公斤
		29394100.01	麻黄碱(麻黄素、盐酸麻黄碱)	公斤
		29394200.01	伪麻黄碱(伪麻黄素、盐酸伪麻黄碱)	公斤
		29394100.02	硫酸麻黄碱	公斤
		29394200.02	硫酸伪麻黄碱	公斤
		29394100.03	消旋盐酸麻黄碱	公斤
		29394900.01	盐酸甲基麻黄碱	公斤
		29394900.02	消旋盐酸甲基麻黄碱	公斤
		29394100.04	草酸麻黄碱	公斤
		13021991.01	供制造医药用麻黄浸膏粉	公斤
		13021992.01	供制造农药用麻黄浸膏粉	公斤
		13021999.01	其他麻黄浸膏粉	公斤
		13021991.02	供制造医药用麻黄浸膏	公斤
		13021992.02	供制造农药用麻黄浸膏	公斤
		13021999.02	其他麻黄浸膏	公斤
		12119049.01	药料用麻黄草粉	公斤
		12119050.01	香料用麻黄草粉	公斤
		12119099.01	其他用麻黄草粉	公斤
		30044090.01	麻黄碱盐类单方制剂(指盐酸麻黄碱片、盐酸麻黄碱注射剂、盐酸伪麻黄碱片、硫酸麻黄碱片)	公斤
		29329300	3,4-亚甲二氧基苯甲醛(胡椒醛、洋茉莉醛)	公斤
		29396100.01	麦角新碱	公斤
		29396200.01	麦角胺	公斤
		29396300.01	麦角酸	公斤
14	蚕丝类	50010010	适于缫丝的桑蚕茧	公斤
		50010090	其他适于缫丝的蚕茧	公斤
		50031000	未梳废丝	公斤
		50039000	其他废丝	公斤

续表

出口许可证		协调制度目录		
序号	商品大类名称	商品编号	商品名称	单位
		50040000	丝纱线(绢纺纱线除外),非供零售用抽丝绢	公斤
		50050010	抽丝绢纺纱线,非供零售用	公斤
		50050090	其他绢纺纱线,非供零售用	公斤
		50020010	桑蚕丝	公斤
		50020020	柞蚕丝	公斤
		50020090	其他生丝	公斤
15	坯绸	50071010	未漂白(包括未练白或练白)或漂白的抽丝机织物	米
		50072011	桑蚕丝机织坯绸,含丝85%及以上	米
		50072021	柞蚕丝机织坯绸,含丝85%及以上	米
		50072031	绢丝机织坯绸,含丝85%及以上	米
16	棉花	52010000	未梳的棉花	公斤
		52030000	已梳的棉花	公斤
	废棉	52021000	废棉纱线(包括废棉线)	公斤
		52029100	棉的回收纤维	公斤
		52029900	其他废棉	公斤
17	锑及其制品	81100020	未锻轧锑	公斤
		81100030	锑废碎料、粉末	公斤
		81100090	其他锑及锑制品	公斤
	锑及其制品:黄埔、北海、天津为指定出口口岸			

特派员办事处核发出口许可证商品（共40种）

出口许可证		协调制度目录		
序号	商品大类名称	商品编号	商品名称	单位
1	活牛	01029000	其他牛,改良种用除外	头
2	活大猪	01039200	50公斤及以上的猪,改良种用除外(大猪)	头
3	活中猪	01039120	10公斤及以上,但50公斤以下的猪,改良种用除外(中猪)	头
4	活乳猪	01039110	10公斤以下的猪,改良种用除外(乳猪)	头
5	活鸡	01059290	其他鸡,重量超过185克但不超过2000克	只
		01059390	其他鸡,重量超过2000克	只
		01059993	珍珠鸡,重量超过185克	只
6	活鸭	01059991	鸭,重量超过185克	只
		01060023	野鸭	只
7	活鹅	01059992	鹅,重量超过185克	只
8	活乳鸽	01060021	食用乳鸽	只
9	牛肉	02011000	鲜、冷整头及半头牛肉	公斤
		02012000	鲜、冷带骨牛肉	公斤

续表

出口许可证		协调制度目录		
序号	商品大类名称	商品编号	商品名称	单位
		02013000	鲜、冷去骨牛肉	公斤
		02021000	冻整头及半头牛肉	公斤
		02022000	冻带骨牛肉	公斤
		02023000	冻去骨牛肉	公斤
		02061000	鲜冷牛杂碎	公斤
		02062900	其他冻牛杂碎	公斤
		02062100	冻牛舌	公斤
		02062200	冻牛肝	公斤
10	猪肉	02031190	其他鲜、冷整头及半头猪肉	公斤
		02031200	鲜、冷带骨猪前腿、猪后腿及其肉块	公斤
		02031900	其他鲜、冷猪肉	公斤
		02032190	其他冻整头及半头猪肉	公斤
		02032200	冻带骨猪前腿、猪后腿及其肉块	公斤
		02032900	其他冻猪肉	公斤
		02063000	鲜、冷猪杂碎	公斤
		02064100	冻猪肝	公斤
		02064900	其他冻猪杂碎	公斤
11	乳猪肉	02031110	鲜、冷整头及半头乳猪肉	公斤
		02032110	冻整头及半头乳猪肉	公斤
12	鸡肉	02071100	整只的鲜或冷的鸡	公斤
		02071200	整只的冻鸡	公斤
		02071300	鲜或冷的鸡，块及杂碎	公斤
		02071400	冻鸡块及杂碎	公斤
13	鸭肉	02073210	整只的鲜或冷的鸭	公斤
		02073310	整只的冻鸭	公斤
		02073510	鲜或冷的鸭块及杂碎	公斤
		02073610	冻鸭块及杂碎(肝除外)	公斤
以上商品均实行全球许可证管理。其中，对港澳出口活牛、活大猪、活中猪、活乳猪、活鸡、牛肉、猪肉、乳猪肉、鸡肉实行配额许可证管理；对澳门出口活鸭、活鹅、活乳鸽、鸭肉实行配额许可证管理。以上商品陆运对港澳部分由广州、深圳特办发证；其余部分由各特办发证				
14	蜂蜜	04090000	天然蜂蜜	公斤
15	大蒜	07032010	鲜或冷藏的大蒜蒜头，不论是否去皮	公斤
		07032090	鲜或冷藏的其他大蒜，不论是否去皮	公斤
16	红小豆	07133210	种用赤豆	公斤
		07133290	其他赤豆	公斤
17	栗子	08024010	鲜或干的板栗，不论是否去壳	公斤
		08024090	鲜或干的其他栗子，不论是否去壳	公斤
		08119010	冷冻栗子，未去壳	公斤

续表

出口许可证		协调制度目录		
序号	商品大类名称	商品编号	商品名称	单位
	对日本出口板栗,山东省和青岛市由青岛特办签发,其余由天津特办签发;对其他市场出口其他栗子由各特办签发。对东南亚出口栗子,北京市、天津市、河北省、山东省、山西省、大连市、青岛市在本省或就近口岸报关;其他省、市、自治区在上述省市各口岸以外的其他口岸报关			
18	茶叶			
	绿茶	09021090	绿茶,内包装每件净重不超过3公斤	公斤
		09022090	绿茶,内包装每件净重超过3公斤	公斤
	特种茶	09021010	花茶(包括其他茶),内包装每件净重＜=3公斤	公斤
		09022010	花茶(包括其他茶),内包装每件净重＞3公斤	公斤
		09023020	普洱茶,内包装每件净重不超过3公斤	公斤
		09024020	普洱茶,内包装每件净重超过3公斤	公斤
	乌龙茶	09023010	乌龙茶,内包装每件净重不超过3公斤	公斤
		09024010	乌龙茶,内包装每件净重超过3公斤	公斤
	乌龙茶由福州特办发福建省,其余由广州特办签发			
	红茶	09023090	红茶(乌龙茶、普洱茶除外),内包装每件净重不超过3公斤	公斤
		09024090	红茶(乌龙茶、普洱茶除外),内包装每件净重超过3公斤	公斤
19	大米	10061010	种用稻谷	公斤
		10061090	其他稻谷	公斤
		10062000	糙米	公斤
		10063000	精米,不论是否磨光或上光	公斤
		10064000	碎米	公斤
20	甘草	12111010	新疆胀果甘草	公斤
		12111090	其他甘草(含东北、西正、梁外甘草等)	公斤
21	蔺草及制品	14019030	蔺草(包括灯芯草)	公斤
		46012021	蔺草制的席子、席料及帘子	公斤
22	苇及苇制品	14019020	芦苇	公斤
		46012031	苇帘	公斤
	苇及苇制品山东省和青岛市由青岛特办签发,其余由天津特办签发			
23	水煮笋	20059031	水煮竹笋罐头,每件容积8公升及以上,包括真空包装	公斤
24	矾土	25083000	耐火粘土(包括矾土、焦宝石及其他耐火粘土)	公斤
		25084000	其他粘土	公斤
		26060000	铝矿砂及其精矿	公斤
25	轻(重)烧镁	25191000	天然碳酸镁(菱镁矿)	公斤
		25199010	熔凝镁氧矿(电熔镁、包括喷补料)	公斤
		25199020	烧结镁氧矿(重烧镁、包括喷补料)	公斤
		25199030	碱烧镁(轻烧镁)	公斤

续表

出口许可证		协调制度目录		
序号	商品大类名称	商品编号	商品名称	单位
	轻(重)烧镁由大连特办签发,西藏出口轻(重)烧镁由成都特办签发。大连、营口、鲅鱼圈、大东港、中山、青岛、天津、长春、满洲里为指定出口口岸			
26	滑石块(粉)	25261020	未破碎及未研粉的滑石	公斤
		25262020	已破碎或已研粉的滑石	公斤
27	氟石块(粉)	25292100	按重量计氟化钙含量在97%及以下的萤石	公斤
		25292200	按重量计氟化钙含量在97%以上的萤石	公斤
28	焦炭	27040010	煤炭制焦炭及半焦炭,不论是否成型(不包括增碳剂)	公斤
29	石蜡	27122000	石蜡,按重量计含油量小于0.75%	公斤
		27129010	微晶石蜡	公斤
30	松香及松脂	38061010	松香及松香渣	公斤
		38061020	树脂酸	公斤
		13019040	松脂	公斤
31	原木	44031000	用油漆、着色剂、杂酚油或其他防腐剂处理的原木	立方米
		44032000	其他方法处理的针叶木原木	立方米
		44034100	深红色红柳桉木、浅红色红柳桉木及巴拷红柳桉木原木	立方米
		44034910	柚木原木	立方米
		44034990	未列名热带木原木	立方米
		44039100	栎木原木	立方米
		44039200	山毛榉木原木	立方米
		44039910	楠木原木	立方米
		44039920	樟木原木	立方米
		44039930	红木原木	立方米
		44039990	其他非针叶木原木	立方米
32	锯材	44061000	未浸渍铁道及电车道枕木	根
		44071000	经纵锯、纵切、刨切或旋切的针叶木木材,厚度超过6毫米	立方米
		44072400	经纵锯、纵切、刨切或旋切的苏里南肉豆蔻木、美洲香桃花心木、巴西胡桃木木材,厚度超过6毫米	立方米
		44072500	经纵锯、纵切、刨节或旋切的深红色红柳桉木、浅红色红柳桉木及巴栲红柳桉木木材,厚度超过6毫米	立方米
		44072600	经纵锯、纵切、刨切或旋切的白柳桉木、白色红柳桉木、白色柳桉木、黄色柳桉木及阿兰木木材,厚度超过6毫米	立方米
		44072910	其他经纵锯、纵切、刨切或旋切的柚木木材,厚度超过6毫米	立方米

续表

出口许可证		协 调 制 度 目 录		
序号	商品大类名称	商品编号	商 品 名 称	单位
		44072990	其他经纵锯、纵切、刨切或旋切的本章子目注释所列热带木木材,厚度超过6毫米	立方米
		44079100	经纵锯、纵切、刨切或旋切的栎木木材,厚度超过6毫米	立方米
		44079200	经纵锯、纵切、刨切或旋切的山毛榉木木材,厚度超过6毫米	立方米
		44079910	经纵锯、纵切、刨切或旋切的樟木、楠木、红木木材,厚度超过6毫米	立方米
		44079990	其他经纵锯、纵切、刨切或旋切的非针叶木木材,厚度超过6毫米	立方米
33	羊绒	51021020	未梳山羊绒	公斤
		51053020	已梳其他山羊绒	公斤
34	无毛绒	51053021	已梳无毛山羊绒	公斤
	羊绒及无毛绒由天津特办签发,西藏出口羊绒及无毛绒不再由成都特办签发			
35	硅锰铁合金	72023000	硅锰铁	公斤
	硅锰铁合金仅对日本和港澳出口实行配额许可证管理			
36	锌及锌基合金	79011100	含锌量在99.99%及以上的未锻轧非合金锌	公斤
		79011200	含锌量低于99.99%的未锻轧非合金锌	公斤
		79012000	未锻轧锌合金	公斤
37	锡及锡基合金	80011000	未锻轧的非合金锡	公斤
		80012010	锡基巴毕脱合金	公斤
		80012020	焊锡	公斤
		80012090	其他锡合金	公斤
38	维生素C	29362700	未混合的维生素C及其衍生物(直接用于注射的小包装针剂〔粉、液体〕除外)	公斤
39	碳化硅	28492000	碳化硅	公斤
40	稀土	25309020	稀土金属矿	公斤
		26122000	钍矿砂及其精矿	公斤
		28053010	未混合或熔合的稀土金属、钪及钇	公斤
		28053090	已混合或熔合的稀土金属、钪及钇	公斤
		28461010	氧化铈	公斤
		28461090	铈的其他化合物	公斤
		28469019	未列名氧化稀土	公斤
		28469020	氯化稀土	公斤
		28469030	氟化稀土	公斤
		28469090	稀土金属、钇、钪及其混合物的其他化合物	公斤
		28469011	氧化钇	公斤
		85051110	稀土永磁体	公斤

（共16种）省级发证机关核发出口许可证商品

出口许可证		协　调　制　度　目　录		
序号	商品大类名称	商品编号	商　品　名　称	单位
1	大闸蟹	03062491	未冻的中华绒毛蟹(大闸蟹)	公斤
	大闸蟹实行全球出口许可证管理,仅对港澳出口实行配额许可证管理,大闸蟹由江苏、安徽、江西、湖北外经贸委签发本省,其余由上海外经贸委签发			
2	食糖	17019910	砂糖	公斤
		17019920	绵白糖	公斤
3	磷片石墨	25041010	磷片天然石墨	公斤
	磷片石墨仅对日本出口实行配额许可证管理			
4	锌矿砂	26080000	锌矿砂及其精矿	公斤
5	锡矿砂	26090000	锡矿砂及其精矿	公斤
6	糠醇	29321300	糠醇及四氢糠醇	公斤
	糠醇仅对韩国出口实行配额许可证管理			
7	桐原木	44039940	泡桐木原木	立方米
8	桐板材	44079920	经纵锯、纵切、刨切或旋切的泡桐木木材,厚度超过6毫米(包括拼板)	立方米
	桐原木及桐板材仅对日本出口实行配额许可证管理			
9	新闻纸	48010000	成卷或成张的新闻纸	公斤
10	棉坯布	52081100	含棉85%及以上未漂白平纹机织物,每平方米重量不超过100克	米
		52081200	含棉85%及以上未漂白平纹机织物,每平方米重量超过100克,但不超过200克	米
		52081300	含棉85%及以上未漂白沾线或四线斜纹机织物,包括双面斜纹机织物,每平方米重量不超过200克	米
		52081900	其他含棉85%及以上未漂白机织物,每平方米重量不超过200克	米
		52091100	含棉85%及以上未漂白平纹机织物,每平方米重量超过200克	米
		52091200	含棉85%及以上未漂白三线或四线斜纹机织物,包括双面斜纹机织物,每平方米重量超过200克	米
		52091900	其他含棉85%及以上未漂白机织物,每平方米重量超过200克	米
	棉坯布仅对日本出口需申领主动配额许可证			
11	抽纱	58042100	化纤机制花边,成卷、成条、成小块图案	公斤
		58042910	丝及绢丝机制花边,成卷、成条、成小块图案	公斤
		58042920	棉机制花边,成卷、成条、成小块图案	公斤
		58042990	其他纺织材料机制花边,成卷、条、小块图案	公斤

续表

出口许可证		协　调　制　度　目　录		
序号	商品大类名称	商品编号	商　品　名　称	单位
		58043000	手工制花边,成卷、成条、成小块图案	公斤
		58101000	不见底布的刺绣品	公斤
		58109100	棉制见底布的刺绣品	公斤
		58109200	化学纤维制见底布的刺绣品	公斤
		58109900	其他纺织材料制见底布的刺绣品	公斤
		58110010	丝及绢丝制经绗缝等方法制被褥状纺织品	公斤
		58110020	毛制经绗缝等方法制被褥状纺织品	公斤
		58110030	棉制经绗缝等方法制被褥状纺织品	公斤
		58110040	化学纤维制经绗缝等方法制被褥状纺织品	公斤
		58110090	其他纺织材料制经绗缝等方法制被褥状纺织品	公斤
		61043100.01	毛制钩编的女式上衣	件
		61043200.01	棉制钩编的女式上衣	件
		61043300.01	合成纤维制钩编的女式上衣	件
		61043900.01	其他纺织材料制钩编的女式上衣	件
		62131010	丝制刺绣手帕	条
		62132010	棉制刺绣手帕	条
		62139010	其他纺织材料制刺绣手帕	条
		63023110	棉制刺绣其他床上用织物制品	公斤
		63023210	化学纤维制刺绣的庆上用织物制品	公斤
		63023921	麻制刺绣的床上用织物制品	公斤
		63023991	其他纺织材料制刺绣的床上用织物制品	公斤
		63025110	棉制刺绣其他餐桌用织物制品	公斤
		63025210	亚麻制刺绣的餐桌用织物制品	公斤
		63025310	化学纤维制刺绣的餐桌用织物制品	公斤
		63031120	棉制钩编的窗帘、帐幔、帘帷及床帷	公斤
		63031220	合成纤维制钩编的窗帘、帐幔、帘帷及床帷	公斤
		63031920	其他纺织材料制钩编窗帘、帐幔、帘帷及床帷	公斤
		63041131	手工钩编的床罩	件
		63041139	非手工钩编的床罩	件
		63041921	棉或麻制刺绣的非针织或钩编的床罩	件
		63041931	化学纤维制刺绣的非针织或钩编的床罩	件
		63041991	其他纺织材料制刺绣的非针织或钩编的床罩	件
		63049131	手工钩编的其他装饰用织物制品	件
		63049139	非手工钩编的其他装饰用织物制品	件
		63049210	棉制刺绣的非针织或钩编的装饰制品	公斤
		63049310	合成纤维制刺绣的非针织或钩编的其他装饰制品	公斤
		63049921	麻制刺绣的非针织或钩编的其他装饰制品	公斤
		65059010	钩编的帽类	个

续表

出口许可证		协 调 制 度 目 录		
序号	商品大类名称	商品编号	商 品 名 称	单位
12	定尺碳素钢板	72084000	铁或非合金钢非卷材,除热轧外未经进一步加工已轧压花纹,未包、镀、涂层	公斤
		72085100	其他热轧及未包、镀、涂层,厚度超过10毫米的铁或非合金钢非卷材	公斤
		72085200	其他热轧及未包、镀、涂层,厚度在4.75毫米及以上,但不超过10毫米的铁或非合金钢非卷材	公斤
		72085300	其他热轧及未包、镀、涂层,厚度在3毫米及以上,不小于4.75毫米的铁或非合金钢非卷材	公斤
		72085400	其他热轧及未包、镀、涂层,厚度小于3毫米的铁或非合金钢非卷材	公斤
		72089000	热轧及未包、镀、涂层,但经进一步加工的宽度在600毫米及以上的铁或非合金钢平板轧材	公斤
		72107000	涂漆或涂塑的铁或非合金钢平板轧材	公斤
		72109000	未列名宽度在600毫米及以上经包、镀、涂层铁或非合金钢平板轨材	公斤
		72111300	热轧及未包、镀、涂层,经四面轧制或在闭合匣内轧制的非卷材,宽度超过150毫米,厚度不小于4毫米,未轧压花纹的铁或非合金钢平板钢材	公斤
		72111400	其他热轧及未包、镀、涂层,厚度在4.75毫米及以上的铁或非合金钢平板轧材	公斤
		72119000	未列名宽度小于600毫米未包、镀、涂层的铁或非合金钢平板轧材	公斤
		72124000	涂漆或涂塑的宽度小于600毫米的铁或非合金钢平板轧材	公斤
		72125000	未列名镀或涂层的,宽度小于600毫米的铁或非合金钢平板轧材	公斤
	定尺碳素钢板仅对美国出口实行配额许可证管理			
13	电风扇	84145110	输出功率不超过125瓦的吊扇	台
		84145120	输出功率不超过125瓦的换气扇	台
		84145130	输出功率不超过125瓦具有旋转导风轮的风扇	台
		84145191	输出功率不超过125瓦的台扇	台
		84145192	输出功率不超过125瓦的落地扇	台
		84145193	输出功率不超过125瓦的壁扇	台
		84145199	输出功率不超过125瓦的其他未列名风机、风扇	台
		84145910	其他吊扇	台
		84145920	其他换气扇	台
		84145990	其他风机、风扇	台
14	电子计算机	84714110	其他巨型、大型及中型机数字式自动数据处理设备	台
		84714120	其他小型机数字式自动数据处理设备	台

续表

出口许可证		协调制度目录		
序号	商品大类名称	商品编号	商品名称	单位
		84714910	系统形式的大型机及中型机	台
		84714920	系统形式的小型机	台
		84715010	巨型、大型及中型机的数字式处理部件	台
		84715020	小型机的数字式处理部件	台
15	黑白电视机及其显像管（包括成套散件）	85281310	显像管屏幕尺寸不超过16厘米的黑白或其他单色电视接收机	台
		85281320	显像管屏幕尺寸超过16厘米，但不超过42厘米的黑白或其他单色电视接收机	台
		85281330	显像管屏幕尺寸超过42厘米，但不超过52厘米的黑白或其他单色电视接收机	台
		85281340	显像管屏幕尺寸超过52厘米的黑白或其他单色电视接收机	台
		85282200	黑白或其他单色的视频监示器	台
		85401200	黑白或其他单色的阴极射线电视显像管	只
16	自行车	87120020	竞赛型自行车	辆
		87120030	山地自行车	辆
		87120041	16、18、20英寸越野自行车	辆
		87120049	其他越野自行车	辆
		87120081	16英寸及以下的未列名自行车	辆
		87120089	其他未列名自行车	辆

国家经济贸易委员会　对外贸易经济合作部　海关总署关于印发1998年机电产品《配额产品目录》和《特定产品目录》的通知

国经贸机〔1998〕3号

1998年1月5日

各省、自治区、直辖市及计划单列市经贸委（经委、计经委），外经贸委（厅、局）、外经贸部驻各地特派员办事处、配额许可证事务局，广东海关分署、各直属海关，国务院有关部门：

根据《机电产品进口管理暂行办法》，现将1998年机电产品《配额产品目录》和《特定产品目录》印发你们，自1998年1月1日起施行。国家经贸委、外经贸部、海关总署《关于印发1997年机电产品〈配额产品目录〉和〈特定产品目录〉的通知》（国经贸机〔1997〕267号）同时废止。

附件：一、1998年配额产品目录

二、1998年特定产品目录

附　件

一、1998年配额产品目录

配额产品目录		协　调　制　度　目　录	
序号	商品名称	商品编号	商　品　名　称
1	汽车及其关键件	87012000	半挂车用的公路牵引车
		87021020	装有柴油发动机的机坪客车
		87021091	30座及以上的装有柴油发动机的机动客车
		87021092	20座及以上至29座的装有柴油发动机的机动客车
		87021093	10座及以上至19座的装有柴油发动机的机动客车
		87029010	其他30座及以上的机动客车
		87029020	其他20座及以上至29座的机动客车
		87029030	其他10座及以上至19座的机动客车
		87031000	雪地行走专用机动车，高尔夫球机动车及类似机动车辆
		87032130	排气量不超过1000毫升的汽油型小轿车
		87032190	排气量不超过1000毫升的汽油型其他载人车辆
		87032230	排气量超过1000毫升，但不超过1500毫升的汽油型小轿车
		87032240	排气量超过1000毫升，但不超过1500毫升的汽油型越野车（4轮驱动）
		87032250	排气量超过1000毫升，但不超过1500毫升的汽油型小客车（9座及以下）
		87032290	排气量超过1000毫升，但不超过1500毫升的汽油型其他主要用于载人的机动车
		87032314	排气量超过1500毫升，但不超过2500毫升的汽油型小轿车
		87032315	排气量超过1500毫升，但不超过2500毫升的汽油型越野车（4轮驱动）
		87032316	排气量超过1500毫升，但不超过2500毫升的汽油型小客车（9座及以下）
		87032319	排气量超过1500毫升，但不超过2500毫升的汽油型其他主要用于载人的机动车
		87032334	排气量超过2500毫升，但不超过3000毫升的汽油型小轿车
		87032335	排气量超过2500毫升，但不超过3000毫升的汽油型越野车（4轮驱动）
		87032336	排气量超过2500毫升，但不超过3000毫升的汽油型小客车（9座及以下）
		87032339	排气量超过2500毫升，但不超过3000毫升的汽油型其他主要用于载人的机动车
		87032430	排气量超过3000毫升的汽油型小轿车

续表

配额产品目录		协 调 制 度 目 录	
序号	商品名称	商品编号	商 品 名 称
		87032440	排气量超过 3000 毫升的汽油型越野车（4 轮驱动）
		87032450	排气量超过 3000 毫升的汽油型小客车（9 座及以下）
		87032490	排气量超过 3000 毫升的汽油型其他载人车辆
		87033130	排气量不超过 1500 毫升的柴油型小轿车
		87033140	排气量不超过 1500 毫升的柴油型越野车（4 轮驱动）
		87033150	排气量不超过 1500 毫升的柴油型小客车（9 座及以下）
		87033190	排气量不超过 1500 毫升的柴油型其他载人车辆
		87033230	排气量超过 1500 毫升，但不超过 2500 毫升的柴油型小轿车
		87033240	排气量超过 1500 毫升，但不超过 2500 毫升的柴油型越野车（4 轮驱动）
		87033250	排气量超过 1500 毫升，但不超过 2500 毫升的柴油型小客车
		87033290	排气量超过 1500 毫升，但不超过 2500 毫升的柴油型其他主要用于载人的机动车
		87033330	排气量超过 2500 毫升的柴油型小轿车
		87033340	排气量超过 2500 毫升的柴油型越野车（4 轮驱动）
		87033350	排气量超过 2500 毫升的汽油型小客车（9 座及以下）
		87033390	排气量超过 2500 毫升的柴油型其他载人车辆
		87039000	未列名主要用于载人的车辆
		87042100	装有柴油发动机，车辆总重量不超过 5 吨的其他货车
		87042230	装有柴油发动机，车辆总重量超过 5 吨，但小于 14 吨的其他货车
		87042240	装有柴油发动机，车辆总重量在 14 吨及以上，但不超过 20 吨的其他货车
		87042300	装有柴油发动机，车辆总重量超过 20 吨的其他货车
		87043100	装在点燃式活塞内燃发动机，车辆总重量不超过 5 吨的其他货车
		87043230	装有点燃式活塞内燃发动机，车辆总重量超过 5 吨，但不超过 8 吨的其他货车
		87043240	装有点燃式活塞内燃发动机，车辆总重量超过 8 吨的其他货车
		87049000	未列名货运机动车辆
		87052000	机动钻探车
		87053000	机动救火车
		87054000	机动混凝土搅拌车
		87059020	机动放射线检查车
		87059030	机动环境监测车
		87059040	机动医疗车
		87059051	航空电源车（频率为 400 赫兹）
		87059059	其他电源车

续表

配额产品目录		协调制度目录	
序号	商品名称	商品编号	商品名称
		87059060	飞机加油车、调温车、除冰车
		87059070	道路（包括跑道）扫雪车
		87059080	石油测井车、压裂车、混沙车
		87059090	未列名特殊用途的机动车辆
		84079090	未列名点燃式活塞内燃发动机
		84082010	输出功率在132.39千瓦（180马力）及以上车辆用压燃式活塞内燃发动机
		84082090	其他车辆用压燃式活塞内燃发动机
		87071000	机动小客车的车身（包括驾驶室）
		84143090	非电动机驱动的制冷设备用压缩机
		84152000	机动车辆上供人使用的空气调节器
2	摩托车及其发动机、车架	87111000	装有往复式活塞内燃发动机，排气量不超过50毫升的摩托车及装有辅助发动机的脚踏车
		8711200	装有往复式活塞内燃发动机，排气量超过50毫升，但不超过250毫升的摩托车及装有辅助发动机的脚踏车
		87113000	装有往复式活塞内燃发动机，排气量超过250毫升，但不超过500毫升的摩托车及装有辅助发动机的脚踏车
		87114000	装有往复式活塞内燃发动机，排气量超过500毫升，但不超过800毫升的摩托车及装有辅助发动机的脚踏车
		87115000	装有往复式活塞内燃发动机，排气量超过800毫升的摩托车及装有辅助发动机的脚踏车
		87119000	未列名摩托车及装有辅助发动机的脚踏车；边车
		84073100	排气量不超过50毫卂的车辆用往复式活塞发动机
		84073200	排气量超过50毫升，但不超过250毫升的车辆用往复式活塞发动机
		84073300	排气量超过250毫升，但不超过1000毫升的车辆用往复式活塞发动机
		87141900	其他摩托车零件、附件（车架）
3	彩色电视机及其显像管	85281291	显示屏幕尺寸不超过42厘米的彩色电视接收机
		85281292	显示屏幕尺寸超过42厘米，但不超过52厘米的彩色电视接收机
		85281293	显示屏幕尺寸超过52厘米的彩色电视接收机
		85282100	彩色视频监视器
		85283010	彩色视频投影机
		85401100	彩色阴极射线电视显像管
		85404000	彩色数据/图形显示管，屏幕萤光点间距小于0.4毫米
4	收、录音机及其机芯	85199910	激光唱机

续表

配额产品目录		协调制度目录	
序号	商品名称	商品编号	商品名称
		85203210	数字音频式盒式磁带型装有声音重放装置的其他录音机
		85203290	数字音频式装有声音重放装置的其他磁带录音机
		85203300	未列名盒式磁带型装有声音重放装置的其他录音机
		85203910	开盘式录音机
		85203990	未列名装有声音重放装置的其他磁带录音机
		85271200	袖珍盒式磁带收放机
		85271300	其他不需外接电源的收录（放）音组合机
		85271900	其他不需外接电源的无线电收音机，包括兼可接收无线电话、电报的设备
		85272100	需外接电源的汽车用收录（放）音组合机
		85272900	其他需外接电源的汽车用无线电收音机
		85273100	其他收录（放）音组合机
		85273200	带时钟的收音机
		85273900	未列名无线电收音机
		85229021	盒式磁带录音机或放声机用走带机构（机芯），不论是否装有磁头
5	电冰箱及其压缩机	84181010	容积超过500升的冷藏－冷冻组合机，各自装在单独外门
		84181020	容积超过200升，但不超过500升的冷藏－冷冻组合机，各自装有单独外门
		84181030	容积不超过200升的冷藏－冷冻组合机，各自装有单独外门
		84182110	容积超过150升的压缩式家用型冷藏箱
		84182120	容积超过50升但不超过150升的压缩式家用型冷藏箱
		84182130	容积不超过50升的压缩式家用型冷藏箱
		84182200	电气吸收式家用型冷藏箱
		84183010	制冷温度在－40℃及以下的柜式冷冻箱，容积不超过800升
		84183021	制冷温度在－40℃以上的柜式冷冻箱，容积超过500升，但不超过800升
		84183029	制冷温度在－40℃以上的柜式冷冻箱，容积不超过500升
		84184010	制冷温度在－40℃及以下的立式冷冻箱，容积不超过900升
		84184021	制冷温度在－40℃以上的立式冷冻箱，容积超过500升，但不超过900升
		84184029	制冷温度在－40℃以上的立式冷冻箱，容积不超过500升
		84185000	其他冷藏或冷冻柜、箱、展示台、陈列箱及似的冷藏箱或冷冻设备
		84143011	电动机额定功率不超过0.4千瓦的冷藏箱或冷冻箱用压缩机
		84143012	电动机额定功率超过0.4千瓦，但不超过5千瓦的冷藏箱或冷冻箱用压缩机
		84143019	电动机驱动的其他制冷设备用压缩机

续表

配额产品目录		协调制度目录	
序号	商品名称	商品编号	商品名称
6	洗衣机	84501200	干衣量不超过 10 公斤的非全自动洗衣机，装有离心甩干机
		84501900	干衣量不超过 10 公斤的其他洗衣机
7	录像设备及其关键件	85211010	磁带型录像机
		85211020	磁带型放像机
		85219010	激光视盘放像机
		85229030	视频信号录制或重放设备的零件、附件（机芯、磁头、磁鼓）
		85253010	特种用途的电视摄像机
		85253090	其他电视摄像机
		85254010	特种用途的静像视频摄像机及其他视频摄录一体机
		85254020	家用型摄录一体机
		85254090	其他静像视频摄像机及其他视频摄录一体机
8	照像机及其机身	90065100	通过镜头取景（单镜头反光式（SLR）），使用胶片宽度不超过 35 毫米的照相机
		90065200	其他使用胶片宽度小于 35 毫米的照相机
		90065300	其他使用胶片宽度为 35 毫米的照相机
		90065900	未列名照相机
9	手表	9101110	原电池或蓄电池驱动仅有机械指示器的手表，表壳用贵金属或包贵金属制成
		91012100	自动上弦的机械手表，表壳用贵金属或包贵金属制成
		91012900	表壳用贵金属或包贵金属制成的其他机械手表
		91021100	其他原电池或蓄电池驱动仅有机械指示器的手表
		91022100	其他自动上弦的手表
		91022900	未列名手表
10	空调器及其压缩机	84151000	独立窗式或壁式空气调节器
		84158110	制冷量不超过 4000 大卡/时，装有制冷装置及一个冷热循环换向阀的空气调节器
		84158210	其他制冷量不超过 4000 大卡/时，装有制冷装置的空气调节器
		84143013	电动机额定功率超过 0.4 千瓦，但不超过 5 千瓦的空气调节器用压缩机
11	录音录像磁带复制设备	85209000	未列名磁带录音机及其他声音录制设备
		85219090	未列名视频信号录制或重放设备
12	汽车起重机及其底盘	87051010	最大起重重量在 100 吨及以上的起重车
		87051090	其他机动起重车
		87060040	汽车起重车底盘、装有发动机
13	电子显微镜	90121000	电子显微镜及衍射设备

续表

配额产品目录		协调制度目录	
序号	商品名称	商品编号	商品名称
14	气流纺纱机	84452020	气流纺纱机
15	电子分色机	90061010	电子分色机

二、1998年特定产品目录

特定产品目录		协调制度目录	
序号	商品名称	商品编号	商品名称
01	功率37千瓦（50匹马力）及以下柴油机	84089092	其他输出功率超过14千瓦，但小于132.39千瓦（180马力）的压燃式活塞内燃发动机
02	离心通风机	84145930	离心通风机
03	斗式提升机	84254990	其他提升机
04	装卸船机	84261120	装船机
		84261131	抓斗式卸船机
		84261139	其他卸船机
05	多用途门机	84263000	门座式起重机及座式旋臂起重机
06	轮胎式起重机和集装箱正面吊	84264110	轮胎式自推进起重机
		84264190	带胶轮的其他自推进起重机械
07	载客电梯	84281010	载客电梯
08	自动扶梯	84284000	自动梯及自动人行道
09	推土机	84291110	发动机输出功率超过235.36千瓦（320马力）的履带式推土机及侧铲推土机
10	震动式压路机	84294011	机重18吨及以上的振动压路机
		84294019	其他机动压路机
11	矿用电铲	84305020	矿用电铲
12	糕点生产线	84381000	糕点加工机器及生产通心粉、面条或类似产品的机器
13	造纸制浆设备	84391000	制造纤维素纸浆的机器
		84392000	纸或纸板的抄造机器
		84393000	纸或纸板的整理机器
14	瓦楞纸板（箱）生产设备	84413090	其他制造箱、盒、管、桶及类似容器的机器，但模制成型机器除外
15	纸浆模塑生产设备	84414000	纸浆、纸或纸板制品模制成型机器
16	胶印机	84431910	平张纸进料式胶印机
		84431990	其他胶印机
17	平网印花机	84435912	平网印刷机
18	清梳联合机	84451100	梳理机

续表

特定产品目录		协调制度目录	
序号	商品名称	商品编号	商品名称
19	精梳机	84451200	精梳机
20	自动络筒机	84454010	自动络筒机
21	整经机	84459000	纺织纱线的其他生产及预处理机器
22	剑杆织机	84463020	织物宽度超过30厘米的剑杆织机
23	片梭织机	84463030	片梭织机
24	非家用缝纫机	84522110	自动平缝机
		84522190	其他自动缝纫机
25	铝电解多功能联合机组	84542010	炉外精炼设备
26	冷室压铸机	84543010	冷室压铸机
27	数控电加工机床	84563010	数控的用放电处理各种材料的加工机床
28	等离子、火焰切割机	84569910	等离子弧切割机
		84569990	其他用化学法、电子束、离子束或离子束等离子弧处理各种材料的加工机床
29	加工中心	84571010	立式加工中心
		84571020	卧式加工中心
		84571030	龙门式加工中心
		84571090	其他加工中心
30	数控卧式车床	84581100	数控卧式车床
31	热模锻压力机	84621090	其他锻造或冲压机床及锻锤
32	木材削片机	84659600	木材、软木、骨、硬质橡胶、硬质塑料或类似硬质材料剖开、切片或刮削机器
33	长材刨片机	84659600	木材、软木、骨、硬质橡胶、硬质塑料或类似硬质材料剖开、切片或刮削机器
34	集散型控制系统	84714991	系统形式的分散型工业过程控制设备
35	水泥生产窑外分解成套设备、立式磨、辊压机	84742010	齿辊式破碎及磨粉机器
		84742090	其他破碎及磨粉机器
36	水泥混凝土搅拌站	84743100	混凝土或砂浆混合机器
37	轮胎外胎成型机	84775900	其他模塑或成型机器
38	烟草加工及制作机器	84781000	烟草加工及制作机器
		84789000	烟草加工及制作机器的零件
39	沥青混凝土摊铺机	84791010	沥青混凝土摊铺机
40	模具（汽车、家用电器）	84804100	金属、硬质合金用注模或压模
41	塑料或橡胶用注模或压模	84807100	塑料或橡胶用注模或压模

续表

特定产品目录		协调制度目录	
序号	商品名称	商品编号	商品名称
42	大型减速机	84834020	行星齿轮减速器
43	电力变压器	85042320	额定容量在400兆伏安及以上的液体介质变压器
44	用户环境载波设备	85175090	未列名有线载波通信设备及有线数字通信设备
45	图文传真机	85172100	传真机
46	电子音频功率放大器	85184000	音频扩大器
47	数字式卫星通讯地面站	85252019	其他卫星地面站设备
48	无线移动通信系统（含蜂窝、集群、无线寻呼、一点多址）	85173013	数字移动通信交换机
		85173091	模拟式移动通信交换机
		85252022	手持（包括车载）式无线电话机
		85252029	其他移动通讯设备
		85252092	移动通信基地站
		85279010	无线寻呼机
49	黑白摄像机	85253090	其他电视摄像机
50	卫星电视地面接收设备	85252011	电视用卫星地面站设备
		85281210	彩色的卫星电视接收机
		85291020	无线电收音机及其组合机、电视接收机用各种天线或天线反射器及其零件
51	电视共用天线及电缆电视分配系统	85291090	品目85.25至85.28所列其他装置或设备用各种天线或天线反射器及其零件
52	消防灭火、报警装置	85311000	防盗或防火报警器及类似装置
53	六氟化硫断路器（含组合电器）	85352900	用于电压不低于72.5千伏线路的自动断路器
54	电缆	85445910	其他电缆，耐压超过80伏，但不超过1000伏
55	光缆	85447000	光缆
56	起拔道捣固车	86040099	铁道及电车道未列名维修或服务车
57	牵引车（除汽车牵引车外）	87019000	未列名牵引车、拖拉机（品目87.09的牵引车除外）
58	电动轮自卸车	87041030	电动轮非公路用货运自卸车
59	油船	89012011	载重量不超过10万吨的成品油船
		89012012	载重量超过10万吨，但不超过30万吨的成品油船
		89012013	载重量超过30万吨的成品油船

续表

特定产品目录		协调制度目录	
序号	商品名称	商品编号	商品名称
		89012021	载重量不超过15万吨的原油船
		89012022	载重量超过15万吨，但不超过30万吨的原油船
		89012023	载重量超过30万吨的原油船
		89012031	容积在2万立方米及以下液化石油气船
		89012032	容积在2万立方米以上液化石油气船
		89012041	容积在2万立方米及以下液化天然气船
		89012042	容积在2万立方米以上液化天然气船
		89012090	其他油船
60	冷藏船	89013000	冷藏船
61	机动货运船舶及客货兼运船舶	89019021	可载标准箱在6000箱及以下机动集装箱船
		89019022	可载标准箱在6000箱以上机动集装箱船
		89019031	载重量在2万吨及以下机动滚装船
		89019032	载重量在2万吨以上机动滚装船
		89019041	载重量不超过15万吨机动散货船
		89019042	载重量超过15万吨，但不超过30吨机动散货船
		89019043	载重量超过30万吨的机动散货船
		89019050	机动多用途船
		89019080	其他机动货运船舶及客货兼运船舶
62	机动捕鱼船、加工船及其他加工保藏鱼类产品的船舶	89020010	机动捕鱼船、加工船及其他加工保藏鱼类产品的船舶
63	拖轮及顶推船	89040000	拖轮及顶推船
64	挖泥船	89051000	挖泥船
65	正射投影仪	90083010	正射投影仪
66	海洋重力仪	90158000	其他大地测量、水道测量、海洋、水文、气象或地球物理用仪器及装置
67	医用超声显像诊断仪	90181210	B型超声波诊断仪
68	牙科治疗设备	90184910	装有牙科设备的牙科用椅
69	直线加速器	90189090	医疗、外科、牙科或兽医用α、β、γ射线的应用设备
70	医用X线诊断机组	90221300	其他，牙科用X射线应用设备
		90221400	其他，医疗、外科或兽医用X射线应用设备
71	X射线探伤仪	90221990	其他X射线的应用设备
72	单光子发射计算机断层扫描装置	90222100	其他医疗、外科或兽医用仪器及器具

续表

特定产品目录		协调制度目录	
序号	商品名称	商品编号	商品名称
	(ECT)		
73	核磁共振波谱仪	90278090	品目90.27所列的其他仪器及装置
74	X射线衍射仪	90301000	离子射线的测量或检验仪器及装置
75	数字频率计	90304010	测试频率在12.4千兆赫兹以下的数字式频率计
76	动平衡机	90311000	机械零件平衡试验机
77	光纤光缆测试仪(含光时域反射计，光纤熔接机，光功率计，光源)	90318010	光纤通信及光纤性能测试仪

对外贸易经济合作部关于棉纱、棉涤纶纱、棉坯布、棉涤纶坯布出口经营管理有关问题的通知

〔1998〕外经贸管出函字第103号

1998年4月15日

各省、自治区、直辖市及计划单列市外经贸委(厅、局)，中国纺织品进出口总公司，中国纺织品进出口商会：

为贯彻中央经济工作会议和全国外经贸工作会议精神，落实《国务院关于纺织工业深化改革调整结构解困扭亏工作有关问题的通知》(国发〔1998〕2号)，适应我国纺织行业出口发展的新形势，支持我国纺织产品开拓国际市场，促进纺织工作的进一步发展，决定对棉纱、绵涤纶纱、棉坯布、棉涤纶坯布(以下简称两纱两布)出口经营体制进行改革。现将有关问题通知如下：

一、从1998年6月1日起，两纱两布出口由经外贸部批准的享有两纱两布出口经营权的各类进出口企业(包括自营出口生产企业)自行对外成交，不再实行统一联合经营。

二、为履行中日政府商定的中方对输日纺织品实行自主管理，使中日经贸关系健康发展，对日本市场出口两纱两布，仍须与日本中大株式会社总代理成交签约；鉴于纺织品贸易的实际情况，取消华润纺织品有限公司、澳门南光纺织品有限公司、韩国环宇贸易株式会社对香港、澳门、韩国市场出口两纱两布的总代理。

三、国家对两纱两布出口仍实行计划配额(日本市场单列)和出口许可证管理。各外经贸部主管部门要严格按照外经贸部下达的两纱两布出口配额进行安排，并支持经营能力强、效益好的外贸企业、生产企业出口；外经贸部授权的发证机关要严格按照出口配额许可证管理的有关规定核发出口许可证。

四、对两纱两布出口许可证发证机关做如下调整(包括外商投资企业出口和各种贸易方式项下出口)：对向欧盟、美国等被动配额地区出口两纱两布由各省级外经贸主管部门核发出口许可证；对向日本和其他国家、地区出口两纱两布，由外经贸部驻各地特派员办事处核发出口许可证。各部委直属总公司仍由配额许可证事务局核发出口许可证。

五、中国纺织品进出口商会全面负责两纱两布出口的协调工作，制订出口价格、市场及客户的具体协调办法，及时向外经贸部报告出口情况及存在的问题，并提出相应的对策措施。

六、各出口经营企业和发证机关应严格执行本通知的各项规定，对违反者将视情节按有关规定进行处理。

七、本通知自1998年6月1日起执行，此前颁布的一切有关两纱两布出口经营管理的办法、规定与本通知的规定不符的，以本通知为准。

国家发展计划委员会、对外贸易经济合作部、海关总署关于调整部分一般配额和特定登记商品进口管理（税号）目录的通知

计经贸〔1998〕803号

1998年5月11日

各省、自治区、直辖市及计划单列市计委（计经委）、外经贸委（厅、局）、外经贸部驻各地特派员办事处、配额许可证事务局，广东分署，各直属海关，国务院有关部门：

根据国务院关税税则委员会和海关总署重新修订的1998年进出口税则以及国家对进口管理的需要，现对一般配额商品和特定登记商品进口管理范围内的腈纶纤维、二醋酸纤维丝束、粮食、农药、彩色感光材料、化纤布等6种商品的税号目录进行调整（详见附表），并就有关事项通知如下：

一、自文件下达之日起，上述6种商品原公布的税号目录一律作废，按调整后的新目录执行。其他21种一般配额商品和特定登记商品进口管理的税号目录仍继续执行原国家计委、外经贸部、海关总署《关于公布调整后的一般配额进口商品目录和特定登记进口商品目录的通知》（计经贸〔1996〕666号）中公布的目录。

二、上述调整税号目录后的商品及未进行调整的其他商品的进口管理政策，仍按照原国家计委、外经贸部、中国人民银行、海关总署、国家外汇管理局联合发布的《一般商品进口配额管理暂行办法》（计经贸〔1994〕421号）、《一般商品进口配额管理暂行办法实施细则》、《特定商品进口自动登记管理暂行办法》（计经贸〔1994〕420号）和原国家计委、外经贸部、海关总署联合发布的《关于实施调整后的一般配额进口商品和特定登记进口商品管理政策通知》（计经贸〔1996〕1177号）的规定执行。

附件：一、国家发展计划委员会一般配额进口商品（税号）修订目录

二、国家发展计划委员会特定登记进口商品（税号）修订目录

附件一

国家发展计划委员会
一般配额进口商品（税号）修订目录

进口许可证		协调制度目录		
序号	商品名称	商品编号	商品名称	单位
4	腈纶纤维	54023990	其他合成纤维长丝变形纱线	公斤
		54024990	其他合成纤维长丝单纱，未加捻或捻度每米不超过50转	公斤
		54025990	其他合成纤维长丝单纱，捻度每米超过50转	公斤
		54026990	未列名合成纤维长丝多股纱线或缆线	公斤
		55013000	聚丙烯腈或变性聚丙烯腈长丝丝束	公斤
		55033000	聚丙烯腈或变性聚丙烯腈短纤，未梳或未经其他纺前加工	公斤
		55063000	聚丙烯腈或变性聚丙烯腈短纤，已梳或经其他纺前加工	公斤
		55093100	含聚丙烯腈或变性聚丙烯腈短纤85%及以上的单纱	公斤
		55093200	含聚丙烯腈或变性聚丙烯腈短纤85%及以上的多股纱线或缆线	公斤
		55096100	含聚丙烯腈或变性聚丙烯腈短纤85%以下主要或仅与羊毛、动物细毛混纺的纱线	公斤
		55096200	含聚丙烯腈或变性聚丙烯腈短纤85%以下主要或仅与棉混纺的纱线	公斤
		55096900	含聚丙烯腈或变性聚丙烯腈短纤85%以下，与其他纤维混纺的纱线	公斤
12	二醋酸纤维丝束	54033310	二醋酸纤维丝束	公斤
		55020010	二醋酸纤维长丝丝束	公斤

附件二

国家发展计划委员会
特定登记进口商品（税号）修订目录

序号	计委分类	协调制度目录		
	商品名称	商品编号	商品名称	单位
1	粮食	10011000	硬粒小麦	公斤
		10019010	种用小麦	公斤
		10019090	其他小麦及混合麦，硬粒小麦除外	公斤
		10059000	玉米，种用除外	公斤
		10061010	种用稻谷	公斤
		10061090	其他稻谷	公斤
		10062000	糙米	公斤
		10063000	精米，不论是否磨光或上光	公斤
		10064000	碎米	公斤
6	彩色感光材料	37013090	其他未曝光的硬片及软片，任何一边超过 255 毫米	平方米
		37019100	其他未曝光的彩色摄影用硬片及软片	平方米
		37023100	未曝光的彩色摄影用无齿孔胶卷，宽度不超过 105 毫米	米
		37024100	未曝光的彩色摄影用无齿孔胶卷，宽度超过 610 毫米，长度超过 200 米	平方米
		37024390	未列名未曝光的无齿孔胶卷，宽度超过 610 毫米，长度不超过 200 米	平方米
		37024490	未列名未曝光的无齿孔胶卷，宽度超过 105 毫米，但不超过 610 毫米	平方米
		37025100	其他未曝光的彩色摄影用胶卷，宽度不超过 16 毫米，长度不超过 14 米	米
		37025200	其他未曝光的彩色摄影用胶卷，宽度不超过 16 毫米，长度超过 14 米	米
		37025410	未曝光的非幻灯片用彩色摄影胶卷，宽度为 35 毫米，长度不超过 2 米	米
		37025490	其他未曝光的非幻灯片用彩色摄影胶卷，宽度超过 16 毫米，但不超过 35 毫米，长度不超过 30 米	米
		37025590	其他未曝光的彩色摄影胶卷，宽度超过 16 毫米，但不超过 35 毫米，长度超过 30 米	米

续表

序号	计委分类	协调制度目录		
	商品名称	商品编号	商品名称	单位
		37025690	未曝光的彩色摄影胶卷，宽度超过 35 毫米	米
		37029100	其他未曝光的胶卷，宽度不超过 16 毫米，长度不超过 14 米	米
		37031010	未曝光成卷的摄影感光纸及纸板，宽度超过 610 毫米	公斤
		37032010	其他未曝光的彩色摄影用感光纸及纸板	公斤
7	农药	29214300	氟乐灵原药	公斤
		29242990	叶蝉散原药	公斤
		29269090	灭扫利原药、来福灵原药、功夫原药	公斤
		29309090	拿扑净原药、杀草丹原药、巴丹原药	公斤
		29329990	呋喃丹原药	公斤
		29332900	扑海因原药	公斤
		29333990	精稳杀得原药、乐斯本原药、莫比朗原药、速克灵原药	公斤
		29339000	精禾草克原药	公斤
		29341000	尼索朗原药	公斤
		29349090	硕丹、韩丹原药	公斤
		38081019	其他零售包装的杀虫剂	公斤
		38081090	非零售包装的杀虫剂	公斤
		38082010	零售包装杀菌剂	公斤
		38082090	非零售包装的杀菌剂	公斤
		38083011	零售包装除草剂	公斤
		38083019	非零售包装除草剂	公斤
		38083099	非零售包装抗萌剂及植物生长调节剂	公斤
		38084000	消毒剂	公斤
11	化纤布	54071010	尼龙或其他聚酰胺高强力纱纺制的机织物	米
		54071020	聚酯高强力纱纺制的机织物	米
		54072000	合成纤维长丝扁条及类似品的机织物	米
		54074100	含尼龙或其他聚酰胺长丝 85% 及以上未漂白或漂白的机织物	米
		54074200	含尼龙或其他聚酰胺长丝 85% 及以上染色的机织物	米
		54074300	含尼龙或其他聚酰胺长丝 85% 及以上色织的机织物	米
		54074400	含尼龙或其他聚酰胺长丝 85% 及以上印花的机织物	米
		54075100	含聚酯变形长丝 85% 及以上未漂白或漂白的机织物	米

续表

序号	计委分类	协调制度目录		
	商品名称	商品编号	商品名称	单位
		54075200	含聚酯变形长丝85%及以上染色的机织物	米
		54075300	含聚酯变形长丝85%及以上色织的机织物	米
		54075400	含聚酯变形长丝85%及以上印花的机织物	米
		54076100	含聚酯非变形长丝85%及以上的机织物	米
		54076900	其他含聚酯长丝85%及以上的机织物	米
		54077100	含其他合成纤维长丝85%及以上未漂白或漂白的机织物	米
		54077200	含其他合成纤维长丝85%及以上染色的机织物	米
		54077300	含其他合成纤维长丝85%及以上色织的机织物	米
		54077400	含其他合成纤维长丝85%及以上印花的机织物	米
		54078100	含合成纤维长丝85%以下主要与或仅与棉混纺的未漂白或漂白机织物	米
		54078200	含合成纤维长丝85%以下主要与或仅与棉混纺的染色机织物	米
		54078300	含合成纤维长丝85%以下主要与或仅与棉混纺的色织机织物	米
		54078400	含合成纤维长丝85%以下主要与或仅与棉混纺的印花机织物	米
		54079100	含合成纤维长丝85%以下的其他未漂白或漂白机织物	米
		54079200	含合成纤维长丝85%以下的其他染色机织物	米
		54079300	含合成纤维长丝85%以下的其他色织机织物	米
		54079400	含合成纤维长丝85%以下的其他印花机织物	米
		54081000	粘胶纤维高强力纱的机织物	米
		54082110	含胶粘纤维长丝85%及以上未漂白或漂白机织物	米
		54082120	含醋酸纤维长丝85%及以上未漂白或漂白机织物	米
		54082190	含其他人造纤维长丝、扁条或类似品85%及以上的未漂白或漂白机织物	米
		54082210	含胶粘纤维长丝85%及以上染色机织物	米
		54082220	含醋酸纤维长丝85%及以上染色机织物	米
		54082290	含其他人造纤维长丝、扁条或类似品85%及以上的染色机织物	米
		54082310	含胶粘纤维长丝85%及以上色织机织物	米
		54082320	含醋酸纤维长丝85%及以上色织机织物	米
		54082390	含其他人造纤维长丝、扁条或类似品85%及以上的色织机织物	米

续表

序号	计委分类	协调制度目录		
	商品名称	商品编号	商品名称	单位
		54082410	含胶粘纤维长丝85%及以上印花机织物	米
		54082420	含醋酸纤维长丝85%及以上印花机织物	米
		54082490	含其他人造纤维长丝、扁条或类似品85%及以上的印花机织物	米
		54083100	含人造纤维长丝85%以下的未漂白或漂白机织物	米
		54083200	含人造纤维长丝85%以下染色机织物	米
		54083300	含人造纤维长丝85%以下色织机织物	米
		54083400	含人造纤维长丝85%以下印花机织物	米
		55121900	其他含聚酯短纤85%及以上机织物	米/公斤
		55122100	含聚丙烯腈或变性聚丙烯腈短纤85%及以上的未漂白或漂白机织物	米/公斤
		55122900	其他含聚丙烯腈或变性聚丙烯腈短纤85%及以上的机织物	米/公斤
		55129100	其他含合成纤维短纤85%及以上的未漂白或漂白机织物	米/公斤
		5512990	其他含合成纤维短纤85%及以上的机织物	米/公斤
		55131110	含聚酯短纤85%以下主要或仅与棉混纺的未漂白平纹机织物，每平方米重量不超过170克	米/公斤
		55131120	含聚酯短纤85%以下主要或仅与棉混纺的漂白平纹机织物，每平方米重量不超过170克	米/公斤
		55131210	含聚酯短纤85%以下主要或仅与棉混纺的未漂白三线或四线斜纹机织物，包括双面斜纹机织物，每平方米重量不超过170克	米/公斤
		55131220	含聚脂短纤85%以下主要或仅与棉混纺的漂白三线或四线斜纹机织物，包括双面斜纹机织物，每平方米重量不超过170克	米/公斤
		55131310	其他含聚酯短纤85%以下主要或仅与棉混纺的未漂白机织物，每平方米重量不超过170克	米/公斤
		55131320	其他含聚酯短纤85%以下主要或仅与棉混纺的漂白机织物，每平方米重量不超过170克	米/公斤
		55131900	其他含合成纤维短纤85%以下主要或仅与棉混纺的未漂白或漂白机织物，每平方米重量不超过170克	米/公斤
		55132100	含聚酯短纤85%以下主要或仅与棉混纺的染色平纹机织物，每平方米重量不超过170克	米/公斤
		55132200	含聚酯短纤85%以下主要或仅与棉混纺的染色三线或四线斜纹机织物，包括双面斜纹机织物，每平方米重量不超过170克	米/公斤

续表

序号	计委分类	协调制度目录		
	商品名称	商品编号	商品名称	单位
		55132300	其他含聚酯短纤85%以下主要或仅与棉混纺的染色机织物，每平方米重量不超过170克	米/公斤
		55132900	其他含合成纤维短纤85%以下主要或仅与棉混纺的染色机织物，每平方米重量不超过170克	米/公斤
		55133100	含聚酯短纤85%以下主要或仅与棉混纺的色织平纹机织物，每平方米重量不超过170克	米/公斤
		55133200	含聚酯短纤85%以下主要或仅与棉混纺的色织三线或四线斜纹机织物，包括双面斜纹机织物，每平方米重量不超过170克	米/公斤
		55133300	其他含聚酯短纤85%以下主要或仅与棉混纺的色织机织物，每平方米重量不超过170克	米/公斤
		55133900	其他含合成纤维短纤85%以下主要或仅与棉混纺的色织机织物，每平方米重量不超过170克	米/公斤
		55134100	含聚酯短纤85%以下主要或仅与棉混纺的印花平纹机织物，每平方米重量不超过170克	米/公斤
		55134200	含聚酯短纤85%以下主要或仅与棉混纺的色织三线或四线斜纹机织物，包括双面斜纹机织物，每平方米重量不超过170克	米/公斤
		55134300	其他含聚酯短纤85%以下主要或仅与棉混纺的印花机织物，每平方米重量不超过170克	米/公斤
		55134900	其他含合成纤维短纤85%以下主要或仅与棉混纺的印花其他机织物，每平方米重量不超过170克	米/公斤
		55141110	含聚酯短纤85%以下主要或仅与棉混纺的未漂白平纹机织物，每平方米重量超过170克	米/公斤
		55141120	含聚酯短纤85%以下主要或仅与棉混纺的漂白平纹机织物，每平方米重量超过170克	米/公斤
		55141210	含聚酯短纤85%以下主要或仅与棉混纺的未漂白三线或四线斜纹机织物，包括双面斜纹机织物，每平方米重量超过170克	米/公斤
		55141220	含聚酯短纤85%以下主要或仅与棉混纺的漂白三线或四线斜纹机织物，包括双面斜纹机织物，每平方米重量超过170克	米/公斤
		55141310	其他含聚酯短纤85%以下主要或仅与棉混纺的未漂白机织物，每平方米重量超过170克	米/公斤
		55141320	其他含聚酯短纤85%以下主要或仅与棉混纺的漂白机织物，每平方米重量超过170克	米/公斤

续表

序号	计委分类	协调制度目录		
	商品名称	商品编号	商品名称	单位
		55141900	其他含合成纤维短纤85%以下主要或仅与棉混纺的未漂白或漂白机织物，每平方米重量超过170克	米/公斤
		55142100	含聚酯短纤85%以下主要或仅与棉混纺的染色平纹机织物，每平方米重量超过170克	米/公斤
		55142200	含聚酯短纤85%以下主要或仅与棉混纺的染色三线或四线斜纹机织物，包括双面斜纹机织物，每平方米重量超过170克	米/公斤
		55142300	其他含聚酯短纤85%以下主要或仅与棉混纺的染色机织物，每平方米重量超过170克	米/公斤
		55142900	其他含合成纤维短纤85%以下主要或仅与棉混纺的染色机织物，每平方米重量超过170克	米/公斤
		55143100	含聚酯短纤85%以下主要或仅与棉混纺的色织平纹机织物，每平方米重量超过170克	米/公斤
		55143200	含聚酯短纤85%以下主要或仅与棉混纺的色织三线或四线斜纹机织物，包括双面斜纹机织物，每平方米重量超过170克	米/公斤
		55143300	其他含聚酯短纤85%以下主要或仅与棉混纺的色织机织物，每平方米重量超过170克	米/公斤
		55143900	其他含合成纤维短纤85%以下主要或仅与棉混纺的色织机织物，每平方米重量超过170克	米/公斤
		55144100	含聚酯短纤85%以下主要或仅与棉混纺的印花平纹机织物，每平方米重量超过170克	米/公斤
		55144200	含聚酯短纤85%以下主要或仅与棉混纺的印花三线或四线斜纹机织物，包括双面斜纹机织物，每平方米重量超过170克	米/公斤
		55144300	其他含聚酯短纤85%以下主要或仅与棉混纺的印花机织物，每平方米重量超过170克	米/公斤
		55144900	其他合成纤维短纤85%以下主要或仅与棉混纺的印花机织物，每平方米重量超过170克	米/公斤
		55151100	含聚酯短纤85%以下主要或仅与粘胶纤维短纤混纺的机织物	米/公斤
		55151200	含聚酯短纤85%以下主要或仅与化学纤维长丝混纺的机织物	米/公斤
		55151300	含聚酯短纤85%以下主要或仅与羊毛或动物细毛混纺的机织物	米/公斤
		55151900	含聚酯短纤85%以下与其他纤维混纺的机织物	米/公斤
		55152100	含聚丙烯腈或变性聚丙烯腈短纤85%以下主	米/公斤

续表

序号	计委分类	协调制度目录		
	商品名称	商品编号	商品名称	单位
			要或仅与化学纤维长丝混纺的机织物	
		55152200	含聚丙烯腈或变性聚丙烯腈短纤 85%以下主要或仅与羊毛或动物细毛混纺的机织物	米/公斤
		55152900	含聚丙烯腈或变性聚丙烯腈短纤 85%以下与其他纤维混纺的机织物	米/公斤
		55159100	其他含合成纤维短纤 85%以下主要或仅与化学纤维长丝混纺的机织物	米/公斤
		55159200	其他含合成纤维短纤 85%以下主要或仅与羊毛或动物细毛混纺的机织物	米/公斤
		55159900	其他含合成纤维短纤 85%以下与其他纤维混纺的机织物	米/公斤
		55161100	含人造纤维短纤 85%及以上的未漂白或漂白机织物	米/公斤
		55161200	含人造纤维短纤 85%及以上的染色机织物	米/公斤
		55161300	含人造纤维短纤 85%及以上的色织机织物	米/公斤
		55161400	含人造纤维短纤 85%及以上的印花机织物	米/公斤
		55162100	含人造纤维短纤 85%以下主要或仅与化学纤维长丝混纺的未漂白或漂白机织物	米/公斤
		55162200	含人造纤维短纤 85%以下主要或仅与化学纤维长丝混纺的染色机织物	米/公斤
		55162300	含人造纤维短纤 85%以下主要或仅与化学纤维长丝混纺的色织机织物	米/公斤
		55162400	含人造纤维短纤 85%以下主要或仅与化学纤维长丝混纺的印花机织物	米/公斤
		55163100	含人造纤维短纤 85%以下主要或仅与羊毛或动物细毛混纺的未漂白或漂白机织物	米/公斤
		55163200	含人造纤维短纤 85%以下主要或仅与羊毛或动物细毛混纺的染色机织物	米/公斤
		55163300	含人造纤维短纤 85%以下主要或仅与羊毛或动物细毛混纺的色织机织物	米/公斤
		55163400	含人造纤维短纤 85%以下主要或仅与羊毛或动物细毛混纺的印花机织物	米/公斤
		55164100	含人造纤维短纤 85%以下主要或仅与棉混纺的未漂白或漂白机织物	米/公斤
		55164200	含人造纤维短纤 85%以下主要或仅与棉混纺的染色机织物	米/公斤
		55164300	含人造纤维短纤 85%以下主要或仅与棉混纺的印花机织物	米/公斤

续表

序号	计委分类	协调制度目录		
	商品名称	商品编号	商品名称	单位
		55164400	含人造纤维短纤 85%以下主要或仅与棉混纺的印花机织物	米/公斤
		55169100	含人造纤维短纤 85%以下与其他纤维混纺的未漂白或漂白机织物	米/公斤
		55169200	含人造纤维短纤 85%以下与其他纤维混纺的染色机织物	米/公斤
		55169300	含人造纤维短纤 85%以下与其他纤维混纺的色织机织物	米/公斤
		55169400	含人造纤维短纤 85%以下与其他纤维混纺的印花机织物	米/公斤
		58013100	化学纤维制不割绒的纬起绒织物	米/公斤
		58013200	化学纤维制割绒的灯芯绒	米/公斤
		58013300	化学纤维制其他纬起绒织物	米/公斤
		58013400	化学纤维制不割绒的经起绒织物（棱纹绸）	米/公斤
		58013500	化学纤维制割绒的经起绒织物	米/公斤
		58013600	化学纤维制绳绒织物	米/公斤
		62011390	化学纤维制男式其他大衣、雨衣、斗蓬及类似品	件
		62019390	化学纤维制男式带风帽的防寒短上衣、防风衣及类似品	件
		62021390	化学纤维制女式其他大衣、雨衣、斗蓬及类似品	件
		62029390	化学纤维制女式带风帽的防寒短上衣、防风衣及类似品	件
		62031200	合成纤维制男式西服套装	套
		62032300	合成纤维制男式便服套装	套
		62033300	合成纤维制男式上衣	件
		62034390	合成纤维制男裤	条
		62041300	合成纤维制女式西服套装	套
		62042300	合成纤维制女式便服套装	套
		62043300	合成纤维制女式上衣	件
		62044300	合成纤维制女式连衣裙	件
		62044400	人造纤维制女式连衣裙	件
		62045300	合成纤维制女式裙子及裙裤	件
		62046300	合成纤维制女裤	条
		62053000	化学纤维制男衬衫	件
		62064000	化学纤维制女衬衫	件
		62113390	化学纤维制其他男式服装	件
		62114300	化学纤维制其他女式服装	件

对外贸易经济合作部关于加强易制毒化学品进口管理的通知

〔1998〕外经贸管发第377号

1998年5月26日

各省、自治区、直辖市及计划单列市外经贸委（厅、局），深圳经发局，各特派员办事处，配额许可证事务局，各部委直属公司，各进出口商会：

为贯彻落实1998年全国禁毒工作领导小组会议精神，进一步加强易制毒化学品进口管理工作，根据我部《易制毒化学品进出口管理暂行规定》（〔1997〕外经贸管发258号），现就加强易制毒化学品进口管理工作通知如下：

一、各省、自治区、直辖市及计划单列市外经贸委（厅、局）（以下简称地方外经贸主管部门）要重视易制毒化学品进口管理工作。在企业申请易制毒化学品进口时要审核：

（一）进口商的进出口经营权，资信情况及经营状况。

（二）申请单位出具的保函，保证不将进口的易制毒化学品用于制造毒品或流入非法制毒渠道，不得转口或复出口。

（三）进口合同或来料加工合同。要求企业如实填报国外客户名称、国别（地区）、地址、电话。

（四）国内最终用户（生产企业）的名称、地址、电话、联系人、购买易制毒化学品的用途、以及消耗数量是否合理。

二、国家各部委直属公司负责审核所属企业的进口申请，审核内容同上。

三、地方外经贸主管部门及国家各部委直属公司向对外贸易经济合作部（以下简称外经贸部）上报申请易制毒化学品进口时，应提供下列文件：

（一）易制毒化学品进口申请表（见附件。该表可复印，由地方外经贸主管部门或各部委直属公司提供给申领企业）。该申请表由企业如实填写，加盖企业公章，一式两份（一份留地方外经贸主管部门或各部委直属公司，一份报外经贸部）。

（二）地方外经贸主管部门或国家各部委直属公司出具的关于企业申请进口易制毒化学品的正式文件。

（三）地方外经贸主管部门或各部委直属公司转报的企业保证该批易制毒化学品仅用于企业正常生产，不用于制毒、不流入非法制毒渠道的保函。

（四）进口合同。以来料加工方式进口易制毒化学品，应提供与外商签订的来料加工合同。

（五）国内用户的详细资料，包括名称、地址、电话、联系人、进口数量、经营范围及该批易制毒化学品的最终用途。

（六）以进料加工、来料加工方式进口易制毒化学品，应提供与国内加工生产企业签订的加工协议。

四、易制毒化学品进口审批程序如下：

（一）外经贸部在收到有效申请后10个工作日内办理审批。对符合规定的签发《外经贸部易制毒化学品进口批复单》，批复单自批复之日起30日内有效，逾期自行作废；对不符合规定的申请将予以退回。

（二）进口企业凭《外经贸部易制毒化学品进口批复单》向外经贸部授权的发证机关申领进口许可证。

五、易制毒化学品进口后的核查。

为加强对易制毒化学品进口后的核查，进口企业应将进口易制毒化学品的销售和使用情况逐月上报所在地方外经贸主管部门或隶属的部委直属公司。地方外经贸主管部门或国家各部委直属以司应督促企业按时上报，并不定期检查企业销售和使用易制毒化学品的情况。对不按时报告的企业，将不再批准其进口易制毒化学品。外经贸部将不定期对地方外经贸主管部门或各部委直属公司易制毒化学品的进口管理情况进行检查。

六、外商投资企业进口易制毒化学品，按照我部颁布的《关于印发〈外商投资企业易制毒化学品进出口审批原则和审批程序〉的通知》(〔1997〕外经贸资三函字第197号）办理。

七、本通知自下发之日起开始执行。

附件：易制毒化学品进口审请表及填写说明

附　件

易制毒化学品进口申请表

1. 申请单位:				2. 进口商:	
3. 进口商地址:				4. 联系人、电话:	
5. 出口国家（地区）:				6. 原产地国家（地区）:	
7. 贸易方式:				8. 商品用途:	
9. 商品名称:				商品编码:	
10. 规格、等级	11. 单位	12. 数量	13. 单价	14. 总值（USD）	15. 折合美元
16. 国外出口商名称	17. 地址				18. 电话
19. 国内最终用户名称	20. 地址				21. 电话

易制毒化学品进口申请表填写说明

1. 申请单位填写申请进口易制毒化学品的企业名称。

2. 进口商填写对外签订进出口合同或来料加工合同的我国有进出口经营权的企业名称及其企业代码，并加盖企业公章。

3. 出口国家（地区）填写最初向我国发货，在中转国不发生任何商业交易的国家、地区。

4. 原产地国家（地区）填写生产该商品的国家（地区）。

5. 商品用途可填写生产用、自用、内销。

6. 数量单位统一为公斤。

7. 单位以美元计价。

8. 国内最终用户为最终使用该批易制毒化学品的生产企业。

中华人民共和国对外贸易经济合作部关于调整8种特定机电产品进行国际招标的通知

〔1998〕外经贸机电函字第119号

1998年12月24日

各部门、地区机电产品进出口办公室：

为加强特定机电产品的国际招标采购工作，经研究决定，原不规定必须进行国际招标的自动扶梯等8种特定产品转为进行国际招标采购的特定产品。

自1999年1月1日起，本文附件所列产品，按特定产品的有关招标规定进行国际招标后，由各地区、部门机电产品进出口办公室转报外经贸部（机电司）办理进口手续。

特此通知。

附件：8种转为进行国际招标的特定产品

附　件

八种转为进行国际招标的特定产品

序号	商品名称	商品编号
1	自动扶梯	84284000
2	数控电加工机床	84563010
3	加工中心	84571010
		84571020
		84571030
		84571090
4	集散型控制系统	84714991.01
5	沥青混凝土摊铺机	84791010
6	水泥生产窑外分解成套设备	84742010.01
	（包括立式磨、辊压机）	84742090.91
7	电力变压器	85042320
8	六氟化硫断路器	85352900.01
	（含组合电器）	

利用外资

中华人民共和国国家旅游局
中华人民共和国对外贸易经济合作部令

第11号

《中外合资旅行社试点暂行办法》已于1998年10月29日经国务院批准，现予发布，自发布之日起施行。

局长　何光暐　　部长　石广生

1998年12月2日

中外合资旅行社试点暂行办法

第一条　为了进一步扩大旅游业的对外开放，促进旅游业的发展，根据《中华人民共和国中外合资经营企业法》和《旅行社管理条例》及有关法律、法规，制定本办法。

第二条　本办法适用于外国公司，企业同中国公司、企业在中国境内设立的中外合资旅行社（以下简称“合资旅行社”）。

第三条　申请设立合资旅行社，中国合营者应当符合下列条件：

（一）为国际旅行社；

（二）申请前3年平均每年外联人数超过3万人天；

（三）申请前3年平均每年旅游业务销售总额超过5000万元；

（四）为中国旅游行业协会的正式会员。

第四条　申请设立合资旅行社，外国合营者应当符合下列条件：

（一）为经营国际旅游的旅行社或拥有全资的经营国际旅游的旅行社的企业；

（二）旅游业务年销售总额5000万美元以上；

（三）加入国际或本国的电脑预订网络，或者已经形成自己的电脑预订网络；

（四）为其本国旅游行业协会的正式会员。

第五条　设立的合资旅行社应当符合以下条件：

（一）注册资本不少于500万元人民币；

（二）企业形式为有限责任公司；

（三）中方出资占注册资本的比例不低于51%；

（四）法定代表人由中方委派；

（五）有符合要求的营业场所、营业设施、经营人员；

（六）合资期限不超过20年。

第六条　合资旅行社按国际旅行社经营入境旅游的规定，交纳旅行社质量保证金。

第七条　合资游行社的审批程序为：

（一）中国合营者向所在地的省（自治区、直辖市）或计划单列市旅游行政管理部门呈报设立合资旅行社的项目建议书和可行性研究报告等文件。省级旅游行政管理部门初审后转报国家旅游局。

中国合营者为中央企业的，由其主管部门初审后转报国家旅游局。

国家旅游局依据国家有关旅游管理的法律、法规对上报文件进行审批。

（二）中国合营者在得到国家旅游局的同意批复后，向所在地的省级外经贸主管部门呈报设立合资旅行社的合同、章程等文件。省级外经贸主管部门初审后转报外经贸部。

中国合营者为中央企业的，由其主管部门初审后转报外经贸部。

外经贸部依照国家有关外商投资的法律、法规对上报文件进行审批。

（三）获得批准同意设立的项目，中国合营者凭外经贸部颁发的《外商投资企业批准证书》和国家旅游局颁发的《旅行社业务经营许可证》，按照规定办理注册登记和税务登记手续。

第八条 申请设方合资旅行社应当提交以下文件：

（一）中国合营者资格证明材料，包括：营业执照副本、旅行社业务经营许可证、申请前3年的业务年检报告、有关旅游行业协会的会员证明；

（二）外国合营者的资格证明材料，包括：注册登记副本、银行资信证明、会计师事务所出具的财务状况证明材料、相关电脑公司提供的入网证明、本国旅游行业协会会员证明、申请前1年的年度报告；

（三）合资旅行社项目建议书；

（四）合资旅行社可行性研究报告；

（五）合资旅行社的合同与章程；

（六）法律、法规和审批机构要求提供的其他材料。

第九条 每个外国合营者只能在中国境内投资设立一家合资旅行社。

第十条 试点阶段暂不允许合资旅行社设立分支机构。

第十一条 合资旅行社可以经营入境旅游业务和国内旅游业务。

第十二条 合资旅行社暂不允许经营中国公民赴外国及香港特别行政区、澳门、台湾地区旅游业务。

第十三条 合资旅行社经营特种旅游项目和到特殊地区旅游的项目，须报国宾旅游局及有关部门审批。

第十四条 合资旅行社不得组织安排含有淫秽、赌博、吸毒内容及其他有害于社会道德和人民身心健康的项目；不得组织含有损害中华人民共和国的国家利益和民族尊严内容的项目；不得组织含有中国法律、法规禁止内容的项目。

第十五条 合资旅行社在中国境内聘用导游员，按国家有关规定办理。

第十六条 合资游行社须接受旅游行政管理部门的行业管理。

第十七条 合资旅行社须按规定向旅游行政管理等有关部门上报财务、会计和统计报表，接受业务检查。

第十八条 合资旅行社的外汇收支按照外商投资企业的有关办法办理。

第十九条 合资旅行社须遵守中华人民共和国法律、法规、受中国法律、法规管辖，其正当经营活动和合法权益受中国法律、法规的保护。

合资旅行社如有违反中国法律、法规的行为，按有关法律、法规处理。

第二十条 违反本办法规定的，由旅游行政管理部门根据《旅行社管理条例》和《旅行社管理条例实施细则》予以处罚。

第二十一条 本规定实施期间，《关于在国家旅游度假区内开办中外合资经营的第一类旅行社的审批管理暂行办法》继续有效。

第二十二条 香港特别行政区、澳门、台湾地区的投资者与国内投资者共同投资开办合资旅行社，参照本规定执行。

第二十三条 本规定由国家旅游局和对外贸易经济合作部负责解释。

第二十四条 本规定自发布之日起实施。

财政部　对外贸易经济合作部　国家税务总局关于1993年12月31日前批准成立的外商投资企业有关税收政策问题的通知

财税字〔1998〕184号
1998年12月14日

各省、自治区、直辖市及计划单列市财政厅(局)，外经贸厅（委、局，外资局、招商局)，国家税务局：

经国务院批准，现就1993年12月31日前批准设立的外商投资企业有关税收政策问题通知如下：

一、根据全国人大常委会《关于外商投资企业和外国企业适用增值税、消费税、营业税等税收暂行条例的决定》，对1993年12月31日前批准设立的外商投资企业超税负返还政策执行到1998年底，不再延长。

二、对1993年12月31日前批准设立的外商投资企业出口货物实行的不征不退政策（即：出口货物实行免税办法，从国内采购原材料照征国内税收，最后一道出口环节免税，进项税额不予抵扣也不退税的办法)，继续执行到2000年底。

三、对1994年1月1日后批准设立的外商投资企业出口货物仍执行现行的出口退税办法。

请遵照执行。

对外贸易经济合作部关于印发《关于解决外商投资企业董事不出席企业董事会会议问题的指导意见》的通知

〔1998〕外经贸法发第302号
1998年4月20日

各省、自治区、直辖市及计划单列市外经贸委（厅、局)：

近日许多地方外经贸主管部门向我部反映，中外合资经营企业、中外合作经营企业和外资企业（以下统称企业）董事不出席董事会（或联合管理机构，下同）会议而致使董事会不能作出有效决策的现象时有发生，为维护企业、企业股东和企业债权人的合法权益，同时减少审批管理部门为解决企业内部纠纷而产生的问题，对外贸易经济合作部依据有关法律、法规，特提出若干指导性意见（见附件)，请各地外商投资企业审批管理部门在处理上述问题时参考使用。

附件：如文

附件一

关于解决企业董事不出席董事会会议问题的指导意见

一、企业应按照有关法律、法规规定，每年至少召开一次董事会会议；董事会临时会议的召集程序，从其合同、章程或有关协议规定。

二、股东超过合资、合作企业合同规定期限不履行或不完全履行其出资义务，其他股东可依据《中外合资经营企业合营各方出资的若干规定》和《外商投资企业投资者股权变更的若干规定》直接向企业原审批机关申请更换股东或变更股权。

三、如果企业股东在合资、合作企业合同及章程规定期限内不委派董事出席企业董事会会议，致使企业董事会会议不能作出有效决议，其他股东可依据合资、合作企业合同有关解决争议方式和程序规定，提请仲裁或诉讼解决。

四、各地外经贸部门在审批企业合同、章程时，应严格把关，注意要求投资者在合同、章程中订明企业董事会议事规则和企业解散的条件和程序，可向企业建议在合资、合作合同和章程有关条款中加入附件二内容或审批机关认为必要的其他条款。

五、对于已批准成立的企业，因严重亏损或其他原因而无法继续经营，确需解散的，且合资、合作一方或数方股东所委派的董事两年以上不出席或不召集董事会会议，致使企业董事会不能作出解散企业的有效决议，经其他股东多次书面催告，仍无任何音信的，经中国公证机关或律师见证，其他股东可向企业原审批机关申请解散企业并提交下列必要文件：

（一）其他股东关于终止合资、合作企业合同及章程的一致申请及有关详情说明；

（二）其他股东所委派的董事关于解散企业的一致决议；

（三）其他股东向不出席董事会的董事发出的催告函；

（四）其他股东对其所述有关详情真实性的保证，该保证将注明：该其他股东向审批机关所陈述的有关详情如与事实不符，将由其连带承担一切责任；

（五）中国公证机关出具的公证或律师出具的见证文件；

（六）合资、合作企业合同及章程；

（七）企业批准证书和营业执照复印件；

（八）审批机关要求报送的其他文件。

审批机关对有关文件认真审查、确认无误后，可酌情予以批准解散该企业。

各地外经贸主管部门在受理此类申请时，应从维护企业、企业股东及企业债权人利益、有利于社会安定出发，根据具体情况，谨慎处理。

六、鉴于目前各地外经贸主管部门对设立企业的审批与颁发批准证书权限有不同规制，如果原审批机关为省级以下外经贸部门，解散企业应征得省级外经贸主管部门的同意。

附件二

企业合同（章程）关于董事会议事规则条款的参考格式

第　条　本公司（企业）营业执照签发之日，为公司董事会成立之日。

第　条　董事会由　　名董事组成，其中甲方委派　　名，乙方委派　名……董事长一名，由　方指定，副董事长　　名，由　　方指定。

第　条　董事任期　年，经委派方继续委派，可以连任。

第　条　董事会是公司的最高权力机构，决定公司的一切重大事宜。

下列事项需由出席董事会会议的董事一致通过决定：

（一）修改公司章程；

（二）解散公司；

（三）调整公司注册资本；

（四）一方或数方转让其在本公司的股权；

（五）一方或数方将其在本公司的股权质押给债权人；

（六）公司合并或分立；

（七）抵押公司资产。

……

第　条　董事长是公司的代定代表人。董事长不能履行其职责时，应授权他人代为履行，董事长未明确授权的，由副董事长代理。

第　条　董事会会议每年至少召开一次（年会），在公司住所或董事会指定的其他地点举行，由董事长召集并主持会议。经　　名（全体董事人数的三分之一）以上的董事提议，董事长应召开董事临时会议。

召开董事会会议的通知应包括会议时间和地点、议事日程，且应当在会议召开的10日前以书面形式发给全体董事。

会议记录归档保存。

第　条　董事会年会和临时会议应当有　　名（全体董事人数的三分之二）以上董事出席方能举行。

每外董事享有一票表决权。

第　条　各方有义务确保其委派的董事出席董事会年会和临时会议。

董事因故不能参加董事会会议，应出具委托书，委托他人代表其出席会议。

第　条　如果一方或数方所委派的董事不出席董事会会议也不委托他人代表其出席会议，致使董事会　　日内不能就法律、法规和本合同（章程）所列之公司重大问题或事项作出决议，则其他方（通知人）可以向不出席董事会会议的董事及委派他们的一方或数方（被通知人），按照该方法定地址（住所）再次发出书面通知，敦促其在规定日期内出席董事会会议。

第　条　前条所述之敦促通知应至少在确定召开会议日期的60日前，以双挂号函方式发出，并应当注明在本通知发出的至少45日内被通知人应书面答复是否出席董事会会议。如果被通知人在通知规定期限内仍未答复是否出席董事会会议，则应视为被通知人弃权，在通知人收到双挂号函回执后，通知人所委派的董事可召开董事会特别会议，即使出席该董事会特别会议的董事达不到举行董事会会议的法定人数，经出席董事会特别会议的全体董事一致通过，仍可就公司之重大问题或事项作出有效决议。

第　条　不在公司经营管理机构任职的董事，不在公司领取薪金。

与举行董事会会议有关的全部费用由公司承担。

对外贸易经济合作部
关于加强外商投资企业审批
管理工作的通知

〔1998〕外经贸资综函字第260号

1998年5月7日

各省、自治区、直辖市及计划单列市外经贸委（厅、局）：

党的十五大和九届人大以后，各地新一届政府都十分重视利用外资工作，都不同程度地采取了一些提高利用外资水平的新措施，改善当地的投资环境，包括简化审批手续，缩短审批时间，实行“一条龙”服务等措施，收到了明显的效果。但也有个别地方违反国家的法律规定，取消对外商投资企业的审批，这不仅损害了我国利用外资法律的严肃性，而且由于未经审批的外商投资企业的合同、章程为无效合同、章程，中外方投资者的权益无法得到保障，一系列法律问题无法解决，给我国利用外资的管理工作带来混乱。为维护我国法律的严肃性和在全国实施的统一性，现就依法加强对外商投资企业审批工作的管理通知如下：

一、中外合资企业法、中外合作企业法、外资企业法是全国人大通过的法律，各地各部门无权自行制定与之相悖的规定，必须严格按照国家有关法律、法规的规定，按现行的审批程序对设立外商投资企业及其合同、章程（包括修改合同、章程）等进行审批。

二、中共中央、国务院最近下发了关于《进一步扩大对外开放、提高利用外资水平的若干意见》（中发〔1998〕6号文），各地区、各部门要认真学习，切实领会文件精神，保证国家利用外资政策能切实得到执行。

三、认真执行中发〔1998〕6号文的各项规定。各级政府要提高办事效率，减少管理层次，做到制度公开，政策透明。提倡一个“窗口”对外，提供优质、规范、方便的服务。结合深化投融资体制改革，改进外资项目的审批方法，简化审批程序。与此同时，各地区、各部门要加强对利用外资工作的统一领导和协调，要认真贯彻党中央、国务院有关利用外资的方针、政策，步调一致，依法行政，不得越权制定地区性和行业性政策，保证全国法律法规的统一和政令畅通。

对外贸易经济合作部 国家工商行政管理局 国家国内贸易局 关于外商投资传销企业转变销售方式有关问题的通知

〔1998〕外经贸资发第455号

1998年6月18日

各省、自治区、直辖市及计划单列市外经贸委（厅、局）、工商行政管理局、商委、财办、商业（贸易）、物资厅（局、集团总公司）：

为贯彻落实《国务院关于禁止传销经营活动的通知》（国发〔1998〕10号），做好原从事传销经营活动的外商投资企业（以下称外商投资传销企业）转变销售方式（以下简称转型）的工作，经国务院批准，现将有关问题通知如下：

一、外商投资传销企业必须转为店铺经营（包括在商店设专柜、将企业产品批发给国内批发商或零售商、自开店铺）。

二、转成店铺经营的企业，分为雇佣推销人员（系指非企业正式雇员，通过为该企业推销产品取得劳动报酬的人员）和不雇佣推销人员两类。

三、转型为不雇佣推销人员企业的条件及程序。

（一）申请转型企业必须符合以下条件：

1. 企业合法批准设立；

2. 企业必须是生产性企业，只能销售本企业生产的产品；

3. 企业在生产经营中无违法行为并已通过1998年联合年检。

（二）转型程序：

1. 合同、章程或批准证书中明确传销或直销业务的企业

（1）企业投资各方需修改合同、章程；

（2）将合同、章程修改协议报原审批机关批准并换发批准证书；

（3）企业凭换发的批准证书到原登记机关办理

变更登记手续。

2. 合同、章程或批准证书中无传销或直销内容的企业可直接到原登记机关办理变更登记手续。

四、转型为雇佣推销人员企业的条件及程序。

（一）申请转型企业必须符合以下条件：

1. 符合第三条第（一）款三个条件；

2. 企业投资总额在1000万美元以上（不包括设立销售分支机构的投资）；

3. 企业外方投资者以从事直销业务为主。

（二）转型程序：

1. 企业投资各方根据转型方案的原则修改合同、章程的有关条款；

2. 企业将合同、章程修改协议依法律程序报外经贸部（转型方案一并上报），抄送国家工商行政管理局和国家内贸局，外经贸部征求上述两部门意见后依法予以审批，并对获批准者换发批准证书；

3. 企业凭换发的批准证书到国家工商行政管理局办理变更登记手续。

（三）企业转型方案应符合以下原则：

1. 企业必须有店铺，明码标价；

2. 企业须制定符合国家各项法规要求的售后服务及顾客退货制度并予公布；

3. 企业应同推销人员签订劳务合同，推销人员在劳务合同授权范围内推销企业产品所产生的法律责任，由企业承担；

4. 推销人员的资格应符合国家有关法律、法规的规定，推销人员应具备原劳动部、内贸部颁发的《推销员职业技术技能标准》（劳部发〔1997〕10号文件）的基本要求；

5. 推销人员不能从企业买断产品，只能按自己直接推销的产品金额计酬；推销人员推销价格应与店铺零售价一致；推销人员只能将产品直接推销给最终消费者；

6. 销售管理人员必须为企业正式职员。

五、政府印发统一的推销人员证。

六、要求转为销售其它企业产品的商业零售企业（包括单体店和连锁店），按国家有关规定报国务院审批。

七、对转企业设立的销售分支机构需重新审核。分支机构是非独立法人的机构，必须自开店铺推销本企业的自产产品。

八、对转型为不雇佣推销人员的企业，有关部门在接到申请后一周内完成各项手续。对转型为雇佣推销人员的企业，有关部门在接到地方外经贸部门上报的全部申报材料后，一个月内予以批复。对上报材料符合上述规定的，批复后15日内完成变更登记手续。

对外经济合作

对外贸易经济合作部 国家工商行政管理局关于审核境内举办对外经济技术展览会主办单位资格的通知

〔1997〕外经贸政发第711号
1998年1月7日

国务院各部委，各直属机构，各省、自治区、直辖市及计划单列市外经贸委（厅、局）、工商行政管理局：

根据《国务院办公厅关于对在我国境内举办对外经济技术展览会加强管理的通知》（国办发〔1997〕25号），为进一步规范在中国境内举办对外经济技术展览会的活动，现就举办对外经济技术展览会的境内主办单位资格审核的有关问题通知如下：

一、举办对外经济技术展览会的境内主办单位，必须具有对外贸易经济合作部（以下简称外经贸部）审核批准的主办资格。

二、除省级、副省级市人民政府或省级外经贸主管部门以及国务院部门以外的境内主办单位，应当具备以下条件：

（一）具有组织招商招展能力和承担举办展览的民事责任能力。

（二）设有专门从事办展的部门或机构，并有相应的展览专业（包括策划、设计、组织、管理及外语）人员，具有完善的办展规章制度。

（三）曾参与承办或协办5个以上较大规模的国际性展览会。

三、上述境内主办单位，应按部门、地区、系统所属，分别向各自上级主管部门（指国务院各部门，各省、自治区、直辖市及计划单列市外经贸主管部门，中国国际贸易促进委员会）申请主办单位资格。经上级主管部门审查同意后，由其上级主管部门报外经贸部审批。申报材料应包括：

（一）上级主管部门的申报文件。

（二）主办单位的申请和资格申报表（详见附件）。

（三）加盖原登记机关印章的企业法人营业执照副本复印件。社团法人或事业单位法人提交社团法人登记证副本复印件或事业单位法人批准文件复印件。

（四）设置专门从事办展部门或机构的文件。

（五）举办展览的规章制度及招展文件（合同）范本。

（六）证明曾承办或协办过较大规模国际性展览会的材料。

（七）其他有关材料。

四、外经贸部对所报材料进行审核，对符合条件的主办单位授予其主办单位资格，并分期分批予以公布。

五、凡取得外经贸部批准文件的主办单位，须在取得批准文件之日起30日内，持批准文件到工商行政管理部门办理登记。

取得主办单位资格的公司、企业或事业单位法人，按《公司登记管理条例》或《企业法人登记管理条例》等有关规定办理；取得主办单位资格的社会团体法人，按民政部、国家工商行政管理局《关于社会团体开展经营活动有关问题的通知》（民社发〔1995〕14号）的有关规定办理。

六、凡未取得外经贸部批准文件，或未依据外经贸部批准文件到工商行政管理部门办理相应登记的主办单位，自本通知发布执行之日起，均不得在中国境内主办对外经济技术展览会。对违反本通知规定的，由外经贸管理部门或工商行政管理部门按照有关法律、法规予以处罚。

七、国务院各部门，各省级、副省级市人民政府，或省级外经贸主管部门在境内举办对外经济技术展览会，按照《国务院办公厅关于对在我国境内举办对外经济技术展览会加强管理的通知》（国办发〔1997〕25号）的有关规定执行。

本通知自发布之日起执行，过去有关规定凡与本通知不符的，以本通知为准。

附件：主办单位资格申报表（略）

对外贸易经济合作部 财政部
关于印发《援外合资合作项目基金管理办法》的通知

〔1998〕外经贸计财发第481号

1998年7月7日

各省、自治区、直辖市及计划单列市外经贸委（厅、局）（含深圳市经发局）、财政厅（局）、各部委直属公司、各驻外经济商务机构：

为了进一步深化援外改革，促进我国与受援国之间的经济技术合作，现将经国务院批准的《援外合资合作项目基金管理办法》印发你们，请遵照执行。执行中有何问题，请及时反映。有关本办法的实施细则，另行下达。

附件：援外合资合作项目基金管理办法

附　件

援外合资合作项目基金管理办法

第一条　为了支持我国企业与受援国企业举办合资合作项目，促进我国与受援国之间的经济技术合作，特设立“援外合资合作项目基金”，并制定本办法。

第二条　援外合资合作项目基金（以下简称“基金”）用于支持我国企业利用受援国当地资源和我国设备、技术，与受援国企业举办合资合作项目及在受援国举办独资、租赁经营等以生产性为主的中小型项目，具体包括：

一、受援国政府将我援款转贷给其企业，我方企业再投入一部分资金，双方合资合作经营的项目；

二、我国政府对外援助建成项目转为双方企业合资合作或由我国企业独资、租赁经营的项目；

三、受援国政府（或主管部门）与我国政府（或主管部门）签订原则协议，同意在政策上或资金上给予支持的项目等。

第三条　“基金”的主要资金来源：

一、自1994年起，我国政府收回的援外贷款；

二、1991年经国务院批准设立的原“多种形式援外专项资金”；

三、本办法第四条所列有偿使用回收的借款本金、“基金”使用费等收入。

第四条 “基金”实行有偿使用、到期归还的办法，并向申请使用“基金”的单位（以下简称借款单位）收取一定的“基金”使用费。“基金”使用费年费率一般为1%－4%，借款期限一般为1－4年，特殊情况最长不超过6年。

第五条 借款单位应是具有法人资格的国有企业、国有控股企业，并具备对外经营条件。借款单位要保证“基金”借款本金和“基金”使用费的按期偿还。

第六条 借款单位申请“基金”数额一般不能超过中方投资额的60%，其余资金自筹解决，并需提供借款项目的技术、经济可行性研究报告和还款担保。

第七条 “基金”由外经贸部和财政部共同管理，实行收支两条线的核算办法。由财政部设“专户存储”，外经贸部单独设立帐户管理。

第八条 外经贸部当年实际收回的援外贷款和“基金”借款本金、使用费等收入应于年度终了后一个月内上缴财政专户存储。

第九条 外经贸部负责援外合资合作项目的立项审批，对外签订协议，向财政部报送“基金”的年度使用计划和“基金”的年度决算，负责项目借款合同的签订、拨款和借款催收，并根据财政部核准的“基金”年度使用计划、决算和有关规定进行帐务处理。

财政部负责审批外经贸部报送的“基金”年度使用计划和决算，并根据审批后的年度计划和外经贸部的申请分季度拨付资金，会同外经贸部对单项借款金额1000万元人民币以上（含1000万元人民币）或等额美元的援外合资合作项目的立项审批。限额以下项目借款由外经贸部审批并抄送财政部备案。

财政部与外经贸部应定期或不定期地检查、监督“基金”的使用、回收和借款项目经济效益情况。

第十条 已批准的借用“基金”的项目，自援外任务书下发之日起2年有效、2年内不能实施，即自动取消。

第十一条 由于战争、自然灾害等不可抗力造成的借款本金和“基金”使用费收不回来的，借款单位及其上级主管部门应及时写出专题报告，经外经贸部审核后报财政部核销。

第十二条 对核“基金”所进行的管理及调研等相关费用，从收取的“基金”使用费中列支。

第十三条 “基金”的实施细则由外经贸部商财政部另行制订。

第十四条 本办法自颁布之日起执行。财政部、外经贸部共同制定的（92）财外字第966号《多种形式援外专项资金管理办法》同时废止。

对外贸易经济合作部关于向台湾地区远洋渔轮派遣渔工劳务有关问题的紧急通知

〔1998〕外经贸合发第514号

1998年7月17日

各省、自治区、直辖市及计划单列市外经贸委（厅、局），各有关国际经济技术合作公司，各驻外经济商务机构：

近年来，向台湾地区远洋渔轮派遣渔工劳务规模不断扩大，取得了一定的经济效益和社会效益，但也出现了一些问题，特别是压价竞争和渔工劳务人员的合法权益受损害等现象时有发生。为切实加强输台渔轮渔工劳务的协调和管理，保护渔工劳务人员的合法权益，现重申有关规定并就有关内容补充通知如下：

一、输台地区远洋渔轮普通渔工劳务工资严格执行每人每月360美元的最低限价，职务船员每人每月工资不得低于相应级别的最低限价（见附件）。

二、经营公司和派出单位收取的服务费标准一律按财政部、外经贸部联合印发的《对外经济合作企业外派人员工资管理办法的补充规定》（财外字〔1997〕8号）执行。除此之外，劳务人员的奖金、加班费和加班工资等一律归已，经营公司不得以任何名义从中扣除或提成。

三、外派渔工劳务合同须按外经贸部拟定的统一合同内容与台方商签，不得更改合同条款或增签其他任何违背合同的协议。合同一式三份，其中一份（正本）报外经贸部备案。合同每页须有小签，落款处要正式签字并加盖公章。

四、各级外经贸主管部门须加强对输台渔工劳务业务的管理，严禁任何未经外经贸部批准的公司擅自经营此项业务。各驻外使（领）馆经济商务参赞处（室）对在其驻在国海域作业的台湾渔轮上的我外派渔工的工作、待遇及收入情况要加强了解，发现渔工劳务人员合法权益受损要及时报国内有关部门查处。

五、经营公司与雇主签订的渔工劳务合同必须经外派渔工本人过目，合同中工资待遇等主要条款必须向渔工解释清楚。如有经营公司被投诉其工资标准待遇和收费标准不符合有关规定和合同，一经查实，将视情节轻重给予处罚，直至取消其经营资格。

六、简化审批手续。合同立项批件的有效期由6个月延长至1年。

本通知自下发之日起执行。

附件：如文

附　件

三等渔船外派职务船员最低限价

职务	限价	职务	限价
船长	1200美元	大管轮	800美元
轮机长	1200美元	二副	400美元
大副	700美元	二管轮	450美元

对外贸易经济合作部 国务院港澳事务办公室关于印发《对澳门地区开展普通劳务合作管理办法》的通知

〔1998〕外经贸合发第430号

1998年7月27日

国务院各有关部委，各有关省、自治区、直辖市及计划单列市外经贸委（厅、局），各有关公司：

《关于对输往澳门地区普通劳务审批管理暂行办法》（〔1996〕外经贸合发82号）执行两年多来，取得了良好的效果，使内地输澳门劳务的管理工作纳入了规范化和制度化的轨道。随着市场和形势的变化，为进一步加强对该项业务的管理，提高工作效率，我们在广泛征求意见的基础上对该办法做了修改和完善，现将修改后的《对澳门地区开展普通劳务合作管理办法》印发给你们，请遵照执行，执行中如有问题请及时向外经贸部合作司反映。1999年澳门回归后，必要时，将根据情况，对此办法做适当修订。

附件：一、对澳门地区开展普通劳务合作管理办法

二、经营公司名单

附件一

对澳门地区开展普通劳务合作管理办法

第一章　总　　则

第一条　为贯彻“一国两制”方针，健康有序地开展输澳劳务业务，维护澳门地区经济发展和社会稳定，特制订本办法。

第二条　输往澳门普通劳务系指根据澳门政府批准引进的从事非专业性工作的内地劳务人员。

第三条　根据国家授权，输澳劳务工作由对外贸易经济合作部（以下称外经贸部）统一归口管理，国务院港澳事务办公室（以下称港澳办）进行政策指导。

第四条　鉴于澳门地区和市场的特殊性，对输澳普通劳务实行限定经营公司数量和总量控制的办法。未经批准的公司一律不得开展对澳劳务合作，确定的经营公司必须严格遵守国家关于输澳劳务的统一政策和规定，服从协调管理，实行公平竞争，禁止经营公司间的压价竞争和中间商介入。

第二章　合同的签订及审批

第五条　输澳普通劳务合同（包括续约合同，下同）统一由中澳服务有限公司（以下称中澳公司）代表经营公司对外以标准合同与雇主直接签订。标准合同的起草及修改由中澳公司负责对外谈判，并报外经贸部批准后使用。

第六条　劳务合同在澳门政府的申报及审批由中澳公司负责办理及协调。合同在内地也实行审批制，新合同及续约合同由经营公司报外经贸部合作司商港澳办澳门司批准后，凭外经贸部合作司批件到有关部门办理劳务人员的任务批件及护照（1999 年 12 月 20 日后为赴澳门通行证）等手续；中澳公司根据外经贸部合作司批件及经营公司所属外经贸主管部门的任务批件协助经营公司办理其输入的劳务人员入澳及在澳居留和工作的合法手续。输澳劳务业务中的人员替换手续在内地由经营公司的上级外经贸主管部门办理。

第七条　经营公司在内地办理输澳劳务合同报批时，须提供以下材料：

（一）公司的申请报告（该报告需包括合同号、雇主名称、所派人数、工作期限等内容）；

（二）中澳公司与雇主签订的劳务合同；

（三）澳门政府批准雇主引进外地劳工的文件；

（四）原批文（续约合同）。

第三章　劳务人员选派

第八条　经营公司按合同要求选派品质好、技术合格、身体健康、能胜任工作的人员赴澳工作。

第九条　劳务人员在内地的招聘由经营公司负责进行，严禁澳门及内地中间商或雇主直接到内地自行招工。

第十条　劳务人员的招聘应实行公平、公开、公正的原则，除经外经贸部批准发布的收费项目和标准外，经营公司不得向应聘人员收取任何额外费用，在澳门的各项收费及标准另行规定。

第十一条　经营公司按照国家《外派劳务人员培训工作管理规定》（〔1996〕外经贸合发第 101 号）对派澳劳务人员进行培训并经考试合格发给《外派劳务培训合格证》后方可派出。

第四章　在澳门的分级管理

第十二条　输澳劳务业务在澳门的管理分三个层次：

（一）中澳公司 是在澳门合法注册的、经外经

贸部批准隶属新华社澳门分社的非营利性劳务管理机构。其任务是在新华社澳门分社领导下，对内协调各地区、各部门驻澳门劳务公司的关系，并对这些公司进行协调管理；对外负责与澳门政府及厂商的联系，办理输澳劳务的各种法律手续。

（二）归口公司 指南粤（集团）有限公司、中福技术服务（澳门）有限公司和南光（集团）有限公司。它们分别代表广东省、福建省和除上述两省以外以及中建、中港、中铁、中智和航空设计院的内地各省、市、自治区及部分中央部属经营公司，并按规定协助中澳公司在澳门对输澳劳务业务的协调和管理工作。

（三）经营公司 经外经贸部商国务院港澳办确定的经营公司具体与雇主洽谈业务并负责管理各自在澳的劳务人员。

第十三条 上述各级管理层应根据各自的职责和管理制度加强自身管理，相互协作、配合并依照分工各尽其责，不得推诿扯皮。各层次的收费标准及办法另行确定。

第十四条 归口公司和经营公司可根据管理工作的需要向外经贸部申请驻澳劳务管理人员专项指标，外经贸部将根据各公司实际在澳劳务人员人数商国务院港澳办后予以批复。

第五章 总量控制与配额确定

第十五条 考虑到澳门地区的特殊性和市场特点，为防止经营公司之间的不正当竞争及中间商的介入，对输澳劳务实行合同人数总量的动态控制，即保持续约合同原则上由原经营公司执行，由外经贸部商国务院港澳办和新华社澳门分社后对澳门政府将向澳门雇主批出的引进内地劳务人员的新合同人数实行主动配额制。中澳公司根据上述原则在上一轮新合同人数总量即将到位时，提出下一轮经营公司劳务配额分配方案报外经贸部商国务院港澳办批准。

第十六条 经上述确定的主动配额即新合同人数总量将根据各经营公司的实际市场份额和经营作风表现按比例进行量化划分，各经营公司将根据获分配的配额人数按规定与雇主洽谈新合同业务，谈妥后由中澳公司对外签订劳务合同，合同中应注明中方经营公司全称和执行人数。

第十七条 上述主动配额即新合同人数总量将根据具体情况随时调整。

第六章 罚 则

第十八条 对违反本办法各条的公司，外经贸部将按情节轻重给予批评、警告、暂停输澳劳务业务及取消其外派劳务经营权等处分。

第十九条 严禁各经营公司利用任何不正当手段游说雇主改变劳务续约合同的经营公司。

第二十条 经营公司在洽谈新合同业务过程中不得出现任何不良行为，禁止利用中间商抢夺新劳务合同的行为出现。一经发现有此类行为的经营公司将立即被取消该公司获分配的所有新合同人数配额，情节特别严重的将被暂停所有输澳劳务业务直至取消其输澳劳务经营权。

第七章 附 则

第二十一条 各地区、各部门过去所制订的有关输澳劳务业务的规定或办法如与本办法有抵触，一律按本办法执行。

第二十二条 本办法由外经贸部负责解释。

第二十三条 本办法自下发之日起执行。

附件二

经营公司名单

1. 中国海外经营合作总公司
2. 中国土木工程总公司
3. 中国建筑工程总公司
4. 中国国际技术智力合作公司

5．中国港湾建设总公司
6．中国铁道建设总公司
7．中国航空工业规划设计研究院
8．中国南光进出口总公司
9．中国四达国际经济技术合作公司
10．中国成套设备进出口（集团）总公司
11．上海对外劳务合作公司
12．中国上海对外经济技术合作公司
13．中国浙江国际经济技术合作公司
14．中国宁波国际经济技术合作公司
15．武汉国际经济技术合作公司
16．北京国际经济技术合作公司
17．中国江苏国际经济技术合作公司
18．扬州国际经济技术合作公司
19．南通国际经济技术合作公司
20．吉林省对外招商建设总公司
21．中国湖北国际经济技术合作公司
22．中国广东国际合作（集团）公司
23．中国广东对外劳务经济合作公司
24．珠海国际经济技术合作公司
25．中国广州国际经济技术合作公司
26．汕头国际经济技术合用公司
27．广东海外建设总公司
28．广州对外经济发展总公司
29．中国深圳国际合作（集团）股份有限公司
30．江门市对外劳动服务公司
31．广东省南粤进出口公司
32．中国福建国际经济技术合作公司
33．福州国际经济技术合作公司
34．福建省对外劳务合作公司
35．中国厦门国际经济技术合作公司
36．泉州国际经济技术合作公司
37．漳州国际经济技术合作公司
38．莆田国际经济技术合作公司
39．中国沈阳国际经济技术合作公司
40．珠海对外劳务合作有限公司

海关、税收

海关总署　外经贸部关于加强对外贸代理业务报关管理的通知

署监〔1998〕611号
1998年9月30日

各外（工）贸总公司、各省、自治区、直辖市、经济特区外经贸委（厅、局），广东分署、各直属海关：

为有效贯彻中国人民银行、国家外汇管理局、对外贸易经济合作部、海关总署、国家工商行政管理局、公安部《关于加强反骗汇工作的通知》（银发〔1997〕557号）有关规定，现就加强对外贸代理业务管理和报关管理的问题通知如下：

一、各外贸公司在代理外贸业务时（不包括以委托人名义从事的代理），必须由代理单位对外签订合同，办理单证、外汇及报关手续，不得以只收取代理费方式，让委托企业（或货主）自带客户、自带货源、自带汇票、自行报关；不得以任何形式出让其名义供他人办理进出口业务中付汇、收汇、报关等手续。

二、外贸代理企业通过专业报关行向海关办理进口报关手续的，应向专业报关行提供委托人的正式委托书和加盖外贸公司印鉴的外贸代理企业委托专业报关行办理报关手续的委托书，专业报关行在向海关办理报关手续时，应同时出具上述正式委托书，外贸代理企业不得将上述委托书交给委托企业（或货主）办理海关报关手续。

三、对违反上述规定办理报关的，海关不予受理。对构成走私违规的，外经贸主管部门按有关规定，给予警告、暂停或取消外贸经营权的处罚，海关根据报关企业管理办法，给予暂停或取消其报关权。

四、各外贸公司要加强对代理业务的管理，切实履行监管职责，积极采取有效措施，防止“四自三不见”现象发生，把防范金融风险同促进外贸代理业务发展有机地结合起来，做到进口商品、供货货主、签约外商等切实到位，有效地打击骗购外汇行为，保证外贸业务的正常发展。

财政部　国家税务总局
关于提高纺织机械出口退税率的通知

财税字〔1998〕107号
1998年6月16日

各省、自治区、直辖市、计划单列市财政厅(局)、国家税务局：

为配合纺织压锭，调整纺机生产结构，鼓励我国的纺机出口，经国务院批准，决定自1998年1月1日至2000年12月31日将纺织机械的出口退税率提高到17%。现将有关问题通知如下：

一、对本通知所列纺机出口企业（具体名单详见附件二）自营（委托）出口的纺织机械，一律按17%的退税率办理退税。

本通知所述的纺机是指棉纺织机械、印染机械及整理、轧光等其他纺织机械的总称。按照现行海关进出口税则分类，纺机共包括67个税号，纺机具体税号及名称详见《纺织机械税号清单》(附件一)。

二、本通知自1998年1月1日起执行〔具体执行日期以“出口货物报关单（出口退税联）”上注明的海关离境日期为准〕。对1998年1月1日至本通知文到之日前，本通知所列纺机出口企业自营（委托）出口的纺织机械，除已办妥退税手续的不作调整外，一律按本通知规定的出口退税率执行。

请遵照执行。

附件：一、纺织机械税号清单

二、列名纺机出口企业名单

附件一

纺织机械税号清单

税　则　号　列	货　　品　　名　　称
84201000	织物轧光机
84435911	圆网印花机
84435912	平网印花机
84440010	合成纤维长丝纺丝机
84440020	合成纤维短丝纺丝机
84440030	人造纤维纺丝机
84440040	化学纤维变形机
84440050	化学纤维切断机
84440090	其他化纤挤压、拉伸、变形或切割机器

续表

税则号列	货品名称
84451100	纺织纤维梳理机
84451200	纺织纤维精梳机
84451300	纺织纤维拉伸机或粗纱机
84451900	纺织纤维的其他预处理机器
84452010	棉细纱机
84452020	气流纺纱机
84452090	其他纺纱机
84453000	并线机或加捻机
84454011	自动络筒机
84454019	其他络纱机
84454090	其他络纱机（包括卷纬机）或摇纱机
84459000	其他生产及处理纺织纱线的机器
84461000	所织织物宽度≤30cm 的织机
84462110	＞30cm 宽的梭织动力地毯织机
84462190	＞30cm 宽的其他梭织动力织机
84462900	＞30cm 宽的梭织非动力织机
84463020	＞30cm 宽的剑杆织机
84463030	＞30cm 宽的片梭织机
84463040	＞30cm 宽的喷水织机
84463050	＞30cm 宽的喷气织机
84463090	＞30cm 宽的其他无梭织机
84471100	圆筒直径≤165mm 的圆型针织机
84471200	圆筒直径＞165mm 的圆型针织机
84472010	经编机
84472020	其他平型针织机
84472030	缝编机
84479011	地毯织机
84479019	其他簇绒机
84479020	绣花机
84479090	编号 8447 其他未列名机器

续表

税则号列	货品名称
84481100	多臂机或提花机
84481900	编号 8444 至 8447 所列机器辅助机器
84482010	喷丝头
84482090	纤维挤压机等及辅助机器的零件
84483100	钢丝针布
84483200	纺织纤维预处理机器的零件、附件
84483310	络筒锭
84483390	其他锭子、锭壳、纺丝环、钢丝圈
84483910	气流环
84483920	电子清纱器
84483930	空气捻接器
84483990	编号 8445 所列机器的其他零、附件
84484100	梭子
84484200	织机用筘，综丝及综框
84484900	织机及其辅助机器用其他零、附件
84484910	接、投梭箱
84484920	引纬、送经装置
84484990	织机及其辅助机器用其它零、附件
84485110	针织机用 28 号以下的弹簧针
84485190	沉降片、其他织针及成圈机件
84485900	编号 8447 机器用的其他零件、附件
84490000	成匹、成形的毡呢制造或整理机器
84512900	松式烘干机
84513000	熨烫机及挤压机（包括熔压机）
84514000	洗涤、漂白或染色机器
84515000	织物的卷绕，退绕，折叠，剪切机器
84518000	编号 8451 所列的其他未列名机器
84519000	编号 8451 所列机器的零件

附件二

列名纺机出口企业名单

序　　号	企　　业　　名　　称
1	常德纺织机械厂
2	国营邯郸纺织机械厂
3	国营郑州纺织机械厂
4	邵阳第二纺织机械厂
5	中国纺织机械工业总公司
6	经纬纺机股份有限公司
7	上海二纺机股份有限公司
8	太平洋机电（集团）公司
9	南通第二纺织机械厂
10	苏州第二纺织机械厂
11	无锡宏源纺织机械制造集团公司
12	浙江三友集团有限公司
13	浙江金鹰纺机有限公司
14	青岛胶南纺织机械厂
15	山东昌邑市纺织机械厂
16	湖北荆沙市纺织机械厂
17	湖北天鹤纺机集团公司
18	山东青岛允春机械公司
19	福建鸿翔机械有限公司
20	顺德市金德纺织机械厂有限公司
21	济南鲁思达纺织机械有限公司
22	中国纺织机械和技术进出口公司
23	中国纺织机械（集团）有限公司
24	中国机械进出口公司
25	中国机械设备进出口公司
26	中国技术进出口公司

续表

序　号	企　业　名　称
27	中国仪器进出口公司
28	中国海外贸易公司
29	中国航空技术进出口公司
30	青岛市机械进出口公司
31	天津市机械进出口公司
32	湖北省机械进出口公司
33	山东省机械进出口公司
34	上海市机械进出口公司
35	河南省机械进出口公司
36	江苏省机械进出口公司
37	浙江省机械进出口公司
38	山西省机械进出口公司
39	河北省机械进出口公司
40	江苏省纺织工业对外贸易公司

对外贸易经济合作部办公厅
关于转发《关于对使用新疆棉生产的
出口产品退税问题的通知》的通知

〔1998〕外经贸计财字第556号

1998年7月28日

各省、自治区、直辖市及计划单列市外经贸委（厅、局），各外贸中心，各部委直属公司：

现将财政部、国家税务总局、海关总署《关于对使用新疆棉生产的出口产品退税问题的通知《（财税字〔1998〕117号）转发给你们，请遵照执行。执行中有何问题，请及时向我部（计财司）反映。

特此通知。

附件：如文

附　件

财政部　国家税务总局　海关总署
关于对使用新疆棉生产的
出口产品退税问题的通知

财税字〔1998〕117号

各省、自治区、直辖市、计划单列市财政厅(局)、国家税务局，广东分署、各直属海关：

经国务院批准，自1998年6月1日起，销售1997年度新疆棉改为实行财政定额补贴办法。为此，财政部制定了《关于印发〈销售1997年度新疆棉花的财政定额补贴办法〉的通知》（财商字〔1998〕336号）。根据上述精神，现对使用新疆棉生产出口产品的退（免）税问题规定如下：

一、从1998年6月1日起，停止执行财政部、国家税务总局、海关总署《关于使用新疆棉生产出口产品实行零税率管理办法的通知》（财税字〔1997〕126号），改为财政定额补贴办法。对企业1998年6月1日以后购买的新疆棉，停止发放《使用新疆棉生产出口纺织品监督证书》(以下简称《监管证书》)，同时，生产出口的纺织原料及制品统一执行11%的出口退（免）税率，纺织原料及制品的范围详见财政部、国家税务总局《关于提高纺织原料及制品出口退税率的通知》（财税字〔1998〕27号）。

二、企业用1998年5月31日以前购买的新疆棉生产出口的产品，凡符合财税字〔1997〕126号文件规定的，仍可继续按该文件的退税监管办法执行。

三、各地国家税务局应对未使用或未发放的《监管证书》进行收缴注销。

以上请遵照执行。

对外贸易经济合作部办公厅
关于转发《国家税务总局关于恢复食糖
出口退税的通知》的通知

〔1998〕外经贸计财字第598号
1998年8月4日

各省、自治区、直辖市及计划单列市外经贸委（厅、局)，各外贸中心，各部委直属公司：

现将《国家税务总局关于恢复食糖出口退税的通知》(国税发〔1998〕118号）转发给你们，请遵照执行。工作中遇到问题，请及时向外经贸部（计财司）反映。

附件：如文

附　件

国家税务总局
关于恢复食糖出口退税的通知

国税发〔1998〕118号

各省、自治区、直辖市和计划单列市国家税务局：

为了解决当前食糖供大于求的问题，鼓励出口，缓解国内市场的压力，根据国务院领导的指示精神，现决定恢复对食糖的出口退税政策。具体通知如下：

一、对出口食糖按9%的退税率办理退税；

二、本通知自1998年8月1日起执行，具体执行日期按“出口货物报关单（出口退税联）”上海关注明的货物离境日期为准。

请遵照执行。

财政部　国家税务总局
关于调高部分机电等产品出口退税率的通知

财税明电〔1998〕002号
1998年8月7日

各省、自治区、直辖市及计划单列市财政厅（局）、国家税务局：

经国务院批准，决定从1998年7月1日起，将七类机电产品、五类轻工产品的出口退税率从9%提高到11%，具体通知如下：

一、七类机电产品包括：

1. 通信设备〔海关商品码为8517，8525，8526，8527（1900+9010+9090）〕

2. 发电及输变电设备〔海关商品码为84041010，8406－（1000），8410，8501，8502，8504（2100－3400）〕

3. 自动数据处理设备（海关商品码为8471，847330，85232010，85044020）

4. 高档家用电器（海关商品码为852812，852821，8528301，8521，85199910，84181020，84181030，84182，84183029，84184029，84151000－84158300，85165000，84501，84502）

5. 农机及工程机械〔海关商品码为84079000，84089091，8409（9191+9199），82084000，84193100，8421（1100+2300），8424（8100+8990+9090），84291190，8432，8433，8434，8436，8437，8701－（2000），8708（3910+4010+5010+6010+9310+9410），87162000，8511（1000+2090+4091+4099+5090+8000），8426（1200+2000+4110+4190+9100+9900），8427，8428（5000+6000+9000），8429－（1190+3010+3090+4019+4090+5200+5900），8430－（3100+3900+4119+4121+4190+4900+5090+6900），8431－（1000），8467，8474－（1000+2000），8705（1010+1090+2000+4000）〕

6. 飞机及航空设备〔海关商品码为8802（1100－4020），8803（1000+2000+3000），84071010，84071020，84091000，8411－（8100+9900），8412（1010+1090+9010+9090），8801，8804，8805，94011000〕

7. 汽车（含摩托车）及零部件〔海关商品码为

8407（3100+3200+3300+3410+3420），8408-（1000+9091），8409（9920+9991+9999），8511-（1000+2090+4091+4099+5090+8000），8512（3000+4000），8702-8704，8705（9010+9090），8706，8707，8708-（3910+4010+5010+6010+9310+9410），8716-（2000），8711，87141，7315112〕

二、五类轻工产品包括：自行车、钟表、照明器具、鞋、陶瓷。

三、本通知自1998年7月1日起执行。具体实施时间按“出口货物报关单（出口退税联）”上注明的海关离境日期为准。为1998年7月1日至本通知文到之日前已出口并已办妥退税手续的上述产品，可不作调整；其他虽已出口但尚未办理退税手续的上述产品，一律按本通知规定的出口退税率执行。

国家税务总局关于提高铝、锌、铅出口退税率的通知

国税发〔1998〕152号

1998年9月23日

各省、自治区、直辖市和计划单列市国家税务局：

为增强铝、锌、铅等产品在国际市场的竞争力，缓解上述产品在国内生产经营的困难，经国务院批准，决定适当提高上述产品的出口退税率。现将有关问题通知如下：

一、铝、锌、铅出口退税率调为11%。铝、锌、铅所对应的海关商品代码和出口退税率计算机文库另行调整后下达。

二、本通知自1998年9月1日起执行。具体执行日期按“出口货物报关单（出口退税联）”上注明的海关离境日期为准。

请遵照执行。

国家税务总局关于提高船舶出口退税率的通知

国税发〔1998〕207号

1998年12月2日

各省、自治区、直辖市和计划单列市国家税务局：

为了缓解亚洲金融危机对我国船舶工业的冲击，支持船舶出口，经国务院批准，现决定进一步提高船舶出口退税率。具体通知如下：

一、船舶出口退税率调为16%；

二、本通知自1998年10月1日起执行。具体执行日期以“出口货物报关单（出口退税联）”上海关注明的货物离境日期为准。

请遵照执行。

对外贸易经济合作部办公厅关于转发《国家税务总局关于利用外国贷款采用国际招标方式国内企业中标的机电产品恢复退税的通知》的通知

〔1998〕外经贸计财字第367号
1998年6月1日

各省、自治区、直辖市及计划单列市外经贸委(厅、局),各外贸中心、各部委直属公司:

现将《国家税务总局关于利用外国贷款采用国际招标方式国内企业中标的机电产品恢复退税的通知》(国税发〔1998〕65号)转发给你们，请遵照执行。执行中有何问题，请及时向部(计财司)反映。

特此通知。

附件：如文

附　件

国家税务总局关于利用外国贷款采用国际招标方式国内企业中标的机电产品恢复退税的通知

国税发〔1998〕65号

各省、自治区、直辖市和计划单列市国家税务局:

为支持我国机电行业的发展，国务院决定对利用外国政府贷款或国际金融组织贷款通过国际招标由国内企业中标的机电产品恢复退税。现将有关事项通知如下:

一、对中标机电产品申报退税所需凭证及审核、审批程序等具体管理办法,依照《国家税务总局关于印发〈出口货物退(免)税管理办法〉的通知》(国税发〔1994〕031号)第十八条等有关规定执行。

中标机电产品生产企业实行“先征后退”管理办法的，负责该企业征税的税务机关对其生产、销售的中标机电产品，视同出口产品按《财政部、国家税务总局关于出口货物恢复使用增值税税收专用缴款书管理的通知》(财税字〔1996〕8号)的有关规定征税并开具“增值税税收(出口货物专用)缴款书”。中标企业在申报办理中标机电产品的退税时，除提供国税发〔1994〕031号文件规定的单证外，还须提供“增值税税收(出口货物专用)缴款书”。

二、本通知自1998年1月1日起执行，以中标货物增值税专用发票的开具时间为准。

国家税务总局　对外贸易经济合作部关于规范出口贸易和退税程序防范打击骗取出口退税行为的通知

国税发〔1998〕84号

1998年6月9日

各省、自治区、直辖市和计划单列市国家税务局、外经贸委（厅、局）：

为进一步支持外贸出口，加快出口退税进度，同时防范和打击骗取出口退税的违法犯罪行为，国家税务总局和外经贸部决定进一步规范出口贸易和出口退税程序。现将有关事项具体通知如下：

一、加强出口贸易管理

（一）出口企业必须端正经营思想。既要努力扩大经营，多创外汇，提高效益，又要遵纪守法，严禁任何形式的弄虚作假。坚决制止少数企业采取“倒汇”手段假冒进出口贸易，骗取退税款的违法犯罪行为，确保对外贸易的健康发展。

（二）出口企业在交易过程中必须做认真细致的工作。要特别注意教育业务人员认真负责地对货源、货物质量、价格以及纳税、客商资信等情况进行认真了解，对交易、仓储、运输、报关等具体出口贸易环节要亲自操作或监管，绝不做“四自三不见”（“客商”或中间人自带客户、自带货源、自带汇票、自行报关和出口企业不见出口产品、不见供货货主、不见外商）的“买单”业务，避免上当受骗。同时内部应建立责任制和奖惩制度，加强制约和处罚。

二、出口退税程序

（一）定期申报。出口企业应建立出口退税凭证收集制度，按期向当地主管出口退税的税务机关申报退税。除中远期结汇的出口货物外，上年度出口退税凡在清算结束前（本年5月31日）应收集齐全，因收集不齐并未申报的，税务机关不再受理该批货物的退税申请。

（二）定期审核、审批退税。税务机关在收到已经外经贸主管部门稽核的退税申报资料后，应及时审核退税单证。对单证齐全真实，且电子信息核对无误的，必须在20个工作日内办完退税审核、审批手续。对有疑问的单证且电子信息核对不上的，要及时发函调查，落实清楚后再办理退税；征税机关应按照国家税务总局的有关规定及时、如实回函，在收到退税机关函调后3个月内必须将函调情况回复发函地退税机关，如因特殊情况确实查不清楚的，应先回函说明暂时查不清的原因以及下次回函的时限。凡经税务机关调查一个生产环节仍查不清、需追溯以往的，应由出口企业负责调查举证，然后报退税机关复核无误后方可退税。举证有误和在本年度退税清算期内不能举证其出口真实有效的，不再办理退税。

三、严格出口退税电子信息审核工作

（一）各地主管出口退税的税务机关应尽快完善出口退税电子化管理，并严格按照有关规定进行审核。除国家税务总局明文规定不进行电子信息审核的出口项目外，对出口企业申报的每一笔退税申请必须与国家税务总局下发的报关单信息、代理出口货物证明信息等进行核对。对确因电子信息原因通不过的退税申请，应适当采用人机结合的办法进行审核。

（二）各级国家税务局应按照出口退税专用税票认证系统的有关规定采集、传递、分发、使用专用税票电子信息，确保电子信息的完整性和正确性。具体办法另行规定。

四、防范和打击骗取出口退税的违法犯罪行为

（一）各级税务部门、外经贸部门必须时刻注意骗取退税的新动向，密切配合，加强协作，提醒和教育企业采取切实可行措施，防范骗取出口退税，避免给企业和国家造成损失。

（二）对从事“四自三不见”买单业务的出口企业，一经发现，无论退税额大小或是否申报退税，一律停止其半年以上的退税权。对采取其他手段骗取退税的，也要按规定严惩不贷，情节严重的，由外经贸部及其授权单位批准，撤销其出口经营权。对有关责任人员，要提请司法机关处理，绝不姑息。

五、本通知自1998年6月1日起执行

以上请遵照执行。

对外贸易经济合作部办公厅关于转发《国家税务总局关于出口货物退（免）税实行按企业分类管理的通知》的通知

〔1998〕外经贸计财字第432号

1998年6月19日

各省、自治区、直辖市及计划单列市外经贸委（厅、局），各外贸中心，各部委直属公司：

现将《国家税务总局关于出口货物退（免）税实行按企业分类管理的通知》（国税发〔1998〕95号）转发给你们，请遵照执行。执行中遇到问题，请及时向外经贸部（计财司）反映。

由于上述通知自7月1日起执行，请你们协助配合当地税务部门抓紧做好出口企业的分类工作。对于进入A、B类企业名单的出口企业，外经贸部需登记备案，请你们务必于6月30日前将企业名单和出口额上报外经贸部（计财司）。

附件：如文

附　件

国家税务总局关于出口货物退（免）税实行按企业分类管理的通知

国税发〔1998〕95号

各省、自治区、直辖市和计划单列市国家税务局：

为了更好地支持出口企业出口创汇，促进我国国民经济的发展，本着既保证出口退税及时、足额到位，又有效防范和打击骗取出口退税违法犯罪行为的原则，国家税务总局决定对出口货物退（免）税实行按企业分类管理、简化退税申报凭证的办法。特通知如下：

一、各主管出口退税的税务机关应对本地区所辖出口企业（包括外商投资企业）进行分类管理，依据其近年来出口退（免）税的实际情况，将出口企业划分为A、B、C、D4类。

（一）A类企业须同时具备以下条件：

1. 必须是生产船舶、大型成套机电设备等生产周期通常在1年以上产品的具有进出口经营权的生产企业；

2. 年创汇额在3000万美元以上；

3. 从未发生过骗税问题；

4. 企业拥有一定规模的资产，如发生骗税案件或错退税款问题，可抵押所退（免）税款；

5. 企业财务制度健全。

（二）B类企业须同时具备以下条件：

1. 连续2年创汇额在3000万美元以上（生产企业可放宽为2000万美元以上）；

2. 近3年来未发生过骗税或涉嫌骗税问题；

3. 企业拥有一定规模的资产，如发生骗税案件或错退税款问题，可抵押所退（免）税款；

4．企业财务制度健全。

（三）C类企业须同时具备以下条件：

1．近3年来未发生过骗税问题；

2．企业财务制度健全。

（四）D类企业是指近3年来曾发生过骗税问题的出口企业。

二、对A类企业实行先预退税后核销的管理办法。A类企业出口的货物，在其退税凭证尚未收集齐全的情况下，可凭出口合同、销售明细帐，按季填具《生产企业自营（委托）出口货物免、抵、退税申报表》或《生产企业出口货物退（免）税申报表》申报退（免）税。经审核无误，主管税务机关可据此办理退（免）税的审核、审批手续。待该企业将有关退税凭证收集齐全后，再予逐笔复审（包括凭证审核、电子信息对审）核销已退（免）税款。所退（免）税款在年度终了后，按出口退税清算的规定进行清算，多退（免）税款予以补缴入中央库，少退（免）税款予以补退。

三、对B类企业实行按简化凭证申报办理退税的管理办法。B类企业出口的货物，在货物报关出口后，可凭出口货物报关单（出口退税专用联）、增值税税收（出口货物专用）缴款书申报退（免）税。其他凭证（即出口收汇核销单、增值税专用发票、出口发票等辅助凭证）可不按月附送，但须装订成册备查。主管出口退税的税务机关经审核（包括凭证审核、电子信息对审）无误，即可办理退（免）税的审批手续。

对B类企业出口货物的出口收汇核销单，实行总量控制、年终清算，如在次年清算结束时尚未核销外汇的，除由外经贸主管部门按规定出具中、远期结汇证明的出口货物外，主管出口退税的税务机关应按比例从已退税款中扣回未核销外汇部分的税款。

四、对C类企业实行单证齐全方可申报办理退税的管理办法。C类企业出口的货物，在货物报关出口后，须将出口货物报关单（出口退税专用联）、增值税税收（出口货物专用）缴款书、出口收汇核销单、增值税专用发票等退税凭证收集齐全后，方可申报退税。主管出口退税的税务机关在认真审核其退税凭证、电子信息的基础上审批退税。

五、对D类企业实行严格的退税申报、审核、审批管理办法。D类企业出口货物退税的申报审批，除按C类企业办法管理外，主管出口退税的税务机关对其退税申报资料须进行严格审核，经调查核实，在确定出口货物的货款确已直接付给销货方且退税凭证、电子信息真实、齐全、无误的基础上审批退税。

六、A类企业名单由各省、自治区、直辖市和计划单列市国家税务局上报国家税务总局，国家税务总局会商外经贸部后审批下达。B类、C类、D类企业名单的确定由各省、自治区、直辖市和计划单列市国家税务局会商同级外经贸委（厅、局）后依据本地实际情况自定。如在一个省、市、自治区范围内符合本通知条件的B类企业不足10户的，可在年出口额3000万美元以下的企业中选定，补足10户。

七、出口企业的分类实行一年一审制。每年年度退税清算结束1个月内，各主管出口退税的税务机关应依上年出口退（免）税实际，对出口企业的分类重新进行调整。其中对建议为A类企业的企业名单，由各省、自治区、直辖市和计划单列市国家税务局于当年6月底前上报总局审批。

八、被确定为A类、B类的出口企业，如有从事骗税业务的，一经发现，自动丧失A类、B类企业申报退税的优惠待遇，除立即转为D类企业管理外，主管出口退税的税务机关还要依据现行有关规定对其进行处罚。

九、出口企业一经确定为D类企业，3年内不得转定为A类、B类、C类企业。

十、各主管出口退税的税务机关应本着实事求是的原则，严格按本通知规定的条件对所辖出口企业进行分类管理。对明知出口企业不符合A类、B类、C类等级条件而有意将该出口企业申请、确定为A类、B类、C类企业的单位，国家税务总局将予以通报批评。

十一、本通知自1998年7月1日起执行。

对外贸易经济合作部办公厅关于转发《关于提高煤炭、钢材、水泥及船舶出口退税率的通知》的通知

〔1998〕外经贸计财字第470号

1998年6月30日

各省、自治区、直辖市及计划单列市外经贸委（厅、局）（含深圳市经发局），各部委直属公司，各外贸中心：

现将财政部、国家税务总局《关于提高煤炭、钢材、水泥及船舶出口退税率的通知》（财税字〔1998〕102号）转发给你们，请遵照执行。

特此通知。

附件：如文

附　件

财政部　国家税务总局关于提高煤炭、钢材、水泥及船舶出口退税率的通知

财税字〔1998〕102号

各省、自治区、直辖市、计划单列市财政厅（局）、国家税务局：

为增强煤炭、钢材、水泥及船舶等产品在国际市场的竞争力，缓解上述四个行业生产经营的困难，经国务院批准，决定适当调高煤炭等四类产品的出口退税率。现将有关问题通知如下：

一、煤炭出口退税率调为9%，煤炭的具体范围仍按财税字〔1997〕14号文件的有关规定执行；

钢材出口退税率调为11%，但对列名企业销售到保税区“以产顶进”国产钢材的退税率仍按财税字〔1998〕53号文件执行；

水泥出口退税率调为11%；

船舶出口退税率调为14%。

二、本通知自1998年6月1日起执行，具体执行日期按“出口货物报关单（出口退税联）”上注明的海关离境日期为准。

请遵照执行。

金 融、外 汇

对外贸易经济合作部办公厅关于转发财政部《关于申请办理出口信用保险若干规定的通知》的通知

〔1998〕外经贸计财字第308号
1998年5月7日

各省、自治区、直辖市及计划单列市外经贸委（厅、局），各外贸中心，本部各直属公司：

现将财政部《关于申请办理出口信用保险若干规定的通知》（财商字〔1998〕103号）转发给你们，请按照执行。执行中有何问题，请及时向我部（计财司）反映。

附件：如文

附 件

财政部关于申请办理出口信用保险若干规定的通知

财商字〔1998〕103号

国务院各部、委，各直属机构，各省、自治区、直辖市、计划单列市人民政府：

我国开办出口信用保险业务十年来，在支持外贸出口和避免出口企业的收汇风险，维护国家利益等方面起到了积极作用。为了加强国家对出口信用保险风险的管理和控制，规范出口信用保险经办机构（以下简称“经办机构”）和出口企业的行为，按国务院要求，现将企业申请办理出口信用保险的有关规定通知如下：

一、我国目前经办出口信用保险的机构是中保财产保险有限公司和中国进出口银行。企业投保出口信用保险业务，一律由这两家经办机构办理。

二、出口信用保险分为以下三种：

（一）短期出口信用保险（简称“短期险”）。短期险承保放帐期在180天以内的收汇风险，主要用于以付款交单（D/P）、承兑交单（D/A）、赊帐（O/A）等商业信用为付款条件的出口。根据实际情况，短期险还可扩展承保放帐期在180天以上、360天以内的出口，以及银行或其他金融机构开具的信用证项下的出口。

（二）中长期出口信用保险（简称“中长期险”），可分为买方信贷保险、卖方信用保险和海外投资保险三大类。中长期险承保放帐期在一年以上、一般不超过10年的收汇风险，主要用于大型机电产品和成套设备的出口，以及海外投资，如以BOT、BOO或合资等形式在境外兴办企业等。

（三）与出口相关的履约保证保险（简称“保证保险”）。保证保险分为直接保证保险和间接保证保险。直接保证保险包括开立预付款保函、出具履约保证保险等；间接保证保险包括承保进口方不合理没收出口方银行保函。

三、短期出口信用保险的申办要求。短期险是以“买方信用限额”为责任上限，由经办机构承担企业收汇风险责任。“买方信用限额”是经办机构根据付款方式对进口方资信调查，对出口企业向某一进口方就某一付款方式将承担的最高保险责任余额。经批准后的“买方信用限额”可循环使用，即：如不发生保险赔偿责任，出口企业可以在收到买方付款后，继续按原定付款方式和约定限额向该进口方出口发货。为此，企业如需办理短期信用保险，应在对外签订出口合同前，向经办机构投保短期险，并将进口方和开证行的英文名称、地址、负责人、联系电话及传真，以及已获知的进口方资信情况提供给经办机构，并办理“买方信用限额”申请手续。待“买方信用限额”批准后，企业可在该限额内组织发货。

四、中长期出口信用保险的申办要求。由于中长期险的保险金额较大，还款期限较长，风险程度相对短期险要大得多。因此，企业在安排中长期出口项目时，要特别注意按规定预先落实保险事宜。出口企业投保中长期险需按下列程序逐一落实：

（一）企业在对外投标或草签中长期出口合同前，至少提前一个月，向经办机构递交《投保申请书》，同时提供下列材料：

1. 项目名称、项目规模、合同金额、项目所在地等；

2. 拟定信贷方式、信贷条件等（进口方一般需要支付15%的预付款）；

3. 进口方名称、地址和资信材料；

4. 借款人或转贷行（在我国提供买方信贷时）名称、地址和资信情况；

5. 还款担保人的名称、地址和资信情况；

6. 出口项目可行性分析报告（包括技术、专利、换汇成本预测、经济效益等）；

7. 进出口双方拟草签的商务合同，或出口企业拟投标书中商务部分；

8. 出口企业的营业执照及要求的其他文件。

（二）经办机构在收到上述《投保申请书》及所附文件后，即对投保项目进行初步审评，如符合国家政策性出口信用保险支持条件，将在四周内出具《承保意向书》。企业可凭此意向书向银行申请信贷。

（三）在进出口双方就商务合同条件、贷款银行与借款人就有关出口信贷协议条款达成一致后，经办机构将对整个项目和全部合同文件进行审定，核定保险费率，并按国家有关规定履行报批手续后出具保险单或签订保险协议。

五、经办机构按国家政策规定，在授权范围内，代表政府办理具体保险业务。为确保国家出口信用保险的正常经营，对出口企业的下列情况，经办机构不得办理保险事宜：

1. 未征得经办机构同意，擅自对外承诺或签署合同；

2. 先出运后投保；

3. 其他不符合国家有关规定的行为。

六、凡违反本通知规定造成的出口经营损失，不论项目和金额大小，一律由出口企业自负。

七、本通知自发布之日起实施。

对外贸易经济合作部办公厅关于转发中国人民银行《关于进一步支持对外经济贸易发展的意见》的通知

〔1998〕外经贸计财字第568号
1998年7月31日

各省、自治区、直辖市及计划单列市外经贸委（厅、局），各外贸中心，各部委直属公司，各部委所属对外经济合作企业：

现将中国人民银行《关于进一步支持对外经济贸易发展的意见》（银发〔1998〕332号）转发你们，并补充通知如下，请一并贯彻执行：

一、各外经贸企业要认真组织学习文件精神，充分认识到在当前形势下进一步加强银贸协作的重要性，加强与银行的沟通和联系，取得银行的理解和支持。

二、针对自身的实际情况，积极与有关银行联系、协商，抓紧落实银行进一步支持对外经济贸易发展的各项政策、措施，制定具体实施办法。

三、要进一步加强资金管理，努力降低成本、费用，提高资金的使用效率。

四、在企业改组、改制过程中，要加强银行债权的保全和维护，制止各种形式逃废银行债务、悬空银行债权的行为。

五、执行中有何问题，请及时向我部（计财司）反映。

附件：如文

附　件

中国人民银行关于进一步支持对外经济贸易发展的意见

银发〔1998〕332号

中国人民银行各省、自治区、直辖市分行、深圳经济特区分行；各国有商业银行，其它商业银行，城市商业银行（由当地人民银行转发）：

为促进对外经济贸易的发展，支持出口多元化战略，确保今年经济增长目标的实现，根据《贷款通则》和中国人民银行《关于改进金融服务，支持国民经济发展的指导意见》，现就有关问题提出如下意见：

一、完善支持对外经贸发展的金融服务体系。为适应对外经济贸易发展的需要，国家银行要进一步加大对外经贸支持的力度。中国银行要继续发挥支持外经贸发展的主渠道作用，促进外经贸企业的更快发展；其他国有商业银行要加大对自营进出口工业企业、农业和乡镇企业以及其他企业出口创汇的支持；城市商业银行等其他金融机构对开户企业的外经贸出口也要给予大力支持；政策性银行要充分发挥自身特点，积极支持机电产品和成套设备等出口。金融机构在支持对外经贸发展中，既要支持外经贸企业的进出口，又要支持其他企业的自营进出口；既要支持国有外贸企业的发展，又要支持非国有外贸企业的发展。

二、适当增加对外经贸企业的贷款。有关银行要适当增加对外经贸企业的贷款，重点支持有效益、信誉好、有稳定经贸关系的进出口企业；鼓励有关金融机构组织国内银团本外币贷款或参与国外银团贷款，支持外经贸企业的发展。

三、对资信良好的企业适当发放信用贷款，增加授信额度。有关银行可根据外经贸企业的特点及其偿债能力、获利能力、经营管理能力、履约情况及发展潜力等因素对外经贸企业的信用进行评定。对经审查、评估，确认资信良好，有偿还贷款保证的企业，按照《商业银行法》的规定，可以实行授信额度管理。

四、支持企业多渠道筹集资本金。对效益好、守信用、还款有保证的外经贸企业，可以比照工业企业的办法发放中期流动资金贷款，帮助其将部分参与流动资金周转的自有资金用于增加效益好的中外合资企业的中方股本；积极支持外经贸企业通过资本市场筹集资金，拓宽资本金来源渠道。

五、运用利率手段支持外经贸发展。商业银行要认真执行中国人民银行的利率政策，对风险小、效益好、守信用、贷款额度大的外经贸企业，利率可以不上浮或少上浮；严禁乱提高存贷款利率。

六、积极为外经贸企业的发展提供保险服务。鼓励国内财产保险公司拓展进出口远洋货物运输保险，作好承保、理赔工作，支持外经贸业务的发展；发挥出口信用保险在支持外贸出口特别是机电设备出口方面的积极作用。经办出口信用保险的机构要严格按照国家风险分类，在核定的国别限额内开展业务，严禁无序竞争、任意降低费率。

七、继续加大对机电产品出口的支持力度。中国人民银行对政策性银行支持机电产品出口的贷款继续实行贷款限额管理，可根据需要适当增加机电产品出口信贷规模。各有关商业银行要认真执行《关于金融系统要进一步做好支持机电产品出口工作的通知》（中国人民银行银发〔1997〕61号）和《关于调整机电产品出口卖方信贷贷款利率的通知》（中国人民银行银发〔1996〕23号），加大对机电产品出口的支持。

八、积极支持企业境外工程承包和到境外投资设厂。对我国企业境外工程承包项目中机电或成套设备50%以上由国内提供的，各有关银行应给予优先支持，其境外分支机构应提供相关的配套服务；对经济效益特别突出的项目，在保证信贷资金安全的前提下，还可适当放宽国内提供的机电或成套设备的比例，但最低不得低于20%。对符合条件的企业到境外投资设厂的，要积极予以支持。特别是对那些产品在国内市场趋于饱和而国外市场前景看好的企业、利用国内设备和零部件到国外进行生产和组装的企业，如其资金不足要优先予以支持。

九、积极支持外商和台、港、澳、侨商投资企业的发展。各银行要根据《外商投资产业指导目录》的要求，优先支持鼓励类企业的资金需要；增加其人民币和外汇贷款；对因受亚洲金融危机影响，资金暂时不能到位但经济效益好的高新技术产业和有利于扩大就业的外商和台、港、澳、侨商投资企业的在建项目，可适当给予信贷支持；要通过改进金融服务帮助外商和台、港、澳、侨商投资企业改善投资环境。

十、支持合理的外贸进口。在支持外贸出口的同时，要支持合理的外贸进口。对符合国家进口政策的产品，特别是国内短缺的资源性产品和高新技术产品的进口，有关银行要积极给予金融支持。

十一、运用“封闭贷款”支持外经贸企业。对暂时亏损，但有订单、还款有保证的外经贸企业，可参照国有工业企业的办法对其发放封闭贷款，经贷款行严格审查后，通过开证、发放打包贷款、押汇、贷款回收等一条龙服务的方式支持其发展。对濒临破产的企业不能发放这类贷款。

十二、防范外经贸贷款中的金融风险。在对外经贸企业提供支持的同时，要依法维护银行贷款自主权，防范金融风险。任何单位或个人不得强迫银行发放贷款或提供担保。对经营性亏损严重、濒临破产、无贷款偿还能力的企业，对以各种形式逃废、悬空银行债务和有意拖欠银行贷款本息的企业，对挪用贷款从事股票、期货交易的企业，对国家法律、法规和产业政策明令禁止或限制支持的项目、企业、产品等，各金融机构必须停止发放新贷款，限期收回已发放的贷款。要加快中央银行贷款登记系统的建设，为商业银行提供贷款信息查询服务，防止企业利用多头开户、多头贷款等手段逃避银行债务。

中国人民银行　外经贸部　国家税务总局
关于对国有亏损外经贸企业实行
封闭贷款有关问题的通知

银发〔1998〕397号

1998年8月31日

中国人民银行各省、自治区、直辖市分行，深圳经济特区分行；各国有独资商业银行；各省、自治区、直辖市及计划单列市外经贸委（厅、局），国家税务局、地方税务局；外经贸部各直属公司：

为了支持国有亏损外经贸企业有订单、有效益、有市场的产品出口和对外工程承包，帮助这些企业实现扭亏增盈，现就有关问题通知如下；

一、各地银行、外经贸主管部门要组织调查，摸清此类企业和产品出口以及对外工程承包等情况，并采取积极措施，支持其有订单、有效益、有市场的产品出口和对外工程承包，帮助企业逐步扭亏为盈，摆脱困境。

二、对亏损的国有外经贸企业有订单、有效益、有市场的产品出口和对外工程承包，各地银行可以比照中国人民银行和国家经贸委《关于支持国有亏损工业企业有销路、有效益产品生产的通知》（银发〔1997〕385号）和中国人民银行、国家经贸委和国家税务总局《关于进一步支持国有亏损工业企业有销路、有效益产品生产的补充通知》（银发〔1998〕265号）的有关精神实行"封闭贷款"，支持外经贸企业的发展。实行"封闭贷款"的企业要对这类出口产品和工程承包项目单独进行成本核算，并在银行设立专户，保证货款和工程款的单独收支、专款专用。

三、各级税务机关要积极参与银行、外经贸主管部门组织的调查，银行、外经贸主管部门确定实施"封闭贷款"的企业及设立专户时，要商得同级税务机关同意。

四、为保证"封闭贷款"的正常运行，在封闭运行期间，有关部门不能用专户的贷款扣取老的欠税、各种费用，企业不能用其支付拖欠的工资，银行也不能在这个帐户上扣收老的欠款和欠息，切实做到对企业所欠的"税、费、薪、贷"一律不得在专户中扣缴。但使用"封闭贷款"所取得的应纳税收入应当缴纳当期税款。

五、封闭贷款实行逐笔核贷的方式，其相应的经营业务结束后，封闭贷款的运行期间即告结束，各单位应按时足额归还贷款本息。

六、各级银行、外经贸主管部门和税务部门要密切配合，加强对此类贷款的管理，保证信贷资金的安全。要把防范金融风险同促进经济发展有机结合起来，支持国有外经贸企业的改革和发展。

对外贸易经济合作部关于印发《对外贸易经济合作部对逃、套汇外经贸企业给予行政处罚的暂行规定》的通知

〔1998〕外经贸计财发第713号
1998年10月9日

各省、自治区、直辖市及计划单列市外经贸委（厅、局）（含深圳市贸发局），各外贸中心，各部委直属公司：

为打击逃、套汇等违法犯罪行为，维护正常的金融外汇管理秩序和进出口管理秩序，根据《国务院关于加强外汇外债管理开展外汇外债检查的通知》和《中华人民共和国外汇管理条例》的有关规定，我部制定了《对外贸易经济合作部对逃、套汇外经贸企业给予行政处罚的暂行规定》，现印发给你们，请认真贯彻执行，并做好宣传工作。本暂行规定自1998年10月1日起执行。

附件：

一、《对外贸易经济合作部对逃、套汇外经贸企业给予行政处罚的暂行规定》

二、最高人民法院关于审理骗购外汇、非法买卖外汇刑事案件具体应用法律若干问题的解释、刑法有关条款、外汇管理条例有关条款

附件一

对外贸易经济合作部对逃、套汇外经贸企业给予行政处罚的暂行规定

第一条 为严厉打击逃、套汇违法行为，根据《中华人民共和国行政处罚法》、《中华人民共和国对外贸易法》、《中华人民共和国外汇管理条例》以及有关法律、法规，特制定本规定。

第二条 本规定所指逃、套汇行为，系指《中华人民共和国外汇管理条例》中列明的，经外汇管理机关认定的逃、套汇行为。

（一）逃汇行为指：违反国家规定，擅自将外汇存放在境外的；不按照国家规定将外汇卖给外汇指定银行的；违反国家规定将外汇汇出或者携带出境的；未经外汇管理机关批准，擅自将外币存款凭证、外币有价证卷携带或者邮寄出境的；其他逃汇行为。

（二）套汇行为指：违反国家规定，以人民币支付或者以实物偿付应当以外汇支付的进口货款或者其他类似支出的；以人民币为他人支付在境内的费用，由对方付给外汇的；未经外汇管理机关批准，境外投资者以人民币或者境内所购物资在境内进行投资的；以虚假或者无效的凭证、合同、单据等向外汇指定银行骗购外汇的；非法套汇的其他行为。

第三条 本规定所指外经贸企业是指外贸公司（包括中外合资外贸公司）、自营进出口生产企业和科研院所、有进出口经营权的商业物资企业、外商投资企业、对外承包劳务企业、加工贸易企业、边贸企业、旅游小额贸易企业等。

第四条 对逃、套汇外经贸企业的行政处罚包括给予警告、暂停或撤销对外贸易经营许可等形式。

第五条 凡经外汇管理机关认定有逃、套汇行为并给予行政处罚的外经贸企业，按本暂行规定给予处罚。

第六条 对外贸易经济合作部或其授权的省

级外经贸主管部门在外汇管理机关依法给予行政处罚的基础上，视情节轻重，对从事、参与套汇的外经贸企业分别给予以下行政处罚：

（一）对套汇金额在50万美元以下的企业，给予暂停3个月对外贸易进口经营许可的处罚。其中，对外商投资企业，通知海关暂停办理其进口业务3个月。

（二）对套汇金额在50万美元以上（含50万美元）、100万美元以下的企业，给予暂停6个月对外贸易进口经营许可的处罚。其中，对外商投资企业，通知海关暂停办理其进口业务6个月。

（三）对套汇金额超过100万美元（含100万美元）的企业，给予撤销对外贸易进口经营许可的处罚。其中，对外商投资企业，通知海关停止办理其进口业务。

第七条 对在代理进口业务中因不按正常贸易程序操作，管理不严而受骗形成套汇、给国家造成损失的外经贸企业，对外贸易经济合作部或其授权的省级外经贸主管部门给予以下处罚：

（一）对造成损失金额在100万美元以下的企业，给予警告处罚并予以通报。

（二）对造成损失金额在100万美元以上（含100万美元）、300万美元以下的企业，给予暂停3个月对外贸易进口经营许可的处罚。

（三）对造成损失金额在300万美元以上（含300万美元）、500万美元以下的企业，给予暂停6个月对外贸易进口经营许可的处罚。

（四）对造成损失金额超过500万美元（含500万美元）的企业，给予撤销对外贸易进口经营许可的处罚。

第八条 对外贸易经济合作部或其授权的省级外经贸主管部门在外汇管理机关依法给予行政处罚的基础上，视情节轻重，对逃汇外经贸企业分别给予以下行政处罚：

（一）对逃汇在100万美元以下的企业，给予警告处罚并予以通报。

（二）对逃汇在100万美元以上(含100万美元)、300万美元以下的企业,给予暂停其3个月对外贸易出口经营许可或单项商品、单项业务的出口经营许可的处罚。其中,对外商投资企业,通知海关暂停办理其出口业务或单项商品、单项业务出口3个月。

（三）对逃汇在300万美元以上（含300万美元）、500万美元以下的企业，给予暂停其6个月对外贸易出口经营许可或单项商品、单项业务的对外贸易出口经营许可的处罚。其中，对外商投资企业，通知海关暂停办理其出口业务或单项商品、单项业务出口6个月。

（四）对逃汇超过500万美元（含500万美元）的企业，给予其撤销对外贸易出口经营许可的处罚。其中，对外商投资企业，通知海关停止办理其出口业务。在海关恢复对外商投资企业办理进出口业务之前，其产品外销仍需按其合同和章程所规定的比例履行义务，可通过外贸代理方式出口。

第九条 对进出口核销达不到外汇管理机关规定的核销比例的外经贸企业，对外贸易经济合作部或其授权的省级外经贸主管部门将对其给予警告处罚并予以通报。对出口收汇核销率低于50%的企业，给予暂停其3个月对外贸易出口经营许可或单项商品、单项业务的出口经营许可的处罚。其中，对外商投资企业，通知海关暂停办理其出口业务或单项商品、单项业务出口3个月。

第十条 对参与上述逃、套汇行为的当事人和企业负责人，将由行政主管部门视其情节轻重予以记过直至撤职或开除公职的处分；构成犯罪的，移送司法机关依法追究刑事责任。

第十一条 对外贸易经济合作部或其授权的省级外经贸主管部门在对逃、套汇外经贸企业作出暂停或撤销对外贸易经营许可的行政处罚之前，应告知企业有要求举行听证的权利；企业要求听证的，对外贸易经济合作部或其授权的省级外经贸主管部门应组织听证。听证结束后，对外贸易经济合作部或其授权的省级外经贸主管部门依据有关法律、法规及听证情况，最终决定是否给予行政处罚。

第十二条 对外贸易经济合作部或其授权的省级外经贸主管部门在作出行政处罚决定后的3个工作日内，将处罚决定书发送企业同时抄送外汇管理机关；无法发送的，公告送达。

第十三条 企业对行政处罚决定不服的，可以按照《行政复议条例》向对外贸易经济合作部行政复议委员会提起行政复议，或按照《中华人民共和国行政诉讼法》提起行政诉讼。

第十四条 本规定由对外贸易经济合作部负责解释。

第十五条 本规定自1998年10月1日起施行。

附件二

最高人民法院关于审理骗购外汇、非法买卖外汇刑事案件具体应用法律若干问题的解释

（1998年9月1日起施行）

为依法惩处骗购外汇、非法买卖外汇的犯罪行为，根据刑法的有关规定，现对审理骗购外汇、非法买卖外汇案件具体应用法律的若干问题解释如下：

第一条 以进行走私、逃汇、洗钱、骗税等犯罪活动为目的，使用虚假、无效的凭证、商业单据或采取其他手段向外汇指定银行骗购外汇的，应当分别按照刑法分则第三章第二节、第一百九十条、第一百九十一条和第二百零四条等规定定罪处罚。

非国有公司、企业或其他单位，与国有公司、企业和其他国有单位勾结逃汇的以逃汇罪的共犯处罚。

第二条 伪造、变造、买卖海关签发的报关单、进口证明、外汇管理机关的核准件等凭证或者购买伪造、变造的上述凭证的，按照刑法第二百八十条第一款的规定处罚。

第三条 在外汇指定银行和中国外汇交易中心及其分中心以买卖外汇，扰乱金融市场秩序，具有下列情形之一的，按照刑法第二百二十五条第（三）项的规定定罪处罚：

（一）非法买卖外汇20万美元以上的；

（二）违法所得5万元人民币以上的。

第四条 公司、企业或者其他单位，违反有关外贸代理业务的规定，采取非法手段，或者明知是伪造、变造的凭证、商业单据，为他人向外汇指定银行骗购外汇，数额在500万美元以上或者违法所得50万元人民币以上的，按照刑法第二百二十五条第（三）项的规定定罪处罚。

居间介绍骗购外汇100万美元以上或者违法所得10万元人民币以上的，按照刑法第二百二十五条第（三）项的规定定罪处罚。

第五条 海关、银行、外汇管理机关工作人员与骗购外汇的行为人通谋，为其提供购买外汇的有关凭证，或者明知是伪造、变造的凭证和商业单据而出售外汇，构成犯罪的，按照刑法的有关规定从重处罚。

第六条 实施本解释规定的行为，同时触犯两个以上罪名的，择一重罪从重处罚。

第七条 根据刑法第六十四条规定，骗购外汇、非法买卖外汇的，其违法所得予以追缴，用于骗购外汇、非法买卖外汇的资金予以没收，上缴国库。

第八条 骗购、非法买卖不同币种的外汇的，以案发时国家外汇管理机关制定的统一折算率折合后依照本解释处罚。

刑 法 有 关 条 款

（1997 年 10 月 1 日起施行）

分则第三章“破坏社会主义市场经济秩序罪”；第二节“走私罪”。

第六十四条 犯罪分子违法所得的一切财物，应当予以追缴或者责令退赔；对被害人的合法财产，应当及时返还；违禁品和供罪所用的本人财物，应当予以没收。没收的财物和罚金，一律上缴国库，不得挪用和自行处理。

第一百九十条 国有公司、企业或者其他国有单位，违反国家规定，擅自将外汇存放境外，或者将境内的外汇非法转移到境外，情节严重的，对单位判处罚金，并对其直接负责的主管人员和其他直接责任人员，处五年以下有期徒刑或者拘役。

第一百九十一条 明知是毒品犯罪、黑社会性质的组织犯罪、走私犯罪的违法所得及其产生的收益，为掩饰、隐瞒其来源和性质，有下列行为之一的，没收实施以上犯罪的违法所得及其产生的收益，处 5 年以下有期徒刑或者拘役，并处或者单处洗钱数额 5% 以上 20% 以下罚金；情节严重的，处 5 年以上 10 年以下有期徒刑，并处洗钱数额 5% 以上 20% 以下罚金：

（一）提供资金帐户的；

（二）协助将财产转换为现金或者金融票据的；

（三）通过转帐或者其他结算方式协助资金转移的；

（四）协助将资金汇往境外的；

（五）以其他方式掩饰、隐瞒犯罪的违法所得及其收益的性质和来源的。

单位犯前款罪的，对单位判处罚金，并对其直接负责的主管人员和其他直接责任人员，处 5 年以下有期徒刑或者拘役。

第二百零四条 以假报出口或者其他欺骗手段，骗取国家出口退税款，数额较大的，处 5 年以下有期徒刑或者拘役，并处骗取税款 1 倍以上 5 倍以下罚金；数额巨大或者有其他严重情节的，处 5 年以上 10 年以下有期徒刑，并处骗取税款 1 倍以上 5 倍以下罚金；数额特别巨大或者有其他特别严重情节的，处 10 年以上有期徒刑或者无期徒刑，并处骗取税款 1 倍以上 5 倍以下罚金或者没收财产。

纳税人缴纳税款后，采取前款规定的欺骗方法，骗取所缴纳的税款的，依照本法第二百零一条的规定定罪处罚；骗取税款超过所缴纳的税款部分，依照前款的规定处罚。

第二百二十五条 违反国家规定，有下列非法经营行为之一，扰乱市场秩序，情节严重的，处 5 年以下有期徒刑或者拘役，并处或者单处违法所得 1 倍以上 5 倍以下罚金；情节特别严重的，处 5 年以上有期徒刑，并处违法所得 1 倍以上 5 倍以下罚金或者没收财产：

（一）未经许可经营法律、行政法规规定的专营、专卖物品或者其他限制买卖的物品的；

（二）买卖进出口许可证、进出口原产地证明以及其他法律、行政法规规定的经营许可证或者批准文件的；

（三）其他严重扰乱市场秩序的非法经营行为。

第二百八十条第一款 伪造、变造、买卖或者盗窃、抢夺、毁灭国家机关的公文、证件、印章的，处 3 年以下有期徒刑、拘投、管制或者剥夺政治权利；情节严重的，处 3 年以上 10 年以下有期徒刑。

外汇管理条例有关条款

(1996年4月1日起施行)

第三十九条　有下列逃汇行为之一的，由外汇管理机关责令限期调回外汇，强制收兑，并处逃汇金额30%以上5倍以下的罚款；构成犯罪的，依法追究刑事责任：

(一) 违反国家规定，擅自将外汇存放在境外的；

(二) 不按照国家规定将外汇卖给外汇指定银行的；

(三) 违反国家规定将外汇汇出或者携带出境的；

(四) 未经外汇管理机关批准，擅自将外币存款凭证、外币有价证券携带或者邮寄出境的；

(五) 其他逃汇行为。

第四十条　有下列非法套汇行为之一的，由外汇管理机关给予警告，强制收兑，并处套汇金额30%以上3倍以下的罚款；构成犯罪的，依法追究刑事责任：

(一) 违反国家规定，以人民币支付或者以实物偿付应当以外汇支付的进口货款或者其他类似支出的；

(二) 以人民币为他人支付在境内的费用，由对方付给外汇的；

(三) 未经外汇管理机关批准，境外投资者以人民币或者境内所购物资在境内进行投资的；

(四) 以虚假或者无效的凭证、合同、单据等向外汇指定银行骗购外汇的；

(五) 非法套汇的其他行为。

第四十八条　境内机构违反外汇核销管理规定，伪造、涂改、出借、转让或者重复使用进出口核销单证的，或者未按规定办理核销手续的，由外汇管理机关给予警告，通报批评，没收违法所得，并处5万元以上30万以下的罚款；构成犯罪的，依法追究刑事责任。

对外贸易经济合作部办公厅关于转发中国进出口银行《关于调整人民币出口卖方信贷利率的通知》的通知

〔1998〕外经贸机电字第25号

1998年8月4日

各省、自治区、直辖市及计划单列市外经贸委（厅、局），机电产品进出口办公室，有关机电外（工）贸总公司：

为进一步促进我国机电产品，特别是大型、成套设备出口，经中国人民银行批准，中国进出口银行决定从1998年7月1日起对现行出口卖方信贷利率确定方式进行改革，并相应调整其利率水平。现将中国进出口银行《关于调整人民币出口卖方信贷利率的通知》（进出银计发〔1998〕191号）转发给你们，并请通知到有关企业。

在当前外贸出口资金仍然比较紧张的情况下，各地机电办要帮助机电出口企业用好这笔资金，积极组织企业做好出口工作，努力完成今年机电产品出口650亿美元的争取目标。

附件：如文

附　件

中国进出口银行关于调整人民币出口卖方信贷利率的通知

进出银计发〔1998〕第191号

各部、室：

根据人民银行银发〔1998〕326号《关于改革机电产品出口卖方信贷利率确定方式的通知》的精神，现就我行人民币出口卖方信贷利率有关问题明确如下：

一、出口卖方信贷利率与中长期贷款利率脱钩，由人民银行确定基准利率，并随国家利率调整而调整。

二、出口卖方信贷利率分两档：第一档为大型成套设备和技术含量高的机电产品（技术含量高的机电产品指1997年11月外经贸部和国家科委制定的中国高技术产品出口目录中的机电产品）利率为5.22%；第二档为其他机电产品，利率为5.85%。两档利率均不分期限。

三、根据我国经济和外贸出口形势，今年出口卖方信贷利率暂不浮动，执行人民银行批准的利率。

四、此次利率调整从1998年7月1日起执行。

附：一、人民币出口卖方信贷利率表

二、关于改革机电产品出口卖方信贷利率确定方式的通知（略）

附件一

人民币出口卖方信贷利率表

单位：年利率%

产　品　分　类	利　　　率
大型成套设备和技术含量高的机电产品	5.22
其他机电产品	5.85

检　验、检　疫

国家进出口商品检验局　国家机电产品进出口办公室关于旧机电产品进口和商品检验的有关规定

国检检联〔1998〕26号
1998年2月8日

各地区商检局，各地区、各部门机电办：

为了更好地贯彻执行国家经济贸易委员会、对外贸易经济合作部、海关总署、国家进出口商品检验局联合发出的“关于加强旧机电产品进口管理的通知”精神，保护环境，保障人民健康和生产安全，现就旧机电产品进口和商检的有关问题规定如下：

一、凡列入《进口商品安全质量许可制度目录》（见附件1）内的旧机电产品，国家机电产品进出口办公室不予批准进口，商检不予备案。国家特殊需要进口的除外。

二、凡被批准可以进口旧机电产品的单位，在签署合同或有约束力的协议时，必须按照国家安全、卫生、环保等法律、法规方面的要求订明该产品的检验依据及各项技术指标等检验条款；对那些涉及国家安全、环保、人身健康的旧机电产品以及大型“二手”成套设备，进口单位应当在对外贸易合同中订明在出口国进行装运前预检验、监装等条款。

三、进口旧机电产品的单位（或收货人）在合同或协议生效后30日内，持合同或协议及国家机电产品进出口办公室签发的有关进口证件复印件向货物使用地商检机构登记。

对于合同中约定须进行装运前预检验、监装的，商检机构可根据需要派出检验人员参加或者组织实施装运前预检验、监装。

四、进口旧机电产品报关之前，进口单位（或收货人）持国家机电产品进出口办公室签发的有关进口证件正本以及有关外贸单据向到货口岸商检机构申请《旧机电产品进口备案书》（见附件2）。

口岸商检机构在受理备案申请后应出具加盖有“已接受登记”印章的《旧机电产品进口备案书》（第一联），并及时将《旧机电产品进口备案书》（第二联）传递给货物使用地商检机构。

五、进口旧机电产品通关之后，进口单位（或收货人）必须在规定的期限内，持发票、装箱单、提运单等必要的单证，向货物使用地商检机构报验。未报经检验的，不准销售、安装和使用。

六、进口旧机电产品的检验按照《商检法》、《商检法实施条例》及商检有关规定执行。

七、本规定自发布之日起执行。

附件一

第一批实施安全质量许可制度的进口商品目录

1. 汽车
2. 摩托车
3. 摩托车发动机
4. 电冰箱（包括食品冷冻箱）
5. 电冰箱压缩机
6. 空调器
7. 空调器压缩机
8. 电视机（包括黑白及彩色电视机）
9. 显像管

（注：上述9种产品自1990年5月1日起实施，未获安全质量许可证者不准进入中国市场）

第二批实施安全质量许可制度的进口商品目录

1. 家用电动洗衣机
2. 真空吸尘器
3. 皮肤及毛发护理器具
4. 电热水器
5. 电烤箱类
6. 微波炉
7. 电饭锅
8. 电熨斗
9. 电灶类
10. 电动食品加工机
11. 液体加热器类
12. 录像机
13. 音响设备
14. 个人计算机
15. 显示器
16. 开关电源
17. 打印机
18. 电动工具
19. 低压电器
20. 电焊机

（注：上述20类产品自1996年10月1日起实施，未获安全质量许可证者不准进入中国市场）

21. 电信终端产品
22. 安全技术防范产品
23. 火灾报警设备
24. 医用X射线诊断设备
25. 血液透析装置
26. 空心纤维透析器
27. 血液净化装置的体外循环管道
28. 心电图机
29. 植入式心脏起搏器
30. 医用超声诊断和治疗设备
31. 汽车用安全玻璃
32. 汽车轮胎
33. 摩托车轮胎
34. 汽车安全带
35. 锅炉
36. 移动式压力容器
37. 固定式压力容器
38. 锅炉压力容器安全附件

（注：上述18类产品自1997年10月1日起实施，未获安全质量许可证者不准进入中国市场）

附件二

中华人民共和国广东进出口商品检验局
旧机电产品进口备案书

第一联　　　　　　　　　　　　　　　　　　　　　　　　　　　　编号：

____________海关：

______________________________公司______年______月______日

向____________________商检局申请旧机电产品进口备案

旧机电产品名称：____，

《配额产品证明》/《进口许可证》编号：______________/______________，

或《机电产品进口证明》编号：____________________________________，

或《机电产品进口登记表》编号：__________________________________，

合同号：____________________，提（运）单号：____________________。

商检局：　　　　　　盖章　　　　　　　　　　　　　　经办人：

　　　　　　　　　　　　　　　　　　　　　　　　　　办理日期：

注：本备案书第一联仅供海关验放进口旧机电产品用，第二联寄收货人所在地商检机构，第三联口岸商检存档用。第四联给进口单位（或收货人）。

对外贸易经济合作部　海关总署国家出入境检验检疫局关于对输美货物的木质包装进行除害处理的紧急通知

〔1998〕外经贸美大发第808号

1998年10月26日

各省、自治区、直辖市及计划单列市外经贸委（厅、局），各部委直属公司，各商会、协会、学会、广东分署，各直属海关，各地“三检”临时协调小组：

1998年9月11日美国农业部长签署一项新法令，要求所有来自中国的木质包装和木质铺垫材料（以下简称木质包装）须附有中国出入境检验检疫机关出具的证书，证明木质包装在进入美国前经过热处理、熏蒸处理或防腐剂处理，或者出口商出具无木质包装的证明。其目的是防止光肩星天牛(Anoplophora glabripennis)传入美国。违规货物将整批禁止入境，或在美方认可的条件下，拆除销毁木质包装。此法令自签署之日起，宽限期为90天。即从1998年12月17日起，离开中国港口、目的地为美国的中国货物将按照新的检疫规定执行，但如果中国货物12月17日前离开中国某个港口后又进入中国另一个港口（包括香港），并于12月17日以后才离港赴美，则以中国货物离开第二个中国港口日期为准。

为保证我输美货物顺利出口，避免经济损失，本着“有效、简化、合理、规范”的原则，现将有关问题紧急通知如下：

一、企业在生产和出口目的地为美国的出口产品中应尽量避免使用木质包装。

二、确须使用木质包装的货物，其包装物在盛装货物之前须向出入境检验检疫机关报检，并按有关规定对木质包装进行热处理、熏蒸处理或防腐剂处理。出入境检验检疫机关按照有关规定对合格者及时出具熏蒸/消毒证书。具体处理方法和标准由国家出入境检验检疫局另文通知。

三、上述使用木质包装的出口货物，由企业向海关出具熏蒸或消毒证书；海关凭相应证书放行。

四、请各地经贸委（厅）立即将本通知转发至各类出口企业。各地经贸部门、海关、出入境检验检疫机关应进一步提高服务意识，加强宣传工作，注意收集我输美货物通关的反馈情况。切实做到为企业服务，促进出口创汇。

五、本通知规定第一条、第二条自11月10日起实施；第三条规定自12月17日起实施。

特此通知。

国家经济贸易委员会　海关总署
国家出入境检验检疫局　对外贸易经济合作部
关于输美货物木质包装除害处理以及改进
包装有关问题的紧急通知

国经贸贸易〔1998〕702号
1998年11月3日

各省、自治区、直辖市、计划单列市及新疆生产建设兵团经贸委（经委、计经委）、外经贸委（厅、局），海关总署广东分署、各直属海关，各地“三检”临时协调小组：

外经贸部、海关总署、国家出入境检验检疫局于10月26日联合下发了《关于对输美货物的木质包装进行除害处理的紧急通知》（外经贸美大发808号），通报了美国为防止光肩星天牛虫害的传入，将对1998年12月17日以后离港的中国输美货物的木质包装和木质铺垫材料（以下简称木质包装）实施新的检疫规定，要求对所有木质包装进行热处理、熏蒸处理或防腐剂处理，否则禁止货物入境或拆除销毁木质包装。

根据国务院领导同志的指示精神，为保证我对美的正常出口贸易，减少和避免经济损失，现就有关问题补充通知如下：

一、各类出口企业，须在严格执行现行框架木箱（GB7284）、普通木箱（GB12464）国家标准的基础上，对输美货物木质包装按规定进行除害处理，并在盛装货物之前向出入境检验检疫机关报检，在办理出口报关手续时，必须向海关递交出入境检验检疫机关出具的熏蒸、消毒等证书，各海关凭证验放，未出具有关证书的，海关不予放行。防虫害处理的具体方法和标准由国家出入境检验检疫局另文通知。各出入境检验检疫机关要加强对输美货物木质包装材料除害处理的监督管理。

二、凡专门生产出口包装物料的企业，除继续执行国家有关部门现行规范标准外，必须按用户要求对输美货物用的木质包装物进行除害处理。

三、有独立包装车间的大中型生产企业，在生产出口目的地为美国的产品时，须对使用的木质包装材料按规定进行除害处理，并在盛装货物前向当地出入境检验检疫机构报验。

四、小型出口企业确须使用木质包装的输美货物，如不具备对木质包装进行除害处理的条件，必须向能对木质包装进行有关处理的专业木材加工企业或有条件的大中型出口企业购买木质包装。各地经贸委要会同当地出入境检验检疫机关，加紧核定一批能对木质包装进行除害处理的专业木材加工企业或大中型企业的名单，以规范小型出口企业对木质包装材料的采购。

五、积极推进木质包装的升级、替代工作。通过逐步推广以及政策引导，鼓励企业采用经济、实惠的新型包装材料。对500公斤以下的出口货物，各出口企业应尽量采用胶合板、瓦楞纸板等替代材料。各地包装管理机构和包装材料生产企业，要加紧研制和生产成本低廉的替代包装物，以满足出口企业的需要。

六、各地经贸委、外经贸委、出入境检验检疫机构要对本地区使用木质包装向美国出口货物的企业进行摸底调查，实行分类指导，加强对企业的宣传，积极帮助企业做好包装物处理，努力保持和扩大我对美出口。

七、中国包装总公司、全国包装改进办公室要尽快提出有关木质包装质量标准的修改方案，国家出入境检验检疫局提出出口木质包装检验检疫方法标准并作试行；待条件成熟后，提交国家质量技术监督局批准后正式颁布执行。请各地包装主管机构抓紧做好有关实施的准备工作。

八、途经香港输美货物的木质包装材料均按上述要求执行。

九、今后如其他国家有类似检疫要求的，也请按上述精神办理。

港　口、运　输

中华人民共和国国务院令

第 243 号

现发布《国务院关于修改〈中华人民共和国海上国际集装箱运输管理规定〉的决定》，自发布之日起施行。

总　理　　朱镕基

1998 年 4 月 18 日

国务院关于修改《中华人民共和国海上国际集装箱运输管理规定》的决定

国务院决定对《中华人民共和国海上国际集装箱运输管理规定》作如下修改：

一、第二条修改为："本规定适用于从事海上国际集装箱运输及与海上国际集装箱运输有关的单位和个人。

"海上国际集装箱运输是指中华人民共和国港口与外国港口之间的海上集装箱运输，包括按照合同约定全程运输为海上国际集装箱运输的中华人民共和国港口之间的区段。"

二、第六条增加两款，分别作为第二款、第三款："经营海上国际集装箱班轮运输，由国务院交通主管部门批准。

"外国企业不得经营中华人民共和国港口之间的海上集装箱班轮运输。"

三、删去第三十一条，增加一条，作为第三十一条："对违反本规定应当给予行政处罚的行为，县级以上交通主管部门应当全面、客观、公正地进行调查，收集有关证据；必要时，可以查看被调查企业的运输单证、财务帐册等有关资料。

"有关单位和个人对县级以上交通主管部门的调查应当予以配合，如实提供有关资料；县级以上交通主管部门应当为被调查企业保守商业秘密。"

四、第三十二条修改为："违反本规定，同时违反国家有关价格管理的法律、法规的，由价格主管部门依照有关法律、法规的规定给予处罚。"

五、第三十三条修改为："违反本规定第十四条、第二十一条的规定，不使用规定的集装箱运输单证，或者不报送集装箱运输统计报表，或者报送集装箱运输统计报表不实的，由县级以上交通主管部门责令改正；拒不改正的，处 5 万元以下的罚款。"

六、第三十四条修改为："违反本规定，有下列行为之一的，由县级以上交通主管部门责令改正；拒不改正的，没收违法所得，并处违法所得 1 倍以上 3 倍以下的罚款；没有违法所得的，按照以下规定处以罚款：

（一）未经批准，擅自经营海上国际集装箱运输、港口装卸、中转站、货运站业务的，处 3 万元以上 30 万元以下的罚款；

（二）未经批准，擅自经营海上国际集装箱班轮运输，属国内区段的集装箱班轮运输的，处 3 万元以上 30 万元以下的罚款；属远洋国际集装箱班轮运输的，处5万元以上50万元以下的罚款；属远洋国际集装箱班轮运输的，处50万元以上500万元以下的罚款。

“违反前款规定，情节严重的，由工商行政管理部门吊销营业执照。”

七、删去第三十五条、第三十六条。

本决定自发布之日起施行。

此外，对部分条文的文字和条文的顺序作相应的调整和修改。

《中华人民共和国海上国际集装箱运输管理规定》根据本决定作相应的修正，重新发布。

中华人民共和国海上国际集装箱运输管理规定

（1990年12月5日中华人民共和国国务院令第68号发布根据1998年4月18日《国务院关于修改〈中华人民共和国海上国际集装箱运输管理规定〉的决定》修正）

第一章　总　　则

第一条　为加强海上国际集装箱运输管理，明确有关各方责任，适应国家对外贸易的需要，制定本规定。

第二条　本规定适用于从事海上国际集装箱运输及与海上国际集装箱运输有关的单位和个人。

海上国际集装箱运输是指中华人民共和国港口与外国港口之间的海上集装箱运输，包括按照合同约定全程运输为海上国际集装箱运输的中华人民共和国港口之间的区段。

第三条　中华人民共和国国务院交通主管部门主管全国海上国际集装箱运输事业。

第四条　海上国际集装箱运输必须贯彻安全、准确、迅速、经济和文明服务的方针，积极发展门到门运输。

第二章　海上国际集装箱运输企业的设立和班轮航线的审批

第五条　海上国际集装箱运输企业是指从事海上国际集装箱运输的航运企业、港口装卸企业及其承运海上国际集装箱的内陆中转站、货运站。

第六条　设立经营海上国际集装箱运输的航运企业，应当经省、自治区、直辖市交通主管部门审核，报国务院交通主管部门审批。

经营海上国际集装箱班轮运输，由国务院交通主管部门批准。

外国企业不得经营中华人民共和国港口之间的海上集装箱班轮运输。

第七条　设立港口国际集装箱装卸企业应当经省、自治区、直辖市交通主管部门审批，报国务院交通主管部门备案。

本规定发布后新设立承运海上国际集装箱的内陆中转站、货运站，应当经设立该企业的主管部门审核同意后，由省、自治区、直辖市交通主管部门审批，报国务院交通主管部门备案。

对外经济贸易系统新设立的承运海上国际集装箱的内陆中转站、货运站的审批办法，由国务院交通主管部门会同国务院对外经济贸易主管部门另行制定。

第八条　设立中外合资经营、中外合作经营的海上国际集装箱运输企业，须经国务院交通主管部门审核同意后，按照有关法律、法规的规定，由国务院对外经济贸易主管部门审批。

第九条　设立经营海上国际集装箱运输的企业，应当具备以下条件：

（一）有与其经营范围和服务对象相适应的运输

船舶、车辆、设备及其他有关设施；

（二）有相应的组织机构、办公场所、专业管理人员；

（三）有与所经营的集装箱运输业务相适应的注册资本和自有流动资金；

（四）国家法律、法规规定的设立企业的其他条件。

第十条 交通主管部门应当根据申请经营海上国际集装箱运输企业的资金来源、设备情况、管理水平、货源情况，审核批准其业务经营范围。

第十一条 交通主管部门应当将批准文件发给获准经营海上国际集装箱运输的企业。取得批准文件的单位，凭该文件向工商行政管理部门申请登记注册，经核准发给营业执照后，方可开业。

设立承运海上国际集装箱的内陆中转站、货运站，还应当向海关办理登记手续。

第三章 货运管理

第十二条 用于海上国际集装箱运输的集装箱，应当符合国际集装箱标准化组织规定的技术标准和有关国际集装箱公约的规定。

集装箱所有人、经营人应当做好集装箱的管理和维修工作，定期进行检验，以保证提供适宜于货物运输的集装箱。

违反本条第二款规定，造成货物损坏或者短缺的，由责任人按照有关规定承担赔偿责任。

第十三条 承运人及港口装卸企业应当保证运载集装箱的船舶、车辆、装卸机械及工具处于良好的技术状况，确保集装箱的运输及安全。

承运人及港口装卸企业违反本条第一款规定，造成货物损坏或者短缺的，应当按照有关规定承担赔偿责任。

第十四条 承运人及港口装卸企业应当按照国家规定使用集装箱运输单证。

第十五条 承运人可以直接组织承揽集装箱货物，托运人可以直接向承运人或者委托货运代理人洽办进出口集装箱货物的托运业务。

第十六条 托运人应当如实申报货物的品名、性质、数量、重量、规格。托运的集装箱货物，必须符合集装箱运输的要求，其标志应当明显、清楚。

第十七条 托运人或者承运人在货物装箱前应当认真检查箱体，不得使用影响货物运输、装卸安全的集装箱。

第十八条 装运粮油食品、冷冻品等易腐食品的集装箱，须经商检机构检验合格后方可使用。

第十九条 集装箱货物运达目的地后，承运人应当及时向收货人发出提货通知，收货人应当在收到通知后，凭提单提货。

收货人超过规定期限不提货或者不按期限归还集装箱的，应当按照有关规定或者合同约定支付货物、集装箱堆存费及支付集装箱超期使用费。

第二十条 海上国际集装箱的运费和其他费用，应当根据国家有关运输价格和费率的规定计收；国家没有规定的，按照双方商定的价格计收。任何单位不得乱收费用。

第二十一条 承运人及港口装卸企业，应当定期向交通主管部门报送运输统计报表。

第二十二条 与海上国际集装箱运输相关的各方应当及时相互提供集装箱运输信息。

第四章 交接和责任

第二十三条 承运人与托运人或者收货人应当根据提单确定的交接方式，在码头堆场、货运站或者双方商定的其他地点办理集装箱、集装箱货物交接。

第二十四条 参加海上国际集装箱运输的承运人、港口装卸企业应当按照下列规定办理集装箱交接：

（一）海上承运人通过理货机构与港口装卸企业在船边交接；

（二）经水路集疏运的集装箱，港口装卸企业与水路承运人在船边交接；

（三）经公路集疏运的集装箱，港口装卸企业与公路承运人在集装箱码头大门交接；

（四）经铁路集疏运的集装箱，港口装卸企业或者公路承运人与铁路承运人在装卸现场交接。

第二十五条 集装箱交接时，交接双方应当检查箱号、箱体和封志。重箱凭封志和箱体状况交接；空箱凭箱体状况交接。

交接双方检查箱号、箱体和封志后，应当作出记录，并共同签字确认。

第二十六条 承运人、港口装卸企业对集装箱、集装箱货物的损坏或者短缺的责任，交接前由交方承担，交接后由接方承担。但如果在交接后180天内，接方能提出证据证明集装箱的损坏或者集装箱货物的损坏或者短缺是由交方原因造成，交方应当承担赔偿责任。法律另有规定的除外。

第二十七条 除法律另有规定外，承运人与托运人应当根据下列规定，对集装箱货物的损坏或者短缺负责：

（一）由承运人负责装箱的货物，从承运人收到货物后至运达目的地交付收货人之前的期间内，箱内货物损坏或者短缺，由承运人负责；

（二）由托运人负责装箱的货物，从装箱托运后至交付收货人之前的期间内，如箱体和封志完好，货物损坏或者短缺，由托运人负责；如箱体损坏或者封志破坏，箱内货物损坏或者短缺，由承运人负责。

承运人与托运人或者收货人之间要求赔偿的时效，从集装箱货物交付之日起算不超过180天，但法律另有规定的除外。

第二十八条 由于托运人对集装箱货物申报不实造成人员伤亡，运输工具、货物自身及其他货物、集装箱损失的，由托运人负责。

第二十九条 由于装箱人的过失，造成人员伤亡，运输工具、其他货物、集装箱损失的，由装箱人负责。

第三十条 集装箱货物发生损坏或者短缺，对外索赔时需要商检机构鉴定出证的，应当依照《中华人民共和国进出口商品检验法》办理。

集装箱、集装箱货物发生短缺，对外索赔时需要理货机构出证的，应当依照有关规定办理。

第五章 罚 则

第三十一条 对违反本规定应当给予行政处罚的行为，县级以上交通主管部门应当全面、客观、公正地进行调查，收集有关证据；必要时，可以查看被调查企业的运输单证、财务帐册等有关资料。

有关单位和个人对县级以上交通主管部门的调查应当予以配合，如实提供有关资料；县级以上交通主管部门应当为被调查企业保守商业秘密。

第三十二条 违反本规定，同时违反国家有关价格管理的法律、法规的，由价格主管部门依照有关法律、法规的规定给予处罚。

第三十三条 违反本规定第十四条、第二十一条的规定，不使用规定的集装箱运输单证，或者不报送集装箱运输统计报表，或者报送集装箱运输统计报表不实的，由县级以上交通主管部门责令改正；拒不改正的，处5万元以下的罚款。

第三十四条 违反本规定，有下列行为之一的，由县级以上交通主管部门责令改正；拒不改正的，没收违法所得，并处违法所得1倍以上3倍以下的罚款；没有违法所得的，按照以下规定处以罚款：

（一）未经批准，擅自经营海上国际集装箱运输、港口装卸、中转站、货运站业务的，处3万元以上30万元以下的罚款；

（二）未经批准，擅自经营海上国际集装箱班轮运输，属国内区段的集装箱班轮运输的，处3万元以上30万元以下的罚款；属近洋国际集装箱班轮运输的，处5万元以上50万元以下的罚款；属远洋国际集装箱班轮运输的，处50万元以上500万元以下的罚款。

违反前款规定，情节严重的，由工商行政管理部门吊销营业执照。

第六章 附 则

第三十五条 本规定自发布之日起施行。

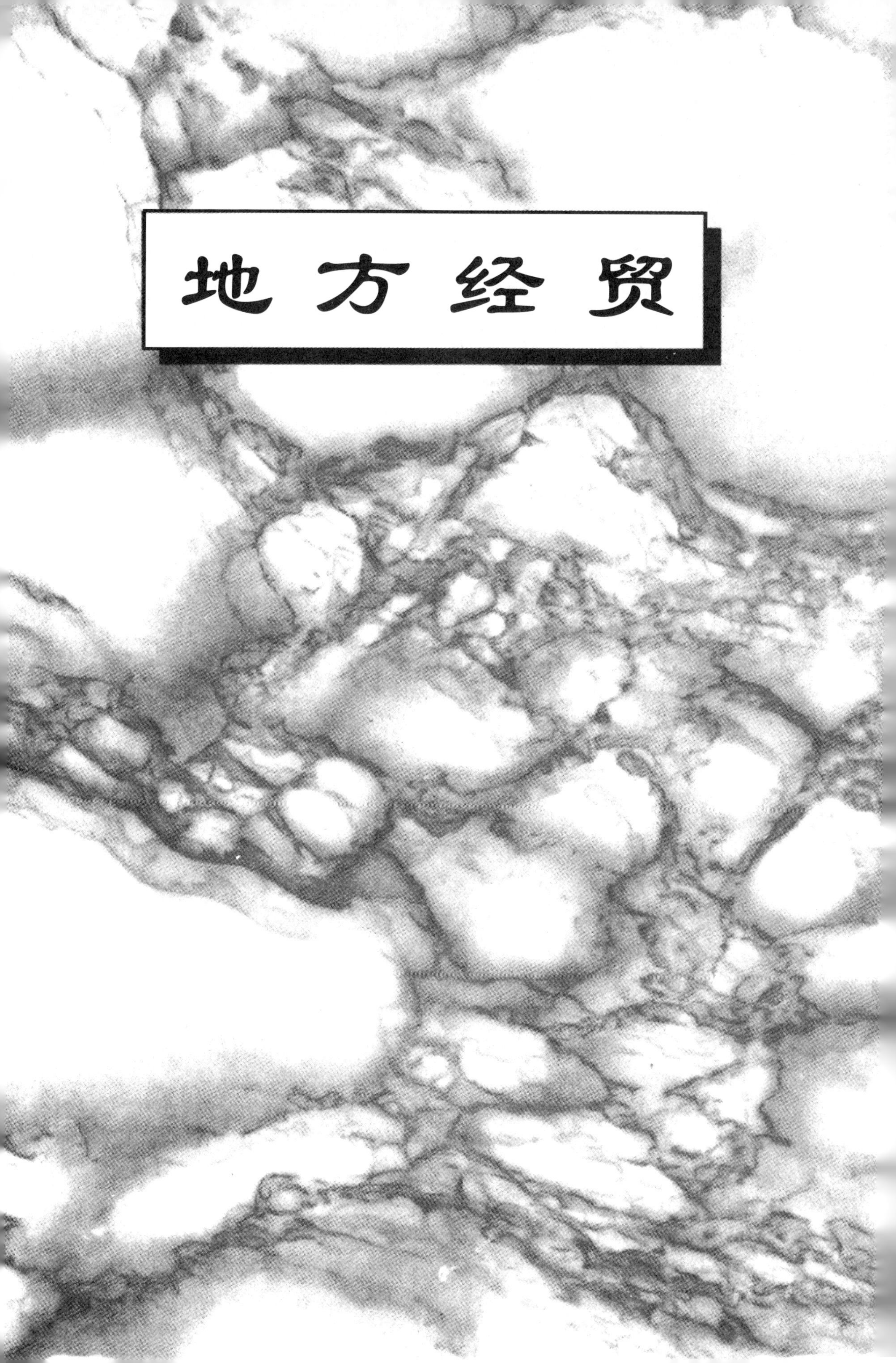

地方经贸

1998年北京市对外经济贸易

北京市对外经济贸易委员会

【对外贸易】

进出口总额 1998年北京市进出口总额650536万美元，比1997年577600万美元增长12.6%。

出口总额 出口总额282896万美元，比1997年246503万美元增长14.7%，占全市国内生产总值2010亿元的11.7%，占全国出口总额的1.54%，居第10位。

出口商品结构 初级产品出口额19302万美元，占出口总额的6.8%，工业制成品出口263594万美元，占出口总额的93.2%。

出口额在500万美元以上的商品情况表

金额分类	商品名称	出口金额	占出口总额
500－1000万美元（36种）	铸造设备、灯具、铸锻件、家用小电器、硅、土建工程机械零件、金属制品、建筑小五金、大米、出版物、电子手表、眼镜片、橡胶拖鞋、针织外衣、生铁、药酒、X光机、镀锌铁皮、化工原料、钼铁、动物性饲料、铝材、工艺美术品、电工产品零配件、喷气式发动机、汽车零件、裘皮及制品、铸铁上水管及配件、酒、钛材、一般中厚钢板、钢琴、塑料公文箱、铸钢件、炼钢设备、钻石坯	25627	9.1%
1000－3000万美元（27种）	电视机及音响设备、食品、无线电收讯机、物理化工仪器、铸铁盖板、丝织品、扬声器、计算机附属设备、照相机、焦炭、箱包、鞋帽、家具、自行车、羽绒裤、羊毛手工打结地毯、日用杂品、耐火材料、电话机、动力机械、螺纹钢、运动鞋、体育用品、键盘、铁路车辆及设备、建筑材料、非金属矿产品	42586	15.15%
3000万美元以上（16种）	通讯设备、皮服装、电子元器件、金首饰、集成电路、电工用具、录像机、钢锭、无线通讯设备、显像管、肉食品、玩具、显示器、针织服装、梭织服装、纺织品	159219	56.3%

出口商品市场 出口商品销往167个国家和地区。

主要出口市场情况表

国别（地区）	出口金额（万美元）	占出口总额（%）
日本	67337	23.8
香港	49131	17.4
欧盟	41952	14.8
美国	39491	13.9
东盟	14717	5.2
韩国	7526	2.7
合计	**220154**	**77.8**

进口总额 进口总额367640万美元，比1997年331100万美元增长11%。

进口商品结构 初级产品进口额43161万美元，占进口总额的11.7%；工业制成品进口额324479万美元，占进口总额的88.3%。

进口额在500万美元以上的商品情况表

金额分类	商品名称	进口金额（万美元）	占进口总额（%）
500－1000万美元（45种）	有色金属成套设备、建筑材料、起重机械、冷冻设备、汽车、化工原料、酒、泵、杂项百货、食品加工机械、有机化工品、复印机零配件、载波机、润滑脂、机床附件、电工产品零配件、钻床、小五金、阀门、紧固件、轻工成套设备、轮胎、染料、冻鱼、冷风机、非金属矿产品、一般中厚钢板、纸、印刷设备、动力机械、可可、水处理设备、汽轮发电机组、图书、钛材、铸锻件、不锈钢板、铜、电线、手表零件、菜油、建材制品、通用机械、油漆、铝制品	30048	8.2%
1000－3000万美元（33种）	铝板、医疗器械、半导体器件、西成药、电缆、鱼粉、塑料制品、发动机、诊断器械及医化用品、豆油、塑料制品设备、电梯、显像管、菌（疫）苗、蓄电池、照相机零件、丙烯腈、粮油食品加工设备、通用机械零配件、腈纶短纤维、飞轮、扣式电池、化纤制品、塑料原料、磨床、革皮制品、杀虫剂、农药、电子设备、环境保护设备、陆地棉、越野车、液晶显示器	55988	15.2%
3000万美元以上（19种）	电子元器件、集成电路、无线通讯设备、通讯设备、电话机零件、铁矿砂、物理化工仪器、电工用具、计算机附属设备、山羊毛、土建工程机械零件、计算机设备、飞机零备件、丝织品、棕榈油、电视机及音响设备、机械除尘设备、低压聚乙烯、玻璃器皿	195596	53.2%

进口商品市场 进口商品来自84个国家和地区。

主要进口市场情况表

国别（地区）	进口金额（万美元）	占进口总额（%）
欧盟	147313	40.1
日本	64656	17.6
美国	43154	11.7
韩国	31384	8.5
香港	19171	5.2
合计	**305678**	**83.1**

技术进出口 1998年北京市技术进出口总额45046万美元，比1997年的38319万美元增长17.6%。其中，签定引进技术和进口设备合同项目195个，比1997年增加27项；合同金额21106万美元，比1997年的19278万美元增长9.5%。签定技术出口合同项目334个，比1997年增加29项；合同金额23940万美元，比1997年的19041万美元增长25.7%。

【利用外资】

1998 年利用外资情况表

利用外资方式	批准签订的合同			实际利用外资	
	项目数（个）	外资金额（万美元）	金额比1997年（±%）	金额（万美元）	金额比1997年（±%）
对外借款	5	890	-74.0	57194	-22.0
外商直接投资	651	409677	143.7	206415	29.6
合资企业	344	61426	-22.6	80726	15.4
合作企业	104	232524	455.5	67515	117.8
外资企业	201	105952	130.0	52761	74.8
外商投资股份制	2	9775			
其他				5413	-81.2
其他形式利用外资				23364	-12.0
合　计	**656**	**410567**	**121.9**	**286973**	**10.7**

外商直接投资行业　外商直接投资项目中，生产型企业 355 家，非生产型企业 296 家。按行业划分：农林牧渔水利业 23 家；工业 319 家；运输邮电业 7 家；商业饮食业 37 家；房地产、公用、居民服务业 213 家（其中：房地产管理 50 家）；其他行业 50 家。

外商直接投资来源　香港 176 家，合同外资额 250019 万美元；美国 120 家，合同外资额 41297 万美元；日本 53 家，合同外资额 21067 万美元；英属维尔京群岛 37 家，合同外资额 9525 万美元；德国 15 家，合同外资额 24989 万美元；荷兰 10 家，合同外资额 3914 万美元；瑞士 6 家，合同外资额 7168 万美元；法国 16 家，合同外资额 11705 万美元；丹麦 1 家，合同外资额 180 万美元；台湾省 55 家，合同外资额 4064 万美元；韩国 40 家，合同外资额 1493 万美元；新加坡 23 家，合同外资额 5006 万美元。

外商直接投资企业生产经营情况　截止 1998 年底，已有 5419 家外商投资企业开业投产，职工总数为 42.6 万人。全年实现总产值 538.80 亿元，比上年增长 10%；销售收入 738.8 亿元，比上年增长 10.5%；缴纳税金总额 52.12 亿元，比上年增长 24.6%。

【对外经济合作】

承包工程和劳务合作　对外承包工程和劳务合作完成营业额 4.58 亿美元，比 1997 年的 5 亿美元下降 8.4%；派出劳务人员 2795 人，与 1997 年的 2793 人持平，年末在外人数为 3645 人。劳务人员分布在斯里兰卡、日本、赤道几内亚、毛里求斯、巴基斯坦、津巴布韦、新加坡、突尼斯、香港、澳门等 60 多个国家和地区。主要对外承包工程项目有新加坡的住房工程，马来西亚电气安装工程，斯里兰卡防水管线工程等。

对外经济技术援助　承担援外项目 8 个。受援国有毛里求斯、刚果、加蓬、贝宁、纳米比亚和赤道几内亚。

接受经济援助　接受国外援助 3 项，金额 244.2 万美元。正在执行的项目 5 个，金额 344 万美元，项目进展顺利。

对外投资　海外举办非贸易型企业 12 家，中方投资 396.95 万美元。这些企业分布在日本、美国、印度尼西亚、蒙古、巴基斯坦、南非、荷兰、罗马尼亚、匈牙利、澳大利亚等 10 个国家和地区。

【其他】

经济技术开发区 北京经济技术开发区批准入区三资企业114家，增长119%；投资额为3.68亿美元，增长37%。实现工业增加值7.2亿元，增长81.8%；销售收入36亿美元，增长46%；出口创汇6416万美元，增长58.9%。

外贸运输 1998年北京市外贸货运总量200.1万吨，比上年下降68.6%。其中出口运量116.8万吨，进口运量83.3万吨；海运量197.3万吨，陆运量2.24万吨，空运量0.55万吨。

涉外旅游 全年接待海外旅游者220万人次，比1997年230万人次下降4.3%；旅游收入23.8亿美元，比1997年22.5亿美元增长5.8%。

1998年天津市对外经济贸易

天津市对外经济贸易委员会

【对外贸易】

进出口总额 1998年天津市进出口总额106.14亿美元比1997年的100.23亿美元增长5.9%。

出口总额 54.99亿美元，比1997年的50.19亿美元增长9.56%，占全市国内生产总值1340.70亿元（161.94亿美元）的33.96%，占全国出口额的2.99%，居第九位。

出口商品结构 初级产品出口额6.02亿美元，占出口总额的10.94%，工业制成品的出口额48.97亿美元，占出口总额的89.06%。其中机电产品出口额为27.09亿美元，占出口总额的49.27%。

出口额在1000万美元以上的商品情况表

金额分类	商品名称	出口金额（万美元）	占出口总额（%）
1000－3000万美元（共17种）	蔬菜、铸锻件、缝纫机、罐头、铝材、工农具、箱包、焦炭、帐篷、各种染料、不锈钢餐具、农药、不锈钢器皿、汽车零件、铸铁制品、电池、铁合金	31012	5.64
3000－5000万美元（共8种）	豆柏、木材、纺织原料、棉布、棉涤纶制品、小五金、橡胶及制品、医药原料	32937	5.98
5000万美元以上（共19种）	水产品、肠衣、棉制品、服装、地毯、工艺品、鞋、体育用品、乐器、家具、钢材、金属制品、有色金属、煤、化工原料、塑料、计算机、照明器材、家电	222589	40.48
合　计	**44种**	**286538**	**52.10**

出口商品市场 出口商品到179个国家和地区。

主要出口市场情况表

国别（地区）	出口金额（亿美元）	占出口总额（%）
美　国	13.02	23.68
日　本	9.15	16.44
香　港	5.88	10.69
德　国	2.91	5.29
英　国	2.22	4.04
法　国	1.14	2.07
台　湾	0.84	1.53
加拿大	0.83	1.51
意大利	0.67	1.22
澳大利亚	0.65	1.18
合　计	**37.31**	**67.85**

进口总额　进口总额51.15亿美元，比1997年的50.91亿美元增长0.47%。

进口商品结构　初级产品进口额5.34亿美元，占进口总额10.4%；工业制成品的进口额45.81亿美元，占进口总额的89.6%。

进口在1000万美元以上的商品情况表

金额分类	商　品　名　称	进口金额（万美元）	占总进口额（%）
1000－5000万美元（37种）	其他植物油、原木、锯材、纸浆、羊毛、纺织用品合成纤维、成品油、合成纤维纱线、棉机织物、涂覆或浸清织物、鞋靴零件、制电灯泡及类似用品、玻璃外壳、未锻造的铜及铜材、废铜、未锻造的铝及铝材、医药品、牛皮革及马皮革、纸及纸板、钢铁或铝制结构体及其部件、活塞式内燃机的零件、制冷设备用压缩机、建筑及采矿用机械、印刷和装订机械、纺织机械、橡胶或塑料加工机械、型模及金属铸造用型箱、阀门、自动数据处理、设备及其部件、电动机及发电机、旋转或电力设备的零件、焊接机器及零件、有线电话电报设备的零附件、录音机及收录音组合机电线和电缆汽车零件、船舶	84640.3	16.55
5000万美元以上（15种）	食用植物油、合成纤长丝织物　钢材、初级形状的聚乙烯、机械提升搬运装运设备及零件、金属加工机床、自动数据处理设备的零件、电视、收音机及无线电讯设备的零附件、通断及保护电路装置、二级管晶体管及类似半导体器件、集成电路及微电子组建、汽车和汽车底盘、计量检测分析自控仪器及器具、塑料制品	177320.23	34.67
合　计	**52种**	**261960.53**	**51.22**

进口商品市场　进口商品来自104个国家和地区。

主要进口市场情况表

国别（地区）	进口金额（亿美元）	占总进口值的（%）
日 本	14.06	27.49
美 国	8.5	16.62
台湾省	3.1	6.06
香 港	3.05	5.96
德 国	1.62	3.17
英 国	0.87	1.70
意大利	0.55	1.08
俄罗斯	0.54	1.06
加拿大	0.48	0.94
澳大利亚	0.37	0.72
合 计	**33.14**	**64.79**

技术进出口 1998年天津市技术进出口总额99.35亿美元，其中签订引进技术和设备合同项目91个，合同金额97.3亿美元；签订技术出口合同项目34个，合同金额2.05亿美元。

【利用外资】

1998年利用外资情况表

利用外资方式	批准签订的合同			实际利用外资	
	项目数（个）	外资金额（亿美元）	金额比1997年（±%）	金 额（亿美元）	金额比1997年（±%）
对外借款	340	13.30	-34.2	53.98	40.8
对外直接投资	859	23.34		25.18	0.3
合资企业	210	6.45			
合作企业	52	7.39			
外资企业	597	9.49			
合 计	**1199**	**36.64**	**-37.16**	**79.16**	**131.26**

外商直接投资行业 农业项目8个，外商投资0.08亿美元；工业及建筑业项目358个，外商投资8.17亿美元；国际贸易及服务项目14个，外商投资3.25亿美元；房地产项目36个，外商投资2.5亿美元；交通运输业项目30个，外商投资7.07亿美元；其它行业13个，外商投资2.28亿美元。

外商直接投资来源 外商直接投资的主要国家和地区。

国别（地区）	项目数（个）	总投资金额（亿美元）	外商投资金额（亿美元）
香 港	182	6.79	5.84
美 国	216	4.08	3.46
韩 国	94	0.47	0.44
日 本	54	0.46	0.35
台 湾	77	0.82	0.78
新加坡	32	1.07	0.996
加拿大	36	0.65	0.62
英属维尔京群岛	34	6.22	5.29
开曼群岛	2	1.04	1.03

（续）

国别（地区）	项目数（个）	总投资金额（亿美元）	外商投资金额（亿美元）
德　国	12	1.22	0.95
萨摩亚独立国	3	0.56	0.56

外商直接投资企业生产情况　1998年天津市已开业的三资企业经营情况统计，完成生产总值824.34亿元，比1997年增长27.5%，其中工业生产总值816.03亿元，占天津市工业总产值的39.1%；销售收入903.44亿元，比1997年增长6.2%；利税总额51.77亿元，比1997年减少7.5%；外商投资企业出口38.24亿美元，比1997年增长21.9%；占全市出口总值的69.54%。

截止1998年底，天津市共计批准外商投资企业12413家，协议投资总额305亿美元，其中协议外资额131.26亿美元，全市累计外资实际到位107.4亿美元。

【对外经济合作】

承包工程和劳务合作　1998年签订对外承包工程和劳务费合作项目937个，金额1.93亿美元，比1997年的1.25亿美元增长54.4%；营业额1.77亿美元，比1997年的2.21亿美元减少19.9%；当年外派劳务4470人，年末在外12074人。派往的主要国家和地区：韩国、新加坡、美国、香港、日本、泰国、新西兰、阿联酋、巴基斯坦、以色列等。承包工程有45项，合同金额1.09亿美元；劳务合约856项合同金额0.77亿美元；设计咨询36项合同金额698万美元。

对外经济援助，1998年天津完成国家下达的对外经济援助项目11个，合同金额4391万元，其中：天津国际经济合作公司项目6个，合同额1231万元；中国成套设备天津分公司项目4个，合同金额160万元；天津轻工对外贸易公司援助物资3000万元。

境外投资　1998年在海外举办企业（含非贸易性企业）21家，总投资8215.41万美元，其中中方投资1690.49万美元。截至1998年底，天津市在海外举办302家企业总投资1.8亿美元，其中中方投资0.76亿美元，涉及主要行业：自行车、化工、塑料、服装、木材加工、贸易、运输、餐饮、医疗服务、劳务合作种植养殖等。

【其他】

经济技术开发区　国内生产总值180.11亿元，比1997年增长19.8%；工业生产总值540.22亿元，比1997年增长20%；出口22.61亿美元，比1997年增长12.8%；总投资14.82亿美元，其中外方投资12.28亿美元；固定资产投人75.35亿元。

天津港保税区　国内生产总值16.2亿元，比1997年增长34.7%，进出口货物总值完成47亿美元，比1997年增长14.6%。批准外商投资企业427家，总投资额5.56亿美元，外资金额5.02亿美元，实际利用外资3.05亿美元。通关出口7.2亿美元比1997年增长9.6%，税收2.66亿元，比1997年增长45.6%。固定资产投资5.6亿元，比1997年增长9.8%。

对外经贸洽谈会　1998年3月8日至3月15日，华北、西北地区十三个省市和计划单列市以及国家科委，在天津体育展览中心，共同举办了“’98中国天津出口商品交易会”。本届交易会共设578个摊位，来自全国27个省市、自治区和计划单列市的434家企业参展，韩国、加拿大、香港、台湾省的21家海外企业也参加了本届交易会。来自世界五大洲62个国家和地区的1508名客商到会，比上届减少11.8%。各参展企业共签订进出口合同6.4亿美元，其中出口成交6.12亿美元与上届持平，技术出口成交2000万美元，新产品成交1476万美元；进口成交2938力美元，比上届减少26.38%。签订利用外资合同8个，协议外资额1.5亿美元。内贸业务成交8904.2万元。本届交易会还开创了国际跨国连锁公司到会采购并举办会中会的新的办会方式，接待了华润集团、澳门南光集团、香港永安百货购物中心、亚洲投资中心、日本宇德运输（株）、法国家乐福公司和荷兰万科隆公司等今20个采购团。

港口运输　1998年天津港共有各类泊位140个，其中万吨级以上的深水泊位48个，年吞吐能力6000万吨，1998年实际完成货物吞吐总量6818万吨，其中完成外贸进出口货物吞吐总量3476万吨，出口量2410.7万吨，进口量1065.3万吨。

涉外旅游 1998年入境的国际旅游人数为30.49万人；旅游收入2.02亿美元，比1997年的1.8亿美元增长12.2%。

1998年河北省对外经济贸易

河北省对外贸易经济合作厅

【对外贸易】

进出口总额 1998年河北省进出口总额为42.27亿美元，比1997年的41.02亿美元增长3.05%。

出口总额 出口总额31.16亿美元，比1997年的32.38亿美元下降3.76%，占全省国内生产总值4238亿元（相当于511.9亿美元）的6.1%，占全国出口额的1.7%，居全国第九位。

出口商品结构 初级产品出口额9.15亿美元，占出口总额的29.36%，工业制成品出口额22.01亿美元，占出口总额的70.64%。

出口额在1000万美元以上商品情况表

金额分类	商品名称	出口金额（万美元）	占出口总额（%）
10000万美元以上（5种）	服装、煤炭、五金制品、原油、化纤布	137620	44.16
5000－10000万美元（5种）	棉布、钢铁、陶瓷产品、塑料制品、肠衣	41709	13.38
1000－5000万美元（14种）	地毯、皮革、维生素C、铝箔、抗菌素、黄金首饰、五氧化二钒、焦炭、纯碱、冻鸡、水泥、电动机、砂轮机、棉纱线	34087	10.94
合　计	**24种**	**213416**	**68.48**

出口商品市场 出口商品销往160个国家和地区。

主要出口市场情况表

国别（地区）	出口金额（万美元）	占全省出口总值比重(%)
日　本	60836	19.52

主要出口市场情况表（续）

国别（地区）	出口金额（万美元）	占全省出口总值比重(%)
欧　盟	59263	19.02

主要出口市场情况表（续）

国别（地区）	出口金额（万美元）	占全省出口总值比重（%）
香　港	44335	14.23
美　国	36076	11.58
韩　国	27177	8.72
台湾省	16110	5.17
合　计	**243797**	**78.24**

进口总额　进口总额 11.11 亿美元，比 1997 年的 8.64 亿美元增长 28.57%。

进口商品结构　初级产品进口额 3.45 亿美元，占进口总额的 31.03%；工业制成品进口额 7.66 亿美元，占进口总额的 68.97%。

进口额在 1000 万美元以上的商品表

金额分类	商品名称	进口金额（万美元）	占进口总额（%）
5000 万美元以上（4 种）	香蕉、钢材、铁矿砂、移动通信站	23658	21.29
1000－5000 万美元（11 种）	机械零件、化肥、磷酸、塑料、合成纤维、皮革、棉花、交换机、玻壳、纸版、印刷品	29462	26.51
合　计	**15 种**	**53120**	**47.80**

进口商品市场　进口商品来自 57 个国家和地区。

主要进口市场情况表

国别（地区）	金　额（万美元）	占进口总额（%）
欧　盟	24960	22.46
日　本	18728	16.85
韩　国	12867	11.58
美　国	11354	10.22
东　盟	6200	5.58
澳大利亚	5065	4.58
台湾省	3302	2.97
巴　西	3093	2.78

主要进口市场情况表（续）

国别（地区）	金　额（万美元）	占进口总额（%）
合　计	**85569**	**77.02**

技术进出口　技术进出口总额 28306 万美元，比 1997 年的 12769 万美元增长 122%，其中，签订引进技术和进口设备合同金额 20139 万美元，比 1997 年的 10681 万美元增长 88.55%；签订技术出口合同金额 8167 万美元，比 1997 年的 2088 万美元增长 291.14%。

【利用外资】

1998 年利用外资情况表

利用外资方式	批准签订的合同			实际利用外资	
	项目数（个）	外资金额（万美元）	金额比1997年（±%）	金额（万美元）	金额比1997年（±%）
对外借款	10	4258	73.10	2370	3.66
外商直接投资	696	126771	13.86	142868	29.80
合资企业	496	64949	8.26	103654	45.04
合作企业	64	27274	-16.43	29427	-10.27
外资企业	136	34548	84.61	9787	68.60
外商其他投资				5109	1993.85
对外发行股票				4500	
补偿贸易				609	149.59
合　计	**706**	**131029**	**15.14**	**150347**	**33.32**

外商直接投资行业　外商直接投资项目中，生产型项目 604 个，非生产型项目 92 个。按行业分，农林牧渔 27 个，采掘业 10 个，制造业 555 个，建筑业 9 个，电力、煤气及水的生产和供应 5 个，房地产业 20 个，交通运输、仓储及邮电通讯业 13 个，批发及零售贸易、餐饮业 13 个，社会服务业 38 个，其他行业 6 个。

外商直接投资来源　外商直接投资来自 52 个国家和地区。投资额居前十位的是：香港，40297 万美元；美国，15206 万美元；日本，12378 万美元；韩国，8570 万美元；台湾省，7864 万美元；新加坡，7807 万美元；加拿大，7387 万美元；澳大利亚，6938 万美元；法国，3241 万美元；意大利，3223 万美元。

外商直接投资企业生产经营情况　截至 1998 年底，全省已开业投产的外商投资企业共 2728 家，职工总数 33.76 万人。1998 年销售（营业）收入 337.66 亿元，比 1997 年的 302.37 亿元增长 11.67%；出口 7.20 亿美元，比 1997 年的 6.32 亿美元增长 13.93%，占全省出口总额的 23.11%。

【对外经济合作】

承包工程和劳务合作　1998 年全省签订对外承包工程和劳务合作合同项目 229 个，金额 10048 万美元，比 1997 年的 5800 万美元增长 73%；营业额 5198 万美元，比 1997 年的 4450 万美元增长 7.6%；当年派出劳务人员 3912 人次，比 1997 年的 3706 人次增长 5.6%；年末在外人数 6412 人，比上年末的 5502 人增长 16.6%。劳务人员分布在新加坡、日本、阿联酋、蒙古、俄罗斯等 40 个国家和地区，承包工程的主要项目及国家是：马里打井与农田整治、菲律宾公路建设、马来西亚厂房建筑等。

接受经济援助　1998 年接受国际援助项目共 9 项，总金额 465 万美元。主要项目是：1. 张家口灾后重建项目；2. 承德修桥项目；3. 献县打井项目；4. 中等职业教育项目。

对外投资　1998 年在海外兴办非贸易型企业 4 家，中方投资 234 万美元，分布在巴新、越南、蒙古等 3 个国家和地区，涉及制药、食品等行业。

【其他】

对外经贸洽谈会　1998 年先后在石家庄、

厦门举办了两次对外经贸洽谈会，到会外商达1800人次，分别来自日本、香港、韩国、新加坡等32个国家和地区，出口成交额达8000万美元。

涉外旅游 1998年共接待境外旅游者32.1万人次，比1997年的30万人次增长6.64%；旅游外汇收入9508万美元，比1997年的8790万美元增长8.17%。

1998年秦皇岛市对外经济贸易

秦皇岛市对外经济贸易合作局

【对外贸易】

1998年河北省秦皇岛市进出口总额37783万美元，比1997年的27719万美元增长36.31%

出口总额27686万美元，比1997年的21688万美元增长27.66%，占全市国内生产总值249.5亿元（相当于30.06亿美元）的9.2%，占全省出口额的6.44%。

出口商品122种，其中，初级产品出口额12077万美元，占出口总额的43.60%；工业制成品的出口额21512万美元，占出口总额的77.70%。出口额在100万美元以上的商品有29种，金额22687万美元，占出口总额的81.94%，比上年增长44.37%；出口额在500万美元以上的商品有13个，出口金额16534万美元，占出口总额的59.72%，比上年增长43.16%；出口额在1000万美元以上的商品有5种，出口金额10974万美元，占出口总额的39.64%，比上年增长75.62%。其中，铝型材出口金额3024万美元，占出口总额的10.92%；钢材出口金额2604万美元，占出口总额的9.40%；革皮服装出口金额2096万美元，占出口总额的7.57%；冻鸡出口金额2019万美元，占出口总额的7.29%；水泥出口金额1231万美元，占出口总值的4.45%。

出口商品销往76个国家和地区，主要分布在亚洲、欧美国家和地区，出口总额25187万美元，占出口总额的90.97%。其中，出口日本9846万美元，占出口总额35.56%；出口韩国5283万美元，占出口总额的19.08%；出口德国3695万美元，占出口总额的13.35%；出口香港2097万美元，占出口总额的7.57%；出口美国2001万美元，占出口总额的7.23%；出口希腊597万美元，占出口金额的2.16%；出口比利时595万美元，占出口金额的2.15%；出口西班牙389万美元，占出口金额的1.41%；出口缅甸379万美元，占出口总额的1.37%；出口俄罗斯305万美元，占出口金额的1.10%。

进口总额10097万美元，比1997年的6031万美元增长67.42%。

进口商品有21个品种，初级产品进口金额4661万美元，占进口总额的46.16%，工业品进口金额5436万美元，占进口总额的53.84%。其中，化工原料进口额4095万美元，占进口总额40.56%；香蕉进口金额3997万美元，占进口金额的39.59%；饲料538万美元占进口金额的5.33%。

进口商品来自16个国家和地区，主要来自亚洲、欧美国家和地区。其中，菲律宾进口金额3195万美元，占进口金额的31.64%；韩国进口金额1687万美元，占进口总额的16.71%；德国进口金额1312万美元，占进口总额的13.00%；日本进口金额1238万美元，占进口金额的12.26%；香港进口金额717万美元，占进口金额的7.1%；美国进口金额657万美元，占进口金额的6.51%。

【技术进出口】

技术进出口总额3804万美元，比上年的2112

万美元增长80.11%，其中，签订引进技术和进口设备项目12个，与1997年相同，合同金额523.73万美元，比1997年的10万美元增长51倍。签订技术出口合同项目2个，合同金额0.76万美元，比1997年的5.3万美元下降85.66%。

【利用外资】

批准外资项目80个，投资总额57836万美元，比1997年的62781.9同期下降7.87%，合同利用外资金额45745万美元，完成年计划的89.80%，比上年同期下降5.6%，直接进入外资19608万美元，完成年计划的82.20%，比上年同期增长7.8%。

外商直接投资的80个项目中，合资企业43个，外资金额18206.05万美元，合作企业9个，外资金额5458.93万美元，外资企业28个，外资金额20701.26万美元。属于生产型项目68个，非生产型项目12个。按行业分：轻工24项，建材9项，机械7项，食品6项，房地产、化工各5项，服务、电子各3项；娱乐、服装各2项，环保、交通、能源、农业、冶金、医药、餐饮、宾馆各1项；其他6项。

外商投资来自18个国家和地区。其中，香港17项，合同外资金额11301.59万美元；韩国16项，合同外资金额4272.86万美元；美国14项，合同外资金额6525.74万美元；日本5项，合同外资金额3197.90万美元；新加坡5项，合同外资金额5240.84万美元；意大利4项，合同外资金额3045万美元；加拿大4项，合同外资金额2624.86万美元；台湾省3项，合同外资金额254.23万美元；法国、俄罗斯各2项，合同外资金额3141.9万美元；澳地利、澳门、德国、菲律宾、土耳其、西班牙、匈牙利、英国各1项，合同外资金额4761.32万美元。

已投产的298家外商投资企业，1998年实现产值570531万元，上缴税金23093.56万元，创汇17507.21万美元，比1997年的12149.04万美元增长44.1%，占全市出口总额的66.51%。

【对外经济合作】

签订对外承包工程和劳务合作合同项目10个，金额2314.64万美元，比1997年的623.83万美元增长265.76%；营业额537.24万美元，比1997年的552万美元下降2.6%；当年派出劳务人员725人次，年末在外人数687人；派往的主要国家和地区蒙古、日本、韩国、印度、泰国、塞内加尔、莫桑比克、新西兰、科威特。

承包工程的主要项目及国别是，秦皇岛市经济技术合作公司在科威特承包两个别墅小区（分别为289栋和294栋两层别墅）和三所中等学校的项目，总承包额1500万美元。

【经济技术开发区】

1998年秦皇岛经济技术开发区投资22846万元，用于开发区的基础设施建设，改善投资环境。

批准利用外资合同45项，合同外资金额34993.79万美元，实际投入外资15998万美元。其中，食品、建筑、饮料、有色金属矿采、娱乐服务各2项、黑色金属冶炼、船舶各3项、房地产4项，化工6项，电子、咨询服务、木材加工、医药、塑料制品、娱乐服务、交通、其他社会服务各1项，其他制造业12项。

批准内联企业277家，总投资5.072亿元。1998年全年实现工业产值34.3574亿元，利税1.1329亿元，创汇14174万美元。

【对外经贸洽谈会】

1998年3月23日在新加坡参加河北省举办的经贸洽谈会，秦皇岛市出口成交额290万美元。

1998年5月18日参加河北省在石家庄举办的经贸洽谈会，秦皇岛市出口成交额1896.45万美元。签订外资合同34项，总投资19416万美元，合同外资金额11527万美元，接待了48个国家和地区的客商132人，接待了国内529个公司，1021人。

1998年8月18日秦皇岛市举办的第十届“北戴河之夏”对外经济技术合作洽谈会既商品交易会，秦皇岛市出口成交额2529.36万美元，签订利用外资合同57项，总投资530069.46万美元，合同外资31270.81万美元，接待了美国、日本、韩国、香港、台湾、新加坡、意大利、澳门等24多个国家和地区的客商730人，其中外商350人，国内客户380人。签订经济技术合同2项，合同额1500万美元。

【港口运输】

全年自营进出口运输总量7755.2万吨，比1997年的7822.1万吨下降0.8%。

秦皇岛有生产泊位28个，港口吞吐能力12045万吨。全年实际完成货运吞吐总量7792.2万吨，其中完成外贸进出口吞吐量2241.8万吨，其中，出口1814.3万吨，进口427.5万吨。

【旅游】

全年接待国内外游客600.61万人次，其中，接待日本、韩国、美国、英国、俄罗斯、新加坡、台湾省、香港、澳门等31个国家和地区的国际游客10.7万人次，比1997年的10.66万人次增长0.37%。其中，港、澳、台同胞和华侨10001人次，国际海员61168人次。全年旅游外汇收入4849.7万美元，比1997年的4682.7万美元，增长了3.55%。接待国内游客589.91万人次，接近上年水平。

1998年山西省对外经济贸易

山西省对外贸易经济合作厅

【对外贸易】

进出口总额　1998年山西进出口总额169974万美元，比1997年195357万美元减少12.99%。

出口总额145202万美元，比1997年164110万美元减少11.52%，占全省国内生产总值1606.7亿元人民币（相当于193.58亿美元）的7.5%，占全国出口总额1837.6亿美元的0.79%。在全省出口总额中，外商投资企业出口完成10617万美元，占出口总额的7.31%，比1997年的14110万美元减少35.74%。

出口商品结构　按国际贸易标准分类：初级产品出口99111万美元，占出口总额的68.26%；工业制成品出口46091万美元，占出口总额的31.74%。

出口商品品种　出口商品508种，出口额在100万美元以上的商品有94种，金额13990万美元，占出口总额的96.35%。

出口额在500万美元以上的商品情况表

金额分类	商品名称	出口金额（万美元）	占出口总额（%）
1亿美元以上（2种）	焦炭	45015	31.00
	煤	45867	31.59

出口额在500万美元以上的商品情况表（续）

金额分类	商品名称	出口金额（万美元）	占出口总额（%）
1000万美元至1亿美元（10种）	金属镁	7344	5.06
	生铁	5508	3.79
	服装	3818	2.63
	钢材	1472	1.01
	棉布	1414	0.97
	核桃仁	1269	0.87
	铝	1215	0.84
	法兰盘	1142	0.79
	活性炭	1100	0.76
	各类机械	1080	0.74
500万至1000万美元（13种）	水管零件	970	0.67
	铸铁件	967	0.66
	鞭炮烟花	739	0.51
	矾土	739	0.51
	玻璃器皿	676	0.46
	镁铁	653	0.45
	锰铁	625	0.43
	磷酸三纳	591	0.41
	芸豆	565	0.39
	柠檬酸	560	0.38
	轮胎	534	0.37
	化纤布	520	0.36
	元明粉	506	0.35
合　计	**25种**	**124889**	**86.01**

出口机电产品131种，金额8339万美元，占出口总额的5.74%，比1997年8570万美元减少2.70%。

出口市场　出口商品销往104个国家和地区。其中出口额在100万美元以上的市场45个，出口金额116512万美元，占出口总额的80.24%。出口额在1000万美元以上的市场23个（见附表）。

主要出口市场情况表

国别（地区）	出口金额（万美元）	占出口总额（%）
美　国	19393	13.36

主要出口市场情况表（续）

国别（地区）	出口金额（万美元）	占出口总额（%）
日　本	19153	13.19
韩　国	12800	8.82
香　港	10516	7.24
瑞　士	6674	4.60
德　国	6157	4.24
印　度	4011	2.76
英　国	3820	2.63
荷　兰	3144	2.17
意大利	2527	1.74
台湾省	2338	1.61

主要出口市场情况表（续）

国别（地区）	出口金额（万美元）	占出口总额（%）
法　国	1956	1.35
菲律宾	1835	1.26
马来西亚	1726	1.19
伊　朗	1717	1.18
土耳其	1475	1.01
南　非	1240	0.85
比利时	1223	0.84
泰　国	1163	0.80
俄罗斯	1069	0.74
印度尼西亚	1090	0.75
加拿大	1003	0.69
合计（22个）	**108516**	**74.73**

进口总额　1998年山西省进口总额24770万美元，比1997年31247万美元减少26.14%。

进口商品结构　按国际贸易标准分类，初级产品进口8466万美元，占进口总额的34.18%；工业制成品进口16306万美元，占进口总额的65.82%。

进口商品品种　进口商品148种，进口额在100万美元以上的商品有38种，金额16322万美元，占进口总额的65.89%。

进口额在500万美元以上的商品情况表

金额分类	商　品　名　称	进口金额（万美元）	占进口总额（%）
1000万美元以上3种	铁矿砂、高压聚乙稀、其它食用油	6814	27.51
500－1000万美元（5种）	其它化工原料、轧钢设备、通用机械零配件、氧化铝、土建工程机械零件	3370	13.60
合　计	**8种**	**10184**	**41.11**

进口商品市场　进口商品来自33个国家和地区。进口额在100万美元以上的市场20个，金额23474万美元，占进口总额的94.76%。其中，进口额在500万美元以上的市场10个（见附表）。

主要进口商品市场情况表

国别（地区）	进口金额（万美元）	占进口总额（%）
美　国	5655	22.83
香　港	4026	16.25
澳大利亚	3903	15.76
德　国	1401	5.66
日　本	1337	5.41

主要进口商品市场情况（续）

国别（地区）	进口金额（万美元）	占进口总额（%）
印　度	1323	5.34
法　国	1208	4.85
韩　国	1118	4.51
意大利	754	3.04
英　国	674	2.73
合计（10个）	**21399**	**86.38**

【技术进出口】

技术引进工作好于上年，全省技术进出口总额为2333.46万美元。签订引进技术和进口设备合同18项，比1997年增加4项；合同金额为2333.46万美元，比1997年693万美元增长236.67%。

技术进口国别（地区）及行业 引进技术和设备来自18国家和地区。主要有：德国6项，金额669.67万美元；法国3项，金额296.96万美元；美国2项，金额49.63万美元；英国2项，金额736.7万美元；俄罗斯2项，金额53万美元；荷兰1项，金额225万美元；挪威1项，金额176万美元；澳大利亚1项，金额82万美元。

引进技术和设备的主要行业分布为：水利工程4项，合同金额769.8万美元；环保检测1项，合同金额176万美元；电信行业4项，合同金额为428.3万美元；机械工业4项，合同金额349万美元；纺织工业2项，合同金额34万美元；高科技行业2项，合同金额352万美元；医疗行业1项，合同金额225万美元。引进技术和设备的主要项目有：山西省电力公司调度局引进微波一点多址设备；山西省邮电管理局引进数据网扩容设备；太原电信局引进帧中继设备、数字通信设备、数字数据网设备；山西省汾河水利管理局引进自动喷灌设备、NLB高压水喷流机泵；山西省引黄工程局引进监理咨询服务合同；山西省心研究所引进心血管造影设备；山西晋城市纺织厂引进纺织机械；山西梅花丝绸服装有限公司引进溢流染色机；山西省铝制品厂引进PVC双壁波纹管生产线；山西煤矿机械厂引进精密磨齿机；介休二机实业股份有限公司引进全自动混凝砌块设备等。

【利用外资】

1998年利用外资情况表

利用外资方式	批准签订的合同			实际利用外资	
	项目数（个）	外资金额（万美元）	金额比1997年（±%）	金额（万美元）	金额比1997年（±%）
对外借款	10	7430	138.14	1540	-13.24
外商直接投资	102	41242	41.85	24451	-8.26
合资企业	68	10198		2089	
合作企业	17	19220		22273	
外资企业	17	11824		89	
合 计	**112**	**48672**	**44.33**	**25991**	**-9.34**

1998年批准签订利用外资合同项目比1997年减少44项，批准签订合同外资金额比1997年增长44.33%；实际利用外资金额比1997年减少13.24%。

外商直接投资 1998年全省批准签订利用外商直接投资合同项目数比1997年减少41项；外商直接投资金额比1997年增长41.85%，实际利用外资金额比1997年减少8.76%。

外商直接投资来源 外商直接投资来自23个国家和地区。其中主要投资者为：香港26项，金额5776万美元；台湾省12项，896万美元；英属维尔京群岛16项，21254万美元；开曼群岛1项，10000万美元；美国16项，1126万美元；德国3项，690万美元；加拿大5项，300万美元；澳大利亚5项，263万美元；马来西亚2项，180万美元；日本6项，147万美元。在外商直接投资项目中，外商投资额在100万美元以上的项目34项。

外商直接投资的102个项目中，生产型项目77项，非生产型项目25项。按行业分：农业牧鱼业1项，金额1万美元，工业73项，金额7745万美元；交通运输邮电通信业5项，金额213万美元；建筑业8项，金额10748万美元；房地产开发与经营业2项，金额111万美元；公用社会服务业

5项，金额3511万美元；商业饮食服务业6项，金额1063万美元；科技服务事业2项，金额223万美元。1998年“三资”企业出口创汇10617万美元，比1997年的14411万美元减少35.74%，占全省出口总额的7.31%。

【对外经济合作】

承包工程和劳务合作 签订对外承包工程和劳务合作合同69项，合同金额4063万美元，比1997年3859万美元增长5.29%；完成营业额2128万美元，比1997年2621万美元减少18.81%；当年派出劳务人员 人次，年末在外人数1501人。劳务人员分布在日本、以色列、新加坡、韩国、阿联酋等13个国家和地区。

对外经济技术援助 承担援外项目2个，项目资金122万美元，受援国家2个，即：山西省技术推广中心在坦桑尼亚承建的中坦联合制厂项目82万美元；山西药研所在多哥承建的同类药业有所公司项目40万美元。正在申请争取的项目：太重公司在蒙古国承建的城市煤气项目1200万美元。该项目也是1999年援外工作的重点。

多、双边经济工作 1998年共争取多、双边援助项目7个，无偿援助资金1853万美元，即：德国无偿援助山西省农林发展土地综合利用项目金额1000万马克，涉及全省10个县；德国无偿援助太原市煤炭深加工型煤项目，共计1500万马克，其中无偿援助500万马克，财政合作1000万马克；加拿大对左权县和顺扶贫项目，无偿援助100万加元；澳大利亚援助大同煤气化公司煤炭深加工项目400万澳元；联合国人口从基金援助沁县妇女参与发展项目30万美元；德国大使馆援助方山县开府乡种羊200只（6.5万元人民币）；日本援助阳曲县希望小学项目1000万日元。

【内陆开放地区】

省会太原市1998年进出口额15167.1万美元，比1997年18195万美元减少16.14%。其中出口完成10444万美元，比1997年10031增长3.95%；进口完成4723万美元，比1997年8164万美元减少42.15%。出口商品78种，比1997年增加1种。出口额在100万美元以上的商品7种，金额4376.3万美元，占出口总额的41.90%。主要出口商品有金属镁出口8211吨，金额1670万美元，比上年增长28.46%；铝锭出口9010吨，金额1215万美元，比上年增长58.27%；焦炭出口120221吨，金额936万美元，比上年增长0.43%；刚玉制品出口金额260万美元，比上年增加171万美元；稀土永磁铁出口9942吨，金额169万美元；棉布出口839万米，金额161万美元，比上年增加92万美元；光纤面板出口金额127万美元。

出口商品销往33个国家和地区。出口额在100万美元以上的市场7个，金额2997万美元，占出口总额的28.70%。主要贸易市场是香港1416万美元，日本481.4万美元，瑞士332万美元，荷兰278万美元，印度187万美元，台湾170.4万美元，英国132.3万美元。

全市（区）外商投资企业进出口总额完成2296万美元，占进出口总额的15.14%。其中出口完成1796万美元，进口完成499.6万美元。

截止1998年底，全市共有外商投资企业913家。其中1998年新批准外商投资企业46家，项目投资总额4.04亿美元，协议外资金额2.84亿美元，外资实际到位额8400万美元。1998年太原地区利用外国政府贷款项目8个，总金额2160万美元。其中，太原市利用外国政府贷款4项，总金额900万美元。项目分别是：清徐县利用丹麦政府贷款引进葡萄汁、酒系列产品生产线；太原铝材厂利用意大利政府贷款引进予涂层机组项目；太原塑料四厂利用意大利政府贷款引进复合软包装生产线；太原口腔医疗中心利用芬兰政府贷款引进PLANNACA牙科设备；太原友谊绿色食品有限公司利用意大利政府贷款引进苹果酒生产线；山西省建筑构件公司利用奥地利政府贷款引进年产30万立方米新型墙体材料生产线；山西省河道管护服务总站利用荷兰政府贷款引进挖泥船项目；山西省汾河管理局利用荷兰政府贷款引进节水改造设备。

【对外经贸洽谈】

一、参加’98香港中国投资贸易洽谈会 1998年6月2日至6月5日在香港展览中心，山西省外经贸厅组团参加了由外经贸部组织举办的’98香港中国投资贸易洽谈会。

山西分团由省晋中地区、长治市、阳泉市等地“三资”企业共计21人组成。会上，山西省出口成交额920万美元；签订意向合同金额3000万港元；成交的主要商品有电石、镁锭、土特产品等。

二、参加’98俄罗斯“中国商品展览会” 1998年8月29日至9月9日在莫斯科索克尼基文化展览中心举办’98俄罗斯“中国商品展览会”。山西分团由省粮油食品进出口公司、省土畜产品进出口公司、省机械进出口公司、省纺织品进出口公司、省对销贸易公司等5家企业共14人组成。会上，山西省达成出口成交意向金额1319万美元。其中，粮油食品类出口成交182万美元，土畜产品类出口成交232万美元，服装类出口成交582万美元等。

三、参加’98圣地亚哥国际贸易博览会。 1998年10月23日至11月1日在智利圣地亚哥国际展览中心举办’98圣地亚哥国际贸易博览会。山西展团由省大晋实业有限公司、省天利实业有限公司、省医药保健品进出口公司、省丝绸进出口公司、中国外贸包装山西公司、省机械进出口公司、省服装针棉织品进出口公司、省技术进出口公司、省新时代进出口公司等9家外贸企业26人组成。会上，山西省出口成交732万美元。其中，服装出口210万美元，工具、健身器材等五金机械成交131万美元，玻璃器皿、童扇等轻工工艺品150万美元，医药保健品30万美元，粮油土畜产品28万美元，活性炭等五矿化工产品183万美元。

【港口、运输】

1998年全省进出口货运总量为1493.97万吨，比1997年1806万吨减少17.28%。其中，出口货运量1330.4万吨，进口货运量163.57万吨。按运输方式分：当年出口海运量1327.48万吨、陆运量2.86万吨、空运量0.06万吨。

1998年内蒙古自治区对外经济贸易

内蒙古自治区对外贸易经济合作厅

【对外贸易】

进出口总额 1998年内蒙古进出口总额13.85亿美元，比1997年的13.10亿美元增长5.73%。

出口总额 出口总额8.23亿美元，比1997年的7.35亿美元增长11.97%，占全区国内生产总值1192亿元（相当于143.99亿美元）的5.7%，占全国出口额的0.45%。

出口商品结构 初级产品出口额19329万美元，占出口总额的23.48%，工业制成品出口额63014万美元，占出口总额的76.52%。

主要出口商品 出口额在1000万美元以上的商品有无毛绒、涤粘混纺布、真丝领带、化纤裤子、羊绒衫、金首饰、钢坯、铝、无烟煤，出口金额20489万美元，占出口总额的24.89%；出口额在500－1000万美元的出口商品有荞麦、蕃茄酱罐头、砂糖、甜菜粕、羊绒围巾、涤棉针织外衣、真丝针织内衣、真丝针织裤子、呢绒西服套装、动力煤、羊毛手工打结地毯、饲料金霉素、混合稀土金属，出口金额11263万美元，占出口总额的13.68%。

出口商品市场 出口商品销往87个国家和地区。

主要出口市场情况表

国别（地区）	出口金额（万美元）	占出口总额（%）
俄罗斯	24884	30.20
香　港	19879	24.10
日　本	12324	15.00
美　国	5079	6.20
蒙　古	4202	5.10
合　计	**66368**	**80.60**

主要进口市场情况表

国别（地区）	进口金额（万美元）	占进口总额（%）
俄罗斯	24872	44.20
蒙　古	14643	26.00
澳大利亚	3369	6.00
德　国	3062	5.40
美　国	1938	3.50
合　计	**47884**	**85.10**

进口总额　进口总额为5.62亿美元，比1997年的5.75亿美元下降2.26%。

进口商品结构　初级产品进口额14529万美元，占进口总额的25.85%；工业制成品的进口额41709万美元，占进口总额的74.15%。

主要进口商品　进口额在1000万美元以上的商品有原木、锯材、废钢、磁铁矿砂、铜精矿砂、氧化铝、氯化钾、复合肥，进口金额19967万美元，占进口总额35.52%；进口额在500－1000万美元的商品有新闻纸、铜、聚氯乙稀，进口金额2239万美元，占进口总额的4.08%。

进口商品市场　进口商品来自27个国家和地区。

边境易货贸易　对俄罗斯、蒙古国的边境易货贸易进出口额39110万美元，比1997年的46710万美元下降16.27%。其中，出口额26186万美元，比1997年的20630万美元增长26.93%；进口额12924万美元，比1997年的26080万美元下降50.44%。主要出口商品有食品制成品、服装、日用杂品、纺织品；主要进口商品有原木、废钢、塑料、化肥。

技术进出口　1998年内蒙古自治区的技术引进设备进出口总额为8168万美元，比1997年的15760万美元下降48.20%。其中，签订引进技术和进口设备合同项目42个，比1997年增加39个；合同金额6613万美元，比1997年的15300万美元下降56.70%。签订技术进口合同项目15个，比1997年增加10个；合同金额1555万美元，比1997年的466万美元增长233.60%。

【利用外资】

1998年利用外资情况表

利用外资方式	批准签订的合同			实际利用外资	
	项目数（个）	外资金额（万美元）	金额比1997年（%）	金　额（万美元）	金额比1997年（%）
政府贷款	12	11860	78		
外商直接投资	91	18786	39	9082	
合资企业	62	10481	183	5631	
合作企业	9	6608	161	1165	26
外资企业	20	1697	－48	2286	
合　计	**103**	**30646**	**52**		

外商直接投资行业 外商直接投资的91个项目中，生产型项目75个，非生产型项目16个。按行业分，主要是制造业、农林牧渔业、社会服务业、采掘业等12个行业。

外商直接投资来源 外商直接投资来自31个国家和地区。主要是：台湾省、香港、美国、澳大利亚、韩国、日本、加拿大。

外商直接投资企业生产经营情况 全年外商直接投资企业出口创汇6804万美元，比1997年的7398万美元下降8%；全年销售收入53亿元，利润9655万元，上缴税款25907万元，从业人员6.8万人。

【对外经济合作】

承包工程和劳务合作 1998年签订对外承包工程和劳务合作合同项目103个，金额4540万美元；完成营业额2393万美元；当年派出劳务人员数2230人次，主要派往俄罗斯和蒙古国。承包工程和劳务合作项目主要分布在俄罗斯、蒙古国、日本，其中，俄罗斯66项，主要是建筑和种植；蒙古国32项，主要是建筑、装璜和种植；日本2项，主要是缝纫。

对外经济技术援助 承担援外项目1个，向蒙古国援助5000万元人民币居民住宅建筑材料，现正在执行当中。

接受经济援助 接受国际双边无偿援助项目7个，金额947.3万美元。

【其他】

对外经贸洽谈会 1998年9月组织参加了厦门中国投资贸易洽谈会，签订外商投资项目21个，协议利用外资金额1.7亿美元。同月举办香港内蒙古自治区招商引资项目洽谈会，签订外商投资项目38个，协议利用外资金额5.4亿美元，出口成交6084万美元。

涉外旅游 1998年入境的外国人数及台港澳同胞36.89万人次，国际旅游外汇收入1.26亿美元，比1997年的1.07亿美元增长17.75%。

1998年辽宁省对外经济贸易

辽宁省对外贸易经济合作厅

【对外贸易】

进出口总额 1998年辽宁省进出口总额127.41亿美元，比1997年的149.08亿美元下降14.5%。

出口总额 出口总额80.52亿美元，比1997年的91.59亿美元下降12.03%，占全省国内生产总值3806亿元（相当于458.6亿美元）的17.6%，居全国第七位。

出口商品结构 初级产品出口额21.71亿美元，占出口总额的27%，工业制成品的出口额58.81亿美元，占出口总额的73%。

出口额在5000万美元以上的商品情况表

金额分类	商品名称	出口金额（万美元）	占出口总额（%）
1亿美元以上（15种）	鱼类、服装、鞋类、钢材、锌、重烧镁、原油、石腊、船舶、集装箱、微电机、复印机零件、电子原器件、家用电器、电视机及音响设备	428399	53.2
5000万美元－1亿美元（15种）	粮谷类、豆类、贝类、木材、棉布、化纤布、小五金、金属制品、铸铁制品、电熔镁、成品油、塑料、医药原料、医疗器械、计算机	92769	11.5
合　计	**30种**	**521168**	**64.7**

出口商品市场　出口商品销往151个国家和地区。

主要出口市场情况表

国别（地区）	出口金额（万美元）	占出口总额（%）
日　本	321862	40.0
美　国	99905	12.4
韩　国	59162	7.3
香　港	34480	4.3
德　国	25066	3.1
新加坡	21171	2.6
朝　鲜	17453	2.2
马来西亚	16839	2.1
荷　兰	15348	1.9
法　国	11937	1.5

主要出口市场情况表（续）

国别（地区）	出口金额（万美元）	占出口总额（%）
英　国	11780	1.5
希　腊	10897	1.4
俄罗斯	10045	1.2
合　计	**655945**	**81.5**

进口总额　进口总额46.89亿美元，比1997年的57.49亿美元下降18.4%。

进口商品结构　初级产品进口额8.44亿美元，占进口总额的18%；工业制成品进口额38.45亿美元，占进口额的82%。

进口额在3000万美元以上的商品情况表

金额分类	商品名称	进口金额（万美元）	占进口总额（%）
1亿美元以上（11种）	水产品、纺织品、钢材、有色金属、原油、塑料、船舶、各类机械、成套设备、电讯设备及器材家用电器	283157	60.4
3000万－1亿美元（10种）	黑色金属、化工原料、航空设备、汽车零件、豆类、饲料、畜产品、纺织原料、纸张、医药原料	48348	10.3
合　计	**21种**	**331505**	**70.7**

主要进口市场情况表

国别（地区）	进口金额（万美元）	占进口总额（%）
日　本	161837	34.5
韩　国	57178	12.2
香　港	30526	6.5
印　尼	24779	5.3
美　国	18498	3.9
澳大利亚	10269	2.2

主要进口市场情况表（续）

国别（地区）	进口金额（万美元）	占进口总额（%）
德　国	7924	1.7
俄罗斯	5227	1.1
蒙　古	5113	1.1
台湾省	4584	1.0
新加坡	4162	0.9
合　计	**330097**	**70.4**

1998 年利用外资情况表

利用外资方式	批准签订的合同			实际利用外资	
	项目数（个）	外资金额（亿美元）	金额比1997年（%）	金　额（亿美元）	金额比1997年（%）
对外借款	13	4.7	－17.6	7.41	148.9
外商直接投资	1708	43.9	0.3	22.3	0.72
合资企业	1027	20.1	－23.9		
合作企业	185	9.7	21.9		
独资企业	495	12.4	37.3		
合作开发	1	1.7	271.6		
外商其他投资		2.1	－61.4	1.7	－68.8
对外发行股票		0.6	－84.5	0.21	－94.5
国际租赁		1.5	－6.5	1.49	－5.7
补偿贸易		0.0		0.0	
加工装配		0.0		0.0	
合　计	**1740**	**50.7**	**－7.9**	**31.41**	**2.7**

1998 年主要行业利用外资统计表

金额单位：亿美元

主　要　行　业	1998 年完成数		截至 1998 年累计数	
	项 目 数	协议外资额	项 目 数	协议外资额
农林牧渔业	951	6.9	69	1.0
石油化工	728	20.6	107	3.0
轻工业	5164	40.4	515	7.3
机械工业	1644	30.8	161	5.5
纺织工业	500	4.5	78	0.6
建材工业	666	11.4	81	2.2
冶金工业	711	13.8	32	1.6

1998年主要行业利用外资统计表（续）

金额单位：亿美元

主 要 行 业	1998年完成数		截至1998年累计数	
	项 目 数	协议外资额	项 目 数	协议外资额
电子工业	734	12.0	66	2.7
餐饮业	1190	13.8	223	3.2
房地产业	710	40.4	82	4.5

技术进出口　1998年，全省技术进出口总额15.5亿美元，比1997年增长19.5%。其中，全省技术引进共签约392项，金额9.2亿美元，比1997年同期增长15.1%；全省技术和成套设备出口签约265项，金额6.3亿美元，比1997年同期增长26.7%。

【利用外资】

外商直接投资企业生产经营情况　到1998年底，全省开业投产外商投资企业已经达到7500家。1998年，全省外商投资企业实际利用外资24亿美元，比上年同期增长了8%，高于全国平均增幅；出口创汇35.4亿美元，比上年同期增长了22%，外商投资企业出口已占全省地方产品出口额的46.6%；实现产值762亿元，比上年同期增长11.1%，约占全省国内生产总值的20%；实现税收46.2亿元，比上年增长15.2%。

【对外经济合作】

承包工程和劳务合作　1998年全省签订对外承包工程与劳务合作合同1173份；新签合同额56681万美元，比上年同期下降10.69%；完成营业额44406万美元，比上所同期增长17.53%；派出劳务25925人，比上年同期增长8.6%，期末在外31717人，比上年同期增长9.01%。外派劳务数量位居全国第二位。对外经济合作领域不断扩大，对外承包工程、劳务合作业务已分布在亚洲、非洲、欧洲及南大地区的近百个国家（地区）。工程承包已签和待签的大项目增多。已签1000万美元以上大项目4个，其中辽宁建设集团签订的苏丹输油管线工程项目6000万美元；在谈的较大承包项目22个，合同额为1.5亿美元。1998年新获外经贸部批准享有对外经营权的企业10家，截至到1998年底，全省对外经济合作公司已达55家，在全国已位居首位。

对外投资　1998年全省在境外兴办非贸易性投资企业10家，总投资3805万美元，其中中方以技术、设备投入额为1410万美元。境外项目主要是大型封头旋压机生产线。预应力钢丝绳生产线及渔业捕捞销售等，分布在俄罗斯、韩国、巴基斯坦、喀麦隆、泰国等国家。截至1998年底，经批准，全省在境外建立非贸易性企业272家。总投资额为2.08亿美元，其中中方投资额为1.04亿美元。

对外经济援助　全省对外援助在建和新建项目共计15项，合同额6.132亿元人民币。其中援外成套项目4项，完成结算金额6964万元人民币，完成计划指标的107%；利用援外优惠贷款在建项目4项，新增7项，新增合同额3.4915亿元人民币。其中利用援外贷款新增2.252亿人民币，超出年度计划125%，与七年同比增长163.7%。新增贷款额度全国排名第二位。接受国际无偿援助在建项目4项，新增3项，新增援款568.6万美元，超出年度计划42%，与上年同比增长65%。

【其他】

开发区建设　1998年全省省级以上开发区新批进区外商投资企业262家，合同外资额14.7亿美元，实际利用外资5.1亿美元，分别占全省15.3%、33.5%、21.3%。1998年省级以上开发区共实现工业总产值550亿元，税收33.9亿元，财政收入26.6亿元，出口创汇18.5亿美元。

大连保税区　1998年全区实现国内生产总

值12.5亿元，比上年增长47%；工业总产值实现6.7亿元，增长48%；市场交易额62亿元，增长31%；合同外资额3.05亿美元，其中500万美元以上的加工项目和仓储项目15个；实际利用外资1亿美元；进出口货物总额8亿元，增长7%；集装箱进出口最7.4万标准箱，增幅27%。到目前区内已累计竣工面积42.52万平方米，在建项目57.63万平方米。

涉外旅游 1998年全省接待境外旅客416540人次，其中外国游客318180人次，海外华侨8951人次，台港澳同胞83523人次。在台港澳游客中，来自台湾的游客为43897人次。1998年全省涉外旅游收入2.624亿美元，比1997年增长1.1%。

1998年沈阳市对外经济贸易

沈阳市对外经济贸易委员会

【对外贸易】

进出口情况 1998年沈阳市进出口总额为11.86亿美元，比1997年的10.52亿美元增12.73%。

出口总额7.26亿美元，比1997年的7.19亿美元增长0.97%，占全市国内生产总值941亿元（相当于113.51亿美元）的6.33%；占全省出口额的9.50%。

出口商品结构 初级产品出口额0.8亿美元，占出口总额的11.7%；工业制成品出口额6.4亿美元，占出口总额的88.3%。

出口额在100万美元以上商品情况表

金额分类	商品名称	出口金额（万美元）	占出口总额（%）
100－500万美元（101种）	高粱、皮帽子、化纤裤子、化纤童装、羊毛手工打结地毯、钓鱼竿、银、焦炭、磺胺嘧啶、车床、风机	18412	25.4
500－100万美元（10种）	鹅鸭绒毛、电熔镁、矿山机械零件、氯霉素盐、锌、铜、呢绒西服套、焊接管件	6750	9.2
1000万美元以上（11种）	化纤纱线、维生素C、汽车蓄电池、电子原器件、轮胎、呢绒西服套、铜、冻鸡、彩色电视机、有线通讯设备、铸铁件	21235	29.3
合　计	**122种**	**46397**	**63.9**

主要出口市场情况表（前 10 名）

国别（地区）	出口金额（万美元）	占出口总额（%）
韩　国	14346	19.8
美　国	13649	18.8
香　港	11324	15.6
日　本	9862	13.6
德　国	4257	5.9
俄罗斯	2977	4.1
荷　兰	1869	2.6
台湾省	1835	2.5
朝　鲜	1732	2.4

主要出口市场情况表（续）（前 10 名）

国别（地区）	出口金额（万美元）	占出口总额（%）
新加坡	1647	2.3
合　计	**63498**	**87.6**

进口总额　进口总额 4.60 亿美元，比 1997 年的 3.33 亿美元增长 38.14%。

进口产品结构　初级产品进口额为 2208 万美元，占进口总额 4.8%；工业制成品进口额 43783 万美元，占进口总额的 95.2%。

进口额在 100 万美元以上的商品情况表

金额分类	商品名称	进口金额（万美元）	占进口总额（%）
100－500 万美元（38 种）	冻鲜虾、冻鸡、棉纱线、绸缎、牛革皮、促进剂、钛白粉、诊断器械	11200	24.4
500－1000 万美元（9 种）	酯化工品、维生素、蓄电池、煤矿机械、酒类设备、聚苯乙稀、土建工程机械	7049	15.3
1000 万美元以上（10 种）	彩色电视和零件、电子原器件、汽车发动机零件、电力成套设备、铜精矿砂、化纤布	20393	44.3
合　计	**57 种**	**38642**	**84.0**

主要进口市场情况表（前 10 名）

国别（地区）	进口金额（万美元）	占进口总额（%）
韩　国	12662	27.5
日　本	10715	23.3
香　港	6392	13.9
美　国	3515	7.6
德　国	3435	7.5
澳大利亚	1586	3.4
台湾省	1456	3.2

主要进口市场情况表（续）（前 10 名）

国别（地区）	进口金额（万美元）	占进口总额（%）
法　国	952	2.1
泰　国	920	2
秘　鲁	574	1.2
合　计	**42207**	**91.7**

技术进出口　1998 年沈阳市技术进出口总额 16730 万美元，比 1997 年的 5,118 万美元增长

326.9%，其中，签订引进技术和进口设备合同146项，合同金额5664万美元，比1997年的1150万美元增长492.5%；签订技术出口合同356项，金额11066万美元，比1997年的3,968万美元增长278.9%。

技术进口 引进技术和设备来自18个国家和地区。其中：从美国引进电导设备、器材及其它成套设备3项，金额为1043万美元；从德国引进成套通用机械1项，金额为300万美元。

技术出口 技术出口项目主要有：向韩国出口各类机械、电子设备等4项，金额为431万美元；向日本出口金属切削机床1项，金额为571万美元；向瑞典出口成套环保设备1项，金额为203万美元。

【利用外资】

1998年利用外资情况

利用外资方式	批准签订的合同			实际利用外资	
	项目数（个）	外资金额（万美元）	金额比1997年（+%）	金额（万美元）	金额比1997年（+%）
对外借款	18	8452	68.94	8452	68.94
外商直接投资	465	75355	-1.26	67505	30.04
合资企业	262	29639	34.49	42001	63.96
合作企业	26	33958	94.80	15998	10.78
外资企业	177	11758	-13.80	9506	13.67
外商其他投资	171	18311	1.48	14940	-5.59
国际租赁	3	14906	-5.81	14906	-5.81
补偿贸易	1	34		34	
加工装备	167	3371	51.92		
合　计	**654**	**102118**	**2.77**	**90897**	**24.96**

外商直接投资行业 在外商直接投资项目中，生产型项目330个，非生产型项目135个。按行业分：农业4个，制造业326个，餐饮娱乐业40个，基础设施类45个，供应业2个，咨询服务业27个，其他行业21个。

外商直接投资来源 外商直接投资来自31个国家和地区。投资额排在前10位的是：英属维尔京群岛13个，21237.91万美元，美国86个，21043.08万美元，香港73个，12160.91万美元，日本46个，5735.17万美元，澳大利亚13个，3379.24万美元，韩国116个，3125.8万美元，台湾省46个，2662.89万美元，荷兰2个，1588.8万美元，比利时1个，920万美元，加拿大24个，756.99万美元。

外商直接投资企业生产经营情况 截至1998年底，已开业投产的外商投资企业1955家，全年总产值176.8亿元，比1997年增长9.7%。出口销售收入33,013万美元，同比增长10.1%。

【对外经济合作】

1998年沈阳累计签订对外工程承包和劳务合作合同7475万美元，比1997年的7021万美元增加6.47%；实现营业额6249万美元，比1997年的5789万美元增加7.95%；派出劳务人员5831人次，比1997年的5303人次增加9.69%；年末在外人数为5360人。劳务人员分布在日本、韩国、俄罗斯、新加坡、塞舌尔、美国、柬埔寨等65个国家和地区。主要对外工程承包项目有塞舌尔住房建筑项目、塞舌尔供水管线项目、布基纳法索住宅建筑项目、扎伊尔农机援助项目、柬埔寨鞋厂项目等。

【其他】

经济技术开发区 1998年沈阳经济技术开发区实现社会总产值146亿元，同比增长22.7%。实现利税总额：10.8亿元，同比增长19.1%。实际利用外资：2.2亿美元，同比增长67%，占全市外资调入总额的22%。实现出口创汇：1.55亿美元，同比增长11%，占全市出口创汇的21.3%。

1998年高新技术产业开发区实现社会总产值121亿元，同比增长21.2%。实现利税总额7.2亿元，同比增长30%。实际利用外资1.6亿美元，同比增长52%，占全市实际利用外资总额的15.8%。

涉外旅游 1998年沈阳市接待海外旅游者18万人次，比1997年增长18.4%；旅游外汇收入9000万美元，比1997年增长27.6%。

1998年大连市对外经济贸易

大连市对外经济贸易委员会

【对外贸易】

进出口总额 1998年辽宁省大连市进出口总额为56.7亿美元，比1997年的50.9亿美元增长11.2%。

出口总额 出口总额34.5亿美元，比1997年的30.1亿美元增长14.5%，占国内生产总值935亿元的30.5%，占全省自营出口总额的45.3%。

出口商品结构 初级产品出口额5.14亿美元，占出口总额的14.9%；工业制成品出口总额29.36亿美元，占出口总额的85.1%。

出口额在1000万美元以上的商品有

服装、运动鞋、成品油、石腊、船舶、集装箱、微电机、复印机零件、电子原器件、录、摄像机散件等53种，出口金额267,251万美元，占出口总额的77.45%。

出口商品市场 出口商品销往114个国家和地区。

主要出口市场情况表

国别（地区）	出口金额（万美元）	占出口总额（%）
香 港	10155	2.94
日 本	202378	58.65
东南亚	27668	8.02
欧 洲	51342	14.88
美 国	27274	7.90
拉丁美洲	1719	0.50
合 计	**320536**	**92.89**

进口总额 进口总额22.2亿美元，比1997年的20.8亿美元增长6.7%。

进口商品结构 初级产品进口额4.56亿美元，占进口总额20.5%；工业制成品的进口额17.64亿美元，占进口总额的79.5%。

进口额在1000万美元以上的商品有：黄大豆、香蕉、冻鱼、服装辅料、钢材、铜材、原油、船用设备和另配件、集装箱材料和另备件、电子原材料等32种，进口金额178,184万美元，占进口金额的80.22%。

主要进口市场情况表

国别（地区）	进口金额（万美元）	占进口总额（%）
香　港	7664	3.45
日　本	128960	58.09
东南亚	29797	13.42
欧　洲	11922	5.37
美　国	5730	2.58
拉丁美洲	427	0.19
合　计	**184500**	**83.1**

技术进出口　1998年大连市技术进出口合同总额4.35亿美元，比1997年的6.53亿美元减少30.6%。其中，签订引进技术和设备合同项目数227个，比1997年增加195个，合同金额2.04亿美元，比1997年的3.7亿美元减少44.8%。签订技术出口合同项目数46个，比1997年减少21个，合同金额2.37亿美元，比1997年的2.87亿美元减少17.4%。

【利用外资】

1998年利用外资情况表

利用外资方式	批准签订的合同			实际利用外资	
	项目数（个）	外资金额（万美元）	金额比1997年（±%）	金额（万美元）	金额比1997年（±%）
对外借款				12225	（97年为0）
外商直接投资	760	251519	-2.1%	115940	-12.1
合资企业	401	121885	-21.4%	58520	-24.7
合作企业	85	26879	-9.0%	18728	+65.4
外资企业	274	102755	+42.0%	38692	-9.9
外商其他投资				4773	-45.1
对外发行股票				4673	-44.0
加工装配				100	-70.6
合　计	**760**	**251519**		**132938**	

外商直接投资行业　外商直接投资项目中生产型项目517个，非生产型项目243个。其中第一产业29个，第二产业480个，第三产业251个。

外商直接投资主要来源情况表

国别（地区）	投资项目数（个）	投资金额（亿美元）
日　本	157	5.8
港　澳	150	5.6
美　国	150	5.0

外商直接投资主要来源情况表（续）

国别（地区）	投资项目数（个）	投资金额（亿美元）
韩　国	122	2.6
台湾省	57	1.3
澳大利亚	27	0.8
荷　兰	3	0.6
英　国	7	0.5
马来西亚	4	0.4
新加坡	17	0.3

外商直接投资企业生产经营情况 至1998年大连市累计有3600家外商投资企业开业投产，与全市已批准外商投资企业总数的46.3%。大部分企业经营状况良好，1998年实现产值364.5亿元，实现涉外税收19.1亿元，出口创汇24.3亿美元，新安排劳动就业人数2万余人。累计实现产值1627.5亿元，上缴税金19.1亿元，出口创汇108.9亿美元。安排劳动就业24万人次。

【对外经济合作】

承包工程和劳务合作 1998年签订对外承包工程和劳务合作合同项目659个，金额1.6亿美元，比1997年的1.4亿美元增长14.3%；营业额1.3亿美元，比1997年的1.1亿美元增长18.2%。当年派出劳务人员10,151人，年末在外10,025人，主要派往日本、韩国、俄罗斯、香港和台湾省等国家和地区。

【其他】

经济技术开发区 大连经济技术开发区，1998年区内新批外商投资企业71家，协议外资金额6.09亿美元。累计批准外商投资企业1,199家，其中496家开业投产。当年实现总产值2.215001亿元，出口创汇额13.41亿美元。全区全年国内生产总值120.8亿元，工业总产值243亿元。

保税区 大连保税区全年完成基础设施投资8,479万元，实现国内生产总值12.5亿元，税收1.5亿元，进出口总额7.9亿美元。

对外经贸洽谈会 '98中国大连出口商品交易会于1998年7月15日至21日在大连星海会展中心举行。共设标准展位660个，来自53个国家和地区的1,710多位客商参加了交易会。在7天的交易会中，共出成交4.11亿美元。交易期间还同时举办了'98大连经济技术洽谈会，共签订利用外资合同金额3.89亿美元。

港口运输 大连港现有泊位71个，当年实现完成货物吞吐量7,515万吨，其中外贸进出口货物吞吐量2,578万吨（出口1,643万吨，进口935万吨）。

涉外旅游 1998年大连共接待海外旅游者20.6万人次，旅游收入1.53亿美元。

1998年吉林省对外经济贸易

吉林省对外贸易经济合作厅

【对外贸易】

进出口总额 吉林省1998年进出口总额为165229万美元，比1997年的185341万美元（海关统计数）下降10.9%。

出口总额 1998年出口总额为74847万美元，比1997年的93209万美元下降19.7%，占全省国内生产总值1564.42亿元的4.0%。

出口商品结构 工业制成品出口50867万美元，占出口总额的67.96%。初级产品出口23980万美元，占出口总额的32.04%。

出口贸易结构 一般贸易45481万美元，占出口总额的60.77%；加工贸易24875万美元，占出口总额的33.23%；其它贸易4491万美元，占出口总额的6.0%。

出口市场结构 亚洲市场占64.32%；欧洲市场占19.43%；北美洲市场占11.57%；非洲市场占2.35%；拉丁美洲市场占1.38%；大洋洲及太平洋岛屿占0.95%。

出口市场 出口销往118个国家和地区。

出口额在 500 万美元以上的商品情况表

金额分类	商品名称	出口金额（万美元）	占出口总额（%）
500－1000 万美元（11 种）	家用或装饰用木制品、药材、鲜冻牛肉、松子仁、钢材、锯材、塑料制品、棉机制物、汽车零件、钢坯及粗锻件、黏土及耐火矿物	8087	10.80
1000 万美元以上（9 种）	服装及衣着附件、纺织纱线制物及制品、冻鸡、家具、未锻造铝及铝材、大米、干豆、蔬菜、汽车及汽车底盘	33230	44.39
合　计	**20 种**	**41317**	**55.19**

主要出口市场情况表

国别（地区）	出口金额（万美元）	占出口总额（%）
日　本	20571	27.48
韩　国	9966	13.32
美　国	7846	10.48
香　港	5039	6.73
朝　鲜	4775	6.38
德　国	3714	4.96
荷　兰	3242	4.33
俄罗斯	1938	2.59
台湾省	1781	2.38
泰　国	1275	1.70
合　计	**60147**	**80.36**

进口总额　1998 年进口总额 90382 万美元，比 1997 年的 92132 万美元下降 1.9%。

进口商品结构　工业制成品进口 73945 万美元，占进口总额的 81.81%；初级产品 16437 万美元，占进口总额的 18.19%。

进口贸易结构　一般贸易 52927 万美元，占进口总额的 58.56%；加工贸易 17411 万美元，占进口总额的 19.26%；其它贸易 20044 万美元，占进口总额的 22.18%。

进口市场结构　亚洲市场占 22.44%；欧洲市场占 57.44%；北美洲市场占 9.20%；非洲市场占 0.78%；拉丁美洲市场占 8.01%；大洋洲及太平洋岛屿占 2.13%。

进口额在 500 万美元以上的商品情况表

金额分类	商品名称	进口金额（万美元）	占进口总额（%）
500－1000 万美元（10 种）	食品加工机械、医疗仪器及器械、通段及保护电路装置、汽车及汽车底盘、初级形状塑料、型模及金属铸造用型箱、锰矿砂、肥料、液泵及液体提升机、纺织用合成纤维	7812	8.64

进口额在500万美元以上的商品情况表（续）

金额分类	商品名称	进口金额（万美元）	占进口总额（%）
1000万美元以上（13种）	汽车零件、计量检测仪器及器具、自动数据处理设备及部件、活塞式内燃机零件、金属加工机床、氧化铝、纺织机械、电线电缆、纸浆、橡胶或塑料加工机械、原木、钢材、铬矿砂。	45968	50.85
合　计	**23种**	**53780**	**59.49**

主要进口市场情况表

国别（地区）	进口金额（万美元）	占进口总额（%）
德　国	39574	43.79
日　本	9651	10.68
美　国	7003	7.75
意大利	6074	6.72
韩　国	4800	5.31
巴　西	4473	4.95
俄罗斯	2713	3.00
墨西哥	2485	2.75
朝　鲜	2242	2.48
澳大利亚	1715	1.90
合　计	**80730**	**89.33**

边境贸易　1998年吉林省边境小额贸易进出口总额为14106万美元，比1997年的24789万美元下降43.0%，其中出口为8708万美元，比1997年下降48%，进口5398万美元，比1997年的8048万美元下降33%。

技术进出口　1998年吉林省共签订技术进出口项目59项，进出口总额11427万美元。其中签订引进技术和进口设备合同项目38项，合同金额7196万美元；签订技术出口合同项目21项，合同金额4231万美元。

【利用外资】

1998年利用外资情况

利用外资方式	批准签订的合同			实际利用外资	
	项目数（个）	外资金额（万美元）	金额比1997年（±%）	金额（万美元）	金额比1997年（±%）
外商直接投资	367	49542	1.6	40917	1.7
合资企业	160	27206	45.9	20473	-29.4
合作企业	35	6896	-60.4	12148	443.5
外资企业	172	15440	21.4	8296	-7.9
合　计	**367**	**49542**	**1.6**	**40917**	**1.7**

外商直接投资行业 1998年外商对吉林省直接投资的367个项目中，生产型项目308个，非生产型项目59个。主要分布在：农、林、牧、渔、水利业21个，工业278个，建筑业9个，商业、饮食、供销仓储业21个，房地产公用服务业4个，科研技术服务事业1个，其他行业33个。

外商直接投资来自24个国家和地区，主要有韩国151项，香港71项、美国43项、日本31项、台湾省22项，来自上述国家和地区的外资金额41995万美元，占全省协议外资金额总额的84.8%。

【对外经济合作】

1998年吉林省共签订对外工程承包和劳务合作项目245个，合同金额14831万美元，完成营业额12850万美元。当年外派劳务人员13.386人，年末累计在外劳务人员26746人次。外派劳务人员主要派往韩国、俄罗斯、美国、新加坡、日本等。

对外经济技术援助 1998年吉林省全年承担援外项目3项，年内共计完成1项。受援国有巴新、加蓬、朝鲜。涉及的行业有森林采伐业和木材加工业，总计金额12200万元人民币。

【其他】

涉外旅游 1998年全省接待海外旅游者13.14万人次，比上年下降34.4%；实现旅游外汇收入3782.6万美元，比上年下降36.3%。

1998年长春市对外经济贸易

长春市对外贸易经济合作局

【对外贸易】

进出口总额 1998年吉林省长春市进出口总额为35534万美元，比1997年的34357万美元增长3.4%。

出口总额 出口总额19270万美元，比1997年的17090万美元增长12.8%，占全市国内生产总值609亿元人民币（相当于73.64亿美元）的2.62%，占吉林省出口总额的14.4%。

出口商品结构 初级产品出口额5775万美元，占出口总额的29.97%；工业制成品出口额13499万美元，占出口总额的70.03%。

出口额在1000万美元以上的商品有焦炭、汽车附配件，两项出口额2296万美元，占出口总额的11.9%；出口额在500万—1000万美元的商品有绿豆、其他纺织品、睛纶衫、点火线圈等，出口额为2869万美元，占出口总额的14.9%；出口额在300万—500万美元的商品有玉米、其他植物性饲料、色布、其他棉针织服装、其他套装、其他皮服装、其他服装、其他工艺美术品、柳制品、桌椅，出口额为3901万美元，占出口总额的20.2%。

出口商品市场 出口商品销往世界73个国家和地区。

主要出口市场情况表

国别（地区）	出口金额（万美元）	占出口总额（%）
日　本	3440	17.85
香　港	3178	16.49
美　国	3070	15.93
韩　国	2046	10.77
德　国	924	4.80
英　国	814	4.22
加拿大	587	3.05

主要出口市场情况表（续）

国别（地区）	出口金额（万美元）	占出口总额（%）
俄罗斯	475	2.47
伊　朗	422	2.19
比利时	404	2.10
合　计	**15360**	**79.71**

进口总额　进口总额16264万美元，比1997年17267万美元减少5.8%。

进口商品结构　初级产品进口额150万美元，占进口总额的0.92%；工业制成品进口额16114万美元，占进口总额的99.08%。

进口额在5000万美元以上的商品为摩托车配件，进口额9974万美元，占进口总额的61.3%。

进口商品市场　进口商品来自25个国家（地区）。

主要进口市场情况表

国别（地区）	进口金额（万美元）	占进口总额（%）
日　本	10320	63.45
美　国	935	5.75
韩　国	769	4.73
香　港	638	3.92
合　计	**12662**	**77.85**

技术进出口　技术进出口总额1076万美元，比1997年1564万美元减少31.2%。其中，签订引进技术和进口设备合同项目数2个，比1997年的6个减少4项；合同金额222万美元，比1997年的518万美元减少57.15%。签订技术出口合同项目16个，比1997年的9项增加7项；合同金额854万美元，比1997年的1046万美元减少57.15%。

【利用外资】

批准签订外商直接投资项目112个，合同外资金额17719万美元，比1997年的22317万美元减少20.61%；实际利用外资13237万美元，比1997年的7500万美元增长76.49%。

在外商直接投资的项目中，合资企业65家，外资金额10079万美元，比1997年的17417万美元减少42.13%；合作企业4家，外资金额1895万美元，比1997年的3950万美元减少52.02%；外资企业43家，金额1263万美元，比1997年的950万美元增长32.95%。

外商直接投资行业　在外商直接投资项目中，生产型项目95个，非生产型项目17个。按行业分：工业91个，农林牧渔水利业4个，建筑、工程、房地产业5个，商业服务业12个。

外商直接投资来源　外商直接投资来自13个国家和地区。投资额居前8位的是：美国17项，金额4939万美元；韩国41项，金额4146万美元；香港10项，金额3059万美元；台湾省4项，金额942万美元；德国2项，金额823万美元；新加坡1项，金额732万美元；加拿大7项，金额567万美元；日本8项，金额514万美元。

外商投资企业生产经营情况　截至1998年底，已开业投产的外商投资企业共421家，职工总数29162人，全年销售（营业）收入42.3亿元，比1997年的32.58亿元增长29.83%；出口创汇5518万美元，比1997年的4300万美元增长28.33%；利税总额2.98亿元，比1997年的2.61亿元增长14.18%。

【对外经济合作】

承包工程和劳务合作　1998年签订对外承包工程和劳务合作项目合同48个，金额3767万美元，比1997年的2904万美元增长29.85%；营业额1785万美元，比1997年的1317万美元增长35.54%；当年派出劳务人员1815人次，年末在外3111人，分别比1997年的1679人次和2231人增长8.1%和39.44%。劳务人员分布在韩国、新加坡、日本、俄罗斯、以色列、柬埔寨、马来西亚等国家。

【其他】

经济技术开发区　长春经济技术开发区

1998年完成固定资产投资11.6亿元，比1997年的10.4亿元增长11.5%。新批入区企业192个，其中外商投资企业52个，合同外资金额6833万美元，实际利用外资6180万美元。截止1998年底，累计兴办外商投资企业267家，其中100家已投产开业。全区全年实现社会总产值160亿元，比1997年的90亿元增长77.78%；出口创汇2273万美元；利税24.5亿元，比1997年的14.5亿元增长68.97%。

长春高新技术产业开发区1998年完成固定资产投资总额6.9亿元，比1997年的4.4亿元增长56.82%。新批入区企业230个，其中外商投资企业27个，合同外资金额7384万美元，实际利用外资6260万美元。截止到1998年底，累计兴办外商投资企业237家，其中76家已投产开业。全区全年实现科工贸总收入130亿元，比1997年的75亿元增长73.33%；出口创汇2016万美元；利税21.8亿元，比1997年的13亿元增长67.69%。

涉外旅游 1998年长春市接待海外旅游者34000人次，比1997年的35346人次下降3.8%；旅游外汇收入1500万美元，比1997年的1544万美元减少2.8%。

1998年黑龙江省对外经济贸易

黑龙江省对外贸易经济合作厅

【对外贸易】

进出口总额 1998年黑龙江省进出口总额为381265万美元，比1997年的358248万美元增长6.42%。

出口总额 出口总额203463万美元，比1997年200183万美元增长1.64%，占全省国内生产总值的5.96%。

出口额在500万美元—1000万美元的商品有羊毛衫、皮鞋、旅行筷子、化工原料、大蒜、锯材、甜菜粕、玉米、飞机、钢材、牛肉罐头、亚麻等29种，出口额19470万美元，占出口总额的9.57%；出口额在1000万美元—5000万美元的商品有大豆、大米、煤、苹果、日用杂品、毛巾被、冻鸡、生铁、健身用品、棉麻混纺布、铝材、芸豆、烤烟、皮鞋、冻牛肉、石蜡、冻猪肉、焦炭、乐器及配件等34种，出口额70671万美元，占出口总额34.73%；出口额在5000万美元以上的商品有计算机附属设备、亚麻细布、纺织品、家用电器及零配件等5种，出口额42280万美元，占出口总额20.78%。

出口商品结构表

项　目	出口额（万美元）	占出口总额（%）	
		1998年	1997年
初级产品	48831	24.0	27.91
工业制成品	154632	76.0	72.09

出口商品市场 出口商品销往117个国家和地区。

主要出口市场情况表

国别（地区）	出口金额（万美元）	占出口总额（%）
俄罗斯	86454	42.20
香　港	20357	9.94
日　本	30978	15.12
韩　国	17700	8.64
台湾省	5446	2.66
巴基斯坦	2255	1.10
德　国	3882	1.90
朝　鲜	1654	0.81
新加坡	1263	0.62

主要出口市场情况表（续）

国别（地区）	出口金额（万美元）	占出口总额（%）
越　南	1880	0.92
马来西亚	342	0.17
印度尼西亚	396	0.19
南　非	2156	1.06
印　度	511	0.25

进口总额　进口总额177802万美元，比1997年158349万美元增加12.28%。

进口商品市场　进口商品来自39个国家和地区。其中从俄罗斯、香港、日本、德国、台湾省、美国、加拿大、法国、意大利、瑞士、乌克兰、乌兹别克斯坦等12个国家和地区进口额为143937万美元，占进口总额的80.95%。

边境贸易　1998年边境贸易进出口总额125721万美元，占全省进出口总额32.97%。其中出口额78372万美元，占全省出口总额38.52%；进口额47349万美元，占全省进口总额的26.63%。

对外经贸洽谈会　1998年6月16日至22日第九届中国哈尔滨经济贸易洽谈会在哈尔滨召开。洽谈会有50个国家和地区的5500多名客商与会，展出商品20大类2万多个品种。成交额45.39亿美元。其中对外贸易合同额23.93亿美元；对外经济技术合作合同额11.8亿美元；利用外资合同额9.66亿美元。

外贸运输　1998年对外贸易运输总量为370.7万吨。其中海运120万吨，陆运130万吨，空运0.7万吨。

涉外旅游　1998年入境外国人340948人次，港澳及台胞42178万人次；旅游外汇收入1.2亿美元，比1997年增长15.7%。

【对外经济合作】

承包工程和劳务合作　1998年签订对外承包工程和劳务合作合同231项，合同金额4.2亿美元，比1997年的3亿美元增长40%。其中承包工程34项，金额6977万美元，派出劳务2577人次；劳务合作191项，金额8477万美元，派出劳务5966人次。劳务人员主要派往俄罗斯、韩国、日本、新加坡、马来西亚、乌克兰、乌兹别克斯坦、以色列、利比亚、南非等国家和地区。

外国政府贷款　1998年签订利用外国政府贷款15项，合同金额5103万美元。其中日本政府第四批贷款1,334万美元，瑞典政府贷款490万美元。

接受经济援助　1998年接受国外政府赠款6项，金额为1,012万美元。其中，东北农业大学接受加拿大政府赠款200万美元；庆林林业局“中芬合作庆林示范林场项目”150万美元；新西兰政府赠款“营造8项人工林项目”500万美元；挪威政府赠款“松花江水质监测项目”150万美元；澳大利亚政府赠款绥滨县“基础教育建设项目”6万美元，桦南县“贫困地区医疗保健项目”6万美元。

【利用外资】

1998年利用外资情况表

利用外资方式	批准签订的合同			实际利用外资	
	项目数（个）	外资金额（万美元）	金额比1997年（±%）	金　额（万美元）	金额比1997年（±%）
外商直接投资	250	80102	+36%	78016	+6
合资企业	123	56728	+56%	58193	+23

1998 年利用外资情况表（续）

利用外资方式	批准签订的合同			实际利用外资	
	项目数（个）	外资金额（万美元）	金额比 1997 年（±%）	金额（万美元）	金额比 1997 年（±%）
合作企业	21	7813	－52%	4976	－70
外资企业	106	11061	＋82%	10347	＋13
对外发行股票		4500		4500	

外商直接投资来源　外商直接投资来自 26 个国家和地区，其中前 10 位的国家有：香港 53 项，投资额 16251 万美元；韩国 50 项，投资额 12797 万美元；美国 40 项，投资额 2998 万美元；台湾省 24 项，投资额 2379 万美元；英国 2 项，投资额 2060 万美元；新加坡 6 项，投资额 1588 万美元；加拿大 13 项，投资额 695 万美元；日本 23 项，投资额 664 万美元；澳大利亚 6 项，投资额 623 万美元；菲律宾 3 项，投资额 562 万美元。

外商直接投资行业　外商投资的 250 个项目中：农业牧渔业 16 项，投资额 2172 万美元；采掘业 2 项，投资额 52 万美元；制造业 177 项，投资额 52447 万美元；电力煤气及生产供应业 5 项，投资额 14317 万美元；交通运输、仓储及邮电通信业 1 项，投资额 1527 万美元；商饮食业 7 项，投资额 165 万美元；房地产 3 项，投资额 1390 万美元；社会服务业 23 项，投资额 1575 万美元。

1998 年哈尔滨市对外经济贸易

哈尔滨市对外贸易经济合作局

【对外贸易】

进出口总额　1998 年哈尔滨市进出口总额为 87500 万美元，比 1997 年的 84802 万美元增长 3.2%。

出口总额　出口总额 41605 万美元，比 1997 年的 48854 万美元下降 14.8%，占全市国内生产总值 816.16 亿元（相当于 98.73 亿美元）的 4.2%；占全省出口额的 20.4%。

出口商品结构　1998 年，哈尔滨市初级产品出口额 5424 万美元，占出口总额的 14.8%；工业制成品出口额 36181 万美元，占出口总额的 85.2%。

出口额在1000万美元以上商品情况表

金额分类	商品名称	出口金额（万美元）	占出口总额（%）
1亿美元以上（1种）	计算机附属设备	14000	33.6
1000万美元至1亿美元（6种）	冻鸡、亚麻细布、棉麻混纺布、棉服装、铝材、发电机组	10356	24.9
合　计	**7种**	**24356**	**58.5**

出口商品市场　出口商品销往89个国家和地区。

主要出口市场情况表

国别（地区）	出口金额（万美元）	占出口总额（%）
韩　国	8852	21.3
美　国	6673	16
香　港	6206	14.9
日　本	6120	14.7
德　国	2247	5.4

主要出口市场情况表（续）

国别（地区）	出口金额（万美元）	占出口总额（%）
巴基斯坦	2132	5.1
越　南	1639	3.9
南　非	1354	3.3
合　计	**35223**	**84.6**

进口总额　1998年哈尔滨市进口总额45941万美元，比1997年的35948万美元增长27.8%。

进口商品结构　初级产品进口额3533万美元，占进口总额的7.7%；工业制成品的进口额42408万美元，占进口总额的92.3%。

进口额在1000万美元以上商品情况表

金额分类	商品名称	进口金额（万美元）	占进口总额（%）
5000万美元以上（2种）	（其他）电子原器件、无线电通讯设备	20192	44
1000－5000万美元（7种）	（其他）电子设备、聚氯乙烯、己内酰胺、（其他）油品、（其他）无线通讯设备、（其他）发动机、氯化钾	9008	19.6
合　计	**9种**	**29200**	**63.6**

进口商品市场　1998年哈尔滨市进口商品市场主要来自27个国家和地区。

主要进口市场情况表

国别（地区）	进口金额（万美元）	占进口总额（%）
韩　国	14834	32.3
俄罗斯	9252	20.1
瑞　典	6264	13.6
香　港	2723	5.9

主要进口市场情况表（续）

国别（地区）	进口金额（万美元）	占进口总额（%）
日　本	2304	5
美　国	1972	4.3
德　国	1742	3.8
合　计	**39091**	**85**

1998 年利用外资情况表

利用外资方式	批准签订的合同			实际利用外资	
	项目数（个）	外资金额（万美元）	金额比1997年（±%）	金　额（万美元）	金额比1997年（±%）
对外借款					
外商直接投资	93	9106	-54.3	15000	-3.8
合资企业	43	3645			
合作企业	10	2949			
外资企业	40	2512			
合　计	**93**	**9106**	**-54.3**	**15000**	**-3.8**

外商直接投资行业　外商直接投资项目中生产型项目 70 个，其中各类加工制造工业 65 个，农业 5 个，非生产型项目 19 个，其中建筑业 3 个，餐饮业 2 个，服务业 14 个。

外商直接投资主要来源　韩国 24 个，金额 3211 万美元；香港 15 个，金额 2429 万美元；美国 17 个，金额 602 万美元；台湾省 8 个，金额 216 万美元；日本 9 个，金额 193 万美元。

外商直接投资企业生产经营情况　1998 年外商投资开业 31 户，实现产值 110 亿元人民币，出口创汇 18300 万美元。

【对外经济合作】

承包工程和劳务合作　1998 年签订对外承包工程和劳务合作合同项目 20 个，金额 14300 万美元，比 1997 年的 40716 万美元减少 64.9%；营业额 8864 万美元，比 1997 年的 6543 万美元增长 35.5%；当年派出劳务人员 1046 人，主要派往俄罗斯、南韩、日本、美国等国家；主要对外承包工程项目有马来西亚联合循环发电机组项目、泰国冰雕、巴基斯坦冰雕。

对外投资　1998 年在海外举办非贸易性企业 6 个，中方投资金额 22.7 万美元，投资国别为莫桑比克、日本。

【其他】

经济技术开发区　1998 年是哈尔滨经济技术开发区各项工作取得蓬勃发展的一年。全年实现工业总产值 48 亿元，比 1997 年增长 12%；财政收入 4.7 亿元，比 1997 年增长 20%。

招商引资取得重大进展。1998 年开发区批准外资企业 28 家，协议外资额 7400 万美元，外资到位额 5084 万美元；引进内联企业 137 家，注册资本 5.7 亿元。统一食品、4G1 发动机、哈飞汽车配套件、斯林百兰床垫等一批大中型生产项目落户开发区。初步形成了以汽车制造、食品加工、制衣纺织、电子、制药为主导的产业结构。

对俄出口加工园区全面启动。对俄出口加工园区是我国第一个以俄罗斯为目标市场的产品加工园区。自成立以来，为实现加工园区、内陆港、保税库、俄罗斯纳霍德卡自由经济区及中国名优产品一条街的联动运作，构筑新的经贸通道，做了大量基础性工作。在香港及深圳、厦门、汕头等沿海城市举办的新闻发布会上，对俄出口加工园区已成为在我市和经济开发区投资的新热点，影响日益扩大，已有中外30余个经贸团组，100余人次来此考察、洽谈。目前，伊达药业、哈飞实业汽车配套件等项目已落户园区。

建设项目再上台阶。全年新开工面积31.5万平方米，竣工面积36万平方米。综合工业区内，顶益食品、旺豪玉米糖等项目已完成主体厂房建设，高美印刷、哈飞汽车配套件、斯林百兰等项目已建成投入生产。管理服务区房地产业持续发展。昆仑商城二期续建、隆马特超市、丰田汽车维修中心相继投入使用，金马大厦已完成主体框架；高尔夫球场也完成了除了草坪外的大部分工程，展示了现代化新城区的雏形和形象。

对外经贸洽谈会 1998年6月15日至21日，第九届中国哈尔滨经济贸易洽谈会在哈尔滨哈洽会会馆举行。我市交易团为大会邀请到会经贸和政府团组外宾1746人，签定对外经济技术合作合同9.8亿美元，比上届增长15.7%，其中：进出口贸易合同金额3.75亿美元，比上界增长2.74%，出口成交2.65亿美元，进口成交1.1亿美元；签订利用外资项目55项，总投资额3.55亿美元，比上届增长49.3%，协议外资额1.93亿美元，比上届增长10.3%；签订对外工程承包和劳务输出项目9项，合同金额1.81亿美元，比上届增长7.1%，合同外派劳务人数268人。签订国内横向经济联合项目113项，合同金额为5.52亿元人民币，折合6688万美元。引进资金2.24亿元人民币，折合2713万美元。签订国内横向经济联合项目金额比上届有所下降。

港口运输 1998年哈尔滨水、陆、空口岸外贸货运量完成14645吨（其中水运完成288吨，空运完成513吨，铁路货运完成13844吨、1295标箱），同比减少18.07%。其中出口8135吨（空运完成110吨，铁路货运完成7737吨、728标箱，水远完成288吨），进口6510吨（空运完成403吨，铁路货运完成6107吨、567标箱）

涉外旅游 1998年入境人数为1324万人，比上年增长10%。其中，外国人9.19万人次，增长8.2%；华侨、港澳台同胞4.05万人次，增长14.5%。旅游外汇收入4021万美元，比上年增长17.6%。

1998年上海市对外经济贸易

上海市对外经济贸易委员会

【对外贸易】

进出口总额 1998年上海市进出口总额为313.44亿美元，比1997年的298.00亿美元增长5.18%。

出口总额 出口总额159.56亿美元，比1997年的150.69亿美元增长5.89%，占全市国内生产总值3688.20亿元（相当于445.59亿美元）的35.82%，占全国出口总额的8.69%，居全国第二位。

出口商品结构 初级产品7.99亿美元，占出口总额的5.01%；工业制成品151.57亿美元，占出口总额的94.99%。

出口额在 5000 万美元以上商品情况表

金额分类	商品名称	出口金额（亿美元）	占出口总额（%）
5000 万－10000 万美元（56 种）	复印机、显示器、紧固件、化纤风衣、女丝绸服装、女内衣、磁带录音机、烟草制卷烟、家用型摄录一体机、皮鞋、滚动轴承、汽车零部件、手工具、体育运动或户外游戏用品及设备、小家电、家具及其零件、床上用品、合成纤维制女式上衣、石油制品、盥洗及厨房毛巾织物、传声器、扬声器，耳机，音频扩大器等，纺织面料鞋、羊毛衫、童婴服装、大型电动机，发电机组及零件、棉染色布、染料、橡胶轮胎、皮革或再生皮革制的衣服及衣着附件、电视机及其零部件、毛制男式西服套装、女式裙子及裙裤、绝缘电线，电缆及其他绝缘电导体、钻石及珠宝首饰、缝纫机、视频信号录制或重放设备及零件、飞机等航空器，航天器、放电灯或放电管用镇流器、塑料包袋、游艺场所，桌上或室内游戏用品、橡胶或塑料鞋、白炽灯泡，放电灯管，弧光灯、计算机器、抗菌素、电视摄像机及零件、铁合金、大中小微型计算机、针织袜、鲜冻鸡、连衣裙、电池、起绒布及绳绒织物、针织手套、铝合金、电气设备的绝缘配件手提式电动工具等。	41.44	25.97
10000 万美元以上（25 种）	集成电路及微电子组件、长西裤、钢材、衬衫、填充的玩具动物、打印机、棉针织 T 恤衫，汗衫及背心、船舶、弹簧床垫、电话机、空调、照相机、塑料或纺织材料作面的提箱、灯具及照明装置、起重机、半导体器件、集装箱（包括运输液体的集装箱）、微型电动机、自行车及零件、合成纤维制男式上衣、塑料制衣服及衣着附件、搪瓷不锈钢器具、电路开关，保护等电气装置、印刷电路、光盘驱动器等。	39.32	24.64
合　计	**81 种**	**80.76**	**50.61**

出口商品市场　出口商品销往 206 个国家和地区。

主要出口市场情况表

国别（地区）	出口金额（亿美元）	占出口总额（%）
日　本	39.81	24.95
美　国	35.64	22.34
香　港	14.78	9.26
德　国	6.19	3.88
英　国	3.83	2.40
新加坡	3.81	2.39

主要出口市场情况表（续）

国别（地区）	出口金额（亿美元）	占出口总额（%）
菲律宾	3.72	2.33
荷　兰	3.32	2.08
台湾省	3.31	2.07
韩　国	3.27	2.05
合　计	**117.68**	**73.75**

进口总额 进口总额153.88亿美元，比1997年的147.31亿美元增长4.46%。

进口商品结构 初级产品20.78亿美元，占进口总额的13.5%；工业制成品133.1亿美元，占进口总额的86.5%。

进口额在5000万美元以上的商品情况表

金额分类	商 品 名 称	进口金额（亿美元）	占进口总额（%）
5000万－10000万美元（29种）	生橡胶、黄大豆、铝废碎料、润滑油脂、皮革、皮革制品及已鞣毛皮、尼龙等聚酰胺长丝>85%染色布、化纤制未列名针织物或钩编织物、数控锻造或冲压机床及锻锤、8456至8461所列机器用的零件、冷凝器为热交换器的压缩式制冷机、载客电梯、大、中、小型计算机及其部件的零件、其他打印机零件、复印设备的其他零件、附件、光端机及脉冲编码调制设备、8517所列其他设备的零件、盒式磁带录音机或放声机的其他零件、8519至8521所列设备的未列名零件、四层以上的印刷电路、其他连接用电气装置、其他电力控制或分配盘、板台等、8535、8536或8537所列装置、其他数字式单片集成电路、混合集成电路、8543所列其他设备及装备的零件、4500>空载重量>15000公斤的、飞机及直升机的其他零件、其他照相机未列名零件等。	20.49	13.32
10000万美元以上（35种）	饲料（不包括未碾磨谷物）、其他油菜子、软木及木材、纸浆及废纸、纺织纤维（羊毛条除外）、未烧结的铁矿砂及其精矿、其他燃料油、有机化学品、染料、鞣料及着色料、医药品、初级形状的塑料、非初级形状的塑料、纸及纸板、非金属矿物制品、钢铁、有色金属、金属制品、动力机械及设备、数字式程控电话或电报交报机的零件、移动通讯基地站、其他电视摄像机的零件、8525至8528所未列名装置或设备、其他半导体器件、其他单片集成电路、集成电路及微电子组件的零件、服装或衣着附件的零件、专业、科学及控制用仪器、摄影器材、光学物品及钟表等。	76.05	49.42
合 计	**64种**	**96.54**	**62.74**

进口商品市场 进口商品来自99个国家和地区。

主要进口市场情况表

国别（地区）	进口金额（亿美元）	占进口总额（%）
日 本	39.19	25.47
美 国	25.25	16.41

主要进口市场情况表（续）

国别（地区）	进口金额（亿美元）	占进口总额（%）
德 国	14.32	9.31
台湾省	10.76	6.99

主要进口市场情况表（续）

国别（地区）	进口金额（亿美元）	占进口总额（%）
韩　国	10.74	6.98
香　港	8.65	5.62
法　国	6.18	4.02
新加坡	4.43	2.88
澳大利亚	4.19	2.72
巴　西	2.83	1.84
合　计	**126.54**	**82.23**

技术进出口　1998年上海市技术进出口总额18.36亿美元，比1997年的15.08亿美元增长21.75%。其中，签订引进技术和进口设备合同项目数940个，比1997年的948个下降0.84%；合同金额10.03亿美元，比1997年的8.44亿美元增长18.84%。签订技术出口合同项目数316个，比1997年的275个增长14.91%；合同金额8.33亿美元，比1997年的6.64亿美元增长25.45%。

技术进口　引进技术和设备来自12个国家和地区。主要有：美国287项，41636万美元；日本134项，28078万美元；德国98项，15944万美元；泰国2项，2468万美元；英国5项，2439万美元；香港202项，2356万美元；法国5项，2215万美元；意大利22项，901万美元；荷兰14项，815万美元；瑞士22项，602万美元；奥地利11项，482万美元；加拿大13项，411万美元。

引进技术和设备的主要行业分布是：机电工业123项，44708万美元；仪表电子工业90项，20417万美元；建筑业19项，14508万美元；冶金工业59项，8421万美元；轻工业21项，2567万美元；石化工业13项，2566万美元；医药工业5项，133万美元。

技术出口　签订技术出口主要有美国、日本、德国、香港、巴拿马、瑞士、新加坡等35个国家和地区。签订技术出口的主要项目有：向德国出口4.8万吨散货船，金额4800万美元；向美国出口集装箱门吊，金额3160万美元；向美国出口图像扫描仪，金额2077万美元等。

【利用外资】

1998年利用外资情况表

利用外资方式	批准签订的合同			实际利用外资	
	项目数（个）	外资金额（万美元）	金额比1997年（±%）	金额（万美元）	金额比1997年（±%）
对外借款					
外商直接投资	1490	584775.90	9.92	363786	－24.3
合资企业	378	252906.28	－7.78	148643	－29
合作企业	278	73115.82	－37.5	48063	－38.7
外资企业	833	149514.20	6.73	127402	－33.6
股份制企业	1	109238.60	6998.02	39678	43.1倍
外商其他投资		256800.00	－10.0	117800	－23.4
合　计	**1490**	**841575.9**	**－1.9**	**481586**	**－28.65**

外商直接投资行业　在外商直接投资的项目中，生产型项目793个，非生产型项目697个。按行业分，农林牧渔水利业14个，工业770个，地质普查和勘探业2个，建筑业7个，交通运输邮电通讯16个，商业饮食物资供销55个，房地产、公用事业256个，卫生体育社会福利4个，教育文

艺广播电视 3 个，科学研究技术服务 1 个，其它行业 362 个。

外商直接投资来源 外商直接投资来自 83 个国家和地区。投资额居前 10 位的是：美国 221 个，15.96 亿美元；德国 39 个，15.18 亿美元；香港 356 个，7.68 亿美元；英属维尔京群岛 81 个，3.38 亿美元；新加坡 85 个，2.67 亿美元；日本 160 个，2.58 亿美元；荷兰 2 个，1.61 亿美元；加拿大 27 个，1.46 亿美元；台湾省 238 个，1.25 亿美元；英国 36 个，0.93 亿美元。

外商直接投资企业生产经营情况 截止 1998 年底，已开业投产的外商投资企业共 12000 多家，外商投资企业经营状况良好，已投产开业的外商企业 1998 年新增合同外资 16.31 亿美元；实现工业总产值 2288.68 亿元，占全市工业总产值的 38.81%；出口创汇 80.32 亿美元，比 1997 年增长 14.71%，占全市出口总额的 50.34%；外商企业从业人员人数占全市职工人数的 24.18%。

【对外经济合作】

承包工程和劳务合作 1998 年上海签对外承包工程和劳务合作合同项目 1010 个，合同金额 71500 万美元，比 1997 年的 63561 万美元增长 12.3%；完成营业额 55800 万美元，比 1997 年的 42208 万美元增长 32.8%；当年派出劳务人员 8180 人次，比 1997 年的 8644 人降低 5.36%，年末在外人数 24165，比 1997 年增长 12%。劳务人员主要分布在日本、塞班岛、新加坡、港澳地区和毛里求斯等国家和地区。主要对外承包工程项目有伊朗 2 台 32.5 万千瓦发电机组，新加坡住宅区工程、香港西北铁路、香港住宅工程、关岛酒店工程等项目。

对外经济技术援助 承担援外项目 2 个，主要是无偿援助物资，总金额 602 万人民币 ，受援国是瓦努阿图、约旦。

接受经济技术援助 接受国外政府贷款、多边和双边无偿援助项目 8 个，总金额 7355.25 万美元。项目是：垃圾焚烧、陇西水厂、上海地籍信息管理系统、地铁营运人员培训等项目。

对外投资 1998 年上海共举办海外非贸易型项目 24 个，总投资 3266 万美元，其中中方投资 2340 万美元。这些企业主要分布在南部非洲等国家和地区。

【其他】

经济技术开发区 1998 年浦东新区外抓形象、内增实力，加快体制创新、产业升级、扩大开放，积极发挥新区的示范、辐射、带动作用。全年浦东新区增加值 708.86 亿元，比上年增长 16.8%；全年完成工业总产值 1421.66 亿元，比上年增长 15.1%；第三产业增加值 283.48 亿元，增长 23.7%；用于固定资产投资 581.22 亿元，增长 15.2%；外贸出口总值 43 亿美元，增长 14.5%；签订外商直接投资项目 554 项，吸引外资合同金额 28.93 亿美元；社会消费品零售总额 178.81 亿元，比上年增长 10.2%。

至 1998 年底，已有 67 个国家和地区在浦东投资了 5472 个项目，累计吸引合同外资 105 亿美元。国际著名跨国公司中，有 88 家在浦东投资了 149 个大项目。证券、人才、产权、商品、粮油、和房地产等要素市场，以及 72 家外资金融机构聚集浦东，陆家嘴金融贸易区、金桥出口加工区、张江高科技园、外高桥保税区、区等重点小区开发加速推进，功能开发进一步加强。

漕河泾新兴技术开发区经过 11 年的开发建设，累计批准外商投资企业 236 家，投资总额为 10 亿美元。1998 年实现工业销售收入 126 亿元，利税 14 亿元，是以信息产业、新材料、现代生物与医药为三大支柱产业，以光电机一体化、航空航天数字程控、计算机及软件等高新技术产业为群体的新兴工业园区。

闵行经济技术开发区创建十四年已建成一个外向型、集约化、综合性的现代化工业园区。到 1998 年底，累计实现工业产值愈 764 亿元，利税 142 亿元；区内已引进 142 个外资项目，技术先进性企业超过 20%。区内企业新开发的激光非金属晶体、血液制品及蛋白素等高技术产品，畅销国际市场。

虹桥经济技术开发区是以外贸中心为主要特征，集展览展示、办公、居住、购物、餐饮娱乐为一体的多功能外向型商贸区。开发 15 年来已累计引进投资项目 102 个，合同额 25.87 亿美元，其中外资 21.23 亿美元。到 1998 年底，有 600 多家中外商社和贸易机构进驻区内，累计营业收入222.48亿元，上缴税金12.91亿元。

保税区 上海外高桥保税区进一步扩大开放，规范管理和优化投资环境，积极推动开发建设的进程，1998年保税区各项综合经济指标持续稳定增长，全年完成国内生产总值63.2亿元，比1997年增长24.2%；实现销售（经营）收入468.3亿元，增长29.9%；完成工业总产值96.8亿元，增长41.8%；全区完成进出口总额29.61亿美元，增长7%，其中出口10.46亿美元，增长45.3%。外高桥保税区日益受到国内外众多船公司的关注，1998年港口吞吐量579.9万吨，增长21.8%；集装箱装卸量67.5万标准箱，增长37.5%；外贸吞吐量451.4万吨，年增长34.2。保税仓储企业货物存储充沛，月均储存量达30万吨，同比增长43.7%。年货运量98.4万吨，增长16.7%。全年批准项目461个，吸引合同外资4.53亿美元，其中外商当年增资1.5亿美元。累计到1998年底，已有109家企业投入生产，比1997年增长22.5%；有11家企业年产值超亿元，12家高科技企业全年完成工业产值73.1亿元，比上年增长33.9%，占工业总产值的76.1%。

对外经贸洽谈会 1998年3月5日～3月14日由上海、江苏、浙江、安徽、福建、江西、山东、南京、宁波9省市共同主办，在上海举办了第八七届中国华东出口商品交易会，外商来自109个国家和地区6518人，成交金额19.65亿美元。

分别在日本、意大利、巴西举办对外经贸洽谈会，成交金额8778.5万美元，签订合同意向5342万美元。

港口运输 1998年，上海港口泊位数317个，港口吞吐能力1.64亿吨。当年实际完成货物吞吐总量16387.8万吨，与1997年的16397.1万吨基本持平。其中，实际完成外贸进出口货物吞吐量4903.8万吨（出口量1879.4万吨，进口量3024.4万吨）。全年本地区外贸运输货运总量为4713万吨，比1997年的2605.1万吨增长80.9%。其中，出口货运量1473万吨，进口货运量3240万吨；按运输方式分：当年海运量4680万吨，空运量19万吨，陆运量14万吨。全年国际集装箱吞吐量为306.6万个国际标准箱，比1997年的252.7万个增长21.32%。

涉外旅游 全年共接待世界各地旅游者152.7万人次，比1997年的165.35万人次下降7.65%，其中，外国人117.6万人次，下降9.6%。旅游外汇收入12.18亿美元，比1997年下降11.09%。

1998年江苏省对外经济贸易

江苏省对外经济贸易委员会

【对外贸易】

进出口总额 1998年江苏省进出口总额为2642600万美元，比1997年的2387700万美元增长11.83%。

出口总额 出口总额为1565100万美元，比1997年的1521800万美元增长11.04%，占全省国内生产总值72008000万元的30.4%，占全国出口总额的11.74%，居全国第三位。

出口商品结构 初级产品出口额70946万美元，占出口总额的4.53%；工业制成品出口额1494163万美元，占出口总额的95.47%。

主要出口商品是梭织服装、计算机、电子元器件、针织服装、化纤布、棉布、玩具、鞋类、家用小电器、棉制品、电视机及音响设备、集装箱及零备件、塑料制品、各类船、手工具、小五金、电动工具、毛纱线、有线通讯设备、化纤制品、金属制品、化纤纱线、电工设备、蔬菜、汽车零件、绸缎、染料中间体、动力机械等，出口额 955917 万美元，占全省出口总额比重 61.08%。

出口商品市场 出口商品销往的主要国家和地区依次为日本、美国、香港、荷兰、德国、韩国、新加坡、英国、台湾省、意大利、法国、加拿大、澳大利亚、比利时、印度、西班牙、孟加拉国、阿联酋、马来西亚、泰国等，金额 1366852 万美元，占全省出口总额的 87.33%。

进口总额 进口总额 1077499 万美元，比 1997 年的 953539 万美元增长 12.99%。

进口商品结构 主要进口商品是自动数据处理设备的零件、制造纸及纸制品用机械、钢材、原油、合成纤维长丝机织物、初级形状塑料、飞机、纺织机械、通断及保护电路装置、集成电路及微电子组件、纸浆、成品油、棉机织物、计量检测分析自控仪器及器具、羊毛、纺织用合成纤维、针织或钩编织物、原木、纸及纸板、金属加工机床等，进口额 526192 万美元，占全省进口总额的 48.83%。

进口商品市场 进口商品主要来自日本、台湾省、韩国、美国、德国、新加坡、泰国、瑞典、芬兰、香港、意大利、印度尼西亚、马来西亚、澳大利亚、荷兰、英国、法国、加拿大等国家和地区，进口额 987845 万美元，占全省进口总额的 91.65%。

技术进出口 1998 年江苏省技术进出口总额 369155 万美元，其中技术出口 277443 万美元，同比增长 34.92%，占全省出口总额的 17.72%；签订引进技术和进口设备合同项目数 97 个，合同金额 91712 万美元。

【利用外资】

1998 年利用外资情况表

利用外资方式	批准签订的合同			实际利用外资	
	项目数（个）	外资金额（万美元）	金额比 1997 年（±%）	金额（万美元）	金额比 1997 年（±%）
对外借款					
外商直接投资	1815	757773	-18.4	665250	7
合资企业	911	233700		316000	
合作企业	128	70400		51100	
外资企业	744	445900		291900	
外商投资股份制	2	7773		6250	
合　计	**1815**	**757773**	**-18.4**	**665250**	**7**

外商直接投资的行业和规模 外商在江苏的投资实现了从第二产业向第一、第二、第三产业全方位投资的转变，从劳动密集型向技术密集型的转变以及下游工业（制造加工业）向上游工业（原材料、基础设施）的转变，投资领域进一步优化。1998 年外商在我省的直接投资仍以第二产业为主，新批协议外资 65.87 亿美元，占全年新批协议外资总额的 86.90%；实际利用外资额 57.86 亿美元，比上年同期增长 9.03%。第三产业吸引外资保持了适度规模，全年新批协议外资额 7.92 亿美元，实际利用外资额 8.31 亿美元，比上年同期增长了 19.11%。

外商直接投资来源 外商直接投资来自 65 个国家和地区。其中，新批协议外资有新加坡 17.19 亿美元，港澳地区 12.30 亿美元，英属维尔京群岛 8.57 亿美元，日本 6.24 亿美元，台湾省 5.70 亿美元，美国 5.68 亿美元。

三资企业生产经营和出口 1998 年全省

新投产开业的三资企业502家，全省三资企业自营出口总值达80.60亿美元，比上年增长20.1%，三资企业自营出口已占全省外贸出口总额的51.48%。全省有自营出口实绩的外商投资企业已达3765家，其中出口超过1000万美元的三资企业达139家，出口超1亿美元的有6家。1998年全省三资企业主营业务收入2062亿元，比上年同期上升16.96%。1998年度全国规模最大的500家外商投资企业中，江苏省占49家。

【对外经济技术合作】

对外承包工程和劳务合作 1998年江苏省签订对外承包工程、劳务合作、设计咨询合同额62500万美元，同比增长31.2%；营业额52200万美元，同比增长35.62%；当年新派劳务人员15800人次，同比增长37.85%；年末在外人数23200人，同比增长54.35%。劳务人员主要派往新加坡、科威特、日本、阿联酋、以色列、毛里求斯、乌干达、津巴布韦、肯尼亚等国家。

对外经济技术援助 承担了对外经援项目8个，完成投资额5479万美元。8个项目分布在厄瓜多尔、加蓬、苏里南、埃及、安哥拉、安提瓜、纳米比亚等7国，项目涉及农田、水利、电力、地质、建筑、制药等行业。

接受国际援助 接受日本援助江苏省17.28亿日元的妇幼卫生保健项目顺利结束，已于1998年11月交付使用；加拿大援助江苏省的“中加江苏中小企业应用管理与环保项目”已开始启动，首批周转金项目开始申请。

对外投资 1998年经批准的江苏海外非贸易企业为17家，总投资2128万美元，其中中方投资1087.9万美元，经营情况良好。

【其他】

经济技术开发区 江苏省已有经国务院批准的11个经济技术开发区和江苏省政府批准的68个经济技术开发区。1998年，新批进区企业3713家，比上年增加830家；进区企业总投资566.7亿元。其中新批外商投资企业557家，合同外资46.30亿美元，占全省新批合同外资总额的61.1%；外商实际出资45.2亿美元，同比增长27.0%，占全省实际利用外资总额的67.7%。开发区企业实现的自营进出口额在全省进出口总额中的比重已达38.6%，其中出口所占比重达30.5%。相当一部分开发区已逐步进入产出期，1998年全省开发区实现技工贸总收入2157.6亿元，比上年增长27.8%；其中工业产品销售收入1523.2亿元，同比增长22.7%。开发区已经成为我省与国际接轨的新兴工业区，也是我省经济发展的重要增长点。此外，开发区还提供了大量的就业岗位。截至1998年底，全省开发区进区企业从业人数已达79.8万人，比上年增加13.7万人。

对外经贸洽谈会 1998年江苏省分别在6个国家举办和参加展览（博览）会，参展企业共139家，成交金额达18.90亿美元，意向成交7309万美元。其中，经外经贸部批准，上半年我省在沙特、日本举办了“江苏省出口商品展览会”，成交了8693.5万美元，意向成交5956.4万美元，接待客户近6000人次。下半年在尼日利亚举办江苏机电产品洽谈会，成交784万美元，意向成交1000.5万美元。主要参展的商品有机械设备、五金矿产、机电、工具、医药保健、轻工、服装、家纺以及畜产品等。

涉外旅游 1998年，江苏省接待海外游客115.4万人次，创汇5.30亿美元，分别比上年增长7.5%和25%。

1998年南京市对外经济贸易

南京市对外经济贸易委员会

【对外贸易】

进出口总额 1998年江苏省南京市进出口总额171282万美元，比1997年的170098万美元增长0.70%。

出口总额 出口总额117422万美元，比1997年的107345万美元增长9.39%；占全市国内生产总值的11.77%；占江苏省出口总额的6.70%。

出口商品结构 初级产品出口额2588万美元，占出口总额的2.20%；工业制成品出口额114834万美元，占出口总额的97.80%。

出口额在1000万美元以上商品情况表

金额分类	商品名称	出口金额（万美元）	占出口总额%
2000万美元以上（10种）	电子元器件、布绒玩具、音响设备、水泥、彩色电视机、工艺玩具、电动工具、显像管、摩托车、组合音响	28082	23.92
1000万－2000万美元（14种）	针织外衣、微型电子计算机、餐具、镁、畜产品、工艺品、有色金属、真丝绸服装、涤粘混纺布、玩具、变压器、整条轮胎、棉服装，其他化工原料	18201	15.50
合　计	**24种**	**46283**	**39.42**

出口商品市场 出口商品销往132个国家和地区。

主要出口市场情况表

国别（地区）	出口金额（万美元）	占出口总额（%）
美　国	28147	23.97
日　本	23254	19.80
香　港	19610	16.70
德　国	7024	5.98
台湾省	6610	5.63
英　国	3063	2.61
瑞　典	2383	2.03
韩　国	2115	1.80
法　国	1881	1.60
荷　兰	1841	1.57

主要出口市场情况表（续）

国别（地区）	出口金额（万美元）	占出口总额（%）
合　计	**95928**	**81.70**

进口总额 进口总额53860万美元，比1997年的62753万美元下降14.17%。

进口商口结构 初级产品进口额1346万美元，占进口额的2.50%；工业制成品进口额52514万美元，占进口总额97.50%。

主要进口商品 化工原料12596万美元，电子原材料10498万美元，电子元器件6875万美元，光纤维通讯设备1280万美元，计算机附属设备1254万美元，有色金属1122万美元，纸1059万美元，电子设备1043万美元。合计35727万美元，占进口总额的66.33%。

进口商品市场 进口商品来自41个国家和地区。其中韩国14669万美元，占进口总额的27.24%；台湾省7762万美元，占14.41%，香港7667万美元，占14.24%；日本6554万美元，占12.17%；荷兰4780万美元，占8.88%；德国2670万美元，占4.96%。瑞典2326万美元，占4.32%；美国2310万美元，占4.29%。合计48738万美元，占90.49%。

【利用外资】

利用外资情况 1998年批准签订外商直接投资合同371项，合同外资金额54247万美元。其中合资企业177项，外资金额23155万美元；合作企业38项，11328万美元；外资企业155项，18560万美元；股份制企业1项，1204万美元。实际利用外资金额74845万美元，比1997年的65443万美元增长14.37%。

外商直接投资行业 在外商直接投资的371个项目中，第一产业项目20个，第二产业项目291个，第三产业项目60个。按行业分，化工医药业37个，机械制造业55个，电子通信业38个，其它制造业137个，房地产业23个，社会服务业28个，农林牧渔业20个，其它33个。

外商直接投资来源 外商直接投资来自37个国家和地区。主要有：香港106个，外资金额16707万美元；台湾省102个，8066万美元；美国60个，7886万美元；英属维尔京群岛8个，6024万美元；日本18个，4702万美元；澳大利亚18个，2318万美元；新加坡9个，1381万美元；荷兰2个，1198万美元；加拿大5个，1126万美元；英国4个，1023万美元。

外商直接投资企业生产经营情况 截止1998年底，已开业投产的外商投资企业共2745家，其中1998年开业的有173家。全年销售(营业)收入351亿元，比1997年286.5亿元增长22.51%；纳税总额18.3亿元，比1997年的16亿元增长14.38%；出口创汇6.41亿美元，比1997年的5.15亿美元增长24.47%，占全市出口总额的54.60%。

【对外经济合作】

承包工程和劳务合作 1998年签订对外承包工程和劳务合作合同128个，合同金额9682万美元，比1997年的9027万美元增长7.62%；完成营业额9029万美元，比1997年的8116万美元增长11.25%；当年派出劳务人员3397人，年末在外5266人。劳务人员分布在卡塔尔、新加坡、莫桑比克、毛里求斯、苏里南、乌干达等50个国家和地区。承包工程的主要项目有：科威特289幢住宅工程项目、科威特360幢住宅工程项目、苏里南政府住宅工程项目、阿联酋低标住宅工程项目。

对外投资 批准在美国、斐济举办非贸易企业3家，中方总投资155万美元。

【其他】

经济技术开发区 南京高新技术开发区全年投入基础设施建设资金22891万元，技工贸销售总额165亿元，比上年增长26.92%；实现利税17亿元，增长13.33%。1998年批准进区外商投资企业23家，合同外资金额2907万美元，出口创汇15452万美元。

对外经贸洽谈会 1998年9月在南京举办“南京金秋经贸洽谈会”，接待了来自44个国家和地区的客商2101人，批准利用外资立项以上项目354个，合同外资金额5.64亿美元。出口成交6503万美元，签订对外承包工程和劳务合作合同6个，合同额1813万美元。

港口运输 南京港拥有生产泊位66个，其中万吨级以上泊位16个，集装箱泊位4个，港口年吞吐能力6700万吨，集装箱吞吐能力30万个标准箱。全年实际完成货物吞吐总量5278万吨，其中外贸货物进出口吞吐量622万吨（出口量189万吨，进口量433万吨）。

涉外旅游 1998年南京市共接待海外旅游者30.52万人次，比1997年的29.91万人次增长2.04%。其中外国人16.94万人次，华侨和港澳台同胞13.58万人次。旅游收入1.47亿美元，比1997年的1.21亿美元增长21.49%。

1998 年连云港市对外经济贸易

连云港市对外经济贸易委员会

【对外贸易】

进出口总额　1998 年连云港市进出口总额为 39273 万美元，比 1997 年的 36957 万美元增长 6.26%。

出口总额　出口总额 35245 万美元，比 1997 年的 33120 万美元增长 6.42%，占全市国内生产总值 32.01 亿美元的 11.01%，其中，一般贸易出口 19503 万美元，外商投资企业出口 15742 万美元。

出口商品结构　在一般贸易出口商品中，初级产品出口额 4148 万美元，占出口总额的 21.46%；工业制成品出口额 15318 万美元，占出口总额的 78.54%；外商投资企业出口商品中，初级产品出口占 58.20%，工业制成品出口占 41.80%。

一般贸易出口额在 3000 万美元以上的为西药原料，出口金额为 3462 万美元，占出口总额的 17.75%；1000 万美元以上的为服装和柠檬酸，出口金额 2330 万美元，占出口总额的 11.95%；500 万美元以上的为水产品，出口额为 645 万美元，占出口总额的 3.31%；200 万美元以上的为铁丝、鞋、元明粉、活性碳、电子元器件、食品、山梨酸、金属钠、杀虫剂、海藻酸钠，出口金额 3130 万美元，占 16%。

出口商品市场　出口商品销往日本、美国、香港、韩国、德国、泰国、马来西亚、新加坡、台湾省、荷兰等 90 多个国家和地区。主要出口市场为：日本 4937 万美元，占一般贸易出口额的 25.31%；美国 3445 万美元，占 17.66%；香港 1768 万美元，占 9.1%；韩国 1743 万美元，占 8.9%；德国 981 万美元，占 5%；泰国 543 万美元，占 2.8%；马来西亚 529 万美元，占 2.7%；新加坡 443 万美元，占 2.3%。

进口总额　进口总额 3928 万美元，比 1997 年的 3837 万美元增长 2.37%；其中，一般贸易进口 2216 万美元；外商投资企业进口 1712 万美元。

进口商品结构　在一般贸易进口中，初级产品进口额 688 万美元，占进口总额的 31%；工业制成品进口额 1528 万美元，占进口总额的 69%。

进口商品市场　一般贸易进口商品来自 11 个国家和地区。主要是：香港 567 万美元，占进口总额的 25.59%；新加坡 408 万美元，占 18.41%；德国 288 万美元，占 13%；韩国 253 万美元，占 11.42%；美国 235 万美元，占 10.6%；日本 172 万美元，占 7.76%。

主要进口商品中，200 万美元以上的有石油沥青、医药原料、酯化工品、油品、进口总额 1011 万美元，占进口总额的 45.62%；100 万美元以上的有牛羊油、油漆、染料、废纸、建筑材料，进口额为 551 万美元，占 24.86%；50 万美元以上的有菜籽粕、设备，进口额 167 万美元，占 7.54%。

1998 年利用外资情况表

利用外资方式	批准签订的合同			实际利用外资	
	项目数（个）	外资金额（万美元）	金额比 1997 年（±%）	金　额（万美元）	金额比 1997 年（±%）
对外借款	7	2114	+349.79	2822	+104.49
外商直接投资	110	9261	+19.84	10308	−2.86

1998 年利用外资情况表（续）

利用外资方式	批准签订的合同			实际利用外资	
	项目数（个）	外资金额（万美元）	金额比 1997 年（±%）	金　额（万美元）	金额比 1997 年（±%）
合资企业	63	2428		6747	
合作企业	1	90		187	
外资企业	46	6743		3374	
外商其他投资	1	15		15	
国际租赁	1	15		15	
合　计	**118**	**11390**	**+20.03**	**13145**	**+7.15**

外商直接投资行业　在外商直接投资的项目中，生产型项目 101 个，非生产型项目 9 个。按行业来分：制造业 92 个，农林牧渔业 9 个，房地产业 4 个，批发零售餐饮服务业 5 个。

外商直接投资来源　外商直接投资来自 14 个国家和地区，主要是：香港 25 个，实际利用外资 2137 万美元；台湾省 32 个，1034 万美元；日本 11 个，2519 万美元；韩国 20 个，534 万美元；美国 8 个，251 万美元。

外商直接投资企业生产经营情况　1998 年全市有 72 家外商投资企业投产，出口创汇 15742 万美元，比 1997 年增长 11.93%，占全市出口总额的 44.66%。

【对外经济合作】

承包工程和劳务合作　1998 年签订对外承包工程和劳务合作合同 70 个，合同金额 6395 万美元，比 1997 年的 5494 万美元增长 16.40%，实际完成营业额 6179 万美元，比 1997 年的 5490 万美元增长 12.55%。当年派出劳务人员 2810 人，年末在外 5180 人，派往国家和地区主要是：新加坡、科威特、阿联酋、日本、韩国、俄罗斯等。

【其他】

经济技术开发区　全年完成固定资产投资 5.08 亿元人民币，比 1997 年下降 28.66%；全区新批利用外资企业 40 个，实际利用外资 6006 万美元，比 1997 年增长 19.52%；全区共完成工业总产值 50.38 亿元人民币，比 1997 年增长 24.64%；实际财政收入 1.74 亿元人民币，比 1997 年增长 3.57%；全区出口总额 1.28 亿美元，比 1997 年增长 18.52%。外商投资企业出口 9608 万美元，比上年增长 19.92%。

对外经贸洽谈会　1998 年 8 月在北京举办"连云港招商引资恳谈会"、20 多个国家的 158 名外宾到会，共签利用外资项目 25 个，总投资 21930 万美元，外经项目 6 个，合同额 3881 万美元，劳务输出 514 人，进出口贸易合同 5 份，成交额 623 万美元。

港口运输　1998 年连云港有生产泊位 26 个，港口吞吐能力 2125 万吨，当年实际完成货物吞吐总量 1775.8 万吨，比 1997 年的 1651.6 万吨增长 7.52%。其中完成外贸进出口货物总量 1006.8 万吨（出口 635.2 万吨，进口 371.5 万吨），下降 0.83%。标准集装箱 91616 个，下降 19%，（其中新亚欧大陆桥过境集装箱 1.21 万个）。

涉外旅游　1998 年入境的外国及台港澳游客 1.3 万人次，旅游外汇收入 450 万美元，比 1997 年的 386 万美元增长 16.58%。

1998年南通市对外经济贸易

南通市对外经济贸易委员会

【对外贸易】

进出口总额 1998年江苏省南通市进出口总额21.84亿美元（海关统计数，下同），比1997年的22.04亿美元下降0.9%。

出口总额 出口总额为13.31亿美元，比1997年有12.42亿美元增长7.2%，占全市国内生产总值620亿元（相当于74.8亿美元）的17.8%，占江苏省出口总额的8.5%，出口总额在江苏省各市中居第3位。

出口商品结构表

项目	出口额（万美元）	占出口总额比重（%）	
		1998年	1997年
初级产品	1.08	8.14	8.29
工业制成品	12.23	91.86	91.72

出口额在1000万美元以上商品情况表

商品名称	出口金额（万美元）	占出口总额（%）
纺织原料服装及纺织制品	70645	53.04
机器电器及零件	14155	10.63
车辆航空器船舶及运输设备	12867	9.67
杂项制品	7614	5.72
鞋帽伞等制品	5099	3.83
化学工业及相关工业产品	4652	3.49
贱金属及制品	3794	2.85
塑料、橡胶及其制品	3776	2.84
生皮皮革、毛皮及制品	2649	1.99
活动物、动物产品	2506	1.88
食品饮料酒及烟草及制品	1930	1.45
植物产品	1727	1.30
合计	**131414**	**98.71**

出口商品市场 出口商品销往119个国家和地区、比上年的106个新增13个。

出口的主要市场表

国别（地区）	出口金额（万美元）	占出口总额（%）
日本	60043	45.1
美国	16019	12.03
香港	8191	6.15
韩国	4491	3.37
英国	3989	3.00
德国	3439	2.58
新加坡	3076	2.31
马来西亚	1807	1.36
台湾省	1804	1.35
法国	1639	1.23
荷兰	1464	1.10
澳大利亚	1152	0.87
泰国	1018	0.76
加拿大	1005	0.75
合计	**109137**	**81.98**

进口总额 1998年南通市进口总额8.53亿美元，比1997年的9.62亿美元下降11.40%。

进口商品结构 初级产品为0.73亿美元，占进口总额的8.57%；工业制成品为7.8亿美元，占进口总额的91.43%。

主要进口商品表

商品名称	进口金额（万美元）	占进口总额（%）
机器电器及零件	29268	34.33
纺织原料服装及纺织制品	27388	32.13

主要进口商品表（续）

商品名称	进口金额（万美元）	占进口总额（%）
化学工业及相关工业产品	7835	9.19
贱金属及制品	4911	5.76
食品饮料酒及烟草及制品	3024	3.55
木及木制品编结材料制品	2707	3.17
塑料、橡胶及其制品	2654	3.11
木浆纸及制品	2322	2.72
矿产品	2159	2.53
合计	**82268**	**96.49**

进口商品市场 进口商品来自40个国家和地区，比上年的43个减少3个。

主要进口市场情况表

国别（地区）	进口金额（万美元）	占进口总额（%）
日本	34395	40.34
美国	18403	21.59
台湾省	9169	10.76
韩国	7701	9.03
印度尼西亚	1903	2.23
香港	1488	1.75
合计	**73059**	**85.70**

【利用外资】

1998年全市协议利用外资金额5.32亿美元，其中1998年以前批准的项目增资金额为2.97亿美元。

1998年利用外资情况表

利用外资方式	批准签订的合同			实际利用外资	
	项目数（个）	外资金额（万美元）	金额比1997年（±%）	金额（万美元）	金额比1997年（±%）
对外借款	3	1960		500	
外商直接投资	119	51222	-8.43	60577	-0.38
合资企业	79	39887	91.47	20180	19.27
合作企业	4	415	-95.55	3118	76.56
外资企业	36	10921	-57.65	14495	-65.59
外商投资股份制				22785	
合计	**122**	**53182**	**-5.01**	**61077**	**0.44**

外商直接投资行业 外商直接投资119个项目中，生产型项目102个，占85.71%，非生产型项目17个，占14.29%。按行业分：服装及其他纤维制造业17个，纺织业14个，化学原料及化学制品制业13个，塑料制品业和普通机械制造业各7个，食品加工业和文教体育用品制造业各5个，娱乐服务业和皮革、毛皮、羽绒制造业各4个，渔业、金属制造业、电子及通信设备制造业、食品制造业、农业、房地产开发与经营业、零售业、仓储业等其他行业43个。

外商直接投资来源 外商直接投资来自29个国家和地区。主要有香港26项，协议外资金额3110万美元；日本14项，金额16006万美元；美国19项，金额5774万美元；台湾省18项，金额621万美元；澳大利亚7项，金额286万美元；韩国5项，金额5519万美元；法国4项，金额132万美元；新加坡3项，金额1680万美元；瑞士2项，金额605万美元；加拿大2项，金额602万美元；英国 1 项，金额 9534 万美元；巴拿马 1 项，金额 2608 万美元；毛里求斯 1 项，金额 1230 万美元等等。

到 1998 年底，南通市累计批准并在册三资企业 2028 家，协议利用外资 31.21 亿美元，实际到资 22.44 亿美元，已有 1478 家外商投资企业开业投产。

外商直接投资企业生产经营情况 1998 年全市外商投资企业（据报送报表的 884 家企业统计）实现主营业务收入 164.92 亿元；出口创汇 12.61 亿美元，比上年增长 12.38%；实现利税 13.36 亿元，增长 3.9%，其中净利润 7.23 亿元，利税超千万元的企业有 17 家，其中净利润超千万元的有 12 家。

【对外经济合作】

承包工程和劳务合作 1998 年签订对外承包工程和劳务合作项目 267 个，合同金额 1.52 亿美元，与上年同口径相比增长 12.4%；完成营业额 1.32 亿美元，与上年同口径相比增长 24.5%；当年派出劳务 4680 人，主要派往新加坡、关岛、塞班岛、毛里求斯等 52 个国家和地区。主要行业涉及建筑业、纺织服装业、远洋捕捞业等。全年签订 500 万美元以上项目 6 个，合同额达 3440 万美元，占全市总数的 22.7%。全市 7 家有对外承包劳务签约权的公司新签合同额 9120 万美元，实现营业额 7693 万美元，分别占全市总数的 60.2%和 58.2%，南通第三建筑安装工程公司、南通第四建筑安装工程公司和南通国际经济技术合作公司在全省近 60 家有权公司中分别列第 2、3 和 14 位。

对外投资 1998 年举办海外非贸易性企业 1 家，中方总投资 9 万美元。

【其他】

经济技术开发区 1998 年南通经济技术开发区完成基础设施投资 4650 万元。区内新批三资企业 11 家（其中投资总额 1000 万美元以上项目 2 个），协议外资金额 1.77 亿美元，实际利用外资 1.6 亿美元。至 1998 年累计兴办三资企业 218 家，协议利用外资 15.45 亿美元，实际利用外资 9.98 亿美元。1998 年全区实现工业总产值 35.7 亿元，比 1997 年增长 13.8%。全区进出口总额 4.9 亿美元，其中出口 2.96 亿美元，比 1997 年增长 4.1%。全区共完成财政收入 1.92 亿元。

对外经贸洽谈会 1998 年 10 月 8 日－10 日，我市举办’98 南通经济技术合作洽谈会，参会国别和地区达 26 个，应邀到会的境外客商达 532 人。世界 500 强企业中有日本三菱、德国西门子等 15 家参会。洽谈会期间共签约利用外资项目 52 个，其中投资总额超千万美元的大项目有 17 个；协议利用外资 2.67 亿美元；签订外贸出口成交额 2778 万美元；签订对外承包工程和劳务合作项目 9 个，合同额 3015 万美元；达成内联合作项目 50 个，协议吸收市外资金 3.72 亿元。

港口运输 1998 年南通港完成旅客吞吐量 168 万人次，比上年下降 37.1%，货物吞吐量 2017 万吨，比上年增长 5.6%，其中外贸吞吐量 360 万吨，增长 4.7%，占全港吞吐量的 17.85%。当年完成集装箱吞吐量 13.03 万标准箱，比上年增长 7.2%，其中国际航线集装箱吞吐量为 3.88 万标准箱，占 29.78%。技术改造项目 7 个，主要有天生港区改造、狼山二期海轮通用泊位及长江港池泊位改造等，项目总投资 8936 万元，全年完成投资 1375 万元。

涉外旅游 1998 年共接待海外旅游者 7.23 万人，比上年的 8.95 万人下降 19.22%。

1998年浙江省对外经济贸易

浙江省对外贸易经济合作厅

【对外贸易】

进出口总额 1998年浙江省进出口总额1485383万美元，比1997年1424379万美元增长4.28%

出口总额 出口总额1086624万美元，比1997年的1008690万美元增长7.73%，占全省国内生产总值4980亿元（相当于601.53亿美元）的18.06%，占全国出口额的5.91%，居全国第四位。

出口商品结构 初级产品出口额124635万美元，占出口总额的11.47%；工业制成品的出口额961989万美元，占出口总额的88.53%。

出口额在5000万美元以上的商品情况表

金额分类	商品名称	出口金额（万美元）	占出口总额（%）
5000万－1亿美元（10种）	轴承、通断及保护电路装置、玩具、茶叶、钢铁或铜制标准紧固件、羽毛及羽绒、汽车零件、肠衣、扬声器、电线和电缆	73300	6.75
1亿美元以上（14种）	服装、纺织品、鞋类、水海产品、旅行用品及箱包、成品油、医药品、手用及机用工具、灯具、塑料制品、蔬菜、家俱、床垫及寝具、合成有机染料	627682	57.76
合　计	**24种**	**700982**	**64.51**

出口商品市场 出口商品销往193个国家和地区。

主要出口市场情况表

国别（地区）	出口金额（万美元）	占出口总额（%）
美　国	204036	18.78
日　本	184293	16.96
香　港	92575	8.52
德　国	54632	5.03
意大利	34389	3.16
荷　兰	33211	3.06
英　国	32422	2.98
韩　国	29606	2.72
法　国	25458	2.34

主要出口市场情况表（续）

国别（地区）	出口金额（万美元）	占出口总额（%）
俄罗斯	20836	1.92
合　计	**711458**	**65.47**

进口总额 进口总额398759万美元，比1997年的415689万美元下降4.07%。

进口商品结构 初级产品进口额103315万美元，占进口总额的25.91%；工业制成品的进口额295444万美元，占进口总额的74.09%。

进口额在 5000 万美元以上的商品情况表

金额分类	商品名称	进口金额（万美元）	占进口总额（%）
5000 万美元 1 亿美元 （11 种）	合成纤维长丝机织物、纸及纸板、合成纤维纱线、橡胶或塑料加工机械、棉机织物、初级形状苯乙烯聚合物、纺织用合成纤维、通断及保护电路装置、成品油、ABS 树脂、纱线织物等后整理机器	82196	20.61
1 亿美元 以上（6 种）	电视、收音机及无线电讯设备的零部件、纺织机械、初级形状的塑料、原油、钢材、纸浆	131422	32.96
合　计	**17 种**	**213618**	**53.57**

进口商品市场　进口商品来自 92 个国家和地区。

主要进口市场情况表

国别（地区）	进口金额（万美元）	占进口总额（%）
日　本	92655	23.24
韩　国	51851	13.00
美　国	49508	12.42
台湾省	31600	7.92
德　国	17757	4.45
意大利	17655	4.43
英　国	14455	3.62
加拿大	12465	3.13

主要进口市场情况表（续）

国别（地区）	进口金额（万美元）	占进口总额（%）
澳大利亚	11234	2.82
印　尼	10563	2.65
合　计	**309743**	**77.68%**

技术进出口　1998 年浙江省技术出口额 24500 万美元，比 1997 年的 30110 万美元下降 18.6%。其中，高科技产品出口 17713 万美元，大型设备、成套设备出口 6795 万美元。

【利用外资】

1998 年利用外资情况表

利用外资方式	批准签订的合同			实际利用外资	
	项目数（个）	外资金额（万美元）	金额比 1997 年（±%）	金额（万美元）	金额比 1997 年（±%）
对外借款	48	41999	-84.3	109448	-89.4
外商直接投资	965	183390	51.6	131802	-12.3
合资企业	581	72335	27.9	60149	-22.7
合作企业	42	48758	122.2	25212	52
外资企业	342	62297	46.5	46441	-16.9
外商其他投资		406	-99.5	406	-99.5

1998 年利用外资情况表（续）

利用外资方式	批准签订的合同			实际利用外资	
	项目数（个）	外资金额（万美元）	金额比 1997 年（±%）	金　额（万美元）	金额比 1997 年（±%）
补偿贸易		30	0	30	0
加工装配		376	-96.3	376	-95.4
合　计	**1013**	**225795**	**-51.9**	**241656**	**-16**

外商直接投资行业　在外商直接投资项目中，生产型项目 817 个，非生产型项目 148 个。按行业分，农林牧渔利业 21 个，制造业 795 个，采掘业 2 个，建筑业 11 个，电力、煤气及水的生产和供应 9 个，交通运输、仓储及邮电通讯业 16 个，批发和零售贸易、餐饮业 17 个，房地产业 21 个，社会服务业 36 个，卫生、体育和社会福利事业 1 个。

外商直接投资来源　外商直接投资来自 73 个国家和地区。合同外资居前几位的依次为：美国 146 个，40928 万美元；香港 306 个，合同外资 36692 万美元；台湾省 170 个，18233 万美元；维尔京群岛 22 个，17028 万美元；欧盟 93 个，15675 万美元。实际利用外资居前几位的依次为：香港 43691 万美元，欧盟 17602 万美元，韩国 13805 万美元，日本 11841 万美元，台湾省 10540 万美元。

外商投资企业生产经营情况　截止 1998 年底，已开业投产的外商投资企业 6795 家，全年销售收入 1144.9 亿元，比 1997 年增长 10.7%，其中出口销售收入 38.2 亿美元，比 1997 年下降 6.2%；盈利总额 38.5 亿元，比 1997 年增长 2%。自营出口 26.8 亿美元，比 1997 年下降 5.2%。

【对外经济技术合作】

承包工程和劳务合作　1998 年浙江省签订对外承包工程和劳务合作合同金额 25205 万美元，比 1997 年增长 52%；完成营业额 30027 万美元，比 1997 年增长 30%；当年派出劳务人员 11100 人次，年末在外人数 18833 人。派往主要国家和地区；新加坡、毛里求斯、美国塞班、日本、柬埔寨及对台渔工。承包工程项目主要有：新加坡大巴窑工程、裕廊西工程、IMPERLAL COURT 工程、乌吉班让工程、后港工程，香港赤柱监仓工程，尼泊尔“中华寺”项目，柬埔寨汽车检测中心工程，关岛 YPAO 商业中心项目，坦桑尼亚商住楼项目，乌干达国家体育场外围道路及旋转门项目等。

对外经济技术援助　承担援外项目 4 个，受援国家和地区尼泊尔、贝宁、中非、密克罗尼西亚，涉及的行业：农业和建筑业。项目建成情况：尼泊尔中华寺已正式完工，进入竣工验收阶段；贝宁马朗维尔垦区恢复项目，已完成 50% 工作量，约 400 万人民币；密克罗尼西亚学院多功能体育馆项目，进入图纸会审阶段；中非勃亚利甲机站恢复和技术合作项目，任务通知书已下达。

接受经济技术援助　杭州应用工程学院中德合作办学项目，接收援助金额 150 万人民币（实物），赴德及新加坡培训人员 12 名。

对外投资　举办海外投资项目 25 个，投资总额 2327 万美元，其中中方投资 1814 万美元。

【其他】

经济技术开发区　国家级开发区和省级经济开发区全年开发土地面积 22.54 平方公里，投入基础设施建设资金 51.36 亿元。全年进区项目 3002 个，其中新批外商投资企业 281 个，合同外资 10.21 亿美元，实际利用外资 7 亿美元。进出口总额 29.57 亿美元，其中出口 19.25 亿美元。

保税区　宁波保税区新批外商投资企业 48 家，合同外资 0.73 亿美元，实际利用外资 0.41 亿美元，完成进出口总额 8.02 亿美元，其中进口

4.99亿美元，出口3.03亿美元。

对外经贸洽谈会 1998年6月在捷克举办浙江出口商品展览会，成交1028万美元；9月在西班牙巴塞罗那举办浙江经贸洽谈会，出口成交1586.9万美元。

港口运输 全省五大港口泊位287个，其中万吨级泊位30个。港口吞吐能力1.48亿吨，当年完成的货物吞吐量1.4亿吨，外贸进出口货物吞吐量4024万吨，其中出口量383万吨，进口3641万吨。

1998年外贸出口货运量423万吨，其中海运集装箱量35万标准箱，比上年增长17%，陆运量6.6万吨，空运量0.8万吨。

涉外旅游 1998年接待的外国人数以及台港澳同胞人数82万人次，比上年增长1.1%。旅游收入3.6亿美元，比上年增长4.7%。

1998年宁波市对外经济贸易

宁波市对外经济贸易委员会

【对外贸易】

进出口总额 1998年浙江省宁波市进出口总额为42.12亿美元，比1997年的46.09亿美元下降8.6%。

出口总额 出口总额29.64亿美元，比1997年29.33亿美元增长1.04%。占全市国内生产总值980亿元的24.99%，占全省出口额的27.28%。

出口商品结构 初级产品出口额3.43亿美元，占出口总额的11.57%；工业制成品出口额26.21亿美元，占出口总额的88.43%。

出口额在1000万美元以上的商品情况表（按业务统计数）

金额分类	商品名称	出口金额（万美元）	占出口总额（%）
5000万美元以上（14种）	棉纱线、针织服装、梭织服装、文教用品、玩具、杂项百货、小五金、车用汽油、塑料制品、轴承基础件、计算机、电子元器件、灯、手工具	158009	45.76
1000万美元 5000万美元（46种）	水煮笋、速冻蔬菜、香菇、冻鱼、冻小虾仁、桔子罐头、茶叶、绵羊毛、毛纱线、化纤纱线、棉布、化纤布、涤纶缝纫线、毯子、绸缎、丝绸制品、皮服装、工艺美术品、蔺草制品、箱类、包袋类、鞋类、体育用品、锁类、眼镜类、钢材、稀土金属、航空煤油、轻柴油、各种染料、染料中间体、农药、橡胶制品、激素、医用敷料、各类船、汽车零件、电工设备、无线通讯设备、电池、望远镜、吸尘器、电筒、电视机及音响设备、电动工具、园艺工具	94685	27.42
合　计	**60种**	**252694**	**73.18**

出口商品市场 出口商品销往167个国家和地区，其中出口额在1000万美元以上的国家和地区有43个，金额28.07亿美元，占出口总额的94.71%。

主要出口市场情况表

国别（地区）	出口金额（万美元）	占出口总额（%）
日　本	50659	17.09
美　国	41070	13.86
香　港	31110	10.49
德　国	13947	4.71
韩　国	13182	4.44
荷　兰	10284	3.47

主要出口市场情况表（续）

国别（地区）	出口金额（万美元）	占出口总额（%）
新加坡	9263	3.13
英　国	8561	2.89
意大利	8273	2.79
澳大利亚	7251	2.45
合　计	**193600**	**65.32**

进口总额 进口总额12.49亿美元，比1997年的16.76亿美元减少25.49%。

进口商品结构 初级产品进口额为5.12亿美元，占进口总额的40.99%，工业制成品的进口额为7.37亿美元，占进口总额的59.01%。

进口额在1000万美元以上的商品情况表（按业务统计数）

金额分类	商品名称	进口金额（万美元）	占出口总额（%）
5000万美元以上（5种）	纸浆类、钢材、原油、塑料原料、化工原料	49954	45.57
10000万美元——5000万美元（19种）	饲料、木材、绵羊毛、长丝、短纤维、服装辅料、纸张、杂项百货、铁矿砂、液化气、铜、铜精矿砂、塑料制品、橡胶及制品、粮油加工机械、轻工成套设备、冶金成套设备、石油成套设备、电子元器件	35058	31.98
合　计	**24种**	**85012**	**77.55**

进口商品市场 进口商品来自72个国家和地区，其中进口额在1000万美元以上的国家和地区有21个，合计金额11.55亿美元，占进口总额的92.54%。

主要进口市场情况表

国别（地区）	进口金额（万美元）	占进口总额（%）
日　本	21925	17.56
韩　国	18944	15.17

主要进口市场情况表（续）

国别（地区）	进口金额（万美元）	占进口总额（%）
台湾省	11838	9.48
美　国	9831	7.87
印度尼西亚	7860	6.30
阿根廷	6164	4.94
澳大利亚	6126	4.91
也　门	3913	3.13
加拿大	3739	2.99

主要进口市场情况表（续）

国别（地区）	进口金额（万美元）	占进口总额（%）
德　　国	3406	2.73
合　计	**93746**	**75.08**

技术进口　1998年浙江省宁波市签订引进技术和进口设备合同项目款66个，合同金额3722万美元，引进项目的国家和地区有11个，其中从瑞典引进项目1个，金额810万美元，澳大利亚引进项目6个，金额779万美元，香港引进项目12个，金额590万美元，德国引进项目10个，金额546万美元，日本引进项目10个，金额306万美元，美国引进项目5个，金额200万美元，瑞士引进项目4个，金额156万美元，台湾引进项目4个，金额162万美元，丹麦引进项目1个，金额80万美元，韩国引进项目1个，金额61万美元，意大利引进项目2个，金额32万美元，涉及的行业分别为电子行业、纺织行业、机械行业、轻工行业和化工行业等。

【利用外资】

1998年利用外资情况表

利用外资方式	批准签订的合同			实际利用外资	
	项目款（个）	外资金额（万美元）	金额比1997年（±%）	金　额（万美元）	金额比1997年（±%）
外商直接投资	281	51198	11.8	50329	−9.2
合资企业	152	19999	−16.8	23132	−9.1
合作企业	14	14353	123.3	10345	72.3
外资企业	115	16846	9.5	16852	−29.6
合　计	**281**	**51198**	**11.8**	**50329**	**−9.2**

外商直接投资行业　在外商直接投资项目中，生产型项目208个，非生产型项目73个。按行业分，主要有机械及金属制品业，塑料制品业，电子及仪器制造业，纺织及服装制造业，食品制造业，建筑业等，外商直接投资来自42个国家和地区，投资居前5位的是，美国37项，合同外资15332万美元，香港106项，合同外资为12790万美元，英属维尔京岛6个，合同外资4733万美元，台湾46个，合同外资为3418万美元，凯曼群岛2个，合同外资3079万美元。

截止1998年底，已开业投产的外商投资企业共1613家，职工总数为19.54万人，全年销售营业收入为319.7亿元，其中自营出口为9.84亿美元，利用总额为9.6亿美元。

承包工程和劳务合作　1998年签订对外承包工程和劳务合作合同287份，金额1.09亿美元，完成营业额1.6亿万美元，比1997年的1.4亿美元增长14.29%；当年派出劳务4500人次，年末在外劳务人员数1.1万人，比上年增长19.6%，劳务人员分布在48个国家和地区，有毛里求斯、新加坡、日本、澳门、沙特、牙买加、西班牙、阿联酋、约旦、柬埔寨、贝宁等。

对外投资　1998年在海外设立贸易型企业3家，非贸易生产型企业7家，境外经贸办事处3家，项目总投资470.37万美元，其中中方投资322.24万美元，这些企业分布美国、匈牙利、日本、俄罗斯、萨摩亚、孟加拉、加纳、秘鲁、德国、澳大利亚等10个国家和地区。

【其他】

经济技术开发区　1998年批准外商投资企

业17家，投资总额18684万美元（含增资），同比增长52%；协议外资14077万美元，同比增长169.4%，合同利用外资17880万美元，实际利用外资15595万美元。全年新批的外商投资项目中以化工专用码头、化工产品加工、仓库、家电、纸品加工为主。投资的来源进一步扩大，现已扩大到31个国家和地区。外资实际到位率明显提高，全年全区34家企业外资到位，其中26家企业的实际外资到位率为100%。1998年全区完成国内生产总值51亿元，同比增长13.8%；实现工业总产值150亿元，同比增长25%；全年外贸出口3.78亿美元，同比增长20%。

保税区 宁波保税区全年新批外商投资企业48家，总投资9390万美元，协议利用外资7291万美元，实际利用外资4148万美元，同比增幅分别为81.8%、29.7%、62.5%、45.5%。保税区优越的财税政策，国际贸易功能和精简高效的办事作风进一步增强了外贸企业投资的吸引力，全年注册国际贸易企业329家，全年完成进出口贸易总额8.02亿美元，其中出口3.03亿美元，进口4.99亿美元，同比分别增长22.5%、18.8%和24.95%。全年新审批仓储项目3个，累计达18个。全年完成进仓货物总值19.2亿元，出仓货物总值20.8亿元。全年固定资产投资额2.5亿元，同比增长103.3%，其中，新增道路面积16780平方米，绿地29021平方米，区容、区貌得到重大改观，区内基础设施配套日臻完善。全区全年实现国内生产总值16.08亿元，工业总产值6.27亿元，利税总额5.76亿元。

对外经贸洽谈会 1998年宁波市外经贸委和市贸促会组织市外经贸企业到德国、日本、美国、南非、香港、澳大利亚、智利、尼日利亚等16个国家和地区参加了38个展销会，由于加大了对国际市场的开拓力度从而有力地促进了我市对外经贸的发展。

港口运输 1998年宁波港货物吞吐量达8701万吨，列全国第二位，比上年增长6%，完成外贸进出口货物吞吐量3504万吨（其中进口3181万吨，出口323万吨），占宁波港吞吐量的40%。全年集装箱吞吐量达35.2万标箱，比上年增长37.1%，列全国第八位。98年9月9日宁波港成功地靠泊32万吨巴哈马籍超大型油轮“莫斯金”号，是迄今为止靠泊我国港口最大吨位的营运船舶。1998年新开通国际集装箱新加坡干线。目前，宁波港每月集装箱班轮已达108班。

涉外旅游 全年接待入境的外国人以及港澳台同胞10万人次，旅游收入4400万美元，比上年增长29.3%。

1998年温州市对外经济贸易

温州市对外贸易经济合作局

【对外贸易】

进出口总额 1998年浙江省温州市进出口总额87941万美元，比1997年的63476万美元增长38.5%。

出口总额 出口总额68329万美元，比1997年的53054万美元增长28.8%，占全市国内生产总值677亿元（相当于82亿美元）的8.3%，占全省出口额的5.7%。

出口商品结构 初级产品出口额4824万美元，占出口总额的7.1%；工业制成品的出口额63505万美元，占出口总额的92.9%。

出口额在1000万美元以上商品情况表

金额分类	商品名称	出口金额（万美元）	占出口总额（%）
2000万美元以上	生牛皮、布胶鞋、皮鞋、打火机、眼镜、电工用具	25943	38
10000－2000万美元	合成革鞋、运动鞋、梭织服装、公文包、建筑小五金、油漆染料、扑热息痛、家用小电器、日用皮制品、塑料制品	13512	19.8
合　计	**16种**	**39455**	**57.8**

出口商品市场　出口商品销往135个国家（地区）。主要出口市场的出口金额52614万美元，占出口总额的77%。

主要出口市场情况表

国别（地区）	出口金额（万美元）	占出口总额（%）
香　港	11598	17
美　国	6003	8.8
日　本	3911	5.7
匈牙利	3323	4.9
法　国	3048	4.5
波　兰	2883	4.2
意大利	2824	4.1
俄罗斯	2268	3.3
西班牙	2220	3.2
德　国	1759	2.6
台　湾	1675	2.5
土耳其	1547	2.3

主要出口市场情况表（续）

国别（地区）	出口金额（万美元）	占出口总额（%）
荷　兰	1528	2.2
巴　西	1526	2.2
阿联酋	1503	2.2
罗马尼亚	1478	2.2
捷　克	1422	2.1
韩　国	1075	1.6
埃　及	1022	1.5
合　计	**52614**	**77**

进口总额　进口总额19612万美元，比1997年的10422万美元增长88.2%。

进口商品结构　初级产品进口额12294万美元，占进口总额的62.6%；工业制成品的进口额7318万美元，占进口总额的37.4%。

主要进口商品的进口金额15127万美元，占进口总额的77.1%。

进口额在500万美元以上商品情况表

金额分类	商 品 名 称	出口金额（万美元）	占出口总额（%）
500万美元以上	液化气、化工原料、塑料原料、牛革皮、钢材、邮电设备、轻工成套设备	15127	77.1

进口商品市场　进口商品来自39个国家（地区）。主要进口市场的进口金额15549万美元，占进口总额的79.3%。

主要进口市场情况表

国别（地区）	进口金额（万美元）	占进口总额（%）
韩　国	7799	39.8

主要进口市场情况表（续）

国别（地区）	进口金额（万美元）	占进口总额（%）
美　国	3061	15.6
香　港	2400	12.2
日　本	1202	6.1
台湾省	1087	5.5
合　计	**15549**	**79.3**

【利用外资】

1998年利用外资情况表

利用外资方式	批准签订的合同			实际利用外资	
	项目数（个）	外资金额（万美元）	金额比1997年（±%）	金　额（万美元）	金额比1997年（±%）
外商直接投资	95	24439	222	3702	-39
合资修企业	60	5560	90	2478	-15
合作企业	3	16045	385	117	-94
外资企业	32	2834	212	837	-6
加工装配	290				

外商直接投资行业　在外商直接投资的95个项目中，生产型项目87个，占91.6%；非生产型项目8个，占8.4%，按行业分，制造业84个，电力业3个，房地产业3个，交通运输仓储业2个，社会服务业2个，娱乐业1个。

外商直接投资来源　外商直接投资来自23个国家和地区。投资额居前6位的是：美国23个：18679万美元，台湾省18个，1559万美元，香港15个，599万美元，法国9个，769万美元，意大利8个，192万美元，荷兰7个，1740万美元。

外商投资企业生产经营情况　截止1998年底，累计批准外商投资企业1321家，项目总投资27.46亿美元，合同外资金额13.73亿美元，实际利用外资4.1亿美元。其中已开业投产的外商投资企业共606家，销售收入64.1亿元，比1997年增长12%；企业盈利3.25亿元，比1997年增长61%；上缴税金3.5亿元，比1997年增长8.4%；直接出口企业220家，比1997年增加12%，自营出口22848万美元，比1997年增长25%。

【对外经济合作】

承包工程和劳务合作　1998年签订对外承包工程和劳务合作项目182个，金额303.7万美元，比1997年的232万美元增长31%；营业额257.6万美元，比1997年的442万美元下降

41.7%；当年派出劳务人员1645人次，年末在外555人。劳务人员主要分布在日本、老挝、坦桑尼亚、罗马尼亚、台湾省（渔轮）等国家和地区；承包工程项目主要有老挝小水电工程。

【对外投资】

1998年温州市在海外举办企业（机构）4家，中方投资额129.63万美元，分别设在巴西、泰国、南非和印尼。

【其他】

温州经济技术开发区 1998年共引进项目78个，固定资产总投资12.33亿元，其中外资项目9个，投资额4413万美元。到1998年底，开发区累计引进项目565个，固定资产总投资59亿元，其中外资项目130个，投资2.75亿美元，合同外资1.42亿美元。开发区东片1.8平方公里，已建成厂房140万平方米，开工投产企业170家。1998年实现国内生产总值12.53亿元，比1997年增长29%；工业总产值29亿元，比1997年增长25%；外贸进出口总额1.61亿美元，比1997年增长63%；财政收入1.62亿元，比1997年增长30%。正在建设的开发区西片2.43平方公里已完成“六通一平”基础设施，已全面铺开厂房建设。省级温州高新技术产业园区位于温州经济技术开发区及其南面扩展区内，规划面积4.33平方公里，由浙江省科委于1998年12月18日批准创建。高新园区同开发区实行两块牌子，一套班子，进行统一开发、统一规划、统一管理。自1999年开始，园区将进入启动开发阶段。

港口运输 温州港口泊位124个，其中万吨级4个，5000－10000吨级4个，5000吨级以下116个，浮筒泊位2个，为万吨级。全年实际完成货物吞吐量621万吨，其中外贸进出口货物吞吐量63万吨，进口39万吨，出口24万吨。国际集装箱吞吐量34351标准箱，其中进口17458标准箱，出口16898标准箱。

涉外旅游 1998年接待外国旅游者、华侨、港澳台同胞4.8万人次，比1997年的4.3万人次增长10.4%；旅游外汇收入2700万美元，比1997年2100万美元增长24.2%。

1998年安徽省对外经济贸易

安徽省对外经济贸易委员会

【对外贸易】

进出口总额 1998年安徽省进出口总额31.20亿美元（外贸业务统计，下同），比1997年的31.16亿美元增长0.1%。

出口总额 出口总额20.15亿美元，比1997年的20.05亿美元增长0.5%，占全省国内生产总值2830亿元（相当于342亿美元）的5.9%，占全国出口额1838亿美元的1.09%。

出口商品结构 初级产品出口额3.36亿美元，占出口总额的16.7%；工业制成品出口额16.79亿美元，占出口总额的83.3%。

出口商品品种共1750种，其中出口额在1000万美元以上的商品40种，出口额12.51亿美元，占全省出口总额的62.1%。

出口商品市场 出口商品销往170个国家（地区）。主要出口市场是欧盟38104万美元，占18.9%；北美34313万美元，占17.0%；日本30999万美元，占15.4%；港澳25503万美元，占12.7%；东盟11629万美元，占5.8%；韩国11250万美元，占5.6%。

出口额在1000万美元以上商品情况表

金额分类	商品名称	出口金额（亿美元）	占出口总额（%）
1000万－5000万美元（35种）	煤、皮服装、生铁、大米、棉布、柠檬酸、化纤布、钢材、蔬菜、其他服装、船舶、羽毛、布绒玩具、电冰箱、羽绒被、千斤顶、天然植物编织品、塑料编织袋、其他医药原料、维生素E、茶叶、灯、手工扎针地毯、铜材、芝麻、机床、运动鞋、各种鞋类、自行车零件、合成革械、自行车、雷达导航设备、小五金、布胶鞋、绸缎	7.43	36.88
5000万－1亿美元（4种）	铜、棉制品、针织服装、轮胎	3.20	15.90
1亿美元以上（1种）	梭织服装	1.87	9.28
合　计	**40种**	**12.51**	**62.1**

进口总额　进口总额11.05亿美元，比1997年的11.11亿美元下降0.5%。

进口商品结构　初级产品进口额0.88亿美元，占进口总额的7.9%；工业制成品进口额10.17亿美元，占进口总额的92.1%。

主要进口商品

进口额在1000万美元以上商品情况表

金额分类	商品名称	进口金额（亿美元）	占进口总额（%）
1000万－5000万美元（9种）	合成纤维、化纤布、塑料原料、化肥农药、纸浆纸张及制品、铜、化工原料、汽车、电车摩托车及零件、电讯设备和器材；	2.69	24.35
5000万－1亿美元（2种）	钢材、邮电通信设备	1.51	13.66
1亿美元以上（3种）	成套设备、铜精矿砂、各类机械	5.72	51.77
合　计	**14种**	**9.92**	**89.78**

进口商品市场　主要进口市场是日本17736万美元，占16.1%；欧盟29695万美元，占26.9%；港澳10567万美元，占9.6%；北美12287万美元，占11.1%；韩国7783万美元，占7.0%。

技术进出口　1998年安徽省技术进出口总

额4.22亿美元，比1997年的4.08亿美元增长3.4%。其中签订引进技术和进口设备合同194项，比1997年增加11项；合同金额3.63亿美元，比1997年的3.61亿美元增长0.7%。签订技术出口合同58项，比1997年增加21项；合同金额0.59亿美元，比1997年的0.47亿美元增长25.0%。主要技术出口项目有船舶、洗衣机生产线、计算机软件、计算机辅助设计（CAD）、硫酸软骨素等生化制品。

【利用外资】

1998年外商投资到位资金情况表

利用外资方式	实际利用外资额（万美元）	比1997年（±%）
合资企业	13917	
合作企业	2973	·
外资企业	10783	
外商其他投资	4557	
合　计	**32230**	**－25.8**

当年新批外商投资企业208家，利用外资合同额2.69亿美元，比1997年的3.85亿美元下降30.1%。其中，新批合资企业109家、0.94亿美元，合作企业17家、0.26亿美元，外资企业80家、1.23亿美元，外商投资股份制企业2家、0.26亿美元。

外商直接投资行业　1998年新批外商直接投资协议项目中，第一、二产业的协议项目159项、协议外商直接投资额22481万美元，第三产业的协议项目49项、协议外商直接投资额4490万美元。

外商直接投资主要行业投向表

行　　业	协议项目数（个）	协议外商投资额（万美元）
粮油食品	28	4343
轻　　工	17	3287

外商直接投资主要行业投向表（续）

行　　业	协议项目数（个）	协议外商投资额（万美元）
机　械	26	3272
房地产	13	2638
化工	11	2572
冶金	16	2457
纺织	28	2183

外商直接投资来源

外商直接投资主要来源国别（地区）表

国别（地区）	协议项目数（个）	协议外商投资额（万美元）
香港	69	8215
台湾省	51	4014
美国	35	2661
新加坡	8	2564
维尔京群岛	4	1298
日本	11	1269
德国	1	1209
英国	1	1010

外商投资企业出口　1998年安徽外商投资企业完成出口额3.83亿美元，比1997年的3.11亿美元增长23.3%；在全省出口总额中的比重由1997年的15.5%上升到19.0%。

【对外经济合作】

承包工程和劳务合作　1998年签订对外承包工程和劳务合作合同额6864万美元，比1997年的7185万美元下降4.4%；完成营业额4926万美元，比1997年的7004万美元下降29.7%；当年派出劳务人员2314人次，年末在外3175人。承包工程和劳务合作的主要市场是新加坡、以色列、日本、斯里兰卡。

【其他】

经济技术开发区　合肥高新技术产业开发

区：到1998年底，进区企业累计511家，协议投资额67.25亿元人民币。其中外商投资企业累计133家，协议利用外资额2.68亿美元，实际利用外资额2.20亿美元。

在国家火炬计划实施十周年之际，合肥高新技术开发区获得国家科技部颁发的“火炬先进管理奖”，区内设立的孵化高新技术企业的创业服务中心被批准为“国家级创业服务中心”。开发区内，中美合资年产120万台无氟电冰箱的生产线已投产，年产40万台空调的企业产销两旺；中国消防产品专业生产基地、年产100万台离子水生成器的合资企业以及一批电子、电器、电机、汽车、化工、药业项目正在建设中。

到1998年底开发区累计建设了130万平方米的标准厂房和配套设施。绿化面积达23.2万平方米，被授予“安微省花园式单位”称号。

开发区实行一区多园建设。区内的德国柏林工业园迎来了德国ALRE－IT公司与中方合资设立的控制技术公司。在区内的中国科大工业园，由中国科大等单位多项科研成果作价入股，与中资、外资合作设立了一批高新技术企业。区内的高科技农业园、留学生园、私营企业园都在积极建设中。

芜湖经济技术开发区：到1998年底，累计批准外商投资项目153项，协议利用外资5.24亿美元。个人电脑、汽车仪表、空调、新型建材等一批较大项目形成批量生产。开发区当年技工贸总收入比上年增长3.3倍。进区企业进出口总额达4015万美元。区内正在筹建国家级标准的高新科技创业服务中心。

对外经贸洽谈会　1998年安徽举办的对外经贸洽谈活动主要有两次：5月16日至25日，安徽经贸代表团参加在法国举办的波尔多国际博览会。会上出口商品成交980万美元；签订招商项目三个，投资总额5100万美元；与15家旅行社开展业务洽谈，并达成组织10个旅游团来安徽旅游的协议；向有关媒体和旅行社赠送了安徽旅游风光录像带和宣传画册2000份。9月20日至10月9日，在美国和加拿大分别举行安徽纽约经济贸易洽谈会，出口商品成交3326亿美元；签订招商项目6个，协议外资6902万美元。

港口运输　全省港口1998年共完成外贸货运量（包括直接外运和转关运输）125万吨，比1997年的135万吨下降7.4%。合肥、黄山两空港运送出入境旅客2.15万人次，比1997年的2.6万人次下降17.3%。自日本至黄山空港的临时直航包机开通。

涉外旅游　接待来省的外国人及港澳台同胞18.4万人次，旅游收入7036.1万美元，比1997年的8206万美元下降14.2%。

1998年福建省对外经济贸易

福建省对外经济贸易委员会

【对外贸易】

进出口总额　1998年依海关统计（下同）福建省进出口总额171.60亿美元，比1997年的181.89亿美元下降5.65%。

出口总额　出口总额99.59亿美元，比1997年的102.65亿美元下降2.98%，占全省国内生产总值（相当于402.22亿美元）的24.76%，占全国出口总额的5.42%，居全国第6位。

出口商品结构　初级产品出口额13.05亿美元，占出口总额的13.10%；工业制成品出口86.54亿美元，占出口总额的86.90%。

主要出口商品　出口额上亿美元的主要商品有17种，包括鱼、甲壳及软体类动物及其制品，蔬菜及水果，有机化学品，软木及木制品，纺纱、织物制成品及有关产品，非金属矿物制品，金属制品，通用工业机械设备及零件，办公用机械及自动数据处理设备，电信及声音的录制及重放装置设备，电力机械、器具及其电气零件，其他运输设备，家具及其零件，旅行用品、手提包及类似品，服装及衣着附件，鞋靴，摄影器材、光学物品及钟表等，合计金额74.81亿美元，占出口总额的75.12%；出口在5000万～1亿美元的主要商品有咖啡、茶、可可、调味料及制品，矿物燃料、润滑油及有关原料，石油产品及有关原料，陆路车辆，无机化学品，医药品，初级形状的塑料，橡胶制品，纸及纸板，有色金属，动力机械及设备，专业、科学控制用仪器和装置等12种，合计金额9.04亿美元，占出口总额的9.07%。

出口商品市场 出口商品销往160个国家和地区。主要出口市场：美国22.02亿美元、日本19.27亿美元、中国香港19.06亿美元、德国5.22亿美元、荷兰2.06亿美元、英国2.03亿美元、新加坡1.95亿美元、意大利1.56亿美元、西班牙1.50亿美元、法国1.30亿美元、菲律宾1.25亿美元、加拿大1.25亿美元、韩国1.02亿美元、澳大利亚1.01亿美元，合计80.51亿美元，占出口总额的80.84%。

进口总额 进口总额72.01亿美元，比1997年的79.24亿美元下降9.12%。

进口商品结构 初级产品进口9.77亿美元，占进口总额的13.57%；工业制成品进口62.24亿美元，占进口总额的86.43%。进口额在1亿美元以上的特大商品有电机、电气、音像设备及其零件，锅炉、机械器具及零件，塑料及其制品，化学纤维长丝，有机化学品，钢铁，化学纤维短丝，生皮及皮革，矿物燃料、矿物油及其产品，航空器，航天器及其零件，纸及纸板，橡胶及其制品，特种机织物，铜及其制品等，合计金额57.17亿美元，占进口总额的79.39%。其中电机、电气、音像设备及其零件，锅炉、机械器具及零件，塑料及其制品，化学纤维长丝等4类商品进口额在3亿美元以上，合计金额37.52亿美元，占进口总额的52.10%。

进口商品市场 进口商品来自92个国家和地区。主要进口市场：中国台湾省21.37亿美元、日本11.98亿美元、韩国9.03亿美元、美国6.29亿美元、德国3.25亿美元、中国香港2.47亿美元、新加坡1.74亿美元、马来西亚1.69亿美元、英国1.45亿美元、印度尼西亚1.39亿美元、泰国1.25亿美元、意大利1.08亿美元、俄罗斯8997万美元、澳大利亚7254万美元、法国5897万美元、芬兰5818万美元等，合计金额65.75亿美元，占进口总额的91.31%。

技术进出口 1998年技术进出口总额1.68亿美元，比1997年的1.19亿美元增长41.18%。其中，签订引进技术进口设备合同29项，合同金额5545万美元，比1997年的3532.32万美元增长56.97%；签订技术出口合同25项，金额1.13亿美元，比1997年的8358.20万美元增长35.20%。

【利用外资】

外商直接投资 新批外商直接投资项目2006个，合同外资金额50.02亿美元，比1997年增长10.23%，实际利用外资金额40.12亿美元，与1997年基本持平。按企业类型分，合资企业420个，合同外资金额10.57亿美元，外商实际利用资8.84亿美元；合作企业45个，合同外资金额3.70亿美元，外商实际利用资5.06亿美元；外商独资企业1541个，合同外资金额35.79亿美元，外商实际利用资26.22亿美元。

外商直接投资行业 在外商直接投资项目中，生产型项目1631个，非生产型375个。按行业分，农林牧渔业168项，采掘业25项，制造业1438项，电力、煤气及水的生产19项，建筑业12项，交通运输、仓储21项，批发和零售贸易98项，房地产业92项，社会服务业115项，卫生、体育和社会福利业1项，科学研究和综合技术服务业1项，其他行业16项。

外商直接投资来源 投资者来自港、澳、台、东南亚和欧美日等56个国家和地区。其中中国香港1110项、合同外资金额24.13亿美元，中国台湾省472项、6.42亿美元，美国73项、3.16亿美元，日本69项、5217万美元，英国18项、7.75亿美元，维尔京群岛16项、2.30亿美元，菲律宾69项、6949万美元，中国澳门42项，5613万美元，新加坡30项、6625万美元，澳大利亚23项、5222万美元，马来西亚14项、3499万美元，阿根廷10项、2125万美元，新西兰7项、609万美元等。

外商直接投资企业生产经营情况 1998年新开业投产的外商投资企业1308家。到1998年底止，全省累计已开业投产的外商投资企业14409家，1998年实现工业产值1220.20亿元，比1997年的1034.90亿元增长17.9%，占全省乡及乡以上工业产值的59.78%；出口54.49亿美元，比1997年的52.99亿美元增长2.84%，占全省出口总额的54.71%。

【对外经济合作】

承包工程和劳务合作 1998年签订对外承包工程和劳务合作合同2858项，合同金额4.39亿美元，比1997年的4.27亿美元增长2.81%。完成营业额5.19亿美元，比1997年的4.83亿美元增长7.45%。1998年派出劳务人数3.19万人次，年末在外劳务人数5.46万人。劳务人员分布在新加坡、中国澳门、中国香港、以色列、柬埔寨、博茨瓦纳、马里、乌拉圭等83个国家和地区。主要对外承包工程项目有马来西亚莫里比吹沙项目、马来西亚岭顶地产、澳大利亚圣捷利湖地产开发、中国香港上水污水处理工程等。

对外经济技术援助 承担派往博茨瓦纳一支医疗队，派出人员32人。

接受经济援助 接受来自联合国儿童基金、世界银行、澳大利亚、英国、比利时等双边和多边援助项目8个，受援金额43.65万美元。主要受援项目有乡村公路建设、妇幼保健、社区与家庭健康促进及儿童营养改进等。

对外投资 1998年新批准在澳大利亚、德国、南非、美国、新加坡、中国香港等地举办海外企业7家，中方投资481万美元。其中生产加工型企业2家，进出口贸易企业2家，工程承包、旅游服务、船务企业各1家，大都是可取得较好经济效益的项目。

【其他】

经济技术开发区 福建省经国务院批准的经济技术开发区有福州经济技术开发区、福清融侨经济技术开发区和福建东山经济技术开发区等。其中东山经济技术开发区继续加强基础设施建设，新建区间道路1.2公里，目前已实现五通一平，水、电、通讯等设施基本配套。开发区重点开发食品、通用器材、水产品和工业城等项目。1998年新批外商投资项目33项，合同外资金额7236万美元，外商实际到资5163.8万美元。1998年开发区出口贸易总额5624万美元，其中外商投资企业出口5399万美元。

对外经贸洽谈会 由福建投资贸易洽谈会更名而来的中国投资贸易洽谈会（简称“9.8”洽谈会），1998年为第二届，9月8日在厦门市举行。本届洽谈会由国家对外经贸部主办、福建省人民政府和厦门市人民政府共同承办、福建省等42个成员单位组成。洽谈会共接待来自港、澳、台、东南亚、欧美、日本、韩国、澳大利亚、新西兰等50多个国家和地区的境外客商6370多人。会上共签订外商投资合同项目1606项，利用外资55.19亿美元；外贸进出口成交10.53亿美元，其中出口成交8.64亿美元，进口成交1.89亿美元。福建省在会上共签订外商投资合同项目960项，利用外资29.55亿美元；进出口成交4.98亿美元，其中出口成交3.89亿美元，进口成交1.09亿美元。

港口运输 沿海主要港口货物吞吐量4517.69万吨，比1997年的4485万吨增长0.73%。

1998年进出口货运总量1743.4万吨，比1997年的1950万吨下降10.59%。其中出口货运量780.57万吨，进口货运量962.9万吨。按运输方式分：海运量1741万吨，陆运量1.76万吨，空运量0.6万吨。

涉外旅游 全年接待观光、探亲访友以及洽谈投资贸易的各类海外人士121.78万人次，比1997年的117.39万人次增长3.74%。其中外国人32.68万人次，比1997年的32.27万人次增长1.27%；港澳同胞48.83万人次，比1997年的50.14万人次下降2.61%；台湾同胞35.36万人次，比1997年的31.10万人次增长13.69%。

1998 年厦门市对外经济贸易

厦门市贸易发展委员会

【对外贸易】

进出口总额 1998 年厦门市进出口总额为 76.14 亿美元。

出口总额 出口总额 42.96 亿美元。

出口商品结构 初级产品出口额 4.5 亿美元，占出口总额 10.6%；工业制成品的出口额 38.4 亿美元，占出口总额的 89.4%。

主要出口市场情况表

国别（地区）	出口金额（万美元）	占出口总额（%）
中国香港	89780	21.93
美国	84570	19.72
日本	79516	18.54
德国	24669	4.75
中国台湾省	14954	3.48
新加坡	10981	2.56
英国	9794	2.28
荷兰	9118	2.13
菲律宾	7270	1.69
韩国	6425	1.50

主要出口市场情况表（续）

国别（地区）	出口金额（万美元）	占出口总额（%）
合　计	**337077**	**78.59**

进口总额 进口总额 33.18 亿美元。

主要进口市场情况表

国别（地区）	进口金额（万美元）	占进口总额（%）
中国台湾省	77601	23.39
日本	52567	15.84
韩国	50603	15.25
美国	33403	10.07
中国香港	17315	5.22
新加坡	12338	3.72
德国	10408	3.14
印度尼西亚	8049	2.42
泰国	7531	2.27
马来西亚	6756	2.10
合　计	**276771**	**83.43**

出口额在 1000 万美元以上商品情况表

金额分类	商品名称	出口金额（万美元）	占出口总额（%）
3000 万美元以上（19 种）	花岗岩碑石或建筑用石及其制品、飞机及直升机的其他零件、电热烤面包器、制作或保藏的（河）鳗鱼，整条或切块的、塑料或塑料制外底及鞋面的其他运动鞋靴、合成纤维帐篷等	116507	27.13

出口额在1000万美元以上商品情况表（续）

金额分类	商 品 名 称	出口金额（万美元）	占出口总额（%）
2000～3000万美元（20种）	瓷制塑像及其他装饰品、草地网球拍、芦笋罐头、其他橡胶或塑料外底，纺织材料鞋面的鞋靴、其他扬声器、机动多用途船等。	48972	11.39
1000～2000万美元（56种）	烟草制的卷烟、未列出名陶制品、彩色电视机，屏幕尺寸>52CM、新的充气橡胶轮胎、其他材料针织或钩编套头衫、开襟衫、马甲等	78557	18.31
合 计	**95种**	**244036**	**56.82**

进口额在1000万美元以上商品情况表

金额分类	商 品 名 称	进口金额（万美元）	占进口总额（%）
3000万美元以上（15种）	飞机及直升机的其他零件、初级形状的聚氯乙烯、轻柴油、聚酯弹力丝、聚酯短纤、对苯二甲酸等	82307	24.82
2000～3000万美元（13种）	8535、8536或8537所列装置、其他初级形状的聚对苯二甲酸乙二酯、8427所列机械的零件、苯乙烯共聚物、铜制绕组电线，提炼豆油所得的其他固体残渣等	30471	9.17
1000～2000万美元（32种）	走带机构（机芯）、其他初级形状的聚苯乙烯、含亚麻85%以下漂白的布、涂无机物的书写、印刷纸、平米重≤150g非合金铝矩形板、片，未列名的塑料制品等	44117	13.28
合 计	**60种**	**156895**	**47.29**

【利用外资】

1998年全市共批准外商投资项目245个，协议外资16.88亿美元，其中独资项目、合资项目、合作项目占协议外资总额的比重分别为75.57%、19.64%和4.8%。第一、二、三、产业的协议外资的比重分别为1.38%、77.15%、21.47%。实际利用资13.91亿美元；1998年新开工投产企业539家。

外商投资行业 外商投资项目中，按行业分：农业8个，工业178个，房地产项目59个。

外商投资来源情况 截至1998年底，在厦门投资的国家和地区30个；1998年欧美投资大幅度上升。来自欧美国家的项目35个，协议外资9.75亿美元，占全市协议外资总额的57.77%，比

1997年同期增加了63.61%。

【对外经济合作】

承包工程和劳务合作 1998年承包工程和劳务合作完成合同额2673万美元，营业额8026万美元，派出人数3297人，年末在外人数8500人，间接利用外资获国家有关部门批准项目3个，金额达1011万美元。

1998年福州市对外经济贸易

福州市对外经济贸易委员会

【对外贸易】

进出口总额 1998年福建省福州市进出口总值348847万美元，比1997年309435万美元，增长12.74%（按业务统计口径）。

出口总额 出口总值232308万美元（按业务统计口径），比1997年202658万美元增长14.63%，占福州市的国内生产总值的22.49%，占全省出口总值19.72%。其中外贸专业公司和工贸出口26822万美元，比1997年同期增长10.04%；外商投资企业出口205486万美元，增长15.26%。

按海关口径，全市出口总值194600万美元，占福州市国内生产总值18.67%，占全省出口总值20.35%；其中外贸工贸出口23300万美元，外商投资企业171300万美元。

出口商品结构 初级产品出口额（按业务口径，以下同）17496万美元，占出口总额的7.53%；工业制成品的出口额214812万美元，占出口总额的92.47%。

出口商品有60多类1000多种，其中主要出口商品有箱包鞋帽45652万美元，光电产品36721万美元，粮油水产23067万美元，文化用品20840万美元，家用电器20028万美元，纺织服装17880万美元，工艺陶瓷17237万美元，化工产品9489万美元，五金矿产8007万美元，钟表4050万美元，医药商品2330万美元，电讯设备1160万美元，机械产品803万美元，共计207264万美元，占出口总额89.22%。

出口商品市场 出口商品销往103个国家和地区。

主要出口市场情况表

国别（地区）	出口金额（万美元）	占出口总额（%）
中国香港	90627	39.01
美　国	47852	20.6
日　本	46931	20.20
中国台湾省	14142	6.09
德　国	11343	4.88
新加坡	1792	0.77
合　计	**212687**	**91.55**

进口总额 116539万美元，比1997年106777万美元增长9.14%。其中外贸企业进口17557万美元，外商投资企业进口98982万美元，分别占进口总额15.07%、84.93%。主要进口商品有化工原料、光电设备、家电设备、轻工业品、纺织丝绸、电讯设备、五金矿产、土畜产品、粮油水产等。进口商品主要来自是中国香港、日本、中国台湾省、美国、马来西亚、德国、澳大利亚、意大利、荷兰、芬兰、印度、印度尼西亚、俄罗斯联邦、韩国、德国、法国、英国、以色列、南非、越南等国家和地区。

【技术进出口】

签订引进技术和进口设备合同6项,合同金额492万美元。引进技术主要来自美国、德国、意大利等国家。引进项目主要分布在机械设备、电机等行业。

【利用外资】

1998年批准签订外商投资企业合同481项,比1997年同期437项递增10.07%。合同外资111031万美元,比1997年92022万美元递增20.7%。其中,合资企业109项,合同外资金额32927万美元;合作企业13项,合同外资金额19577万美元;外资企业359项,合同外资金额58827万美元。外商投资企业全年实际利用外资90384万美元,比1997年97848万美元递减7.6%。

外商直接投资行业 外商直接投资的481项中,制造业291项,农牧业23项,采掘业6项,建筑业6项,交通运输4项,批发零售78项,房地产31项,社会服务42项。其中生产型、出口创汇型项目占83.78%。

外商直接投资来源 投资者主要来自中国香港、中国澳门、中国台湾省、日本、菲律宾、缅甸、泰国、马来西亚、新加坡、印尼、韩国、苏丹、匈牙利、罗马尼亚、英国、冰岛、奥地利、巴拿马、多米尼加、阿根廷、维尔京群岛、加拿大、美国、百慕大、澳大利亚、新西兰、西萨摩亚等27个国家和地区。其中中国香港266项,金额66655万美元;中国澳门16项,金额1442万美元;中国台湾省75项,金额6835万美元;日本35项,金额1454万美元;维尔京群岛12项,金额21086万美元;美国25项,金额4519万美元;菲律宾9项,金额1018万美元;泰国3项,金额1005万美元;西萨摩亚2项,金额1291万美元;澳大利亚9项,金额1652万美元。

生产经营情况 1998年有228家外商投资企业开业投产,至1998年底累计已开业投产2863家,工业产值366.50亿元,占全市工业总产值的33.99%;出口创汇205486万美元,比1997年178284万美元增长15.26%,占福州市出口总额的88.45%。

【对外经济合作】

签订对外承包合同和劳务合作合同684项,合同金额5466万美元,比1997年增长1.2%;完成营业额6284万美元,比1997年增长8.1%;全年外派劳务人员6659人次;年末在外劳务8381人,主要派往新加坡、中国台湾省(渔工)、中国澳门、中国香港、也门、日本、马来西亚、孟加拉、印尼、越南、马尔代夫、柬埔寨、菲律宾、以色列、毛里求斯、南非、塞浦路斯、莱索托、喀麦隆、毛里塔尼亚、赤道几内亚、加纳、贝宁、多哥、几内亚、乌干达、利比利亚、塞舌尔、博茨瓦纳、摩尔多瓦、马绍尔、匈牙利、保加利亚、英国、土耳其、俄罗斯、阿塞拜疆、丹麦、圣马丁岛、捷克、苏里南、希腊、罗马尼亚、美国、加拿大、牙买加、墨西哥、阿根廷、玻利维亚、澳大利亚、新西兰、斐济、巴布亚新几内亚等53个国家和地区,从事建筑、渔工、海员、服装、机械、综合工业、电子、缝纫、餐饮等业务。

在境外兴办非贸易企业累计17家。

【其他】

经济技术开发区 1998年福州经济技术开发区充分发挥国家级开发区、保税区、台商投资区和高科技园区区位的优势。面对亚洲金融危机和国际金融市场持续动荡,趋利避害,及时调整政策,加大软硬环境建设力度,合理有效利用外资,提高对外商投资企业管理水平,保证了开发区外向型经济稳步加速增长。1998年新批外商投资项目103项,总投资41320万美元,合同外资30017万美元,分别完成年计划的135%、165%和200%。实际利用外资1.9亿美元,四项外经贸指标均居福州市五区八县(市)之首。1998年全区实现国内生产总值66.5亿元。

福州保税区在面临国家对保税区政策调整情况下,依靠自身努力,做好三方面工作。一是加大招商力度,突出抓项目、抓"台球"、抓港澳促增资;二是以功能开发为导向,加快保税区各项功能开发;三是抓软环境建设,强化为企业服务质量,促进保税区经济进一步发展。1998年共审批项目91项,完成年计划130%;项目总投资7220万美元,完成年计划103%；进出口货物总值11321万美元，社会生产总值27196万元。

地处福清市的国家级融侨开发区、元洪投资区，同样深受亚洲金融危机的冲击。他们“求新应变”，在招商方面采取多元化招商战略，积极拓展日欧美，突出“四个强化，抓好一个加强”，即强化以商引商，强化网上招商，强化社会招商，强化二次招商。加强软硬环境建设。促进开发区外向型经济健康发展。

融侨开发区龙头企业不断壮大，行业支柱已经形成，仅11家电子行业完成产值42亿元人民币；产业链逐步完善，形成了以冠捷电子为中心的十多家企业为骨干的电子产业群体。1998年工业产值达101亿元人民币，与1997年同期增长17.4%，完成税收1.2亿元；1998年新批外商投资项目20家，总投资3500万美元，增资18家5000万美元；实现出口7.9亿美元，比1997年增长11%。

元洪投资区已初步形成化工、钢铁、食品等为龙头的工业区，成为闽江口经济圈迅速崛起的一支重要工业生产基地。1998年累计新批项目26个，合同外资4.74亿美元，实际利用资2.04亿美元，出口4022万美元，实现工业产值7.5亿人民币。

海峡两岸（福州）农业合作试验区成立近两年来，发展势头良好，农业投资规模和领域进一步扩大；农业技术交流和合作进一步发展，榕台农产品贸易进一步活跃。榕台农业合作项目由单一农产品生产，向加工销售等领域延伸，从单项向产业整体配套发展。现有福州市台资农产品加工业100多家，福州市农业出口供货可达180亿人民币。

对外经贸洽谈会 1998年5月，在福州举办的中国福州国际招商月、9月福州代表团参加在厦门举办的’98中国投资贸易洽谈会，福州接待了来自中国香港、中国澳门、中国台湾省、美国、加拿大、德国、英国、法国、意大利、瑞士、西班牙、葡萄牙、阿根延、玻利维亚、泰国、马来西亚、菲律宾、印度、澳大利亚、新加坡、日本、韩国、以色列等近40个国家和地区的4000多名客商、一百多个财团和代表。两场招商会国别多，层次高，规模大，人数多。洽谈会和招商月的国际性尤为突显，项目层次明显提高，项目结构明显优化。新项目开发有新的突破，生产性项目和基础项目、农业综合开发项目、市场建设项目有新的突破和新的发展，投资区域和投资者有新的拓展。招商月、洽谈会期间共签订外商投资项目合同474项，总投资21.15亿美元，协议外资17.36亿美元。

港口运输 福州港目前共有大小生产性泊位129个，其中万吨级以上深水泊位13个，最大吨级泊位3万吨，港口吞吐量1758万吨，1998年实际进出口货物总运量1287万吨，其中外贸进出口吞吐量431万吨，出口265万吨，进口166万吨。

涉外旅游 抓住香港回归、两岸直航试点、长乐国际机场通航的良好机遇，积极拓展福州旅游事业。旅游项目招商取得显著成效，在福州国际招商月期间举办永泰旅游招商专场、’98第二届中国投资贸易洽谈会福州旅游招商专场、农业观光生态旅游招商专场上，共签约外商投资项目54个，总投资6.86亿美元。1998年共接待国内游客约467万人次，营业收入15.5亿元人民币；接待境外游客22.41万人次，其中外国游客70795人次，港澳同胞49342人次，台湾同胞90681人次。创汇1.1亿美元。

1998年江西省对外经济贸易

江西省对外贸易经济合作厅

【对外贸易】

进出口总额 1998年江西省进出口总额187982万美元，比1997年的185602万美元增长1.28%。

出口总额 出口总额165109万美元，比1997年的163080万美元增长1.24%，占全省的国内生产总值1850亿元（相当于223.46亿美元）的7.39%，占全国出口额的0.9%。

出口商品结构 出口商品58个大类259个小类1201个品种。初级产品28202万美元，占出口总额的17.08%；工业制成品136907万美元，占出口总额的82.92%。出口额在100万美元以上商品141种，金额为141746万美元，占出口总额的85.85%。

出口额在1000万美元以上商品表

金额分类	商品名称	出口金额（万美元）	占出口总额（%）
1000万～5000万美元（23种）	棉制品、抗菌素药、珠宝首饰、羽绒服装、化纤布、铁合金、医药原料、仲钨酸铵、日用瓷、稀土金属、茶叶、工艺美术品、活大猪、皮劳保手套、铜、麻布、羽绒制品、电子元器件、汽车零件、松香、丝绸制品、塑料制品、化纤制品	44955	27.22
5000万美元以上（5种）	针织服装、梭织服装、棉布、大米、鞭炮烟花	60224	36.48
合　计	**28种**	**105179**	**63.70**

出口商品市场 出口商品销往150个国家和地区，比1997年增加12个。出口额在100万美元以上市场68个，金额为162120万美元，占出口总额的98.18%，其中出口额在1000万美元以上的重点市场18个，金额为141537万美元，占出口总额的85.72%。

主要出口市场情况表

金额单位：万美元

国别（地区）	出口金额	占出口总额（%）	出口额比1997年（±）%
中国香港	71035	43.02	-16.48
美国	15835	9.59	25.33
日本	14486	8.77	18.16
德国	6645	4.02	7.75
韩国	5523	3.35	-20.56
印度尼西亚	4414	2.67	164.79
菲律宾	3672	2.22	717.82
英国	2878	1.74	4.50
荷兰	2817	1.71	-2.63
阿联酋	2053	1.24	-19.21
合　计（10个）	**129358**	**78.33**	**879.47**

进口总额 进口总额22873万美元，比1997年的22522万美元增长1.56%。

进口商品结构 进口商品197种，比1997年增加63种。初级产品进口额为3111万美元，占进口总额的13.60%；工业制成品进口额为19762万美元，占进口总额的86.40%。进口额在100万美元以上商品计35种，计13874万美元，占进口总额的60.66%，其中进口500万美元以上的8种主要商品是铜合金、豆粕、化工原料、纸浆、黑色金属矿产品、矿山机械、钢材和化纤布，计7339万美元，占进口总额的32.09%。

进口商品市场 进口商品来自29个国家和地区，进口额在100万美元以上市场19个国家和地区，金额为22366万美元，占进口总额的97.78%，其中中国香港4915万美元，占进口总额的21.49%、日本4251万美元，占18.59%、英国3920万美元，占17.14%、美国2528万美元，占11.05%。

技术进出口 1998年技术进出口总额13966万美元，比1997年的12736万美元，增长9.65%。其中签订技术引进和进口设备合同33项，比1997年增加18项，合同金额3223万美元，比1997年的7460万美元下降56.80%。签订技术出口合同635项，比1997年增加301项，合同金额10743万美元，比1997年的5276万美元增长103.62%。实际履行合同604项、金额9592万美元，比1997年增长113%。

【利用外资】

1998年利用外资情况表

利用外资方式	批准签订的合同			实际利用外资	
	项目数（个）	外资金额（万美元）	金额比1997年（±%）	金额（万美元）	金额比1997年（±%）
对外借款	5	20295	286.42	13142	3.41
外国政府贷款	1	1515	278.75	5715	163.61
国际金融组织贷款	3	17660	638.29	6007	0.18
外国银行商业贷款	1	1120	-54.47	1420	-68.62
外商直接投资	334	41919	-34.95	46493	-2.67
合资企业	129	15380	-36.36	21791	-6.25
合作企业	28	4969	-56.04	5679	114.54
独资企业	177	21570	-5.98	19023	19.89
外商其他投资	3	230	-99.00	11230	130.55
补偿贸易	2	124		124	72.22
加工装配	1	106	-96.05	106	-86.73
对外发行股票				11000	175.00
合　计	**342**	**62444**	**-32.62**	**70865**	**8.44**

外商直接投资行业 在外商直接投资行业中，生产型项目240个、非生产型项目102个。按行业分：签约合同中制造业192个，22027万美元，占35.28%；建筑业10个，1737万美元，占27.81%；房地产业39个，7687万美元，占12.31%；社会服务业49个，5441万美元，占8.71%；农林牧业26个，2760万美元，占4.42%；采掘业、电力煤气业、地质勘查业、交通

运输业、批发零售业、卫生体育、教育文化、科学研究等行业26个，7164万美元，占11.47%。在1998年实际进资中，制造业345个，36196万美元，占51.08%；建筑业23个，13157万美元，占18.57%；房地产业84个，8014万美元，占11.31%；社会服务业64个，3892万美元，占5.49%；农林牧业39个，1890万美元，占2.67%；交通运输业7个，1354万美元，占1.91%；卫生体育3个，1290万美元，占1.28%；采掘业、电力煤气业、地质勘查业、批发零售业、教育文化等行业45个，5073万美元，占7.16%。

外商直接投资来源 外商签约直接投资来自23个国家和地区，投资额居前七位是：中国香港24511万美元，占39.25%；美国5339万美元，占8.55%，中国台湾省5268万美元，占8.44%；加拿大2876万美元，占4.61%；荷兰1130万美元，占1.81%；日本1030万美元，占1.65%；中国澳门784万美元，占1.26%。

外商直接投资企业生产经营情况 1998年全省有130家外商投资企业投产开业。截至1998年底，全省累计批准外商投资企业4700家，其中投产开业的1429家。外商投资企业生产出口商品164种。销往46个国家和地区，出口创汇37293万美元，比1997年的32583万美元增长14.46%，占全省出口总额的比重由1997年的19.98%上升到1998年的22.59%，提高2.5个百分点。1998年实现销售（营业）收入66.43亿元，缴纳税金2.96亿元，利润0.8亿元，从业人员64136人，其中外籍员工431人。

【对外经济合作】

承包工程和劳务合作 1998年新签对外承包工程和劳务合作合同103项，比1997年增加5项，合同金额7725万美元，比1997年7555万美元增长2.25%，完成营业额7615万美元，比1997年7270万美元增长4.75%，1998年派出劳务人员2033人，年末在外人数4097人，比1997年增加397人。承包工程主要项目有：吉尔吉斯坦的中国商品城、马里的体育场、马来西亚的住宅和多哥的培训工程项目。

对外经济技术援助 承担对外援助项目3个，受援国家及其项目是：埃塞俄比亚的低造价住房项目、斐济的乡村供电项目和赤道几内亚的毕可莫水电站第9期技术维修项目。年末在外工程技术人员61人。

接受经济援助 接受国际组织援助项目5个，金额679.2万美元，比1997年增长69.8%。接受援助的项目是：德国援助江西灾后重建项目500万马克、日本援助修水乡村公路项目1000万日元、德国援助余干县金山嘴乡小学项目2.5万马克、联合国儿基会灾后紧急救援项目5万美元和德国援助南昌大学食品中试车间项目600万马克。

【其他】

商新技术产业开发区 南昌国家级高新技术产业开发区1998年经济快速发展。1998年技工贸总收入完成38亿元，比1997年增长46.15%，比建区初增长133倍；实现工业销售收入25亿元，增长37.36%；创利税3.2亿元，增长45.45%。签订利用外资合同金额2236万美元，实际利用外资2528万美元，增长13.82%；签订利用内资合同4.95亿元，实际利用内资3.83亿元，增长204.94%。1998年出口创汇1078万美元，增长34.75%。

对外经贸洽谈会 1998年5月5日至6日，江西省，98江西招商引资（深圳）新闻发布会取得丰硕成果。五百三十余位客商到会，共签订合同项目125项，合同外资额4.32亿美元，项目平均外资额343万美元，外资比例达86.2%。此外分别参加华交会、广交会、厦交会、巴西圣保罗中国商品展览会、圣彼得堡国际消费品展览会、意大利米兰马契夫秋季博览会、沙特中国商品展览会以及出国推销共成交出口商品4.53亿美元，占1998年出口成交额的36.92%。

港口运输 1998年长江九江港有12个泊位，港口年吞能力1250万吨。1998年因长江洪水曾一度封航，实际完成货物吞吐总量348万吨，其中完成外贸进出口货物吞吐量为5.4万吨，其中出口量4.09万吨，进口量1.31万吨。1998年江西省外贸运输货运总量83.00万吨，比1997年增长5.2%，其中出口量56.30万吨、进口量26.70万吨，按运输方式分：海运量68.80万吨、空运量306吨、陆运量14.20万吨。

涉外旅游 1998年江西省接待旅游、参观、访问及从事各项交流活动的外国人、海外侨胞和台港澳同胞11.4923万人次，比1997年的13.3443万人次减少1.852万人次，下降13.88%；旅游外汇收入4284万美元，比1997年的4456.54万美元减少172.54美元，下降3.87%。

1998年山东省对外经济贸易

山东省对外经济贸易委员会

【对外贸易】

进出口总额 1998年山东省进出口总额为166.29亿美元，比1997年的175.54亿美元下降5.3%。

出口总额 出口总额103.6亿美元，比1997年的108.8亿美元下降4.8%，占全省的国内生产总值7162亿元人民币(相当于864亿美元)的12.0%，占全国出口总额的5.6%，居全国第五位。

出口商品结构 初级产品出口额23.3亿美元，占出口总额的22.5%；工业制成品出口额80.3亿美元，占出口总额的77.5%。出口额在5000万美元以上的商品有：冻鸡、水海产品、冻鱼、蔬菜、鲜干水果及坚果、花生及花生仁、食用油籽、煤、轮胎、棉纱线、棉机织物、地毯、水泥、玻璃制品、家用陶瓷器皿、生铁及镜铁、钢材、锁、电视及无线电讯零附件、集装箱、汽车零件、家具、旅行用品及箱包、服装、鞋类、塑料制品、玩具、棉坯布等。出口额在3000万～5000万美元的商品有：黏土及其它耐火矿物、合成短纤85%及以上的纱线、人造短纤机织物、棉浴巾、钢坯及粗锻件、钢铁管配件等。出口额在1000万～3000万美元的商品有：原油、鲜冻兔肉、冻虾仁、辣椒、啤酒、肠衣、药材、烤烟、生丝、天然石墨、焦炭、合成有机染料、抗菌素、医用敷料、家用及装饰用木制品、丝绸、塑料编织带、珍珠及宝石、半宝石、铜材、钢铁及铜制标准紧固件、纺织机械、金属加工机床、轴承、电动机及发电机、原电池、静止式变流器、扬声器、收录机、电容器、电线和电缆、船舶、手表、医疗器械、带编织品、人造花、锯材、坯绸等。

出口商品市场 1998年出口商品销往185个国家和地区。

主要出口市场表

国别（地区）	出口金额(万美元)	占出口总额(%)
日本	299525	28.9
美国	203187	19.6
韩国	124103	12.0
中国香港	61130	5.9
德国	43567	4.2
荷兰	22880	2.2
俄罗斯	17885	1.7
英国	17264	1.7
意大利	14359	1.4
中国台湾省	14205	1.4
合　计	**818105**	**79.0**

进口总额 进口总额62.7亿美元，比1997年的66.8亿美元下降6.1%。

进口商品结构 进口额在5000万美元以上的商品有：机械、成套设备、电器及电子产品、塑料、牛皮革、纺织用合成纤维、钢材、针织或钩编织物、铁矿砂、计量监测分析仪器、合成纤维、长丝机织物、合成纤维纱线、纸及纸板、原棉、纸浆、天然橡胶、塑料制品、谷物及谷粉、棉机织物、食用植物油。进口额在3000万～5000万美元的商品有：肥料、农药、纺织用人造纤维、医疗器械、钻石等。进口额在1000万～3000万美元的商品有：裘皮及制品、睛纶长丝、棉纱布、服装、文体用品、电工设备、箱包鞋帽等。

进口商品市场 进口商品来自73个国家和地区。

主要进口市场表

国别（地区）	进口金额（万美元）	占进口总额（%）
韩国	226573	36.1
日本	105703	16.9
美国	57938	9.2
法国	27279	4.4
俄罗斯	20544	3.3
中国台湾省	20293	3.2
中国香港	18425	2.9
澳大利亚	14975	2.4
意大利	14900	2.4
西班牙	10708	1.7
合　计	**517338**	**82.5**

技术进出口 1998年山东省签订技术出口合同272项，合同金额32123.72万美元，技术出口项目主要分布在机械、电子、化工、材料、交通运输、能源、医药、轻纺等行业。出口过1000万美元的商品有：发电机组、工程机械、船舶、石英谐振器、合成蒽醌。

【利用外资】

1998年利用外资情况表

利用外资方式	批准签订的合同			实际利用外资	
	项目数（个）	外资金额（万美元）	金额比1997年（±%）	金　额（万美元）	金额比1997年（±%）
外商直接投资	1366	221866	-32	222262	-13
合资企业	650	78022	-10	115436	-11
合作企业	85	41345	-74	30295	52
独资企业	630	101499	70	74563	-25
合作开发	1	1000	-66	1968	162
外商其他投资		74956	15	57525	5
补偿贸易		6473	-27	4395	2
加工贸易		2470	-88	479	-97
对外发行股票		31363	18	30399	14
国际租赁		34650	252	22252	126
合　计	**1366**	**296822**	**-24**	**279787**	**-8**

外商直接投资行业 在外商直接投资项目中，第一产业项目54个，第二产业项目1098个，第三产业项目214个。按行业划分：农林牧渔水利业54个；采掘业6个；制造业1074个；建筑业13个；交通运输邮电业4个；商业餐饮业98个；房地产业35个；社会服务业48个；其他行业29个。

外商直接投资来源 外商直接投资来源的国家和地区主要有中国香港258个，合同金额5.8亿美元；韩国342个，合同金额2.9亿美元；美国188个，合同金额2.8亿美元；维尔京群岛17个，合同金额2.3亿美元；中国台湾省164个，合同金额1.6亿美元；日本124个，合同金额1.0亿元。

外商直接投资企业生产经营情况 截至1998年底，全省累计开业投产外商投资企业10245家，1998年实现销售收入1370.6亿美元，出口创汇52.3亿美元，比1997年增长1.5%，占全省出口总额的50.4%。

【对外经济合作】

承包工程和劳务合作 签订对外承包工程和劳务合作项目1296项，合同额7.4亿美元，比1997年的5.7亿美元增长34.0%，完成营业额4.7亿美元，比1997年的3.6亿美元增长27.8%。1998年外派劳务人员18898人次，年末在外人数29121人，分别比上年增长2.7%和9.4%。项目主要分布在韩国、日本、新加坡、中国香港、以色列等国家和地区，涉及建筑、水产、电子、渔业、服装、宾馆服务、石油工程等行业。

接受经济援助 接受国际援助项目1个，金额40万马克。

对外投资 全省海外企业建设紧紧围绕"管理"和"发展"两条主线开展工作，取得积极成果。1998年新批海外企业(机构)41家，总投资额980.4万美元。其中贸易型企业13家，投资额307万美元；非贸易型企业12家，投资额567万美元；代表机构16家。截止1998年底，全省海外企业(机构)总数已达621家，累计境外投资总额2.3亿美元，分布在世界的66个国家和地区，投资合作领域已从单一的贸易型发展到加工装配型和实业开发型。

【其他】

经济技术开发区 1998年全省各类经济开发区新批利用外资项目407项，比1997年增长3%；合同外资额9.3亿美元，下降2%；实际使用外资9.2亿美元，增长2%；出口17.5亿美元，增长4%。上述四项指标分别占全省总数的29.8%、31.3%、33.0%和13.3%，增长率分别高出全省17；22；10和4个百分点。全省经济开发区完成工业总产值561.4亿元，上交利税49.0亿元，实现销售收入254.9亿元，分别比1997年增长18.7%、38.1%和21.3%，实现财政收入11.4亿元。

港口运输 山东省对外开放口岸29个，港口年吞吐能力1.5亿吨，1998年完成货物吞吐量1.15亿吨，其中完成外贸货物运输4950.5万吨，进口货物运量2641.1万吨，出口货物货运量2309.4万吨。

涉外旅游 1998年共接待境外旅游者60.82万人次，比1997年的58.5万人次增长4.0%。旅游外汇收入2.19亿美元，比1997年增长7.7%。

1998年青岛市对外经济贸易

青岛市对外经济贸易委员会

【对外贸易】

进出口总额 1998年山东省青岛市进出口总额59亿美元，比1997年的52.2亿美元增长13.5%。

出口总额 出口总额38.27亿美元，比1997年的33.85亿美元增长13%，约占全市国内生产总值880亿元（相当于106.4亿美元）的36%；占全省出口总额103.6亿美元的36.9%。

出口商品结构 初级产品出口额6.7亿美元，占出口总额的17.5%；工业制成品出口额31.56亿美元，占出口总额的82.5%。

出口额在 2000 万美元以上商品情况表

金额分类	商品名称	出口金额（万美元）	占出口总额比重（%）
2000～3000 万美元（12 种）	轮胎 棉坯布 健身用品 塑料编织布 钠化合物 涤棉针织外衣 化纤服装 女内衣 全皮包 帐篷 电视机及音响设备 变压器	34264	8.9
3000～5000 万美元（11 种）	肉食 速冻蔬菜 工农具 冻鱼 冻贝 肉罐头 纯涤纶布 棉毛衫裤 布胶鞋 钢材 空调器	43567	11.4
5000 万美元以上（11 种）	冻鱼片 生牛皮 化纤布 棉针织服装 皮服装 发制品 运动鞋 布绒玩具 集装箱 计算机散件 电冰箱	133543	34.9

出口商品市场 出口商品销往 147 个国家和地区。主要出口市场情况如表：

出口商品前 8 大市场情况表

国别（地区）	出口金额（万美元）	占全市出口比重（%）
韩国	113527	29.65
日本	98688	25.77
美国	79756	20.83
中国香港	19061	4.98
德国	9542	2.49
法国	5687	1.49
新加坡	3767	0.98
沙特	3745	0.98

进口总额 进口总额 20.68 亿美元，比 1997 年的 18.35 亿美元增长 12.7%。

进口商品结构 其中工业制成品 181987 万美元，占进口总额的 85.37%。

进口额在 2000 万美元以上商品情况表

金额分类	商品名称	进口金额（万美元）	占进口总额比重（%）
3000 万美元以上（15 种）	冻鱼、革皮及制品、电子元器件、长丝、计算机、化纤布、电子原材料、塑料制品	141753	68.5

进口额在 2000 万美元以上商品情况表（续）

金额分类	商品名称	进口金额（万美元）	占进口总额比重（%）
	管材、船舶、家用小电器、纸浆纸张及制品、短纤维、服装辅料、杂项百货		

进口市场情况 青岛市进口商品来自 37 个国家和地区。主要进口市场情况如表：

进口商品前 8 大市场

国别（地区）	进口金额（万美元）	占进口总额比重（%）
韩国	129127	62.4
日本	36344	17.6
美国	21564	10.4
中国香港	8847	4.3
中国台湾省	3431	1.7
俄罗斯	1617	0.8
比利时	1485	0.7
德国	1361	0.7

【利用外资】

1998 年青岛市共批准利用外资项目 563 个，按可比口径（以下均同）比 1997 年下降 10.1%；合同外资 10.4 亿美元，比 1997 年增长 20.8%，实际利用外资8.48亿美元，比1997年下降6.5%。

1998年来青岛直接投资的国家和地区达到67个，按合同外资额，排在前六位的依次是：中国香港2.3亿美元；韩国2亿美元；美国1.3亿美元；日本0.7亿美元；中国台湾省0.6亿美元；百慕大地区0.6亿美元。

截至1998年底，青岛市累计投产开工的外商投资企业2919家，出口26.5亿美元，比1997年增长19.5%；缴纳税金15.1亿元，比1997年增长52.5%；实现销售收入414.1亿元，比1997年增长13.2%，累计吸纳社会劳动力35万人。

1998年利用外资情况表（新统计口径）

利用外资方式	批准签订的合同			实际利用外资	
	项目数（个）	外资金额（亿美元）	金额比1997年（±%）	金额（亿美元）	金额比1997年（±%）
对外借款	10	0.5	14	1.0	225
外商直接投资	553	9.84	37	7.3	-12.88
合资企业	163	2.43	18	2.6	5.45
合作企业	39	1.52	66	0.3	-3.25
外资企业	351	5.91	40	4.5	-21.3
合　计	**563**	**10.4**	**20.8**	**8.4**	**6.5**

外商直接投资分行业表（新统计口径）

行　　业	项目数（个）	合同外资（万美元）
农、林、牧、渔业	21	1417
其中：农业	8	605
制造业	386	67705
其中：纺织业	11	510
化学原料及制品	32	4334
医药制造业	3	1635
普通机械制造业	14	2077
专用设备制造业	10	1205
电子及通信设备制造业	15	10067
建筑业	5	1345
交通运输、仓储及邮电通信业	2	851
批发和零售贸易、餐饮业	77	4285
房地产业	15	9001
其中：房地产开发与经营业	14	8997
社会服务业	18	4352
教育、文化及广播电影电视	1	25
其它行业	28	9467
合　计	**553**	**98448**

【对外经济技术合作】

1998年签订对外承包工程和劳务合作合同378份，合同金额0.6亿美元，比1997年增长了10.1%；营业额0.5亿美元，比1997年增长15.2%；1998年派出劳务4394人次，比1997年下降1.4%；期末在外人数7151人，比1997年增长25.2%。劳务派往的国家和地区有54个，主要是：韩国、新加坡、日本、巴拿马、尼日利亚、利比利亚、西班牙等。

【其他】

经济技术开发区　①基础设施建设：截至1998年底，全社会基础设施投资累计119亿元人民币，其中区属基础设施投资15.1亿元人民币，建成了一批大型能源、交通设施和其它配套设施。主要有前湾港，一期工程已投产6个泊位，年吞吐能力2200万吨，二期工程年吞吐能力510万吨，已建成目前国内唯一能停靠第五代集装箱专用泊位；黄岛油港有两个码头，年输油能力3000万吨，可停泊20～30万吨级油轮；胶黄铁路、环胶州湾高速公路、轮渡、黄岛发电厂等均已建成并投入使用；区内道路、供水、供热、排水、通信等基础设施日益完善。1998年固定资产完成投资额307650万元，项目投资完成额136222万元，区属基础设施投资额23525万元。②招商引资：截至1998年底，全区累计批准外资项目1048个，合同总投资25.8亿美元，合同利用外资19.3亿美元，实际利用外资9.6亿美元，投资的国家和地区已达47个，千万美元以上大项目69个，世界500强大公司中有11家落户开发区。其中1998年共批准外商投资项目108个，合同利用外资2.8亿美元，实际利用外资2.1亿美元，新批1000万美元以上的项目14个。1998年全区三资企业实现工业总产值49.5亿元，出口创汇3.14亿美元，涉外税收8000余万元，从业人员占现有职工总数的40%。

保税区 青岛保税区于1992年经国务院批准设立。总体规划面积2.5平方公里，1993年3月正式封关作业。该区一期内已经完成“七通一平”，供水、供电、供气和通讯等问题得到全面解决。二期内路基回填、夯实工程及“三水”管网工程已完成，目前已具备外租条件。保税仓储方面，仓储面积达8万平方米，设施一流的大型仓储企业菱光物流正式投入使用。1998年共批准外商投资项目84个，总投资7260万美元，合同外资6767万美元。目前从事出口加工贸易企业达71家。

港口运输 青岛港现共有生产用泊位49个，其中万吨级以上的30个。港口实际综合能力为8432万吨。1998年当年实际完成货物吞吐总量为7044万吨。

涉外旅游 1998年青岛市接待海外游客14.4万人次，台港澳同胞5.6万人次，涉外旅游收入10230万美元，比1997年增长4.3%。

98中国青岛对外经济贸易洽谈会

98中国青岛对外经贸洽谈会于1998年7月8日至12日举行。青岛代表团外贸成交9500万美元，其中外贸企业成交8436万美元，占88.8%；三资企业出口成交1064万美元，占11.2%。青岛市进口成交394万美元。利用外资共签订合同、协议183项，对外经济技术合作共签订合同2份，合同金额420万美元，合同派出劳务350人。

青岛市代表团经贸洽谈和成交签约的主要特点有：一是进出口企业成交活跃，精品、家电产品成交比重大增。青岛市参展的36家进出口企业累计成交6990万美元，占青岛市成交总数的73.6%。海尔冰箱、空调，澳柯玛冰柜、等精品成交占青岛市总成交的49.2%。家电产品成交额占青岛市总成交的43.4%。二是新客户、新市场成交增加，技术成交取得突破。在全部出口成交额中，新客户成交占22.1%，新产品成交占36.6%。三是项目质量水平有所提高，大项目和老企业嫁接项目较多。本届洽谈会上，总投资过千万美元的大项目29个，外资金额达到48148万美元。四是重点开放区域吸引外资突出，高科园、开发区仍为投资热点，一批基础设施、工业生产性大项目分别在这些重点开放区域落户。五是轻纺、机电行业投资较为集中，外商独资项目比重较大。六是亚洲国家和地区的投资有所下降，欧洲国家和地区的投资所占比重上升。

亚太经济合作组织（APEC）服务贸易研讨会

亚太经济合作组织（APEC）服务贸易研讨会于1998年5月4日至8日在青岛举行。来自澳大利亚、文莱、智利、中国、中国香港、印度尼西亚、日本、韩国、马来西亚、菲律宾、新加坡、中国台北、泰国、美国、巴布亚新几内亚等15个亚太经合组织（APEC）成员经济体及世界贸易组织（WTO）的39位专家及学员参加了本次研讨会。中华人民共和国对外经济贸易合作部副部长龙永图到会并致开幕辞。研讨会就《服务贸易总协定》（GATS）内容、WTO与APEC的服务贸易政策、金融服务自由化、发达经济体和发展中经济体执行GATS的情况及将来可能采取的自由化措施、服务自由化带来的问题及风险预警等问题进行了研讨。

1998年烟台市对外经济贸易

烟台市对外经济贸易委员会

【对外贸易】

进出口总额 据海关统计，烟台市1998年进出口总额22.3亿美元，与1997年的21.6亿美元相比增长3.2%。

出口总额 出口总额为12.84亿美元，比1997年的13.79亿美元下降6.9%，占烟台市国内生产总值的14.4%，占全省出口总额的11.9%。

出口商品结构 出口商品有十七大类六百多个品种，其中初级产品出口额4.1亿美元，占出口总额的31.9%；工业制成品出口额8.7亿美元，占出口总额的69.1%。

出口额在1000万美元以上的商品情况表

金额分类	商品分类	出口金额（万美元）	占出口总额（%）
1亿美元以上（3种）	服装、水产品、机电产品	44693	34.8
5000～1亿美元（2种）	蔬菜、纺织品	16700	13
1000～5000万美元（15种）	水泥、锁头、水果、玩具、化工产品、家电、家俱、汽车零件、鞋类等	31828	24.8
合计	20种	93221	72.6

出口商品市场 出口商品销往117个国家和地区，比1997年增长12个。

主要出口市场情况表

国别（地区）	出口金额（万美元）	占出口总额（%）
日本	45981	35.8
美国	23719	18.5
韩国	17704	13.8
中国香港	5331	4.2
德国	3379	2.6
中国台湾省	2052	1.6
新加坡	1883	1.5
澳大利亚	1943	1.5
菲律宾	1306	1.0
马来西亚	1330	1.0

进口总额 1998年进口总额为9.4亿美元，比1997年的7.8亿美元增长20.5%。

进口商品结构 初级产品进口额为3.19亿美元，工业制成品进口额为6.21亿美元，分别占进口总额的33.9%、66.1%。

进口商品市场 进口商品来自42个国家和地区。

主要进口市场情况表

国别（地区）	进口金额（万美元）	占进口总额（%）
韩国	35152	37.4
日本	25414	27
美国	3903	4.2
澳大利亚	3296	3.5
加拿大	2750	2.9
俄罗斯	1888	2
中国台湾省	1816	1.9
马来西亚	1628	1.7
中国香港	1090	1.2

技术进出口 1998年烟台市签订进口设备合同金额5.78万美元，比1996年增长近十倍，引进项目主要来自韩国、日本、德国、中国香港、美国、意大利等国家和地区。

【利用外资】

1998年利用外资情况表

利用外资方式	批准签订的合同			实际利用外资	
	项目数（个）	外资金额（万美元）	金额比1997年（±%）	金额（万美元）	金额比1997年（±%）
对外借款	3	2595	63.3	2915	43.7
外商直接投资	175	30703	-13.6	45800	22.1
合资企业	113	17888	-7.8	36850	44.1
合作企业	5	3212	-54	1418	-64.9
外资企业	57	9602	5.1	7532	-4.4
国际租赁	2	1800	-54.8	1455	-49.4
加工装配	-	-4	-	-	-
合 计	180	35102	-30	50170	8.8

外商直接投资行业 在外商直接投资的175个项目中，生产型项目172项，非生产型项目3项。按行业划分，农业35项，工业168项，第三产业3项。

外商直接投资来源 外商投资来自20个国家和地区。主要有：中国香港39项，合同外资12322万美元；韩国34项，1529万美元；中国台湾省23项，4055万美元；美国23项，1323万美元，日本21项，1789万美元。

外商直接投资企业生产经营情况 1998年共有30家外商投资企业投产，烟台市累计投产的外商投资企业达到1860家，1998年完成销售收入237亿元人民币，实现利润4.6亿元人民币，税收7亿元人民币，出口8.4亿美元。

【对外经济合作】

承包工程与劳务合作 1998年共签订对外承包工程与劳务合作103项，合同额7327万美元，比1997年的6467万美元增长13.3%；营业额4919万美元，比1997年的4464万美元增长10.1%；共派出各类劳务人员2700人次，比1997年的2404人次增长12.4%；年末在外人数达到2734人，比1997年的2359人增长15.9%。对外经济合作涉及的国家和地区主要有日本、韩国、中国香港、新加坡、美国、中国台湾省、玻利维亚、巴巴多斯、以色列、厄立特里亚、尼泊尔、也门等。

【其他】

经济技术开发区 烟台经济技术开发区1998年完成固定资产投资25亿元人民币。批准外引内联项目72个，总投资1.2亿美元，其中外商投资项目39个，合同外资额0.9亿美元，比1997年下降38.5%；实际利用外资2.5亿美元，比1997年增长24.7%。1998年新投产企业18家，其中外商投资企业16家。

到1998年底，烟台开发区累计完成固定资产投资115亿元人民币；共批准外引内联项目687个，总投资26亿美元，其中外商投资项目470个，合同外资额23.3亿美元，实际利用外资9.8亿美元。累计开业投产企业208家，其中外商投资企业155家。1998年，全区共实现国内生产总值31.4亿元人民币，财政收入1.8亿元人民币，利税4.6亿元人民币，出口创汇2亿美元。

港口运输 烟台港现有生产型泊位33个，其中万吨级以上泊位15个，港口设计年吞吐能力1146万吨。龙口港是全国最大的地方港口，现有生产型泊位17个，其中万吨级以上泊位5个，港口设计年吞吐能力635万吨。1998年烟台、龙口港完成货物吞吐量2000万吨，其中完成外贸进出口货运总量690万吨，出口量270万吨，国际集装箱突破10万标箱，在长江以北各港口中列第四位。

对外经贸洽谈会 1998年10月8日至14日，在烟台市举办了第二届APEC中小企业技术交流暨展览会。本次交展会由国家经贸委、国外外经贸部与亚太经合组织主办，山东省人民政府协办；烟台市人民政府承办。参会参展的有APEC21个成员、准成员及国内二十多个省、市、自治区，参展的有中外企业近千家，展位总数达到1056个，参会的中外客商三万多人，其中海外客商近4000人。山东省共签订利用外资项目合同、协议和意向252个，总投资21亿美元，外资额14.7亿美元，其中烟台市204个，总投资15亿美元，外资额9.9亿美元；进出口贸易合同总额11.7亿美元，出口成交9.3亿美元，其中烟台市8.8亿美元，出口6.5亿美元；国内贸易成交额13.1亿元，其中烟台市2.5亿元；烟台市对外劳务合作签约项目7项，合同额2293万美元。外派劳务880人。本次交展会签订的25个千万美元以上的大项目，外资额7.6亿美元。

涉外旅游 1998年共接待观光旅游的外国人和港澳同胞12万人次，旅游外汇收入4708万美元，比1997年增长49.37%。

1998年河南省对外经济贸易

河南省对外经济贸易合作厅

【对外贸易】

进出口总额 据郑州海关统计，1998年，河南省进出口总额为173138万美元，比1997年下降8.7%。占全国进出口总额的0.53%。

出口总额 出口总额为118669万美元，比1997年下降7.8%。占全省国内生产总值4330亿元的2.27%，占全国出口总值的0.65%。

出口商品结构 初级产品出口额为38923.43万美元，占出口总额的32.8%；工业制成品出口额为79745.57万美元，占出口总额的67.2%。

出口额在500万美元以上的商品情况表

金额分类	商品名称	出口金额（万美元）	占出口总额（%）
5000万美元以上（2种）	假发、假眉毛及类似品，未锻轧的非合金铝	13405	11.30

出口额在500万美元以上的商品情况表（续）

金额分类	商品名称	出口金额（万美元）	占出口总额（%）
1000万～5000万美元（22种）	活大猪、人造刚玉、瓷餐具、冻牛肉、碳化硅、丝毯及其他铺地制品、钼铁、冻猪肉、革制品、毛皮制品、棉布、圣诞灯、腈纺棉纱、滚珠轴承、焦炭及半焦炭、未锻轧镁、铜锌合金板、片及带、棉制品、化纤服装、棉织服装、抗菌素、劳动布	35739	30.12
500万～1000万美元（23种）	桐木材、烤烟、镁、未精梳纤维纱、羊肠衣、棉包装袋、化纤布、聚酰胺—6弹力丝、铸铁、味精、尼龙帘子布、冻整头猪肉、芝麻、陶瓷餐具、蓄电池、未锻轧非合金锌、生铁锭、块、精炼铅、猪鬃、鞋靴、玩具、棉印花床单、棉线、粘胶纤维纱	18145	15.30
合　计	**47种**	**67289**	**56.72**

出口商品市场　出口商品销往一百四十多个国家和地区。

主要出口市场情况表

国别（地区）	出口金额（万美元）	占出口总额（%）
美国	22036.30	18.57
日本	13981.09	11.78
德国	6927.32	5.84
俄罗斯	5278.64	4.44
韩国	5134.12	4.33
荷兰	3380.59	2.84
意大利	2787.07	2.35
中国香港	2279.45	1.92
阿拉伯酋长国	2228.28	1.88
中国台湾省	2166.78	1.83
新加坡	2011.85	1.69

主要出口市场情况表（续）

国别（地区）	出口金额（万美元）	占出口总额（%）
比利时	1804.29	1.52
印度	1799.77	1.57
合　计	**71815.55**	**60.56**

进口总额　进口商品总额54469万美元，比1997年的60351万美元下降10.8%，占全国总额的0.39%。

进口商品结构　初级产品进口额8443万美元，占进口总额的15.50%；工业制成品进口额64026万美元，占进口总额的84.50%。

进口额在500万美元以上的商品情况表

金额分类	商品名称	进口金额（万美元）	占进口总额（%）
1000万美元以上（10种）	氧化铝、尼龙66盐、陆地棉、通讯设备、机械器具、玉米、棉羊皮、烟草机械、牛皮、铜材	20017	36.75

进口额在500万美元以上的商品情况表（续）

金额分类	商品名称	进口金额（万美元）	占进口总额（%）
500万～1000万美元（16种）	纤维长丝、机器零件、木薯干、重油、玻璃机械、腈基化合物、铁矿砂、塑料机械、冷冻箱压缩机、耐火建材、谷氨酸、钻石、灯类封装机、非合金铝、脉冲编码调制设备、汽轮机	10687	19.62
合　计	**26种**	**30704**	**56.37**

进口商品市场　进口商品来自55个国家和地区。

主要进口市场情况表

国别（地区）	进口金额（万美元）	占进口总额（%）
美国	8517.83	15.64
澳大利亚	6217.31	11.41
中国香港	6048.12	11.10
日本	5309.92	9.75
荷兰	2878.58	5.28
韩国	2753.17	5.05
德国	2734.33	5.02
英国	1779.13	3.27

主要进口市场情况表（续）

国别（地区）	进口金额（万美元）	占进口总额（%）
比利时	1722.72	3.16
法国	1642.54	3.02
合　计	**39603.65**	**72.71**

技术进出口　1998年河南省技术进出口总额为6010.7万美元。其中出口4969万美元，进口1041.7万美元。

【利用外资】

1998年利用外资情况表

利用外资方式	批准签订的合同			实际利用外资	
	项目数（个）	外资金额（万美元）	金额比1997年（±%）	金　额（万美元）	金额比1997年（±%）
外商直接投资	341	53003	-13.3	62177	-10.2
合资企业	240	29109		32488	
合作企业	25	11149		16621	
外资企业	76	12745		12545	
合　计	**341**	**53003**	**-13.3**	**62177**	**-10.2**

外商直接投资行业　河南省外商直接投资　　协议项目涉及40多个行业。生产型项目287个，

合同外资金额42463万美元，占总合同外资金额的80.11%，其中，农、林、牧、渔业类18个，采掘业7个，制造业252个，电力、煤气及水的生产和供应业10个，建筑业5个，交通运输、仓储及邮电通讯业1个；非生产型项目49个，合同外资金额14577万美元，占合同外资金额的27.5%。其中，商业、饮食业9个，金融保险业1个，房地产业15个，社会服务业19个，卫生、体育和社会福利业2个，教育、文化、广播电影视业1个，其他行业2个。

外商直接投资来源 外商直接投资来源于49个国家和地区。主要国家和地区是：中国香港118个，外资金额26929万美元；中国澳门115个，外资金额26644万美元；美国48个，外资金额9061万美元；维尔京群岛4个，外资金额5411万美元；新加坡12个，外资金额3568万美元；中国台湾省58个，外资金额2524万美元；开曼群岛3个，外资金额2277万美元；加拿大12个，外资金额1565万美元；欧盟18个，外资金额1392万美元；日本18个，外资金额1039万美元。

外商直接投资生产经营情况 截止1998年底，河南省建成投产（开业）企业2000余家，从业职工30多万人；销售（营业）收入235.27亿元，比1997年332.3亿元下降29.2%；出口24684万美元，比1997年出口22887万美元增长7.85%；税收16.4亿元，比1997年15.6亿元增长5.12个百分点。

【对外经济合作】

承包工程和劳务合作 1998年与二十多个国家和地区签订对外承包工程和劳务合作项目120个，合同金额11148万美元，比1997年增长4%；其中，承包工程项目30个，合同金额8750万美元；劳务合作项目64个，合同金额1960万美元；设计咨询项目26个，合同金额438万美元。完成营业额6994万美元，比1997年的6500万美元增长7.6%，1998年派出劳务人员8126人比1997年增长3%，年末在外人数达11368人，比1997年末增加280人，分布在14个国家和地区。主要集中在日本、新加坡、韩国、马来西亚、塞内加尔、尼泊尔、中国台湾省等国家和地区。承包工程主要有：马来西亚根登房建工程、泥泊尔108公路项目、拉普尔灌溉工程、巴基斯坦输变电工程等。

【接受外援】

1998年接受国际组织及双边援助项目共计4个。（1）为渑池县申请小额贷款31万元人民币；（2）为西峡县申请到澳大利亚援助小额贷款51万元人民币；（3）为郑州市供电局申请到新西兰政府“亚洲发展便利”项目200万美元援助；（4）为商城县积极申请德国民间组织EZE第三期40万马克的综合扶贫开发项目。

经济技术开发区 1998年郑州高新技术产业开发区固定资产投资28856万元，累计投资额64.3亿元。开工投产企业21家，累计166家。1998年实现技工贸收入82亿元，比1997年增长24.24%。1998年批准外商投资企业12家，协议外资金额3289万美元，比1997年1997万美元增长64.69%，出口创汇3286万美元。

洛阳高新技术产业开发区 1998年完成固定资产投资3.21亿元，区内企业达483家。1998年完成技工贸总收入45.1亿元，比1997年增长12.75%。新批三资企业9家，合同金额859万美元。全区出口创汇5098.42万美元，进口到货1095.59万美元。

对外经济洽谈会 1998年4月6日至12日，在阿尔及利亚阿尔及尔市举办了'98中国河南经贸文化活动。五十多家有进出口经营权的企业参加了本次文化周经贸洽谈活动。阿各界人士到会十分活跃，此次活动周签订出口合同467万美元。不少新获权企业结识了客户，为发展业务创造了条件。

涉外旅游 1998年共接待境外旅游者27.4万人次，比1997年增长3.78%；旅游外汇收入10001万美元，比1997年5.28%。其中来自台港澳地区同胞12.9万人次。

1998年湖北省对外经济贸易

湖北省对外经济贸易合作厅

【对外贸易】

进出口总额 1998年湖北省进出口总额349191万美元，比1997年的328268万美元增长6.8%。

出口总额 出口总额280468万美元，比1997年的253103万美元增长10.8%，占全省国内生产总值3704.21亿元（相当于447.91亿美元）的6.26%，占全国出口总额的1.53%。

出口商品结构 初级产品出口23876万美元，占出口总额的8.5%；工业制成出口256592万美元，占出口总额的91.5%。

出口额在1000万美元以上商品情况表

金额分类	商品名称	出口金额（万美元）	占出口总额（%）
1000～7000万美元（56种）	大米、食用植物油籽、芝麻、活大猪、冻猪肉、罐头、木材、白肋烟人造丝、棉坯布、棉色布、棉色织布、化纤坯布、人造棉布、汗衫背心、棉裤子、棉衬衫、棉牛仔服装、尼龙针织服装、涤棉针织服装、化纤裤子、化纤夹克、化纤大衣、化纤羽绒外衣、金首饰、中厚钢板、薄钢板、钢坯、高纯铜、磷酸五钠黄磷、白石腊、整套轮胎、维生素、医用纱布、船用甲板机械、滚装船汽车、汽车零件、动力机械、冶金成套设备、公路和桥梁设备、电线电站锅炉、通用机械、无线通讯设备、计算机、光纤维通讯设备、干电池、电子原器件、家用小电器、麻裤子、呢绒西服套、呢绒西服上衣、化纤衬衫、电视机及音响设备	105972	37.78
1亿美元以上（1种）	集装箱船	10056	3.58
合　计	**57种**	**116028**	**41.36**

出口商品市场 出口商品销往153个国家和地区。

主要出口市场情况表

国别（地区）	出口金额（万美元）	占出口总额（%）
中国香港	103427	36.88
日本	31327	11.17
美国	24765	8.83
德国	18216	6.49
中国台湾省	8181	2.92
韩国	6713	2.39
荷兰	5515	1.97
法国	5418	1.93
意大利	4382	1.56

主要出口市场情况表（续）

国别（地区）	出口金额（万美元）	占出口总额（%）
英国	3283	1.17
合　计	**211227**	**75.31**

进口总额　进口总额68741万美元，比1997年的75165万美元下降8.55%。

进口商品结构　初级产品进口额14176万美元，占进口总额的20.6%；工业制成品进口54565万美元，占进口总额的79.4%。

进口额在1000万美元以上的商品情况表

金额分类	商　品　名　称	进口金额（万美元）	占进口总额（%）
1000～3000万美元（12种）	木材、棉布、化纤布、铁球团矿砂、化工原料、化肥、天然橡胶、矿山机械船用动力和机电设备、粮油加工机械、邮电通讯设备、电讯设备及器材	21925	31.89
3000～7000万美元（3种）	纺织原料、精纺织品、铜精矿砂	16264	23.66
合　计	**15种**	**38189**	**55.55**

进口商品市场　进口商品来自41个国家和地区。

主要进口市场情况表

国别（地区）	进口金额（万美元）	占进口总额（%）
日本	16651	24.22
中国香港	9365	13.62
澳大利亚	7264	10.57
美国	7103	10.33
韩国	3798	5.53
德国	3713	5.4
南非	3578	5.21
加拿大	2836	4.13

主要进口市场情况表（续）

国别（地区）	进口金额（万美元）	占进口总额（%）
意大利	1915	2.79
丹麦	1055	1.53
合　计	**57278**	**83.32**

技术进出口　1998年湖北技术进出口总额52071.7万美元，比1997年的35278万美元增长47.6%。其中，技术和设备进口项目13个，比1997年减少18项；合同金额6445万美元，比

1997年的11416万美元减少43.54%；技术出口项目55个，比1997年减少18项，合同金额45626.7万美元，比1997年的23862万美元增长91.21%。

【利用外资】

1998年利用外资情况表

利用外资方式	批准签订的合同			实际利用外资	
	项目数（个）	外资金额（万美元）	金额比1997年（%）	金额（万美元）	金额比1997年（%）
对外借款	2	3950	-73.13	9673	-51.63
外商直接投资	330	51596	-20	92012	3.16
合资企业	176	14289	-52.42	55406	9.33
合作企业	24	20550	-1.38	10601	-27.95
外资企业	130	16757	25.95	26005	9.24
外商其他投资		19295	8	9355	6
对外发行股票		5104		5408	
加工装配		13891	-5	3947	25
合　计	**332**	**74841**	**-22.59**	**111040**	**-5.89**

外商直接投资行业　在外商直接投资中，生产型项目231个，非生产型项目99个。按行业分：农林牧渔业13个，采掘出4个，制造业199个，电力煤气及水供应业3个，建筑业10个，交通运输仓储业2个，批发零售贸易餐饮业9个，金融保险业1个，房地产业29个，社会服务业53个，教育文化艺术广播2个，其它行业5个。

外商直接投资来源　外商直接投资来源于34个国家和地区。主要有中国香港135项28553万美元，美国51项9428万美元，加拿大9项4322万美元，新加坡22项，2533万美元，中国台湾省45项2035万美元，英国12项1212万美元，中国澳门9项1078万美元。

外商直接投资企业生产经营情况　截至1998年底，外商直接投资已开业投产的企业有2650家，销售营业收入315亿元人民币，比1997年增长74.17%，其中出口销售收入53141万美元，比1997年增长20%。

【对外经济合作】

承包工程和劳务合作　1998年签订对外承包工程和劳务合作合同项目188个，金额17392万美元，比1997年的23500万美元下降25.99%；1998年派出劳务2340人次，年末在外人数4933人。劳务人员派往的主要国家和地区有新加坡、沙特阿拉伯、保加利亚、罗马利亚、美国、日本、中国香港、中国澳门等。承包工程的主要项目有上海世界金融中心和北京信息枢纽中心（境内国际招标项目）2个。

对外经济技术援助　承担援外项目5个，受援的国家有喀麦隆、缅甸、古巴、佛得角、吉布堤等。涉及的行业：工业、建筑业和养殖业。全年外派援外人数120人，年末在外人数120人。

接受多边、双边经济援助　接受外国援助项目2个，即德国救灾款和联合国儿童基金款共225万美元。

对外经贸洽谈　1998年湖北采取“派出去，请进来”的办法，洽谈贸易，扩大交流，先后派人赴英国、法国、美国、澳大利亚、新西兰等国考察市场；接待来自法国、比利时、荷兰、韩国、美国、德国、新加坡、中国台湾省等国家和地区的经贸考察团，工商代表团 11 批 80 人次洽谈合作项目；先后在法国波尔多举办国际博览会，在喀麦隆杜阿拉市举办"湖北出口销售会"；在湖北举办"98 湖北省（美国）对外经贸洽谈会"。积极组织外国企业来湖北举办展览会，先后举办了湖北（武汉）第十四届国际先进医疗仪器设备展览会和第四届武汉国际制冷、空调、采暖、通风、食品冷冻技术设备展览会以及'98 三峡国际焊接展览会等。通过这些博览会、展览会，开展对外经贸洽谈，不仅增进了双方的了解，扩大了交流与合作，而且为湖北省扩大了利用外资，引进了先进技术。1998 年共签订利用外资项目 9 个，投资总额 4.48 亿美元，协议外资额 2.6 亿美元，出口合同 2100 万美元；引进先进设备 200 多万美元，国内成交 4500 万人民币。

港口运输　1998 年湖北外贸出口货运总量 125.2 万吨，比 1997 年同期减少 34.28%，其中海运量 112.1 万吨，比 1997 年同期减少 35.94%；陆运量 13.1 万吨，比 1997 年同期减少 15.48%；空运量 445 吨，比 1997 年同期减少 9.92%。

涉外旅游　1998 年共接待国外及台、港、澳同胞 29 万人次，旅游外汇收入 8800 万美元，比 1997 年的 15000 万美元下降 41.33%。

1998 年武汉市对外经济贸易

武汉市对外经济贸易委员会

【对外贸易】

进出口总额　1998 年武汉市进出口总额 181，418 万美元，比 1997 年的 161，448 万美元增长 12.36%。

出口总额　出口总额 108，214 万美元，比 1997 年的 94，109 万美元增长 15%，占武汉市国内生产总值 1016 亿元人民币（相当于 122.41 亿美元）的 8.84%，占全国出口总额的 0.589%。

出口商品结构　初级产品出口额 5070 万美元，占出口总额的 4.69%；工业制成品的出口额 103144 万美元，占出口总额的 95.31%。

出口额在 1000 万美元以上商品情况表

金额分类	商品名称	出口金额（万美元）	占出口总额（%）
10000 万美元以上（2 种）	服装、钢材	38554	35.63
3000 万～7000 万美元（2 种）	船舶、光纤维通讯设备	11077	10.24
1000 万～3000 万美元以上（15 种）	棉布、棉涤轮布、人造棉布、有色金属、化工原料、染料、医用敷料、医疗器械、电站锅炉、冶金成套设备、公路和桥梁设备、无线通讯设备、电池、光学仪器、家用电器	25510	23.58
合　计	**19 种**	**75141**	**69.45**

出口商品市场 出口商品销往 121 个国家和地区。

主要出口市场表

国别（地区）	出口金额（万美元）	占出口总额（%）
中国香港	39384	36.39
美国	10637	9.83
中国台湾省	6686	6.18
德国	6369	5.84
日本	5237	4.84
俄罗斯	3614	3.34

主要出口市场表（续）

国别（地区）	出口金额（万美元）	占出口总额（%）
韩国	3418	3.16
荷兰	2780	2.57
瑞典	2278	2.11
新加坡	2091	1.93
合　计	**82444**	**76.19**

进口总额 进口总额 73205 万美元，比 1997 年的 67，339 万美元增长 8.71%。

【利用外资】

1998 年利用外资情况表

利用外资方式	批准签订的合同			实际利用外资	
	项目数（个）	外资金额（万美元）	金额比 1997 年（%）	金　额（万美元）	金额比 1997 年（%）
对外借款	3	25186		46086	
外商直接投资	148	41038	5.7	45397	0.1
合资企业	70	11236		16965	
合作企业	18	22036		8197	
外资企业	60	7766		20235	
外商其他投资	104	9793		11725	
国际租赁	0	0		1920	
加工贸易	104	9793		9805	
合　计	**255**	**76017**		**103208**	

外商直接投资行业 外商直接投资项目中生产型项目 96 个，非生产型项目 52 个。按行业分，工业 86 个，建筑业 5 个，房地产公用服务业 39 个，科研技术服务事业 3 个，其它行业 9 个。

外商直接投资来源 外商直接投资来自 16 个国家和地区。投资额居前五位的是：中国香港，24761 万美元；新加坡，3589 万美元；美国，2168 万美元；加拿大，1157 万美元；中国澳门，411 万美元。

外商直接投资企业生产经营情况 1998 年外商直接投资企业的开发投产项目 63 个。目前，绝大多数企业生产经营状况良好，1998 年实现销售收入 190 亿元人民币，比 1997 年增长 32%；实现税收 12.7 亿元人民币，比 1997 年增长 51%；出口创汇 15，125 万美元。比 1997 年增长 50.5%。

【对外经济合作】

承包工程和劳务合作 1998年签订对外工程承包和劳务合作合同121个，金额14832万美元，比1997年的8216万美元增长80.5%；营业额5206万美元，比1997年的4224万美元增长23.2%；1998年派出劳务人员1655人次，年末在外3019人，派往的主要国家和地区是：新加坡、中国香港、中国澳门、毛里求斯、韩国、中国台湾省、孟加拉、越南、俄罗斯、罗马尼亚；承包工程的主要项目和国别是津巴布韦国际刑警总部、津巴布韦再保险公司综合大楼、境内国际招标秦皇岛复合磷肥厂、境内国际招标上海信息枢纽装饰工程等。

对外经济技术援助 1998年承担援外项目3个，受援国家和地区是：佛得角、塞拉利昂、圣卢西亚，涉及建筑业、物资采购及施工监理等行业。目前，援佛得角国家图书馆建设进展顺利，即将竣工；援塞拉利昂农机具供货项已采购完毕，在港待命启运；援圣卢西亚施工监理人员正在执行任务。1998年派出援外人员30人，年末在外30人。

对外投资 1998年在海外举办非贸易性企业2家，中方投资金额704万美元，其中，武汉拖拉机厂在喀麦隆投资200万美元；汇凯集团在尼泊尔投资484万美元。

港口运输 1998年武汉有港口泊位59个，港口吞吐能力1346.56万吨，1998年实际完成的货物吞吐总量1377.7万吨，完成外贸进出口货物吞吐量15.3万吨。1998年武汉地区外贸运输货物总量84.48万吨，比1997年减少36.4%，其中，按运输方式分：1998年海运进口货物量14.54、出口货物量62.12，分别比1997年下降48.4%和36%；1998年空运进口货物量3135万吨，比1997年增长10%，1998年空运出口货物量450万吨，比1997年下降50%；1998年陆运进口货物量2.55万吨，比1997年增长84.8%，1998年陆运出口货物量4.88万吨，比1997年下降28.7%。

涉外旅游 1998年入境的外国人和台港澳同胞13万人次，旅游收入84，000万美元，比1997年的10，984.3万美元下降57.9%。

1998年湖南省对外经济贸易

湖南省对外经济贸易委员会

【对外贸易】

进出口总额 1998年湖南省进出口贸易总额为307655万美元，比1997年的328366万美元下降6.25%。

出口总额 1998年全省出口总额220214万美元，比1997年的232922万美元下降5.46%，占全省国内生产总值3211.4亿元的5.68%。

出口商品结构 初级产品33211万美元，占出口总额的15.08%，比1997年的12.67%提高2.41个百分点；工业制成品187003万美元，占出口总额的84.92%，比1997年的87.33%下降2.41个百分点。其中：机电产品出口33646万美元，占出口总额的15.28%，比1997年的33854万美元下降0.61%。

出口额500万美元以上商品情况表

金额分类	商　品　名　称	出口金额（万美元）	占出口总额（%）
1000万美元以上（41种）	大米、活大猪、冻猪肉、咸荞头、食品罐头、茶叶、鞭炮烟花、猪肠衣、革皮及制品、苎麻纱线、棉布、麻布、化纤布、棉制品、丝制品、服装、陶瓷、箱包、鞋类、文体用品、钢材、生铁、铁合金、铸铁制品、锡、氧化锑、铅、锌、锰、硅、钠化合物、硫酸锰、电解二氧化锰、塑料制品、肝素钠、汽车摩托车及零件、电工设备、成套设备、电子元器件、家用电器、手工具	162033	-7.85
500万～1000万美元（28种）	桐油、香料及香料油、竹筷、烟草、动物纤维、棉麻混纺纱线、化纤纱线、化纤制品、丝绸制品、纸张纸浆、锑、锌合金、铅锌矿砂、仲钨酸铵、锌粉、无定型石墨、贝化合物、锌化合物、硫脲、氧化锌、中药材、双烯醇酮醋酸脂、解热镇痛药、动力机械、工业轴承、硬质合金、珠宝首饰	20273	-15.44
合　计	**69种**	**182306**	**-8.76**

出口商品市场　1998年出口销往144个国家和地区，比1997年增加2个。主要市场有：港澳地区67991万美元，占出口总额30.86%；美国35841万美元，占出口总额16.28%；欧共体30447万美元，占出口总额13.83%；日本23433万美元，占出口总额10.64%；东盟6国16849万美元，占出口总额7.65%；独联体及东欧3564万美元，占出口总额1.62%，对以上六大市场共出口178125万美元，占全省出口总额80.89%，比1997年增长4.64%，比重提高0.69个百分点。

出口主要国别（地区）表（前10位）

金额单位：万美元

国别（地区）	出口额	比重（%）
中国香港	66488	30.19
美国	35841	16.28
日本	23433	10.64
德国	10142	4.61
韩国	10128	4.60
荷兰	7018	3.19

出口主要国别（地区）表（前10位）（续）

金额单位：万美元

国别（地区）	出口额	比重（%）
新加坡	6132	2.78
菲律宾	5949	2.70
中国台湾省	5330	2.42
英国	3728	1.69

进口总额　1998年全省进口到货总额87441万美元，比1997年的95444万美元下降8.39%。

进口商品结构　初级产品进口额17114万美元，占进口总额的19.57%；工业制成品进口额70327万美元，占进口总额的80.43%。按其产品性质分类，生产资料82546万美元，占94.40%；生活资料4895万美元，占5.60%。

进口额 500 万美元以上商品情况表

金额分类	商品名称	进口金额（万美元）	占进口总额（%）
1000 万美元以上（20 种）	水产品、饲料、猪肠衣、木材、烟草辅料、纺织原料、纺织品、钢材、铁矿砂、铬矿砂、铝、铝矿砂、氧化铝、化肥农药、汽车电车摩托车及零件、土建工程机械、成套设备、计算机、有线通讯设备、电子元器件	64449	73.71
500 万～1000 万美元（10 种）	棕榈油、服装、纸张纸浆、废钢、铜、钾化合物、醇醛化工品、塑料原料、医疗器械、卷烟机	6775	7.75
合　计	**30 种**	**71224**	**81.45**

进口商品市场　进口商品来自 47 个国家和地区，主要进口市场有中国香港、美国、德国、日本、澳大利亚、以色列、韩国、法国、中国台湾省等 10 个国家和地区。

主要进口市场情况表

国别（地区）	进口额	比重（%）
中国香港	19572	22.38
美国	17397	19.90
德国	7125	8.15
日本	6542	7.48
澳大利亚	5573	6.37
以色列	3508	4.01
韩国	3261	3.73
法国	3044	3.48
中国台湾省	2728	3.12
瑞士	2265	2.59

技术进出口　1998 年湖南省共对外签订技术进出口合同项目 118 个，合同金额 31676.84 万美元，比 1997 年的 29039 万美元增长 9.08%；实际完成 30909 万美元，比 1997 年的 24683 万美元增长 25.22%。其中：签订技术引进和进口设备合同项目 62 个，比 1997 年减少 28 个；合同金额 24904.03 万美元，比 1997 年的 22709 万美元增长 9.67%；实际用汇 24904 万美元，比 1997 年的 18767 万美元增长 32.6%。签订技术出口合同项目 56 个，比 1997 年减少 4 个；合同金额 6772.81 万美元，比 1997 年的 6329.65 万美元增长 7%；年内收汇 6005 万美元，比 1997 年的 5380 万美元增长 11.62%，收汇率为 88.66%。

技术设备进口主要来自的国家和地区有美国、日本、英国、瑞士、韩国、意大利、以色列、德国、奥地利、澳大利亚、中国香港和中国台湾省等。技术设备出口的主要国家和地区有埃及、孟加拉国、缅甸、菲律宾、巴基斯坦、马来西亚、印度尼西亚、越南、土耳其、德国、美国、日本、肯尼亚、新加坡、中国香港、中国澳门和中国台湾省等。

技术引进项目分布在邮电、纺织、机械、石化、电子、轻工、粮食、烟草、冶金、建材等十多个行业。其中，引进项目金额最多的是：邮电行业 12 个项目，11108.1 万美元；轻纺行业十个项目，7725.99 万美元；机械行业 24 个项目，2375.82 万美元，石化行业 5 个项目，2310.69 万美元。这些重点技术项目的引进，对促进湖南科学技术进步和产业、产品结构的调整起到了积极作用。

【利用外资】

1998 年，湖南共批准利用外资项目 421 个（未含加工装配项目），比 1997 年 416 个（未含加工装配项目647个）增加5个；合同利用外资金额143026万美元，比1997年的97810万美元增长46.23%；实际利用外资金额100918万美元，比1997年的100799万美元增长0.02%。其中，直接利用外资项目416个，比1997年增加9个，合同利用外资金额122149万美元，比1997年增长37.10%；实际利用外资金额97913万美元，比1997年增长2.44%。

1998年利用外资情况表

利用外资方式	批准签订的合同			实际利用外资	
	项　目（个）	外资金额（万美元）	金额比1997年（±%）	金　额（万美元）	金额比1997年（±%）
对外借款	5	20877	46.23	3005	-42.45
外商直接投资	416	109492	27.30	81816	-10.78
合资企业	171	28299	15.34	36829	-22.41
合作企业	48	34225	-2.73	17432	-9.25
外资企业	197	46968	78.65	27555	10.07
外商其他投资		12657	210.67	16097	215.38
补偿贸易				31	-90.49
加工装配		12657	240.24	16066	252.69
合　计	**421**	**143026**	**45216.00**	**100918**	**0.12**

注：加工装配未列项目个数

外商直接投资行业　外商直接投资项目中，属于生产型的336个，合同外资金额97386万美元，实际利用外资金额72400万美元；属于非生产型的80个，合同外资金额12106万美元，实际利用外资金额9416万美元。这些项目分布在十大行业：农林牧副渔业27个项目，合同外资金额7183万美元，实际利用外资金额2980万美元；制造业232个项目，合同外资金额35659万美元，实际利用外资金额41805万美元；建筑业23个项目，合同外资金额18356万美元，实际利用外资金额11674万美元；采掘业6个项目，合同外资金额1725万美元，实际利用外资金额876万美元；电力、煤气及水的生产和供应业19个项目，合同外资金额19402万美元，实际利用外资金额3565万美元；交通运输、仓储及邮电通讯业3个项目，合同外资金额2651万美元，实际利用外资金额586万美元；房地产业26个项目，合同外资金额12410万美元，实际利用外资金额3704万美元；批发和另售贸易、餐饮业17个项目，合同外资金额1004万美元，实际利用外资金额1463万美元；社会服务业63个项目，合同外资金额10856万美元，实际利用外资金额7589万美元；教育、文化、艺术及广播电影、电视业合同外资金额246万美元，实际利用外资金额354万美元。

外商直接投资来源　1998年湖南直接利用外资来源于32个国家和地区。外商投资金额排前十位的是：中国香港214个项目，合同外资金额43524万美元，实际外资金额33082万美元；美国28个项目，合同外资金额6109万美元，实际外资金额7819万美元；中国台湾省84个项目，合同外资金额6408万美元，实际外资金额6200万美元；英国4个项目，合同外资金额3352万美元，实际外资金额5864万美元；日本2个项目，合同外资金额4579万美元，实际外资金额4275万美元；维尔京群岛16个项目，合同外资金额25612万美元，实际外资金额6020万美元；加拿大9个项目，合同外资金额2445万美元，实际外资金额2089万美元；中国澳门13个项目，合同外资金额1761万美元，实际外资金额2277万美元；马来西亚3个项目，合同外资金额4672万美元，实际外资金额

1484万美元；德国3个项目，合同外资金额3541万美元，实际外资金额1122万美元。

外商直接投资企业生产经营情况 1998年，全省累计投产开业的外商投资企业共二千多家，其中有进出口实绩的272家，1998年共完成进出口总额57045万美元，比1997年下降25.85%，其中出口42139万美元，比1997年下降9.59%；销售收入194亿元，比1997年增长14.12%；实现税收8.94亿元，比1997年增长31.47%。1998年外商投资企业生产经营状况比较好，获得全国外商投资企业"双优"的共13家：湖南火炬有色金属有限公司、湖南华联瓷业有限公司、湖南湘进电化有限公司、维用——长城电器有限公司、岳阳先龙皮革制有限公司、华南彩色印刷制品有限公司、湖南黎海微电机有限公司、翔鹏精细化工有限公司、湖南兴联箱包有限公司、郴州东江嘉兴针织厂、湖南新丰纤维制品有限公司、湖南国龙饲料有限公司、湖南凯美特干冰有限公司。

【对外经济合作】

承包工程与劳务合作 1998年对外承包劳务继续保持了较好的发展势头，湖南省16家外经企业共对外签订承包劳务合同项目388个，合同总金额12743万美元，完成营业额10563万美元，1998年派出人数1868人（次），年末在外人数3265人，与1997年相比较，除合同额下降43.73%外，其它三项分别增长26.76%、14.60%和26.35%。对外承包劳务项目分布在中国香港、中国澳门、日本、韩国、越南、菲律宾、泰国、新加坡、马来西亚、印度等74个国家和地区。

对外经济技术援助 1998年湖南正在执行的援外项目13个，合同总金额13102.5万元人民币，其中1998年新增项目6个，援外金额8612万元人民币。援外项目主要分布在阿尔及利亚、坦桑尼亚、喀麦隆、白俄罗斯、越南等国家和地区。项目进展顺利，得到受援国的好评。

接受经济援助 1998年湖南正在执行的国际双边和多边的无偿受援项目38个，受援总金额6999.05万美元。其中，1998年新增项目23个，受援金额3257.3万美元。主要项目是：世界粮食计划署的紧急救灾粮食援助项目，受援金额2800万美元；德国援助的灾后重建项目（17个子项目），受援金额298万美元；联合国开发计划署援助的湘西UNDP扶贫项目，受援金额100万美元。这些受援项目对湖南灾后重建工作发挥了重要作用。

【其他】

对外经贸洽谈 1998年10月17日至20日，由国务院侨办和湖南省政府在长沙联合举办的"'98中国中西部地区对外经济技术合作洽谈会"取得圆满成功。有五十多个国家和地区的二千余名客商和14个省、市、自治区及5个特邀城市的七千五百多名代表参加了洽谈会；参观展览的人数达三万多人次，洽谈会上共对外签约的项目285个，总投资达81.1亿美元，利用外资54.54亿美元。其中，合同项目122个，合同外资金额13.96亿美元，协议项目91个，协议外资17.63亿美元，意向项目72个，意向外资22.94亿美元；外贸出口成交16864.3万美元；对外承包劳务签订合同项目5个，合同金额7176万美元；技术进出口签订合同项目7个，合同金额4685万美元。湖南省在这次洽谈会上成绩居于中西部地区各省市自治区首位，共对外成交出口贸易额16864.3万美元；签订利用外资合同项目54个，合同外资金额9.05亿美元；签订对外承包劳务合同项目5个，合同总金额7176万美元；签订技术进出口合同项目7个，合同总金额4685万美元。

涉外旅游 1998年湖南旅游业在东南亚金融危机的负面影响下，仍保持了继续增长的发展势头。1998年接待境外旅游者34.86万人次，比1997年的30.16万人次增长15.58%；涉外旅游创汇1.56亿美元，比1997年的1.4亿美元增长11.43%。接待国内旅游者4200万人次，国内旅游收入87亿元人民币，分别比1997年增长5%和27.94%。连接湘西北大动脉的长石铁路通车以后，大大缩短了长沙至张家界的旅游时间，加之长益高速公路的开通和长沙至常德高速公路的加紧建设，使得制约旅游业的交通"瓶颈"得到相应缓解，促进了全省旅游业的发展。

1998年广东省对外经济贸易

广东省对外经济贸易委员会

【对外贸易】

进出口总额 据海关统计，1998年广东省进出口总额1298.27亿美元，比1997年的1300.97亿美元下降0.21%。

出口总额 出口总额756.40亿美元，比1997年的745.41亿美元增长1.47%，占全国出口总额的41.2%，居全国首位。

出口商品结构 初级产品的出口额39.85亿美元，占出口总额的5.27%；工业制成品的出口额716.55亿美元，占出口总额的94.73%。

出口额在1000万美元以上的商品情况表

金额分类	海关统计的商品名称	出口金额（万美元）	占出口总额（%）
5亿美元以上（19）种	硬盘驱动器、其他玩具、显示器、黄金制首饰及其零件、无绳电话机等	1856084	24.54
1亿～5亿美元（131种）	填充的玩具动物、圣诞节用品、棉制未列名针织物或钩编织物、激光唱机、激光打印机等	2781148	36.77
5000万～1亿美元（153种）	塑料制衣服及衣着附件、其他稳压电源、真空吸尘器、电熨斗、其他活鱼等	1082293	14.31
1000万～5000万美元（568种）	氯化钾、扫描仪、未列名食品、松香、无线寻呼机等	1269473	16.78
合　计	**871种**	**6988998**	**92.40**

出口商品市场 出口商品销往212个国家和地区。

主要出口市场情况表

国别（地区）	出口金额（万美元）	占出口总额（%）
中国香港	2，651，211	35.05
美国	1，895，697	25.06
欧共体	999，701	13.21
日本	696，302	9.21
中国台湾省	170，890	2.26
新加坡	163，983	2.17

主要出口市场情况表（续）

国别（地区）	出口金额（万美元）	占出口总额（%）
加拿大	81363	1.08
韩国	80113	1.06
合　计	**6739260**	**89.10**

进口总额 进口总额541.87亿美元，比1997年的555.56亿美元下降2.46%。

进口商品结构 初级产品进口额53.52亿美元，占进口总额的9.88%；工业制成品进口额488.35亿美元，占进口总额的90.12%。

进口额在1000万美元以上的商品情况表

金额分类	海关统计的商品名称	进口金额（万美元）	占进口总额（%）
5亿美元以上（12种）	大中小型计算机及其部件的零件、其他单片集成电路、初级形状的聚丙烯、其他燃料油等	932007	17.20
1亿～5亿美元（84种）	其他经鞣制或复鞣的牛皮革及马皮革、混合集成电路、轻柴油、初级形状的可发性聚苯乙烯等	1611484	29.74
5000万～1亿美元（131种）	聚对苯二甲酸乙二脂切片、镍镉蓄电池、蓝湿牛坡、钛白粉等	945597	17.45
1000万～5000万美元（561种）	每层都漂白的未经涂布的多层纸及纸、其他大豆、板材热轧机、激光打印机等	1255137	23.16
合　计	**788种**	**4744225**	**87.55**

进口商品市场 进口商品来自142个国家和地区。

主要进口市场情况表

国别（地区）	进口金额（万美元）	占进口总额（%）
日本	1154594	21.31
中国台湾省	1074578	19.83
韩国	539807	9.96
美国	458626	8.46
欧共体	418087	7.72
中国香港	415915	7.68
新加坡	203483	3.75
泰国	133207	2.46
合　计	**4398297**	**81.17**

技术进出口 1998年广东省技术进出口总额35.45亿美元，比1997年的19.64亿美元增长80.5%。其中，签订技术引进合同115项，比1997年的117项下降1.71%；合同金额11.78亿美元，比1997年11.85亿美元下降0.59%。签订技术出口合同331项，比1997年的286项增长15.73%；合同金额23.67亿美元，比1997年的7.79亿美元增长2.04倍。

【利用外资】

1998 年利用外资情况表

利用外资方式	批准签订的合同			实际利用外资	
	项目数（个）	外资金额（万美元）	金额比1997年（±%）	金额（万美元）	金额比1997年（±%）
对外借款	89	185226	+176.94	204474	+56.01
外商直接投资	4349	916180	+19.11	1202005	+2.64
合资企业	1107	224442	+7.91	346565	−10.32
合作企业	642	254892	+4.53	454796	+22.96
外资企业	2596	430662	+37.07	392427	−5.38
外商投资股份制	4	6184	+93.19	8217	
外商其他投资	11021	136396	+6.19	103466	−12.59
对外发行股票		2300		2300	−91.14
国际租赁				179	
补偿贸易	26	3560	−13.97	2085	−42.80
加工装配	10995	130536	+5.01	98902	+11.42
合　计	**15459**	**1237802**	**+28.33**	**1509945**	**+6.30**

外商直接投资行业　在新批准的 4349 个外商直接投资项目中，生产性项目占近 80%。按行业分，农、林、牧、渔业 121 个，采掘业 13 个，制造业 3225 个，电力、煤气及水的生产和供应业 15 个，建筑业 38 个，交通运输、仓储及邮电通讯业 65 个，批发和零售贸易、餐饮业 119 个，房地产业 149 个，社会服务业 365 个，卫生、体育和社会福利业 11 个，教育、文化艺术及广播电影电视业 2 个，科学研究和综合技术服务业 144 个，其他行业 82 个。

外商直接投资来源　外商直接投资来自 49 个国家和地区。其中中国香港 3029 个，合同外资金额 470154 万美元；维尔京群岛 240 个，226863 万美元；中国台湾省 498 个，38971 万美元；新加坡 76 个，31074 万美元；日本 43 个，30687 万美元；美国 169 个，20900 万美元；开曼群岛 15 个，14956 万美元；德国 11 个，13390 万美元；巴哈马 8 个，8699 万美元；荷兰 8 个，7295 万美元。

外商直接投资企业生产经营情况　截至 1998 年底广东省登记注册的外商投资企业有 57665 家，其中投产开业的近 5 万家。广东省外商投资企业出口总额 391.83 亿美元，占全省出口总额的 51.80%。大批技术先进的外商投资企业经济效益有所提高。

【对外经济合作】

承包工程和劳务合作　1998 年签订对外承包工程和劳务合作合同项目 2405 个，金额 26658 万美元，比 1997 年的 39800 万美元下降 33%；营业额 32329 万美元，比 1997 年的 25700 万美元增长 26%。1998 年派出劳务人员 15058 人次，年末在外 21382 人。

接受经济援助　1998 年获德国、澳大利亚等国提供的援助项目 4 项，金额共 74 万元人民币，主要用于贫困地区的医疗、教育及山区的饮用水工程等。其中乳源瑶族自治县大坪乡用澳大利亚政府援助 30 万元建设的饮水项目，解决了四千多农民的饮用水问题。

【其他】

经济技术开发区 广州、湛江、大亚湾、南沙经济技术开发区各项建设取得新成就。其中惠州市大亚湾经济技术开发区 1998 年批准外商投资企业 108 家，合同外资额 9.03 亿美元，实际利用外资 3.83 亿美元；全区出口总额 4055 万美元，其中外商投资企业出口 3269 万美元。

保税区、高新技术产业开发区 深圳沙头角、深圳福田、深圳盐田港、广州、汕头、珠海保税区和深圳科技工业园、广州天河、中山“火炬”、惠州仲恺、佛山、珠海高新技术产业开发区等的整体效益进一步提高。其中佛山高新技术产业开发区 1998 年完成基建投资 9441 万元，基础设施更为完善；1998 年实际利用外资 1580 万美元，产品出口 1.23 亿美元。中山“火炬”高新技术产业开发区 1998 年新建 11 万伏变电站 1 座，新建道路总面积 11.92 万平方米，年内新批准合同外资额 13008.3 万美元，实际利用外资 9074.8 万美元，产品出口 3.8 亿美元。惠州仲恺高新技术产业开发区 1998 年完成基础设施建设投资 1.1 亿元，1998 年批准合同外资额 1383 万美元，实际利用外资 650 万美元；全区出口总额 2.76 亿美元。

对外经贸洽谈会 1998 年 8 月 5～8 日在香港展览中心举办广东高新技术洽谈会，共接洽来自港、台、澳以及美国、日本、德国、法国、澳大利亚、挪威等数十个国家和地区的客商 6696 人次，洽谈公司 2893 家。共签订利用外资合同 762 个，合同外资金额 39.06 亿美元；签订协议 310 个，协议外资金额 16.97 亿美元；签订意向书 315 个，意向外资金额 14.92 亿美元。出口成交 12.3 亿美元。10 月 6～9 日在美国洛彬矶举办广东经济技术贸易洽谈会，三天半时间共接洽了美国各州及加、英、法、澳、日等国家和地区的客商 3620 人次，签订外商直接投资合同 123 个，金额 13.92 亿美元；贸易成交 8.2 亿美元。

港口运输 1998 年广东省沿海主要港口完成货物吞吐总量 12866 万吨，比 1997 年的 12384 万吨增长了 4%。

涉外旅游 1998 年入境旅客 5157.04 万人次，其中外国人 203.79 万人次，华侨 4.91 万人次，港澳台胞 4948.34 万人次。广东省旅游外汇收入 29.42 亿美元，比 1997 年的 28.01 亿美元增长 5%。

1998 年广州市对外经济贸易

广州市对外经济贸易委员会

【对外贸易】

进出口总额 1998 年广州市进出口总额为 129.43 亿美元，(海关数，不可比。业务数 130.63 亿美元，比 1997 年 116.4 亿美元增长 12.54%)。

出口总额 出口总额 75.2 亿美元（海关数。业务数 80.18 亿美元，比 1997 年 75.38 亿美元增长 6.36%）。占广州市国内生产总值 1844.09 亿元的 33.76%，占全省出口总额的 9.3%。

出口商品结构 初级产品出口总额 2.756 亿美元（业务数），占出口总额的 3.34%；工业制成品的出口总额 77.24 亿美元（业务数），占出口总额的 96.56%。

出口额在 1000 万美元以上的商品情况表（业务数）

金额分类	商品名称	出口金额（亿美元）	占出口总额（%）
1 亿美元以上（18 种）	纺织品、服装、鞋类、表类、首饰、宝石、包袋、玩具、塑料制品、各类船集装箱、各类机械、有线通讯设备、电子元器件、照相机、家用小电器机、音响设备、其他家用电器	53.1	66.23
5 千万～1 亿美元（16 种）	水产品、皮革及制品、其他工艺品、文体用品、办公用品及设备、纸制品、家具、金属器皿、杂项百货、钢材、金属制品、小五金、化工原料、橡胶及制品、计算机、自行车类	10.92	13.62
1 千万美元～5 千万美元（42 种）	粮油、活畜禽、肉食、蔬菜、食品制成品、咖啡制品、香调料及香料油、山货木材、纺织原料、陶瓷类、人造花、其他工艺美术品、藤制品、箱类、帽类、体育用品、乐器、玻璃器皿、保温瓶类、钟类、清洁用品、日用剪刀、理发用具、灯具、眼镜类、日用皮制品、铸铁制品、其他黑色金属、有色金属矿产品、有色金属材及制品、贵稀金属、建筑材料其他金属矿产品、油漆、油墨及染料、医药原料、汽车、电车、摩托车及零件、成套设备、无线通讯设备、电子设备及仪器、光学仪器、工农具	10.34	12.9
合　计		**74.36**	**92.75**

主要出口市场情况表（业务数）

国别（地区）	出口金额（亿美元）	占出口总额（%）
中国香港	61.69	76.94
美国	6.41	8
日本	2.18	2.72
德国	1.27	1.58
比利时	1.19	1.48
新加坡	0.68	0.85
英国	0.59	0.74
中国台湾省	0.42	0.52
澳大利亚	0.42	0.52

进口总额　进口总额为 54.23 亿美元（海关数，不可比。业务数 50.45 亿美元，比 1997 年的 41.02 亿美元增长 24%）。

进口商品结构　初级产品进口额 0.94 亿美元（业务数），占进口总额的 1.86%；工业制成品的进口总额 49.51 亿美元（业务数），占进口总额的 98.14%。

主要进口商品情况表（业务数）

商品名称	进口金额（亿美元）	占进口总额（%）
纺织品	6.95	13.78
塑料	5.32	10.55
电信设备及器材	3.68	7.29
畜产品	3.39	6.72
有色金属	3.03	6.01
黑色金属	2.67	5.29
工艺品类	2.58	5.11
纸浆纸张及制品	2.02	4
汽车、电车、摩托车及零件	1.43	2.83

主要进口商品情况表（业务数）（续）

商品名称	进口金额（亿美元）	占进口总额（%）
化工原料	1.36	2.7
日用杂品	1.32	2.7
各类机械	1.32	2.7
橡胶及制品	1.2	2.38
船舶	1.18	2.34

主要进口市场情况表（业务数）

国别（地区）	进口金额（亿美元）	占进口总额（%）
中国香港	40.58	80.44
日本	2.82	5.59
中国台湾省	2.09	4.14
比利时	0.96	1.90
美国	0.69	1.37

主要进口市场情况表（业务数）（续）

国别（地区）	进口金额（亿美元）	占进口总额（%）
瑞典	0.50	1.00
新加坡	0.40	0.79
泰国	0.27	0.54
澳大利亚	0.23	0.46
德国	0.22	0.44
合计	**48.76**	**96.65**

技术进出口 1998年广州市技术进出口总额为10.97亿美元，比1997年6.472亿美元增长69.5%。其中：签订引进技术和设备合同项目80个，比1997年的50个增加30个；合同金额6.95亿美元，比1997年的2.972亿美元增长134%。签订技术出口合同项目175个，比1997年的88个增加87个，合同金额4.02亿美元，比1997年的3.5亿美元增长10.02%。

【利用外资】

1998年利用外资情况表

单位：万美元

利用外资方式	批准签订的合同			实际利用外资	
	项目数（个）	外资金额（万美元）	金额比1997年（±%）	金额（万美元）	金额比1997年（±%）
对外借款		31394	－20.67	31394	－20.67
外商直接投资	643	193178	13.75	271608	9.39
合资企业	136	49037	50.96	59304	－7.61
合作企业	193	84112	－16.06	151389	21.74
外资企业	314	60029	61.64	60915	2.46
外商其他投资	343	20486	36.36	1465	－18.7
加工贸易	343	20486	38.75	1286	－18.7
合计	**986**	**245058**	**11.43**	**304467**	**5.11**

外商直接投资行业 外商直接投资项目中生产型项目436个，占总数的67.81%。

外商直接投资来源 外商直接投资的国家和地区有40个。

外商直接投资来源情况表

单位：万美元

国别	项目数		合同利用外资		实际利用外资		项目平均投入金额
	个数	比重%	金额	比重%	金额	比重%	
中国香港	377	58.6	102497	53.1	162023	59.7	271.9
维尔京群岛	63	9.8	44438	23.0	44845	16.5	705.37
日本	10	1.6	8128	4.2	172894	6.4	812.3
中国台湾省	88	13.7	7369	3.8	6069	2.2	83.74
英国	3	0.5	6075	3.1	3928	1.4	2025
新加坡	15	2.3	5518	2.9	4052	2.5	367.9
开曼群岛	3	0.5	4000	2.1	548	0.2	1333.3
毛里求斯	1	0.2	3273	1.7	2170	0.8	3273
澳大利亚	8	1.2	3215	1.7	1306	0.5	401.9
中国澳门	7	1.1	2124	1.1	5992	2.2	303.4
其他	68	10.6	6541	3.4	23381	8.6	96.19
合　计	**643**	**100.0**	**193178**	**100.0**	**271608**	**100.0**	**300.4**

【对外经济合作】

承包工程和劳务合作　1998 年签定对外承包工程和劳务合作合同项目 1516 个，金额 918 万美元，比 1997 年 6730 万美元下降 86.36%；对外劳务营业额 2185 万美元，增长 13.2%，对外承包工程营业额 1927 万美元，下降 20.4%。1998 年派出劳务人员 1309 人次，增长 13.3%，年末在外人数 2283 人。

对外投资　1998 年在海外开办企业数为 9 家，投资金额 472.65 万美元，投资的国家和地区有美国、新西兰、澳大利亚、法国、新加坡、泰国、柬埔寨、中国香港等。

【其他】

广州经济技术开发区　1998 年广州经济技术开发区完成工业总产值 231.5 亿元人民币，比 1997 年增长 16.63%；合同利用外资 7.54 亿美元，比 1997 年增长 5.17%；实际利用外资 4.32 亿美元，比 1997 年增长 11.6%。出口总额 5.6 亿美元，比 1997 年增长 11.6%。

广州高新技术产业开发区　1998 年广州高新技术产业开发区与广州经济技术开发区“合署办公”，实行“一套人马，两块牌子”的运作形式。工业总产值 44.4 亿元人民币，出口创汇 7794 万美元。

广州保税区　1998 年是广州保税区历年来经济发展最好的一年，主要由于国家出台了一系列政策如打击走私、以产顶进及保税汽车政策等使保税区的投资环境更具吸引力，和保税区建设趋于完善。1998 年广州保税区引进外资项目 59 个，投资总额 9828 万美元，比 1997 年增长 59%；进口货值 15611 万美元，比 1997 年增长 20%，出口货值 11341 万美元，比 1997 年增长 43%。

广州南沙经济技术开发区　1998 年广州南沙经济技术开发区经济稳步增长，1998 年实现国内生产总值20.5亿元人民币，比1997年增长16.4%；进口总值1.27亿美元，比1997年增长21.2%，出口总值1.63亿美元，比1997年增长10.3%。引进外资项目31个，合同利用外资8514万美元，比1997年增长146%，实际利用外资2075万美元，比1997年下降43.2%。

对外经济洽谈会 1998年3月9日～25日，广州市经贸代表团赴加拿大、美国进行经贸交流活动，举行了5场招商项目洽谈会，签订了总投资额1.03亿美元，合同利用外资9000万美元的合作项目一批。

8月5日～8日，广州组团参加在香港举行的广东高新技术项目洽谈会，签订项目57个，总投资额6.096亿美元，利用外资4.053亿美元。

10月6日～9日，由广州市常务副市长伍亮率领的广州代表团参加了美国洛杉矶98广州经济技术贸易洽谈会。签订利用外资项目34个，总投资额3.83亿美元，利用外资金额3.193亿美元。

港口运输 1998年广州港口货物吞吐量8716万吨，比1997年增长3.9%；其中进口5531.73万吨，比1997年增长4.65%，出口3184.45万吨，比1997年增长3.52%。

涉外旅游 1998年入境的外国人数以及港澳台同胞人数为133.32万人次，比1997年减少40.85%。旅游外汇收入10.63亿美元，比1997年增长4.1%。

1998年深圳市对外经济贸易

深圳市贸易发展局

进出口贸易 1998年深圳市外贸克服亚洲金融危机的影响，仍保持一定的增长，外贸进出口总值452.76亿美元，比1997年增长0.6%；其中出口总值264.24亿美元，比1997年增长3.6%，进口总值188.52亿美元，比1997年下降3.4%。出口总额占全国的比重14.4%，比1997年提高0.4个百分点。出口总值中，一般贸易出口24.15亿美元，下降26.33%；加工贸易出口227.7亿美元，增长7.12%。进出口总值、出口总值、进口总值三项指标连续六年居全国大中城市首位，荣获省政府颁发的外贸出口贡献奖，同时，作为“1998年在扩大出口和利用外资方面成绩突出的地方外经贸主管部门”受到外经贸部的表彰。

1998年深圳市对外贸易的主要特点是：

（一）贸易顺差扩大。1998年我市外贸顺差达75.5亿美元，比1997年增长23%。

（二）一般贸易出口下降，加工贸易出口稳定增长。一般贸易1998年出口24.15亿美元，比1997年下降26.33%；加工贸易出口227.7亿美元，比1997年增长7.12%，增幅比1997年回落5.3个百分点。

（三）国有外贸企业出口下降，外商投资企业出口稳定增长。国有外贸企业全年出口111.4亿美元，比1997年下降2.8%；外商投资企业全年出口1526亿美元，比1997年增长7.76%。

（四）机电产品出口占主导地位，保持增长。从出口的商品结构看，1998年深圳市机电产品出口达到153.58亿美元，占全市出口比重58.18%，比1997年增长8.48%。其中科技含量高的电讯器材保持较高增长，1998年出口80.6亿美元，增长13.6%。

（五）远洋贸易出口稳定增长。从出口的市场结构看，按运抵国口径统计，1998年远洋贸易出口达到36.53亿美元，比1997年增长18.39%，占深圳市出口比重达13.84%。从市场分布看，对日本、韩国出口下降，对欧美和东盟出口保持增长。按消费国口径统计，1998年深圳对美国、欧盟、东盟出口分别为767354万美元、389317万美元、134973万美元，增长6.01%、3.75%和11.3%；对日本、韩国出口分别为310159万美元、18673万美元，比1997年下降4.98%和20.86%。

（六）1998年累计进口188.5亿美元，比1997

年下降3.4%，持续负增长。虽然进口总值负增长，但占进口总值77.84%的加工贸易有所回升，1998年累计进口146.95亿美元，比1997年增长0.23%。

1998年深圳市进出口的十大贸易伙伴（国家和地区，按消费国口径统计）依次是：美国96亿美元、中国香港85.64亿美元、日本79.65亿美元、中国台湾省43.03亿美元、新加坡20.50亿美元、韩国14.05亿美元、德国14.02亿美元、英国11.72亿美元、荷兰8.47亿美元、泰国7.97亿美元。

出口企业构成 1998年深圳市国有一般贸易出口受金融危机影响最深，1998年出口24.15亿美元，下降26.33%，占深圳市出口总额的9.15%。外商投资企业出口稳定增长，1998年出口152.6亿美元，增长7.76%，占出口总额的57.8%。"三来一补"企业出口87亿美元，增长4.7%，占出口总额的33%。

出口贸易方式 一般贸易出口24.15亿美元，下降26.33%；加工贸易出口227.7亿美元，增长7.12%，占出口总额的86%；其中来料加工出口87亿美元增长4.71%，进料加工出口140.7亿美元，增长8.67%。保税贸易出口（含保税仓和保税区出口）12亿美元，增长12.1%。

出口商品结构 1998年深圳市机电产品出口153.57亿美元，增长8.48%。深圳市出口264亿美元，其中机电产品占153.57亿美元，占全市出口总值58.18%。深圳市最大的出口商品类别为：电讯设备及器材（计算机及配件、通讯器材和电子元器件）出口80.6亿美元，占深圳市出口总值30.5%；文体用品（办公文教体育用品、玩具和旅游用品）出口26.1亿美元，增长9.13%，占出口总值9.8%。出口超10亿美元的商品有8种，依次是电讯设备器材、文体用品、箱包及鞋帽16.2亿美元、家用电器16亿美元、服装14.4亿美元、各类机械12亿美元、钟表10.4亿美元、塑料10.3亿美元。

出口市场结构 至1998年底，深圳与世界上一百五十多个国家和地区建立了经济贸易往来关系，在全球三十多个国家和地区设立了一百多家贸易机构。出口市场分布，主要是出口香港地区227亿美元（运抵国口径，包括转口贸易），占出口总值86%，其中经香港地区转口其他市场的出口占53.5%，在香港地区本地消费和再加工的占32.5%。直接远洋贸易增长迅速，共出口36.53亿美元，增长18.39%，占出口总额的比重由1997年的12%上升为13.84%。深圳十大出口市场（按消费国口径）依次是：美国76.73亿美元、中国香港73.82亿美元、日本31.01亿美元、德国10.63亿美元、英国9.79亿美元、新加坡9.24亿美元、荷兰7.39亿美元、中国台湾省7.28亿美元、法国4.73亿美元、澳大利亚3.33亿美元。

进口市场结构 1998年进口总值188.5亿美元。其中日本位居首位，进口48.63亿美元，占进口总值25.76%，其次是中国台湾省，进口35.74亿美元，占进口总值18.93%，第三位是美国，进口19.26亿美元，占进口总值10.21%。以下分别是：韩国12.18亿美元、中国香港11.81亿美元、新加坡11.26亿美元、泰国6.33亿美元、马来西亚4.52亿美元、德国3.38亿美元、法国3.11亿美元。

进口商品结构 进口商品结构以生产资料为主，进口的十大商品种类分别是：电讯设备及器材57.24亿美元、塑料23.37亿美元、各类机械13亿美元、黑色金属10.88亿美元、纸浆纸张及制品9.35亿美元、有色金属9.32亿美元、纺织品6.95亿美元、未分类商品5.89亿美元、钟表5.06亿美元、化工原料4.96亿美元。

主要进口市场情况表

国别（地区）	进口金额（万美元）	占进口总额（%）
日本	486371	25.76
中国台湾省	357438	18.93
美国	192677	10.21
韩国	121898	6.46
中国香港	118114	6.26
新加坡	112638	5.97
泰国	63304	3.35
马来西亚	45260	2.40
德国	33877	1.79
法国	31125	1.65

主要出口市场情况表

国别（地区）	出口金额（万美元）	占出口总额（%）
美国	767354	29.07
中国香港	738289	27.97
日本	310159	11.75
德国	106366	4.03
英国	97991	3.71
新加坡	92453	3.50
荷兰	73901	2.80
中国台湾省	72864	2.76
法国	47312	1.79
澳大利亚	33315	1.26

出口超1亿美元商品种类

单位：万美元

序号	名　　称	出口额
1	电讯设备及器材	805695
2	文体用品	261042
3	箱包及鞋帽	162135
4	家用电器	159921
5	服装	143939
6	各类机械	119417
7	钟表	103965
8	塑料	103644
9	成套设备	87758
10	纺织品	66400
11	未分类商品	61360
12	日用杂品	61478
13	工艺品类	51146
14	家具类	50590
15	黑色金属	41284
16	照相制版及电影器材	27058
17	自行车类	23170
18	纸浆、纸张及制品	22112
19	船舶	20005
20	日用五金器皿	18269
21	陶瓷类	17428
22	出版物	16121
23	石油及制品	15861

出口超1亿美元商品种类（续）

单位：万美元

序号	名　　称	出口额
24	非金属矿产品及制品	15678
25	化工原料	13772
26	有色金属	13490
27	电子设备及仪器	12305
28	光学仪器	12150
29	食用动物及其产品	11576
30	粮油	10490

进口超1亿美元商品种类

单位：万美元

序号	名　　称	进口额
1	电讯设备及器材	572427
2	塑料	233756
3	各类机械	129954
4	黑色金属	108833
5	纸浆、纸张及制品	93545
6	有色金属	93292
7	纺织品	69536
8	未分类商品	58958
9	钟表	50611
10	化工原料	49602
11	丝织品	40416
12	成套设备	36574
13	石油及制品	36321
14	航空设备	35984
15	木材	25469
16	非金属矿产品及制品	24311
17	畜产品	23690
18	粮油	19535
19	照相制版及电影器材	16034
20	化肥、农药	15370
21	油漆、油墨及染料	14965
22	家用电器	11922
23	服装	10350

对外经济合作　1998年深圳市积极拓展海外市场，1998年新签对外经济合作合同金额971

万美元，下降143.15%，完成营业额1334万美元，增长80.13%；签对外承包工程和劳务合作合同项目120个，金额2619万美元，下降4.9%，完成营业额4196万美元，增长79.0%，在外企业人数850人。深圳市共有驻外企业212家，投资总额12.9亿美元，主要投资在贸易、房地产、通讯、电子及制造等行业，分布在北美、中国香港、独联体地区。

1998年珠海市对外经济贸易

珠海市对外经济贸易委员会

【对外贸易】

进出口总额 1998年珠海市进出口总额为59.17亿美元，比1997年的55.22亿美元增长7.2%

出口总额 出口总额29.95亿美元，比1997年的29.65亿美元增长1%，占全省出口总额的4%。

出口商品结构 初级产品出口额0.4亿美元，占出口总额的1.3%；工业制成品的出口额29.6亿美元，占出口总额的98.7%。

出口额在1000万美元以上的商品情况表

金额分类	商品名称	出口金额（万美元）	占出口总额（%）
1亿美元以上（5种）	服装、各类机械、电讯设备、照相电影器材、家用电器	163018	54.43
5000万～1亿美元（4种）	纺织品、箱包及鞋帽、文体用品、钟表	51137	17.07
1000万～5000万美元（16种）	食用动物及产品、食品及制成品、陶瓷、工艺品类、日用五金器皿、日用杂品、黑色金属、有色金属、非金属矿产品、化工原料、医药原料、船舶、成套设备、工农具、塑料、缝纫机类	49426	16.5
合　计	**25种**	**263581**	**88.01**

出口商品市场 出口商品销往122个国家和地区。

主要出口市场情况表

国别（地区）	出口金额（万美元）	占出口总额（%）
中国香港	190965	63.76
中国澳门	23269	7.77
荷兰	21335	7.12
美国	8789	2.96
日本	7474	2.50
瑞士	3269	1.09
俄罗斯	2673	0.89
德国	2175	0.73
柬埔寨	2100	0.67

主要出口市场情况表（续）

国别（地区）	出口金额（万美元）	占出口总额（%）
新加坡	1615	0.54
合　计	**263575**	**88.01**

进口总额　进口总额29.22亿美元，比1997年的25.56亿美元增长14.3%。

进口商品结构　初级产品进口额9.1亿美元，占进口总额的31%；工业制成品的进口额20.1亿美元，占进口总额的69%。

进口额达1000万美元以上的商品情况表

金额分类	商品名称	进口金额（万美元）	占进口总额（%）
1亿美元以上（5种）	石油制品、电讯设备、各类机械、黑色金属、塑料	157596	53.93
5000万～1亿美元（5种）	有色金属、钟表、化工原料、纸浆纸张、纺织品	33552	11.48
1000万～5000万美元（16种）	食品制成品、饲料、矿产品、木材、纺织原料、丝织品、服装、非金属矿产品及制品、西成药、航空设备、油漆、油墨及染料、铁路与车辆及设备、汽车、电车、摩托车及零件、成套设备、照相制版及电影器材家用电器	35248	12.06
合　计	**26种**	**226396**	**77.48**

进口商品市场　进口商品来自34个国家和地区。

主要进口市场情况表

国别（地区）	进口金额（万美元）	占进口总额（%）
中国香港	181200	62.01
伊　朗	40324	13.80
中国澳门	17875	6.12
日　本	13744	4.70

主要进口市场情况表（续）

国别（地区）	进口金额（万美元）	占进口总额（%）
美　国	6290	2.15
瑞　士	3280	1.12
韩　国	2985	1.02
伊拉克	1647	0.56

主要进口市场情况表（续）

国别（地区）	进口金额（万美元）	占进口总额（%）
英国	1579	0.54
阿根廷	1191	0.41
合　计	**270115**	**92.44**

【利用外资】

珠海市新批利用外资合同300项，合同利用外资5.22亿美元，实际利用外资11.06亿美元，比1997年增长8.1%。

1998年利用外资情况表

利用外资方式	批准签订的合同			实际利用外资	
	项目数（个）	外资金额（万美元）	金额比1997年（±%）	金　额（万美元）	金额比1997年（±%）
对外借款	64	40032	2.6	40032	2.6
外商直接投资	207	37891	-34.5	69570	12.9
合资企业	58	6930	-48.7	17793	0.1
合作企业	21	11992	-34.7	23069	3.9
外资企业	128	18969	-26.1	28708	32.5
外商投资股份制		354			
外商其它投资	29	1056	-31.3	1055	-38.8
补偿贸易	0	0		0	
来料加工	29	1056	-30.7	1055	-38.4
合　计	**300**	**78979**	**19.8**	**110657**	**8.1**

外商直接投资行业　1998年外商直接投资的207个项目中，属生产型项目159个，非生产型项目48个。按行业分，农林牧渔13项，制造业146项，电力、煤气及水的生产供应业1项，建筑业3项，交通运输、仓储及邮电通信业4项，批发和零售贸易、餐饮业10项，房地产业9项，社会服务业20项，卫生体育和社会福利业1项。

外商直接投资来源　外商直接投资来自16个国家和地区，项目主要有来自中国香港78个，合同利用外资15631万美元；中国台湾省28个，合同利用外资473万美元；美国14个，合同利用外资1661万美元；维尔京群岛12个，合同利用外资10654万美元；新加坡7个，合同利用外资2340万美元；日本4个，合同利用外资4573万美元；德国2个，合同利用外资426万美元；英国2个，合同利用外资230万美元；澳大利亚2个，合同利用外资849万美元；开曼群岛2个，合同利用外资407万美元；西萨摩亚2个，合同利用外资2470万美元；卢森堡1个，合同利用外资13万美元；玻利维亚1个，合同利用外资113万美元；巴哈马1个，合同利用外资1972万美元。

外商直接投资企业生产经营情况　截至1998年底，已开业投产的外商投资企业共2578家，1998年总产值302.77亿元人民币，比1997年的299.55亿元人民币增长18.92%；出口销售收入18.0353亿美元，比1997年的18.96亿美元下降4.9%。

【对外经济合作】

承包工程和劳务合作　1998年签订对外承包工程和劳务合作合同147个，与1997年持平；

合同金额5086万美元，比1997年的3407万美元增长49.3%；营业额4205万美元，比1997年的3173万美元增长32.5%；年末在外劳务人员有2839人，比1997年的2721人增加了118人，对外承包工程和劳务人员主要是在中国澳门，其次是越南和柬埔寨。

技术进出口 1998年珠海市技术出口金额21115万美元，其中成套设备生产线出口2个，金额78万美元，三资企业高新技术产品出口20137万美元。1997年出口项目结汇491万美元。出口市场主要集中在中国香港和东南亚的柬埔寨及缅甸。

【其他】

高新技术开发区 珠海国家高新技术产业开发区1998年工业总产值为20.48亿元人民币，比1997年增长12.5%；税利总额8690万元人民币，比1997年增长11.4%；全区高新技术企业和技术含量较高企业的产品产值达4.6亿元人民币，占全区工业总产值的22.5%，比1997年增长27.8%。1998年实际利用外资5729万美元，比1997年减少5%。新批外资企业17家，内联企业20家，注册资金3.25亿元人民币。截至1998年底，累计开发面积8.05平方公里，竣工面积236.4万平方米，各项基础建设投资达3.29亿元。

保税区 1999年5月8日，珠海保税区顺利通过了海关总署的验收，正式开关运作，这标志着珠海保税区开发建设进入了一个全新的阶段。目前已有中国香港、中国澳门、中国台湾省、美国、日本、德国、新加坡、韩国等国家和地区的外商前来考察洽谈，现已运作或正在兴建的项目有：珠海保税区良品计划仓储有限公司、宝丽杜邦建材有限公司、西门子松下电子珠海保税区有限公司、丽珠合成制药厂、珠海保税区置成实业发展有限公司、珠海保税区新中港通讯设备有限公司、珠海保税区建设开发有限公司等。在谈项目十多个，意向性项目四十多个，呈现良好的发展趋势。

涉外旅游 1998年珠海市宾馆共接待过夜国际游客697166人次，比1997年增长14.47%。在国际游客中，外国人69796人次，比1997年增长17.53%；港澳同胞505271人次，比1997年增长17.32%；台湾同胞121584人次，比1997年增长3.16%；华侨515人次，比1997年下降53%；国际旅游外汇收入3.32亿美元，占旅游总收入的45.6%，比1997年增长1%。

1998年汕头市对外经济贸易

汕头市对外经济贸易委员会

【对外贸易】

进出口总额 按海关统计，1998年汕头市进出口总值66.10亿美元，比1997年68.73亿美元下降13.7%。

出口总额 出口总值34.49亿美元，比1997年的42.32亿美元下降18.5%。按贸易方式分，一般贸易出口13.36亿美元，比1997年减45.8%；加工贸易出口195902万美元，比1997年增12.59%；其它15444万美元，比1997年增460%。出口总值占全市国内生产总值423.05亿元（相当于51.16亿美元）的67.4%，占全省出口总额的4.6%。

出口商品结构

出口额在500万美元以上的商品情况表

金额分类	商品名称	出口金额（万美元）	占出口总额（%）
500万～1000万美元（3种）	人造花、铜、贵金属或包贵金属的首饰	2432	0.7
1000万～5000万美元（5种）	纸及纸板、钢材、美容化妆品及护肤品、家具、铝	15925	4.6
5000万～1亿美元（3种）	陶瓷、旅行用品及箱包、鞋类	22627	6.6
1亿美元以上（6种）	服装及衣着附件、机电产品、塑料制品、纺织纱线、织物及制品、玩具、渔农产品	257136	74.5
合　计	**17种**	**298119**	**86.4**

出口商品市场　出口商品销往130个国家和地区。

主要出口市场情况表

国别（地区）	出口金额（万美元）	占出口总额（%）
中国港澳	232123	67.3
美　国	18986	5.5
日　本	12133	3.5
新加坡	8204	2.4
南　非	7441	2.2
印　度	6851	2.0
英　国	5645	1.6
中国台湾省	4895	1.4
韩　国	4841	1.4
越　南	4039	1.2
合　计	**305158**	**88.5**

进口总额　进口总额31.61亿美元，比1997年下降7.7%。主要进口商品20种，金额24.98亿美元，占进口总额79%。

进口商品结构

进口1000万美元以上的商品表

金额分类	商品名称	进口金额（万美元）	占进口总额（%）
1000～5000万美元（8种）	己内酰胺、塑料制品、棉机织物、针织或钩编织物、羊毛（包括羊毛条）、医药品、涂复或浸渍塑料的织物、纺织用人造纤维	20644	6.53

进口1000万美元以上的商品表

金额分类	商品名称	进口金额（万美元）	占进口总额（%）
5000万～1亿美元（5种）	鱼农产品、铜、合成纤维长丝机织物、仅由木质薄板制的胶合板、成品油	38280	12.1
1亿美元以上（7种）	初级形态的塑料、机电产品、钢材、纸及纸板（未切成形的）、塑料薄膜、铝、合成纤维纱线	190903	60.4
合　计	**23种**	**249827**	**79**

进口商品市场　进口商品来自80个国家和地区。

主要进口市场情况表

国别（地区）	进口金额（万美元）	占进口总额（%）
韩　国	103227	32.7
日　本	37288	11.8
中国台湾省	33929	10.7
中国香港	24310	7.7
美　国	16372	5.2
俄罗斯	15292	4.8
印度尼西亚	14912	4.7
马来西亚	13603	4.3

主要进口市场情况表（续）

国别（地区）	进口金额（万美元）	占进口总额（%）
德　国	7459	2.4
泰　国	6877	2.2
合　计	**273269**	**86.5**

【利用外资】

汕头市签订利用外资项目302项，合同外资金额4.95亿美元，实际利用外资10.39亿美元。

1998年利用外资情况表

利用外资方式	批准签订的合同			实际利用外资	
	项目数（个）	外资金额（万美元）	金额比1997年（±%）	金额（万美元）	金额比1997年（±%）
对外借款	5	5209	60.28	7729	23.45
外商直接投资	215	40032	4.9	94104	0.43
合资企业	42	6082	47.82	18135	35.05
合作企业	41	15374	32.24	40169	18.81
外资企业	132	18576	24.85	35800	11.97
外商其他投资	82	4296	5.87	2070	78.14

1998 年利用外资情况表（续）

利用外资方式	批准签订的合同			实际利用外资	
	项目数（个）	外资金额（万美元）	金额比1997年（±%）	金 额（万美元）	金额比1997年（±%）
国际租赁					
补偿贸易	26	3560	0.84	1404	148.94
加工装配	56	736	24.44	666	11.37
合 计	**302**	**49537**	**7.75**	**103903**	**2.75**

外商直接投资行业 在外商直接投资的215个项目中，属生产型项目170项，非生产型项目45个。按行业分，农林牧渔业12项，制造业170项，交通运输、仓储及邮电通信业4项，批发和零售贸易、餐饮业1项，房地产6项，社会服务业3项，卫生、体育和社会福利业1项，其它行业18项。

外商直接投资来源 外商直接投资来自12个国家和地区。合同外资额居前十位的是：中国香港167项，23095万美元；维尔京群岛4017万美元（增资）；新加坡11项，3633万美元；巴哈马2970万美元（增资）；中国台湾省22项，2496万美元；英国1280万美元（增资）；加拿大2项，848万美元；马来西亚1项，582万美元；法国3项，313万美元；美国6项，294万美元。

外商直接投资企业生产经营情况 截至1998年底，已批准的外商投资企业共5089家，1998年总产值为150.91亿元，比1997年123.33亿元增长7.82%；销售（营业）收入141.67亿元，比1997年114.05增长24.2%，其中出口销售收入12.57亿美元，比1997年增长34.9%，三资企业盈亏总额11466万元，比1997年盈利3226万元增长255.4%。

【保税区】

1998年汕头保税区坚持“实业兴区”发展战略，加大政策宣传力度，经济运行呈健康发展态势。1998年共引进实业性项目36家，投资总额36139万美元协议利用外资总额22409万美元，批准成立企业181家，比1997年增长57.39%，其中，外商投资企业28家，比1997年增长33%；投资总额12347万美元，比1997年增长15%；合同外资7596万美元，比1997年增长147%；内资企业150家，比1997年增长76.48%；投资总额和注册资本总额为37875万元，比1997年增长53.22%。其中，私营企业107家，注册资本26683万美元。1998年进出口贸易总额1.66亿美元，比1997年减少2.4%；工业产值现行价3.8亿美元，1997年增长18.7%。

【对外经济合作】

1998年对外签订劳务合作合同8个，合同金额180万美元，营业额219万美元，1998年派出劳务人员169人，年末在外人数443人。

劳务人员主要派往中国澳门、越南、毛里求斯、泰国、新加坡、马来西亚、牙买加、柬埔寨、圣卢西亚、美国、日本、科威特等国家和地区，主要从事制衣、毛织、建筑、饮食、捕捞、维修等工作。

【港口运输】

汕头港共有5000吨以上泊位28个，其中万吨以上泊位9个，最大靠泊能力3.5万吨。1997年实际完成货物吞吐量1300万吨，比1997年1360万吨下降4.5%，其中，完成外贸进出口货物吞吐量1290万吨（进口1167万吨，出口123万吨）。

1998年湛江市对外经济贸易

湛江市对外经济贸易委员会

【对外贸易】

进出口总额 1998年湛江市进出口总额150420万美元，比1997年80508万美元增长86.84%。

出口总额 出口总额41411万美元，比1997年45125万美元下降8.23%，占全市国内生产总值365.4亿元（相当于44.13亿美元）的9.38%。占全省出口总额0.55%。

出口商品结构 初级产品8593万美元，占出口总额20.75%，工业制成品32818万美元，占出口总额79.25%，比1997年增长6.28%。

出口额在1000万美元以上商品情况表

金额分类	商 品 名 称	出口金额（万美元）	占出口总额（%）
1000万～3000万美元（4种）	石油及制品、工农具类、化工产品类、五金矿产类	6985	16.87
3000万美元以上（7种）	纺织丝绸类、轻工业品类、家电设备、服装类、土产畜产类、精油食品类、工艺品类	32869	79.37
合 计	**11种**	**39854**	**96.24**

出口商品市场 出口商品销往84个国家和地区。

主要出口市场情况表

国 别（地区）	出口金额（万美元）	占出口总额（%）
中国香港	24104	58.21
美 国	3862	9.33
日 本	3795	9.16
中国台湾省	964	2.33
越 南	902	2.18
德 国	880	2.13
韩 国	807	1.95
新加坡	678	1.64
法 国	622	1.50
荷 兰	425	1.03
合 计	**37039**	**89.44**

进口总额 进口总额109009万美元，比1997年35383万美元增长208.1%

进口商品结构 初级产品进口额104593万美元，占进口总额95.95%；工业制成品进口额

4416 万美元，占进口总额 4.05%。

进口额在 500 万美元以上商品情况表

金额分类	商品名称	进口金额（万美元）	占进口总额（%）
500 万～1000 万美元（1 种）	五金矿产类（钢材）	657	0.60
1000～3000 万美元（3 种）	粮油食品类（小麦） 纺织丝绸类（棉花） 化工产品原料（丙烯）	6348	5.82
3000 万美元以上（2 种）	原油、液化石油汽	99912	91.65
合计	**6 种**	**106917**	**98.07**

进口商品市场 进口商品来自 21 个国家和地区

主要进口市场情况表

国别（地区）	进口金额（万美元）	占进口总额（%）
澳大利亚	86173	79.05
也门	10408	9.55
中国香港	8461	7.76
美国	991	0.91
日本	155	0.14
中国澳门	110	0.10
俄罗斯	103	0.09
南非	83	0.03
比利时	30	0.03
中国台湾省	27	0.02
合计	**106541**	**97.74**

技术进出口 1998 年湛江市技术进出口总额 1213.7 万美元，比 1997 年的 1641.53 万美元下降 26.06%

技术进出 签订技术引进合同 3 个，合同金额 869.56 万美元，比 1997 年的 829 万美元增长 4.89%。引进技术来自法国和芬兰。行业系轻工和化肥生产。

技术出口 签订技术设备出口合同 7 个，合同金额 344.14 万美元，比 1997 年的 812.53 万美元下降 57.65%，主要出口设备带技术的项目有生产酒精、方便面、腰果加工成套设备、农用运输车、高压电器设备等。分别出口到英国、越南、马来西亚、伊朗和中东地区的国家。

【利用外资】

外商直接投资行业 在外商直接投资的 37 个项目中，生产型项目 33 个，非生产型项目 4 个。按行业分，渔业 2 个，制造业 31 个，建筑业 1 个，房地产业 1 个，餐饮业 1 个，社会服务业 1 个。

外商直接投资来源 按批准的合同统计，外商直接投资来自 13 个国家和地区。主要有中国香港 26 个，2947 万美元；芬兰 1 个，443 万美元；美国 2 个，438 万美元；中国台湾省 4 个，339 万美元；新加坡 2 个，189 万美元；加拿大 1 个，16 万美元；法国 1 个，10 万美元。

外商直接投资企业生产经营情况 截至 1998 年底，已开业投产的外商投资企业 558 家，1998 年销售（营业）收入 55.54 亿元，比 1997 年下降 9.6%。其中，出口销售收入 7916 万美元，比1997年下降54%。外商投资企业盈利总额11417万元，比1997年下降43.2%，亏损总额27800万元，比1997年增长18.3%。湛江市外商投资企业盈亏相抵利润总额－16383万元，比1997年的3378万元增长385%。

1998年利用外资情况表

利用外资方式	批准签订的合同			实际利用外资	
	项目数（个）	外资金额（万美元）	金额比1997年（±%）	金　额（万美元）	金额比1997年（±%）
外商直接投资	37	5507	－50.7	10494	3.9
合资企业	17	2490	－67.0	6011	－10.9
合作企业	7	375	－75.9	2906	9.8
外资企业	13	2642	－27.3	1577	121.8
加工装配	42			20	
合　计	**79**	**5507**	**－51.5**	**10514**	**4，19**

【其他】

1998年湛江市经济技术开发区工业总产值60.76亿元，比1997年增长7.9%。固定资产投资完成总额10772万元，比1997年下降37.7%，其中：基本建设投资1300万元。

1998年新批准外商直接投资项目15个，合同外资金额5167万美元，比1997年下降23%，实际利用外资6972万美元，比1997年下降34.2%。投产的外商投资企业89家，1998年工业产值36.25亿元，占全区工业总产值59.66%。全区外贸进出口总额8999万美元，其中：出口额8360万美元，比1997年下降22.6%；进口额639万美元。比1997年下降84.89%。

对外经贸洽谈会　1998年湛江市积极组织和参加对外招商引资洽谈活动，先后参加了在东莞市举办的1998广东台商投资介绍会、在香港举办的1998广东高新技术项目洽 谈会，在美国举办的1998广东（洛杉机）经济技术贸易洽谈会。大力宣传湛江投资环境，加强同工商界、跨国公司的联系，引进了一批基础设施、科技含量较高的项目，取得较好成果，共签订利用外资合同、协议58个，总投资额44305万美元，协议利用外资29308万美元。湛江市参加第83届和84届广州中国出口商品交易会，共成交出口金额4900万美元，比1997年的5100万美元下降3.92%。

港口运输　湛江市共有港口码头泊位128个，港口吞吐能力2874万吨，其中，万吨以上泊位24个，最大靠泊能力7万吨，1998年完成货物吞吐量2190万吨，比1997年的2428.4万吨下降9.8%。其中外贸进出口货物吞吐量928.7万吨（出口265.3万吨，进口663.4万吨），占全年货物吞吐量42.4%。

涉外旅游　1998年湛江市接待来自18个国家和中国香港、澳门、台湾省地区的境外旅游者5.32万人次，比1997年3.98万人次增长33.67%。旅游收入42516万元，比1997年44867万元下降5.24%。

1998年广西壮族自治区对外经济贸易

广西壮族自治区对外贸易经济合作厅

【对外贸易】

进出口总额 1998年广西壮族自治区进出口总额298378万美元，比1997年的306821万美元下降2.8%。

出口总额 出口总额241817万美元，比1997年的238266万美元增长1.5%。其中一般贸易出口202574万美元，占出口总额的68%，比1997年减少2.4%；易货贸易出口24991万美元，占出口总额的12.3%，比1997年增长2.8%；进料加工出口22318万美元，比1997年增长64.4%，占出口总额的9.2%；来料加工出口14161万美元，比1997年下降40.6%，占出口总额的5.9%。1998年出口总额占广西壮族自治区国内生产总值2181.88亿元的9.2%，比1997年减少0.36个百分点。

出口商品结构 初级产品出口额40445万美元，占出口总额的16.7%；工业制成品出口额201372万美元，占出口总额的83.3%；其中机电产品出口额21087万美元，占出口总额的8.3%。

出口额在1000万美元以上的商品有32种，出口金额141572万美元，占出口总额的58.54%。

出口额在1000万美元以上的商品情况表

金额分类	商品名称	出口金额（万美元）	占出口总额（%）
1000万－2000万美元（14种）	棉布、活猪、锰铁、收录两用机、牛革皮、纸张、锡材、干电池、除草剂、电子元器件、柴油机、塑料、生铁、宝石	19198	7.94
2000万－3000万美元（7种）	硅、硅锰合金、滑石块（粉）氧化锌、锌、金首饰、木材	16501	6.82
3000万美元以上（11种）	服装、锡、松香、陶瓷、人造棉布、重晶石、水泥、罐头、鞭炮烟花、鞋、真丝领带	105873	43.78
合　计	**32种**	**141572**	**58.54**

出口商品市场 出口商品销往 118 个国家和地区。其中十大主要出口市场出口额 216341 万美元，占出口总额的 89.47%。

主要出口市场情况表

国别（地区）	出口金额（万美元）	占出口总额（%）
中国香港	117378	48.54
越　南	43699	18.07
美　国	18435	7.62
日　本	11902	4.92
荷　兰	6755	2.79
中国台湾省	5134	2.12
德　国	5083	2.10
英　国	3084	1.28

主要出口市场情况表（续）

国别（地区）	出口金额（万美元）	占出口总额（%）
泰　国	2543	1.05
法　国	2328	0.96
合　计	**216341**	**89.47**

进口总额 进口总额 56561 万美元，比 1997 年的 68555 万美元下降 17.5%。

进口商品结构 初级产品进口额 17575 万美元，占进口总额的 31.1%；工业制成品进口额 38985 万美元，占进口总额的 68.9%。

进口额在 500 万美元以上的商品有 14 种，进口金额 18744 万美元，占进口总额的 33.14%。

进口额在 500 万美元以上商品情况表

金额分类	商品名称	进口金额（万美元）	占进口总额（%）
500－1000 万美元（4 种）	鱼粉、豆油、菜油、液化石油气	2899	5.13
1000 万美元以上（10 种）	棕榈油、豆粕、硬锰砂、钢材、纸张、铁矿砂、电子元器件、录音机零件、钻石、塑料	15845	28.01
合　计	**14 种**	**18744**	**33.14**

进口商品市场 进口商品来自 41 个国家和地区。其中十大主要进口市场进口额 49893 万美元，占进口总额的 88.21%。

主要进口市场情况表

国别（地区）	进口金额（万美元）	占进口总额（%）
中国香港	20743	36.67
越　南	13447	23.77
日　本	3292	5.82
美　国	2586	4.57

主要进口市场情况表

国别（地区）	进口金额（万美元）	占进口总额（%）
德　国	2320	4.1
南　非	1980	3.5
芬　兰	1569	2.77
意大利	1396	2.47
加　蓬	1351	2.39
澳大利亚	1209	2.14
合　计	**49893**	**88.21**

边境贸易 据广西壮族自治区外经贸厅统计，1998年广西壮族自治区对越边境贸易进出口总额36740万美元，比1997年的35734万美元增长2.8%，占广西壮族自治区进出口总额的12.3%。其中出口额24991万美元，比1997年的21550万美元增长16%，占广西壮族自治区出口总额的10.33%；进口额11749万美元，比1997年的14184万美元下降17.2%，占广西壮族自治区进口总额的20.8%。

【利用外资】

1998年，广西壮族自治区批准签订外商投资项目合同266个，比1997年减少23个；其中合资项目101个，合作项目60个，独资项目105个。合同外资额6.42亿美元，比1997年的14.7亿美元下降56.3%；实际直接利用外资金额8.86亿美元，比1997年的8.8亿美元增长0.68%。

1998年利用外资情况表

利用外资方式	批准签订的合同			实际利用外资	
	项目数（个）	外资金额（万美元）	金额比1997年（±%）	金 额（万美元）	金额比1997年（±%）
外商直接投资	266	64242	-56.33	88613	0.68
合资企业	101	10862		30947	
合作企业	60	28059		17623	
外资企业	105	25321		40043	
外商投资股份制					
合作开发					
其他					
合 计	**266**	**64242**		**88613**	

外商直接投资行业 在1998年批准的外商直接投资项目中，生产型项目202项，合同外资额44416万美元；非生产型项目64项，合同外资额19806万美元。按行业分，农、林、牧、渔业21项，合同外资额3680万美元；采掘业3项，37万美元；制造业154项，16306万美元；电力、煤气及水的生产和供应业6项，14084万美元；建筑业10项，7584万美元；交通运输、仓储业8项，2725万美元；餐饮业5项，55万美元；房地产业22项，6304万美元；社会服务业28项，8981万美元；教育、文化艺术业1项，91万美元；科学研究和综合技术服务业3项，1994万美元；其它行业5项，2381万美元。与1997年相比，制造业项目增长，能源、基础设施项目下降，基础设施建设和工业制造业仍是外资主要投向。

外商直接投资来源 外商直接投资来自中国香港、中国台湾省、美国、加拿大、法国、越南、泰国、英国、维尔京群岛等23个国家和地区。其中合同外资额较大的国家和地区有：中国香港133项，合同外资额23977万美元；中国台湾省43项，5579万美元；美国16项，4738万美元；加拿大11项，1726万美元；维尔京群岛10项，11607万美元；法国3项，5106万美元；越南3项，4690万美元；泰国2项，1220万美元；英国2项，1047万美元；毛里求斯1项，1562万美元。

【对外经济合作】

承包工程和劳务合作 1998年广西壮族自治区签订对外承包工程和劳务合同作项目84个，合同总金额7493万美元，比1997年的12122万美元下降38.2%；完成营业额2854万美元，比1997年下降28%；年末在国（境）外劳务人员840人，比1997年减少1456人。对外承包和劳务合作业务主要分布在中国澳门、越南、柬埔寨、泰国、马来西亚、孟加拉国、巴基斯坦、斯里兰卡、肯尼亚、安哥拉、纳米比亚、法属波里尼西亚等22个国家和地区。

接受经济援助 1998年，广西壮族自治区新获批准的接受国际无偿援助项目11个，援助金额97万美元。同时，日本政府无偿援助广西壮族自治区粮食增产项目、联合国开发署无偿援助广西壮族自治区扶贫项目以及一批接受国际无偿援助项目继续顺利实施。

对外投资 1998年广西壮族自治区在境外举办非贸易性企业三家，合同总额218万美元；其中中方协议投资145万美元，占合同总额的66.5%。这三家企业分布在澳大利亚、新加坡和马来西亚。主要生产销售兽用药品、建筑机械以及开采矿山等。

【其他】

对外经贸洽谈会 1998年广西壮族自治区组织了五次重大的招商洽谈活动。分别是：8月赴英国伦敦招商会，9月参加厦门’98第二届中国投资贸易洽谈会，10月在广东东莞举办’98广西壮族自治区对外经济技术合作交流会，11月在德国汉堡举办’98广西壮族自治区投资贸易洽谈会，12月在南宁举办广西壮族自治区成立四十周年大庆经贸洽谈会。五次招商会共鉴订外商投资项目合同165个，合同外资额7.75亿美元；鉴订协议172项，协议外资额17.6亿美元；内联141项，总投资额53亿美元。

港口运输 1998年广西壮族自治区外贸运输总量643.1万吨，比1997年下降4.88%。其中出口量390.1万吨，进口量253万吨。按运输方式分，海运量620.42万吨，陆运量22.67万吨，空运量124吨。

涉外旅游 1998年广西壮族自治区共接待国（境）外旅游人数52.43万人次，比1997年下降8.5%。其中接待国外游客27.94万人次，比1997年下降17.9%。1998年国际旅游收入11.95亿元，比1997年的14.8亿元下降19.3%

1998年北海市对外经济贸易

北海市对外贸易经济合作局

【对外贸易】

进出口总额 1998年广西壮族自治区北海市进出口总额为14409.7万美元，比1997年的15858万美元减少9.1%。

出口总额 1998年全市出口总额10529万美元，比1997年的8375万美元增长25.72%，占全市国内生产总值126.09亿元（相当于152302万美元）的6.91%，占广西壮族自治区出口总额24.2亿美元的4.35%。

出口商品结构 初级产品出口额551万美元，占出口总额的5.23%；工业制成品出口额9978万美元，占全市出口总额的94.77%。

出口额在100万美元以上的商品情况表

金额分类	商品名称	出口金额（万美元）	占出口总额（%）
1000万美元以上（3种）	鞭炮烟花、皮革及制品、除草剂	7066	67.11
100万美元～1000万美元（12种）	梭织服装、纺织品、针织服装、杀虫剂、日用杂品、水产品、汽车零件、集装箱、过磷酸钙、瓷土、有色金属、塑料制品	2774	26.34
合计	**15种**	**9840**	**93.35**

主要出口商品市场情况表

国别（地区）	出口金额（万美元）	占出口总额（%）
中国香港	6243	59.29
美国	2721	25.84
越南	808	7.67
日本	279	2.65
孟加拉国	160	1.52
合计	**10211**	**96.97**

进口总额 1998年全市进口总额3881万美元，比1997年7483万美元下降48.14%。

进口商品结构 初级产品进口额922万美元，占进口总额的23.76%，工业制成品进口总额2959万美元，占进口总额76.24%。

进口额在50万美元以上的商品情况表

金额分类	商品名称	进口金额（万美元）	占进口总额（%）
1000万美元以上（1种）	农药	1252	32.26
100万～1000万美元（5种）	畜产品、电子成套设备、化工原料、棕榈油、棉布	2013	51.87
50万～100万美元（4种）	废纸、卫生洁具设备、低压聚乙烯、液化石油气	302	7.78
合计	**10种**	**3567**	**91.91**

主要进口商品市场情况表

国别（地区）	进口金额（万美元）	占进口总额（%）
中国香港	2953	76.09
日　本	522	13.45
越　南	150	3.86
美　国	86	2.22
合　计	**3711**	**95.62**

【利用外资】

1998年全市共批准签订利用外资项目合同24个,比1997年的18个增长33.33%。新批项目合同投资总额8802万美元,比1997年的11527万美元下降23.6%,合同外资额6078万美元,比1997年的2207万美元增长175.4%,实际利用外资5440万美元,比1997年的4502万美元增长20.8%。其中:中外合资项目13个,合同外资金额807万美元,合作项目2个,合同外资金额1425万美元,独资项目9个,合同外资金额3846万美元。

外商直接投资行业　外商直接投资项目中生产型项目20个,非生产型项目4个,按行业划分;工业制造业12项、渔业2项、建筑业3项、房地产业2项、社会服务业4项、煤气生产业1项。

外商直接投资来源　外商直接投资主要来自亚洲、欧洲、北美洲、拉丁美洲四大洲13个国家和地区，具体为：中国香港13项，合同外资金额1422万美元，实际利用外资金额1522万美元；台湾1项，合同外资金额12万美元，实际外资金额945万美元；越南、新加坡、马来西亚3个东南亚联盟国家3项，合同外资金额2635万美元，实际外资金额9万美元；日本1项，合同外资金额56万美元，实际外资金额56万美元；韩国1项，合同外资金额29万美元；德国、意大利二个欧盟国家2项，合同外资金额98万美元，美国、加拿大、委内瑞拉、维尔京群岛共4项，合同外资金额1956万美元，实际外资金额236万美元。

外商直接投资企业生产经营情况　截至1998年底，全市开业投产经营并参加年检的外商投资企业260家，比1997年的324家减少64家。投资总额115638万美元，全年出口总额5001万美元，比1997年的5864万美元下降14.72%，资产总额882573万元，负债总额632023万元，长期负债总额112751万元，纳税总额4595万元，从业人员10997人，其中外籍职工人数354人，外资到位率44.27%。

对外商贸洽谈会　1998年9月、10月、12月，北海市分别在福建厦门、广东东莞、广西南宁参与广西壮族自治区组织和举办的大型招商会和商贸洽谈会，共签订利用外资项目13项，其中合同类10项，合同投资总额11192万美元，外资额9958万美元，协议类项目3个，投资总额20512万美元，外资额9800万美元。

【对外经济合作】

承包工程和劳务合作　1998年签订对外承包工程和劳务合作合同项目2个，合同总金额97万美元，比1997年的60万美元减少65%。当年共派出各类劳务人员6人，年末在国（境）外各类劳务人员达32人，主要派驻国别为柬埔寨。

对外投资　1998年北海对外投资项目主要为柬埔寨农业综合开发项目，已由北海海外经济技术合作公司累计完成投资近200万美元，目前项目已完成了土地租用手续，进入对外招商和全面开发启动阶段。

【其他】

港口运输　1998年北海市港口吞吐总量为301万吨，比1997年的266万吨增长13.16%，其中完成外贸进出口货物吞吐总量130.42万吨，比1997年的131.04万吨下降0.47%（出口量69.65万吨，比1997年的75.74万吨减少8.04%，进口量为60.77万吨，比1997年的55.3万吨增长5.47%）。

涉外旅游　1998年北海市旅游业取得新成绩，所经营的北海—越南海防、下龙湾国际旅游航线正式投入运营，目前运营正常，市场前景看好。全年入境到北海观光旅游及考察的国内外游客达257万人次，比1997年的228万人次增长12.72%，旅游总收入6.73亿元，比1997年的5.8亿元增长16.03%，其中接待境外旅游人数1.03

万人次，比1997年的7846人次增长31.28%，国际旅游外汇收入270.03万美元，比1997年的252万美元增长7.14%。

1998年海南省对外经济贸易

海南省商贸经济合作厅

【对外贸易】

进出口总额 1998年海南省进出口总额为190913万美元，比1997年的194901万美元下降2.05%。

出口总额 出口总额88463万美元，比1997年88966万美元下降0.56%，占全省国内生产总值438.92亿元（相当于53.02亿美元）的16.69%。

出口商品结构 初级产品出口额18439万美元，占出口总额的20.84%；工业制成品出口额70024万美元，占出口总额的79.16%。

出口商品涉及57个大类996种。

出口额在1000万美元以上商品情况表

金额分类	商品名称	出口金额（万美元）	占出口总额（%）
10000万美元以上（1种）	天然气	11903	13.46
5000～10000万美元（2种）	西成药、其他生化药物	15514	17.54
1000～5000万美元（8种）	木材、硅锰合金、工艺品、锡锭、木家具、玩具、锑、硅	10577	11.97
合　计	**11种**	**37994**	**42.97**

出口商品市场 出口商品销住129个国家（地区）。

主要出口市场情况表

国别（地区）	出口金额（万美元）	占出口总额（%）
中国香港	29737	33.62
美　国	8527	9.64
日　本	6871	7.77
越　南	3112	3.52

主要出口市场情况表（续）

国别（地区）	出口金额（万美元）	占出口总额（%）
荷　兰	2098	2.37
韩　国	1889	2.14
德　国	1879	2.12
英　国	1533	2.74

主要出口市场情况表（续）

国别（地区）	出口金额（万美元）	占出口总额（%）
中国台湾省	1028	1.73
法　国	1011	1.14
合　计	**57685**	**65.21**

进口总额　1998年海南进口总额102450万美元，比1997年的105935美元下降3.28%。

进口商品结构　进口商品涉及29个大类54种商品。其中，初级产品进口额13144万美元，占进口总额12.83%；工业制成品进口额89306万美元，占进口总额的87.17%。

主要进口商品情况表

金额分类	商　品　名　称	进口金额（万美元）	占进口总额（%）
10000万美元以上（4种）	钢铁；航空器及其零件；锅炉、机器、机械器具及其零件；蛋白类物质、改性淀粉、胶	59484	58.06
1000－10000万美元的（11种）	有机化学品；矿物燃料及矿物油；电机、电气设备及其零件；肥料；动、植物油；药品；车辆及其零附件；塑料及其制品；谷物；木及木制品	32905	32.12
合　计	**15种**	**92389**	**90.18**

进口商品市场　进口商品来自27个国家（地区）。

主要进口市场情况表

国别（地区）	进口金额（万美元）	占进口总额（%）
美　国	32873	32.09
日　本	13983	13.65
俄罗斯	13716	13.39
韩　国	9392	9.17
新加坡	4117	4.02
意大利	3706	3.62
台湾省	3451	3.37
德　国	2838	2.77

主要进口市场情况表（续）

国别（地区）	进口金额（万美元）	占进口总额（%）
香　港	2263	2.21
泰　国	1846	1.80
马来西亚	1623	1.58
荷　兰	1262	1.23
越　南	1246	1.22
加拿大	1241	1.21
合　计	**93557**	**91.32**

技术进出口　1998年海南省技术进出口合同总额为8884万美元，比1997年的1299万美元增长584%。其中签订引进技术和进口设备合同项目数1个，合同金额166万美元，比1997年的1139万美元下降85%。签订技术出口合同项目数1个，合同金额8718万美元，比1997年的160万美元增长5348%。

【利用外资】

1998 年利用外资情况表

利用外资方式	批准签订的合同			实际利用外资	
	项目数（个）	外资金额（万美元）	金额比 1997 年（±%）	金 额（万美元）	金额比 1997 年（±%）
对外借款	10	20100	-	38000	-7.32
外商直接投资	174	14321	-49	71715	1.65
合资企业	52	7629	-56	27136	-9.11
合作企业	7	826	-80	1472	-13.00
外资企业	115	5866	-14	38379	6.53
外商投资股份制企业	-	-	-	4728	58.66
合 计	358	34421	20051	109715	-1.65

1998 年外商直接投资主要行业情况表

投 资 产 业	项目数	外资金额	外商直接投资总额（%）
第一产业	54	6294	8.78
其中：农业	36	1453	2.03
第二产业	72	21362	29.78
其中：（一）工业	64	20937	29.19
采掘业	2	144	0.20
制造业	62	20793	28.99
（二）建筑业	8	425	0.59
第三产业	48	44059	61.44
其中：交通运输仓储业	3	3626	5.06
批零贸易餐饮业	7	2551	3.56
房地产业	9	10600	14.78
其他服务行业	29	27282	38.04
合 计	174	71715	100

外商直接投资分国别（地区）主要情况表

国别（地区）	项目数	外资金额（万美元）	占外商直接投资总额（%）
中国香港	59	30788	42.93
美 国	8	12616	17.59
中国台湾省	55	8576	11.96
日 本	8	4131	5.76

外商直接投资分国别（地区）主要情况表（续）

国别（地区）	项目数	外资金额（万美元）	占外商直接投资总额（%）
英 国	6	1867	2.60
中国澳门	3	1864	2.35
泰 国	5	1289	1.80
马来西亚	3	830	1.16

【对外经济合作】

承包工程和劳务合作 1998年签订对外承包工程和劳务合作合同项目3个，合同金额80.46万美元，比1997年的843万美元下降90%；营业额676.82万美元，比1997年的92.3万美元增长813%。1998年共派出劳务21人（次），年末在外人数58人。

对外经济技术援助 承担援外项目5个，合同金额为6280万元人民币，受援国别和项目分别是柬埔寨的一个农业中学项目（2265万元人民币），援加纳职业技术培训中心项目（1174万元人民币）、援朝鲜2万吨化肥项目（2522万元人民币）、援马耳他一般物资项目（287万元人民币）。

接受经济援助 接受国际无偿援助项目3个，援助金额743万美元。受援项目和金额分别是日本援助的海南省粮食增产项目，受援金额539万美元；海南省少数民族示范中学项目，金额为100万美元。澳大利亚政府援助的海南省昌江县王下乡饮水工程项目，金额4.3万美元。

对外投资 1998年共在海外举办企业和办事处2个，投资金额40万美元，投资国别为斯里兰卡和马其顿。

【其他】

港口运输 1998年完成外贸进出口货运量412万吨，比1997年的640万吨下降35.6%，其中进口运量138万吨，下降29.7%，出口运量274万吨，下降38.2%。

涉外旅游 全年宾馆接待游客过夜人数855.97万人次，比上年增长8.1%，其中接待海外游客39.42万人次，比上年下降43.4%。全年海外旅游者消费7.99亿元，下降4.9%。

1998年重庆市对外经济贸易

重庆市对外经济贸易委员会

【对外贸易】

进出口总额 1998年重庆市进出口总额为103370万美元，比1997年的163178万美元下降38.4%。

出口总额 出口总额51395万美元，比1997年的78489万美元下降34.1%，占全市国内生产总值1434亿元的2.98%。

出口商品结构 初级产品出口额为5867万美元，占出口总额的11.42%；工业制成品的出口额为45528万美元，占出口总额的88.58%。

出口额在500万美元以上的商品情况表

金额分类	商 品 名 称	出口金额（万美元）	占出口总额（%）
500万～1000万美元（8种）	棉针织女三角裤、化纤男防寒上衣、双筒望远镜、未锻轧锌、胱氨酸骨粉及骨废料、重氮化合物、纯铝板材	5544	10.79

出口额在500万美元以上的商品情况表（续）

金额分类	商品名称	出口金额（万美元）	占出口总额（%）
1000万美元以上（6种）	聚乙烯醇、棉针织女长裤、肝素纳、摩托车、热轧非卷材、猪鬃	8119	15.80
合计	**14种**	**13663**	**26.58**

出口商品市场 出口商品销往128个国家和地区。

主要出口市场情况表

国别（地区）	出口金额（万美元）	占出口总额（%）
香港	15773	30.69
日本	6294	12.25
美国	5565	10.83
德国	2991	5.82
韩国	2134	4.15
荷兰	2134	4.15
意大利	1659	3.23
英国	1018	1.98
合计	**37568**	**73.10**

进口总额 进口总额为51975万美元，比1997年的84689万美元下降42.11%。

进口商品结构 初级产品进口额为3616万美元，占进口总额的6.96%，工业制成品进口额为48359万美元，占进口总额的93.04%。

进口额在500万美元以上的商品情况表

商品分类	商品名称	进口金额（万美元）	占进口总额（%）
500万～2000万美元（2种）	有机化学品、塑料及其制品	1375	2.65
2000万～20000万美元（6种）	钢铁及其制品、汽车及其零件、金属矿砂、光学仪器及设备、电气设备及其零件、橡胶及其制品	17684	34.02
20000万美元以上（1种）	机器设备及其零件	28952	55.70
合计	**9种**	**48011**	**92.37**

进口商品市场 进口商品来自38个国家和地区。

主要进口市场情况表

国别（地区）	进口金额（万美元）	占进口总额（%）
日　本	29585	56.92
中国香港	4007	7.71
德　国	3092	5.95
美　国	3031	5.83
澳大利亚	2778	5.34
意大利	1328	2.56
中国台湾省	1210	2.33
韩　国	1010	1.94
合　计	**46041**	**88.58**

【利用外资】

全市外商直接投资实际到位资金和合同外资分别比上年增长11%和3%。诺基亚、ABB、爱立信、施格兰、美标、利宝、罗克威尔等世界著名跨国公司也来渝投资，截至1998年底，世界500强企业中已有26户来渝落户，其中有16户投资兴办了26个项目。

1998年利用外资情况表

利用外资方式	批准签订的合同			实际利用外资	
	项目数（个）	外资金额（万美元）	金额比1997年（±%）	金　额（万美元）	金额比1997年（±%）
对外借款	5	25861	52.8	9026	-75.2
外商直接投资	222	47577	3.39	43107	11.46
合资企业	129	26305	45.93	28586	73.54
合作企业	7	4599	-74.89	4493	-71.64
外资企业	86	16673	72.35	10028	57.72
外商其他投资	36	1661	-88.27	1572	-86.21
加工装配	36	1661	-58.95	1572	-49.73
合　计	**263**	**75099**	**-2.6**	**53705**	**-37.9**

外商直接投资行业　在外商直接投资项目中，生产型项目139个，非生产型项目83个。合同外资在1000万美元以上的行业分布为：农林牧渔业5个；合同外资金额1087万美元；制造业120个，合同外资金额2.4亿美元；建筑业13个，合同外资金额3124万美元；批发和零售贸易、餐饮业11个，合同外资金额1184万美元；房地产业40个，合同外资金额1.07亿美元；社会服务业23个，合同外资金额6505万美元。

外商直接投资来源　外商直接投资来自28个国家和地区。投资额居前5位的国家和地区是：香港87项，1.49亿美元；日本12项，8957万美元；美国24项，4739万美元；新加坡18项，3440万美元；台湾省34项，3205万美元。

外商直接投资企业生产经营情况　1998年外商直接投资企业出口创汇7058万美元，比1997年增长6.04%，涉外税收11.38亿元，比1997年增长75.08%。

【对外经济合作】

承包工程和劳务合作　1998年签订对外承包工程的劳务合作合同项目24个，合同金额1969万美元，比1997年的2725万美元下降27.74%；当年派出劳务人员1308人次，年末在外人数1838人。对外劳务承包分布在35个国家和地区，主要有马来西亚、新加坡、印度尼西亚、阿尔及利亚、苏丹、罗马尼亚、西萨摩亚、美国和新西兰等；主要承包工程项目有马来西亚蒲种商品广场、阿尔及利亚旅馆、苏丹道路、马来西亚住宅楼等。由重庆国际公司组织实施的总投资为2.06亿元人民币的我国经援项目——阿尔及利亚首都机场宾馆竣工，被外经贸部评为优良工程。

对外投资 1998年批准重庆市在海外举办非贸易企业2家。分别是重庆市经济协作总公司投资240万美元与缅甸蝎厂业有限公司合资组建的曼德勒陵铃摩托车有限公司和重庆华伟机车制造有限公司以生产设备、零部件占总投资75%的形式与越南进出口开发投资公司合作组建的“越南华伟摩托车制造厂”，生产、销售民用摩托车。

【其他】

经济技术开发区 1998年重庆经济技术开发区兴办外商投资企业11家，合同外资金额5262万美元，实际利用外资5003万美元。截止1998年底，开发区累计兴办外商投资企业249家，投资总额5.84亿美元，协议外资金额3.84亿美元，实际使用外资金额3.41亿美元。其中投资300万美元以上的大中型工业项目44个，目前已有来自台湾省、香港、日本、美国、新加坡等二十多个国家和地区的企业前来投资建厂。一批技术起点高、产品竞争力强的项目已在开发区落户，初步形成以机动车及零部件、电子通讯、生物制品、食品工业为主的企业群。

高新技术产业开发区 1998年重庆高新技术产业开发区兴办外商投资企业24家，合同外资金额6894万美元，实际利用外资4055万美元。截至1998年底，开发区累计兴办外商投资企业247家，投资总额8.48亿美元，协议外资金额3.4亿美元。亚洲、欧洲、大洋洲、北美洲许多科技企业前来投资，产品涉及电子、通讯、光电技术、仪器仪表、生物工程、精细化工、计算机、新材料、环保与节能等高新技术领域。

港口运输 1998年重庆进出口货物运输总量为116万吨，其中进口运量为102万吨，出口运量为14万吨。

涉外旅游 全市接待旅游、参观访问及从事各项活动的海外游客16.37万人，其中港澳台同胞2万人，分别比1997年下降38%和39%，旅游外汇收入0.88亿美元，下降16%。

1998年四川省对外经济贸易

四川省对外贸易经济合作委员会

【对外贸易】

进出口总额 1998年，四川省对外贸易实现平稳增长。全省进出口总额285888万美元，比1997年的271540万美元增长5.28%。其中，出口总额167464万美元，比1997年的164429万美元增长1.85%；进口总额118423万美元，比1997年的107111万美元增长10.56%，占全国进口总额的0.76%。出口占全省国内生产总值3580.3亿元（相当于432.46亿美元）的3.86%，占全国出口总额的0.64%。

出口商品结构 初级产品出口额37524万美元，占出口总额的22.4%，比1997年的41958万美元下降3.1个百分点。工业制成品的出口额为129941万美元，占出口总额的77.6%，比1997年的出口122476万美元增长3.1个百分点。机电产品出口额为40475万美元，占出口总额的24.2%，比1997年增长13.9%。

出口商品1亿美元以上的有5种，5000万至1亿美元之间的商品有8种，1000万美元至5000万美元之间的商品有16种。

出口额在1000万美元以上的商品情况表

金额分类	商品名称	出口金额（万美元）	占出口总额（%）
1亿美元以上（5种）	服装、化工原料、纺织品成套设备、钢材	63642	38
5000万美元～1亿美元（8种）	冻猪肉、纺织原料、丝织品、铁合金、有色金属、医药原料、各类机械、电讯设备及器材	54251	32.40
1000万美元～5000万美元（16种）	蔬菜、干菜制品、罐头、白酒、猪肠衣、鹅鸭绒毛、木材、烟草、丝类、鞋类、日用杂品、稀有金属及矿产品、中药材、航空设备、家用电器、工农具	38840	23.19
合　计	**29种**	**156733**	**93.59**

出口商品市场　1998年，四川省出口商品销往126个国家和地区，主要出口市场是：中国香港、日本、美国、伊朗、俄罗斯、德国、韩国、中国台湾省、荷兰和印度，上述10个国家和地区出口总额合计为131135万美元，占出口总额的78.31%。附四川商品输往的主要国家和地区。

出口商品输往主要国家（地区）

单位：万美元

国别（地区）	出口金额（万美元）	占出口总额（%）
中国香港	28619	17.09
日　本	26563	15.86
美　国	23606	14.10
伊　朗	10181	6.08
俄罗斯	9530	5.69
德　国	7450	4.45
韩　国	7417	4.43
台湾省	6543	3.91
荷　兰	5420	3.24
印　度	3806	2.27
意大利	2839	1.70
新加坡	2751	1.64

出口商品输往主要国家（地区）（续）

单位：万美元

国别（地区）	出口金额（万美元）	占出口总额（%）
法　国	2723	1.63
瑞　士	2316	1.38
菲律宾	2157	1.29
泰　国	2147	1.28
越　南	1850	1.10
澳大利亚	1579	0.94
英　国	1572	0.94
缅　甸	1541	0.92
加拿大	1505	0.90
印度尼西亚	1329	0.79
孟加拉国	1205	0.72
巴基斯坦	1177	0.70
合　计	**155826**	**93.05**

进口商品结构　1998年全省初级产品进口额5392万美元，占进口总额的4.6%；工业制成品进口额为113031万美元，占进口总额的95.4%。

进口额在1000万美元以上的商品有17种，进口额为102787万美元，占进口总额的86.80%。

进口额在1000万美元以上的商品情况表

金额分类	商品名称	进口金额（万美元）	占进口总额（%）
1亿美元以上（3种）	航空设备、电子元器件、成套设备	61646	52.06
5000万美元～1亿美元（2种）	电工设备、塑料	14968	12.64
1000万美元～5000万美元（23种）	化工原料、钢材、有色金属材及制品、金属制品、电子仪器、通用机械、黑色金属矿产品、纸浆、豆粕、物理化工仪器、包装机械、有色金属矿产品小五金、日用杂品、计算机、合成纤维、印刷制板器材、纸张、金属切削机床、土建工程机械、纸制品、橡胶制品、服装辅料	26173	22.10
合　计	**28种**	**102787**	**86.80**

进口商品市场　进口商品来自世界39个国家和地区，其中名列前10位的国家和地区是：日本、香港、美国、法国、德国、韩国、瑞士、澳大利亚、新加坡、台湾省。上述10个国家和地区的进口商品合计为107079万美元，占进口总额的90.42%。

进口商品主要来源国家（地区）

金额单位：万美元

国别（地区）	进口金额（万美元）	占进口总额（%）
日　本	25606	21.62
中国香港	24307	20.53
美　国	19220	16.23
法　国	16043	13.55
德　国	8964	7.57
韩　国	3823	3.23
瑞　士	2989	2.52
澳大利亚	2478	2.09
新加坡	1859	1.57
中国台湾省	1790	1.51
意大利	1685	1.42

进口商品主要来源国家（地区）（续）

金额单位：万美元

国别（地区）	进口金额（万美元）	占进口总额（%）
英　国	1542	1.30
加拿大	1526	1.29
阿根廷	957	0.81
西班牙	685	0.58
瑞　典	587	0.50
乌克兰	563	0.48
合　计	**114624**	**96.79%**

技术进出口　1998年全省签订引进技术和进口设备合同32个，合同金额2359.8万美元。

【利用外资】

截至1998年底，四川省累计合同利用外资117亿美元，实际利用外资58亿美元。其中，1998年合同利用外资157696万美元，同比增长18%，实际利用外资106477万美元，同比增长21.4%，新批外商投资企业233家。

利用外资情况表

利用外资方式	批准签订的合同			实际利用外资	
	项目数（个）	外资金额（万美元）	金额比1997年（±%）	金额（万美元）	金额比1997年（±%）
对外借款		**79373**	**+47**	**49500**	**+10**
外商直接投资	**233**	**71215**	**+28.8**	**50400**	**+102.8**
合资企业	130	49825	+58.38	22399	+45.66
合作企业	17	10786	+43.53	8224	+252.66
外资企业	86	10604	−34.99	6625	−7.16
外商其他投资		**7108**	**−70.7**	**6577**	**−63.1**
合　计		**157696**	**+18**	**106477**	**+21.4**

1998年四川省外商投资企业外资来源国别和地区主要是：香港（占49.52%）、美国（占14.2%）、台湾省（占8.83%）、新加坡（占4.65%）、日本（占3.43%）、维尔京群岛（占3.03%）、英国（占1.83%）、澳大利亚（占1.76%）、泰国（占1.40%）、德国（占1.40%）。外商投资行业分布主要在：工业（占64.7%）、城市建设（占17.2%）、能源交通通讯（占9.1%）、服务教育（占6.7%）、农林水利（占2.3%）。

1998年四川省共批准外商直接投资项目233项。其中生产型项目188个，非生产型项目45个。

外商直接投资分行业情况表

金额单位：万美元

行　业	项目数量（家）	合同利用外资额	实际到位外资额
农林牧渔业	8	102	432
采掘业	3	1100	1975
制造业	166	57485	18953
电力煤气及水生产和供应业	4	3838	5101
建筑业	7	1776	2169
交通运输仓储及邮电通信业	3	1053	18
批发零售贸易餐饮业	10	482	606
房地产业	11	19791	3501
社会服务业	20	2900	4247
科学研究和综合技术服务业			15
卫生体育和社会福利			9
教育文化艺术广播			22
其他行业	1	500	200

外商直接投资分国别情况表

金额单位：万美元

国　别（地区）	项　目 数量（个）	合同利用 外资额	实际到位 外资额
中国香港	77	18184	15134
中国澳门	2	74	
中国台湾省	46	1392	1657
泰　国		-2259	85
马来西亚	3	36	8
新加坡	10	3095	2713
印　尼	3	53	48
日　本	14	5306	630
毛里求斯	1	1500	
韩　国	5	144	98
德　国	3	3396	2252
罗马尼亚	1	500	150
瑞　典	2	32	
法　国	5	139	70
意大利	3	135	86
荷　兰	4	711	475
英　国	2	206	139
比利时			5
挪　威	1	2450	1611
瑞　士	1	3	
巴哈马			1148
英属维尔京群岛	12	4954	5517
开曼群岛			100
加拿大	4	133	526
美　国	31	28484	2404
百慕大			125
澳大利亚	7	3101	3243
奥 地利			360
俄罗斯		33	
巴　西	1	32	32
西印度群岛	1	1020	5
西萨摩亚	1	1358	12
境外机构	1	-908	
联合国及其他国际组织	1	135	

注：因有几个项目的外方投资者不止一个，故分国别的项目总数大于233。

1998年全省外商投资企业完成进出口总额为　　45615万美元。其中出口25069万美元，比1997

年出口 22195 万美元增长 12.9%，外商投资企业 1998 年实现销售收入 197.8 亿元人民币，上缴税金 10.28 亿元人民币，为社会提供就业机会 17 万个。

【对外经济合作】

承包工程和劳务合作 1998 年，四川省新签对外承包工程和劳务输出合同项目 117 个，比 1997 年减少 30 个。其中，承包工程合同 30 个，劳务输出合同 87 个。新签对外承包劳务合作合同总金额 30748 万美元，比 1997 年减少 9354 万美元。其中，承包工程合同额为 21085 万美元，劳务输出合同额为 9663 万美元。全年完成营业额 22460 万美元，比 1997 年减少 681 万美元。其中，承包工程完成 18975 万美元，劳务输出完成 3485 万美元。当年四川省共派出劳务 9083 人次，比 1997 年减少 134 人次，派往的主要国家和地区是：越南、尼泊尔、赞比亚、印度尼西亚、叙利亚、老挝、日本、台湾省、俄罗斯、坦桑尼亚、肯尼亚、塞班、新加坡、阿联酋、柬埔寨、斐济、蒙古、美国、科威特、以色列、沙特、菲律宾、巴西、乌兹别克斯坦、马来西亚和土耳其。承包工程的主要项目及国别（地区）是：肯尼亚西卡蒙 1200 套房建一期工程；老挝川圹公路改建项目、沙湾那吉——巴色段公路改建项目、巴色公路改建项目、万象市政道路改建 4100 项目、万象市政道路改建 4200 项目；缅甸中国驻缅甸大使馆官邸项目；尼泊尔中国援尼泊尔体育设施游泳场项目；巴基斯坦 PEAM 项目；缅甸农业林业综合开发项目。

1998 年四川省对外新签合同额、完成营业额和派出劳务人次均较上年有不同程度的下降，其主要原因是：四川省对外经济技术合作业务 70% 集中在亚洲市场，受亚洲金融危机的冲击，四川省在亚洲市场的外经业务受到很大影响，在该地区的业务量锐减。由于亚洲国家和地区的本币大幅贬值，在建承包工程项目效益下降，劳务收入损失较大。

接受经济援助 1998 年，四川省除执行现有项目外，又争取到 4 项外国政府和国际组织的无偿援助，受援金额 204 万美元。具体项目是：1、日本政府援助四川省广安和仪陇县医院装备（2 亿日元）。2、日本政府援助四川省巴中地区保健院建设（9 万美元）。3、新西兰政府援助四川省康定饮水工程建设（15 万元）。4、新西兰政府援助四川省仪陇县农民培训中心建设。

1998 年成都市对外经济贸易

成都市对外贸易经济合作委员会

【对外贸易】

进出口总额 1998 年四川省成都市进出口总额为 5.07 亿美元，比 1997 年的 4.92 亿美元增长 3.1%。

出口总额 出口总额 3.57 亿美元，比 1997 年的 3.51 亿美元增长 1.5%。占全市国内生产总值 1103 亿元人民币（相当于 133.05 亿美元）的 2.68%，占全国出口总额的 0.19%

出口商品结构 初级产品 7390 万美元，占出口总额的 20.7%；工业制成品 28284 万美元，占出口总额的 79.3%。

出口额在100万美元以上的商品情况表

金额分类	商品名称	出口金额（万美元）	占出口总额（%）
100～500万美元（40种）	食用植物油、其他食用动物及其产品：蔬菜、罐头、蜂蜜、饲料、鬃尾、板及制品、动物纤维、合成纤维、棉布、绸缎、汽车零件、动力机械、矿山机械、起重机械、通用机械、轴承基础件、土建工程机械、电池、观察仪器、专用仪器仪表、量具、刃具、硬质合金及制品、手工具、羽绒服装、其他服装、其他地毯及装饰挂毯、包装类、有色金属矿产品、建材制品、铝化合物、醇、醛、化工品、塑料制品、各种染料、植物药材、未分类商品。	9622	26.95
500～1000万美元（8种）	生化药物、电工设备、梭织服装、成材、鞋类、针织服装、电视机及散件、肉食	5982	16.77
1000万美元以上（12种）	航空设备及零件、钢材、电子元器件、皮服装、抗菌素类药、肠衣、棉布、化纤布、其他金属化合物、羽绒及制品、干菜及制品、钠化合物	18432	51.67
合　计	**60种**	**34036**	**95.34**

出口商品市场　出口商品销往87个国家和地区。

主要出口市场情况表

国别（地区）	出口金额（万美元）	占出口总额（%）
美　国	7658	21.5
香　港	6462	18.1
日　本	5431	15.2
德　国	2890	8.1
俄罗斯	1883	5.3
台湾省	1462	4.1
意大利	1077	3.0

主要出口市场情况表（续）

国别（地区）	出口金额（万美元）	占出口总额（%）
韩　国	824	2.3
菲律宾	732	2.1
英　国	685	1.9

进口总额　进口总额15041万美元，比1997年的14061万美元增长7.0%。

进口商品结构　初级产品722万美元，占进口总额的4.8%；工业制成品14319万美元，占95.2%。

进口额在200万美元以上的商品情况表

金额分类	商品名称	进口金额（万美元）	占进口总额（%）
200～500万美元（16种）	塑料制品，服装辅料，电子原材料，土建工程机械，航空设备及零件，纸张，焦、油化工品，小五金，自动化仪表，废钢，电子设备，通用机械，其他化工原料，液化气，钾化物，稀有金属及其矿产品	5065	33.67
500～1000万美元（2种）	钢材、纸浆类	1459	9.7
1000万美元以上（3种）	轻工成套设备、塑料原料、有色金属材料及制品	5780	38.43
合　计	**21种**	**12304**	**81.8**

进口商品市场　进口商品来自24个国家和地区。

主要进口市场情况表

国别（地区）	进口金额（万美元）	占进口总额（%）
中国香港	5114	34
美　国	3444	22.9
日　本	2153	14.3
德　国	1115	7.4
加拿大	709	4.7
韩　国	597	4.0

主要进口市场情况表（续）

国别（地区）	进口金额（万美元）	占进口总额（%）
新加坡	417	2.8
法　国	319	2.1
英　国	199	1.3
台湾省	180	1.2

技术进出口　1998年成都市实现技术和设备进口合同金额3161万美元，比1997年的3747万美元减少15.6%。

【利用外资】

1998年利用外资情况表

利用外资方式	批准签订的合同			实际利用外资	
	项目数（个）	外资金额（万美元）	金额比1997年（±%）	金额（万美元）	金额比1997年（±%）
对外借款	3	2805	23	1200	266
外商直接投资	131	26711	70	14892	33
合资企业	71	14171	107	7449	5.5
合作企业	10	6377	114	3992	102
外资企业	50	6163	5.7	3451	60
合　计	**134**	**29516**	**64.5**	**16092**	**38.6**

外商直接投资行业 在外商直接投资项目中，制造业项目98个，协议外资金额19994万美元；第三产业项目20个，协外金额2888万美元。

外商直接投资来源 外商直接投资来自25个国家和地区。投资居前5位的国家和地区是：香港43个，10302万美元；日本9个，5243万美元；美国20个，4535万美元；新加坡7个，2071万美元；英属维尔京群岛7个，1570万美元。

截至到1998年底，成都市累计批准外商投资企业2301家，协议外资金额30.07亿美元，实际利用外资12.44亿美元。1998年三资企业进出口总额达16180万美元，其中出口额为9645万美元，比1997年增加3.4%。

【对外经济合作】

承包工程和劳务合作 1998年成都市共签订对外承包工程、劳务合作合同13份，合同金额1670.20万美元，比1997年增长11.32倍，其中，承包工程600万美元，劳务合作1070.20万美元；完成营业额610万美元，比上年增长1.24倍。全年外派劳务1020人次，比上年增长2.1倍。主要派往新加坡、越南、沙特阿拉伯、科威特、日本、以色列。

【其他】

经济技术开发区 1998年成都经济技术开发区实现合同外资金额1435.26万美元，实际利用外资351万美元。截止1998年底，全区累计实现合同外资金额8017.2万美元，实际利用外资5243.7万美元。

1998年成都高新技术产业开发区批准利用外资项目34个，协议外资3234.48万美元，比1997年增长18%，实际到位外资2753.46万美元，比1997年增长24.5%。1998年新批的34个项目中，500万美元以上项目3个，其中1000万美元以上2个。

涉外旅游 1998年成都市共接待海外旅游者18.68万人次，较1997年增加2.57%。旅游外汇收入6832.05万美元，比1997年的6206万美元增加10.08%。

1998年贵州省对外经济贸易

贵州省对外贸易经济合作厅

【对外贸易】

进出口总额 1998年按业务统计，贵州省进出口总额70926万美元，比1997年的69126万美元增长2.6%。

出口总额 出口总额44303万美元，比1997年的49729万美元下降10.9%，占全省国内生产总值843亿元（相当于1019347万美元）的4.3%；占全国出口额的0.24%。

出口商品结构 初级产品出口额8956万美元，占出口总额的20.2%；工业制品的出口额35375万元，占出口总额的79.8%。

出口额在1000万美元以上商品情况表

金额分类	商　品　名　称	出口金额（万美元）	占出口总额（%）
3000万美元以上（3种）	铁合金、磷矿石粉、黄磷	15283	34.5
2000—3000万美元（2种）	烤烟、轮胎	4378	9.9
1000—2000万美元（9种）	服装、化纤布、硅铁、硅锰合金、锌、矾土、焦炭、化肥、磨料	12586	28.4
合　计		**32247**	**72.8**

出口商品市场　出口商品销往93个国家和地区。

主要出口商品市场情况表

国别（地区）	出口金额（万美元）	占出口总额（%）
香　港	8243	18.6
日　本	6566	14.8
韩　国	4812	10.9
美　国	4086	9.2
台湾省	1308	3.0
俄罗斯	1287	2.9
缅　甸	1173	2.6
荷　兰	1142	2.5

主要出口商品市场情况表（续）

国别（地区）	出口金额（万美元）	占出口总额（%）
英　国	1039	2.3
印　度	926	2.1
合　计	**30582**	**69.0**

进口总额　进口总额26623万美元，比1997年的19397万美元增长37.3%。

进口商品结构　初级产品进口额14502万美元，占进口总额的54.5%；工业制成品的进口额12288万美元，占进口总额的46.2%。

进口额在1000万以上商品情况表

金额分类	商　品　名　称	进口金额（万美元）	占进口总额（%）
2000万美元以上（4种）	油菜籽、豆粕、黑金属（钢材）、电讯设备及器材	15002	56.3
1000—2000万美元（7种）	黄大豆、二醋酸烟用丝束、纸张、黑金属矿产品、天然橡胶、卷烟机、成套设备	8897	33.4
合　　计		**23899**	**89.7**

进口商品市场 进口商品来自28个国家和地区。

主要进口商品市场情况表

国别（地区）	进口金额（万美元）	占进口总额（%）
美　国	6421	24.1
香　港	3924	14.7
澳大利亚	3530	13.3
德　国	1953	7.3
印　度	1882	7.1

主要进口商品市场情况表（续）

国别（地区）	进口金额（万美元）	占进口总额（%）
法　国	1705	6.4
阿根廷	1556	5.8
日　本	1302	4.9
意大利	993	3.7
加拿大	870	3.3
合　计	**24136**	**90.6**

【利用外资】

1998年利用外资情况表

利用外资方式	批准签订的合同			实际利用外资	
	项目数（个）	外资金额（万美元）	金额比1997年（±%）	金　额（万美元）	金额比1997年（±%）
外商直接投资	**73**	**15312**	**52.1**	**4535**	**-8.9**
合资企业	33	2872	-31.5	3042	173.3
合作企业	10	7154	79.8	443	-83.1
外资企业	30	5286	178.8	1050	-14.6
合　计		**15312**	**52.1**	**4535**	**-8.9**

外商直接投资行业 外商直接投资的73个项目中生产型项目55个，非生产型项目18个。按行业分：农林牧渔业4个、采掘业5个、制造业41个、电力煤气及水供应业2个、建筑2个、地勘1个、房地产5个、社会服务12个、其他行业1个。

外商直接投资来源 外商直接投资来自17个国家和地区。主要投资的国家和地区及金额（以万美元为单位）有：香港6404、加拿大3499、美国1330、缅甸723、马来西亚485、韩国482、德国365、台湾省313、日本200、英属维尔京群岛137、澳大利亚110、法国102。

【对外经济合作】

承包工程和劳务合作 1998年签订对外承包工程和劳务合作合同项目22个，合同金额8769万美元，比1997年的1272万美元增长589.4%；完成营业额956万美元，比1997年的1071万元下降10.7%；当年派出劳务人员360人，年末在外人数219人，派往的国家和地区主要有：越南、柬埔寨、孟加拉、巴林、肯尼亚、新加坡、印度。承包工程项目涉及的国家有：老挝的零散工程和菲律宾的公路桥梁工程项目。

接受经济援助 接受国际经济组织及双边援助的项目6个，金额1262万人民币。

【其他】

经济技术开发区 贵阳高新技术产业开发区是贵州省的经国家科委批准的国家级开发区，位于贵州省贵阳市新天寨镇，规化面积11.32平方公里。1998年，高新开发区完成工业总产值210000万元，比上年增长16.7%；实现利税总额11000万元，较上年下降37.1%；创汇700万美元，较上年下降40.6%。基础设施建设项目投资总额6621万元，较上年增长36.7%；完成投资额5600万元，较上年增长57.5%；招商引资合同资金总额21800万元，比上年下降57.3%，实际到位资金15000万元，较上年增长80.7%。继1996、1997年一批大企业、大公司在开发区落户以来，1998年又有中韩合资企业——东朝化工冶金有限公司，注册资金500万美元；赤天化集团投资4580万元，建设年产25000吨奶油生产线等两家企业来开发区落户。另外全国八大电子软件园之一的托普集团，也初步达成在高新开发区建立西部软件园贵州分园的协议；中美合资汇美数码影像有限公司也即将落户高新开发区。

对外经贸洽谈会 第二届中国投资贸易洽谈会于1998年9月8日—12日在福建厦门举行，贵州省投资贸易洽谈团组成了9个分团和9个地州市代表团共350余人。5家进出口公司组成外贸分团参加。全省招商引资共签订外资项目和内联项目18个，总投资47414.5万美元，其中外资项目12个，总投资45576.5万美元，协议引进外资30715万美元，分列42个参会代表团第13位和第15位。对外贸易出口成交金额386.6万美元，成交类别涉及五矿、机电、土畜产、纺织、粮油食品等大类产品。其中：土畜产品（土畜公司）92.1万美元、化工产品（化工公司）117.5万美元、五矿产品（五矿公司）53.2万美元、纺织产品（纺织公司）72.8万美元、机电产品（基地公司）51.0万美元。出口国和地区是：港澳22.8万美元、台湾101.2万美元、东盟8.9万美元、日本12.8万美元、欧共体61.2万美元，其他179.7万美元。

港口运输 1998年贵州省外贸货物运输总量217万吨，比1997年197万吨增长10.2%；其中出口运量112万吨，比1997年增长3.7%；进口运量105万吨，比上年增长18.0%。

涉外旅游 1998年贵州省共接待国内国外旅游者1895.13万人次，其中外国人6.8万人次，港澳同胞3.82万人次，台胞4.52万人次，分别比上年增长12.8%、8.8%、22.2%，旅游外汇收入4831.18万美元；国内旅游者1880万人次，旅游国内收入35.14亿元，省旅游企业实现税金4268.66万元。

1998年云南省对外经济贸易

云南省对外贸易经济合作厅

【对外贸易】

进出口总额 1998年云南省进出口总额203499万美元，比1997年201111万美元增长1.2%。

出口总额 出口总额126299万美元，比1997年的121425万美元增长4%，占全省国内生产总值的5.8%，占全国出口总额的0.69%。

出口商品结构表

项　目	出　口　额（万美元）	占出口总额比重（%）		
		1998年	1997年	+、-百分点
初级产品	39171	31	30.7	0.3
工业制成品	87128	69	69.3	-0.3

出口100万美元以上的商品有87种，金额102018万美元，占出口总额的80.8%。其中出口1000万美元以上的商品有：卷烟、黄磷、锡、铁路设备、铝、服装、烤烟、糖制品设备、钢材、铅、松茸、焊锡、磷酸、石蜡、双筒望远镜、红茶、磷矿石粉、香料烟、棉绦纶布、磷酸二铵、棉纱、磷酸五钠、锌、车床、芸豆等25种，金额82125万美元，占出口总额的65%；出口500万—1000万美元的商品13种，金额8808万美元，占出口总额的7%；出口100万—500万美元的商品49种，金额11085万美元，占出口总额的8.8%。

出口商品市场　出口商品销往104个国家和地区，主要出口商品市场见下表：

主要出口商品市场情况表

国别（地区）	出口金额（万美元）	占出口总额（%）	比1997年（±%）
香　港	30422	24.1	-0.5
缅　甸	27613	21.9	-0.1
日　本	11394	9	-13.4
美　国	6790	5.4	25.1
越　南	6241	4.9	21.4
韩　国	2411	1.9	2.2

进口总额　进口总额77200万美元，比1997年的79686万美元下降3.1%。

进口商品结构表

项　目	进　口　额（万美元）	占进口总值比重（%）		
		1998年	1997年	+、-百分点
初级产品	10874	14.1	11	3.1
工业制成品	66326	85.9	89	-3.1

进口100万美元以上的商品70种，金额59725万美元，占进口总额的77.4%。进口1000万美元以上的商品有：飞机、集成电路、醋酸烟用丝束、铜精矿砂、氧化铝、电子计算机散件、照像器材、原木、化工成套设备、铜版纸、磁铁矿砂、钢材、卷烟机、包装机械、铁路车辆及设备、印刷机等16种，金额40815万美元，占进口总额的52.9%；进口500万—1000万美元的商品12种，金额8516万美元，占进口总额的11%；进口100万—500万美元的商品42种，金额10394万美元，占进口总额的13.5%。

进口商品市场　进口商品来自40个国家和地区，主要进口商品市场见下表：

主要进口商品市场情况表

国别（地区）	进口金额（万美元）	占进口总额（%）	比1997年（±%）
美　国	22820	29.6	78.6
香　港	17283	22.4	-32.4
西　欧	15907	20.6	-35.7
韩　国	3870	5	123.6
缅　甸	3259	4.2	0.6

边境贸易　1998年全省边境小额贸易进出口总额13089万美元，比1997年的7413万美元增长76.6%。其中，出口8896万美元，比1997年的4201万美元增长111.8%；进口4193万美元，

比1997年的3212万美元增长30.5%。主要出口商品有：钢材、石蜡、棉布、棉涤纶布、棉纱、锌、电池、柴油机、水果、水泥、成品油、石膏、啤酒等；主要进口商品有：原木、铁矿砂、锯材、铬矿砂、竹、叶、棕制品等。

技术进出口 1998年共签订技术引进和进口设备合同24项，合同总额4094万美元，比1997年同期减少55%。主要是烟草、电力、轻工、冶金、有色、化工、机械等方面的技术和设备，引进项目主要来自德国、美国、意大利、瑞士、英国等。其中，包括三份专有技术转让合同，金额22万美元。

【利用外资】

1998年利用外资情况表

利用外资方式	批准签订的合同			实际利用外资	
	项目数（个）	外资金额（万美元）	金额比1997年（±%）	金额（万美元）	金额比1997年（±%）
对外借款					
外商直接投资	119	33039	23.6	14568	-12.1
合资企业	66				
合作企业	19				
外资企业	34				

外商直接投资项目中生产型项目97项，非生产型项目22项。按行业分，农林牧渔业10项，采掘业5项，制造业76项，电力、煤气及水的生产和供应2项，交通运输、仓储及邮电通讯业1项，卫生、体育和社会福利业1项，教育、文艺及广播电影电视业1项，批发和零售贸易、餐饮业1项，房地产业7项，社会服务业13项，科学研究和综合技术服务业1项，其他行业1项。

外商直接投资来自香港、台湾省、美国、泰国、日本、英属维尔京群岛、澳门、加拿大、德国、意大利、澳大利亚、马来西亚、英国、韩国、瑞士、法国、缅甸等17个国家和地区。

协议外资额居前十位的国家及地区依次为：香港48项，14066万美元；美国13项，5484万美元；英属维尔京群岛2项，3200万美元；德国2项，2210万美元；台湾省12项，438万美元；缅甸5项，331万美元；日本4项，245万美元；加拿大1项，244万美元；泰国3项，235万美元；澳门1项163万美元。

【对外经济合作】

承包工程和劳务合作 1998年对外签订合同83项，总金额31000万美元，比1997年的9805万美元增长316%。营业额10000万美元，比1997年的9519万美元增长5.3%。当年派出劳务人员833人，年末在外人数760人。派往主要国家和地区为越南、老挝、缅甸、柬埔寨、泰国、马来西亚、巴基斯坦等；承包工程的主要项目为老挝ADB公路建设，水电站、民用建筑等。

对外经济技术援助 1998年承担援外项目4个，总金额3000万美元，项目为老挝文化中心、老挝万荣水泥厂二期工程、援越建筑工程设备、也门亚丁五金厂租赁。

接受经济援助 1998年接受国际组织及双边援助项目9个，金额500万美元，主要来自日本、新西兰、澳大利亚等。

【其他】

对外经贸洽谈会 1998年8月8日—15日，在昆明举办了'98中国昆明出口商品交易会，到会境外客商、来宾达8000余人，分别来自57个国家和地区。其中缅甸、老挝、越南、泰国、马来西亚、新加坡、美国、英国、法国、意大利、德国、日本、韩国等13个国家和香港特别行政区的参展展位150个。交易会各项业务成交总额18.168亿美元，其中：出口7.19亿美元（含外商投资企业1733万美元）；进口2.32亿美元（含境外来展150万美元）；利用外资7.88亿美元；对外承包工程和劳务合作18项，金额0.72亿美元。

海外旅游 1998年入境的外国人及台港澳同胞76.09万人次，旅游外汇收入26100万美元，比1997年的26400万美元下降1.1%。

1998年西藏自治区对外经济贸易

西藏自治区对外贸易经济合作厅

【对外贸易】

进出口总额 西藏自治区1998年对外贸易进出口总额为10963万美元，比1997年的11833万美元下降7.35%。

出口总额 出口总额4587万美元，比1997年的5010万美元下降8.44%；占全区国内生产总值91.18亿元人民币的4.16%

出口商品结构 初级产品出口额为307万美元，占出品总额的6.69%；工业制成品出口额为4280万美元，占出口总额的93.31%。

出口商品市场 出口商品主要销往：香港，1670万美元，占出口总额的36.41%；韩国，1440万美元，占出口总额的31.39%；美国，635万美元，占出口总额的13.84%；南非，466万美元，占出口总额的10.16%；巴西160万美元，占出口总额的3.49%。

进口总额 进口总额6376万美元，比1997年的6823万美元下降6.55%。

进口商品结构 初级产品进口额233万美元，占进口总额的3.65%；工业制成品进口额6143万美元，占进口总额的96.35%。

进口商品市场 进口商品主要来自：俄罗斯，1015万美元，占进口总额的15.92%；韩国，484万美元，占进品总额的7.59%；日本，305万美元，占进口总额的4.78%；澳大利亚，220万美元，占进口总额的3.45%；尼泊尔，214万美元，占进口总额的3.36%；香港134万美元，占进口总额的2.10%。

边境贸易 1998年全区边境贸易进出口额为2349万美元，比1997年的360万美元增长552.50%，主要的进出口商品有农产品、畜产品、纺织品、轻工业品、机电产品、建材、医药等。

【利用外资】

外商投资概况 1998年外商在西藏自治区的投资项目8个，协议利用外资2463万美元，比1997年的1668万美元增长47.66%，其中中外合资项目7个，外商投资2424万美元；外商独资企业1个，外商投资39万美元。

外商直接投资行业 外商投资项目中生产型企业2个，非生产型企业6个；其中机电行业项目2个，服务业项目3个，环境保护项目1个，运输行业项目1个，食品加工项目1个。

外商直接投资来源 外资分别来自4个国家和地区。其中香港投资项目4个，投资额1714万美元；尼泊尔投资项目2个，投资额147万美元；英国投资项目1个，投资额600万美元；美国投资项目1个，投资额0.6万美元。

【对外经济合作】

接受经济援助 1998年西藏自治区共接受国际援助项目9个，援助金额988万美元，援助国别来自联合国儿童基金会，欧盟等国际组织及新西兰政府，援助项目涉及农牧林业综合开发，妇幼保健、教师培训等行业。

【其他】

涉外旅游 1998年西藏自治区共接待境外游客及台港澳同胞9.6万多人次，旅游收入3302万美元，比1997年的3172万美元增长4.10%。

1998年陕西省对外经济贸易

陕西省对外贸易经济合作厅

【对外贸易】

进出口总额 1998年陕西省进出口总额20.51亿美元，比1997年的18.76亿美元增长18.3%。

出口总额 全省出口总额11.77亿美元，比1997年的13.49亿美元下降4.4%。

进口总额 全省进口总值8.74亿美元，比1997年的5.28亿美元增长73.9%。

主要进出口市场情况表

金额单位：美元

国别（地区）	金　　额
香　港	460507343
台湾省	25394895
日　本	300497590
伊　朗	25136975
土耳其	39689424
韩　国	89816984
德　国	73481811
意大利	47065731
荷　兰	50442347
比利时	83610487

主要进出口市场情况表（续）

金额单位：美元

国别（地区）	金　　额
英　国	51572248
瑞　典	41139803
俄罗斯	37396317
美　国	179062223
澳大利亚	23781241

1000万美元以上进口商品

金额单位：美元

商　品　名　称	金　　额
合成纤维	18184947
黑色金属	21448061
有色金属	41894233
化工原料	33315153
医药原料	71737700
汽车、电车、摩托车及零件	36668689
各类机械	46855829
成套设备	110628159
电讯设备及器件	63016077

主要出口市场情况表

金额单位：美元

国家（地区）	金　　额
香港	337909700
日本	178285305
美国	132619496
马来西亚	17470145
新加坡	19717757
印度	20021932
伊朗	25136975
土耳其	39458807
阿联酋	20135507
韩国	66824117
德国	54098970
意大利	35037167
荷兰	49276827
英国	39988646
俄罗斯	29405337

1000 万美元以上出口商品

金额单位：美元

商　品　名　称	金　　额
飞机零备件	12411532
滚动轴承	27486430
工业轴承	27421381
油田勘探设备	22241160
石油成套设备	24838232
电子成套设备	15293988
电子元器件	82641743
显像管	61673761
果汁	19444780
绒毛	10017506
坏布	55171243
动物纤维	14627473
棉涤绒布	63389607
人造棉布	35970385
服装	231010868
工艺品	18837630
箱包及鞋帽	12998131
日用五金器皿	25160692
日用杂品	13801900
有色金属	126619547
铁合金	34323180

1000 万美元以上出口商品（续）

金额单位：美元

商　品　名　称	金　　额
煤炭及煤制品	32063935
化工原料	29315151
医药原料	22549237
航空设备	13947223
各类机械	104873713
轴承基础件	33591934
电工设备	13046509
成套设备	42879813
电讯设备及器材	92850832
工农具	40735281
缝纫机类	21562664
金属制品	13333262
文体用品	14641223
玩具	13007918
稀有金属及矿产品	21979267
通用机械	14076003
豆类	11965257
食用植物及其产品	17410317
食品制成品	28299751
棉制品	18489164
棉布	74039898
化纤布	104659927
丝织品	12540203
氧化钼	50065073
锌	16158784

【经济技术合作】

技术进出口　全省共签定技术出口合同 30 个，合同金额 6093 万美元，收汇 2195 万美元。主要市场为亚洲发展中国家以及英国、美国、日本、比利时等发达国家，涉及的行业主要有冶金、机械、化工、航空、电子等。注册技术引进合同 14 项，合同金额 627 万美元。

对外承包劳务　全年共签订对外承包劳务合同 102 份，合同金额 6348 万美元，完成营业额 8684 万美元，年末在外人数 1898 人。承包劳务主要涉及建筑、纺织、服装、机械、电子、商业餐饮、医疗卫生、教育和设计咨询等领域，主要市场有六十多个国家和地区。

接受国际无偿援助 全省正在执行的国际无偿援助项目15个，受援金额2019万美元。比利时政府无偿援助陕西贫困地区社会经济综合发展项目，于1998年11月3日比利时首相访陕时由中比两国政府正式签署，受援金额约合7350万元人民币，是我省迄今为止争取到的最大的受援项目。

【利用外资】

1998年我省共批准外商直接投资项目196个，总投资额81196万美元，合同外资额37582万美元，实际使用外资30010万美元。其中合资项目127个，合同外资额10920万美元，实际外资金额20413万美元；合作项目34个，合同外资额20037万美元，实际外资金额4324万美元；外资项目35个，合同外资额6625万美元，实际外资金额5273万美元。

新批项目投资来源国别地区情况为：港澳台地区项目总数102个（香港73个，澳门6个，台湾23个），占项目总数的52%；东亚及东南亚地区项目22个（马来西亚1个，新加坡3个，文莱1个，日本11个，缅甸2个，韩国4个），占项目总数的11%；欧美地区项目58个（德国4个，法国3个，意大利1个，比利时2个，英国4个，希腊1个，罗马尼亚非1个，俄罗斯1个，乌克兰1个，立陶宛1个，秘鲁1个，维尔京群岛7个，加拿大3个，美国29个），占项目总数的29%；大洋洲项目16个（澳大利亚15个、新西兰1个），占项目总数的8%。

新批项目中工业性项目仍然是主要组成部分，占新批项目总数的70%，农业项目占新批项目总数的2.5%，房地产项目占新批项目总数的8%，服务业项目占新批项目总数的10.7%。

新批项目利用外资平均规模191.74万美元。利用外资项目质量提高。1998年全省共批准总投资在500万美元以上项目38个，占项目总数的19.39%。其中2000万美元以上的项目13个，占项目总数的6.6%；1000万美元以上项目15个，占项目总数的7.7%；且大项目中生产性项目所占比重较大。投资国别地区发生较大变化。由于金融危机的影响，东亚及东南亚地区的投资大幅下降，而美洲、大洋洲的投资有所增加来我省投资国别不断增多，1998年又有一批国家客商前来投资。这些新增投资的国家是：乌克兰、希腊、文莱、罗马尼亚、缅甸。到目前为止，来我省投资国别已增到56个。

利 用 外 资 统 计 快 报

1998年01～12月

填报单位：陕西省外经贸厅

地方代码：610000

金额单位：万美元

利用外资方式	本年批准外资情况		本年实际利用外资
	项　目　数	合同利用外资金额	
总计	**209**	**70167**	**67809**
一、对外借款	**13**	**32585**	**37799**
外国政府贷款	13	32585	14895
国际金融组织贷款			7904
外国银行商业贷款			15000
二、外商直接投资	**196**	**37582**	**30010**
中外合资企业	127	10920	20413
中外合作企业	34	20037	4324
外资企业	35	6625	5273

利用外商直接投资行业报表（分投资方式）

金额单位：万美元

行　　业	外商直接投资合计		
	项目数	合同外资	实际外资
总计	**196**	**37582**	**30010**
农、林、牧、渔业	5	232	542
采掘业	7	758	471
制造业	138	18849	18287
电力、煤气及水的生产和供应业	3	6217	172
建筑业	2	127	863
交通运输、仓储及邮电通信业	1	99	
批发和零售贸易、餐饮业	3	345	266
房地产业	16	6270	5790
社会服务业	21	4685	3312
卫生、体育和社会福利业			67
教育、文化艺芳及广播电影电视业			10
其他行业			230

对外经贸洽谈活动　组织省内企业参加春、秋两次出口商品广州交易会，共成交25.164万美元。另外，还组织企业分别参加了’98中国东西部投资与贸易洽谈会、’98天津出口商品交易会、’98华东出口商品交易会、’98昆明出口商品交易会。这些小交会共有37家企业参展，共成交21.530万美元。为了积极开拓海外市场，还成功举办了’98日本香川陕西省经贸洽谈会，出口成交3100万美元。组织省内4家企业参加了外经贸部主办的’98莫斯科中国商品展览会。参加了外经贸部主办的’98第二届中国投资贸易洽谈会，签订利用外资项目13个，项目总投资3543万美元，协议外资361万美元，签订技术出口合同421万美元。

1998年西安市对外经济贸易

西安市对外贸易经济合作局

【对外贸易】

进出口总额　陕西省西安市1998年进出口总额31999万美元，比1997年的46084万美元下降30.56%。

出口总额　出口总额24240万美元，比1997年的33057万美元下降26.67%，占全市国内生产总值560亿元（相当于67.64亿美元）的3.58%；占全省出口总额117600万美元的20.61%。

出口商品结构　初级产品出口额2133万美元，占出口总额的8.80%；工业制成品的出口额22107万美元，占出口总额的91.20%。

出口额 200 万美元以上的商品情况表

金额分类	商 品 名 称	出口金额（万美元）	占出口总额（%）
200—500 万美元（7 种）	无毛绒、针织外衣、棉涤坯布、搪瓷器皿、皮劳保手套、高压断路器、风机	2162	8.92
500—1000 万美元（5 种）	铁制玩具、玻璃器皿、铸铁制品、轴承、电子元器件	3741	15.43
2000 万美元以上（1 种）	缝纫机头	2176	8.98
合 计	**13 种**	**8079**	**33.33**

出口商品市场 出口商品销往 104 个国家（地区）。

主要出口国家（地区）情况表

国家（地区）	出口金额（万美元）	占出口总额的（%）
香 港	5659	23.35
日 本	3856	15.91
美 国	2859	11.80
德 国	1243	5.13
意大利	1212	5.00
英 国	867	3.58
印 度	716	2.95
马来西亚	676	2.79
荷 兰	537	2.22
新加坡	519	2.14
合 计	**18144**	**74.85**

进口总额 进口总额 7759 万美元，比 1997 年的 13027 万美元下降 40.44%。

进口商品结构 初级产品进口额 236 万美元，占进口总额的 3.04%；工业制成品的进口额 7523 万美元，占进口总额的 96.96%。

进口额 200 万美元以上的商品情况表

金 额 分 类	商 品 名 称	进口金额（万美元）	占进口总额（%）
200—500 万美元（6 种）	合成纤维、钢材、电子仪器缝纫机零件、粮油食品加工设备、电子设备	2014	25.96
500 万美元以上（4 种）	铝化合物、无线电通讯设备、航空设备、轻工成套设备	2374	30.59
合 计	**10 种**	**4388**	**56.55**

进口商品市场　进口商品来自23个国家(地区)。

主要进口国家（地区）情况表

国家（地区）	进口金额（万美元）	占进口总额的%
日　本	2125	27.39
香　港	1421	18.31
美　国	855	11.02
德　国	599	7.72
英　国	521	6.71
澳大利亚	503	6.48
意大利	497	6.41
韩　国	323	4.16
加拿大	230	2.96
台湾省	168	2.17
合　　计	**7242**	**93.34**

【利用外资】

1998年利用外资情况表

利用外资方式	批准签订的合同			实际利用外资	
	项目数（个）	外资金额（万美元）	金额比1996年（±%）	金　额（万美元）	金额比1996年（±%）
外商直接投资	112	29185	13.49	22146	0.27
合资企业	58	5880	-51.35	13340	-3.87
合作企业	29	16731	106.38	4459	23.62
外资企业	25	6574	19.05	4347	-4.94
外商其他投资					
补偿贸易				140	-30.00
合计	**112**	**29185**	**13.49**	**22286**	**1.04**

注：批准签订的合同中外资金额按新统计口径。

外商直接投资行业　在外商直接投资项目中，生产型项目83个，非生产型项目29个。按行业分，农林牧渔水利业1个，工业82个，房地产管理业11个，服务业12个，咨询服务业3个，其他行业3个。

外商直接投资来源　外商直接投资来自21个国家（地区）。投资额前10位的是：香港37个，12728万美元；台湾省13个，6000万美元；美国20个，5342万美元；澳大利亚5个，4403万美元；维尔京群岛6个，4173万美元；德国3个，2828万美元；澳门4个，2218万美元；缅甸2个，554万美元；加拿大2个，362万美元；新加坡3个，322万美元。

外商直接投资企业生产经营情况　截止1998年底，已开业投产的外商投资企业共654家，全年完成销售收入35亿元，其中出口销售收入6038万美元，比1997年增长8.6%；完成税收5亿元。

【对外经济合作】

承包工程和劳务合作　1998年签订对外承包工程和劳务合作合同项目30个，金额2034万美元，比1997年的3959万美元下降48.62%；营业额3618万美元，比1997年的3205万美元增长12.89%；当年派出劳务人员473人，年末在外人数为931人，主要分布在印尼、泰国、马来西亚、菲律宾、新加坡、毛里求斯、日本、阿联酋、沙特阿拉伯、莫桑比克、吉尔吉斯斯坦、孟加拉、塞班等国家和地区。

主要对外承包工程项目有苏丹公路、马来西亚输电线路、莫桑比克使馆大楼项目等。

对外投资 1998年在海外举办企业1个，中方投资金额90万美元，投资国为吉尔吉斯斯坦。

【其他】

【经济技术开发区】

西安高新技术产业开发区1998年完成基建投资11.28亿元，完成开工面积68.9万平方米，完成竣工面积63.2万平方米。新批外商投资项目36个，合同外资金额10654万美元，实际进资6973万美元。截止1998年，外商投资企业累计达到345家。

1998年，西安高新技术产业开发区完成技工贸总收入140亿元，比上年增长38.34%。随着西安大唐电信有限公司、金花股份公司等一批规模大、技术含量高的项目入区投产，使电子、通讯、制冷、机电一体化等产业规模迅速扩大。西安高新技术产业开发区已成为我国首批向亚太经济合作组织成员特别开放的四个科技园之一。

为了促进更多的上市公司在高新区投资发展高新技术产业，1998年4月，西安高新区与国家科技部合作，成功地举办了全国首次上市公司投资高新技术产业研讨会及项目推介会。会后有一批上市公司踊跃与高新区内企业洽谈合作项目，其中秦川发展股份公司已出资1000万元投资IC卡防伪系统项目。

【对外经贸洽谈会】

’98中国西安投资与贸易洽谈会于1998年9月12日至17日在西安举行。来自香港、日本、美国、英国、法国、德国、韩国、加拿大、澳大利亚、新西兰、马来西亚、泰国、瑞典、俄罗斯、比利时、丹麦等23个国家和地区的商社、协会共1400余人参加了本届洽谈会。

本届洽谈会，西安市共签订外商直接投资合同项目116个，合同总额8.48亿美元，其中外资额6.03亿美元；签订进出口合同总额5395万美元，其中出口成交5286万美元，进口成交109万美元。

【涉外旅游】

全年接待海外旅游者48万人次，与1997年持平。旅游外汇收入1.94亿美元，比1997年的2亿美元下降3%。

1998年甘肃省对外经济贸易

甘肃省对外贸易经济合作厅

【对外贸易】

进出口总额 1998年甘肃省进出口总额53895万美元，比1997年55421万美元下降2.97%。

出口总额 出口总额41546万美元，比1997年的4.08亿美元，增长1.68%，占全省国内生产总值870亿元（相当于105亿美元）的3.95%。

出口商品结构 初级产品5266万美元，占出口总额的12.7%，工业制成品36280万美元，占出口总额的87.3%。

出口额在 1000 万美元以上的商品情况表

金额分类	商品名称	出口金额（万美元）	占出口总额（%）
1000 万—4000 万美元（4 种）	石墨电极、铝、锌、稀土	6803	16.39
4000 万美元以上（3 种）	镍、铁合金、服装	17300	41.68
合计	**7 种**	**24103**	**58.07**

主要出口市场情况表

国别（地区）	出口金额（万美元）	占出口总额（%）
日本	9103	21.93
香港	8884	21.40
美国	6430	15.49
韩国	3256	0.78
德国	1858	0.44
新加坡	1514	0.36
意大利	1258	0.30
伊朗	776	0.19
台湾省	722	0.17
越南	654	0.16
英国	604	0.15
泰国	574	0.14
合计	**35633**	**85.86**

出口商品市场 出口商品销售 96 个国家和地区。

进口总额 1998 年 12349 万美元，比 1997 年 1.46 亿美元下降 18.69%。

进口商品结构 初级产品 2848 万美元，占进口总额的 23.06%；工业制成品 9501 万美元，占进口总额的 76.94%。

进口额在 400 万美元以上的商品情况表

金额分类	商品名称	出口金额（万美元）	占出口总额（%）
400 万—1000 万美元（4 种）	绵羊毛、纸张、塑料、焦、油化工	2224	18.08
1000 万美元以上（4 种）	成套设备、铜精矿砂、动力机械、氧化铝	8520	69.26
合计	**8 种**	**10744**	**87.35**

进口商品商场 进口商品来自 21 个国家和地区。

主要进口市场情况表

国别（地区）	进口金额（万美元）	占进口总额（%）
香　港	3694	31.03
澳大利亚	1724	14.01
美　国	1505	12.24
德　国	1277	10.38
日　本	1139	9.2
瑞　士	932	7.6
俄罗斯	425	3.5
合　计	**10696**	**87.96**

技术进出口　1998年甘肃省技术进出口总额7812.31万美元，比1997年3201.48万美元增加59.01%。其中技术出口4384.15万美元。其组成为：1、成套设备出口额429.20万美元；2、利用外政府贷款项下采用国际招标方式国内企业中标的机电成套设备额3954.95万美元。

技术引进　1998年技术进口总额3438.16万美元。其组成为：1、第四批日元贷款项目通过国际招标从国外引进额为264万美元；2、利用外国政府贷款项技术引进额2420.85万美元；3、审批技术引进和设备进口合同13个，合同总金额753.31万美元，比1997年11项增加2项。

【利用外资】

1998年新批准设立外商投资企业68户，比1997年62家增加了6家，总投资21133万美元，实际利用外资7665万美元，比1997年的10722万美元减少3057万美元，截止1998年底我省外商投资企业累计达1424家，总投资24亿美元，其中外资额10.45亿美元。

1998年利用外资情况表

利用外资方式	批准签订的合同			实际利用外资	
	项目数（个）	外资金额（万美元）	金额比1996年（±%）	金　额（万美元）	金额比1996年（±%）
外商直接投资					
合资企业	34	2138	－20	1354	－24
合作企业	11	2645	5	1363	2
外资企业	23	3581	－7	1147	－11
合　　计	**68**	**8364**	**－22**	**3864**	**－33**

【对外经济合作】

承包工程和劳务合作　1998年甘肃签订对外承包工程58项，比1997年增长20.83%；合同金额20100万美元，比1997年增长5.24%，实现营业额3668万美元比1997年的3224万美元增长10.3%。派出各类劳务人员908人，主要项目：科特迪瓦国家剧场、露天剧场、几内亚总统府工程。

接受多、双边无偿援助　1998年接受多、双边无偿援助项目64项，增长6项；协议金额3647.44万美元，比1997年3504.5万美元，增长3.9%，执行金额832.12万美元，比1997年833.7万美元下降0.18%；主要项目分布：1、联合国组织（多边）援助30项，主要项目：联合国儿童基金会援助贫困地区社会发展项目，促进贫困地区初等教育、妇女参与发展、新生儿破伤风防治；联合国开发署援助河西沙漠综合治理与利用、黄土高原农机具研究与推广、干旱、半干旱农业，农村发展扶贫项目；联合国人口基金会援助榆中生殖健康教育。2、友好国家（双边）援助项目33项，日本援助的兰州徐家山绿化与水土保持、民族中学民族教育；澳大利亚援助榆中上庄人畜饮水项目；加拿大国际发展署援助的甘肃综合扶贫项目，欧洲联盟援助甘肃喷灌培训中心、甘肃省贫困地区农村基础教育项目等。3、民间组织援助1项，爱德基金援助和政、积石山县失学儿童重建校园项目。

对外投资 境外非贸易性投资项目执行32项，合同额2423万美元。

【其他】

对外经贸洽谈会 1998年甘肃省继续通过省市联合与国家五部委协办的办会方式，主办了“兰交会”共有中外宾客八百多人到会，签订合同81940万元，促成外资项目22项，产权项144项，引进外资4124万美元，主要项目有：投资1.8亿元生产物固氮肥，建设甘肃黑河龙首水电站、驼鸟良种繁育中心、武威梨花梨果生产线、敦煌天然气工程、泾川县8000吨浓缩果汁生产线、张掖2000吨脱水菜扩建、金川镍钴金属盐项目、高台面粉厂扩建等。

【涉外旅游】

1998年全年接待涉外游客12.24万人次，比1997年11.3万人次，增长7.67%，旅游外汇收入3018万美元，比1997年2637.23万美元，增长12.62%。

高新技术开发区 兰州高新技术开发区1998年完成技工贸收入20.5亿万比1997年15亿元增长26.82%，总产值16.2亿元，比1997年11亿元增长32.09%；上缴税收0.9亿元，出口收汇430万美元，比1997年259万美元增长39.76%。

1998年青海省对外经济贸易

青海省对外贸易经济合作厅

【对外贸易】

进出口总额 1998年青海省进出口总额为11405万美元，比1997年的16478万美元下降了30.78%。

出口总额 出口总额10431万美元，比1997年的12440万美元下降16.15%，占全省国内生产总值220.4亿元（相当于26.69亿美元）的3.91%；占全国出口总额的0.06%。

出口商品结构 初级产品出口额2425万美元，占出口总额的23.20%；工业制成品的出口额为8007万美元，占出口总额的76.80%。

出口额在200万美元以上的商品情况表

金额分类	商品名称	出口金额（万美元）	占出口总额（%）
1000万美元以上（2种）	铅锭 硅铁	1223 1010	11.72 9.68

出口额在200万美元以上的商品情况表（续）

金额分类	商品名称	出口金额（万美元）	占出口总额（%）
500万—1000万美元（3种）	碳化硅 金属硅 镁锭	868 677 589	8.32 6.49 5.65
200万—500万美元（10种）	氯化镁、铝锭、铸铁件、锌锭、蚕豆、领带、虫草、无毛绒、其他锁、其他化工原料	3054	29.28
合计	**15种**	**7421**	**71.14**

出口商品市场 出口商品销往50个国家和地区。

主要出口市场情况表

国别（地区）	出口金额（万美元）	占出口总额（%）
日本	2308	22.13
香港	2023	19.39
韩国	1540	14.76
美国	1514	14.51
比利时	442	4.24
英国	433	4.15

主要出口市场情况表（续）

国别（地区）	出口金额（万美元）	占出口总额（%）
德国	291	2.79
合计	**8551**	**81.98**

进口总额 进口总额974万美元，比1997年的4038万美元下降75.88%。

进口商品结构 初级产品进口额409万美元，占进口总额的42.00%；工业制成品的进口额为565万美元，占进口总额的58.00%。

进口额在100万美元以上的商品情况表

金额分类	商品名称	进口金额（万美元）	占进口总额（%）
100万—200万美元（3种）	其他短纤维 铬矿砂 其他电讯设备及器材	111 126 168	11.40 12.94 17.25
200万—500万美元（1种）	氧化铝	230	23.61
合计	**4种**	**635**	**65.20**

进口商品市场 进口商品国别和地区10个。

主要进口市场情况表

国别（地区）	进口金额（万美元）	占进口总额（%）
香　港	202	20.74
印　度	126	12.94
德　国	176	18.07
瑞　典	107	10.99
澳大利亚	230	23.61
合　计	**841**	**86.34**

【利用外资】

1998 年利用外资情况表

利用外资方式	批准签订的合同		
	项目数（个）	外资金额（万美元）	金额比 1997 年（±%）
对外借款	8	2548	355
外商直接投资	24	7583.9	44
合资企业	7	1129.75	-63
合作企业	6	1152.85	-44
外资企业	11	5301.3	3005
合　计	**32**	**10131.9**	**73.37%**

外商直接投资行业　生产型项目 15 个，非生产型项目 9 个；能源 2 个，建材 1 个，冶炼 1 个，纺织 5 个，房地产开发 1 个，服务性行业 3 个，其他 11 个。

外商直接投资来源　香港 14 个项目，协议外资 3445.77 万美元；澳门 1 项，670.12 万美元；加拿大 2 项，600 万美元；挪威 1 项，81.88 万美元；美国 3 项，2625.3 万美元；台湾省 1 项，13.25 万美元；澳大利亚 1 项，50.60 万美元；新西兰 1 项，75 万美元；日本 1 项，20.48 万美元。

【对外经济合作】

接受经济援助　新接受国际双边援助项目 2 个，合计受援金额 100.72 万美元。分别是：澳大利亚政府援助青海省玉树藏族自治州囊谦县香达乡人畜引水工程项目 1 个，受援金额 0.72 万美元，资金当年到位，运转正常；日本国援助青海省师范大学民族教育器材装备项目 1 个，受援助金额 100 万美元（1.2 亿日元）。

【其他】

涉外旅游　1998 年全省接待境外旅游人数 1.66 万人次，比 1997 年增长 29.6%。其中外国游客 9724 人次，增长 3.2%；港澳台同胞 6561 人次，增长 93.1%。旅游外汇收入 276 万美元，比 1997 年 271.7 万美元增长 1.6%。

1998年宁夏回族自治区对外经济贸易

宁夏回族自治区对外经济贸易厅

【对外贸易】

进出口总额 1998年宁夏回族自治区进出口总额为31728万美元，比1997年的30283万美元增长4.8%。

出口总额 出口总额为28650万美元，比1997年的25203万美元增长13.7%，占全区国内生产总值的10.4%，占全国出口总额的0.16%。

出口商品结构 初级产品出口额为7373万美元，占出口总额的25.7%；工业制成品出口额为21277万美元，占出口总额的74.3%。

出口额在100万美元以上的商品情况表

金额分类	商品名称	出口金额（万美元）	占出口总额（%）
1000万美元以上（9种）	无烟煤、钽制品、铝、镁、无毛绒、硅铁、铸铁件、羊绒衫、碳化硅及磨料	16152	56.4
500万—1000万美元（3种）	双氰胺、活性炭、轮胎	2184.8	7.6
100万—500万美元（8种）	四环素、电石、焦炭、枸杞、衬衫、柠檬酸、石灰氮、硫脲	2401	8.4
合计	**20种**	**20737.8**	**72.4**

出口商品市场 出口商品主要销往76个国家和地区。

主要出口市场情况表

国别（地区）	出口金额（万美元）	占出口总额（%）
美国	6035	21
日本	5327	18.6
香港	2629	9.2
英国	2457	8.6
德国	2036	7.1
法国	1485	5.2
以色列	1170	4.1

主要出口市场情况表（续）

国别（地区）	出口金额（万美元）	占出口总额（%）
韩国	1114	3.9
荷兰	1031	3.6
新加坡	777	2.7
加拿大	707	2.5
合计	**24768**	**86.5**

进口总额 进口总额为3073.5万美元，比1997年的5080万美元下降39.4%。

进口商品结构 初级产品的进口额为

813.9万美元，占进口总额的26.4%；工业制成品的进口额为2264.6万美元，占进口总额的73.6%。

主要进口商品情况表

金额分类	商品名称	进口金额(万美元)	占出口总额(%)
500万—1000万美元（2种）	钽铌矿砂、氧化铝	1389.4	45.2
100万—500万美元（6种）	成套设备、油漆、医疗器械、纸浆及纸制品、天然橡胶、农药	1326.5	43.2
合　计	**8种**	**2715.9**	**88.4**

进口商品市场　进口商品来自20个国家和地区。

主要进口市场情况表

国别（地区）	进口金额(万美元)	占进口总额%
香　港	833.1	27.1
美　国	791.6	25.8
日　本	507.2	16.5
瑞　典	284.9	9.3
合　计	**2416.8**	**78.6**

技术进出口　1998年全自治区签订技术进口合同16项，合同总额2707万美元，比1997年的1602万美元增长69%。

【利用外资】

1998年利用外资情况表

利用外资方式	批准签订的合同			实际利用外资	
	项目数(个)	外资金额(万美元)	金额比1997年（±%）	金额(万美元)	金额比1997年（±%）
对外借款	5	10600	538.2	5153	92.3
外商直接投资	36	5203	386.3	1856	176.6
合资企业	18	2199	251.3	371	-4.9
合作企业	5	2677	1015.4	1197	398.8
外资企业	13	327	60.3	288	602.4
外商其他投资	4	267	-88.4	26	-98.9
加工装配					
合　计	**45**	**16070**	**219.7**	**7035**	**24.6**

外商直接投资行业 外商直接投资项目中，生产型项目18个，非生产型企业18个。

外商直接投资来源 外商投资项目来自18个国家和地区，其中香港12项，合同金额3760万美元，实际使用外资1082万美元；台湾省6项，合同外资金额131万美元，实际使用外资111万美元；美国1项，合同外资金额600万美元，实际使用210万美元。

外商直接投资企业生产经营情况 1998年外商投资企业生产经营状况良好。全自治区已经投产的二百多家外商投资企业，效益普遍较好。1998年全区外商投资企业实现销售收入187896万元，实现利润2665万美元，出口创汇2851万美元，占全区出口总额的10%。

【对外经济合作】

承包工程和劳务合作 1998年全自治区签订对外承包工程和劳务合同项目3个，金额580万美元。当年派出劳务人员113个，派往的主要国家是日本、赞比亚、卢旺达、乌干达等。

接受经济援助 接受国外援助项目4个，总金额1000万美元。项目是：日本援助的自治区医院项目，加拿大援助的同心和海原县扶贫项目，澳大利亚援助的彭阳县、泾源县卫生项目，欧盟援助的自治区农业厅项目等。

对外投资 1998年批准在境外投资项目1个，中方投资额2.6万美元，是中蒙合资企业。

【其他】

对外经贸洽谈会 1998年9月在银川举办中国宁夏投资暨东西部合作洽谈会，签订引资合同1.4亿美元。

港口运输 1998年全自治区完成进出口货运量100万吨，与1997年基本持平，其中出口量为90万吨，进口量为10万吨。按运输方式分：海运97万吨，陆运3万吨。

涉外旅游 1998年入境的外国人及港澳同胞5069人次，增长19.6%。旅游收入141.6万美元，比1997年的133万美元增长6.5%。

1998年新疆维吾尔自治区对外经济贸易

新疆维吾尔自治区对外贸易经济合作厅

【对外贸易】

进出口总额 1998年新疆维吾尔自治区进出口总额15.32亿美元，比1997年的14.47亿美元增长5.87%。

出口总额 出口总额80789.7万美元，比1997年的66611万美元，增长21.29%，占全区国内生产总值的6%，占全国出口总额的0.44%。

出口商品结构 初级产品出口额17692万美元，占出口总额的21.9%；工业制成品63088万美元，占78.1%。

出口额在1000万美元以上的商品情况表

金额分类	商品名称	出口金额（万美元）	占出口总额（%）
4000万美元以上（2种）	日用杂品、蕃茄酱罐头	11989	14.84
2000—4000万美元（7种）	家具、化纤服装、精梳、棉纱、纯涤纶布、羊绒衫、焦炭、鞋	18299	22.65
1000—2000万美元（12种）	酒精、农膜、方便面、棉毛衫、裤、棉坯布、肠衣、棉色布、烤烟、尼龙衫裤、食糖、铝合金等	15411	19.08
合　计	**21种**	**45699**	**56.57**

出口商品市场　出口商品销往79个国家和地区。

主要出口市场情况表

国别（地区）	出口金额（万美元）	占出口总额（%）
吉尔吉斯斯坦	17127.1	21.2
哈萨克斯坦	16673.8	20.64
香　港	15624.4	19.34
日　本	5837.1	7.23
美　国	4596.7	5.69
俄罗斯	2542.1	3.15

主要出口市场情况表（续）

国别（地区）	出口金额（万美元）	占出口总额（%）
乌兹别克斯坦	2381.5	2.95
合　计	**64782.7**	**80.2**

进口总额　722424.6万美元，比1997年的78120万美元下降7.29%。

进口商品结构　初级产品进口额11834.5万美元，占进口总额的16.3%；工业制成品64590.1万美元，占83.7%。

进口额在100万美元以上的商品情况表

金额分类	商品名称	进口金额（万美元）	占进口总额（%）
1000万美元以上（16种）	钢材、化肥、铝、铜、棉花、其他化工原料、铝材、石油成套设备、新闻纸、牛皮、铜材、棉短绒、球团矿、废钢、羊毛、汽车	55845	77.10

进口额在 100 万美元以上的商品情况表（续）

金额分类	商品名称	进口金额（万美元）	占进口总额（%）
500—1000 万美元（8 种）	无机酸、有线通讯设备、绵羊皮、计算机、石油、机械、低压聚乙烯、酯化工品、钠化合物	6241	8.62
100—500 万美元（28 种）	医疗器械、桑蚕茧、木材、其他电讯设备、医药原料、碳酸锂、动力机械、亚麻、油漆、地震仪、铜炉渣、纸浆、其他各类机械、电力成套设备、无线通讯设备等	6104	8.43
合　计	**52 种**	**68190**	**94.15**

进口商品来自 37 个国家和地区。

主要进口市场情况表

国别（地区）	进口金额（万美元）	占进口总额 %
哈萨克斯坦	39350	54.33
香　港	7270	10.04
美　国	5551	7.66
俄罗斯	5075	7.01
乌兹别克斯坦	3636	5.02
吉尔吉斯斯坦	3073	4.24
日　本	2332	3.22
合　计	**66287**	**91.52**

【边境贸易】

1998 年，全区边境贸易进出口总额 86953.3 万美元，占全区进出口总额的 56.75%，比 1997 年的 74994 万美元增长 15.95%。其中出口额 37599.3 万美元，增长 63.74%。出口的主要商品有：酒精、化纤布、服装、鞋类、塑料原料及制品等。进口额 49354 万美元，比 1997 年的 52031 万美元下降 5.15%。进口的主要商品有：钢材、化肥、铜、铝、棉花、牛皮等。

技术进出口　1998 年，全区签订引进技术和进口设备合同项目 6 个，比上年增加 1 个；合同金额 3252.21 万美元，比 1997 年的 1277.5 万美元增加 1.55 倍。

【利用外资】

1998 年利用外资情况表

利用外资方式	批准签订的合同			实际利用外资	
	项目数（个）	外资金额（万美元）	金额比 1997 年（±%）	金额（万美元）	金额比 1997 年（±%）
外商直接投资	46	13827	235.04	2167	-12.34
合资企业	28	5943		986	
合作企业	5	2087			
外资企业	13	5797		1181	
合　　计	**46**	**13827**	**235.04**	**2167**	**-12.34**

外商直接投资行业　外商直接投资的 46 个项目中，生产型项目 41 个，占 89.13%；非生产型项目 5 个，占 10.87%。按行业划分：农林牧渔业 3 项、工业 38 项、服务业 4 项、其他行业 1 项。

外商直接投资来源　外商直接投资分别来自 13 个国家和地区。主要有香港特别行政区 13 项，金额 6500 万美元；澳门 1 项，400 万美元；台湾省 2 项，53 万美元；泰国 3 项，152 万美元；马来西亚 4 项，500 万美元；新加坡 3 项，114 万美元；韩国 4 项，391 万美元；塞拉利昂 1 项，200 万美元；英国 1 项，51 万美元；维尔京群岛 3 项，3063 万美元；加拿大 1 项，8 万美元；美国 6 项，1679 万美元；澳大利亚 4 项，716 万美元。

外商直接投资企业生产经营情况　全年外商投资企业出口创汇 10922.4 万美元，比上年增长 45.17%，占全区出口总额的 13.52%。

【对外经济合作】

承包工程和劳务合作　1998 年全区签订对外承包工程和劳务合同 3 个，金额 91.6 万美元，比上年下降 27%，营业额 276.3 万美元，比上年增长 102.6%；当年派出劳务人员 312 人，年末回国 287 人。派往的主要国家是：苏丹、沙特阿拉伯、哈萨克斯坦。承包的主要项目是：哈萨克斯坦阿克纠宾斯克油田钻井工程，分包苏丹喀士穆炼油厂工程土建部分。

对外经济技术援助　1998 年承担援外项目 4 个，总金额 1.18 亿元人民币。受援国家和地区是：乌克兰、阿塞拜疆、哈萨克斯坦、巴基斯坦。涉及的行业有：轻工、纺织、加油站、电子计算机，目前这些项目均在建设中。

接受经济援助　接受外国政府和国际经济援助项目 3 个，总金额（折合）295.6 万美元。其中：日本政府无偿援助“少数民族地区中等学校、教育器材装备”项目 1.2 亿日元。澳大利亚政府无偿援助我区“塔里木河流域生态环境项目”300 万澳元，加拿大驻华社团为和田市乡村妇女活动中心捐赠 35 万元人民币。

对外投资　1998 年全区批准在境外兴办企业 5 家，总投资额 182.2 万美元，其中中方投资 143.2 万美元，比 1997 年的 440.8 万美元下降 67.51%。这些企业主要分布在哈萨克斯坦、吉尔吉斯斯坦、塔吉克斯坦。

【其他】

经济技术开发区　1998 年乌鲁木齐高新技术产业开发区完成基础设施投资额 1060 万元。新批生产型项目 18 个，总投资额 3.06 亿元，其中：三资企业 13 个，投资额 2.78 亿元，注册资本 1.73 亿元。项目涉及新型建材、金属加工、风力发电等行业。整个开发区内企业全年共实现工业总产值 4.512 亿元，实现税收 9132 万元；财政收入 5366 万元。外贸完成进出口总额 2235 万美元，其中进口523万美元；出口1712万美元。内贸销售额59857万元。

1998年乌鲁木齐经济技术开发区完成基础设施投资额1762万元。新批生产型项目26个，总投资额8.7亿元人民币，其中：三资企业8个，投资额7563.2万美元，注册资本3298万美元。项目涉及金属制品、精细化工、生物农药、高档针织服装、化妆品等行业。整个开发区内企业全年共实现工业总产值5亿元人民币，比1997年的4.08亿元人民币增长22.5%。实现税收7636万元人民币；财政收入5110万元人民币。1998年外贸完成进出口总额3073万美元，其中进口417万美元；出口2656万美元。内贸销售额39641万元人民币。

1998年伊宁市边境经济合作区完成基础设施投资额330万元。新批生产型项目4个，总投资额189万元。项目涉及电器制造、服装、建材、饲料等行业。整个开发区企业全年共实现工业总产值2873.51万元，实现税收473万元；财政收入697.25万元。外贸完成出口额159万美元。内贸销售额267万元。

1998年塔城市边境经济合作区完成基础设施投资额50.4万元。新批项目3个，总投资额1623万元。项目涉及房屋建设和商业。整个开发区企业全年共实现工业总产值5922万元。外贸完成进出口总额507万美元，其中进口288万美元；出口219万美元。

1998年博乐市边境经济合作区完成基础设施投资额288.35万元。新批生产型项目1个，总投资额1500万元。整个开发区内企业1998年全年共实现工业总产值2.13亿元，实现税收2585万元；财政收入1465.54万元。外贸完成进口14.17万美元。

对外经贸洽谈会 1998年9月1日至9月8日在乌鲁木齐举办的'98乌鲁木齐对外经济贸易洽谈会，有四十多个国家和地区以及国内28个省、区、市一万多名客商和政府官员到会。成交总额12.87亿美元，其中出口成交5.11亿美元。进口订货4.67亿美元，对外经济技术合作项目3.099亿美元；国内贸易和经济技术合作项目合同成交76.21亿元人民币，其中商贸成交35.65亿元人民币，经济技术合作项目成交40.56亿元人民币。

1998年新疆维吾尔自治区在哈萨克斯坦、澳大利亚、吉尔吉斯斯坦分别举办了3次大型对外经贸洽谈会，签订贸易合同总金额合计达1121.61万美元；合同意向610万美元；零售商品1.6万美元。

港口运输 全区已经国家批准开放的陆路口岸16个，已建成开通的12个，货物吞吐能力为520万吨。当年完成货物运输总量306.34万吨，比1997年的214.77万吨增长42.64%，其中：出口货物运量78.15万吨；进口货物运量228.19万吨。

涉外旅游 1998年全区接待入境旅游和旅游购物者25.65万人次，旅游外汇收入8046万美元，比1997年的7115.20万美元增长13.08%。

1998年香港对外贸易

外经贸部台港澳司

受亚洲金融危机的影响，1998年香港整体经济处于艰难的调整时期，对外贸易也表现欠佳。据香港特区政府统计，1998年香港对外贸易总额为27767.41亿港元，比上年下降9.6%；其中总出口13476.49亿港元，比上年下降7.4%；进口14290.92亿港元，比上年下降11.5%。香港的进出口出现了全面下滑的罕见局面。

【港产品出口】

1998年港产品出口额为1884.54亿港元，比上年下降10.9%。主要出口市场中，由于祖国内地消费不旺，加之内地生产水平的提高，以当地产品代替进口货物需求，港产品对内地出口出现了大幅下滑，全年港产品出口内地560.66亿港元，比上年下降12.2%；美国经济持续稳健增长，带动进口增加，在港产品主要出口市场中，对美出口降幅最小，为-0.4%，货值548.42亿港元；港产品出口到英国、德国和台湾省也出现下跌。在日本，由于经济长期陷于低迷，企业盈利进一步下降，收入和就业情况持续恶化，消费信心进一步减弱，港产品对日出口在上年下跌6.1%的基础上大跌39.5%，仅为64.35亿港元。

1998年港产品主要出口市场情况表

国家或地区	金 额（亿港元）	比上年（%）	占 总 值	
			1998年	1997年
出口总计	1884.54	-10.9	100.0	100.0
五大市场				
中国内地	560.66	-12.2	29.8	30.2
美国	548.42	-0.4	29.1	26.1
英国	100.58	-6.2	5.3	5.1
德国	98.05	-5.0	5.2	4.9
台湾省	65.05	-7.5	3.5	3.3

【转口贸易】

1998年香港转口贸易额为11591.95亿港元，在上年增长5%的基础上下降了6.9%，主要原因是世界贸易增长的减慢、国际需求萎缩及香港新机场7、8月份空运货物服务的局部受阻。转口贸易占香港对外贸易总额的比重由1997年的40.53%微升至98年的41.75%。

内地仍为香港最大的转口来源地和转口市场。1998年香港转口内地商品6912.19亿港元，较上年下降4.5%；海外经港转口运往内地商品4073.66亿港元，较上年下降8.2%。两者均扭转了上年增长的态势。前者主要是因为海外市场需求的萎缩导致内地经港出口商品的减少；后者是因为内地加工贸易政策的调整和进口货物需求的放缓。此外，香港离岸贸易的发展也是重要原因之一。

1998年香港主要转口市场情况表

国家或地区	金 额（亿港元）	比上年（%）	占 总 值	
			1998年	1997年
转口总值	11591.95	-6.9	100.0	100.0
五大市场				
中国内地	4073.66	-8.2	35.1	35.7
美国	2598.56	-0.6	22.4	21.0
日本	641.94	-17.4	5.5	6.2
英国	422.59	+8.2	3.6	3.1
德国	421.16	-9.0	3.6	3.7

1998 年香港主要转口商品来源地情况表

国家或地区	金　额（亿港元）	比上年（%）	占总值	
			1998 年	1997 年
五大来源地				
中国内地	6912.19	-4.5	59.6	58.1
日本	1238.79	-7.4	10.7	10.8
台湾省	717.82	-13.9	6.2	6.7
美国	545.30	-12.9	4.7	5.0
韩国	396.37	-0.1	3.4	3.2

【进口】

1998 年香港进口总额为 14290.92 亿港元，同比下降了 11.5%，扭转了连续几年增长的势头。主要原因是香港本地经济的收缩导致的内部需求缩减所致。1998 年香港的消费开支自 1974 年石油危机以来首次下跌，跌幅为 6.6%；整体投资连续 4 年取得双位数字增长后，首次回落 5.8%。此外，由于港产品出口大幅下跌，进口留用的原料及半制成品也大幅下降。1998 年香港进口降幅大于出口降幅致使香港的贸易逆差由 1997 年的 1591.41 亿港元降至 814.43 亿港元。

1998 年香港主要进口国家或地区情况表

国家或地区	金　额（亿港元）	比上年（%）	占总值	
			1998 年	1997 年
进口总额	14290.92	-11.5	100.0	100.0
其中：				
中国内地	5538.24	-5.1	38.8	36.1
日本	1866.52	-19.1	13.1	14.3
美国	1110.67	-16.6	7.8	8.2
台湾省	1037.90	-16.7	7.3	7.7
韩国	713.50	-5.4	5.0	4.7

1998年台湾省对外经济贸易

外经贸部台港澳司台湾处

【对外贸易】

1998年台湾省进出口贸易总额为2153.8亿美元，比1997年的2365.1亿美元下降8.9%，占1998年台湾“GNP”2623亿美元的82.11%，与1997年的82.9%大体相当。其中出口1106.4亿美元，比1997年的1220.8亿美元下降9.4%，进口1047.4亿美元，比1997年的1144.2亿美元下降8.5%，全年贸易顺差59.0亿美元，比1997年的76.6亿美元减少22.9%。截止到1998年底，台湾外汇储备达903.4亿美元，比1997年的835亿美元增加68.4亿美元。

出口商品结构 1998年台湾省出口商品结构与1997年相比，农产品、农产加工品、重化工业产品和非重化工业产品出口均大幅度减少。1998年台湾省农产品出口3.2亿美元，占出口总值的0.3%，比1997年的3.8亿美元减少0.6亿美元；农产加工品出口16.3亿美元，占出口总值的1.5%，比1997年的21.7亿美元减少5.4亿美元；重化工业产品出口711.0亿美元，占出口总值的64.3%，比1997年的767.5亿美元减少62.9亿美元；非重化工业产品出口375.8亿美元，占出口总值的34.0%，比1997年的427.8亿美元减少52.0亿美元。

1998年台湾省出口商品结构

单位：亿美元

	1998年		1997年		增减比较	
	金 额	%	金 额	%	金 额	%
出口总额	1106.4	100.0	1220.8	100.0	-114.4	-9.4
农产品	3.2	0.3	3.8	0.3	-0.6	-15.4
农产加工品	16.3	1.5	21.7	1.8	-5.4	-24.8
重化工业产品	711.0	64.3	767.5	62.9	-56.4	-7.4
非重化工业产品	375.8	34.0	427.8	35.0	-52.0	-12.2

资料来源：台湾省“财政部”进出口贸易统计

1998年台湾省出口商品金额列前三位的分别是机械用具及其设备、电机设备及其零件、塑胶及其制品，占全年出口总额的27.0%、23.0%和5.3%。

1998年台湾省主要出口商品

单位：亿美元

	1998年		1997年		增减比较	
	金额	%	金额	%	金额	%
出口总额	1106.4	100.0	1220.8	100.0	-114.4	-9.4
1、机械用具及其零件	298.6	27.0	318.4	26.1	-19.8	-6.2
2、电机设备及其零件	254.5	23.0	271.5	22.2	-17.1	-16.3

1998年台湾省主要出口商品（续）

单位：亿美元

	1998年		1997年		增减比较	
	金额	%	金额	%	金额	%
3、塑胶及其制品	59.0	5.3	66.4	5.4	-7.3	-11.1
4、运输设备	43.8	4.0	48.1	3.9	-4.3	-9.1
5、钢铁制品	35.1	3.2	37.1	3.0	-2.1	-5.6
6、人造纤维丝	33.2	3.0	37.3	3.1	-4.1	-10.9
7、钢铁	29.0	2.6	29.3	2.4	-0.3	-1.1
8、针织品	28.2	2.5	30.2	2.5	-2.0	-6.7
9、家具	20.6	1.9	22.8	1.9	-2.2	-9.8
10、光学仪器	19.8	1.8	21.7	1.8	-1.9	-8.6

资料来源：台湾省“财政部”进出口贸易统计。

进口商品结构 1998年台湾省进口商品除资本设备呈增长外，其余均呈下降。资本设备进口243.1亿美元，占进口总值的23.2%，比1997年的217.3亿美元增加25.8亿美元；农工原料进口668.3亿美元，占进口总值的63.8%，比1997年的771.3亿美元减少103.0亿美元；消费品进口135.9亿美元，占进口总值的12.0%，比1997年的155.6亿美元减少19.7亿美元。

1998年台湾省进口商品结构

单位：亿美元

	1998年		1997年		增减比较	
	金　额	%	金　额	%	金　额	%
进口总额	1047.4	100.0	1144.2	100.0	-96.8	-8.5
资本设备	243.1	23.2	217.3	19.0	25.8	11.9
农工原料	668.3	63.8	771.3	67.4	-103.0	-13.4
消费品	135.9	13.0	155.6	13.6	-19.7	-12.6

资料来源：台湾省“财政部”进出口贸易统计。

1998年台湾省进口商品金额列前三位的分别是电机设备及其零件、机械用具及其零件、矿物燃料，占全年进口总额的24.2%、16.9%和6.4%；进口增长幅度最大的前三位商品分别是航空器、机械用具及其零件、电机设备及其零件，与1997年相比分别增长65.7%、9.5%和1.4%。

1998年台湾省主要进口商品

单位：亿美元

	1998年		1997年		增减比较	
	金　额	%	金　额	%	金　额	%
进口总额	1047.4	100.0	1144.2	100.0	-96.9	-8.5
1、电机设备及其零件	253.0	24.2	249.6	21.8	3.4	1.4
2、机械用具及其零件	176.9	16.9	161.6	14.1	15.3	9.5
3、矿物燃料	67.1	6.4	90.9	7.9	-23.8	-26.1

1998 年台湾省主要进口商品（续）

单位：亿美元

	1998 年		1997 年		增减比较	
	金　额	%	金　额	%	金　额	%
4、特殊制品	51.2	4.9	55.1	4.8	-3.9	-7.0
5、光学仪器	49.1	4.7	60.3	5.3	-11.2	-18.6
6、有机化学品	45.7	4.4	55.4	4.8	-9.7	-17.5
7、钢铁	43.4	4.1	54.5	4.8	-11.1	-20.3
8、运输设备	27.9	2.7	33.5	2.9	-5.6	-16.7
9、塑胶及其制品	27.2	2.6	30.8	2.7	-3.6	-11.6
10、航空器	22.2	2.1	13.4	1.2	8.8	65.7

资料来源：台湾省“财政部”进出口贸易统计

进出口贸易市场　1998 年台湾省的主要出口市场是美国、香港、欧盟、东盟六国（新加坡、泰国、马来西亚、印尼、菲律宾、越南）和日本，出口金额分别占台湾省全年出口总额的 26.6%、22.5%、16.7%、10.6% 和 8.4%；主要进口国家和地区为日本、美国、欧盟、东盟六国和韩国，进口金额分别占台湾省全年进口总额的 25.8%、18.8%、16.9%、12.0% 和 5.4%，而从香港的进口只占台湾省全年进口的 1.9%。

1998 年台湾省的贸易顺差主要来自香港和美国，分别达到 228.9 亿美元和 97.0 亿美元，贸易逆差则主要来自日本、韩国和法国，分别为 176.9 亿美元、41.8 亿美元和 39.5 亿美元。

1998 年台湾省出口市场中增长最多的国家和地区是墨西哥、意大利、德国、荷兰和奥地利，增幅分别达到 23.2%、18.9%、10.7%、1.7% 和 1.2%；而台湾省从菲律宾、奥地利、韩国、法国和泰国的进口增长最多，增幅分别达到 32.6%、31.9%、12.9%、12.7% 和 2.1%。

台湾省与祖国大陆的贸易情况　1998 年台湾省与大陆贸易总额为 225.11 亿美元，比 1997 年下降 7.9%，其中输出估计金额为 184.0 亿美元，下降 10.3%，输入金额为 41.11 亿美元，增长 5.0%，贸易顺差 142.9 亿美元。

1998 年台湾省输出到大陆的商品主要包括电机设备及其零件、机械用具及其零件、塑胶及其制品、人造纤维丝、钢铁及工业用纺织物，合计 114.19 亿美元，占台湾省输出大陆商品金额的 62.1%；台湾省自大陆输入的商品集中于电机设备及其零件、钢铁、机械设备及其零件、矿物燃料与矿油及其蒸馏产品、石料、涂敷料、石灰及水泥等，合计 24.96 亿美元，占台湾省自大陆输入商品金额的 56.7%。

赵春

1998 年台湾省与大陆经香港转口间接贸易

单位：亿美元

		1998 年	1997 年
台湾省“海关统计”	贸易总额	225.1	244.5
	年增率	-7.9	10.00
	输出总额（推估值）	184	205.18
	年增率	-10.3	7.20
	输入总额	41.1	39.15
	年增率	5	28.00
香港海关统计值：转口输出总额		83.64	85.7

1998 年台湾省与大陆经香港转口间接贸易（续）

单位：亿美元

	1998 年	1997 年
年增率	-13.90	0.00
转口输入总额	16.55	17.43
年增率	-5.10	10.20
转口贸易差额	67.09	79.71
年增率	-15.80	-2.00

资料来源：台湾省“经济部”国贸局两岸经香港转口间接贸易统计

【利用外资】

海外华侨和外国人在台湾直接投资

1998 年海外华侨和外国人在台湾省的直接投资件数与 1997 年相比均有较大增长，增幅分别为 20.45% 和 35.37%，但投资金额均呈下降，分别下降 62.99% 和 18.76%。按行业分，制造业、金融保险业和商业领域的投资金额列前三位。

1998 年海外华侨和外国人在台湾省直接投资

单位：万美元

	1998 年		1997 年	
	金额	年增率（%）	金额	年增率（%）
对台湾省投资总额	329471	-22.78	426663	72.68
海外华侨投资额	14339	-62.99	38747	127.32
外国人投资额	315132	-18.76	386187	68.61
按行业：农林渔牧业				
工业	191309	-17.11	230797	
矿业及土石采取业	253	301.59	63	
制造业	186529	-18.24	229261	
水电燃气业	788			
建筑营造业	3739	153.84	1473	
服务业	422224	117.49	194138	
商业	47618	-7.39	51417	
运输及仓储业	5317	-53.2	11360	
金融保险业	103004	88.94	54516	
其他及个有服务业	26629	-65.35	76845	

资料来源：台湾省“经济部”核准侨外投资统计。

台商对外投资　1998 年经台湾省“经济部”核准的对外投资金额（不含到祖国大陆投资）达到 32.96 亿美元，比 1997 年增长 13.91%。美国、新加坡、泰国、越南和香港是台商投资金额列前五名的国家和地区，金融保险业、制造业和商业是台商对外投资金额最多的三个行业。

1998 年台湾省核准对外投资

单位：千美元

	1998 年	1997 年
总额	3296302	2893826
年增率	13.91	33.64
按地区：美国	598666	547416
日本	29596	32342
香港	68643	141593
新加坡	158176	230310
泰国	131186	57546
马来西亚	19736	85088
印度尼西亚	19541	55861
菲律宾	38777	127022
越南	110078	85414
欧洲	33828	58508
大洋州	8470	78437
按行业：农林渔牧业	5203	22026
矿业及土石采取业	2676	17578
制造业	1038551	966128
水电燃气业		
建筑营造业	1669	2743
商业	290191	503796
运输及仓储业	58333	233982
金融保险业	1788760	997461
其他	110919	150112

资料来源：台湾省“经济部”核准对外投资统计。

台商在祖国大陆的投资　1998 年经台湾省“经济部”核准的台商到大陆投资金额为 20.35 亿美元，比 1997 年的 43.34 亿美元下降 53.1%，显示了“戒急用忍”大陆经贸政策和亚洲金融危机对台商到大陆投资的影响较大。台商到大陆投资以电力电子业、金属基本工业和精密器械业为主，而广东、江苏、福建则是台商投资金额最多的三个省份。

1998 年台湾省对大陆投资

单位：万美元

	1998 年	1997 年
核准对大陆投资总额	203462	433431
按行业：食品饮料业	7004	33307
塑胶制品业	6418	34912
金属基本工业	12685	39597

1998 年台湾省对大陆投资（续）

单位：万美元

	1998 年	1997 年
电力电子业	75898	87504
精密器械业	7462	24725
其他	93995	213386
按地区：广东	82442	172090
福建	15079	47223
江苏	69475	124730
海南	1300	3798
河北	9242	23357
东北地区	1050	6277
其他	24874	55956

资料来源：台湾省“经济部”核准对大陆投资统计。

1998 年澳门对外经济贸易

外经贸部国际经济贸易合作研究院

【对外贸易】

据澳门政府统计，1998 年澳门对外贸易总值为 326.8 亿元（澳门元，下同，约合 40.95 亿美元），比 1997 年（337 亿元）下降 3.02%。其中进口总值为 155.96 亿元（约折合 19.54 亿美元），较 1997 年（166 亿元）下降 6.1%；出口总值为 170.83 亿元（约折合 21.41 亿美元），比 1997 年（171.3 亿元）下跌 0.3%。其中澳门本地产品出口值 149.04 亿元（约折合 18.67 亿美元），比 1997 年（150 亿元）下降 1.0%。澳门出口贸易下跌主要与亚洲金融危机后部分国家的进口需求减少，澳门产品对外竞争力下降，出口产品价格下跌等因素有关。进口下降主要由于澳门经济持续衰退，各支柱产业在调整中面临诸多困难，内需疲软，通货紧缩所致。澳门内需的持续下降，使其对外贸易出现 15 亿元的顺差，较 1997 年的顺差增长 183%。

1998 年澳门对外贸易情况表

项　　目	金　额（亿澳门元）	比 1997 年（±%）	1997 年比 1996 年（±%）	占　总　值（%）
对外贸易总值	326.8	-3.02	5.87	100
其中：				
进口总值	155.9	-6.1	4.19	48.95
出口总值	170.8	-0.3	7.75	52.26
本地产品出口值	149.04	-1	12.14	45.61
转口值	21.8	4.7	-15.48	6.67

近年澳门的经济与外贸正处于调整时期，其出口商品结构主要是劳动密集型的加工产品。纺织品及成衣是澳门出口的主要商品，1998 年出口总值为 144.42 亿元（约 18.10 亿美元），比 1997 年（145.65 亿元）下跌 0.8%，占澳门出口总值的 84.5%。

1998 年澳门产品主要出口市场情况表

项　　目	金　额（亿澳门元）	比 1997 年（±%）	1997 年比 1996 年（±%）	占　总　值（%）
纺织品及成衣	144.42	-0.8	13.07	84.5
鞋类	3.83	18.7	7.1	2.2
玩具	0.94	3.7	7.1	1.9
电子	0.15	-6.6	-29.1	0.09

澳门最大的出口市场是美国。1998 年对美国的出口货值为 81.41 亿元（约 10.20 亿美元），比 1997 年增长 5.1%，占澳门出口总值的 47.7%；出口到欧盟的货值为 52.10 亿元（约 6.53 亿美元），较 1997 年下降 7.5%，占澳门出口比重由 1997 年的 32.9%下降到 30.5%。1998 年澳门对内地出口较上年增长 4.1%，占澳门出口比重为 6.8%。澳门对香港出口比 1997 年下降 1.1%。

1998 年澳门产品主要出口市场情况表

国别（地区）	金　额（亿澳门元）	比 1997 年（±%）	1997 年比 1996 年（±%）	占　总　值（%）
欧盟（15 国）	52.10	-7.5	5.0	30.5
美国	81.41	5.1	20.78	47.4

1998 年澳门产品主要出口市场情况表（续）

国别（地区）	金额（亿澳门元）	比 1997 年（±%）	1997 年比 1996 年（±%）	占总值（%）
香港	13.01	-1.1	-21.9	7.6
内地	11.57	4.1	-12.3	6.8

1998 年澳门进口仍集中于亚太地区，其中主要国家和地区为中国内地、香港及日本等。中国内地是澳门最大的进口市场，占其进口比重的 32.6%，香港地区占 23.7%，日本占 7.7%。1998 年澳门从中国内地、香港、日本进口货值分别为 50.29 亿元（约 6.38 亿美元）、36.97 亿元（约 4.63 亿美元）、12.08 亿元（约 1.51 亿美元），分别比 1997 年增长 7.4%、下降 11.5% 及 14.8%。1998 年澳门自中国台湾省的进口比重由上年的 9.6%上升为 9.9%。中国内地、香港、台湾省对澳门的出口总额占澳门进口总额的 66.2%。此外，澳门的主要进口国家还有欧盟、美国等。欧盟及美国对澳门的出口总值占澳门进口总值的 15.2%。

1998 年澳门主要进口市场情况表

国别（地区）	金额（亿澳门元）	比 1997 年（±%）	1997 年比 1996 年（±%）	占总值（%）
内地	50.92	7.4	24.2	32.6
香港	36.97	-11.5	-9.7	23.7
台湾省	15.37	0.0	9.6	9.9
日本	12.08	-14.8	-0.9	7.7
欧盟（15 国）	16.41	-20.0	-6.0	10.5
美国	7.33	-29.7	11.0	4.7

【旅游】

据澳门政府统计，1998 年赴澳门的游客人数达695 万人次，比 1997 年的 700 万人次下降了 0.7%。主要客源来自中国内地、香港、台湾省、日本和韩国。其中内地及香港游客达 527 万人次，比 1997 年增加了 6.8%。因受台湾省经济及金融波动影响，台湾省赴澳门游客为 82.2 万人次，较 1997 年下降 9.3%。

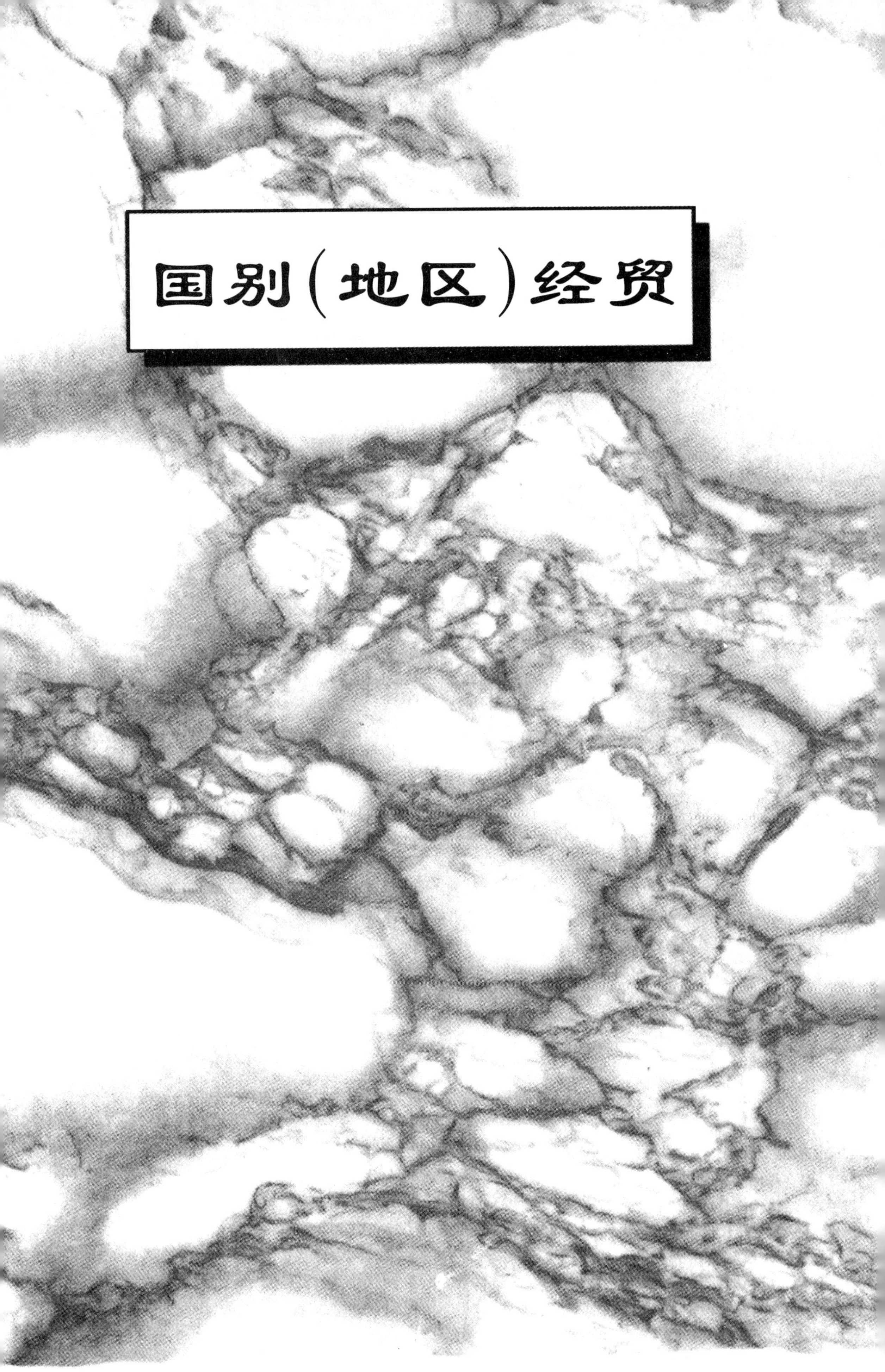

国别（地区）经贸

1998年中国内地与港、澳地区的经济贸易关系

对外贸易经济合作部台港澳司综合处

1998年，亚洲金融危机的不利影响和香港经济的艰难调整给祖国内地和香港特区的经贸合作带来了前所未有的困难；在这一年，迎接澳门回归的各项工作在有条不紊地进行，祖国内地与澳门的经贸合作在原有的基础上继续稳步发展，为两地的经贸合作注入了新的生机与活力。

一、进出口贸易

据我海关统计，1998年内地与香港进出口贸易额为454.12亿美元，比上年下降10.6%，占当年我进出口总额的14.02%；其中内地对香港出口387.53亿美元，比上年下降11.5%，占当年我出口总额的21.09%；内地从香港进口66.58亿美元，比上年下降4.7%，占当年我进口总额的4.8%。香港仍为内地第三大贸易伙伴和最大的出口市场，但出现了两地贸易总额、内地对港出口额和内地自港进口额齐步下降的罕见局面。另据特区政府统计，内地仍为香港最大的转口来源地和转口市场。1998年香港转口内地商品6912.19亿港元，较上年下降4.5%；海外经港转口运往内地商品4073.66亿港元，较上年下降8.2%。

1998年，内地与澳门进出口总额为8.70亿美元，比上年增长13.8%；其中内地对澳门出口7.74亿美元，比上年增长16.4%；内地自澳门进口1.23亿美元，比上年增长0.1%。

据海关统计，1998年内地对香港出口的前20种主要商品为：机电产品（119.13亿美元），服装及衣着附件（93.02亿美元），纺织纱线、织物及制品（46.44亿美元），贵金属或包贵金属的首饰（11.06亿美元），玩具（8.30亿美元），塑料制品（8.09亿美元）旅行用品及箱包（6.74亿美元），鞋类（6.64亿美元），集装箱（5.57亿美元），家具（3.93亿美元），手表（3.60亿美元），通断及保护电路装置（2.93亿美元），活猪（2.65亿美元），电动机及发动机（2.59亿美元），未锻造的铝及铝材（2.55亿美元），电视、收音机及无线电讯设备的零附件（2.54亿美元），钢材（2.45亿美元），电扇（2.40亿美元），二极管、晶体管及类似半导体器件（2.36亿美元），未锻造的铜及铜材（2.32亿美元）。上述20种商品的出口额合计335.31亿美元，占当年内地对香港出口的86.5%。1998年内地对澳门出口超过1千万美元的商品有服装及衣着附件，纺织纱线、织物及制品，机电产品、塑料制品，玩具，活猪和鞋类。

1998年内地从香港进口的前20种主要商品为：机电产品（31.81亿美元），集成电路及微电子组件（4.04亿美元），棉机织物（3.70亿美元），合成纤维长丝机织物（1.93亿美元），二极管、晶体管及类似半导体器件（1.71亿美元），针织及钩编织物（1.63亿美元），自动数据处理设备的零件（1.47亿美元），纸及纸板（1.43亿美元），钟表机芯及钟表零件（1.37亿美元），通断及保护电路装置（1.34亿美元），自动数据处理设备及其部件（1.17亿美元），初级形状的塑料（1.09亿美元），合成纤维纱线（0.97亿美元），塑料制品（0.95亿美元），有线电话电报设备的零附件（0.91亿美元），计量检测分析自控仪器及器具（0.81亿美元），电动机及发动机（0.81亿美元），电视、收音机及无线电讯设备的零部件（0.78亿美元），未锻造的铜及铜材（0.75亿美元），橡胶或塑料加工机械（0.70亿美元）。上述20种商品的进口额合计59.37亿美元，占当年内地从香港进口的89.2%。1998年内地从澳门进口超过1千万美元的商品有针织或钩编织物、机电产品和棉机织物。

二、投资

投资方面，根据外经贸部业务统计，香港仍是内地吸引境外投资的首要来源地。1998年内地吸引香港直接投资项目数7830个（占同期我吸引外资项目总数的39.5%），同比下降6.8%；合同港资金额165.16亿美元（占同期我合同外资总金额的31.7%），同比下降9.4%；实际使用港资

187.90亿美元（占同期我实际利用外资总金额的41.2%），同比下降8.9%”截止1998年底，内地吸引香港直接投资项目数累计178947个，占同期我吸引外资总数的55.1%；合同港资金额2965.13亿美元，占同期我吸引外资合同总额的51.8%；实际利用港资金额1387.17亿美元，占同期我实际利用外资总额的51.9%。

1998年内地吸引澳门直接投资项目264个，同比下降0.75%；合同澳门资金金额3.30亿美元，同比下降8.02%；实际使用澳门金额4.38亿美元，同比上升11%。截止1998年底，澳门对内地直接投资项目6164个，合同澳门资金金额89.06亿美元，实际利用澳门资金金额33.44亿美元。按内地实际使用外资金额来源地排序，澳门排第10位。

三、承包工程和劳务合作

根据外经贸部业务统计，1998年内地新签对港承包工程、劳务合作和设计咨询合同1342份，合同金额20.17亿美元，完成营业额21.42亿美元，年末在港人数为22335，分别占同期对外承包工程和劳务合作总数的5.2%、17.1%、21.1%和6.3%。1998年内地对澳门新签承包工程、劳务合作及设计咨询合同数792份，合同金额2.66亿美元，营业额2.60亿美元，年末在澳门人数27,508。

四、重要经贸往来

1998年是香港回归祖国的第一年，也是澳门即将回归祖国的最后一年。在这一年，祖国内地和港澳地区的经贸团组往来密切。6月份，外经贸部石广生部长应香港政策研究所的邀请出席了“香港经济论坛”并发表演讲；随后石部长出席了庆祝香港回归祖国一周年的庆典活动；10月份，石部长应“香港明天更好基金”的邀请赴港出席了“中国·香港迈向21世纪论坛”并发表演讲。外经贸部在香港举办了第五届中国投资贸易洽谈会暨投资政策研讨会。1998年外经贸部接待港澳地区的经贸团组28个，其中部领导会见的有香港特别行政区贸易署代表团、香港贸发局高级经济代表团、香港总商会和欧盟、印度、英国驻香港的商会等12个代表团。澳门贸易投资促进局也拜访了外经贸部。

五、对祖国内地与港澳地区经贸合作的展望

展望1999年内地与香港的经贸交流，我们认为，两地的经贸合作虽然基础稳固，发展余地较大，但形势依然严峻，仍然面临许多困难和挑战。在贸易方面，世界市场需求萎缩，贸易壁垒的增多，将影响内地商品通过香港转口海外市场。内地直接远洋贸易比重仍将上升，经港转口比重将继续下将。世界经济和贸易增长的放缓影响了香港经济的恢复，而香港内部投资和消费需求疲弱必然影响我对港的出口。因此，1999年内地对港出口难以乐观，估计两地贸易仍将出现负增长。但内地从香港进口由于内地扩大内需和增加投资的政策见效而可能维持一定规模。

在利用港资方面，1999年内地吸引港资的水平很难高于上年。香港企业过去通常可利用香港股市集资或向香港银行借贷，以扩大在内地的投资规模，但在今后的一段时间内，将不容易以类似方式获得资金，这将影响港商往内地投资。在香港股市持续低迷，投入市场的资金明显减少的环境下，红筹、国企股企业在港上市集资难度加大。当亚洲金融危机平息，受冲击东南亚国家局势稳定后，其经营成本相应下降，对外来投资的限制也会减少，大量的收购合并机会增加了对港商的吸引力，从而分散了其原本投资于内地的资金。

展望祖国内地与澳门的经贸合作，我们认为，两地经贸合作具有良好稳固的基础。随着澳门即将回归，澳门的经济环境将会不断改善。中葡友好合作关系以及祖国内地经济持续、快速、健康发展，将有助于澳门旅游、贸易、金融、房地产业的发展。由于澳门1999年基础设施建设和贸易、旅游业的发展，内地与澳门贸易可望进一步扩大。充分结合澳门在国际联系、市场开发、信息交流、资金筹集等方面的优势，内地与澳门的经济合作将迈出新的步伐。澳门对内地投资会发展到新的领域，并保持一定规模。

1998年中国与日本的经济贸易关系

对外贸易经济合作部亚洲司一处

一、双边贸易情况

1. 中日贸易统计

1998年中日贸易总额为578.99亿美元，同比下降4.8%。其中，出口296.62亿美元，同比下降6.7%，进口282.07亿美元，同比下降2.7%，中方顺差14.85亿美元。1998年中日贸易额占我国对外贸易额的17.9%，日本连续六年保持我国第一大贸易伙伴地位。

2. 中日技术贸易

据外经贸部业务统计，1998年，中国从日本引进技术设备共1386项，同比增长40.5%，合同总金额为20.9亿美元，同比下降38.3%，日本在中国技术引进国别中仅次于美国和德国，居第3位。

3. 主要进出口商品情况

1998年中国对日主要出口商品依次为：纺织原料及制品87.2亿美元，占对日出口总额的29.4%，同比下降6.03%；机电、车辆及光学仪器类77.1亿美元，同比增长5.4%；粮油食品类45.6亿美元，同比下降4.8%。

1998年中国自日主要进口商品为：机电、车辆及光学仪器类161.39亿美元，占自日进口总额的57.2%，同比下降1.3%；贱金属（钢铁等）及其制品36.5亿美元，同比下降3.2%；纺织原料及制品27.5亿美元，同比下降14.3%。

4. 中日大米贸易问题

1994年，日本因国内大米歉收，首次从国外紧急进口254.5万吨大米。应日本政府请求，我国政府责成中国粮油食品进出口总公司紧急组织货源。经过努力，分批向日本出口了107.2万吨大米，占日本进口总量的42%。根据关贸总协定乌拉圭回合达成的协议，日本将从1995年度起逐步开放大米市场，进口数量将从1995年的42万吨递增至2000年的80万吨。日本是世界有名的大米高价市场，因此，美国等很多国家政府首脑均在进口大米份额问题上对日本施压。在此情况下，日本政府对大米进口采取了一般进口招标和SBS招标两种方式进口（一般进口招标是由政府划定进口国别和数量，此种方式占日本大米进口量的90%，1998年该项下我中标仅1万吨，占一般进口招标的1.95%，少于其他国家；SBS招标是由民间进口，政府规定数量，但对国别、品种不加限制，1998年该项下我中标6.2万吨，占SBS的51.67%)，实际上是对我带有明显歧视性的做法，严重地影响了我大米对日出口所占份额，1998年我对日大米出口仅为7.2万吨。就此，我国政府曾多次对日提出交涉，要求其迅速改变歧视性作法，本着公平、公正的态度进行大米进口招标。

二、中日资金合作情况

1. 日本对华直接投资

亚洲地区仍是日本企业海外投资的重点，中国是日资关注的热点国家之一。截至1998年12月，我国共批准日本企业对华投资项目数17602个，合同外资金额325.43亿美元，实际使用金额219.12亿美元，占全国利用外商直接投资比例分别为5.42%、5.68%和8.20%，1998年1月～12月，日本对华直接投资项目数为1198个，合同外资金额27.49亿美元，实际使用金额34.00亿美元，占全国利用外商直接投资的比例分别为6.05%、5.28%和7.48%。日本对华直接投资实际投入金额居我国利用外资国别首位，今后中日两国在技术资金密集型领域以及中西部地区的资金合作可望有更大发展。

2. 中日政府资金合作

第四批日元贷款自1998年度起采用新的贷款利率和贷款条件，普通项目年利率为1.8%，一般环保项目为1.3%，特殊环保项目为0.75%；普通项目和一般环保项目贷款条件不变，特殊环保项目为还款期40年（含10年宽限期），均不附带采购条件。目前双方已就第四批日元贷款后两年（1999

年～2000年）金额为3900亿日元，即年平均额为1950亿日元和28个项目达成协议。

1997年3月底，日方宣布解除对华无偿援助冻结，双方就南京妇幼保健中心项目（17.28亿日元）达成协议。1997年度就6个项目签约换文，金额共计63.33亿日元。1998年度（到1999年3月）已签订两个项目，金额约16亿日元，近期还将有几个项目签约换文。

三、双边经贸往来

1998年9月中日高层经济磋商在北京举行，会议由外经贸部孙广相副部长主持。双方就亚洲经济问题、中日两国经济情况、金融财政政策及中日经贸合作等问题坦率交换了意见。

9月外经贸部石广生部长率团访日，出席中日投资促进机构联席会议。

11月石广生部长随江主席访问日本。除参加江主席访日活动外，石部长同高村正彦外相就“国家级贫困县医疗器材装备”项目进行换文，还提请日方就“大连海事大学教育培训器材无偿援助”项目积极考虑，优先安排。

1998年中国与东盟国家的经济贸易关系

对外贸易经济合作部亚洲司二处

自1997年下半年亚洲金融危机爆发以来，东盟国家的经济遭受巨大冲击，我与东盟的经贸合作也受到了严重影响。

一、双边贸易

1998年，中国与东盟九国（新加坡、印尼、马来西亚、泰国、菲律宾、文莱、越南、缅甸和老挝）的双边贸易全面大幅滑坡，全年贸易总额为234.8亿美元，比上年下降6.2%；其中我出口109.2亿美元，比上年下降13.6%；我进口125.6亿美元，比上年微增1.2%。我对东盟国家出口除菲律宾比上年增长12%外，其他均大幅减少，其中我对印尼、泰、马、新等四国的出口额分别比上年下降36.4%、23.5%、16.9%和9.1%。我机电产品对东盟的出口额及比重都有所提高。全年出口总额达49.7亿美元，比上年增长5.3%，占我出口总额的比重由上年的39%上升到45.5%。

二、经济技术合作

1998年，东盟仍为中国引进外资的重要来源，实际外资投入仍继续增长，但来华投资协议金额明显下降。全年来华投资项目共994项，同比下降21%；合同外资金额为39.3亿美元，同比下降29%；实际使用外资金额42.2亿美元，同比增长23%。其中新加坡、马来西亚、泰国和菲律宾四国当年来华投资合同金额同比分别下降33%、34%、11%和20%。

我与东盟国家承包工程和劳务合作相对受危机影响较小。1998年我与东盟国家共签订承包劳务、设计咨询合同2120份，同比下降21.3%；合同额达22.66亿美元，同比增长2.1%；营业额16.8亿美元，同比增长1.6%。

中国继续向有关国家提供力所能及的援助。1998年，中国分别向越南和老挝提供了1100万和1000万元人民币的无偿援助，向印尼提供价值300万美元药品的无偿援助。同时我进出口银行和印尼财政部签订了向印尼提供2亿美元出口信贷的框架协议。

三、重要经贸往来

1998年，中国与东盟各国政府继续保持着频繁密切的高层经贸往来。

1月，外经贸部副部长李国华和新贸工部常秘许文远在京共同主持了中国—新加坡贸易、投资和经济合作磋商会第三次会议。双方各自介绍了国内经济形势，回顾了自上次磋商会议来双边经贸合作发展情况，并就亚洲金融危机及今后如何进一步扩大合作交换了意见。应新方要求，国家经贸委企业司副司长刘春生向新方介绍了我国有企业改革情况。

4月，应吴仪国务委员的邀请，泰国副总理兼商业部长苏帕猜率团访华。朱镕基总理会见了苏帕猜一行。吴仪国务委员与苏帕猜举行了会谈，外交部唐家璇部长、外经贸部石广生部长、贸促会俞晓松会长分别会见和宴请了苏帕猜一行。石广生部长还与苏帕猜分别代表各自政府签署了《中华人民共和国政府与泰王国政府关于贸易、投资和经济技术合作的谅解备忘录》。

5月，应外经贸部石广生部长的邀请，马来西亚初级产品工业部长林敬益率团访华。吴仪国务委员会见了林敬益一行。林敬益分别与国家经贸委盛华仁主任、国家计委增培炎主任、外经贸部刘山在副部长举行了会谈，就进口马来西亚棕榈油等问题交换了意见。

6月，应菲律宾贸工部邀请，外经贸部副部长刘山在率政府经贸代表团访问了菲律宾，同菲贸工部长帕多举行了会谈，重点就我向菲律宾出口大米事进行了磋商。刘副部长还拜会了埃斯特拉达总统、阿罗育副总统和西亚松外长等，并主持了中技（菲律宾）机电产品有限公司的开业典礼。代表团还同菲粮食署签署了《中华人民共和国对外贸易经济合作部和菲律宾共和国粮食署关于中菲粮食贸易谅解备忘录》。

1998年中国与南亚及部分西亚国家的经济贸易关系

对外贸易经济合作部亚洲司三处

一、双边贸易

1998年，中国与南亚八国（印度、巴基斯坦、孟加拉国、尼泊尔、斯里兰卡、马尔代夫、阿富汗、不丹）的贸易总额为39.18亿美元，较上年下降2.15%，其中我出口25.86亿美元，进口13.32亿美元，分别较上一年下降了2.56%和1.33%。这是中国同南亚国家的贸易首次出现下降的现象。其原因有，（一）受亚洲金融危机影响，东南亚国家低价出口产品夺走了我部分市场；（二）印巴经济不景气，核试爆及所受国际制裁又进一步加重了其财经困难，我同其贸易也相应受到影响。如1998年中印贸易额仅为19.22亿美元，增长5%，与前几年平均30%的增长率相比，增幅剧减。我对印出口10.16亿美元，进口9.06亿美元，同比分别增长了8.9%和0.9%。除增幅减缓外，中印贸易的另一特点是基本趋于平衡。中巴贸易额为9.13亿美元，下降14.6%，主要是我出口下降了24%，为5.24亿美元，进口则有2.6%的增长，达3.89亿美元，双边贸易不平衡状况有所改善。中国同其他南亚国家的贸易额有增有减，呈现分化之势。

中国对南亚国家出口的主要商品有机电产品、化工原料及产品、医药原料、生丝、焦炭、煤、钢材、水泥、纺织品等；中国从南亚国家进口的主要商品有铁矿砂、铬矿石、石油、豆粕、皮革、原棉等。

1998年我同西亚三国（土耳其、伊朗、塞浦路斯）的贸易额为19.98亿美元，我出口13.96亿美元，进口6.02亿美元，分别较上年增长17.53%、26.91%和0.3%。其中我对伊朗贸易额为12.15亿美元，创历史最好水平，我出口6.57亿美元，进口5.58亿美元；对土贸易额为7.01亿美元，我出口6.59亿美元，进口只有4278万美元。其特点是我对伊、土出口有较大增长，但自土进口严重萎缩，贸易不平衡问题日益突出；对伊贸易增长主要是地铁等大项目设备出口陆续到货，今后如无项目跟上，不排除贸易额回落的可能。

我对上述三国出口主要商品有纺织品、机电产品及成套设备、五矿及化工产品、仪器仪表、工农具等；主要进口商品有原油、钢材、铬矿石等。

二、经济技术合作

1998年我同南亚国家新签承包劳务合同226

项，合同金额 76461 万美元，营业额 69010 万美元，派出劳务人员 2592 人。新签技术出口合同 35 项，合同金额 3.4 亿美元。西亚三国新签承包劳务合同 101 项，合同金额 21645 万美元，营业额 34635 万美元，在外劳务人员 1087 人。该地区继续保持我技术出口和承包工程重要地区和市场的地位。

1998 年，中国政府继续向南亚部分国家提供力所能及的援助，同尼泊尔、斯里兰卡、马尔代夫等国政府签订了新的援助协议，新提供的援款金额为 1.74 亿元人民币。

三、重要经贸往来

1998 年 1 月，巴基斯坦总理谢里夫访华期间与贸促会在北京举办了投资研讨会，安民部长助理出席会议并讲话；2 月 16 日，吴仪部长会见了来访的土耳其外长杰姆及随同访问的企业家代表团；4 月，外经贸部刘山在副部长率政府经贸代表团访问了尼泊尔、斯里兰卡，马尔代夫等国，并同尼财政部共同举行了中尼经贸联委会第八次会议；10 月，外经贸企业协会与孟加拉驻华使馆共同举办经贸投资研讨会，杨文生部长助理出席会议并讲话。

1998 年中国与西亚国家的经济贸易关系

对外贸易经济合作部西亚非洲司一处

一、双边贸易

本文所指的西亚国家是沙特阿拉伯、阿拉伯联合酋长国、科威特、巴林、卡塔尔、阿曼、约旦、叙利亚、黎巴嫩、巴勒斯坦、伊拉克、以色列、也门共 13 个国家。1998 年我国与这些国家的贸易又有较大幅度增长，据我海关统计，双边进出口贸易额为 60.6 亿美元，比 1997 年下降了 5.3%。其中，我国出口 34.1 亿美元，比 1997 年增长 9.5%：我国进口 26.4 亿美元，比 1997 年下降 19.3%。

1998 年我国对这一地区出口额最大的国家是阿联酋，达 12.9 亿美元，占我国对这一地区出口总额的 37.8%，其次是沙特，达 8.9 亿美元，占 26.3%，以色列达 3.53 亿美元，占 10.3%。

我国从这一地区进口额最大的国家是沙特，达 8.04 亿美元，占我国从这一地区进口总额的 30.4%，其次是阿曼 7.06 亿美元，占 26.7%，也门 5.24 亿美元，占 19.8%。

我国对西亚地区出口的主要商品是机电产品（约 11.39 亿美元，占我对这一地区出口总额的 33.4%），服装和纺织品（约 9.66 亿美元，28.3%，其中服装 5.74 亿美元，纺织品 3.93 亿美元）。除此之外，我对西亚地区鞋类出口达 1.78 亿美元，轮胎出口达 1.14 亿美元。

1998 年中国从西亚地区进口原油 1243 万吨，达 15.2 亿美元，比 1997 年减少了 28%。原油已成为中国从本地区进口额最大的商品，随着中国国民经济的发展，中国对原油的需求会愈来愈大，原油将会在中国与本地区国家的经贸合作中起一定程度的主导作用。中国从该地区进口的其他主要商品有成品油、塑料、乙二醇、化肥、铝等。

我国对西亚地区的出口贸易虽然金额不少，但与这些国家的进口贸易的总额相比，仅占 2.3%，所占份额仍很少，因此市场潜力很大。双边贸易有较大的互补性，西亚地区的原油、成品油、化肥、石化产品和铝锭等，是我国需求较多的商品。因此，我应紧紧抓住这一地区形势继续趋向缓和的时机，调整我出口产品结构，加大出口商品在这一地区的宣传力度，同时继续贯彻以质取胜和大经贸战略，积极拓展我国在西亚地区的市场。西亚地区的原油储量占世界原油储量的一半以上，做好与这一地区国家的经贸合作工作对中国具有长远的战略意义。

1998 年中国与西亚地区国家签署的主要经贸协定有：2 月份，中国和也门政府投资保护协定。

二、经济技术合作

（一）承包劳务

近两年中国与西亚国家的经济合作的深度和广度都有了进一步明显的拓展。中国与这一地区的经济合作不再局限于派遣普通劳务和承建一般土木工程项目，而是逐步扩展到了技术含量高、难度大的项目上，出现了工程承包带动中国大型机电设备出口的可喜局面。

据统计，截止 1998 年底，中国公司在西亚地区国家累计签订承包劳务合同 4080 份，合同金额 61.32 亿美元，完成营业额 42.37 亿美元。其中 1998 年新签承包劳务合同 438 项，合同金额 5.97 亿美元，比 1997 年增长 14.3%，完成营业额 3.25 亿美元，比 1997 年增长 41.2%。1998 年在西亚十三国执行合同的中国承包劳务人员有 23923 人。

1998 年在该地区承包工程超过 5000 万美元的大项目有两个：中国电子系统工程总公司同沙特中东电信公司（METCO）签署了承建沙特微波通信外线项目合同金额 2 亿美元；天津水泥设计院同也门亚哈毕公司签署了在也门建水泥生产线项目的合同，合同金额 5249 万美元。

（二）对外援助

1998 年，中国向也门、巴勒斯坦提供了经济援助，并执行了向伊拉克提供电力设备配件、水泵、药品原料，向约旦提供机械设备及管线，承担了援巴勒斯坦法学院大楼三项目。目前，援叙利亚哈马棉纺厂更新梳棉设备项目正在建设中。另外中国还向沙特、阿曼、伊拉克、约旦、巴勒斯坦提供了多边技术援助，共有 27 名学员参加了各类技术培训班。

（三）双向投资

近两年，中国公司和企业在西亚地区国家建立的独资、合资工厂逐渐增多，主要集中在阿联酋，许多项目取得了较好的经济效益，如在阿联酋的现代塑料厂、拉丝厂、编织厂、沙迦眼镜框厂等，但也都不同程度地面临着各种费用、原材料价格上涨、竞争日趋激烈的问题。1998 年中国公司在西亚地区新投资的项目有湖南海外国际公司在阿联酋与阿治曼酋长国合资的“意特拉”中东轮胎厂项目和山东龙口发达童车有限公司在约旦独资设立的“约旦哈希姆王国（中国）麦利达有限公司”。

此外，中国石油天然气集团在苏丹投资开发油田、建炼厂及铺设输油管道的业务取得明显进展。

1998 年，沙特、科威特和以色列在华的项目投资也取得新进展。其中以色列联合发展有限公司、死海钾肥厂与中方公司于 1998 年 11 月 25 日签订合资兴建中以青海钾肥有限公司的合同，共建青海钾肥二期工程，总投资 46.4 亿人民币。注册资本 13.6 亿人民币，外方出资占注册资本的 33.3%。

三、重要经贸往来

1998 年我国加强了与西亚地区国家的经贸往来，西亚地区国家也更加重视与中国经贸关系的发展，加强了与我经贸合作的力度。1998 年，我与该地区有以下重要活动：

1998 年 2 月，也门总统萨利赫访华，双方签署了经济技术协定和两国政府投资保护协定，两国企业家举行了经贸洽谈会；3 月，摩洛哥工商部国务秘书访华，在上海举办摩洛哥经贸周；5 月，以色列总理内塔尼亚胡访华，两国企业家举行了贸易洽谈会；6 月，沙特商业大臣访华；8 月，利比亚工矿部长助理访华，举行两国混委会跟踪会议；10 月，沙特王储访华，随行的沙特财经大臣与孙广相副部长举行了对口会谈，并签署了两国经贸合作谅解备忘录；12 月摩洛哥首相访华，双方签署了经济技术合作协议；1998 年 5 月，杨文生部长助理率政府经贸代表团访问以色列。

1998年中国与非洲国家的经济贸易关系

西亚非洲司协调处

1998年是中非经贸合作不同寻常的一年。由于亚洲金融危机不断加深蔓延，国际经济、金融形势持续动荡，我国对外贸易，特别是出口面临严峻挑战，对日、韩及东南亚等一些主要市场的出口都出现了下滑；1998年非洲的经济形势也难尽人意，许多国家赖以生存的农矿初级产品出口价格一直下降，使得外汇收入明显减少，国际收支趋向恶化，间接影响了其进口的规模。面对不利的内外部经济环境，党中央国务院加大了贯彻实施“市场多元化”战略和“两种市场，两种资源”方针的力度，采取积极有效措施，使中非经贸合作保持了健康平稳的发展势头，可谓“风景这边独好”。1998年中非经贸合作成绩表现在：

一、双边贸易势头良好

据海关统计，1998年中国与非洲双边贸易总额达55.36亿美元，比上年下降2.4%，但我对非出口40.6亿美元，比上年增长了26.5%，我从非进口14.77亿美元，比上年减少40.1%。1998年中非贸易有几个显著的特点。

1. 出口增势继续强劲，进口下降比较明显

1998年对非出口的增长势头进一步加快，增幅高于1997年24.9%的水平，高出同期全国出口增长率26个百分点。

由于木材、原棉、原油等资源性产品的进口减少，我从非进口下降幅度比较明显，与1997年增长41.4%的情况形成鲜明对比，这也成为制约1998年双边贸易总额增长的主要原因。

2. 商品结构进一步优化。

初级产品比重下降，电信、电子等技术含量高的产品逐渐进入非洲市场，机电产品已大大超过纺织和轻工产品，成为对非洲出口最重要的商品，1998年我出口机电产品14.80亿美元，占对非出口总额的36%，而纺织品和服装仅占22.89%。

3. 企业界多种形式贸易合作进一步扩大。

到1998年止，我在非共有贸易机构和代表处150多家，越来越多的国内企业派团组访非，与企业直接洽谈，通过举办展销会、进行现货现售等多种形式，使越来越多的中国产品打入非洲市场，同时，随着对非利用优惠贴息贷款援助项目和互利合作项目的开展，我技术和成套设备出口有了长足进展，形成了在大经贸的范畴内援助、贸易和互利合作共同发展、相互促进的大好局面，摆脱了以往单纯“为贸易而贸易”的单一格局。

4. 一批新的贸易国别增长点逐渐形成。

98年我在非洲的10大贸易伙伴是南非、埃及、尼日利亚、苏丹、摩洛哥、安哥拉、科特迪瓦、加蓬、贝宁和津巴布韦，中国与这10个国家的贸易总额已占中非贸易总额的71.6%。与我双边贸易额在1亿美元以上的非洲国家已增加到14个。

二、对非援助进展顺利

非洲是我对外援助的重点地区之一。自1995年我开始实施以援外方式多样化和援外资金来源多元化、推动中国企业和受援国企业直接合作为中心内容的援外方式改革以来，我援外新方式受到广大非洲国家的欢迎。截至1998年底，我在非洲与23个国家签订了31笔优惠贷款框架协议，接受优惠贷款的国家占我对非援助国家的41%，同时，我国企业还在18个非洲国家承担了32个援外合资合作项目，其中20个项目已经实施，多数项目已取得较好的经济和社会效益。

三、互利合作成绩斐然

1998年我在非洲国家开展的多种形式互利经济合作也取得了丰硕成果。中国公司从承揽中小型工程项目，发展到承建上千万美元的大项目或过亿美元的特大型项目；对非劳务合作从派遣建筑工人、医务人员、海员等低级劳务到输出从事飞机维修、企业管理、软件开发和教育培训等在内的各种中高级专门人才。规模从小到大，项目领域不断拓展，技术含量越来越高，截止1998年末，我国在

非洲累计签订承包劳务业务合同8586份，合同总金额122.26亿美元，完成营业额89.61亿美元，后两项分别占我国对外承包劳务合作业务合同总金额的14.64%和15.35%，目前在非人数43888人。

四、对非投资初见成效

1. 1998年我国政府积极鼓励企业到非洲国家投资办厂，开展境外带料加工贸易业务，这是我国开展对外投资的一种新形式，是我国企业以国内成熟的技术和设备及适用的原材料到国外办厂，其产品应适合当地市场需要，并根据国际市场需求出口，这项业务极大地拓宽了中非经贸合作的渠道。目前，国内企业已在非洲11个国家开展了这项业务，总投资额超过2200多万美元，主要从事我具有较强优势的家电、轻工、机电和服装加工等行业，这些项目带动了原材料、散件、零配件的出口，取得了较好的经济和社会效益，成为我对非出口新的增长点。

2.1998年我国政府确定在非洲建立的11个投资开发贸易促进中心的建设工作也顺利开展，中心的宗旨是为我国企业开拓非洲市场提供诸如保税存仓、报关保险、运输旅行、结汇结算、法律会计、经贸咨询、安全保障等全方位服务。通过“中心”的桥梁作用，1998年一些合资合作项目已经开始实施，一些公司开展了存仓分拨、商品展示等业务，逐步打开了非洲市场。

1998年的中非经贸合作正朝经营方式多样化、经营主体多元化的方向发展，并在许多领域取得了积极成果，但仍存在巨大潜力，也面临困难和风险，目前存在的主要问题是开拓非洲市场经营秩序和规避非洲政治和金融风险及扩大从非进口的问题。我们要抓住机遇，直面挑战，再挖潜力，用不懈的努力求得更大发展。

1998年中国与欧洲联盟国家的经济贸易关系

外经贸部欧洲司四处

1998年，中国与欧盟国家的双边关系得到了不断改善与加强。双方高层领导高度重视中欧关系的发展，频繁的高层互访对促进双边关系起到了重要的作用。欧盟注意到中国国际地位和作用的上升，赞赏中国在亚洲金融危机中树立的负责任大国的形象以及为稳定地区经济和世界经济作出的巨大贡献，更加重视中国作为未来世界大国的地位和潜在的巨大市场，同时愿意支持中国继续为稳定亚洲经济发挥积极作用。中国与欧盟经济技术合作发展总体呈持续快速增长态势，双边贸易额逐年增长。

一、双边贸易

据中国海关统计，1998年，中欧双边进出口达488.6亿美元，比上年增长13.6%；其中我出口281.5亿美元，增长18.1%，进口207.2亿美元，增长7.9%。欧盟成为我国第三大贸易伙伴，居日本、美国之后，香港之前。

1998年，中国在与欧盟各成员国的贸易中，与德国的贸易仍居第一位，达143.5亿美元，比上年增长了13.2%，其他国家依次为英国（65.8亿美元，增长13.6%）、法国（60.3亿美元，增长8.1%）、荷兰（60亿美元、增长9.4%）、意大利（48.5亿美元，增长3.5%）、瑞典（26.7亿美元，增长46.5%）、比利时（25.2亿美元，增长10.5%）、西班牙（20亿美元，增长11.3%）、芬兰（15.8亿美元，增长64.8%）、丹麦（7.8亿美元，增长8%）、奥地利（4.8亿美元，增长6.2%）、希腊（4.1亿美元，增长29.2%）、爱尔兰（3亿美元，增长54.5%）、葡萄牙（2.3亿美元，增长7.9%）、卢森堡（0.8亿美元，增长60.7%）。

在欧盟成员国中，德国、荷兰、英国、法国、意大利和比利时是中国前6位出口市场，排序与上年没有变化，共占中国对欧盟总出口的85.9%；而德国、法国、意大利、瑞典、英国、芬兰则是中国前6位进口来源国，占中国从欧盟进口的85.6%。

二、来华投资

1998年，欧盟来华直接投资项目数为994项，协议金额59.1亿美元，实际投入43.0亿美元，协议金额和实际投入分别比1997年增长39.8%和3.1%。截止1998年年底，欧盟成员国来华投资项目数达9330项，协议外资金额363.5亿美元，实际投入174.1亿美元。欧盟对华投资继续保持项目平均规模大，技术含量高，经济和社会效益好的特点。

三、双边经济技术合作

（一）引进技术

欧盟国家是中国引进先进技术、设备的最大供应者。截止1998年底，中国从欧盟成员国引进技术共8564项，合同总金额约455.2亿美元，占我国同期引进技术总额的45.1%。其中1998年，我自欧盟引进技术共1700项，合同总金额约75.3亿美元，占我国同期引进技术总额的46%，远高于1997年的29%。

（二）贷款合作

欧盟是中国利用外国政府贷款较集中的地区。截止1998年年底，欧盟成员国及官方金融组织累计向中国提供政府贷款协议金额约152.77亿美元，占外国政府和官方金融组织向中国提供贷款总额的36.2%。其中1998年，欧方提供贷款协议金额10.1亿美元，占全国同期的34%。

（三）其他合作

中欧双方在培训、科技、发展援助等领域开展了广泛的合作，如欧盟继续为我培养高级翻译人员、双方合资成立的中欧工商管理学院运转良好。目前，中欧双方在混委会下成立了经贸、科技、环保、能源、信息通迅技术5个工作组，使上述领域的合作机制化。在1998年6月召开的中欧混委会期间，石广生部长和欧盟委员会副主席布里坦爵士签署了《中欧金融领域合作谅解备忘录》以及“辽宁综合环保”、“中欧环境管理合作”、“白朗农业综合开发”和“职业培训”等四个合作项目的财政协议。10月，欧盟委员会桑特主席访华期间，双方签署了《欧盟与中国航空和通信合作领域的工业合作谅解备忘录》，以及“中欧立法和司法合作”，“欧盟支持中国加入世贸组织”等合作项目的财政协议。12月，中欧间签署了《中国与欧盟科技合作协定》。自1993年以来，我共接受欧盟委员会及其成员国对华无偿援助约计4亿美元。

四、重要经贸往来

1998年，中国与欧盟的经贸合作是在良好的政治气氛中发展的。全年中国和欧盟高层互访十分频繁，欧盟九位国家元首或政府首脑以及欧盟委员会主席相继来访，其中意大利总统、爱尔兰总理和比利时首相以及欧盟委员会主席都是近十年来首次访华。年初，李鹏总理、李瑞环主席、李岚清副总理分别出访欧盟国家，就中国加入世贸组织和双边经贸关系问题在高层与欧方交换了意见。4月，新当选的朱镕基总理出访英国、法国并出席了在伦敦召开的第二届亚欧会议。会议期间，朱镕基总理与欧盟轮值主席国英国首相布莱尔及欧盟委员会主席桑特举行了中欧领导人首次会晤，双方确立了面向21世纪长期、稳定的合作伙伴关系和中欧领导人年度会晤机制。4月，欧盟理事会通过决议，将中国从“非市场经济”国家的名单上删除，随后通过了《与中国建立全面伙伴关系》的政策文件。这是1995年以来欧盟发表的第三份专门针对对华关系的政策性文件，表示要把对华关系提升到与美、俄、日同等重要的地位，标志着中欧经贸关系进入了一个成熟、稳定的发展阶段。6月，外经贸部石广生部长访问欧盟、奥地利和比利时，就中国加入世贸组织和双边经贸关系与对方全面地交换了意见，在中国加入世贸组织问题上，欧盟愿于1999年年底以前结束与中方的谈判。在双边贸易方面也取得了一些重大进展：欧盟决定恢复中国三家兔肉加工厂对欧出口权；取消对中国输欧玻璃器皿和玩具的单边数量限制；决定派专家来华考察禽、兔肉生产加工情况，为其进一步取消禁令作技术准备；经过三轮磋商，中欧于11月签署了第六个双边纺织品协议。

在此背景下，虽然1998年中国外经贸面临亚洲金融危机进一步蔓延、负面影响不断扩大的严峻挑战，中国对欧盟出口、从其吸收直接投资和引进技术仍实现了较大幅度的增长，从而使中欧双边经贸合作保持了高水平的发展。

五、中欧经贸关系中的主要问题

1．不公正的贸易政策

欧盟仍对中国实行不公正的贸易政策，反倾销法中对我国有企业存在明显歧视，维持对我鞋、陶餐具、瓷餐具等三类输欧商品的单方面歧视性数量限制等，影响了我扩大对欧盟出口。

2. 利用技术标准阻止我部分农产品对欧出口

欧盟自1996年8月以中国相关产品生产、养殖、加工及检验检疫的总体条件及监管状况不符合要求为由，相继停止从我进口禽肉和部分水产品。我有关部门和企业按欧盟法规努力进行了整改并协调解决了欧盟特别关心的技术问题，但欧盟至今未解除对我上述产品对欧出口的禁令，影响了我对欧出口。

3. 削弱对我普惠制优惠待遇

欧盟于1995年开始分三阶段实施为期10年的新普惠制，限制竞争力强的国家和地区享受该待遇，而把优惠给予最穷的发展中国家。我部分产品已在第一阶段方案中毕业。

4. 与我加入世贸组织谈判无实质进展

虽然欧盟对我加入世贸组织一直保持积极姿态，但其提出的要价也超出了我国目前的承受能力，中欧在我加入世贸组织的谈判中未获突破性进展。

1998年中国与独联体国家的经济贸易关系

外经贸部欧洲司二处

据中国海关统计，1998年中国与独联体国家的贸易总额为67.40亿美元，比1997年下降10.1%。其中，中国出口24.01亿美元，比1997年下降0.3%；进口43.38亿美元，比1997年下降14.7%，中国逆差19.37亿美元。

中国向独联体国家主要出口服装、鞋类等轻纺产品、食品和机电产品等；自这些国家主要进口化肥、钢材、棉花、有色金属、木材等原材料性商品。

目前中国在这些国家注册的合（独）资企业约2300 家，主要从事进出口贸易、服务性行业，生产型企业数量不多，涉及石油开采、家电组装、服装生产、食品加工、通讯等领域。

1998年中国与独联体国家新签劳务、工程承包合同527项，合同金额25211万美元，完成营业额15371万美元。至1998年底，在外人数11911人。

1998年，中国国家主席江泽民对哈萨克斯坦进行了访问，哈萨克斯坦总理巴尔金巴耶夫、吉尔吉斯斯坦总统阿卡耶夫，外长伊马拉利耶夫、土库曼斯坦总统尼亚佐夫、乌兹别克斯坦副总理尤努索夫、乌克兰外长塔拉修克、白俄罗斯国民大会上院主席施普克、下院主席马洛费耶夫、国家科委主席盖肖诺夫、外长安东诺维奇、格鲁吉亚外长梅纳加里什维利分别访问了中国。上述高层互访对加深相互间了解，增进友谊，进一步扩大中国与上述国家间的经济贸易合作起到了积极的推动作用。

1998年2月，中国外经贸部部长吴仪会见了来访的吉尔吉斯坦外交部长伊马纳利耶夫，同月，外经贸部副部长石广生参加江泽民主席与来访的吉尔吉斯总统之间举行的会谈，并代表我国政府签署了中吉经贸合作协定、向吉提供1亿元人民币政府贷款协定和向吉提供500万元人民币无偿援助的换文。4月，陈新华副部长率中国政府经贸代表团访问了吉尔吉斯斯坦、哈萨克斯坦、土库曼斯坦，主持召开了中国与哈、吉政府间经贸合作委员会例会。5月，石广生部长参加朱镕基总理与来访的哈萨克斯坦总理巴尔金巴耶夫的会谈，并会见了随访的中哈经贸合作委员会哈方主席、哈交通运输部长卡利耶夫一行。同月，孙振宇副部长会见了来访的爱沙尼亚外长伊尔维斯。6月，杨文生部长助理率中国政府经贸代表团访问了乌克兰、阿塞拜疆、塔吉克斯坦，签署了中国向乌克兰提供500万元人民币、向阿、塔分别提供300万元人民币无偿援助的换文。7月，张祥副部长分别在北京和明斯克主持召开了中国和乌克兰政府间经贸合作委员会例会。

10月，张祥副部长率团访问白俄罗斯，主持召开了中国与白俄罗斯政府间经贸合作委员会例会。同月，杨文生部长助理会见了来华出席中爱第三次混委会的爱沙尼亚外交部副国务秘书库尔一行。12月，石广生部长会见了来华访问的乌克兰外长塔拉修克。上述会见会谈中，双方着重就双边经贸关系中的具体问题广泛交换了意见。

（一）中国与独联体重点国家和地区的经贸关系分述如下：

俄罗斯是中国在独联体国家中的第一大贸易伙伴，也是近年来我在全球的第八大贸易伙伴，中俄贸易在我国对外贸易发展中起着比较重要作用。双边经贸合作基础良好，发展相对平稳。1998年中俄贸易额为54.8亿美元，比上年下降10.5%，其中中国向俄出口18.4亿美元，比上年下降9.7%，进口36.4亿美元，比上年下降10.9%。1998年两国毗邻地区贸易额上升较快。中国对俄出口以轻纺产品和食品为主，自俄进口的主要商品有钢材、化肥、成品油、木材等。两国进出口商品结构虽仍以传统商品为主，但机电和高新技术产品比例有所增加。

目前中俄相互投资规模不大，在俄中资企业约1300家，总投资5000多万美元，主要从事进出口贸易、微电子、通讯、服装加工、家用电器组装、餐饮业、木材加工、农业等。俄罗斯在中国投资项目约900个，实际投入约1.5亿美元，主要涉及汽车、农机组装、维修和零配件加工、化工、建材、食品加工和餐饮服务等。

1998年中国与俄罗斯劳务、工程承包合作与上年相比略有增长，全年新签合同481项，合同金额21375万美元，完成营业额12256万美元，在外劳务人员17136人。

1998年，中国与俄罗斯签订自俄技术引进合同总额19.21亿美元，中国自俄进口的技术产品主要涉及军工、核电、航空、电子等领域。中国对俄罗斯技术出口规模不大，1998年上半年签订对俄技术出口合同金额30.3万美元，出口技术产品主要涉及电子、冶金、机械、轻工、船舶和通讯等领域。

1998年中俄贸易虽然受到两国市场需求变化及地区性金融危机等因素较大影响，但仍保持了双边合作的总体规模。

1998年中国与中亚地区的经贸合作进一步发展，尤其是中国出口大幅增长，使往年中国巨额逆差局面得以改变。1998年中国与中亚地区贸易额达9.56亿美元，比1997年增长9.9%，其中中国出口4.56亿美元，比上年增长83.6%，中国进口5亿美元，比上年下降18.5%，中国逆差0.44亿美元（1997年中国逆差达3.73亿美元）。

中国自中亚进口商品主要有棉花、短绒、羊毛、牛羊皮、钢材、化肥、石油、有色金属和黑色金属等，出口商品主要有食品、轻纺产品、机械产品、日用消费品等。

哈萨克斯坦、吉尔吉斯斯坦和乌兹别克斯坦分别为中国在独联体国家中第二、第四和第五大贸易伙伴，贸易额分别为6.36亿美元、1.98亿美元和0.9亿美元。

中国在中亚地区共注册合（独）资企业700多家，但是运营的不到200家，其他的基本上或关门，或有名无实。投资领域主要涉及贸易、餐饮、建筑、农业种植、宾馆、商店等。1998年起，双方一些大型及长线投资项目开始实施，如石油开采、输油管道铺设、造纸、汽车组装等。

1998年中国与中亚地区劳务、工程承包合作方面全年新签合同19项，合同金额3190万美元，完成营业额2334万美元，在外劳务人员713人。

截至目前，中国向中亚地区共提供13笔政府商品和援外优惠贷款，总金额7亿元人民币。

乌克兰是中国在独联体国家中的第三大贸易伙伴。1998年中乌贸易额2.75亿美元，比上年下降36.8%，其中中国出口0.90亿美元，比上年下降10.8%，进口1.85亿美元，比上年下降44.7%。中国对乌出口商品以服装和纺织品、耐火材料等为主，进口商品主要有钢材、化肥等。中国在乌注册的企业60多家。

（二）中国与独联体国家经贸合作中存在的问题

1. 商品结构单一

中国出口以传统的轻纺产品和食品为主，而进口以原材料性商品为主。单一的商品结构易受市场需求变化及两国相关产业政策调整的影响，这已成为双边贸易发展的制约因素。

2. 贸易方式不正规

中国与独联体银行间无直接账户往来，信用证等符合国际贸易规范的支付方式很少采用，现钞贸易、易货贸易仍占很大比重，中方贸易人员多为个体户和小商贩，基本从事“倒爷”贸易，造成中国与独联体国家的贸易方式极不正规。

3. 双方对各自优势和互补性了解不够

目前双方企业对对方国家的优势行业和优势产品还很不了解，各自优势未充分反映在双边经贸合作中，这也是双边贸易规模不大、进出口商品结构单一、双边经贸合作没有大的突破的重要原因之一。

4. 独联体国家企业支付能力下降

受俄罗斯金融危机的影响，独联体国家企业进口支付能力进一步下降，双边贸易中往往要求中方货到付款甚至售后付款，给中方向这些国家出口带来极大困难。

5. 独联体国家投资经营环境欠佳

独联体各国法律法规多变，法治不严，社会治安不好，官员腐败，中国企业及经贸人员的财产、人身安全和合法权益不能得到充分保障，对中国企业开拓独联体市场的信心和积极性产生了消极影响。

6. 中国商品形象问题

各国独立之初，市场处于饥饿状态，双方倒爷将许多中国假冒伪劣商品贩运到独联体国家，严重损害了中国商品形象，加之中国企业缺乏品牌意识，不愿为商品做广告。因此，重塑中国商品在上述国家消费者中的形象的任务还很重。

7. 双边经贸合作服务体系不完善

目前中国与独联体国家在银行、信贷、保险、贸易结算等方面的服务机制尚不尽完善，双方企业难以利用各种融资手段开展经贸业务和合作，在一定程度上制约了一些项目的实施，不利于经贸合作的健康稳定发展。

1998 年中国与欧洲其他国家的经济贸易关系

外经贸部欧洲司办公室

一、中国和瑞士的经贸关系

瑞士是最早承认中国的西方国家之一。1950 年 9 月 14 日，两国建交。1974 年 12 月，两国签订了贸易协定并成立了贸易混合委员会，至今已先后在北京和伯尔尼召开过 14 次会议。两国经济贸易关系发展顺利。

瑞士是我在西欧除欧盟外最大的贸易伙伴。在我国同瑞士的贸易中，转口贸易占有一定比重。根据我海关统计，1998 年中瑞双边贸易额为 14.30 亿美元，比 1997 年下降 3.8%；其中我国出口 6.34 亿美元，增长 3.4%，商品以纺织原料及其制品、钟表及其零件、矿产品和化工产品为主；我国进口 7.96 亿美元，下降 8.8%，商品以机电设备、珠宝首饰、贵金属制品、光学医疗仪器、钟表和化工产品为主。

中瑞两国的财政合作稳步发展。自 1984 年至今，瑞士政府已向我提供了四笔政府贷款，总计 3.5 亿瑞士法郎。到目前为止，已建成和在建的项目有 60 多个，其中绝大多数项目进展顺利，取得了较好的社会和经济效益。

随着双边贸易的发展，瑞士企业在华投资的步伐也不断加快。汽巴精化和雀巢等一批瑞士大公司相继和我国在医药制造和食品工业领域成立了数家合资企业。同时，瑞士中小企业的对华投资也日渐活跃。1998 年，我国共批准瑞商对华投资项目 42 个，协议瑞资 2.57 亿美元，实际投入 2.23 亿美元。截至 1998 年底，我国已累计批准瑞士在华投资项目 369 个，协议瑞资金额 16.32 亿美元，实际投入金额 8.62 亿美元。瑞士在华投资项目主要集中在电梯、医药、化工、机械和饮食服务等领域。投资区域主要在沿海开放城市和经济特区。

为促进中瑞企业，尤其是中小企业之间建立合资企业及开展其他形式的合作，1997 年 12 月 11 日，中瑞双方正式签署了关于建立中瑞合资企业项目融资基金的有关文件（简称“合作基金”SSPF)。基金首期规模3125万瑞士法郎，中瑞双方所占比例为2:8。“合作基金”由中瑞双方专家组成的投资委员会委托开发银行国际基金管理部进行管理。1998年1月，“合作基金”正式在华成立。

瑞士还一直是我国技术引进的主要来源国之一。1998年中国批准从瑞士技术引进合同108个，金额约2.21亿美元。从1979年至1998年，我累计批准从瑞技术引进合同640个，金额约14.1亿美元。

二、中国与挪威的经济贸易关系

中挪两国于1954年10月5日建立外交关系以来签订了一系列贸易协议和协定。目前，中挪经贸关系良好，挪商对华投资的兴趣不断增强，挪政府向中国提供的优惠贷款保持在稳定的水平，金融、技术、海运等方面的合作也在发展。

据中国海关统计，1998年中挪双边贸易额为6.35亿美元，同比下降33%。其中中国对挪出口3.3亿美元，同比下降41.9%；进口3.05亿美元，同比下降19.6%。

1986年至1998年底，中国与挪威共签订技术设备引进合同52个，合同金额1.3亿美元，引进的技术和设备主要用于邮电、电子、机械、交通、轻工、农业和环保等方面。其中1998年引进技术设备项目13个，合同金额2326万美元。

中国自1986年开始使用挪威政府混合贷款。至1998年底，中挪双方共签订贷款协议金额2.53亿美元，其中1998年签订贷款协议金额2100万美元。中国使用挪威混合贷款的领域主要是能源、通讯、轻工、农业、城市建设、运输等。

挪威对华投资起步晚、规模小，金额少。1998年，中国共批准挪威在华投资项目11个，协议挪资金额3602万美元，实际投入金额2592万美元。截至1998年底，中国累计批准挪威在华投资项目79个，协议挪资金额1.91亿美元，实际投入金额1.3亿美元。挪在华投资的领域主要是：航运、电子、机械、通讯及化工等。

三、中国同中、东欧国家的经贸关系

波兰、匈牙利、捷克、斯洛伐克、罗马尼亚、南斯拉夫、斯洛文尼亚、克罗地亚、波黑、马其顿*、保加利亚、阿尔巴尼亚等十二个中东欧国家是我国的传统贸易伙伴。90年代以来，随着贸易方式的改变，我与中东欧国家的经贸合作开始在市场经济条件下，按照国际贸易规则进行，经贸合作逐步得到恢复和发展。1998年我国同中东欧各国的贸易总额达到19.6亿美元，比上年增长14.2%，其中我出口18.3亿美元，进口约1.3亿美元。我在中东欧地区的最大贸易伙伴是波兰，1998年中波贸易额8.14亿美元，贸易额最小的是波黑，仅33万美元。

我向中东欧国家主要出口商品有：轻纺产品、土畜、化工、焦炭和机电产品；主要进口商品有：化肥、钢材、铜、汽车、机械、化工和医药产品。

除传统的一般贸易外，我同中东欧各国还在相互投资、生产技术合作和大型项目建设方面开展了合作。我国在这些国家的投资约1.6亿美元，主要集中在匈牙利、波兰、罗马尼亚。我在这些国家投资的项目大多为贸易企业、餐馆、批发和零售公司，生产性企业少，且经营状况不佳。中东欧国家对华投资总金额虽然比我向这些国家投资的金额小，但有的企业达到了一定规模，如波兰与我河北省合资建立的锅炉生产企业。

除波黑外，我同中东欧各国均签订了双边《经贸合作协定》和《投资保护协定》，除波黑、马其顿外，我同中东欧各国均签订了《避免双重征税协定》，另外，我同波兰、克罗地亚等国签订了《海运协定》、同捷克签订了《海关合作协定》。

为及时研究解决经贸合作中存在的问题，探讨扩大和深化双边合作的方式和途径，促进经贸合作关系的不断发展，我与中东欧大多数国家成立了部级或司局级政府间经贸合作委员会。1998年，我分别与罗马尼亚（正部级）、波兰、南斯拉夫、保加利亚（副部级）、捷克、斯洛伐克、克罗地亚、斯洛文尼亚（司局级）举行了双边经贸混委会。

1998年外经贸部张祥副部长率中国政府经贸代表团出访波兰、捷克、斯洛伐克、克罗地亚、斯洛文尼亚。匈牙利政府经济内阁主席兼经济部长奇甘、罗马尼亚工贸部长、保加利亚贸易旅游部长、南斯拉夫外贸部长等访华，这些政府间高层交往为进一步活跃我与有关国家的经贸合作起到了积极的推动作用。

目前我与中东欧国家经贸合作中存在的主要问题有：(1）贸易不平衡状况比较严重，我与各国贸易存在较大顺差，但由于这些国家产品在质量和技术水平方面竞争力等方面原因，扩大进口难度较大；(2) 双方相互投资、生产合作尚属起步阶段，数量不多，规模较小，经贸合作亟待由单纯贸易向投资合作等深层次转变和发展；(3) 波兰等国开始以市场保障、反倾销等措施限制进口我部分产品，如鞋、打火机、自行车、纺织品等，对我有关产品的出口造成困难。

* 马其顿与台湾1999年1月签署所谓“建交公报”后，我国政府于2月9日宣布中止与马其顿的外交关系。

1998年中国与美国的经济贸易关系

对外贸易经济合作部美洲大洋洲司三外

一、双边贸易

1998年是中美经贸关系继续发展的一年。根据中国海关统计，1998年，中美双边贸易额为549.1亿美元，比上年增长12.1%。其中中国对美出口379.8亿美元，增长16.1%；自美进口169.6亿美元，增长4.0%；对美贸易顺差210.2亿美元，比上年增长28%。

1998年中国对美出口的商品主要是：机电产品（163.40亿美元）、服装（37.48亿美元）、鞋类（43.17亿美元）、玩具（27.84亿美元）、塑料制品（11.97亿美元）、家具（10.40亿美元）、纺织纱线、织物及制品（9.56亿美元）、旅行用品及箱包（5.85亿美元）、医药品（3.63亿美元）、装饰用陶瓷制品（2.47亿美元）、原油（2.16亿美元）。

1998年中国自美进口的商品主要是：机电产品（94.18亿美元）、肥料（12.15亿美元）、初级形状的塑料（5.69亿美元）、纸及纸浆（5.46亿美元）、食用植物油（2.58亿美元）、牛皮革和马皮革（1.87亿美元）、原棉（1.73亿美元）、医疗仪器及器械（1.45亿美元）、原木（1.16亿美元）。

随着两国经贸关系的发展，两国间的技术贸易正步入一个新时期。据统计，1998年中国自美引进技术价值30亿美元，双方合作领域更加广泛，合作方式更加灵活。1998年3月20日（中美两国政府关于和平利用核能合作协定》的正式启动将有助于两国进一步拓宽经济技术合作的领域。

二、双边投资

1998年，美国对华投资项目数2215个，协议美资金额62.1亿美元，实际投入美资39.1亿美元，分别比上年增长1.2%、25.8%和20.8%。截至1998年底，美对华投资项目累计26581个，协议美资金额462.8亿美元，实际投入美资214.1亿美元。近年来，美国对华投资领域广阔，涉及机械、冶金、石油、电子、通讯、化工、纺织、轻工、食品、农业、医药、房地产、以及金融、保险、外贸、会计、货运代理等试点开放的行业。其中许多在华美资企业经营状况良好，陆续追加投资。

近年来，中国在美国开设的贸易型和非贸易型公司也呈增长趋势。截止1998年底，经批准的我国在美国投资举办的海外企业共计555家，协议投资总额约7.15亿美元，中方投资总额约4.98亿美元，涉及的行业有工业、科技、承包、服装、农业、餐馆、食品、旅游、金融、保险、运输等等。

三、双边经贸合作及重要经贸往来

1998年6月，应江泽民主席邀请，克林顿总统对中国进行了正式友好访问。访问期间，中美双方就双边经贸关系中的一系列问题进行了广泛深入的讨论，表示将在平等互惠的基础上，进一步加强交流与合作，共同推动中美经贸关系的发展。双方签署了《中美和平利用核技术合作协定》，并签署了总额约31.2亿美元的商贸合同。中美两国首脑互访对中美两国加深了解，增进友谊，扩大共识，发展合作，推动两国关系进入一个新的发展阶段产生了积极的影响；同时，对扩大两国在经贸领域的合作，促进中美经贸关系的健康发展，也起到了有力的推动作用。

1998年，中美经贸交往频繁。4月，外经贸部孙振宇副部长与美国商务部副部长阿伦共同主持了中美商贸联委会项下第一次副部长级中期磋商；5月，中美经济联委会第十一次会议在华盛顿举行，财政部项怀诚部长与美国财政部部长鲁宾共同主持；12月，中美两国举行了第十二次商贸联委会会议，外经贸部石广生部长率中国政府经贸代表团赴华盛顿同美商务部部长戴利共同主持了此次会议，就各自关心的问题进行讨论，促进中美两国在有关行业的经济技术合作。这次联委会会议是中美两国首脑实现互访后两国举行的首次高级经贸会议，中美双方对此次会议极为重视，此次会议取得了积极有效的成果，为推动两国经贸关系继续向前发展创造了条件。

四、中美经贸关系中存在的主要问题

中美经贸关系中新的机遇层出不穷，新的矛盾甚至摩擦也不断出现。面对新机遇，积极运筹，妥善处理中美经贸关系中出现的问题和摩擦，对促进双边贸易和经济合作的稳定、健康发展至关重要。

（一）最惠国待遇问题

最惠国待遇问题曾长期困扰中美经贸关系的发展。最惠国待遇是贸易伙伴间相互给予的基本待遇，也是“中美贸易关系协定”的核心条款和发展中美经贸关系的基本保证。1998年6月25日美国会通过了将最惠国待遇更名成“正常贸易关系”(NTR)的议案，7月22日，美国总统克林顿签署了此议案，从而正式生效。但该议案仍未改变年度审议的法律程序，仍受到杰克逊－瓦尼克修正案的制约。

近年来，越来越多的有识之士已经认识到，只有永久性解决这一问题，才能将中美经贸关系建立在一个坚实稳定的基础上。美国有关方面应从当前现实出发，尊重两国人民的根本利益和愿望，取消年度审议的做法，永久解决最惠国待遇问题，为双边经贸关系的发展奠定一个长期、稳定的基础。

（二）中国加入世贸组织问题

中国加入世贸组织不仅符合中国的利益，也符合世界各国的利益。世界贸易组织是一个建立在国际公认规则之上的国际性组织，中国加入世界贸易组织的要求充分显示了中国承担国际义务的信心和决心。1998年中美双方在中国加入WTO问题上进行了频繁的磋商。在6月克林顿总统访华前夕，中美之间就中国加入WTO问题举行了密集的双边磋商，取得了一些进展。但终因美方要价过高而未达成协议。无论中国加入与否，中国都将继续改革开放。这个问题久拖不决不利于中美经贸关系的稳定发展，也不利于双边关系的发展。美国作为世界贸易组织的重要缔约方，在中国加入世界贸易组织这一问题上，应该明事理、晓大义，信守诺言，切实发挥积极作用。

（三）美方对中国输美货物木质包装检疫问题

1998年9月11日，美国农业部长签署一项新法令，要求所有来自中国的木质包装和木质铺垫材料（以下简称木质包装）须附有中国出入境检验检疫机关出具的证书，证明木质包装在进入美国前经过热处理、熏蒸处理或特定处理，或者出口商出具无木质包装的证明。美方单方面采取的这一不合理的严厉措施不仅不符合世贸组织有关动植物卫生检疫措施协议中关于无歧视性、科学性及对贸易影响最小的原则，还严重影响中美贸易的正常进行，损害两国经贸合作。美方这一规定引起了中方极大的关注。在中方多次交涉下，美方将12月17日到港实施时间推迟为离港实施时间，并同意考虑中方提出的其他处理方法。美方应从维护两国贸易的大局出发，寻求妥善办法，解决星天牛问题。

（四）美对华反倾销问题

自1980年到1998年底，美国已对中国输美商品提起反倾销调查案件66件，近年来呈不断上升的趋势。反倾销案件的不断增多严重阻碍了中国商品向美国的正常出口，影响了中美两国正常的双边经贸关系的健康发展。在对华反倾销调查中，美国继续视中国为“非市场经济国家”的情况成为中国政府十分关切的问题。美国政府应正确了解中国的社会发展状况，改变将中国视为非市场经济国家、采用歧视性的替代国方法来计算倾销幅度的做法，公正合理地处理反倾销案件。

（五）出口管制问题

美国自“冷战”以来一直维持着严格的技术出口管制，不仅影响了中国的技术进口，更限制了美国自身出口优势的发挥。1998年6月中美双方就访问最终用户一事达成谅解。这是中方在出口管制问题上采取的最为积极灵活的措施。美方应对中方的安排作出积极的反应，改变对中国歧视性的出口管制政策，采取切实有效措施放宽乃至取消对华高技术出口限制。

在相互尊重、平等协商、互谅互让的基础上处理双边经贸关系中存在的问题是发展和促进国与国之间经贸关系的基本原则。经验告诉我们，如果将经贸问题作为一国国内政治的筹码，或采取单方面措施，不仅无助于问题的解决，反而会对中美经贸关系甚至双边关系的发展带来不利影响。双方只有排除非贸易因素的影响，以积极务实的态度解决前进道路上的问题，中美经贸关系的发展才能走向成熟、健康稳定之路。

1998年中国与加拿大的经济贸易关系

对外贸易经济合作部美洲大洋洲司二处

一、双边贸易

据中国海关统计，1998年中加双边贸易额达43.7亿美元，比上年增长11.6%，创历史最高纪录；其中中国对加拿大出口21.3亿美元，增长11.7%；从加进口22.4亿美元，增长11.5%。加拿大为中国第十大贸易伙伴，中国是加第四大贸易伙伴。

中国从加进口的主要商品有机电产品（6.4亿美元）、粮食（141万吨、2.6亿美元）、纸浆（56万吨、2.5亿美元）、钾肥（199万吨、2.5亿美元）、纸及纸板（11万吨、5862万美元）等，以上各项合计占从加进口总额的64.8%。进口增长较快的商品主要有飞机、电讯设备及零附件、自动数据处理设备及附件、食用植物油等商品。进口降幅较大的商品主要有小麦、矿砂、纸及纸板及化工原料等。

中国对加出口的主要商品有机电产品（6.9亿美元）、服装（3.7亿美元）、塑料制品（1.6亿美元）、鞋类（1.3亿美元）、纺织品（1.2亿美元）、旅行用品和箱包（1.1亿美元）、玩具（6505万美元）等。机电产品出口额继续列居首位，占出口总额32.5%；纺织服装合计占23.1%，轻工类产品表现出一定增长潜力，对加出口商品结构进一步改善。1998年2月，中加双方经过谈判，就今后三年两国纺织品贸易的配额安排达成了协议，这有助于中国对加出口服装、纺织口的平稳发展。

二、经济技术合作

1. 相互投资

1998年加拿大在华新设投资项目414个，协议外资金额9.53亿美元，实际利用3.5亿美元。截止1998年底，共批准加拿大在中国直接投资项目3982项，协议加资金额63.72亿美元，加方实际投入17.67亿美元。加拿大投资企业分布在广东、上海、江苏、福建、山东、河北、北京、陕西、安徽、新疆、海南等20多个省市自治区。覆盖的行业有石油开发 、机械、电子、通讯、化工、轻工、食品、纺织、农业、水产养殖、房地产、服务业等。生产性项目约占总数的80%。

1998年经外经贸部批准在加新设的投资企业有2家，中方协议投资总额约60万美元。至1998年底，经外经贸部批准或在外经贸部备案的中国在加拿大投资兴办的贸易和非贸易性机构共121家，中方协议投资总额为3300万美元，涉及的行业有资源开发、工业生产、建筑承包、农牧渔业、餐饮业、科技文化交流、交通运输、咨询服务等。

2. 贷款合作

自1986年至1998年，加政府通过其出口发展公司（EDC）共对华提供五批优惠混合贷款，总计承诺金额22.6亿美元。1997年开始执行第五批贷款协议，加方承诺向中国提供一笔与7500万加元等值的美元的无息贷款，有效期两年，还款期四十年（含十五年宽限期）。该笔贷款与出口信贷混合使用，占合同总价的42%，混合后贷款总额为1.79亿加元（约合1.3亿美元）。到1998年底，已有20个项目向EDC提出申请并签署商务合同，涉及金额1.04亿美元；其中8个项目已经生效，金额为3500万美元。

3. **加对华援助**

中加两国从1982年起开始进行发展合作，1983年中加两国政府签署《中国和加拿大政府关于发展合作总协定》。双方已进行了三个周期的合作，涉及农业、林业、能源、交通、通讯、环保、人才开发、扶贫等多个领域，到1998年底项目总数已达83个，加方投入资金5.5亿加元（约合4.1亿美元）。其中已完成合作项目52个，正在执行的项目31个，另外还有4个项目正在规划中。中加合作项目为中国培养了大批的有用人才，通过加方的技术转让和关键仪器设备的引进，使许多项目部门在技术和管理水平上都有了不同程度的提高，取得了良好的经济和社会效益。

三、重要经贸往来

1998年3月，加拿大国际贸易部长马奇率企业家代表团访华，与石广生部长举行双边会谈，李鹏委员长和李岚清副总理分别会见了马奇。

9月，加拿大亚太国务部长陈卓愉应邀率企业家代表团访华，孙振宇副部长在北京会见了陈卓愉一行。加代表团还参加了在厦门举行的第二届’98投资贸易洽谈会。同月，中加经贸联委会第15次会议在北京举行，由孙振宇副部长和加外交国贸部副部长莱特共同主持。

11月，加总理克雷蒂安来华访问，这是他继1994年、1996年两度访华后第三次率大型企业代表团访华。同时，加国贸部长马奇再次应外经贸部邀请访华。克雷蒂安和马奇均参加了加中贸易理事会在北京举行的大型活动。孙振宇副部长会见了马奇一行。

1998年中国与拉美国家的经济贸易关系

对外贸易经济合作部美洲大洋洲司一处

一、中拉贸易略有下降，但双边贸易额仍维持相当规模，我对拉美出口保持增长势头

1998年，受亚洲金融危机影响，中拉贸易与上年相比略有下降。根据中国海关统计，去年中拉贸易总额为83.1亿美元，同比下降0.8%。其中我对拉美出口53.2亿美元，同比增长15.5%，我从拉美进口29.8亿美元，同比下降20.7%。我对拉美出口增长率继续高于同年我国对外出口平均增长率。在对各大洲出口中，我对拉美出口增长率位于非洲和北美洲之后居第三位。

在拉美主要贸易伙伴中，中国与巴西、阿根廷、巴拿马和智利的双边贸易额均超过10亿美元，分别为22.19亿美元、12.74亿美元、10.49亿美元和10.41亿美元。与墨西哥的双边贸易额达8.4亿美元，与秘鲁、古巴、委内瑞拉、乌拉圭、厄瓜多尔、和哥伦比亚的双边贸易额均超过1亿美元。在上述国家中，中国对巴西和巴拿马出口均超过10亿美元，在上年基础上继续保持3.9%和3.7%的增速。此外，我对墨西哥、乌拉圭、委内瑞拉、玻利维亚以及安提瓜和巴布达、特立尼达和多巴哥、苏里南等加勒比国家和哥斯达黎加、洪都拉斯等中美洲国家的出口也有较大幅度的增长。1998年我国对拉美出口的大宗商品有机电产品（20亿美元）、服装和纺织品（15亿美元）、医药和化工品（3.3亿美元）、轻工产品（2.9亿美元）以及谷物和蔬菜（7000万美元）。

1998年我从拉美进口降幅较大，但仍保持一定水平。从巴西进口为11.3亿美元，同比下降23.9%，从阿根廷和智利进口分别为7.2亿美元和4.2亿美元，同比分别增长0.3%和1.5%。从秘鲁和墨西哥进口分别为2.9亿美元和1.5亿美元，同比分别下降53.6%和20%。我从乌拉圭和委内瑞拉等国的进口也有较大幅度的下降。1998年中国从拉美进口的主要商品有矿产品（4.9亿美元）、鱼粉（1.9亿美元）、原油（1.3亿美元）、羊毛

(1.07亿美元)、机电产品（1亿美元)、钢材（1亿美元)、植物油（0.95亿美元)、食糖（0.95亿美元)、纸浆（0.93亿美元）和皮革（0.8亿美元)。

二、双边经济技术合作取得进展

1998年中国新天公司在墨西哥的农业综合开发项目取得初步成功，在古巴的水稻种植项目继续获得进展。在哥伦比亚的金城摩托车组装厂在原有规模上扩大生产。此外，上海广电集团在阿根廷的彩电生产厂、北方公司在阿根廷的小型货车厂、南京跃进汽车公司在阿根廷的汽车装配厂以及长江经济联合发展（集团）公司在墨西哥的纺织城项目等也正在实施中。

1998年，我国在拉美国家建立投资项目23个，其中中方投资3678万美元。同期，拉美国家在华投资项目777个，合同外资金额73亿美元，实际投资金额45.6亿美元。其中维尔京群岛在华投资项目622个，合同外资金额61.5亿美元，实际投资金额40亿美元；开曼群岛在华投资项目41个，合同外资金额7.9亿美元，实际投资金额3.2亿美元；巴哈马在华投资项目19个，合同外资金额2.2亿美元，实际投资金额8077万美元；巴拿马在华投资项目18个，合同外资金额6503万美元，实际投资金额7004万美元；阿根廷在华投资项目17个，合同外资金额2511万美元，实际投资金额128万美元。

1998年，中国企业共在拉美签订承包工程合同41份，合同总金额1亿美元，完成营业额4925万美元；签订劳务合作合同150份，合同总金额4837万美元，完成营业额4076万美元；签订设计咨询合同7份，合同金额90万美元，完成营业额50万美元。1998年中国共向拉美国家提供6.5亿元人民币援助，其中无偿援助8300万元人民币，无息贷款5000万元人民币，优惠贷款5亿元人民币。

1998年，中国与苏里南、圭亚那、牙买加和古巴签订了优惠贷款框架协议。向古巴、玻利维亚、苏里南、圭亚那、秘鲁、特里尼达和多巴哥、圣卢西亚、巴哈马、哥伦比亚、牙买加、厄瓜多尔、安提瓜和巴布达、墨西哥提供了无息贷款援助或无偿援助。此外，中国还向巴西、智利、圭亚那、哥伦比亚、厄瓜多尔、洪都拉斯和危地马拉提供了多边技术援助，共有13名学员参加了各类技术培训。

三、双方继续保持经贸领域高层频繁互访

1998年，国务院吴邦国副总理对委内瑞拉、秘鲁、哥伦比亚和阿根廷四国进行了正式友好访问，我部张祥副部长随同出访。此外，我部孙振宇副部长、张祥副部长、高虎城部长助理、杨文生部长助理先后率团访问了古巴、智利、墨西哥、哥伦比亚、厄瓜多尔、乌拉圭、巴西、阿根廷、巴拿马、巴哈马、圣卢西亚和苏里南等国。中国与墨西哥、委内瑞拉、巴西、阿根廷、古巴和乌拉圭共同召开了双边经贸混合委员会，与南方共同市场举行了第二次磋商。与此同时，苏里南总统、乌拉圭副总统、牙买加总理、智利外长和农业部长、墨西哥外长、巴西外长、委内瑞拉副外长和古巴经济合作与外国投资部副部长等相继访华，就发展双边经贸关系与中方交换了意见，这些高层交往起到了增进了解、加深友谊和推动合作的作用。

1998年中国与澳大利亚、新西兰的经济贸易关系

对外贸易经济合作部美洲大洋洲司二处

一、中国与澳大利亚经济贸易关系

（一）双边贸易

据中国海关统计，1998年中澳双边贸易额为50.3亿美元，比上年下降了5.2%。其中，中国对澳出口23.4亿美元，比上年增长13.9%，中国从澳进口26.9亿美元，比上年下降17.2%。澳继续

保持中国第9大贸易伙伴的地位。

1998年，中国对澳出口的主要商品和金额为：机电产品7.19亿美元，服装6.12亿美元，纺织品1.92亿美元，鞋类9193万美元，塑料制品6931万美元，旅行用品及箱包3978万美元，玩具3665万美元等。其中，机电产品出口再次超过服装成为中国对澳出口的第一大商品，这说明中国出口商品的结构进一步得到优化。

中国从澳进口的商品大多数为原料性商品，主要有：铁矿砂2557万吨，金额6.87亿美元；羊毛9万吨，金额3.71亿美元；氧化铝107万吨，金额2.33亿美元；机电产品1.75亿美元；谷物106万吨，金额1.72亿美元；原棉4531万美元；铝1.30亿美元；铜矿砂27万吨，金额9864万美元；钢材13万吨，5956万美元；煤118万吨，5116万美元；锰矿砂34万吨，3386万美元；食糖8万吨，金额1603万美元等。其中，粮食、羊毛、原棉、铁矿砂等进口量比上年均有较大幅度的下降，主要是因为中国国内粮食丰收、纺织工业改造以及钢铁市场疲软，这些方面的进口需求减少。

（二）经济合作

1. 双向投资。1998年，中国新批澳在华直接投资项目452个，协议澳资6.99亿美元，实际投入2.72亿美元。澳大利亚康联保险集团于4月份获准在上海筹建一家合资寿险公司。截至1998年底，中国累计批准澳在华直接投资项目3468个，澳方协议投资额52.07亿美元，实际投入15.40亿美元。投资行业分布在农业、建材、纺织、电子、服务业等领域。澳大利亚是中国吸收外资的主要来源地之一。

截至1998年底，中国在澳设立的各种贸易性机构和生产性企业共计169家，中方协议投资额为3.65亿美元。澳大利亚已成为中国在海外投资最多的国家之一。

2. 技术合作。自1981年10月中澳两国政府正式签署《中澳技术合作促进发展计划协定》以来，由于两国政府的重视及双方的共同努力，中澳技术合作进展顺利，成果显著。十几年来，合作领域不断扩大，已涉及农业、林业、牧业、能源、矿产、交通、纺织、建材、教育、卫生、审计、城市改造等方面。截至1998年底，双方已完成合作项目71个，正在执行项目27个，澳方投入资金3亿多澳元。

澳政府1998/99年度财政预算中对华援款部分有所增加，但同时取消了对华优惠贷款。中澳两国贷款合作已告结束，技术合作则将继续发展。

（三）重要经贸访问

外经贸部孙振宇副部长于7月访澳，同澳外交贸易部秘书长卡尔弗特共同主持了中澳经济联委会中期磋商。

二、中国与新西兰经济贸易关系

（一）双边贸易

1998年，中国和新西兰的经贸关系继续发展。据中国海关统计，1998年中新双边贸易额达6.85亿美元，比上年增长8.4%；其中中国对新出口2.75亿美元，比上年下降2.5%，从新进口4.10亿美元，增长17.5%。

从商品结构看，1998年中国从新西兰进口的主要商品多是原料性产品，包括羊毛1.17亿美元(4.2万吨)，纸及纸板3039万美元，纸浆1559万美元，饲料用鱼粉1200万美元，原木1192万美元等。其中羊毛仍是中国从新进口的最大商品，但占从新进口总额的比重有所降低，为28.5%。

中国对新西兰的出口商品仍以轻工产品为主，包括：服装9296万美元，纺织品2939万美元，鞋类797万美元，塑料制品791万美元，玩具500万美元等。近几年中国对新西兰的机电产品出口增长很快，1998年中国向新出口机电产品价值6250万美元，比上年增长7.6%，对新出口商品结构得到进一步改善。

（二）经济技术合作

1. 相互投资

1998年，中国新批新西兰来华投资项目51个，协议金额2156万美元，实际投入2664万美元。截至1998年底，中国批准新西兰在华投资项目总数为422个，协议金额3.01亿美元，实际投入1.61亿美元。目前新西兰在华投资的行业主要分布在农林、轻工、纺织、冶金、食品加工、计算机、服务业等领域。

截至1998年底，中国在新西兰设立的各种贸易性机构和生产性企业近20家，投资额超过8亿美元。其中最大的项目包括中国对外贸易运输总公司经营的威尼达林业公司和中信公司与新西兰雄狮公司和新西兰BRIERLEY投资公司组成的财团买下的新西兰森林公司。目前新西兰已成为中国在海外最大的投资目的地之一。

2. 技术合作

自1989年以来，新西兰共向中国提供了1000多万新元的无偿援助，用于对中国经济不发达地区的扶贫，并将其先进的农牧业技术和设备介绍到中国，收到了很好的经济和社会效益。1997/98年度，新西兰援华资金额度为200万新元，援助项目主要分为综合扶贫、体制改革研讨和促进双边投资合作等三大类。其中，1998年完成扶贫项目17个，使用新方援助金额51.5万新元。

（三）高层经贸互访

1998年7月，外经贸部孙振宇副部长率团访问了新西兰，与新西兰外交贸易部副秘书长比斯利共同主持了中新经贸联委会第20项会议；10月，新西兰外长麦金农访华，与吴仪国务委员就进一步推动两国经贸关系进行了商谈。

北京爱立信移动通信有限公司

Beijing Ericsson Mobile Communications Co., Ltd

北 京爱立信移动通信有限公司(BMC)，是1995年8月由中国邮电工业总公司(PTIC)、瑞典爱立信集团和香港永兴企业公司共同投资兴建的中外高新技术合资企业。主要生产、销售移动电话；通信系统；承揽系统网络交钥匙工程服务；提供手机和系统的售后服务。公司投资总额为2800万美元，注册资金为2000万美元。

北京爱立信移动通信有限公司成立近四年来，业务迅速发展，取得了令人瞩目的成就。1998年销售额达34.8亿元人民币，员工人数超过600人。

总经理：柏力

Managing Director:

Robert J Parris

副总经理：于民

Deputy Managing Director:

Yu Min

Beijing Ericsson Mobile Communications Co., Ltd (BMC) is a ghtech joint venture set up by the China ational Posts & Telecommunications dustry Corporation (PTIC), Sweden LM ricsson in Sweden and Hong Kong Yeung hing Enterprise in August.1995,mainly anufacturing and selling mobile phones, SM system, Providing turnkey services oject required to mobile cellular and fixed lecommunication networks, offering tersale service for both mobile phones and stems. Its total investment is US$28 million id registered capital is US$20 million.

With four years development, BMC has own very fast with its business and has ade remarkable achievements. Total venue in 1998. reached RMB¥ 3.48 llon. And there are over 600 staff nployees by BMC.

地址：北京市顺义区天竺空港工业区
A区天柱西路

邮编：101312

电话：+86 10 6457 1188

传真：+86 10 6457 5729

电子邮件：Li.tao@bmc.ericsson.se

Add: Beijing Ericsson Mobile Communications Co.,Ltd
Tian Zhu West Road.

P.C: 101312

Tel: +86 10 6457 1188

Fax: +86 10 6457 5729

E-mail: Li.tao@bmc.ericsson.se

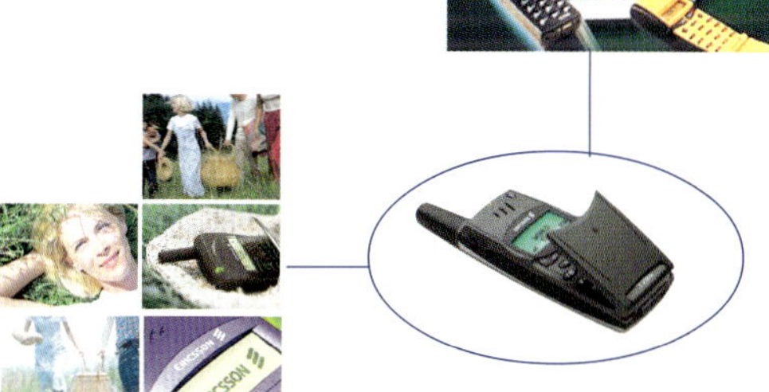

仙妮蕾德®

董事长陈得福博士、总裁陈徐爱莲医学博士伉俪合影

仙妮蕾德国际机构是研发生产天然浓缩草本植物品、美容护肤化妆品和家居用品的美资跨国公司，由华人陈得福博士伉俪在1982年创办于美国犹他州，现设在加州洛杉矶地区的多伦斯市。经过17年的稳步仙妮蕾德事业已遍及全球30个国家和地区，并拥有方尺以上的高科技厂房和数百万的消费者。

仙妮蕾德创办人兼董事长的陈得福博士是专业和国际知名的草本学家，总裁陈徐爱莲亦是拥有美国的医学博士。陈博士伉俪以其专业知识及经验亲自研制天然的对人体健康有益的仙妮蕾德产品。

仙妮蕾德国际机构分别于1993年和1995年在广州津设立了分公司，投资总额超过3000万美元，注册资1325.3万美元，已全部到位，经营期限50年。目前，在全国各地的600余家授权经销店，以指定的统一价码销售仙妮蕾德产品。

仙妮蕾德产品是基于中国古代的再生哲理及五千养文化的理念，结合并运用西方的高科技，选用优质本植物经萃取，以高度浓缩精制而成。仙妮蕾德在中产的产品分为三个系列达200多个品种：吃得健康 喝康 — 仙妮蕾德草本营养饮食品系列，是老少皆宜的品；家居健康 — 欣美™家庭用品以及个人护理产品系列，包括各类洗涤剂、草本牙膏等浓缩产品，为现代家庭生活提供健康和方便；仪容健康 — 蔻蒂森™个人保养护肤及化妆品系列，助您缔造自然、时尚的蕴生之美。

天津公司外景
Sunrider Products in China

仙妮蕾德广州有限公司
广州市天河北路中信广场5304-5306室
邮政编码：510620
电话：(020)38770808
传真：(020)38770052

Sunrider (Guangzhou) Ltd.
Room 5304-5306, CITIC PLAZA,
233 Tianhe North Road
Guangzhou, China 510620
Tel:(020)38770808
Fax:(020)38770052

仙妮蕾德天津有限公司
天津市经济技术开发区黄海路161号
邮政编码：3000457
电话：(020)25321333
传真：(020)25321331

Sunrider (Tianjin) Ltd.
161 Huang Hai Road,
TEDA
Tianjin, China 300457
Tel: (022)25321333
Fax:(022)25321331

www. sunrider. com

UNRIDER® INTERNATIONAL

Sunrider® International ("Sunrider"), founded by Drs. Tei Fu d Oi-Lin Chen in 1982 in Utah, USA and currently headquartered Torrance, California, USA, is one of the world's largest multinational rporations specializing in the manufacturing and marketing of rbal products - food and beverage, beauty care and household oducts. With 17 years of stable and continuous growth, Sunrider esently does business in 30 countries and regions with over a lion consumers world-wide. It has its own high-tech manufacturing nts in the U.S., China, Singapore and Taiwan area with over one lion square feet of state-of-the-art production facilities.

Dr. Tei Fu Chen, Sunrider's founder and chairman of the board, a pharmacist and world-renowned herbalist while Dr. Oi-Lin Chen, esident of Sunrider, is a licensed medical doctor in the U.S. gether, the Chens personally oversee the research, development d manufacture of Sunrider's herb-based products designed for althy living.

Sunrider entered the China market when it established its angzhou office in 1993; the Tianjin office opened subsequently in 95. Total investment in China exceeded US$30,000,000 while gistered and paid-in capital was US$13,253,000. Sunrider was granted operation rights in China for 50 years and currently, Sunrider products are exclusively sold in over 600 Sunrider authorized stores throughout China at company-designated fixed prices.

美国总部外景
Sunrider World Headquarters in USA

国总部厂房一景
unrider Plant in USA

Sunrider products are manufactured based on the ancient Philosophy of Regeneration. Combining Chinese herbal knowledge with the most advanced modern technology, Sunrider creates unique herbal formulations to help nourish and cleanse the body so that it can achieve its own natural balance.With over 200 products available in China, Sunrider's highly-concentrated herbal products can be divided into three groups,

- Sunrider's nutritional herbal and beverage line, with products like NuPlus, Calli and Fortune Delight, is designed to improve people's eating habits and is suitable for all ages.
- The SunSmile household and personal care line includes such products as herbal toothpaste and all-purpose cleansers and is designed for every day convenience as well as to enable users to live a more healthy lifestyle.
- The Kandesn line of skin care and cosmetic products, including such products as Supreme Emulsion, Moisturizing Lip Colors and Protective Foundation, helps bring out the natural beauty within you.

德产品图片
er Products in China

北京建工集团

SYNOPSIS OF BCEG

北京建工集团是一家由300余家企业组成的集设计、科研、施工、建筑安装、材料供应为一体的，具有工程总承包、房地产开发经营以及国际工程承包、对外贸易资格和实力的跨行业、跨地区经营的大型企业集团。集团现有员工5万多人，其中各类专业技术人员11791人，具有高级职称的近500人。年竣工能力达200多万平方米。1995年，中华人民共和国国家统计局等权威单位公布"中国的脊梁"——国有企业500强，建工集团荣列第224位。

北京建工集团成立46年来共完成各类大中型建筑6500余万平方米。先后建成了人民大会堂、北京工人体育场、北京图书馆新馆、长城饭店、中央彩电中心、东方广场、恒基中心、新世界中心、国际金融中心等一大批标志性建筑，长安街上90%的建筑均出自建工集团之手。现已获鲁班奖25个，居全国建筑企业之首。

北京建工集团还积极开拓国际市场，先后在巴基斯坦、桑给巴尔、斯里兰卡、博茨瓦纳、泰国、马来西亚、澳门等国家和地区承建了大批建筑工程。1994年建工集团在中国500家最大服务业企业国际经济技术合作中排序第10位，1995年、1996年、1997年、1998年连续被评为全球最大225家国际承包商之一。

The Beijing Construction Engineering Group (hereinafter referrded to as BCEG) is a giant enterprise group, composed of more than 300 companies and factories, engaging in architectural design, scientific research, construction, equipment installation, building material supply as an organic whole. It is highly qualified and powerful in general contractor, real estate development and operation, international engineering contract and foreign trade, and is able to execute trans-regional and inter-trade operation. BCEG possesses over 50,000 employees, among whom 11,791 are various professionals and about 500 have been awarded senior professional titles. Its annual project completion amounts to 2,000,000 square meters. In 1995, the State Statistics Bureau assessed 500 backbone state-run enterprises in China and BCEG was ranked 224th among them.

BCEG has completed during 46 years of construction a total floor space of more than 65 moillion square meters of various types of large and medium-sized buildings, among which are the significant buildings in Beijing, such as the Great Hall of the People, the Beijing Worker's Stadium, the New National Library Complex of Beijing, the Beijing Great Wall Hotel, the China Central Television (CCTV)Transmission Tower, the Oriental Plaza, the Beijing Henderson Center, the New World Center, the Beijing International Financial Buildion, etc. 90 percent of Buildings in the Chang An Street of Beijing were undertaken by BCEG.BCEG has been awarded 23 special Luban prizes, the topmost prizewinner in construction enterprises of China.

BCEG has also actively developed the international market and has undertaken and accomplished a great number of overseas projects successively in teens of countries and regions such as Pakistan, Zanzibar, Sri Lanka, Botswana, Thailand, Malaysia, Macao, etc. BCEG was listed 10th among 500 the most gigantic service enterprises in China in international economic and technological cooperation in 1994, and elected one of the 225 top gigantic international construction contractors in the world successively in 1995, 1996, 1997, and 1998 by ENR.

地址：中国北京复外南礼士路19号

Add: No.19 Nanlishi Road Fuxingmenwai, Beijing

电话 (Tel): 8610-68018218　　传真 (Fax): 8610-68015032

法人代表：张兴

中国万宝工程公司

CHINA WANBAO ENGINEERING CORP.

国万宝工程公司（简称万宝公司）是1985年经中华人民共和国政，从事对外工程承包、劳务合作、境内外投资和进出口业务的国际术合作公司。

宝公司前身从五十年代起，先后在10多个国家承建80多个不同种外经济援助项目。自1985年公司正式成立以来，在十几个国家承多个工业项目和电站、铁路、公路桥梁、建筑、市政设施、环保项目。万宝公司累计对外工程承包总额16亿美元，同世界各国和行了广泛的经济技术合作和贸易往来。

宝公司总部设在北京，在国内外设有数十个代表处。万宝公司资产亿元人民币，注册资本4.74亿人民币。与境内外各银行、金融机切的业务联系，有广泛的融资渠道和良好的商业信誉。万宝公司是）家大型外经企业之一，并连续几年进入美国《工程新闻记录》全球225家大型国际承包商之列。万宝公司具有国家工程施工总级企业资质和国家机电设备成套单位甲级企业资质。万宝公司是中贸易促进委员会、中国对外承包工程商会、中国机电产品进出口商单位。

宝公司业务范围广泛，经营方式多样，主要业务有：承包国内外各、能源、交通、土木工程、供水工程、环保工程项目，提供各种类司层次的劳务，在境内外投资，开展联合承包以及各种方式的经济作。

国万宝工程公司本着“平等互利、讲求实效、形式多样、共同发展”，愿意进一步加强同海内外各界的业务联系与合作，为各国和各地济贸易的发展提供良好的服务。

China Wanbao Engineering Corporation (CWBEC), established in 1985, is a renowned state-owned corporation engaged in international economic and technical co-operation and is authorized by the Chinese government to undertake overseas engineering contracting, investment, labor co-operation, as well as import and export business.

Since the 1950's, China Wanbao Engineering Corporation had undertaken over 80 projects in various countries around the world. Starting from its formal establishment in 1985, CWBEC has contracted over 50 industrial projects in more than 10 countries in such sectors as power plant, railway, highway, civil engineering and construction, and environmental protection. Over the years, CWBEC has scored project contracting value of some 1.6 billion U.S. dollars, and has conducted a wide range of trade and economic and technical co-operation with many countries and regions in the world.

Headquartered in Beijing, China Wanbao Engineering Corporation boasts dozens of representative offices around the world. CWBEC's registered capital is 474 million RMB yuan (equivalent to about 57 million U.S. dollars), while its total assets have exceeded 2.5 billion RMB yuan (about 300 million U.S. dollars). Enjoying a remarkable reputation and commercial credit standing, CWBEC has various channels available for fund-raising. CWBEC is one of the 50 largest engineering enterprises in China. In the past a few years, China Wanbao Engineering Corporation has consecutively ranked among the Top 225 International Contractors recognized by the U.S. Engineering News Record (ENR). CWBEC holds top qualifications issued by the government for construction and the supply of complete set of mechanical and electrical equipment. China Wanbao Engineering Corporation is also members of the China Council for Promotion of International Trade, the China Chamber of International Contract Engineering, and China Import & Export Chamber of Mechanical and Electrical Product.

CWBEC conducts a wide range of business in diversified forms. The Corporation's main business includes: contracting various kinds of industrial, energy, transportation, water supply, civil engineering and environment protection projects, providing labor service of various types at different levels, establishing joint ventures by investing both at home and abroad, and undertaking joint contracting and other forms of economic & technical co-operation.

Adhering to the principle of "maintaining equality and mutual benefits, emphasizing practical results, diversity of forms and common progress", CWBEC aims at further tightening business ties with all domestic and overseas partners and rendering faithful services to promote economic & trade development in the world.

朗首都德黑兰城郊电气化铁路工程。电气化铁路全长43同额1.17亿美元。是由万宝公司提供设计、电力系统、信号控制系统、机车、车辆及全部设备的安装调试直至的“交钥匙”工程。主运营段于1999年3月竣工。

n a total length of 43 km and contracting value 17 million, the Tehran Suburban Electrified Railway is a "turn-key" Project for which CWBEC supplies design,procures,installs and hands over power ,telecommunication & signal control systems, ves and passenger cars.Its major section started operation in March, 1999.

海南海口世纪大桥正在沉井

The Laying Down of the Open Caisson for the Haikou Century Bridge in Hainan.

泰国PTA化工厂自备电站。该电站装机容量55MW，全部操作均由自动控制系统控制。

The Self-supplied Power Station Project at PTA Factory Plant in Thailand.The installed capacity of the station is 55 MW. The station is operated by an automatic control system.

事长：李德　　副董事长：顾永春
经理：王筱
总经理：江继久　李成杰　李建民
总会计师：李映红
址：中国北京广安门南街甲12号
编：100053
话：(8610)63529988　传真：(8610)63540392
子信箱：cnwanbao@public3.bta.net.cn

Chairman: Li De　　Vice Chairman: Gu Yongchun
President: Wang Xiao
Vice Presidents: Jiang Jijiu, Li Chengjie, Li Jianmin
Deputy Chief Accountant: Li Yinghong
Add: 12A Guang An Men Nan Jie,Beijing, P.R.China
Post Code: 100053　P.O.Box: Beijing 2932, China
Tel: (86-10)63529988　Fax: (86-10)63540392
Telex: 22985 CNWB CN
E-mail: cnwanbao@public 3.bta.net.cn

NOKIA
CONNECTING PEOPLE
诺基亚
诺基亚科技
让你的今天与未来更加丰富多彩

江西省建筑工程总公司

China Jiangxi Construction Engineering Corporation

江西省建筑工程总公司是江西建工集团的核心企业。集施工、安装、设计、房地产开发、装潢、人才培训于一体的大型综合性经济实体。具有国家一级工程总承包资质，拥有资产10.15亿元，各类专业技术人员3500人。在国内、外承建了大批工业与民用建筑。

本公司经外经贸部批准具有对外经营权。业务分布于赞比亚、南非、厄立特里亚、科威特、伊拉克、新加坡等国家，取得了很好的经济效益和社会信誉，积累了丰富的国内，国外工程承包和劳务合作经验。公司以“优质、守约”为宗旨，竭诚为国内和世界各地区服务。

As a core enterprise of Jiangxi Construction Enginering Group, Jiangxi Construction Engineering Corp. is a Large-scaled comprehensive enterprise engaging in construction, installation, design, real-estate development, decoration and personnel training. It has best granted with national first-class qualification and endowment as a man contractor, with the assets of 1.015 billion yuan and 3500 various kinds of technical professionals. It has been constructing a number of civil and industrial buildings at home or aboard.

With the approval by the Ministry of Foreign Trade and Economic Cooperation of P.R.C., it enjoys the foreign management power with its business ranging in Zambia, South Africa, Eritrea, Kuwait, Iraq, Singapore and other countries and has achieved considerable economic benefit and social reputation and accumulated rich experience in project contracting and labor service cooperation at home or aboard. According to the management policy “respecting contract, ensuring quality”, it will provide good service to domestic and foreign customers.

地址：中国江西省南昌市北京西路176号
Add: No.176 Beijing West Rd. Nanchang, China
传真(Fax): (0791)-6214173
电话(Tel): (0791)-6274174/6275433/6254215
E-mail: jxcec@public. nc. jx. cn

厄立特里亚红海贸易大楼，由江西省建筑工程总公司承建。

联合国驻赞比亚办公大楼，由江西省建筑工程总公司承建。

赞比亚钦格拉玉米加工厂，是我国经援工程，由江西省建筑工程总公司承建。

江西省博物馆新馆：建筑面积35,000M²，是跨世纪的雄伟工程，由江西省建筑工程总公司承包。

北京八达岭高速公路发展有限公司

BEIJING BADALING EXPRESSWAY DEVELOPMENT CO.,LTD.

北京八达岭高速公路发展有限公司，是由北京市公路桥梁建设公司和香港卡姆瑞斯发展有限公司共同出资设立的合资企业。公司注册资本为6.6亿元人民币，开发、建设和经营北京八达岭高速公路马甸桥至昌平路段(32.5公里)以及该路段的加油站、餐饮服务、广告载体和沿线土地开发等业务。公司是1998年度北京市十大中外合资企业之一。公司经营的八达岭高速公路路段是北京西北出境方向的惟一通道，也是通往举世闻名的八达岭长城和明十三陵的必经之路。

Beijing Badaling Expressway Development Co., Ltd is joint-venture co-invested by Beijing Road & Bridge orporation and Comrich Development Limited, HK. The gistered capital of the company is RMB 660,000,000 yuan. ne company is in charge of developing, constructing and perating the section from Madian bridge to Changping 2.5km) of the Beijing Badaling expressway and the gas ations, restaurants, advertisement carriers and land evelopment along the way of the section. The company was one of the ten biggest joint-ventures in Beijing in 1998. The section of Badaling expressway operated by the company is the only exit of the north-west of Beijing and is the only way to the Great Wall of Badaling section and the Thirteen Tombs of the Ming dynasty.

事长：刘长乐
经理：王　泽
话：(010)62510506, 62510508, 62510509
真：(010)62510504
址：http: //www.bdlgl.com.cn
址：北京海淀路165号南门凤凰会馆403号
编：100080

Director: Liu Changle
General manager: Wang Ze
TEL: (010)62510506, 62510508, 62510509
Fax: (010)62510504
Web Site:http://www.bdlgl.com.cn
Add: Rom 403, Phoenix Mansion,#165 South Gate, Haidian Road, Beijing, P.R. China
P.C: 100080

大连日清制油有限公司
Dalian Nisshin Oil Mills, Ltd.

大连日清制油有限公司是1988年9月成立，1990年10月正式投产的中日合资植物油生产企业，每年可加工大豆等油料20万吨左右，是我国制油行业规模较大的合资企业。

投资方为5家：大连经济技术开发区经济技术发展公司、日清制油株式会社、三菱商事株式会社、丸红株式会社、野村·中国投资株式会社；总投资额4,004.25万美元；注册资本1,700万美元（中方占投资比例3.5%、日方占投资比例96.5%）；合资年限25年；占地面积82,930平方米；建筑面积28,000平方米。

主要产品：大豆粕、一级大豆油、大豆色拉油、大豆精炼油、调和油、工业用·食用磷脂等。

Dalian Nisshin Oil Mills, Ltd., a sino-Japanese invested enterprise producing vegetable oil, was established in Sep, 1988 and formally went into production in Oct, 1990. It is a large scale jointventure in vegetable oil production field in China with a capacity of processing about 200,000 M/Ts of soybeans and other oil crops.

Here are some of its briefs:

1.Five investors: Dalian E.T.D.Z. Development company, Nisshin Oil Mills, Ltd., Mitsubish Corporation, Marubeni Corporation, Nomura China Investment co., ltd.

2.Total investment amount: US$40,042,500.00

3.Registered capital: US$17,000,000.00 (96.5% of it from Japanese side)

4.Jointly investment period: 25 years

5.Covered area: 82,930 square metres

6.Construction area: 28,000 square metres

7.Main products: soybean meal, Class-A soybean oil, soybean salad oil, refined soybean oil, quality cooking oil, phosphatide for industry or edibles.

广州轻出集团有限公司
GUANGZHOU LIGHT HOLDINGS LIMITED

地址：中国广州市长堤大马路八十七号　Add: No.87 the Bund, Guangzhou, China
电话(Tel): 83337704　83337522　传真(Fax): (020)83337697　邮编(Zip Code): 510120
Internet: http://www.gzli.com　E-mail: gzlicom@public.guangzhou.gd.cn
CIET Net: http://www.ec.com.cn　E-mail: gzliieg@ciet.cn.net

企业集团领导班子　Leaders of GZLI

一九九七年十月，经广州市人民政府批准，以原广州轻工业品进出口(集团)公司为主体、改组为广州轻出集团有限公司。通过国有资产授权，将原广州机械进出口公司、广州五金矿产进出口公司、广州市对外贸易广告展览公司作其全资企业，共同组建的广州轻出集团，是广州市按现代企业制度组建的第一家外经贸企业集团，共有全资、控股、参股和关联企业50多家。

广州轻出集团有限公司以投资效益最大化为原则，以国有资产经营为主体，资产连接为纽带，从价值形态上经营管理广州市国有资产管理委员会授权范围内的国有资产，使国有资产保值增值；以市场为导向，发挥集团群体优势，多元化、全方位开拓经营，目标是发展成为以贸易为龙头、服务为补充、实业为基础、金融为后盾，集工、农、科、金于一体的跨行业、跨地区、跨国的综合商社式的企业集团。

广州轻出集团有限公司经营范围：轻工产品、纺织品、工艺品、五金矿产、土畜产、化工机械、粮油食品、医药保健品及其原辅材料的进出口、代理进口、转口贸易；经营上述进出口商品的国内调拨、加工、收购、批发、零售。承办中外合资经营、合作生产业务；承办来料加工、来样加工、来件装配业务，开展补偿贸易业务、运输、仓储及保税业务、包装装璜业务。旅游服务。

On the approval of Guangzhou municipal government in October, 1997, former Guangzhou Light Industrial Products Imp. & Exp(Group) Corp. has been reformed as the main part of Guangzhou Light Holdings Limited (GZLI).GZLI was authorized to organize the former Guangzhou Machinery Imp.& Exp.Corp., Guangzhou Metals & Minerals Imp. & Exp. Corp. and Guangzhou Foreign Trade Advertising Exhibition Corp. as her wholly-invested enterprises,and form Guangzhou Light Group.It is the first foreign trade enterprise group built up in the way of modern enterprise system.The group has more than 50 members of enterpises.

The business scope of GZLI includes: import & export of light industrial products; textiles,arts and crafts items; metals & minerals; native products, animal by-products; chemical & machinery; cereal, oil and foodstuffs; medicine and health products; materials; agent service of import; entrepot trade, allocating; purchasing; processing; wholesale and reail; Sino-foreign joint venture; co-production; processing with supplied materials and samples; assembling of supplied parts;compensation trade; transportation and storage; bond business; packing design; tourism and etc.

Tiger Head

中国驰名商标：虎头商标(用于电池)
China Well-Known Trademark:
Tiger Head(Used for Battery)
注册人：广州轻工业品进出口(集团)公司
Registered by: Guangzhou Light Industrial Products Imp.& Exp. (Group) Corp.

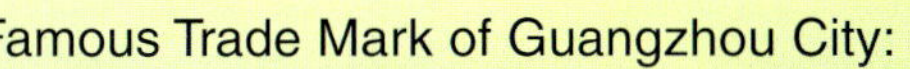
Famous Trade Mark of Guangzhou City:

"Diamond" Lock

"Triangle" Electric Rice Cooker

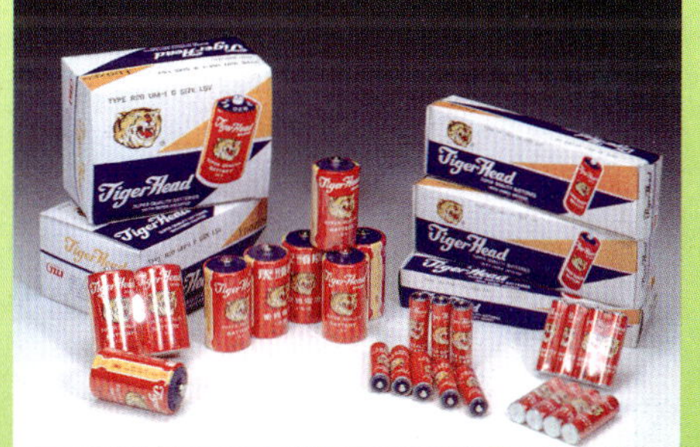

深圳市龙岗区对外经济发展有限公司

Shenzhen Longgang Foreign Economic Development Co.Ltd.

法人代表，总经理：黄抗成

本公司是一九九三年成立的以对外经济贸易为主的独立法人国有独资企业。

公司主要管理和协调龙岗区境内的"三来一补"、"三资"、自营、内联企业项目，是深圳市政府批准的龙岗区境内为外商服务的唯一的商务单位。主要为外商投资办厂提供咨询、协议签约、生产合同签订、结汇、报关等"一条龙"服务。公司设于深圳市笋岗东路1002号宝安广场C座17、18楼。公司拥有工业区，可为外商提供环境优美、交通便利的工业厂房。公司电话:(0755)5170948。

公司下属的深圳市顺意得报关有限公司设于宝安广场A座17楼B、D室，下设沙湾、布吉、盐田港等报关行，为外商办理报关工作；电话:(0755)5170608。

公司拥有进出口权，下属的贸易分公司设于宝安广场A座21楼C、D室，经营进出口业务。电话:(0755)5170133。

总经理：黄抗成

Shenzhen Longgang Foreign Economic Development Co. Ltd.,founded in 1993, is an independent state-owned corporation mainly dealing with foreign econorny and trade.

The Corporation is to manage and to coordinate all projects of processing & assembling enterprises, independent ventures and joint ventures, private sectors and inland linked enterprises within Longgang District.It is the sole commercial affairs organization approved by Shenzhen Municipal Government, serving foreign businessmen in Longgang District. The Corporation provides foreign investors with connected sequence services such as counseling, making contracts, converting foreign exchange, making a customs declaration and so on. The Corporation is located on 17/F & 18/F, Section C, Bao'an Plaza, No.1002 Shungang East Road, Shenzhen. The Corporation owns an industrial estate itself. This area boasts a sound environment and has transport facilities. Factory sites in this place are waiting for foreign investors. Tel:(0755)5170948

Shenzhen Shunyida Customs Declaration Co. Ltd. is one of its subsidiaries in Room B & D 17/F, Section A Bao'an Plaza. It distributes customs declaration agencies in Shawan, Shatoujia Buji, Wenjingdn and Yantian Port. These branches makes customs declarations for foreign investors. Tel:(0755)5170608

The Corporation has been entitled to import & export rights. One of its subsidiaries, in Room C & D 21/F, Section A Bao'an Plaza, operates import & export business for the corporation itself as well as its clients. Tel:(0755)5170133

General Manager:

Huang Kangcheng

贸易分公司1999年1-6月份已完成市府下达的一般贸易出口创汇任务的114%

公司员工为外商提供优质服务

环境优美、交通便利的工业区

报关公司为外商提供快捷的代理报关

河北圣仑进出口集团公司

HEBEI SHENGLUN IMP. & EXP. (GROUP) CORP.

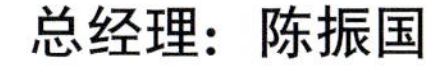

总经理：陈振国

General Manager: Chen Zhenguo

河北圣仑进出口集团公司是由原河北省服装进出口公河北省针棉织品进出口公司组建的集团型企业。

公司主要经营男、女、童各种面料的春、夏、秋、冬服及棉织品、针织品、家用纺织品等产品，远销全世界99个家和地区。“莲花池”、“晚香玉”、“瑞香”、“足球”牌出商品，在海内外享有盛誉。我公司新注册的“圣仑”牌商已在梭织服装、针织服装及家用纺织品等出口产品上使将与商家、客户见面。

我公司欢迎海内外贸易界人士及我公司的新老朋友来来电，来人洽谈业务增进贸易往来。

HEBEI SHENGLUN IMP. & EXP. (GROUP))RP. is incorporated with former Hebei Knitwear Home Textiles I/E Corp. and former Hebei rments I/E Corp.

We mainly deal with the export of garments men, ladies and children, sweaters, knit ars, cotton textiles and home textiles ich sell well in more than 99 countries and gions. Some famous brands such as)TUS POND", "TUBEROSE", "DAPHNE" d "FOOTBALL" enjoy great fame at home d abroad. The newly registered brand HENGLUN" has been used on our nmodities and it will meet customers soonly.

We warmly welcome ures of trade at me and abroad d all the friends our Corporation contact with us and velop the business ween us.

地址：中国 石家庄和平西路499号圣仑大厦 邮编：050061

电话：0311-7043793 传真：0311-7042790，7042775

E-Mail: Knit@public. sj. he. cn Hebg@public. sj. he. cn

青岛国际人才技术合作公司

Qingdao International Personnel & Technical Cooperation Co.

青岛国际人才技术合作公司是由青岛市政府、国家劳动部于1987年批准成立的，是青岛市从事国际劳务输出和劳务合作的专职机构。是经国家外经贸部批准的有对外经济技术合作签约权的外经企业。它的上级主管部门是青岛开源热力总公司。总公司位于青岛市东部开发区，拥有固定资产1.5亿元人民币。为进一步拓展国际市场、发展外向型经济，总公司以开源热力公司为基础，以青岛国际人才技术合作公司为窗口，大力发展国际劳务输出、国际承包工程、经济技术合作和商贸合作业务。

青岛国际人才技术合作公司将以其集团公司的国际化、多元化、现代化、实业化的优势，以其规范化的管理和优质的服务恭候国内、国外各界朋友的到来。

总经理：周昀

公司总经理在日本招商会上致词

公司在新加坡举办业务恳谈会

公司领导到新加坡看望劳务人员

QINGDAO INTERNATIONAL PERSONNEL & TECHNICAL COOPERATION CO. Being established in 1987 with the approval of Qingdao Municipal and The Ministry of Labour,P.R.C. QINGDAO INTERNATIONAL PERSONNEL & TECHNICAL COOPERATION CO. (QIPTCC) is a specialized organization engaged in international personnel export and cooperation, and a foreign oriented enterprise.It possesses the rights authorized by Ministry of Foreign Trade & Economic Co-operation and Qingdao Foreign Economic & Trade Commission to sign contracts concerning foreign economic & technical cooperation as well. The higher authority of QIPTCC is Qingbao Labour Administrative Bureau Kaiyuan Heat & Power Corporation,which is located in Eastern Development Zone with fixed assets of RMB ¥150 million. In order to promote overseas market and develop foreign oriented economy, it is taking Kaiyuan Heat & Power Corp. as foundation and QIPTCC as main strength to carry out international labour exporting,international contracted projects, economic & technical cooperation and trade cooperation as well.

QIPTCC is awaiting all friends from both dometic and overseas respectfully with the group's internationalization, diversification, modernization and industry superiority, and with its standard management and high quality service.

General Manager: Zhou Yun

地　址：中国青岛山东路15号
电　话：(0532)5828955 5811473 5829409
传　真：(0532)5829409
邮　编：266071

Add: No.15,Shandong,Road Qingdao,China
Tel: (0532)5828955 5811473 5829409
Fax: (0532)5829409
Post code: 266071

泰达—未来工业的起点

TEDA-Start Point of Future Industry

天津经济技术开发区于1984年12月6日经中华人民共和国国务院批准成立，为中国首批国家开发区之一。天津经济技术开发区（TEDA）又称泰达。

经过无数泰达人十几年的开发建设，天津开发区投资环境日臻完善，经济实力迅猛发展，已成为中国乃至整个亚洲颇具吸引力的投资区域。截止1999年6月，天津开发区累计批准来自世界67个国家和地区的外商投资企业3164家，吸引投资总额115亿美元，世界工业企业100强中，已有25家在这里投资。天津开发区的税收、工业总产值、吸引外资额等14项主要经济指标在全国开发区中居于首位。15年来，天津开发区坚持走发展现代工业的道路，制定高科技产业政策，嫁接国外先进技术，致力增育中国的新兴产业。目前，天津开发区已形成了电子、机械、生物医药、食品四大产业群、形成了以移动通讯设备、电子计算机、数控机床、人工胰岛素、工业用酶制剂、方便食品等为代表的拳头产品，一批国际知名公司如摩托罗拉、雀巢、可口可乐、诺和诺德、SEW、霍尼韦尔、丰田、三星云集这里。这四大产业群在国内技术领先、科技含量高、市场覆盖面广，在天津开发区经济发展中占有80%的比重，使天津开发区成为天津市的经济引擎。

面对新世纪的到来，天津开发区制定了建设“面向21世纪的现代化工业新城区”的目标，决心把天津开发区建设成为中国投资成本低、服务水平高、投资环境好的现代化工业区。泰达新一轮投资环境、城区环境、人文环境等全方位园区综合建设工程已拉开了帷幕。相信在不久的将来，一个以现代化工业为基础，现代化管理为支撑，现代化生活为标志的新城区一定会呈现在世界的东方，呈现在渤海之滨。

The Tianjin Economic-Technological Development Area (T one of the first batch of state-level development areas, was estab on December 6,1984 with the approval of the State Council People's Republic of China.

With its well-developed investment envionment and swift eco development as a result of more than ten years' construction, now is the most attractive area to investors in China,and ev Asia. By the end of June 1999, there are 3164 foreign-fu enterprises from 67 countries and regions with the total fo investment of US$11.5 billion. Also, 25 enterprises which are list of the world top 100 set up factories in the area. 14 major eco indicators of TEDA, such as tax revenue, total production valu foreign invest value, rank the first among China's develop areas.In the past 15 years, TEDA focused on developing m industries and promoting China's new industrial sectors by formu high-tech industrial policy and importing foreign adva technology.Up till now,four industrial groups have taken shape in in the fields of electronics,machinery, bio-pharmaceutics and represented by mobile telecommu tion equipment,compu numerical cont machine to synthe insu st enzy fast foods other compet products. A lot of world famous companies established their brar in TEDA, such as Motorola, Nestle, Coca Cola, SEW, Hone Toyota, Samsung and etc. Total production value of the four ind groups account for 80% that of TEDA, and make TEDA the eco engine of Tianjin because of its advanced technologies, high tec contents and high market share in the country.

In the course of marching to the 21st century, TEDA will de into a modern industrial area with the lowest investment cos highest service level and the best investment environment in C Now, TEDA is concentrating on new construction engineering co to improve investment and community environment of the area expected that a new urban area with modern industries, m management and modern life will emerge on the bank of Bohai Orient in future.

投资咨询机构:

天津开发区公共关系部　电话：86-22-25328112

传真：86-22-25201440

天津开发区经济发展局　电话：86-22-25201313

传真：86-22-25201412

天津开发区北京办事处

地址：北京市建国门内大街7号光华长安大厦二座532

电话：86-10-65129980　传真：86-10-651012

国际互联网网址：http://www.teda.gov.cn

重庆长安铃木汽车有限公司

CHONGQING CHANGAN SUZUKI AUTOMOBILE CO., LTD.

重庆长安铃木汽车有限公司是专业生产奥拓轿车系列产品的中日合资企业，公司于1993年5月由长安汽车有限责任公司与日本铃木株式会社、日商岩井株式会社合资组建，投资总额19085万美元。到1995年9月公司冲压、焊接、涂装、总装四大生产线相继建成投产，形成了年产奥拓轿车5万辆的生产能力。

1998年，国家计委、国家经贸委批准了奥拓轿车15万辆项目。公司通过对生产线的扩建改造，目前已形成年产奥拓轿车10万辆的生产能力，并通过加大资金及技术投入，进一步开发性能优良、小排量(1L左右)的经济型轿车，形成并完善奥拓轿车系列产品。

公司引进国际通行的“精益生产”方式，实行先进的“准时制”生产和“零库存”管理，推行全员“5S”管理，坚持高起点、专业化、大批量的生产方式，依靠高素质的员工队伍以及严格的产品配套质量保证制度，保证生产出品质优秀、用户喜爱的产品。

址：中国重庆市巴南区鱼洞镇
编：631321
D: Yudong, Banan District, Chongqing, China
话(TEL)：(023)66223204，66222884
真(FAX)：(023)66222722
挂：巴南区(1575)

华东电力对外经济贸易公司

EAST CHINA ELECTRIC POWER FOREIGN ECONOMIC & TRADE CORPORATION

华东电力对外经济贸易公司是经国家批准成立的综合性涉外企业，系中国华东电力集团的全资国有企业，归口经营中国华东电力集团企业的外经贸业务。中国华东电力集团是国家第一批试点的55家大中型企业集团之一，集电力生产、建设、设计、修造、科研、教育、多元化经营于一体。集团1998年拥有固定资产原值达1582亿元，至1998年末集团所在的华东电网装机容量达47579兆瓦，年统调发电量1829.42亿千瓦时，为中国极大型的跨省电网。公司具有较强的电力机械、辅助设备等产品及技术出口能力。1990年以来，计有输电线路铁塔、金具、电气仪表、施工机械、大型载重平板车、保温制品、水泥、水产品等出口到欧洲、美洲、亚洲等国家和地区。随着电力工业的迅速发展，集团将有一批重大发、供电建设项目利用外资，引进先进设备和技术。

经营范围：经营集团成员企业生产、建设、科研所需原辅材料、机械设备、仪器仪表、零配件等商品及相关技术的进口和产品、技术的出口业务；承办集团成员企业的中外合资经营、合作生产及开展"三来一补"业务，承包本行业国外工程和境内外资工程，对外派遣本行业工程技术服务的劳务人员。

对外经济合作意向：1.代理集团内进出口项目；2.国内外各种类型发电厂（水电、火电）及输配电工程建设的总承包（或交钥匙方式）；3.受外商委托进行产品销售代理；4.提供相关的技术服务及劳务输出。

East China Electric Power Foreign Economic & Trade Corporation (EEF) is a government-approved, comprehensive, foreign-oriented enterprise,financed completely by East China Electric Power Group Corporation (ECEPGC). It operates the foreign trade business of member enterprises under the jurisdiction of East China Electric Power Group (ECEPG). ECEPG,the largest transprovincial power network in China,is one of the nation's first lot 55 giant enterprise groups,centralizing the electric power production, construction, design,repair,manufacturing, scientific research,education and pluralistic management into one unit.The fixed assets owned by the Group attained more than 158.2 billon RMB yuan in 1998.By the end of 1998 the total installed capacity in the network was 47579 MW,and the yearly generation under the central dispatch amounted to 182.94 billion kwh.The corporation has strong capability in power machinery,auxiliaries and technology export business.Since 1990 a number of transmission line towers, metallic appliances,electric meters, construction machinery, large heavy flatbeds,insulation products,cement and aquatic products have been exported to Europe, America, Asia, etc.With rapid development of electric power industry, ECEPG will use foreign capital and imported advanced equipment and technologies in a big batch of major power generation and supply projects.

Scope of business:Dealing with raw auxiliary materials,electrical and mechanical equipment, instruments and meters,spare parts required in production, construction and scientific research of the Group's member enterprises, importing relevant technologies and exporting products and technologies. Undertaking joint ventures and cooperative productions, and developing the business of assembling customers components according to their own samples and drawings, as well as compensation trade. Contracting for internal projects invested by foreign capital and projects abroad,dispatching engineering and technical service laborers and teams for the projects and production of electric power trade.

Intention of economic cooperation: Firstly to be an agent of the Group to do business of import & export businesses; Secondly to undertake contracts or turnkey projects in the field of different types of power plants (hydroelectric or thermal-electric) transmission and distribution both in foreign countries and in China;Thirdly to act as an agent of foreign customers to sell their mechanical and electrical products; fourthly to provide relevant technical services and dispatch labors.

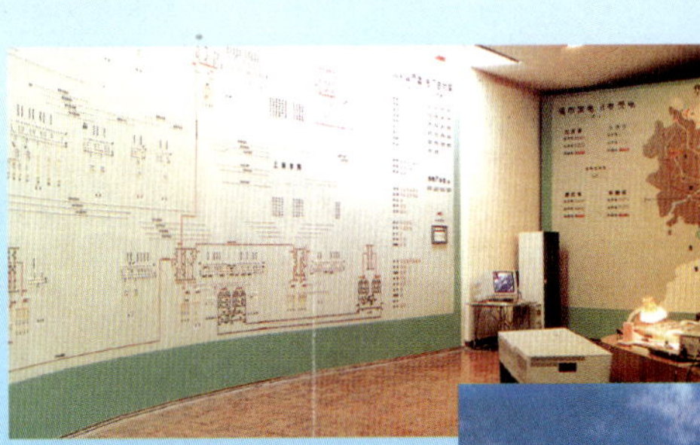

华东电网总调度大厅

法人代表：陈维恒　总经理

地址：上海市徐家汇路101号百汇大厦12楼

邮编：200023　电话:(021) 63010313　传真:(021)63010378

Legal Representative: Chen Weiheng General Manager

Add: 12th Floor,Baihui Building,101 Xujiahui Road, Shanghai

post code: (021)200023　Tel:(021) 63010313　Fax: 63010378

望亭发电

上海贝尔有限公司

SHANGHAI BELL COMPANY LIMITED

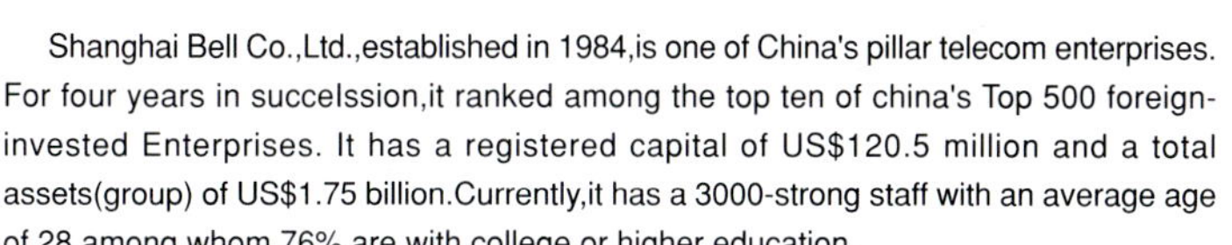

成立于1984年的上海贝尔有限公司(SHANGHAI BELL COMPANY LIMITED),经过多年的努力,成为了我国通信产业的龙头。近几年来,其产量、销售收入等生产经营业绩始终在同行业中保持前茅。

上海贝尔注册资本为1.2亿美元,是我国较早的合资企业之一。15年来,上海贝尔累计实现产值512亿元,销售收入282亿元,上缴税金61亿元,出口创汇1.3亿美元。1998年,上海贝尔销售收入又创新高,达95亿元。1989年至1994年,连续六年跻身中国十佳合资企业行列。

成立15年来,上海贝尔为改善我国人民的通信条件,发挥了巨大的作用。其主营产品之一的S12程控交换机,自1985年为我国开通第一个程控交换局至今,已装备了我国4500个交换局,市场占有率超过三分之一,是我国通信网的重要支撑。

顺应全球信息化的大趋势,上海贝尔又积极拓宽产品领域,开发、生产出移动通信(移动基站、CDMA系统)、数据通信(帖中继、宽带)、接入网、多媒体终端等通信信息产品,它们为我国信息化建设中发挥了重要作用,在国家骨干网及包括北京、上海在内的各省、市、区的网络上,向大众提供了多种多样的宽带多媒体信息业务。为我国人民创造出信息时代全新的工作、生活、学习、通信方式,是上海贝尔现在的发展目标。

15年来,上海贝尔构筑了遍布全国的营销服务网络,并在东南亚、欧洲设立了多个分支机构,负责销售及服务工作;采纳国际先进的MRP Ⅱ管理系统,现已起用更先进的ERP管理系统;在"引进、消化、吸收"的基础上,每年投入大量资金,不断加大自主创新力度,拥有了国家技术中心、博士后科研工作站和海外科研中心。

15年来,上海贝尔建立了具有世界先进水平的信息产业生产基地。其S12数字程控交换系统,1995年通过了国际国内三家权威单位联合组织的ISO 9001质量体系认证。在此基础上,又开发了S12系统的综合业务数字网(ISDN)、智能网(IN)和虚拟交换(CENTREX)等新业务,以多方面满足国内、国际通信和信息市场日益增长的需求。

15年来,上海贝尔在通信行业充分发挥了带头和幅射作用,创造了良好的社会效益。上海贝尔始终注重国产化工作,S12程控交换机的综合国产化率已达76%。通过国产化工作,大幅度降低了产品成本,为平抑国内市场交换机价格发挥了关键作用。通过国产化工作带动了上海及国内其它地区近百家企业共同发展。很多企业因上海贝尔的订单扭亏为盈,更多企业因此实现了技术、产品、管理等方面的进步。目前,上海贝尔每年在上海地区的采购额已超过6.5亿元人民币。国内配套企业超过80家,为社会提供了2万个就业机会。此外,上海贝尔一直坚持进行无偿的技术推广和培训工作,除了建立现代化的培训中心为用户提供集中培训外,还独创了"集装箱移动培训站",巡回全国各地,免费上门培训。

上海贝尔之所以能在短短的15年内成为中国通信产业的支柱企业,其根本原因就是在改革开放的政策指引下,以市场为导向,以用户为中心,成功地走出了一条引进、消化、吸收、创新相结合的发展道路。在不久前举办的"改革开放20年以来利用外资成果展"上,国家领导人视察了上海贝尔的展台,并通过上海贝尔生产的ISDN可视电话和在上海的公司常务副总裁冯大慈亲切通话,称赞"上海贝尔搞得很好"。

展望未来,上海贝尔任重道远。到2000年,上海贝尔的销售收入将超百亿元,其中20%来自出口。上海贝尔终将发展成为国际一流、极具竞争实力的信息产业型高科技企业集团。

Shanghai Bell Co.,Ltd.,established in 1984,is one of China's pillar telecom enterprises. For four years in succelssion,it ranked among the top ten of china's Top 500 foreign-invested Enterprises. It has a registered capital of US$120.5 million and a total assets(group) of US$1.75 billion.Currently,it has a 3000-strong staff with an average age of 28,among whom 76% are with college or higher education.

Shanghai Bell provides sophisticated products in five categories,ranging from S12 switching systems,GSM,DataCom ,AN to multimedia terminals,among which S12 accounts for 1/3 of China's switching market.It owns a HW and SW manufacturing plant which is among the first-rate in the world and the largest in China.Shanghai Bell has also built up a strong R&D and a nation-wide sales team,each with a staff of about 1,000.The R&D capability of Shanghai Bell is greatly re-enforced with the establishment of a state-level design center,a postdoctoral work station and a European R&D center,etc.. Shanghai Bell has set up 30 branch companies or offices across China and in other countries such as DPRK,Vietnam and the Philippines,etc.. The sales revenue in 1998 for the whole group reached US$1.22 billion and annual output US$2.4 billion.Up to date,Shanghai Bell has turned in an accumulative tax of US$735 million and earned an accumulative US$120 million of foreign currency.

地址:上海市浦东金桥出口加工区宁桥路388号

No.388, Ningqiao Rd, Pudong Jingqiao, Shanghai, P.R. China

电话:(021)58541240　传真:(021)58540791

法人:李大来 Li Dalai

延边海外经济技术合作公司

Yanbian Overseas Economic & Technology Cooperation Company

向世界各国派遣各类工程、生产及服务行业的普通劳务和技术劳务，拥有广泛的劳动力资源。开办专业技术培训学校，根据雇主的要求培养输送各类优秀的专业技术工人。在有关国家设立办事处，协调管理劳务人员，得到了雇主的认可。承办各类商品和技术及设备的进出口业务，承办中外合资经营、合作生产业务，创办了一批境内外合资、合作企业。

With have a rich labor resorce, we can supply ordinary and technical labor service to all kinds of projects,production a service business of all the countries in the world.We have set up professional technical training schools, training and sendi nearly all kinds of excellent professional workers according to the requirements of employers.We have offices in many countrie to coordinate and manage our Laborers,which is accepted by our employers. We are also engaged in the importing and exporti business of various kinds of commodities, technology and equipment,Sino-foreign joint ventures ,cooperative production business,a we have set up many joint ventures and cooperation business in and outside China.

出国劳务人员登船
Boarding of laborers to go abroad

国内部
Domestic Department

微机室
Computer Room

地址：吉林省延吉市局子街85号 电话：0433 - 2524911 0433 - 2511875 传真：0433 - 2511
Add：85 Juzi Street, Yanji City, Jilin ,China Tel：0433 - 2524911 0433 - 2511875 Fax：0433 - 2511

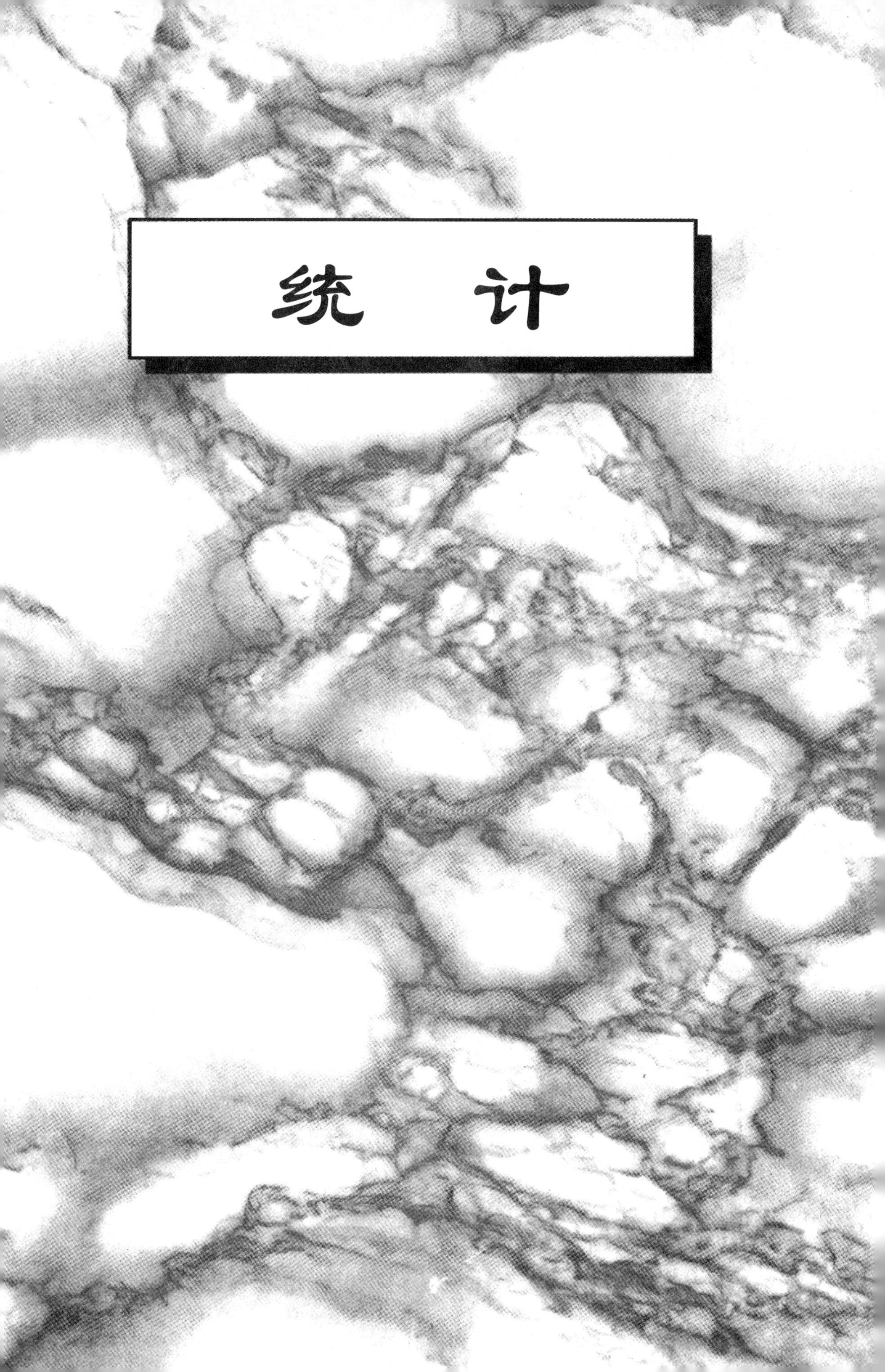

统　计

1993—1998年中国对外贸易进出口情况

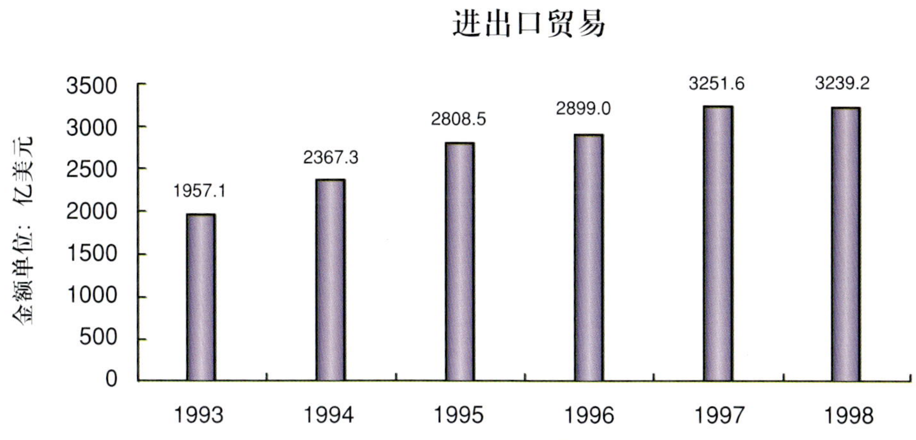

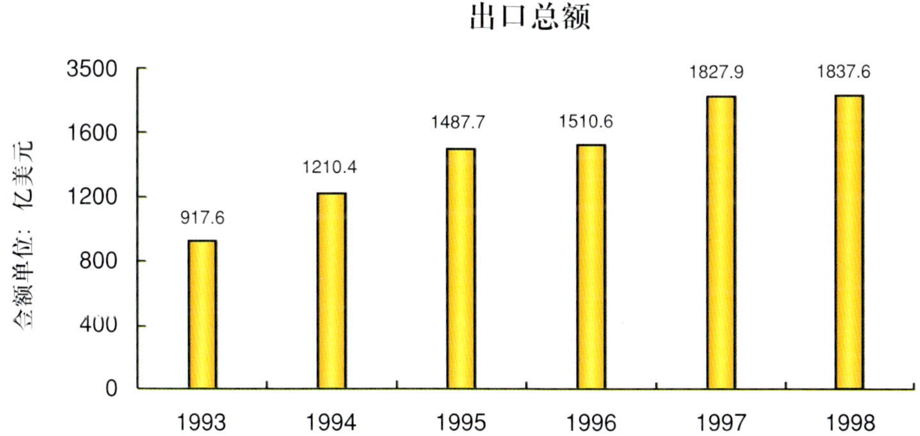

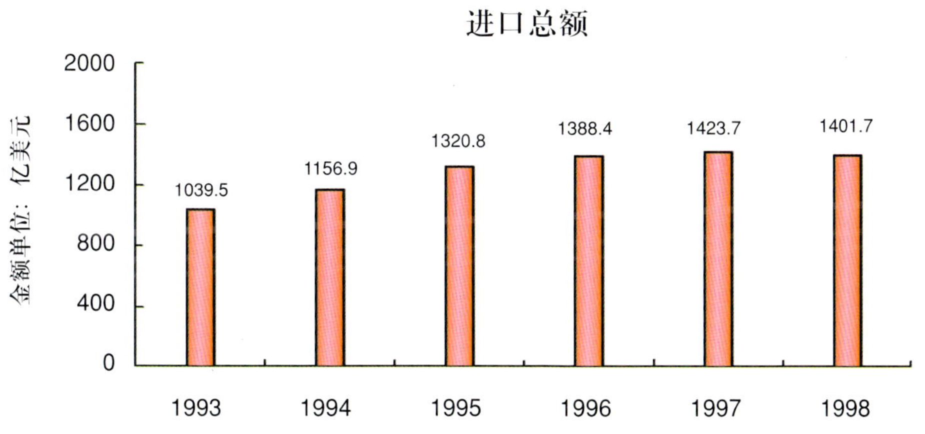

1998 年中国对外贸易构成情况(一)

按《国际贸易标准分类》划分

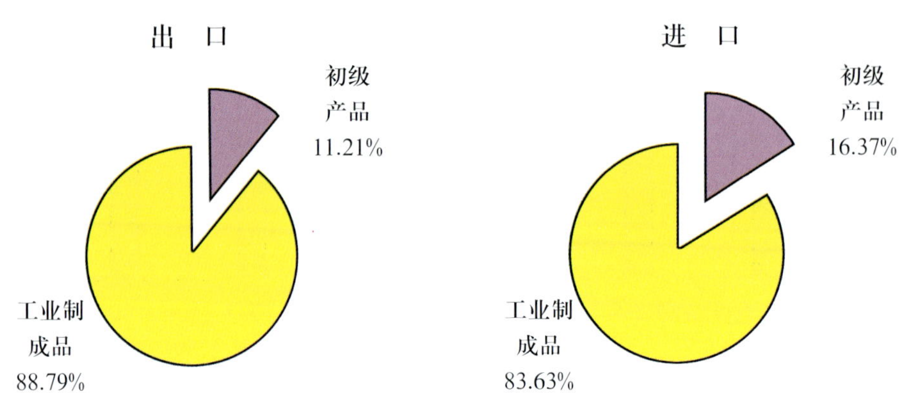

按贸易方式划分

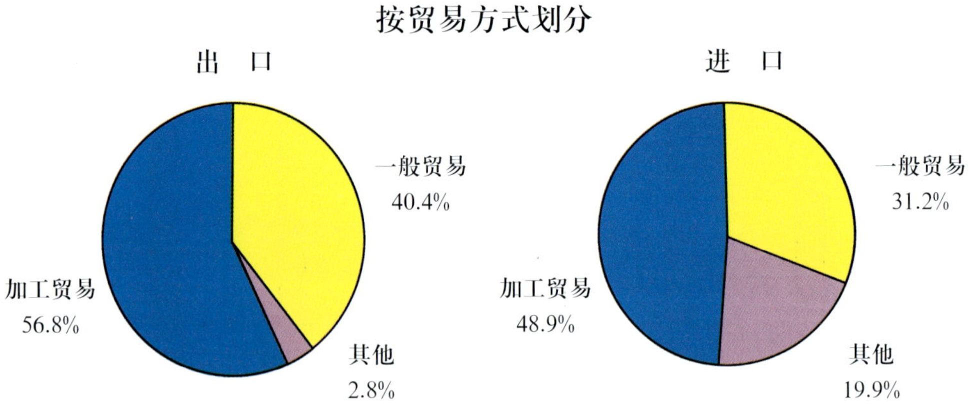

按企业性质划分

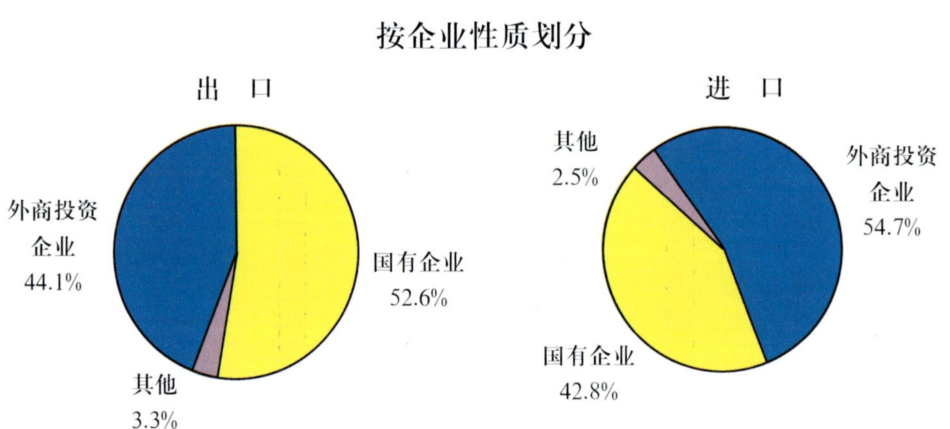

1998 年中国对外贸易构成情况(二)

按主要贸易伙伴划分

出 口

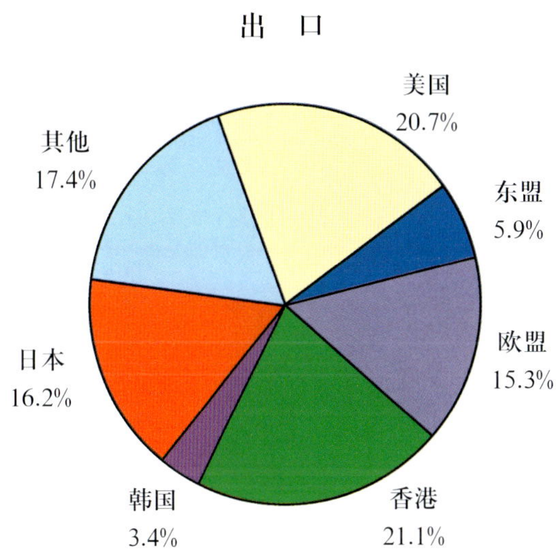

进 口

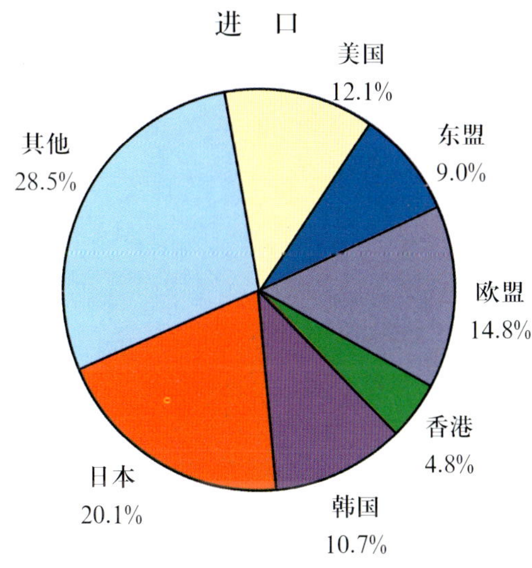

1998 年中国对外贸易构成情况（三）

按主要省市划分

出　口

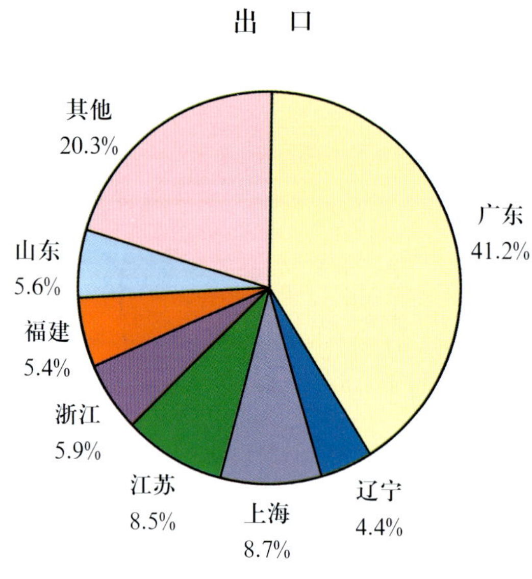

进　口

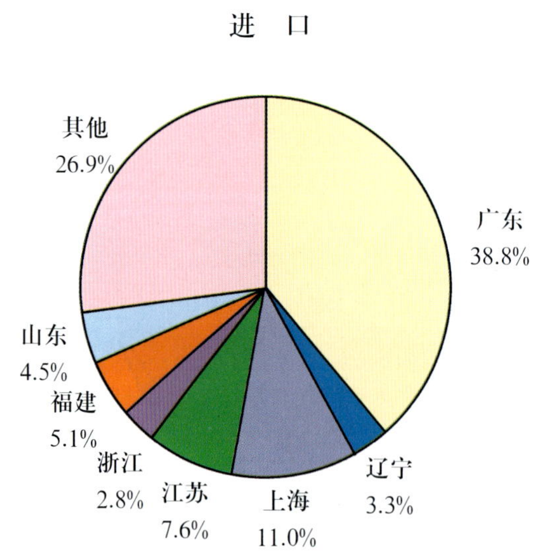

1993年—1998年中国实际利用外资情况

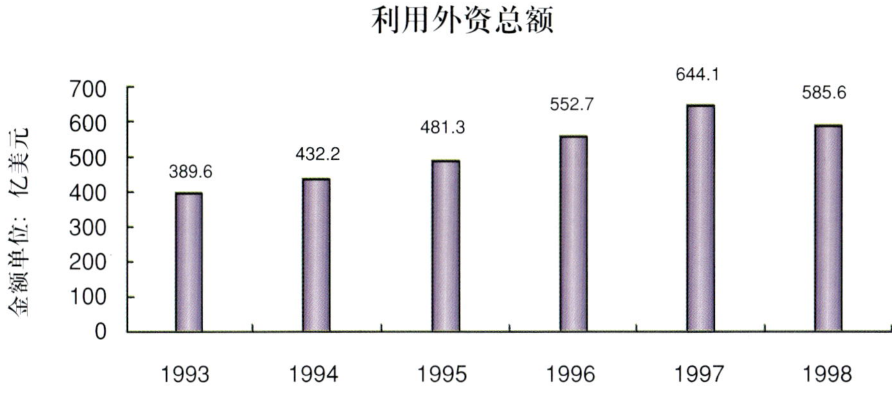

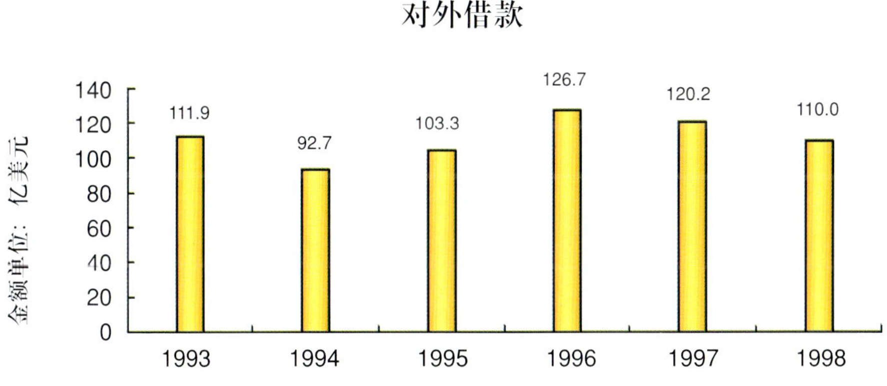

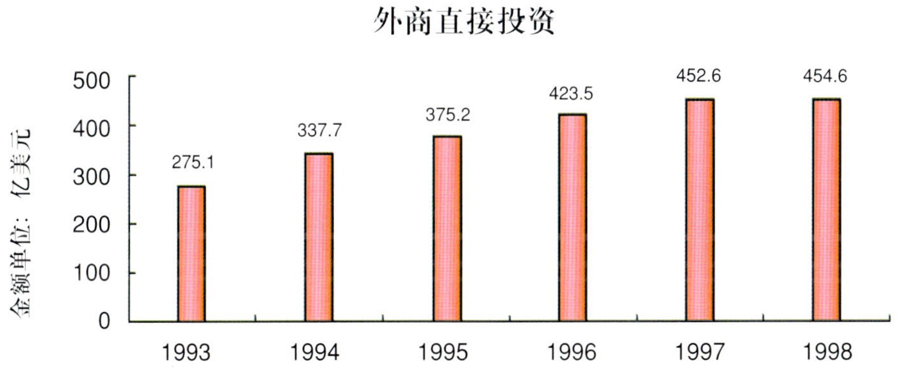

1998年实际利用外资构成

按利用外资方式划分

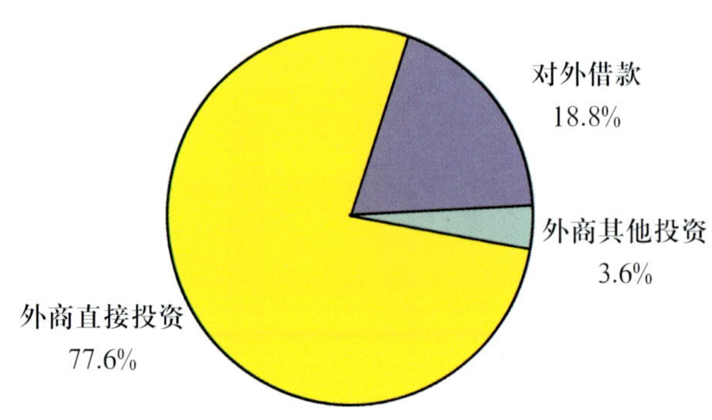

按主要投资方划分（外商直接投资）

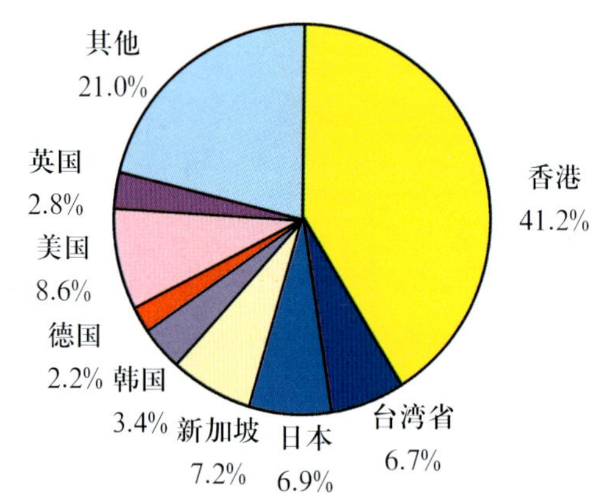

按主要利用外资省市划分（外商直接投资）

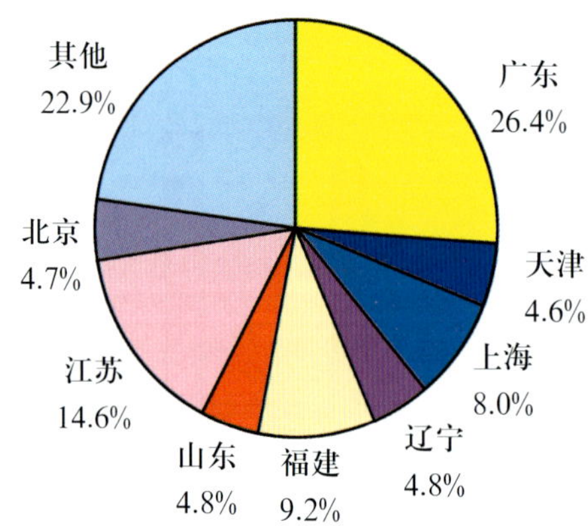

1993年—1998年中国批准签订利用外资协议（合同）情况

项目个数

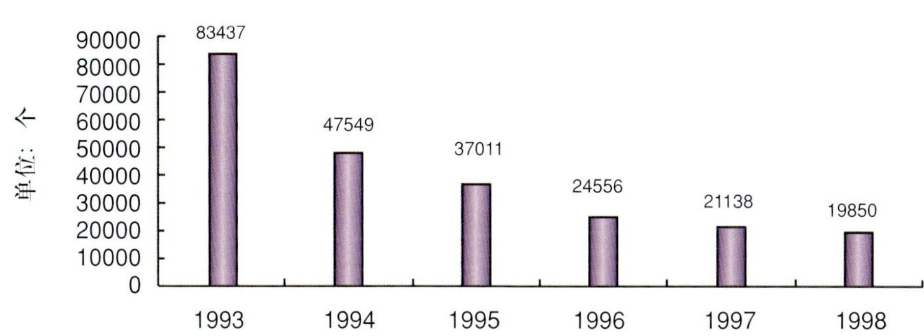

协议（合同）金额

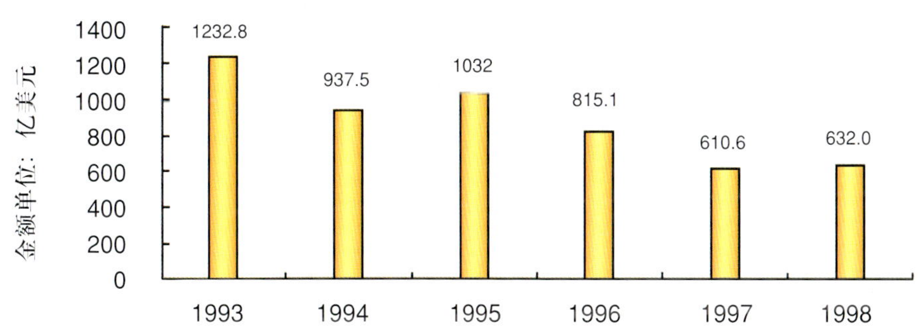

1993 年— 1998 年中国签订对外经济合作合同情况

承包工程合同额

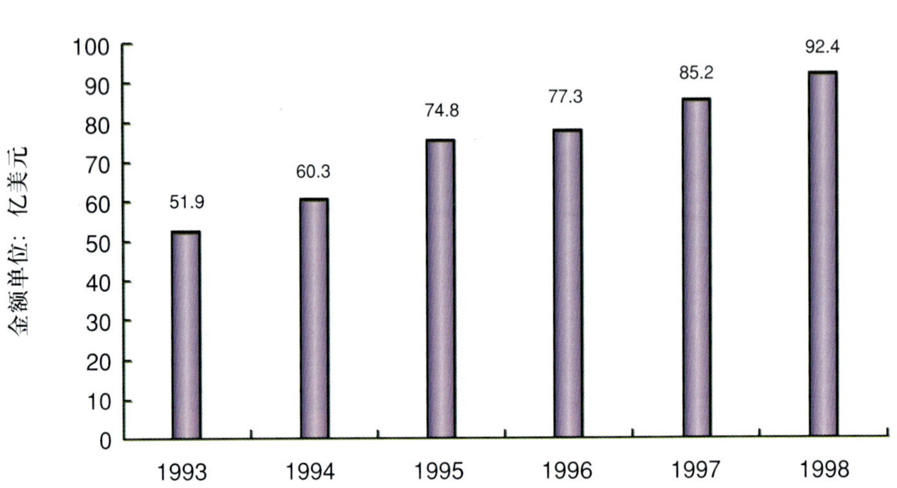

劳务合作合同额

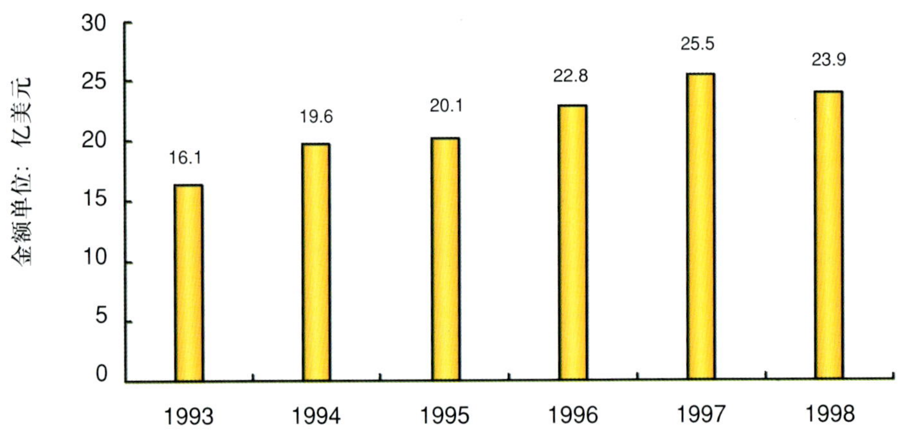

1993 年— 1998 年中国对外经济合作实际完成情况

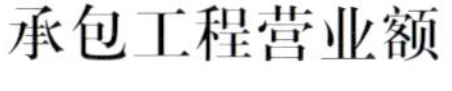

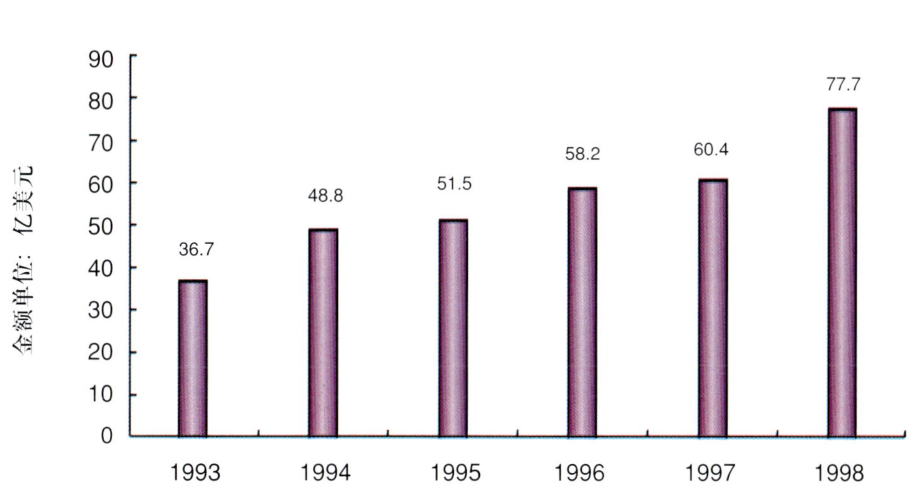

劳务合作营业额

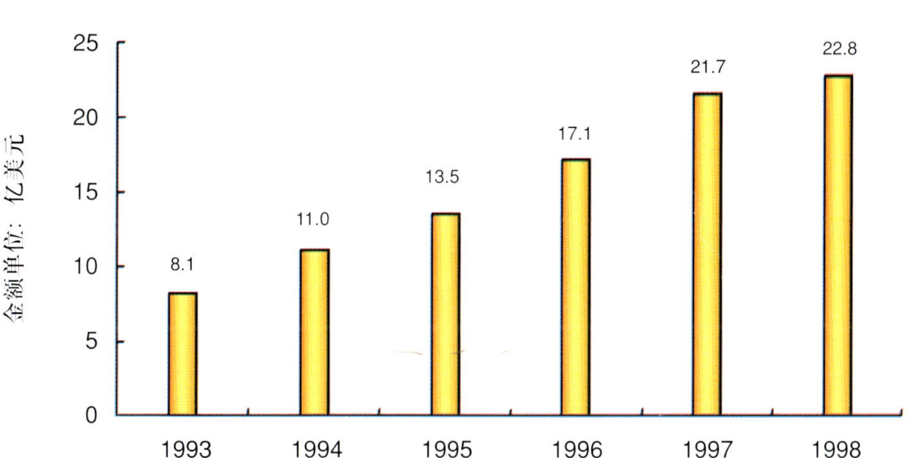

1998年中国签订对外经济合作合同构成情况

按合作方式划分

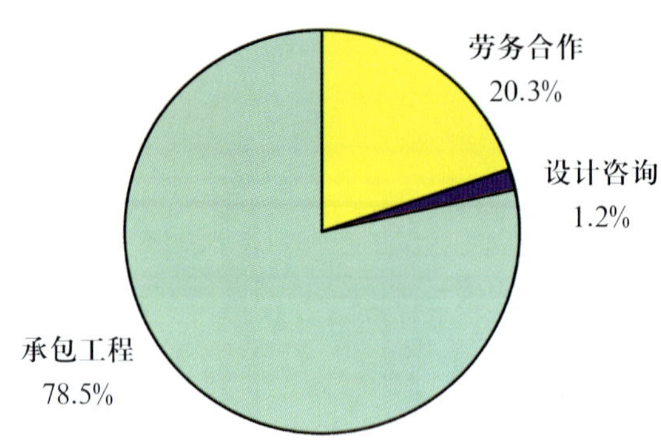

按主要国家（地区）划分

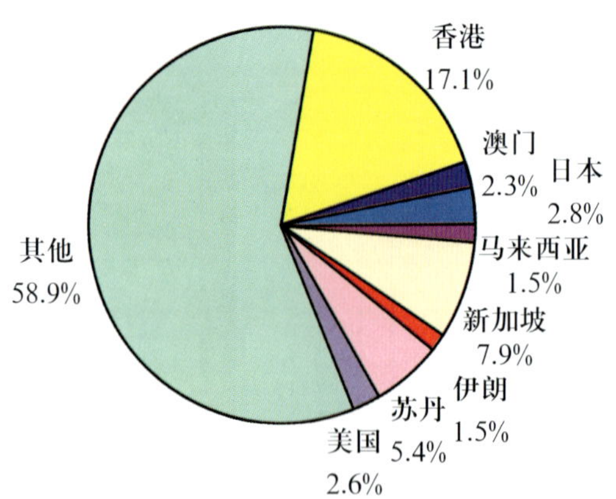

1998 年中国实际完成对外经济合作构成情况

按合作方式划分

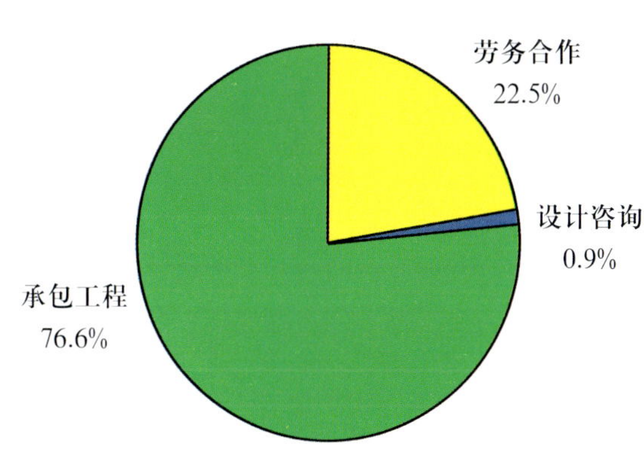

按主要国家（地区）划分

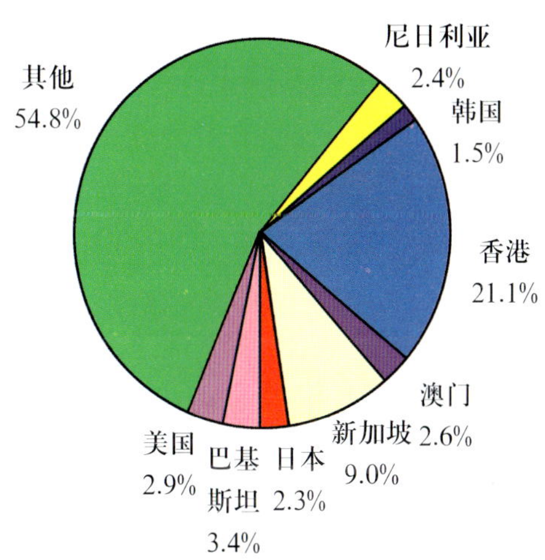

1980年—1998年中国进出口总额

金额单位:亿美元

年 份	进出口总额	出口额	进口额
1980	381.4	181.2	200.2
1981	440.2	220.1	220.1
1982	416.2	223.2	192.8
1983	436.1	222.2	213.9
1984	535.5	261.4	274.1
1985	696.0	273.5	422.5
1986	738.4	309.4	429.0
1987	826.5	394.4	432.1
1988	1028.0	475.2	552.8
1989	1116.8	525.4	591.4
1990	1154.4	620.9	533.5
1991	1356.3	718.4	637.9
1992	1655.3	849.4	805.9
1993	1957.1	917.6	1039.5
1994	2367.3	1210.4	1156.9
1995	2808.5	1487.7	1320.8
1996	2899.0	1510.7	1388.3
1997	3251.6	1827.9	1423.7
1998	3239.3	1837.6	1401.7

1980年—1998年中国进出口总额指数

(1980=100)

年 份	进出口总额	出口额	进口额
1980	100.0	100.0	100.0
1981	115.4	121.5	109.9
1982	109.1	123.2	96.3
1983	114.3	122.6	106.8
1984	140.4	144.3	136.9
1985	182.5	150.9	211.0
1986	193.6	170.8	214.3
1987	216.7	217.7	215.8
1988	269.5	262.2	276.1
1989	292.8	289.9	295.4
1990	302.7	342.7	266.5
1991	355.6	396.5	318.6
1992	434.0	468.8	402.5

1980年—1998年中国进出口总额指数

(1980=100)

年　份	进出口总额	出口额	进口额
1993	513.1	506.4	519.2
1994	620.7	668.0	577.9
1995	736.4	821.0	659.7
1996	760.1	833.7	693.5
1997	852.3	1008.3	711.1
1998	856.5	1005.8	717.0

1980年—1998年中国进出口总额增长速度

(比上年增长%)

年　份	进出口总额	出口额	进口额
1980			
1981	15.4	21.5	9.9
1982	-5.4	1.4	-12.4
1983	4.8	-0.4	10.9
1984	22.8	17.6	28.1
1985	30.0	4.6	54.2
1986	6.1	13.1	1.5
1987	11.9	27.5	0.7
1988	24.4	20.5	27.9
1989	8.7	10.6	7.0
1990	3.4	18.2	-9.8
1991	17.5	15.7	19.6
1992	22.0	18.2	26.3
1993	18.2	8.0	28.9
1994	21.0	31.9	11.3
1995	18.6	22.9	14.2
1996	3.2	1.5	5.1
1997	12.1	20.9	2.5
1998	-0.4	0.5	-1.5

1980年—1998年中国出口总额占世界出口总额的比重和位次

金额单位:亿美元

年　份	世界出口总额	中国出口总额	中国出口总额占世界出口总额比重%	位次
1980	19,906	181.2	0.9	26
1981	19,724	220.1	1.1	19
1982	18,308	223.2	1.2	17
1983	18,078	222.2	1.2	17
1984	19,019	261.4	1.4	18
1985	19,277	273.5	1.4	17
1986	21,157	309.4	1.5	16
1987	24,969	394.4	1.6	16
1988	28,382	475.2	1.7	16
1989	30,361	525.4	1.7	14
1990	34,700	620.9	1.8	15
1991	35,300	718.4	2.0	13
1992	37,000	849.4	2.3	11
1993	36,870	917.6	2.5	11
1994	41,683	1,210.4	2.9	11
1995	50,200	1,487.7	3.0	11
1996	52,540	1,510.7	2.9	11
1997	54,550	1,827.9	3.3	10
1998	54,050	1,837.6	3.4	9

1990 年—1998 年中国出口商品构成

(按《国际贸易标准分类》)

金额单位：亿美元

年份	出口总额	初级产品		1、食品及主要供食用的活动物		2、饮料及烟草		3、非食用原料（燃料除外）		4、矿物资料、润滑油及有关原料		5、动、植物油脂及腊	
		金额	比重%	金额	比重%	金额	比重%	金额	比重%	金额	比重%	金额	比重%
1990	620.9	158.9	25.6	66.1	10.6	3.4	0.5	35.4	5.7	52.4	8.4	1.6	0.4
1991	718.4	161.5	22.5	72.3	10.1	5.3	0.7	34.9	4.9	47.5	6.6	1.5	0.2
1992	849.4	170.0	20.0	83.1	9.8	7.2	0.8	31.4	3.7	46.9	5.5	1.4	0.2
1993	917.6	166.7	18.2	84.1	9.2	9.0	1.0	30.5	3.3	41.1	4.5	2.0	0.2
1994	1,210.4	197.1	16.3	100.2	8.3	10.0	0.8	41.3	3.4	40.6	3.4	5.0	0.4
1995	1,487.7	214.9	14.4	99.5	6.7	13.7	0.9	43.8	2.9	53.4	3.6	4.5	0.3
1996	1,510.7	219.3	14.5	102.3	6.8	13.4	0.9	40.5	2.7	59.3	3.9	3.8	0.3
1997	1,827.9	239.3	13.1	110.5	6.0	10.5	0.6	41.9	2.3	69.9	3.8	6.5	0.4
1998	1,837.6	206.0	11.2	106.2	6.0	9.8	0.5	35.2	1.9	51.8	3.0	3.1	0.2

1990年—1998年中国进口商品构成

（按《国际贸易标准分类》）

金额单位：亿美元

年份	工业制成品		1、化学品及有关产品		2、按原料分类的制成品		3、机械及运输设备		4、杂项制品		5、没有分类的其他产品	
	金额	比重%	金额	比重%	金额	比重%	金额	比重%	金额	比重%	金额	比重%
1990	434.9	81.6	66.5	12.5	89.1	16.7	168.4	31.6	21.0	3.9	89.9	6.9
1991	529.6	83.0	92.8	14.5	104.9	16.4	196.0	30.7	24.4	3.8	111.5	21.1
1992	673.3	83.6	111.6	13.8	192.7	23.9	313.1	38.8	55.9	6.9	--	--
1993	897.3	86.3	97.1	9.3	285.4	27.5	449.9	43.3	64.9	6.2	--	--
1994	992.2	85.8	121.3	10.5	280.8	24.3	515.6	44.6	67.7	5.9	6.8	0.6
1995	1,076.7	81.5	173.0	13.1	287.7	21.8	526.4	39.8	82.7	6.3	6.9	0.5
1996	1,134.0	81.7	181.1	13.0	313.9	22.6	547.7	39.5	84.8	6.1	6.5	0.5
1997	1,137.4	79.9	193.0	13.6	322.2	22.6	527.6	37.1	85.5	6.0	9.1	0.6
1998	1,172.1	83.6	201.7	19.4	310.7	22.2	567.7	40.5	84.6	6.0	7.5	0.5

1990年—1998年中国出口商品构成

（按《国际贸易标准分类》）

金额单位：亿美元

年份	工业制成品		1、化学品及有关产品		2、按原料分类的制成品		3、机械及运输设备		4、杂项制品		5、没有分类的其他产品	
	金额	比重%	金额	比重%	金额	比重%	金额	比重%	金额	比重%	金额	比重%
1990	461.8	74.4	37.3	6.0	125.8	20.3	55.9	9.0	126.9	20.4	116.3	18.7
1991	556.9	77.0	38.2	5.3	144.6	20.1	71.5	10.0	166.2	23.1	136.5	19.0
1992	679.4	80.0	43.5	5.1	161.4	19.0	132.2	15.6	342.3	40.3	--	--
1993	750.9	81.8	46.2	5.0	164.0	17.8	152.9	16.7	387.8	42.3	--	--
1994	1,013.3	83.7	62.3	5.1	232.2	19.2	219.3	18.1	499.4	41.3	0.1	0
1995	1,272.8	85.6	90.9	6.1	322.4	21.7	313.9	21.1	545.5	36.7	0.1	0
1996	1,291.4	85.5	88.8	5.9	285.1	18.9	353.1	23.4	564.3	37.3	0.1	0
1997	1,587.7	86.9	102.3	5.6	344.1	18.9	437.0	23.9	704.3	38.5	0.1	0
1998	1,631.6	88.8	103.2	5.6	323.8	17.6	502.3	27.3	702.2	38.2	0.1	0

1990 年—1998 年中国进口商品构成

（按《国际贸易标准分类》）

金额单位：亿美元

年份	出口总额	初级产品		1、食品及主要供食用的活动物		2、饮料及烟草		3、非食用原料（燃料除外）		4、矿物燃料、润滑油及有关原料		5、动、植物油脂及腊	
		金额	比重%	金额	比重%	金额	比重%	金额	比重%	金额	比重%	金额	比重%
1990	533.5	98.6	18.3	33.4	6.2	1.6	0.3	41.1	7.7	12.7	2.3	9.8	1.8
1991	637.9	108.3	17.0	28.0	4.4	2.0	0.3	50.0	7.8	21.1	3.3	7.2	1.1
1992	805.9	132.6	16.4	31.5	3.9	2.4	0.3	57.7	7.2	35.7	4.4	5.3	0.6
1993	1,039.5	142.2	13.7	22.1	2.1	2.5	0.3	54.4	5.2	58.2	5.6	5.0	0.5
1994	1,156.9	164.7	14.2	31.2	2.7	0.7	0.1	74.4	6.4	40.3	3.5	18.1	1.6
1995	1,320.8	244.1	18.5	61.3	4.6	3.9	0.3	101.6	7.7	51.3	3.9	26.0	2.0
1996	1,388.4	254.4	18.3	56.7	4.1	5.0	0.4	107.0	7.7	68.8	4.9	17.0	1.2
1997	1,423.7	286.2	20.1	43.0	3.0	3.2	0.2	120.1	8.4	103.1	7.2	16.8	1.2
1998	1,401.7	229.5	16.4	37.9	2.7	1.8	--	107.2	7.7	67.7	4.8	14.9	1.1

1998年中国进出口分国家、地区总值表

金额单位:万美元

国家、地区	1998			1997		
	进出口	出口	进口	进出口	出口	进口
总值	**32,392,341**	**18,375,711**	**14,016,630**	**32,505,745**	**18,269,664**	**14,236,081**
亚洲	**18,523,504**	**9,818,039**	**8,705,464**	**19,731,733**	**10,892,078**	**8,839,655**
香港	4,541,163	3,875,321	665,842	5,077,103	4,378,076	699,027
澳门	87,044	74,748	12,296	76,474	64,189	12,285
台湾省	2,049,917	386,956	1,662,961	1,983,821	339,648	1,644,173
东南亚国家联盟	2,348,213	1,092,110	1,256,103	2,436,295	1,203,085	1,233,210
文莱	915	914	1	3,331	3,331	
印度尼西亚	362,792	117,122	245,670	451,419	184,061	267,358
马来西亚	426,432	159,635	266,797	441,531	191,993	249,538
菲律宾	201,311	150,116	51,195	166,618	133,911	32,707
新加坡	815,433	393,004	422,429	878,356	431,905	446,451
泰国	356,087	114,807	241,280	351,476	150,030	201,446
越南	124,579	102,844	21,736	143,564	107,854	35,710
缅甸	58,090	51,886	6,204	64,350	57,009	7,341
老挝	2,573	1,783	790	2,875	2,293	582
阿富汗	2,455	2,434	21	3,308	3,248	61
巴林	5,704	2,971	2,733	4,043	2,532	1,511
孟加拉国	68,715	66,068	2,647	75,025	69,590	5,435
不丹	28	28		17	17	
柬埔寨	16,187	11,369	4,818	12,069	7,568	4,501
塞浦路斯	8,122	8,059	62	4,363	4,243	120
朝鲜	41,302	35,571	5,731	65,629	53,468	12,161
印度	192,230	101,660	90,570	183,032	93,306	89,726
伊朗	121,502	65,669	55,832	103,222	49,642	53,580
伊拉克	16,453	10,467	5,986	9,320	5,898	3,422
以色列	52,382	35,279	17,103	35,626	25,654	9,972
日本	5,789,918	2,969,199	2,820,720	6,081,280	3,181,982	2,899,298
约旦	15,981	13,568	2,413	13,491	11,159	2,332
科威特	23,015	11,030	11,985	17,040	9,344	7,696
黎巴嫩	14,853	14,828	25	13,001	12,991	9
马尔代夫	59	54	5	33	33	
蒙古	24,329	6,254	18,075	25,190	6,365	18,825
尼泊尔	7,210	6,688	522	6,774	5,808	966
阿曼	74,589	3,942	70,646	136,246	1,696	134,549
巴基斯坦	91,276	52,376	38,900	106,787	68,871	37,916
巴勒斯坦	866	865	1	320	312	8
卡塔尔	6,133	1,621	4,513	13,309	1,494	11,815

1998年中国进出口分国家、地区总值表

金额单位:万美元

国家、地区	1998			1997		
	进出口	出口	进口	进出口	出口	进口
沙特阿拉伯	169,973	89,614	80,358	167,997	85,409	82,588
韩国	2,126,433	626,898	1,499,536	2,404,547	911,627	1,492,920
斯里兰卡	29,858	29,279	579	25,489	24,552	936
叙利亚	17,588	17,441	148	15,452	15,130	322
土耳其	70,190	65,911	4,278	62,123	55,671	6,453
阿拉伯酋长国	145,244	129,080	16,164	138,495	130,048	8,447
也门共和国	63,036	10,670	52,365	75,111	10,022	65,089
中国	301,526		301,526	292,377		292,377
亚洲其他国家	12	12		99	99	
非洲	**553,587**	**405,933**	**147,654**	**567,066**	**320,687**	**246,379**
阿尔及利亚	11,680	11,668	12	11,298	11,297	2
安哥拉	19,036	3,666	15,370	63,252	2,902	60,350
贝宁	15,713	15,364	349	11,840	10,962	878
博茨瓦那	1,124	1,124		301	254	47
布隆迪	209	209		39	39	
喀麦隆	6,757	1,892	4,865	11,093	1,255	9,838
加那利群岛	1,762	1,762		1,734	1,712	22
佛得角	197	196		41	41	
中非	107	106	1	191	84	108
塞卜泰	134	134		97	97	
乍得	15	15		263	103	160
科摩罗	12	12		22	22	
刚果	8,807	4,674	4,133	16,408	1,209	15,199
吉布提	3,092	3,092		1,345	1,344	
埃及	60,653	57,484	3,169	52,090	46,420	5,670
赤道几内亚	7,185	294	6,891	8,082	334	7,749
埃塞俄比亚	6,875	6,827	48	5,561	5,498	63
加蓬	15,733	1,016	14,717	31,906	592	31,313
冈比亚	5,064	5,064		4,182	4,182	
加纳	12,007	11,155	852	8,870	8,617	253
几内亚	3,813	3,718	95	7,074	3,476	3,598
几内亚比绍	145	145		176	72	104
科特迪瓦	17,613	15,207	2,406	12,410	9,240	3,171
肯尼亚	11,971	11,821	149	13,354	13,235	118
利比里亚	2,778	2,778		7,363	7,350	13
利比亚	9,314	7,160	2,154	9,664	7,971	1,693
马达加斯加	3,447	3,273	175	2,992	2,673	319

1998年中国进出口分国家、地区总值表

金额单位:万美元

国家、地区	1998			1997		
	进出口	出口	进口	进出口	出口	进口
马拉维	251	251		291	225	66
马里	2,925	2,439	486	4,137	1,389	2,748
毛里塔尼亚	1,076	955	121	1,178	1,137	41
毛里求斯	6,651	6,588	63	4,814	4,800	14
摩洛哥	25,160	16,554	8,606	16,220	11,884	4,336
莫桑比克	1,377	1,334	43	1,668	1,595	73
纳米比亚	1,699	923	777	1,159	720	439
尼日尔	741	741		216	185	31
尼日利亚	38,468	35,726	2,742	32,705	31,642	1,063
留尼汪	448	448		453	453	
卢旺达	402	212	191	299	233	66
圣多和普林	6	6		11	11	
塞内加尔	4,376	4,336	40	3,413	3,370	43
塞舌尔	132	132		105	105	
塞拉利昂	441	441		409	409	
索马里	22	18	5	77	48	29
南非	155,827	86,722	69,105	157,389	78,427	78,962
西撒哈拉	4	4		4	4	
苏丹	35,104	34,958	147	13,379	11,078	2,301
坦桑尼亚	7,967	6,998	969	10,210	8,448	1,762
多哥	6,223	5,909	314	7,705	6,925	780
突尼斯	12,971	8,393	4,579	9,730	7,465	2,264
乌干达	1,092	1,078	13	1,165	991	174
布基纳法索	939	514	426	175	157	18
扎伊尔	6,325	6,100	224	3,140	2,949	191
赞比亚	2,835	2,213	622	3,719	1,068	2,651
津巴布韦	13,273	10,487	2,787	10,275	2,816	7,459
莱索托	902	899	3	494	494	
梅利利亚	172	172		239	239	
斯威士兰	234	234		66	66	
厄立特里亚	263	260	4	313	313	
非洲其他国家	39	37	2	261	61	200
欧洲	**5,973,511**	**3,342,877**	**2,630,634**	**5,471,419**	**2,896,471**	**2,574,948**
欧洲共同体	4,886,322	2,814,790	2,071,532	4,300,397	2,381,148	1,919,249
比利时	251,951	164,110	87,841	227,802	135,975	91,827
丹麦	77,629	45,744	31,885	71,874	37,218	34,656
英国	658,407	463,219	195,187	579,166	381,338	197,828

1998年中国进出口分国家、地区总值表

金额单位:万美元

国家、地区	1998			1997		
	进出口	出口	进口	进出口	出口	进口
德国	1,434,755	735,392	699,363	1,267,041	649,046	617,995
法国	602,749	282,276	320,473	557,162	232,878	324,284
爱尔兰	30,201	19,627	10,573	19,540	12,775	6,765
意大利	485,437	257,734	227,703	468,745	223,735	245,009
卢森堡	8,222	3,671	4,551	5,118	2,110	3,007
荷兰	599,522	516,151	83,370	547,721	440,463	107,258
希腊	40,642	38,594	2,048	31,449	24,788	6,661
葡萄牙	22,756	20,060	2,696	21,072	16,603	4,468
西班牙	200,410	152,388	48,022	179,996	124,472	55,524
奥地利	48,340	21,141	27,198	45,487	19,974	25,512
芬兰	157,847	31,855	125,992	95,747	27,043	68,704
瑞典	267,455	62,826	204,629	182,479	52,730	129,749
冰岛	1,266	536	730	1,397	471	927
列支敦士登	41	41		44	34	10
挪威	63,450	32,996	30,454	94,658	56,803	37,855
瑞士	142,955	63,399	79,556	148,552	61,305	87,247
阿尔巴尼亚	884	883		664	664	
安道尔	157	157		142	142	
保加利亚	4,799	4,518	280	4,797	3,138	1,659
直布罗陀	376	376		320	196	124
匈牙利	40,986	39,705	1,281	32,211	29,639	2,572
马耳他	2,703	2,529	175	1,787	1,755	32
摩纳哥	202	172	30	117	115	1
波兰	81,453	75,867	5,586	70,538	67,336	3,202
罗马尼亚	25,966	23,975	1,991	24,852	17,605	7,246
圣马力诺	11	10		4	4	
爱沙尼亚	1,468	692	776	1,067	802	264
拉脱维亚	2,178	1,359	820	677	556	120
立陶宛	2,408	2,369	39	1,640	1,376	264
格鲁吉亚	773	613	161	408	79	329
亚美尼亚	84	78	6	37	37	
阿塞拜疆	131	115	16	1,566	147	1,419
白俄罗斯	1,734	646	1,088	4,262	1,684	2,578
哈萨克斯坦	63,554	20,468	43,086	52,741	9,463	43,278
吉尔吉斯斯坦	19,810	17,241	2,569	10,662	7,060	3,602
摩尔多瓦	70	19	51	114	35	80
俄罗斯	548,123	184,037	364,086	611,895	203,283	408,612

1998 年中国进出口分国家、地区总值表

金额单位:万美元

国家、地区	1998			1997		
	进出口	出口	进口	进出口	出口	进口
塔吉克斯坦	1,923	1,104	819	2,023	1,105	918
土库曼斯坦	1,252	1,029	222	1,524	1,163	361
乌克兰	27,505	9,011	18,494	43,527	10,104	33,423
乌兹别克斯坦	9,025	5,788	3,236	20,292	6,153	14,139
南斯拉夫联盟共和国	3,333	2,882	450	2,347	1,960	387
斯洛文尼亚共和国	3,608	3,411	196	2,236	1,848	387
克罗地亚共和国	2,027	1,987	40	2,526	1,324	1,203
捷克共和国	29,196	26,590	2,605	27,845	24,994	2,852
斯洛伐克共和国	3,457	3,224	233	3,371	2,765	606
马其顿共和国	251	238	12	157	156	1
波斯尼亚－黑塞哥维那共和国	33	20	13	21	21	
拉丁美洲	**831,215**	**532,299**	**298,916**	**837,571**	**460,646**	**376,924**
安提瓜和巴布达	224	215	9	16	11	5
阿根廷	127,450	55,004	72,446	118,749	46,528	72,221
阿鲁巴岛	257	257		258	258	
巴哈马	2,786	2,786		4,893	4,890	3
巴巴多斯	205	205		157	157	
伯利兹	210	184	26	165	139	26
玻利维亚	754	746	8	503	378	125
博内尔				4	4	
巴西	221,867	108,556	113,310	253,307	104,410	148,898
开曼群岛	20	20		46	46	
智利	104,135	61,990	42,145	97,717	56,206	41,511
哥伦比亚	10,097	9,275	822	7,297	6,959	338
多米尼加	4,657	4,634	23	4,500	4,496	4
哥斯达黎加	6,329	4,645	1,684	2,411	2,275	136
古巴	22,128	12,736	9,392	25,582	15,619	9,964
库腊索岛	1,227	1,227		1,211	1,211	
多米尼加	6,191	6,158	33	3,996	3,990	5
厄瓜多尔	14,704	7,393	7,311	15,774	5,781	9,993
法属圭亚那	85	85		34	33	
格林纳达	24	23	1	3	3	
瓜德罗普	57	57		59	59	
危地马拉	9,534	9,497	37	7,415	7,376	39
圭亚那	597	552	45	643	643	
海地	944	944		722	722	

1998 年中国进出口分国家、地区总值表

金额单位:万美元

国家、地区	1998			1997		
	进出口	出口	进口	进出口	出口	进口
洪都拉斯	5,958	5,861	97	4,126	4,043	83
牙买加	6,425	4,632	1,793	3,195	3,182	13
马提尼克	35	35		22	22	
墨西哥	83,681	68,935	14,747	59,798	41,367	18,430
蒙特塞拉特	2	2		8	8	
尼加拉瓜	1,834	1,834		1,394	1,394	1
巴拿马	104,875	104,756	119	101,157	100,999	158
巴拉圭	8,026	7,841	186	8,578	8,511	67
秘鲁	39,540	10,726	28,814	71,853	9,762	62,091
波多黎各	3,629	3,595	34	2,576	2,555	21
萨巴						
圣卢西亚	57	57		8	8	
圣马丁岛	55	55		23	23	
圣文森特和格林纳丁斯	561	536	26	711	685	26
萨尔瓦多	4,432	4,424	8	3,482	3,482	
苏里南	949	850	99	626	564	62
特立尼达和多巴哥	1,671	1,671		1,079	1,076	3
特克斯群岛	12	10	2	10	10	
乌拉圭	16,500	12,047	4,453	17,920	8,773	9,147
委内瑞拉	18,290	17,043	1,247	15,458	11,904	3,555
英属维尔京群岛	107	107		2	2	
圣其茨尼维	1	1		18	18	
拉丁美洲其他国家	92	91	1	64	64	
北美洲	**5,930,284**	**4,010,439**	**1,919,845**	**5,290,710**	**3,460,132**	**1,830,578**
加拿大	436,486	212,766	223,720	391,213	190,505	200,708
美国	5,493,699	3,797,587	1,696,112	4,899,290	3,269,480	1,629,810
格陵兰	26	13	13	73	15	58
百慕大	72	72		128	125	3
北美洲其他国家	2	2		7	7	
大洋洲	**580,150**	**266,124**	**314,027**	**607,044**	**239,650**	**367,393**
澳大利亚	502,976	234,166	268,809	530,259	205,491	324,768
库克群岛	27	27		14	14	
斐济	1,785	1,385	400	2,014	1,999	15
盖比群岛	13	13		36	36	
马克萨斯	2	2		15	15	
瑙鲁	2	2		2	2	

1998年中国进出口分国家、地区总值表

金额单位:万美元

国家、地区	1998			1997		
	进出口	出口	进口	进出口	出口	进口
新喀里多尼	252	251	1	221	221	
瓦努阿图	130	110	19	116	116	
新西兰	68,493	27,501	40,992	63,178	28,239	34,939
诺福克岛	17	15	1	9	9	
巴布亚新几内亚	5,244	1,904	3,340	10,298	2,629	7,669
社会群岛	101	101		101	101	
所罗门群岛	564	110	454	109	106	
汤加	51	51		58	58	
土阿莫土				1	1	
萨摩亚	124	115	9	123	123	
基里巴斯	131	131		203	203	
图瓦卢	8	8		2	2	
密克罗尼西亚联邦	17	17		45	45	
马绍尔群岛共和国	29	29		52	52	
贝劳共和国	48	48		123	123	
大洋洲其他国家	137	137		66	66	
其他国家(地区)	**90**		**90**	**203**		**203**

1998年中国出口主要商品数量金额

金额单位:万美元

品名	单位	1998		1997	
		数量	金额	数量	金额
总值	**金额**		**18,375,711**		**18,269,664**
粮谷	公吨	8,886,399	157,618	8,331,641	131,681
大米	公吨	3,745,387	92,506	937,602	26,265
玉米	公吨	4,686,261	53,164	6,607,213	85,752
高粱	公吨	18,607	246	111,985	1,550
大麦	公吨	8,356	217	6,567	196
荞麦	公吨	106,337	2,474	106,690	2,470
谷子	公吨	18,597	446	21,560	574
面粉	公吨	268,967	7,389	457,060	12,531
豆类	公吨	642,205	28,042	779,315	33,992
黄大豆	公吨	169,874	6,339	185,719	7,325
蚕豆	公吨	17,574	580	69,161	1,997
绿豆	公吨	114,279	6,598	76,466	5,860

1998年中国出口主要商品数量金额

金额单位:万美元

品　　名	单位	1998		1997	
		数量	金额	数量	金额
红小豆	公吨	53,438	2,428	36,763	1,943
芸豆	公吨	222,850	9,851	368,736	15,184
扁豆	公吨	26,310	722	17,861	513
食用植物油	公吨	309,314	22,545	822,878	54,813
花生油	公吨	10,165	1,199	8,602	1,060
豆油	公吨	185,891	13,475	555,770	36,861
芝麻油	公吨	4,171	767	4,016	657
食用植物油籽	公吨	439,694	26,982	414,546	26,156
花生仁	公吨	148,573	11,273	124,980	10,578
花生果	公吨	66,296	4,278	46,367	3,261
芝麻	公吨	44,471	4,424	40,649	4,153
葵花籽	公吨	8,550	612	15,811	817
工业用油	公吨	35,903	5,839	53,764	8,064
桐油	公吨	21,176	2,963	29,021	4,803
工业用油籽	公吨	24,797	1,020	28,305	1,360
活畜禽	金额		44,101		47,590
活大猪	头	1,748,965	25,880	1,772,246	26,576
活中猪	头	433,502	2,967	487,640	3,324
活牛	头	74,491	4,107	65,455	3,551
活鸡	万只	4,114	9,154	4,611	8,980
活鸭	万只	89	255	354	1,017
活鸽	万只	211	272	362	469
肉食	金额		113,953		129,911
冻猪肉	公吨	104,975	18,082	103,386	19,472
冻牛肉	公吨	43,041	7,266	31,494	5,386
冻山羊肉	公吨	2,756	396	1,039	211
冻兔肉	公吨	15,029	2,660	29,105	6,356
冻驴马肉	公吨	451	212	834	323
冻鸡	公吨	274,443	46,017	295,663	55,498
冻鸭	公吨	4,499	701	4,682	846
咸腊肉	公吨	912	310	1,328	478
灌腊肠	公吨	9,742	2,146	10,256	2,089
鲜蛋	万个	57,755	1,875	73,324	2,528
鸡蛋	万个	54,899	1,803	69,987	2,431
皮蛋	万个	9,643	592	9,536	822
咸蛋	万个	17,510	758	11,915	722
苹果	公吨	170,329	6,456	188,420	7,749

1998年中国出口主要商品数量金额

金额单位:万美元

品名	单位	1998		1997	
		数量	金额	数量	金额
桔柑橙	公吨	161,159	4,612	209,127	7,111
梨	公吨	112,675	3,503	120,371	5,276
香蕉	公吨	16,660	559	14,748	536
荔枝	公吨	2,990	290	4,788	622
荸荠	公吨	11,125	586	11,572	542
西瓜	公吨	47,001	693	23,249	523
栗子	公吨	38,581	6,903	31,551	6,365
柿饼	公吨	6,561	731	6,214	1,079
蜜饯	公吨	41,229	4,886	45,585	6,375
蜜枣	公吨	5,933	598	7,285	927
核桃仁	公吨	9,969	2,851	12,506	3,741
苦杏仁	公吨	5,797	1,092	7,524	1,567
松子仁	公吨	4,897	4,909	1,828	2,287
腰果仁	公吨	708	226	507	137
白果	公吨	2,586	923	4,049	1,575
红枣	公吨	19,943	2,268	18,848	2,734
山核桃仁	公吨	9,969	2,851	12,506	3,741
蔬菜	公吨	2,034,171	148,779	1,689,980	149,090
土豆	公吨	37,134	515	32,721	464
洋葱	公吨	128,860	2,890	45,294	796
萝卜	公吨	41,350	1,117	16,666	540
鲜姜	公吨	53,059	3,681	44,044	4,983
蕃茄	公吨	28,025	634	28,444	598
大蒜	公吨	157,627	8,450	162,557	9,771
咸蕨菜	公吨	6,285	622	4,494	514
榨菜	公吨	17,755	829	16,206	764
速冻蔬菜	公吨	262,746	27,462	213,250	22,400
黑木耳	公吨	4,781	1,920	4,833	2,178
金针菜	公吨	1,928	204	2,121	275
蘑菇	公吨	45,149	10,866	31,806	11,448
蘑菇干片	公吨	14,981	5,853	15,972	6,880
辣椒干	公吨	52,983	4,810	45,829	5,696
辣椒粉	公吨	6,340	953	7,123	1,488
笋干丝	公吨	2,467	1,113	2,671	1,341
水产品	金额		173,668		188,548
大闸蟹	公吨	207	437	411	1,151
活鳗鱼	公吨	5,929	4,859	5,043	4,923

1998 年中国出口主要商品数量金额

金额单位:万美元

品　　名	单位	1998		1997	
		数量	金额	数量	金额
冰鲜鱼	公吨	62,150	13,672	61,233	17,743
冻鱼	公吨	120,404	20,977	124,519	29,237
冻鱼片	公吨	226,253	46,321	153,333	34,003
冻对虾	公吨	5,160	4,838	4,633	5,531
冻鲜虾	公吨	19,212	2,506	14,773	2,997
冻小虾	公吨	33,567	14,072	38,424	16,369
冻虾仁球	公吨	3,659	3,390	3,072	3,568
冻小虾仁	公吨	25,298	11,245	26,510	11,977
鱼翅	公吨	2,005	3,174	2,421	3,265
海蜇皮	公吨	3,842	1,570	3,746	1,918
猪肉罐头	公吨	33,394	5,914	37,117	6,553
牛肉罐头	公吨	7,489	1,196	24,270	4,322
菠罗罐头	公吨	52,730	3,210	19,610	1,226
桔子罐头	公吨	112,234	7,954	98,497	8,321
桃子罐头	公吨	31,543	2,676	30,471	2,700
荔枝罐头	公吨	4,787	652	7,559	931
蘑菇罐头	公吨	137,745	13,038	143,799	14,293
蕃茄酱罐头	公吨	92,345	6,628	106,668	6,338
芦笋罐头	公吨	78,813	9,300	55,564	6,563
核桃仁罐头	公吨	967	397	1,014	449
花生米罐头	公吨	2,192	314	3,994	630
糖	金额		12,321		13,279
砂糖	公吨	409,428	11,220	337,162	11,592
原糖	公吨	13,509	521	13,039	545
啤酒	公吨	56,412	2,629	72,400	3,390
米酒及黄酒	公吨	16,352	2,266	13,548	2,025
葡萄酒	公吨	4,385	767	3,267	677
果汁	公吨	116,197	8,836	66,044	7,190
食盐	公吨	332,649	1,266	235,058	953
味素	公吨	10,735	1,520	12,935	1,913
酱油	公吨	47,705	2,522	47,654	2,737
醋	公吨	7,989	470	6,854	362
鲜奶	公吨	24,495	1,820	26,129	1,915
奶粉	公吨	8,408	1,366	7,843	1,493
炼乳	公吨	2,412	345	3,217	465
花生制品	公吨	105,972	11,873	110,433	13,810
蜂蜜	公吨	78,678	8,307	48,217	6,538

1998 年中国出口主要商品数量金额

金额单位:万美元

品　　名	单位	1998		1997	
		数量	金额	数量	金额
淀粉	公吨	32,131	1,624	61,806	3,033
麦麸	公吨	14,554	213	57,422	684
豆粕	公吨	18,493	462	19,677	623
甜菜粕	公吨	592,514	4,539	367,967	4,298
棉子仁饼粕	公吨	52,508	679	332,301	4,658
玉米蛋白粉	公吨	29,048	297	33,716	357
混合饲料	金额		9,730		11,329
鱼粉	公吨	1,473	222	1,488	44
骨粉	公吨	13,946	312	13,445	296
茶叶	公吨	217,437	37,028	202,464	33,248
红茶	公吨	69,591	10,263	87,145	12,315
绿茶	公吨	111,685	18,065	78,775	12,442
花茶	公吨	15,645	3,712	15,285	3,197
乌龙茶	公吨	17,134	4,277	18,156	4,708
咖啡	公吨	2,685	739	14,461	2,163
可可	公吨	18,966	4,380	18,307	5,649
八角	公吨	2,490	312	2,494	435
胡椒	公吨	645	234	3,595	1,441
薄荷脑	公吨	1,804	2,612	765	3,002
香茅油	公吨	1,071	390	1,037	389
桂油	公吨	627	1,304	392	880
山苍子油	公吨	606	467	397	385
桉叶油	公吨	2,811	992	3,690	1,220
松油	公吨	24,650	1,256	30,638	2,338
香叶油	公吨	73	229	101	516
天然樟脑(粉、块)	公吨	7,524	1,297	7,159	1,761
柠檬酸	公吨	130,008	11,707	127,763	11,948
松香	公吨	254,145	13,568	204,729	15,942
明胶	公吨	3,056	503	2,636	407
蜂蜡	公吨	2,591	808	7,172	1,557
鞭炮烟花	公吨	137,432	22,131	116,628	19,752
蚊香	公吨	10,008	1,001	9,895	1,083
神纸(土纸)	公吨	79,780	7,676	92,564	10,507
观赏鱼	金额		304		438
猎鬃	公吨	12,293	8,383	11,077	7,277
马鬃尾	公吨	1,532	735	1,783	792
鬃刷	万把	33,120	4,824	36,459	5,719

1998年中国出口主要商品数量金额

金额单位:万美元

品　　名	单位	1998		1997	
		数量	金额	数量	金额
肠衣	公吨	45,502	34,278	48,369	36,916
猪肠衣	公吨	32,647	20,670	35,941	21,954
绵羊肠衣	公吨	6,469	10,160	5,634	11,018
山羊肠衣	公吨	1,045	1,647	1,346	2,329
鹅鸭绒毛	公吨	30,232	17,074	20,781	18,642
羽绒睡袋	个	402,351	1,047	385,922	936
骨粒粉	公吨	70,025	1,671	66,506	1,649
猪革皮	公吨	5,504	5,513	4,650	4,766
羊革皮	公吨	1,635	2,839	1,559	2,895
牛革皮	公吨	47,609	25,556	45,961	24,048
生牛皮	公吨	33,938	1,285	43,520	2,600
原木	立方米	31,926	1,246	63,319	2,946
桐原木	立方米	9,395	303	15,883	505
锯材	立方米	254,545	11,439	387,170	19,305
胶合板	立方米	176,857	6,496	437,886	15,154
梧桐木拼板	公吨	50,654	9,051	51,601	9,363
箱板	金额		1,573		1,878
木板门	公吨	70,548	7,196	65,246	7,010
烟类	金额		57,836		65,760
烟草	公吨	106,289	18,202	88,952	19,589
烤烟	公吨	85,969	16,355	69,643	16,982
烟草制品	金额		37,392		43,619
卷烟	万支	2,286,031	37,392	2,472,757	43,497
烟草辅料	金额		2,242		2,552
棉花	公吨	45,115	5,631	1,480	393
苎麻	公吨	1,650	679	2,690	1,188
麻袋	万条	552	230	2,027	168
茧类	金额		570		1,172
桑蚕茧	公吨	591	559	1,123	1,149
丝类	金额		35,195		42,745
桑蚕丝	公吨	8,481	19,909	10,120	25,307
柞蚕丝	公吨	534	1,007	755	1,628
羊毛	公吨	15,659	5,867	21,934	8,731
羊绒	公吨	2,003	10,005	2,257	15,142
兔毛	公吨	2,808	4,044	4,029	8,141
纺织品	金额		1,200,729		1,288,911
棉纱线	件	735,159	42,086	843,551	48,457

1998年中国出口主要商品数量金额

金额单位:万美元

品　名	单位	1998		1997	
		数量	金额	数量	金额
麻纱线	件	142,635	9,896	161,649	11,379
亚麻纱线	件	31,100	3,121	39,025	3,949
棉麻混纺纱线	件	14,181	361	17,503	364
苎麻纱线	件	88,569	5,904	96,700	6,516
毛纱线	件	258,162	40,149	322,976	48,008
棉涤纶纱线	件	19,612	946	28,366	1,407
棉布	万米	221,206	213,225	234,976	234,602
坯布	万米	82,122	51,281	88,064	63,831
漂布	万米	11,386	9,227	11,509	10,507
色布	万米	63,801	69,943	62,220	67,952
花布	万米	17,796	13,068	25,616	18,680
色织布	万米	43,966	67,029	45,602	71,350
其他棉布	万米	2,134	2,677	1,966	2,282
麻布	万米	16,968	28,977	17,337	29,548
浴巾	打	9,776,852	17,632	9,782,551	18,016
毛巾被	条	6,768,643	3,324	20,134,975	10,406
床单	条	28,025,219	7,983	30,649,004	9,070
床罩	条	21,243,057	6,527	11,231,056	5,187
棉毯	条	12,278,684	6,533	12,817,160	7,780
毛毯	条	10,369,187	12,300	10,244,298	14,590
纤维毯	条	887,138	487	727,079	441
绸缎	万米	12,110	38,268	15,310	47,975
服装	金额		3,005,720		3,175,368
日用瓷	金额		66,550		67,849
日用陶	金额		5,656		5,479
美术陶瓷	金额		60,856		62,209
建筑陶瓷	金额		10,200		10,847
陶瓷砖	金额		7,572		9,269
卫生洁具	金额		2,417		1,328
地毯及装饰毯	金额		44,165		45,464
宝石	金额		32,091		30,498
钻石	金额		26,529		22,883
养殖珍珠	公斤	368,151	5,517	329,208	5,726
天然植物编织品	金额		46,339		58,183
稻草制品	金额		4,175		4,941
藤制品	金额		5,241		5,802
柳制品	金额		9,152		11,303

1998年中国出口主要商品数量金额

金额单位:万美元

品名	单位	1998		1997	
		数量	金额	数量	金额
竹编制品	金额		8,709		11,414
鞋类	金额		839,179		853,571
帽类	金额		45,466		41,940
圆珠笔	打	97,220,425	5,893	57,185,565	4,297
铅笔	公斤	20,271,284	5,547	27,322,104	6,977
电子计算器	台	385,107,371	45,709	328,567,315	42,517
乒乓球	万个	14,769	570	19,116	751
玩具	金额		514,246		504,078
电动玩具	金额		3,213		2,160
机械玩具	金额		46,984		57,814
智力玩具	金额		5,402		5,298
布绒玩具	金额		140,659		118,828
童车	金额		2,345		2,483
乐器	金额		30,715		27,967
钢琴	台	36,170	3,849	32,407	3,067
口琴	打	642,852	653	454,953	485
手风琴	架	74,055	320	47,495	290
提琴	套	435,748	1,121	335,957	977
管乐器	个	85,975	470	73,041	345
铜响乐器	金额		669		314
电子乐器	金额		10,673		11,391
帐篷	顶	13,711,624	24,669	11,688,632	23,219
太阳伞	个	17,136,477	9,628	13,216,900	7,017
纸浆类	公吨	19,786	935	22,307	1,150
纸张	公吨	240,857	19,893	214,987	18,762
纸制品	公吨	762,878	87,581	821,423	89,385
玻璃器皿	金额		12,565		12,050
保温瓶类	金额		14,676		14,613
钟类	金额		50,037		50,521
闹钟	个	186,031,586	15,759	177,485,839	18,125
表类	金额		98,167		98,991
机械手表	个	26,638,790	5,423	39,046,410	8,699
电子手表	个	830,479,361	92,744	792,943,051	90,292
家具类	金额		219,026		181,806
清洁用品	金额		3,517		2,468
香皂	公吨	10,927	1,736	11,926	1,940
肥皂	公吨	6,689	460	16,655	642

1998年中国出口主要商品数量金额

金额单位:万美元

品名	单位	1998		1997	
		数量	金额	数量	金额
牙膏	公吨	18,286	3,468	12,817	2,410
化妆品	金额		10,871		7,538
美容用品	金额		7,988		4,647
护发美发用品	金额		2,369		2,212
香水	金额		235		144
锁类	公吨	138,161	36,401	140,110	39,961
灯具	金额		148,798		131,804
衡器类	金额		8,539		7,757
皮手套	打付	46,468,053	37,210	47,214,591	41,077
钢材	公吨	3,565,997	168,698	4,619,391	193,505
钢坯	公吨	1,644,296	35,143	3,631,198	84,535
钢锭	公吨	528,586	10,994	515,022	12,314
废钢	公吨	24,922	651	68,251	1,334
铁丝	公吨	124,955	6,544	140,408	7,979
铝矿砂	公吨	84,258	711	160,645	1,388
铅矿砂	公吨	34,371	465	25,681	243
锌矿砂	公吨	201,325	2,714	381,309	6,923
钼矿砂	公吨	4,567	2,080	2,819	1,412
生铁	公吨	2,444,244	33,642	5,550,109	82,256
铁合金	公吨	959,958	69,931	1,062,887	73,530
钨铁	公吨	3,617	1,571	2,210	975
钼铁	公吨	31,739	17,204	24,458	14,895
锰铁	公吨	130,658	5,634	145,847	7,234
铬铁	公吨	102,083	7,248	98,069	7,503
硅铁	公吨	265,981	14,536	208,067	12,924
钒铁	公吨	2,308	3,780	1,949	2,476
锡	公吨	53,573	26,695	41,087	20,521
锑	公吨	22,365	3,060	31,034	5,628
硫化锑	公吨	5,636	741	13,910	1,887
氧化锑	公吨	28,062	3,871	28,329	5,872
铜	公吨	131,903	21,834	96,446	20,339
铜合金	公吨	2,336	486	735	270
铝	公吨	237,756	33,696	163,151	25,437
铅	公吨	250,941	14,152	197,893	13,245
锌	公吨	370,612	38,816	543,841	63,769
镍	公吨	15,051	7,762	4,748	3,408
镁	公吨	85,036	18,407	67,074	15,216

1998年中国出口主要商品数量金额

金额单位:万美元

品名	单位	1998		1997	
		数量	金额	数量	金额
钼	公吨	546	458	303	435
铋	公吨	1,344	911	1,603	948
铬	公吨	3,418	2,044	3,736	2,167
锰	公吨	73,214	8,072	63,471	7,563
铝合金	公吨	89,142	11,073	85,311	11,446
锌合金	公吨	12,282	1,415	13,167	1,408
氧化铝	公吨	32,613	936	12,773	471
氧化钼	公吨	17,147	7,448	21,983	10,948
三氧化钨	公吨	3,668	1,985	1,363	788
仲钨酸铵	公吨	12,675	5,918	14,596	7,412
铜材	公吨	93,143	30,393	99,440	32,053
铜管	公吨	8,825	2,982	6,294	2,076
铜棒	公吨	10,177	1,742	5,687	1,251
铜丝	公吨	21,336	4,451	27,564	6,671
铝材	公吨	109,354	24,272	100,328	22,022
铝板	公吨	22,688	5,768	18,337	5,033
铝管	公吨	1,047	435	827	321
铝丝	公吨	2,078	379	3,079	555
铝箔	公吨	20,841	5,468	13,963	3,946
铅材	公吨	6,361	484	1,752	184
锌材	公吨	9,952	979	5,938	631
镍材	公吨	1,127	643	1,299	808
镁材	公吨	3,673	725	4,410	876
锡材	公吨	7,028	3,492	4,384	2,077
银	公斤	88,574	1,402	26,688	400
钯	公斤	2,515	2,088	3,121	1,683
钯合金	公斤	2,515	2,088	3,121	1,683
水泥	公吨	8,199,725	29,046	11,684,542	44,571
平板玻璃	平方米	36,450,929	9,738	39,865,588	9,442
重烧镁	公吨	1,198,985	12,446	1,372,824	15,403
白云石	公吨	357,394	567	469,467	731
鳞片石墨	公吨	123,298	3,848	105,768	3,692
无定形石墨	公吨	57,455	439	64,255	621
滑石块	公吨	385,273	2,482	453,608	2,777
滑石粉	公吨	311,210	3,109	524,721	4,893
长石块	公吨	608,501	1,091	591,265	1,122
轻烧镁	公吨	310,606	3,270	401,738	4,191

1998年中国出口主要商品数量金额

金额单位:万美元

品　　名	单位	1998		1997	
		数量	金额	数量	金额
硼石块	公吨	1,315,972	12,947	1,293,672	12,963
重晶石	公吨	1,774,289	6,868	2,926,955	9,833
煤	公吨	27,995,790	106,779	26,427,559	113,253
焦炭	公吨	11,463,981	79,839	10,580,693	79,096
电力	万度	717,364	44,630	290,910	46,075
石油及制品	金额		246,880		428,931
原油	公吨	15,600,712	152,745	19,828,880	273,413
成品油	公吨	4,360,976	73,891	5,585,850	120,136
汽油	公吨	1,819,730	28,081	1,780,425	36,095
煤油	公吨	921,877	20,243	722,995	20,77
轻柴油	公吨	984,769	16,325	2,288,915	46,567
重柴油	公吨	12,286	1,809	14,066	1,771
润滑油脂	公吨	22,190	1,603	104,560	3,750
液化石油气	公吨	502,177	8,261	399,007	7,776
磷酸	公吨	94,287	3,970	90,604	4,305
氢氟酸	公吨	9,808	512	4,433	269
金属钠	公吨	1,551	247	874	152
烧碱	公吨	262,142	4,465	229,078	4,654
纯碱	公吨	705,537	8,069	622,812	8,124
硫化碱	公吨	60,651	1,224	66,155	1,503
次亚磷酸钠	公吨	6,924	1,185	6,144	1,227
氯化钠	公吨	332,649	1,266	235,058	953
氯化钾	公吨	452,094	4,881	587,010	6,064
氯酸钾	公吨	7,975	491	7,467	485
硝酸钾	公吨	5,515	209	4,245	184
硫酸钾	公吨	21,473	472	10,755	209
高锰酸钾	公吨	10,396	1,040	10,176	1,136
碳酸钙	公吨	23,963	232	44,392	265
电石(碳化钙)	公吨	62,937	2,030	66,786	2,325
氯化钙	公吨	55,681	717	57,452	835
硫酸钡	公吨	17,253	401	16,363	378
碳酸钡	公吨	174,499	3,808	152,130	3,581
电解二氧化锰	公吨	17,149	1,488	16,335	1,326
氯化镍	公吨	1,676	383	177	37
碳酸镁	公吨	19,045	1,116	21,347	1,509
氯化镁	公吨	57,621	812	36,731	384
硫酸铝	公吨	26,071	277	36,184	401

1998年中国出口主要商品数量金额

金额单位:万美元

品　　名	单位	1998		1997	
		数量	金额	数量	金额
工业氢氧化铝	公吨	40,552	823	44,617	701
钼酸铵	公吨	795	466	829	574
硝酸钴	公吨	29,159	1,038	24,892	1,019
氧化钴	公吨	287	739	204	339
钨酸	公吨	547	229	541	241
钨酸钠	公吨	1,508	459	1,268	425
氢氧化锂	公吨	1,913	606	992	364
五氧化二钒	公吨	7,586	8,213	6,465	4,831
碳酸锶	公吨	43,207	2,046	40,910	2,106
工业硝酸铵	公吨	47,997	874	35,556	724
氯化铵	公吨	171,202	1,405	216,771	2,162
磷酸氢二铵	公吨	68,007	1,553	33,568	727
活性碳	公吨	104,745	5,626	220,357	6,234
液氯	公吨	11,639	387	6,848	192
石蜡	公吨	593,032	24,678	387,880	19,040
石油焦	公吨	984,355	5,786	657,550	4,161
锻烧焦	公吨	180,042	2,774	89,805	1,587
沥青焦	公吨	18,063	322	10,250	204
石油沥青	公吨	166,318	985	188,654	987
煤焦沥青	公吨	85,835	1,371	56,401	878
甲醇(木精)	公吨	47,472	786	7,161	216
乙醇(酒精)	升	105,652,309	4,342	140,725,001	7,040
乙二醇	公吨	5,176	309	23,578	1,279
环乙醇	公吨	105,685	4,398	140,745	7,093
糠醇	公吨	33,792	3,648	30,026	3,470
糠醛	公吨	56,389	4,203	38,416	3,087
甲酸(蚁酸)	公吨	5,632	303	4,968	347
苯甲酸	公吨	12,034	1,568	9,650	1,231
水杨酸	公吨	2,959	741	2,552	693
草酸(乙二酸)	公吨	23,885	1,209	21,148	1,191
酒石酸	公吨	1,707	283	1,513	245
己二酸	公吨	1,564	217	2,908	382
癸二酸	公吨	14,555	3,195	12,833	2,674
对苯二甲酸	公吨	12,431	783	31,042	1,800
丙烯酸酯	公吨	9,670	735	6,180	379
对苯二酚	公吨	785	234	511	168
乙烯	公吨	6,794	249	34,589	1,647

1998 年中国出口主要商品数量金额

金额单位:万美元

品　　名	单位	1998		1997	
		数量	金额	数量	金额
丁二烯	公吨	11,488	452	3,155	137
双氰胺	公吨	12,843	1,837	13,521	1,996
三聚氰胺	公吨	23,348	3,956	18,168	2,449
己内酰胺	公吨	24,304	3,351	17,084	2,136
纯苯	公吨	26,956	563	52,025	1,460
粗苯	公吨	35,192	514	55,373	1,125
二甲苯(含邻间对)	公吨	69,463	2,048	120,861	5,645
防老剂	公吨	5,212	1,172	3,585	900
催化剂	公吨	3,897	1,359	3,511	908
塑料	金额		521,611		488,752
高压聚乙烯	公吨	14,219	980	14,551	1,165
低压聚乙烯	公吨	20,779	1,540	14,911	1,302
聚丙烯	公吨	28,302	1,881	19,242	1,481
ABS 树脂	公吨	28,933	3,636	56,431	7,311
电木粉(酚醛树脂)	公吨	11,056	978	11,328	1,092
电玉粉	公吨	7,155	576	6,290	546
聚氯乙烯(树脂)	公吨	42,796	3,888	54,354	5,112
聚苯乙烯	公吨	127,843	10,650	182,098	16,554
聚四氟乙烯	公吨	911	650	1,044	718
环氧树脂	公吨	3,831	812	2,599	494
聚碳酸脂	公吨	23,096	5,630	19,895	4,947
塑料雨衣	公吨	161,068	37,908	137,130	33,210
塑料雨帽	打	20,597,495	1,898	18,993,245	1,474
尼龙牙刷	罗	4,140,737	3,457	3,123,755	2,889
各种染料	公吨	131,690	49,727	127,284	52,759
硫化染料	公吨	21,724	2,602	22,804	3,083
还原染料	公吨	11,387	7,717	11,801	8,154
直接染料	公吨	6,236	2,539	6,802	3,053
酸性染料	公吨	16,071	6,795	13,255	5,968
盐基染料	公吨	7,228	3,862	7,719	4,597
活性染料	公吨	4,316	2,862	5,926	4,018
分散染料	公吨	58,853	20,539	52,529	20,500
增白粉	公吨	1,516	560	1,137	549
二萘酚(B 萘酚)	公吨	12,458	1,331	11,243	1,664
苯胺	公吨	1,395	607	1,266	710
二苯胺	公吨	951	558	1,082	485
甲萘胺(1-萘胺)	公吨	7,308	1,716	7,036	1,960

1998 年中国出口主要商品数量金额

金额单位:万美元

品　　名	单位	1998		1997	
		数量	金额	数量	金额
三聚氯氰	公吨	11,759	2,472	9,180	2,302
立德粉	公吨	70,186	2,370	60,046	2,197
钛白粉	公吨	31,967	3,251	23,717	2,455
氧化锌	公吨	57,445	4,800	55,743	4,764
群青	公吨	4,059	239	3,659	240
油漆	公吨	74,210	11,820	75,148	10,599
油墨	公吨	9,178	2,999	9,411	2,990
化肥	公吨	1,342,851	16,811	1,758,623	22,660
尿素	公吨	125,051	1,861	350,505	6,005
氯化钾	公吨	452,094	4,881	587,010	6,064
硝铵(硝酸铵)	公吨	47,997	874	35,556	724
过磷酸钙	公吨	238,818	2,437	171,532	1,665
硫酸钾	公吨	21,473	472	10,755	209
农药	公吨	107,479	32,530	87,595	30,935
除草剂	公吨	34,418	13,318	29,108	12,838
杀虫剂	公吨	43,890	10,170	43,911	12,381
天然橡胶	公吨	19,043	1,383	39,316	4,793
合成橡胶	公吨	29,486	2,609	31,357	3,293
轮胎	金额		64,210		56,645
整套轮胎	万套	7,397	57,516	7,497	50,069
轮胎内胎	万条	7,963	5,191	7,887	5,389
胶管	公吨	8,419	1,680	10,655	1,791
运输带	公吨	2,927	882	3,614	985
传动带	公吨	4,012	1,289	3,837	1,201
乳胶手套	万付	86,397	6,227	76,596	5,699
甘草	公吨	3,917	496	4,767	613
半夏	公吨	636	570	549	431
虫草	公吨	7	414	31	1,693
菊花	公吨	2,444	412	1,989	564
黄芪	公吨	3,291	458	4,220	655
当归	公吨	1,349	204	2,235	333
枸杞	公吨	3,936	837	4,206	913
党参	公吨	1,001	296	1,749	517
茯苓	公吨	3,245	519	3,665	617
白术	公吨	1,904	270	3,202	672
姜黄	公吨	1,909	271	2,006	832
动物药材	金额		1,702		1,746

1998年中国出口主要商品数量金额

金额单位:万美元

品　　名	单位	1998		1997	
		数量	金额	数量	金额
鲜王浆	公斤	2,163,323	1,546	3,141,992	1,434
槟榔	公吨	9,868	6,111	9,228	4,182
片仔癀	公斤	1,595	610	2,496	1,075
清凉油	公斤	3,110,292	1,472	2,335,745	1,191
药酒	金额		395		993
抗菌素药	公吨	30,381	52,931	25,536	53,861
磺胺药	公吨	9,574	7,804	8,904	7,810
磺胺嘧啶	公斤	1,221,495	1,000	1,292,145	1,186
磺胺二甲基嘧啶	公斤	2,182,572	1,422	2,080,388	1,543
维生素	金额		29,785		23,277
医疗器械	金额		32,382		30,119
体温表	万支	3,550	2,123	4,669	2,442
血压表	万支	952	7,542	979	7,622
听诊器	万个	229	241	133	188
心电瞬时记录仪	台	9,574	1,547	13,289	1,889
注射器	万支	18,647	882	13,764	713
注射针头	金额		425		414
畜牧专用器械	金额		340		277
医用敷料	金额		25,545		24,787
各类船	艘	30,158	173,160	18,668	161,848
客船	艘	35	2,008	53	4,034
客货船	艘	403	120,279	544	122,661
冷藏船	艘	1	1,540	4	1,235
挖泥船	艘	135	1,129	84	529
拖轮	艘	70	4,466	61	2,994
渔船	艘	115	3,239	44	729
海洋平台	金额		12,421		26
集装箱	只	569,706	158,689	329,521	102,806
飞机	架	31	10,610	49	2,815
汽车	辆	9,833	15,470	13,401	18,891
载重汽车	辆	6,951	6,417	8,522	7,959
小轿车	辆	1,592	1,916	2,914	3,843
客车	辆	743	2,694	1,257	4,860
汽车底盘	金额		267		91
摩托车	辆	110,143	6,460	92,940	6,226
摩托车零件	金额		8,822		8,395
汽车零件	金额		53,049		44,721

1998 年中国出口主要商品数量金额

金额单位:万美元

品　　名	单位	1998		1997	
		数量	金额	数量	金额
显像管	万只	615	25,619	453	18,486
集成电路	金额		115,004		93,180
电线电缆	公吨	363,381	97,983	303,428	86,977
蓄电池	金额		47,346		34,670
铅酸蓄电池	万个	1,454	7,267	1,066	5,802
起重机械	台	10,965,597	39,129	11,961,685	32,885
金属切削机床	台	2,255,084	23,507	2,493,102	28,150
车床	台	38,123	6,615	41,354	7,587
钻床	台	566,261	3,629	734,965	4,344
镗床	台	979	262	2,889	765
磨床	台	1,519,752	4,091	1,660,211	5,646
铣床	台	3,243	1,058	4,449	1,419
铸造机械	台	8,831,114	4,896	7,497,000	2,621
木工机械	台	451,745	3,371	313,277	2,805
各种泵	金额		105,866		100,471
滚动轴承	套	850,993,241	44,542	789,824,113	41,150
纺织机械	台	121	221	80	306
印刷机械	金额		2,849		3,000
制革制鞋机械	金额		205		135
金属轧机	金额		3,667		3,838
玻璃加工机械	金额		931		163
橡胶或塑料加工机械	金额		9,072		11,031
烟草加工机械	金额		233		206
电动机及发电机	万台	200,488	129,022	184,782	122,473
发电机组	台	12,826	6,176	10,987	3,699
电动机和发电机零件	金额		17,061		18,745
有线电话电报交换机	台	110,175,329	155,565	102,248,422	122,815
有线电话电报交换机零件	金额		32,757		24,995
计算机	金额		706,797		536,371
微型电子计算机	台	248,111	20,397	179,742	12,255
显示器	台	17,381,051	173,777	9,931,121	121,485
打印机	台	11,050,770	97,839	7,013,557	80,930
键盘	个	177,220,758	52,726	123,757,928	40,431
磁盘	万片	62,915	8,263	71,377	9,568
文字处理机	金额		4,055		3,965
有线通讯设备	金额		188,322		147,811
电话机	台	106,861,882	130,412	100,106,587	94,796

1998 年中国出口主要商品数量金额

金额单位:万美元

品　　名	单位	1998		1997	
		数量	金额	数量	金额
各种电子交换机	金额		1,551		3,238
载波机	台	1,196,803	5,451	14,681	1,125
传真机	台	1,291,746	17,725	1,727,069	23,435
复印机	台	1,508,751	62,009	1,423,691	66,366
调制解调器	台	11,168	2,575	834	560
雷达	金额		1,045		2,630
电台对讲机	金额		8,311		8,674
电池	金额		42,711		40,297
测绘仪器	金额		13,731		12,225
望远镜	金额		17,689		16,494
放大镜	只	12,060,241	433	13,742,544	480
照相机	架	67,465,551	99,400	65,589,906	92,533
照相机零件	金额		7,763		8,404
彩色冲洗扩印系统	金额		639		1,065
自行车类	金额		109,917		101,914
自行车	辆	17,825,640	61,507	14,617,906	51,789
自行车外胎	条	40,432,021	5,193	47,831,988	6,779
自行车内胎	条	61,632,928	2,936	62,003,784	3,306
自行车零配件	金额		43,295		43,905
缝纫机类	金额		27,669		27,069
缝纫机	金额		23,590		22,355
家用缝纫机	台	3,157,512	10,187	3,086,902	10,204
工业缝纫机	台	895,070	13,403	901,033	12,152
缝纫机零件	金额		4,078		4,714
缝纫机针	金额		516		532
电风扇	台	151,846,680	72,974	131,634,054	71,667
吊扇	台	24,145,831	32,836	21,345,041	30,983
台扇	台	11,781,226	8,401	13,185,659	10,117
落地电扇	台	9,510,221	10,786	8,515,958	9,125
排风扇	台	1,023,597	1,391	1,506,725	891
电冰箱	台	881,914	7,179	793,647	6,592
洗衣机	台	525,320	5,050	705,008	6,720
空调器	台	683,317	16,419	513,757	11,428
吸尘器	台	18,095,204	23,614	18,864,198	19,861
空气加湿器	台	2,719,854	2,316	2,585,138	1,747
空气干燥器	台	5,003	557	17,016	422
电水壶	个	32,954,444	15,673	31,863,112	14,509

1998年中国出口主要商品数量金额

金额单位:万美元

品名	单位	1998		1997	
		数量	金额	数量	金额
电炉	个	18,099,616	10,571	15,588,312	9,331
电热水器	个	4,465,976	1,792	3,894,396	1,737
电面包烤炉	台	38,727,881	31,211	36,656,070	27,685
电吹风	个	50,041,175	11,449	54,225,484	11,961
电动剃须刀	个	13,999,652	7,167	15,547,478	7,102
电熨斗	个	28,256,221	13,293	31,348,047	14,450
电筒	个	374,403,485	12,707	373,434,699	13,336
台灯	金额		29,783		27,866
吊灯	金额		25,398		21,549
节日灯	金额		40,629		32,403
卤钨灯	万只	26,477	9,000	22,531	8,735
收音机	台	121,452,947	28,202	134,820,635	32,791
录音机	金额		221,097		214,883
收录两用机	台	24,206,528	8,387	25,785,363	10,689
电视机及散件	金额		68,665		65,431
彩色电视机	台	4,388,198	52,590	4,289,598	50,554
黑白电视机	台	5,815,482	16,075	4,764,772	14,877
录像机	台	7,934,754	42,005	6,479,024	39,343
摄像机	台	355,432	9,586	193,236	5,633
音箱	万台	91,533	66,874	88,162	59,081
组合音响	万套	15	558	43	1,238
录像带	万盒	28,849	16,212	30,876	22,864
耳塞机	万个	31,360	10,657	29,324	10,771
麦克风	个	145,135,383	3,935	139,060,312	4,713
量具	金额		10,097		10,269
刃具	金额		3,734		3,244
磨具	金额		4,550		5,691
砂布	公吨	3,662	560	5,021	864
电动工具	金额		59,451		53,898
电钻	个	14,779,517	26,059	12,393,435	25,603
各种锤	金额		5,169		5,529
各种钳	金额		9,105		9,474
各种扳手	金额		5,235		6,292
各种螺丝批	金额		5,213		4,858
各种钻	金额		4,094		2,954
各种锉和刀	金额		21,113		20,837
各种锯和锯条	金额		8,629		8,279

1998年中国出口主要商品数量金额

金额单位:万美元

品　　名	单位	1998		1997	
		数量	金额	数量	金额
农具	金额		8,910		8,062
出版物	金额		22,604		18,540

1998年中国进口主要商品数量金额

金额单位:万美元

品　　名	单位	1998		1997	
		数量	金额	数量	金额
总值	**金额**		**14,016,630**		**14,236,081**
粮谷	公吨	3,883,057	71,602	4,165,275	91,619
大米	公吨	243,815	11,996	326,345	13,982
小麦	公吨	1,489,403	27,857	1,860,612	36,829
玉米	公吨	250,613	3,174	414	17
大麦	公吨	1,519,141	24,097	1,874,182	38,232
面粉	公吨	58,903	1,549	61,192	1,601
豆类	公吨	3,294,343	82,713	3,001,254	87,440
黄大豆	公吨	3,192,594	80,481	2,875,907	84,293
豌豆	公吨	78,417	1,742	112,179	2,755
绿豆	公吨	6,448	199	4,531	160
食用植物油	公吨	2,055,237	129,877	2,748,097	150,457
花生油	公吨	8,723	847	10,670	971
豆油	公吨	829,189	52,124	1,225,160	68,464
菜油	公吨	246,291	15,292	311,782	17,453
玉米油	公吨	1,536	113	1,901	166
食用植物油籽	公吨	4,604,676	122,124	2,953,530	87,013
花生仁	公吨	3,354	198	3,210	206
芝麻	公吨	11,316	597	14,289	745
葵花籽	公吨	10,768	597	3,442	141
油菜籽	公吨	1,386,413	40,246	55,134	1,583
工业用油	公吨	298,051	19,309	489,110	27,316
蓖麻油	公吨	41,417	3,085	22,790	1,820
亚麻油	公吨	11,876	526	37,931	1,825
椰子油	公吨	48,763	3,131	16,168	1,103
棕榈油	公吨	166,718	10,571	376,710	20,282
工业用油籽	公吨	1,209	261	5,603	111
活畜禽	金额		5,447		4,102
活羊	头	1,868	341	604	89
肉食	金额		14,467		15,247
冻猪肉	公吨	15,789	682	2,758	176
冻牛肉	公吨	3,548	506	2,590	323
冻绵羊肉	公吨	9,192	490	4,050	237
冻鸡	公吨	193,621	10,741	204,760	12,749
苹果	公吨	8,587	281	11,542	349
桔柑橙	公吨	3,989	137	5,820	170
梨	公吨	8,523	231	364	11

1998 年中国进口主要商品数量金额

金额单位:万美元

品　　名	单位	1998		1997	
		数量	金额	数量	金额
香蕉	公吨	539,093	16,312	546,938	14,570
菠萝	公吨	22,492	524	17,893	349
葡萄	公吨	7,023	330	4,795	222
西瓜	公吨	13,879	276	4,766	115
榛子	公吨	1,602	108	2,244	59
腰果仁	公吨	471	104	732	190
红枣	公吨	4,016	328	38,033	2,511
蔬菜	公吨	80,486	3,527	68,511	2,816
速冻蔬菜	公吨	20,983	794	21,160	736
水产品	金额		66,635		54,372
活鳗鱼	公吨	64	150	10	1
活鳗鱼苗、种	公斤	88,934	3,407	111,383	3,979
冰鲜鱼	公吨	8,699	700	5,913	576
冻鱼	公吨	572,344	42,910	393,875	30,352
冻鱼片	公吨	2,711	249	1,385	319
冻对虾	公吨	4,439	1,832	4,736	1,822
冻小虾	公吨	10,704	2,549	9,249	2,799
冻虾仁球	公吨	652	548	527	559
冻小虾仁	公吨	1,281	417	1,266	521
鱼翅	公吨	4,236	2,475	4,391	2,481
糖	金额		14,516		22,877
砂糖	公吨	59,618	2,033	71,323	2,630
原糖	公吨	445,291	12,367	702,980	19,918
啤酒	公吨	33,143	2,150	28,846	1,362
葡萄酒	公吨	51,563	3,831	40,897	3,756
果汁	公吨	11,973	913	12,517	853
食盐	公吨	4,432	104	6,299	149
味素	公吨	6,313	616	8,233	672
酱油	公吨	16,165	2,878	13,789	2,771
鲜奶	公吨	8,884	326	10,083	392
奶粉	公吨	31,053	3,901	27,908	1,915
淀粉	公吨	83,365	2,851	80,279	3,048
麦麸	公吨	36,359	386	64,955	605
豆粕	公吨	3,733,302	86,374	3,469,508	98,040
菜籽饼粕	公吨	107,246	1,274	53,366	759
玉米蛋白粉	公吨	11,077	473	9,655	440
木薯干片	公吨	300,501	3,172	277,803	2,675

1998年中国进口主要商品数量金额

金额单位:万美元

品名	单位	1998		1997	
		数量	金额	数量	金额
混合饲料	金额		6,099		5,882
鱼粉	公吨	416,188	31,168	985,234	62,819
骨粉	公吨	154,003	5,841	40,907	1,508
茶叶	公吨	1,185	246	911	110
红茶	公吨	345	161	185	42
咖啡	公吨	4,973	1,122	1,527	263
可可	公吨	37,645	6,419	48,333	7,113
薄荷脑	公吨	790	857	344	547
松香	公吨	1,400	250	2,033	299
明胶	公吨	1,469	810	1,339	706
神纸(土纸)	公吨	1,869	111	323	95
肠衣	公吨	65,319	4,835	114,404	6,661
猪肠衣	公吨	14,836	1,899	11,229	1,539
绵羊肠衣	公吨	10,989	1,425	8,468	960
鹅鸭绒毛	公吨	1,366	1,256	1,980	2,021
猪革皮	公吨	9,605	9,720	10,181	11,379
羊革皮	公吨	8,840	22,482	9,886	24,488
牛革皮	公吨	445,231	152,832	464,598	170,420
生猪皮	公吨	15,632	1,889	15,411	1,972
生牛皮	公吨	204,355	23,938	188,749	24,008
绵羊皮	公吨	62,759	6,309	47,169	5,502
水貂皮	公吨	987	2,846	683	2,341
原木	立方米	4,823,042	59,909	4,470,669	67,779
锯材	立方米	1,678,992	34,692	1,324,675	26,782
胶合板	立方米	1,691,113	54,363	1,488,500	60,550
梧桐木拼板	公吨	53,817	3,733	22,988	1,509
箱板	金额		150		176
木板门	公吨	1,748	242	2,243	347
烟类	金额		10,571		25,440
烟草	公吨	6,708	3,510	15,135	8,441
烤烟	公吨	6,004	3,236	11,383	6,477
烟草制品	金额		6,954		16,831
卷烟	万支	343,980	6,933	722,567	16,705
烟草辅料	金额		107		169
棉花	公吨	209,418	35,697	782,976	139,383
麻袋	万条	519	186	26	10
茧类	金额		204		365

1998 年中国进口主要商品数量金额

金额单位:万美元

品　　名	单位	1998		1997	
		数量	金额	数量	金额
桑蚕茧	公吨	744	183	1,389	261
丝类	金额		1,331		1,076
羊毛	公吨	168,606	60,300	207,203	78,945
羊绒	公吨	775	893	1,439	2,036
纺织品	金额		1,094,971		1,209,150
棉纱线	件	2,092,500	74,142	2,035,761	71,655
麻纱线	件	91,537	3,343	115,811	4,397
亚麻纱线	件	22,038	922	29,138	1,529
苎麻纱线	件	62,263	2,209	79,022	2,580
毛纱线	件	282,557	20,994	377,132	26,085
棉涤纶纱线	件	119,613	3,279	85,970	2,591
棉布	万米	138,395	133,841	144,689	145,023
坯布	万米	33,997	24,106	30,966	22,723
漂布	万米	8,978	6,754	11,353	9,086
色布	万米	53,328	55,385	55,876	57,961
花布	万米	5,635	8,646	6,704	11,036
色织布	万米	35,052	37,028	38,090	41,396
其他棉布	万米	1,404	1,922	1,700	2,821
麻布	万米	8,449	15,741	8,892	14,229
绸锻	万米	3,951	11,428	4,961	14,733
服装	金额		106,592		110,550
日用瓷	金额		199		239
建筑陶瓷	金额		4,291		6,957
陶瓷砖	金额		2,965		5,153
卫生洁具	金额		1,223		1,634
地毯及装饰毯	金额		2,191		3,126
宝石	金额		35,579		34,119
钻石	金额		30,115		26,246
养殖珍珠	公斤	68,532	565	67,744	349
天然植物编织品	金额		447		598
鞋类	金额		29,043		35,834
帽类	金额		114		189
圆珠笔	打	4,216,486	315	3,909,056	306
铅笔	公斤	1,232,784	245	1,494,159	265
电子计算器	台	4,175,799	392	5,312,213	347
玩具	金额		6,947		5,306
电动玩具	金额		324		144

1998 年中国进口主要商品数量金额

金额单位:万美元

品　　名	单位	1998		1997	
		数量	金额	数量	金额
机械玩具	金额		125		305
智力玩具	金额		180		240
乐器	金额		7,007		6,876
钢琴	台	3,027	272	2,086	182
铜响乐器	金额		119		9
纸浆类	公吨	2,199,310	92,368	1,541,584	74,792
纸张	公吨	5,754,765	300,781	5,507,907	280,404
纸制品	公吨	558,688	65,483	723,601	73,009
玻璃器皿	金额		7,871		8,596
保温瓶类	金额		244		270
钟类	金额		16,324		17,916
表类	金额		4,504		4,494
机械手表	个	968,492	1,882	2,379,097	1,799
电子手表	个	11,667,454	2,623	14,147,394	2,694
家具类	金额		9,274		7,554
清洁用品	金额		335		362
香皂	公吨	5,659	425	3,032	355
肥皂	公吨	2,430	107	2,714	121
牙膏	公吨	761	133	887	148
去污粉	公斤	1,050,524	139	1,087,790	109
化妆品	金额		3,246		2,352
美容用品	金额		2,264		1,801
护发美发用品	金额		705		406
香水	金额		141		81
锁类	公吨	8,347	3,488	8,007	3,358
灯具	金额		5,452		5,726
衡器类	金额		1,931		2,600
钢材	公吨	12,415,481	628,677	13,228,294	652,017
钢坯	公吨	661,657	14,896	316,180	8,530
钢锭	公吨	29,171	1,753	78,595	2,531
废钢	公吨	2,018,655	21,378	1,828,759	21,548
铁丝	公吨	167,505	10,542	159,459	10,419
铁矿砂	公吨	51,770,715	146,776	55,105,835	161,484
铬矿砂	公吨	711,544	8,089	894,001	11,078
锰矿砂	公吨	1,179,051	9,033	1,316,784	12,375
铜矿砂	公吨	1,182,867	45,831	937,776	42,116
镍矿砂	公吨	1,813	355	2,662	250

1998 年中国进口主要商品数量金额

金额单位:万美元

品　　名	单位	1998		1997	
		数量	金额	数量	金额
钴矿砂	公吨	2,787	781	494	104
铝矿砂	公吨	148,533	539	137,131	334
铅矿砂	公吨	236,034	4,226	118,330	2,037
锌矿砂	公吨	52,508	1,274	166,503	5,433
铬矿砂	公吨	711,544	8,089	894,001	11,078
钼矿砂	公吨	10,843	2,807	6,992	2,288
生铁	公吨	43,052	2,138	42,132	1,914
铁合金	公吨	6,974	1,356	28,999	1,120
硅铁	公吨	2,749	149	8,968	396
镍铁	公吨	635	143	262	41
锡	公吨	2,988	1,121	2,650	863
水银	公吨	524	212	481	180
锑	公吨	2,782	356	2,675	358
硫化锑	公吨	3,853	199	7,396	372
氧化锑	公吨	1,038	224	502	163
铜	公吨	1,226,635	73,751	1,009,803	77,985
铜合金	公吨	9,892	1,964	11,410	2,141
铝	公吨	203,208	27,647	230,229	28,253
铅	公吨	15,414	772	13,999	711
锌	公吨	12,091	1,157	10,800	1,034
镍	公吨	4,983	2,341	1,116	523
铬	公吨	598	125	1,815	295
铝合金	公吨	103,780	12,070	58,662	8,283
锌合金	公吨	75,385	7,515	61,171	6,112
氧化铝	公吨	1,574,909	35,422	1,094,407	23,866
铜材	公吨	546,625	137,470	484,679	127,382
铜管	公吨	30,705	11,343	24,553	9,871
铜棒	公吨	122,884	22,873	111,839	22,144
铜丝	公吨	207,875	44,088	179,209	39,864
铝材	公吨	341,294	84,492	312,099	78,940
铝板	公吨	216,860	47,923	209,071	45,764
铝管	公吨	12,224	4,130	8,780	3,719
铝丝	公吨	1,956	752	1,870	603
铝箔	公吨	35,592	16,394	24,671	13,895
铅材	公吨	4,734	484	4,564	445
锌材	公吨	63,475	4,567	61,399	4,379
镍材	公吨	8,175	4,693	6,708	4,083

1998 年中国进口主要商品数量金额

金额单位:万美元

品　　名	单位	1998		1997	
		数量	金额	数量	金额
镁材	公吨	145	113	151	144
锡材	公吨	13,463	4,280	14,560	4,605
银	公斤	156,546	3,035	125,458	2,229
钯	公斤	537	167	1,800	96
钯合金	公斤	537	167	1,800	96
水泥	公吨	179,775	1,143	168,736	1,769
平板玻璃	平方米	17,361,645	8,977	15,092,090	10,361
鳞片石墨	公吨	1,482	177	514	52
滑石粉	公吨	8,797	363	8,006	357
长石块	公吨	20,256	744	11,121	509
煤	公吨	1,582,133	6,845	1,998,608	9,562
石油及制品	金额		650,369		1,001,472
原油	公吨	27,322,632	327,454	35,469,701	545,621
成品油	公吨	21,739,869	240,518	23,794,877	368,206
汽油	公吨	14,867	314	84,290	1,836
煤油	公吨	1,290,823	19,774	1,380,655	30,280
轻柴油	公吨	3,104,241	44,777	7,374,667	150,306
重柴油	公吨	40,058	8,353	45,378	8,326
润滑油脂	公吨	175,961	20,465	171,389	19,377
石脑油	公吨	779,492	12,379	810,594	15,968
液化天然气	公吨	41,442	787	108,427	2,985
液化石油气	公吨	4,781,684	81,542	3,586,358	84,641
硫酸	公吨	297,227	909	128,929	551
硝酸	公吨	1,577	133	1,373	92
磷酸	公吨	152,321	3,915	103,815	2,733
硼酸	公吨	47,631	2,510	43,931	2,297
烧碱	公吨	26,403	814	31,379	758
纯碱	公吨	84,238	1,293	110,730	1,796
硝酸钠	公吨	10,297	180	21,640	426
氯化钠	公吨	4,432	104	6,299	149
氰化钠	公吨	14,213	1,656	18,095	2,502
氯化钾	公吨	5,120,377	60,627	4,625,909	53,216
硫酸钾	公吨	534,354	11,459	628,128	12,711
氢氧化钾	公吨	10,528	767	8,072	592
碳酸钙	公吨	69,313	2,083	98,918	2,795
电解二氧化锰	公吨	5,585	796	4,388	333
氯化镍	公吨	1,667	222	1,407	192

1998 年中国进口主要商品数量金额

金额单位:万美元

品　　名	单位	1998		1997	
		数量	金额	数量	金额
氧化镍	公吨	1,642	857	2,272	1,096
碳酸镁	公吨	1,532	158	2,312	206
氯化镁	公吨	9,074	188	1,895	42
工业氢氧化铝	公吨	2,351	166	1,968	262
氧化钴	公吨	52	137	150	291
工业硝酸铵	公吨	31,393	346	246,906	2,767
氯化铵	公吨	7,130	229	3,200	80
磷酸二氢铵	公吨	84,858	1,790	80,620	1,478
磷酸氢二铵	公吨	5,440,556	125,472	4,641,787	108,169
活性碳	公吨	1,692	328	1,517	333
硫磺	公吨	241,132	1,205	384,070	2,249
溴素	公吨	1,920	171	1,892	183
石蜡	公吨	13,046	1,032	12,899	930
石油焦	公吨	58,517	546	2,233	108
锻烧焦	公吨	6,808	377	4,202	231
沥青焦	公吨	18,850	928	21,237	1,041
石油沥青	公吨	871,601	11,126	759,859	10,234
煤焦沥青	公吨	109,660	1,578	123,830	1,888
甲醇(木精)	公吨	704,531	8,403	241,744	4,998
乙醇(酒精)	升	1,746,500	126	2,910,010	153
乙二醇	公吨	308,172	13,447	199,289	12,915
丁醇(正丁醇)	公吨	104,892	4,224	65,698	3,577
季戊四醇	公吨	1,246	148	354	43
环乙醇	公吨	1,794	139	2,935	162
甲醛	公吨	2,521	142	3,326	146
甲酸(蚁酸)	公吨	3,339	164	1,152	76
甲酸钠	公吨	21,554	408	4,743	146
苯甲酸	公吨	694	173	429	121
冰醋酸(乙酸)	公吨	135,396	4,869	95,863	5,084
己二酸	公吨	22,080	2,313	12,386	942
对苯二甲酸	公吨	728,742	26,861	478,704	28,095
丙烯酸酯	公吨	80,372	6,654	58,883	5,661
丙酮	公吨	67,149	2,595	48,978	2,024
环己酮	公吨	21,203	1,176	15,953	843
苯酚(石碳酸)	公吨	37,197	2,400	61,877	4,391
间苯二酚(雷锁辛)	公吨	2,335	473	1,665	268
二氯甲烷	公吨	35,524	1,794	32,565	1,831

1998 年中国进口主要商品数量金额

金额单位:万美元

品　　名	单位	1998		1997	
		数量	金额	数量	金额
二氯乙烷	公吨	133,793	2,300	5,736	208
三氯甲烷(氯仿)	公吨	43,687	2,541	38,751	2,746
三氯乙烷	公吨	5,211	310	6,397	355
环乙烷	公吨	1,389	110	1,155	86
乙烯	公吨	32,848	1,269	289	30
丙烯	公吨	67,469	2,063	21,888	907
丁二烯	公吨	41,141	1,039	19,549	780
苯乙烯	公吨	583,395	23,812	439,984	22,466
三氯乙烯	公吨	12,250	709	12,179	672
丙烯腈	公吨	99,031	4,891	39,559	3,041
乙二胺	公吨	5,737	840	4,918	780
双氰胺	公吨	448	113	308	100
三聚氰胺	公吨	3,763	420	3,870	469
己内酰胺	公吨	175,850	22,118	138,662	17,381
纯苯	公吨	74,414	1,593	54,829	1,602
甲苯	公吨	369,380	8,357	402,093	11,818
二甲苯(含邻间对)	公吨	204,741	5,609	401,986	16,066
粗萘(工业萘)	公吨	21,831	563	26,863	922
四氢呋喃	公吨	2,974	856	1,502	400
羧甲基纤维素	公吨	884	330	482	238
防老剂	公吨	77,261	13,174	77,687	11,626
催化剂	公吨	26,444	9,847	33,543	10,681
塑料	金额		1,045,876		1,020,026
高压聚乙烯	公吨	650,436	42,080	564,150	43,962
低压聚乙烯	公吨	1,810,737	120,744	1,718,869	132,980
聚丙烯	公吨	1,544,122	99,147	1,252,910	94,802
ABS 树脂	公吨	1,069,033	108,356	1,030,979	106,405
电木粉(酚醛树脂)	公吨	51,406	6,344	46,682	5,916
电玉粉	公吨	6,756	660	4,542	492
聚氯乙烯(树脂)	公吨	1,605,107	106,648	1,201,193	90,354
聚苯乙烯	公吨	2,603,173	230,133	2,619,656	235,113
聚四氟乙烯	公吨	8,534	2,160	7,397	2,268
环氧树脂	公吨	72,510	16,964	58,650	13,182
聚碳酸脂	公吨	108,507	19,580	82,024	14,334
醇酸树脂	公吨	31,406	3,236	33,574	3,353
塑料雨衣	公吨	42,192	1,472	2,747	1,438
各种染料	公吨	36,832	15,410	38,405	15,335

1998年中国进口主要商品数量金额

金额单位:万美元

品　　名	单位	1998		1997	
		数量	金额	数量	金额
硫化染料	公吨	717	110	1,337	189
还原染料	公吨	952	453	1,347	594
直接染料	公吨	6,498	1,900	7,200	2,043
酸性染料	公吨	4,357	2,373	3,494	2,274
盐基染料	公吨	2,058	737	2,593	1,010
活性染料	公吨	10,167	4,983	11,307	5,255
分散染料	公吨	7,452	3,285	7,433	2,751
增白粉	公吨	2,345	962	2,039	599
二甲基苯胺	公吨	293	139	474	286
苯胺	公吨	4,819	406	5,501	367
三聚氯氰	公吨	11,580	748	3,035	328
钛白粉	公吨	79,766	12,283	92,119	9,592
氧化锌	公吨	9,875	1,019	9,330	990
油漆	公吨	156,969	33,327	170,830	34,882
油墨	公吨	18,790	7,983	18,849	6,869
化肥	公吨	13,871,429	250,567	16,489,103	299,494
尿素	公吨	119,104	1,722	3,419,647	61,854
氯化钾	公吨	5,120,377	60,627	4,625,909	53,216
硝铵(硝酸铵)	公吨	31,393	346	246,906	2,767
硝酸钠	公吨	10,297	180	21,640	426
硫酸钾	公吨	534,354	11,459	628,128	12,711
农药	公吨	44,173	18,614	48,583	16,571
除草剂	公吨	24,995	11,528	23,491	9,447
杀虫剂	公吨	10,679	3,387	11,689	3,445
天然橡胶	公吨	430,079	31,928	429,877	45,760
合成橡胶	公吨	513,622	46,552	453,284	46,900
再生胶	公吨	2,898	285	3,086	294
轮胎	金额		3,546		4,314
整套轮胎	万套	321	2,050	349	2,056
轮胎内胎	万条	128	105	261	218
胶管	公吨	2,355	1,611	2,309	1,329
运输带	公吨	3,125	1,763	2,911	1,751
传动带	公吨	1,352	1,208	951	1,060
乳胶手套	万付	3,095	240	4,975	261
槐米	公吨	578	168	259	68
动物药材	金额		296		428
鲜王浆	公斤	42,386	255	91,737	305

1998年中国进口主要商品数量金额

金额单位:万美元

品　名	单位	1998		1997	
		数量	金额	数量	金额
血竭	公吨	938	109	1,101	147
槟榔	公吨	9,894	883	7,628	491
丁香	公吨	2,385	172	2,103	160
抗菌素药	公吨	2,325	20,249	2,101	9,581
磺胺药	公吨	3,706	428	6,555	464
维生素	金额		3,900		3,556
医疗器械	金额		39,567		33,322
血压表	万支	66	3,075	32	4,968
心电瞬时记录仪	台	2,169	750	659	1,097
体外反搏装置	万个		205		234
注射器	万支	2,414	153	1,693	84
注射针头	金额		467		473
畜牧专用器械	金额		880		2,590
医用敷料	金额		626		483
各类船	艘	968	12,163	1,013	25,372
客船	艘	38	931	37	2,836
客货船	艘	252	5,730	279	5,197
冷藏船	艘	3	356	3	291
挖泥船	艘	17	1,493	12	1,129
拖轮	艘	30	1,133	32	999
渔船	艘	20	634	8	112
集装箱	只	1,203	633	1,026	459
飞机	架	81	260,279	73	257,604
汽车	辆	39,375	81,512	47,779	69,074
载重汽车	辆	4,634	10,090	7,016	12,726
小轿车	辆	27,498	42,489	35,345	32,101
客车	辆	4,608	9,558	3,325	8,189
汽车底盘	金额		1,224		2,100
摩托车零件	金额		3,956		6,529
汽车零件	金额		93,499		93,249
显像管	万只	596	46,527	581	37,335
集成电路	金额		477,824		364,178
电线电缆	公吨	246,721	92,484	231,912	90,502
蓄电池	金额		37,971		29,848
铅酸蓄电池	万个	174	605	275	618
起重机械	台	38,125	23,179	39,897	27,406
金属切削机床	台	79,112	139,077	104,684	158,459

1998年中国进口主要商品数量金额

金额单位:万美元

品　　名	单位	1998		1997	
		数量	金额	数量	金额
车床	台	7,320	12,527	8,977	14,319
钻床	台	6,026	4,879	7,617	5,217
镗床	台	605	6,012	1,572	4,644
磨床	台	13,875	20,080	21,434	22,607
齿轮加工机床	台	301	2,823	360	1,888
螺纹加工机床	台	2,595	1,424	2,693	1,352
铣床	台	4,622	7,579	6,595	8,343
刨床	台	317	168	550	346
插床	台	46	107	45	505
拉床	台	231	764	74	681
铸造机械	台	2,800,022	11,504	3,148,365	16,272
木工机械	台	26,782	13,689	50,025	22,116
各种泵	金额		104,991		101,571
滚动轴承	套	376,280,681	23,192	329,088,637	23,708
纺织机械	台	4,871	12,643	1,164	11,694
印刷机械	金额		42,533		50,901
制革制鞋机械	金额		8,142		11,710
金属轧机	金额		34,283		34,800
玻璃加工机械	金额		12,516		24,405
橡胶或塑料加工机械	金额		92,601		130,156
烟草加工机械	金额		20,890		20,632
电动机及发电机	万台	73,904	58,044	70,511	55,929
发电机组	台	12,502	31,893	14,513	60,087
电动机和发电机零件	金额		61,438		58,748
有线电话电报交换机	台	1,113,176	136,582	1,098,293	20,201
有线电话电报交换机零件	金额		91,176		100,620
计算机	金额		181,010		113,452
大、中型电子计算机	台	54	3,600	34	4,341
小型电子计算机	台	780	4,609	838	3,268
微型电子计算机	台	49,513	7,584	23,354	4,683
显示器	台	1,544,810	8,182	681,077	10,056
打印机	台	934,736	23,262	306,388	7,504
键盘	个	3,185,662	1,958	3,245,685	1,686
磁盘	万片	21,481	7,968	25,053	2,263
文字处理机	金额		376		93
有线通讯设备	金额		227,758		120,822
电话机	台	871,837	16,595	939,835	2,337

1998 年中国进口主要商品数量金额

金额单位:万美元

品　　名	单位	1998		1997	
		数量	金额	数量	金额
各种电子交换机	金额		47,028		4,759
载波机	台	115,298	66,280	40,995	10,671
传真机	台	82,747	1,215	95,497	1,475
复印机	台	20,859	2,379	16,040	1,762
调制解调器	台	27,833	8,371	18,872	2,941
雷达	金额		3,068		4,434
导航设备	金额		2,314		2,244
电台对讲机	金额		213		76
电池	金额		25,122		22,529
测绘仪器	金额		12,241		11,994
望远镜	金额		1,214		942
放大镜	只	921,250	127	777,874	118
照相机	架	92,672	688	98,680	944
照机相零件	金额		47,073		48,975
彩色冲洗扩印系统	金额		185		156
自行车类	金额		13,595		12,040
自行车	辆	28,398	135	17,556	61
自行车外胎	条	2,865,455	442	3,228,343	393
自行车零配件	金额		12,970		11,448
缝纫机类	金额		15,969		23,837
缝纫机	金额		10,333		16,498
家用缝纫机	台	211,915	1,139	116,892	770
工业缝纫机	台	134,888	9,194	210,822	15,728
缝纫机零件	金额		5,635		7,338
缝纫机针	金额		117		105
电风扇	台	20,768,682	8,462	14,459,406	9,174
排风扇	台	207,345	585	148,276	742
电冰箱	台	16,398	435	17,373	551
洗衣机	台	40,710	866	34,390	732
空调器	台	5,954	235	10,506	395
吸尘器	台	69,584	376	284,482	550
空气加湿器	台	10,572	720	11,081	774
空气干燥器	台	12,453	5,267	13,653	9,014
电炉	个	80,426	309	166,144	558
电热水器	个	257,114	1,637	152,345	986
煤气热水器	台	29,208	234	45,656	280
洗碗机	台	3,704	215	2,359	211

1998年中国进口主要商品数量金额

金额单位:万美元

品　　名	单位	1998		1997	
		数量	金额	数量	金额
消毒柜	台	1,844	712	2,105	633
电熨斗	个	116,092	188	46,674	128
台灯	金额		167		95
吊灯	金额		490		778
卤钨灯	万只	1,091	721	862	755
收音机	台	167,845	182	257,629	76
录音机	金额		3,025		3,823
电视机及散件	金额		13,175		17,158
彩色电视机	台	303,434	13,041	422,583	17,016
黑白电视机	台	10,842	134	15,466	142
投影电视机	台	1,250	356	216	313
录像机	台	8,880	683	57,529	895
摄像机	台	26,216	1,626	23,186	1,685
音箱	万台	42,384	8,561	46,378	9,080
组合音响	万套	4	280	7	399
录像带	万盒	17,361	8,905	9,468	5,476
耳塞机	万个	5,410	2,181	4,413	1,273
麦克风	个	156,523,478	2,736	130,509,043	1,956
量具	金额		1,657		1,687
刃具	金额		5,381		5,313
磨具	金额		5,485		5,846
砂布	公吨	2,267	823	1,784	754
电动工具	金额		6,688		7,250
电站	个	45,024	150	67,698	427
各种锤	金额		104		113
各种钳	金额		351		358
各种扳手	金额		1,118		979
各种螺丝批	金额		175		140
各种钻	金额		167		60
各种锉和刀	金额		940		1,128
各种锯和锯条	金额		904		1,007
出版物	金额		11,130		7,653

1998年中国出口主要商品输往地

粮谷

输往地	1998		1997	
	数量(公吨)	金额(美元)	数量(公吨)	金额(美元)
总值	**8,886,399**	**1,576,182,797**	**8,331,641**	**1,316,808,315**
巴林	10	2,820		
孟加拉国	120	306,450		90
缅甸	7,703	1,729,237	490	173,728
朝鲜	404,304	75,975,715	1,021,802	192,210,982
香港	114,939	43,020,795	114,549	43,940,312
印度	11,996	2,762,493		
印度尼西亚	1,405,384	318,030,312	724,900	91,744,496
伊朗	268,745	28,213,982		
伊拉克	98,690	29,123,695	124,035	40,936,326
以色列	100	37,659	342	127,091
日本	400,353	90,532,814	313,279	68,590,444
科威特	20	4,305		
老挝	524	127,230	152	50,873
澳门	1,844	655,231	819	340,178
马来西亚	1,253,653	145,888,848	1,278,079	161,637,628
蒙古	36,255	9,400,701	72,666	20,287,451
巴基斯坦	500	241,610	178	65,831
菲律宾	1,453,734	325,110,066	410,860	69,804,113
新加坡	1,411	379,932	33,535	4,822,497
韩国	2,640,937	324,966,870	3,625,208	472,215,083
斯里兰卡	83,527	9,495,807	51,264	6,575,605
泰国	1,106	412,686	478	136,718
土耳其	41	9,532	11,540	3,515,210
阿拉伯联合酋长国	536	162,687	200	56,000
越南	72,691	11,869,221	11,045	4,024,805
台湾省	17,410	2,279,709	14,284	2,190,986
佛得角	500	230,155	1	253
吉布提	4	1,080		
赤道几内亚	3,150	709,065		
加纳	28,050	6,451,500	26,279	5,413,448
几内亚	23,625	5,315,625	12,637	2,610,896
科特迪瓦	179,941	41,706,564	99,991	20,470,931
利比亚	73,164	25,682,380	65,831	25,486,020
毛里求斯	11,420	2,948,600	115	54,790
尼日利亚	1	720		
南非	334	106,875	20	5,200

1998 年中国出口主要商品输往地

粮谷

输 往 地	1998		1997	
	数量(公吨)	金额(美元)	数量(公吨)	金额(美元)
苏丹	1	720	530	197,829
坦桑尼亚	35,824	9,253,919		
布基纳法索	19,788	4,511,561		
莱索托	200	41,286		
比利时	2,412	603,680	7,838	1,923,445
丹麦	83	32,721	91	39,239
英国	2,215	813,759	3,226	1,073,062
德国	1,101	543,404	996	501,572
法国	31	17,348	39	18,539
意大利	1,372	307,133	1,063	325,570
荷兰	13,808	3,079,466	19,366	4,372,046
葡萄牙	74	11,046	107	22,980
西班牙	9	3,040	4,019	1,034,876
奥地利	4	1,480	41	27,945
波兰	19,999	5,283,200		
罗马尼亚	3	2,775	8,050	2,044,700
哈萨克斯坦	1,052	372,299	7,224	2,646,195
吉尔吉斯斯坦	891	348,970	657	266,935
俄罗斯	25,806	8,038,117	68,849	18,905,721
塔吉克斯坦	8	1,975	900	298,320
乌兹别克斯坦	120	40,823	900	478,444
南斯拉夫	1	558		
斯洛文尼亚共和国	17,843	4,602,276		
安提瓜和巴布达	5	1,510		
阿根廷	15	6,250		
巴西	10	7,626	2	1,200
智利	26	6,530	1	1,018
哥斯达黎加		293		
古巴	145,375	33,573,108	84,625	18,219,675
巴拿马	4	2,025		
加拿大	339	154,798	300	152,464
美国	815	393,437	634	333,665
澳大利亚	206	98,745	288	130,748
新西兰	61	46,947	78	50,956
巴布亚新几内亚	180	87,001	100	36,150
其他			107,140	26,217,036

1998 年中国出口主要商品输往地

豆类

输往地	1998		1997	
	数量(公吨)	金额(美元)	数量(公吨)	金额(美元)
总值	**642,205**	**280,422,194**	**779,315**	**339,923,887**
孟加拉国	59	12,142		
缅甸	279	38,238	379	92,530
朝鲜	41,253	11,089,935	29,400	8,236,473
香港	12,199	4,475,892	10,123	4,717,180
印度	37,868	12,589,213	12,746	4,555,920
印度尼西亚	5,222	1,424,259	6,655	2,383,202
伊拉克	28,806	17,632,199	15,780	9,354,998
以色列	379	147,336	1,235	568,120
日本	217,208	113,280,047	244,236	127,809,762
约旦	726	265,071	1,368	539,460
科威特	426	173,836	557	261,865
黎巴嫩	1,221	671,631	1,284	705,060
澳门	102	38,887	116	58,007
马来西亚	8,012	2,773,431	7,911	3,312,782
尼泊尔	28	8,856	40	13,851
巴基斯坦	23,131	8,367,334	19,047	6,682,616
菲律宾	9,053	3,277,899	8,156	3,596,050
卡塔尔	20	7,450	20	7,712
沙特阿拉伯	327	91,188	268	85,658
新加坡	2,811	1,094,541	3,361	1,446,282
韩国	36,905	10,393,562	17,565	6,911,885
斯里兰卡	765	245,025		
泰国	1,342	492,122	1,329	519,865
土耳其	6,292	3,069,069	30,871	11,202,339
阿拉伯联合酋长国	848	345,017	449	226,046
也门共和国	9,273	3,318,438	8,032	2,628,186
越南	4,076	1,849,052	970	444,925
台湾省	17,728	6,873,256	13,089	6,670,204
阿尔及利亚	200	105,500	1,350	283,500
安哥拉	1,852	796,231	10,139	3,347,309
博茨瓦那		68		
刚果	145	81,550		
埃及	4,963	1,902,573	21,025	5,955,301
加纳	1	202		
利比亚	2,830	1,471,366	718	129,226
毛里求斯	424	194,485	101	40,607

1998年中国出口主要商品输往地

豆类

输往地	1998		1997	
	数量(公吨)	金额(美元)	数量(公吨)	金额(美元)
摩洛哥	298	71,489	1,185	489,777
尼日利亚		20		
南非	43,366	16,641,410	45,394	16,826,705
苏丹	61	17,622	500	138,500
突尼斯	59	26,347		
扎伊尔	223	90,141	120	48,850
比利时	18,620	7,115,019	15,811	6,763,385
丹麦	40	22,980		
英国	4,599	2,675,324	4,614	3,242,288
德国	2,132	1,064,782	904	423,672
法国	5,827	2,238,957	7,290	2,820,361
爱尔兰	20	15,539	60	48,400
意大利	19,375	9,269,806	44,381	15,125,611
荷兰	7,926	4,324,375	6,714	4,185,370
希腊	514	319,493	79	84,511
葡萄牙	5,923	2,541,324	5,244	2,340,758
西班牙	3,323	1,508,079	4,359	1,944,809
奥地利	60	47,899	40	28,000
波兰	120	72,000	218	128,784
罗马尼亚	2	1,400		
瑞典	5	2,250	20	10,400
瑞士	60	29,314	8	20,182
吉尔吉斯斯坦	33	12,859		
俄罗斯	30	15,062	256	130,282
塔吉克斯坦	600	246,042	120	47,640
土库曼斯坦	120	46,200		
乌兹别克斯坦	300	115,500	496	193,638
斯洛文尼亚共和国	21	11,361	116	56,730
阿根廷	327	188,341	189	103,950
伯利兹		180		90
巴西	17,819	4,820,072	8,057	3,376,459
智利	119	69,988	139	105,610
哥伦比亚	5,370	2,629,633	14,859	6,477,124
多米尼加共和国	420	130,200		
危地马拉	140	65,800	677	246,621
墨西哥	203	107,222	136	101,830
乌拉圭	260	171,364	284	149,240

1998年中国出口主要商品输往地

豆类

输往地	1998		1997	
	数量(公吨)	金额(美元)	数量(公吨)	金额(美元)
委内瑞拉	11,373	4,600,907		
加拿大	3,459	2,136,371	2,426	1,652,246
美国	12,116	8,250,560	8,818	6,442,089
澳大利亚	82	61,341		41
新西兰	90	50,720	37	26,586
其他			137,444	53,356,427

蔬菜

输往地	1998		1997	
	数量(公吨)	金额(美元)	数量(公吨)	金额(美元)
总值	**2,034,171**	**1,487,788,793**	**1,689,980**	**1,490,902,495**
巴林	112	76,280	70	81,660
孟加拉国	78	20,659	6	1,776
文莱	265	147,182	150	96,215
缅甸	2,654	1,060,644	1,611	823,982
柬埔寨	47	28,189	2	6,853
塞浦路斯	15	13,760	10	12,400
朝鲜	340	369,429	640	437,117
香港	456,706	107,094,111	412,606	152,744,828
印度	1	16,211	217	123,502
印度尼西亚	21,894	8,881,821	50,049	31,758,978
伊朗	40	13,000		
以色列	1,550	1,340,164	992	1,347,201
日本	850,164	918,198,624	670,011	867,670,814
约旦	176	110,277		
科威特	552	406,763	1,161	856,694
老挝	2,684	641,887	1,986	565,989
黎巴嫩	167	112,241	179	165,543
澳门	27,469	7,240,261	23,846	1,785,196
马来西亚	35,185	14,061,359	19,602	16,010,560
蒙古	11,138	1,447,617	9,078	1,060,578
尼泊尔	2,710	747,183	143	102,104
阿曼	578	413,699	582	415,981
巴基斯坦	1,219	624,910	7	8,918
菲律宾	10,960	2,939,764	1,625	2,003,854
卡塔尔	16	12,341	16	12,341

1998年中国出口主要商品输往地

蔬菜

输往地	1998		1997	
	数量(公吨)	金额(美元)	数量(公吨)	金额(美元)
沙特阿拉伯	3,652	2,163,394	2,074	1,231,145
新加坡	83,550	27,241,226	62,441	32,502,137
韩国	61,179	48,703,636	60,341	77,321,505
斯里兰卡	945	318,159	284	144,897
叙利亚	104	133,831	58	50,399
泰国	3,576	4,728,497	3,433	6,178,680
土耳其	499	652,504	1,041	1,278,193
阿拉伯联合酋长国	13,497	7,877,589	18,255	11,261,043
也门共和国	191	108,687	319	90,938
越南	24,070	4,996,480	14,683	2,649,951
台湾省	23,375	23,396,619	20,529	27,112,022
阿尔及利亚	64	114,628	1	5,304
博茨瓦那	1	783		
埃及	138	146,675		
加纳	3	1,088		425
几内亚	170	199,360		
肯尼亚	89	47,039		
利比亚	20	5,103		
马达加斯加		155		
毛里求斯	59	69,076	142	158,424
摩洛哥	80	42,500	20	79,615
纳米比亚	12	5,736		94
塞拉利昂		19		
南非	1,498	1,325,292	1,431	1,982,277
苏丹	57	17,728	61	21,362
突尼斯	14	13,630		
比利时	6,000	7,424,541	3,797	4,955,667
丹麦	546	619,489	442	521,446
英国	9,698	8,640,813	6,328	6,959,955
德国	36,257	45,084,151	26,514	35,436,089
法国	17,547	24,848,715	14,784	22,629,688
爱尔兰	64	66,824		
意大利	21,018	34,441,537	15,834	23,034,389
荷兰	45,429	33,024,290	44,395	32,584,429
希腊	246	233,315	297	376,352
葡萄牙	770	590,935	227	261,737
西班牙	4,982	4,649,356	2,928	3,167,622

1998 年中国出口主要商品输往地

蔬菜

输往地	1998		1997	
	数量(公吨)	金额(美元)	数量(公吨)	金额(美元)
奥地利	16	48,469	5	33,335
保加利亚	188	138,812	216	168,578
芬兰	263	207,843	267	266,747
匈牙利	61	50,505	17	28,590
马耳他	16	21,440	85	71,319
挪威	513	737,723	104	381,888
波兰	818	789,270	267	396,756
罗马尼亚	629	425,585	69	34,352
瑞典	1,130	1,239,805	823	750,082
瑞士	782	2,244,236	1,496	2,822,317
拉脱维亚	20	29,120	9	13,334
立陶宛	109	74,581	17	7,482
白俄罗斯	92	94,656	128	260,884
哈萨克斯坦	437	213,014	141	30,777
吉尔吉斯斯坦	23	12,500	173	97,042
俄罗斯	116,834	19,729,903	104,892	17,009,486
塔吉克斯坦		604		
乌克兰	141	82,241	68	42,418
南斯拉夫	27	23,191		
斯洛文尼亚共和国	40	29,083		
克罗地亚共和国	10	7,883		
捷克共和国	14	20,680	3	9,794
斯洛伐克共和国	2	1,069		
阿根廷	2,755	1,710,961	892	1,141,876
阿鲁巴岛	40	20,200		1,384
伯利兹	1	844	1	504
玻利维亚	1	2,109		
巴西	23,074	13,643,254	34,171	21,026,641
智利	333	245,799	140	215,518
哥伦比亚	6,645	3,553,935	3,831	2,449,893
多米尼克	508	208,280	578	406,000
哥斯达黎加	284	168,184	186	162,134
古巴	64	45,380	350	577,500
多米尼加共和国	2,237	2,893,383	180	126,000
厄瓜多尔	329	180,435		
危地马拉	123	71,250	184	134,860
圭亚那		2,247		

1998年中国出口主要商品输往地

蔬菜

输往地	1998		1997	
	数量(公吨)	金额(美元)	数量(公吨)	金额(美元)
洪都拉斯	92	47,513	29	23,203
墨西哥	163	147,437	1	519
巴拿马	178	141,210	137	137,173
秘鲁	399	244,711	2	15,852
波多黎各	112	102,135	90	127,159
苏里南	18	19,844	10	8,254
特立尼达和多巴哥	193	117,750	348	262,260
乌拉圭	169	155,664	53	66,915
委内瑞拉	249	271,148	149	198,263
加拿大	12,894	10,073,877	9,795	9,788,848
美国	68,121	71,753,526	29,818	48,332,518
澳大利亚	6,212	7,015,108	4,302	6,220,088
新西兰	672	762,911	537	707,554
巴布亚新几内亚	6	7,609	10	13,043
其他	18	8,100	159	244,486

水产品

输往地	1998		1997	
	数量	金额(美元)	数量	金额(美元)
总值		**1,736,683,979**		**1,885,477,087**
孟加拉国		1,700		1,809
文莱		9,315		36,718
柬埔寨		161		
朝鲜		15,291		233,213
香港		215,154,130		239,699,635
印度		152,107		75,044
印度尼西亚		205,601		854,848
伊朗		28,492		84,782
以色列		615,948		56,347
日本		737,104,505		895,899,736
约旦		2,180		
澳门		6,504,649		6,982,768
马来西亚		2,809,643		4,482,957
蒙古		1,700		6,391
菲律宾		320,803		1,509,275
沙特阿拉伯		186,659		

1998 年中国出口主要商品输往地

水产品

输往地	1998		1997	
	数量	金额(美元)	数量	金额(美元)
新加坡		6,717,506		8,683,546
韩国		170,754,977		253,361,825
斯里兰卡		33,770		63,108
泰国		7,068,924		5,210,895
土耳其		288,037		33,137
阿拉伯联合酋长国		29,179		5,555
越南		142,414		589,227
台湾省		38,342,973		52,387,045
留尼汪		128,071		
塞内加尔		38,880		
南非		298,388		827,924
苏丹		5		
比利时		11,246,904		18,307,854
丹麦		5,687,912		2,403,414
英国		10,626,577		9,338,662
德国		113,381,863		33,660,899
法国		20,158,201		31,356,877
意大利		2,128,419		1,235,140
卢森堡		24		75,090
荷兰		22,383,758		12,634,725
希腊		2,514,196		2,713,553
葡萄牙		4,316,648		2,317,520
西班牙		64,475,647		38,593,425
奥地利		2,061		4,059
芬兰		4,944,440		631,393
匈牙利		1,801		243,148
马耳他		27,219		
挪威		736,299		2,241,685
波兰		2,129,089		159,362
罗马尼亚		29,552		
瑞典		4,619,950		3,694,230
瑞士		176,471		17,423
立陶宛		205,511		
哈萨克斯坦		17,278		
俄罗斯		23,578,834		27,084,433
乌克兰		72		
捷克共和国		543,382		64,897

1998年中国出口主要商品输往地

水产品

输往地	1998		1997	
	数量	金额(美元)	数量	金额(美元)
斯洛伐克共和国		22,294		
阿根廷		134		6,132
玻利维亚		363		
智利		4		1,888
墨西哥		350,683		373,202
巴拿马		2,928		1,568
波多黎各		392,034		71,540
乌拉圭		320,084		
委内瑞拉		2,566		4,802
加拿大		20,744,539		15,672,584
美国		230,189,188		208,731,684
澳大利亚		2,129,836		2,157,323
斐济		59,952		41,990
新西兰		691,050		182,444
巴布亚新几内亚		889,708		
其他		500		368,356

茶叶

输往地	1998		1997	
	数量(公吨)	金额(美元)	数量(公吨)	金额(美元)
总值	**217,437**	**370,275,800**	**202,464**	**332,477,112**
阿富汗	4,414	4,964,917	7,209	8,020,580
缅甸	44	37,634	131	80,476
柬埔寨	4	30,994	14	71,001
香港	11,700	22,849,082	14,189	29,146,114
印度	542	855,630	883	1,520,680
印度尼西亚	857	908,679	1,490	1,292,690
伊朗	124	128,603	1,104	2,635,401
伊拉克	9,816	18,671,139	5,138	6,047,038
以色列	30	56,915	33	68,684
日本	20,833	48,168,992	24,051	56,324,092
澳门	265	473,658	301	546,329
马来西亚	1,203	2,610,047	1,537	2,748,716
蒙古	643	536,887	454	457,656
尼泊尔	17	55,002	39	19,029
巴基斯坦	5,369	5,813,661	9,644	13,141,714

1998 年中国出口主要商品输往地

茶叶

输往地	1998		1997	
	数量(公吨)	金额(美元)	数量(公吨)	金额(美元)
菲律宾	44	129,438	31	68,869
沙特阿拉伯	967	2,342,755	363	989,124
新加坡	2,017	4,654,683	1,891	5,061,292
韩国	213	262,754	302	548,485
斯里兰卡	534	608,030	227	361,953
叙利亚	59	65,867	585	496,145
泰国	257	529,785	258	531,235
土耳其	1	8,452	1	8,508
阿拉伯联合酋长国	5,021	7,099,820	4,841	8,946,236
也门共和国	1,164	1,411,923	847	867,717
越南	71	68,270	25	47,817
阿尔及利亚	6,308	12,861,040	606	1,064,990
贝宁	9	19,780	54	102,470
喀麦隆		240	119	80,514
乍得	42	32,487		
刚果	45	100,100		
吉布提	13	10,128	48	34,106
埃及	714	1,037,498	958	1,840,041
加蓬	35	75,241	190	473,324
冈比亚	4,177	8,490,154	3,374	7,295,121
加纳	126	291,788	17	39,000
几内亚	1,850	3,178,939	859	2,079,842
科特迪瓦	2,622	5,538,456	1,357	3,011,863
肯尼亚	550	609,447	1,169	1,034,632
利比里亚	138	238,602	12	26,160
利比亚	551	913,848	2,705	5,000,560
马里	7,069	13,466,275	2,116	4,651,992
毛里塔尼亚	998	1,802,586		
毛里求斯	3	12,333	2	6,448
摩洛哥	15,447	24,077,692	13,933	21,031,358
尼日尔	130	244,080		
尼日利亚	4,990	2,926,944	4,351	2,519,409
留尼汪	1	4,500		
塞内加尔	12,632	24,176,108	7,908	16,926,548
南非	3	6,882		
多哥	4,369	7,904,087	3,482	5,570,430
突尼斯	4,297	6,484,140	5,834	8,002,124

1998 年中国出口主要商品输往地

茶叶

输往地	1998		1997	
	数量(公吨)	金额(美元)	数量(公吨)	金额(美元)
比利时	3,728	8,277,727	1,847	3,258,412
丹麦	329	590,415	455	725,946
英国	7,590	11,932,964	8,898	11,717,627
德国	6,526	13,217,501	5,723	11,531,706
法国	15,179	29,531,051	5,170	11,496,207
爱尔兰	547	1,016,640	5	2,832
意大利	325	644,676	68	128,160
荷兰	3,564	7,689,521	2,793	5,212,034
希腊	17	24,354	9	20,805
西班牙	1,190	2,721,694	5,034	7,174,859
奥地利		1,099		
芬兰	41	104,807	34	76,142
直布罗陀	9	27,541	23	41,717
匈牙利	2	8,677	2	8,011
挪威	3	9,733	2	4,529
波兰	3,286	5,881,679	2,835	4,814,737
瑞典	10	32,518	8	22,916
瑞士	3	28,277		610
立陶宛	118	102,713	21	14,145
白俄罗斯	134	189,388		
哈萨克斯坦	1,154	1,687,165	288	405,900
吉尔吉斯斯坦	103	160,650		
俄罗斯	6,780	9,994,485	8,204	11,463,035
塔吉克斯坦	59	52,180		
土库曼斯坦	2,244	2,224,459	307	312,081
乌克兰	1,927	2,379,743	647	960,988
乌兹别克斯坦	9,872	12,052,690	15,584	19,167,059
捷克共和国	4	14,297		3,359
阿根廷	5	30,857		
阿鲁巴岛		670		
巴西	1	6,045	1	5,757

1998 年中国出口主要商品输往地

茶叶

输往地	1998		1997	
	数量(公吨)	金额(美元)	数量(公吨)	金额(美元)
智利	2	12,410	108	250,014
巴拿马	26	47,428	26	48,132
秘鲁	6	39,567	2	18,378
加拿大	468	1,148,119	591	1,580,332
美国	17,888	18,429,646	17,326	18,278,637
百慕大	10	19,850		
澳大利亚	535	1,536,421	1,084	2,018,185
新西兰	425	559,151	360	416,458
其它			331	459,889

纺织品

输往地	1998		1997	
	数量	金额(美元)	数量	金额(美元)
总值		**12,007,289,886**		**12,889,109,261**
阿富汗		1,150,843		1,895,821
巴林		9,156,695		6,415,859
孟加拉国		353,296,844		323,482,966
文莱		261,282		273,813
缅甸		67,888,240		79,813,760
柬埔寨		28,417,808		10,011,348
塞浦路斯		16,033,930		10,327,753
朝鲜		21,767,511		22,505,529
香港		4,465,875,908		5,137,702,706
印度		42,712,350		31,305,785
印度尼西亚		72,447,046		91,105,207
伊朗		10,394,777		6,966,224
伊拉克		1,219,155		
以色列		33,297,025		17,906,325
日本		1,284,641,157		1,481,775,189
约旦		14,024,295		10,781,073

1998年中国出口主要商品输往地

纺织品

输往地	1998		1997	
	数量	金额(美元)	数量	金额(美元)
科威特		12,708,247		11,586,461
老挝		2,174,780		2,766,885
黎巴嫩		14,291,712		18,444,333
澳门		118,982,665		107,080,359
马来西亚		81,172,812		100,650,018
马尔代夫		278,693		124,438
蒙古		7,595,443		6,153,217
尼泊尔		19,537,308		12,328,501
阿曼		7,001,390		8,730,678
巴基斯坦		8,476,433		8,073,264
巴勒斯坦		259,480		118,899
菲律宾		121,227,092		110,949,228
卡塔尔		5,078,932		6,211,867
沙特阿拉伯		72,261,140		86,300,849
新加坡		203,583,103		305,968,823
韩国		740,399,525		992,317,792
斯里兰卡		115,787,288		98,697,873
叙利亚		15,787,193		13,844,544
泰国		124,198,527		124,434,455
土耳其		107,419,423		130,230,787
阿拉伯联合酋长国		173,040,593		162,528,746
也门共和国		6,109,276		4,347,589
越南		122,497,242		142,210,962
台湾省		72,807,130		76,727,780
阿尔及利亚		16,244,500		10,302,004
安哥拉		4,176,968		3,610,107
贝宁		89,017,635		63,718,665
博茨瓦那		52,897		69,158
布隆迪		143,230		63,610
喀麦隆		2,014,475		1,207,460
加那利群岛		8,853,672		6,704,733
佛得角		73,844		26,583
中非共和国		53,600		105,000
塞卜泰(休达)		453,785		357,431
乍得		4,834		158,016
刚果		3,353,887		6,435,770
吉布提		3,081,007		1,032,026

1998 年中国出口主要商品输往地

纺织品

输往地	1998		1997	
	数量	金额(美元)	数量	金额(美元)
埃及		40,880,190		41,925,754
赤道几内亚		28,675		2,249
埃塞俄比亚		4,846,978		6,146,884
加蓬		383,776		746,311
冈比亚		30,796,923		26,849,201
加纳		19,537,217		16,621,848
几内亚		1,975,458		2,525,112
几内亚(比绍)		170,552		81,526
科特迪瓦		35,174,032		20,317,557
肯尼亚		21,944,390		32,870,086
利比里亚		413,497		865,907
利比亚		12,919,954		12,337,386
马达加斯加		12,398,951		12,606,639
马拉维		453,402		531,959
马里		3,101,640		2,898,205
毛里塔尼亚		2,423,065		1,840,048
毛里求斯		36,426,714		23,106,377
摩洛哥		17,435,110		7,661,867
莫桑比克		1,766,530		880,788
纳米比亚		467,568		308,700
尼日尔		3,849,509		781,489
尼日利亚		13,325,471		9,950,381
留尼汪		126,748		141,208
卢旺达		112,122		1,639
塞内加尔		5,848,643		5,147,980
塞舌尔		43,368		87,484
塞拉利昂		609,303		167,034
南非		78,728,926		80,762,444
苏丹		4,988,662		4,419,667
坦桑尼亚		10,874,890		8,854,091
多哥		19,565,853		27,883,948
突尼斯		7,618,174		6,099,293
乌干达		281,478		999,443
扎伊尔		6,412,007		15,900,318
赞比亚		1,315,445		2,115,946
津巴布韦		5,081,902		7,616,315
莱索托		1,792,127		835,835

1998年中国出口主要商品输往地

纺织品

输往地	1998		1997	
	数量	金额(美元)	数量	金额(美元)
梅利利亚		190,479		78,671
斯威士兰		1,468,421		
比利时		98,553,883		114,202,888
丹麦		12,369,849		12,074,535
英国		127,111,922		122,966,784
德国		256,617,190		212,224,505
法国		108,771,835		80,821,314
爱尔兰		1,238,651		1,937,692
意大利		174,366,932		155,165,980
卢森堡		128,310		78,968
荷兰		58,581,692		55,973,079
希腊		24,656,685		20,570,758
葡萄牙		15,177,390		15,089,499
西班牙		50,454,765		38,472,418
阿尔巴尼亚		2,896,887		2,813,061
安道尔		55,812		53,298
奥地利		6,455,117		4,431,287
保加利亚		779,237		508,120
芬兰		3,698,028		3,346,169
直布罗陀		1,005,333		1,554,688
匈牙利		28,705,259		19,909,719
冰岛		1,331,068		680,360
马耳他		2,937,020		2,602,948
摩纳哥		64,608		6,254
挪威		12,424,921		11,179,951
波兰		34,582,973		31,003,559
罗马尼亚		28,750,084		16,920,377
瑞典		11,420,030		10,044,894
瑞士		9,890,945		8,637,247
爱沙尼亚		229,980		100,706
拉脱维亚		3,390,284		482,106
立陶宛		1,786,378		1,494,637
格鲁吉亚		29,303		13,500
亚美尼亚		200,690		1,531
阿塞拜疆		204,165		498,120
哈萨克斯坦		21,384,240		3,159,778
吉尔吉斯斯坦		47,625,058		38,891,978

1998年中国出口主要商品输往地

纺织品

输往地	1998		1997	
	数量	金额(美元)	数量	金额(美元)
俄罗斯		83,825,507		121,659,028
塔吉克斯坦		2,729,870		1,651,855
土库曼斯坦		106,519		1,027
乌克兰		12,163,424		10,460,171
乌兹别克斯坦		2,294,880		2,264,619
南斯拉夫		2,318,070		1,700,133
斯洛文尼亚共和国		1,958,652		1,257,931
克罗地亚共和国		951,722		1,103,952
捷克共和国		7,445,852		3,816,893
斯洛伐克共和国		1,007,882		927,671
马其顿共和国		878,492		318,564
安提瓜和巴布达		168,267		975
阿根廷		35,957,510		27,508,414
阿鲁巴岛		50,240		167,964
巴哈马		37,630		38,400
巴巴多斯		527,081		353,419
伯利兹		25,666		58,133
玻利维亚		585,001		78,132
巴西		46,997,789		50,653,482
开曼群岛		4,656		
智利		60,801,393		64,604,229
哥伦比亚		2,979,271		1,925,147
多米尼克		20,434,872		19,466,039
哥斯达黎加		10,170,035		5,736,589
古巴		7,782,093		8,612,064
库腊索岛		1,281,592		2,131,209
多米尼加共和国		35,519,222		23,406,426
厄瓜多尔		3,734,363		3,760,808
危地马拉		40,838,355		33,321,668
圭亚那		941,295		683,216
海地		4,184,906		3,479,806
洪都拉斯		40,970,359		26,270,337
牙买加		20,378,296		13,098,985
墨西哥		29,091,675		17,718,650
尼加拉瓜		13,674,683		11,179,310
巴拿马		102,979,377		128,833,408
巴拉圭		4,421,663		3,709,052

1998年中国出口主要商品输往地

纺织品

输往地	1998		1997	
	数量	金额(美元)	数量	金额(美元)
秘鲁		7,332,553		5,936,316
波多黎各		491,993		942,667
圣卢西亚		3,928		12,414
圣马丁岛		154,402		
圣文森特和格林纳丁斯		44,311		34,928
萨尔瓦多		25,514,830		20,728,173
苏里南		1,238,469		798,049
特立尼达和多巴哥		3,734,254		2,895,376
乌拉圭		5,165,898		4,529,178
委内瑞拉		9,830,162		10,344,255
加拿大		117,987,285		113,581,154
美国		751,354,774		689,278,215
百慕大		13,639		2,052
澳大利亚		188,938,270		174,647,924
库克群岛		3,406		
斐济		5,677,474		7,048,680
瑙鲁		2,055		
新喀里多尼亚		278,419		586,637
瓦努阿图		55,414		68,615
新西兰		28,729,318		32,397,948
巴布亚新几内亚		2,320,773		2,826,221
社会群岛		620,593		619,061
所罗门群岛		77,629		117,001
汤加		2,708		1,952
萨摩亚		32,855		33,717
基里巴斯		69,619		3,038
图瓦卢		53,840		
密克罗尼西亚联邦		33,393		200,678
马绍尔群岛共和国		7,666		13,549
贝劳共和国		278		30,435
其他		862,228		1,704,755

1998年中国出口主要商品输往地

棉纱线

输往地	1998		1997	
	数量(件)	金额(美元)	数量(件)	金额(美元)
总值	**735,159**	**420,864,608**	**843,551**	**484,571,712**
孟加拉国	370	219,732	749	402,800
缅甸	26,750	14,090,875	19,710	11,753,409
柬埔寨	77	23,615	11	6,336
朝鲜	613	263,157	615	318,943
香港	588,526	336,554,956	663,666	372,677,687
印度	918	408,553		
印度尼西亚	49	41,325	328	270,056
伊朗	201	171,035		
以色列	39	34,257	288	302,488
日本	56,576	32,971,682	82,943	52,849,997
科威特	15	20,802	21	30,585
老挝	1	2,148	2	819
黎巴嫩	91	40,588	30	25,907
澳门	4,496	1,668,645	893	491,589
马来西亚	3,422	2,212,653	3,447	2,355,413
蒙古	590	346,660	1,076	628,849
尼泊尔	33	14,460		
阿曼	12	17,300	26	36,833
巴基斯坦	14	21,173	38	18,628
菲律宾	2,190	1,137,477	4,128	2,184,179
卡塔尔	2	2,799		
沙特阿拉伯	9	3,730	1	1,060
新加坡	1,049	594,034	5,190	3,145,226
韩国	28,129	16,838,672	31,865	19,133,480
斯里兰卡	396	358,207	385	311,434
叙利亚	151	178,169	80	40,268
泰国	3,375	1,701,093	6,319	3,889,642
土耳其	110	44,000	88	86,687
阿拉伯联合酋长国	281	274,452	259	292,068
也门共和国	80	92,127	26	31,641
越南	11	16,532	516	235,037
台湾省	54	34,475	1,453	846,017
贝宁	302	181,361	36	38,911
喀麦隆	111	46,200		
刚果	49	33,850	111	74,424
加蓬	1	288		

1998 年中国出口主要商品输往地

棉纱线

输 往 地	1998		1997	
	数量(件)	金额(美元)	数量(件)	金额(美元)
加纳	225	116,476	213	148,377
几内亚	63	33,978		
科特迪瓦	694	415,609	387	282,518
肯尼亚	4	7,648		
利比亚	2,931	2,078,290	550	413,280
马达加斯加	43	29,707	32	49,875
毛里求斯	73	102,051	147	155,775
尼日利亚	1,272	820,114	665	511,219
留尼汪	2	2,756	2	2,641
塞内加尔	9	10,119	56	38,640
南非	61	44,040	8	11,350
苏丹	72	65,550	30	39,784
坦桑尼亚	111	46,549	49	40,320
多哥	104	69,807		
突尼斯	1,836	979,855	703	402,052
扎伊尔	167	107,542	300	229,568
比利时	150	70,400	1,054	682,617
丹麦	2	2,195		
英国	33	48,252	8	16,892
德国	244	237,195	450	322,838
法国	8	12,483	7	11,343
意大利	65	68,355	84	64,602
荷兰	14	17,017		
西班牙	2,620	1,020,311	2,086	716,208
阿尔巴尼亚		10		
保加利亚		1		
芬兰	2	3,378	4	6,541
匈牙利	2	1,296	91	54,904
冰岛	122	75,019	83	56,166
马耳他		75		
波兰	10	3,233	11	17,860
瑞典	2	3,420	2	5,760
瑞士		35		
哈萨克斯坦	4	3,925		
捷克共和国	18	3,564		
巴西	22	11,362	45	63,252
智利	132	171,591	682	479,660

1998年中国出口主要商品输往地

棉纱线

输往地	1998		1997	
	数量(件)	金额(美元)	数量(件)	金额(美元)
古巴	193	121,890		
厄瓜多尔	86	100,644	156	203,002
危地马拉	75	127,269	42	73,690
圭亚那	33	45,942		
海地	10	13,594		
洪都拉斯	22	37,051	13	22,045
牙买加	19	13,846		
巴拿马	11	14,327		
秘鲁		30		
苏里南	42	59,782	12	18,886
特立尼达和多巴哥	12	20,347	2	3,800
加拿大	201	236,273	256	319,471
美国	2,150	1,623,201	8,249	4,819,401
澳大利亚	1,667	767,808	997	474,040
斐济	423	327,636	1,050	899,583
新西兰	7	10,678	133	88,774
其他			595	344,555

棉布

输往地	1998		1997	
	数量(万米)	金额(美元)	数量(万米)	金额(美元)
总值	**221,206**	**2,132,250,017**	**234,976**	**2,346,024,846**
阿富汗	10	126,569		
巴林	428	6,191,061	185	3,276,484
孟加拉国	10,533	123,715,516	9,829	125,129,914
缅甸	751	5,859,123	958	7,385,027
柬埔寨	591	8,112,124	197	2,359,569
塞浦路斯	232	2,319,264	47	651,342
朝鲜	102	569,886	146	904,508
香港	99,619	1,073,469,129	106,895	1,199,161,901
印度	661	9,618,296	275	3,755,133
印度尼西亚	1,650	20,247,182	1,527	17,992,343
伊朗	9	180,904	21	272,113
以色列	205	2,933,136	108	1,761,111
日本	17,172	102,835,584	22,408	157,117,768
约旦	168	2,030,807	57	388,376

1998 年中国出口主要商品输往地

棉布

输往地	1998		1997	
	数量(万米)	金额(美元)	数量(万米)	金额(美元)
科威特	356	3,120,433	196	1,721,189
老挝	29	353,713	57	630,320
黎巴嫩	80	1,246,100	127	1,824,597
澳门	1,638	26,270,536	1,628	23,718,700
马来西亚	1,848	19,597,587	2,631	26,838,517
蒙古	192	2,425,765	138	1,657,591
尼泊尔	143	1,336,895	58	725,391
阿曼	198	2,472,978	280	3,673,040
巴基斯坦	68	768,511	78	1,216,542
菲律宾	2,387	26,059,377	2,206	21,833,601
卡塔尔	271	3,272,382	326	4,413,472
沙特阿拉伯	190	1,431,411	238	2,190,132
新加坡	6,332	40,557,860	10,202	70,048,313
韩国	14,954	84,235,999	9,230	68,152,953
斯里兰卡	2,252	24,254,846	1,776	23,676,651
叙利亚	3	66,751	8	110,617
泰国	1,516	13,421,848	1,718	15,120,052
土耳其	1,041	9,607,063	1,874	19,613,605
阿拉伯联合酋长国	1,121	12,669,520	1,082	13,235,069
越南	1,287	13,405,829	988	12,912,760
台湾省	221	2,340,775	332	3,471,449
阿尔及利亚	13	147,538	21	294,791
安哥拉	392	2,460,037	378	2,463,864
贝宁	3,618	39,865,598	1,689	19,787,663
布隆迪	11	109,060		
喀麦隆	68	356,779	29	184,977
加那利群岛	26	225,942	170	778,516
刚果	152	875,537	773	4,860,821
埃及	1,290	15,598,156	1,273	17,410,500
埃塞俄比亚	1	34,266	2	55,040
加蓬	4	69,030	48	359,380
冈比亚	1,962	15,055,497	2,319	16,835,678
加纳	1,321	8,372,633	801	6,977,244
几内亚	62	447,070	185	1,229,083
科特迪瓦	1,970	15,485,838	1,541	12,508,590
肯尼亚	1,244	8,509,640	2,729	20,005,329
利比里亚	11	58,200	105	690,720

1998 年中国出口主要商品输往地

棉布

输往地	1998		1997	
	数量(万米)	金额(美元)	数量(万米)	金额(美元)
利比亚	50	348,024	261	2,327,609
马达加斯加	70	1,167,719	62	980,363
马里	362	2,079,223	401	2,272,392
毛里塔尼亚	103	402,782	186	788,802
毛里求斯	977	24,523,171	766	15,915,142
摩洛哥	111	1,785,114	9	235,060
莫桑比克	18	186,233		
纳米比亚	18	103,581		
尼日尔	557	3,440,065	26	129,374
尼日利亚	156	1,577,951	218	3,027,648
塞内加尔	241	1,650,153	290	2,247,935
塞拉利昂	68	461,776	18	126,536
南非	639	6,677,629	982	10,790,420
苏丹	24	223,008	36	294,730
坦桑尼亚	608	3,759,700	723	4,756,987
多哥	626	5,050,695	1,757	12,910,714
突尼斯	78	601,024	84	958,550
扎伊尔	88	586,813	1,356	8,865,177
赞比亚	67	370,721	186	1,270,227
津巴布韦	193	1,866,623	321	3,092,260
莱索托	26	466,163	10	202,897
比利时	2,511	24,436,049	2,976	29,287,570
丹麦	80	846,405	142	1,217,378
英国	1,549	13,705,329	2,192	19,985,925
德国	883	7,551,457	891	7,966,779
法国	895	9,014,193	1,181	10,629,414
爱尔兰	1	11,272	12	193,083
意大利	1,018	10,684,949	647	6,663,570
荷兰	493	4,313,026	707	5,925,995
希腊	54	520,156	57	468,180
葡萄牙	51	792,048	20	146,503
西班牙	336	2,959,754	367	3,065,624
阿尔巴尼亚	31	277,683	33	291,259
奥地利	80	581,782	43	350,007
芬兰	3	30,683	7	60,720
匈牙利	23	434,831	19	264,898
冰岛		2,431	18	108,005

1998 年中国出口主要商品输往地

棉布

输往地	1998		1997	
	数量(万米)	金额(美元)	数量(万米)	金额(美元)
马耳他	80	701,509	5	52,373
摩纳哥	2	32,746		
挪威	586	3,765,371	595	4,022,477
波兰	29	316,947	56	787,778
罗马尼亚	10	66,732	3	21,634
瑞典	36	283,376	59	566,084
瑞士	64	588,430	24	278,800
爱沙尼亚	3	22,704	3	40,172
拉脱维亚		4,590		
立陶宛	10	241,317	10	250,950
亚美尼亚	2	18,722		766
俄罗斯	51	660,577	19	374,572
乌克兰	425	4,535,141	207	2,228,862
南斯拉夫	25	349,669	9	169,383
斯洛文尼亚共和国	39	433,089	20	247,617
克罗地亚共和国	10	78,108	15	188,921
捷克共和国	2	48,598	20	164,113
斯洛伐克共和国	6	60,664		
马其顿共和国	42	536,395	34	318,564
阿根廷	79	691,056	151	1,933,194
玻利维亚	5	64,561	3	30,555
巴西	1,652	10,485,726	2,115	13,407,988
智利	254	3,167,009	256	3,607,153
哥伦比亚	21	309,744	24	370,623
多米尼克	307	3,621,008	506	5,756,831
哥斯达黎加	106	936,926	37	385,612
古巴	235	1,680,754	197	1,569,611
多米尼加共和国	852	9,602,730	494	5,649,932
厄瓜多尔	10	143,547	3	44,038
危地马拉	1,408	16,741,299	1,217	15,041,494
圭亚那	15	52,592	17	119,987
海地	71	717,074	119	1,578,653
洪都拉斯	1,585	17,575,602	909	9,732,681
牙买加	351	8,056,037	260	4,926,671
墨西哥	294	3,177,765	80	1,189,030
尼加拉瓜	837	10,641,153	838	9,370,533
巴拿马	243	2,925,351	232	2,624,355

1998 年中国出口主要商品输往地

棉布

输往地	1998		1997	
	数量(万米)	金额(美元)	数量(万米)	金额(美元)
巴拉圭	27	291,232	33	431,253
秘鲁	12	193,115	14	237,291
波多黎各	18	150,000	65	573,964
萨尔瓦多	689	8,506,065	528	7,130,843
苏里南	73	492,491	33	215,273
特立尼达和多巴哥	33	339,972	27	317,114
乌拉圭	12	98,260	38	352,164
委内瑞拉	97	1,569,295	134	1,794,184
加拿大	1,224	12,504,775	1,468	15,597,340
美国	11,908	77,158,344	14,235	104,948,959
澳大利亚	3,394	35,616,393	2,243	22,528,262
斐济	180	1,075,048	236	1,478,482
新喀里多尼亚	1	4,290	3	15,543
瓦努阿图	2	10,243		
新西兰	160	2,022,717	227	2,443,639
巴布亚新几内亚	118	528,865	183	911,541
社会群岛	1	7,816	11	66,322
基里巴斯		6,040		
其他	12	54,640	74	730,586

绸缎

输往地	1998		1997	
	数量(万米)	金额(美元)	数量(万米)	金额(美元)
总值	**12,110**	**382,676,024**	**15,310**	**479,746,837**
阿富汗		13,134		
孟加拉国	1	28,890		2,750
文莱		8,207	1	51,566
塞浦路斯	2	132,041	2	90,567
香港	4,784	163,828,301	6,978	229,103,120
印度	314	7,345,776	465	10,940,859
印度尼西亚	2	98,738	4	168,212
以色列	9	285,946	6	80,258
日本	1,142	26,482,756	1,203	33,164,276
约旦	1	5,006	4	47,429
科威特	2	51,217	3	83,909
黎巴嫩	1	24,350	2	43,910

1998年中国出口主要商品输往地

绸缎

输往地	1998		1997	
	数量(万米)	金额(美元)	数量(万米)	金额(美元)
澳门	3	98,488	3	97,941
马来西亚	62	1,535,555	193	5,022,997
尼泊尔	306	6,594,356	187	4,833,425
巴基斯坦	1	13,750	18	99,488
菲律宾	20	353,637	13	351,750
沙特阿拉伯	225	4,172,322	183	2,935,821
新加坡	108	2,806,371	484	13,695,499
韩国	2,473	79,293,135	2,898	92,662,305
斯里兰卡		3,600	2	119,089
叙利亚	2	50,838	1	48,179
泰国	2	67,547		32,485
土耳其	28	784,249	57	1,747,034
阿拉伯联合酋长国	119	3,178,927	123	2,965,374
越南	2	70,859	2	77,232
台湾省	8	325,493	4	114,623
塞卜泰(休达)	5	203,696		
埃及	1	36,903	26	1,058,439
肯尼亚		5,145		
摩洛哥	143	2,813,263	68	1,556,460
南非	1	22,665	2	58,523
突尼斯	9	128,351	11	206,034
丹麦	8	324,929	5	262,614
英国	75	2,739,488	77	2,779,962
德国	265	7,958,085	294	9,110,230
法国	168	4,467,528	148	4,101,068
爱尔兰	1	21,173	1	16,946
意大利	772	25,428,123	1,113	35,811,615
荷兰	12	301,794	18	623,581
希腊	7	217,946	3	130,141
西班牙	13	281,562	9	231,723
奥地利	4	100,389	3	89,571
芬兰	2	64,382	4	150,427
匈牙利		59,341		
波兰	35	771,354	31	672,630
罗马尼亚	4	32,515		26,902
瑞典	2	83,544	2	39,900
瑞士	69	1,825,186	139	3,861,984
哈萨克斯坦	7	151,800		

1998年中国出口主要商品输往地

绸缎

输往地	1998		1997	
	数量(万米)	金额(美元)	数量(万米)	金额(美元)
吉尔吉斯斯坦	476	20,895,013	185	8,238,944
俄罗斯	1	58,441	1	47,203
乌克兰	2	106,395		
乌兹别克斯坦	1	38,640		5,611
南斯拉夫	2	94,574	2	85,419
斯洛文尼亚共和国	2	74,733	1	11,177
克罗地亚共和国		6,061		
斯洛伐克共和国		90		
阿根廷		17,361		2,675
巴西	1	44,638	2	74,719
智利	1	13,234		
多米尼克		390		
墨西哥	1	15,829	10	303,200
巴拿马	1	18,590		
加拿大	6	235,032	13	394,152
美国	370	14,529,697	274	10,051,245
澳大利亚	21	691,310	18	599,347
新西兰	6	143,345	6	137,587
其他			10	417,710

服装

输往地	1998		1997	
	数量	金额(美元)	数量	金额(美元)
总值		**30,057,203,416**		**31,753,677,284**
阿富汗		90,113		429,473
巴林		2,867,265		2,596,942
孟加拉国		9,322,266		9,168,923
不丹		5,206		88,713
文莱		101,811		129,782
缅甸		1,408,726		2,563,602
柬埔寨		13,930,484		5,642,810
塞浦路斯		3,873,746		2,945,774
朝鲜		1,841,249		4,285,478
香港		9,302,036,225		11,600,238,817
印度		36,286,317		1,028,761

1998年中国出口主要商品输往地

服装

输往地	1998		1997	
	数量	金额(美元)	数量	金额(美元)
印度尼西亚		4,371,386		7,615,847
伊朗		1,796,868		447,367
以色列		22,659,757		13,330,201
日本		7,447,414,477		7,725,021,413
约旦		14,824,084		11,730,024
科威特		35,808,283		24,988,948
老挝		21,588		335,515
黎巴嫩		18,092,846		10,651,791
澳门		237,902,164		211,541,811
马来西亚		36,342,783		29,805,741
马尔代夫		46,899		
蒙古		1,134,079		2,180,405
尼泊尔		2,951,420		1,501,457
阿曼		955,591		506,951
巴基斯坦		1,621,664		3,772,336
巴勒斯坦		83,368		69,779
菲律宾		13,726,531		17,019,507
卡塔尔		815,733		361,487
沙特阿拉伯		292,319,448		239,820,339
新加坡		243,826,729		226,145,461
韩国		516,616,682		737,386,601
斯里兰卡		6,219,515		4,444,658
叙利亚		660,400		1,460,594
泰国		16,408,676		33,064,852
土耳其		9,286,789		8,205,335
阿拉伯联合酋长国		176,057,250		166,122,988
也门共和国		8,511,093		9,042,116
越南		157,509,822		143,719,318
台湾省		192,316,632		172,224,064
阿尔及利亚		12,672,509		4,272,207
安哥拉		9,096,754		2,322,541
贝宁		2,304,051		2,550,059
博茨瓦那		1,260,394		158,977
布隆迪		24,665		
喀麦隆		1,055,646		1,396,970

1998年中国出口主要商品输往地

服装

输往地	1998		1997	
	数量	金额(美元)	数量	金额(美元)
加那利群岛		5,897,561		7,416,444
佛得角		85,920		33,730
中非共和国		386,014		174,556
塞卜泰(休达)		453,349		316,634
乍得		39,790		
刚果		27,680,530		144,007
吉布提		4,142,066		2,427,244
埃及		110,806,901		86,821,623
赤道几内亚		7,049		16,253
埃塞俄比亚		3,402,440		2,518,584
加蓬		122,892		9,231
冈比亚		207,622		296
加纳		1,678,618		2,726,492
几内亚		5,246,427		1,612,678
几内亚(比绍)		28,909		16,865
科特迪瓦		1,096,535		1,093,334
肯尼亚		13,896,814		6,353,224
利比里亚		254,856		112,351
利比亚		13,154,868		18,133,906
马达加斯加		1,150,475		1,003,686
马拉维		11,100		12,114
马里		385,865		
毛里塔尼亚		405,553		1,053,535
毛里求斯		575,696		627,202
摩洛哥		16,902,959		15,001,398
莫桑比克		795,649		67,945
纳米比亚		484,009		540,779
尼日尔		55,209		198,934
尼日利亚		5,475,206		1,951,750
留尼汪		79,058		52,491
卢旺达		432,733		654,951
塞内加尔		118,648		66,635
塞舌尔		48,391		12,633
塞拉利昂		13,003		3,651
南非		108,330,814		101,646,570
西撒哈拉		3,175		
苏丹		1,520,525		1,160,731

1998 年中国出口主要商品输往地

服装

输 往 地	1998		1997	
	数量	金额(美元)	数量	金额(美元)
坦桑尼亚		360,301		390,731
多哥		6,238,368		7,799,955
突尼斯		5,547,248		5,447,362
乌干达		263,207		342,188
扎伊尔		8,610,999		900,016
赞比亚		14,974,094		112,232
津巴布韦		223,286		604,601
莱索托		123,302		
梅利利亚		563,700		420,476
斯威士兰		30,206		66,458
比利时		102,357,076		94,631,433
丹麦		109,720,765		103,428,188
英国		399,684,412		375,077,489
德国		908,867,889		953,816,794
法国		334,115,011		286,329,604
爱尔兰		14,597,446		9,285,355
意大利		375,649,828		339,596,525
卢森堡		10,132,628		7,575,533
荷兰		271,773,452		253,636,625
希腊		22,715,158		17,976,851
葡萄牙		11,798,966		10,803,073
西班牙		159,631,025		137,108,809
阿尔巴尼亚		2,860,932		643,811
安道尔		761,644		1,276,525
奥地利		42,209,949		40,866,649
保加利亚		11,705,222		6,882,361
芬兰		72,659,623		61,319,679
直布罗陀		18,988		260,991
匈牙利		164,910,739		131,012,746
冰岛		1,305,392		1,012,336
马耳他		8,897,898		2,369,147
摩纳哥		271,491		51,130
挪威		104,203,970		91,298,181
波兰		313,440,423		314,750,998
罗马尼亚		61,344,793		33,149,345
瑞典		152,372,567		155,460,846
瑞士		218,195,933		184,734,701

1998 年中国出口主要商品输往地

服装

输 往 地	1998		1997	
	数量	金额(美元)	数量	金额(美元)
爱沙尼亚		2,849,937		4,546,880
拉脱维亚		1,928,695		1,356,194
立陶宛		10,009,037		5,612,193
格鲁吉亚		147,491		23,516
亚美尼亚		435,915		268,662
阿塞拜疆		76,318		113,442
白俄罗斯		169,623		3,943,533
哈萨克斯坦		44,797,545		3,300,094
吉尔吉斯斯坦		30,839,539		5,120,669
摩尔多瓦		57,397		117,675
俄罗斯		888,539,868		879,213,117
土库曼斯坦		621,966		447,885
乌克兰		16,849,562		23,781,235
乌兹别克斯坦		3,230,783		3,306,556
南斯拉夫		7,850,448		3,696,356
斯洛文尼亚共和国		10,658,791		5,754,133
克罗地亚共和国		9,218,182		4,856,990
捷克共和国		132,970,658		109,619,091
斯洛伐克共和国		14,395,206		15,313,630
马其顿共和国		662,129		59,611
波斯尼亚—黑塞哥维那		39,318		114
安提瓜和巴布达		32,479		
阿根廷		54,161,309		42,236,380
阿鲁巴岛		770,739		555,150
巴哈马		1,678,350		1,988,975
巴巴多斯		34,200		11,825
伯利兹		9,253		9,718
玻利维亚		151,079		13,326
巴西		153,459,393		165,177,504
开曼群岛		826		6,532
智利		175,957,396		145,631,215
哥伦比亚		2,644,024		1,651,817
多米尼克		1,431,725		1,092,594
哥斯达黎加		692,211		196,730
古巴		8,710,761		3,433,470
库腊索岛		6,395,713		4,051,450
多米尼加共和国		4,832,792		2,508,327

1998年中国出口主要商品输往地

服装

输往地	1998		1997	
	数量	金额(美元)	数量	金额(美元)
厄瓜多尔		7,882,001		950,597
法属圭亚那		33,675		6,331
格林纳达		84,250		
危地马拉		13,109,947		8,632,931
圭亚那		267,629		577,517
海地		46,790		102,473
洪都拉斯		963,754		864,770
牙买加		11,117,904		6,306,912
马提尼克		4,617		14,429
墨西哥		43,457,695		40,693,213
尼加拉瓜		2,195,473		187,658
巴拿马		417,125,700		351,679,101
巴拉圭		4,622,981		5,972,207
秘鲁		7,030,771		4,472,554
波多黎各		363,653		539,476
圣卢西亚		29,100		4,586
圣马丁岛		173,130		
萨尔瓦多		1,526,741		2,053,228
苏里南		290,846		200,603
特立尼达和多巴哥		709,066		231,693
特克斯和凯科斯群岛		3,944		
乌拉圭		15,431,360		10,032,378
委内瑞拉		21,950,715		9,656,343
加拿大		365,760,385		320,173,252
美国		3,747,916,055		3,591,853,300
格陵兰		50,097		43,989
百慕大		552,299		803,812
澳大利亚		611,986,685		532,198,386
库克群岛		77,518		25,474
斐济		2,096,738		936,382
盖比群岛		2,326		39,717
马克萨斯群岛		3,123		
新喀里多尼亚		290,085		217,677
瓦努阿图		37,711		14,958
新西兰		92,982,444		94,369,495
诺福克岛		45,197		
巴布亚新几内亚		1,973,224		2,424,458

1998年中国出口主要商品输往地

服装

输往地	1998		1997	
	数量	金额(美元)	数量	金额(美元)
社会群岛		27,259		22,566
所罗门群岛		53,263		46,525
汤加		11,316		10,290
萨摩亚		45,020		83,239
图瓦卢		21,250		
马绍尔群岛共和国		4,436		7,330
贝劳共和国		10,080		
其他		529,361		1,451,909

日用瓷

输往地	1998		1997	
	数量	金额(美元)	数量	金额(美元)
总值		**665,500,783**		**678,487,487**
阿富汗		72,675		591,194
巴林		454,341		291,143
孟加拉国		644,217		674,836
文莱		7,122		147,365
缅甸		832,902		1,000,209
柬埔寨		1,314,649		1,968,570
塞浦路斯		1,773,817		1,707,440
朝鲜		4,138		13,541
香港		25,541,369		27,514,645
印度		199,202		248,930
印度尼西亚		1,447,003		9,526,639
伊朗		581,071		2,638,463
以色列		14,112,125		10,246,703
日本		9,141,753		9,397,095
约旦		6,432,068		4,379,994
科威特		2,374,631		1,626,424
老挝		37,490		37,693
黎巴嫩		14,542,817		12,070,652
澳门		109,520		379,562
马来西亚		3,184,995		6,383,447
马尔代夫		35		
蒙古		2,626		54,924

1998年中国出口主要商品输往地

日用瓷

输往地	1998		1997	
	数量	金额(美元)	数量	金额(美元)
尼泊尔		69,840		101,350
阿曼		92,355		151,215
巴基斯坦		3,142,803		4,535,754
巴勒斯坦		25,754		46,575
菲律宾		6,606,156		15,620,644
卡塔尔		90,729		156,705
沙特阿拉伯		11,307,148		11,237,752
新加坡		4,589,386		5,274,976
韩国		1,216,242		3,090,603
斯里兰卡		2,928,579		609,475
叙利亚		60,958		22,418
泰国		497,706		2,002,240
土耳其		11,165,902		10,346,988
阿拉伯联合酋长国		27,768,498		24,173,600
也门共和国		511,114		426,851
越南		1,736,575		3,884,119
台湾省		1,358,234		1,000,961
阿尔及利亚		7,727,959		6,433,695
安哥拉		238,908		318,408
贝宁		75		25,896
喀麦隆		902,806		524,035
佛得角		26,591		55,570
刚果		39,581		93,894
吉布提		237,641		70,327
埃及		18,597,592		14,757,360
埃塞俄比亚		770,107		641,955
加蓬		129,785		27,785
加纳		225,783		507,550
几内亚		119,784		115,897
几内亚(比绍)		55,800		5,680
科特迪瓦		267,211		120,781
肯尼亚		4,381,145		2,920,041
利比里亚		1,824		53,466
利比亚		368,826		212,969
马达加斯加		74,177		97,230
马拉维		22,598		16,800
马里		25,041		

1998年中国出口主要商品输往地

日用瓷

输往地	1998		1997	
	数量	金额(美元)	数量	金额(美元)
毛里求斯		710,555		562,525
摩洛哥		13,206,866		8,007,384
莫桑比克		51,967		107,447
尼日尔		989		12,859
尼日利亚		2,471,666		2,693,781
留尼汪		44,238		
卢旺达		10,064		
南非		22,985,967		36,944,769
苏丹		1,053,079		1,618,457
坦桑尼亚		1,468,606		1,805,214
多哥		8,500		8,059
突尼斯		4,258,349		9,168,575
乌干达		370,691		629,137
扎伊尔		114,141		127,831
赞比亚		167,928		142,425
津巴布韦		210,810		233,376
比利时		4,713,177		6,159,468
丹麦		1,374,776		1,467,077
英国		13,108,436		17,983,475
德国		27,384,439		21,184,643
法国		11,744,261		10,505,701
爱尔兰		510,283		420,681
意大利		20,985,526		18,784,846
荷兰		17,943,479		19,525,852
希腊		3,610,987		4,260,667
葡萄牙		4,634,042		3,870,279
西班牙		9,220,660		10,140,600
阿尔巴尼亚		52,964		118,968
安道尔		13,745		
奥地利		1,702,443		2,154,085
保加利亚		809,925		148,874
芬兰		464,332		938,320
匈牙利		330,795		403,200
冰岛		12,799		3,429
马耳他		69,296		61,323
摩纳哥		8,124		
挪威		2,806,753		3,135,380

1998 年中国出口主要商品输往地

日用瓷

输往地	1998		1997	
	数量	金额(美元)	数量	金额(美元)
波兰		1,118,850		414,694
罗马尼亚		1,022,393		442,123
瑞典		2,154,147		2,776,093
瑞士		667,133		1,005,990
爱沙尼亚		53,099		
拉脱维亚		257,104		123,815
立陶宛		300,407		20,526
亚美尼亚		6,798		
哈萨克斯坦		1,173,759		57,052
吉尔吉斯斯坦		159,594		447,753
俄罗斯		2,078,271		1,633,692
土库曼斯坦		1,275		
乌克兰		236,669		100,118
乌兹别克斯坦		30,480		51,385
南斯拉夫		141,634		881,859
斯洛文尼亚共和国		322,421		226,209
克罗地亚共和国		203,417		439,076
捷克共和国		542,989		577,640
斯洛伐克共和国		42,124		50,662
安提瓜和巴布达		11,250		
阿根廷		10,955,319		11,716,131
巴哈马		5,262		
巴巴多斯		36,680		28,148
玻利维亚		64,357		20,163
巴西		4,590,185		5,416,220
智利		12,759,120		13,551,719
哥伦比亚		1,427,276		1,374,269
多米尼克		4,349,929		3,539,173
哥斯达黎加		1,132,715		360,435
古巴		119,819		32,723
库腊索岛		16,609		14,280
多米尼加共和国		749,553		750,593
厄瓜多尔		3,190,645		5,061,919
瓜德罗普		11,017		46,800
危地马拉		4,851,787		4,021,358
圭亚那		38,697		63,634
海地		165,989		206,948

1998 年中国出口主要商品输往地

日用瓷

输往地	1998		1997	
	数量	金额(美元)	数量	金额(美元)
洪都拉斯		550,106		677,162
牙买加		790,720		1,230,976
墨西哥		3,983,130		3,223,450
尼加拉瓜		150		
巴拿马		17,632,828		17,301,150
巴拉圭		99,840		202,790
秘鲁		6,378,158		7,523,664
波多黎各		2,153,892		675,445
圣马丁岛		800		79
萨尔瓦多		291,646		225,732
苏里南		3,298		4,772
特立尼达和多巴哥		192,574		166,312
乌拉圭		1,904,002		1,949,885
委内瑞拉		5,482,137		2,128,520
加拿大		24,648,144		21,790,815
美国		169,615,464		164,447,010
澳大利亚		15,483,996		13,560,604
斐济		354,071		348,508
新喀里多尼亚		5,311		11,083
瓦努阿图		8,431		
新西兰		1,945,144		3,126,585
巴布亚新几内亚		128,532		277,907
所罗门群岛		12,747		
汤加		8,230		
贝劳共和国		80		
其他		11,142		252,097

地毯及装饰毯

输往地	1998		1997	
	数量	金额(美元)	数量	金额(美元)
总值		**441,650,842**		**454,636,007**
巴林		12,617		77,120
文莱		51,370		13,685
缅甸		5,330		
柬埔寨		80		1,835
塞浦路斯		288,529		394,221

1998年中国出口主要商品输往地

地毯及装饰毯

输往地	1998		1997	
	数量	金额(美元)	数量	金额(美元)
朝鲜		62,043		9,873
香港		14,423,802		14,321,257
印度尼西亚		117,760		68,797
以色列		459,220		259,903
日本		60,351,093		88,917,974
约旦		253,429		162,610
科威特		843,009		1,197,186
老挝		5,565		
黎巴嫩		1,181,984		1,209,832
澳门		60,487		37,115
马来西亚		439,982		716,224
蒙古		498,413		58,458
尼泊尔		7,930		
阿曼		194,226		106,714
巴基斯坦		19,235		45
菲律宾		71,515		55,634
卡塔尔		247,908		
沙特阿拉伯		7,800,177		6,607,027
新加坡		623,931		1,624,703
韩国		653,157		2,254,505
斯里兰卡		1,208		
泰国		360,406		304,148
土耳其		5,580,804		7,605,836
阿拉伯联合酋长国		9,458,505		6,860,730
也门共和国		58,439		4,678
越南		17,186		4,225
台湾省		1,836,088		871,609
阿尔及利亚		19,065		13,318
贝宁		8,654		481
喀麦隆		776		
埃及		2,862,291		2,227,220
加纳		5,861		760
肯尼亚		3,470		
利比亚		150		63,673
马达加斯加		3,720		
毛里求斯		796,987		469,268
留尼汪		7,990		8,472

1998 年中国出口主要商品输往地

地毯及装饰毯

输　往　地	1998		1997	
	数量	金额(美元)	数量	金额(美元)
南非		354,948		666,110
突尼斯		3,379		15,191
比利时		4,483,218		4,401,931
丹麦		281,756		329,225
英国		28,589,806		30,625,010
德国		49,708,692		52,669,857
法国		3,698,580		3,646,128
爱尔兰		14,110		77,213
意大利		15,093,369		16,050,952
卢森堡		18,390		1,134
荷兰		7,866,092		7,593,297
希腊		1,045,678		1,444,819
葡萄牙		4,304,809		3,327,523
西班牙		4,246,839		2,143,779
阿尔巴尼亚		32,400		
奥地利		1,134,938		944,666
保加利亚		284,847		25,227
芬兰		79,671		143,977
匈牙利		162,557		73,599
冰岛		141,432		
马耳他		52,626		
挪威		151,707		258,647
波兰		314,495		336,051
罗马尼亚		161,547		184,376
瑞典		1,164,621		1,509,436
瑞士		3,634,609		4,807,356
拉脱维亚		5,339		9,000
立陶宛		29,171		11,229
哈萨克斯坦		14,371		
吉尔吉斯斯坦		49,181		
俄罗斯		1,306,125		610,166
乌克兰		46,940		
乌兹别克斯坦		64,700		
南斯拉夫		128,349		210,664
斯洛文尼亚共和国		58,898		6,158
克罗地亚共和国		35,042		
捷克共和国		27,331		19,819

1998年中国出口主要商品输往地

地毯及装饰毯

输往地	1998		1997	
	数量	金额(美元)	数量	金额(美元)
斯洛伐克共和国		60,186		43,035
马其顿共和国		28,844		
波斯尼亚—黑塞哥维那		400		
阿根廷		630,972		486,692
巴哈马		42,712		
玻利维亚		4,856		
巴西		2,166,181		2,173,677
智利		184,299		26,200
圭亚那		21,327		56,740
墨西哥		561,587		398,002
巴拿马		21,251		
巴拉圭		4,460		97,004
乌拉圭		65,565		10,477
委内瑞拉		58,907		57,648
加拿大		6,483,192		5,389,889
美国		189,907,131		174,272,777
澳大利亚		2,388,273		2,523,332
斐济		790		
瑙鲁		100		
新西兰		516,180		189,586
巴布亚新几内亚		13,097		1,051
贝劳共和国		5,577		
其他				244,221

鞋类

输往地	1998		1997	
	数量	金额(美元)	数量	金额(美元)
总值		**8,391,789,934**		**8,535,710,365**
巴林		716,552		607,448
孟加拉国		319,248		383,790
文莱		137,823		186,485
缅甸		1,165,083		2,729,303
柬埔寨		1,579,380		321,021
塞浦路斯		1,148,284		457,836
朝鲜		921,681		946,648
香港		663,822,819		571,234,988

1998 年中国出口主要商品输往地

鞋类

输往地	1998		1997	
	数量	金额(美元)	数量	金额(美元)
印度		4,064,485		2,919,374
印度尼西亚		6,068,200		7,551,721
伊朗		1,587,404		474,126
伊拉克		84,678		85,498
以色列		21,866,062		15,968,559
日本		727,828,074		777,300,965
约旦		14,300,487		8,094,108
科威特		4,869,964		3,668,194
老挝		80,249		69,193
黎巴嫩		10,529,548		8,439,084
澳门		23,705,989		21,302,361
马来西亚		9,820,480		21,574,136
马尔代夫		16,347		83,417
蒙古		155,457		1,064,881
尼泊尔		3,603,055		2,383,844
阿曼		102,937		278,632
巴基斯坦		1,661,107		1,785,290
巴勒斯坦		52,463		260,904
菲律宾		19,529,456		21,091,014
卡塔尔		70,388		142,671
沙特阿拉伯		62,193,529		65,831,739
新加坡		15,265,851		28,625,005
韩国		91,493,414		160,410,922
斯里兰卡		457,989		325,819
叙利亚		214,900		54,816
泰国		9,063,202		12,013,587
土耳其		10,817,289		12,043,616
阿拉伯联合酋长国		56,143,974		77,682,018
也门共和国		6,232,440		5,979,933
越南		11,521,180		11,783,943
台湾省		65,508,246		66,800,602
阿尔及利亚		9,922,709		12,177,717
安哥拉		6,056,845		9,527,890
贝宁		1,896,232		1,107,475
博茨瓦那		1,150,245		277,681
喀麦隆		1,413,751		1,088,959
加那利群岛		141,027		138,456

1998 年中国出口主要商品输往地

鞋类

输 往 地	1998		1997	
	数量	金额(美元)	数量	金额(美元)
佛得角		232,227		121,470
中非共和国		6,813		251,031
塞卜泰(休达)		214,548		87,288
乍得		29,983		
刚果		2,742,715		1,812,235
吉布提		4,125,465		2,093,219
埃及		27,000,105		29,085,224
赤道几内亚		40,627		34,135
埃塞俄比亚		1,684,534		3,907,453
加蓬		723,938		385,096
冈比亚		4,452,705		3,336,366
加纳		6,363,416		6,674,354
几内亚		3,809,706		4,457,312
几内亚(比绍)		27,146		6,170
科特迪瓦		11,071,681		8,047,006
肯尼亚		2,638,529		3,937,063
利比里亚		404,126		253,590
利比亚		7,563,174		9,586,303
马达加斯加		2,033,071		3,662,841
马拉维		130,170		249,167
马里		682,715		1,433,058
毛里塔尼亚		1,309,085		1,625,898
毛里求斯		1,228,771		1,850,371
摩洛哥		924,449		1,431,532
莫桑比克		3,587,540		6,843,324
纳米比亚		1,817,034		1,124,738
尼日尔		185,789		11,885
尼日利亚		9,519,922		6,421,000
留尼汪		234,563		314,948
卢旺达		167,874		248,822
塞内加尔		2,830,195		2,505,257
塞舌尔		74,284		128,688
塞拉利昂		339,902		325,782
索马里		103,609		34,989
南非		46,193,506		59,887,129
苏丹		642,683		3,090,053
坦桑尼亚		2,237,902		5,773,287

1998 年中国出口主要商品输往地

鞋类

输往地	1998		1997	
	数量	金额(美元)	数量	金额(美元)
多哥		11,206,134		9,994,744
突尼斯		10,901,254		9,470,499
乌干达		118,243		101,882
布基纳法索		202,108		239,775
扎伊尔		1,435,068		2,718,870
赞比亚		789,798		1,799,764
津巴布韦		291,336		1,793,100
莱索托		5,765,328		1,801,979
梅利利亚		91,980		1,150,116
斯威士兰		16,742		154,795
厄立特里亚		43,340		19,836
比利时		114,832,736		125,611,881
丹麦		8,780,138		11,150,593
英国		117,429,900		112,023,879
德国		183,095,466		250,001,780
法国		108,025,017		100,826,031
爱尔兰		4,429,440		3,803,603
意大利		87,720,888		80,965,149
荷兰		92,896,556		83,831,403
希腊		16,376,028		15,743,564
葡萄牙		11,909,387		9,102,552
西班牙		68,662,682		81,951,555
阿尔巴尼亚		1,007,104		641,020
奥地利		8,899,710		12,185,465
保加利亚		5,987,242		2,885,831
芬兰		19,573,379		19,559,240
直布罗陀		5,175		
匈牙利		64,576,180		78,419,424
冰岛		116,931		162,157
马耳他		734,918		948,238
摩纳哥		221,516		240,681
挪威		8,518,276		9,807,994
波兰		132,715,017		113,366,089
罗马尼亚		76,112,590		61,211,919
瑞典		15,670,039		16,191,174
瑞士		6,914,647		5,823,456
爱沙尼亚		710,626		279,347

1998 年中国出口主要商品输往地

鞋类

输往地	1998		1997	
	数量	金额(美元)	数量	金额(美元)
拉脱维亚		679,825		379,201
立陶宛		1,182,745		494,257
格鲁吉亚		68,048		6,000
亚美尼亚		1,080		12,298
阿塞拜疆		73,542		
白俄罗斯		29,665		2,005,443
哈萨克斯坦		37,078,394		1,632,785
吉尔吉斯斯坦		42,896,055		1,072,990
俄罗斯		164,174,460		204,892,790
土库曼斯坦		80,012		113,595
乌克兰		7,895,145		4,113,376
乌兹别克斯坦		1,274,651		930,206
南斯拉夫		3,382,121		2,292,740
斯洛文尼亚共和国		2,587,382		3,170,157
克罗地亚共和国		2,114,219		2,323,280
捷克共和国		34,736,490		25,971,105
斯洛伐克共和国		8,714,807		4,504,774
马其顿共和国		113,059		439,544
波斯尼亚—黑塞哥维那		14,369		
安提瓜和巴布达		1,759		
阿根廷		22,055,156		16,955,044
阿鲁巴岛		260,360		65,280
巴哈马		39,535		40,608
巴巴多斯		19,794		13,893
伯利兹		129,966		63,774
玻利维亚		1,078,708		1,412,542
巴西		30,560,583		35,321,689
开曼群岛		32,160		455,031
智利		76,003,956		75,391,963
哥伦比亚		3,652,440		2,927,613
多米尼克		1,038,802		714,771
哥斯达黎加		3,513,074		2,748,530
古巴		5,614,412		7,548,602
库腊索岛		1,581,338		3,451,690
多米尼加共和国		653,304		219,661
厄瓜多尔		4,283,116		1,988,750
瓜德罗普		34,864		37,609

1998年中国出口主要商品输往地

鞋类

输往地	1998		1997	
	数量	金额(美元)	数量	金额(美元)
危地马拉		4,179,844		2,993,053
圭亚那		374,350		1,356,839
海地		51,058		
洪都拉斯		1,037,695		737,932
牙买加		1,277,223		2,288,132
马提尼克		17,280		
墨西哥		780,331		1,118,915
尼加拉瓜		82,018		
巴拿马		138,229,471		172,869,193
马拉圭		5,852,129		6,343,581
秘鲁		1,488,822		1,629,594
波多黎各		2,197,648		2,335,608
萨尔瓦多		3,415,565		3,302,587
苏里南		358,582		570,855
特立尼达和多巴哥		855,562		922,887
乌拉圭		12,740,302		11,754,528
委内瑞拉		10,989,329		13,028,165
加拿大		127,166,978		138,550,388
美国		4,317,317,806		4,329,282,216
澳大利亚		91,926,200		94,032,186
库克群岛		2,940		7,331
斐济		1,017,021		1,494,012
盖比群岛		60		
马克萨斯群岛		11,558		
瑙鲁		2,610		2,730
新喀里多尼亚		225,275		133,230
瓦努阿图		29,611		7,269
新西兰		7,966,699		10,819,091
巴布亚新几内亚		768,744		1,136,226
社会群岛		22,613		
所罗门群岛		87,374		73,857
汤加		1,918		38,517
萨摩亚		93,954		52,712
基里巴斯		5,032		
马绍尔群岛共和国		3,996		
贝劳共和国		1,250		2,854
其他		103,746		821,148

1998 年中国出口主要商品输往地

玩具

输往地	1998		1997	
	数量	金额(美元)	数量	金额(美元)
总值		**5,142,463,692**		**5,040,779,570**
阿富汗		10,063		70,333
巴林		596,527		632,786
孟加拉国		217,594		327,824
文莱		35,260		79,270
缅甸		580,669		1,057,236
柬埔寨		51,402		58,364
塞浦路斯		1,512,229		1,342,965
朝鲜		29,956		142,455
香港		829,599,424		1,040,899,730
印度		1,302,446		1,372,331
印度尼西亚		1,479,107		9,962,811
伊朗		90,088		73,231
以色列		7,670,735		6,468,530
日本		251,942,010		253,238,905
约旦		939,711		735,382
科威特		2,226,397		2,045,496
老挝		36,168		39,435
黎巴嫩		2,202,887		1,510,259
澳门		26,083,016		2,751,452
马来西亚		6,565,926		6,746,894
马尔代夫		1,440		802
蒙古		78,567		13,374
尼泊尔		41,371		102,137
阿曼		14,508		20,782
巴基斯坦		750,506		963,833
巴勒斯坦		14,456		40,751
菲律宾		4,271,654		5,908,161
卡塔尔		59,636		91,177
沙特阿拉伯		14,308,290		11,834,536
新加坡		18,451,219		16,564,046
韩国		37,771,269		47,515,701
斯里兰卡		347,153		369,601
叙利亚		115,942		151,590
泰国		4,741,913		9,125,591
土耳其		9,012,880		8,966,095
阿拉伯联合酋长国		24,649,775		33,794,596

1998 年中国出口主要商品输往地

玩具

输往地	1998		1997	
	数量	金额(美元)	数量	金额(美元)
也门共和国		148,120		122,669
越南		3,098,897		1,088,922
台湾省		24,372,509		20,910,408
阿尔及利亚		271,363		133,539
安哥拉		87,702		56,735
博茨瓦那		1,100		3,707
喀麦隆		19,377		46,483
加那利群岛		69,378		142,469
佛得角		3,346		
中非共和国		16,129		103,985
乍得		9,887		
刚果		13,506		550
埃及		7,565,669		9,791,403
埃塞俄比亚		13,548		32,173
加蓬		3,693		
加纳		95,419		69,593
几内亚		14,740		9,476
科特迪瓦		102,581		181,255
肯尼亚		53,866		64,195
利比里亚		821		16,914
马达加斯加		137,731		182,918
毛里求斯		165,907		190,645
摩洛哥		2,018,057		2,334,793
莫桑比克		51,511		
纳米比亚		7,148		27,235
尼日尔		14,096		
尼日利亚		162,010		132,287
留尼汪		14,333		19,802
塞内加尔		71,140		15,073
塞舌尔		6,342		17,354
索马里		6,909		
南非		7,559,621		7,093,564
苏丹		5,542		13,370
坦桑尼亚		1,822		21,286
突尼斯		639,652		731,032
赞比亚		898		7,670
津巴布韦		12,261		11,578

1998年中国出口主要商品输往地

玩具

输往地	1998		1997	
	数量	金额(美元)	数量	金额(美元)
比利时		27,381,849		27,701,539
丹麦		8,309,978		7,368,629
英国		216,443,324		204,443,165
德国		187,695,728		182,609,417
法国		94,027,370		95,975,465
爱尔兰		2,721,659		1,484,278
意大利		81,224,205		78,790,292
卢森堡		144,913		543,130
荷兰		54,974,417		55,376,324
希腊		10,730,571		9,455,291
葡萄牙		7,487,166		7,244,475
西班牙		53,442,636		49,350,804
阿尔巴尼亚		314,063		84,320
奥地利		3,085,054		3,606,580
保加利亚		1,369,682		558,733
芬兰		3,902,676		4,310,591
直布罗陀		28,550		6,587
匈牙利		1,964,498		1,402,658
冰岛		75,150		41,553
马耳他		146,031		249,965
摩纳哥		45,687		41,895
挪威		3,655,059		4,609,151
波兰		14,179,258		11,517,198
罗马尼亚		3,055,855		1,455,196
瑞典		7,939,355		7,778,450
瑞士		4,346,985		4,880,275
爱沙尼亚		60,874		15,084
拉脱维亚		36,508		60,900
立陶宛		279,755		116,842
格鲁吉亚		13,804		
阿塞拜疆		22,912		290,975
白俄罗斯		35,346		133,540
哈萨克斯坦		5,491,275		817,124
吉尔吉斯斯坦		1,153,272		20,482
摩尔多瓦		9,141		420
俄罗斯		18,262,359		22,137,226
乌克兰		1,798,481		1,404,970

1998 年中国出口主要商品输往地

玩具

输往地	1998		1997	
	数量	金额(美元)	数量	金额(美元)
乌兹别克斯坦		99,352		79,359
南斯拉夫		603,122		238,155
斯洛文尼亚共和国		733,385		302,350
克罗地亚共和国		499,881		422,668
捷克共和国		2,467,452		2,514,370
斯洛伐克共和国		896,749		966,472
马其顿共和国		26,632		6,580
波斯尼亚—黑塞哥维那		55,542		30,496
阿根廷		26,624,469		26,543,696
阿鲁巴岛		11,640		
伯利兹		243		775
玻利维亚		89,701		85,867
巴西		35,387,210		30,408,468
智利		22,054,541		20,738,691
哥伦比亚		2,377,961		1,163,024
多米尼克		425,701		140,245
哥斯达黎加		870,971		431,517
古巴		251,644		405,296
摩腊索岛		60,426		
多米尼加共和国		536,350		340,909
厄瓜多尔		1,950,296		2,403,565
法属圭亚那		16,930		
危地马拉		514,543		549,679
圭亚那		16,782		36,739
海地		38,448		
洪都拉斯		274,364		265,608
牙买加		87,778		38,525
墨西哥		11,566,814		7,870,482
尼加拉瓜		5,147		262,637
巴拿马		7,888,890		6,094,075
巴拉圭		10,659,179		11,928,343
秘鲁		1,634,569		1,916,103
波多黎各		2,238,804		910,245
萨尔瓦多		119,295		92,080
苏里南		54,825		54,670
特立尼达和多巴哥		259,768		108,585
乌拉圭		5,205,313		3,602,249

1998年中国出口主要商品输往地

玩具

输往地	1998		1997	
	数量	金额(美元)	数量	金额(美元)
委内瑞拉		4,410,857		2,427,777
加拿大		65,048,615		62,738,876
美国		2,783,991,980		2,509,271,948
格陵兰		7,834		6,700
百慕大		20,160		20,709
澳大利亚		36,650,330		44,818,623
库克群岛		22,078		586
斐济		23,887		41,204
瑙鲁		6,234		2,392
新喀里多尼亚		30,008		35,981
瓦努阿图		1,567		300
新西兰		4,999,698		5,327,241
诺福克岛		5,887		
巴布亚新几内亚		100,787		289,188
社会群岛		4,778		
所罗门群岛		1,082		648
汤加		2,264		
贝劳共和国		332		
其他		36,326		369,805

纸制品

输往地	1998		1997	
	数量(公吨)	金额(美元)	数量(公吨)	金额(美元)
总值	**762,878**	**875,813,271**	**821,423**	**893,852,945**
阿富汗	12	19,626	4	4,928
巴林	63	68,499	117	126,264
孟加拉国	3,207	4,063,038	3,981	4,993,411
文莱	86	101,593	45	88,404
缅甸	564	514,320	449	457,732
柬埔寨	347	783,304	689	1,887,199
塞浦路斯	24	41,459	30	97,528
朝鲜	1,065	1,255,306	1,271	877,531
香港	357,876	355,263,318	460,622	409,087,548
印度	1,149	1,855,672	68	87,484
印度尼西亚	2,396	2,421,876	2,304	3,134,785
伊朗	6	18,583	11	41,767

1998年中国出口主要商品输往地

纸制品

输往地	1998		1997	
	数量(公吨)	金额(美元)	数量(公吨)	金额(美元)
伊拉克	2	16,297		
以色列	639	1,009,268	253	673,379
日本	45,514	86,646,254	48,088	94,515,147
约旦	140	248,611	351	541,439
科威特	577	664,059	877	744,893
老挝	321	697,013	220	488,562
黎巴嫩	54	173,141	95	258,920
澳门	28,355	21,963,598	18,313	12,254,019
马来西亚	8,213	10,151,148	14,848	19,934,183
蒙古	348	270,583	391	449,300
尼泊尔	51	47,737	63	65,613
阿曼	36	29,401	131	73,144
巴基斯坦	262	331,577	219	394,201
菲律宾	2,966	3,183,116	5,049	7,190,868
卡塔尔	79	110,730	77	140,722
沙特阿拉伯	2,268	2,789,651	2,694	3,001,627
新加坡	24,546	34,652,699	30,737	51,254,584
韩国	3,086	4,073,395	5,194	7,602,912
斯里兰卡	244	236,814	153	225,145
叙利亚	16	40,084	70	134,779
泰国	6,950	9,814,624	8,050	8,204,787
土耳其	153	343,326	84	251,780
阿拉伯联合酋长国	933	1,307,205	994	1,405,489
也门共和国	61	64,059	102	131,380
越南	2,747	3,167,473	3,144	3,264,227
台湾省	48,261	31,165,453	47,720	32,398,541
阿尔及利亚	133	237,848	11	23,059
安哥拉	7	64,481		
贝宁	158	163,351	72	73,887
布隆迪		977		
喀麦隆	6	14,599	5	14,721
加那利群岛		2,022		
佛得角	1	750		
刚果	402	533,108	34	43,153
吉布提	178	225,683	46	54,978
埃及	378	634,771	200	399,963
赤道几内亚		121		

1998 年中国出口主要商品输往地

纸制品

输往地	1998		1997	
	数量(公吨)	金额(美元)	数量(公吨)	金额(美元)
埃塞俄比亚	223	260,966	327	499,674
加蓬	3	826		
冈比亚	2	3,156		
加纳	84	122,681	21	30,354
几内亚	43	108,980		32
科特迪瓦	31	61,902	12	27,070
肯尼亚	60	92,660	28	74,250
利比里亚	7	4,671	1	1,272
利比亚	166	214,309	56	54,550
马达加斯加	47	65,866	25	61,787
马拉维	9	13,236		
马里		4,807		
毛里求斯	84	111,485	27	50,271
摩洛哥	50	155,518	56	91,222
莫桑比克	18	24,591	4	3,725
尼日尔	1	22,500	1	16,950
尼日利亚	370	612,976	318	589,204
留尼汪	91	85,373	59	75,032
塞内加尔	1	1,349	1	564
塞舌尔		400	1	4,142
塞拉利昂	45	62,015	49	65,315
南非	1,559	2,370,510	920	1,412,602
苏丹	63	82,755	123	215,804
坦桑尼亚	283	412,879	33	84,891
突尼斯	36	62,528	37	104,758
乌干达	18	19,804	14	16,967
扎伊尔	323	369,987	150	240,452
赞比亚		417		
津巴布韦	14	8,785	8	16,345
厄立特里亚	2	2,558		
比利时	1,463	4,137,163	1,115	2,425,589
丹麦	644	932,065	685	1,114,081
英国	26,252	32,137,982	18,280	22,522,766
德国	11,286	19,129,865	10,341	16,155,838
法国	5,617	9,175,940	5,749	9,429,542
爱尔兰	34	42,909	79	122,988
意大利	5,003	7,089,392	2,073	4,234,391

1998年中国出口主要商品输往地

纸制品

输往地	1998		1997	
	数量(公吨)	金额(美元)	数量(公吨)	金额(美元)
卢森堡	30	46,773	48	89,088
荷兰	11,658	10,700,880	6,930	8,875,744
希腊	426	939,663	202	655,940
葡萄牙	248	366,342	264	549,982
西班牙	4,771	6,290,919	1,252	2,766,723
阿尔巴尼亚	10	38,430	3	2,299
奥地利	387	893,406	399	752,949
保加利亚	31	71,361	27	245,138
芬兰	570	781,820	1,120	1,180,205
匈牙利	152	210,622	59	65,535
马耳他	15	17,233	13	21,698
挪威	328	513,414	225	286,760
波兰	683	972,882	513	506,759
罗马尼亚	150	293,861	113	376,310
瑞典	772	1,693,744	1,128	1,859,772
瑞士	330	721,105	460	1,222,243
爱沙尼亚	15	23,776		450
拉脱维亚	76	74,919	125	247,882
立陶宛	101	76,584	9	10,817
白俄罗斯	1	564		102
哈萨克斯坦	554	801,737	210	187,929
吉尔吉斯斯坦	415	891,294	46	176,112
摩尔多瓦	1	729		210
俄罗斯	4,157	4,582,424	3,867	5,146,568
塔吉克斯坦	52	138,320		
土库曼斯坦	5	25,894	2	7,122
乌克兰	132	174,480	78	130,351
乌兹别克斯坦	37	19,753	26	52,589
南斯拉夫	50	43,828	26	51,310
斯洛文尼亚共和国	28	59,506	27	63,189
克罗地亚共和国	13	8,829	6	3,545
捷克共和国	25	41,610	48	72,580
斯洛伐克共和国	155	122,959	50	41,077
马其顿共和国		2,020		
阿根廷	1,088	1,532,587	508	868,942
阿鲁巴岛		419		
巴哈马	7	37,465	1	10,766

1998 年中国出口主要商品输往地

纸制品

输往地	1998		1997	
	数量(公吨)	金额(美元)	数量(公吨)	金额(美元)
巴巴多斯	2	2,548		
伯利兹	20	30,875	1	3,328
玻利维亚		2,126		513
巴西	2,157	1,965,029	1,551	1,906,999
智利	367	689,223	282	470,424
哥伦比亚	82	119,538	17	70,736
多米尼克	5	50,224	34	76,853
哥斯达黎加	35	34,857	1	8,129
古巴	245	614,237	175	542,518
多米尼加共和国	33	83,896	3	23,540
厄瓜多尔	27	64,471	80	120,008
法属圭亚那	1	734		
瓜德罗普		140		140
危地马拉	43	59,870		2,850
圭亚那		331	1	2,660
海地	4	8,775		
洪都拉斯	35	26,271	1	5,070
牙买加	7	8,530	34	38,063
墨西哥	235	474,219	632	759,384
巴拿马	334	459,224	128	361,857
巴拉圭	272	393,616	247	332,864
秘鲁	3	12,127	14	34,675
波多黎各	21	26,901	3	6,767
萨尔瓦多	3	5,800	3	9,452
苏里南	9	20,436	3	4,723
特立尼达和多巴哥	2	1,939	3	7,605
乌拉圭	282	309,223	60	141,204
委内瑞拉	64	110,311	19	35,193
加拿大	7,688	9,465,072	4,876	5,686,480
美国	112,607	154,457,261	88,592	118,283,494
澳大利亚	11,237	11,811,788	7,374	9,943,950
斐济	54	67,997	465	527,443
瑙鲁		6		
瓦努阿图	2	2,174	47	47,118
新西兰	624	967,201	360	751,330
巴布亚新几内亚	80	121,570	79	123,534
所罗门群岛	8	9,654	9	10,132

1998年中国出口主要商品输往地

纸制品

输 往 地	1998		1997	
	数量(公吨)	金额(美元)	数量(公吨)	金额(美元)
汤加	2	3,495	5	9,547
萨摩亚	2	1,310		
马绍尔群岛共和国		693		
其他			64	139,265

家具类

输 往 地	1998		1997	
	数量	金额(美元)	数量	金额(美元)
总值		**2,190,259,333**		**1,818,062,875**
阿富汗		910		
巴林		199,963		76,314
孟加拉国		21,303		23,736
文莱		224,289		1,539,064
缅甸		21,394		47,688
柬埔寨		12,124		35,772
塞浦路斯		338,766		153,275
朝鲜		327,417		359,546
香港		392,732,684		359,549,395
印度		49,590		274,774
印度尼西亚		1,464,962		5,238,348
以色列		1,772,207		1,301,377
日本		225,386,347		242,942,648
约旦		198,137		263,119
科威特		890,432		712,225
黎巴嫩		605,392		314,379
澳门		6,420,388		8,012,816
马来西亚		1,993,125		3,965,085
蒙古		625,086		236,030
尼泊尔		3,149		404,794
阿曼		1,268,412		376,034
巴基斯坦		68,433		55,074
巴勒斯坦		19,546		65,760
菲律宾		1,234,068		2,111,025
卡塔尔		141,961		156,565
沙特阿拉伯		4,987,136		4,008,276
新加坡		37,390,758		37,689,292

1998年中国出口主要商品输往地

家具类

输往地	1998		1997	
	数量	金额(美元)	数量	金额(美元)
韩国		9,839,342		25,053,814
斯里兰卡		304,529		200,016
叙利亚		29,007		35,720
泰国		3,200,762		2,467,006
土耳其		386,652		268,972
阿拉伯联合酋长国		8,183,182		7,267,324
也门共和国		65,279		13,072
越南		337,392		157,069
台湾省		70,938,727		78,941,576
阿尔及利亚		416,380		305,217
安哥拉		45,884		58,013
贝宁		16,146		
博茨瓦那		276		2,219
布隆迪		900		
喀麦隆		33,735		55,183
加那利群岛		70,047		66,365
佛得角		464		11,325
乍得		77		
刚果		600		
吉布提		63,511		
埃及		289,215		346,210
埃塞俄比亚		1,089		661,175
加蓬		133,303		
冈比亚		361		10,479
加纳		151,997		39,743
几内亚		2,926		3,300
几内亚(比绍)		120,096		
科特迪瓦		14,401		67,097
肯尼亚		258,244		7,074
利比里亚		479		329
利比亚		11,019		683,357
马达加斯加		53,470		42,106
毛里塔尼亚		12,875		
毛里求斯		142,000		83,020
摩洛哥		396,714		378,163
莫桑比克		5,712		8,241
纳米比亚		56,635		37,217

1998 年中国出口主要商品输往地

家具类

输往地	1998		1997	
	数量	金额(美元)	数量	金额(美元)
尼日尔		15,857		
尼日利亚		113,908		152,823
留尼汪		199,369		183,278
卢旺达		14,901		9,698
塞内加尔		4,568		3,000
塞舌尔		142,345		1,500
南非		3,316,582		2,790,149
苏丹		1,418,030		83,036
坦桑尼亚		22,343		25,419
多哥		3,314		
突尼斯		42,889		110,474
扎伊尔		75,255		5,676
赞比亚		36,807		6,804
津巴布韦		35,102		56,538
斯威士兰		86		
比利时		18,324,679		16,360,907
丹麦		4,664,176		3,198,052
英国		72,340,204		49,487,807
德国		38,918,928		40,310,978
法国		45,209,659		38,435,176
爱尔兰		1,292,777		1,069,405
意大利		21,042,705		14,551,150
卢森堡		615,848		64,233
荷兰		41,363,979		33,117,459
希腊		2,503,014		2,677,422
葡萄牙		2,019,992		1,713,841
西班牙		13,852,209		12,172,096
阿尔巴尼亚		6,270		27,405
奥地利		455,586		647,797
保加利亚		27,858		1,223
芬兰		1,250,288		883,910
匈牙利		304,897		74,706
冰岛		43,642		88,364
马耳他		121,690		266,132
摩纳哥		80		
挪威		1,715,188		1,310,917
波兰		448,619		433,040

1998 年中国出口主要商品输往地

家具类

输往地	1998		1997	
	数量	金额(美元)	数量	金额(美元)
罗马尼亚		102,051		50,773
瑞典		8,247,674		5,032,781
瑞士		850,771		435,288
爱沙尼亚		38,482		14,495
拉脱维亚		463		6,474
立陶宛		13,212		
哈萨克斯坦		532,206		57,510
吉尔吉斯斯坦		49,058		720
俄罗斯		4,408,948		2,815,601
乌克兰		20,567		282,229
乌兹别克斯坦		55,406		9,122
南斯拉夫		25,482		5,164
斯洛文尼亚共和国		33,971		
克罗地亚共和国		13,491		
捷克共和国		43,867		68,457
安提瓜和巴布达		446		7,893
阿根廷		3,136,935		2,285,979
阿鲁巴岛		13,328		
巴巴多斯		7,386		30,030
伯利兹		6,412		
巴西		2,905,605		1,916,423
智利		3,779,915		3,215,346
哥伦比亚		490,413		290,395
多米尼克		958,818		446,264
哥斯达黎加		160,169		90,555
古巴		61,652		86,346
库腊索岛		159,040		103,871
多米尼加共和国		670,593		339,701
厄瓜多尔		337,345		95,466
瓜德罗普		53,190		90,104
危地马拉		50,682		39,152
圭亚那		9,867		51,703
海地		35,417		
牙买加		67,503		103,879
墨西哥		1,320,552		595,299
巴拿马		2,902,381		1,396,514
巴拉圭		50,310		123,304

1998年中国出口主要商品输往地

家具类

输往地	1998		1997	
	数量	金额(美元)	数量	金额(美元)
秘鲁		319,476		382,405
波多黎各		1,452,373		1,234,566
萨尔瓦多		34,225		56,097
苏里南		46,952		19,377
特立尼达和多巴哥		31,441		39,832
乌拉圭		975,175		675,853
委内瑞拉		1,464,217		592,076
加拿大		30,294,569		24,782,151
美国		1,040,431,826		730,903,163
格陵兰		3,665		
百慕大		14,454		2,766
澳大利亚		34,274,665		27,758,597
斐济		6,458		60,031
瑙鲁		295		
新喀里多尼亚		58,167		31,334
瓦努阿图		8,892		6,385
新西兰		3,078,504		3,613,571
诺福克岛		34,477		26,191
巴布亚新几内亚		30,733		30,210
社会群岛		37,838		6,155
所罗门群岛		1,822		6,156
汤加		12,620		2,918
萨摩亚		6,087		
马绍尔群岛共和国		27,727		1,655
贝劳共和国		16,661		24,762
其他		37,355		216,558

钢材

输往地	1998		1997	
	数量(公吨)	金额(美元)	数量(公吨)	金额(美元)
总值	**3,565,997**	**1,686,980,064**	**4,619,391**	**1,935,047,856**
阿富汗	10	7,908	20	11,107
巴林	618	385,552	2,015	950,979
孟加拉国	21,539	12,399,928	9,048	6,342,555
文莱	1,329	351,202	18,619	5,592,346
缅甸	55,645	29,426,538	49,728	23,077,509

1998年中国出口主要商品输往地

钢材

输 往 地	1998		1997	
	数量(公吨)	金额(美元)	数量(公吨)	金额(美元)
柬埔寨	65,053	16,782,949	59,405	16,493,127
塞浦路斯	1,065	598,322	292	238,175
朝鲜	34,077	12,769,861	11,189	6,881,575
香港	621,160	244,512,559	749,267	301,731,901
印度	31,438	22,096,744	74,540	38,738,090
印度尼西亚	46,809	23,287,004	130,569	56,200,241
伊朗	14,801	14,233,540	22,145	16,901,568
伊拉克	525	435,235	220	159,057
以色列	14,449	6,324,309	3,369	3,457,777
日本	397,261	154,152,076	627,150	240,093,613
约旦	6,192	3,885,618	3,356	1,399,564
科威特	4,341	2,634,109	5,104	3,849,122
老挝	689	225,301	390	154,215
黎巴嫩	5,793	2,782,418	5,279	2,822,333
澳门	10,595	4,579,464	14,952	6,376,116
马来西亚	55,524	21,762,483	240,177	86,177,439
蒙古	8,351	3,808,706	1,029	594,192
尼泊尔	1,449	567,688	190	103,737
阿曼	87	41,419	63	41,116
巴基斯坦	24,615	14,132,394	26,740	15,224,939
巴勒斯坦	73	103,502	76	99,463
菲律宾	31,946	14,014,452	77,287	30,479,581
卡塔尔	686	446,200	983	624,076
沙特阿拉伯	23,843	8,906,648	27,188	13,526,114
新加坡	68,840	38,526,482	176,600	82,468,357
韩国	145,122	54,679,097	1,094,334	350,897,820
斯里兰卡	5,353	3,206,109	6,493	2,814,600
叙利亚	27,392	16,710,823	18,671	12,440,469
泰国	30,164	12,472,923	208,994	67,235,314
土耳其	64,154	21,570,317	3,595	2,394,342
阿拉伯联合酋长国	23,709	16,089,567	30,754	19,575,899
也门共和国	2,545	1,533,737	2,438	1,282,877
越南	43,780	15,427,000	27,292	11,088,559
台湾省	100,782	63,539,890	96,089	64,009,021
阿尔及利亚	852	774,363	1,372	1,968,646
安哥拉	100	98,880		
贝宁	127	49,770	44	24,028

1998 年中国出口主要商品输往地

钢材

输往地	1998		1997	
	数量(公吨)	金额(美元)	数量(公吨)	金额(美元)
博茨瓦那	11,251	7,312,927	1,258	1,262,633
布隆迪	1,238	872,730		
喀麦隆	244	193,725	76	91,141
加那利群岛	8	25,818		
刚果	338	141,905		
吉布提	2,689	788,896	175	107,424
埃及	27,695	17,059,907	28,728	17,344,949
埃塞俄比亚	2,806	1,019,846	689	384,235
加蓬	49	78,722	246	275,867
冈比亚	41	26,240	21	15,924
加纳	912	519,584	302	192,734
几内亚	30	8,625	96	46,461
科特迪瓦	746	529,543	444	296,294
肯尼亚	1,135	753,590	840	756,172
利比亚	387	744,950	492	644,740
马达加斯加	439	234,371	443	225,551
马里	6	12,604	62	25,668
毛里塔尼亚	77	31,856	77	58,337
毛里求斯	447	282,398	603	327,701
摩洛哥	1,270	784,157	711	574,742
莫桑比克	393	165,431	82	76,268
尼日利亚	2,538	2,368,192	2,895	2,312,771
卢旺达	40	17,600	2	2,117
塞内加尔	535	333,827	330	211,227
塞舌尔	1	718	16	14,705
南非	12,611	20,101,959	2,766	3,104,943
苏丹	237,828	185,054,788	9,782	5,782,186
坦桑尼亚	649	317,339	3,544	2,160,076
多哥	120	59,376	1,341	471,582
突尼斯	794	556,843	583	451,582
乌干达	20	11,660	19	14,424
扎伊尔	101	79,309	16	8,017
赞比亚	6	5,968	76	54,471
津巴布韦	1,084	534,049	206	156,044
比利时	139,426	51,512,681	72,720	25,123,102
丹麦	1,066	4,635,600	933	1,719,429
英国	65,925	29,114,434	70,305	31,612,634

1998 年中国出口主要商品输往地

钢材

输往地	1998		1997	
	数量(公吨)	金额(美元)	数量(公吨)	金额(美元)
德国	11,238	15,374,428	9,349	14,720,542
法国	11,189	6,380,161	5,877	4,514,378
爱尔兰	346	584,995	239	485,417
意大利	69,895	33,082,748	42,328	20,965,362
卢森堡	5	836		
荷兰	34,917	12,646,207	2,508	2,982,925
希腊	2,187	2,269,562	1,108	1,359,232
葡萄牙	5,034	1,987,078	534	487,049
西班牙	58,145	20,624,871	19,412	8,693,817
奥地利	16	67,833		35
芬兰	227	288,549	191	272,034
匈牙利	450	607,872	546	739,602
冰岛		43		
马耳他	180	170,168	143	77,205
挪威	105	134,146	40	33,999
波兰	816	1,335,766	686	832,884
罗马尼亚	136	136,941	41	70,936
瑞典	5,353	1,653,769	121	184,226
瑞士	51	54,193	41	25,276
哈萨克斯坦	41	9,853		
吉尔吉斯斯坦	318	109,908	68	74,314
俄罗斯	826	1,054,606	4,436	5,446,591
塔吉克斯坦	166	60,598		
土库曼斯坦	141	272,668		7
乌克兰		5,381	6,686	2,662,103
乌兹别克斯坦	900	287,100		
南斯拉夫	245	856,611	16	19,174
斯洛文尼亚共和国	60	33,880		
克罗地亚共和国	15	21,071		
捷克共和国	21	35,758	17	21,456
斯洛伐克共和国	59	61,943	1	508
马其顿共和国	7	27,891		
阿根廷	3,013	4,842,115	1,984	2,423,089
巴哈马	8	10,770		
巴巴多斯	28	15,549	24	13,629
伯利兹	21	18,535		
玻利维亚	33	22,831		

1998年中国出口主要商品输往地

钢材

输往地	1998		1997	
	数量(公吨)	金额(美元)	数量(公吨)	金额(美元)
巴西	4,803	3,069,047	4,086	3,294,880
智利	1,980	1,651,942	2,004	2,258,671
哥伦比亚	3,357	3,779,475	915	1,082,951
多米尼克	82	121,615	112	143,618
哥斯达黎加	115	111,917	111	110,911
古巴	2,758	2,021,525	1,157	810,579
库腊索岛	95	68,345		
多米尼加共和国	399	482,540	166	193,970
厄瓜多尔	1,262	1,256,564	1,300	1,466,772
危地马拉	180	138,644	80	73,537
圭亚那	60	41,831	206	235,511
海地	176	105,685		
洪都拉斯	96	99,807	98	125,824
牙买加	3,459	4,054,040	157	93,973
墨西哥	9,382	3,871,408	123	195,655
尼加拉瓜	126	85,221	9	10,804
巴拿马	286	167,510	152	120,690
巴拉圭	54	61,862	9	9,939
秘鲁	836	873,964	594	854,721
波多黎各	124	127,916	4,137	2,190,703
圣卢西亚	270	137,133		
圣文森特和格林纳丁斯	87	57,358		
萨尔瓦多	189	102,366	173	116,278
苏里南	42	26,151	29	15,280
特立尼达和多巴哥	8,466	2,656,743	127	82,519
乌拉圭	174	169,863	72	117,606
委内瑞拉	4,217	3,899,494	2,310	3,043,398
加拿大	39,101	20,343,951	33,437	16,217,819
美国	726,441	328,659,116	399,301	223,757,672
澳大利亚	41,411	16,111,510	41,442	19,345,030
斐济	143	64,826	159	115,759
瓦努阿图	131	36,957	270	78,666
新西兰	1,544	704,264	2,077	1,111,462
巴布亚新几内亚		153	10	13,392
所罗门群岛	1	1,045	8	4,575
萨摩亚	126	45,425		
马绍尔群岛共和国		362		

1998年中国出口主要商品输往地

钢材

输往地	1998		1997	
	数量(公吨)	金额(美元)	数量(公吨)	金额(美元)
其他			221	201,191

水泥

输往地	1998		1997	
	数量(公吨)	金额(美元)	数量(公吨)	金额(美元)
总值	**8,199,725**	**290,457,117**	**11,684,542**	**445,714,935**
孟加拉国	365,451	9,122,766	2,551,341	84,091,983
文莱	44,421	1,569,431	275,566	11,662,288
缅甸	140,586	5,126,467	388,638	13,917,096
朝鲜	5,411	232,778	5,948	257,631
香港	1,406,349	59,024,428	1,155,216	51,436,851
印度	7,000	287,000		
印度尼西亚	141	13,338	146,547	5,335,869
伊朗	80	11,048		
日本	142,343	4,567,084	86,298	3,478,886
老挝	1,498	81,245	4,363	250,929
澳门	151,195	5,770,957	491,696	19,834,761
马来西亚	8,389	374,912	1,243,994	46,463,897
蒙古	6,966	320,357	670	42,345
巴基斯坦	579	75,822	213	21,624
菲律宾	55,773	2,075,997	504,471	19,618,023
新加坡	425,413	12,849,551	1,059,724	40,514,413
韩国	195,735	6,225,323	1,695,361	65,881,391
斯里兰卡	27,925	914,075	168,460	7,047,662
也门共和国	132,179	3,733,114	239,302	7,856,144
越南	3,961	173,330	820,044	33,667,468
台湾省	1,115,672	32,138,853	27,913	1,097,039
贝宁	11,001	330,030		
喀麦隆	13,000	377,000		
刚果	20,000	609,985		
冈比亚	9,500	275,090		
加纳	22,000	719,400		
几内亚	19,112	582,901	41,000	1,394,000
马里	3	1,039		
毛里塔尼亚	30,050	966,584	15,750	511,875

1998年中国出口主要商品输往地

水泥

输往地	1998		1997	
	数量(公吨)	金额(美元)	数量(公吨)	金额(美元)
尼日尔	1	125		
尼日利亚	63,020	1,798,688	9	530
南非	200	18,000	19	719
苏丹	14	959		
厄立特里亚	15,906	477,180		
比利时	38	780		
英国		30		12
德国	2	53		3
法国		80		
意大利	160	28,000	140	28,450
荷兰	1,646	161,242	229	27,029
希腊	250	30,000	60	7,800
葡萄牙	60	7,370		
西班牙	50	12,250	52	7,290
俄罗斯	8,347	434,839	16,365	1,007,282
美国	3,682,699	136,034,868	659,868	26,896,486
澳大利亚	57,399	2,493,449	761	86,710
瓦努阿图	23	9,329		
新西兰	8,148	398,918	8,000	313,000
马绍尔群岛共和国	30	1,052		
其他			76,525	2,957,449

焦炭

输往地	1998		1997	
	数量(公吨)	金额(美元)	数量(公吨)	金额(美元)
总值	**11,463,981**	**798,389,639**	**10,580,693**	**790,964,300**
孟加拉国	11,951	1,246,997	7,193	785,087
不丹	4,479	259,760		
缅甸	2,060	137,322	1,991	188,906
朝鲜	84,127	5,860,330	48,875	3,378,409
香港	42,444	2,170,533	15,541	884,540
印度	1,373,827	95,349,803	1,906,143	135,808,185
印度尼西亚	20,651	2,318,503	41,059	3,308,722
伊朗	190,095	13,330,762	109,892	7,696,812
以色列	32	4,022		
日本	1,053,715	79,449,794	1,181,546	97,240,549

1998年中国出口主要商品输往地

焦炭

输 往 地	1998		1997	
	数量(公吨)	金额(美元)	数量(公吨)	金额(美元)
约旦	114	7,676		
黎巴嫩	35	3,724		
澳门	472	20,500	361	34,330
马来西亚	37,707	2,261,639	47,857	3,196,483
蒙古	500	56,503	183	33,054
巴基斯坦	20,414	2,027,175	22,653	1,821,235
菲律宾	16,736	1,484,283	18,403	1,662,175
卡塔尔	20	2,800		
新加坡	2,400	229,360	9,266	712,396
韩国	120,067	9,912,543	164,435	14,385,535
斯里兰卡	100	10,320	47	5,188
叙利亚	100	16,000		
泰国	52,650	4,136,515	48,460	4,384,705
土耳其	312,525	21,696,630	470,524	35,334,019
越南	4,588	301,856	400	29,851
台湾省	95,469	7,568,921	99,694	8,659,716
埃及	57,018	3,961,611	41,624	2,906,920
南非	485,292	34,128,618	324,597	24,088,016
坦桑尼亚	184	16,275		
比利时	582,995	37,578,397	328,314	23,583,634
英国	510,705	34,596,073	499,239	36,652,507
德国	369,780	25,351,935	309,156	23,161,008
法国	789,310	53,868,795	469,436	35,350,321
意大利	525,588	38,305,495	223,531	17,297,997
荷兰	368,681	22,712,314	293,723	22,187,264
希腊	5,000	375,000		
西班牙	3,234	210,000	21,595	1,641,234
保加利亚	105,868	7,027,599	15,847	1,168,853
挪威	112,750	7,134,631	93,267	6,761,178
瑞典	268,279	18,715,670	208,996	15,743,045
瑞士	719,120	51,618,078	1,058,195	81,102,751
俄罗斯	162	13,932	285	98,793
巴西	1,250,046	82,201,380	826,094	57,019,854
墨西哥	332,805	23,087,192	137,324	8,239,971
秘鲁	225,578	15,770,496	97,111	6,970,124
加拿大	29,498	1,913,300		
美国	1,232,794	87,317,232	1,222,422	92,079,108

1998年中国出口主要商品输往地

焦炭

输往地	1998		1997	
	数量(公吨)	金额(美元)	数量(公吨)	金额(美元)
澳大利亚	42,017	2,621,345	53,258	3,971,624
其他			162,156	11,390,201

成品油

输往地	1998		1997	
	数量(公吨)	金额(美元)	数量(公吨)	金额(美元)
总值	**4,360,976**	**738,906,453**	**5,585,850**	**1,201,360,778**
巴林	79	45,540		
孟加拉国	28	14,820	621	89,009
文莱	401	157,787	374	147,717
缅甸	23,112	5,383,621	22,116	5,022,117
柬埔寨	2,081	357,225	66	14,285
塞浦路斯	27,628	3,738,539	26,508	4,984,938
朝鲜	149,757	25,723,252	109,600	26,861,426
香港	829,953	127,282,031	1,698,748	341,850,199
印度	4,319	582,828	43,630	6,582,317
印度尼西亚	1,876	814,857	76,880	16,444,361
伊朗	4,976	1,664,382	34,536	8,376,623
以色列	2,547	969,403	2,435	959,354
日本	250,298	35,265,282	411,572	88,923,665
约旦	26	15,340	26	16,092
科威特	32	7,025		
老挝	3	2,055	116	38,798
黎巴嫩	13	7,313	13	7,212
澳门	46,114	7,183,796	45,186	9,012,192
马来西亚	7,990	2,689,330	32,222	7,511,741
蒙古	7,231	1,938,365	3,969	1,269,932
尼泊尔	1,963	766,345	1,647	625,734
巴基斯坦	3,790	1,282,278	4,528	1,751,310
菲律宾	70,718	11,190,095	50,320	11,290,709
新加坡	909,648	138,231,755	758,278	156,174,681
韩国	586,766	95,879,389	642,166	139,030,381
斯里兰卡	2,920	482,107	2,910	601,308
泰国	42,973	9,980,423	52,336	17,183,594
土耳其	2,669	328,791	5,402	903,343
阿拉伯联合酋长国	6,303	1,196,599	88	53,086

1998年中国出口主要商品输往地

成品油

输 往 地	1998		1997	
	数量(公吨)	金额(美元)	数量(公吨)	金额(美元)
也门共和国	1,083	217,090	359	102,531
越南	522,752	73,843,049	536,893	113,503,505
台湾省	184,096	32,059,401	211,428	46,403,006
阿尔及利亚	204	28,836		
埃及	587	100,991	470	123,743
赤道几内亚	3	3,356	76	31,587
埃塞俄比亚	823	334,963	659	273,420
几内亚	5	4,504		
利比里亚	24,483	3,668,830	32,145	5,306,192
马里	5	11,682	4	6,852
毛里求斯	4	2,880	17	11,159
苏丹	2	1,799	300	89,096
坦桑尼亚	20	3,200	90	23,040
比利时	1,185	216,560	250	53,250
丹麦	1,651	318,927	1,075	291,269
英国	11,491	4,515,300	14,392	5,154,176
德国	39,189	14,655,126	35,209	13,436,908
法国	26,741	9,908,668	21,685	8,411,092
意大利	12,916	5,025,007	12,549	4,751,237
荷兰	12,928	4,236,864	9,577	3,425,100
希腊	14,353	1,954,137	12,597	2,463,927
奥地利	11,190	4,194,364	8,377	3,272,087
芬兰	5,641	2,162,439	6,603	2,428,978
匈牙利	608	221,027		
马耳他	11,073	1,860,950	11,403	2,120,430
挪威	2,178	395,673	5,963	1,347,522
波兰	2,992	995,048	3,120	1,142,378
罗马尼亚	1,679	601,660	3,301	815,663
瑞典	10,559	3,948,866	10,593	4,104,918
瑞士	25,188	9,551,262	25,427	9,577,174
格鲁吉亚	688	258,340		
白俄罗斯	474	185,082	2,306	562,308
哈萨克斯坦	1,772	681,551	2,280	903,887
吉尔吉斯斯坦	591	226,632	36	15,660
俄罗斯	78,167	13,585,762	127,095	25,967,354
土库曼斯坦	44	17,355		
乌克兰	3,920	1,329,739	3,313	1,150,734

1998 年中国出口主要商品输往地

成品油

输往地	1998		1997	
	数量(公吨)	金额(美元)	数量(公吨)	金额(美元)
乌兹别克斯坦	1,085	415,013	1,200	461,933
南斯拉夫	2,413	919,161		
斯洛伐克共和国	30	4,800		
安提瓜和巴布达	696	68,931	427	62,852
巴哈马	9,059	1,141,786	13,734	2,476,544
伯利兹	7,268	1,005,988	4,255	659,415
危地马拉	5	3,335		
洪都拉斯	2,642	413,180	2,608	497,207
巴拿马	167,218	28,411,444	188,901	33,944,268
圣文森特和格林纳丁斯	35,676	5,091,491	40,155	6,735,062
加拿大	17,073	6,445,270	15,051	5,912,675
美国	99,109	22,775,677	73,655	21,736,763
澳大利亚	18,792	7,336,260	49,114	11,941,872
瓦努阿图	579	102,969	253	43,784
巴布亚新几内亚	33	32,000	203	58,787
马绍尔群岛共和国	969	116,541	1,566	327,891
其他	828	115,154	68,838	13,505,418

塑料

输往地	1998		1997	
	数量	金额(美元)	数量	金额(美元)
总值		**5,216,105,056**		**4,887,521,066**
阿富汗		508,502		394,233
巴林		739,942		463,701
孟加拉国		3,633,366		3,303,161
不丹		5,206		
文莱		261,445		338,008
缅甸		1,844,583		1,195,516
柬埔寨		561,693		733,975
塞浦路斯		1,100,128		964,826
朝鲜		15,427,527		14,882,737
香港		1,312,668,043		1,549,349,676
印度		17,052,280		7,823,874
印度尼西亚		13,382,605		16,502,071
伊朗		3,091,789		2,205,147
伊拉克		1,511,774		2,811

1998 年中国出口主要商品输往地

塑料

输往地	1998		1997	
	数量	金额(美元)	数量	金额(美元)
以色列		10,307,155		8,010,799
日本		448,355,358		418,843,810
约旦		3,151,610		1,966,842
科威特		2,801,173		1,624,396
老挝		22,342		32,089
黎巴嫩		5,084,285		4,099,764
澳门		32,422,883		15,495,804
马来西亚		21,009,471		25,057,210
马尔代夫		12,231		31,832
蒙古		1,586,118		712,923
尼泊尔		245,694		92,449
阿曼		157,448		78,399
巴基斯坦		8,628,033		7,713,567
巴勒斯坦		160,256		428,627
菲律宾		24,473,328		30,788,068
卡塔尔		93,525		112,354
沙特阿拉伯		17,432,286		12,362,565
新加坡		55,453,197		60,596,096
韩国		58,457,621		81,234,542
斯里兰卡		2,373,635		2,020,350
叙利亚		2,723,048		1,664,115
泰国		33,435,247		46,069,733
土耳其		10,333,367		6,028,228
阿拉伯联合酋长国		24,415,184		22,001,547
也门共和国		1,043,150		1,123,293
越南		24,704,649		12,870,442
台湾省		74,381,812		62,275,835
阿尔及利亚		2,213,864		930,825
安哥拉		759,578		414,996
贝宁		333,456		108,888
博茨瓦那		48,022		450
喀麦隆		335,670		331,615
加那利群岛		175,213		363,470
佛得角		59,885		14,066
中非共和国		60,182		45,540
塞卜泰(休达)		5,088		765
乍得		4,807		1,244

1998 年中国出口主要商品输往地

塑料

输往地	1998		1997	
	数量	金额(美元)	数量	金额(美元)
刚果		701,813		412,022
吉布提		276,397		36,758
埃及		15,976,155		10,260,302
赤道几内亚		9,989		5,568
埃塞俄比亚		488,483		331,749
加蓬		145,156		7,631
冈比亚		116,653		50,594
加纳		874,269		451,275
几内亚		188,093		135,477
几内亚(比绍)		4,888		
科特迪瓦		1,348,205		371,252
肯尼亚		1,119,552		1,188,789
利比里亚		52,018		120,484
利比亚		460,804		192,222
马达加斯加		585,050		325,885
马拉维		4,510		
马里		9,535		45,770
毛里塔尼亚		40,634		70
毛里求斯		669,728		746,000
摩洛哥		4,197,663		2,275,210
莫桑比克		81,104		184,469
纳米比亚		444,390		186,962
尼日尔		17,385		102,130
尼日利亚		4,542,758		3,694,710
留尼汪		136,019		51,054
卢旺达		80,930		16,620
塞内加尔		184,867		240,883
塞舌尔		76,776		46,683
塞拉利昂		40,153		15,937
南非		23,783,410		13,242,090
苏丹		5,499,727		9,971,380
坦桑尼亚		871,651		682,626
多哥		107,117		62,080
突尼斯		2,414,501		1,368,256
乌干达		40,194		58,903
扎伊尔		668,722		462,567
赞比亚		111,131		22,164

1998年中国出口主要商品输往地

塑料

输往地	1998		1997	
	数量	金额(美元)	数量	金额(美元)
津巴布韦		527,736		235,780
莱索托		500		
梅利利亚		6,450		
比利时		48,511,277		39,206,310
丹麦		14,982,289		16,136,690
英国		265,604,809		193,589,063
德国		201,698,318		169,190,101
法国		109,584,043		105,056,401
爱尔兰		5,801,522		5,381,789
意大利		87,032,251		67,669,014
卢森堡		11,647,885		7,793,982
荷兰		140,832,364		120,654,616
希腊		10,507,749		9,023,086
葡萄牙		7,251,431		6,523,612
西班牙		57,723,005		46,794,548
阿尔巴尼亚		159,418		117,524
安道尔		10,186		4,394
奥地利		3,850,445		3,344,131
保加利亚		899,351		242,747
芬兰		11,044,163		9,685,226
匈牙利		1,707,190		1,120,743
冰岛		175,009		253,688
马耳他		355,889		214,165
摩纳哥		266,927		5,498
挪威		11,262,217		7,414,708
波兰		12,011,500		8,613,677
罗马尼亚		7,364,943		4,180,428
圣马力诺		14,504		1,114
瑞典		29,085,757		22,819,806
瑞士		6,672,738		7,391,733
爱沙尼亚		111,068		18,780
拉脱维亚		545,663		365,070
立陶宛		480,323		232,618
格鲁吉亚		7,053		70
亚美尼亚		280		
阿塞拜疆		333		
白俄罗斯		6,288		388,364

1998 年中国出口主要商品输往地

塑料

输往地	1998		1997	
	数量	金额(美元)	数量	金额(美元)
哈萨克斯坦		6,046,352		4,662,828
吉尔吉斯斯坦		3,045,574		1,693,211
摩尔多瓦		427		2,864
俄罗斯		24,068,864		25,532,631
塔吉克斯坦		915,670		
土库曼斯坦		64,629		101,363
乌克兰		2,023,226		722,516
乌兹别克斯坦		21,058,035		13,837,304
南斯拉夫		403,576		129,215
斯洛文尼亚共和国		386,263		91,975
克罗地亚共和国		138,087		60,998
捷克共和国		3,419,333		1,963,504
斯洛伐克共和国		357,963		171,095
马其顿共和国		191,498		59,744
波斯尼亚—黑塞哥维那		11,712		2,070
安提瓜和巴布达		12,302		363
阿根廷		17,489,252		8,809,524
阿鲁巴岛		5,405		22,111
巴哈马		53,833		12,095
巴巴多斯		185,146		96,834
伯利兹		23,765		2,696
玻利维亚		27,077		59,119
巴西		25,207,928		26,242,260
智利		17,253,259		9,882,433
哥伦比亚		1,716,502		1,109,890
多米尼克		342,203		458,518
哥斯达黎加		607,316		239,711
古巴		2,049,199		2,783,827
库腊索岛		134,356		181,023
多米尼加共和国		575,572		474,671
厄瓜多尔		2,714,848		1,559,625
法属圭亚那		28,000		30,285
格林纳达		4,128		553
瓜德罗普		6,467		48,046
危地马拉		775,084		333,992
圭亚那		301,036		259,165
海地		112,988		68,615

1998 年中国出口主要商品输往地

塑料

输往地	1998		1997	
	数量	金额(美元)	数量	金额(美元)
洪都拉斯		123,647		80,600
牙买加		630,817		939,939
马提尼克		4,617		
墨西哥		9,665,499		6,264,303
尼加拉瓜		127,846		51,298
巴拿马		15,901,836		10,143,643
巴拉圭		3,019,907		1,674,556
秘鲁		1,886,383		1,489,701
波多黎各		2,891,740		2,064,024
圣卢西亚		13,253		11,880
圣马丁岛		17,915		21,900
萨尔瓦多		281,156		364,519
苏里南		181,795		121,659
特立尼达和多巴哥		394,969		185,866
乌拉圭		4,064,479		2,203,845
委内瑞拉		3,774,558		2,591,601
加拿大		175,044,683		138,713,587
美国		1,418,742,890		1,205,933,663
格陵兰		42,953		7,938
澳大利亚		83,444,607		77,685,492
斐济		573,850		724,938
瑙鲁		3,049		1,182
新喀里多尼亚		137,983		75,577
瓦努阿图		22,290		2,664
新西兰		9,569,690		8,687,194
巴布亚新几内亚		299,966		404,644
社会群岛		30,225		76,719
所罗门群岛		32,939		36,144
汤加		11,886		13,694
萨摩亚		72,645		57,557
密克罗尼西亚联邦		12,103		
马绍尔群岛共和国		52,299		35,252
贝劳共和国		43,882		21,541
其他		67,766		383,950

1998年中国出口主要商品输往地

各种染料

输往地	1998		1997	
	数量(公吨)	金额(美元)	数量(公吨)	金额(美元)
总值	**131,690**	**497,269,310**	**127,284**	**527,588,807**
阿富汗	47	127,350		
孟加拉国	2,440	4,231,730	1,850	3,002,318
缅甸	555	1,100,568	538	1,406,320
朝鲜	97	382,023	54	206,219
香港	12,222	48,624,864	14,754	68,217,350
印度	3,061	13,228,630	2,697	13,008,240
印度尼西亚	7,634	20,317,997	10,248	32,512,329
伊朗	2,230	7,171,263	3,069	9,736,834
以色列	32	240,908	68	335,305
日本	8,619	33,275,763	8,104	34,113,735
约旦	116	642,206	91	336,733
澳门	11	52,207	3	13,355
马来西亚	349	1,474,515	294	1,066,148
尼泊尔	21	138,160	23	108,903
巴基斯坦	5,296	12,928,416	3,856	10,448,037
菲律宾	227	940,277	248	1,089,517
沙特阿拉伯	4	8,149	66	186,510
新加坡	840	4,352,552	1,252	6,651,943
韩国	20,141	65,222,570	18,392	68,116,594
斯里兰卡	68	298,128	110	396,397
叙利亚	664	2,177,364	555	2,595,439
泰国	3,424	9,813,257	3,651	11,815,330
土耳其	1,407	7,100,471	1,523	6,985,784
阿拉伯联合酋长国	318	1,041,760	351	1,349,704
也门共和国	14	65,235	9	39,189
越南	1,835	5,416,654	1,212	3,899,638
台湾省	13,907	50,779,047	12,268	51,914,030
阿尔及利亚	9	45,859	21	98,550
贝宁	9	45,574		
吉布提	1	10,932	2	14,102
埃及	1,698	4,965,780	1,370	3,474,677
埃塞俄比亚	12	76,487	13	80,555
加纳	4	44,992	3	31,401
几内亚	25	90,814		
科特迪瓦	197	857,343	29	116,694
肯尼亚	55	195,841	10	42,341

1998年中国出口主要商品输往地

各种染料

输往地	1998		1997	
	数量(公吨)	金额(美元)	数量(公吨)	金额(美元)
马里	8	19,480	14	126,266
毛里求斯	162	404,551	141	610,571
摩洛哥	310	1,055,048	259	849,684
莫桑比克	10	61,001		
尼日利亚	312	1,367,163	249	1,237,643
南非	301	1,528,354	76	297,674
苏丹	29	89,142	37	132,514
坦桑尼亚	23	47,340	4	15,819
突尼斯	29	45,477	61	141,665
津巴布韦	12	85,319	5	6,081
斯威士兰	35	104,974		
比利时	885	4,419,812	1,189	6,834,589
英国	4,437	19,022,056	4,017	19,308,927
德国	3,831	21,704,231	2,241	10,438,122
法国	206	1,118,963	86	598,801
爱尔兰	20	92,844	11	118,700
意大利	3,372	11,989,334	3,344	12,261,536
荷兰	5,204	30,915,138	5,751	32,934,526
希腊	267	1,176,718	267	967,218
葡萄牙	448	527,257	441	534,446
西班牙	1,843	5,680,394	1,575	4,730,583
奥地利	1	11,787	1	9,235
芬兰	10	58,318	29	40,900
匈牙利	10	19,136		5,623
波兰	128	422,122	98	509,095
瑞典	37	89,832	85	387,420
瑞士	2,442	14,199,773	2,130	11,827,760
哈萨克斯坦	3	25,088	25	116,500
吉尔吉斯斯坦		402		
俄罗斯	83	190,746	82	151,196
捷克共和国		762		
斯洛伐克共和国		382		389
阿根廷	964	2,656,073	1,003	3,418,306
巴西	2,520	7,883,325	2,314	9,992,020
智利	111	476,363	108	460,765
哥伦比亚	285	856,780	272	901,295
多米尼克		167		458

1998 年中国出口主要商品输往地

各种染料

输　往　地	1998		1997	
	数量(公吨)	金额(美元)	数量(公吨)	金额(美元)
哥斯达黎加		500		
厄瓜多尔	156	449,557	136	356,961
危地马拉	187	268,531	240	352,488
圭亚那	1	4,150		
海地		1,615		
墨西哥	1,550	4,850,627	879	2,896,373
巴拿马	101	343,596	60	289,913
秘鲁	96	406,873	72	186,090
波多黎各		3,234		
乌拉圭	45	126,758	3	13,509
委内瑞拉	103	443,240	96	540,582
加拿大	339	1,263,021	262	1,196,761
美国	12,654	61,061,017	12,284	66,015,639
澳大利亚	523	2,162,302	399	1,706,404
新西兰	7	48,210	49	306,765
巴布亚新几内亚	1	4,741		2,600
其他			156	348,174

各类船

输　往　地	1998		1997	
	数量(艘)	金额(美元)	数量(艘)	金额(美元)
总值	**30,158**	**1,731,599,433**	**18,668**	**1,618,483,887**
孟加拉国	1	436,050		
文莱	4	925		
缅甸	128	25,238,347	82	58,699,303
柬埔寨	1	100		
塞浦路斯	3	29,701,075		
朝鲜	12	23,034	11	217,116
香港	404	154,461,626	582	182,564,225
印度	10	108,777	162	207,437
印度尼西亚	79	54,391,190	21	4,054,300
以色列	4	1,040	36	7,760
日本	12,923	22,979,347	10,482	59,138,901
黎巴嫩	16	23,750		
澳门	76	2,097,700	18	458,283
马来西亚	16	152,197,900	8	105,150,010

1998年中国出口主要商品输往地

各类船

输往地	1998		1997	
	数量(艘)	金额(美元)	数量(艘)	金额(美元)
蒙古	2	4,824		
菲律宾	4	38,667,198	30	36,691,184
新加坡	181	226,307,475	237	178,201,052
韩国	378	3,719,332	354	15,817,001
斯里兰卡	5	6,506,300		
泰国	28	8,521,667	6	12,220,706
阿拉伯联合酋长国	78	156,146	64	129,138
越南	13	40,752	104	176,852
台湾省	829	3,514,291	71	2,679,917
加蓬	8	2,770,000	2	1,326,000
加纳	1	12,493		
科特迪瓦	4	482		
利比里亚	3	19,220,096	4	63,022,000
苏丹	1	337,265	15	70,726
比利时	111	79,771		
丹麦	374	78,683,460	420	28,491,301
英国	1,636	89,616,863	496	27,688,179
德国	1,211	374,959,294	629	229,913,896
法国	3,754	66,323,306	441	112,360
爱尔兰	3	23,119,488	1	7,706,496
意大利	1,070	531,535	303	318,213
荷兰	2,314	763,990	1,758	2,878,844
希腊	567	89,900,571	200	37,547
葡萄牙	100	21,613	200	40,557
西班牙	544	3,113,464	100	23,131
奥地利	40	7,800		
直布罗陀	1	2,650,000		
马耳他	21	2,450		
挪威	1,436	81,400,258	309	343,295,562
瑞典	165	105,395	290	65,366
俄罗斯	9	293,000		
斯洛文尼亚共和国	1	258,400		
捷克共和国	1	20,737,700	103	62,232,462
斯洛伐克共和国	87	24,684		
巴哈马	1	22,000,000	2	42,100,000
哥伦比亚	2	2,630,946		
墨西哥	115	15,050		

1998年中国出口主要商品输往地

各类船

输 往 地	1998		1997	
	数量(艘)	金额(美元)	数量(艘)	金额(美元)
巴拿马	41	69,327,893	45	79,604,320
加拿大	63	5,414,749	31	65,092,861
美国	998	44,670,811	466	2,790,523
澳大利亚	235	3,371,649	92	511,094
新西兰	46	136,111	55	10,165
其他			438	4,739,099

集装箱

输 往 地	1998		1997	
	数量(只)	金额(美元)	数量(只)	金额(美元)
总值	**569,706**	**1,586,890,412**	**329,521**	**1,028,063,532**
朝鲜	1	2,537	100	195,000
香港	182,458	557,380,470	188,145	575,830,794
印度	6,174	14,668,962	2,868	6,742,523
印度尼西亚	1,251	3,461,230		
以色列	990	2,154,400	620	1,137,000
日本	10,346	33,304,319	7,998	23,105,729
科威特	385	850,775		
马来西亚	216	812,260	365	808,625
巴基斯坦	14	27,500		
菲律宾	583	2,693,695		
新加坡	1,575	9,561,126	1,893	10,203,692
韩国	108,626	301,630,813	59,207	194,103,302
泰国	1,347	4,166,890		
阿拉伯联合酋长国	2	3,900		
台湾省	47,191	131,990,793	20,980	62,959,520
喀麦隆	40	362,325		
埃及	88	245,520		
南非	1	19,000		
比利时	3,452	11,307,494	419	1,430,694
丹麦	3,704	7,748,804	3,050	5,347,800
英国	25,837	52,558,201	6,952	17,099,307
德国	51,837	123,517,460	12,838	30,622,205
法国	7,948	18,552,195	842	5,467,250
意大利	512	3,587,417	501	2,143,650
荷兰	577	5,927,888	1,329	13,255,415

1998年中国出口主要商品输往地

集装箱

输往地	1998		1997	
	数量(只)	金额(美元)	数量(只)	金额(美元)
西班牙	232	2,199,693		
瑞典	36	211,200	298	890,650
瑞士	5,535	12,504,364		
阿根廷	177	1,964,700	100	830,000
巴西	130	1,485,000		
古巴	8	8,000	69	70,100
巴拿马	9,506	20,534,201	3,400	7,707,000
乌拉圭	25	268,186		
加拿大	68	421,400	40	272,000
美国	96,897	250,343,674	13,981	50,056,974
澳大利亚	1,610	9,038,460	1,300	7,457,078
新西兰	327	1,375,560	332	3,134,300
其他			1,894	7,192,924

汽车

输往地	1998		1997	
	数量(辆)	金额(美元)	数量(辆)	金额(美元)
总值	9,833	154,700,682	13,401	188,907,288
孟加拉国	86	1,573,072	9	328,482
缅甸	286	5,762,402	333	4,292,976
柬埔寨	53	347,640	209	1,965,522
塞浦路斯	16	115,416	4	29,500
朝鲜	993	7,155,613	2,310	15,505,790
香港	949	34,616,416	2,677	73,012,561
印度	31	609,444	17	52,378
印度尼西亚	3	679,000	11	382,000
伊朗	17	13,270,719		
以色列	3	7,518		
日本	48	741,344	168	1,928,725
约旦	1	9,225	87	653,026
科威特	17	236,573	93	624,636
老挝	145	1,351,750	333	4,258,527
黎巴嫩	95	639,600	63	464,100
蒙古	79	1,621,971	107	1,502,204
尼泊尔	75	811,304	24	203,517
阿曼	24	201,519		

1998年中国出口主要商品输往地

汽车

输往地	1998		1997	
	数量(辆)	金额(美元)	数量(辆)	金额(美元)
巴基斯坦	2	56,109	103	6,227,312
菲律宾	58	781,016	143	1,147,653
沙特阿拉伯	475	4,075,672	1,277	12,615,396
韩国	82	3,454,544	19	315,230
斯里兰卡	3	21,308	1	8,000
叙利亚	64	259,790	100	304,000
泰国	1	23,976	6	272,885
土耳其	19	4,501,040		
阿拉伯联合酋长国	40	1,083,586	259	3,333,058
也门共和国	12	116,749	89	689,889
越南	255	4,195,963	358	4,024,077
台湾省	8	134,000		
安哥拉	7	233,550		
博茨瓦那	4	37,067		
布隆迪	2	39,990		
喀麦隆	16	234,230	27	373,646
刚果	4	146,736	2	26,178
埃及	1,313	5,506,862	493	3,220,209
赤道几内亚	15	386,002	9	266,346
埃塞俄比亚	211	2,983,105	106	1,205,851
冈比亚	6	36,000		
加纳	64	1,421,403	27	92,012
几内亚	33	517,794	19	244,532
科特迪瓦	96	1,003,717	145	1,918,118
肯尼亚	31	1,081,309	162	2,520,704
利比里亚	2	4,334		
马达加斯加	39	610,863	7	50,266
马里	17	559,264	6	98,748
毛里塔尼亚	4	81,320		
摩洛哥	18	247,864	42	260,753
莫桑比克	6	52,307	18	252,000
纳米比亚	12	85,200		
尼日利亚	106	3,705,302	73	1,769,017
塞内加尔	8	51,375		
塞舌尔	1	7,463	4	80,179
塞拉利昂	15	92,900		
南非	772	8,470,155	251	2,909,839

1998 年中国出口主要商品输往地

汽车

输往地	1998		1997	
	数量(辆)	金额(美元)	数量(辆)	金额(美元)
苏丹	240	7,896,140	522	13,034,703
坦桑尼亚	153	2,291,268	301	7,422,083
乌干达	52	1,266,760	69	1,113,928
扎伊尔	100	1,863,846	1	29,119
赞比亚	10	31,562	14	140,335
津巴布韦	90	1,193,703	9	80,441
厄立特里亚	151	1,319,197	9	72,316
比利时	1	10,800		
英国	17	218,166	14	447,210
德国	7	1,024,602	2	298,216
法国	17	165,914		
意大利	7	54,300	24	25,600
荷兰	1	125,540	24	27,755
西班牙	8	24,000		
马耳他	8	42,344	44	319,649
波兰	2	72,500		
罗马尼亚	1	14,785	5	25,598
瑞典	6	99,500	1	14,000
格鲁吉亚	6	1,849,398		
阿塞拜疆	1	57,190		
哈萨克斯坦	20	242,113		
吉尔吉斯斯坦	4	35,600	2	15,797
摩尔多瓦	2	6,945		
俄罗斯	62	1,000,030	3	66,817
塔吉克斯坦	16	466,807	18	389,121
土库曼斯坦	2	48,193	3	527,472
乌克兰	4	100,072	2	9,303
乌兹别克斯坦	3	24,797		
南斯拉夫	5	18,340		
安提瓜和巴布达	13	154,215		
阿根廷	1,583	10,025,062	865	5,548,323
巴哈马	1	8,800		
巴巴多斯	5	68,367		
玻利维亚	124	2,210,400		
巴西	11	43,019	2	171,151
智利	3	78,908	61	716,250
哥伦比亚	11	30,515	6	54,000

1998年中国出口主要商品输往地

汽车

输往地	1998		1997	
	数量(辆)	金额(美元)	数量(辆)	金额(美元)
哥斯达黎加	3	57,222		
古巴	6	50,316	414	1,234,389
多米尼加共和国	42	268,917	103	756,297
厄瓜多尔	6	68,254		
危地马拉	11	59,298	8	20,377
圭亚那	8	21,018		
尼加拉瓜	3	28,500	6	22,235
巴拿马	1	9,500	4	42,693
巴拉圭	57	346,980	33	194,630
秘鲁	22	56,098	120	906,066
圣马丁岛	6	15,804		
苏里南	5	137,605	4	41,747
乌拉圭	68	536,394	161	1,276,981
委内瑞拉	27	352,273		
加拿大	1	30,000	3	20,600
美国	70	1,942,697	59	431,371
澳大利亚	1	5,315		
新西兰	1	250,000	3	85,900
基里巴斯	4	185,000		
密克罗尼西亚联邦	2	45,402		
其他			291	3,894,973

汽车零件

输往地	1998		1997	
	数量	金额(美元)	数量	金额(美元)
总值		**530,486,376**		**447,211,451**
阿富汗		453,827		171,100
巴林		22,869		28,572
孟加拉国		479,801		583,404
文莱		90		273
缅甸		1,574,632		2,100,045
柬埔寨		22,063		209,161
塞浦路斯		689		
朝鲜		159,622		78,142
香港		11,608,453		14,587,468
印度		233,425		355,759

1998年中国出口主要商品输往地

汽车零件

输往地	1998		1997	
	数量	金额(美元)	数量	金额(美元)
印度尼西亚		2,306,651		5,972,187
伊朗		111,248		352,604
伊拉克		125,000		
以色列		1,691,163		458,263
日本		105,847,905		92,951,194
约旦		437,690		313,872
科威特		115,509		234,567
老挝		115,573		154,847
黎巴嫩		199,621		124,356
澳门		1,876		4,033
马来西亚		2,549,895		7,884,687
蒙古		106,866		257,556
尼泊尔		152,966		33,572
阿曼		27,196		12,710
巴基斯坦		1,456,076		3,435,245
菲律宾		3,614,823		7,219,594
卡塔尔		20,573		66,154
沙特阿拉伯		1,786,419		1,512,643
新加坡		4,678,387		12,903,922
韩国		1,886,422		4,607,572
斯里兰卡		874,732		1,218,967
叙利亚		271,821		369,189
泰国		3,993,083		10,846,684
土耳其		1,155,214		445,193
阿拉伯联合酋长国		3,996,993		4,658,465
也门共和国		180,069		512,086
越南		4,618,448		3,994,944
台湾省		8,728,842		8,525,351
阿尔及利亚		783,121		417,058
安哥拉		4,575		
贝宁		3,176		15,466
博茨瓦那		69,278		
布隆迪		3,600		
喀麦隆		117,238		55,526
吉布提		14,081		
埃及		2,503,967		1,029,377
埃塞俄比亚		149,141		487,802

1998 年中国出口主要商品输往地

汽车零件

输往地	1998		1997	
	数量	金额(美元)	数量	金额(美元)
加蓬		601		
冈比亚		7,380		744
加纳		516,071		122,916
几内亚		131,223		9,011
科特迪瓦		329,767		541,429
肯尼亚		371,893		241,936
利比里亚		22,070		
马达加斯加		31,012		1,928
马里		77,353		98,808
毛里塔尼亚		30,999		
毛里求斯		39,707		8,007
摩洛哥		140,001		53,372
莫桑比克		6,700		
纳米比亚		15,405		72,306
尼日利亚		2,574,650		2,186,918
留尼汪		12,516		
卢旺达		3,398		13,177
塞舌尔		531		
南非		4,830,741		4,608,396
苏丹		348,477		1,035,887
坦桑尼亚		791,026		680,220
多哥		4,815		1,168
突尼斯		73,900		156,941
乌干达		35,210		175,913
扎伊尔		3,586		
赞比亚		22,056		11,040
津巴布韦		164,856		592,148
厄立特里亚		42,138		1,620
比利时		1,046,812		769,742
丹麦		725,720		582,032
英国		8,310,267		7,366,496
德国		19,711,067		6,206,220
法国		6,472,445		4,283,903
爱尔兰		287,559		117,898
意大利		9,144,057		6,027,544
荷兰		4,258,276		2,363,656
希腊		552,218		638,339

1998年中国出口主要商品输往地

汽车零件

输往地	1998		1997	
	数量	金额(美元)	数量	金额(美元)
葡萄牙		157,205		112,580
西班牙		18,252,979		1,989,922
阿尔巴尼亚		39,609		20,809
奥地利		166,040		188,489
保加利亚		128,536		4,644
芬兰		319,193		324,059
匈牙利		563,024		861,111
冰岛		29,469		
马耳他		6,282		26,211
挪威		202,664		355,992
波兰		308,938		258,254
罗马尼亚		18,263		85,544
瑞典		636,319		660,811
瑞士		81,744		35,082
拉脱维亚		40,692		
立陶宛		1,742		
哈萨克斯坦		96,261		
俄罗斯		113,220		91,180
塔吉克斯坦		51,350		675
土库曼斯坦		226,969		233,830
乌克兰		8,241		85,867
乌兹别克斯坦		80		
南斯拉夫		400		
斯洛文尼亚共和国		78,083		19,365
捷克共和国		102,393		23
安提瓜和巴布达		600		
阿根廷		1,418,086		685,862
巴巴多斯		7,552		
玻利维亚		108,072		37,620
巴西		734,490		3,224,279
智利		961,910		500,183
哥伦比亚		635,424		183,982
多米尼克		41,273		58,209
哥斯达黎加		70,312		68,465
古巴		1,659,024		1,373,584
多米尼加共和国		35,475		58,686
厄瓜多尔		558,989		544,562

1998年中国出口主要商品输往地

汽车零件

输往地	1998		1997	
	数量	金额(美元)	数量	金额(美元)
危地马拉		80,689		95,555
洪都拉斯		84,569		
牙买加		5,661		
墨西哥		536,318		285,583
巴拿马		706,554		351,532
巴拉圭		122,566		67,180
秘鲁		464,981		439,797
波多黎各		35,608		33,850
圣马丁岛		1,104		
苏里南		6,514		1,097
乌拉圭		155,488		125,968
委内瑞拉		997,507		790,754
加拿大		25,164,975		11,252,660
美国		237,236,542		189,138,631
澳大利亚		6,169,803		3,892,801
新喀里多尼亚		2,193		318
新西兰		389,413		304,882
巴布亚新几内亚		21,485		42,386
所罗门群岛		4,300		
基里巴斯		48,000		71,799
其他				67,453

电线电缆

输往地	1998		1997	
	数量(公吨)	金额(美元)	数量(公吨)	金额(美元)
总值	**363,381**	**979,828,560**	**303,428**	**869,769,264**
巴林	5	9,243		
孟加拉国	1,137	2,898,673	366	1,237,351
文莱	16	18,108		
缅甸	879	2,968,143	1,170	3,485,442
柬埔寨	307	669,387	17	86,304
塞浦路斯	58	189,166	1,935	3,701,856
朝鲜	239	708,417	267	899,564
香港	80,074	174,282,331	84,721	185,291,831
印度	446	993,926	2,837	8,328,255
印度尼西亚	894	1,925,555	1,763	5,054,273

1998 年中国出口主要商品输往地

电线电缆

输往地	1998		1997	
	数量(公吨)	金额(美元)	数量(公吨)	金额(美元)
伊朗	2,296	11,276,952	232	1,873,753
伊拉克	4	17,243		
以色列	443	740,602	188	412,866
日本	45,625	266,367,260	34,539	235,179,801
约旦	203	284,857	23	65,273
科威特	206	350,207	92	202,814
老挝	17	50,192	23	73,013
黎巴嫩	304	535,960	34	74,428
澳门	445	999,394	349	931,478
马来西亚	2,530	7,439,227	1,764	8,583,026
蒙古	110	325,931	233	551,585
尼泊尔	48	189,933	69	224,308
阿曼	28	60,031	24	49,248
巴基斯坦	4,875	10,371,626	8,579	28,673,079
菲律宾	1,552	2,996,416	798	2,376,595
卡塔尔	39	83,599	12	27,694
沙特阿拉伯	896	1,415,812	576	1,061,858
新加坡	16,080	38,428,660	12,118	35,076,670
韩国	15,601	45,378,743	13,714	61,311,657
斯里兰卡	259	603,328	191	404,596
叙利亚	818	4,098,229	326	2,177,626
泰国	2,621	6,835,405	1,885	4,638,239
土耳其	116	195,540	27	43,652
阿拉伯联合酋长国	2,969	4,961,708	1,435	2,929,336
也门共和国	407	649,135	797	1,704,354
越南	549	1,806,383	869	2,541,195
台湾省	30,707	72,656,148	28,896	65,362,804
阿尔及利亚	267	456,307	83	176,787
安哥拉	2	3,430		96
贝宁	61	75,978	66	131,746
博茨瓦那		70	4	12,629
喀麦隆	11	28,786		
刚果	38	80,540		
吉布提		2,095	3	9,815
埃及	354	683,714	128	289,913
赤道几内亚	10	22,967	2	6,341
埃塞俄比亚	30	63,175	12	47,754

1998年中国出口主要商品输往地

电线电缆

输往地	1998		1997	
	数量(公吨)	金额(美元)	数量(公吨)	金额(美元)
加蓬	33	94,597		
冈比亚		117		
加纳	52	104,555	33	72,444
几内亚	2	4,978		
科特迪瓦	64	172,323	43	106,091
肯尼亚	46	108,556	32	113,043
利比里亚	14	48,439		
利比亚	34	46,305		
马达加斯加	83	88,037	60	117,485
马里	3	41,978		
毛里塔尼亚	1	5,634		
毛里求斯	51	91,765	17	52,023
摩洛哥	454	739,135	192	340,586
莫桑比克		200	1	2,726
纳米比亚		1,822		
尼日利亚	532	891,435	560	993,675
塞舌尔	7	18,221		
南非	493	776,746	303	554,351
苏丹	13	71,093	75	322,052
坦桑尼亚	1	3,171	1	300
多哥	11	27,727	10	22,652
突尼斯	22	27,669	57	111,368
赞比亚	7	33,344	2	1,320
津巴布韦	2	15,651		
比利时	1,069	2,111,469	371	720,810
丹麦	232	556,564	70	240,129
英国	11,440	17,650,263	8,345	12,303,394
德国	17,518	39,650,541	11,541	24,866,267
法国	3,844	8,422,688	5,707	10,244,000
爱尔兰	375	1,544,464	61	399,690
意大利	2,085	3,874,951	1,073	2,087,288
卢森堡	4	6,346		304
荷兰	2,663	4,912,440	1,763	3,472,755
希腊	372	609,017	251	295,228
葡萄牙	152	251,801	42	87,693
西班牙	1,212	3,828,006	828	2,468,424
阿尔巴尼亚	7	12,439	25	78,961

1998年中国出口主要商品输往地

电线电缆

输往地	1998		1997	
	数量(公吨)	金额(美元)	数量(公吨)	金额(美元)
奥地利	116	274,290	82	167,584
保加利亚	229	532,783	80	202,683
芬兰	185	362,283	27	81,733
匈牙利	596	1,467,687	917	1,836,318
冰岛	2	3,865		
马耳他	41	121,766	74	109,149
挪威	242	464,076	251	463,115
波兰	412	630,207	129	169,129
罗马尼亚	9	15,755		810
瑞典	1,317	8,650,768	569	1,241,655
瑞士	242	477,237	118	138,893
拉脱维亚	30	62,989	1	431
立陶宛	57	106,084	5	9,370
阿塞拜疆		108		
白俄罗斯	10	13,499		8
哈萨克斯坦	10	45,172	2	6,644
吉尔吉斯斯坦		150		
俄罗斯	247	767,582	529	2,622,743
塔吉克斯坦	6	4,335		
土库曼斯坦	10	46,394		
乌克兰	66	126,516		
南斯拉夫	15	28,180	5	46,090
斯洛文尼亚共和国	28	68,545		5
克罗地亚共和国	4	9,396		
捷克共和国	562	672,137	400	433,968
斯洛伐克共和国	14	19,970		
安提瓜和巴布达	3	17,000		
阿根廷	185	249,905	141	186,132
玻利维亚	2	2,895		
巴西	844	1,436,191	233	761,366
智利	655	1,109,891	370	658,433
哥伦比亚	146	291,174	58	155,777
多米尼克	140	370,868	16	43,826
哥斯达黎加	29	55,391		
古巴	47	241,365	116	575,488
多米尼加共和国	47	104,763		
厄瓜多尔	58	142,972	26	62,308

1998年中国出口主要商品输往地

电线电缆

输往地	1998		1997	
	数量(公吨)	金额(美元)	数量(公吨)	金额(美元)
危地马拉	10	11,921		
圭亚那	45	135,694	10	25,113
海地	11	27,050		
牙买加	1	6,827		
墨西哥	906	2,506,231	133	592,798
尼加拉瓜	2	4,338		
巴拿马	204	407,798	157	322,291
巴拉圭	8	7,884	14	34,955
秘鲁	65	113,932	15	37,894
波多黎各	35	105,133	23	58,992
苏里南	126	528,482	21	9,987
特立尼达和多巴哥	1	2,414	2	4,584
乌拉圭	18	33,455	16	19,385
委内瑞拉	109	238,941	21	46,971
加拿大	2,089	4,065,064	1,269	3,262,825
美国	91,090	189,028,101	61,756	121,665,298
澳大利亚	4,012	10,254,240	2,928	7,885,620
斐济		56		
盖比群岛	58	111,205		
新西兰	473	755,245	203	333,570
巴布亚新几内亚	27	447,189		836
密克罗尼西亚联邦		152		
其他			79	108,513

金属切削机床

输往地	1998		1997	
	数量(台)	金额(美元)	数量(台)	金额(美元)
总值	**2,255,084**	**235,073,457**	**2,493,102**	**281,497,252**
巴林	1	9,291	7	72,146
孟加拉国	2,543	1,073,418	5,488	464,778
文莱	69	23,891	11	41,751
缅甸	280	4,067,651	218	3,309,090
柬埔寨	94	166,229	232	118,481
塞浦路斯	143	58,018	196	476,091
朝鲜	19	190,350	21	205,174
香港	63,890	18,161,660	11,932	18,106,990

1998年中国出口主要商品输往地

金属切削机床

输往地	1998		1997	
	数量(台)	金额(美元)	数量(台)	金额(美元)
印度	767	2,280,499	571	2,745,404
印度尼西亚	446	1,364,141	28,795	23,557,037
伊朗	5,923	6,996,500	3,018	4,893,384
以色列	301	348,458	1,387	193,991
日本	33,684	8,201,906	34,524	9,403,413
约旦	676	160,967	2,180	152,764
科威特	63	47,038	3	8,400
老挝	20	18,362	18	102,886
黎巴嫩	690	127,458	2,872	1,253,930
澳门	67	149,417	158	318,899
马来西亚	5,060	3,018,918	18,828	20,076,767
蒙古	18	7,282	16	17,184
尼泊尔	9	27,277	23	241,954
巴基斯坦	241	2,204,532	1,116	904,699
菲律宾	4,084	786,884	5,043	6,235,711
沙特阿拉伯	7,621	1,028,801	3,515	936,360
新加坡	1,244	5,020,394	5,270	6,715,930
韩国	70	526,421	1,717	3,452,199
斯里兰卡	2,447	400,771	3,344	405,420
叙利亚	582	815,528	798	565,348
泰国	2,245	12,751,974	7,094	4,950,583
土耳其	17,172	733,690	13,137	1,163,365
阿拉伯联合酋长国	6,422	1,058,602	4,409	1,050,671
也门共和国	115	300,023	501	292,235
越南	7,699	3,503,586	6,271	4,012,757
台湾省	3,836	2,180,607	1,081	1,380,040
阿尔及利亚	16	55,733	153	795,009
博茨瓦那	13	24,231	3	630
喀麦隆	14	278,756	2	23,333
吉布提	10	20,164	6	120,408
埃及	3,261	2,452,988	3,990	3,524,876
埃塞俄比亚	251	259,342	649	993,154
加蓬	18	31,677	1	14,900
加纳	175	244,204	124	307,802
几内亚	4	17,579	2	16,919
科特迪瓦	459	393,904	136	57,535
肯尼亚	374	56,336	231	32,187

1998 年中国出口主要商品输往地

金属切削机床

输往地	1998		1997	
	数量(台)	金额(美元)	数量(台)	金额(美元)
利比里亚	1	560		
马达加斯加	22	30,070	1	400
马里	7	15,563	1	6,810
毛里塔尼亚	3	36,520		
毛里求斯	103	35,233	495	43,813
摩洛哥	1,539	72,396	335	57,570
纳米比亚	6	2,237	6	8,427
尼日利亚	113	774,645	95	957,643
塞舌尔	3	1,435	6	164
塞拉利昂	5	17,617		
南非	18,727	3,585,664	18,489	4,416,358
苏丹	87	5,379,082	215	154,981
坦桑尼亚	14	12,206	1	547
突尼斯	1,291	137,614	1,237	103,871
津巴布韦	31	27,761	75	112,841
比利时	33,856	2,550,758	18,235	1,336,012
丹麦	5,207	667,521	9,298	514,418
英国	127,124	14,287,930	188,159	7,824,457
德国	360,618	18,094,379	340,918	19,511,394
法国	116,926	3,464,268	126,406	3,462,494
爱尔兰	314	119,055	751	165,875
意大利	63,434	5,036,456	101,994	6,493,075
荷兰	94,935	4,019,931	105,779	4,096,264
希腊	1,950	425,101	1,226	202,954
葡萄牙	8,019	801,513	6,845	752,249
西班牙	41,738	2,019,417	27,598	1,527,200
阿尔巴尼亚	3	4,600		
奥地利	15,651	1,207,191	19,665	964,806
芬兰	9,157	530,157	7,833	431,113
匈牙利	3,810	104,422	3	6,481
冰岛	9	870	1	8,520
马耳他	105	9,447		
挪威	10,031	461,348	12,351	489,325
波兰	7,467	671,752	12,145	785,040
瑞典	21,066	961,153	19,100	1,022,169
瑞士	5,483	799,484	5,680	301,768
哈萨克斯坦	12	22,199	20	68,683

1998年中国出口主要商品输往地

金属切削机床

输往地	1998		1997	
	数量(台)	金额(美元)	数量(台)	金额(美元)
吉尔吉斯斯坦	1	1,084	1	3,000
俄罗斯	2,373	118,916	16	20,437
塔吉克斯坦	9	2,533		
斯洛文尼亚共和国	7	20,949	10	66,682
克罗地亚共和国	1	5,000	1	12,030
捷克共和国	352	38,594		
阿根廷	29,953	5,396,336	26,484	4,606,691
伯利兹	2	10,753		
玻利维亚	915	179,858	13	29,528
巴西	76,299	2,840,472	89,080	2,704,952
智利	13,135	1,671,488	17,459	1,705,244
哥伦比亚	1,992	737,695	3,493	612,725
多米尼克	2	474		
哥斯达黎加	176	5,412		
厄瓜多尔	2,725	329,502	1,891	199,061
危地马拉	627	232,637	96	39,480
洪都拉斯	15	51,651	49	72,234
墨西哥	10,114	3,007,433	1,321	2,559,755
尼加拉瓜	2	24,226	2	149,225
巴拿马	36	123,919	52	5,953
巴拉圭	585	41,539	1,845	98,443
秘鲁	8,807	767,537	5,000	12,032,824
萨尔瓦多	59	150,284		
特立尼达和多巴哥	5	21,388	3	8,101
乌拉圭	7,072	806,783	6,775	552,747
委内瑞拉	10,653	689,585	13,381	758,702
加拿大	126,680	8,813,350	141,467	7,881,475
美国	774,910	53,189,587	896,298	56,933,251
澳大利亚	57,338	6,940,883	78,989	9,012,132
斐济	1	120	2	1,704
瓦努阿图	1	3,520	3	8,558
新西兰	8,121	768,062	14,439	1,365,771
巴布亚新几内亚	31	21,746	4	40,045
汤加	1	2,500		
萨摩亚	1	821		
基里巴斯	80	23,807		
其他			874	476,195

1998 年中国出口主要商品输往地

照相机

输往地	1998		1997	
	数量(架)	金额(美元)	数量(架)	金额(美元)
总值	**67,465,551**	**994,004,682**	**65,589,906**	**925,329,284**
巴林	615,069	3,082,321		
孟加拉国	851	36,355	1,410	62,820
缅甸	2	748	1	276
塞浦路斯	1,040	8,244		
香港	10,227,066	177,571,206	10,777,895	161,082,867
印度	70,592	1,369,284	131,988	893,865
印度尼西亚	5,000	29,500	51,225	241,449
以色列	26,182	216,756	20,015	227,382
日本	10,816,554	204,979,994	4,968,837	264,818,948
约旦	19,580	297,062	11,296	137,770
科威特	19,935	193,562	16,350	201,209
黎巴嫩	4,770	59,650	5,170	93,970
澳门	131,373	677,545	17,689	152,933
马亚西亚	1,072,756	9,285,185	1,115,947	13,386,777
尼泊尔	320	11,365		
阿曼	50,500	492,340	20,080	370,036
巴基斯坦	13,070	43,842	6,500	71,442
巴勒斯坦	2,500	18,300		
菲律宾	5,632	34,666	4,000	17,153
沙特阿拉伯	15,320	121,730	23,264	318,482
新加坡	1,309,086	30,030,512	2,614,945	29,596,400
韩国	164,570	5,143,602	562,420	18,580,238
斯里兰卡	17	4,960	38	5,030
叙利亚	5,640	94,004	3,150	54,043
泰国	999	44,252	23,253	135,133
土耳其	77,303	746,633	58,200	650,659
阿拉伯联合酋长国	2,688,162	22,049,645	1,563,821	13,066,228
越南	16,546	267,290	8,976	157,886
台湾省	1,356,001	10,929,945	3,028,159	23,267,113
喀麦隆	20	193		
加那利群岛	1,220	43,894	950	34,680
埃及	1,350	30,748	4,282	27,577
肯尼亚	4	1,619		
摩洛哥	1	62		
塞舌尔	150	755		
塞拉利昂	2	1,508		

1998年中国出口主要商品输往地

照相机

输往地	1998		1997	
	数量(架)	金额(美元)	数量(架)	金额(美元)
南非	10,843	98,578	33,321	231,967
突尼斯	9,042	164,180	1,200	5,696
比利时	1,666,128	39,873,937	750,065	15,763,012
丹麦	29,328	735,307	40,253	860,340
英国	1,036,706	21,664,901	2,322,206	29,082,475
德国	12,413,555	124,827,188	7,227,751	61,666,776
法国	829,496	17,281,137	1,062,295	19,416,409
爱尔兰	3,000	114,000	360	2,039
意大利	241,077	3,694,846	413,232	4,677,891
荷兰	1,742,325	39,845,703	1,295,091	30,973,511
希腊	38,867	643,589	32,568	425,894
葡萄牙	7,364	214,616	27,873	122,272
西班牙	308,821	6,680,930	3,641,715	12,870,281
安道尔	150	4,912	100	4,157
奥地利	6,920	311,214	2,820	121,985
芬兰	285,639	3,877,600	258,984	6,036,372
匈牙利	20,791	469,190	65,149	273,945
冰岛	160	7,208		
挪威	7,005	175,739	8,919	301,571
波兰	230,102	2,396,510	149,459	1,180,165
罗马尼亚	100	350		
瑞典	56,242	1,435,145	52,144	1,504,433
瑞士	20,205	776,688	51,760	564,223
爱沙尼亚	500	1,658		
立陶宛	23,092	477,597	2,760	16,034
俄罗斯	77,939	522,001	454,642	5,387,554
南斯拉夫	135	2,136	160	2,473
捷克共和国	7,183	32,432	23,961	270,930
阿根廷	205,201	3,004,596	86,184	1,725,321
巴西	148,374	1,439,282	106,967	924,926
智利	311,684	1,729,558	70,592	547,943
哥伦比亚	34,706	800,939	24,868	154,265
墨西哥	620,947	5,320,389	343,992	2,216,980
巴拉圭	22,000	196,086	159,200	1,308,934
秘鲁	2,000	1,404	130	1,833
委内瑞拉	34,855	278,706	5,510	39,846
加拿大	224,572	6,527,176	262,822	6,059,671

1998年中国出口主要商品输往地

照相机

输往地	1998		1997	
	数量(架)	金额(美元)	数量(架)	金额(美元)
美国	17,946,257	238,270,224	21,177,338	189,478,336
澳大利亚	109,936	2,108,107	162,339	2,725,743
新西兰	13,121	79,646	2,572	23,022
其他			228,743	907,693

自行车

输往地	1998		1997	
	数量(辆)	金额(美元)	数量(辆)	金额(美元)
总值	**17,825,640**	**615,069,023**	**14,617,906**	**517,888,231**
阿富汗	96,683	3,921,146	161,240	6,826,558
巴林	6,124	179,343	5,201	157,775
孟加拉国	117,747	4,317,641	128,392	4,715,682
缅甸	37,425	1,068,437	114,154	3,934,562
柬埔寨	1,803	48,455	8,903	346,665
塞浦路斯	1,651	37,425	630	11,328
朝鲜	13,260	470,290	13,141	467,602
香港	939,700	25,619,298	273,807	8,892,311
印度	11,279	238,208	1,925	77,795
印度尼西亚	335	11,428	354,171	14,442,283
伊朗	143,791	4,568,588	26,070	765,018
以色列	54,810	1,477,292	35,077	1,037,494
日本	1,298,872	77,700,594	1,212,811	79,036,890
约旦	33,787	640,345	39,250	623,778
科威特	61,343	1,436,891	41,194	1,067,584
老挝	2,724	112,745	1,208	54,113
黎巴嫩	65,223	1,358,272	75,358	1,457,260
澳门	325	8,722	2,206	56,987
马来西亚	16,339	269,824	65,752	1,291,566
马尔代夫	690	10,230	1,710	31,321
蒙古	57	1,152	20	574
尼泊尔	7,095	257,402	7,147	267,290
巴基斯坦	25,161	892,972	15,904	467,922
菲律宾	17,470	352,206	93,789	2,030,723
卡塔尔	780	31,347	2,742	119,627
沙特阿拉伯	378,700	7,301,162	310,647	5,910,739
新加坡	34,637	1,083,081	66,851	2,407,755

1998 年中国出口主要商品输往地

自行车

输往地	1998		1997	
	数量(辆)	金额(美元)	数量(辆)	金额(美元)
韩国	292,828	7,006,918	427,824	14,633,552
斯里兰卡	42,550	952,514	23,164	532,473
泰国	610	14,452	611	36,235
土耳其	5,000	91,000	5,439	78,285
阿拉伯联合酋长国	991,728	18,439,342	769,222	15,586,895
也门共和国	10,850	221,817	11,235	246,308
越南	15,557	934,880	9,695	389,805
台湾省	25,546	558,423	902	21,585
阿尔及利亚	18,008	413,320	785	34,328
安哥拉	14,862	374,745	8,762	220,689
贝宁	12,924	589,632	8,063	332,193
博茨瓦那	4,788	93,868	20	740
喀麦隆	3,205	73,910	4,944	100,485
中非共和国	3,523	308,596		
刚果	1,612	69,197		
埃及	124,299	4,242,630	87,191	3,477,067
赤道几内亚	250	10,068	2,270	87,240
埃塞俄比亚	17,457	726,536	18,570	706,544
加蓬	1,156	29,447	1,900	38,990
冈比亚	2,876	109,457	770	30,288
加纳	153,652	5,738,139	160,886	6,331,242
几内亚	11,724	370,752	6,067	169,991
科特迪瓦	18,643	352,243	5,734	137,946
肯尼亚	40,057	1,203,245	25,289	950,634
利比亚	1,032	15,652		
马达加斯加	10,131	367,704	4,575	193,197
毛里求斯	13,355	290,192	14,617	338,734
摩洛哥	61,766	1,678,356	34,258	841,194
莫桑比克	700	24,337	2,477	56,716
纳米比亚	2,140	42,268	1,454	49,615
尼日利亚	87,702	2,926,066	72,230	2,430,826
塞内加尔	1,109	30,755	985	17,260
塞舌尔	695	15,305	224	6,064
塞拉利昂	3,226	101,914	4,648	184,292
南非	311,107	7,276,951	136,258	2,423,697
苏丹	31,107	1,128,570	49,227	2,055,691
坦桑尼亚	53,052	2,054,232	190,570	8,121,929

1998 年中国出口主要商品输往地

自行车

输往地	1998		1997	
	数量(辆)	金额(美元)	数量(辆)	金额(美元)
多哥	7,226	308,327	16,776	703,504
突尼斯	10,374	173,667		
乌干达	5,144	204,234	7,122	288,105
扎伊尔	2,640	103,999	2,337	99,054
津巴布韦	8,231	269,113	5,561	228,602
比利时	2,601	103,709	1,514	81,090
丹麦	191	11,482	241	14,450
英国	10,047	255,342	1,157	105,670
德国	62,289	1,527,886	83,940	3,741,263
法国	1,907	53,598	6,731	329,982
爱尔兰	275	18,250		
意大利	323	33,981	1,967	72,477
荷兰	54,499	866,984	3,239	85,048
希腊	88,454	1,757,987	27,595	573,543
葡萄牙	2,080	22,630	980	25,933
西班牙	6,109	127,606	5,955	206,120
阿尔巴尼亚	3,423	95,206		
奥地利	3,508	137,545	5,174	295,396
保加利亚	11,807	191,480	9,618	176,779
芬兰	12,582	208,320	3,621	66,706
匈牙利	88,255	1,553,093	84,683	1,892,770
冰岛	211	25,950	161	11,902
马耳他	600	10,939	1,992	37,014
挪威	95,298	1,610,143	87,724	1,457,881
波兰	70,995	2,352,826	42,192	879,763
罗马尼亚	80,394	1,851,443	13,982	350,483
瑞典	342	7,420	2,458	119,716
瑞士	9,057	509,848	7,612	441,281
爱沙尼亚	3,086	57,487		
拉脱维亚	8,899	180,607	7,835	170,580
立陶宛	25,508	484,727	17,610	394,881
哈萨克斯坦	12,205	393,197	1,419	25,780
吉尔吉斯斯坦	2,282	45,654	1,170	19,563
俄罗斯	31,408	973,426	13,957	555,722
乌克兰	47,134	1,859,107		
乌兹别克斯坦	510	27,540	1,920	41,038
南斯拉夫	1,212	18,777		

1998 年中国出口主要商品输往地

自行车

输往地	1998		1997	
	数量(辆)	金额(美元)	数量(辆)	金额(美元)
斯洛文尼亚共和国	4,600	83,400	6,410	120,940
克罗地亚共和国	14,870	365,666	18,306	544,460
捷克共和国	18,780	707,058	10,679	460,297
阿根廷	28,110	463,976	22,890	434,316
阿鲁巴岛	390	21,757		
巴哈马	1,150	23,500		
伯利兹	2,735	77,280	1,146	32,480
玻利维亚	17,106	708,555	2,905	66,381
巴西	95,643	1,449,505	241,805	4,525,141
开曼群岛	2,576	154,642		
智利	445,047	8,308,875	209,075	4,900,337
哥伦比亚	8,250	120,853	8,650	95,150
多米尼克国	70,843	1,151,576	48,439	840,684
哥斯达黎加	49,552	1,044,673	23,183	434,182
古巴	17,372	626,602	4,573	152,536
库腊索岛	2,626	103,726	430	23,220
多米尼加共和国	101,615	1,662,700	83,757	1,371,148
厄瓜多尔	101,079	1,932,141	104,814	2,204,624
危地马拉	34,527	652,918	19,598	374,511
圭业那	13,772	396,695	3,150	95,661
洪都拉斯	25,565	595,854	24,326	632,271
牙买加	12,657	347,705	7,651	227,501
墨西哥	53,939	790,980	15,000	294,915
巴拿马	1,002,100	22,171,353	1,234,785	24,226,296
巴拉圭	52,573	1,012,686	31,100	688,046
秘鲁	40,270	860,296	55,223	1,269,836
波多黎各	17,920	362,953	13,025	260,060
萨尔瓦多	15,358	283,757	15,073	273,903
苏里南	4,722	149,203	4,300	128,840
特立尼达和多巴哥	13,901	237,311	6,194	113,868
乌拉圭	56,049	897,965	68,016	980,840
委内瑞拉	182,538	3,888,896	60,349	1,210,454
英属维尔京群岛	15,967	948,746		
加拿大	335,358	12,415,389	129,241	4,575,084
美国	7,645,682	307,947,754	5,721,002	219,267,888
澳大利亚	704,122	27,951,497	716,957	32,097,362
斐济	2,025	43,117	2,333	66,343

1998年中国出口主要商品输往地

自行车

输往地	1998		1997	
	数量(辆)	金额(美元)	数量(辆)	金额(美元)
新路里多尼亚	210	6,787	552	29,035
瓦努阿图	1,382	60,703	590	27,451
新西兰	71,902	3,087,360	59,766	3,285,429
巴布亚新几内亚	10,960	222,945	16,318	515,502
基里巴斯	50	4,100	325	10,260
马绍尔群岛共和国	3	109	50	1,675
其他			7,511	175,276

电风扇

输往地	1998		1997	
	数量(台)	金额(美元)	数量(台)	金额(美元)
总值	**151,846,680**	**729,742,354**	**131,634,054**	**716,666,540**
巴林	4,427	64,646	3,741	79,076
孟加拉国	25,694	154,350	11,509	116,221
缅甸	21,713	418,253	85,057	954,792
柬埔寨	7,846	178,403	4,153	39,451
塞浦路斯	6,261	30,934	7,350	94,423
朝鲜	42,383	442,355	6,264	112,152
香港	46,154,317	240,409,891	48,214,508	242,253,788
印度	10,722	25,631	7,509	1,724,494
印度尼西亚	230,258	489,698	876,091	3,576,195
伊朗	266	2,827,438	30,255	404,249
伊拉克	74	196,249	1,800	22,333
以色列	310,858	1,252,512	151,410	834,472
日本	17,261,783	44,402,895	11,987,590	39,931,849
约旦	94,155	886,731	79,275	819,801
科威特	13,310	202,027	6,089	67,696
老挝	10	32,282	5	993
黎巴嫩	162,383	1,576,336	177,650	1,989,230
澳门	48,718	628,311	18,037	262,441
马来西亚	439,831	2,173,310	713,963	3,725,040
马尔代夫	2,306	21,212	1,250	11,696
蒙古	5	5,091	38	446
尼泊尔	19,548	288,368	5,013	46,552
阿曼	11,017	106,221	10,725	60,556
巴基斯坦	28,984	292,141	14,768	1,620,091

1998年中国出口主要商品输往地

电风扇

输往地	1998		1997	
	数量(台)	金额(美元)	数量(台)	金额(美元)
菲律宾	350,049	1,851,185	318,077	1,945,384
卡塔尔	6,474	49,207	2,766	32,407
沙特阿拉伯	592,556	5,982,560	365,025	4,075,111
新加坡	2,260,874	6,455,731	1,664,871	7,440,686
韩国	1,600,280	1,309,550	1,253,886	1,534,608
斯里兰卡	26,771	307,838	20,198	264,130
叙利亚	49,757	431,531	2	30,600
泰国	7,175,899	3,428,385	1,101,738	1,002,938
土耳其	109,679	652,908	237,312	1,781,865
阿拉伯联合酋长国	1,504,836	15,072,351	637,641	6,503,248
也门共和国	8,228	73,069	2,755	43,511
越南	218,217	2,361,756	111,604	1,275,314
台湾省	10,914,445	6,437,672	11,757,345	8,072,939
阿尔及利亚	53,222	437,553	1,400	16,073
安哥拉	9,938	49,843		
贝宁	7,179	40,453	940	7,627
喀麦隆	26,971	103,406	13,386	167,187
中非共和国	2,966	12,131		
刚果	85,998	261,899	835	10,772
吉布提	8,975	79,983	320	3,551
埃及	342,830	3,763,785	276,563	2,717,269
埃塞俄比亚	1,808	14,610		
加蓬	3,723	140,968	3,000	27,568
冈比亚	4	144		
加纳	90,947	680,806	24,041	244,152
几内亚	300	3,328		
几内亚(比绍)	550	5,349		
科特迪瓦	12,717	107,310	16,835	170,660
肯尼亚	4,196	46,968	2,174	31,909
马达加斯加	969	8,129	3	11
马里	686	6,302	50	3,641
毛里求斯	10,165	125,218	9,304	113,557
摩洛哥	10,191	94,858	26,274	308,358
莫桑比克	680	7,020		
尼日尔	8	29,925		
尼日利亚	721,124	7,968,457	465,786	5,260,029
留尼汪	8,208	74,001	510	7,261

1998 年中国出口主要商品输往地

电风扇

输往地	1998		1997	
	数量(台)	金额(美元)	数量(台)	金额(美元)
塞内加尔	1,057	12,412	10,601	79,968
塞舌尔	738	10,605	700	10,250
南非	319,855	2,377,600	264,830	1,619,405
苏丹	13,315	139,595	10,010	107,009
坦桑尼亚	6	14,738	510	4,214
突尼斯	96,490	875,383	29,999	344,666
扎伊尔	1,408	5,632	900	11,897
赞比亚	2	34		
津巴布韦	7,014	169,162		
比利时	155,587	1,328,979	246,437	1,852,457
丹麦	279,501	474,983	189,452	182,227
英国	4,759,592	14,526,761	2,794,396	11,012,542
德国	1,043,128	4,614,137	1,518,934	9,043,563
法国	2,472,177	9,662,132	1,595,335	9,998,203
意大利	612,719	1,354,404	665,145	3,676,553
荷兰	957,518	2,696,500	1,126,444	3,634,635
希腊	128,174	1,070,622	99,694	920,388
葡萄牙	43,206	228,464	64,860	453,555
西班牙	584,054	2,680,757	641,382	3,976,692
奥地利	132,112	346,558	201,140	577,340
保加利亚	1,950	24,454		
芬兰	108,125	485,026	4,548	15,940
匈牙利	1	102	736	9,516
马耳他	6,252	76,798	1,645	19,555
挪威	50,706	251,882		
波兰	19,057	48,178	110,986	341,965
罗马尼亚	950	6,508	4,259	65,767
瑞典	108,731	654,978	63,867	435,631
瑞士	6,416	74,826	41,693	264,797
爱沙尼亚	40	600		
俄罗斯	25,275	93,012	22,530	174,350
南斯拉夫	202	57	980	473
斯洛文尼亚共和国	3,011	583		
克罗地亚共和国	4,000	4,000		
捷克共和国	5,500	1,043	1,783	5,926
马其顿共和国	1	1,107		
阿根廷	770,834	6,938,303	721,794	7,490,615

1998年中国出口主要商品输往地

电风扇

输往地	1998		1997	
	数量(台)	金额(美元)	数量(台)	金额(美元)
阿鲁巴岛	100	1,150		
巴巴多斯	1,200	11,430	740	17,765
伯利兹	550	7,298		
玻利维亚	4,335	56,132		
巴西	394,842	1,984,187	154,779	1,624,475
智利	139,010	677,552	131,264	1,236,704
哥伦比亚	22,458	111,610		
多米尼克	34,795	391,945	31,000	336,805
哥斯达黎加	20,587	42,663	4,779	28,146
古巴	318,757	3,608,917	150,739	1,846,103
多米尼加共和国	16,244	151,760	1,600	8,262
厄瓜多尔	7,810	50,861	39,648	499,134
瓜德罗普	1,810	18,516		
危地马拉	5,892	49,998	5,480	19,393
圭亚那	8,774	93,448		
海地	1,720	20,683		
洪都拉斯	15,955	122,637		
牙买加	28,399	196,939		
墨西哥	686,278	6,422,128	277,366	3,350,701
巴拿马	479,826	4,032,884	317,475	3,542,573
巴拉圭	225,601	3,207,809	211,438	3,222,604
秘鲁	37,960	393,704	49,091	610,892
波多黎各	198,087	1,173,677	138,346	342,230
萨尔瓦多	6,668	15,410		
苏里南	5,743	16,370		
特立尼达和多巴哥	6,168	79,199	2,400	30,691
乌拉圭	25,448	243,406	66,940	716,733
委内瑞拉	19,413	189,758	20,071	134,280
加拿大	318,135	1,339,669	761,418	6,740,788
美国	43,039,347	277,490,384	36,080,756	273,073,886
澳大利亚	1,888,436	20,205,605	1,987,427	20,695,404
库克群岛	408	8,968		
新喀里多尼亚	8,603	97,245	6,650	83,768
瓦努阿图	1,230	13,016		
新西兰	33,998	367,532	13,000	165,814
巴布亚新几内亚	1,630	17,007	1,234	14,346
社会群岛	1,500	16,200		

1998 年中国出口主要商品输往地

电风扇

输 往 地	1998		1997	
	数量(台)	金额(美元)	数量(台)	金额(美元)
所罗门群岛	10	118		
贝劳共和国	680	6,242	392	4,704
其他	280	2,908	15,740	149,837

1998 年中国进口主要商品来源地

小麦

来 源 地	1998		1997	
	数量(公吨)	金额(美元)	数量(公吨)	金额(美元)
总值	**1,489,403**	**278,570,132**	**1,860,612**	**368,285,026**
马来西亚	1	500		
叙利亚		35		
南非	5,621	1,011,780		
乌克兰	3	18,963		
墨西哥		22		15
加拿大	961,661	179,826,254	1,334,290	257,930,499
美国	319,002	57,876,513	187,591	41,133,982
澳大利亚	203,115	39,836,065	245,792	53,007,631
其他			92,939	16,212,899

黄大豆

来 源 地	1998		1997	
	数量(公吨)	金额(美元)	数量(公吨)	金额(美元)
总值	**3,192,594**	**804,805,878**	**2,875,907**	**842,928,118**
印度		299		
印度尼亚西亚	4	2,117		
日本	9	8,563	38	16,251
新加坡		925		
韩国		55		
俄罗斯	64,961	11,396,735	54,863	9,082,982
阿根廷	391,111	95,490,250		
巴西	941,207	238,791,758	439,882	138,009,372
乌拉圭	27,449	6,414,746		
加拿大	17,355	6,442,493	14,215	4,683,714
美国	1,750,012	446,167,602	2,366,482	691,027,700
澳大利亚		215	98	23,955
新西兰	86	16,568		
其他	400	73,552	329	84,144

1998 年中国进口主要商品来源地

食用植物油

来 源 地	1998		1997	
	数量(公吨)	金额(美元)	数量(公吨)	金额(美元)
总值	**2,055,237**	**1,298,769,892**	**2,748,097**	**1,504,572,202**
香港	32,489	16,465,876	19,576	10,382,722
印度	1,737	1,196,885		
印度尼西亚	188,466	111,177,376	291,479	146,328,919
日本	704	880,372	2,905	2,418,107
马来西亚	741,217	476,635,889	873,657	467,166,729
菲律宾	6,150	4,397,115		
新加坡	10,088	6,714,341	23,816	13,606,451
韩国	4,080	2,782,057	202	285,690
泰国	1,974	985,778	5,008	2,109,478
越南	31,465	21,280,775	29,913	17,591,918
台湾省	165	190,419	92	118,619
摩洛哥	5	9,504		
南非	424	334,532	966	710,872
比利时	5,007	3,665,845		
丹麦	1,200	819,792		
英国		155	99	76,610
德国	86,849	54,525,982	196,019	111,064,497
法国	16	17,840	27	34,442
意大利	34	68,662	6	7,275
荷兰	111,003	72,064,662	86,612	49,118,442
西班牙	8,975	5,507,067		77
瑞典	212	1,692,600	215	1,719,200
阿根廷	202,813	128,919,997	202,375	113,068,855
巴西	161,962	101,571,304	638,637	352,005,515
加拿大	44,597	28,404,805	25,349	14,040,460
美国	412,937	257,837,287	323,539	185,488,122
澳大利亚	122	125,236	1,003	617,246
新西兰	40	50,142	2	2,733
其他	506	447,597	26,599	16,609,223

1998年中国进口主要商品来源地

食用植物油籽

来　源　地	1998		1997	
	数量(公吨)	金额(美元)	数量(公吨)	金额(美元)
总值	**4,604,676**	**1,221,237,766**	**2,953,530**	**870,125,924**
缅甸	2,660	1,180,499	3,444	1,804,136
香港	22	14,789		115
印度	8,182	4,661,589	11,689	6,139,032
印度尼西亚	540	242,120	75	14,301
伊朗	40	9,196		
日本	133	96,560	170	73,972
马来西亚	186	82,392	18	15,889
蒙古	76	18,720		
巴基斯坦	105	67,026		
菲律宾	58	39,672	8	5,028
新加坡	13	24,865	9	17,480
韩国	1,074	596,329		388
泰国	164	72,995	41	25,173
越南	943	383,691	2,724	1,347,534
台湾省	409	74,484	228	75,139
埃塞俄比亚	199	136,881		
苏丹	545	302,277	434	229,927
德国	133,141	39,373,958	32	7,544
法国	232,775	69,447,748	11,953	3,612,560
瑞典		8		
俄罗斯	65,901	11,520,075	55,327	9,144,020
阿根廷	391,111	95,490,250	97	26,130
巴西	941,207	238,791,758	439,882	138,009,372
乌拉圭	27,449	6,414,746		
委内瑞拉	57	40,008		
加拿大	946,387	274,612,639	14,216	4,684,435
美国	1,760,057	451,912,482	2,369,714	692,399,618
澳大利亚	90,523	25,393,430	42,786	12,179,280
新西兰	86	16,568	18	17,053
其他	634	220,011	666	297,798

1998年中国进口主要商品来源地

糖

来 源 地	1998		1997	
	数量	金额(美元)	数量	金额(美元)
总值		**145,160,106**		**228,768,237**
缅甸		347,413		48,721
香港		361,464		1,041,627
印度尼西亚		136		383
日本		2,427,434		3,269,538
马来西亚		231,824		1,374,177
尼泊尔		87,933		331,324
沙特阿拉伯		84,114		
新加坡		1,091,616		67,721
韩国		13,870,334		17,553,751
泰国		12,532,324		51,742,116
台湾省		138,998		147,452
南非		385,303		34,748
比利时		624,166		304,290
英国		1,310,370		1,707,325
德国		301,567		246,634
法国		267,381		22,088
西班牙		91		6
瑞士		2,002		
巴西		5,933,277		687,471
古巴		88,852,904		99,235,352
美国		136,775		216,966
澳大利亚		16,029,137		44,862,610
其他		143,543		5,873,937

胶合板

来 源 地	1998		1997	
	数量(立方米)	金额(美元)	数量(立方米)	金额(美元)
总值	**1,691,113**	**543,632,030**	**1,488,500**	**605,498,312**
缅甸	115	28,980	1,143	140,758
柬埔寨	957	210,583		
香港	1,684	672,506	5,298	1,859,115
印度	2,044	508,906	1,594	801,927
印度尼西亚	920,345	309,113,657	720,978	322,241,493
日本	2,903	1,174,314	6,442	2,838,286
约旦		7		

1998年中国进口主要商品来源地

胶合板

来源地	1998		1997	
	数量(立方米)	金额(美元)	数量(立方米)	金额(美元)
马来西亚	669,189	187,637,375	637,662	222,405,921
马尔代夫	2	567		
菲律宾	11	10,403	24	17,880
新加坡	2,969	1,281,422	7,298	4,641,944
韩国	54,292	30,018,527	40,202	29,896,248
泰国	3,338	1,179,676	8,980	2,007,908
越南	665	211,341	1,896	545,904
台湾省	17,991	5,923,387	26,769	8,417,472
南非	33	12,592	51	12,039
比利时	481	111,490	1,151	238,699
丹麦	42	16,964		
英国	1,064	394,537	1,176	394,409
德国	1,101	693,854	3,857	1,482,385
法国	191	55,277	349	87,420
意大利	97	75,118	1,094	445,647
荷兰	102	76,175	157	138,501
西班牙	34	65,794	63	45,033
奥地利	285	70,925	85	27,886
芬兰	954	721,627	2,879	781,788
瑞典	327	258,347	209	134,936
瑞士	39	13,725		
俄罗斯	306	335,309	75	57,058
巴西	21	19,114	35	47,593
智利	85	30,688	452	91,202
加拿大	1,263	277,026	918	664,477
美国	3,683	1,079,571	8,901	2,249,582
澳大利亚	2,274	544,368	3,365	897,004
新西兰	675	189,843	1,507	448,096
其他	1,551	618,035	3,890	1,439,701

棉花

来源地	1998		1997	
	数量(公吨)	金额(美元)	数量(公吨)	金额(美元)
总值	**209,418**	**356,972,376**	**782,976**	**1,393,827,827**
阿富汗	81	86,768		
缅甸	50	17,500	50	69,804

1998年中国进口主要商品来源地

棉花

来 源 地	1998		1997	
	数量(公吨)	金额(美元)	数量(公吨)	金额(美元)
香港	66	130,053	3	3,944
印度	5,520	8,769,674	26,328	40,775,847
印度尼西亚	151	150,827	191	321,883
以色列	100	267,622	22	49,186
日本	552	984,664	1,326	2,459,223
马来西亚		71		32
尼泊尔		524		164
巴基斯坦	2,444	3,162,581	1,237	1,955,976
韩国	597	3,023,587	2,758	6,676,214
叙利亚	1,049	1,369,356	1,493	2,524,313
泰国		310	1	997
土耳其	340	569,254		
阿拉伯联合酋长国	507	927,918	3,404	6,359,489
也门共和国	531	1,322,150	53	142,243
台湾省	389	367,730	193	226,893
贝宁	1,962	3,489,858	4,930	8,778,936
喀麦隆	1,449	2,556,550	20,166	36,096,839
埃及	199	612,380	417	1,213,910
科特迪瓦	4,491	8,021,375	11,653	20,880,890
马里	2,899	4,769,757	16,221	27,468,499
尼日利亚	799	1,320,418	5,550	9,055,520
苏丹	222	395,322	12,304	19,484,454
坦桑尼亚	5,101	7,958,508	9,103	14,246,525
多哥	1,840	3,122,366	4,144	7,679,943
乌干达	18	26,104	1,093	1,739,525
布基纳法索	2,532	4,258,756	100	181,129
津巴布韦	132	264,876	1,107	2,092,907
德国		43		
法国	6	8,368	42	48,477
意大利		17	1	10,563
瑞士	47	117,227	1,101	1,992,589
阿塞拜疆	50	90,678	8,444	14,055,698
哈萨克斯坦	4,101	6,233,405	23,789	35,542,134
吉尔吉斯斯坦	1,914	2,609,133	2,889	4,017,629
俄罗斯	1,638	2,435,774	12,449	20,548,984
塔吉克斯坦	3,478	5,847,540	3,124	5,070,688
土库曼斯坦	1,029	1,803,475	2,982	3,513,193

1998年中国进口主要商品来源地

棉花

来源地	1998		1997	
	数量(公吨)	金额(美元)	数量(公吨)	金额(美元)
乌兹别克斯坦	16,047	25,998,525	76,084	133,198,313
阿根廷	2,035	2,732,986	1,258	2,150,369
墨西哥	6,195	10,451,577	14,009	24,571,965
秘鲁	1,250	3,679,076	3,213	8,676,408
美国	107,161	186,120,346	392,795	716,126,377
澳大利亚	30,444	50,896,227	101,196	187,833,777
其他	1	1,120	15,758	25,985,368

羊毛

来源地	1998		1997	
	数量(公吨)	金额(美元)	数量(公吨)	金额(美元)
总值	**168,606**	**602,996,523**	**207,203**	**789,450,254**
香港	77	332,074	182	684,342
日本	834	6,312,410	1,963	15,121,740
马来西亚	536	3,340,324	590	3,746,873
蒙古	4,661	2,316,795	11,070	5,307,336
韩国	677	2,947,857	1,127	9,129,374
泰国	1,016	6,629,456	1,160	9,297,665
台湾省	3,690	16,817,126	3,791	21,337,551
南非	1,215	5,625,409	1,163	6,178,585
莱索托	6	29,064		
英国	3,764	9,874,603	2,909	9,785,343
德国	372	2,962,426	312	2,634,791
法国	200	1,586,382	358	1,818,578
爱尔兰	1,703	4,461,656	1,132	3,346,902
意大利	180	2,214,271	140	1,496,947
荷兰	54	109,102	43	107,500
西班牙	63	139,408	125	311,834
哈萨克斯坦	4,374	2,751,091	17,018	10,701,511
吉尔吉斯斯坦	1,374	1,106,279	4,537	3,741,353
俄罗斯	1,672	1,508,096	5,336	7,462,929
阿根廷	2,874	10,951,890	4,737	18,813,148
智利	123	480,790	848	2,412,242
秘鲁	305	2,485,496	34	256,416
乌拉圭	5,416	22,230,360	16,662	71,162,035
美国	891	4,716,626	1,603	8,908,400

1998年中国进口主要商品来源地

羊毛

来源地	1998		1997	
	数量(公吨)	金额(美元)	数量(公吨)	金额(美元)
澳大利亚	89,916	371,413,404	99,227	469,853,812
新西兰	41,854	116,960,764	30,743	104,181,932
其他	761	2,693,364	394	1,650,515

纺织品

来源地	1998		1997	
	数量	金额(美元)	数量	金额(美元)
总值		**10,949,707,019**		**12,091,495,766**
孟加拉国		2,181,861		377,650
不丹		83		
缅丹		310		
柬埔寨		228,516		
塞浦路斯		32,759		
朝鲜		136,631		254,354
香港		1,335,150,722		1,501,246,094
印度		147,577,645		141,583,403
印度尼西亚		142,703,328		124,650,244
伊朗		79,320		964,480
以色列		161,860		204,252
日本		2,102,600,054		2,439,374,790
约旦		6,040		989
科威特		104		70
黎巴嫩		242		81
澳门		70,104,489		94,800,137
马来西亚		81,945,684		143,147,959
蒙古		25,503		22,684
尼泊尔		216,299		237,942
阿曼		197,908		144
巴基斯坦		350,570,905		335,228,472
菲律宾		3,588,138		3,679,416
沙特阿拉伯		158,975		276,718
新加坡		19,474,986		24,089,619
韩国		2,141,340,546		2,494,841,224
斯里兰卡		469,444		1,390,083
泰国		89,728,310		99,545,091
土耳其		1,120,040		605,605

1998年中国进口主要商品来源地

纺织品

来 源 地	1998		1997	
	数量	金额(美元)	数量	金额(美元)
阿拉伯联合酋长国		1,876,630		2,691,488
越南		5,947,191		7,555,088
台湾省		3,032,847,342		3,106,025,354
吉布提		4,973		806
埃及		30,842		6,592
加纳		7,904		20,113
肯尼亚		35,450		11,200
马达加斯加		24,989		115,504
毛里求斯		3,032		37,706
莫桑比克		14,000		9,107
南非		2,633,997		2,227,741
苏丹		426,509		1,436,152
乌干达		55		
扎伊尔		10		
比利时		3,167,482		3,553,945
丹麦		754,589		914,368
英国		28,824,519		31,809,400
德国		32,858,977		36,989,433
法国		16,899,856		15,053,569
爱尔兰		506,847		532,080
意大利		133,415,021		159,975,020
卢森堡		5,744,934		14,175,435
荷兰		6,641,354		3,909,096
希腊		29,799		1,576
葡萄牙		785,793		1,561,209
西班牙		4,178,776		3,880,167
奥地利		2,415,633		1,921,708
保加利亚		86,718		152,297
芬兰		1,608,219		1,963,377
匈牙利		66,578		59,108
冰岛		929		323
马耳他		1,034		
挪威		453,811		552,025
波兰		121,522		198,569
罗马尼亚		493,721		436,291
瑞典		1,793,957		1,734,131
瑞士		4,148,142		4,945,035

1998年中国进口主要商品来源地

纺织品

来源地	1998		1997	
	数量	金额(美元)	数量	金额(美元)
爱沙尼亚		118,029		544
拉脱维亚		150,158		
立陶宛		1,074		
白俄罗斯		299,502		4,542
哈萨克斯坦		43,333		30,867
吉尔吉斯斯坦		269,686		633,253
摩尔多瓦		3,341		398
俄罗斯		1,755,679		3,227,830
塔吉克斯坦		118		1,122,715
乌兹别克斯坦		2,542,258		40,384
南斯拉夫		103,964		
斯洛文尼亚共和国		92,778		90,719
捷克共和国		323,221		370,244
阿根廷		31,750		2,625,449
巴西		413,322		11,361,510
智利		724,781		285,781
哥伦比亚		33,756		62,080
多米尼克		174		
古巴		10,365		430
厄瓜多尔		4,496		
法属圭亚那		3,266		3,592
危地马拉		188,098		43,450
牙买加		21,945		
墨西哥		4,371,792		6,233,945
巴拿马		5,461		163,582
巴拉圭		18,506		90,803
秘鲁		379,231		1,949,139
萨巴		400		
萨尔瓦多		138		
乌拉圭		237,903		1,786,354
委内瑞拉		410,195		1,682,365
加拿大		18,613,140		38,247,923
美国		123,749,412		167,027,085
澳大利亚		24,550,515		28,066,486
新西兰		2,738,199		4,366,887
巴布亚新几内亚		54,935		
所罗门群岛		5,121		

1998年中国进口主要商品来源地

纺织品

来 源 地	1998		1997	
	数量	金额(美元)	数量	金额(美元)
其他		988,785,140		1,011,000,895

棉纱线

来 源 地	1998		1997	
	数量(件)	金额(美元)	数量(件)	金额(美元)
总值	**2,092,500**	**741,421,862**	**2,035,761**	**716,552,182**
香港	226,953	82,132,997	196,456	68,274,632
印度	379,817	125,416,223	370,611	132,210,522
印度尼西亚	119,229	39,806,369	78,815	28,463,690
伊朗	83	36,191		
日本	13,325	13,434,735	16,311	14,486,063
澳门	13,679	5,152,257	14,979	6,419,862
马来西亚	17,469	6,026,639	12,570	4,182,616
巴基斯坦	689,931	215,575,073	704,391	223,238,860
菲律宾	1,013	411,910	223	77,084
新加坡	573	196,797	691	182,156
韩国	68,424	33,530,169	57,222	28,792,257
斯里兰卡	182	41,644	6	29,735
泰国	47,660	23,278,858	52,740	21,485,209
土耳其	304	120,785	28	4,631
阿拉伯联合酋长国	100	47,213		
越南	232	52,349	35	25,898
台湾省	82,135	30,281,414	63,095	23,241,648
吉布提	16	3,807		
南非	146	31,946	38	11,001
苏丹	1,186	426,509	3,370	1,436,152
比利时	7	2,448		
丹麦	1	1,650		671
英国	335	331,424	167	198,554
德国	144	249,497	172	252,780
法国	1,403	478,332	132	186,381
爱尔兰	4	10,541		
意大利	1,385	1,475,247	1,587	1,685,420
荷兰	13	1,807	19	15,671
葡萄牙	1	12,893		
西班牙	5	2,386		782

1998年中国进口主要商品来源地

棉纱线

来源地	1998		1997	
	数量(件)	金额(美元)	数量(件)	金额(美元)
奥地利	34	11,963		
芬兰	70	84,262	143	170,421
瑞典	41	37,739		1,304
瑞士	277	103,344	6	1,942
哈萨克斯坦	124	38,333	17	5,270
吉尔吉斯斯坦	359	110,664	1,193	324,662
俄罗斯	67	13,821	1,927	733,284
塔吉克斯坦		29	2,607	1,095,263
乌兹别克斯坦	6,119	2,542,258	91	40,384
巴西	189	90,654	311	93,191
墨西哥	18	3,962		
秘鲁	20	33,678	133	60,837
加拿大	403	104,148	300	105,147
美国	4,715	1,825,544	1,878	709,336
澳大利亚	6,705	2,869,531	2,251	1,207,369
新西兰	6	2,595	12	7,808
其他	407,596	154,979,227	451,231	157,093,689

棉布

来源地	1998		1997	
	数量(万米)	金额(美元)	数量(万米)	金额(美元)
总值	**138,395**	**1,338,408,587**	**144,689**	**1,450,234,705**
孟加拉国		752		
缅甸		310		
塞浦路斯	3	29,310		
香港	40,885	345,245,041	46,205	402,911,289
印度	2,555	15,345,400	645	5,666,763
印度尼西亚	1,199	12,406,297	736	10,020,369
伊朗		1,160		8,022
日本	15,433	315,481,589	15,085	328,735,488
澳门	2,840	15,670,874	4,180	24,848,884
马来西亚	96	1,212,294	97	1,064,608
巴基斯坦	16,089	126,580,055	11,041	100,447,236
菲律宾		6,029	14	180,767
沙特阿拉伯	3	38,497	9	44,383
新加坡	93	1,549,906	141	1,426,826

1998 年中国进口主要商品来源地

棉布

来 源 地	1998		1997	
	数量(万米)	金额(美元)	数量(万米)	金额(美元)
韩国	5,137	56,452,558	7,698	90,962,108
斯里兰卡	30	183,347		22
泰国	542	8,210,985	544	9,449,119
土耳其	1	12,246	1	25,048
阿拉伯联合酋长国	140	1,798,036	195	2,691,344
越南	13	265,718	5	107,365
台湾省	15,524	136,373,225	17,677	158,246,700
埃及		268		
毛里求斯		3,032	3	37,706
南非	193	1,758,220	154	1,410,551
扎伊尔		10		
比利时	10	294,150	12	314,845
丹麦	1	12,742	4	34,314
英国	28	354,192	57	654,186
德国	68	1,439,759	92	3,148,841
法国	37	837,827	21	416,441
爱尔兰	2	26,076		1,219
意大利	242	8,433,155	166	5,583,774
荷兰	6	161,836	9	270,098
葡萄牙	4	222,648	6	250,267
西班牙	8	280,956	12,	266,802
奥地利	3	77,551	2	141,825
保加利亚		1,985		
芬兰	2	55,303		23,456
挪威	2	20,343	4	16,837
波兰	1	15,160		
罗马尼亚		7,623		
瑞典	4	57,959	12	78,627
瑞士	11	251,264	6	438,118
爱沙尼亚		1,216		
哈萨克斯坦	23	5,000	8	25,597
吉尔吉斯斯坦	49	159,022	109	273,728
俄罗斯		1,843	2	33,678
捷克共和国	2	99,188	1	55,402
巴西	12	199,132	18	280,421
智利	1	64,246		
厄瓜多尔		4,179		

1998 年中国进口主要商品来源地

棉布

来源地	1998		1997	
	数量(万米)	金额(美元)	数量(万米)	金额(美元)
法属圭亚那		3,266		
牙买加	1	20,574		
墨西哥	1	42,995		
萨尔瓦多		138		
加拿大	54	1,243,688	21	463,611
美国	452	5,716,986	491	6,066,028
澳大利亚	48	1,048,482	18	337,406
新西兰		24		86
巴布亚新几内亚		1,473		
其他	36,546	278,621,447	39,188	292,774,500

服装

来源地	1998		1997	
	数量	金额(美元)	数量	金额(美元)
总值		**1,065,922,727**		**1,105,500,970**
孟加拉国		2,259,204		4,188,218
柬埔寨		2,141,917		409,307
朝鲜		156,494		1,255,864
香港		495,488,991		421,580,530
印度		7,298,786		3,844,309
印度尼西亚		526,317		780,100
以色列		54,927		31,602
日本		327,885,908		397,499,637
约旦		100		46
科威特		277		375
黎巴嫩		3,008		
澳门		17,075,005		10,989,745
马来西亚		1,789,443		1,681,145
蒙古		2,504,620		310,127
尼泊尔		2,043		11,150
巴基斯坦		7,097		48,851
菲律宾		2,336,836		2,439,395
沙特阿拉伯		243		
新加坡		1,202,337		1,302,651
韩国		76,224,729		113,358,158
斯里兰卡		37,170		186,211

1998年中国进口主要商品来源地

服装

来源地	1998		1997	
	数量	金额(美元)	数量	金额(美元)
泰国		1,178,778		1,895,376
土耳其		9,044		1,103
阿拉伯联合酋长国		9,896		8,899
越南		2,160,183		1,446,880
台湾省		58,586,604		60,513,524
埃及		5,896		
埃塞俄比亚		47		
摩洛哥		146		
南非		13,190		20,845
津巴布韦		35		39
比利时		101,714		114,248
丹麦		340,680		374,977
英国		2,632,248		1,951,794
德国		2,983,168		3,228,468
法国		2,083,812		1,492,344
爱尔兰		3,615		43,897
意大利		12,452,255		8,229,018
卢森堡		523		9,024
荷兰		210,894		232,332
希腊		25,052		6,102
葡萄牙		36,514		25,273
西班牙		969,387		282,822
奥地利		69,407		47,157
芬兰		86,510		184,928
匈牙利		970		15
冰岛		5		
摩纳哥		209		
挪威		61,820		48,215
波兰		63,846		43,860
罗马尼亚		12,836		
瑞典		197,510		188,959
瑞士		379,147		917,103
吉尔吉斯斯坦		17,735		20,820
俄罗斯		109,065		15,761
斯洛文尼亚共和国		77		
捷克共和国		80		195,755
阿根廷		5,933		

1998年中国进口主要商品来源地

服装

来源地	1998		1997	
	数量	金额(美元)	数量	金额(美元)
巴西		10,361		27,107
智利		218		35
哥伦比亚		13,245		106
哥斯达黎加		187		
牙买加		921		
墨西哥		17,656		428
巴拿马		480		11,341
秘鲁		22,832		30
乌拉圭		226		21
委内瑞拉		20		
加拿大		658,529		641,854
美国		7,736,044		11,531,303
澳大利亚		6,366,185		8,940,489
新西兰		79,126		155,325
其他		29,212,414		42,735,972

鞋类

来源地	1998		1997	
	数量	金额(美元)	数量	金额(美元)
总值		**290,429,462**		**358,340,322**
缅甸		100,283		
塞浦路斯		984		
香港		8,419,826		12,019,206
印度		43,606		174,526
印度尼西亚		2,973,975		2,371,139
伊朗		227		
以色列		115		
日本		10,468,471		9,340,185
澳门		35,001		86,291
马来西亚		137,861		212,544
尼泊尔		2,674		10,627
巴基斯坦		3,959		9,910
菲律宾		123,389		58,800
新加坡		310,723		307,267
韩国		115,763,947		149,291,667
斯里兰卡		101,275		216,209

1998年中国进口主要商品来源地

鞋类

来 源 地	1998		1997	
	数量	金额(美元)	数量	金额(美元)
泰国		891,451		850,126
土耳其		2,160		
阿拉伯联合酋长国		31,735		
越南		862,226		1,431,264
台湾省		81,056,600		113,407,438
纳米比亚		14		231
塞内加尔		90		
南非		904		38
比利时		21,308		10,020
丹麦		40,794		4,763
英国		980,105		1,403,119
德国		911,579		776,406
法国		559,127		490,242
意大利		9,019,658		5,786,478
荷兰		122,282		147,590
希腊		285		
葡萄牙		29,789		1,475
西班牙		638,781		624,693
奥地利		28,256		
芬兰		259,084		142,565
匈牙利		4,305		56,297
挪威		224		
波兰		3,088		
罗马尼亚		23,183		
瑞典		14,223		49,181
瑞士		63,705		37,998
捷克共和国		88,338		757
阿根廷		245,448		10,874
巴西		702,267		333,656
智利		4,345		
哥伦比亚		15,910		
巴拿马		100		
加拿大		249,566		50,674
美国		52,611,253		54,591,605
澳大利亚		138,235		56,335
斐济		775		
其他		2,321,953		3,978,126

1998 年中国进口主要商品来源地

纸张

来 源 地	1998		1997	
	数量(公吨)	金额(美元)	数量(公吨)	金额(美元)
总值	**5,574,765**	**3,007,806,346**	**5,507,907**	**2,804,036,914**
缅甸	3	2,086		
朝鲜	44	24,600		
香港	320,954	142,399,107	320,872	145,071,704
印度	2,365	1,148,461	1,800	1,077,854
印度尼西亚	751,491	350,615,571	430,386	235,153,258
伊朗	1	361	157	79,690
以色列	3	5,422	1	920
日本	494,910	343,654,522	404,940	285,336,227
黎巴嫩		164		
澳门	233	140,527	3,126	1,059,093
马来西亚	18,356	10,657,227	13,540	7,438,158
马尔代夫	127	49,502		
菲律宾	13,233	7,675,026	5,700	2,776,563
沙特阿拉伯	43	14,452		
新加坡	23,748	11,681,775	17,763	9,199,003
韩国	1,137,336	661,941,081	995,179	535,482,205
泰国	279,862	98,639,562	132,512	51,961,389
土耳其	420	434,286	541	428,416
越南	2,951	1,382,437	1,512	612,601
台湾省	609,285	293,737,688	707,555	329,489,445
索马里	7	3,891	98	49,318
南非	25,569	11,388,633	26,802	10,490,449
比利时	4,931	3,765,851	8,056	4,633,868
丹麦	310	663,718	208	210,629
英国	27,827	43,198,633	24,133	32,479,125
德国	78,127	54,222,439	116,246	61,264,395
法国	27,425	22,380,874	38,554	26,200,971
爱尔兰		3,223	1	19,649
意大利	7,224	7,424,489	10,438	11,931,361
卢森堡	3	10,938	65	189,774
荷兰	59,468	24,721,088	67,552	27,186,900
葡萄牙	559	327,434	712	454,735
西班牙	5,177	13,673,306	5,668	11,184,118
奥地利	9,478	5,685,494	15,684	8,933,520
芬兰	89,236	73,517,833	89,284	69,487,467
匈牙利	5	3,534	10	7,832

1998年中国进口主要商品来源地

纸张

来 源 地	1998		1997	
	数量(公吨)	金额(美元)	数量(公吨)	金额(美元)
挪威	16,593	10,462,341	9,457	5,608,347
波兰	539	229,631	5,047	2,630,449
罗马尼亚	91	64,369	367	255,181
瑞典	88,664	48,951,772	74,300	41,349,386
瑞士	3,182	1,922,461	2,238	1,838,116
白俄罗斯	37	35,040		
哈萨克斯坦	270	159,429	782	399,081
俄罗斯	141,763	61,695,330	120,074	53,591,267
南斯拉夫	40	23,278		
捷克共和国	68	103,108	77	98,444
阿根廷	46	18,102	111	91,060
巴西	11,819	5,215,267	27,090	11,588,756
智利	4	2,756	2,712	1,299,232
牙买加	51	43,746		
墨西哥	51	104,831	246	206,413
巴拿马	24	6,170		67
特克斯和凯科斯群岛	2	17,874		
加拿大	113,314	58,328,624	251,987	118,958,611
美国	1,138,897	544,980,106	1,328,856	606,348,538
澳大利亚	154,460	47,281,995	157,353	50,330,430
新西兰	70,186	30,380,724	41,314	18,149,871
诺福克岛	7	13,523		
其他	23,949	12,570,534	46,801	21,403,028

纸制品

来 源 地	1998		1997	
	数量(公吨)	金额(美元)	数量(公吨)	金额(美元)
总值	**558,688**	**654,829,112**	**723,601**	**730,085,579**
孟加拉国		1,687		1,921
柬埔寨	3	10,743		
塞浦路斯		34		
朝鲜	3	5,048		
香港	138,652	125,809,308	179,728	151,821,549
印度	90	103,443	46	120,561
印度尼西亚	21,190	12,349,047	26,401	15,263,379
伊朗	14	9,101	1	664

1998 年中国进口主要商品来源地

纸制品

来 源 地	1998		1997	
	数量(公吨)	金额(美元)	数量(公吨)	金额(美元)
以色列	35	75,602	25	102,780
日本	70,006	137,218,869	87,275	135,065,582
科威特	2	1,001		
黎巴嫩		362	12	3,035
澳门	1,097	1,137,475	1,756	1,555,843
马来西亚	2,709	3,037,574	2,577	2,572,780
蒙古		140		
尼泊尔		107		118
巴基斯坦	1	2,655		1,329
菲律宾	211	344,265	232	876,525
沙特阿拉伯	4	3,727	132	63,482
新加坡	4,043	8,964,200	8,266	9,597,042
韩国	92,512	97,585,459	129,185	113,443,616
斯里兰卡	1	2,043	3	18,290
泰国	3,866	3,181,822	3,033	1,750,941
土耳其	14	5,021	1	11,577
阿拉伯联合酋长国	114	51,238	26	13,857
越南	6	3,913	1	5,227
台湾省	111,068	114,299,480	130,591	133,284,040
贝宁		30		
加纳		39		26
毛里求斯		416		170
莫桑比克	30	11,800		90
南非	2,193	1,027,657	1,402	776,160
突尼斯	34	15,004		64
比利时	833	2,099,545	1,312	2,155,331
丹麦	2,247	3,450,087	957	1,931,184
英国	3,068	6,820,688	2,560	5,656,318
德国	4,133	8,882,742	7,121	9,222,302
法国	5,164	7,792,038	6,947	9,238,705
爱尔兰	44	339,623	10	72,285
意大利	1,322	3,494,868	2,288	3,061,263
卢森堡	38	63,692	80	221,489
荷兰	1,512	3,045,213	1,067	2,525,177
希腊		1,192	1	7,427
葡萄牙	80	57,546	102	61,320
西班牙	363	663,766	119	258,313

1998年中国进口主要商品来源地

纸制品

来源地	1998		1997	
	数量(公吨)	金额(美元)	数量(公吨)	金额(美元)
奥地利	967	1,875,933	681	1,215,182
芬兰	3,183	2,138,293	4,594	3,248,590
匈牙利	2	13,209	1	2,658
挪威	138	207,640	145	269,867
波兰		10,619	3	23,226
瑞典	1,301	2,002,034	2,331	2,531,074
瑞士	198	881,790	510	1,514,771
白俄罗斯		5,506		
俄罗斯	175	354,369	2	8,546,986
乌克兰		40,833		
南斯拉夫		749		
斯洛文尼亚共和国	7	20,432		331
克罗地亚共和国		12		
捷克共和国	1	6,807	6	18,388
马其顿共和国		1,900		
阿根廷	8	21,126	10	6,752
巴西	146	112,724	276	152,290
智利	1	1,766	1	2,645
危地马拉		149		207
牙买加		231		5,015
墨西哥	37	94,482	16	36,388
巴拉圭		33		155
秘鲁		650		
波多黎各		915		
乌拉圭		104		53
加拿大	4,058	3,338,915	4,010	2,590,542
美国	50,149	68,736,696	64,095	66,749,514
澳大利亚	1,492	2,970,701	3,353	3,055,126
新西兰	748	545,111	982	533,540
巴布亚新几内亚		19		
其他	29,374	29,476,054	49,329	38,820,517

1998 年中国进口主要商品来源地

钢材

来 源 地	1998		1997	
	数量(公吨)	金额(美元)	数量(公吨)	金额(美元)
总值	**12,415,481**	**6,286,773,774**	**13,228,294**	**6,520,168,638**
缅甸	35	14,301		
朝鲜	2,037	881,993	4,317	1,289,816
香港	34,566	28,289,216	49,659	42,066,571
印度	12,421	8,891,179	72,976	21,157,679
印度尼西亚	108,388	34,700,118	6,140	2,269,966
伊朗	150	171,213	472	203,205
以色列	20	99,205	87	118,022
日本	3,606,412	2,311,577,201	3,947,912	2,512,384,985
科威特		346		
澳门	7	9,668	12	9,445
马来西亚	56,940	33,012,031	13,541	8,949,703
蒙古	105	21,000	72	11,532
菲律宾	3,345	1,639,522	6,076	1,960,566
卡塔尔	90	19,164		
沙特阿拉伯	703	231,086	1,258	467,773
新加坡	8,716	11,137,442	12,126	14,252,684
韩国	2,531,003	1,276,290,273	1,694,459	966,632,996
叙利亚		11		
泰国	58,239	33,345,111	61,288	34,012,826
土耳其	11,623	3,504,646	16,596	4,909,905
阿拉伯联合酋长国	3	7,492	123	228,751
越南	1,191	572,316	6,938	3,252,952
台湾省	1,826,698	1,034,872,636	1,504,709	864,242,420
埃及	10	15,144	11,772	3,917,146
赤道几内亚	2	3,659		
肯尼亚	1	310		
利比亚	161	168,237		
南非	24,445	11,136,660	26,499	14,390,440
苏丹		181		25
比利时	28,350	26,261,567	36,429	32,216,747
丹麦	543	1,281,206	1,144	3,239,449
英国	66,300	43,238,080	95,417	93,647,154
德国	156,118	165,443,574	175,348	173,083,989
法国	39,812	53,571,702	45,663	48,599,055
爱尔兰	62	84,617		4,804
意大利	15,292	19,126,303	37,978	39,374,601

1998年中国进口主要商品来源地

钢材

来 源 地	1998		1997	
	数量(公吨)	金额(美元)	数量(公吨)	金额(美元)
卢森堡	2,441	1,426,535	2,173	1,413,959
荷兰	11,751	7,536,500	15,806	10,275,320
希腊	51	43,533	14	32,558
葡萄牙	2	7,234	1	11,012
西班牙	22,684	26,036,615	26,952	18,495,329
奥地利	14,932	12,530,155	10,042	9,306,473
芬兰	3,012	2,764,317	2,175	5,286,823
匈牙利		5	4,533	1,223,601
冰岛		30		
挪威	15,620	11,003,129	3,906	4,104,796
波兰	4,191	824,702	17,568	5,215,184
罗马尼亚	16,996	5,508,455	15,567	5,290,838
瑞典	11,833	18,014,421	24,001	22,188,939
瑞士	251	1,179,502	144	1,160,338
立陶宛	16	4,506	9,854	2,321,489
白俄罗斯	5,428	1,625,497	18,507	6,009,072
哈萨克斯坦	854,473	185,702,221	864,793	222,149,123
俄罗斯	2,038,248	500,966,838	2,939,381	771,305,010
乌克兰	361,760	92,398,553	846,272	212,721,309
南斯拉夫	298	87,763	3,002	1,053,480
捷克共和国	408	125,413	905	540,655
阿根廷	70,602	52,576,653	73,301	44,233,260
巴西	37,483	15,266,016	113,292	42,933,865
智利	64	60,800		
瓜德罗普	1	258		
危地马拉		297		
墨西哥	8,355	7,331,191	45,959	22,402,403
巴拉圭	1	702		
秘鲁	11	5,256	29	18,688
特立尼达和多巴哥	2	1,182		
加拿大	7,508	4,259,363	3,882	2,363,320
美国	60,887	119,060,086	77,334	103,460,108
澳大利亚	132,944	59,562,416	129,587	57,065,416
新西兰	162	98,225	1,682	1,004,130
其他	139,248	61,146,994	148,619	59,686,933

1998 年中国进口主要商品来源地

铁矿砂

来源地	1998		1997	
	数量(公吨)	金额(美元)	数量(公吨)	金额(美元)
总值	**51,770,715**	**1,467,762,617**	**55,105,835**	**1,614,839,812**
缅甸	1	18	848	23,087
朝鲜	82,770	1,363,841	167,673	3,035,135
香港	12,066	407,956	59	5,567
印度	6,940,559	187,164,606	6,609,219	186,127,523
印度尼西亚		6	55,308	1,660,219
日本	2	1,310		28
马来西亚	53,346	1,400,925	95,962	2,973,781
韩国	2	2,829	3	118
越南	155,253	2,033,659	94,925	1,405,186
台湾省	3	1,744	2	1,080
南非	5,657,525	151,411,810	5,310,470	145,856,571
英国	15	390	10	1,341
德国	20,981	699,187		64
法国	66	10,956	300	51,200
瑞典	151,510	7,566,878	285,869	14,282,381
格鲁吉亚	48,503	1,567,307	52,500	2,373,669
哈萨克斯坦	356,266	16,231,379	353,901	16,000,157
巴西	8,958,232	281,597,950	7,814,876	245,274,318
秘鲁	2,744,986	96,506,770	2,362,113	85,465,348
委内瑞拉	139,852	3,917,609	267,286	7,213,437
加拿大	622,170	23,798,793	730,636	27,425,090
美国	1	962		223
澳大利亚	25,567,496	686,901,601	30,971,967	858,360,815
新西兰	259,101	5,171,205	219,066	4,391,384
其他	11	2,926	252,844	12,912,090

铜矿砂

来源地	1998		1997	
	数量(公吨)	金额(美元)	数量(公吨)	金额(美元)
总值	**1,182,867**	**458,312,575**	**937,776**	**421,163,938**
缅甸	4,602	566,559	4,670	907,675
朝鲜	5,884	584,510	5,647	698,607
印度尼西亚	23,220	12,361,968	5,492	634,834
伊朗	14,996	5,755,538		
日本		335		

1998年中国进口主要商品来源地

铜矿砂

来 源 地	1998		1997	
	数量(公吨)	金额(美元)	数量(公吨)	金额(美元)
马来西亚	325	119,852	7	1,150
蒙古	318,055	113,462,441	254,326	116,702,810
菲律宾	22,065	7,591,313	90	26,940
泰国	1,603	344,554		
土耳其	30,289	8,602,814	56,904	19,232,789
越南	4,810	1,057,090	1,627	362,847
南非	897	135,409		
意大利	2,909	954,090	499	96,265
西班牙	10,397	2,949,639	13,633	4,355,525
波兰	6,099	2,620,850		
瑞典	3,091	953,388		
哈萨克斯坦	39	22,637	337	128,060
俄罗斯	7,431	1,753,604	23,392	7,478,515
斯洛伐克共和国	8,630	1,427,826		
阿根廷	10,550	4,516,694		
巴西	405	153,748	1,399	507,820
智利	314,615	145,848,654	212,260	112,703,471
墨西哥	6,364	2,437,322	9,278	3,481,947
秘鲁	49,151	17,168,602	22,791	10,964,685
加拿大	63,677	25,537,364	118,089	52,312,420
美国	554	170,968	41,231	17,935,531
澳大利亚	267,596	98,637,513	140,003	60,951,552
巴布亚新几内亚	4,615	2,577,293		
其他			26,100	11,680,495

铜

来 源 地	1998		1997	
	数量(公吨)	金额(美元)	数量(公吨)	金额(美元)
总值	**1,226,635**	**737,513,936**	**1,009,803**	**779,853,914**
缅甸	10	5,304	116	56,106
朝鲜	474	906,350	445	804,225
香港	55,583	25,370,433	38,003	24,121,891
印度	42	7,122	22	24,224
印度尼西亚	1,078	1,249,729	269	173,281
日本	381,051	123,822,128	196,825	86,989,417
黎巴嫩	139	218,761	21	5,097

1998 年中国进口主要商品来源地

铜

来源地	1998		1997	
	数量(公吨)	金额(美元)	数量(公吨)	金额(美元)
马来西亚	2,111	1,616,161	1,179	801,108
蒙古	849	1,267,593	1,002	1,523,363
阿曼	680	1,204,400		
菲律宾	35,308	64,036,592	15,485	26,205,699
沙特阿拉伯	293	487,406	472	888,002
新加坡	13,927	23,311,909	14,820	29,598,434
韩国	64,348	103,121,052	13,756	20,682,364
泰国	1,879	3,493,524	2,090	3,826,580
阿拉伯联合酋长国	23	42,375		
越南	836	1,505,668	1,882	3,519,956
台湾省	12,969	16,947,577	15,632	16,007,765
南非	2,574	4,551,716	13,559	27,871,727
赞比亚	2,248	4,103,022	10,808	24,802,354
津巴布韦	41	80,247	1,238	2,955,085
比利时	3,629	828,538	18,531	6,135,144
英国	4,681	7,787,713	6,580	7,385,939
德国	13,931	8,287,512	20,610	20,961,679
法国	375	616,516	688	441,971
意大利	368	155,628	3,305	3,015,196
荷兰	21,912	6,231,125	23,317	17,190,638
希腊	43	6,510	337	37,294
葡萄牙	4	258		
西班牙	483	290,783	78	183,427
奥地利	508	927,731		
保加利亚	21	48,254	43	53,515
芬兰	98	166,807	758	459,521
挪威	145	28,743	59	38,204
波兰	13,000	23,207,983	45	62,546
罗马尼亚	96	34,466	20	32,624
瑞典	967	193,062	1,456	618,409
瑞士	536	805,963	1,382	2,468,853
哈萨克斯坦	39,605	56,924,376	28,454	39,089,591
吉尔吉斯斯坦	1,877	2,304,282	6,317	7,853,717
俄罗斯	14,793	19,497,409	35,793	41,354,585
阿根廷	339	194,347	362	446,214
巴西	1,981	3,795,710	154	313,806
智利	52,241	90,990,035	70,862	153,038,968

1998年中国进口主要商品来源地

铜

来源地	1998		1997	
	数量(公吨)	金额(美元)	数量(公吨)	金额(美元)
厄瓜多尔	19	9,626	39	35,288
墨西哥	386	568,809	59	86,402
秘鲁	2,641	3,333,816	6,419	11,616,778
委内瑞拉	384	391,093	231	304,031
加拿大	5,282	1,297,798	4,616	2,441,482
美国	458,087	122,150,262	435,047	171,317,012
澳大利亚	11,247	8,610,060	10,976	11,945,524
新西兰	407	255,592	224	197,400
其他	87	197,060	5,416	9,871,478

铝

来源地	1998		1997	
	数量(公吨)	金额(美元)	数量(公吨)	金额(美元)
总值	**203,208**	**276,467,498**	**230,229**	**282,534,718**
巴林	100	111,321	99	159,163
缅甸	3,000	3,460,380		
朝鲜	1,335	1,468,131	1,117	1,251,671
香港	3,213	4,112,673	10,066	12,979,883
印度	47	36,403	1,385	2,195,788
印度尼西亚	2,426	3,430,833	2,900	4,164,041
日本	1,310	2,168,972	1,272	1,904,989
马来西亚	521	723,534	274	410,256
蒙古	113	93,392	11	8,115
菲律宾	439	723,623		
新加坡	10	14,000	2,176	3,104,093
韩国	1,566	1,890,326	1,839	2,876,319
阿拉伯联合酋长国	1,417	2,369,014	1,806	2,998,363
台湾省	4,179	6,682,998	4,277	7,712,851
南非	994	1,361,584	518	765,923
比利时	22	23,876		
德国	494	533,568	1,497	1,843,646
法国		1,327	62	92,984
意大利	21	28,119		
荷兰	178	256,427	1	9,419
瑞典	131	206,446	907	1,405,706
爱沙尼亚	150	210,000		

1998年中国进口主要商品来源地

铝

来源地	1998		1997	
	数量(公吨)	金额(美元)	数量(公吨)	金额(美元)
白俄罗斯	20	39,427		
哈萨克斯坦	212	197,319	700	680,165
吉尔吉斯斯坦	189	152,250		
俄罗斯	127,719	168,969,736	157,883	176,238,360
巴西	649	878,543	1,130	1,418,598
加拿大	619	850,883	843	1,178,722
美国	1,576	1,800,103	1,659	2,050,974
澳大利亚	45,324	65,975,617	36,497	54,957,534
新西兰	18	31,921		
其他	5,217	7,664,752	1,310	2,127,155

铜材

来源地	1998		1997	
	数量(公吨)	金额(美元)	数量(公吨)	金额(美元)
总值	**546,625**	**1,374,704,204**	**484,679**	**1,273,820,020**
缅甸	1	713		
朝鲜	4	8,959		
香港	22,020	64,507,399	23,910	76,074,792
印度	26	49,446	25	59,974
印度尼西亚	3,475	7,238,698	2,303	5,274,308
伊朗	51	97,665	18	125,141
以色列	4	20,583		1,040
日本	116,400	349,553,829	116,615	345,673,176
澳门	8	19,718	36	66,682
马来西亚	8,690	29,399,100	5,702	15,808,736
菲律宾	142	607,336	42	143,483
卡塔尔		168		
沙特阿拉伯	422	980,168	946	2,114,197
新加坡	2,162	8,185,526	1,495	5,496,437
韩国	111,507	242,386,167	70,969	172,032,329
泰国	1,636	6,845,521	1,179	8,086,693
土耳其	3,278	7,324,519	3,311	7,406,880
阿拉伯联合酋长国		4,466	105	271,320
越南	44	111,531		
台湾省	198,543	447,119,673	173,244	415,710,427
南非	1,334	2,453,122	1,868	3,835,366

1998年中国进口主要商品来源地

铜材

来源地	1998		1997	
	数量(公吨)	金额(美元)	数量(公吨)	金额(美元)
比利时	624	2,114,956	1,750	4,736,365
丹麦	12	169,612	3	11,061
英国	1,189	5,055,746	1,874	8,475,221
德国	9,092	26,361,537	8,005	22,178,223
法国	3,706	11,329,383	3,575	10,715,643
爱尔兰	102	1,339,965	40	426,236
意大利	1,320	2,558,443	2,039	4,642,231
卢森堡	85	824,830	63	533,794
荷兰	1,834	6,432,714	2,442	7,116,227
希腊		199		
葡萄牙	1	1,714		
西班牙	79	345,983	7	72,670
奥地利	38	605,674	23	146,149
芬兰	227	668,103	96	225,642
挪威	41	78,311	13	15,772
波兰	906	1,469,958	117	187,111
瑞典	898	3,287,234	1,482	3,114,363
瑞士	97	681,078	159	569,179
哈萨克斯坦	5	6,175	4	7,486
俄罗斯	406	656,406	2,511	4,557,950
捷克共和国	1	17,573		5,234
阿根廷		116	300	450,000
巴西	37	171,690	574	1,056,880
智利	655	1,220,867	10	21,222
墨西哥	17	102,098		
秘鲁	20	38,748		
加拿大	542	1,879,058	935	3,551,084
美国	7,057	29,842,336	5,068	24,011,381
澳大利亚	16,826	34,741,859	15,377	37,549,075
新西兰	30	127,963	26	288,498
萨摩亚	2	4,878		
其他	31,032	75,654,690	36,417	80,974,342

1998年中国进口主要商品来源地

铝材

来源地	1998		1997	
	数量(公吨)	金额(美元)	数量(公吨)	金额(美元)
总值	**341,294**	**844,917,833**	**312,099**	**789,401,992**
巴林	5,299	10,318,786	2,708	5,853,746
香港	9,226	24,190,192	9,990	26,935,098
印度	32	85,274	194	409,298
印度尼西亚	1,674	4,418,487	2,700	6,918,119
以色列	13	125,224	33	654,927
日本	101,996	258,461,707	76,486	210,375,749
澳门	52	97,334	28	52,389
马来西亚	5,236	9,582,753	1,999	5,020,037
菲律宾	42	81,840	33	131,098
沙特阿拉伯	11	25,052		
新加坡	2,676	8,906,142	3,200	14,728,515
韩国	45,165	111,885,863	47,462	119,061,373
泰国	311	393,732	140	334,660
土耳其	186	345,510	181	529,093
阿拉伯联合酋长国	157	258,985	276	540,063
台湾省	62,618	143,205,553	53,636	127,087,016
南非	843	1,020,108	575	558,185
比利时	1,343	4,233,891	1,664	4,895,462
丹麦	74	310,363	15	18,197
英国	3,007	10,142,762	1,914	6,816,540
德国	10,575	29,455,383	9,724	27,792,541
法国	10,366	28,065,158	11,942	30,258,847
爱尔兰		289	48	236,949
意大利	573	3,169,069	783	2,899,986
荷兰	2,594	9,071,199	1,457	4,444,075
希腊	1,429	2,094,841	942	1,690,890
西班牙	6	36,445	421	1,505,953
奥地利	3	15,999	8	11,175
芬兰	1	7,510	103	146,915
冰岛	2	3,024		
挪威	1	387	57	275,824
波兰	19	73,097		
罗马尼亚		116		
瑞典	8,180	18,473,572	605	1,431,501
瑞士	112	328,896	141	680,385
俄罗斯	1,052	1,512,410	556	670,207

1998年中国进口主要商品来源地

铝材

来 源 地	1998		1997	
	数量(公吨)	金额(美元)	数量(公吨)	金额(美元)
巴西	29	110,288	52	159,846
墨西哥	7	12,234		
巴拿马		81		243
巴拉圭	49	54,764		
加拿大	1,270	2,106,864	517	1,157,729
美国	33,361	92,954,120	58,750	131,077,127
澳大利亚	27,346	60,822,205	17,081	43,362,847
新西兰	145	817,368	57	136,220
其他	4,216	7,642,956	5,620	10,543,167

原油

来 源 地	1998		1997	
	数量(公吨)	金额(美元)	数量(公吨)	金额(美元)
总值	**27,322,632**	**3,274,537,489**	**35,469,701**	**5,456,210,767**
香港	1	1,785	64,459	10,801,828
印度尼西亚	3,387,144	386,614,968	6,585,351	1,065,458,822
伊朗	3,619,989	415,914,820	2,756,718	418,408,734
伊拉克	607,352	59,835,233	239,010	34,116,020
日本	55,336	5,251,052	1	935
科威特	282,285	36,813,361	68,790	11,118,229
马来西亚	451,096	55,667,060	230,296	37,568,706
蒙古	5,615	561,490		
阿曼	5,793,430	704,309,160	9,033,023	1,343,614,897
巴基斯坦	26,096	3,032,131	96,333	15,238,855
沙特阿拉伯	1,807,618	193,861,505	499,908	72,698,646
新加坡		5	144,206	21,784,324
泰国	132,350	16,826,778	103,739	18,281,608
阿拉伯联合酋长国	514,506	65,884,702	48,438	7,516,516
也门共和国	4,043,151	520,806,221	4,055,011	641,870,361
越南	865,899	109,806,765	1,499,143	248,098,473
安哥拉	1,104,985	153,453,062	3,836,639	603,131,937
刚果	382,400	40,074,642	979,956	147,829,116
埃及	198,714	21,292,684	286,514	40,203,435
赤道几内亚	243,204	33,339,986	204,919	29,335,875
利比亚	138,383	21,371,086	70,003	10,999,454
尼日利亚	123,238	17,633,820		

1998年中国进口主要商品来源地

原油

来源地	1998		1997	
	数量(公吨)	金额(美元)	数量(公吨)	金额(美元)
德国		190		
挪威	489,779	55,900,761	987,052	145,163,751
哈萨克斯坦	409,153	39,280,484	44,891	4,713,583
俄罗斯	144,578	15,845,529	475,257	66,415,636
阿根廷	1,057,144	130,603,434	1,108,515	148,065,797
加拿大	162,822	24,044,406		41
美国	853,713	96,072,344	753,658	114,801,564
澳大利亚	353,856	42,203,060	325,486	52,319,359
巴布亚新几内业亚	68,792	8,234,965	323,736	48,465,592
其他			648,648	98,188,673

成品油

来源地	1998		1997	
	数量(公吨)	金额(美元)	数量(公吨)	金额(美元)
总值	**21,739,869**	**2,405,175,867**	**23,794,877**	**3,682,055,026**
巴林	88,156	12,306,243	26,768	6,841,815
缅甸	12	3,189		
朝鲜	51,226	6,889,282	236,478	31,932,196
香港	107,362	51,042,247	94,832	55,642,245
印度	36,522	2,358,921	97,322	20,423,305
印度尼西亚	426,777	46,919,429	185,651	21,454,328
伊朗	1	92	50,560	4,846,692
以色列	5	5,365		
日本	1,921,988	201,050,020	2,546,757	366,242,890
科威特	43,372	9,335,362	127,955	26,263,682
马来西亚	553,714	53,681,807	239,311	31,999,529
巴基斯坦	2	2,301	5	5,048
菲律宾	93,745	9,237,587	280,819	32,196,293
沙特阿拉伯	40,447	4,513,414	165,835	34,600,120
新加坡	7,515,761	850,682,328	9,785,063	1,645,125,837
韩国	9,139,357	900,247,597	5,763,642	850,333,031
斯里兰卡	13,458	1,991,740	28,275	5,658,752
泰国	21,541	3,412,943	15,393	2,533,902
阿拉伯联合酋长国	43,708	4,441,537	33,231	7,723,887
越南	71,113	5,431,427	17,381	3,148,123
台湾省	152,663	32,428,369	160,589	33,107,753

1998年中国进口主要商品来源地

成品油

来源地	1998		1997	
	数量(公吨)	金额(美元)	数量(公吨)	金额(美元)
南非	170	88,365	5,258	554,531
比利时	2,190	2,631,297	1,523	1,972,750
丹麦	60	76,228	22	43,463
英国	3,170	4,438,519	7,933	7,246,287
德国	3,632	7,963,394	2,675	4,509,623
法国	6,637	8,171,000	8,069	10,329,094
意大利	120	303,183	26,973	7,025,916
荷兰	4,067	7,460,437	2,567	3,072,437
希腊	14	18,635	14	10,080
西班牙	908	1,301,907	971	1,276,245
奥地利		1,516		1,676
挪威		1,171		2,476
瑞典	1,176	339,999	897	479,372
瑞士	996	348,984	24	75,084
白俄罗斯	1,300	117,000	986	99,026
俄罗斯	904,719	87,606,237	3,459,921	343,174,669
乌克兰	1	150,000		
马其顿共和国		762		
巴西	28	51,884	31	93,848
墨西哥		401		641
巴拉圭	770	55,055		
加拿大	148	323,544	5,134	1,529,943
美国	416,519	70,931,573	270,364	86,684,969
澳大利亚	35,221	7,100,064	46,419	12,297,352
新西兰	24,153	4,046,710		163
其他	12,936	5,666,802	99,230	21,495,953

塑料

来源地	1998		1997	
	数量	金额(美元)	数量	金额(美元)
总值		**10,458,763,363**		**10,200,259,934**
孟加拉国		466		47,164
缅甸		8,578		5,652
柬埔寨		492		
塞浦路斯		5		
朝鲜		126,711		122,026

1998年中国进口主要商品来源地

塑料

来 源 地	1998		1997	
	数量	金额(美元)	数量	金额(美元)
香港		301,955,265		330,481,427
印度		3,196,829		5,466,760
印度尼西亚		152,305,856		78,985,015
伊朗		10,284,378		9,692,035
以色列		2,949,948		2,904,999
日本		2,078,113,021		2,208,785,685
约旦		26,654		5,301
科威特		49,650,277		1,254,699
老挝		32,963		8,605
黎巴嫩		213		58
澳门		1,000,144		1,896,294
马来西亚		179,916,279		159,022,142
马尔代夫		90		
蒙古		1,486		
尼泊尔		46,232		23,255
阿曼		68,388		
巴基斯坦		41,226		50,678
菲律宾		9,190,764		4,642,956
卡塔尔		39,813,138		61,172,164
沙特阿拉伯		180,394,471		181,625,694
新加坡		359,941,706		268,766,473
韩国		2,535,936,356		2,208,551,562
斯里兰卡		140,502		140,173
泰国		419,307,252		254,013,807
土耳其		789,238		348,566
阿拉伯联合酋长国		4,247,361		7,466,939
也门共和国		3,415		27,298
越南		1,389,949		711,728
台湾省		2,487,194,786		2,520,854,898
埃及		833		939,738
赤道几内亚		33		
加纳		142		
利比里亚		277		5,666
尼日利亚		145,175		17,054
塞内加尔		524		
南非		9,189,315		12,244,073
苏丹		57,074		38,342

1998年中国进口主要商品来源地

塑料

来 源 地	1998		1997	
	数量	金额(美元)	数量	金额(美元)
突尼斯		1,246		
乌干达		108,250		484
比利时		74,876,090		69,542,151
丹麦		1,664,092		1,271,825
英国		40,195,859		45,354,889
德国		156,351,960		165,685,372
法国		59,808,663		65,544,673
爱尔兰		1,004,457		1,408,853
意大利		36,724,779		37,634,184
卢森堡		12,705,040		9,575,410
荷兰		58,341,003		66,419,663
希腊		115,731		521,870
葡萄牙		4,004,623		10,308,482
西班牙		11,822,302		18,660,925
阿尔巴尼亚		1,355		
奥地利		2,147,138		1,639,373
保加利亚		18,971		3,633
芬兰		11,488,678		14,159,914
匈牙利		2,017,191		5,548,846
冰岛		3,424		269
列支敦士登		93		710
挪威		2,972,309		4,709,226
波兰		367,601		828,323
罗马尼亚		26,019		1,570,292
瑞典		21,125,791		16,580,137
瑞士		9,186,792		11,268,749
立陶宛		41,059		
哈萨克斯坦		75,060		
俄罗斯		87,658,446		138,834,960
乌克兰		19,846		
斯洛文尼亚共和国		5,572		351
克罗地亚共和国		4,378		64,943
捷克共和国		290,975		261,557
斯洛伐克共和国		408		
阿根廷		2,760,342		3,902,009
巴西		18,048,048		22,970,410
智利		402,942		21,498

1998 年中国进口主要商品来源地

塑料

来源地	1998		1997	
	数量	金额(美元)	数量	金额(美元)
哥伦比亚		180,640		591,313
危地马拉		208		39,904
海地		271		194
牙买加		568		
墨西哥		7,780,317		15,697,353
巴拿马		916		25,634
巴拉圭		66,081		151,239
乌拉圭		17,981		5,426
委内瑞拉		770		
加拿大		58,996,554		91,430,191
美国		784,743,627		902,448,771
澳大利亚		39,507,532		33,267,464
新西兰		2,078,122		3,193,733
诺福克岛		1,364		
巴布亚新几内亚		371		
土阿莫土群岛		24		
其他		121,533,672		118,795,805

化肥

来源地	1998		1997	
	数量(公吨)	金额(美元)	数量(公吨)	金额(美元)
总值	**13,871,429**	**2,505,671,727**	**16,489,103**	**2,994,935,833**
缅甸	50	8,154		
朝鲜	164	25,062		
香港	81	54,012	401	107,677
印度		319		
印度尼西亚	16,197	2,084,731	45,546	9,174,242
以色列	218,814	27,312,206	236,343	27,014,534
日本	259	221,047	262	837,483
约旦	203,907	24,071,600	201,231	22,615,741
马来西亚	1	968	15	4,886
蒙古	11,864	1,305,052		
新加坡	26	22,525	1	1,360
韩国	42,269	9,098,264	52,899	10,773,309
泰国	14	3,001	8	58,140
越南	14,800	1,826,000	5,000	625,000

1998年中国进口主要商品来源地

化肥

来源地	1998		1997	
	数量(公吨)	金额(美元)	数量(公吨)	金额(美元)
台湾省	45,753	9,805,652	92,452	18,539,228
摩洛哥	319,567	71,918,611	164,010	36,950,218
突尼斯	54,629	12,385,063		
比利时	123,380	26,687,152	160,768	37,554,396
丹麦	129,979	28,292,502	167,440	37,093,080
英国	9	3,103	5,258	1,203,055
德国	288,456	58,516,923	276,585	55,382,174
法国	18,579	3,474,573	54,949	12,539,730
意大利	3	4,054	19	7,762
荷兰	389	413,337	52,385	13,236,085
希腊	52,411	10,709,169	231,418	56,090,624
西班牙	18,000	3,780,000	56,748	12,701,633
奥地利	1	9,973		
芬兰	38,795	8,450,451	123,959	30,236,609
挪威	333,110	65,663,570	291,729	58,659,408
瑞士	4	14,320	1	9,162
拉脱维亚	49,336	5,734,403		
哈萨克斯坦	30,536	4,863,277	142,476	23,175,061
俄罗斯	4,485,269	637,861,997	6,251,494	961,251,786
乌克兰	26,999	3,077,938	319,099	53,053,459
乌兹别克斯坦	3,611	608,566	29,310	5,018,771
智利	83,692	22,888,152	49,255	13,645,495
加拿大	1,992,155	249,394,878	1,742,617	217,119,509
美国	5,267,986	1,214,993,533	4,867,229	1,122,876,168
澳大利亚	32	18,104	60	76,664
新西兰	2	784		
其他	297	68,701	868,137	157,303,384

天然橡胶

来源地	1998		1997	
	数量(公吨)	金额(美元)	数量(公吨)	金额(美元)
总值	**430,079**	**319,281,527**	**429,877**	**457,603,020**
缅甸	580	429,793	58	42,047
柬埔寨	7,296	5,734,593	2,691	2,834,431
香港	21	11,364	73	89,915
印度尼西亚	34,988	26,812,450	34,379	38,718,268

1998年中国进口主要商品来源地

天然橡胶

来 源 地	1998		1997	
	数量(公吨)	金额(美元)	数量(公吨)	金额(美元)
日本	460	350,597	840	822,681
马来西亚	62,567	49,776,603	78,015	84,788,738
菲律宾	4,947	3,601,523	6,347	7,055,106
新加坡	2,177	1,601,551	4,080	4,661,374
韩国	2,325	2,013,908	1,761	2,871,082
斯里兰卡	304	233,680	204	327,870
泰国	281,903	203,685,576	278,241	292,913,618
越南	25,491	19,174,321	11,774	11,743,464
台湾省	6,336	5,239,189	10,609	9,963,591
科特迪瓦	75	45,122	45	27,073
尼日利亚	181	128,326		
英国	65	36,301	2	1,835
德国	16	23,549	38	50,172
法国	2	2,448		51
意大利	4	1,896		26
荷兰	15	18,320	31	39,669
俄罗斯	85	145,935		
美国	111	92,196	225	196,486
其他	129	122,286	461	455,523

合成橡胶

来 源 地	1998		1997	
	数量(公吨)	金额(美元)	数量(公吨)	金额(美元)
总值	**513,622**	**465,517,420**	**453,284**	**469,004,990**
香港	5,702	5,834,665	7,297	8,123,983
印度尼西亚	3,686	2,313,404	4,260	3,721,796
伊朗	5,804	3,704,036	8,658	6,441,049
日本	107,800	132,619,019	98,577	127,484,802
澳门	2	11,337	12	13,602
马来西亚	2,822	1,992,583	3,464	3,056,645
菲律宾	4	2,961	46	42,354
卡塔尔		254		
沙特阿拉伯	20	12,914	1	1,615
新加坡	1,618	3,052,812	1,761	3,689,526
韩国	78,644	68,150,655	74,982	76,243,710
斯里兰卡	165	380,399		206

1998年中国进口主要商品来源地

合成橡胶

来源地	1998		1997	
	数量(公吨)	金额(美元)	数量(公吨)	金额(美元)
泰国	9,330	6,411,478	8,292	6,436,587
阿拉伯联合酋长国	58	116,311	21	16,279
越南	35	18,552	115	138,816
台湾省	184,156	146,608,509	159,994	138,733,612
南非	349	344,962	1,603	1,590,849
比利时	2,777	5,115,490	2,606	4,088,712
丹麦		1,497	18	30,088
英国	44,904	10,060,533	4,574	8,380,802
德国	3,899	7,153,339	4,585	5,670,290
法国	6,424	7,390,212	9,971	10,680,966
意大利	848	1,581,765	2,169	3,642,807
卢森堡	13	44,204		
荷兰	558	730,911	2,976	2,994,577
西班牙	401	413,139	1,365	1,619,725
奥地利		982	1	4,674
芬兰		843		6
挪威		800		
波兰	13	37,050		
瑞典	69	187,559	62	129,631
瑞士		856	232	185,092
拉脱维亚	1,332	2,302,178		
白俄罗斯	79	94,480	46	32,485
俄罗斯	18,461	16,285,509	22,343	19,388,853
巴西	134	144,500	204	226,017
墨西哥	2,590	2,080,911	1,874	1,527,739
加拿大	6,263	10,414,861	5,224	7,678,521
美国	19,704	26,299,878	21,059	23,115,016
澳大利亚	133	93,708	123	142,263
新西兰	24	32,890	20	29,534
其他	4,798	3,474,474	4,748	3,701,761

医疗器械

来源地	1998		1997	
	数量	金额(美元)	数量	金额(美元)
总值		**395,673,251**		**333,215,085**
香港		8,395,795		8,751,531

1998年中国进口主要商品来源地

医疗器械

来源地	1998		1997	
	数量	金额(美元)	数量	金额(美元)
印度		524,997		355,910
印度尼西亚		12,192		10,262
以色列		18,421,768		2,553,438
日本		103,551,600		112,053,395
马来西亚		1,881,664		4,507,214
菲律宾		93,649		15,301
新加坡		4,734,415		4,088,003
韩国		3,768,993		1,752,744
泰国		870,877		715,629
台湾省		1,733,192		2,052,235
比利时		1,470,762		159,365
丹麦		1,888,038		1,846,051
英国		4,572,647		1,543,258
德国		51,529,131		45,852,697
法国		7,657,866		3,365,220
爱尔兰		206,537		68,206
意大利		3,169,576		6,599,773
荷兰		15,629,478		16,299,449
希腊		2,020		7,021
西班牙		134,253		5,155,648
奥地利		2,810,933		454,749
芬兰		3,072,853		2,390,367
匈牙利		14,084		
挪威		635,213		479,213
波兰		15,112		
瑞典		5,602,322		4,785,849
瑞士		1,582,864		773,012
俄罗斯		30,278		20,707
南斯拉夫		150,537		
巴西		64,366		39,580
哥伦比亚		2,434		48,313
古巴		289		
多米尼加共和国		112,898		25,061
墨西哥		18,942		30,360
波多黎各		3,935		
加拿大		344,252		405,207
美国		143,437,483		97,483,437

1998 年中国进口主要商品来源地

医疗器械

来源地	1998		1997	
	数量	金额(美元)	数量	金额(美元)
澳大利亚		400,420		365,656
新西兰		11,016		17,599
其他		7,113,570		8,143,625

各类船

来源地	1998		1997	
	数量(艘)	金额(美元)	数量(艘)	金额(美元)
总值	**968**	**121,631,206**	**1,013**	**253,720,580**
香港	207	9,034,193	205	10,231,958
日本	171	23,324,291	242	50,202,005
澳门	12	258,170	3	71,100
马来西亚	6	692,735		
新加坡	3	803,698	9	396,866
韩国	80	9,099,778	13	124,668,619
泰国	2	2,000		
台湾省	7	561,192	34	406,101
丹麦	15	470,099	8	248,835
英国	4	25,777	6	515,291
德国	68	34,948,419	59	7,746,913
法国	3	4,088	15	16,795
荷兰	11	9,957,940	10	9,794,692
希腊	2	112,020	4	230,001
西班牙	4	326,862	2	1,204,888
芬兰	1	280,005		
马耳他	1	600,000		
挪威	25	8,654,477	7	478,938
波兰	4	11,350		
俄罗斯	31	557,650	3	480,000
伯利兹	1	258,437	1	258,200
巴拿马	2	515,878	1	258,200
圣文森特和格林纳丁斯	1	258,261	1	258,200
加拿大	20	9,091,697	168	514,096
美国	180	3,587,160	95	1,834,571
澳大利亚	13	40,120	7	20,300,134
新西兰	4	436,778	1	3,928
其他	90	7,718,131	119	23,600,249

1998年中国进口主要商品来源地

飞机

来 源 地	1998		1997	
	数量(架)	金额(美元)	数量(架)	金额(美元)
总值	**81**	**2,602,789,125**	**73**	**2,576,044,950**
德国	1	42,864,528		
法国	25	959,942,171	24	1,219,375,047
瑞典	4	7,367,728		
俄罗斯	12	317,678,409	18	34,581,106
加拿大	3	80,215,373	2	53,732,451
美国	36	1,194,720,916	29	1,268,356,346

汽车

来 源 地	1998		1997	
	数量(辆)	金额(美元)	数量(辆)	金额(美元)
总值	**39,375**	**815,116,351**	**47,779**	**690,736,460**
缅甸	2	14,600		
香港	10	423,954	10	158,072
日本	31,177	533,980,346	21,545	369,091,009
菲律宾	22	1,698,443		
新加坡	3	729,336	6	600,469
韩国	2,155	34,159,225	3,354	43,064,092
泰国	2	42,770		
台湾省	99	1,817,177	90	2,844,732
比利时	6	752,795	3	59,659
英国	146	5,686,649	117	6,246,417
德国	1,329	89,544,531	768	44,493,149
法国	1,029	11,673,979	16,827	87,269,624
意大利	48	2,777,531	51	4,365,309
荷兰	4	407,940	12	1,603,538
奥地利	8	1,320,991	21	7,027,020
芬兰	5	1,816,926	9	4,404,426
匈牙利	2	21,053	1	68,887
罗马尼亚	100	340,000	1,307	3,488,049
瑞典	664	18,603,578	604	13,880,173
瑞士	19	2,529,532	1	430,919
白俄罗斯	11	1,151,291	16	1,973,000
俄罗斯	35	9,968,834	785	6,754,114
乌克兰	15	6,640,000		
捷克共和国	120	3,706,767	145	4,618,095

1998 年中国进口主要商品来源地

汽车

来 源 地	1998		1997	
	数量(辆)	金额(美元)	数量(辆)	金额(美元)
巴西	4	65,000		
加拿大	26	566,812	48	2,047,234
美国	2,303	82,627,359	1,491	77,986,497
澳大利亚	31	2,048,932	7	1,074,312
其他			561	7,187,664

汽车零件

来 源 地	1998		1997	
	数量	金额(美元)	数量	金额(美元)
总值		**934,985,338**		**932,485,958**
香港		2,056,995		599,422
印度		51,882		731,514
印度尼西亚		20,988		62,541
以色列		3		4,579
日本		114,036,253		167,622,549
澳门		5		
马来西亚		140,327		333,987
巴基斯坦		84		316
菲律宾		43,880		233,520
沙特阿拉伯		245		203
新加坡		773,953		1,129,679
韩国		7,489,976		13,592,202
斯里兰卡		106,691		
泰国		1,634,327		2,686,797
土耳其		32,220		43,337
阿拉伯联合酋长国		23		
越南		112		
台湾省		5,029,602		7,709,327
南非		125,757		9,990
突尼斯		2,009		
比利时		640,882		1,427,058
丹麦		7,215		1,169
英国		39,080,020		17,294,123
德国		533,761,897		511,608,093
法国		143,272,590		63,114,688
意大利		18,472,747		14,907,553

1998年中国进口主要商品来源地

汽车零件

来源地	1998		1997	
	数量	金额(美元)	数量	金额(美元)
荷兰		3,392,518		265,429
希腊		92		
葡萄牙		508,910		6,186
西班牙		5,289,808		864,016
奥地利		469,836		1,607,793
芬兰		209,826		80,996
匈牙利		319,689		325,219
挪威		729		5,549
波兰		14,737		11,922
罗马尼亚		26,922		68,325
瑞典		13,023,493		7,347,128
瑞士		84,687		348,168
白俄罗斯		1,890,973		981,472
俄罗斯		371,206		852,387
乌克兰		733,818		15,279
捷克共和国		1,021,941		1,546,810
斯洛伐克共和国		54,170		119,092
巴西		2,523,011		27,202,862
墨西哥		33,298		73,275
加拿大		1,195,281		561,852
美国		35,975,257		86,846,991
澳大利亚		1,010,863		121,585
新西兰		554		622
其他		53,036		120,353

集成电路

来源地	1998		1997	
	数量	金额(美元)	数量	金额(美元)
总值		**4,778,243,261**		**3,641,777,378**
朝鲜		446,154		4,739,624
香港		455,745,844		362,975,996
印度		69,361		222,819
印度尼西亚		2,239,866		506,954
以色列		181,798		39,901
日本		1,617,506,457		1,552,341,899
澳门		5,653,625		246,150

1998 年中国进口主要商品来源地

集成电路

来源地	1998		1997	
	数量	金额(美元)	数量	金额(美元)
马亚西亚		241,785,200		129,150,268
阿曼		5,704		3,021
菲律宾		71,226,080		23,269,257
新加坡		261,101,202		175,606,073
韩国		356,197,186		285,921,548
泰国		36,985,729		25,743,740
土耳其		1,164,576		
阿拉伯联合酋长国		10,899		76,378
也门共和国		1,000		
越南		37,500		
台湾省		791,070,473		558,816,767
埃及		41,428		
毛里塔尼亚		1,228		
摩洛哥		1,106,854		87,757
南非		56,545		63,480
比利时		32,577,773		38,063,192
丹麦		90,132		49,237
英国		14,761,083		18,371,198
德国		73,550,835		27,679,607
法国		28,392,687		18,417,465
爱尔兰		9,244,370		1,324,752
意大利		5,166,887		2,488,932
卢森堡		54		
荷兰		5,852,836		8,604,981
希腊		18,943		
葡萄牙		1,331,160		143,764
西班牙		237,484		1,851,110
奥地利		1,247,701		882,571
芬兰		68,296,058		4,492,542
匈牙利		1,377		
马耳他		1,050,366		131,088
摩纳哥		1,173		
挪威		448,968		1,024
波兰		2,386		
瑞典		4,940,076		6,943,692
瑞士		913,372		2,607,308
立陶宛		10,040		7,935

1998 年中国进口主要商品来源地

集成电路

来源地	1998		1997	
	数量	金额(美元)	数量	金额(美元)
白俄罗斯		522,123		
俄罗斯		11,380,931		1,045,620
乌克兰		15,977		2,006
捷克共和国		10,982		
巴西		14,639		1,018
智利		3,819		
哥斯达黎加		1,248,006		
墨西哥		3,304,299		1,674,186
巴拿马		67,512		
秘鲁		675		
加拿大		13,924,312		12,373,892
美国		621,421,114		359,388,648
澳大利亚		105,417		211,726
新西兰		74,388		28,721
其他		35,378,597		15,179,531

金属切削机床

来源地	1998		1997	
	数量(台)	金额(美元)	数量(台)	金额(美元)
总值	**79,112**	**1,390,772,572**	**104,684**	**1,584,587,419**
缅甸	1	30,000		
朝鲜	4	2,799,570		
香港	6,183	22,859,936	9,139	29,481,878
印度尼西亚	8	128,501	65	268,631
以色列	22	211,963	10	321,986
日本	12,882	480,252,545	20,919	508,826,536
马来西亚	571	3,667,762	389	2,359,814
菲律宾	49	932,150	44	306,797
新加坡	481	10,546,536	610	10,550,846
韩国	4,356	99,570,367	4,566	63,452,547
泰国	276	2,289,128	297	3,464,743
土耳其	1	18,796	2	22,653
越南	5	2,017	14	14,251
台湾省	45,604	279,385,911	54,521	372,568,822
南非	3	25,888	1	2,153,407
比利时	156	11,338,365	194	15,880,982

1998年中国进口主要商品来源地

金属切削机床

来源地	1998		1997	
	数量(台)	金额(美元)	数量(台)	金额(美元)
丹麦	20	105,296	79	1,215,185
英国	448	17,703,870	713	27,363,137
德国	1,553	195,524,372	1,871	193,554,375
法国	135	5,673,988	304	38,571,005
爱尔兰	1	337,368	4	99,845
意大利	545	71,960,650	918	87,972,443
卢森堡	1	1,268	2	191,764
荷兰	74	6,055,998	116	5,699,367
葡萄牙	3	20,300	23	156,387
西班牙	330	18,493,257	435	14,464,200
奥地利	14	1,557,951	20	5,300,276
芬兰	23	1,831,058	17	1,182,041
波兰	2	5,000	1	7,566
瑞典	122	2,514,229	107	12,069,447
瑞士	491	24,867,201	681	34,678,564
白俄罗斯	4	464,396		
吉尔吉斯斯坦	12	4,200		
俄罗斯	174	13,222,187	90	13,942,819
乌克兰	2	6,200	10	561,769
捷克共和国	11	1,688,480	6	1,173,169
斯洛伐克共和国	1	1,828	1	179,260
巴西	9	214,702	17	512,179
墨西哥	8	27,328	9	23,238
加拿大	81	4,423,087	48	2,010,651
美国	2,102	101,614,102	4,213	120,892,884
澳大利亚	113	3,344,193	451	4,163,511
新西兰	1	548,000	3	1,868
其他	2,230	4,502,628	3,774	8,926,576

铸造机械

来源地	1998		1997	
	数量(台)	金额(美元)	数量(台)	金额(美元)
总值	**2,800,022**	**115,043,468**	**3,148,365**	**162,717,971**
香港	8,430	1,351,381	5,177	1,638,346
印度	3,900	10,100		
以色列	113	198,115		

1998年中国进口主要商品来源地

铸造机械

来源地	1998		1997	
	数量(台)	金额(美元)	数量(台)	金额(美元)
日本	605,502	34,743,619	622,584	50,295,581
马来西亚	1,217	23,833		
菲律宾	2	58		
新加坡	915	54,975	22,005	89,985
韩国	130,320	4,609,950	26,527	500,084
泰国	6,153	9,689		
台湾省	209,415	8,888,244	304,607	14,361,795
比利时	25,189	1,409,861	14,988	399,999
丹麦	11,130	448,956	1,877	165,792
英国	44,022	6,554,486	341	1,456,029
德国	1,153,741	25,429,854	1,311,349	39,251,853
法国	6,892	754,673	11,402	238,021
意大利	22,652	11,135,593	69,609	19,852,521
卢森堡	81,468	3,158,966		
荷兰	25,916	213,390	5	1,254,000
西班牙	4,546	55,225	76,557	4,782,472
奥地利	16,329	1,262,012	584	1,021,230
芬兰	6,298	490,322	454	417,628
瑞典	15	248,770	2,649	296,508
瑞士	23,032	4,019,682	77,264	8,966,944
白俄罗斯	1	43,000	3	384,200
摩尔多瓦	1,609	364,000		
俄罗斯	55	395	5	546,540
捷克共和国	1,540	19,808	640	21,104
墨西哥	560	3,652		
加拿大	196,477	272,221	2,648	106,964
美国	209,422	8,673,827	434,259	15,650,484
澳大利亚	2,927	114,123	2,209	698,319
新西兰	80	27		
其他	154	480,661	160,622	321,572

橡胶或塑料加工机械

来源地	1998		1997	
	数量	金额(美元)	数量	金额(美元)
总值		**926,007,754**		**1,301,559,413**
香港		70,014,110		85,113,529

1998 年中国进口主要商品来源地

橡胶或塑料加工机械

来 源 地	1998		1997	
	数量	金额(美元)	数量	金额(美元)
印度		284,215		73,315
印度尼西亚		653,989		7,279,032
以色列		241,829		5,294
日本		208,080,728		364,429,271
澳门		2,366		25,968
马来西亚		2,636,095		1,942,436
菲律宾		167,022		619,032
新加坡		10,945,645		16,535,180
韩国		48,045,866		46,641,807
斯里兰卡		23,540		2,756
泰国		1,858,628		4,334,214
台湾省		226,042,252		328,236,518
比利时		2,562,588		2,279,480
丹麦		252,367		599,829
英国		9,486,333		16,323,402
德国		117,540,781		129,379,997
法国		18,790,093		40,429,673
爱尔兰		25,224		240,000
意大利		128,308,529		112,278,743
卢森堡		30,175		164,198
荷兰		4,505,395		13,246,456
西班牙		285,978		11,098,472
奥地利		9,597,106		22,007,442
芬兰		875,683		1,988,010
匈牙利		700		
挪威		10,450		274,690
瑞典		1,166,448		1,530,753
瑞士		11,907,820		7,118,112
摩尔多瓦		95,000		
俄罗斯		302,314		914,972
巴西		107,910		61,668
墨西哥		7,733		8,614
加拿大		11,097,338		15,002,642
美国		34,103,518		55,381,345
澳大利亚		2,458,931		2,364,025
新西兰		41,603		355,057
其他		3,451,452		13,273,481

1998 年中国进口主要商品来源地

烟草加工机械

来 源 地	1998		1997	
	数量	金额(美元)	数量	金额(美元)
总值		208,903,959		206,318,684
香港		8,570		23,861
日本		1,260,055		29,686
新加坡		4,222		26,469
韩国		1,035		11,301
泰国		6		
台湾省		4,065		273,113
丹麦		33,241		1,714
英国		25,034,986		75,665,887
德国		56,333,046		66,359,325
法国		5,299		289,102
意大利		115,645,256		40,314,316
瑞典		96,816		4,443
瑞士		79,925		140,383
巴西		117,554		7,873,600
美国		10,274,977		14,964,242
其他		4,906		341,242

电动机及发电机

来 源 地	1998		1997	
	数量(万台)	金额(美元)	数量(万台)	金额(美元)
总值	**73,904**	**580,438,698**	**70,511**	**559,290,913**
巴林		26		
朝鲜		972		
香港	16,076	80,601,845	16,112	66,680,727
印度	30	108,756	2	67,185
印度尼西亚	428	5,674,926	205	2,755,617
以色列	2	18,023		7,058
日本	13,909	144,376,618	18,625	187,496,755
黎巴嫩		146		
澳门	4	9,975	28	48,187
马来西亚	2,781	32,569,498	1,485	22,858,989
阿曼	4	28,918		
菲律宾	72	3,374,947	2	67,029
沙特阿拉伯		172		252
新加坡	1,232	10,011,416	539	7,522,517

1998 年中国进口主要商品来源地

电动机及发电机

来源地	1998		1997	
	数量(万台)	金额(美元)	数量(万台)	金额(美元)
韩国	642	14,962,238	726	18,323,453
泰国	1,295	20,165,279	1,092	14,039,736
土耳其		60		117
阿拉伯联合酋长国	26	66,538		40
越南	8	37,861	12	36,967
台湾省	6,869	49,250,201	6,490	48,172,642
埃及		20		
南非		4,653		6,405
比利时	1	2,848,803		222,225
丹麦		1,120,737		564,882
英国	14	8,793,059	36	5,807,598
德国	340	28,117,042	200	37,106,115
法国	8	5,634,749	10	3,954,889
爱尔兰		1,857		18,685
意大利	69	8,510,736	68	7,937,875
荷兰	135	3,042,103	158	2,111,434
希腊		2,007		
西班牙	5	1,278,707	2	1,548,505
奥地利		5,699,641		90,252
芬兰	11	5,925,801		1,836,095
匈牙利		24,112		4,426
挪威		344,382		53,154
波兰		20,404		2,352
瑞典	73	5,348,177	17	2,282,671
瑞士	25	1,848,238	1	1,461,595
俄罗斯		68,924		1,811,248
乌克兰		5,740,835		1,510,000
捷克共和国		11,953		11,650
斯洛伐克共和国		15,481		4,133
巴西	6	983,214	2	597,668
智利	9	365,120		
加拿大	20	3,367,049	4	1,143,188
美国	146	30,311,782	260	31,639,151
澳大利亚		787,982		2,028,071
新西兰	2	146,893		11,900
其他	29,664	98,815,822	24,435	87,447,475

1998年中国进口主要商品来源地

发电机组

来 源 地	1998		1997	
	数量(台)	金额(美元)	数量(台)	金额(美元)
总值	**12,502**	**318,927,169**	**14,513**	**600,867,131**
香港	192	3,078,332	1,099	8,965,842
印度	411	85,535	1,636	260,570
印度尼西亚	44	12,300	1	25,000
日本	5,961	34,759,717	3,968	65,438,120
马来西亚	6	41,948	16	417,317
新加坡	213	8,489,120	300	7,685,191
韩国	1,672	11,136,677	3,199	9,604,307
台湾省	270	5,823,484	301	8,938,150
比利时	4	3,904,596	1	175,276
丹麦	56	7,572,683	197	50,031,566
英国	1,106	57,920,510	1,062	35,880,280
德国	120	13,926,343	118	22,023,045
法国	80	2,072,139	151	60,108,400
意大利	242	1,676,961	22	8,594,648
荷兰	21	3,959,000	10	37,047,538
奥地利	5	6,485,226		
芬兰	51	21,032,943	20	21,327,631
挪威	4	1,265,744	7	2,662,733
波兰	3	34,239		
罗马尼亚	1	3,075,866		
瑞典	33	1,332,461	65	2,714,741
瑞士	1	51,620	1	87,939
俄罗斯	2	1,015,656	3	749,892
加拿大	81	1,871,450	67	3,602,367
美国	1,700	115,485,748	2,145	118,934,554
澳大利亚	213	12,592,368	103	5,152,839
其他	10	224,503	21	130,439,185

有线电话电报交换机零件

来 源 地	1998		1997	
	数量	金额(美元)	数量	金额(美元)
总值		**911,755,040**		**1,006,204,665**
香港		91,129,344		59,556,326
印度		28,788		29,248
印度尼西亚		1,057,029		475,012

1998年中国进口主要商品来源地

有线电话电报交换机零件

来源地	1998		1997	
	数量	金额(美元)	数量	金额(美元)
以色列		10,870,637		1,044,237
日本		156,945,245		190,126,130
澳门		5,610		14,364
马来西亚		2,182,818		5,667,166
菲律宾		580,034		175,214
新加坡		3,629,059		649,312
韩国		23,942,992		49,056,565
泰国		1,437,806		80,739
土耳其		34,705		30,392
越南		451		
台湾省		53,416,093		57,090,360
南非		406		
比利时		11,690,022		32,296,865
丹麦		20,649		69,928
英国		8,045,202		7,748,299
德国		102,797,503		80,372,594
法国		54,917,523		32,794,309
爱尔兰		166,041		477,050
意大利		5,350,465		6,340,773
卢森堡		12,431		
荷兰		20,107,332		26,435,968
葡萄牙		13,678		
西班牙		6,270,340		7,491,239
奥地利		3,035,272		1,736,786
芬兰		44,755,260		11,347,896
匈牙利		4,751		
挪威		1,054,956		275,679
波兰		765,019		37,493
瑞典		87,606,711		191,990,026
瑞士		3,029,885		900,802
斯洛文尼亚共和国		41		
捷克共和国		454		
阿根廷		4,846		402,639
巴西		13,246		232,784
智利		18		
墨西哥		57,993		
巴拿马		775		

1998年中国进口主要商品来源地

有线电话电报交换机零件

来源地	1998		1997	
	数量	金额(美元)	数量	金额(美元)
特克斯和凯科斯群岛		51		
加拿大		60,694,189		111,170,543
美国		149,832,721		123,791,695
澳大利亚		2,654,329		2,849,549
新西兰		1,200,977		110,524
其他		2,391,343		3,336,159

计算机

来源地	1998		1997	
	数量	金额(美元)	数量	金额(美元)
总值		**1,810,096,712**		**1,134,521,320**
朝鲜		95,195		149,754
香港		116,958,162		74,556,957
印度		17,300		10,700
印度尼西亚		8,185,574		340,661
伊朗		118		
以色列		2,545,314		866,275
日本		324,214,376		253,512,310
澳门		13,990		20,000
马来西亚		49,234,969		65,176,334
菲律宾		35,473,709		17,114,002
新加坡		209,499,320		82,399,833
韩国		46,675,864		20,776,885
泰国		62,919,706		30,717,293
阿拉伯联合酋长国		2,300		
台湾省		139,455,727		93,529,559
安哥拉		950		
比利时		2,952,198		4,718,433
丹麦		1,044,405		1,251,804
英国		16,127,411		9,903,113
德国		43,741,558		18,444,240
法国		15,965,871		9,017,078
爱尔兰		4,225,606		985,126
意大利		9,840,348		6,201,159
荷兰		607,415		2,755,931
葡萄牙		500		32,599

1998 年中国进口主要商品来源地

计算机

来源地	1998		1997	
	数量	金额(美元)	数量	金额(美元)
西班牙		15,979,647		226,545
奥地利		79,155		502,937
保加利亚		409		
芬兰		7,475,093		1,383,895
匈牙利		1,410,812		1,521,970
挪威		2,876,763		186,428
瑞典		8,654,896		5,025,674
瑞士		1,118,446		1,858,405
白俄罗斯		557,144		
俄罗斯		280,782		2,000
乌克兰		484		
巴西		1,259		382
哥斯达黎加		68,550		
墨西哥		1,049,971		633,763
波多黎各		904		656
加拿大		24,847,817		16,535,718
美国		598,285,564		378,381,929
澳大利亚		5,659,541		5,816,650
新西兰		33,051		26,827
其他		51,873,538		29,937,495

有线通讯设备

来源地	1998		1997	
	数量	金额(美元)	数量	金额(美元)
总值		**2,277,576,710**		**1,208,219,646**
香港		98,545,496		66,448,374
印度		28,788		29,248
印度尼西亚		1,057,029		476,752
以色列		56,591,016		6,359,864
日本		333,677,194		244,457,845
澳门		5,610		2,441,622
马来西亚		2,588,828		5,887,475
菲律宾		589,194		235,033
新加坡		4,158,772		789,677
韩国		25,651,964		59,477,010
泰国		4,677,811		104,039

1998 年中国进口主要商品来源地

有线通讯设备

来 源 地	1998		1997	
	数量	金额(美元)	数量	金额(美元)
土耳其		121,321		30,392
阿拉伯联合酋长国		130		
越南		451		
台湾省		57,959,366		59,735,480
南非		406		
比利时		14,604,378		37,253,231
丹麦		37,377		361,884
英国		58,376,862		20,004,877
德国		260,905,671		93,181,719
法国		75,230,668		44,579,736
爱尔兰		4,165,787		558,836
意大利		51,602,730		9,405,620
卢森堡		12,431		
荷兰		26,906,690		26,822,422
葡萄牙		13,678		
西班牙		12,716,990		7,527,881
奥地利		3,816,400		1,784,810
芬兰		132,408,211		19,016,639
匈牙利		4,751		
挪威		1,465,138		2,271,489
波兰		765,019		37,493
瑞典		334,209,168		203,555,429
瑞士		6,551,642		2,420,872
俄罗斯		599		73,894
斯洛文尼亚共和国		41		
捷克共和国		454		
阿根廷		4,846		402,639
巴西		35,270		237,204
智利		142,494		142,430
墨西哥		57,993		
巴拿马		775		
特克斯和凯科斯群岛		51		
加拿大		147,501,576		123,778,515
美国		544,649,258		156,623,849
澳大利亚		7,133,037		6,082,768
新西兰		1,200,977		110,524
其他		7,402,372		5,512,074

利用外资统计简要文明

中国利用外资统计资料分类，是按我国现行《利用外资统计制度》规定确定的，由对外贸易经济合作部根据国内各地方、各部门的利用外资统计报表汇总而成。

外商投资企业名录因版面有限，本统计资料只提供在中国境内设立的部分外商投资企业。

本统计资料中，各表所列利用外资项目个数，是指依法批准的外国政府和国际金融组织的项目贷款个数、各外商投资企业个数以及海洋石油合作勘控开发合同个数，其他方式签订的利用外资协议（合同）只汇总金额，未计算项目个数。

利用外资的国家（地区），是指外资来源或投资者的法人注册地所在的国家或地区。在统计分类时，除政府贷款按贷款国家名称统计外，其他方式吸收的外资按外国公司、企业或其他经济组织以其法人注册所在地国家（地区）统计。

“协议外资金额”是指对外已正式签订或批准的协议（合同）规定，可供我国使用的贷款金额和应由外商提供的项目投资。

“实际利用外资金额”是指利用外资协议（合同）的实际执行金额，包括现汇、实物和双方同意计价投资的劳务、技术等无形资本。

利用外资金额统一以美元计算，其他各种货币按业务发生时美元对各种货币的汇率折算为美元。

1998 年中国利用外资统计表

金额单位：万美元

方式	批准利用外资协议(合同)		实际使用外资金额
	项目个数	外资金额	
总计	**19,850**	**6,320,054**	**5,855,749**
一、对外借款	51	838,500	1,100,000
外国政府贷款	51	5,000	290,000
国际金融组织贷款		285,600	300,000
出口信贷		190,000	184,000
外国银行商业贷款		257,900	226,000
对外发行债券		100,000	100,000
二、外商直接投资	19,799	5,210,205	4,546,275
合资经营企业	8,107	1,728,631	1,834,840
合作经营企业	2,003	1,165,570	971,904
外资企业	9,673	2,175,270	1,646,963
外商投资股份制企业	9	132,984	70,682
合作开发	7	7,750	17,886
其他		271,349	4,000
三、外商其他投资		62,493	209,474
国外发行股票		49,556	62,229
国际租赁		10,033	37,337
补偿贸易		149,267	6,480
加工装配			103,428

1998 年中国实际利用外资分国家(地区)统计表

金额单位:万美元

国家(地区)	合　计	对外借款	外商直接投资	外商其他投资
总值	**5,855,749**	**1,100,000**	**4,546,275**	**209,474**
香港	1,939,983		1,850,836	89,147
澳门	43,924		42,157	1,767
台湾省	305,123		291,521	13,602
越南	1,414		1,414	
菲律宾	17,927		17,927	
泰国	20,538		20,538	
马来西亚	34,057		34,049	8
新加坡	340,397		340,397	
文莱	183		183	
印度尼西亚	6,897		6,897	
朝鲜	510		510	

1998年中国实际利用外资分国家(地区)统计表

金额单位:万美元

国家(地区)	合　计	对外借款	外商直接投资	外商其他投资
老挝	112		112	
柬埔寨	370		290	80
蒙古	103		103	
日本	344,407		340,036	4,371
缅甸	511		511	
巴基斯坦	119		119	
孟加拉	17		17	
印度	557		557	
阿富汗	212		212	
伊朗	56		56	
土耳其	99		99	
塞浦路斯	425		425	
叙利亚	8		8	
约旦	12		12	
巴勒斯坦	10		10	
伊拉克	7		7	
沙特	30		30	
科威特	59		59	
阿联酋	175		175	
阿曼	878		878	
韩国	180,430		180,320	110
以色列	712		712	
亚洲其他国家	1,925		1,925	
埃及	14		14	
利比亚	12		12	
突尼斯	3,027		3,027	
摩洛哥	5		5	
塞内加尔	350		350	
几内亚	39		39	
几内亚(比绍)	642		642	
科特迪瓦	4		4	
利比里亚	20		20	
塞拉利昂	215		215	
尼日利亚	326		326	
布隆迪	36		36	
乌干达	15		15	
毛里求斯	10,050		10,050	
博茨瓦纳	23		23	

1998年中国实际利用外资分国家(地区)统计表

金额单位:万美元

国家(地区)	合 计	对外借款	外商直接投资	外商其他投资
莱索托	25		25	
南非	860		860	
纳米比亚	190		190	
非洲其他国家	23		23	
德国	73,673		73,673	
法国	71,489		71,489	
意大利	27,457		27,457	
荷兰	71,882		71,882	
比利时	2,804		2,804	
卢森堡	1,151		1,151	
英国	117,486		117,486	
丹麦	6,266		6,266	
芬兰	3,930		3,930	
瑞典	23,342		13,342	10,000
奥地利	2,113		2,113	
希腊	30		30	
西班牙	5,383		5,383	
葡萄牙	867		867	
波兰	94		94	
匈牙利	1,073		1,073	
捷克	507		507	
保加利亚	171		171	
阿尔巴尼亚	1,117		1,117	
罗马尼亚	1,441		1,441	
南斯拉夫	645		645	
挪威	2,592		2,592	
瑞士	22,882		22,882	
马耳他	57		57	
列支敦士登	63		63	
斯洛伐克	180		180	
俄罗斯	1,936		1,936	
乌克兰	46		46	
白俄罗斯	106		106	
哈萨克斯坦	12		12	
吉尔吉斯斯坦	6		6	
欧洲其他国家	132		132	
墨西哥	198		198	
洪都拉斯	287		287	

1998 年中国实际利用外资分国家(地区)统计表

金额单位:万美元

国家(地区)	合 计	对外借款	外商直接投资	外商其他投资
哥斯达黎加	510		510	
巴拿马	7,004		6,990	14
多米尼加共和国	45		45	
牙买加	55		55	
巴巴多斯	53		53	
委内瑞拉	86		86	
巴西	2,021		2,021	
厄瓜多尔	87		87	
秘鲁	861		861	
玻利维亚	510		510	
智利	483		483	
巴拉圭	70		70	
阿根廷	128		128	
乌拉圭	14		14	
巴哈马	8,077		8,077	
特克斯和凯科斯群岛	39		39	
维尔京群岛	403,134		403,134	
安提瓜	12		12	
伯利兹	130		130	
开曼群岛	32,423		32,423	
加拿大	31,652		31,652	
美国	417,355		389,844	27,511
百慕大群岛	11,447		11,447	
澳大利亚	27,832		27,197	635
新西兰	2,664		2,664	
西萨摩亚	12,641		12,641	
斐济	13		13	
库克群岛	402		402	
马绍尔群岛	66		66	
东萨摩亚	13		13	
其他太平洋岛屿	1,883		1,883	
大洋洲其他国家	8,490		8,490	
其他	1,186,068	1,100,000	23,839	62,229

1998年中国实际利用外资分省市统计表

金额单位:万美元

省 市	合 计	对外借款	外商直接投资	外商其他投资
总计	**5,855,749**	**1,100,000**	**4,755,749**	
北京市	216,800		216,800	
天津市	211,361		211,361	
河北省	142,868		142,868	
山西省	24,451		24,451	
内蒙古自治区	9,082		9,082	
辽宁省	240,624		219,045	21,579
大连市	120,723		115,940	4,783
吉林省	40,917		40,917	
黑龙江省	52,639		52,639	
上海市	366,774		360,150	6,624
江苏省	663,179		663,179	
浙江省	134,012		131,802	2,210
宁波市	50,329		50,329	
安徽省	27,673		27,673	
福建省	421,211		421,211	
厦门市	138,121		138,121	
江西省	46,496		46,496	
山东省	273,100		220,274	52,826
青岛市	72,830		72,830	
河南省	61,654		61,654	
湖北省	103,649		97,294	6,355
湖南省	81,816		81,816	
广东省	1,303,160		1,201,994	101,166
深圳市	197,205		166,357	30,848
广西壮族自治区	88,613		88,613	
海南省	71,715		71,715	
四川省	37,248		37,248	
重庆市	43,107		43,107	
贵州省	4,535		4,535	
云南省	14,568		14,568	
陕西省	30,010		30,010	
甘肃省	3,864		3,864	
青海省				
宁夏回族自治区	1,856		1,856	
新疆维吾尔族自治区	2,167		2,167	

1998年中国批准签订外商投资协议(合同)分国家(地区)统计表

金额单位:万美元

国家(地区)	合计		对外借款		外商直接投资		外商其他投资	
	项目个数	合同外资金额	项目个数	合同外资金额	项目个数	合同外资金额	项目个数	合同外资金额
总值	**19,850**	**6,320,054**	**51**	**838,500**	**19,799**	**5,210,205**		**271,349**
香港	7,805	1,882,634			7,805	1,761,328		121,306
澳门	264	32,915			264	30,718		2,197
台湾省	2,970	311,827			2,970	298,168		13,659
越南	4	4,790			4	4,790		
菲律宾	86	14,446			86	14,437		9
泰国	136	28,099			136	28,023		76
马来西亚	144	32,731			144	32,591		140
新加坡	566	300,367			566	300,152		215
文莱	1	2,856			1	2,856		
印度尼西亚	43	8,422			43	8,379		43
朝鲜	12	422			12	422		
老挝		29				29		
柬埔寨	8	1,394			8	1,314		80
蒙古	10	623			10	623		
日本	1,198	289,530			1,198	274,899		4,371
缅甸	14	1,934			14	1,934		
巴基斯坦	6	619			6	619		
孟加拉	2	35			2	35		
印度	5	1,388			5	1,388		
伊朗	2	98			2	98		
土耳其	7	748			7	748		
黎巴嫩	1	20			1	20		
塞浦路斯	4	613			4	613		
叙利亚	1	45			1	45		
约旦	3	46			3	46		
巴勒斯坦	1	10			1	10		
也门	1	20			1	20		
沙特	1	5			1	5		
科威特	1	10			1	10		
阿联酋	11	291			11	291		
韩国	1,309	168,135			1,309	164,085		4,050
以色列	5	66			5	66		
埃及	2	19			2	19		
苏丹	1	20			1	20		
利比亚	1	280			1	280		

1998年中国批准签订外商投资协议(合同)分国家(地区)统计表

金额单位:万美元

国家(地区)	合计		对外借款		外商直接投资		外商其他投资	
	项目个数	合同外资金额	项目个数	合同外资金额	项目个数	合同外资金额	项目个数	合同外资金额
阿尔及利亚	2	43			2	43		
摩洛哥	3	20			3	20		
科特迪瓦	1	40			1	40		
多哥		21			5	21		
塞拉利昂	5	336			1	336		
喀麦隆	1	20			1	20		
赤道几内亚	1	11			1	11		
坦桑尼亚	1	70			22	70		
毛里求斯	22	23,081			3	23,081		
马达加斯加	3	233			1	233		
莱索托	1	16			1	16		
赞比亚	1	2			28	2		
南非	28	3,589			2	3,589		
纳米比亚	2	195			1	195		
非洲其他国家	1	7			208	7		
德国	208	237,467			201	237,467		
法国	201	48,884			126	48,884		
意大利	126	19,177			97	19,177		
荷兰	97	56,268			22	56,268		
比利时	22	2,405				2,375		30
卢森堡	6	1,892			6	1,892		
英国	220	168,209			220	168,209		
丹麦	13	4,922			13	4,922		
爱尔兰	5	836			5	836		
芬兰	10	19,331			10	19,331		
瑞典	35	43,717			35	16,819		26,898
奥地利	19	3,340			19	3,340		
希腊	2	50			2	50		
西班牙	33	14,098			33	14,098		
葡萄牙	5	327			5	320		7
波兰	9	615			9	615		
匈牙利	31	2,216			31	2,216		
捷克	13	2,267			13	2,267		
保加利亚	4	144			4	144		
罗马尼亚	20	2,205			20	2,205		
冰岛	1	28			1	28		

1998年中国批准签订外商投资协议(合同)分国家(地区)统计表

金额单位:万美元

国家(地区)	合计		对外借款		外商直接投资		外商其他投资	
	项目个数	合同外资金额	项目个数	合同外资金额	项目个数	合同外资金额	项目个数	合同外资金额
挪威	11	3,602			11	3,602		
瑞士	43	26,188			43	26,177		11
马耳他	1	80			1	80		
摩纳哥	1	3			1	3		
直布罗陀	1	42			1	42		
斯洛伐克	4	607			4	607		
俄罗斯	73	2,166			73	2,166		
乌克兰	6	76			6	76		
白俄罗斯	1	14			1	14		
乌兹别克斯坦	3	44			3	44		
哈萨克斯坦	2	2,992			2	2,992		
吉尔吉斯斯坦	1	10			1	10		
立陶宛	1	19			1	19		
拉脱维亚	1	38			1	38		
墨西哥	4	336			4	336		
洪都拉斯	1	17			1	17		
哥斯达黎加	2	113			2	113		
巴拿马	18	6,503			18	6,503		
多米尼加共和国	2	4			2	4		
牙买加	3	40			3	40		
巴巴多斯	1	37			1	37		
委内瑞拉	6	232			6	232		
圭亚那	1	10			1	10		
巴西	9	210			9	210		
厄瓜多尔	2	18			2	18		
秘鲁	6	662			6	662		
玻利维亚	9	913			9	913		
智利	4	186			4	186		
巴拉圭	2	22			2	22		
阿根廷	17	2,511			17	2,511		
乌拉圭	2	24			2	24		
巴哈马	19	22,130			19	22,130		
维尔京群岛	622	615,054			622	613,613		1,441
圣基茨和尼维斯	1	10			1	10		
伯利兹	3	64			3	64		
开曼群岛	41	79,286			41	79,286		

1998 年中国批准签订外商投资协议(合同)分国家(地区)统计表

金额单位:万美元

国家(地区)	合计		对外借款		外商直接投资		外商其他投资	
	项目个数	合同外资金额	项目个数	合同外资金额	项目个数	合同外资金额	项目个数	合同外资金额
苏里南	1	7			1	7		
拉美洲其他国家	1	2,533			1	2,533		
加拿大	416	94,679			416	94,679		
美国	2,238	671,282			2,238	648,373		22,909
百慕大群岛	7	12,144			7	12,144		
澳大利亚	452	70,915			452	69,899		1,016
新西兰	51	2,156			51	2,156		
西萨摩亚	64	40,264			64	40,201		63
斐济	1	75			1	75		
瑙鲁	1	13			1	13		
汤加		500				500		
库克群岛	1	500			1	500		
巴布亚新几内亚	7	1,102			7	1,102		
基里巴斯	2	150			2	150		
瓦努阿图		3,831				3,831		
马绍尔群岛	6	2,689			6	2,689		
其他太平洋岛屿	4	3,839				3,839		
大洋洲其他国家	1	42				42		
其他	78	907,501	51	838,500	27	6,508		62,493

1998 年中国批准签订利用外资协议(合同)分省市统计表

金额单位:万美元

省、市	合计		对外借款		外商直接投资		外商其他投资	
	项目个数	合同外资金额	项目个数	合同外资金额	项目个数	合同外资金额	项目个数	合同外资金额
总计	**19,850**	**6,320,054**	**51**	**838,500**	**19,799**	**5,210,205**		**271,349**
北京市	651	409,692			651	409,692		
天津市	859	307,598			859	307,598		
河北省	696	126,771			696	126,771		
山西省	101	40,929			101	40,929		
内蒙古自治区	91	13,039			91	13,039		
辽宁省	1,703	461,971			1,703	438,014		23,957
大连市	760	255,958			760	251,519		4,439

1998年中国批准签订利用外资协议(合同)分省市统计表

金额单位:万美元

省、市	合计		对外借款		外商直接投资		外商其他投资	
	项目个数	合同外资金额	项目个数	合同外资金额	项目个数	合同外资金额	项目个数	合同外资金额
吉林省	367	49,542			367	49,542		
黑龙江省	250	55,496			250	55,496		
上海市	1,490	591,175			1,490	584,551		6,624
江苏省	1,817	757,764			1,817	757,764		
浙江省	965	185,600			965	183,390		2,210
宁波市	281	50,329			281	50,329		
安徽省	206	24,300			206	24,300		
福建省	2,006	500,150			2,006	500,150		
厦门市	245	168,811			245	168,811		
江西省	334	41,928			334	41,928		
山东省	1,364	289,391			1,364	220,186		69,205
青岛市	553	98,448			553	98,448		
河南省	341	53,003			341	53,003		
湖北省	330	68,655			330	52,502		16,153
湖南省	416	109,492			416	109,492		
广东省	4,348	1,049,625			4,348	915,529		134,096
深圳市	1,391	230,178			1,391	203,475		166,357
广西壮族自治区	266	64,242			266	64,242		
海南省	174	14,321			174	14,321		
四川省	233	71,215			233	71,215		
重庆市	222	47,577			222	47,577		
贵州省	73	15,312			73	15,312		
云南省	119	33,039			119	33,039		
陕西省	196	37,582			196	37,582		
甘肃省	68	8,364			68	8,364		
青海省	24	7,897			24	7,897		
宁夏回族自治区	36	5,203			36	5,203		
新疆维吾尔族自治区	46	13,827			46	13,827		

1998年中国批准签订外商投资协议(合同)分行业统计表

金额单位:万美元

行业	合计		对外借款		外商直接投资		外商其他投资
	项目个数	外资金额	项目个数	外资金额	项目个数	外资金额	
总计	**19,850**	**6,320,054**	**51**	**838,500**	**19,799**	**5,210,205**	**271,349**
农林牧渔业	876	120,420			876	120,420	
采掘业	168	85,223			168	85,223	
制造业	13,477	3,236,632			13,477	3,082,722	153,910
电力煤气及水的生产和供应业	142	196,812			142	196,812	
建筑业	318	175,011			318	175,011	
交通运输仓储及邮电业	274	279,675			274	230,119	49,556
批发零售餐饮业	1,184	131,352			1,184	131,352	
金融保险业							
房地产业	834	664,752			834	664,752	
社会服务业	1,634	301,193			1,634	301,193	
卫生体育和社会福利业	40	14,174			40	14,174	
教育文化艺术及广播电影电视业	14	2,212			14	2,212	
其他行业	720	1,029,098	51	838,500	669	190,598	

1998年中国实际利用外资分行业统计表

金额单位:万美元

行业	合计	对外借款	外商直接投资	外商其他投资
总计	**5,855,749**	**838,500**	**4,546,275**	**209,474**
农林牧渔业	62,375		62,375	
采掘业	57,809		57,809	
制造业	2,699,411		2,558,238	111,173
电力煤气及水的生产和供应业	310,279		310,279	
建筑业	206,423		206,423	
交通运输仓储及邮电业	201,671		164,513	37,158
批发零售餐饮业	118,149		118,149	
金融保险业	4,000		4,000	
房地产业	641,006		641,006	
社会服务业	296,315		296,315	
卫生体育和社会福利业	9,724		9,724	
教育文化艺术及广播电影电视业	6,830		6,830	
其他行业	1,006,395	838,500	106,752	61,143

1998年中国最大500家外商投资企业名录

金额单位:万元人民币

编号	企业名称	销售额
1	上海大众汽车有限公司	2631635
2	摩托罗拉(中国)电子有限公司	1964108
3	华能国际电力股份有限公司	1181292
4	深圳希捷科技有限公司	837522
5	长飞光纤光缆有限公司	766287
6	康佳集团股份有限公司	634337
7	广东核电合营有限公司	607238
8	上海贝尔电话设备制造有限公司	499372
9	一气－大众汽车有限公司	487969
10	广州宝洁有限公司	484559
11	希捷国际科技(无锡)有限公司	470486
12	大连西太平洋石油化工有限公司	469038
13	上海轮胎橡胶(集团)股份有限公司	430661
14	中国国际海运集装箱(集团)有限公司	429268
15	北京吉普汽车有限公司	413369
16	深圳三洋华强能源有限公司	408645
17	北京诺基亚移动通信有限公司	397863
18	庆铃汽车股份有限公司	382414
19	上海三菱电梯有限公司	381904
20	南通远洋船务工程有限公司	380890
21	南京依维柯汽车有限公司	344448
22	神龙汽车有限公司	342667
23	富士康(昆山)电脑接插件有限公司	324214
24	五羊－本田摩托(广州)有限公司	321038
25	南海油脂工业(赤湾)有限公司	313038
26	佳能珠海有限公司	286693
27	山西晓山煤化有限公司	275460
28	上海大江(集团)股份有限公司	274510
29	苏州飞利浦消费电子有限公司	268960
30	和德(集团)有限公司	263791
31	北京·松下彩色显像管有限公司	259769
32	深圳三洋华强激光电子有限公司	258782
33	爱普生技术(深圳)有限公司	255969
34	沈阳金杯客车制造有限公司	253621
35	东莞福安纺织印染有限公司	253214
36	厦门华侨电子企业有限公司	251097
37	北京爱立信移动通信有限公司	250000
38	广东高路华电视机有限公司	249932

1998年中国最大500家外商投资企业名录

金额单位:万元人民币

编号	企业名称	销售额
39	上海联华超市有限公司	240329
40	中国天津奥的斯电梯有限公司	240227
41	上海申美饮料食品有限公司	239656
42	吉林德大有限公司	236707
43	卓越织造(广州)有限公司	235400
44	广州钢铁股份有限公司	234343
45	冠捷电子(福建)有限公司	233779
46	上海永新彩色显像管有限公司	229867
47	浙江青鸿国际电脑有限公司	226477
48	南京熊猫电子股份有限公司	225418
49	湛江东兴石油企业有限公司	223143
50	河南新飞电器有限公司	221288
51	福建大丰投资集团有限公司	221141
52	南京金城机械有限公司	220368
53	上海索广电子有限公司	213953
54	广州福地彩色显像管股份有限公司	211968
55	华懋双汇实业(集团)有限公司	208929
56	翔鹭涤纶纺纤(厦门)有限公司	206772
57	福建省南靖万利达电子有限公司	206123
58	TCL王牌电器(惠州)有限公司	206106
59	中山市嘉华电子有限公司	205177
60	北京国际交换系统有限公司	198838
61	天津三美电机有限公司	197822
62	北京北大方正电子有限公司	197482
63	友利电电子(深圳)有限公司	197216
64	理光(深圳)工业发展有限公司	195202
65	杭州娃哈哈食品有限公司	194952
66	深圳创维-RGB电子有限公司	188788
67	徐州维维食品饮料有限公司	188449
68	华飞彩色显示系统有限公司	186196
69	广东健力宝集团有限公司	184097
70	中国惠普有限公司	182007
71	信华精机有限公司	179177
72	三洋电机(蛇口)有限公司	178870
73	深圳开发科技股份有限公司	176981
74	深圳三九药业有限公司	174449
75	福建恒安集团有限公司	174000
76	长城国际信息产品(深圳)有限公司	172256

1998年中国最大500家外商投资企业名录

金额单位:万元人民币

编号	企业名称	销售额
77	西安杨森制药有限公司	171854
78	上海夏普电器有限公司	171413
79	天津顶益国际食品有限公司	170507
80	广州广船国际股份有限公司	168218
81	佳能大连办公设备有限公司	167601
82	江苏春兰制冷设备股份有限公司	167215
83	夏普办公设备(常熟)有限公司	164587
84	正大集团(天津)实业有限公司	160472
85	江铃汽车股份有限公司	159135
86	上海白猫有限公司	158539
87	中国国际贸易中心有限公司	155133
88	松下电器(中国)有限公司	154440
89	哈尔滨哈飞汽车制造有限公司	153326
90	国际商业机器中国有限公司	153202
91	张家港保税区东海粮油工业有限公司	151633
92	江苏富士通通信技术有限公司	148560
93	东莞三星电机有限公司	147170
94	福建中银国际实业有限公司	145537
95	深圳赛格日立彩色显示器有限公司	144016
96	青岛啤酒股份有限公司	143853
97	安利(中国)日用品有限公司	143482
98	苏州罗技电子有限公司	142539
99	合肥美菱股份有限公司	141366
100	哈尔滨双太电子实业有限公司	140685
101	天津华利汽车有限公司	139704
102	上海伊藤忠商事有限公司	139550
103	江铃五十铃汽车有限公司	139236
104	深圳妈湾电力有限公司	138225
105	重庆长安铃木汽车有限公司	135485
106	雅达电子有限公司	134015
107	陕西渭河发电有限公司	132536
108	上海自动化仪表股份有限公司	129541
109	天津三星电机有限公司	129483
110	LG曙光电子有限公司	126529
111	上海汽轮机有限公司	126180
112	顺德市顺达电脑厂有限公司	125973
113	河南安阳彩色显像管玻壳有限公司	124662
114	福建永恩投资(集团)有限公司	124577

1998年中国最大500家外商投资企业名录

金额单位:万元人民币

编号	企业名称	销售额
115	惠州三星电子有限公司	124494
116	仙妮蕾德(广州)有限公司	123672
117	华强三洋电子有限公司	122307
118	本溪北龙炼铁有限公司	121398
119	杭州中策像胶(股份)有限公司	121086
120	葫芦岛东方铜业有限公司	120895
121	恩倍福显示器(东莞)有限公司	120162
122	广州珠江电力有限公司	119431
123	本溪北龙钢铁(集团)有限公司	119128
124	江苏利港电力有限公司	119051
125	海南航空股份有限公司	118848
126	洛阳北方易初摩托车有限公司	118137
127	杭州松下家用电器有限公司	117525
128	上海美蓓亚精密机电有限公司	117483
129	青岛三美电机有限公司	116999
130	光大木材工业深圳有限公司	116967
131	深圳长科国际电子有限公司	116570
132	中美天津史克制药有限公司	116265
133	佛山普立华照相机有限公司	115616
134	厦门灿坤实业股份有限公司	115200
135	上海利华有限公司	115185
136	洛阳春都实业有限公司	114206
137	上海金马房地产有限公司	113869
138	厦门正新橡胶工业有限公司	113517
139	银川中策(长城)橡胶有限公司	113214
140	日本电产(大连)有限公司	113193
141	张家港润忠钢铁有限公司	111884
142	上海-易初摩托车有限公司	111828
143	上海嘉士德-华海金属制品有限公司	111588
144	哈尔滨东安微型汽车发动机有限公司	111201
145	首钢日电电子有限公司	111077
146	索尼精密部件(惠州)有限公司	110988
147	深圳南方中集集装箱制造有限公司	110800
148	深圳创华合作有限公司	110114
149	广西玉柴机器股份有限公司	110000
150	伟创力实业(深圳)有限公司	109757
151	上海朗讯科技通信设备有限公司	109252
152	北京轻型汽车有限公司	109228

1998年中国最大500家外商投资企业名录

金额单位:万元人民币

编号	企业名称	销售额
153	顺德格兰仕电器厂有限公司	109008
154	北海粮油工业(天津)有限公司	107299
155	北京飞机维修工程有限公司	106931
156	上海旭电子玻璃有限公司	106604
157	深圳南天油粕工业有限公司	105887
158	惠阳联想电脑有限公司	105836
159	信华(中国)机械有限公司	105781
160	开平中晖复合纤维母粒有限公司	105769
161	中外合作佛斯弟摩托车有限公司	105668
162	厦门中鹭植物油有限公司	105340
163	奥林巴斯(深圳)工业有限公司	104266
164	黄河铝业有限公司	104254
165	江西华丽美莎纺织品有限公司	103592
166	青岛正大有限公司	103530
167	金利来(中国)服饰皮具有限公司	103040
168	内蒙古鄂尔多斯羊绒制品股份有限公司	102829
169	秦皇岛首钢板材有限公司	101784
170	珠海天草电子有限公司	101517
171	合肥荣事达洗衣机有限公司	101319
172	北京燕莎友谊商城有限公司	101112
173	南太电子(深圳)有限公司	100814
174	上海延锋汽车饰件有限公司	100026
175	江阴兴澄钢铁有限公司	98283
176	惠普计算机产品(上海)有限公司	98004
177	天津本田摩托有限公司	97957
178	青岛朗讯科技通讯设备有限公司	97215
179	天津三星电子有限公司	97205
180	福建日立电视机有限公司	95205
181	麦科特玛骐摩托车有限公司	94836
182	厦门华夏国际电力发展有限公司	94533
183	赛特集团有限公司	94442
184	广州市东峻房产有限公司	93745
185	东芝复印机(深圳)有限公司	93405
186	广州岩谷贸易有限公司	93334
187	营口渤海油脂有限公司	93283
188	南通中集顺达集装箱有限公司	93026
189	株洲南方雅马哈摩托车公司	93000
190	上海太平洋百货有限公司	92944

1998年中国最大500家外商投资企业名录

金额单位:万元人民币

编号	企业名称	销售额
191	中国迅达电梯有限公司	92853
192	东风金狮轮胎有限公司	92523
193	顺德市伦教首饰钻石加工厂	92257
194	上海上菱电器股份有限公司	91889
195	上海易初通用机器有限公司	91600
196	南京爱立信通信有限公司	91505
197	高明市高丰纺织染联合企业有限公司	91396
198	万宝至马达大连有限公司	91303
199	杭州顶益国际食品有限公司	91155
200	上海百事可乐饮料有限公司	90252
201	广州镇达玩具有限公司	89286
202	安利(中国)有限公司	89000
203	上海联合利华牙膏有限公司	88814
204	上海海欣集团股份有限公司	88760
205	广州进道集装箱有限公司	88570
206	南通天生港发电有限公司	88130
207	番禺创信鞋业有限公司	87831
208	康惠(惠州)电子实业有限公司	87571
209	长春长铃摩托车有限公司	86974
210	顺德惠而浦蚬华微波制品有限公司	86942
211	上海日立电器有限公司	86535
212	江阴振华港口机械有限公司	86000
213	天津雅马哈电子乐器有限公司	85603
214	苏州明基电脑有限公司	85347
215	北京市华远房地产股份有限公司	85216
216	上海振华港口机械有限公司	84845
217	上海福海(木业)企业有限公司	83682
218	扬州通运集装箱有限公司	83536
219	上海 JVC 电器有限公司	83455
220	天津通广三星电子有限公司	83187
221	茉织华实业(集团)有限公司	82942
222	番禺潭洲裕纺织印有限公司	82679
223	上海外高桥保税区开发股份有限公司	82304
224	深圳国威电子有限公司	82131
225	宁波益普资讯设备有限公司	82022
226	广州正大万客隆(佳景)有限公司	81589
227	乐金电子(惠州)有限公司	81577
228	南通醋酸纤维有限公司	81368

1998年中国最大500家外商投资企业名录

金额单位:万元人民币

编号	企业名称	销售额
229	厦门松下音响有限公司	81020
230	肇庆市万亚电子实业有限公司	80526
231	上海益昌薄板有限公司	79929
232	正大岳阳有限公司	78748
233	湖南火炬有色金属有限公司	78700
234	北京富华建设发展有限公司	78519
235	厦门进雄企业有限公司	78212
236	丹东阿尔派电子有限公司	78022
237	上海新福木业有限公司	77936
238	北京大发正大有限公司	77192
239	牧田(中国)有限公司	76904
240	杭州娃哈哈饮料有限公司	76857
241	百威(武汉)国际啤酒有限公司	76588
242	广东正大康地有限公司	76105
243	北京首钢宝生带钢有限公司	75909
244	广州宝洁纸品有限公司	75471
245	京光华长安大厦有限公司	75468
246	海润国际广告有限公司	75269
247	东芝大连有限公司	74760
248	乐金电子(天津)电器有限公司	74654
249	飞利浦光磁电子(上海)有限公司	74592
250	番禺精艺针织有限公司	74403
251	爱立信(中国)有限公司	74296
252	上海新亚(集团)股份有限公司	73992
253	重庆建设-雅马哈摩托车有限公司	73966
254	西门子(中国)有限公司	73928
255	南通正大有限公司	73479
256	松下·万宝(广州)压缩机有限公司	73253
257	天津正大饲料科技有限公司	73079
258	中国南玻集团股份有限公司	72963
259	上海物资贸易中心股份有限公司	72922
260	青岛世原鞋业有限公司	72892
261	上海远东集装箱有限公司	72857
262	东莞普思电子有限公司	72422
263	深圳赛格中康股份有限公司	72154
264	明达塑胶(福建)有限公司	72070
265	中兴投资(中国)有限公司	71903
266	正大康地(蛇口)有限公司	71858

1998 年中国最大 500 家外商投资企业名录

金额单位:万元人民币

编号	企业名称	销售额
267	正大康地(深圳)有限公司	71431
268	永新－沈阳化工有限公司	70966
269	好孩子儿童用品有限公司	70908
270	上海花王有限公司	70890
271	汕头海洋第一聚苯树脂有限公司	70855
272	开封正大有限公司	70724
273	广州造纸有限公司	70690
274	三水健力宝富特容器有限公司	70430
275	上海新格有色金属有限公司	70384
276	广东现代集装箱制造有限公司	70235
277	箭牌口香糖有限公司	70117
278	东莞德永佳纺织制衣有限公司	69958
279	上海第一八佰伴有限公司	69635
280	四川嘉里粮油工业有限公司	69629
281	上海华源股份有限公司	69602
282	中波轮船股份公司	69491
283	上海派克电气有限公司	69381
284	陕西康佳电子有限公司	68985
285	青岛嘉里植物油有限公司	68975
286	高标准实业(深圳)有限公司	68904
287	珠海经济特区美星制鞋有限公司	68861
288	中国南山开发(集团)股份有限公司	68792
289	上海日立家用电器有限公司	68734
290	广州市东迅房地产发展有限公司	68523
291	深圳观澜湖高尔夫球会有限公司	68153
292	广州珠江轮胎有限公司	67918
293	肇庆蓝带啤酒卢堡有限公司	67805
294	徐州华润电力有限公司	67162
295	南京华新电线电缆有限公司	67036
296	东莞致力电脑有限公司	66957
297	上海庄臣有限公司	66750
298	甘肃靖远第二发电有限公司	66608
299	辽宁大成农牧实业有限公司	66150
300	杭州中萃食品有限公司	66128
301	福建省德胜联建(集团)有限公司	65624
302	吉联(吉林)石油化学有限公司	65500
303	沈阳沈海热电有限公司	65488
304	张家港永新钢铁有限公司	65382

1998 年中国最大 500 家外商投资企业名录

金额单位:万元人民币

编 号	企 业 名 称	销 售 额
305	宁波保税区国联有限公司	65252
306	聊城嘉明实业有限公司	65014
307	珠海松下马达有限公司	64978
308	广州京安豹汽车有限公司	64874
309	杭州大厦有限公司	64804
310	太平洋塑胶(福建)有限公司	64697
311	郑州日产汽车有限公司	64666
312	惠州王牌视听电子有限公司	64569
313	内蒙古伊泰煤炭股份有限公司	64541
314	仪化佛山聚酯有限公司	64383
315	美国通用电器塑料中国有限公司	64317
316	广州雅芳有限公司	64008
317	上海耀华皮尔金顿玻璃股份有限公司	63910
318	甘肃兰炼中旅石化有限公司	63887
319	江苏双良特灵溴化锂制冷机有限公司	63653
320	湖南湘钢华光线材有限公司	63601
321	天津天美汽车配件有限公司	63528
322	上海动力设备有限公司	63142
323	合肥江淮汽车有限公司	63080
324	东洲油脂工业(广州)有限公司	62507
325	舟山兴业有限公司	62374
326	南京东方化工有限公司	62371
327	上海太平国际货柜有限公司	62262
328	天津宝洁有限公司	62232
329	上海友谊华侨股份有限公司	62130
330	重庆奥妮化妆品有限公司	62055
331	天津福津木业有限公司	61988
332	珠海经济开发区红塔仁恒纸业有限公司	61513
333	北京松下通信设备有限公司	61427
334	常熟通润机电有限公司	60975
335	南京中萃食品有限公司	60932
336	仙妮蕾德(天津)企业有限公司	60877
337	才众电脑(深圳)有限公司	60689
338	至卓飞高线路板(深圳)有限公司	60512
339	深圳金威啤酒有限公司	60271
340	河南新中益电力有限公司	60164
341	北京月坛大厦房地产开发有限公司	60000
342	青岛进道冷冻集装箱有限公司	59991

1998年中国最大500家外商投资企业名录

金额单位:万元人民币

编号	企业名称	销售额
343	广州东方电力有限公司	59202
344	中国海外建筑(深圳)有限公司	59170
345	欧姆龙(大连)有限公司	58600
346	山东松下映像产业有限公司	58590
347	3M中国有限公司	58335
348	双城雀巢有限公司	58333
349	嘉陵-本田发动机有限公司	58237
350	南益集团(福建)有限公司	58197
351	建泰橡胶(深圳)有限公司	57973
352	松下·万宝(广州)空调器有限公司	57849
353	北京贵友大厦有限公司	57828
354	江阴博丰钢铁有限公司	57553
355	武进大众钢铁有限公司	57067
356	佛山市荣宝资讯企业有限公司	56913
357	沈阳华润雪华啤酒有限公司	56874
358	中国华录松下录像机有限公司	56806
359	北京可口可乐饮料有限公司	56686
360	广州南方大厦有限公司	56602
361	东莞生益敷铜板股份有限公司	56493
362	天津可口可乐饮料有限公司	56478
363	伟立吉泰电子(深圳)有限公司	56414
364	杭州西湖电子实业有限公司	56297
365	上海麦克林电子有限公司	56212
366	广州荣诚鞋业有限公司	56105
367	高明市高丰针织企业有限公司	55953
368	深圳百仕达实业有限公司	55794
369	青岛泰光制鞋有限公司	55391
370	可比雅工业发展(深圳)有限公司	55139
371	珠海醋酸纤维有限公司	55123
372	深圳聚友实业有限公司	55086
373	广州海丰鞋业有限公司	54866
374	世界塑胶餐垫(宝安)有限公司	54756
375	上海嘉里粮油工业有限公司	54582
376	厦门台和电子有限公司	54476
377	英业达集团(上海)电子技术有限公司	54383
378	包头鹿金羊绒制品有限公司	54341
379	北京燕莎中心有限公司	54336
380	大东-骏通(东莞)电子有限公司	54277

1998 年中国最大 500 家外商投资企业名录

金额单位:万元人民币

编 号	企 业 名 称	销 售 额
381	安徽佳通轮胎有限公司	54256
382	TCL 通讯设备股份有限公司	54188
383	上海制皂有限公司	54065
384	广东天贸(集团)股份有限公司	53949
385	哈尔滨阿斯宝化纤有限公司	53890
386	蛇口南顺面粉有限公司	53846
387	北京松下电子部品有限公司	53621
388	新利实业(深圳)有限公司	53514
389	东莞汇勋电器制品有限公司	53500
390	长营电器(深圳)有限公司	53484
391	成都电缆股份有限公司	53482
392	济南轻骑铃木摩托车有限公司	53395
393	苏州迅达电梯有限公司	53358
394	上海肯德基有限公司	53352
395	福建清禄鞋业有限公司	53163
396	广州万邦鞋业有限公司	53104
397	无锡八佰伴商贸中心有限公司	53000
398	广州欣昌鞋业有限公司	52934
399	米尺(番禺)电线有限公司	52456
400	大连中集集装箱制造有限公司	52366
401	荣成国泰轮胎有限公司	52283
402	上海纳铁福传动轴有限公司	52283
403	三菱重工金羚空调器有限公司	52226
404	河南莲花味之素有限公司	52062
405	威海威东航运有限公司	51619
406	丹东饭山显示器有限公司	51566
407	合肥正大有限公司	51520
408	武汉广场管理有限公司	51404
409	北京 JVC 电了产业有限公司	51359
410	湖南旺旺食品有限公司	51306
411	莱州大东服装有限公司	51289
412	广州花园酒店	51148
413	中国大酒店	51141
414	通用电气嘉宝照明有限公司	51126
415	从化东麟钻石有限公司	51097
416	防城港新海油脂工业有限公司	51096
417	湖北汉新发电有限公司	50982
418	金桐石油化工有限公司	50963

1998 年中国最大 500 家外商投资企业名录

金额单位:万元人民币

编号	企业名称	销售额
419	飞利浦亚明照明有限公司	50948
420	厦门厦杏摩托有限公司	50919
421	厦新电子有限公司	50636
422	上海联吉合纤有限公司	50492
423	天津三星光电子有限公司	50436
424	中讯电子(昆山)有限公司	50343
425	上海合众－开利空调设备有限公司	50317
426	海尔梅洛尼(青岛)洗衣机有限公司	50242
427	上海建设路桥机械设备有限公司	50082
428	镇泰(广州)有限公司	50078
429	上海申佳铁合金有限公司	50049
430	宜兴乐祺纺织印染有限公司	50042
431	东南(福建)汽车工业有限公司	50017
432	东莞诺基亚移动电话有限公司	49816
433	石家庄棉二锦宏纺织有限公司	49761
434	铭基食品有限公司	49589
435	广东健力宝天然饮品有限公司	49482
436	昆明醋酸纤维有限公司	49277
437	金隆铜业有限公司	49276
438	上海施乐复印机有限公司	48971
439	上海先进半导体制造有限公司	48942
440	佛山市沙口发电厂有限公司	48819
441	帝闻电子(深圳)有限公司	48724
442	厦门 TDK 有限公司	48593
443	天津星湖实业有限公司	48567
444	维德木业(苏州)有限公司	48536
445	上海华新电线电缆有限公司	48527
446	上海建伍电子有限公司	48391
447	秦皇岛正大有限公司	48382
448	无锡夏普电子元器件有限公司	48332
449	武汉可口可乐饮料有限公司	48241
450	东莞胜美达(太平)电机有限公司	48104
451	北京麦当劳食品有限公司	47873
452	斯大精密(大连)有限公司	47784
453	南宁正大畜牧有限公司	47781
454	广东南方镀锌板有限公司	47678
455	天津日电电子通信工业有限公司	47648
456	本溪北龙烧结有限公司	47314

1998年中国最大500家外商投资企业名录

金额单位:万元人民币

编号	企业名称	销售额
457	南京金鹰国际实业有限公司	47282
458	汤盛音响(东莞)有限公司	47271
459	日立电梯(广州)有限公司	47245
460	中山中粤马口铁工业有限公司	47154
461	烟台鹏晖铜业有限公司	47136
462	上海瑞侃电缆附件有限公司	47098
463	番禺世门手袋有限公司	47067
464	上海通惠－开利空调设备有限公司	46927
465	金铃电器有限公司	46823
466	深圳中华自行车(集团)股份有限公司	46760
467	深圳南油(集团)有限公司	46701
468	上海小糸车灯有限公司	46695
469	上海开开实业股份有限公司	46618
470	捷安特(中国)有限公司	46490
471	辉瑞制药有限公司	46286
472	上海闵行联合发展有限公司	46210
473	白天鹅宾馆	46200
474	南海发电一厂有限公司	45976
475	北洋集装箱有限公司	45901
476	粤海(番禺)石油化工储运开发有限公司	45877
477	深圳王利电机有限公司	45796
478	上海中集冷藏箱有限公司	45765
479	汕头经济特区春源实业(集团)有限公司	45726
480	江苏春兰动力制造有限公司	45710
481	济南卢堡啤酒有限公司	45563
482	杭州旺旺食品有限公司	45528
483	双喜轮胎工业股份有限公司	45475
484	无锡松下冷机有限公司	45378
485	上海水仙电器股份有限公司	45318
486	广州华凌空调设备有限公司	45278
487	南京港泰电子有限公司	45119
488	时机防盗系统(中国)有限公司	45107
489	宝吉工艺品(深圳)有限公司	44997
490	正大(中国)投资有限公司	44921
491	马华隆(潮阳)纺织有限公司	44878
492	翠宁电子(深圳)有限公司	44869
493	青岛三湖制鞋有限公司	44819
494	江阴苏龙发电有限公司	44710

1998 年中国最大 500 家外商投资企业名录

金额单位:万元人民币

编 号	企 业 名 称	销 售 额
495	北京巴布科克·威尔科克斯有限公司	44664
496	上海德加拉电器有限公司	44543
497	捷家宝电器(深圳)有限公司	44385
498	廊坊华美粮油食品有限公司	44376
499	中法合营王朝葡萄酿酒有限公司	44166
500	北京百盛轻工发展有限公司	43988

1998 年中国对外承包工程和劳务合作合同额分国家(地区)总值

金额单位:万美元

国家(地区)	合 计	承包工程	劳务合作	设计咨询
合 计	**1177323**	**924316**	**238960**	**14047**
亚洲:	**690016**	**532231**	**154764**	**3021**
香港	201726	182677	18773	276
澳门	26584	13033	13379	172
台湾省	11379	465	10834	80
朝鲜	2664	2572	92	0
越南	7467	6279	1094	94
老挝	15051	14768	274	9
柬埔寨	4446	1121	3293	32
蒙古	7180	6359	818	3
日本	33169	240	32737	192
菲律宾	5363	4504	859	0
缅甸	52332	49183	2971	178
泰国	27804	27026	777	1
马来西亚	17788	16218	1560	10
新加坡	92446	58916	33526	4
文莱	3925	3856	69	0
印度尼西亚	4414	1773	2637	4
巴基斯坦	37224	37035	152	37
孟加拉国	22314	21103	1163	48
印度	2433	1944	98	391
尼泊尔	10166	9826	29	311
斯里兰卡	3903	3606	294	3
马尔代夫	421	0	421	0
伊朗	17887	16687	54	1146
土耳其	1107	1012	94	1

1998 年中国对外承包工程和劳务合作合同额分国家(地区)总值

金额单位:万美元

国家(地区)	合 计	承包工程	劳务合作	设计咨询
塞浦路斯	2651	2160	491	0
叙利亚	2076	2050	26	0
黎巴嫩	4	0	4	0
约旦	924	907	17	0
巴勒斯坦	15	0	0	15
也门共和国	16915	16860	55	0
伊拉克	540	533	7	0
沙特阿拉伯	23114	20734	2380	0
科威特	7149	3690	3459	0
巴林	24	0	24	0
卡塔尔	412	0	412	0
阿拉伯联合酋长国	6471	4409	2062	0
阿曼	1177	0	1177	0
韩国	10391	53	10324	14
以色列	8960	632	8328	0
非洲:	**201912**	**187064**	**14414**	**434**
埃及	2104	2075	29	0
苏丹	63584	62576	739	269
利比亚	1092	356	736	0
突尼斯	48	0	47	1
阿尔及利亚	8313	7856	457	0
摩洛哥	1783	872	909	2
毛里塔尼亚	1942	619	1323	0
塞内加尔	3052	3038	14	0
冈比亚	149	100	49	0
几内亚(比绍)	2600	2600	0	0
马里	9489	9456	30	3
几内亚	4477	3833	641	3
加纳	1227	717	493	17
科特迪瓦	8824	8780	42	2
布基纳法索	221	220	1	0
贝宁	335	172	155	8
尼日尔	1252	1216	32	4
利比里亚	285	0	285	0
塞拉利昂	2356	2236	120	0
多哥	567	567	0	0
尼日利亚	13189	12646	540	3
喀麦隆	1347	1176	171	0

1998年中国对外承包工程和劳务合作合同额分国家(地区)总值

金额单位:万美元

国家(地区)	合　计	承包工程	劳务合作	设计咨询
赤道几内亚	142	83	59	0
加蓬	1791	1421	370	0
刚果	384	367	1	16
扎伊尔	1337	1336	1	0
佛得角	254	252	0	2
圣多美和普林西比	114	114	0	0
布隆迪	77	77	0	0
卢旺达	1198	1117	81	0
埃塞俄比亚	8750	8686	51	13
索马里	3	3	0	0
吉布提	1247	1217	23	7
肯尼亚	2512	2304	208	0
乌干达	1522	1487	35	0
坦桑尼亚	2441	2303	104	34
塞舌尔	4704	4562	142	0
毛里求斯	6516	1279	5231	6
科摩罗	3	3	0	0
马达加斯加	1914	1271	636	7
安哥拉	2381	2371	0	10
莫桑比克	452	445	7	0
赞比亚	12040	12010	30	0
津巴布韦	7751	7702	49	0
斯威士兰	5	0	5	0
博次瓦纳	6303	6132	168	3
莱索托	921	708	213	0
南非	6177	5996	181	0
纳米比亚	1935	1929	6	0
厄里特里亚	802	778	0	24
欧洲:	**48923**	**23880**	**24623**	**420**
波兰	877	839	27	11
匈牙利	140	1	139	0
捷克共和国	49	0	49	0
保加利亚	150	0	150	0
阿尔巴尼亚	379	350	29	0
罗马尼亚	1150	50	1100	0
德国	2930	586	2226	118
南斯拉夫	2952	2782	170	0
法国	757	6	750	1

1998 年中国对外承包工程和劳务合作合同额分国家(地区)总值

金额单位:万美元

国家(地区)	合　计	承包工程	劳务合作	设计咨询
意大利	336	114	222	0
荷兰	470	408	55	7
比利时	114	0	109	5
卢森堡	16	0	13	3
英国	6130	3962	2047	121
爱尔兰	1	0	1	0
丹麦	125	0	109	16
芬兰	34	30	2	2
瑞典	4161	4090	43	28
挪威	1705	1490	215	0
冰岛	5	0	5	0
瑞士	111	0	107	4
奥地利	109	14	95	0
希腊	423	0	423	0
马耳他	59	35	0	24
西班牙	320	0	320	0
葡萄牙	60	0	60	0
俄罗斯	21375	8524	12771	80
乌克兰	483	0	483	0
白俄罗斯	1	0	1	0
乌兹别克斯坦	167	0	167	0
哈萨克斯坦	77	50	27	0
摩尔多瓦	62	0	62	0
吉尔吉斯斯坦	2744	215	2529	0
塔吉克斯坦	202	194	8	0
立陶宛	2	0	2	0
拉脱维亚共和国	42	40	2	0
格鲁吉亚共和国	100	100	0	0
斯洛文尼亚共和国	105	0	105	0
拉丁美洲:	**15303**	**10376**	**4837**	**90**
墨西哥	538	200	332	6
危地马拉	69	0	69	0
洪都拉斯	26	0	26	0
萨尔瓦多	81	0	81	0
尼加拉瓜	91	0	91	0
巴拿马	1391	16	1375	0
古巴	171	152	18	1
多米尼加共和国	11	0	11	0

1998年中国对外承包工程和劳务合作合同额分国家(地区)总值

金额单位:万美元

国家(地区)	合 计	承包工程	劳务合作	设计咨询
牙买加	1369	510	859	0
特立尼达和多巴哥	3	0	3	0
巴巴多斯	948	948	0	0
委内瑞拉	1430	1430	0	0
圭亚那	489	437	52	0
巴西	101	0	101	0
厄瓜多尔	780	482	298	0
秘鲁	181	12	139	30
玻利维亚	212	193	19	0
智利	180	180	0	0
阿根廷	719	13	705	1
乌拉圭	93	59	34	0
巴哈马	46	0	46	0
特克斯和凯科斯群岛	4	0	4	0
英属维尔京	35	0	35	0
安提瓜	3669	3667	0	2
圣卢西亚	658	607	3	48
圣文森特格	23	0	23	0
伯利兹英属	150	0	150	0
苏里南	1822	1470	350	2
圣马丁	13	0	13	0
北美洲:	**32178**	**11107**	**20390**	**681**
加拿大	1454	322	1132	0
美国	30566	10785	19100	681
美国塞班	158	0	158	0
大洋洲及太平洋岛屿小计:	**14963**	**9969**	**4790**	**204**
澳大利亚	7272	6591	533	148
新西兰	514	323	191	0
西萨摩亚	212	98	111	3
汤加	7	0	7	0
斐济	510	4	500	6
巴布亚新几内亚	1021	931	78	12
所罗门群岛	22	22	0	0
瓦努阿图	112	99	13	0
法属波利尼西亚	12	0	12	0
马绍尔群岛	73	0	38	35
密克罗尼西亚	3714	1544	2170	0
东萨摩亚	117	0	117	0

1998年中国对外承包工程和劳务合作合同额分国家(地区)总值

金额单位:万美元

国家(地区)	合　计	承包工程	劳务合作	设计咨询
其它太平洋岛屿	1042	41	1001	0
贝劳	335	316	19	0
其它小计:	**174028**	**149689**	**15142**	**9197**
其它	**5183**	**3625**	**1558**	**0**
国境内	**168845**	**146064**	**13584**	**9197**

1998年中国对外承包工程和劳务合作营业额分国家(地区)总值

金额单位:万美元

国家(地区)	合　计	承包工程	劳务合作	设计咨询
合　计	**1013381**	**776856**	**227625**	**8900**
亚洲:	**606556**	**457611**	**146894**	**2051**
香港	214228	190087	23976	165
澳门	25975	14524	11223	228
台湾省	10992	500	10341	151
朝鲜	555	524	26	5
越南	6572	5547	961	64
老挝	7278	6982	288	8
柬埔寨	2562	914	1623	25
蒙古	2740	2196	541	3
日本	23328	154	22950	224
菲律宾	10737	10508	229	0
缅甸	16532	15422	983	127
泰国	13705	13105	589	11
马来西亚	14236	13130	1083	23
新加坡	91461	49259	42173	29
文莱	3003	2906	97	0
印度尼西亚	4493	2526	1962	5
巴基斯坦	34042	33530	248	264
孟加拉国	18526	17986	526	14
印度	5087	4497	561	29
尼泊尔	6516	6415	60	41
斯里兰卡	4509	4283	223	3
马尔代夫	330	2	328	0
伊朗	33474	33179	54	241
土耳其	790	502	265	23
塞浦路斯	371	103	268	0
叙利亚	381	378	3	0

1998年中国对外承包工程和劳务合作营业额分国家(地区)总值

金额单位:万美元

国家(地区)	合　　计	承包工程	劳务合作	设计咨询
黎巴嫩	15	0	15	0
约旦	583	434	149	0
巴勒斯坦	53	40	5	8
也门共和国	6389	6245	144	0
伊拉克	1501	1501	0	0
沙特阿拉伯	1767	1256	511	0
科威特	19320	15950	3020	350
巴林	6	0	6	0
卡塔尔	252	231	21	0
阿拉伯联合酋长国	3770	2287	1483	0
阿曼	100	0	100	0
韩国	15069	54	15005	10
以色列	5308	454	4854	0
非洲:	**167841**	**150917**	**16325**	**599**
埃及	98	63	35	0
苏丹	39453	38521	757	175
利比亚	1151	268	883	0
突尼斯	398	391	6	1
阿尔及利亚	8844	8294	506	44
摩洛哥	1834	872	960	2
毛里塔尼亚	2472	1426	1046	0
塞内加尔	3052	3044	8	0
冈比亚	145	96	49	0
几内亚(比绍)	2687	2687	0	0
马里	8379	8335	29	15
几内亚	3648	3217	429	2
加纳	1583	1047	526	10
科特迪瓦	6054	6010	42	2
布基纳法索	579	579	0	0
贝宁	746	587	151	8
尼日尔	306	290	12	4
利比里亚	1700	0	1700	0
塞拉利昂	2318	2296	22	0
多哥	2667	1901	766	0
尼日利亚	24254	23434	651	169
喀麦隆	1102	1009	93	0
赤道几内亚	1126	1039	80	7
乍得	93	92	1	0

1998年中国对外承包工程和劳务合作营业额分国家(地区)总值

金额单位:万美元

国家(地区)	合　计	承包工程	劳务合作	设计咨询
加蓬	4993	4616	377	0
刚果	133	123	3	7
扎伊尔	1221	1216	4	1
佛得角	222	222	0	0
圣多美和普林西比	44	44	0	0
布隆迪	87	74	13	0
卢旺达	1982	1857	125	0
埃塞俄比亚	2063	2046	11	6
索马里	3	3	0	0
吉布提	834	814	17	3
肯尼亚	5833	5712	109	12
乌干达	1238	1219	19	0
坦桑尼亚	4315	4156	135	24
塞舌尔	2812	2739	72	1
毛里求斯	5953	552	5395	6
科摩罗	5	5	0	0
马达加斯加	1911	1439	470	2
安哥拉	83	67	7	9
莫桑比克	494	472	22	0
赞比亚	957	933	24	0
马拉维	229	229	0	0
津巴布韦	8936	8891	45	0
斯威士兰	108	30	78	0
博次瓦纳	4523	4379	141	3
莱索托	1264	1120	138	6
南非	805	471	328	6
纳米比亚	1751	1702	29	20
厄里特里亚	353	288	11	54
欧洲:	**32946**	**16500**	**16009**	**437**
波兰	95	58	27	10
匈牙利	207	0	207	0
捷克共和国	40	0	40	0
保加利亚	163	0	163	0
阿尔巴尼亚	133	132	1	0
罗马尼亚	835	55	780	0
德国	2520	721	1608	191
南斯拉夫	1627	1586	41	0
法国	1066	384	669	13

1998 年中国对外承包工程和劳务合作营业额分国家(地区)总值

金额单位:万美元

国家(地区)	合　　计	承包工程	劳务合作	设计咨询
意大利	940	760	154	26
荷兰	527	382	112	33
比利时	72	0	67	5
卢森堡	21	0	18	3
英国	6262	4083	2080	99
丹麦	129	10	92	27
芬兰	28	20	8	0
瑞典	111	0	99	12
挪威	1296	1205	91	0
冰岛	1	0	1	0
瑞士	91	0	87	4
奥地利	241	6	235	0
希腊	446	0	446	0
马耳他	156	93	63	0
西班牙	468	0	468	0
葡萄牙	29	0	29	0
圣马力诺	24	0	24	0
俄罗斯联邦	12256	4792	7450	14
乌克兰	363	66	297	0
白俄罗斯	1	0	1	0
乌滋别克斯坦	54	0	54	0
哈萨克斯坦	111	50	61	0
摩尔多瓦	92	0	92	0
吉尔吉斯斯坦	256	150	106	0
塔吉克斯坦	200	90	110	0
土库曼斯坦	1713	1713	0	0
立陶宛	1	0	1	0
拉脱维亚共和国	40	40	0	0
阿塞拜缰共和国	225	4	221	0
格鲁吉亚共和国	100	100	0	0
斯洛文泥亚共和国	6	0	6	0
拉丁美洲:	**9051**	**4925**	**4076**	**50**
墨西哥	59	0	53	6
危地马拉	164	100	64	0
洪都拉斯	35	0	35	0
萨尔瓦多	36	0	36	0
尼加拉瓜	74	0	74	0
巴拿马	1982	16	1966	0

1998 年中国对外承包工程和劳务合作营业额分国家(地区)总值

金额单位:万美元

国家(地区)	合　计	承包工程	劳务合作	设计咨询
古巴	355	273	81	1
多米尼加共和国	4	0	4	0
牙买加	1083	510	573	0
特立尼达和多巴哥	106	101	5	0
巴巴多斯	834	801	28	5
委内瑞拉	1125	1125	0	0
哥伦比亚	20	20	0	0
圭亚那	48	20	28	0
巴西	47	47	0	0
厄瓜多尔	685	654	31	0
秘鲁	91	3	82	6
玻利维亚	242	193	49	0
智利	21	15	6	0
巴拉圭	25	0	25	0
阿根廷	646	13	632	1
乌拉圭	96	47	48	1
巴哈马	13	0	13	0
英属维尔京	38	0	38	0
安提瓜	240	232	0	8
圣卢西亚	52	12	27	13
圣文森特格	11	0	11	0
伯利兹英属	59	0	59	0
苏里南	859	743	107	9
圣马丁	1	0	1	0
北美洲:	**30292**	**8607**	**21351**	**334**
加拿大	744	426	318	0
美国	29489	8181	20974	334
美国塞班	59	0	59	0
大洋洲及太平洋岛屿:	**20085**	**14024**	**5942**	**119**
澳大利亚	6000	5657	284	59
新西兰	425	0	425	0
西萨摩亚	109	65	40	4
汤加	2	0	2	0
斐济	334	4	323	7
巴布亚新几内亚	7022	6431	583	8
基里巴斯	6	0	6	0
所罗门群岛	24	12	12	0
瓦努阿图	23	22	1	0

1998年中国对外承包工程和劳务合作营业额分国家(地区)总值

金额单位:万美元

国家(地区)	合计	承包工程	劳务合作	设计咨询
法属波利尼西亚	1	0	1	0
马绍尔群岛	110	13	56	41
密克罗尼西亚	3196	1096	2100	0
东萨摩亚	456	0	456	0
其它太平洋岛屿	1618	0	1618	0
厄里特立亚	58	58	0	0
贝劳	701	666	35	0
其他小计	**146610**	**124272**	**17028**	**5310**
其他	**5612**	**3521**	**2091**	**0**
国境内	**140998**	**120751**	**14937**	**5310**

1998年中国对外承包工程和劳务合作合同分公司总值

名称	合同数(份)	合同额(万美元)			
		合计	承包工程	劳务合作	设计咨询
合计	**25955**	**1177323**	**924316**	**238960**	**4047**
中央合计	**4420**	**599977**	**554617**	**41625**	**3735**
中国建筑工程总公司	208	159704	158977	643	84
中国广播电视国际经济技术合作公司	4	247	247	0	0
中国冶金建设集团总公司	12	4793	4793	0	0
中国商业对外经济技术合作公司	9	79	2	77	0
中国水产(集团)总公司	11	2330	2240	90	0
中国国际技术智力合作公司	1990	17171	0	17037	134
中国路桥(集团)总公司	30	33517	33437	80	0
中国土木工程集团公司	93	25219	23352	1567	300
中国港湾建设(集团)总公司	31	24042	23333	685	24
中国海外工程总公司	109	14505	14029	476	0
中国水利电力对外公司	15	8088	8088	0	0
中国石化工程建设公司	1	150	150	0	0
中国化学工程(集团)公司	6	808	720	88	0
中国轻工业对外经济技术合作公司	76	2120	483	1637	0
中国电子国际经济技术合作公司	27	793	667	126	0
中国地质工程公司	18	11286	11286	0	0
中国国际展览公司	19	152	152	0	0
中国国际工程和材料公司	10	883	670	213	0
中国航空技术国际工程公司	22	2463	2463	0	0
中国国际计算机软件工程公司	37	72	0	72	0
中国林业国际合作公司	4	932	17	915	0

1998年中国对外承包工程和劳务合作合同分公司总值

名　　称	合同数(份)	合同额(万美元)			
		合计	承包工程	劳务合作	设计咨询
中国建材工业对外经济技术合作公司	21	6994	6725	269	0
中国万宝工程公司	25	21964	21910	54	0
中国交远国际经济技术合作公司	26	929	30	899	0
国华国际工程承包公司	3	1252	1200	52	0
中国海员对外经济技术合作公司	20	573	0	573	0
中国石油工程建设(集团)公司	6	50554	50487	67	0
中国四达国际经济技术合作公司	290	1286	0	1286	0
中国中原对外工程公司	2	3500	3500	0	0
中海国际石油工程有限责任公司	5	1795	1795	0	0
中国国际工程咨询公司	15	37	0	2	35
中国体育国际经济技术合作公司	10	438	348	85	5
中国海外贸易总公司	20	960	0	960	0
中国国际企业合作公司	5	23	0	23	0
中国电子系统工程总公司	1	20000	20000	0	0
中国铁道建筑总公司	26	4089	3387	622	80
中国化工建设总公司	18	4358	4347	5	6
五洲工程设计研究院	21	360	0	0	360
中国海外经济合作总公司	15	2014	1964	50	0
中国机械设备进出口总公司	18	21865	21865	0	0
中国寰球化学工程公司	13	16696	16567	0	129
中国机械对外经济技术合作公司	21	752	588	164	0
远大国际经济合作有限责任公司	6	208	205	3	0
中国有色金属建设股份有限公司	17	14053	13341	712	0
中国海洋工程公司	12	355	0	355	0
中国医疗卫生对外经济合作公司	175	526	72	454	0
中国纺织工业对外经济技术合作公司	15	266	265	1	0
中国北方工业公司	1	0	0	0	0
长城国际经济技术合作有限公司	13	1087	1026	61	0
中化国际工程贸易公司	25	119	0	119	0
中国航空工业规划设计院	20	258	0	0	258
中国仪器进出口总公司	25	8	0	8	0
中国通信建设总公司	1	109	109	0	0
中远对外劳务合作公司	57	2170	0	2170	0
中国成套设备进出口集团总公司	264	17844	11467	6377	0
中国对外建设总公司	3	7	7	0	0
轻工业部规划设计院	17	88	0	5	83
北京有色冶金设计研究总院	3	91	45	3	43
燕兴国际经济技术合作公司	6	242	0	242	0

1998年中国对外承包工程和劳务合作合同分公司总值

名　　称	合同数(份)	合同额(万美元)			
		合计	承包工程	劳务合作	设计咨询
中国铁路工程公司	125	24389	23196	298	895
中国新兴工程建筑房地产开发总公司	2	52	0	52	0
北京煤炭设计研究院(集团)	3	1023	0	0	1023
中国技术进出口总公司	4	4939	4939	0	0
北京钢铁设计研究院	7	139	0	0	139
中国电力技术进出口公司	14	1826	1305	521	0
华北电力设计院	2	20	0	0	20
中国安能建设总公司	4	3224	3224	0	0
中国京冶建设工程承包公司	1	1145	1145	0	0
中外园林建设总公司	4	165	63	97	5
中纺人力资源开发有限公司	1	30	0	30	0
中国电子工程设计院	1	100	100	0	0
广播电影电视部设计院	2	3	0	0	3
建设部建筑设计院	2	12	0	4	8
核工业第二研究设计院	6	40	0	0	40
中交公路规划设计院	1	5	0	0	5
中国地质勘查技术院	11	130	130	0	0
中煤建设集团公司	5	9549	9379	170	0
中国国际人才开发中心	176	349	18	331	0
中水远洋渔业有限责任公司	9	12795	12020	775	0
北京建隆建筑工程联合公司	5	4478	4478	0	0
北京市地质矿产勘查开发总公司	1	6	0	0	6
中国机械工业安装总公司	6	842	842	0	0
华北电力国际经贸公司	1	248	248	0	0
中设国际工程有限公司	26	2008	2008	0	0
中国工程与农业机械进出口总公司	11	15541	15541	0	0
北京中水远洋渔业发展公司	7	2245	2245	0	0
中国新星石油公司	10	7450	7380	20	50
地方合计	21535	577346	369699	197335	10312
北京市	180	25527	18797	6233	497
中国北京国际经济合作公司	108	2915	2573	342	0
北京市建筑工程总公司	27	6936	6528	408	0
北京市政工程总公司	2	1429	1420	9	0
北京市政工程设计研究院	10	360	0	8	352
北京市建筑设计院	4	145	0	0	145
北京住宅开发建设集团总公司	5	6244	6244	0	0
首钢总公司国际经贸部	2	285	156	129	0
四通国际经济技术合作公司	4	73	0	73	0

1998年中国对外承包工程和劳务合作合同分公司总值

名　称	合同数（份）	合同额(万美元)			
		合计	承包工程	劳务合作	设计咨询
北京市外国企业服务总公司	11	5261	0	5261	0
北京城乡建设集团总公司	2	575	575	0	0
北京市第二房修工程公司	2	58	55	3	0
中国燕山联合对外贸易有限公司	2	916	916	0	0
北京八仙房地产开发公司	1	330	330	0	0
天津市	937	19295	10908	7690	697
中国天津国际经济技术合作公司	537	10030	2726	7304	0
天津立达国际劳务工程公司	1	108	0	108	0
天津水泥工业设计研究院	1	5249	5249	0	0
铁道部第三勘测设计院	14	94	0	87	7
中国天辰化学工程公司	39	2316	2184	4	128
机械部第五设计研究院	11	171	66	0	105
天津港海员对外服务公司	9	104	0	104	0
天津市政设计研究院	4	420	0	0	420
天津市亿利达集团有限公司	7	11	0	11	0
天津市化工设计院	10	75	38	0	37
天津机械进出口集团有限公司	13	5	0	5	0
水利部天津水利水电勘测设计研究院	5	7	0	7	0
大港油田集团有限责任公司	15	645	645	0	0
天海集团股份有限公司	22	19	0	19	0
天津系列外企业	249	41	0	41	0
河北省	229	10048	5187	4726	135
中国河北国际经济技术合作公司	42	1001	121	880	0
石家庄国际经济技术合作公司	49	1115	0	1115	0
北方设计研究院	3	45	0	0	45
河北公路工程建设集团有限公司	1	150	150	0	0
河北建工集团有限责任公司	44	964	0	964	0
核工部第四设计研究院	1	5	0	0	5
唐山国际工程总公司	4	1323	1200	123	0
中国耀华玻璃(集团)公司	5	31	31	0	0
化工部第一勘察设计院	2	16	16	0	0
中国第二十二冶金建设公司	3	35	35	0	0
张家口对外劳务工程公司	23	561	0	561	0
河北电力勘测设计研究院	5	1270	885	385	0
秦皇岛国际经济技术合作公司	4	85	0	0	85
地矿河北工程勘测公司	7	251	251	0	0
邢台对外合作公司	3	104	0	104	0
保定国际经济技术合作公司	4	166	0	166	0

1998年中国对外承包工程和劳务合作合同分公司总值

名　　称	合同数(份)	合同额(万美元)			
		合计	承包工程	劳务合作	设计咨询
承德对外经济合作公司	7	320	0	320	0
唐山对外合作公司	12	39	0	39	0
铁道部建场工程局	5	1648	1648	0	0
河北省进出口公司	2	14	0	14	0
中油管道建设有限责任公司	1	850	850	0	0
河北国际供销合作总公司	2	55	0	55	0
山西省	69	3898	2645	1119	134
中国山西国际经济技术合作公司	12	491	487	4	0
山西省建筑工程总公司	5	835	0	835	0
太原市国际经济技术合作公司	15	153	0	153	0
太原钢铁(集团)公司	1	15	15	0	0
山西省电力公司	7	344	344	0	0
山西省送变电工程公司	2	610	610	0	0
山西省公路桥梁工程总公司	4	588	588	0	0
化工部第二设计院	10	433	430	0	3
山西四建集团有限公司	3	76	0	76	0
煤炭部太原设计研究院	6	9	0	8	1
太原重型机器进出口公司	1	2	2	0	0
山西省电力勘测设计院	1	130	0	0	130
中国第十三冶金建设公司	2	212	169	43	0
内蒙古自治区	103	4541	1667	2862	12
中国内蒙古国际经济技术合作公司	11	854	604	250	0
冶金部包头钢铁设计研究院	2	12	0	0	12
呼伦贝尔盟国际经济技术合作公司	16	622	0	622	0
满洲里国际经济技术合作公司	30	653	0	653	0
内蒙古电力集团公司	2	403	403	0	0
二连浩特国际经济技术合作公司	7	280	47	233	0
锡林郭勒国际经济技术合作公司	6	265	0	265	0
额尔古纳国际经济技术合作公司	6	75	0	75	0
内蒙古高等院校科技开发集团	5	125	0	125	0
二连浩特市边境贸易总公司	4	283	176	107	0
额尔古纳市边境贸易公司	2	59	0	59	0
新巴尔虎右旗边境贸易公司	2	5	0	5	0
满洲里东方国际贸易股份有限公司	4	140	0	140	0
内蒙古大兴安岭林管进出口	1	230	230	0	0
呼和浩特国际经济技术合作公司	1	118	0	118	0
包头兴业集团股份有限公司	1	85	0	85	0
满洲里第一建筑工程公司	2	207	207	0	0
内蒙古农牧业科技开发公司	1	125	0	125	0

1998年中国对外承包工程和劳务合作合同分公司总值

名　　称	合同数（份）	合同额(万美元)			
		合计	承包工程	劳务合作	设计咨询
辽宁省	1155	46865	26326	20156	383
中国辽宁国际合作(集团)股份有限公司	176	9363	5944	3419	0
辽宁省建设集团公司	4	7868	7868	0	0
辽宁国际建设工程集团公司	6	74	19	55	0
鞍山国际经济技术合作公司	12	822	0	822	0
抚顺对外建设经济合作(集团)股份公司	14	376	170	206	0
本溪对外经济技术合作总公司	7	504	0	504	0
丹东国际经济技术合作公司	7	217	0	217	0
营口国际经济技术合作公司	2	2	0	2	0
鞍山焦化耐火材料设计院	3	10	0	2	8
东北电力集团进出口公司	1	30	30	0	0
鞍山冶金设计研究院	2	219	0	0	219
锦州华锦国际经贸股份有限公司	28	69	48	21	0
铁岭国际经济技术合作公司	1	9	0	9	0
辽宁华曦集团	6	222	0	222	0
辽阳国际经济技术合作公司	28	1086	0	930	156
鞍钢集团国际经济贸易公司	1	59	59	0	0
辽河石油勘探局	6	382	310	72	0
朝阳建设集团有限公司	9	804	726	78	0
抚顺市第二建筑工程公司	7	33	0	33	0
辽宁省国际劳务交流有限公司	5	32	0	32	0
本钢集团国际经济贸易有限公司	13	218	0	218	0
鞍山市对外建设工程承包集团公司	3	305	305	0	0
沈阳市	114	7349	4491	2858	0
中国沈阳国际经济技术合作公司	110	6018	3951	2067	0
沈阳对外经济建设总公司	2	515	0	515	0
煤炭工业部沈阳设计研究院	1	276	0	276	0
中国建筑东北设计研究院	1	540	540	0	0
人连市	700	16812	6356	10456	0
中国大连合作(集团)股份有限公司	431	12349	5967	6382	0
瓦房店市国际工程公司	2	30	30	0	0
辽宁省大连海洋渔业集团公司	24	344	0	344	0
大连经济技术开发区劳务公司	97	305	0	305	0
大连工程总承包公司	1	100	100	0	0
大化国际经济贸易公司	6	304	0	304	0
大连华南国际经济技术合作公司	3	472	101	371	0
大连港国际经济技术合作公司	9	159	0	159	0
大连渤海建筑集团有限公司	2	155	0	155	0

1998年中国对外承包工程和劳务合作合同分公司总值

名　　称	合同数(份)	合同额(万美元)			
		合计	承包工程	劳务合作	设计咨询
大连远洋船员管理公司	26	644	0	644	0
中国外运大连公司	34	170	0	170	0
大连海运集团国际劳务合作公司	4	80	0	80	0
中国成套设备进出口大连公司	6	26	0	26	0
大连水产远洋渔业公司	12	810	0	810	0
大连亿达国际合作公司	3	158	158	0	0
中国商业对外经济合作公司大连分公司	4	13	0	13	0
辽宁成大股份公司	6	67	0	67	0
中国辽宁国际合作大连开发总公司	30	626	0	626	0
吉林省	245	14830	3349	11477	4
中国吉林国际经济技术合作公司	14	449	77	372	0
吉林市对外经济技术合作公司	5	654	0	654	0
延边对外经济技术合作公司	15	607	49	558	0
珲春国际经济技术合作公司	7	117	2	115	0
吉林化学工业进出口公司	10	411	0	411	0
吉林冶金建设公司	3	65	0	65	0
吉林省对外招商建设总公司	16	1476	361	1115	0
延边海外经济技术合作公司	7	651	0	651	0
吉林建设开发集团公司	3	264	264	0	0
吉林省对外经济技术合作公司	7	225	0	225	0
吉林国际人才交流公司	23	216	0	216	0
吉林省对外经济发展公司	14	1367	0	1367	0
延边国际经济技术合作公司	4	633	0	633	0
吉林化工工程公司	4	272	265	3	4
吉林省农业对外合作公司	51	1011	0	1011	0
吉林省新创对外工程公司	1	191	191	0	0
吉林省工程建设有限公司	1	1200	1200	0	0
吉林化工(集团)建设公司	10	958	940	18	0
珲春对外经贸公司	2	297	0	297	0
长春国际经济技术合作公司	33	1048	0	1048	0
长春建工集团总公司	1	531	0	531	0
长春对外劳务合作公司	6	1320	0	1320	0
长春对外经济技术合作公司	8	867	0	867	0
黑龙江省	229	42490	34005	8477	8
中国黑龙江国际经济技术合作公司	18	4579	1947	2632	0
黑龙江国际工程技术合作公司	6	126	99	27	0
黑龙江东方集团国际经济技术合作公司	1	187	0	187	0
黑龙江省森林工对外经济贸易公司	3	197	0	197	0

1998 年中国对外承包工程和劳务合作合同分公司总值

名　　称	合同数（份）	合同额(万美元)			
		合计	承包工程	劳务合作	设计咨询
中国煤碳国际经济技术合作黑龙江公司	4	44	12	32	0
哈尔滨铁路局对外经济技术合作公司	8	645	294	351	0
齐齐哈尔国际经济技术合作公司	2	50	50	0	0
牡丹江国际经济技术合作公司	8	189	0	189	0
东宁宏达经济贸易公司	3	106	0	106	0
东宁国际经济技术合作公司	73	2513	0	2513	0
东宁边境经济贸易公司	1	18	0	18	0
密山市经济技术合作公司	6	127	0	127	0
绥芬河国际经济技术合作公司	12	470	0	470	0
同江国际经济技术合作公司	10	328	0	328	0
黑河国际经济技术合作公司	13	640	501	139	0
伊春市边境贸易公司	4	121	0	121	0
萝北边境贸易公司	1	33	0	33	0
饶河县边境贸易公司	1	11	0	11	0
黑龙江农垦对外贸易公司	1	18	0	18	0
绥芬河东成经济贸易有限公司	1	1972	1972	0	0
东宁欣荣经济贸易公司	2	68	0	68	0
东宁良丰经济贸易公司	1	6	0	6	0
同江市北江有限公司	2	27	0	27	0
黑河祥云经济贸易公司	1	68	0	68	0
绥芬河华城国际经济公司	1	474	0	474	0
同江松江经济贸易公司	1	18	0	18	0
黑河奥特实业发展有限公司	1	63	63	0	0
绥芬河兴建经济贸易公司	3	149	0	149	0
绥芬河京鹏经济贸易公司	1	897	897	0	0
黑河龙港经济贸易公司	1	11	0	11	0
黑河龙飞对外经济贸易公司	1	221	221	0	0
同江红利红经济贸易公司	1	43	0	43	0
哈尔滨市	37	28071	27949	114	8
哈尔滨对外经济技术合作公司	14	89	34	55	0
哈尔滨国际经济技术合作公司	12	63	0	55	8
哈尔滨中建工程公司	8	890	886	4	0
哈尔滨电站工程责任有限公司	3	27029	27029	0	0
上海市	9674	71065	46038	20948	4079
中国上海外经(集团)有限公司	249	20118	6189	11189	2740
上海对外劳务合作公司	120	1546	0	1546	0
上海对外建设公司	2	976	972	4	0
上海机械进出口(集团)有限公司	1	36	0	36	0

1998年中国对外承包工程和劳务合作合同分公司总值

名　　称	合同数(份)	合同额(万美元)			
		合计	承包工程	劳务合作	设计咨询
上海机械设备进出口公司	4	39	0	39	0
上海建筑设计研究院	5	159	0	0	159
上海轻工业设计研究院	12	30	0	0	30
上海电气(集团)总公司	2	8412	8412	0	0
上海市对外服务公司	8752	5685	0	5685	0
上海轻纺工业对外经济技术合作公司	33	997	0	997	0
上海金山石油化工工程公司	5	1330	1330	0	0
上海核工程研究设计院	1	3	0	0	3
上海医药设计院	4	98	0	0	98
中船第九设计研究院	12	84	0	0	84
华东建筑设计研究院	9	148	0	0	148
上海机电设计研究院	5	399	0	0	399
宝钢集团国际经济贸易公司	1	10	0	0	10
华东电力对外经济贸易公司	1	9	0	9	0
上海成套设备进出口公司	312	425	0	425	0
上海建工(集团)总公司	43	18893	18893	0	0
上海市政工程设计研究院	3	408	0	0	408
上海航空工业(集团)公司	8	133	0	133	0
上海水产(集团)公司	5	35	0	35	0
上海东方国际(集团)有限公司	60	809	120	689	0
上海浦东国际经济技术合作公司	15	143	0	143	0
中国华源集团有限公司	1	3	0	3	0
上海隧道工程股份有限公司	5	1292	1292	0	0
上海建筑装饰(集团)总公司	1	194	194	0	0
上海住总(集团)总公司	1	8636	8636	0	0
上海黄埔对外经济技术合作	2	15	0	15	0
江苏省	659	62485	38206	24277	2
中国江苏国际经济技术合作公司	171	16349	12950	3399	0
江苏省建筑工程总公司	20	1413	547	866	0
南通国际经济技术合作公司	32	1595	736	859	0
连云港国际经济技术合作公司	9	2705	0	2705	0
镇江国际经济技术合作公司	20	333	0	333	0
扬州国际经济技术合作公司	42	1262	447	815	0
苏州国际经济技术合作公司	34	704	151	553	0
无锡国际经济技术合作公司	1	5	0	5	0
常州国际经济技术合作(集团)有限公司	22	774	112	662	0
盐城国际经济技术合作公司	7	1552	0	1552	0
徐州国际经济技术合作公司	3	91	20	71	0

1998年中国对外承包工程和劳务合作合同分公司总值

名　　称	合同数(份)	合同额(万美元)			
		合计	承包工程	劳务合作	设计咨询
淮阴国际经济技术合作公司	20	2185	1500	685	0
江苏建达建设股份有限公司	3	1845	1845	0	0
江苏省建筑材料工业总公司	10	764	478	286	0
南化集团永利进出口公司	1	37	37	0	0
张家港国际经济技术合作公司	2	812	0	812	0
江苏公路桥梁工程公司	16	639	633	6	0
江苏水利外经公司	1	131	131	0	0
南京化学工业集团公司设计院	1	2	0	0	2
启东市对外经济技术合作公司	7	108	0	108	0
南通第四建筑安装工程公司	5	1811	1781	30	0
南通市第三建筑安装工程公司	6	3212	0	3212	0
武进市建设工程公司	4	1645	1620	25	0
江苏地质工程有限公司	4	59	59	0	0
江苏农业对外经济技术合作公司	9	168	0	168	0
常熟国际经济技术合作公司	14	205	0	205	0
江苏省建筑安装工程股份有限公司	1	290	290	0	0
无锡建筑工程公司	2	192	192	0	0
吴县国际经济技术合作公司	3	199	172	27	0
苏州建筑控股集团	30	1676	1676	0	0
南通建筑工程总承包公司	21	1044	42	1002	0
徐州建筑安装工程公司	6	289	0	289	0
南通苏中建筑安装工程公司	7	917	0	917	0
江都市建筑工程总公司(集团)	9	1045	793	252	0
江苏省泰兴市第一建筑安装工程公司	3	287	287	0	0
江苏省对外交流公司	17	163	0	163	0
江苏河海疏浚工程集团公司	1	2209	2209	0	0
中设江苏公司	5	2489	2420	69	0
常州市对外经济技术贸易集团公司	3	938	30	908	0
江苏天目安装集团公司	7	1235	1203	32	0
盐城市天虹建筑工程总公司	10	1416	316	1100	0
南通市第六建筑安装工程公司	34	907	0	907	0
南京市	36	6783	5529	1254	0
南京国际经济技术合作公司	23	3221	2287	934	0
南京海外建筑工程公司	4	1775	1775	0	0
南京市住宅建设总公司	1	787	787	0	0
南京大地建设(集团)股份有限公司	8	1000	680	320	0
浙江省	691	26190	15903	10112	175
中国浙江国际经济技术合作公司	217	4099	2151	1948	0

1998年中国对外承包工程和劳务合作合同分公司总值

名　　称	合同数(份)	合同额(万美元)			
		合计	承包工程	劳务合作	设计咨询
浙江省建工集团有限责任公司	27	5761	5123	638	0
杭州国际经济技术合作公司	8	379	0	379	0
温州国际经济技术合作公司	17	101	81	20	0
绍兴国际经济技术合作公司	14	849	0	849	0
舟山国际经济技术合作公司	81	53	0	53	0
丽水国际经济技术合作公司	27	280	11	269	0
湖州对外经济技术合作有限公司	5	60	0	60	0
金华对外经济技术合作有限公司	14	80	0	80	0
台州国际经济技术合作公司	28	169	162	7	0
嘉兴市对外经济技术合作有限公司	1	31	0	31	0
浙江省粮油食品进出口股份有限公司	15	178	0	178	0
机械工业部第二设计研究院	3	190	188	0	2
电力工业部华东勘测设计研究院	4	173	0	0	173
浙江中大对外经济技术合作有限公司	8	325	0	325	0
浙江东方集团股份有限公司	1	9	0	9	0
浙江舜杰建筑集团股份有限公司	23	470	115	355	0
诸暨市建筑安装工程公司	1	450	450	0	0
上虞第六建筑工程公司	3	600	400	200	0
宁波市	194	11933	7222	4711	0
中国宁波国际合作(集团)有限公司	110	1544	0	1544	0
宁波天地集团股份有限公司	29	1206	59	1147	0
宁波市进出口公司	8	1223	0	1223	0
宁波国际建设经贸公司	3	127	39	88	0
宁波市建筑安装集团总公司	8	943	833	110	0
鄞县进出口公司	20	599	0	599	0
龙元建设集团股份有限公司	10	3259	3259	0	0
宏润建设集团股份有限公司	6	3032	3032	0	0
安徽省	134	6864	2436	4347	81
安徽国际经济技术合作公司	21	1104	127	974	3
蚌埠玻璃工业设计研究院	2	231	225	0	6
化工部第三设计院	4	66	0	0	66
安徽省外经建设(集团)公司	8	1120	106	1014	0
合肥对外经济技术合作公司	20	334	61	273	0
冶金部马鞍山钢铁设计研究院	3	6	0	0	6
安徽建工集团有限公司	5	1312	56	1256	0
芜湖国际经济技术合作公司	5	156	0	156	0
冶金部第十七冶金建设公司	1	360	360	0	0
合肥建筑集团公司	1	102	102	0	0

1998年中国对外承包工程和劳务合作合同分公司总值

名称	合同数(份)	合同额(万美元)			
		合计	承包工程	劳务合作	设计咨询
中国化学工程第三建筑公司	12	744	744	0	0
安徽省电力建设二公司	2	411	411	0	0
宿县地区国际经济技术合作公司	2	518	0	518	0
安徽轻工进出口股份有限公司	1	3	0	3	0
安庆国际经济技术合作公司	2	51	0	51	0
安徽省对外劳务开发中心	41	57	0	57	0
煤炭部合肥设计研究院	1	25	25	0	0
铁道部第四工程局	2	219	219	0	0
马鞍山钢铁国际贸易公司	1	45	0	45	0
福建省	2858	43919	19436	24357	126
中国福建国际经济技术合作公司	748	5057	2133	2924	0
福州国际经济技术合作公司	616	4345	80	4265	0
福建省对外劳务合作公司	257	4078	0	4078	0
福建福通对外经济技术合作公司	5	945	0	945	0
福建省水利水电勘测设计院	1	54	0	0	54
福建省建筑设计院	8	269	202	0	67
福建华源国际贸易经济合作公司	55	387	0	387	0
中国武夷实业总公司	17	12025	12025	0	0
莆田国际经济技术合作公司	23	1360	0	1360	0
中国泉州国际经济技术合作集团有限公司	385	1111	0	1111	0
中国漳州国际经济技术合作公司	230	1896	245	1651	0
福建厦门轮船总公司	5	1770	0	1770	0
宁德国际经济技术合作公司	172	86	0	86	0
三明国际经济技术合作公司	10	189	0	189	0
南平国际经济技术合作公司	13	65	0	65	0
龙岩国际经济技术合作公司	1	135	0	135	0
福建省轮船总公司	6	108	0	108	0
福州市劳务技术合作公司	34	623	0	623	0
福州壮安发展有限公司	5	74	0	74	0
福建省投资企业公司	7	2008	1961	47	0
福建省金福集团公司	14	108	0	108	0
福建省对外劳务咨询服务中心	8	207	0	207	0
福建中旅对外劳务合作公司	22	86	0	86	0
福建省外国机构服务中心	10	95	0	95	0
福建华旅对外劳务合作公司	2	74	0	74	0
福建三木集团股份有限公司	26	401	0	401	0
莆田对外经济技术合作公司	32	310	0	310	0
福州市建筑设计院	3	5	0	0	5

1998 年中国对外承包工程和劳务合作合同分公司总值

名　　称	合同数（份）	合同额（万美元）			
		合计	承包工程	劳务合作	设计咨询
福建省人才开发中心	4	30	0	30	0
福建轻纺工业经济技术公司	9	75	0	75	0
福建省对外经贸服贸公司	8	199	0	199	0
泉州市对外经济技术服务公司	10	270	0	270	0
福建省工业设备安装有限公司	12	2802	2790	12	0
中国厦门国际经济技术合作公司	67	1684	0	1684	0
厦门建隆发集团公司	21	383	0	383	0
厦门经济特区船务有限公司	4	184	0	184	0
厦门国贸集团有限公司	2	307	0	307	0
厦门经济特区对外贸易集团公司	3	97	0	97	0
厦门诚毅船务公司	3	17	0	17	0
江西省	103	7724	3694	4021	9
中国江西国际经济技术合作公司	48	3002	514	2479	9
南昌对外工程总公司	4	822	815	7	0
江西省建筑工程总公司	8	300	287	13	0
南昌国际经济技术合作公司	21	1544	818	726	0
江西省轻工业对外经济技术合作公司	4	145	0	145	0
赣州国际经济技术合作公司	10	978	343	635	0
萍乡矿务局建筑安装总公司	2	527	527	0	0
宜春海程经贸发展有限公司	4	390	390	0	0
吉安对外经济技术合作公司	2	16	0	16	0
山东省	1040	48596	27611	20963	22
中国山东国际经济技术合作公司	41	6043	3716	2327	0
齐鲁建设集团公司	19	1107	1097	10	0
山东省国泰集团公司	5	320	307	0	13
山东省建筑工程总公司	6	2300	2300	0	0
山东省外商投资服务公司	16	506	0	506	0
山东省劳务合作公司	255	1120	0	1120	0
山东省水产企业集团公司	7	2210	0	2210	0
山东省五金矿产进出口公司	2	87	0	87	0
济南钢铁集团总公司	1	160	0	160	0
山东省物产进出口公司	16	52	0	52	0
莱芜钢铁总厂	2	126	80	46	0
山东对外贸易集团有限公司	2	6	0	6	0
黄河工程局	1	1300	1300	0	0
山东省纺织品进出口公司	2	9	0	9	0
威海国际经济技术合作公司	53	3853	423	3430	0
烟台国际经济技术合作公司	95	3916	1510	2406	0

1998年中国对外承包工程和劳务合作合同分公司总值

名称	合同数(份)	合同额(万美元)			
		合计	承包工程	劳务合作	设计咨询
烟台市建筑工程公司	3	2600	2480	120	0
潍坊国际经济技术合作公司	31	408	110	298	0
淄博国际经济技术合作公司	33	508	381	127	0
济南国际经济技术合作公司	2	325	265	60	0
日照国际经济技术合作公司	26	2377	910	1467	0
临沂国际经济技术合作公司	1	30	0	30	0
济宁国际经济技术合作公司	3	30	0	30	0
泰安国际经济技术合作公司	14	2099	742	1357	0
东营国际经济技术合作公司	12	501	0	501	0
潍坊建筑安装工程公司	16	524	17	507	0
济南四建集团责任有限公司	4	1170	1150	20	0
荣成市对外经济技术合作公司	17	378	0	378	0
威海火炬高技术开发区进出口公司	14	87	0	87	0
烟台二建实业股份有限公司	2	520	400	120	0
淄博建筑工程公司	3	500	450	50	0
潍坊柴油机厂进出口公司	12	1085	1043	42	0
济南轻骑集团进出口公司	4	269	0	269	0
诸城市建筑工程公司	9	2143	1795	348	0
菏泽地区对外经济技术合作	7	134	0	134	0
威海市进出口集团公司	5	21	0	21	0
中国水产烟台海洋渔业公司	3	293	0	293	0
山东省电力公司	3	1259	1259	0	0
胜利油田管理局	26	1680	1680	0	0
德州市国际经济技术合作公司	3	99	0	99	0
泰安建筑工程公司	28	1882	1247	635	0
青岛市	236	4559	2949	1601	9
中国青岛国际经济技术合作公司	96	2327	1720	607	0
青岛建设集团公司	21	1237	1229	8	0
青岛市五金矿产机械进出口公司	43	496	0	496	0
青岛国际人才技术合作公司	56	156	0	156	0
青岛海洋渔业公司	8	214	0	214	0
青岛海尔国际贸易有限公司	3	8	0	8	0
青岛市建筑设计研究院	3	9	0	0	9
青岛国际交流中心	6	112	0	112	0
河南省	91	5858	2745	2696	417
中国河南国际经济技术合作公司	42	2309	601	1708	0
河南省水利电力对外公司	10	239	0	239	0
河南省对外劳务合作公司	5	687	0	687	0

1998 年中国对外承包工程和劳务合作合同分公司总值

名　　称	合同数(份)	合同额(万美元)			
		合计	承包工程	劳务合作	设计咨询
河南省建设工程公司	13	1210	1164	46	0
郑州国际经际技术合作公司	4	16	0	16	0
洛阳国际经际技术合作公司	1	830	830	0	0
邮电部设计院	2	33	0	0	33
洛阳石油化工工程公司	1	150	0	0	150
机械部第四设计研究院	10	174	0	0	174
中原石油勘探局外经外贸总公司	1	150	150	0	0
河南交通规划勘察设计院	2	60	0	0	60
湖北省	188	17394	13622	3172	600
中国湖北国际经济技术合作公司	5	633	623	10	0
湖北建材工贸(集团)公司	1	80	0	80	0
湖北大地国际经济技术合作有限公司	4	227	191	36	0
黄石国际经济技术合作公司	13	32	0	32	0
湖北晴川国际海员劳务开发公司	14	103	0	103	0
孝感国际经济技术合作建筑有限公司	3	15	0	15	0
湖北省建筑工程集团有限公司	13	579	579	0	0
湖北省国际劳务合作有限公司	8	513	172	341	0
电力工业部中南电力设计院	5	279	0	0	279
武汉地质勘察基础工程(集团)总公司	1	101	101	0	0
武汉市	121	14832	11956	2555	321
中国武汉国际经济技术合作公司	65	6413	4298	2115	0
中国五环化学工程公司	6	2402	2402	0	0
武汉建工集团有限公司	4	186	186	0	0
武汉钢铁设计研究院	6	281	80	0	201
中国第一冶金建设公司	4	908	908	0	0
铁道部第四勘测设计院	6	39	0	2	37
煤碳部武汉设计院	3	88	5	0	83
武汉凌云集团有限责任公司	11	4175	4077	98	0
长江航运集团对外经济技术合作总公司	16	340	0	340	0
湖南省	166	4621	3749	741	131
中国湖南国际经济技术合作公司	16	554	485	47	22
湖南省公路桥梁建设公司	2	824	824	0	0
湖南建筑工程集团总公司	3	1410	1410	0	0
湖南省进出口公司	10	95	0	95	0
湖南环球(集团)公司	10	278	0	278	0
长沙冶金设计院	3	32	0	0	32
长沙轻工设计院	3	77	0	0	77
湖南建筑设计院	2	0	0	0	0

1998 年中国对外承包工程和劳务合作合同分公司总值

名　　称	合同数(份)	合同额(万美元)			
		合计	承包工程	劳务合作	设计咨询
岳阳第四化建公司	1	360	360	0	0
湖南机械集团进出口公司	4	8	0	8	0
电力中南设计院	8	70	70	0	0
湖南株州海外国际合作有限公司	63	28	0	28	0
华隆进出口公司	41	885	600	285	0
广东省	2300	31145	19919	10841	385
中国广东国际合作(集团)公司	183	5116	2209	2907	0
广东对外劳务经济合作公司	271	3446	0	3446	0
广东海外建设总公司	2	2600	2600	0	0
广东省源大水利水电集团有限公司	6	9210	9210	0	0
珠海国际经济技术合作公司	73	4007	3250	757	0
汕头国际经济技术合作公司	2	71	0	71	0
江门市对外劳动服务公司	94	2168	0	2168	0
广东省南粤进出口公司	29	42	0	42	0
中山国际经济技术合作公司	4	945	945	0	0
广州市	1516	919	405	514	0
中国广州国际经济技术合作公司	1480	280	98	182	0
广州对外经济发展总公司	33	332	0	332	0
广州建筑总公司 *	2	265	265	0	0
广州工程总承包集团有限公司	1	42	42	0	0
深圳市	120	2621	1300	936	385
中国深圳国际合作(集团)股份有限公司	27	115	0	115	0
深圳市对外劳动服务公司	50	622	0	622	0
深圳市国际人才劳务经济发展有限公司	25	159	0	159	0
深圳市建设投资控股公司	3	1340	1300	40	0
深圳市建筑设计总院	15	385	0	0	385
广西自治区	84	7492	6974	518	0
中国广西国际经济技术合作公司	61	279	61	218	0
南宁国际经济技术合作公司	4	173	0	173	0
广西对外建筑工程总公司	2	492	492	0	0
北海海外经济技术合作公司	2	97	0	97	0
防城港国际经济技术合作有限责任公司	3	2188	2186	2	0
广西公路桥梁工程总公司	1	1870	1870	0	0
广西水利水电对外有限责任公司	4	575	575	0	0
梧州国际经济技术合作公司	5	1694	1694	0	0
广西地矿建设工程发展中心	1	28	0	28	0
凭祥市对外经济技术合作公司	1	96	96	0	0
海南省	3	81	81	0	0

1998年中国对外承包工程和劳务合作合同分公司总值

名称	合同数（份）	合同额（万美元）			
		合计	承包工程	劳务合作	设计咨询
中国海南国际经济技术合作公司	3	81	81	0	0
重庆市	23	1967	1437	257	273
中国重庆国际经济技术合作公司	10	308	286	19	3
重庆对外建设总公司	4	403	383	20	0
宝钢集团重庆钢铁设计研究院	4	271	1	0	270
涪陵国际经济技术合作公司	3	232	14	218	0
重庆海外建筑工程承包有限公司	2	753	753	0	0
四川省	115	23422	17162	5479	781
中国四川国际合作股份有限公司	9	858	820	38	0
中国华西企业公司	1	4	4	0	0
四川东方电力设备联合公司	2	12536	12536	0	0
中国华西工程设计建设总公司	3	118	0	36	82
中国成达化学工程公司	4	418	415	0	3
四川公路桥梁工程总公司	1	680	680	0	0
四川省外经实业股份公司	42	1208	0	1208	0
四川省电力进出口公司	3	19	15	4	0
中国化学工程第七建设公司	3	445	445	0	0
铁道部第二设计院	3	696	0	0	696
川铁国际经济技术合作公司	10	1435	1283	152	0
成都市建筑工程总公司	6	729	0	729	0
绵阳国际经济技术合作有限公司	3	967	964	3	0
四川省劳务开发公司	18	2272	0	2272	0
中国成都国际经济技术合作公司	7	1037	0	1037	0
贵州省	11	8769	8645	124	0
铁道部第五工程局	4	445	445	0	0
贵州省桥梁工程公司	7	8324	8200	124	0
云南省	83	31016	29625	377	1014
中国云南国际经济技术合作公司	21	1128	1048	41	39
昆明国际经济技术合作公司	1	10	0	10	0
云南建工集团总公司	2	200	200	0	0
云南公路桥梁工程总公司	1	2402	2402	0	0
中国有色金属工业第十四冶金建设公司	1	30	0	30	0
云南地矿勘查工程总公司（集团）	2	292	12	0	280
云南省化学工业建设公司	1	58	58	0	0
云南省铁路总公司	2	1049	1049	0	0
云南德宏国际经济技术合作公司	11	1540	1515	25	0
云南省机械进出口公司	1	60	60	0	0
云南省机械设备进出口公司	1	17000	17000	0	0

1998年中国对外承包工程和劳务合作合同分公司总值

名 称	合同数(份)	合同额(万美元)			
		合计	承包工程	劳务合作	设计咨询
电力部昆明勘测设计研究院	4	577	0	0	577
德宏州进出口公司	9	1372	1012	242	118
云南省云岭工业进出口公司	1	132	132	0	0
瑞丽勐卯商号	2	642	642	0	0
裕丰商号	7	890	890	0	0
昆明永峰装饰工业有限公司	2	1649	1649	0	0
版纳州勐腊县养护段	4	141	141	0	0
版纳州勐腊县对外经济技术公司	1	24	24	0	0
版纳州勐腊县种子公司	0	1	0	1	0
版纳州勐腊县乡镇企业局	1	15	15	0	0
版纳州勐腊糖厂	1	27	0	27	0
版纳州勐海县农业局	3	87	86	1	0
版纳州勐海县储运公司	1	78	78	0	0
版纳州南腊商行	1	13	13	0	0
版纳州勐海报关行	1	32	32	0	0
瑞丽市进出口公司	1	1567	1567	0	0
陕西省	100	5888	4529	1012	347
中国陕西国际经济技术合作公司	18	314	16	257	41
秦海国际工程公司	1	136	125	11	0
机械部第七设计院	17	225	160	0	65
化工部第六设计院	3	967	790	0	177
西北勘测设计院	2	3	0	3	0
交通部第一公路设计院	2	41	0	0	41
西北电力集团对外公司	1	18	0	18	0
陕西省机械设备进出口公司	1	1000	1000	0	0
华山国际工程公司	15	929	904	25	0
西飞集团公司	1	16	0	16	0
煤碳工业部西安设计研究院	3	30	0	7	23
中国计算机软件工程公司西安分公司	5	176	0	176	0
西安市	31	2033	1534	499	0
西安国际技术贸易公司	30	1083	584	499	0
西安电力机械进出口公司	1	950	950	0	0
甘肃省	59	4963	4657	306	0
中国甘肃国际经济技术合作公司	8	288	0	288	0
甘肃建筑工程总公司	14	3983	3983	0	0
甘肃对外经济发展公司	6	118	100	18	0
甘肃地质工程总公司	31	574	574	0	0
新疆自治区	6	393	346	47	0

1998年中国对外承包工程和劳务合作合同分公司总值

名　　称	合同数(份)	合同额(万美元)			
		合计	承包工程	劳务合作	设计咨询
中国新疆国际经济技术合作公司	1	10	0	10	0
新疆机械化工五金矿产轻工进出口公司	2	87	50	37	0
新疆生产建设兵团	3	296	296	0	0
新天国际经济技术合作公司	3	296	296	0	0

1998年中国对外承包工程和劳务合作营业额分公司总值

金额单位:万美元

名　　称	合　计	承包工程	劳务合作	设计咨询
合计	**1013381**	**776856**	**227625**	**8900**
中央合计	**545020**	**498026**	**44269**	**2725**
中国建筑工程总公司	194388	193655	576	157
中国广播电视国际经济技术合作公司	1427	1427	0	0
中国冶金建设集团总公司	2940	2940	0	0
中国商业对外经济技术合作公司	64	2	62	0
中国水产(集团)总公司	2264	2162	102	0
中国国际技术智力合作公司	13756	0	13670	86
中国路桥(集团)总公司	22015	21626	389	0
中国土木工程集团公司	32148	29626	2363	159
中国港湾建设(集团)总公司	26086	26076	0	10
中国海外工程总公司	13279	12726	553	0
中国水利电力对外公司	19664	19664	0	0
中国石化工程建设公司	1049	1014	35	0
中国化学工程(集团)公司	477	460	13	4
中国轻工业对外经济技术合作公司	1251	227	1024	0
中国电子国际经济技术合作公司	967	904	63	0
中国地质工程公司	4252	4252	0	0
中国国际展览公司	152	152	0	0
中国国际工程和材料公司	548	500	48	0
中国光大国际经济技术合作公司	270	270	0	0
中国航空技术国际工程公司	1057	966	91	0
中国国际计算机软件工程公司	57	0	57	0
中国林业国际合作公司	15	0	15	0
中国建材工业对外经济技术合作公司	2995	2585	410	0
中国万宝工程公司	13175	13175	0	0
中国交远国际经济技术合作公司	919	372	547	0

1998年中国对外承包工程和劳务合作营业额分公司总值

金额单位:万美元

名 称	合 计	承包工程	劳务合作	设计咨询
国华国际工程承包公司	8	7	1	0
中国海员对外经济技术合作公司	2378	0	2378	0
中国石油工程建设(集团)公司	48446	48404	42	0
中国四达国际经济技术合作公司	79	0	79	0
中国中原对外工程公司	8834	8834	0	0
中海国际石油工程有限责任公司	838	838	0	0
中国国际工程咨询公司	55	1	3	51
中国体育国际经济技术合作公司	363	314	44	5
中国海外贸易总公司	458	0	458	0
中国国际企业合作公司	108	0	108	0
中国电子系统工程总公司	1253	1253	0	0
中国铁道建筑总公司	3909	3383	446	80
中国化工建设总公司	4073	4062	5	6
五洲工程设计研究院	207	3	0	204
中国海外经济合作总公司	1486	1482	4	0
中国机械设备进出口总公司	4313	4313	0	0
中国寰球化学工程公司	3303	2765	0	538
中国机械对外经济技术合作公司	1441	1235	206	0
远大国际经济合作有限责任公司	150	150	0	0
中国有色金属建设股份有限公司	4673	3857	816	0
中国海洋工程公司	1125	1052	73	0
中国医疗卫生对外经济合作公司	526	72	454	0
中国纺织工业对外经济技术合作公司	348	329	19	0
中国北方工业公司	1429	1429	0	0
长城国际经济技术合作有限公司	294	289	5	0
中化国际工程贸易公司	56	0	56	0
中国航空工业规划设计院	108	0	0	108
中国仪器进出口总公司	8	0	8	0
中国通信建设总公司	112	89	23	0
中远对外劳务合作公司	12163	0	12163	0
中国成套设备进出口集团总公司	13690	8621	5069	0
中国对外建设总公司	104	104	0	0
轻工业部规划设计院	76	0	2	74
北京有色冶金设计研究总院	61	45	3	13
燕兴国际经济技术合作公司	144	0	144	0
中国铁路工程公司	15662	14746	170	746
中国新兴工程建筑房地产开发总公司	6	4	2	0
中国机械进出口(集团)有限公司	1377	1377	0	0

1998 年中国对外承包工程和劳务合作营业额分公司总值

金额单位:万美元

名　称	合　计	承包工程	劳务合作	设计咨询
北京煤炭设计研究院(集团)	179	0	0	179
中国技术进出口总公司	3888	3888	0	0
北京钢铁设计研究院	124	0	0	124
中国电力技术进出口公司	3889	3490	399	0
华北电力设计院	79	0	1	78
中国安能建设总公司	474	474	0	0
中国京冶建设工程承包公司	146	146	0	0
中外园林建设总公司	163	63	95	5
中纺人力资源开发有限公司	10	0	10	0
中国电子工程设计院	60	60	0	0
广播电影电视部设计院	2	0	0	2
建设部建筑设计院	2	0	0	2
核工业第二研究设计院	25	0	0	25
中交公路规划设计院	4	0	0	4
建设部综合勘察研究院	10	10	0	0
中国地质勘查技术院	113	113	0	0
中煤建设集团公司	9549	9379	170	0
中机中电设计研究院	41	32	0	9
中国国际人才开发中心	48	14	34	0
中水远洋渔业有限责任公司	13096	12355	741	0
北京建隆建筑工程联合公司	1040	1040	0	0
北京市地质矿产勘查开发总公司	150	144	0	6
中国机械工业安装总公司	235	235	0	0
华北电力国际经贸公司	230	230	0	0
中设国际工程有限公司	8410	8410	0	0
中国工程与农业机械进出口总公司	4534	4534	0	0
北京中水远洋渔业发展公司	2906	2906	0	0
中国新星石油公司	6734	6664	20	50
地方合计	468361	278830	183356	6175
北京市	31012	24405	6080	527
中国北京国际经济合作公司	3552	3355	197	0
北京市建筑工程总公司	4281	3831	450	0
北京市政工程总公司	2649	2624	25	0
北京市政工程设计研究院	461	0	8	453
北京市建筑设计院	74	0	0	74
北京住宅开发建设集团总公司	6483	6483	0	0
北京城建集团总公司	4878	4878	0	0
首钢总公司国际经贸部	3018	2891	127	0

1998年中国对外承包工程和劳务合作营业额分公司总值

金额单位:万美元

名　　称	合　计	承包工程	劳务合作	设计咨询
四通国际经济技术合作公司	63	0	63	0
北京市外国企业服务总公司	5210	0	5210	0
北京城乡建设集团总公司	318	318	0	0
北京市第二房修工程公司	25	25	0	0
天津市	17733	10640	6733	360
中国天津国际经济技术合作公司	7297	1922	5375	0
天津立达国际劳务工程公司	930	0	930	0
天津建工集团总公司	6235	6235	0	0
铁道部第三勘测设计院	53	0	50	3
中国天辰化学工程公司	1145	961	59	125
机械部第五设计研究院	124	22	0	102
天津港海员对外服务公司	15	0	15	0
天津市政设计研究院	110	0	0	110
天津市亿利达集团有限公司	14	0	14	0
天津市化工设计院	47	38	0	9
天津天航海员技术服务公司	122	0	122	0
水利部天津水利水电勘测设计研究院	11	0	0	11
大港油田集团有限责任公司	1462	1462	0	0
天海集团股份有限公司	17	0	17	0
天津系列外企业	151	0	151	0
河北省	5097	2486	2499	112
中国河北国际经济技术合作公司	613	189	424	0
石家庄国际经济技术合作公司	399	0	399	0
北方设计研究院	25	0	0	25
河北公路工程建设集团有限公司	70	70	0	0
河北建工集团有限责任公司	377	0	377	0
核工部第四设计研究院	5	0	0	5
唐山国际工程总公司	453	0	453	0
化工部第一勘察设计院	4	4	0	0
中国第二十二冶金建设公司	35	35	0	0
张家口对外劳务工程公司	250	0	250	0
河北电力勘测设计研究院	134	7	127	0
秦皇岛国际经济技术合作公司	82	0	0	82
地矿河北工程勘测公司	174	169	5	0
邢台对外合作公司	35	0	35	0
保定国际经济技术合作公司	65	0	65	0
承德对外经济合作公司	149	0	149	0
唐山对外合作公司	180	0	180	0

1998年中国对外承包工程和劳务合作营业额分公司总值

金额单位：万美元

名　　称	合　计	承包工程	劳务合作	设计咨询
铁道部建场工程局	1007	1007	0	0
河北省进出口公司	3	0	3	0
中油管道建设有限责任公司	1005	1005	0	0
河北国际供销合作总公司	32	0	32	0
山西省	2099	1454	632	13
中国山西国际经济技术合作公司	494	398	96	0
山西省建筑工程总公司	408	6	402	0
太原市国际经济技术合作公司	66	0	66	0
太原钢铁(集团)公司	87	87	0	0
山西省电力公司	132	132	0	0
山西省送变电工程公司	425	425	0	0
山西省公路桥梁工程总公司	103	103	0	0
化工部第二设计院	103	100	0	3
山西四建集团有限公司	44	0	44	0
煤炭部太原设计研究院	5	0	5	0
太原重型机器进出口公司	1	1	0	0
山西省电力勘测设计院	10	0	0	10
中国第十三冶金建设公司	221	202	19	0
内蒙古自治区	2394	957	1432	5
中国内蒙古国际经济技术合作公司	335	259	76	0
冶金部包头钢铁设计研究院	5	0	0	5
呼伦贝尔盟国际经济技术合作公司	417	32	385	0
满州里国际经济技术合作公司	516	300	216	0
内蒙古电力集团公司	183	183	0	0
二连浩特国际经济技术合作公司	210	18	192	0
锡林郭勒国际经济技术合作公司	115	0	115	0
额尔古纳国际经济技术合作公司	82	0	82	0
内蒙古高等院校科技开发集团	83	0	83	0
二连浩特市边境贸易总公司	189	151	38	0
额尔古纳市边境贸易公司	20	0	20	0
新巴尔虎右旗边境贸易公司	4	0	4	0
满州里东方国际贸易股份有限公司	98	0	98	0
内蒙古大兴安岭林管进出口公司	5	5	0	0
呼和浩特国际经济技术合作公司	120	0	120	0
满州里第一建筑工程公司	9	9	0	0
内蒙古农牧业科技开发公司	3	0	3	0
辽宁省	38126	22096	15538	492
中国辽宁国际合作(集团)股份有限公司	8160	5883	2277	0

1998 年中国对外承包工程和劳务合作营业额分公司总值

金额单位:万美元

名　称	合　计	承包工程	劳务合作	设计咨询
辽宁省建设集团公司	3000	3000	0	0
辽宁国际建设工程集团公司	74	19	55	0
鞍山国际经济技术合作公司	697	22	675	0
抚顺对外建设经济合作(集团)股份公司	1303	466	837	0
本溪对外经济技术合作总公司	347	0	347	0
丹东国际经济技术合作公司	80	0	80	0
营口国际经济技术合作公司	5	0	5	0
鞍山焦化耐火材料设计院	18	0	2	16
东北电力集团进出口公司	3181	3170	11	0
鞍山冶金设计研究院	30	0	0	30
锦州华锦国际经贸股份有限公司	17	9	8	0
铁岭国际经济技术合作公司	7	0	7	0
辽宁华曦集团	116	0	116	0
辽阳国际经济技术合作公司	608	0	566	42
鞍钢集团国际经济贸易公司	46	46	0	0
中国第三冶金建设公司	60	0	60	0
辽河石油勘探局	17	7	10	0
朝阳建设集团有限公司	866	788	78	0
抚顺市第二建筑工程公司	45	0	45	0
辽宁省国际劳务交流有限公司	17	0	17	0
本钢集团国际经济贸易有限公司	218	0	218	0
沈阳市	5681	2656	2625	400
中国沈阳国际经济技术合作公司	5078	2622	2456	0
沈阳对外经济建设总公司	170	34	136	0
煤炭工业部沈阳设计研究院	33	0	33	0
中国建筑东北设计研究院	400	0	0	400
大连市	13533	6030	7499	4
中国大连合作(集团)股份有限公司	11191	5870	5321	0
瓦房店市国际工程公司	20	20	0	0
辽宁省大连海洋渔业集团公司	290	0	290	0
大连经济技术开发区劳务公司	31	0	31	0
大连工程总承包公司	80	80	0	0
大化国际经济贸易公司	47	0	47	0
大连华南国际经济技术合作公司	436	30	406	0
大连港国际经济技术合作公司	23	0	23	0
大连渤海建筑集团有限公司	20	0	20	0
大连远洋船员管理公司	427	0	427	0
中国外运大连公司	5	0	5	0

1998年中国对外承包工程和劳务合作营业额分公司总值

金额单位:万美元

名称	合计	承包工程	劳务合作	设计咨询
大连海运集团国际劳务合作公司	20	0	20	0
中国成套设备进出口大连公司	53	0	53	0
大连水产远洋渔业公司	691	0	691	0
大连亿达国际合作公司	30	30	0	0
中国商业对外经济合作公司大连分公司	2	0	2	0
辽宁成大股份公司	13	0	13	0
中国辽宁国际合作大连开发总公司	154	0	150	4
吉林省	12848	3114	9729	5
中国吉林国际经济技术合作公司	3560	811	2749	0
吉林市对外经济技术合作公司	177	0	177	0
延边对外经济技术合作公司	476	36	440	0
珲春国际经济技术合作公司	88	2	86	0
吉林化学工业进出口公司	148	0	148	0
吉林冶金建设公司	123	0	123	0
吉林省对外招商建设总公司	361	95	265	1
延边海外经济技术合作公司	1761	0	1761	0
吉林建设开发集团公司	132	132	0	0
吉林省对外经济技术合作公司	53	0	53	0
吉林国际人才交流公司	293	0	293	0
吉林省对外经济发展公司	705	0	705	0
延边国际经济技术合作公司	112	0	112	0
吉林化工工程公司	73	66	3	4
吉林省农业对外合作公司	724	0	724	0
吉林省新创对外工程公司	199	199	0	0
吉林省工程建设有限公司	690	690	0	0
吉林化工(集团)建设公司	1102	1083	19	0
珲春对外经贸公司	289	0	289	0
长春国际经济技术合作公司	785	0	785	0
长春建工集团总公司	180	0	180	0
长春对外劳务合作公司	99	0	99	0
长春对外经济技术合作公司	718	0	718	0
黑龙江省	14470	9943	4513	14
中国黑龙江国际经济技术合作公司	720	0	720	0
黑龙江国际工程技术合作公司	658	293	365	0
黑龙江省森林工对外经济贸易公司	30	0	30	0
中国煤炭国际经济技术合作黑龙江公司	30	9	21	0
哈尔滨铁路局对外经济技术合作公司	455	455	0	0
黑龙江省瑞驰建设公司	159	159	0	0

1998年中国对外承包工程和劳务合作营业额分公司总值

金额单位:万美元

名　称	合　计	承包工程	劳务合作	设计咨询
牡丹江国际经济技术合作公司	117	0	117	0
东宁宏达经济贸易公司	33	0	33	0
东宁国际经济技术合作公司	1530	0	1530	0
东宁边境经济贸易公司	18	0	18	0
密山市经济技术合作公司	110	0	110	0
绥芬河国际经济技术合作公司	247	0	247	0
同江国际经济技术合作公司	320	0	320	0
黑河国际经济技术合作公司	247	170	77	0
伊春市边境贸易公司	104	0	104	0
萝北边境贸易公司	30	0	30	0
饶河县边境贸易公司	11	0	11	0
虎林边境贸易公司	3	0	3	0
东宁欣荣经济贸易公司	65	0	65	0
东宁良丰经济贸易公司	6	0	6	0
同江市北江有限公司	27	0	27	0
黑河祥云经济贸易公司	68	0	68	0
绥芬河华城国际经济公司	160	0	160	0
同江松江经济贸易公司	18	0	18	0
黑河奥特实业发展有限公司	60	60	0	0
绥芬河兴建经济贸易公司	69	0	69	0
绥滨边境经济贸易公司	9	0	9	0
黑河龙港经济贸易公司	25	0	25	0
黑河龙飞对外经济贸易公司	220	220	0	0
同江红利红经济贸易公司	43	0	43	0
哈尔滨市	8878	8577	287	14
哈尔滨对外经济技术合作公司	52	0	52	0
哈尔滨国际经济技术合作公司	245	0	231	14
哈尔滨中建工程公司	570	566	4	0
哈尔滨电站工程责任有限公司	8011	8011	0	0
上海市	55721	34503	19973	1245
中国上海外经(集团)有限公司	14800	6579	8011	210
上海对外劳务合作公司	1431	0	1431	0
上海对外建设公司	144	138	6	0
上海机械进出口(集团)有限公司	6	0	6	0
上海机械设备进出口公司	39	0	39	0
上海建筑设计研究院	54	0	0	54
上海轻工业设计研究院	30	0	0	30
上海电气(集团)总公司	5320	5320	0	0

1998年中国对外承包工程和劳务合作营业额分公司总值

金额单位:万美元

名　　称	合　计	承包工程	劳务合作	设计咨询
上海市对外服务公司	6108	0	6108	0
上海轻纺工业对外经济技术合作公司	2372	0	2372	0
上海金山石油化工工程公司	1499	1499	0	0
上海核工程研究设计院	205	0	0	205
上海医药设计院	99	0	0	99
中船第九设计研究院	84	0	0	84
华东建筑设计研究院	105	0	0	105
上海纺织建筑设计研究院	63	0	0	63
上海机电设计研究院	322	0	0	322
宝钢集团国际经济贸易公司	10	0	0	10
华东电力对外经济贸易公司	17	0	17	0
上海成套设备进出口公司	788	0	788	0
上海建工(集团)总公司	16045	16039	6	0
上海市政工程设计研究院	63	0	0	63
上海航空工业(集团)公司	42	0	42	0
上海水产(集团)公司	408	0	408	0
上海东方国际(集团)有限公司	554	0	554	0
上海浦东国际经济技术合作公司	77	0	77	0
中国华源集团有限公司	106	0	106	0
上海隧道工程股份有限公司	1894	1894	0	0
上海建筑装饰(集团)总公司	90	90	0	0
上海住总(集团)总公司	2944	2944	0	0
上海黄埔对外经济技术合作	2	0	2	0
江苏省	52526	35155	17355	16
中国江苏国际经济技术合作公司	14475	12386	2089	0
江苏省建筑工程总公司	1380	478	902	0
南通国际经济技术合作公司	1360	591	769	0
连云港国际经济技术合作公司	1811	391	1420	0
镇江国际经济技术合作公司	100	0	100	0
扬州国际经济技术合作公司	401	84	317	0
苏州国际经济技术合作公司	668	151	517	0
无锡国际经济技术合作公司	356	281	75	0
常州国际经济技术合作(集团)有限公司	404	0	404	0
盐城国际经济技术合作公司	873	0	873	0
徐州国际经济技术合作公司	127	20	107	0
淮阴国际经济技术合作公司	1634	998	636	0
江苏建达建设股份有限公司	2203	2203	0	0
江苏省建筑材料工业总公司	465	368	97	0

1998年中国对外承包工程和劳务合作营业额分公司总值

金额单位:万美元

名　称	合　计	承包工程	劳务合作	设计咨询
南化集团永利进出口公司	205	205	0	0
张家港国际经济技术合作公司	439	0	439	0
江苏公路桥梁工程公司	836	722	114	0
江苏水利外经公司	118	118	0	0
南京化学工业集团公司设计院	134	130	0	4
启东市对外经济技术合作公司	3	0	3	0
南通第四建筑安装工程公司	2302	2137	165	0
南通市第三建筑安装工程公司	3000	700	2300	0
武进市建设工程公司	2126	2124	2	0
江苏地质工程有限公司	415	415	0	0
江苏农业对外经济技术合作公司	120	0	120	0
常熟国际经济技术合作公司	122	0	122	0
江苏省建筑安装工程股份有限公司	521	307	214	0
无锡建筑工程公司	807	807	0	0
江苏省矿业总承包公司	861	861	0	0
吴县国际经济技术合作公司	2	0	2	0
苏州建筑控股集团	1920	1920	0	0
南通建筑工程总承包公司	637	32	605	0
徐州矿务集团有限公司	49	0	37	12
徐州建筑安装工程公司	26	0	26	0
南通苏中建筑安装工程公司	700	0	700	0
江都市建设工程总公司(集团)	191	145	46	0
江苏省对外交流公司	107	0	107	0
中设江苏公司	1819	1750	69	0
常州市对外经济技术贸易集团公司	800	30	770	0
江苏天目安装集团公司	424	411	13	0
盐城市天虹建筑工程总公司	467	233	234	0
南通市第六建筑安装工程公司	453	0	453	0
南京市	6665	4157	2508	0
南京国际经济技术合作公司	2265	1783	482	0
南京海外建筑工程公司	2127	1885	242	0
南京市住宅建设总公司	20	20	0	0
南京大地建设(集团)股份有限公司	2253	469	1784	0
浙江省	31843	14838	16792	213
中国浙江国际经济技术合作公司	4046	585	3461	0
浙江省建工集团有限责任公司	3502	2608	894	0
浙江省机械设备进出口总公司	2234	2234	0	0
浙江省建筑设计研究院	10	0	0	10

1998年中国对外承包工程和劳务合作营业额分公司总值

金额单位:万美元

名 称	合 计	承包工程	劳务合作	设计咨询
杭州国际经济技术合作公司	300	0	300	0
温州国际经济技术合作公司	49	29	20	0
绍兴国际经济技术合作公司	724	119	604	1
舟山国际经济技术合作公司	156	0	156	0
丽水国际经济技术合作公司	108	5	103	0
湖州对外经济技术合作有限公司	50	0	50	0
金华对外经济技术合作有限公司	309	0	309	0
台州国际经济技术合作公司	319	279	40	0
嘉州市对外经济技术合作有限公司	2	0	2	0
浙江省粮油食品进出口股份有限公司	139	0	139	0
机械工业部第二设计研究院	209	207	0	2
电力工业部华东勘测设计研究院	200	0	0	200
浙江中大对外经济技术合作有限公司	274	0	274	0
浙江舜杰建筑集团股份有限公司	65	24	41	0
诸暨市建筑安装工程公司	450	450	0	0
上虞第六建筑工程公司	394	262	132	0
宁波市	18303	8306	10267	0
中国宁波国际合作(集团)有限公司	2968	0	2968	0
宁波天地集团股份有限公司	3177	374	2803	0
宁波市进出口公司	2990	1120	1870	0
宁波国际建设经贸公司	4446	2074	2372	0
宁波市建筑安装集团总公司	1006	1006	0	0
鄞县进出口公司	254	0	254	0
龙元建设集团股份有限公司	1588	1588	0	0
宠润建设集团股份有限公司	1874	1874	0	0
安徽省	4933	2800	1857	276
安徽国际经济技术合作公司	892	202	670	20
蚌埠玻璃工业设计研究院	49	23	0	26
化工部第三设计院	53	0	0	53
安徽省外经建设(集团)公司	535	253	277	5
合肥对外经济技术合作公司	340	0	340	0
冶金部马鞍山钢铁设计研究院	167	2	0	165
蚌埠国际经济技术合作公司	207	198	9	0
安徽建工集团有限公司	231	76	155	0
安徽省水利水电勘察设计院	4	0	0	4
芜湖国际经济技术合作公司	163	35	128	0
冶金部第十七冶金建设公司	50	50	0	0
安徽建筑设计研究院	9	0	6	3

1998年中国对外承包工程和劳务合作营业额分公司总值

金额单位:万美元

名称	合计	承包工程	劳务合作	设计咨询
合肥建筑集团公司	10	10	0	0
中国化学工程第三建筑公司	1601	1601	0	0
安徽省电力建设二公司	109	102	7	0
宿县地区国际经济技术合作公司	175	0	175	0
安徽轻工进出口股份有限公司	2	0	2	0
安庆国际经济技术合作公司	79	0	79	0
安徽省对外劳务开发中心	7	0	7	0
煤炭部合肥设计研究院	10	10	0	0
铁道部第四工程局	238	238	0	0
马鞍山钢铁国际贸易公司	2	0	2	0
福建省	51877	15617	36116	144
中国福建国际经济技术合作公司	8954	1549	7405	0
福州国际经济技术合作公司	4873	80	4793	0
福建省对外劳务合作公司	4378	300	4078	0
福建福通对外经济技术合作公司	980	0	980	0
福建省水利水电勘测设计院	44	0	0	44
福建省建筑设计院	230	146	0	84
福建华源国际贸易经济合作公司	466	0	466	0
中国武夷实业总公司	11029	11029	0	0
莆田国际经济技术合作公司	1096	0	1096	0
中国泉州国际经济技术合作集团有限公司	1405	9	1396	0
中国漳州国际经济技术合作公司	2443	290	2153	0
福建厦门轮船总公司	359	0	359	0
宁德国际经济技术合作公司	473	0	473	0
三明国际经济技术合作公司	87	0	87	0
南平国际经济技术合作公司	40	0	40	0
福建省华洋水产集团公司	83	0	83	0
龙岩国际经济技术合作公司	55	0	55	0
福建省轮船总公司	111	0	111	0
福州市劳务技术合作公司	391	0	391	0
福州壮安发展有限公司	499	0	499	0
福建省投资企业公司	123	0	123	0
福建省金福集团公司	549	0	549	0
福建省对外劳务咨询服务中心	443	0	443	0
福建中旅对外劳务合作公司	188	0	188	0
福建省外国机构服务中心	208	0	208	0
福建华旅对外劳务合作公司	251	0	251	0
福建三木集团股份有限公司	507	0	507	0

1998年中国对外承包工程和劳务合作营业额分公司总值

金额单位:万美元

名　　称	合　计	承包工程	劳务合作	设计咨询
莆田对外经济技术合作公司	626	0	626	0
福州市建筑设计院	16	0	0	16
福建省人才开发中心	17	0	17	0
福建轻纺工业经济技术公司	34	0	34	0
福建省对外经贸服贸公司	344	0	344	0
泉州市对外经济技术服务公司	322	0	322	0
福建省工业设备安装有限公司	2224	2214	10	0
中国厦门国际经济技术合作公司	6087	0	6087	0
厦门建隆发集团公司	526	0	526	0
厦门经济特区船务有限公司	88	0	88	0
厦门国贸集团有限公司	605	0	605	0
厦门经济特区对外贸易集团公司	104	0	104	0
厦门特贸有限公司	501	0	501	0
厦门经贸船务公司	38	0	38	0
厦门诚毅船务公司	80	0	80	0
江西省	7050	4031	2995	24
中国江西国际经济技术合作公司	2950	1099	1827	24
南昌对外工程总公司	1280	1270	10	0
江西省建筑工程总公司	579	322	257	0
南昌国际经济技术合作公司	500	132	368	0
南昌有色冶金设计研究院	150	150	0	0
江西省轻工业对外经济技术合作公司	400	0	400	0
赣州国际经济技术合作公司	474	371	103	0
萍乡矿务局建筑安装总公司	187	172	15	0
宜春海程经贸发展有限公司	515	515	0	0
吉安对外经济技术合作公司	15	0	15	0
山东省	33204	15460	17712	32
中国山东国际经济技术合作公司	3599	2254	1345	0
齐鲁建设集团公司	1250	1237	13	0
山东省国泰集团公司	83	57	0	26
山东省建筑工程总公司	1560	1500	60	0
山东省外商投资服务公司	175	0	175	0
山东省劳务合作公司	876	0	876	0
山东省水产企业集团公司	1800	0	1800	0
山东省五金矿产进出口公司	87	0	87	0
济南钢铁集团总公司	66	0	66	0
山东省物产进出口公司	9	0	9	0
莱芜钢铁总厂	96	64	32	0

1998 年中国对外承包工程和劳务合作营业额分公司总值

金额单位:万美元

名　称	合　计	承包工程	劳务合作	设计咨询
山东对外贸易集团有限公司	2	0	2	0
黄河工程局	62	62	0	0
山东省纺织品进出口公司	1	0	1	0
威海国际经济技术合作公司	2901	176	2725	0
烟台国际经济技术合作公司	2051	119	1932	0
烟台市建筑工程公司	2249	2151	98	0
潍坊国际经济技术合作公司	784	0	784	0
淄博国际经济技术合作公司	525	261	264	0
济南国际经济技术合作公司	426	208	218	0
日照国际经济技术合作公司	1197	0	1197	0
临沂国际经济技术合作公司	327	120	207	0
济宁国际经济技术合作公司	16	0	16	0
泰安国际经济技术合作公司	1363	733	630	0
东营国际经济技术合作公司	237	0	237	0
潍坊建筑安装工程公司	562	129	433	0
济南四建集团责任有限公司	375	355	20	0
荣成市对外经济技术合作公司	281	0	281	0
威海火炬高技术开发区进出口公司	130	0	130	0
烟台二建实业股份有限公司	443	400	43	0
淄博建筑工程公司	408	187	221	0
潍坊柴油机厂进出口公司	1126	876	250	0
济南轻骑集团进出口公司	144	0	144	0
枣庄国际经济技术合作公司	48	0	48	0
诸城市建筑工程公司	788	713	75	0
菏泽地区对外经济技术合作	27	0	27	0
威海市进出口集团公司	10	0	10	0
中国水产烟台海洋渔业公司	173	80	93	0
山东省电力公司	258	258	0	0
胜利油田管理局	1599	1596	3	0
德州市国际经济技术合作公司	42	0	42	0
泰安建筑工程公司	1010	537	473	0
青岛市	4038	1387	2645	6
中国青岛国际经济技术合作公司	2112	11	2101	0
青岛建设集团公司	1400	1376	24	0
青岛市五金矿产机械进出口公司	158	0	158	0
青岛国际人才技术合作公司	171	0	171	0
青岛海洋渔业公司	162	0	162	0
青岛海尔国际贸易有限公司	7	0	7	0

1998年中国对外承包工程和劳务合作营业额分公司总值

金额单位:万美元

名　称	合　计	承包工程	劳务合作	设计咨询
青岛市建筑设计研究院	6	0	0	6
青岛国际交流中心	22	0	22	0
河南省	7085	4130	2580	375
中国河南国际经济技术合作公司	1838	600	1238	0
河南省水利电力对外公司	1100	395	705	0
河南省对外劳务合作公司	647	35	612	0
河南省建设工程公司	532	513	19	0
郑州国际经济技术合作公司	5	0	5	0
洛阳国际经济技术合作公司	748	747	1	0
邮电部设计院	189	0	0	189
洛阳石油化工工程公司	75	0	0	75
机械部第四设计研究院	48	0	0	48
洛阳有色金属加工设计院	135	132	0	3
中原石油勘探局外经外贸总公司	1708	1708	0	0
河南交通规划勘察设计院	60	0	0	60
湖北省	9537	6095	2909	533
中国湖北国际经济技术合作公司	855	606	249	0
湖北建材工贸(集团)公司	40	0	40	0
湖北大地国际经济技术合作有限公司	169	166	3	0
黄石国际经济技术合作公司	111	0	111	0
葛洲坝水利水电工程集团公司	1567	1567	0	0
中国有色第十五冶金建设公司	43	43	0	0
湖北晴川国际海员劳务开发公司	73	0	73	0
孝感国际经济技术合作建筑有限公司	21	0	21	0
湖北省建筑工程集团有限公司	592	592	0	0
湖北省国际劳务合作有限公司	33	7	26	0
电力工业部中南电力设计院	279	0	0	279
铁道部大桥工程局	475	465	0	10
武汉地质勘察基础工程(集团)总公司	71	71	0	0
武汉市	5208	2578	2386	244
中国武汉国际经济技术合作公司	2523	367	2156	0
中国五环化学工程公司	754	754	0	0
武汉建工集团有限公司	442	442	0	0
武汉钢铁设计研究院	235	70	0	165
中国第一冶金建设公司	469	469	0	0
铁道部第四勘测设计院	58	0	3	55
华中电力国际经贸公司	42	42	0	0
煤炭部武汉设计院	32	8	0	24

1998年中国对外承包工程和劳务合作营业额分公司总值

金额单位:万美元

名　　称	合　计	承包工程	劳务合作	设计咨询
武汉凌云集团有限责任公司	339	323	16	0
武汉船用机械厂	47	0	47	0
长江航运集团对外经济技术合作总公司	162	0	162	0
中国出口商品基地武汉公司	5	3	2	0
武汉市市政工程总公司	100	100	0	0
湖南省	9868	9178	488	202
中国湖南国际经济技术合作公司	1587	1265	304	18
湖南省公路桥梁建设公司	1547	1547	0	0
湖南建筑工程集团总公司	1083	1077	6	0
湖南省进出口公司	89	0	89	0
湖南环球(集团)公司	44	0	44	0
长沙冶金设计院	93	0	0	93
长沙轻工设计院	28	0	0	28
湖南建筑设计院	12	0	0	12
岳阳第四化建公司	748	748	0	0
湖南机械集团进出口公司	1	0	1	0
电力中南设计院	80	35	0	45
中国水利水电第八工程局	2000	2000	0	0
湖南交通国际工程合作公司	2306	2306	0	0
湖南株州海外国际合作有限公司	10	0	10	0
华隆进出口公司	234	200	34	0
430115	6	0	0	6
广东省	29295	16514	12448	333
中国广东国际合作(集团)公司	3836	2018	1818	0
广东对外劳务经济合作公司	4900	0	4900	0
广东海外建设总公司	3170	3162	8	0
广东省建筑工程总公司	1545	1545	0	0
广东省源大水利水电集团有限公司	2566	2566	0	0
珠海国际经济技术合作公司	3380	3150	230	0
汕头国际经济技术合作公司	96	0	92	4
江门市对外劳动服务公司	1316	0	1316	0
广东省南粤进出口公司	42	0	42	0
中山国际经济技术合作公司	134	134	0	0
广州市	4114	1927	2187	0
中国广州国际经济技术合作公司	2327	657	1670	0
广州对外经济发展总公司	543	26	517	0
广州珠江实业集团有限公司	931	931	0	0
广州建筑总公司 *	302	302	0	0

1998 年中国对外承包工程和劳务合作营业额分公司总值

金额单位:万美元

名 称	合 计	承包工程	劳务合作	设计咨询
广州工程总承包集团有限公司	11	11	0	0
深圳市	4196	2012	1855	329
中国深圳国际合作(集团)股份有限公司	2019	1587	432	0
深圳市对外劳动服务公司	941	0	941	0
深圳市国际人才劳务经济发展有限公司	466	0	466	0
深圳市建设投资控股公司	441	425	16	0
深圳市建筑设计总院	329	0	0	329
广西自治区	2854	2775	79	0
中国广西国际经济技术合作公司	451	447	4	0
南宁国际经济技术合作公司	558	505	53	0
广西对外建筑工程总公司	245	245	0	0
北海海外经济技术合作公司	16	1	15	0
防城港国际经济技术合作有限责任公司	607	600	7	0
广西公路桥梁工程总公司	507	507	0	0
广西水利水电对外有限责任公司	379	379	0	0
广西地矿建设工程发展中心	35	35	0	0
凭祥市对外经济技术合作公司	56	56	0	0
海南省	677	677	0	0
中国海南国际经济技术合作公司	677	677	0	0
重庆市	3099	2404	422	273
中国重庆国际经济技术合作公司	1785	1409	373	3
重庆对外建设总公司	500	500	0	0
宝钢集团重庆钢铁设计研究院	349	79	0	270
万县市国际经济技术合作公司	29	0	29	0
涪陵国际经济技术合作公司	12	10	2	0
重庆钢铁(集团)有限责任公司	18	0	18	0
重庆海外建筑工程承包有限公司	406	406	0	0
四川省	22459	18355	3487	617
中国四川国际合作股份有限公司	2134	759	1374	1
中国华西企业公司	1617	1609	8	0
四川东方电力设备联合公司	12990	12990	0	0
中国华西工程设计建设总公司	7	0	0	7
中国成达化学工程公司	272	174	4	94
四川公路桥梁工程总公司	819	709	110	0
四川省外经实业股份公司	83	0	83	0
四川省电力进出口公司	155	153	2	0
中国化学工程第七建设公司	110	110	0	0
铁道部第二设计院	515	0	0	515

1998年中国对外承包工程和劳务合作营业额分公司总值

金额单位：万美元

名　称	合　计	承包工程	劳务合作	设计咨询
川铁国际经济技术合作公司	1891	1851	40	0
成都市建筑工程总公司	114	0	114	0
四川省劳务开发公司	1253	0	1253	0
中国成都国际经济技术合作公司	499	0	499	0
贵州省	956	950	6	0
中国贵州国际经济技术合作公司	1	0	1	0
铁道部第五工程局	850	850	0	0
贵州省桥梁工程公司	105	100	5	0
云南省	10001	9770	122	109
中国云南国际经济技术合作公司	630	597	8	25
昆明国际经济技术合作公司	6	0	6	0
云南建工集团总公司	114	114	0	0
云南公路桥梁工程总公司	5071	5071	0	0
中国有色金属工业第十四冶金建设公司	454	450	4	0
中国云南水利水电昆明国际公司	855	855	0	0
云南地矿勘查工程总公司(集团)	145	17	70	58
云南省化学工业建设公司	50	50	0	0
云南省铁路总公司	283	283	0	0
云南德宏国际经济技术合作公司	932	920	12	0
云南省机械设备进出口公司	40	40	0	0
电力部昆明勘测设计研究院	26	0	0	26
文山州国际股份有限公司	23	23	0	0
云南省云岭工业进出口公司	60	60	0	0
瑞丽勐卯商号	287	287	0	0
裕丰商号	513	513	0	0
昆明永峰装饰工业有限公司	143	143	0	0
版纳州勐腊县养护段	121	121	0	0
版纳州勐腊县对外经济技术公司	10	10	0	0
版纳州勐腊县种子公司	1	0	1	0
版纳州勐腊县乡镇企业局	15	15	0	0
版纳州勐腊糖厂	20	0	20	0
版纳州勐海县农业局	87	86	1	0
版纳州勐海县储运公司	70	70	0	0
版纳州南腊商行	13	13	0	0
版纳州勐海报关行	32	32	0	0
陕西省	7750	6693	802	255
中国陕西国际经济技术合作公司	200	10	175	15
秦海国际工程公司	315	305	10	0

1998年中国对外承包工程和劳务合作营业额分公司总值

金额单位:万美元

名　　称	合　计	承包工程	劳务合作	设计咨询
机械部第七设计院	121	81	0	40
化工部第六设计院	302	234	6	62
西北勘测设计院	2	0	1	1
交通部第一公路设计院	111	0	0	111
西北电力集团对外公司	38	2	36	0
陕西省机械设备进出口公司	9	0	9	0
华山国际工程公司	2949	2934	15	0
西飞集团公司	16	0	16	0
煤炭工业部西安设计研究院	29	0	3	26
中国计算机软件工程公司西安分公司	39	0	39	0
西安市	3619	3127	492	0
西安国际技术贸易公司	720	235	485	0
西安电力机械进出口公司	2892	2892	0	0
西安市机械进出口公司	7	0	7	0
甘肃省	3502	3470	32	0
中国甘肃国际经济技术合作公司	215	202	13	0
甘肃建筑工程总公司	2913	2913	0	0
甘肃对外经济发展公司	41	22	19	0
甘肃地质工程总公司	333	333	0	0
新疆自治区	345	320	25	0
中国新疆国际经济技术合作公司	20	0	20	0
新疆建筑工程总公司	202	202	0	0
新疆机械化工五金矿产轻工进出口公司	55	50	5	0
新疆生产建设兵团	68	68	0	0
新天国际经济技术合作公司	68	68	0	0

1998年末中国在外从事对外承包工程和劳务合作的人数

单位:人

名　　称	合　计	承包工程	劳务合作	设计咨询
合　计	**352125**	**61077**	**290771**	**277**
中央合　计	**72585**	**30798**	**41725**	**62**
中国建筑工程总公司	5535	4616	909	10
中国广播电视国际经济技术合作公司	30	30	0	0
中国冶金建设集团总公司	118	103	15	0
中国商业对外经济技术合作公司	54	0	54	0
中国水产(集团)总公司	1122	807	315	0

1998年末中国在外从事对外承包工程和劳务合作的人数

单位:人

名　　称	合　计	承包工程	劳务合作	设计咨询
中国国际技术智力合作公司	3970	0	3969	1
中国路桥(集团)总公司	1647	1006	641	0
中国土木工程集团公司	4605	1648	2957	0
中国港湾建设(集团)总公司	1963	1878	85	0
中国海外工程总公司	3215	1075	2140	0
中国水利电力对外公司	1054	1050	4	0
中国石化工程建设公司	12	8	4	0
中国化学工程(集团)公司	343	334	0	9
中国轻工业对外经济技术合作公司	1193	6	1187	0
中国电子国际经济技术合作公司	156	0	156	0
中国地质工程公司	303	303	0	0
中国国际工程和材料公司	42	14	28	0
中国光大国际经济技术合作公司	88	31	57	0
中国航空技术国际工程公司	707	359	348	0
中国林业国际合作公司	19	0	19	0
中国建材工业对外经济技术合作公司	1452	57	1395	0
中国万宝工程公司	427	425	2	0
中国交远国际经济技术合作公司	763	239	524	0
国华国际工程承包公司	2	0	2	0
中国海员对外经济技术合作公司	2917	0	2917	0
中国石油工程建设(集团)公司	5931	5900	31	0
中国四达国际经济技术合作公司	4106	0	4106	0
中国中原对外工程公司	749	749	0	0
中海国际石油工程有限责任公司	134	134	0	0
中国国际工程咨询公司	16	5	1	10
中国体育国际经济技术合作公司	51	27	24	0
中国海外贸易总公司	624	0	624	0
中国国际企业合作公司	260	0	260	0
中国电子系统工程总公司	1670	1670	0	0
中国铁道建筑总公司	818	70	748	0
中国化工建设总公司	186	180	0	6
中国海外经济合作总公司	117	68	49	0
中国机械设备进出口总公司	236	236	0	0
中国机械对外经济技术合作公司	230	25	205	0
远大国际经济合作有限责任公司	100	71	29	0
中国有色金属建设股份有限公司	1317	824	493	0
中国海洋工程公司	883	0	883	0
中国医疗卫生对外经济合作公司	173	3	170	0

1998 年末中国在外从事对外承包工程和劳务合作的人数

单位:人

名　称	合　计	承包工程	劳务合作	设计咨询
中国纺织工业对外经济技术合作公司	101	75	26	0
长城国际经济技术合作有限公司	33	27	6	0
中化国际工程贸易公司	152	0	152	0
中国航空工业规划设计院	3	0	0	3
中国仪器进出口总公司	25	0	25	0
中国通信建设总公司	12	12	0	0
中远对外劳务合作公司	9949	0	9949	0
中国成套设备进出口集团总公司	5027	873	4154	0
中国对外建设总公司	11	11	0	0
燕兴国际经济技术合作公司	225	0	225	0
中国铁路工程公司	968	833	123	12
中国新兴工程建筑房地产开发总公司	63	45	18	0
中国机械进出口(集团)有限公司	465	465	0	0
北京钢铁设计研究院	1	0	0	1
中国电力技术进出口公司	1229	710	519	0
华北电力设计院	3	1	0	2
中国安能建设总公司	25	25	0	0
中国京冶建设工程承包公司	13	13	0	0
中外园林建设总公司	20	0	20	0
中纺人力资源开发有限公司	127	0	127	0
广播电影电视部设计院	1	0	0	1
建设部建筑设计院	11	0	4	7
建设部综合勘察研究院	5	5	0	0
中煤建设集团公司	520	520	0	0
中机中电设计研究院	4	4	0	0
中国国际人才开发中心	125	0	125	0
中水远洋渔业有限责任公司	3052	2161	891	0
北京建隆建筑工程联合公司	5	5	0	0
北京市地质矿产勘查开发总公司	18	18	0	0
中国机械工业安装总公司	365	365	0	0
华北电力国际经贸公司	5	5	0	0
中设国际工程有限公司	219	219	0	0
中国工程与农业机械进出口总公司	249	249	0	0
北京中水远洋渔业发展公司	167	167	0	0
中国新星石油公司	49	39	10	0
地方合　计	279540	30279	249046	215
北京市	3647	2233	1408	6
中国北京国际经济合作公司	737	113	624	0

1998年末中国在外从事对外承包工程和劳务合作的人数

单位:人

名　称	合　计	承包工程	劳务合作	设计咨询
北京市建筑工程总公司	296	0	296	0
北京市政工程总公司	171	165	6	0
北京市政工程设计研究院	3	1	2	0
北京市建筑设计院	8	2	0	6
北京住宅开发建设集团总公司	1293	1293	0	0
北京城建集团总公司	139	139	0	0
首钢总公司国际经贸部	481	380	101	0
四通国际经济技术合作公司	359	0	359	0
北京市外国企业服务总公司	20	0	20	0
北京城乡建设集团总公司	72	72	0	0
中国燕山联合对外贸易有限公司	28	28	0	0
北京八仙房地产开发公司	40	40	0	0
天津市	12074	478	11590	6
中国天津国际经济技术合作公司	7479	394	7085	0
天津立达国际劳务工程公司	1877	0	1877	0
天津建工集团总公司	112	0	112	0
天津市建筑设计院	2	0	2	0
天津水泥工业设计研究院	9	9	0	0
铁道部第三勘测设计院	20	0	20	0
机械部第五设计研究院	37	0	37	0
天津港海员对外服务公司	219	0	219	0
天津市亿利达集团有限公司	9	0	9	0
天津天航海员技术服务公司	184	0	184	0
中国成套天津公司	28	0	28	0
天津机械进出口集团有限公司	11	0	11	0
水利部天津水利水电勘测设计研究院	16	0	10	6
大港油田集团有限责任公司	75	75	0	0
天海集团股份有限公司	140	0	140	0
天津系列外企业	1856	0	1856	0
河北省	6412	952	5458	2
中国河北国际经济技术合作公司	737	16	721	0
石家庄国际经济技术合作公司	1628	0	1628	0
北方设计研究院	2	0	0	2
河北公路工程建设集团有限公司	40	40	0	0
河北建工集团有限责任公司	658	0	658	0
唐山国际工程总公司	466	0	466	0
中国耀华玻璃(集团)公司	69	69	0	0
中国第二十二冶金建设公司	1	1	0	0

1998年末中国在外从事对外承包工程和劳务合作的人数

单位:人

名　　称	合　计	承包工程	劳务合作	设计咨询
张家口对外劳务工程公司	1228	0	1228	0
河北电力勘测设计研究院	253	4	249	0
地矿河北工程勘测公司	203	203	0	0
邢台对外合作公司	25	0	25	0
保定国际经济技术合作公司	72	0	72	0
承德对外经济合作公司	103	0	103	0
唐山对外合作公司	277	0	277	0
铁道部建场工程局	186	186	0	0
河北省进出口公司	10	0	10	0
中油管道建设有限责任公司	433	433	0	0
河北国际供销合作总公司	21	0	21	0
山西省	1304	143	1159	2
中国山西国际经济技术合作公司	623	42	579	2
山西省建筑工程总公司	370	0	370	0
太原市国际经济技术合作公司	61	0	61	0
山西省电力公司	7	0	7	0
山西省公路桥梁工程总公司	17	17	0	0
山西四建集团有限公司	88	0	88	0
煤炭部太原设计研究院	2	0	2	0
太原重型机器进出口公司	42	11	31	0
中国第十三冶金建设公司	94	73	21	0
内蒙古自治区	1392	324	1068	0
中国内蒙古国际经济技术合作公司	149	0	149	0
呼伦贝尔盟国际经济技术合作公司	454	60	394	0
满州里国际经济技术合作公司	177	30	147	0
内蒙古电力集团公司	13	13	0	0
二连浩特国际经济技术合作公司	146	40	106	0
锡林郭勒国际经济技术合作公司	30	0	30	0
额尔古纳国际经济技术合作公司	150	0	150	0
内蒙古高等院校科技开发集团	3	0	3	0
二连浩特市边境贸易总公司	27	21	6	0
额尔古纳市边境贸易公司	35	0	35	0
满州里东方国际贸易股份有限公司	45	0	45	0
内蒙古大兴安岭林管进出口	44	44	0	0
满州里第一建筑工程公司	116	116	0	0
内蒙古农牧业科技开发公司	3	0	3	0
辽宁省	26623	3349	23262	12
中国辽宁国际合作(集团)股份有限公司	5528	314	5213	1

1998 年末中国在外从事对外承包工程和劳务合作的人数

单位:人

名　　称	合　计	承包工程	劳务合作	设计咨询
辽宁省建设集团公司	1099	763	336	0
辽宁国际建设工程集团公司	82	10	72	0
鞍山国际经济技术合作公司	915	144	771	0
抚顺对外建设经济合作(集团)股份公司	870	32	838	0
本溪对外经济技术合作总公司	948	0	948	0
丹东国际经济技术合作公司	375	0	375	0
营口国际经济技术合作公司	227	4	225	-2
东北电力集团进出口公司	284	284	0	0
鞍山冶金设计研究院	7	0	0	7
锦州华锦国际经贸股份有限公司	274	189	85	0
铁岭国际经济技术合作公司	193	0	193	0
辽宁华曦集团	685	0	685	0
辽阳国际经济技术合作公司	761	16	745	0
鞍钢集团国际经济贸易公司	66	33	33	0
中国第三冶金建设公司	179	179	0	0
辽河石油勘探局	344	218	126	0
朝阳建设集团有限公司	161	42	119	0
抚顺市第二建筑工程公司	55	0	55	0
辽宁省国际劳务交流有限公司	491	0	491	0
本钢集团国际经济贸易有限公司	97	0	97	0
鞍山市对外建设工程承包集团公司	3	0	3	0
沈阳市	3009	638	2371	0
中国沈阳国际经济技术合作公司	2857	638	2219	0
沈阳对外经济建设总公司	65	0	65	0
煤炭工业部沈阳设计研究院	83	0	83	0
中国建筑东北设计研究院	4	0	4	0
大连市	9970	483	9481	6
中国大连合作(集团)股份有限公司	5076	336	4740	0
瓦房店市国际工程公司	4	4	0	0
辽宁省大连海洋渔业集团公司	725	0	725	0
大连经济技术开发区劳务公司	686	0	686	0
大化国际经济贸易公司	21	0	21	0
大连华南国际经济技术合作公司	436	117	319	0
大连港国际经济技术合作公司	365	0	365	0
大连渤海建筑集团有限公司	165	0	165	0
大连远洋船员管理公司	565	0	565	0
中国外运大连公司	361	0	361	0
大连海运集团国际劳务合作公司	256	0	256	0

1998年末中国在外从事对外承包工程和劳务合作的人数

单位:人

名 称	合 计	承包工程	劳务合作	设计咨询
中国成套设备进出口大连公司	51	0	51	0
大连水产远洋渔业公司	682	0	682	0
大连亿达国际合作公司	26	26	0	0
中国商业对外经济合作公司大连分公司	16	0	16	0
辽宁成大股份公司	55	0	55	0
中国辽宁国际合作大连开发总公司	480	0	474	6
吉林省	21359	1502	19847	10
中国吉林国际经济技术合作公司	4666	51	4615	0
吉林市对外经济技术合作公司	213	0	213	0
延边对外经济技术合作公司	1287	94	1193	0
珲春国际经济技术合作公司	129	12	117	0
吉林化学工业进出口公司	373	0	373	0
吉林冶金建设公司	55	0	55	0
吉林省对外招商建设总公司	2009	536	1463	10
延边海外经济技术合作公司	2551	0	2551	0
吉林建设开发集团公司	33	33	0	0
吉林省对外经济技术合作公司	521	0	521	0
吉林国际人才交流公司	1729	0	1729	0
吉林省对外经济发展公司	3277	0	3277	0
延边国际经济技术合作公司	154	0	154	0
吉林化工工程公司	90	81	9	0
吉林省农业对外合作公司	336	0	336	0
吉林省工程建设有限公司	500	500	0	0
吉林化工(集团)建设公司	190	190	0	0
珲春对外经贸公司	135	0	135	0
长春国际经济技术合作公司	1094	5	1089	0
长春建工集团总公司	237	0	237	0
长春对外劳务合作公司	92	0	92	0
长春对外经济技术合作公司	1688	0	1688	0
黑龙江省	4508	1375	3128	5
中国黑龙江国际经济技术合作公司	1009	170	839	0
黑龙江国际工程技术合作公司	870	134	736	0
黑龙江东方集团国际经济技术合作公司	78	0	78	0
黑龙江省森林工对外经济贸易公司	120	0	120	0
中国煤炭国际经济技术合作黑龙江公司	52	2	50	0
哈尔滨铁路局对外经济技术合作公司	818	673	145	0
齐齐哈尔国际经济技术合作公司	110	110	0	0
牡丹江国际经济技术合作公司	24	0	24	0

1998年末中国在外从事对外承包工程和劳务合作的人数

单位:人

名　　称	合　计	承包工程	劳务合作	设计咨询
东宁宏达经济贸易公司	24	0	24	0
东宁国际经济技术合作公司	222	0	222	0
密山市经济技术合作公司	12	0	12	0
绥芬河国际经济技术合作公司	17	0	17	0
黑河国际经济技术合作公司	176	176	0	0
伊春市边境贸易公司	4	0	4	0
绥芬河华城国际经济公司	208	0	208	0
黑河奥特实业发展有限公司	43	43	0	0
哈尔滨市	721	67	649	5
哈尔滨对外经济技术合作公司	114	0	114	0
哈尔滨国际经济技术合作公司	540	0	535	5
哈尔滨电站工程责任有限公司	67	67	0	0
上海市	24116	975	23108	33
中国上海外经(集团)有限公司	11590	218	11372	0
上海对外劳务合作公司	4748	0	4748	0
上海对外建设公司	16	18	-2	0
上海机械进出口(集团)有限公司	45	0	45	0
上海电气(集团)总公司	110	110	0	0
上海市对外服务公司	1208	0	1208	0
上海轻纺工业对外经济技术合作公司	3075	0	3075	0
上海核工程研究设计院	33	0	0	33
华东电力对外经济贸易公司	7	0	7	0
上海成套设备进出口公司	1024	0	1024	0
上海建工(集团)总公司	143	122	21	0
上海航空工业(集团)公司	215	0	215	0
上海水产(集团)公司	649	0	649	0
上海东方国际(集团)有限公司	503	0	503	0
上海浦东国际经济技术合作公司	158	0	158	0
中国华源集团有限公司	69	0	69	0
上海隧道工程股份有限公司	193	193	0	0
上海建筑装饰(集团)总公司	51	51	0	0
上海住总(集团)总公司	263	263	0	0
上海黄埔对外经济技术合作	16	0	16	0
江苏省	23517	5811	17706	0
中国江苏国际经济技术合作公司	5280	1261	4019	0
江苏省建筑工程总公司	816	137	679	0
南通国际经济技术合作公司	1477	464	1013	0
连云港国际经济技术合作公司	1405	0	1405	0

1998年末中国在外从事对外承包工程和劳务合作的人数

单位:人

名　称	合　计	承包工程	劳务合作	设计咨询
镇江国际经济技术合作公司	185	0	185	0
扬州国际经济技术合作公司	690	104	586	0
苏州国际经济技术合作公司	1001	0	1001	0
无锡国际经济技术合作公司	294	46	248	0
常州国际经济技术合作(集团)有限公司	280	0	280	0
盐城国际经济技术合作公司	465	0	465	0
徐州国际经济技术合作公司	136	0	136	0
淮阴国际经济技术合作公司	516	12	504	0
江苏建达建设股份有限公司	17	17	0	0
江苏省建筑材料工业总公司	51	8	43	0
南化集团永利进出口公司	2	2	0	0
张家港国际经济技术合作公司	385	0	385	0
江苏公路桥梁工程公司	217	83	134	0
启东市对外经济技术合作公司	114	0	114	0
南通第四建筑安装工程公司	284	120	164	0
南通市第三建筑安装工程公司	1889	201	1688	0
武进市建设工程公司	91	80	11	0
江苏地质工程有限公司	47	47	0	0
江苏农业对外经济技术合作公司	50	0	50	0
常熟国际经济技术合作公司	152	0	152	0
江苏省建筑安装工程股份有限公司	311	119	192	0
江苏省矿业总承包公司	353	353	0	0
吴县国际经济技术合作公司	40	26	14	0
苏州建筑控股集团	25	25	0	0
南通建筑工程总承包公司	257	11	246	0
徐州矿务集团有限公司	39	0	39	0
徐州建筑安装工程公司	197	0	197	0
南通苏中建筑安装工程公司	523	0	523	0
江都市建设工程总公司(集团)	329	271	58	0
江苏省泰兴市第一建筑安装工程公司	17	17	0	0
江苏省对外交流公司	74	0	74	0
中设江苏公司	16	0	16	0
常州市对外经济技术贸易集团公司	869	10	859	0
江苏天目安装集团公司	35	0	35	0
盐城市天虹建筑工程总公司	314	0	314	0
南通市第六建筑安装工程公司	394	0	394	0
南京市	3880	2397	1483	0
南京国际经济技术合作公司	2704	1962	742	0

1998年末中国在外从事对外承包工程和劳务合作的人数

单位:人

名　　称	合　计	承包工程	劳务合作	设计咨询
南京海外建筑工程公司	493	362	131	0
南京大地建设(集团)股份有限公司	683	73	610	0
浙江省	18975	1083	17886	6
中国浙江国际经济技术合作公司	3333	335	2998	0
浙江省建工集团有限责任公司	455	219	236	0
浙江省机械设备进出口总公司	17	17	0	0
杭州国际经济技术合作公司	386	0	386	0
温州国际经济技术合作公司	102	13	89	0
绍兴国际经济技术合作公司	1091	12	1079	0
舟山国际经济技术合作公司	271	0	271	0
丽水国际经济技术合作公司	317	11	306	0
湖州对外经济技术合作有限公司	72	0	72	0
金华对外经济技术合作有限公司	213	0	213	0
台州国际经济技术合作公司	142	38	104	0
嘉兴市对外经济技术合作有限公司	12	0	12	0
浙江省粮油食品进出口股份有限公司	153	0	153	0
电力工业部华东勘测设计研究院	7	0	1	6
浙江中大对外经济技术合作有限公司	78	0	78	0
浙江东方集团股份有限公司	16	0	16	0
浙江舜杰建筑集团股份有限公司	225	5	220	0
诸暨市建筑安装工程公司	38	0	38	0
上虞第六建筑工程公司	112	69	43	0
宁波市	11935	364	11571	0
中国宁波国际合作(集团)有限公司	2871	0	2871	0
宁波天地集团股份有限公司	3026	120	2906	0
宁波市进出口公司	2906	19	2887	0
宁波国际建设经贸公司	2605	31	2574	0
宁波市建筑安装集团总公司	218	192	26	0
鄞县进出口公司	307	0	307	0
宏润建设集团股份有限公司	2	2	0	0
安徽省	3175	473	2697	5
安徽国际经济技术合作公司	668	19	645	4
安徽省外经建设(集团)公司	685	186	499	0
合肥对外经济技术合作公司	351	0	351	0
蚌埠国际经济技术合作公司	50	40	10	0
安徽建工集团有限公司	570	22	548	0
芜湖国际经济技术合作公司	136	0	136	0
冶金部第十七冶金建设公司	40	40	0	0

1998年末中国在外从事对外承包工程和劳务合作的人数

单位:人

名　称	合　计	承包工程	劳务合作	设计咨询
安徽省建筑设计研究院	4	0	3	1
中国化学工程第三建筑公司	125	125	0	0
安徽省电力建设二公司	11	3	8	0
宿县地区国际经济技术合作公司	322	0	322	0
安徽轻工进出口股份有限公司	1	0	1	0
安庆国际经济技术合作公司	107	0	107	0
安徽省对外劳务开发中心	41	0	41	0
铁道部第四工程局	38	38	0	0
马鞍山钢铁国际贸易公司	26	0	26	0
福建省	54618	119	54497	2
中国福建国际经济技术合作公司	10789	0	10789	0
福州国际经济技术合作公司	6007	95	5912	0
福建省对外劳务合作公司	7083	0	7083	0
福建福通对外经济技术合作公司	2084	0	2084	0
福建省建筑设计院	4	2	0	2
福建华源国际贸易经济合作公司	804	0	804	0
中国武夷实业总公司	22	22	0	0
莆田国际经济技术合作公司	1937	0	1937	0
中国泉州国际经济技术合作集团有限公司	2552	0	2552	0
中国漳州国际经济技术合作公司	4510	0	4510	0
福建厦门轮船总公司	663	0	663	0
宁德国际经济技术合作公司	664	0	664	0
三明国际经济技术合作公司	141	0	141	0
南平国际经济技术合作公司	418	0	418	0
福建省华洋水产集团公司	141	0	141	0
龙岩国际经技术合作公司	71	0	71	0
福建省轮船总公司	226	0	226	0
福州市劳务技术合作公司	737	0	737	0
福州壮安发展有限公司	898	0	898	0
福建省投资企业公司	93	0	93	0
福建省金福集团公司	574	0	574	0
福建省对外劳务咨询服务中心	691	0	691	0
福建中旅对外劳务合作公司	465	0	465	0
福建省外国机构服务中心	623	0	623	0
福建华旅对外劳务合作公司	553	0	553	0
福建三木集团股份有限公司	739	0	739	0
莆田对外经济技术合作公司	1365	0	1365	0
福建省人才开发中心	25	0	25	0

1998年末中国在外从事对外承包工程和劳务合作的人数

单位:人

名　　称	合　计	承包工程	劳务合作	设计咨询
福建轻纺工业经济技术公司	53	0	53	0
福建省对外经贸服贸公司	581	0	581	0
泉州市对外经济技术服务公司	605	0	605	0
中国厦门国际经济技术合作公司	4563	0	4563	0
厦门建隆发集团公司	1061	0	1061	0
厦门经济特区船务有限公司	122	0	122	0
厦门国贸集团有限公司	1511	0	1511	0
厦门经济特区对外贸易集团公司	156	0	156	0
厦门特贸有限公司	858	0	858	0
厦门经贸船务公司	151	0	151	0
厦门诚毅船务公司	78	0	78	0
江西省	4070	309	3755	6
中国江西国际经济技术合作公司	2327	57	2264	6
南昌对外工程总公司	140	114	26	0
江西省建筑工程总公司	272	19	253	0
南昌国际经济技术合作公司	419	27	392	0
南昌有色冶金设计研究院	2	0	2	0
江西省轻工业对外经济技术合作公司	647	0	647	0
赣州国际经济技术合作公司	182	34	148	0
萍乡矿务局建筑安装总公司	26	17	9	0
宜春海程经贸发展有限公司	41	41	0	0
吉安对外经济技术合作公司	14	0	14	0
山东省	24255	2478	21773	4
中国山东国际经济技术合作公司	2463	97	2366	0
齐鲁建设集团公司	342	328	14	0
山东省国泰集团公司	5	4	0	1
山东省建筑工程总公司	112	0	112	0
山东省外商投资服务公司	311	0	311	0
山东省劳务合作公司	1394	0	1394	0
山东省水产企业集团公司	897	0	897	0
山东省五金矿产进出口公司	101	0	101	0
济南钢铁集团总公司	60	0	60	0
莱芜钢铁总厂	11	7	4	0
山东对外贸易集团有限公司	3	0	3	0
威海国际经济技术合作公司	2048	0	2045	3
烟台国际经济技术合作公司	2135	24	2111	0
烟台市建筑工程公司	291	277	14	0
潍坊国际经济技术合作公司	693	0	693	0

1998 年末中国在外从事对外承包工程和劳务合作的人数

单位:人

名　称	合　计	承包工程	劳务合作	设计咨询
淄博国际经济技术合作公司	410	96	314	0
济南国际经济技术合作公司	381	10	371	0
日照国际经济技术合作公司	1373	0	1373	0
临沂国际经济技术合作公司	423	27	396	0
济宁国际经济技术合作公司	14	0	14	0
泰安国际经济技术合作公司	1662	236	1426	0
东营国际经济技术合作公司	459	0	459	0
潍坊建筑安装工程公司	759	19	740	0
济南四建集团责任有限公司	34	34	0	0
荣成市对外经济技术合作公司	345	0	345	0
威海火炬高技术开发区进出口公司	128	0	128	0
烟台二建实业股份有限公司	25	0	25	0
淄博建筑工程公司	50	13	37	0
潍坊柴油机厂进出口公司	172	98	74	0
济南轻骑集团进出口公司	220	0	220	0
枣庄国际经济技术合作公司	35	0	35	0
诸城市建筑工程公司	354	264	90	0
菏泽地区对外经济技术合作	61	0	61	0
威海市进出口集团公司	29	0	29	0
中国水产烟台海洋渔业公司	283	0	283	0
胜利油田管理局	108	103	5	0
德州市国际经济技术合作公司	88	0	88	0
泰安建筑工程公司	799	256	543	0
青岛市	5177	585	4592	0
中国青岛国际经济技术合作公司	3067	20	3047	0
青岛建设集团公司	614	565	49	0
青岛市五金矿产机械进出口公司	556	0	556	0
青岛国际人才技术合作公司	439	0	439	0
青岛海洋渔业公司	487	0	487	0
青岛海尔国际贸易有限公司	4	0	4	0
青岛国际交流中心	10	0	10	0
河南省	8418	3608	4780	30
中国河南国际经济技术合作公司	3631	116	3515	0
河南省水利电力对外公司	703	1	702	0
河南省对外劳务合作公司	3173	2724	449	0
河南省建设工程公司	141	80	61	0
郑州国际经际技术合作公司	40	0	40	0
洛阳国际经济技术合作公司	63	50	13	0

1998年末中国在外从事对外承包工程和劳务合作的人数

单位:人

名　　称	合　计	承包工程	劳务合作	设计咨询
洛阳石油化工工程公司	2	0	0	2
机械部第四设计研究院	2	0	0	2
洛阳有色金属加工设计院	419	404	0	15
中原石油勘探局外经外贸总公司	233	233	0	0
河南交通规划勘察设计院	11	0	0	11
湖北省	4916	565	4324	27
中国湖北国际经济技术合作公司	1065	72	993	0
湖北建材工贸(集团)公司	15	0	15	0
湖北大地国际经济技术合作有限公司	22	9	13	0
黄石国际经济技术合作公司	86	0	86	0
葛州坝水利水电工程集团公司	149	149	0	0
中国有色第十五冶金建设公司	6	6	0	0
湖北晴川国际海员劳务开发公司	93	0	93	0
孝感国际经济技术合作建筑有限公司	24	0	24	0
湖北省建筑工程集团有限公司	68	68	0	0
湖北省国际劳务合作有限公司	352	150	202	0
铁道部大桥工程局	6	0	0	6
武汉地质勘察基础工程(集团)总公司	11	11	0	0
武汉市	3019	100	2898	21
中国武汉国际经济技术合作公司	2320	30	2290	0
中国五环化学工程公司	21	5	0	16
武汉建工集团有限公司	79	7	72	0
武汉钢铁设计研究院	4	0	0	4
中国第一冶金建设公司	40	40	0	0
铁道部第四勘测设计院	3	0	2	1
华中电力国际经贸公司	3	3	0	0
煤碳部武汉设计院	3	3	0	0
武汉凌云集团有限责任公司	33	0	33	0
武汉船用机械厂	4	0	4	0
长江航运集团对外经济技术合作总公司	479	0	479	0
中国出口商品基地武汉公司	18	0	18	0
武汉市市政工程总公司	12	12	0	0
湖南省	2058	409	1628	21
中国湖南国际经济技术合作公司	903	179	713	11
湖南省公路桥梁建设公司	44	36	8	0
湖南建筑工程集团总公司	10	5	5	0
湖南省进出口公司	161	0	161	0
湖南环球(集团)公司	320	0	320	0

1998 年末中国在外从事对外承包工程和劳务合作的人数

单位:人

名　　称	合　计	承包工程	劳务合作	设计咨询
长沙冶金设计院	2	0	0	2
湖南建筑设计院	4	0	0	4
岳阳第四化建公司	30	30	0	0
湖南机械集团进出口公司	14	0	14	0
电力中南设计院	4	0	0	4
中国水利水电第八工程局	96	96	0	0
湖南交通国际工程合作公司	63	63	0	0
湖南株洲海外国际合作有限公司	166	0	166	0
华隆进出口公司	241	0	241	0
广东省	19391	579	18812	0
中国广东国际合作(集团)公司	4851	127	4724	0
广东对外劳务经济合作公司	6131	0	6131	0
广东海外建设总公司	47	17	30	0
广东省建筑公程总公司	47	47	0	0
广东省源大水利水电集团有限公司	95	95	0	0
珠海国际经济技术合作公司	1154	123	1031	0
汕头国际经济技术合作公司	155	0	155	0
汕尾市对外劳动服务公司	94	0	94	0
江门市对外劳动服务公司	3256	0	3256	0
广东省南粤进出口公司	563	0	563	0
中山国际经济技术合作公司	21	21	0	0
珠海劳动服务公司	97	0	97	0
广州市	2283	149	2134	0
中国广州国际经济技术合作公司	1856	103	1753	0
广州对外经济发展总公司	394	13	381	0
广州珠江实业集团有限公司	15	15	0	0
广州建设总公司 *	14	14	0	0
广州工程总承包集团有限公司	4	4	0	0
深圳市	597	0	597	0
中国深圳国际合作(集团)股份有限公司	272	0	272	0
深圳市对外劳动服务公司	57	0	57	0
深圳市国际人才劳务经济发展有限公司	238	0	238	0
深圳市建设投资控股公司	30	0	30	0
广西自治区	840	430	410	0
中国广西国际经济技术合作公司	402	107	295	0
南宁国际经济技术合作公司	127	66	61	0
广西对外建筑工程总公司	167	120	47	0
防城港国际经济技术合作有限责任公司	94	92	2	0

1998年末中国在外从事对外承包工程和劳务合作的人数

单位:人

名　　称	合　计	承包工程	劳务合作	设计咨询
广西公路桥梁工程总公司	21	21	0	0
广西水利水电对外有限责任公司	16	16	0	0
广西地矿建设工程发展中心	13	8	5	0
海南省	58	58	0	0
中国海南国际经济技术合作公司	58	58	0	0
重庆市	1435	173	1262	0
中国重庆国际经济技术合作公司	726	73	653	0
重庆对外建设总公司	242	70	172	0
宝钢集团重庆钢铁设计研究院	7	7	0	0
万县市国际经济技术合作公司	403	0	403	0
涪陵国际经济技术合作公司	38	18	20	0
重庆钢铁(集团)有限责任公司	14	0	14	0
重庆海外建筑工程承包有限公司	5	5	0	0
四川省	8980	995	7985	0
中国四川国际合作股份有限公司	4010	175	3835	0
中国华西企业公司	103	97	6	0
四川东方电力设备联合公司	186	186	0	0
中国华西工程设计建筑总公司	50	0	50	0
四川公路桥梁工程总公司	141	57	84	0
四川省外经实业股份公司	1118	0	1118	0
四川省电力进出口公司	20	17	3	0
中国化学工程第七建设公司	116	116	0	0
川铁国际经济技术合作公司	437	328	109	0
成都市建筑工程总公司	81	0	81	0
绵阳国际经济技术合作有限公司	66	19	47	0
四川省劳务开发公司	1827	0	1827	0
中国成都国际经济技术合作公司	825	0	825	0
贵州省	106	68	38	0
中国贵州国际经济技术合作公司	18	0	18	0
铁道部第五工程局	33	33	0	0
贵州省桥梁工程公司	55	35	20	0
云南省	770	585	163	22
中国云南国际经济技术合作公司	134	68	64	2
昆明国际经济技术合作公司	8	0	8	0
云南建工集团总公司	22	22	0	0
云南公路桥梁工程总公司	10	10	0	0
中国有色金属工业第十四冶金建设公司	29	21	8	0
云南地矿勘查工程总公司(集团)	84	3	81	0

1998年末中国在外从事对外承包工程和劳务合作的人数

单位:人

名　称	合　计	承包工程	劳务合作	设计咨询
云南省铁路总公司	285	285	0	0
云南德宏国际经济技术合作公司	25	23	2	0
云南省机械进出口公司	10	10	0	0
电力部昆明勘测设计研究院	20	0	0	20
云南省云岭工业进出口公司	20	20	0	0
瑞丽勐卯商号	33	33	0	0
裕丰商号	77	77	0	0
昆明永峰装饰工业有限公司	13	13	0	0
陕西省	1655	473	1171	11
中国陕西国际经济技术合作公司	311	78	224	9
秦海国际工程公司	45	35	10	0
化工部第六设计院	2	0	0	2
西北勘测设计院	7	6	1	0
西北电力集团对外公司	14	3	11	0
陕西省机械设备进出口公司	6	0	6	0
华山国际工程公司	294	250	44	0
西飞集团公司	17	0	17	0
煤碳工业部西安设计研究院	5	0	5	0
中国计算机软件工程公司西安分公司	60	0	60	0
西安市	894	101	793	0
西安国际技术贸易公司	875	93	782	0
西安电力机械进出口公司	8	8	0	0
西安市机械进出口公司	11	0	11	0
甘肃省	581	509	67	5
中国甘肃国际经济技术合作公司	173	115	53	5
甘肃建筑工程总公司	240	240	0	0
甘肃对外经济发展公司	38	24	14	0
甘肃地质工程总公司	130	130	0	0
新疆自治区	287	223	64	0
中国新疆国际经济技术合作公司	9	0	9	0
新疆建筑工程总公司	222	222	0	0
新疆机械化工五金矿产轻工进出口公司	56	1	55	0

中国批准海外投资企业统计表

金额单位:万美元

国别(地区)	截至1998年批准		1998年批准	
	企业数量	中方投资	企业数量	中方投资
合　计	**2396**	**258383.1**	**266**	**25901.7**
香港	197	23049.7	25	1283.1
澳门	49	5741	12	1019.7
朝鲜	5	127.1	1	16.3
韩国	18	986.5	1	103.5
日本	86	1604.1	0	-44.6
蒙古	28	303.3	4	23.3
越南	10	504.3	2	222
老挝	7	247.1		
柬埔寨	27	3472.2	5	587.7
缅甸	12	597.6	1	253
泰国	136	6723.4	2	80
马来西亚	78	3159.9	8	561.6
新加坡	79	2874.4	12	1112
印度尼西亚	42	3033.4	5	1085.6
文莱				
菲律宾	29	1083	0	83.2
尼泊尔	3	61		
不丹				
锡金				
巴基斯坦	12	522		
印度	4	198	1	149.5
孟加拉	29	1041.6	1	4.4
斯里兰卡	11	382.8	2	67.8
马尔代夫				
伊朗	2	6.7	1	6
阿富汗				
土耳其	7	850.7		
塞浦路斯	3	31.5		
也门	8	418.4		
沙特阿拉伯	2	81	0	75
巴林				
卡塔尔	1	21		
阿联酋	20	816.5		
阿曼	1	4.6		
叙利亚	2	63.2	2	63.2
黎巴嫩				

中国批准海外投资企业统计表

金额单位:万美元

国别(地区)	截至1998年批准		1998年批准	
	企业数量	中方投资	企业数量	中方投资
约旦	5	114.2	0	59.1
伊拉克				
科威特	3	81.3		
以色列	1	6		
巴勒斯坦				
俄罗斯	259	9957.7	25	250
白俄罗斯	2	223	1	212
乌克兰	16	219	5	99.3
拉脱维亚	2	564		
爱沙尼亚	1	1.8	1	1.8
立陶宛	1	91		
摩尔多瓦				
阿塞拜疆				
亚美尼亚				
格鲁吉亚 *	2	95	2	95
乌兹别克斯坦	12	535	9	364.3
哈萨克斯斯坦	25	782.2	11	612.7
吉尔吉斯坦	12	817.4	6	671.6
塔吉克斯坦	3	248	2	188
土库曼斯坦	2	30	2	30
阿尔巴尼亚	1	250		
英国	11	725	1	49.8
爱尔兰				
法国	15	998	1	50.3
德国	32	1111	2	178.9
瑞士	4	300	1	100.5
荷兰	15	628	3	99.1
比利时	6	162.1		
卢森堡	1	20		
奥地利	7	203.9		
摩纳哥				
圣马力诺				
葡萄牙	3	229.5		
西班牙	12	411.7		
安道尔				
意大利	6	298.6		
马耳他	6	180.6		

中国批准海外投资企业统计表

金额单位:万美元

国别(地区)	截至1998年批准		1998年批准	
	企业数量	中方投资	企业数量	中方投资
希腊				
冰岛				
丹麦	2	34.9		
瑞典	6	185.6	1	1.5
芬兰	1	23.6		
挪威	2	65.1		
波兰	4	64.1		
捷克	3	55.9		
斯洛伐克				
保加利亚	1	25		
匈牙利	14	643	3	278.2
罗马尼亚	4	261	1	50
南斯拉夫	1	5	1	5
马其顿				
克罗地亚				
斯洛文尼亚				
波黑共和国				
埃及	7	1576.6	1	696.5
利比亚	1	10	1	10
阿尔及利亚	1	35		
突尼斯	1	21		
摩洛哥	11	103.6	1	20
毛塔	2	177.5		
马里	3	2824.8		
苏丹	7	1081.5		
埃塞俄比亚	2	174.3		74.3
肯尼亚	14	859.2	0	129.6
索马里				
吉布提				
厄立特里亚	2	97.3		
坦桑尼亚	9	2082.4	0	586
乌干达	8	343		
赞比亚	10	4322.9	3	3254.6
莫桑比克	2	108		
马拉维				
布隆迪	2	71.8		
卢旺达	4	285.1	2	27

中国批准海外投资企业统计表

金额单位:万美元

国别(地区)	截至1998年批准		1998年批准	
	企业数量	中方投资	企业数量	中方投资
马达加斯加	13	222.8	0	-10.9
科摩罗				
毛里求斯	19	722.7	2	39.5
留尼旺				
刚果(民)	6	824.2	1	4.2
刚果	1	2		
中非	5	178.6		
乍得	1	17	0	8.6
塞内加尔	3	24.3		
冈比亚	5	175	0	30
几内亚比绍	1	420	-1	-6.6
几内亚	3	578	1	218
塞拉利昂	2	114.7		
利比里亚	7	736.8		
科特迪瓦	10	1217.3	3	626.6
布基纳瓦索	1	3		
加纳	6	279.1	3	79.1
多哥	3	111	0	65
贝宁	1	98.8		
尼日尔	2	102		
尼日利亚	22	2048	2	779.1
喀麦隆	11	893.9	2	482
赤道几内亚	3	798.5		
加蓬	9	1037.5	2	193
佛得角	3	60		
南非	50	5421	11	829.5
纳米比亚	6	732.5	2	560
津巴布韦	6	2991.1	2	29.6
安哥拉	1	198		
博茨瓦纳	4	208.5	1	98
莱索托	6	62.4	1	4
斯威士兰				
塞舌尔	1	15		
巴西	23	4205	3	158.3
阿根廷	15	514	2	159
乌拉圭	2	28		
智利	6	2087	0	-160.5

中国批准海外投资企业统计表

金额单位:万美元

国别(地区)	截至1998年批准		1998年批准	
	企业数量	中方投资	企业数量	中方投资
秘鲁	9	12072	2	24.2
哥伦比亚	4	130	2	93.5
委内瑞拉	4	182	1	9.5
巴拉圭				
厄瓜多尔	14	390	2	13.4
圭亚那	3	511	1	49.8
法属圭亚那	1	388		
玻利维亚	14	558	1	217.9
苏里南				
墨西哥	32	2592	3	938.2
古巴				
牙买加	2	130		
安提瓜和巴布达	3	130		
巴巴多斯	1	20	0	-106
特立尼达和多巴哥				
百慕大	4	1351.2	2	850
开曼群岛	4	100	4	100
洪都拉斯	2	198	1	98
巴拿马	6	95	0	19.5
伯利兹	2	142	-1	-15.4
哥斯达黎加	1	30	-1	-60
维尔京群岛	10	36	10	36
多米尼加共和国	3	91.2		
密克罗尼西亚	1	10		
巴哈马	3	106		
波利尼西亚	2	38		
美国	274	40104	17	2563
加拿大	82	35645	4	487.3
澳大利亚	96	32921	-2	-13.5
新西兰	15	4588	1	213.9
巴布亚新几内亚	16	4327	5	986.3
斐济	13	713	0	134.2
瓦努阿图	9	497	-1	-20.8
西萨摩亚	5	171	4	95.5
所罗门群岛	3	54.3	3	54.3
新喀里多尼亚				
贝劳	4	106.5		

1998年中国对外援助成套项目建成及提供单项设备情况

行 业	建成项目	建设规模	国 家
公用民用建筑	政府办公楼	建设面积8000平方米	贝宁
	住房项目	建设面积2684平方米	吉布提
	村民住宅	建筑面积2213.91平方米	巴布亚新几内亚
	邮政分拣中心	建筑面积2000平方米	刚果(金)
	机场旅馆	建筑面积26492平方米,331套客房	阿尔及利亚
	国家会议中心	占地面积16984平方米,建筑面积6369.88平方米	莱索托
文教体育卫生	新建教学楼	建筑面积2688平方米	塞舌尔
	增建教学楼	建筑面积3914平方米	塞舌尔
	小学校	建筑面积787平方米	加蓬
	综合工艺学校宿舍	建筑面积2300平方米	塞舌尔
	农业中学	新建校舍5616平方米,修复校舍1100平方米	柬埔寨
更新改造大修	兽医学校修复		卢旺达
	水库修复		尼日尔
	电子计分牌	更换双色LED牌	贝宁
	外交部办公楼维修	空调、线路和家具	吉布提
水利电力	水电站加固		老挝
	水资源勘探		尼日尔
	扬水站	总功率1000千瓦	纳米比亚
交通运输	公路桥	全长1152.4米,正桥长577米	孟加拉
	色迪河桥	全长244米,宽11.4米跨度140米斜桥	尼泊尔
农牧渔业	平原整治	整治面积53公顷,建筑面积427平方米	几内亚
	农业试验站	提供机械,派6名专家,试种2.3公顷	巴布亚新几内亚
工业	水泥厂	年产3万吨水泥立窑	秘鲁
	碾米机厂房	建筑面积380平方米	卢旺达

1998年中国对外援助建成成套项目进行技术合作情况

行 业	项目数	派出专家人数	国 家
农牧渔业	9	46	坦桑尼亚、刚果、毛利塔尼亚、佛得角、毛里求斯、古巴、几内亚、玻利维亚
公用民用建筑	12	63	马里、尼日尔、塞拉利昂(2)、刚果(金)、多哥、乌干达、柬埔寨、毛里塔尼亚、喀麦隆、肯尼亚、津巴布韦
文教体育卫生	9	51	巴基斯坦、柬埔寨、多哥、厄瓜多尔、瓦努阿图(2)萨摩亚、尼泊尔、基里巴斯
交通运输	3	40	赤道几内亚、坦桑尼亚、毛里塔尼亚
水利电力	3	12	几内亚、赤道几内亚、安提瓜和巴布达
广播通讯	3	9	几内亚、赤道几内亚、桑给巴尔
能源开发	2	37	朝鲜、坦桑尼亚
轻纺工业	4	27	塞拉利昂、哥伦比亚(2)、厄瓜多尔
合 计	45	285	

1998年中国承担援外成套项目和单项设备情况

行 业	项目数	国 家
农牧渔业	3	刚果、纳米比亚、加蓬
公用民用建筑	17	吉不提(2)莫桑比克、桑给巴尔、贝宁、几内亚、马里(2)、乌干达、圣卢西亚、斯里兰卡、(2)、纳米比亚、马绍尔、南非、苏里南、肯尼亚
文教卫生	7	巴勒斯坦、塞舌尔、贝宁、厄立特里亚、马里、埃及、卢旺达
交通运输	4	埃及、安提瓜和巴布达、库克群岛、肯尼亚、尼日尔、几内亚
水利电力	2	尼日尔、几内亚
能源	2	坦桑尼亚、乌干达
邮电通讯	3	几内亚、中非、布隆迪
轻工业	5	埃及(2)、乌干达、塔吉克斯坦、巴基斯坦

1998年中国承担援外技术合作项目情况

行 业	项目数	国 家
农牧渔业	5	毛里求斯、贝宁、毛里塔尼亚、中非(2)
文教体育卫生	6	瓦努阿图(3)、多哥、马绍尔、基里巴斯
手工业	2	厄瓜多尔、哥伦比亚
交通运输	3	毛利求斯、毛里塔尼亚(2)
工业及民用建筑	5	喀麦隆(2)、肯尼亚、贝宁、马里

1998年中国承担援外技术合作项目情况

行　业	项目数	国　家
水利电力	2	老挝、几内亚
邮电通讯	2	桑给巴尔、几内亚

大事记

1998 年中国对外经济贸易活动大事记

1 月

1997 年 12 月 28 日－1998 年 1 月 1 日 石广生副部长陪同钱其琛副总理兼外长访问南非。1 日，石副部长参加了中南建交公报签署仪式，并与南非外交部帕哈德副外长分别代表各自政府签署中南政府促进并鼓励相互投资协定和我向南提供 2500 万美元无偿援助的换文。

5 日 吴仪部长会见伊拉克议长哈马迪。双方表示今后进一步加强经贸及石油领域的合作。

6 日 吴仪部长会见德国西门子公司董事长兼德国经济亚太委员会主席冯必乐博士，双方就西门子中国有限公司增资、西门子公司管理培训中心和第七届德国经济亚太会议等问题交换意见。

8 日 孙振宇副部长会见美国雷曼兄弟公司副董事长李学民（Sherman Lewis）。李向孙副部长通报了该公司与我五矿公司纠纷案的进展情况，并表示愿与五矿公司通过谈判解决双方的纠纷。

孙振宇副部长会见美国前商务部长、现任美国梅尔·布朗·普莱特律师事务所合伙人米基·坎特（Micky Kantor），双方就中美经贸关系及其事务所业务交换意见。

9 日 陈新华副部长分别会见意大利驻华使馆公使代办奈利先生和西班牙驻华大使莱尼亚，就欧盟将我从“非市场经济国家”名单中排除做交涉工作，并阐述我方立场。

12 日 吴仪部长与来访的英贸工大臣玛格丽特·贝克举行小范围会谈，并共同主持召开第二届中英经贸联委会，双方就如何进一步加强双边经贸合作进行磋商。

13 日 吴仪部长会见并宴请即将离任的新加坡驻华大使郑东发，双方就中新经贸关系的有关问题交换意见。

吴仪部长会见法国驻华大使毛磊，重点就欧盟将我从“非市场经济国家”名单中排除等问题向法方做交涉工作。双方还就中法经贸合作等问题交换意见。

杨文生部长助理会见并宴请俄罗斯联邦移民总局代表团，双方就《中俄短期劳务合作协定》进行正式会谈。

14 日－24 日 吴仪部长率中国经贸代表团访问斐济和萨摩亚两国。19 日，吴部长会见斐济参议长兼代总统伊洛伊洛（H.E.Ratu Josefa Iloilo）和总理布兰卡（Sitiveni Buraka）；21 日，吴部长会见萨摩亚国家元首马列托亚第二殿下（Malietoa Tanumafili II）和总理托菲劳（Tofilau Eti Alesana），就双边进一步扩大经贸合作举行对口会谈，并在当地参观中国援建项目。

刘山在副部长在北京会见马拉维新闻部长姆帕苏，就发展双边贸易及中马建交进程交换意见。

16 日－26 日 龙永图首席谈判代表率团赴美国，出席在波士顿、华盛顿、旧金山举行的中国融入世界经济研讨会。

19 日 吴仪部长与斐济外交和外贸部部长贝雷纳多·乌尼博博分别代表各自政府就我国向斐济提供 200 万元人民币无偿援助事在苏瓦换文确认。

刘山在副部长会见以会长樱内义雄为团长的日本国际贸易促进协会第 26 届访华团。应日方要求刘副部长向其介绍中国经济和对外贸易的总体形势，并希望中日双方共同努力，广开合作领域，克服东南亚金融危机带来的负面影响，将中日经贸合作关系全面推向 21 世纪。

孙振宇副部长会见美国联邦参议员蒂姆·哈金森（Tim Hutchinson），双方就双边经贸关系、东南亚金融危机及其对中国的影响交换意见。

孙振宇副部长会见美国媒体国际集团董事长约翰·克鲁吉先生（John Kluge）及其一行。孙副部长对克鲁吉先生不断扩大在华投资表示赞赏，并对其因长期致力于促进中美交流而荣获马可·波罗奖表示祝贺。

安民部长助理会见并宴请以冯永祥先生为团长的香港总商会中国委员会访京团。安助理就客人关心的国企改业、开放第三产业等问题作详细介绍。

联合国人口基金执行局会议批准了人口基金在1998年～2000年内向我国提供2000万美元资助贫困地区的生殖健康、计划生育服务、妇女参与发展等活动的方案。

19日—21日 石广生副部长率中国政府代表团出席会议在俄布拉戈维申斯克市举行的中俄边境和地方经贸合作常设工作小组第二次会议。会议前石副部长与俄经济部第一副部长沙波瓦里杨茨就发展两国边境地方经贸合作问题交换意见。会议期间成立了两国毗邻省、区和州、边区组成的边境地方经贸合作协调委员会，并批准了委员会章程。21日中俄双方签署会议纪要。

20日 吴仪部长与萨摩亚副总理兼财政、贸工商部部长图伊莱帕·塞伊莱莱·马利勒高伊分别代表各自政府就我国向萨摩亚提供500万元人民币无偿援助用于小学校增加建筑面积事在阿皮亚换文确认。

20日 刘山在副部长与贝宁外交与合作部长皮埃尔·奥分别代表各自政府在北京签署《中华人民共和国向贝宁共和国政府提供无息贷款的协定》，并就我承担会议大厦项目、向贝宁无偿提供200万美元现汇援助及提供1200辆自行车事在北京分别换文确认。

孙振宇副部长会见美国联邦参议员约翰·洛克菲勒（John Rockefeller）。洛向孙副部长表达了西弗吉尼亚州希望与天津建立友好合作关系的良好愿望。孙副部长向美方介绍中国贸易体制现状，并就中国加入世贸组织问题与对方交换看法。

20日—21日 李国华副部长与新加坡贸工部常务秘书许文远在北京共同主持召开中新贸易、投资和经济合作磋商会第三次会议。双方分别介绍各自国内经济形势，回顾了自上次磋商会以来双边经贸合作发展情况，并就东南亚金融危机及进一步扩大双边经贸合作问题交换意见。

21日 刘山在副部长会见贝宁环境、住房和城市规划部长纳代伊，双方就洛科萨医院中国医生住房地皮问题交换意见，并签署《关于在贝宁建立中国经济贸易发展中心的议定书》。

22日 联合国儿童基金组织向我河北地震灾区提供5万美元援助，用于购买药品及其他儿童保健器具。

23日 联合国人口基金向我河北地震灾区提供用于购买帐篷、药品等救灾物资的5万美元援助。

26日 刘山在副部长会见埃及驻华大使赫纳米，双方就有关建设苏伊士西北经济特区事交换意见。

2 月

1月30日—2月4日 龙永图首席谈判代表陪同李岚清副总理出席达沃斯世界经济论坛年会。

1月31日—2月18日 陈新华副部长陪同李岚清副总理出席瑞士达沃斯世界经济论坛年会并访问瑞士、西班牙、比利时、欧盟总部、丹麦和俄罗斯。13日，陈新华副部长在丹麦同丹麦外交部助理常务秘书里斯—约恩森进行会谈，就双边经贸合作问题广泛交换意见。16日－18日，陈新华副部长陪同李岚清副总理访问俄罗斯期间参加中俄总经理定期会晤委员会第二次会议及经贸合作分委会第一次会议。

5日 孙振宇副部长会见以社长森下洋一为团长的日本松下电器产业株式会社访华团。双方就进一步加强合作等问题交换意见。

6日 石广生副部长会见荷兰驻华大使伍思德。双方就李鹏总理访问荷兰，以及荷兰经济大臣威伊尔斯访华问题交换意见。

8日—10日 全国对外经济贸易工作会议在北京举行。李鹏总理、吴邦国副总理以及国务委员罗干等接见了全体与会代表；朱镕基副总理到会并作了重要讲话；吴仪部长在开幕大会上作题为“以十五大精神为指针，认清形势克服困难，增强责任感，全面完成各项外经贸任务”的报告。来自全国各省、自治区、直辖市、计划单列市外经贸委（厅、局）和外经贸部各直属单位及国务院有关部委、部分直属部委外经贸公司、自营进出口生产企业、有进出口经营权的科研院所的负责同志共200多人参加会议。

10日 龙永图首席谈判代表会见美国助理贸易代表卡西迪。双方就中国加入世贸组织所存在的关税减让和服务业开放等方面的问题举行会谈。

11日 龙永图首席谈判代表会见日本通产省经济局局长大岛。双方就双边经济合作方面的问题交换看法。

杨文生部长助理会见几内亚总统特使、几计划合作部长马马杜·塞爱·迪亚洛。双方就我国政府援助几内亚总统府附加工程事进行会谈。

高虎城部长助理会见摩根士丹利公司首席经济学家 Stethen S.Roach。双方就东南亚金融危机和中国证券业的发展等方面的问题交换意见。

11日—15日 孙振宇副部长与巴基斯坦外交秘书沙姆沙德·艾哈迈德分别代表各自政府在北京签署我国政府向巴提供5000万元人民币无偿援助的经济技术合作协定。

孙振宇副部长会见美国孟山都公司农业公司副总裁阿诺德·唐纳德（Arnold Donald）。双方就发展在农业方面的合作交换意见。

12日 吴仪部长会见吉尔吉斯斯坦共和国外交部长伊马纳利耶夫，双方就进一步加深和扩大双边经贸合作等问题交换意见。

孙振宇副部长会见新西兰新任驻华大使彼德·亚当斯（Peter Adams）。双方就双边经贸合作现状交换意见。

龙永图首席谈判代表会见联合国人口基金新任驻华代表伯梅斯特。双方就中国与人口基金未来合作事宜进行会谈。

杨文生部长助理与几内亚计划合作部长塞鲁·迪亚洛分别代表各自政府就我国政府在援款项下承担几内亚总统府补充工程事在北京换文确认。

杨文生部长助理会见博茨瓦纳外交部长蒙帕蒂·梅拉费。双方就双边经贸关系中的具体问题交换意见，并分别代表各自政府就我国政府向博茨瓦纳政府提供3000万元人民币无偿援助事换文确认。

安民部长助理会见日本外务省经济合作局审议官西田恒夫，双方就中日环保合作和日元贷款执行率问题交换意见。

安民部长助理出席中国贸促会与巴基斯坦投资局共同在北京召开的中国巴基斯坦经贸投资研讨会。

12日—17日 石广生副部长陪同李鹏总理访问卢森堡、荷兰。

13日 李国华副部长出席朝鲜驻华使馆为金正日56岁诞辰举行的招待会。

16日 吴仪部长与欧盟委员会副主席布里坦，着重就中国加入世贸组织中的服务贸易以及中欧双边经贸关系问题举行正式会谈。会谈结束后，吴部长与布里坦签署中欧村务管理培训、中欧统计合作、中欧公共采购合作三个项目协议，总金额1600万欧币。

吴仪部长会见土耳其外长杰姆及随同来访的企业家代表团一行。双方就加强了解、增进政府间及企业间的交流、扩大经济合作规模、促进双边经贸发展等问题交换意见。

刘山在副部长参加江泽民主席与来访的也门总统萨利赫举行的大组会谈，并分别与也门计划发展部长阿卜杜·高达尔·阿卜杜·拉赫曼·巴杰迈勒和工业部长艾哈迈德·穆罕默德·苏凡代表各自政府签署两国政府经济技术合作协定和两国政府鼓励与相互保护投资协定。

16日 龙永图首席谈判代表出席外经贸部在北京举行的中国与经合组织对话评估会，并发表讲话。

安民部长助理会见台湾学者于宗先、侯家驹及夫人、叶万安、魏蕚等一行。安助理向客人介绍了大陆经济状况，双方并就共同关心的东南亚金融危机及对海峡两岸影响进行探讨。

17日 孙振宇副部长会见美国恒康国际控股公司总裁兼首席执行官徐伟士（Derek Chilvers）。客人表达了在华开展保险业务的愿望。

17日—18日 陈新华副部长陪同李鹏总理参加中俄总理第三次定期会晤。

17日—20日 外经贸部在广西北海召开全国外经贸运输工作会议。刘向东部长助理出席会议并作题为“调动一切积极因素，做好外经贸储运工作”的报告。各省、自治区、直辖市及计划单列市外经贸委的主要负责人或运输处长计99人参加会议。

18日 孙振宇副部长会见莫桑比克外交与合作部长莱昂纳多·桑托斯·西蒙。双方就进一步扩大双边经贸合作交换意见，并签署中国政府向莫桑比克政府提供200万元人民币无偿援助的换文。

孙振宇副部长会见美国康宇公司总裁 Larry Aeillo。客人介绍了在华投资项目情况，孙副部长对该公司来华投资表示赞赏并介绍了我国相关政策和情况。

孙广相部长助理会见新加坡淡马锡集团副总裁

陈福金、陈文隆。孙助理向客人介绍了中新两国经贸发展的进展情况，并正式邀请该集团出席今年9月在厦门举行的中国投资贸易洽谈会。

19日－24日 龙永图首席谈判代表出席在澳大利亚举行的世界经济与多边贸易体制高级研讨会，并就中国经济发展形势和加入世贸组织谈判的情况发表演讲。

20日 吴仪部长会见荷兰新任驻华大使伍思德。伍通报了李鹏总理访问荷兰情况及成都机场项目进展，并谈及荷经济大臣威伊尔斯访华问题。

吴仪部长会见葡萄牙驻华大使卡塔里诺。吴部长就欧盟改变我非市场定论问题向葡方进行交涉，双方还就如何进一步发展双边经贸关系交换意见。

孙广相部长助理会见由外交部、贸工部官员组成的菲律宾官员代表团，双方就发展中菲经贸合作问题交换意见。

23日 吴仪部长会见来访的荷兰经济大臣威伊尔斯。双方就双边经贸关系及有关问题交换意见。会后，吴仪部长会见随同来访的荷兰企业界领导人，向客人介绍了我国经贸形势和投资政策，并回答企业家提问。

安民部长助理会见台湾力霸公司总经理王令楣女士一行。安助理就客人提出拟在长沙投资一事介绍了我吸收外（台）投资的相关政策。

24日 石广生副部长陪同李岚清副总理会见荷兰经济大臣威伊尔斯一行。

刘山在副部长参加江泽民主席与来访的意大利总统的会谈。

孙振宇副部长与荷兰经济大臣威伊尔斯共同出席中荷企业间协议签字仪式。

孙振宇副部长会见加拿大原子能公司总裁瑞德·莫登（Reid Morden）一行。双方就双边核能合作、秦山核电站三期工程进展及加拿大国内坎杜型核电站机组运行的有关问题交换意见。

25日 孙振宇副部长会见马来西亚金狮集团总裁钟廷森等。客人介绍了该集团目前在华投资情况及今后投资计划。孙副部长对其来华投资表示欢迎，并介绍了我国吸引外资的政策。

刘向东部长助理会见爱尔兰外交部长戴维安德鲁斯一行。双方就双边经贸合作问题交换意见。

26日 孙振宇副部长会见美国驻华使馆临时代办麦克海（Mac Cahill）。客人就美贸易副代表费希尔信中所提的美方关心的问题陈述了美方的关注和立场，孙副部长对此进行解释并递交致副代表的复函。

刘山在副部长会见喀麦隆工商发展国务部长贝洛·布巴·马伊加里。双方就双边经济合作等问题进行交谈。27日，双方签署两国政府关于建立杜阿拉经济开发区的备忘录。

27日 吴仪部长会见喀麦隆工商发展国务部长贝洛·布巴·马伊加里。双方就双边经贸合作及中国在喀麦隆建立经济开发区问题交换意见。

孙广相部长助理会见孟加拉新任驻华大使。孙助理首先对大使的到任表示欢迎，双方并就双边经贸合作中存在的具体问题交换意见。

3 月

2日 刘山在副部长会见埃赛俄比亚驻华大使巴莱玛。双方就进一步发展两国经贸关系交换意见。

3日 孙振宇副部长会见美国宝洁公司副总裁威林。威林向孙副部长介绍宝洁公司为延长中国最惠国待遇以及中国加入世贸组织所做的工作，以及该公司与中国企业开展技术合作的情况。

5日 杨文生部长助理会见塞舌尔外交部首席秘书巴耶特一行，双方就中塞经贸关系中的具体问题交换意见。

8日 孙振宇副部长会见来访的德国联邦议会经济合作与发展委员会代表团，并就双边经贸合作等问题交换意见。

9日 吴仪部长会见来访的奥地利副总理兼外长许瑟尔、奥联邦商会主席马德塔那及企业家代表团。双方就发展双边经贸关系和具体合作项目交换意见。

孙振宇副部长与日本驻华大使佐腾嘉恭分别代表各自政府在日本政府第二次无偿援助7.2亿日元用于我国少数民族地区中等学校教育器材装备项目的换文上签字。

安民部长助理会见以香港特别行政区贸易署长黎年先生为团长的香港特区贸易署访京团。双方就发展经贸方面的工作进行会谈。

10日 石广生部长会见美国副贸易代表费希尔，双方就双边经贸关系的有关问题交换意见。

11日 龙永图首席谈判代表与美贸易副代表

费希尔举行会谈。双方就中国1998年加入世贸组织谈判的前景及美方特别关心的关税出价、农产品关税配额，以及服务贸易等问题交换意见，双方同意应加速谈判，为克林顿总统访华解决中国加入WTO问题奠定基础。

13日 杨文生部长助理会见并宴请几内亚渔业畜牧业部长巴里·布巴卡一行。几内亚客人是为即将于5月在几内亚首都科那克里举行的项目招商会来华进行宣传。

孙广相部长助理与朝鲜驻华大使朱昌骏分别代表各自政府签订关于中国供朝鲜部分原油改供柴油的换文。

16日 石广生部长会见香港嘉里建设有限公司联席董事总经理洪敬南先生，双方就嘉里集团对华投资等问题进行商谈。

安民部长助理会见以司徒伟先生为团长的香港印度商会代表团。安助理就内地吸引外资政策、与香港经贸关系的发展等问题与客人交换意见。

19日 刘山在副部长与来访的埃及贸供部第一国务秘书兼驻外商务机构主席哈马迪率领的苏伊士湾西北经济特区技术代表团举行会谈。20日，双方签署会谈纪要。

20日 石广生部长会见法国前总理雷蒙·巴尔及来华参加第四届中法经济研讨会的法国企业家。石部长向客人介绍我国外经贸形势及鼓励外资政策，并就双方共同关心的问题交换意见。

陈新华副部长会见来访的加拿大鲍尔公司总裁兼中加贸易理事会主席德马雷一行。双方就加拿大企业界扩大与在中国贸易投资合作交换意见。

23日 陈新华副部长会见意大利意达太尔电信公司董事长普莱巴尼一行。客人介绍了公司与中国的合资、合作的状况，双方并就如何扩大在华业务交换意见。

陈新华副部长会见瑞士丰泰保险公司公关部经理施乐山先生，并出席该公司向四川省广安县扶贫捐款的协定签字仪式。

陈新华副部长会见以香港贸发局副总裁林天福先生为团长的香港广告业京、沪考察团一行27人，并就两地广告业间加强交流与合作交换意见。

刘向东部长助理会见瑞士荣格集团董事长荣格先生。刘助理向客人介绍我国十五大、九届人大一次会议及外经贸形势，并希望荣格集团积极开展对华合作。

23日—27日 孙振宇副部长和古巴外贸部长布里萨斯在哈瓦那共同主持召开中、古经委混委会第10次会议，并分别代表各自政府签署关于我国向古巴提供5000万元人民币无息贷款、1000万元人民币无偿援助和1亿元人民币优惠贷款的协定。

24日 石广生部长会见加拿大驻华使馆大使贝详。双方就加拿大国贸部长访华事进行商谈。

龙永图首席谈判代表会见澳大利亚外交贸易部副部长哈威特。双方就双边经贸关系中的加入世贸组织、经济合作与援助等问题交换意见。

孙广相部长助理会见美驻华使馆公使麦克海。客人向孙助理提交了美商务部戴利部长致石广生部长的信函，通报了美方三位部长拟相继来访的意向及美将可能对中国纺织品进行三倍扣减的打算。孙助理向客人表明了中方的有关立场。

24日—25日 杨文生部长助理与几内亚外交部长拉明·卡马拉分别代表各自政府就我国向几内亚无偿提供400万元人民币物资援助、无偿提供10万美元现汇财政援助事在北京分别换文确认。

24日—26日 外经贸部在北京召开全国外经贸审计工作会议。会议的主要内容是总结1997年工作、交流经验、研究部署1998年工作。国家审计署金基鹏副审计长、刘山在副部长到会作重要讲话，驻部审计局陈克勤副局长作工作报告和总结讲话。国家出入境检验检疫局、各省（自治区、直辖市）及计划单列市外经贸委（厅、局）和部直属企业分管审计工作的领导以及审计部门负责人共90多人参加会议。

25日 刘山在副部长出席西非国家经济共同体十国驻华大使在科特迪瓦使馆联合举行的午餐会并发表题为"中非经贸合作"的书面讲话。

陈新华副部长会见以拉托维亚外交部第二政治司司长叶德戈尔·斯库亚为团长的来华参加中国—拉托维亚政府经贸混委会第二次会议的拉托维亚代表团。双方就进一步发展双边经贸关系、联合利用欧亚大陆桥开展四国联运、加强两国企业界联系等问题交换意见。

26日 刘山在副部长会见以副社长后藤又三为团长的日本日商岩井株式会社代表团。刘副部长向客人介绍我国新一届政府制定的方针政策，双方并就进一步扩大在华贸易等问题交换意见。

孙广相部长助理会见美国商务部副部长赖因斯。双方就有关出口管制问题交换意见。

27 日 龙永图首席谈判代表分别会见联合国前驻华代表贺尔康和美驻华公使麦克海。

28 日 龙永图首席谈判代表率中国政府代表团赴日内瓦参加中国加入世贸组织工作组第七次会议。会议期间，与美国、欧盟、日本、加拿大、巴西等十几个国家进行双边磋商。

29 日 孙广相部长助理会见加纳贸易投资促进代表团，并在“加纳政府和企业家贸易投资促进报告会”上发表讲话。

30 日 石广生部长和莫桑比克外交与合作部部长莱昂那多·桑托斯·西蒙分别代表各自政府在北京签署关于我国向莫桑比克提供3000万元人民币无偿援助的经济技术合作协定和关于我国向莫桑比克提供1亿元人民币优惠贷款的框架协议，并就我国帮助莫桑比克建设外交部办公楼项目换文确认。

31 日 石广生部长会见法国外贸国务秘书董杜率领的企业家代表团，双方就共同关心的问题交换意见。

刘山在副部长会见并宴请加纳贸易投资促进代表团，双方就进一步加强双边经贸关系交换意见。

刘山在副部长与来访的莫桑比克工业经贸旅游部长巴洛伊举行对口会谈，双方就双边经贸关系等问题交换意见。

陈新华副部长与来访的法国外贸国务秘书董杜进行会谈。双方就双边经贸关系中的主要问题交换意见，并共同出席“中国的改革；中法经贸合作的新跃进”研讨会。

4　月

3 月 15 日－4 月 1 日 孙振宇副部长率政府经贸代表团访问巴西、智利和古巴。18 日，在巴西圣保罗主持’98 中国出口商品展览会开幕式，并拜会圣保罗州副州长阿尔科明。19 日，出席智利中国工商旅游协会揭幕仪式并发表讲话。20 日，与智利代副外长进行工作会谈。25 日，与古巴外贸部长卡布里萨斯共同主持中国古巴经贸混委会第十次会议，并与外资部代部长玛尔塔·洛玛斯进行工作会谈。26 日，拜会古巴国务委员会副主席部长会议执行秘书拉赫。27 日，与古巴外贸部长卡布里萨斯共同签署中国政府向古巴政府提供1000 万元人民币无偿援助、5000 万元人民币无息贷款和 1 亿元人民币贴息贷款的协议及会谈纪要。

3 月 28 日－4 月 2 日 石广生部长会见以贸工部长欧文为团长的南非政府经贸访华代表团。双方就进一步扩大双边经贸合作和交流交换意见并达成广泛共识。

2 日 刘山在副部长会见并宴请以摩洛哥工业、贸易和手工业部秘书长穆萨达克为团长的政府代表团。双方就双边经贸关系交换意见。

3 日 安民部长助理会见日本海外经济协力基金内田富夫理士。双方就日元贷款的有关问题交换意见。

3 月 31 日－4 月 4 日 石广生部长陪同朱镕基总理出访英国，并出席在伦敦举行的第二届亚欧首脑会议。2 日，陪同朱总理出访欧盟并会晤欧盟轮值主席国英国首相布莱尔、欧盟委员会主席桑特等中欧领导人。3 日－4 日，出席在伦敦举行的第二届亚欧会议，并分别会见越南贸易部长张廷延、菲律宾贸工部长鲍蒂斯塔。

5 日－7 日 石广生部长陪同朱镕基总理访问法国。7 日，与法国经济、财政和工业部长斯特劳斯·卡恩进行对口会谈，就双边经贸合作交换意见。

6 日 孙振宇副部长会见美国商务部前助理部长帮办麦肯蒂。双方就美一些公司在华业务及投资计划交换意见。

孙振宇副部长会见澳大利亚驻华大使石励。双方就双边经贸合作及亚洲金融危机等问题交换意见。

孙振宇副部长会见加拿大农业和食品部长范克利夫。双方就两国农业合作有关问题交换意见。

孙振宇副部长会见萨尔瓦多常驻联合国代表里卡多．卡斯达涅达．柯梅霍。双方就发展中国和拉美、中国和萨尔瓦多经贸关系交换意见。

陈新华副部长会见美国耐克公司副总裁何好景。客人通报了该公司在华的业务以及面临的假冒商标问题。陈副部长阐明中方在保护知识产权问题上的原则立场，并鼓励耐克公司继续扩大在华投资。

杨文生部长助理会见孟加拉国驻华大使法鲁克。杨助理就孟方使用我优惠贷款的一些问题阐明意见。

7 日 刘山在副部长会见斯里兰卡驻华大使万德松特。双方就进一步发展双边经贸关系交换意见，并就中国政府经贸代表团访问斯里兰卡等事宜进行交谈。

8 日 石广生部长与坦桑尼亚外交与国际合作部长贾卡亚·姆里绍·基奎特分别代表各自政府在北京签署我国政府向坦桑尼亚政府提供3000万元人民币无偿援助的经济技术合作协定。

石广生部长与桑给巴尔政府总统办公室计划和投资国务部长阿里·珠马·沙穆胡纳分别代表各自政府就我国政府向桑给巴尔政府提供500万元人民币无偿援助事换文确认。

孙振宇副部长会见美国雷曼兄弟公司董事长刘易斯。双方就东南亚金融危机、美国金融机构合并以及雷曼公司与我五矿公司纠纷等问题交换意见。

8 日－10 日 安民部长助理率我部部分司局的有关人员参加在厦门举办的第二届对台出口商品交易会及期间我部召开的全国部分省市对台经贸工作座谈会，并作重要讲话。会后，参观考察厦门、漳州等地的合资企业。

9 日 石广生部长与来访的坦桑尼亚外交与合作部长基奎特举行对口会谈。双方就双边经贸关系中的具体问题交换意见。

石广生部长会见保加利亚贸旅部副部长赫·米哈依洛夫斯基率领的中国保加利亚经贸混委会保方代表团。双方就发展双边经贸关系交换意见。

刘山在副部长在新加坡主持召开驻东南亚经商参赞片会。驻日本、韩国、东盟、柬埔寨等12个国家经济商务参赞（含部分领事）和部有关司局的负责同志出席会议。会议以面对东南亚金融危机，如何采取措施确保今年我国与本地区的经贸合作为中心议题。

孙振宇副部长会见来访的智利农业部长卡洛斯·姆拉迪尼。双方就农产品贸易、WTO、APEC等问题交换意见并强调加强沟通，协调立场，维护切身利益。

3 月 29 日－4 月 10 日 龙永图首席谈判代表率中国代表团赴日内瓦参加世贸组织中国工作组第七次会议，并与美国、欧盟、日本、加拿大、巴西等世贸组织主要成员进行加入世贸组织的双边磋商。

7 日－10 日 中国保加利亚经贸混委会第七届会议在北京举行。7日，孙振宇副部长与保加利亚贸旅部副部长赫·米哈依洛夫斯基共同主持混委会全体会议。10日，双方签署会议议定书。

13 日 石广生部长会见美国商务部副部长阿伦。石部长向客人阐明中方对贸易不平衡问题的态度和立场。

石广生部长会见美国驻华大使尚慕杰。客人就美国总统克林顿访华前美方关心的经贸问题以及美国贸易代表巴舍夫斯基访华提出看法，石部长就中美贸易关系阐述中方观点。

孙振宇副部长与美国商务部副部长阿伦共同主持中美商贸联委会项下第一次副部长级磋商。双方就双边经贸关系中的具体问题交换意见。

高虎城部长助理赴朝鲜驻华使馆参加朝鲜使馆为金日成诞辰86周年举行的宴会。

14 日 高虎城部长助理会见埃及亚历山大企业家代表团。双方就双边经贸关系交换意见。

15 日 李国华副部长与朝鲜驻华大使朱昌骏分别代表各自政府就我国政府向朝鲜政府无偿提供10万吨粮食和2万吨化肥事在北京换文确认。

孙振宇副部长会见以冯国经博士为团长的香港贸发局代表团。孙副部长向客人介绍了东南亚金融危机对内地进出口和利用外资的影响，双方并就共同关心的问题交换意见。

高虎城部长助理会见以会长柴田稔为团长的日本纺织协会第15次访华团。双方就双边经贸关系中的具体问题交换意见。

16 日 龙永图首席谈判代表会见美国驻华公使麦克海。双方就中国加入世贸组织谈判以及中美双边磋商交换意见。

孙广相部长助理会见来访的苏丹能源矿产部长阿瓦德·艾哈迈德·贾兹一行。双方就双边经贸关系交换意见。

高虎城部长助理会见乌兹别克驻华大使阿利莫夫。双方就召开中乌经贸混委会第二次例会问题交换意见。

17 日 石广生部长会见来访的加拿大国际合作部部长玛尔露女士。双方就发展双边援助合作情况交换意见，并签署中国加拿大妇女合作、农村综合发展和扶贫、邮电数据通信培训三个援助项目备忘录。

石广生部长会见泰国副总理兼商业部长素帕猜，并分别代表各自政府签署谅解备忘录。

刘山在副部长与尼泊尔财政部秘书帕特拉依分

别代表各自政府在加德满都签署关于我国政府向尼泊尔政府提供3000万元人民币无偿援助的经济技术合作协定，并就我国向尼（泊尔）中（国）非政府合作论坛尼方委员会提供40万元人民币启动资金事换文确认。

孙振宇副部长会见澳大利亚前总理弗雷泽。双方就亚洲金融危机等问题交换意见。

龙永图首席谈判代表与美国助理贸易代表卡西迪就中国加入世贸组织问题进行非正式磋商，为美国贸易代表巴舍夫斯基访华作准备。

10日－20日 陈新华副部长率中国政府经贸代表团访问吉尔吉斯坦、哈萨克斯坦、土库曼斯坦。10日－13日，率团赴吉尔吉斯坦，与吉尔吉斯坦外长伊马纳科夫共同主持召开中吉经贸混委会第三次例会，并签署会议纪要。13日，会见吉尔吉斯坦总理朱马利耶夫。14日－16日，率团赴哈萨克斯坦，与哈萨克斯坦外长共同主持召开中哈经贸混委会第四次例会，并签署会议纪要。15日，会见哈第一副总理兼国家投资委员会主席江多索夫。17日，在土库曼斯坦会见土贸易部副部长阿塔耶夫及外经部代表。18日，会见土库曼斯坦副总理艾多格德耶夫，就发展中土经贸关系和成立两国政府间经贸混委会问题交换意见。同日，主持召开我驻中亚五国经商参赞片会，研究和部署经贸合作问题。

20日 石广生部长与来访的丹麦发展合作大臣尼尔森举行会谈。双方就恢复两国财政、经贸合作等问题交换意见并签署中国丹麦关于混合贷款安排协议的谅解备忘录。

刘山在副部长与斯里兰卡司法部长兼财政部副部长皮里斯分别代表各自政府在科伦坡签署关于我国政府向斯里兰卡政府提供3000万元人民币无偿援助的经济技术合作协定。

孙广相部长助理会见以斯洛文尼亚经济关系和发展部双边司司长博·施科达率领的中斯经贸混委会斯方代表团。双方就发展双边经贸关系交换意见。

安民部长助理会见香港雇主联合会代表，向客人介绍了有关情况。

杨文生部长助理与吉布提外交和国际合作部部长穆罕默德·穆萨·谢海姆分别代表各自政府在吉布提签署我国向吉布提提供2000万元人民币无偿援助的经济技术合作协定，并就我国援建吉布提外交部办公楼及1991年3月26日中吉两国政府经济技术协定规定的贷款延长使用期事分别换文确认。

21日 石广生部长与来访的乌干达第一副总理兼外长卡特加亚举行会谈。双方就双边经贸关系中的具体问题交换意见并签署中国政府向乌干达政府提供500万元人民币无偿援助的换文。

李国华副部长会见佛得角经济协调部长罗萨里奥。双方就双边经贸合作交换意见并签署中国、佛得角两国投资保护协定。

孙广相部长助理会见芬兰外交部副国务秘书雷夫·法格纳斯及芬兰混委会代表团。双方就东南亚金融危机及我国目前的经济形势交换意见。

21日 杨文生部长助理与吉布提计划、财政和经济部长亚辛·艾尔米·布赫分别代表各自政府在吉布提签署我国援助吉布提55套民用住房项目的交接证书。

22日 石广生部长与土耳其国务部长厄欣·切莱比在北京共同主持中土经贸联委会第十二次会议。

石广生部长与葡萄牙经济部长皮纳·莫拉举行会谈。双方就中葡混委会等双边经贸问题交换意见。

石广生部长会见瑞士苏黎士保险公司董事长兼总裁胡仁夫一行。双方就双边金融保险、东南亚金融危机等问题交换意见。

孙振宇副部长会见英国壳牌集团董事布宏达。双方就壳牌在华业务等问题交换意见。

陈新华副部长参加葡萄牙产品与技术展览会开幕式及中葡经贸研讨会。

龙永图首席谈判代表与陪同美国贸易代表巴舍夫斯基访华的助理贸易代表卡西迪就中国加入世贸组织和双边经贸关系等问题进行会谈。

23日 刘山在副部长与马尔代夫外交部副部长沙拉赫·施哈伯分别代表各自政府在马累签署关于我国政府向马尔代夫政府提供500万元人民币无偿援助的经济技术合作协定。

孙振宇副部长会见美国中国物产公司总裁费普斯。双方就克林顿总统访华以及双边经贸合作中的具体问题交换意见。

孙振宇副部长与赞比亚外交部长瓦卢·比塔分别代表各自政府就我国政府向赞比亚政府提供200万元人民币无偿援助事在北京换文确认。

24日 孙振宇副部长会见几内亚比绍外交合作部长费尔南多·德尔芬·达·席尔瓦。双方就双边经贸合作举行会谈，并签署中国与几内亚比绍政府经济技术合作协定等协议。同日，孙副部长与席尔瓦分别代表各自政府就我国政府向几内亚比绍政府提供3000万元人民币无偿援助事在北京换文确认。

孙振宇副部长会见美国IBM公司副总裁克利斯·克恩。双方就进一步开展电子商务法律等方面合作的问题进行探讨。

刘向东部长助理在广州会见美国商务代表团，介绍我国出口商品交易会发展情况，并陪同参观广州出口商品交易会。

23日－25日 石广生部长会见美国贸易代表巴舍夫斯基。双方就中国加入WTO及其双边经贸关系问题交换意见。

24日 杨文生部长助理与厄立特里亚卫生部长萨勒赫·迈基分别代表各自政府在阿斯马拉签署关于我国向厄立特里亚提供3000万元人民币无偿援助的经济技术合作协定，并就撤销陶瓷厂改建项目和将贷款余额用于为医院项目提供医疗设备事分别换文确认。

25日 龙永图首席谈判代表与美国助理贸易代表卡西迪进行贸易代表巴舍夫斯基访华期间的第二轮双边磋商。

刘向东部长助理在广州会见以经济协调部长罗萨里奥为团长的弗得角经贸代表团。双方就双边经贸合作交换意见，并陪同代表团参观广州出口商品交易会。

27日 石广生部长参加江泽民主席与来访的吉尔吉斯总统之间举行的会谈，并与吉尔吉斯工贸部长阿卜迪卡雷科夫分别代表各自政府签署中吉经贸合作协定、向吉尔吉斯提供1亿元人民币政府贴息优惠贷款的框架协议；与吉尔吉斯外交部长伊马纳利耶夫分别代表各自政府就我国政府向吉尔吉斯政府提供500万元人民币无偿援助事换文确认。

龙永图首席谈判代表会见联合国发展计划署驻朝鲜代表莱梅尔。莱梅尔先生通报了朝鲜近年的受灾、抗灾及国际社会向朝鲜供粮情况，同时邀请中国参加由联合国开发署在日内瓦召开的朝鲜农业恢复问题国际圆桌会议。

龙永图首席谈判代表会见来北京参加第七届德国经济界亚太会议的德国技术合作公司总经理埃森布拉特勒博士。双方就双边技术合作中的有关问题交换意见。

孙广相部长助理会见冰岛混委会代表团。双方就扩大双边经贸合作等问题交换意见。

安民部长助理会见德国安联保险集团董事长舒尔特·诺勒博士。双方就共同关心的问题交换意见。

安民部长助理会见德国复兴银行董事REZCH一行。双方就共同关心的问题交换意见。

安民部长助理会见台湾国民党社会工作会副主任、香港台湾贸易有限公司董事长马爱珍及随行人员。双方就共同关心的问题交换意见。

28日 石广生部长在第七届德国经济亚太会议开幕式上作演讲，并与德国联邦经济部长莱克斯洛特进行对口会谈。

13日－28日 刘山在副部长率政府经贸代表团出访尼泊尔、斯里兰卡和马尔代夫。15日－17日，访问尼泊尔，与尼泊尔财政秘书共同主持召开中国尼泊尔经贸联委会第八次会议。16日，拜会尼泊尔国王比兰德拉、首相柯伊拉腊、财政大臣玛哈特和商业大臣瓦格尔。17日，签署我国政府向尼政府提供3000万元人民币无偿援助的协定。20日，与斯里兰卡副财长皮里斯、商贸部长维克拉马拉特纳分别举行会谈，就进一步扩大双边经贸合作交换意见，并与斯里兰卡副财长皮里斯签署我国政府向斯里兰卡政府提供3000万元人民币无偿援助的协定。21日，会见斯里兰卡总统库马拉通加。23日，会见马尔代夫总统加尧姆，并签署我国政府向马尔代夫政府提供500万元人民币无偿援助的协定。

5 月

4日 石广生部长会见以会长木村一三为团长的日本日中经贸中心访华团。双方就双边经贸合作的具体问题交换意见。

安民部长助理会见台湾东吴大学余德培博士。安助理向客人介绍了大陆的有关对台政策，双方并就保护知识产权、加入WTO以及金融等问题交换意见。

6日 石广生部长会见西班牙外交大臣马图斯特。双方就如何进一步发展中（国）西（班牙）经贸关系、落实李岚清副总理访西时提出的中西合作三年规划建议及共同开发第三国市场等问题交换意见。

陈新华副部长会见塞舌尔副总统米歇尔。双方就鼓励中国企业去塞投资办厂、发展转口分拨业务等问题交换意见。

孙广相副部长会见阿富汗副外长阿卜杜拉。双方就阿富汗当前局势和双边经贸合作等问题交换意见。

7日 石广生部长参加朱镕基总理与来访的哈萨克斯坦总理巴尔金巴耶夫的会谈。

石广生部长会见智利外长何塞·米格尔·因苏尔萨。双方就共同关心的贸易、经济合作和相互投资等问题交换意见。

孙广相部长助理会见韩国汉城论坛代表团一行。双方就双边经贸合作中共同关心的问题交换意见。

8日 石广生部长会见中国哈萨克斯坦经贸合作委员会哈方主席、交通运输部长卡利耶夫一行。双方就进一步发展双边经贸合作的有关问题交换意见。

4日—8日 龙永图首席谈判代表赴青岛出席APEC服务贸易研讨会。

5日—8日 由我部和国家税务总局联合召开的全国税贸协作会议在广州举行。刘山在副部长和国家税务总局程法光副局长主持会议并分别在大会上讲话。会议的主题是：研究加强出口退税工作、完善出口退税办法的具体措施，加快退税进度，缓解和化解亚洲金融危机的负面影响，确保出口的稳定增长。各省、自治区、直辖市及计划单列市外经贸委（厅、局）和国家税务总局、中央有关部门及部门企业代表约150人参加会议。

11日 石广生部长会见瑞典工贸大臣松德斯特伦一行。双方就双边经贸关系中共同关心的有关问题交换意见。

刘山在副部长和埃塞俄比亚贸易和工业部长卡萨洪·阿耶勒分别代表各自政府就我国向埃塞俄比亚提供500万元人民币无偿援助事在北京换文确认。

孙振宇副部长会见爱沙尼亚外长伊尔维斯。双方就双边经贸合作的有关问题交换意见。

孙振宇副部长会见帕劳共和国国务部长萨比诺·阿纳斯塔西奥一行。双方就推动双边经贸合作有关问题交换意见，并分别代表各自政府签署我国向帕劳提供100万元人民币无偿援助和资助帕劳举办密克罗尼西亚运动会的换文。

12日 石广生部长会见保加利亚贸易旅游部长瓦西列夫。双方就双边经贸关系的有关问题交换意见。

13日 孙广相副部长会见利比亚副外长穆吉贝尔一行。双方就加强经贸合作等问题交换意见。

14日 高虎城部长助理会见马其顿经济部常务副部长佩特罗舍夫斯基，并出席“科佳”电站合同签字仪式。

15日 孙振宇副部长会见美国波音中国公司新任总裁博睿。双方就波音公司进一步发展对华业务交换意见。

高虎城部长助理会见法国标致—雪铁龙公司总裁福尔兹一行。双方就双边经贸合作及中法合资神龙汽车项目的有关情况交换意见。

高虎城部长助理会见波兰铜业公司董事长谢维斯基一行。双方就进一步扩大双边的经贸合作、促进贸易的平稳发展交换意见。

18日 石广生部长会见卢森堡经济大臣戈贝尔斯。双方就双边经贸关系、亚洲金融危机、欧元启动等共同关心的问题交换意见。

孙振宇副部长与苏里南外交部长斯奈德斯分别代表各自政府在北京签署关于我向苏里南提供1亿元人民币优惠贷款的框架协议，并就我国向苏里南提供500万元人民币无偿援助事和我国同意承担援助苏里南低造价住房项目可行性考察事分别换文确认。

19日 石广生部长会见美国全美保险集团公司总裁兼首席执行官顾史克。双方就我国金融保险市场开放 及东南亚金融危机对我国的影响交换意见。

20日 孙振宇副部长会见日本外务审议官原口幸市。客人通报了此次八国集团首脑会议的有关亚洲金融危机、中国加入世贸组织等问题。孙副部长对以上问题表明看法，双方并就双边服务贸易谈判问题交换意见。

18日—20日 龙永图首席谈判代表率团出席在日内瓦举行的世贸组织第二届部长会议和多边贸易体制50周年庆祝大会。

8日—20日 安民部长助理率团访问芬兰、瑞典和西班牙。11日，拜会芬兰财政部长斯基马坦、并会见北欧投资银行高级副行长丁斯坦，13日，会见瑞典外交部国务秘书克劳森，18日，会见西班牙经济财政部国务秘书费尔南德斯，并代表各自政府就沈阳机场项目、四川农村电话项目和沪宁高速公路交通控制项目签署政府间贷款协议。

20日－22日 杨文生部长助理出席在安徽召开的落实优惠贷款项目座谈会，并做重要讲话。

25日 石广生部长会见马来西亚初级产品工业部长林敬益。双方就双边经贸合作中的具体问题交换意见。

孙振宇副部长会见由德克萨斯州众议员欧蒂斯率领的美国众院访华团。孙副部长应邀向客人介绍了中国改革开放的成绩和经验。

孙振宇副部长和委内瑞拉副外长卡洛斯·比维罗在北京共同主持中委第三届经贸混委会开幕式。双方并就双边经贸关系的发展情况和进一步促进经贸合作等问题交换意见。

陈新华副部长出席德国安联保险集团为我部系统举办的企业经营管理模式介绍会开幕式并发言。

张祥副部长会见英国商联保险公司副总裁托尼·怀恩特一行。双方就我外资政策、服务业开放等问题交换意见。

何晓卫部长助理会见斯威士兰亲王马希塞拉一行。双方就在一般贸易、合资经营、承包劳务、资源开发等领域加强合作交换意见。

26日 陈新华副部长参加朱镕基总理与来访的以色列总理内塔尼亚胡举行的大组会谈。

张祥副部长会见瑞典爱立信集团公司董事长阮魁森博士和总裁兼首席执行官倪尔升一行。双方就双边经贸合作的有关问题交换意见。

张祥副部长会见丹麦A.P.穆勒集团总裁索登伯格。双方就双边经贸关系的具体问题交换意见。

安民部长助理会见以林树哲先生为团长的香港泉州同乡总会访京团。双方就共同关心的问题交换意见。

28日 张祥副部长会见德国经济亚太委员会中国工作组主席赫劳约斯。双方就共同关心的问题交换意见。

张祥副部长会见美国福特汽车公司董事长乔德曼。双方就福特公司进一步扩大在华投资交换意见。

18日－28日 孙广相副部长率中国政府经贸代表团访问毛里塔尼亚、尼日尔、马里。

18日－20日，访问毛里塔尼亚。毛里塔尼亚总统、总理分别会见代表团。18日，孙副部长与毛里塔尼亚外交合作部长穆罕默德·埃尔·哈桑·乌尔德·勒巴特分别代表各自政府在努瓦克肖特签署我国向毛里塔尼亚提供3000万元人民币无偿援助的经济技术合作协定，并出席我国援助毛里塔尼亚总统府办公楼的奠基仪式。21日－23日，访问尼日尔。尼日尔总统、总理分别会见代表团。21日，孙副部长与尼日尔外交和非洲一体化部长玛芒·桑博·西迪库分别代表各自政府在尼亚美签署关于我国向尼日尔提供1500万元人民币无偿援助的经济技术合作协定和我国向尼日尔提供5000万元人民币优惠贷款的框架协议。26日－28日，访问马里。马里总统、总理分别会见代表团。27日，孙副部长与马里外长西迪贝签署我国向马里提供2000万元人民币无偿援助的协定。

29日 刘山在副部长会见伊拉克总统特使、石油部长拉希德将军。双方着重就石油换食品协定、合作开发油田、召开第十届经贸混委会等事宜交换意见。

6 月

1日 张祥副部长会见英国电讯公司董事会主席埃恩·瓦伦斯爵士一行。双方就中英两国电信业的发展和中国电信业开放等问题交换意见。

2日 石广生部长会见津巴布韦国务部长姆西帕率领的贸易投资旅游代表团。双方就双边经贸合作关系交换意见。

石广生部长会见欧盟委员会驻华代表团大使魏根深、比利时驻华大使马利国和奥地利驻华大使齐格勒，向客人通报他出访奥地利、比利时、欧盟的背景及拟达到的目标。

刘山在副部长、高虎城部长助理主持部出口领导小组第六次会议。

陈新华副部长会见日本日中经济协会丸山元喜专务理事。双方就双边加强合作、面对亚洲金融危机的挑战、新世纪提出的一系列新问题以及半官方组织合作问题交换意见。

2日－5日 安民部长助理率团赴香港参加我部举办的“香港’98中国投资贸易洽谈会暨政策研讨会”。安助理在港期间，分别会见香港特别行政区政府工商局局长周德熙、香港中华厂商会和香港总商会等商会的香港有关知名人士，双方就发展内地与香港的经济关系交换意见。安助理还就亚洲金融危机及中国对外经济贸易的最新发展发表演说。

3日 孙广相副部长出席津巴布韦贸易投资旅

游研讨会开幕式并就中津贸易投资关系问题做专题演讲。

3日－12日 石广生部长率中国政府经贸代表团访问奥地利、比利时和欧盟总部。4日，石部长会见奥国民议会议长菲舍尔；同奥经济部长举行正式会谈，并会见奥联邦商会主席马德塔纳及60多位奥企业家代表。5日，石部长会见奥生产和开发设计特种车辆SDP公司董事长考赫，并参观优斯特公司。8日，石部长与比利时副首相兼财政外贸大臣梅斯达德举行会谈，双方就中比、中欧经贸关系的发展以及东南亚金融危机交换意见并共同签署1998年比利时向中国提供2亿比郎的政府贷款协议。9日，石部长与欧盟委员会副主席布里坦一起出席“’98中欧经贸洽谈会”开幕式，并就我国宏观经济形势和外经贸发展发表演讲；石部长前往比利时王宫拜会比利时王储兼比利时外贸局名誉主席菲利普亲王，并在首相官邸拜会比利时首相阿纳，还分别会见比利时瓦隆大区首席大臣科利尼翁、弗拉芒大区首席大臣范登布兰德和布鲁塞尔首都大区外贸大臣格里普；11日，石部长与布里坦共同主持中欧第十六届混委会，双方就双边经贸关系的发展及存在的问题、东南亚金融危机、欧元等问题交换意见，并签署《中欧金融领域合作谅解备忘录》以及辽宁综合环保、中欧环境管理合作、西藏白朗农业综合开发和职业培训等四个项目的财政协议。

5日 陈新华副部长会见韩国对外经济政策研究院代院长洪裕洙一行。双方就韩国金融危机及双方经贸关系交换意见。

8日 孙振宇副部长会见来访的加拿大曼尼托巴省副省长詹姆斯·道尼（James Downey）及其所率企业家代表团。孙副部长介绍当前中国经济形势及中加经贸合作的有关情况，双方就加强在能源、农业、教育和贸易等领域的互利合作交换意见。

安民部长助理会见台湾远东集团董事长徐旭东一行。安助理回答客人关心的问题并鼓励远东集团扩大在大陆的投资。

8日－28日 杨文生部长助理出访乌克兰、阿塞拜疆和塔吉克斯坦三国。12日，杨助理与乌克兰对外经济联络和贸易部副部长奥列依尼克分别代表各自政府就我国向乌克兰提供500万元人民币无偿援助事在基辅换文确认；18日，杨助理与阿塞拜疆第一副总理阿巴索夫分别代表各自政府在巴库签署我向阿塞拜疆提供6000万元人民币优惠贷款的框架协议，并就我向阿塞拜疆提供300万元人民币无偿援助事换文确认；23日，杨文生部长助理与塔吉克斯坦经济和经济联络部长乌斯曼分别代表各自政府在杜尚别签署我向塔吉克斯坦提供1亿元人民币优惠贷款的框架协议。同日，杨助理还与塔吉克斯坦国家合同贸易委员会副主席纳日米金诺夫分别代表各自政府就我国向塔吉克斯坦提供500万元人民币无偿援助事在杜尚别换文确认。

9日 孙振宇副部长会见智利农业部副部长让·雅克·杜哈特（Jean Jacques Duhart）一行。双方就双边经贸关系、农产品贸易、中国入世等问题交换意见。孙副部长还简要介绍中方对亚洲金融危机的看法及目前在吸引外资方面所面临的形势。

陈新华副部长会见朝鲜对外经济委员会李成禄副委员长。双方就双边经贸关系问题交换意见。

龙永图首席谈判代表会见乌拉圭驻日内瓦大使。双方就中国入世问题进行磋商。

张祥副部长参加江泽民主席与意大利总统路易奇·斯卡尔法罗的会谈，并出席欢迎宴会。

马秀红部长助理约见德国工商会北京代办处代表金德乐先生，介绍第二届厦门投资贸易洽谈会的筹备情况，希望其多向德国企业介绍宣传此次洽谈会。

10日 安民部长助理会见以夏迪为团长的香港欧盟商会代表团。双方就回归后香港的发展及欧盟对华反倾销等问题交换意见。

安民部长助理会见萨秉达主席率领的香港总商会高级代表团。双方就中国加入WTO谈判进程和内地对外商开放服务业领域的情况交换意见。

15日 孙振宇副部长会见立陶宛副外长别尔诺斯塔。双方就两国经贸合作的有关问题交换意见。

15日－27日 石广生部长率中国代表团就中国加入WTO问题与美国代表团在北京进行磋商。

16日 龙永图首席谈判代表会见日本新任驻华大使谷野作太郎。双方就日本对华无偿援助事交换意见。

张祥副部长会见南联盟塞尔维亚共和国矿业能源部部长乔希奇。双方就发展双边经贸关系等问题交换意见。

17日 石广生部长会见英国渣打银行集团董事会主席祈泽林一行，双方就亚洲的经济、金融形势，中国的外贸发展等问题交换意见。

孙振宇副部长会见俄罗斯联合银行行长兼董事长普罗霍洛夫一行，双方就中俄银行界合作情况及双边经贸领域的有关问题交换意见。

18日 石广生部长会见挪威工贸部国务秘书伯格女士。石部长介绍我国企业改革情况及我加入WTO进程。

19日 张祥副部长和挪威工贸部国务秘书伯格女士共同主持中挪第13次混委会。双方就如何扩大经贸合作交换意见。

22日 高虎城部长助理会见印尼亚太资源集团主席陈江河一行。高助理简要介绍中国吸引外资情况、政策及对亚洲经济前景的看法。

何晓卫部长助理会见刘道贯主席率领的香港顾问工程师协会代表团。

22日—23日 龙永图首席谈判代表率中国代表团赴马来西亚古晋参加APEC贸易部长会议。会议就进一步推进APEC贸易投资自由化、便利化及APEC与WTO等议题进行讨论。

23日 石广生部长与布隆迪对外关系和合作部部长塞弗兰·恩塔翁维基耶分别代表各自政府就我向布隆迪提供200万元人民币人道主义物资援助事在北京换文确认。双方还就双边经贸关系问题交换意见。

何晓卫部长助理会见埃及社会发展基金会秘书长侯塞因·贾迈勒一行。双方就发展我部与基金会的关系交换意见。

24日 我部召开传达中共中央对台工作会议精神大会，安民部长助理到会做重要讲话。

26日 孙振宇副部长会见韩国轮胎社长曹忠焕。双方就韩国轮胎扩大在华投资问题交换意见。

27日 刘山在副部长会见罗马尼亚经贸咨询公司总裁莫古良努，表示积极支持罗经贸咨询公司同中方有关企业的经贸合作。

30日 张祥副部长会见克罗地亚驻华大使斯特雷尼亚。双方就进一步发展两国经贸关系交换意见。斯特雷尼亚大使再次邀请石广生部长和张祥副部长访问克罗地亚。

7　月

1日 何晓卫部长助理会见法国国际咨询公司副总裁考尼克一行。

2日 孙振宇副部长会见加拿大宏利保险公司副总裁业荣达（Victor Apps）一行。双方就中加保险合作项目、中国保险市场对外开放等问题交换意见。

3日 孙振宇副部长会见美国外交政策协会主席保罗福特（Paul Ford）一行。双方就中美经贸关系及纽约外资洽谈会事宜交换意见。

3日—11日 孙振宇副部长率团访问新西兰和澳大利亚。在新期间，孙副部长与新外交贸易部副秘书长比斯利（Alastair Bisley）共同主持第20次中新经贸联委会，会后拜会新国贸部长史密斯（Lockwood Smith）；在澳期间，孙副部长与澳大利亚外交贸易部秘书长卡尔弗特（Ashton Calvert）共同主持中澳经济联委会中期磋商，拜会澳贸易部长议会秘书长布朗希尔参议员（Senator David Brownhill）和澳副总理兼贸易部长费希尔（Tim Fischer），在悉尼主持召开中国驻南太主要国家经商处室负责人片会。

6日 石广生部长会见英国副首相普雷斯科特一行。双方就双边经贸合作及欧盟对华商品市场开放等问题交换意见。

7日 龙永图首席谈判代表赴天津出席中日无偿资金合作“天津代谢病防治中心”项目的开业典礼。

8日 龙永图首席谈判代表会见香港立法会议员、香港贸发局理事黄宜弘博士率领的“京港服务贸易合作研讨会”港方代表，双方就内地服务业的发展与开放、内地与香港加强服务业合作等问题交换意见。

10日 孙振宇副部长会见美国前总统安全事务助理斯考克罗夫特（Scowcroft）。双方就洛阳春都火腿肠项目交换意见。

13日 石广生部长与巴勒斯坦总统府秘书长塔伊卜·阿卜杜·拉海姆分别代表各自政府在北京签署我向巴勒斯坦提供1000万元人民币无偿援助的两国经济技术合作协定。

高虎城部长助理出席安联保险集团为我部直属企业负责人举办的第三期企业经营管理模拟培训班开幕式并致辞。

14日 石广生部长分别参加江主席、朱总理与俄罗斯联邦总理基里延科的会见。

孙振宇副部长会见美国泰森食品公司(Tyson Food)总裁约翰·泰森(John Tyson)。双方就泰森在华投资、开展合作事交换意见。

孙振宇副部长会见洛阳春都火腿肠美投资方Tudor公司总裁道尔顿(Dalton),双方就投资纠纷问题交换意见。

孙振宇副部长会见美国、加拿大记者代表团。孙副部长介绍中国经济发展和中美经贸关系发展情况并回答记者提出的有关问题。

孙振宇副部长出席在澳大利亚驻华使馆举行的中澳技术合作公共部门能力建设项目启动会。孙副部长代表中国政府签署项目备忘录。

张祥副部长会见欧盟委员会驻华代表团魏根深大使。双方就恢复我鸡肉对欧出口、海运、知识产权、欧元等问题进行会谈。

张祥副部长会见轩尼诗集团总裁纳瓦尔,并就我酒类进口关税问题作解释。

14日－24日 龙永图首席谈判代表率中国代表团赴日内瓦出席中国工作组第八次会议,并与18个WTO成员国代表就市场准入问题进行双边磋商。

15日 张祥副部长与日本驻华大使谷野作太郎分别代表双方政府在北京签署中日无偿资金合作“中国营造汉江上游水土保护林器材装备”项目的政府换文。

张祥副部长会见来访的瑞士人寿保险和养老金公司代表团。张副部长介绍中国的保险市场,并就中瑞在金融、保险领域开展合作等问题与客人交换意见。

何晓卫部长助理与布隆迪驻华大使恩迪古马根格·热尔韦分别代表各自政府就我向布无偿提供气象设备事在北京换文确认。

15日－17日 孙振宇副部长会见经合组织副秘书长重原久美春一行。

16日 孙振宇副部长会见美国哥伦比亚广播公司董事长乔丹(Michael Jordan,原西屋公司董事长)。乔丹介绍西屋公司重组情况,孙副部长表示西屋公司重组不会影响同中国的合作关系。

17日 石广生部长主持召开1998年第三次部长办公会议。会议讨论建立机关职工养老保险有关问题、修改后的《出口商品配额招标办法》及《出口商品配额招标办法实施细则》。

孙广相副部长会见来华参加中国—阿尔及利亚政治磋商的阿外交部部长级代表穆萨维。

孙广相副部长会见摩洛哥新任驻华大使米蒙·迈赫迪,双方就加强两国贸易、投资和技术合作交换意见。

孙广相副部长会见赞比亚驻华大使并简要介绍出访赞比亚的目的。

张祥副部长出席由中国改革开放论坛、欧盟货币统一协会和中国国际经济技术交流中心联合举办的“欧元启动及对中国经济的影响”报告会开幕式并致辞。

马秀红部长助理出席联合国儿童基金发起的“为儿童捐一美元”活动。

22日 石广生部长、孙振宇副部长、高虎城部长助理主持召开出口领导小组第七次会议。与会各单位汇报本单位上半年在扩大出口和利用外资方面所做的主要工作和下半年的打算。石部长对下半年工作提出具体要求。

张祥副部长会见法国总理外事顾问里佩尔,双方就中法经贸合作中共同关心的问题,尤其就今年9月法总理若斯潘访华经贸方面的准备工作交换意见。

22日－24日 张祥副部长在北京出席APEC贸易与环境问题国际研讨会。

23日 孙振宇副部长会见美国进出口银行董事长兼行长哈蒙(James Harmon)。双方就美进出口银行如何进一步对华提供贷款问题交换意见。

23日－24日 中乌(克兰)经贸混委会第四次会议在北京举行。会议由张祥副部长与乌对外经济联络和贸易部副部长奥列依尼克主持。双方就进一步发展中乌经贸合作等问题深入交换意见。

23日－31日 以外经贸部孙广相副部长为团长、财政部李延龄副部长为副团长的中国政府经贸代表团对肯尼亚、赞比亚和津巴布韦三国进行友好访问。23日－25日,访问肯尼亚。23日,孙副部长与肯财政部部长尼亚切分别代表各自政府在内罗毕签署我向肯提供3500万元人民币无息贷款的经济技术合作协定,并就我承担基玛——恩姆苏茨威公路建设项目和向肯提供1000万元人民币无偿援助用于维修肯莫伊国际体育中心事分别在内罗毕换文确认;27日－28日,访问赞比亚。孙副部长与赞财政部副部长分别代表各自政府在卢萨卡签署我向赞提供2000万元人民币无偿援助的经济技术合作协定，并就我为赞6省安装调频发射机的可行性考察事换文确认；30日－31日，访问津巴布韦。31日，孙广相副部长与津巴布韦财政部副部长穆·奇纳玛萨分别代表各自政府在哈拉雷签署我向津提供2亿元人民币优惠贷款的框架协议、我向津提供500万元人民币无偿援助弥补瓦利水坝灌溉项目费用超支的换文和我向津提供500万元人民币无偿援助用于实施双方商定的项目或提供一般物资的换文。

24日 孙振宇副部长会见美国蒙山都公司副董事长鲍勃·德尔夫斯（Bob Delfs）。双方就该公司对华开展合作事宜交换看法。

安民部长助理会见台湾朋友沈秉康先生。安助理对沈先生关心和积极推动两岸贸易表示赞赏，并介绍两岸贸易的有关情况。

马秀红部长助理会见德国赫斯特公司董事韦哲豪，向客人介绍今年9月在厦门举行的“中国投资洽谈会”的情况、东南亚金融危机对我国外贸出口和吸引外资所产生的影响和我国所采取的措施。

27日 孙振宇副部长会见来访的意大利贝萨罗省省督迪巴利率领的贝萨罗省商会代表团一行。双方就进一步加强两国企业的联系等问题交换意见。

龙永图首席谈判代表参加上海中欧管理学院组织召开的市场竞争国际研讨会。

28日 石广生部长主持召开1998年第四次部长办公会议。会议讨论关于咨询公司代表我部所持国贸中心股份的转移问题。

29日 石广生部长会见法国农业部长勒邦塞克一行。双方就经贸领域合作交换意见。石部长就欧盟对我农产品设限问题进行严正交涉。

孙振宇副部长会见西班牙蒙德拉贡集团总裁坎塞洛，听取该集团在华开展业务情况。

30日－31日 龙永图首席谈判代表参加我部举办的“亚欧会议经贸合作政策研讨会”并作重要讲话。

8　月

7月26日－8月17日 张祥副部长率政府经贸代表团访问乌拉圭、巴拿马和墨西哥三国。期间，与乌政府探讨中乌羊毛贸易中存在的问题，考察巴拿马贸易中心运营情况并主持中墨第十次经贸混委会。

3日 何晓卫部长助理出席并主持“中国—非洲经济官员研修班”开学典礼。吴仪国务委员、石广生部长到会并讲话。

4日 龙永图首席谈判代表会见以日立制作所株式会社社长金井务为团长的日本日立集团访华团。龙首席谈判代表介绍我国今后外资政策和加入世贸组织后在分销等服务贸易领域放宽限制的有关政策。金井社长表示今后将大力发展高新技术、环保等领域的对华投资合作，为中日经贸合作的发展继续作出努力。

4日－7日 利比亚工矿部长助理阿里·法利斯·阿维德率团参加在北京召开的中利混委会跟踪委员会会议。期间，刘山在副部长、何晓卫部长助理分别会见利比亚客人，双方详细商讨上届混委会会议纪要落实情况和下届混委会准备情况。

6日 杨文生部长助理会见澳大利亚北部地区交通、铁道、港口部长库尔塔（Barry Coulter）一行，双方就两国经贸合作以及我机械进出口（集团）有限公司参与澳亚铁路项目投标等议题交换意见。

7日 石广生部长主持召开1998年第五次部长办公会议。会议研究双边经贸关系问题和子弟学校借款问题。

石广生部长会见伊朗驻华大使马拉耶克。双方就发展中国家经济发展、中伊经贸合作、核领域项目及中伊经贸联委会等问题广泛交换意见。

石广生部长会见巴基斯坦驻华大使依·哈克先生。哈克大使表达进一步发展双边贸易的愿望并重点提出第11届中巴经贸联委会召开时间的问题。石部长回答哈克大使的问题并表达邀请巴财长访华的愿望。

石广生部长会见新西兰驻华大使安德岩（Perer Adams）。双方就近期中新关系、双边经贸关系及中国加入WTO问题交换意见。

石广生部长会见埃及驻华大使贾拉勒博士。双方就进一步加强两国经贸关系交换意见。

石广生部长会见津巴布韦驻华大使塔瓦亚先生，双方就中津经贸关系和中非关系交换意见。

孙振宇副部长参加中国政府与联合国儿童基金联合在北京举行的本周期合作方案中期审评会议。孙副部长在开幕式上致词。

8日 张祥副部长作为我国政府特使参加哥伦

比亚新总统就职仪式。

10日 张祥副部长作为我国政府特使参加厄瓜多尔新总统就职仪式。

11日 孙广相副部长会见日本住金物产株式会社社长几佐田隆二一行。双方就亚洲金融危机、日元贬值、中国经济运行等问题交换意见。

12日 何晓卫部长助理会见并宴请塞舌尔土地应用和住宅部长艾尔奈斯达夫妇。双方就促进两国经贸合作等问题交换意见。

14日 孙振宇副部长会见美国内布拉斯加州州长本杰明·纳尔森（Benjamin Nelson）一行。双方就双边经贸合作问题交换意见。

17日 何晓卫部长助理与吉布提驻华大使拉沙德·法拉赫分别代表各自政府就我向吉提供200万元人民币无偿援助事在北京换文确认。

18日 孙广相副部长会见日本宝酒造株式会社社长大宫久一行。孙副部长听取客人介绍企业基本情况、业务动态及与中国的经贸合作，表示欢迎其在北京合资设厂。

19日 石广生部长主持召开1998年第六次部长办公会议。会议听取部机关后勤工作并研究有关问题。

杨文生部长助理宴请以色列建筑承包商访华团。杨助理介绍我国对外开展经济合作的情况并表达我进一步扩大与以色列合作的愿望。

20日 石广生部长会见日本新任驻华大使谷野作太郎。石部长表示希望早日就WTO问题、亚洲金融危机问题及双边经贸合作等问题与日本通产大臣举行对口会谈。谷野表示日方希望在江主席访日期间，两国首脑就共同努力推动中国在2000年前加入WTO发表声明。谷野建议在江主席访日前举行中日高层经济磋商，就日元、人民币走势等问题坦率交换意见。

石广生部长会见韩国新任驻华大使全丙铉，双方就中韩经贸关系和东南亚金融危机交换意见。

刘山在副部长会见韩国新任驻华大使全丙铉，双方就刘副部长率中国政府经贸代表团访问韩国的有关事宜交换意见。

21日 何晓卫部长助理会见由科特迪瓦总理府办公室副主任尼亚尔·卡巴女士和科驻华大使科南·科拉莫率领的代表团一行。双方就促进两国经贸合作等问题交换意见。

24日—28日 改革开放以来第一部集中反映我国外经贸事业发展的大型电视专题片《走向世界的历程》制作完成，并在中央电视台黄金时段连续播出。社会各界对此反响热烈。

本片由外经贸部国际贸易经济合作研究院和中央电视台合作完成，是外经贸调研与电视报道相结合的一次创新性尝试，也是新中国成立以来外经贸系统第一次大规模的、成系列的电视宣传报道活动。

25日 石广生部长陪同李岚清副总理会见法国经济财政和工业部长多米尼克·斯特劳斯—卡恩，双方就进一步发展两国经贸合作进行交谈。同日，石部长与卡恩部长举行对口会谈。双方就中法经贸关系中共同关心的问题，尤其是为9月法国总理若斯潘来访在经贸方面的准备工作交换意见。石部长还就欧盟对我出口设限问题与法方进行交涉。

孙广相副部长会见马里财政部长苏马亚·西塞一行。马财长此次访华旨在邀请中国参加将于9月上旬在日内瓦举行的为马里寻求国际援助的圆桌会议。

孙广相副部长会见阿尔及利亚驻华大使阿明·赫尔比。双方就进一步推动两国经贸合作交流交换意见。大使先生表达阿方希望孙副部长于今年访阿的强烈愿望。

26日 孙振宇副部长会见加拿大驻华大使贝祥（Edward Balloch）。双方就国内形势、双边经贸关系以及加企业在华投资的有关问题交换意见。

26日—30日 刘山在副部长率中国政府经贸代表团访问韩国，就我向韩提供专项信贷、扩大对韩粮食出口事与韩方进行协商。

27日 石广生部长会见以日中经济协会名誉会长今井敬为最高顾问、会长渡里杉一郎为团长的1998年度日中经济协会大型访华团。石部长对日方所关心的当前中国经济情况及东南亚金融危机中我外经贸采取的措施进行说明。日方介绍当前日本国内恢复经济的情况并对我部分地区发生严重水灾表示慰问。

龙永图首席谈判代表会见德国工业联合会干事冯·瓦腾贝格，向客人介绍我国经济形势、我国政府为保持人民币稳定、促进经济持续快速增长所采取的政策措施及我入世的有关情况。

安民部长助理会见台湾统派学者王小波，双方就台湾当局的大陆政策、亚洲金融危机对祖国大陆经济的影响及两岸经贸交流等议题交换看法。

安民部长助理会见台湾鹏发股份有限公司洪迈德先生，双方就促成台湾电力公司购买大陆煤炭签订长约事交换意见。

何晓卫部长助理会见卢旺达驻华大使鲁加巴·西拉斯，双方就双边经贸合作等问题交换意见。

28日 龙永图首席谈判代表会见美国白宫国家安全事务委员会亚太事务高级主任李侃如（Kenneth Lieberthal）一行。双方就中国入世问题交换意见。

孙广相副部长会见由新任社长吉野浩行、前任社长川本信彦率领的日本本田技研株式会社访华代表团。

31日 石广生部长参加江主席与土库曼斯坦总统尼亚佐夫的会谈。石部长代表我国政府与土政府萨尔贾耶夫副总理签署《中土关于成立政府间经贸合作委员会的协定》，与土政府库尔班穆拉托夫副总理签署《中土政府关于中国向土库曼斯坦提供优惠贷款的框架协定》、《中国政府向土库曼斯坦政府提供无偿援助的换文》。

孙振宇副部长会见加拿大永明人寿保险公司高级副总裁依夫·兰诺威（Yves Laneuville）。双方就该公司在华业务拓展计划、中国保险市场开放、互助基金开放等问题交换意见。

孙振宇副部长会见加拿大亚太国务部长陈卓愉（Raymond Chan）及所率企业家代表团，双方就发展中加经贸合作关系问题进行探讨。

9　月

8月31日－9月2日 刘山在副部长率中国政府经贸代表团访问菲律宾。期间，刘副部长同菲贸工部部长帕多（Jose Trinidad Pardo）、副部长维拉佛黛女士举行会谈，还拜会菲总统约瑟夫·E·埃斯特拉达（Josephejercito Estarada）、副总统阿罗育女士（Gloria Magapagal Arroyo）、外长西亚松（Domingol. Siazon Jr）。9月1日刘副部长主持中技（菲律宾）机电产品有限公司开业典礼。

8月31日－9月5日 张祥副部长赴俄罗斯参加“’98中国商品展览会”。9月1日，张副部长检查布展工作，并分别拜会俄工贸部代副部长卡拉斯金和俄工商会副主席切斯诺科夫，双方互相通报当前各自的经济形势并就进一步发展双边经贸关系交换意见；9月2日，张副部长出席展览会开幕式和开幕酒会；9月3日，张副部长主持召开驻莫斯科中资企业座谈会，听取企业工作汇报，介绍国内经济发展及外经贸情况并对办好海外企业提出要求。

1日 部党组全体成员出席外经贸部机构改革及定岗分流培训动员大会。石部长作动员报告。

3日 孙振宇副部长会见美国农业部助理部长邓恩。美方向孙副部长通报美国即将对中国输美产品木质包装材料实施新的检疫规定一事。

杨文生部长助理与巴哈马外交部长珍尼特·博斯特威克分别代表各自政府就我向巴提供200万元人民币无偿援助事在拿骚换文确认。

4日 孙振宇副部长会见并宴请古巴商会会长萨尔萨曼蒂（Salsamendi）一行。双方就中古经贸关系的发展，特别是商会组织在推动双边经贸合作中发挥作用等问题交换看法。

孙振宇副部长会见美国中华团体工商联合会回国经贸考察团。孙副部长向对方介绍中国当前经济发展形势以及利用外资的有关情况。

孙广相副部长出席1998年威海中韩经贸工作研讨会并作重要讲话。

安民部长助理会见台湾奇美公司许春华副总经理。安助理对奇美公司通过外经贸部向灾区捐款100万港币表示感谢。

7日 石广生部长在厦门会见应邀参加’98投资贸易洽谈会的科威特工业总局副局长优素夫·巴哈尔一行。石部长感谢巴哈尔副局长率团出席此次洽谈会并就中科经贸领域的合作与科方交换意见。

刘山在副部长赴朝鲜驻华使馆参加朝方为庆祝朝鲜建国50周年而举行的宴会。

8日 孙振宇副部长会见即将卸任回国的古巴驻华使馆商务参赞佩尼亚维尔（Penalver）。

8日－23日 张祥副部长随吴邦国副总理访问委内瑞拉、秘鲁、哥伦比亚和阿根廷等拉美四国。期间，张副部长分别与有关国家的外经贸主管部门负责人进行对口会谈，并代表中国政府签署向秘鲁政府提供500万元人民币无偿援助的换文和向哥伦比亚政府提供500万元人民币无偿援助的换文。

10日 受石广生部长委托，刘山在副部长主持召开1998年第七次部长办公会议。会议研究贯彻落实《中共中央办公厅国务院办公厅关于增收节支制止浪费支援抗洪救灾工作的通知》（中办发〔1998〕20号）的具体措施。

石广生部长会见并宴请联合国贸易和发展会议秘书长鲁本斯·里库佩罗。双方就国际形势、贸发会议与中国的合作等问题交换意见。

孙振宇副部长会见由美国半导体协会董事长桑德斯率领的信息产业结构代表团。双方就信息业在经济发展中的作用、中国加入ITA协议及WTO的有关问题交换意见。

孙振宇副部长会见前美助理贸易谈判代表李森智。孙副部长阐述中国加入世贸组织的原则和立场，美方介绍美政府内部在中国加入WTO问题上的考虑。

孙振宇副部长会见加拿大驻华大使贝祥（Howard Balloch）和加小麦局驻华代表。加方代表加小麦局向中国水灾地区捐赠100万元人民币。

安民部长助理会见以香港振华集团执行董事王振声先生为团长的香港新界总商会北京访问团。双方就中国加入WTO的进程、港商在内地投资的政策等问题交换意见。

11日　石广生部长、刘山在副部长、孙振宇副部长、高虎城部长助理主持召开出口工作领导小组第八次会议。会议检查第七次出口领导小组会议定事项的落实情况，分析当前外贸出口形势，并就下一步出口工作作具体安排。

杨文生部长助理与圣卢西亚外交和国际贸易部长乔治·奥德伦分别代表各自政府在卡斯特里签署中国政府向圣卢西亚政府提供无息贷款的协定。

14日　孙振宇副部长会见芝加哥第一国民银行高级副总裁博睿（Barry Sabloff）一行。双方就外商来华投资、美国经济形势及亚洲金融危机等问题交换意见。

孙广相副部长主持中日高层经济磋商会议。双方就亚洲经济问题、中日两国经济情况、金融财政政策及中日经贸合作等问题坦率交换意见。

张祥副部长与秘鲁司法部长、代理外交部长阿尔弗雷多·基斯佩服·科雷亚分别代表各自政府就我向秘提供500万元人民币无偿援助事在利马换文确认。

15日　孙振宇副部长会见美国前参议员考佩斯基。双方就中国加入WTO和中美经贸关系有关问题交换意见。

孙振宇副部长会见爱尔兰企业、贸易和就业部国务部长汤姆·基特。双方就进一步发展中爱两国经贸关系的有关问题交换意见。

孙广相副部长会见英前首相希思。双方就东南亚金融危机对中国外经贸的影响以及我吸引外资政策等问题交换意见。

16日　孙广相副部长会见中非共和国外交国务部长让·梅特·亚彭德一行。双方就双边经贸合作问题交换意见并分别代表各自政府就我向中非无偿提供150万元人民币一般物资事在北京换文确认。

17日　孙振宇副部长会见古巴驻华大使格拉（Guerra）。双方就中国加入世贸组织双边市场准入谈判、1999年中古贸易方式和中国以贷款方式向古巴糖工业提供总价值为1.15亿美元的设备和物资等问题交换意见。

孙振宇副部长会见旧金山湾区世贸中心主席郑可欣女士。郑女士表示希望石广生部长能够出席明年在旧金山举行的世贸中心协会年会。

龙永图首席谈判代表会见德国驻华大使赛康德，并接受赛康德递交的2500万马克灾区重建赠款。

龙永图首席谈判代表会见英国科技国务大臣盛博理勋爵。双方签署《中英洁净煤和煤的有效利用研究与开发合作项目备忘录》。

龙永图首席谈判代表分别会见比利时驻华大使马利国和卢森堡驻华大使舒梅，就欧盟对华棉坯布反倾销案进行交涉。卢大使告卢已改变立场，从支持征税改为反对征税。

张祥副部长与哥伦比亚外交部长吉列尔莫·费尔南德斯·德索托分别代表各自政府就我向哥提供500万元人民币无偿援助事在圣菲波哥大换文确认。

安民部长助理会见台湾威京集团主席沈庆京一行。双方就近期亚洲经济形势、香港股市、人民币币值等共同关心的问题交换意见。

21日　孙振宇副部长在北京大学出席“世贸组织与中国农产品贸易政策国际研讨会”并致辞。研讨会由我部主办，许多国家和国际组织代表参加。

孙振宇副部长与来访的美国商务副部长阿伦举行中美商贸联委会中期磋商。双方就中美经贸关系的有关问题及第十二次中美商贸联委会的有关准备工作进行会谈。

高虎城部长助理会见法国萨理德会计师事务所总裁。双方就该公司与利安达会计师事务所的合作事宜交换意见。

22 日　孙振宇副部长会见安哥拉人民运动总书记洛波一行，双方就进一步发展两国经贸合作关系交换意见。

23 日　石广生部长会见美国商务副部长阿伦。双方就东南亚金融危机、中美经贸关系及即将举行的第十二次中美商贸联委会的有关议题交换意见。

石广生部长、安民部长助理会见英国怡和集团主席亨利·凯瑟克。双方就亚洲经济形势及对香港特别行政区的影响、怡和集团在中国内地业务发展等问题交换意见。

孙广相副部长会见沙特驻华大使。双方就中沙间加强经济技术合作（特别是在承包工程、劳务合作方面）以及举行中沙第二届混委会等事直接交换意见。

24 日　石部长参加朱镕基总理和法国若斯潘总理的会谈。会后与法国财政、经济和工业部长卡恩签署《中法财政议定书》。

25 日　孙振宇副部长在北京图书大厦出席由外经贸部主办的英首相布莱尔所著《新英国》中译本首发式。

龙永图首席谈判代表参加在上海举行的“环太平洋经济论坛”98 年会。龙首席谈判代表就我国当前经贸形势及我国参加多边和区域合作做主旨发言。

马秀红部长助理会见法国兰格赛公司总裁罗德意。马助理介绍我吸引外资的政策，并就兰格赛公司申请在华建立低压电器物流中心事与法方交换意见。

28 日　石广生部长会见中远香港（集团）公司总裁张大春、汇丰投资银行主席兼行政总裁韦智理先生率领的香港工商金融界高层管理人员（清华大学研修班学员）一行十六人。双方就中国经济形势及中国加入 WTO 等问题交换意见。

张祥副部长会见比利时驻华大使马利国。马告比在欧盟对华棉坯布反倾销案上已从支持征税改为弃权，从而可以阻止欧盟对华棉坯布征收反倾销税。

29 日　孙振宇副部长与加拿大外交国贸部莱特副部长（Robert G.Wrighr）在北京共同主持中国—加拿大第十五次经贸联委会。双方就上届联委会以来的双边经贸合作交换意见。

孙振宇副部长会见美国福特汽车公司副董事长布克。双方就中美经贸关系、东南亚金融危机和福特公司对华开展合作问题交换看法。

30 日　孙振宇副部长会见基里巴斯交通部常务秘书陶阿巴（Taakei Taoaba）。双方就促进两国经贸合作尤其是船舶和飞机贸易交换意见。

龙永图首席谈判代表会见联合国儿童基金驻华代表贾德先生并接受该基金向我水灾地区提供的约144.5 万美元的援助。上述援款是由儿童基金香港委员会和美国国际发展署通过联合国儿童基金会提供的。

10　月

4 日　中国财政部长项怀诚在华盛顿举行的世行会议上重申，中国的人民币不会贬值。**同日**　中国人民银行行长戴相龙在 IMF 会议上呼吁，发达国家应承担起支持亚洲经济复苏的责任，维护主要货币间的汇率稳定，刺激本国需求。

5 日－17 日　外经贸部部长助理马秀红率中国投资贸易洽谈代表团分别访问丹麦、荷兰和瑞典。

6 日　中国进出口银行在京举行“1998 年金融债券市场化发行推介会暨承销主协议”签字仪式，这是该行首次在国内以市场化方式发行金融债券。

8 日　上海证券交易所与伦敦证券交易所谅解备忘录的续签仪式在上海举行，正在中国访问的英国首相布莱尔出席仪式。同日　首家获得在华营业执照的英国保险公司——皇家太阳联合保险公司上海分公司在浦东金融中心正式开业，布莱尔首相出席开业典礼。

17 日　中英民用航空谅解备忘录在京签署。

10 日－15 日　中国越南经贸合作委员会第二次会议在京举行，外经贸部首席谈判代表龙永图和越南贸易部副部长梅文瑜共同主持会议，龙永图建议，两国共 同努力，发展大宗商品贸易，丰富双边贸易形式并大力发展边境贸易。

12 日－14 日　由外经贸部副部长张祥率领的中国代表团和由经济部副部长布瓦什契克为团长的波兰代表团在华沙举行中波经贸混委会第八次例会。双方代表就彻底解决和清算两国在记账贸易时期遗留下来的财务差额问题进行磋商，对此达成共识并签订议定书。

13 日　中国欧盟工业合作协议项下的中欧航空项目第一阶段合作在京举行闭幕式。

14日 中国海关总署与中国日本商会在京召开恳谈会。

15日 国务院副总理李岚清在京会见美国商会会长兼首席执行官托马斯·多诺霍一行。

15日—30日 第84届中国出口商品交易会在广州举行，到会客商70019名，成交额110亿美元。其中，对欧盟、美国、海湾8国成交情况较好，对日本、韩国和东南亚成交呈恢复性增长，对拉美、原苏东地区及台湾省成交不理想。**16日** 外经贸部副部长孙振宇在广州举行的"国际市场战略研讨会"上表示，中国已初步形成外向型经济。

20日 江泽民主席在京分别会见法国布依格集团董事长马丹·布依格一行和丹麦马士基集团董事长马士基·穆勒一行。

21日—23日 台湾同胞投资保护法制理论与实践探讨会在江苏昆山举行。外经贸部部长助理安民在会上透露我国政府进一步推动台胞投资祖国大陆的7点新措施。

22日 江泽民主席在京会见美国大通银行前董事长戴维·洛克菲勒。

26日 中韩第七次经贸联委会、中国希腊第五届经贸混委会在京分别举行。

27日 中国科学技术部与美国国际数据集团在京签署合作备忘录，决定共同在我国发展高新技术风险投资基金。今后7年，美国国际数据集团将据此向中国高新技术企业投资10亿美元。

29日 李岚清副总理在京与今天开始访华的欧盟主席桑特进行会谈。会后，双方签署《中国与欧盟在航空与通信领域的工业合作谅解备忘录》、《中欧立法与司法合作》的财政协议、《欧盟支持中国加入世贸组织》的财政协议。**同日** 中国人民银行行长戴相龙在会晤桑特时表示，明年人民币汇率保持稳定是有基础的。**30日** 江泽民主席、李鹏委员长、朱镕基总理分别会见欧盟主席桑特。

29日 国务委员吴仪在京分别会见新西兰外交贸易部长唐·麦金农和由主席弗里特兹·克诺尔率领的海地工商会代表团。

30日 李岚清副总理在京会见美国英特尔公司总裁贝瑞特。

30日 中国人民银行和国家外汇管理局正式联合公布《关于停办外汇调剂业务的通知》。通知决定：自1998年12月1日起，在全国范围内取消外商投资企业外汇调剂业务，外商投资企业的外汇买卖均纳入银行结售汇体系。

31日 根据中国人民银行决定，扩大对小企业贷款利率的浮动幅度这项措施即日开始实施。

11 月

1日—2日 第十次上海市国际企业家咨询会议召开，本次会议主题是金融风险管理。

2日 李岚清副总理在京会见美国戴尔计算机公司董事长兼首席执行官迈克·戴尔一行。

3日 外经贸部部长石广生在京会见比利时首相让－吕克·德阿纳。石广生部长表示，西方社会对中国在世界经济中所起的作用不要低估，但对中国经济的发展水平更要实事求是地认识。**同日** "中比陕西社会——经济综合扶贫项目"财政协议在西安签署，正在访华的比利时首相德阿纳和陕西省省长程安东出席签字仪式。

4日 外经贸部副部长孙广相在京会见美国ABC公司、美国收账局有限公司和美国高级商务信用资料有限公司董事长贺海威一行，双方就国际贸易信用风险管理方面的合作进行探讨。

5日 李岚清副总理在京与西班牙第二副首相兼经济财政大臣拉托举行会谈。

5日 外经贸部首席谈判代表龙永图在京表示，中国加入世贸组织的立场没有改变。

9日 国务委员吴仪在京会见雀巢集团行政总裁彼得·包必达一行。

10日 中国——乌拉圭第九届经贸混委会在京举行。外经贸部副部长孙振宇和乌拉圭牧农渔业部副部长德圣·马丁主持会议并进行会谈。

13日 中国东方航空公司和全日空航空公司在东京签订以代码共享为核心的总体合作协议，这是中日两家航空公司之间首次进行此类合作。

15日 中国人民银行管理体制改革正式开始启动。根据方案，中国人民银行撤消32个省、自治区、直辖市分行，组建9个跨行政区的分行。

17日—18日 APEC第六次领导人非正式会议在马来西亚首都吉隆坡举行。**17日** 江泽民主席在参加工商咨询理事会代表对话会上强调，APEC要加强经济技术合作；**18日** APEC第六次领导人非正式会议开幕，江泽民主席就促进国际金融稳定发展和推动建立国际金融新秩序提出三点主张：加强国际合作，制止金融危机蔓延，为受这场危机冲击的国家和地区恢复经济增长创造有利的外部环境；改革和完善国际金融体制，确保国际金融市场安全有序运行；尊重有关国家和地区为这场危机自主作出的选择。并宣布中国将拨款1000万美元设立“中国APEC科技产业合作基金”

18日 中国化工进出口总公司和中国银行在京签署《银企合作协议》，据此中国银行会向中化公司海内外企业提供本外币折算最高可达100亿元人民币的信用额度。

19日－21日 加拿大总理克雷蒂安访华。

20日 国家发展计划委员会主任曾培炎和加拿大国际贸易部长塞尔焦·马尔基在京出席中加47项、价值7.2亿加元的贸易协定签字仪式。项目涉及电讯、交通、水利、医疗、机械、农业、食品加工、环保、发电等领域，签约加方多是中小企业。

20日 针对美国商务部高级官员近日指责中国出口退税政策，外经贸部新闻发言人胡楚生明确表示，中国政府近期虽提高了部分商品出口退税率，但仍然没有超过法定征税率，胡根本不能视为出口补贴，更不是人民币变相贬值。

20日 经过5天谈判，中国政府纺织品协议代表团与欧盟委员会代表团在比利时布鲁塞尔达成第六个双边纺织品协议。根据协议，欧盟将相应增加中国纺织品对欧盟出口的配额总量。

23日 李鹏委员长在京会见ABB集团总裁兼首席执行官林道先生。

25日 根据最近在美国纽约举行的350余家跨国公司税收、金融和财务执行总裁会议的评选，中国被推选为海外最佳投资国之一。

27日 “改革开放20年以来利用外资成果展”在京开幕。

27日 李岚清副总理在京会见荷兰财政大臣赫里特·扎尔姆。

12　月

2日 国务委员吴仪在京会见埃塞俄比亚商业与工业部长萨胡纳·阿耶莱时说，中国将鼓励企业到埃塞俄比亚进行加工装配项目。

3日 朱镕基总理在京会见摩洛哥王国政府首相阿卜杜拉－拉赫曼·尤素福。会后双方出席中摩两国政府经济技术合作、动植物检疫合作、民用航空运输等协议的签字仪式。

3日 外经贸部、科技部联合正式发布《限制出口技术管理办法》及经国务院批准的《中国禁止出口、限制出口技术目录》。

3日 世界贸易组织公布1997年世界贸易进出口排名，中国商品出口额进入10强，进口额保持在第12位；服务贸易出口中国排名第16位，进口中国位居第10位。

5日 国务委员吴仪在驻外经商参赞工作会议上指出，要通过大力推动赴境外开展带料加工项目等方式，培育外贸出口新的增长点。

8日 中化总公司在美国成功发行2亿美元商业票据。

8日 外经贸部新闻发言人胡楚生就欧盟可能继续维持对我国输欧家禽贸易禁令一事表示，中方按照欧盟“区域化管理”的法律要求，对重点地区投入数亿元人民币进行企业整改和体系建立与完善，对欧盟提出的问题逐一改进。欧盟兽医专家考察团提交的报告仍然认为，中国的防疫、检疫体系和质量保证体系不符合欧盟要求，因此可能继续维持其贸易禁令，这只能充分反映欧盟利用技术壁垒妨碍正常贸易的真实意图。

9日 外经贸部、财政部、国家税务总局正式联合发布就1993年12月31日前批准成立的外商投资企业的有关税收政策问题的通知。

10日 针对美国穆迪评级公司近日公布中国进出口银行的外币长期债务信用级别由A3降至Baal，该行负责人表示，财务报表显示中国进出口银行资产状况良好，穆迪评级公司认为“政策性银行因执行国家政策导致财政状况恶化”不符合事实。

11日 全国经贸工作会议在京召开，国务委员吴仪在会上要求切实搞好6个方面的工作，加大出口力度。

15日 石广生部长率领中国政府经贸代表团赴美参加中美商贸联委会。

16日 石广生部长在华盛顿会见美国贸易代表巴尔舍夫斯基，双方就中国加入世贸组织等问题交换意见。

17日－18日 中美商贸联委会第12次会议在华盛顿举行。石广生部长和美国商务部长威廉·戴利共同主持。

18日 石广生部长在和美国商务部长戴利举行的联合记者招待会上表示，根据GATT主席声明，作为中国的一个单独关税区，台湾省不得先于我方加入WTO。

22日 外经贸部正式公布对3家骗汇的进出口企业撤消其对外贸易经营许可的决定。

25日 外交部副部长杨文昌和日本驻华大使谷野作太郎分别代表本国政府在京签署1998年度日元贷款政府换文。**同日** 财政部副部长金立群和日本海外经济协会基金总裁篠沢恭助在东京签署1998年度日元贷款协议。

26日 1997年中国最大500家外商投资企业排序揭晓。按1997年销售额（营业额）排序，名列前3位的依次是上海大众汽车有限公司、摩托罗拉（中国）电子有限公司、华能国际电力股份有限公司。

29日 中国人民银行和国家外汇管理局正式公布，自1999年1月1日起，中国的金融机构、企业及个人在与欧元区11国的经贸、金融等往来中可以接受和使用欧元。

29日 国家外汇管理局正式发出《关于欧元启动后外汇管理有关问题的通知》，对境内机构将欧元区原11国货币账户转换为欧元账户、保留欧币账户并新开一个欧元账户以及外债指标、外汇统计报表、欧元挂牌汇率等有关问题作出规定和说明。

29日 第9届全国人大常委会第6次会议通过《中华人民共和国证券法》。

29日 全国供应港澳鲜活冷冻商品管理改革工作会议在京召开。

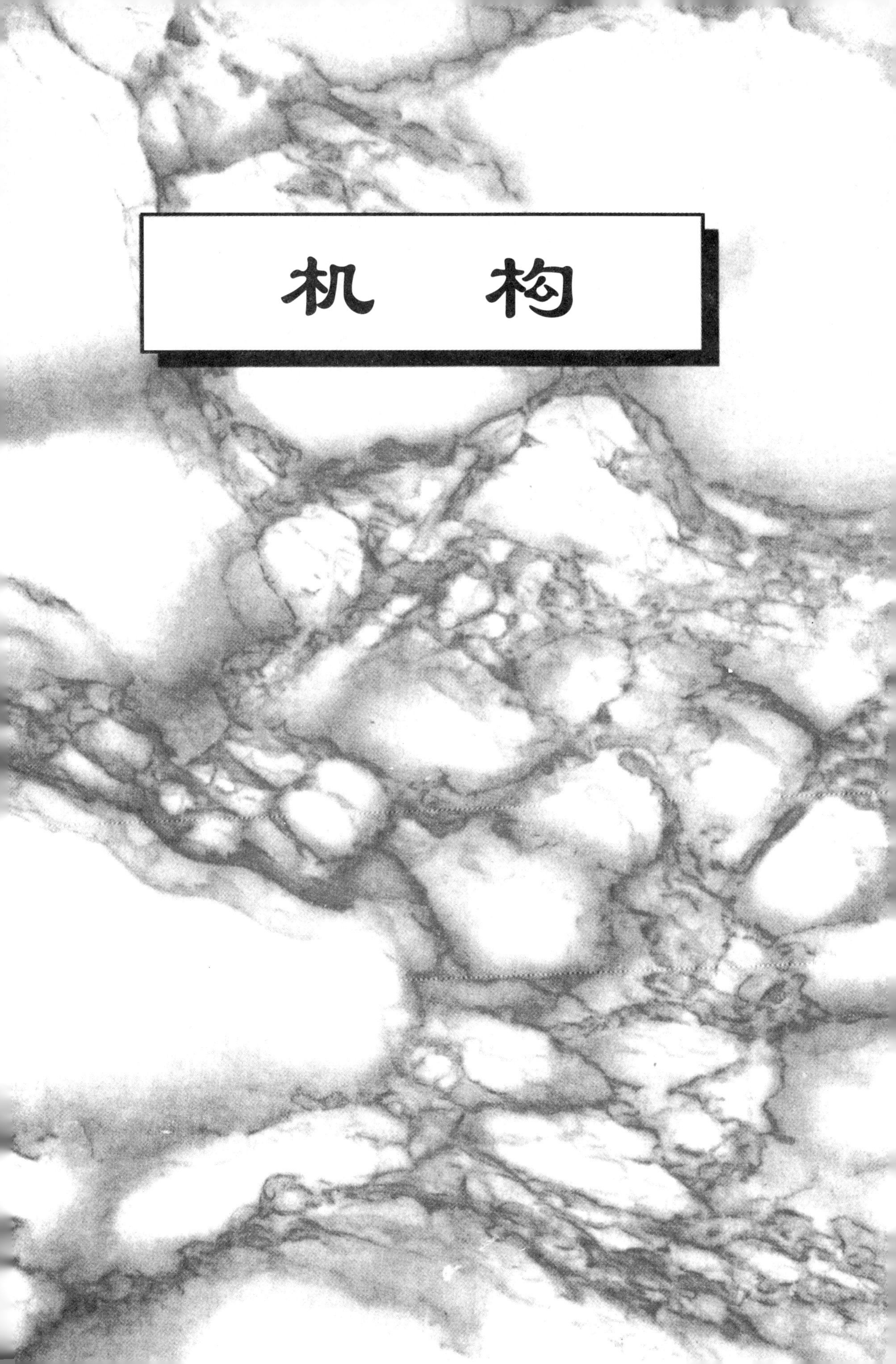

机　　构

中国驻外经济商务机构

亚　洲

中华人民共和国驻蒙古国大使馆经济商务参赞处

地 址：NO. 5. FRIENDSHIP STREET，ULAN BATOR，MONGOLIA
电话：009761－323940
传真：009761－311943

中华人民共和国驻朝鲜民主主义人民共和国大使馆经济商务参赞处

地址：KINMAEULI DONG，MAO LANG BONG DISTRICT，PYONGYANG，DEMOCRATIC PEOPLE'S REPUBLIC OF KOREA
电话：00850－2－3813119，00850－2－3813120
传真：00850－2－3813422，00850－2－3813425

中华人民共和国驻大韩民国大使馆经济商务参赞处

地址：大韩民国汉城特别市中区新堂2洞406－2号
邮编：100－452
电话：00822－2537521，2537522，2537523
传真：00822－2537524

中华人民共和国驻釜山总领事馆经济商务室

地址：600－015大韩民国釜山市中区中央洞5街50番（半岛投资金融BLDG.6层）
电话：008251－4414890，008251－4414891
传真：008251－4414892

中华人民共和国驻日本国大使馆经济商务参赞处

地址：テ106日本国东京都港区南麻布5丁目8番16号
电话：0081－3－3440－2011
传真：0081－3－3446－8242

中华人民共和国驻福冈总领事馆经济商务室

地址：テ810日本国福冈市中央区地行浜1－3－3
电话：0081－92－713－1121
传真：0081－92－781－8906

中华人民共和国驻大阪总领事馆经济商务室

地址：テ550日本国大阪市西区勒本町3－9－2
电话：0081－6－4459481，0081－6－4459471
传真：0081－6－4459476

中华人民共和国驻札幌总领事馆经商室

地址：テ064日本国札幌市中央区南13条西23－5－1
电话：0081－11－563－5563
传真：0081－11－563－1818

中华人民共和国驻越南社会主义共和国大使馆经济商务参赞处

地 址：SO NHA 46. 52 PHO HOANG DIEU，HANOI，VIET NAM
电话：00844－8232845
传真：00844－8234286

中华人民共和国驻胡志明市总领事馆经济商务室

地址：SO NHA 39 NGNYEN THI MINH KHAI Q. 1
电话：00848－8292463
传真：00848－8231142

中华人民共和国驻老挝人民民主共和国大使馆经济商务参赞处

地 址：RUELLE VATNAK MUONG SISATTANAK，VIENTIANE，LAOS
信箱：NO. 898，VIENTIANE，LAOS
电话：00856－21－315101，00856－21－315107
传真：00856－21－315106

中华人民共和国驻柬埔寨王国大使馆经济商务参赞处

地址：NO. 156 BLC MAO TSETUNG，PHNOM PENH，CAM BODIA
电话：00855－23－720923
传真：00855－23－720924

中华人民共和国驻缅甸联邦大使馆经济商务参赞处

地 址：NO. 53，PYIDAUNGSU YEIKTHA ROAD，RANGOON，MYANMAR
电话：0095－1－222800，0095－1－221399
0095－1－221398
传真：0095－1－220386

中华人民共和国驻曼德勒总领事馆经济商务室

地址：CONNER OF ZZND & 63RD STREET，MANDALAY，MYANMAR
电话：0095－2－227176，0095－2－270403

中华人民共和国驻泰王国大使馆经济商务参赞处

地址：CHINESE EMBASSY IN THAILAND，NO. 57，RACHADAPISAKE ROAD，DINDAENG，BANGKOK，10310 THAILAND
电话：0066－2－2457038，0066－2－2472122
0066－2－2474506
传真：0066－2－2472123，0066－2－2474506

中华人民共和国驻宋卡总领事馆经济商务室

地 址：9 SADAO ROOD，SONGKHLA 9000THAILAND
电话：0066－74－322034，325045
传真：0066－74－323772

中华人民共和国驻马来西亚大使馆经济商务参赞处

地 址：NO. 39，JALAN UIU KELANG，68000 AMPANG SELANGOR DARUL EHSAN，MALAYSIA
电话：0060－3－4513226，0060－3－4513555
传真：0060－3－4513233

中华人民共和国驻古晋总领事馆经济商务室

地 址：340 FORTUNE GARDEN，LORONG 5，JALAN STAMPIN TIMUR，OFF KUCHING BY － PASS，93350 KUCHING，SARAWAK，MALAYSIA
电话：0060－82－461344
传真：0060－82－461424

中华人民共和国驻新加坡共和国大使馆经济商务参赞处

地 址：70 － 76，DALVEY ROAD，SINGAPORE 1025
电话：0065－7343360，0065－7343307
传真：0065－7338590
电传：RS36878 CHICRO

中华人民共和国驻菲律宾共和国大使馆经济商务参赞处

地址：NO. 10，FLAME TREE ROAD，SOUTH FORBES PARK，MAKATI CITY 1200，METRO MANILA，PHILIPPINES
电话：0063－2－8195991，0063－2－8195992
0063－2－8939067
传真：0063－2－8184553
电传：22363 CHCOF PH

中华人民共和国驻宿务总领事馆经济商务室

地 址：4 TH FL. EURD PACIFIC BLDG，F. GONZALES COMPOUND，CAMPUTHAW ST. LAHUG CEBU CITY，6000，THE PHILIPPINES
电话：006332－2316217，006332－2316218
006332－2316219

传真：006332－2315697
节假日值班电话：006332－2548727
006332－2548728

中华人民共和国驻印度尼西亚共和国大使馆经济商务参赞处

地址：JL. PERMATA HIJAU RAYA，BLOKS，KAV. 4－5－6，JAKARTA SELATAN 12210，INDONESIA
电话：0062－21－5495347，0062－21－5301372
传真：0062－21－5301382

中华人民共和国驻文莱大使馆经济商务处

地址：SIMPANG 462，LOT38868，KG SUNGAI TILONG，JALAN MUARA NEGARA BRUNEI DARUSSALAM
电话：00673－2－336077
传真：00673－2－335163

中华人民共和国驻尼泊尔王国大使馆经济商务参赞处

地址：P. O. BOX 4234 NAXAL，KATHMANDU，NEPAL
电话：00977－1－418972，00977－1－414672
传真：00977－1－415091

中华人民共和国驻孟加拉人民共和国大使馆经济商务参赞处

地址：FLOT NO. 15. PARK ROAD，BLOCK－I，BARIDHARA，DHAKA，BANGLADESH
电话：00880－2－885272，00880－2－883313
00880－2－605728
传真：00880－2－883082
电传：675602 CECOF BG

中华人民共和国驻印度共和国大使馆经济商务参赞处

地址：NO. 50. D－SHANTIPATH CHANAKYAPURI NEW DELHI－110021，INDIA
电话：0091－11－4672687
传真：0091－11－6111099
电传：5166250 SINO IN

中华人民共和国驻孟买总领事馆经济商务室

地址：P. O. BOX 189，GPO，MUMDAI 400001，INDIA
电话：0091－22－4973091
传真：0091－22－4963310

中华人民共和国驻斯里兰卡民主社会主义共和国大使馆经济商务参赞处

地址：120/3A，WIJERAMA MAWATHA，COLOMBO 07，SRILANKA
电话：00941－684576－7，8041，8012
传真：00941－684578，00941－684579

中华人民共和国驻巴基斯坦伊斯兰共和国大使馆经济商务参赞处

地址：P. O. BOX 2601，HOUSE NO. 11，STREET NO. 19，F8/2，ISLAMABAD，PAKISTAN
电话：0092－51－252426
传真：0092－51－256887

中华人民共和国驻卡拉奇总领事馆经济商务室

地址：43－6－B，BLOCK 6，P. E. C. H. S. KARACHI
电话：0092－21－4530523，0092－21－4530526
传真：0092－21－4530525

中华人民共和国驻伊朗伊斯兰共和国大使馆经济商务参赞处

地址：NO. 180，FARMANIEH AVE.，TEHRAN，IRAN
电话：0098－21－2292284
传真：0098－21－2292283
电话：213237 COMO IR

中华人民共和国驻科威特大使馆经济商务参赞处

地址：MISHRIF，BLOCK 4，STREET 7，HOUSE NO. 4
信箱：P. O. BOX 25713 SAFAT，13118 SAFAT，

KUWAIT
电话：00965－5390239，5396160
传真：00965－5390291，5386404

中华人民共和国驻沙特阿拉伯王国
大使馆经济商务参赞处

地址：P. O. BOX 99882，RIYADH 11625，SAUDI ARABIA
电话：00966－1－4655655，00966－1－4622485
传真：00966－1－4629617

中华人民共和国驻吉达
总领事馆经济商务室

地址：AL－ANDALUS ROAD，ANDALUS DIST.（2）P. O. BOX 51373 JEDDAH 21543，SAUDI ARABIA
电话：00966－2－6605430
传真：00966－2－6606546

中华人民共和国驻巴林国
大使馆经济商务处

地 址：VILLA 1710，ROAD 7332 373，BILAD ALQADEEM MANAMA，STATE OF BAHRAIN
信箱：P. O. BOX 5260 MANAMA，BAHRAIN
电话：00973－233339
传真：00973－272790

中华人民共和国驻卡塔尔国
大使馆经济商务参赞处

地 址：63，AL－SHAM STREET，WEST BAY AREA，DOHA，QATAR
信箱：17514 DOHA，QATAR
电话：00974－835680
传真：00974－835184
电传：5120 CHINEM DH

中华人民共和国驻阿拉伯联合酋长国
大使馆经济商务参赞处

地址：AL FALAH STREET，IOTH LANE，35－1 SECTER
信箱：P. O. BOX 25455 ABU DHABI－U. A. E.
电话：00971－2－765525
传真：00971－2－764402

中华人民共和国驻迪拜
总领事馆经济商务室

地址：P. O. BOX 9374 DUBAI，THE UNITED ARAB EMIRATES
电话：00971－4－448032，00971－4－449445
传真：00971－4－448099
电传：46268 COMOF EM

中华人民共和国驻阿曼苏丹国
大使馆经济商务参赞处

地址：SHATI AL－QURUM，WAY3021，HOUSE NO. 1784
信箱：3315 RUWIS MASCAT，SULTANATE OF OMAN
电话：00968－697804
传真：00968－697482

中华人民共和国驻也门共和国
大使馆经济商务参赞处

地址：P. O. BOX 10285，SANA，YEMEN
电话：00967－1－275339，00967－1－275411
传真：00967－1－272298

中华人民共和国驻亚丁
总领事馆经济商务室

地址：KHORMAKSAY，ADEN，YEMEN
信箱：P. O. BOX 6160 KHORMAKSAY，ADEN，YEMEN
电话：00967－2－232630
传真：00967－2－231377

中华人民共和国驻伊拉克共和国
大使馆经济商务参赞处

地 址：P. O. BOX 15097 AL－YARMUK，BAGHDAD，IRAQ
电话：00964－1－5567897，00964－1－5562740
传真：00964－1－5417628

中华人民共和国驻阿拉伯叙利亚
共和国大使馆经济商务参赞处

地址：P. O. BOX 2455，DAMASCUS，SYRIA
电话：00963－11－6133008
传真：00963－11－6133019
电传：（0492）413217 CHINEC SY

中华人民共和国驻黎巴嫩共和国大使馆经济商务参赞处

地址：72，RUE NICOLAS IBRAHIM SURSOCK，RAMLET ELBAIDA，BEIRUT，LEBANON
信箱：P. O. BOX 114－5098，BEIRUT
电话：00961－1－822493
传真：00961－1－822492
电传：CHINCO 21344 LE

中华人民共和国驻约旦哈希姆王国大使馆经济商务参赞处

地址：NO. 21，ZAHRAN ST. SOUTHERN UM UTHAINA，AMMAN，JORDAN
信箱：423 UM ESSOMAQ & KHELDA，AMMAN，11821，JORDAN
电话：00962－6－5516194，00962－6－5518195
传真：00962－6－5537417

中华人民共和国驻以色列国大使馆经济商务参赞处

地址：NO. 94，NAMIR ROAD，TEL－AVIV 62337，ISRAEL
电话：00972－3－5444915，00972－3－5444917
传真：00972－3－5444918

中华人民共和国驻塞浦路斯共和国大使馆经济商务参赞处

地址：17 AGAPINOR STREET，1706，NICDSIA，CYPRUS
信箱：P. O. BOX 7088，NICOSIA，CYPRUS
电话：00357－2－375252
传真：00357－2－376699
电传：4910 CHINA COF CY

中华人民共和国驻土耳其共和国大使馆经济商务参赞处

地址：ALI FUAT BASGIL MAHALLESI，HATIR SOKAK NO. 16 06700 GAZIOSMANPASA，ANKARA－TURKEY
电话：0090－312－4377107
传真：0090－312－4466762
电传：46387 CHCM TR

中华人民共和国驻伊斯坦布尔总领事馆经济商务室

地址：MEMDUH PASA YALISI KIRECBURNU MAH. MISIRH CAD. SARIYER，ISTANBUL
电话：0090－212－2992631
传真：0090－212－2992632
电传：26906 CCGT TR

中华人民共和国驻巴勒斯坦民族权力机构办事处

电话：00972－7－825068，00972－5－864215
传真：00972－7－825058

非　洲

中华人民共和国驻阿拉伯埃及大使馆经济商务参赞处

地址：22，BAHGAT ALY STREET，ZAMALEK，CAIRO，EGYPT
电话：0020－2－3404316，3417423
传真：0020－2－3412094，0020－2－3408728

中华人民共和国驻大阿拉伯利比亚人民社会主义民众国大使馆经济商务参赞处

地址：NEAR THE PETROL STATION NO. 37，KALKALISH STREET，TRIPOLI，LIBYA
信箱：P. O. BOX 6310 ANDALUS，TRIPOLI
电话：00218－21－4831234
传真：00218－21－4831225，00218－21－4831877

电传：20392 CHINOM LY

中华人民共和国驻突尼斯共和国大使馆经济商务参赞处

地址：ROUTE DE LA MARSA KMG EL AOUINA 2405 CITE TAIEB MHIRI TUNIS, TUNISIE
电话：00216－1－849453/845805
传真：00216－1－841996

中华人民共和国驻阿尔及利亚民主人民共和国大使馆经济商务参赞处

地址：34，BD，DES MARTYRS，ALGER，ALGERIE
电话：00213－2－691865/693189
传真：00213－2－692362/691865
电传：66193 BCCAC DE

中华人民共和国驻摩洛哥王国大使馆经济商务参赞处

地址：2，RUE MEKKI EL－BITAOURI SOUISSI－RABATMAROC
电话：00212－7－754940，00212－7－752718
传真：00212－7－756966，636682
电传：32745 M

中华人民共和国驻毛里塔尼亚伊斯兰共和国大使馆经济商务参赞处

地 址：B. P. 5534 NOUAKCHOTT，MAURITANIE
电话：00222－2－51205
传真：00222－2－58634

中华人民共和国驻马里共和国大使馆经济商务参赞处

地址：B. P. 1614，BAMAKO，MALI
电话：00223－223823
传真：00223－229019

中华人民共和国驻佛得角共和国大使馆经济商务参赞处

地 址：C. P. NO. 8，PRAIA；ACHADA DE SANTO ANTONIO PRAIA REPUBLICA DE CABO VERDE
电话：00238－623029
传真：00238－623007
scec@mail. cvtelecom. cv

中华人民共和国驻几内亚共和国大使馆经济商务参赞处

地址：B. P. 714 CONAKRY，REDUBLIQUE DE GUINEE
电话：（224）464366
传真：001－212－4794818

中华人民共和国驻塞拉利昂共和国大使馆经济商务参赞处

地 址：28，KONG HARMAN ROAD，FREETOWN，SIERRA LEONE
信 箱：P. O. BOX 778，FREETOWN，SIERRA LEONE
电 话：00232 － 22 － 240075（ECONOMIC SECTION），00232－22－240086，00232－22－240490（COMMERCIAL SECTION）
传真：00232－22－240086

中华人民共和国驻科特迪瓦共和国大使馆经济商务参赞处

地 址：06 B. P. 206 ABIDJAN 06 COTED’IVOIRE
电话：00225－420102
传真：00225－426373

中华人民共和国驻加纳共和国大使馆经济商务参赞处

地址：P. O. BOX M344 AIRPORT RESIDENTIAL AREA ACCRA，GHANA
电话：00233－21－777462，00233－21－772541
传真：00233－21－777462，00233－21－772541
电传：091－2116 EMBCHA GH
jshchu@ghana. com

中华人民共和国驻多哥共和国大使馆经济商务参赞处

地址：11，RUE TEVI－BENISSAN A TOKOIN－LYCEE

信箱：B. P. 4714－LOME－TOGO
电话：00228－215470，00228－215243
传真：00228－218390，00228－215470

中华人民共和国驻贝宁共和国
大使馆经济商务参赞处

地址：ROUTE NO. 2 DE I' AEROPORT ZONE DES AMBASSADES COTONOU，BENIN
信箱：08－0167 08－0462 COTONOU，BENIN
电话：00229－301909，00229－301097
传真：00229－301639

中华人民共和国驻尼日利亚联邦共和国
大使馆经济商务参赞处

地址：161A，ADEOLA ODEKU STREET，VICTORIA ISLAND，LAGOS，NIGERIA
信箱：P. O. BOX 72697 V/I，LAGOS
电话：00234－1－2612414，00234－1－2612404
传真：00234－1－2612414
ecochnemb@alpha. linkserve. com

中华人民共和国驻喀麦隆共和国
大使馆经济商务参赞处

地址：B. P. 11608 YAOUNDE CAMEROUN 或 B. P. 4019
电话：00237－209522，00237－203191
传真：00237－203191
电传：AMBACHINE 3321 KN

中华人民共和国驻杜阿拉
总领事馆经济商务室

地址：B. P. 4391－DOUALA，CAMEROUN
电话：00237－425437
传真：00237 422268

中华人民共和国驻赤道几内亚共和国
大使馆经济商务参赞处

地址：CALLE DE INDEPENDENCIA 26 － B － 2 CONSEJERO ECONOMICO－COMERCIAL DE LA EMBAJADA DE LA REPUBLICA POPULAR CHINA EN LA REPUBLICA DE GUINEA ECUATORIAL
信箱：P. O. BOX MALABO NO 44，GUINEA ELUATORIAL
电话：00240－9－3440
传真：00240－9－3459

中华人民共和国驻乍得共和国
大使馆经济商务参赞处

地址：P. O. BOX 165 N' DJAMENA，TCHAD
电话：00235－523321（办公室）522405（住处）
传真：00235－523063（办公室）523684（使馆）

中华人民共和国驻苏丹共和国
大使馆经济商务参赞处

地址：P. O. BOX 1425 KHARTOUM－SUDAN
电话：00249－11－272274，00249－11－224816
传真：00249－11－272274
电传：22806 CHINCC SD

中华人民共和国驻埃塞俄比亚
大使馆经济商务参赞处

地址：HIGH ER 24，KEBELE 13，HOUSE，NO. 729 JIMMA ROAD，ADDIS ABABA，ETHIOPIA
信 箱：P. O. BOX 5643，ADDIS ABABA，ETHIOPIA
电 话：002511 － 712266（COMMERCIAL SECTION）002511－202315 (ECONOMIC SECTION)
传真：002511－711611，002511－710059

中华人民共和国驻吉布提共和国
大使馆经济商务参赞处

地址：RUE DE NAIROBI，HERON，DJIBOUTI
信箱：B. P. 4001 DJIBOUTI
电话：00253－350575
传真：00253－354174
电传：CHINADJI 5926DJ

中华人民共和国驻肯尼亚共和国
大使馆经济商务参赞处

地址：NGONG ROAD，NAIROBI，KENYA
信箱：P. O. BOX 28190，47030，NAIROBI
电话：00254－2－712120，00254－2－721434
传真：00254－2－713451，00254－2－711029

中华人民共和国驻乌干达共和国
大使馆经济商务参赞处

地址：P. O. BOX 8858 KAMPALA，UGANDA
电话：00256－41－220570，00256－41－220572，00256－41－220578
传真：00256－41－220379

中华人民共和国驻坦桑尼亚
联合共和国经济商务参赞处

地 址：PLOT NO 3621，MSASANI ROAD，DARES SALAAM（ECONOMIC），TANZANIA
电话：00255－51－668198，668243，667863
传真：00255－51－666177
电传：41036 CHINEMBA

中华人民共和国驻桑给巴尔
领事馆经济商务室

地址：P. O. BOX 1200 ZANZIBAR，TANZANIA
电话：0255－054－30816
传真：0255－054－30816

中华人民共和国驻卢旺达共和国
大使馆经济商务参赞处

地址：B. P. 519 OU 182，KIGALI，RWANDA
电话：00250－75629
传真：00250－75629

中华人民共和国驻布隆迪共和国
大使馆经济商务参赞处

地址：SUR LA PARCELLE 675 A VUGIZO，BUJUMBURA，BURUNDI
信箱：B. P. 6287，BUJUMBURA，BURUNDI
电话：00257－224246，00257－222558
传真：00257－221962
电传：5137 BCCHINE BDI

中华人民共和国驻扎伊尔共和国
大使馆经济商务参赞处

地 址：466，AV COLONEL LUKUSA，KINSHASA/GOMBE，ZAIRE
信箱：B. P. 20659 KIN 15，KINSHASA－ZAIRE
电话：00243－12－26210，00243－12－83076，00243－12－46507
传真：001－212－3769255/00243－8803962
jingshang@ic. cd

中华人民共和国驻刚果共和国
大使馆经济商务参赞处

地 址：AVENUE MONSEIGNEUR AUGOUARD，BRAZZAVILLE，CONGO
信箱：B. P. 2838，BRAZZAVILLE，CONGO
电话：00242－830952
传真：00242－837702/00242－810120
00871761661271

中华人民共和国驻加蓬共和国
大使馆经济商务参赞处

地址：B. P. 3914 LIBREVILLE，GABON
电话：00241－722279，00241－722282
传真：00241－738887，00241－722283
becacg@internetgabon. com

中华人民共和国驻圣多美和普林西比
民主共和国大使馆经济商务参赞处

地址：AV. PRES. KWAME N’KRUMAH NO. 24A（B），SAOTOME
信箱：C. P. 142 REPUBLICA DEMDCRATICA DE SAO TOME E PRINCIPE
电话：00239－12－22187，00239－12－21550
传真：00239－12－21785

中华人民共和国驻安哥拉人民共和国
大使馆经济商务参赞处

地址：RUA FERNAO MENDES PINTO NO. 26/28 BAIRRO ALVALADE，LUANDA，ANGOLA
信箱：CAIXA POSTAL NO 704
电话：00244－2－322803
传真：00244－2－322803

中华人民共和国驻中非共和国
大使馆经济商务参赞处

电话：00236－614682
传真：00236－614358

手机：00236－640252

中华人民共和国驻赞比亚共和国
大使馆经济商务参赞处

地址：UNITED NATIONS AVENUE，LUSAKA，ZAMBIA
信箱：P．O．BOX 31205 LUSAKA，ZAMBIA
电话：00260－1－253601，00260－1－262363，00260－1－264123
电传：CHINEB ZA41360
传真：00260－1－262363，00260－1－253001，251157

中华人民共和国驻莫桑比克共和国
大使馆经济商务参赞处

地址：AV．DO ZIMBABWE N．1088，MAPUTO，MOCAMBIQUE；AV．DE KIM IL SUNG N．974，MAPUTO，MOCAMBIQUE
信箱：C．P．2545，MAPUTO，MOCAMBIQUE；C．P．1105，MAPUTO，MOCAMBIQUE
电话：00258－1－491879，00258－1－490306
传真：00258－1－491879，00258－1－490306

中华人民共和国驻科摩罗伊斯兰
共和国大使馆经济商务参赞处

地址：B．P．442 MORONI，COMORES
电话：00269　732937
传真：00269－732866

中华人民共和国驻马达加斯加民主
共和国大使馆经济商务参赞处

地址：B．P．4094，TANANARIVE 101，REPUBLIQUE DE MADAGASCAR B．P．43 IVATO A L ＊ AEROPORT TANANARIVE，MADAGASCAR
电话：00261－20－2244623
传真：00261－20－2244529，00261－20－2245223

中华人民共和国驻塞舌尔共和国
大使馆经济商务参赞处

地 址：P．O．BOX 680，VICTORIA，SEYCHELLES
电话：00248－266808
传真：00248－266866

中华人民共和国驻毛里求斯共和国
大使馆经济商务参赞处

地 址：HAPPY VALLEY，SAINT CLEMENT STREET，CUREPIPE，MAURITIUS
电话：00230－4549113，00230－6755635
传真：00230－4540362，00230－6743523
电传：4829 CHINCOM IW

中华人民共和国驻津巴布韦共和国
大使馆经济商务参赞处

地址：10，CORK ROAD，AVONDALE，HARARE，ZIMBABWE
信箱：P．O．BOX 40，HARARE，ZIMBABWE；P．O．BOX 1340，HARARE，ZIMBAWE
电话：00263－4－730516，00263－4－735194
传真：00263－4－700264，00263－4－735252

中华人民共和国驻博茨瓦纳共和国
大使馆经济商务参赞处

地址：3097 NORTH RING ROAD，GABORONE，BOTSWANA
信箱：P．O．BOX 1031 GABORONE BOTSWANA
电话：00267－353270，00267－352209
传真：00267－300156

中华人民共和国驻纳米比亚共和国
大使馆经济商务参赞处

地 址：66 GEVERS STREET，WINDHOEK，NAMIBIA
纳米比亚共和国温得和克市杰瓦大街 66 号
信箱：P．O．BOX 21350
电话：00264－61－222702
00264－61－220210，221460
传真：00264－61－221325

中华人民共和国驻厄立特里亚
大使馆经济商务参赞处

地 址：ERITREA ASMARA ZONE 4 ADM．02 STREET NO702 HOUSE NO．74 P．O．BOX；204

电话：002911－182273
传真：002911－182200

中华人民共和国驻莱索托王国
大使馆经济商务参赞处

电话：00266－316544
传真：00266－312059

中华人民共和国驻利比里亚共和国
大使馆经济商务参赞处

地 址：EID COMPOUND，MAMBA POINT，MONROVIA，LIBERIA
信箱：P．O．BOX T．O．BOX 10－2895 1000 MONROVIA，LIBERIA
电话：00231－226186
传真：00231－227787

中华人民共和国驻尼日尔共和国
大使馆经济商务参赞处

地 址：BOITE POSTALE：10777 NIAMEY，REPUBLIQUE DUNIGER
电话：00227－752859/722101/722126－
传真：00227－722106/723285

中华人民共和国驻南非共和国
大使馆经济商务参赞处

地 址：797 PARK STREET，CLYDESDALE，(HATFIELD) PRETORIA，0083，RSA
电话：0027－12－3440428
传真：0027－12－3440439

美　洲

中华人民共和国驻加拿大大使馆
经济商务参赞处（渥太华）

地 址：511－515 ST．PATRICK STREET，7893511 OTTAWA，ONTARIO，CANADA KIN 5H3
信箱：P．O．BOX 8953
电话：001－613－7893513
传真：001－613－7893515
电传：053－3770 CHINAEMBA OTT

中华人民共和国驻温哥华
总领事馆经济商务室

地 址：3380 GRANVILLE STREET，VANCOUVER，B．C．CANADA，V6H 3K3
电话：001－604－7364021
传真：001－604－7364343
电传：04－54659

中华人民共和国驻多伦多
总领事馆经济商务室

地 址：240 ST．GEORGE STREET，TORONTO，ONTARIO，CANADA，M5R 2P4
电话：001－416－3246455
传真：001－416－3246468

中华人民共和国驻美利坚合众国
大使馆经济商务参赞处

地 址：2133 WISCONSIN AVENUE，NW．WASHINGTON D．C．，20007，U．S．A．
电话：001－202－625－3380，001－202－625－3360
传真：001－202－337－5864，001－202－337－5845

中华人民共和国驻旧金山
总领事馆经济商务室

地址：1450 LAGUNA STREET，SAN FRANEISCO，CA94115，U．S．A．
电话：001－415－5634858，001－415－5634874
传真：001－415－5630494
电传：497021 CCSF

中华人民共和国驻纽约
总领事馆经济商务室

地址：520 12TH AVENUE，NEW YORK，N．Y．

10036
电话：001－212－3307427，001－212－3307428，001－212－3307426
传真：001－212－5020248

中华人民共和国常驻联合国代表团

地址：WEST. 66TH STREET NEW YORK，N. Y. 10023
电话：001－212－8700300，001－213－7873838
电传：424465 PRC 423727

中华人民共和国驻洛杉矶总领事馆经济商务室

地址：501 SHATTO PLACE，SUITE 300，LOS ANGELES，CA 90020，U. S. A.
电话：001－213－3800587，001－213－3800669
传真：001－213－3801961

中华人民共和国驻休斯敦总领事馆经济商务室

地址：3417 MONTROSE BOULEVARD，HOUSTON，TEXAS 77006，U. S. A.
电话：001－713－5244064，001－713－5240780，001－713－5240778
传真：001－713－5247656

中华人民共和国驻芝加哥总领事馆经济商务室

地址：100 WEST ERIE STREET，CHICAGO，IL. 60610. U. S. A.
电话：001－312－8030115
传真：001－312－8030114

中华人民共和国驻墨西哥合众国大使馆经济商务参赞处

地址：CALLE PLATON NO. 317，COL POLANCO MEXICO；D. F. 11560 MEXICO. D. F.
电话：0052－5－2808592，0052－5－2802970
传真：0052－5－2804847，0052－5－2821646
电传：1763515 OCCHME

中华人民共和国驻古巴共和国大使馆经济商务参赞处

地址：LA，CALLE 42. NO. 313，5 AVENIDA MIRAMAR PLAYA，CIUDAD DE LA HABANA，CUBA
电话：0053－7－332585
传真：0053－7－331021

中华人民共和国驻牙买加大使馆经济商务参赞处

地址：8，SEAVIEW AVE，KINGSTON 10，JAMAICA W. I.
电话：001－809－9276816
传真：001－809－9787780

中华人民共和国驻安提瓜和巴布达大使馆经济商务参赞处

地址：MCKINNONS WAY，ST. JOHN'S，ANTIGUA，W. I.
信箱：P. O. BOX 1355，ST. JOHN'S，ANTIGUA
电话：001－809－4626414
传真：001－809－4620986

中华人民共和国驻巴巴多斯大使馆经济商务参赞处

地址：CORAL ISLE APARTMENTS，MAXWELL COAST ROAD，CHRIST CHURCH，BARBADOS，W. I.
信箱：P. O. BOX 34A，CHRIST CHURCH，BARAADOS
电话：001－246－4283384
传真：001－246－4285860

中华人民共和国驻特立尼达和多巴哥共和国大使馆经济商务参赞处

地址：40 ELIZABETH STREET，ST. CLAIL，PORT OF SPAIN，TRINIDAD，W. I.
电话：001－809－6285556
传真：001－809－6288020

中华人民共和国驻哥伦比亚共和国大使馆经济商务参赞处

地址：CALLE 71 NO. 2A－41 SANTAFE DE BO-

GOTA，COLOMBIA
电话：0057－1－2115411
传真：0057－1－2178985

中华人民共和国驻委内瑞拉共和国
大使馆经济商务参赞处

地 址：QUINTA LA ORQUIDEA CALLE SAN FRANCISCO DESVIACION SAN PEDRO URB. PRADOS DEL ESTE APARTADO 80520，ZONA POSTAL 1080－A CARACAS，VENEZUELA
电话：0058－2－9761678，0058－2－9762896
传真：0058－2－9784864

中华人民共和国驻圭亚那合作共和国
大使馆经济商务参赞处

地址：52 BRICKDAM，GEORGETOWN. COOPERATIVE REPUBLIC OF GUYANA
电话：00592－2－69965，00592－2－67428
传真：00592－2－64308

中华人民共和国驻苏里南共和国
大使馆经济商务参赞处

地址：120 PLUTOS TRAAT－SURINAME DISTRICT PARAMARIBO
信 箱：P. O. BOX 8116，PARAMARIBO IN SURINAME
电话：00597－450490，00597－451281
传真：00597－452560

中华人民共和国驻厄瓜多尔共和国
大使馆经济商务参赞处

地址：AV. ATAHUALPA NO. 349 Y AV. AMAZONAS QUITO，ECUADOR
信箱：17－11－5143
电话：00593－2－444362
传真：00593－2－444364
电传：0308－22614 ECHINA ED

中华人民共和国驻秘鲁共和国
大使馆经济商务参赞处

地址：AV. JAVIER PRADO OESTE 2496，MAGDALENA DEL MAR，LIMA，PERU
信箱：P. O. BOX 170140，LIMA 17，PERU
电话：0051－14－619536
传真：0051－14－619855

中华人民共和国驻巴西联邦共和国
大使馆经济商务参赞处

地 址：SHIS QI 11，CONJUNTO 3，CASA 16，LAGO SUL，CEP；71625－230，BRASILIA－DF，BRASIL
电话：0055－61－2481446，0055－61－2484582
传真：0055－61－2482139

中华人民共和国驻圣保罗
总领事馆经济商务室

地址：RUA ESTADOS UNIDOS，1071－JARDIM AMERICA－CEP 01437 SAO PAULO－SP－BRASIL
电话：0055－11－2829877，8522663
传真：0055－11－30641813
电传：1139911 CGRH BR

中华人民共和国驻里约热内卢
总领事馆经济商务室

地 址：RUA MUNIZ BARRETOTS BOTAFOGO，KIO DE JANEIRD CEP 22251－090
电话：0055－21－5514878
传真：0055－21－5515736，5514533

中华人民共和国驻玻利维亚共和国
大使馆经济商务参赞处

地址：CALLE 25 CALACOTO NO. 33 LA PAZ－BOLIVIAZ
电话：00591－2－794567
传真：00591－2－797577

中华人民共和国驻智利共和国
大使馆经济商务参赞处

地址：CASILLA 3417 AV. PEDRO DE VALDIVIA 1032. PROVIDENCIA, SANTIAGO, CHILE
信箱：CASILLA 3417，SANTIAGO，CHILE
电话：0056－2－2239988，2232465
传真：0056－2－2232465

中华人民共和国驻阿根廷共和国
大使馆经济商务参赞处

地址：LA PAMPA 3410 BUENOS AIRES，ARGENTINA
电话：0054－1－5541258，5542613
手机：4456536
传真：0054－1－5538939

中华人民共和国驻乌拉圭东岸共和国
大使馆经济商务参赞处

地址：RAMBLE REPUBLICA DEL PERU 727/101
信箱：P. O. BOX 18966
电话：00598－2－710852
传真：00598－2－704810
电传：00598－2－23323CHIEMBA

中国巴拿马贸易发展办事处

地 址：TORRE GLOBAL BANK，PISO 22，CALLE 50，PANAMA
电话：00507－2654061，2654062
传真：00507－2654051，2130265

中华人民共和国贸促会驻
圣多明各商务代表处

地 址：CALLE REPOBLACION FORESTAL NO. 7，EDIFICIO DON SAMUEL，LOS MILLONES，APARTADO POSTAL 3513，SANTO DOMINGO，REPUBLICA DOMINICANA
电话：001－809－5662620，5667063
传真：001－809－5662620

大 洋 洲

中华人民共和国驻澳大利亚
大使馆经济商务参赞处

地址：15 CORONATION DRIVE YARRALUMLA，ACT 2600CANBERRA，AUSTRALIA
电话：0061－6－2734785
传真：0061－6－2735189
电传：CHIEM AA 62489

中华人民共和国驻悉尼
总领事馆经济商务室

地址：68 GEORGE STREET，REDFERN，NEW SOUTH WALES 2016，AUSTRALIA
电话：0061－2－6987788，0061－2－6987838
传真：0061－2－6987373

中华人民共和国驻墨尔本
总领事馆经济商务室

地址：75－77 IRVING ROAD，TOORAK，VIC. 3142，AUSTRALIA
电话：0061－3－95095547
传真：0061－3－98220320

中华人民共和国驻珀斯
总领事馆经济商务室

地址：3RD FLOOR，AUSTRALIA PLACE，15－17 WILLIAM STREET，PERTH W. A. 6000，AUSTRALIA
电话：0061－9－3218193
传真：0061－9－3218457

中华人民共和国驻新西兰
大使馆经济商务参赞处

地 址：104A KOROKORO ROAD，LOWER HUTT，P. O. BOX. 12342，THORNDON，WELLINGTON，NEW ZEALAND
电话：00644－5870407
传真：00644－5870407

中华人民共和国驻奥克兰
总领事馆经济商务室

地址：30－32 ALPERS AVE. EPSOM，AUCKLAND，NEW ZEALAND
电话：0064－9－5224424
传真：0064－9－5224407

中华人民共和国驻巴布亚新几内亚
大使馆经济商务参赞处

地 址：P. O. BOX 5411，BOROKO NCD，PAPUA NEW GUINEA
电话：00675－3255392，3251190
传真：00675－3253169

中华人民共和国驻瓦努阿图共和国
大使馆经济商务参赞处

地址：PRIVATE MAIL BAG 071，PORT VILA，VANUATU
电话：00678－24565
传真：00678－22730

中华人民共和国驻斐济共和国
大使馆经济商务参赞处

地址：147 QUEEN ELIZABETH DRIVE，SUVA，FIJI
电话：00679－304564
传真：00679－300950

中华人民共和国驻基里巴斯共和国
大使馆经济商务参赞处

地址：P. O. BOX 30，TARAWA，KIRIBATI
电话：00686－21313
传真：00686－21378

中华人民共和国驻密克罗尼西亚联邦
大使馆经济商务参赞处

地址：P. O. BOX 1836 KOLONIA，POHNPEI，FEDERATED STATES OF MICRONESIA 96941
电话：00691－320－5072
传真：00691－320－5074

中华人民共和国驻马绍尔群岛共和国
大使馆经济商务参赞处

地 址：P. O. BOX 1378，MAJURO 960，THE REPUBLIC OF THE MARSHALL ISLANDS
电话：00692－2475505
传真：00692－2477511

中华人民共和国驻西萨摩亚
大使馆经济商务参赞处

地 址：PRIVATE BAG，VAILIMA，APIA，WESTERN SAMOA
电话：00685－20802
传真：00685－21115

欧 洲

中华人民共和国驻冰岛共和国
大使馆经济商务参赞处

地址：VIDIMELUR 25，REYKJAVIK，ICELAND
信 箱：P. O. BOX 7290，REYKJAVIK，ICELAND
电话：00354－1－5526322
传真：00354－1－5623922

中华人民共和国驻丹麦王国
大使馆经济商务参赞处

地址：REGARDS ALLE 12，2900 HELLERUP，COPEN－HAGEN，DENMARK
电话：0045－39611013，0045－39611092
传真：0045－39612913
电传：27019 CHEM DK

中华人民共和国驻挪威王国
大使馆经济商务参赞处

地 址：INKOGNITOGATEN 11，0258 OSLO，NORWAY
电话：0047－22－560270，0047－22－438666
0047－22－447230
传真：0047－22－447230

中华人民共和国驻瑞典王国
大使馆经济商务参赞处

地址：RINGVAGEN 56 181 34 LIDINGO，SWEDEN
电话：0046－8－7674083，0046－8－7679625
0046－8－7678740
传真：0046－8－7318404
电传：16490 CHINO S

中华人民共和国驻芬兰共和国大使馆经济商务参赞处

地址：VAHANITYNTIE 4 00570 HELSINKI 57，FINLAND
电话：00358－9－6848416，00358－9－6849641
传真：00358－9－6849595
电传：126055 CHINA SF

中华人民共和国驻俄罗斯联邦大使馆经济商务参赞处

地址：ULITSA DRUZHBA 6，MOSCOW，RUSSIA
电话：007－095－1431544，007－095－9382111
传真：007－095－9382005
电传：413981 CHINA SU

中华人民共和国驻哈巴罗夫斯克总领事馆经济商务室

地址：STADION IM LENINA，HABAROVSK，RUSSIA
电话：007－4212－348586，007 4212－399466
传真：007－4212－338390
电传：141255 CGKHB SU

中华人民共和国驻阿塞拜疆共和国大使馆经济商务参赞处

地址：巴库布，第·阿利耶瓦大街，94号
电话：007－3712－623437，007－3712－625567
传真：007－3712－0078922，0099412
电传：（065）116583 KTP UZ SU

中华人民共和国驻亚美尼亚共和国大使馆经济商务参赞处

地址：875048 EREVAN，NORK 9 STREET，HOUSE 89
电话：007－8852－651935，651311
传真：007－8852－151153

中华人民共和国驻格鲁吉亚共和国大使馆经济商务参赞处

地址：第比利斯市，奥谢吉斯卡亚大街，3号
电话：007－8832－936189，932893
传真：0049－5151－13057 NO. 192
0049－5151－8635

中华人民共和国驻白俄罗斯共和国大使馆经济商务参赞处

地址：31/2 KRASNOZ VEZDNAYA STR. 220071，MINSK，BELORUSSIA
电话：00375－0172－370211
传真：00375－0172－100391

中华人民共和国驻乌克兰大使馆经济商务参赞处

地址：250035 STREET RECHINAY 3，KIEV，UKRAINE
电话：380－44－2948810，2947710
传真：380－44－2948040

中华人民共和国驻乌兹别克斯坦共和国大使馆经济商务参赞处

地址：700170 15，SOROK LET KOMSOMOLA，TASHKENT
电话：007－3712－682642
传真：007－3712－891246，672340

中华人民共和国驻哈萨克斯坦共和国大使馆经济商务参赞处

地址：480016 ST. TULEBAEVA 26，ALMA－ATA，KAZAKHSTAN
电话：007－3272－327681，007－3272－651114
传真：007－3272－392007

中华人民共和国驻吉尔吉斯共和国大使馆经济商务参赞处

地址：6，MANAS ST. BISHKEK，720017，KIRGHIZSTAN
电话：007－3312－224732
传真：007－3312－620148
电传：788－245136 CHTRD KH

中华人民共和国驻塔吉克斯坦
共和国大使馆经济商务参赞处

地 址：35，TAJIKISTAN 40 YERS ST. DUSHANBE
电话：007－3772－273414，007－3772－273228
007－3772－231859
传真：007－3772－211859

中华人民共和国驻土库曼斯坦
大使馆经济商务参赞处

地址：ASHGABAT，BERZENGI，HOTEL ASIA
电话：00993－1－2－510180 转 215，218
传真：00993－1－2－520101
电传：116556 CHINA SU

中华人民共和国驻拉脱维亚
大使馆经济商务处

电话：00371－7－322322
传真：00371－7－243124

中华人民共和国驻爱沙尼亚
共和国大使馆经济商务参赞处

地址：KUMALASE 6，EE0009 TALLINN，ESTONIA
电话：00372－2－518018
传真：00358－49－200186

中华人民共和国驻立陶宛共和国
大使馆经济商务参赞处

地址：BLINDZIU 34，2004 VILNIUS，LITHUANIA
电话：00370－2－722259/722375/722223
传真：00370－2－722161

中华人民共和国驻摩尔多瓦
大使馆经济商务参赞处

地址：基希讷乌市，电视中心区，弗卢摩依萨大街，31 34 号
电话：007－3732－212549，007－3732－443505
传真：445928

中华人民共和国驻波兰共和国
大使馆经济商务参赞处

地 址：BIURO RADCY HANDLOWO－KEONOMICZNEGO PRZY AMBASADZIE CHINSKIEJ REPUBLIKI LUDOWEJ WPOLSCE UL. BONIFRATERSKA 100－203 WARSZWA
电话：0048－22－313861，0048－22－313836
传真：0048－22－6354211
电传：813589 CHINA PL

中华人民共和国驻捷克共和国
大使馆经济商务参赞处

地址：VELVYSLSNECTVI CINSKE LI DOVE REPUBLIKY OBCHODNI ODDELENI PELLEOVA 22 16000 PRAHA 6－BUBENEC
电话：0042－2－24311324
传真：0042－2－323252

中华人民共和国驻斯洛伐克共和国
大使馆经济商务参赞处

地址：JESENESKEHO 7，811，01，BRATISLAVA，SLOVENSKA REPUBLIKA
电话：0042－7－322103
传真：0042－7－367208

中华人民共和国驻匈牙利共和国
大使馆经济商务参赞处

地 址：1068 BUDAPEST，BENCZUR U. 17，HUNGARY
电话：0036－1－3225242
传真：0036－1－3229067
电传：22－7733 CHIBE H

中华人民共和国驻德意志联邦共和国
大使馆经济商务参赞处

地 址：FRIEDRICH－EBERT－STR. 59 53177 BONN BAD GODESBERG F. R. GERMANY
电话：0049－228－955940
传真：0049－228－356781

中华人民共和国驻德意志联邦

共和国大使馆柏林办事处

地 址：ARNOLD - ZWEIG - STR. 5 13189 BERLIN，GERMANY
电话：0049-30-4723118
传真：0049-30-4710230

中华人民共和国驻
汉堡总领事馆经济商务室

地 址：ELBCHAUSSEE 268 22605. HAMBURG，GERMANY
电话：0049-40-82276012，0049-40-82276016
传真：0049-40-8227602
电传：21 2811 GKCHH-D

中华人民共和国驻奥地利共和国
大使馆经济商务参赞处

地址：A-1030 WIEN，METTERNICHGASSE 4
电话：0043-1-7143140
传真：0043-1-7130037

中华人民共和国常驻联合国
工业发展组织代表处

地址：UNTERE DONAUSTRASSE 41，1020 VIENNA，AUSTRIA
电话：00431-2163367
00431-2169380（下班后）
传真：00431-2169389

中华人民共和国常驻维也纳联合国
和其他国际组织代表团

地 址：POETZLEINSDORFER STRASSE 42 1180 VIENNA，AUSTRIA
电话：0043-0222-471364，0043-0222-478338

中华人民共和国驻瑞士联邦
大使馆经济商务参赞处

地 址：7. J. V. WIDMANNSTRASSE，3074 MURI，BERN，SCHWEIZ
电话：0041-31-9511401，0041-31-9511402
0041-31-9511403
传真：0041-31-9510575
电传：912629HBCH CH

中华人民共和国驻联合国日内瓦办事处
和瑞士其他国际组织代表团

地址：CHEMIN DE SURVILLE 11 1213 PETIT-LANCY，GENEVA，SWITZERLAND
电话：0041-22-7937013，0041-22-7933270
传真：0041-22-7937014

中华人民共和国驻荷兰王国
大使馆经济商务参赞处

地址：GROOT HAESEBROEKSEWEG 2A 2243 EA WASSENAAR，THE NETHERLANDS
电话：0031-（0）70-5115559
传真：0031-（0）70-5115206

中华人民共和国驻比利时王国
大使馆经济商务参赞处

地 址：BOULEVARD GENERAL JACQUES 19 1050 BRUXELLES，BELGIQUE
电话：0032-2-6404006，0032-2-6404210
传真：0032-2-6403595
电传：23328 AMCHIN B

中华人民共和国驻欧洲
共同体经济商务参赞处

地址、电话、传真、电传：（同驻比利时商务处）

中华人民共和国驻卢森堡大公国
大使馆经济商务参赞处

地 址：BOULEVARD GENERAL JACQUES 19 1050 BRUXELLES，BELGIQUE
电话：0032-36404006，0032-2-6404210，
0032-2-6404006
传真：0032-2-6403595
电传：23328 AMCHIN B

中华人民共和国驻大不列颠及北爱尔兰
联合王国大使馆经济商务参赞处

地址：CLEVELAND COURT，1 - 3 LEINSTER GARDENS，LONDON W2 6DP，THE UNITED KINGDOM
电话：0044-171-7238923，0044-171-2620253
0041-171-2623911
传真：0044-171-7062777

电传：896440 CLEFSL G

中华人民共和国驻爱尔兰
大使馆经济商务参赞处

地 址：77，AILESBURY ROAD，DUBLIN 4，IRELAND
电话：00353－1－2600580
传真：00353－1－2696966
电传：91834 COCE EI

中华人民共和国驻法兰西共和国
大使馆经济商务参赞处

地址：21，RUE DE L' AMIRAL D' ESTAING 75016 PARIS FRANCE
电话：0033－1－47201747，0033－1－47209416
传真：0033－1－47234831

中华人民共和国驻西班牙王国
大使馆经济商务参赞处

地址：ARTURO SORIA 142，PISO 2 － A 28043 MADRID，ESPANA
电话：0034－1－4135892，0034－1－4132776
传真：0034－1－5194675
电传：22808 EMCHI E MADRID

中华人民共和国驻葡萄牙共和国
大使馆经济商务参赞处

地址：RUA ANTONIO DE SALDANHA，42 1400，LISBOA，PORTUGAL
电话：00351－1－3011947
传真：00351－1－3014950

中华人民共和国驻意大利共和国
大使馆经济商务参赞处

地址：00135 ROMA VIA DELLA CAMILLUCCIA，613 ITALIA
电话：0039－6－36308534，0039－6－36303856
传真：0039－6－36308552
电传：622162 CINAC I

中华人民共和国驻米兰
总领事馆经济商务室

地址：VIA PALEOCAPA，4－2－21 MILANO，ITALIA
电话：0039－2－72021905，0039－2－72021988
传真：0039－2－86452219

中华人民共和国驻马耳他共和国
大使馆经济商务参赞处

地址：CASA VERDALA，SACRED HEART AVENUE，ST. JULIANS，MALTA
电话：00356－330840
传真：00356－310072，00356－344730

中华人民共和国驻南斯拉夫联盟
共和国大使馆经济商务参赞处

地址：VASILIJA GACESE 5，11000 BELGRADE，YUGOSLAVIA
电话：0038－111－651630
传真：0038－111－650726
电传：12492 CNCCO YU

中华人民共和国驻斯洛文尼亚共和国
大使馆经济商务参赞处

地址：MALCI BELICEVE 123 1000 LJUBLJANA，REPUBLIC OF SLOVENIA
电话：00386－61－272759
传真：00386－61－1233838

中华人民共和国驻克罗地亚共和国
大使馆经济商务参赞处

地 址：BUKOVACKA C. 177 1000 ZAGREB，CROATIA
电话：00385－41－242888
传真：00385－41－243287

中华人民共和国驻罗马尼亚
大使馆经济商务参赞处

地址：SOSEAUA NORDULUI NO. 2，BUCHAREST，ROMANIA
电话：0040－1－6335040，0040－1－6331923，0040－1－6331732
传真：0040－1－3129786，0040－1－3127523
电传：11324 CHIAB R

中华人民共和国驻保加利亚共和国大使馆经济商务参赞处

地址：SOFIA 3，9，"PLER DEGELDER" STR，1113，SOFIA，BULGARIA
电话：00359－2－724988，00359－2－9712032
传真：00359－2－9712416

中华人民共和国驻阿尔巴尼亚共和国大使馆经济商务参赞处

地址：RRUGA SKENDERBEJ NR. 57，TIRANE，ALBANIA
电话：00355－42－32077
传真：00355－42－32077

中华人民共和国驻希腊共和国大使馆经济商务参赞处

地址：DIADOCHOU PAVLOU 7，P，PSYCHIKO，154 52 ATHENS，GREECE
电话：0030－1－6727492
传真：0030－1－6741575
电传：226848 CPRC GR

中华人民共和国驻马其顿共和国大使馆经济商务参赞处

地址：ST. OSLO 22－B 91000 SKOPJE，REPUBLIC OF MACEDONIA
邮政编码：91000 电话：0038991－362680
传真：0038991－362803

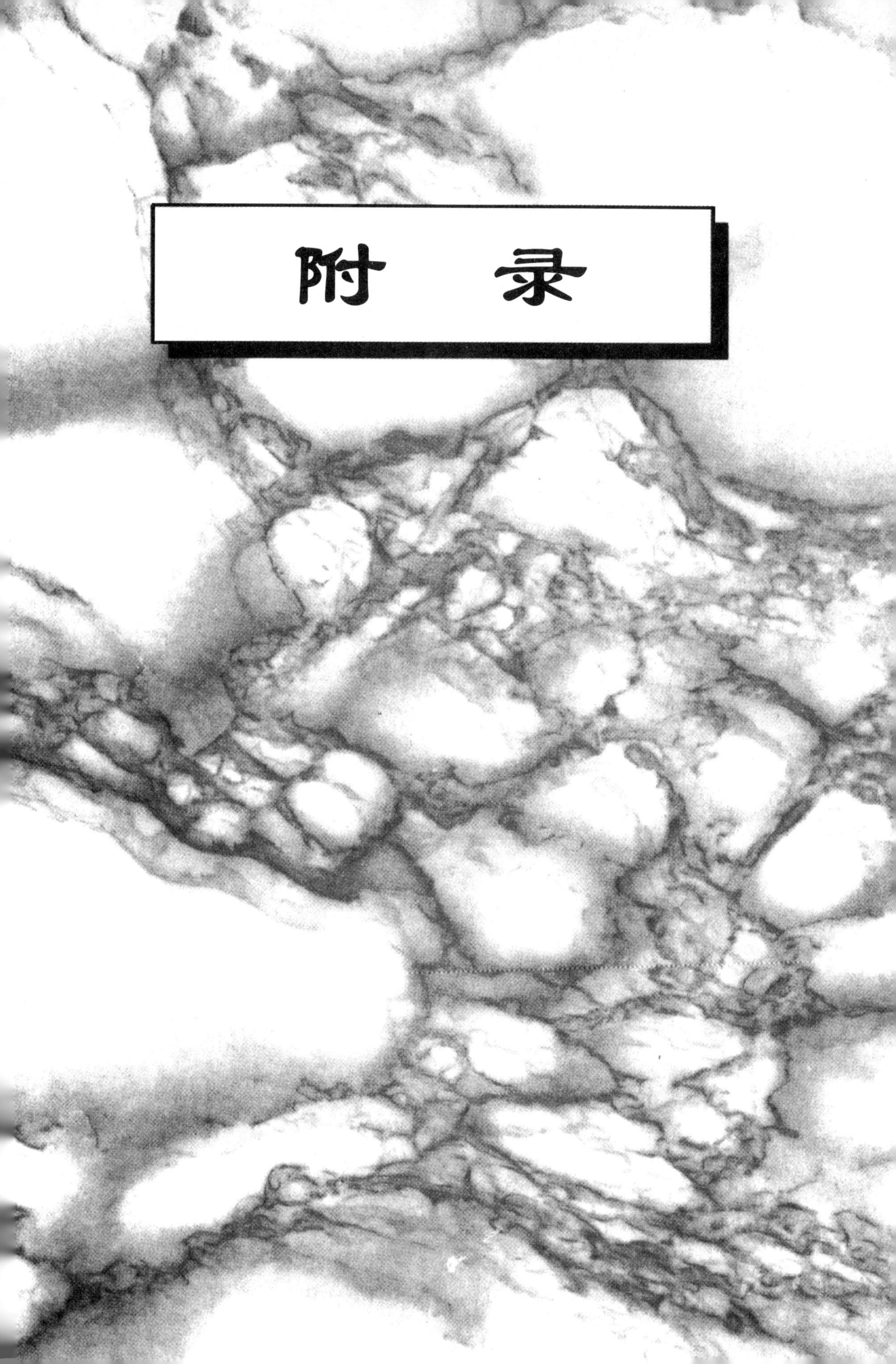

附　　录

第一部分

中国国民经济基本情况统计(一)

(1985 年－1998 年)

指　　标	单　位	绝　对　数					1998 年为以下年份%			
		1985	1990	1995	1997	1998	1985	1990	1995	1997
国内生产总值	亿元	8964.4	18547.9	58478.1	74772.4	79552.8	330.8	226.6	128.5	107.8
第一产业	亿元	2541.6	5017.0	11993.0	13968.8	14298.7	169.3	138.0	112.6	103.5
第二产业	亿元	3866.6	7717.4	28537.9	36770.3	39149.8	464.6	302.3	135.7	109.2
工业	亿元	3448.7	6858.0	24718.3	31752.3	33540.9	477.5	307.2	136.1	108.9
建筑业	亿元	417.9	859.4	3819.6	5018.0	5608.9	358.2	262.1	131.1	112.0
第三产业	亿元	2556.2	5813.5	17947.2	24033.3	26104.3	316.0	201.9	125.6	107.6
＃运输邮电业	亿元	406.9	1147.5	3054.7	4525.5	5029.3	360.8	225.7	133.3	108.0
商业	亿元	878.4	1419.7	4932.3	6281.5	6609.6	221.4	176.8	123.1	107.7
人均国内生产总值	元/人	853	1634	4854	6079	6404	279.5	206.7	124.5	106.7
固定资产投资										
全社会固定资产投资总额	亿元	2543.2	4517.0	20019.3	24941.1	28457.5	1119.0	630.0	142.2	114.1
基本建设投资	亿元	1074.4	1703.8	7403.6	9917.0	11904.3	1108.0	698.7	160.8	120.0
财政总收入	亿元	2004.8	2937.1	6242.2	8651.1	9853.0	491.5	335.5	157.8	113.9
财政总支出	亿元	2004.3	3083.6	6823.7	9233.6	10771.0	537.4	349.3	157.8	116.7
交通、邮电										
货物周转量	亿吨公里	18365	26207	35730	38212	37855	206.1	144.4	105.9	99.1
沿海主要港口货物吞吐量	万吨	31154	48321	80166	90822	92237	296.1	190.9	115.1	101.6
旅客周转量	亿人公里	4437	5628	9002	10019	10559	238.0	187.6	117.3	105.4
邮电业务总量	亿元	29.60	81.65	988.85	1773.29	2431.21	4311.4	1563.1	245.9	137.1
商业和物价										
社会消费品零售额	亿元	3801.4	7250.3	20620.0	27298.9	29152.5	264.8	225.0	135.8	109.6
年末城乡集市贸易点	个	61337	72579	82892	87105	89177	145.4	122.9	107.6	102.4
农产品收购价格总指数	上年=100	108.6	97.4	119.9	95.5	92.0				
商品零售物价指数	上年=100	108.8	102.1	114.8	100.8	97.4				
全国居民消费价格总指数	上年=100	109.3	103.1	117.1	102.8	99.2				

中国国民经济基本情况统计(二)

(1985 年 - 1998 年)

指标	单位	绝对数					1998 年为以下年份 %			
		1985	1990	1995	1997	1998	1985	1990	1995	1997
城市居民消费价格指数	上年 = 100	111.9	101.3	116.8	103.1	99.4				
农村居民消费价格指数	上年 = 100	107.6	104.5	117.5	102.5	99.0				
外贸、旅游										
进出口总额	亿美元	696.0	1154.4	2808.6	3251.6	3239.3	465.4	280.6	115.3	99.6
出口总额	亿美元	273.5	620.9	1487.8	1827.9	1837.6	671.9	296.0	123.5	100.5
进口总额	亿美元	422.5	533.5	1320.8	1423.7	1401.7	331.8	262.7	106.1	98.5
实际利用外资	亿美元	46.47	102.89	481.33	644.08	585.57	1260.1	569.1	121.7	90.9
对外借款	亿美元	26.88	65.34	103.27	120.21	110.00	409.2	168.4	106.5	91.5
外商直接投资及其他	亿美元	19.59	37.55	378.06	523.87	475.57	2427.6	1266.5	125.8	90.8
接待外来旅游人数	万人	1783.3	2746.2	4638.7	5758.8	6347.8	356.0	231.2	136.8	110.2
外国人	万人	137.0	174.7	588.7	742.8	710.8	518.8	406.9	120.7	95.7
港澳台同胞	万人	1637.8	2562.4	4038.4	5006.1	5624.9	343.4	219.5	139.3	112.4
旅游收入外汇	亿美元	12.5	22.2	87.3	120.7	126.0	1008.0	567.6	144.3	104.4
科学、教育、文化										
国家级重大科学技术成果	项	10476	26829	31099	30566	28000	267.3	104.4	90.0	91.6
国有企业事业单位专业技术人员在校学生:	万人	781.7	1080.9	1913.4	2049.5	2091.4	267.5	193.5	109.3	102.0
普通高等学校	万人	170.3	206.3	290.6	317.4	340.9	200.2	165.2	117.3	107.4
成人高等学校	万人	172.5	166.6	257.0	272.5	282.2	163.6	169.4	109.8	103.6
普通中学	万人	4706.0	4586.0	5371.0	6017.9	6301.0	133.9	137.4	117.3	104.7
中等专业学校	万人	157.1	224.4	372.2	465.4	498.1	317.1	222.0	133.8	107.0
成人中等学校	万人	547.0	1529.4	5646.3	6078.1	6676.0	1220.5	436.5	118.2	109.8
成人初等学校	万人	833.8	2282.1	778.3	616.1	538.6	64.6	23.6	69.2	87.4
小学	万人	13370	12241	13195.2	13995.4	13953.8	104.4	114.0	105.7	99.7
艺术表演团体	个	3317	2805	2682	2663	2635	79.4	93.9	98.2	98.9
文化馆	个	2965	2955	2886	2901	2915	98.3	98.6	101.0	100.5

中国国民经济基本情况统计(三)

(1985 年－1998 年)

指标	单位	绝对数					1998 年为以下年份%			
		1985	1990	1995	1997	1998	1985	1990	1995	1997
公共图书馆	个	2344	2527	2615	2661	2721	116.1	107.7	104.1	102.3
广播电台	座	213	635	1202	1363					
电视台	座	202	509	837	923					
全国性和省级报纸出版	亿份	199.8	160.5	178.9	186.5	196.0	98.1	122.1	109.6	105.1
各类杂志出版	亿册	25.6	17.9	23.4	24.4	25.4	99.2	141.9	108.5	104.1
图书出版	亿册	66.7	56.4	63.2	73.1	72.4	108.5	128.4	114.6	99.0
卫生、体育										
医院病床	万张	222.9	262.4	283.6	290.3	291.4	130.7	111.1	102.8	100.4
专业卫生技术人员	万人	341.1	389.8	425.7	439.8	442.4	129.7	113.5	103.9	100.6
♯医生	万人	141.3	176.3	191.8	198.5	200.0	141.5	113.4	104.3	100.8
护师、护士	万人	63.7	97.5	112.6	119.8	121.9	191.4	125.0	108.3	101.8
获得世界体育冠军	项	42	54	98	87	77	183.3	142.6	78.6	88.5
打破体育世界纪录	项	5	14	13	29	31	620.0	221.4	238.5	106.9
举办县以上运动会	万次	2.7	3.0	2.8	2.7	2.7	100.0	89.4	96.4	100.0
人民生活										
农民平均每人纯收入	元	397.6	686.3	1577.7	2090.1	2162.0	205.7	166.6	113.6	105.8
城市居民人均可支配收入	元	739.1	1510.2	4283.0	5160.3	5425.1	169.8	146.8	119.1	104.4
年末职工人数	万人	12358	14059	14908	14668	12337	99.8	87.8	82.8	84.1
职工工资总额	亿元	1382.8	2951.1	8100.0	9405.3	9296.5	188.4	146.1	102.9	99.4
职工平均工资	元	1148	2140	5500	6470	7479	182.5	162.1	122.0	116.3
年末城乡人民储蓄存款余额	亿元	1622.6	7119.8	29662.3	46279.8	53407.5	3291.5	750.1	180.1	115.4
城镇人均住房面积	平方米	5.2	6.7	8.1	8.8	9.3	178.8	138.8	114.8	105.7
农村人均住房面积	平方米	14.7	17.8	21.0	22.5	23.7	161.2	133.1	112.9	105.3
人口										
年末全国人口	万人	105851	114333	121121	123626	124810	117.9	109.2	103.0	101.0

中国国民经济基本情况统计(四)

(1985 年－1998 年)

指　标	单　位	绝　对　数					1998 年为以下年份%			
		1985	1990	1995	1997	1998	1985	1990	1995	1997
年人口出生率	‰	21.04	21.06	17.12	16.57	16.03				
年人口死亡率	‰	6.78	6.67	6.57	6.51	6.50				
年人口自然增长率	‰	14.26	14.39	10.55	10.06	9.53				

注:1.表中的数字,均未包括台湾省。

2.本表价值指标绝对数按当年价格计算,国内生产总值、邮电业务总量、社会消费品零售总额、农民平均每人纯收入、城镇居民人均可支配收入、职工工资总额、职工平均工资发展速度均按可比价格计算。

3.国内生产总值是指物质生产部门和非物质生产部门的增加值之和,是一个国家(或地区)所有常住单位在核算期内生产活动的最终成果。

4.邮电业务总量 1985、1990 年按 1980 年不变价格计算,1995 年以后按 1990 年不变价格计算。

5.农村和城市居民平均每人收入,是根据家庭抽样调查得出的。职工工资总额包括发给职工的物价补贴。1998 年职工人数为在岗职工。

6.表中的出口、进口总额系中国海关统计数字。

资料来源:《中国统计年鉴》1986－1998、《中国统计摘要》1999。

(国家统计局综合司资料处)

1985年—1998年中国长期与短期外债的结构与增长

项目/年度		1985	1986	1987	1988	1989	1990	1991	1992	1993	1994	1995	1996	1997	1998
外债余额(亿美元)		158.3	214.8	302.0	400.0	413.0	525.5	605.6	693.2	835.7	928.1	1065.9	1162.8	1309.7	1460.4
中长期外债	余额(亿美元)	94.1	167.1	244.8	326.9	370.3	457.8	502.6	584.7	700.2	823.9	946.8	1021.7	1128.2	1287.0
	比上年增长(%)		77.6	46.5	33.5	13.3	23.6	9.8	16.4	20.0	17.7	14.9	7.9	10.4	14.1
	占总余额的比例(%)	59.0	77.8	81.0	81.7	89.7	87.1	83.0	84.4	83.8	88.8	88.8	87.9	86.1	88.1
短期外债	余额(亿美元)	64.2	47.7	57.2	73.1	42.7	67.7	103.0	108.5	135.5	104.2	119.1	141.1	181.4	173.4
	比上年增长(%)		-25.7	19.9	27.8	-41.6	58.5	52.2	5.2	24.3	-23.1	14.3	18.4	28.6	-4.4
	占总余额的比例(%)	41.0	22.2	19.0	18.3	10.3	12.9	17.0	15.6	16.2	11.2	11.2	12.1	13.9	11.9

(国家外汇管理局资本项目司)

1985 年—1998 年中国外债流动与国民经济、外汇收入

项目/年度	1985	1986	1987	1988	1989	1990	1991	1992	1993	1994	1995	1996	1997	1998
1 外债流入（亿美元）	83.3	87.2	92.1	142.3	174.3	164.8	188.6	152.2	273.7	343.3	391.1	309.5	431.0	456.6
2 比上年增长（%）	－－	4.7	5.6	54.5	22.5	－5.5	14.4	－19.3	79.8	25.4	13.9	－20.9	39.3	5.9
3 外债流出（亿美元）	8.4	62.3	51.2	72.8	170.2	96.2	127.9	134.3	182.5	250.6	317.1	224.7	324.2	424.8
4 比上年增长（%）		641.7	－17.8	42.2	133.7	－43.5	33.0	5.0	35.9	37.3	26.5	－29.1	44.3	31.0
5 外债净流入（亿美元）	74.9	24.9	40.9	69.5	4.1	68.6	60.7	17.9	91.2	92.7	74.0	84.8	106.8	31.8
6 国内生产总值（亿元人民币）	8964.4	10202.2	11962.5	14928.5	16909.2	18547.9	21617.8	26638.1	34634.4	46759.4	58478.1	67884.6	74772.4	79553.0
7 外债流出/国内生产总值	0.3	2.1	1.6	1.8	3.8	2.5	3.1	2.8	3.0	4.6	4.5	2.8	3.6	4.4
8 外汇收入（亿美元）	282.5	297.8	391.7	459.1	478.2	573.7	659.0	788.2	865.6	1189.3	1472.4	1716.8	2072.5	2075.9
9 偿债率（%）	2.7	15.4	9.0	6.5	8.3	8.7	8.5	7.1	10.2	9.1	7.6	6.0	7.3	10.9

注：1. 从 1998 年开始，原使用的“国民生产总值”数据调整为“国内生产总值”数据，以前年份数据均按《中国统计提要一九九八》中公布数据进行了调整。计算负债率时按当年年平均汇率折美元。

2. 外债流出指当年发生的还本付息额。

3. 从 1998 年开始，本报表中外汇收入指国际收支口径的货物和服务收入，以前年份数据均据此进行了调整。

（国家外汇管理局资本项目司）

1985年—1998年中国外债与国民经济、外汇收入

项目/年度	1985	1986	1987	1988	1989	1990	1991	1992	1993	1994	1995	1996	1997	1998
1 外债余额（亿美元）	158.3	214.8	302.0	400.0	413.0	525.5	605.6	693.2	835.7	928.1	1065.9	1162.8	1309.6	1460.4
2 比上年增长（%）	30.9	35.7	40.6	32.5	3.3	27.2	15.2	14.5	20.6	11.1	14.8	9.1	12.6	11.5
3 国内生产总值(亿元人民币)	8964.4	10202.2	11962.5	14928.5	16909.2	18547.9	21617.8	26638.1	34634.4	46759.4	58478.1	67884.6	74772.4	79553.0
4 比上年增长（%）	25.0	13.8	17.3	24.8	13.3	9.7	16.6	23.2	30.1	35.0	25.1	16.1	10.1	6.4
5 负债率(%)	5.2	7.3	9.4	10.0	9.2	13.5	14.9	14.4	13.9	17.1	15.2	14.2	14.5	15.2
6 外汇收入（亿美元）	282.5	297.8	391.7	459.1	478.2	573.7	659.0	788.2	865.6	1189.3	1472.4	1716.8	2072.5	2075.9
7 比上年增长（%）	--	5.4	31.5	17.2	4.2	20.0	14.9	19.6	9.8	37.4	23.8	16.6	20.7	0.2
8 债务率(%)	56.0	72.1	77.1	87.1	86.4	91.6	91.9	87.9	96.5	78.0	72.4	67.7	63.2	70.4

注:1.从1998年开始,原使用的“国民生产总值”数据调整为“国内生产总值”数据,以前年份数据均按《中国统计提要一九九八》中公布数据进行了调整。计算负债率时按当年年平均汇率折美元:

2.第四行“比上年增长”是按可变价格计算。

3.从1998年开始,本报告中外汇收入指国际收支口径的货物和服务收入,以前年份数据均据此进行了调整。

（国家外汇管理局资本项目司）

1998 年我国外汇市场人民币对主要外币月平均汇率

外币单位	货币	月平均汇率												年平均
		1	2	3	4	5	6	7	8	9	10	11	12	
100	美元	827.91	827.91	827.92	827.92	827.90	827.97	827.98	827.99	827.90	827.78	827.78	827.79	827.91
100	英镑	1358.12	1360.13	1375.05	1384.71	1355.66	1365.61	1362.03	1353.15	1392.36	1401.83	1376.62	1383.11	1372.37
100	加拿大元	574.38	576.98	584.69	579.25	573.38	565.40	557.64	540.25	543.46	536.51	537.17	536.48	558.80
100	德国马克	457.21	457.54	453.56	456.15	466.58	462.01	460.60	463.21	485.71	504.93	492.23	495.39	471.26
100	荷兰盾	405.62	406.18	402.41	405.03	414.03	409.87	408.50	410.75	430.59	450.30	436.55	439.54	418.28
100	瑞士法郎	562.91	567.06	556.77	549.67	560.64	554.38	546.92	553.73	590.01	619.36	597.85	607.91	572.27
100	比利时法郎	22.15	22.18	21.98	22.11	22.63	22.40	22.33	22.47	23.54	24.50	23.88	24.03	22.85
100	法国法郎	136.49	136.59	135.30	136.09	139.15	137.80	137.35	138.17	144.92	150.59	146.79	147.70	140.58
100	意大利里拉	0.4643	0.4639	0.4505	0.4616	0.4730	0.4689	0.4669	0.4693	0.4914	0.5101	0.4973	0.5002	0.4765
100	瑞典克朗	103.74	102.75	103.96	105.73	107.63	104.65	103.58	101.89	104.83	105.29	103.34	102.55	104.16
100	挪威克朗	110.95	109.90	109.24	109.92	111.69	109.34	108.57	107.34	109.44	111.27	111.09	108.87	109.80
100	丹麦克朗	120.10	120.12	118.99	119.57	122.45	121.24	120.86	121.60	127.50	132.34	129.52	130.22	123.71
100	奥地利先令	65.03	65.02	64.44	64.77	66.27	65.64	65.40	65.78	69.03	71.81	69.95	70.37	66.96
100	日元	6.3667	6.5842	6.4433	6.2811	6.1517	5.8981	5.8894	5.7253	6.1369	6.8667	6.8917	7.0247	6.3488
100	新加坡元	474.37	498.35	511.85	516.93	506.08	489.03	485.19	472.03	479.44	506.57	505.98	501.27	495.59
100	澳大利亚元	542.46	556.62	555.13	540.98	522.24	500.07	512.78	488.66	486.94	513.16	525.67	511.96	521.39
100	港币	107.00	107.03	106.96	106.88	106.90	106.95	106.85	106.86	106.78	106.72	106.81	106.80	106.88
100	欧洲货币单位	903.04	903.93	899.23	904.24	919.28	912.56	909.87	913.69	955.78	995.29	968.39	972.73	929.84

（国家外汇管理局国际收支司）

1998 年末全国所欠债务简表

金额单位:万美元

债务人/债务类型	外国政府贷款	国际金融组织贷款	国外银行及其它金融机构贷款	买方信贷	向国外出口商‘国外企业或私人借款	在华外资银行贷款	对外发行债券	延期付款	海外私人存款	国际金融租赁	补偿贸易中用现汇偿还的债务	其它	合计
国务院有关部委	1345883.33	2236319.74	44947.40				531810.00	5181.51					4164141.98
国内银行	893791.07		905884.82	1161185.84	26878.10	16027.78	300582.60	77311.62	15941.07	117.00			3397719.89
非银行金融机构			367972.39	4887.08	754.77	88988.56	335661.28		752.05	1778.30			800794.43
租赁公司			94395.47	2460.00	2432.63	50717.76		3067.97		14403.22			167477.05
外商投资企业	293.64	56059.60	1107174.16	118950.59	1682012.31	1431137.71	74974.70	34210.66		15414.08	774.57	2908.48	4523910.50
国内企业	647.73	3000.00	133463.65	9503.56	23213.80	41210.81		51293.48		1273637.14	14157.25		1550127.42
其他			130.00									17.50	147.50
合计	2240615.78	2295379.34	2653967.89	1296987.07	1735291.61	1628082.63	1243028.58	171065.22	16693.12	1305349.74	14931.82	2925.98	14604318.79

（国家外汇管理局资本项目司）

第二部份

世界部分国家和地区国内生产总值(一)

金额单位:亿美元

国别(地区) \ 年份	1985	1987	1988	1989	1990	1991	1992	1993	1994	1995	1996	1997
美国	40387.0	45399.0	49004.0	52508.0	57438.0	59167.0	62444.0	65581.0	69470.0	72654.0	76616.0	81109.0
德国	7419.3	12590.6	11763.2	13097.0	15036.2	17195.5	19693.9	19082.4	20460.3	24140.7	23524.7	21027.0
日本	15981.0	28212.6	29513.6	27619.2	29700.9	34021.2	37194.2	42750.1	46889.7	51373.6	45951.6	41926.7
英国	5161.8	7923.6	8530.5	8283.7	9835.8	10185.9	10573.9	9477.6	10247.5	11115.2	11589.2	12882.5
法国	6216.2	9993.6	9465.4	10642.2	11954.3	12010.1	13222.3	12496.6	13310.0	15350.9	15387.9	13924.5
沙特阿拉伯	861.3	735.5	761.4	830.0	1046.7	1180.4	1232.0	1185.2	1201.7	1256.9	1365.4	1461.7
意大利	4829.3	8413.6	8361.2	9393.9	10939.8	11507.3	12191.7	9851.3	10163.1	10880.3	12136.9	11453.8
加拿大	3420.3	4243.7	5080.2	5620.6	5738.0	5904.5	5709.6	5525.6	5472.0	5742.1	6048.2	6256.3
荷兰	1534.6	2478.8	2287.6	2530.4	2835.4	2899.9	3219.2	3117.4	3342.9	3952.8	3925.5	3604.8
比利时	941.4	1570.9	1489.9	1686.8	1937.5	1985.5	2248.5	2140.4	2322.2	2736.8	2682.3	2425.2
瑞典	1137.9	1750.3	1810.1	1979.4	2297.6	2393.3	2475.6	1858.1	1984.3	2313.0	2517.4	2277.6
瑞士	1098.0	1993.0	1784.6	1877.8	2284.0	2327.1	2434.9	2367.4	2613.9	3074.0	2951.5	2552.9
印度	2155.5	2587.6	2647.5	2681.7	3059.5	2712.2	2723.7	2658.8	3071.0	3450.7	3603.9	…
印度尼西亚	862.2	756.5	820.9	930.4	1061.4	1166.2	1391.2	1580.1	1768.9	2021.3	2273.7	2149.9
中国台湾	732.5	1159.0	1284.3	1539.7	1627.4	1917.4	2144.6	2242.9	2467.3	2559.3	2747.7	2513.2
澳大利亚	1568.3	2044.4	2731.8	2833.1	2948.0	2966.7	2928.0	2855.5	3271.0	3536.1	3953.3	3939.3
韩国	921.8	1415.3	1946.1	2194.9	2536.7	2941.8	3079.4	3328.2	3808.2	4563.6	4845.7	4425.4
中国	2664.4	3038.6	3780.1	3388.3	3877.7	4060.9	4690.1	5987.7	5466.1	7113.2	8343.1	9177.2
墨西哥	1275.0	874.7	1711.8	1922.1	2470.4	2905.3	3636.1	4032.0	4217.2	2867.0	3300.5	4025.3
中国香港	334.4	475.9	552.8	629.7	726.2	833.4	1006.4	1159.6	1308.2	1392.2	1541.2	1736.0
新加坡	176.9	202.5	248.5	294.6	374.5	435.7	496.8	583.7	708.5	851.6	927.5	963.2
西班牙	1829.5	3316.0	3539.8	4105.4	4919.6	5286.0	5773.1	4789.6	4838.2	5596.3	5822.1	5320.5
巴西	2279.5	3030.8	3504.6	4821.7	4429.1	4045.0	4092.0	4405.3	5464.9	7039.1	7749.5	8041.1

世界部分国家和地区国内生产总值(二)

金额单位:亿美元

国别(地区) \ 年份	1985	1987	1988	1989	1990	1991	1992	1993	1994	1995	1996	1997
挪威	659.7	900.9	887.8	939.4	1154.5	1177.6	1263.1	1161.1	1229.3	1466.0	1581.5	1533.6
阿联酋	270.2	237.0	236.7	272.7	336.4	339.1	354.1	4.0	32.8	148.5	222.1	251.9
委内瑞拉	598.7	468.6	603.8	344.8	486.0	534.6	604.2	600.5	584.2	773.9	705.4	884.3
尼日利亚	723.6	262.9	271.3	293.8	324.3	327.0	317.8	315.9	414.4	…	…	…
奥地利	780.3	1316.8	1246.6	1415.9	1584.3	1650.0	1872.1	1827.1	1959.3	2310.0	2280.7	2060.3
丹麦	685.8	1147.9	1065.0	1161.0	1291.2	1294.4	1471.0	1388.3	1518.2	1809.4	1839.6	1700.5
芬兰	612.2	980.4	1041.8	1199.8	1348.1	1189.1	1064.4	844.5	978.3	1259.2	1249.6	1198.3
马来西亚	319.6	319.4	334.6	379.5	427.7	481.4	583.1	641.8	725.0	873.1	991.7	978.8
波兰	706.6	536.9	589.5	822.1	589.8	764.8	843.6	860.0	926.0	1190.5	1345.7	1356.2
科威特	223.2	230.9	204.3	244.6	181.8	110.1	198.6	239.7	248.0	265.6	310.8	303.7
罗马尼亚	519.6	615.1	596.4	554.0	382.5	288.5	195.8	263.8	300.7	354.8	351.4	348.4

资料来源:国际货币基金组织《国际金融统计》(月报和年报)
中国台湾省《统计月报》
中国香港《香港统计月报》

(对外贸易经济合作部国际贸易经济合作研究院文献信息中心)

世界主要国家(地区)外汇储备(一)

(期末数)

金额单位:亿美元

年份 国别(地区)	1988	1990	1991	1992	1993	1994	1995	1996	1997	1998
世界	6650.60	8445.29	8945.72	9408.04	10366.75	11200.74	13758.47	15681.11	16535.90	15596.99
日本	905.14	694.87	617.58	618.88	887.20	1151.46	1724.43	2073.35	2078.66	2032.15
德国	533.24	629.67	575.17	858.87	727.27	722.19	777.94	758.03	698.53	641.33
新加坡	168.61	275.35	339.31	396.61	480.66	578.90	683.49	764.91	708.83	744.18
美国	173.60	521.90	459.30	400.10	415.30	412.20	491.00	382.90	308.10	360.00
西班牙	354.01	493.89	642.95	441.76	397.98	401.82	324.91	558.79	660.23	524.90
英国	411.20	329.30	387.30	340.90	346.30	385.30	391.80	371.20	288.80	273.60
瑞士	240.45	292.21	290.02	324.40	316.50	335.54	346.85	367.75	368.99	383.46
荷兰	145.42	160.28	162.40	202.37	296.69	327.16	310.60	241.19	218.81	175.36
马来西亚	61.34	93.27	104.21	167.84	268.14	248.88	229.45	261.56	200.13	247.28
巴西	69.71	74.30	80.20	225.20	306.02	370.69	497.07	583.22	508.26	425.78
泰国	59.97	132.47	172.87	200.12	240.78	288.84	354.63	371.92	256.97	284.34
意大利	325.00	601.76	454.95	249.66	251.40	301.07	329.42	440.64	534.31	254.47
中国	175.48	285.94	426.64	194.43	211.99	516.20	735.79	1050.29	1398.90	1449.59
中国香港 *	…	…	…	351.70	429.90	492.50	554.00	638.10	928.00	…
中国台湾	…	724.41	824.05	823.06	835.73	924.54	903.10	880.38	835.02	…
法国	223.59	340.67	282.92	243.84	200.08	235.20	231.42	231.20	270.97	387.53
加拿大	135.17	158.02	140.79	93.82	104.71	102.19	126.29	180.28	151.22	199.11
挪威	121.73	143.03	122.09	111.01	186.42	179.92	211.09	252.36	220.74	169.27
澳大利亚	129.89	156.05	158.94	105.36	104.70	107.06	113.40	139.67	160.99	141.33
韩国	123.40	144.59	133.06	166.40	197.04	250.32	319.28	332.37	197.10	519.63
沙特阿拉伯	112.19	85.82	97.37	45.61	56.82	58.88	71.01	52.95	59.44	60.14
丹麦	102.24	100.63	68.07	104.77	97.91	84.44	102.62	133.66	181.57	137.53
比利时	83.06	111.21	110.68	128.25	104.74	128.84	146.80	153.80	145.19	157.63

世界主要国家(地区)外汇储备(二)

(期末数)

金额单位:亿美元

国别(地区) \ 年份	1988	1990	1991	1992	1993	1994	1995	1996	1997	1998
瑞典	77.52	173.65	174.76	219.59	183.72	225.27	229.39	181.72	96.56	124.20
墨西哥	48.85	94.46	171.40	183.94	248.86	61.01	152.50	191.76	281.36	314.61
奥地利	67.11	87.54	96.55	115.06	138.66	160.08	178.67	218.61	186.05	299.18
芬兰	58.75	92.12	71.08	47.74	49.93	100.51	92.93	62.05	75.32	85.08
印度	41.48	12.05	35.80	54.61	98.07	193.86	174.67	197.42	243.24	269.58
印度尼西亚	49.48	73.53	91.51	101.81	109.88	118.20	133.06	178.20	160.88	224.01
葡萄牙	50.83	142.52	202.61	187.69	154.81	151.06	153.15	153.59	151.30	150.67
阿联酋	41.41	42.76	50.48	54.22	58.06	63.61	70.12	76.79	80.27	86.64
以色列	40.16	62.75	62.79	51.27	63.82	67.92	81.19	114.13	203.32	226.75
希腊	35.23	33.06	50.82	46.33	76.34	143.22	146.11	173.37	124.41	171.88
智利	31.16	60.68	70.41	91.67	96.39	130.87	141.37	147.81	169.91	150.49
哥伦比亚	30.94	40.49	58.66	72.36	72.85	74.53	77.24	91.83	89.79	75.23
委内瑞拉	29.75	83.11	103.97	92.88	85.31	73.93	56.88	111.24	140.00	116.12
新西兰	28.24	40.71	28.72	29.29	31.95	35.61	42.45	57.71	42.73	…
爱尔兰	47.25	48.49	53.20	30.80	55.79	57.45	81.78	77.15	60.20	86.22

注: * 不包括黄金贮备。

资料来源: 国际货币基金组织《国际金融统计》(月刊和年鉴)。
中国台湾《统计月报》

(对外贸易经济合作部国际贸易经济合作研究院文献信息中心)

世界主要国家(地区)黄金储备(一)

(期末数)

单位:万盎司

年份 国别(地区)	1985	1988	1989	1990	1991	1992	1993	1994	1995	1996	1997	1998
世界	95145	94665	94104	93901	93801	92881	92310	91904	90976	90755	89057	96526
美国	26265	26187	26193	26191	26191	26184	26179	26173	26170	26166	26164	26161
德国	9518	9518	9518	9518	9518	9518	9518	9518	9518	9518	9518	11898
瑞士	8328	8328	8328	8328	8388	8328	8328	8328	8328	8328	8328	8328
法国	8185	8185	8185	8185	8185	8185	8185	8185	8185	8185	8189	10237
意大利	6667	6667	6667	6667	6667	6667	6667	6667	6667	6667	6667	8336
荷兰	4394	4394	4394	4394	4394	4394	3505	3477	3477	3477	2707	3383
比利时	3418	3367	3023	3023	3023	2504	2504	2504	2504	1532	1532	952
日本	2423	2423	2423	2423	2423	2423	2423	2423	2423	2423	2423	2423
奥地利	2114	2115	2066	2039	2003	1993	1860	1834	1199	1075	787	964
西班牙	1465	1404	1572	1561	1562	1562	1562	1562	1563	1563	1563	1954
印度	940	1045	1045	1069	1128	1135	1146	1180	1278	1278	1274	1149
委内瑞拉	1146	1146	1146	1146	1146	1146	1146	1146	1146	1146	1146	976
黎巴嫩	922	922	922	922	922	922	922	922	922	922	922	922
澳大利亚	793	793	793	793	793	793	790	790	790	790	256	256
葡萄牙	2023	1607	1605	1583	1587	1606	1606	1607	1607	1607	1607	2009
英国	1903	1900	1899	1894	1889	1861	1845	1844	1843	1843	1842	2300
加拿大	2011	1714	1610	1476	1296	994	605	389	341	309	309	249
希腊	412	340	340	340	343	343	344	345	346	347	364	362
芬兰	191	196	200	200	200	200	200	200	160	160	160	200
丹麦	163	163	164	165	166	166	164	163	165	166	169	214
瑞典	607	607	607	607	607	607	607	607	470	470	472	472
沙特阿拉伯	460	460	460	460	460	460	460	460	460	460	460	460
南非	484	347	308	409	647	665	476	420	425	379	399	400

世界主要国家(地区)黄金储备(二)

(期末数)

单位:万盎司

国别(地区) \ 年份	1985	1988	1989	1990	1991	1992	1993	1994	1995	1996	1997	1998
土耳其	386	382	378	409	416	405	403	382	375	375	375	375
科威特	254	254	254	254	254	254	254	254	254	254	254	254
泰国	249	248	248	248	248	247	247	247	247	247	247	247
巴基斯坦	190	195	195	195	196	202	204	205	205	206	207	208
菲律宾	148	284	245	289	337	280	322	289	358	465	499	543
中国	1270	1270	1270	1270	1270	1270	1270	1270	1270	1270	1270	1270
印度尼西亚	310	310	310	310	311	310	310	310	310	310	310	310
马来西亚	234	235	237	235	235	239	239	239	239	239	235	235
阿根廷	437	437	437	423	412	437	437	437	437	437	36	36
巴西	310	273	298	457	202	223	293	371	458	369	303	460
智利	…	182	175	186	186	187	187	186	186	186	186	122
秘鲁	195	171	197	221	183	182	130	112	112	111	111	110
乌拉圭	262	261	261	240	226	203	170	170	172	174	176	178
罗马尼亚	382	145	217	221	225	231	237	263	270	282	302	322

资料来源:国际货币基金组织《国际金融统计》(月报和年鉴)

(对外贸易经济合作部国际贸易经济合作研究院文献信息中心)

世界部分国家(地区)商品贸易额(一)

国别(地区) \ 金额 \ 年份	1990			1992			1993			1994	
	总额	出口	进口	总额	出口	进口	总额	出口	进口	总额	出口
世界	69815.52	34250.43	35565.09	74558.81	36610.19	37948.62	73863.11	36513.47	37349.64	84309.00	41688.07
发达的市场经济国家	50287.14	24551.42	25735.72	53365.96	26363.57	27002.39	51059.85	25666.11	25393.74	57643.51	28862.87
发展中的市场经济国家	15859.33	7985.57	7873.76	19272.80	9302.20	9970.60	20821.95	9874.05	10947.90	23883.18	11448.30
石油输出国组织	2863.01	1766.80	1096.21	3338.32	1783.16	1555.16	3370.27	1776.68	1593.59	3334.33	1812.95
最不发达国家	377.74	150.29	227.45	390.01	152.16	237.85	394.05	144.80	249.25	421.83	160.70
其他国家	3669.06	1713.45	1955.61	1920.06	944.43	975.63	1981.32	973.31	1008.01	2782.31	1376.90
美洲	13623.68	6277.08	7346.60	14961.23	6841.93	8119.30	15433.12	6631.84	8801.28	18006.33	7961.70
美国	9105.79	3935.92	5169.87	10020.86	4481.63	5539.23	10682.11	4647.73	6034.38	12018.42	5126.27
加拿大	2508.81	1276.34	1232.47	2637.09	1344.41	1292.68	2842.21	1451.82	1390.39	3204.56	1653.80
巴西	539.38	314.14	225.24	588.61	357.93	230.68	663.37	385.97	277.40	795.55	435.58
阿根廷	164.29	123.53	40.76	271.07	122.35	148.72	299.02	131.18	167.84	371.86	156.59
智利	160.51	83.73	76.78	201.36	100.07	101.29	203.24	91.99	111.25	234.29	116.04
哥伦比亚	123.56	67.66	55.90	134.33	69.17	65.16	169.48	71.16	98.32	203.02	84.19
墨西哥	582.78	271.31	311.47	758.66	277.30	481.36	798.11	301.88	496.23	955.12	345.32
委内瑞拉	252.26	177.83	74.43	284.88	143.43	141.45	268.05	145.36	122.69	262.04	169.12
秘鲁	67.01	32.31	34.70	83.45	34.84	48.61	83.74	35.15	48.59	112.46	45.55
哥斯达黎加	34.38	14.48	19.90	42.82	18.41	24.41	48.81	19.95	28.86	52.68	22.43
危地马拉	28.12	11.63	16.49	38.27	12.95	25.32	39.39	13.40	25.99	41.26	15.22
古巴	116.55	49.10	67.45	42.35	20.50	21.85	32.65	12.75	19.90	34.40	13.85
多米尼加	27.97	7.35	20.62	30.63	5.62	25.01	29.47	5.11	24.36	32.70	6.44
牙买加	30.82	11.58	19.24	27.23	10.48	16.75	32.04	10.71	21.33	34.32	12.11
特立尼达和多巴哥	30.69	19.60	11.09	28.59	16.91	11.68	31.25	16.62	14.63	29.96	18.66
荷属安的列斯	29.31	17.90	21.41	34.27	15.59	18.68	32.30	12.83	19.47	31.34	13.76
巴拿马	18.79	3.40	15.39	25.26	5.02	20.24	27.41	5.53	21.88	29.87	5.83
萨尔瓦多	18.45	5.82	12.63	22.97	5.98	16.99	26.44	7.32	19.12	34.18	8.44
乌拉圭	30.36	16.93	13.43	37.48	17.03	20.45	39.71	16.45	23.26	46.99	19.13
厄瓜多尔	45.76	27.14	18.62	55.08	30.07	25.01	54.66	29.04	25.62	75.10	38.20
洪都拉斯	17.66	8.31	9.35	18.39	8.02	10.37	19.44	8.14	11.30	18.98	8.42
欧洲	36273.22	17791.09	18482.13	36095.18	17719.77	18375.41	32681.93	16553.65	16128.28	37605.34	19124.54
德国 a	7549.90	4099.58	3450.32	8259.74	4227.06	4032.68	7287.61	3826.31	3461.30	8138.21	4290.75
法国	4433.76	2101.69	2332.07	4707.88	2319.13	2388.75	4069.81	2062.31	2007.50	4667.11	2360.72
英国	4098.76	1853.26	2245.50	4121.80	1905.42	2216.38	3878.80	1815.59	2063.21	4301.81	2040.09
意大利	3523.66	1703.83	1819.83	3666.20	1781.64	1884.56	3160.54	1677.46	1483.08	3606.10	1974.31
荷兰	2582.72	1317.87	1264.85	2750.26	1403.56	1346.70	2638.69	1391.27	1247.42	2968.71	1555.54

金额单位:亿美元

1995		1996			1997			1997 比 1996 增减%			1998 *		
出口	进口	总额	出口	进口	总额	出口	进口	总额	出口	进口	总额	出口	进口
49698.98	50460.62	104849.62	51708.25	53141.37	108204.49	53403.20	54801.29	3.2	3.3	3.1	109350.00	53750.00	55600.00
34178.87	33863.41	70404.40	35182.01	35222.39	71965.72	35967.36	35998.36	2.2	2.2	2.2	…	…	…
13763.19	14751.96	30475.68	14607.21	15868.47	32049.44	15470.13	16579.31	5.2	5.9	4.5	…	…	…
2058.00	1804.98	4071.17	2238.38	1832.79	4193.91	2326.21	1867.70	3.0	3.9	1.9	…	…	…
191.56	310.81	516.27	186.42	329.85	532.18	190.23	341.95	3.1	2.0	3.7	…	…	…
1756.92	1845.25	3969.55	1919.03	2050.52	4189.33	1965.71	2223.62	5.5	2.4	8.4	…	…	…
9211.69	11121.52	21750.00	9891.21	11858.79	24070.53	10801.79	13268.80	10.7	9.2	11.9	…	…	…
5847.43	7708.52	14470.98	6250.73	8220.25	15877.16	6886.97	8990.19	9.7	10.2	9.4	16276.00	6830.00	9446.00
1922.04	1680.53	3765.98	2016.36	1749.62	4153.08	2144.28	2008.80	10.3	6.3	14.8	4193.00	2143.00	2050.00
465.06	537.83	1047.09	477.62	569.47	1179.94	529.87	650.07	12.7	10.9	14.2	1120.00	510.00	610.00
209.67	201.22	475.73	238.11	237.62	558.65	255.16	303.49	17.4	7.2	27.7	566.00	252.00	314.00
161.37	159.14	331.81	153.53	178.28	367.35	168.75	198.60	10.7	9.9	11.4	…	…	188.00
101.26	138.53	242.71	105.87	136.84	269.00	115.22	153.78	10.8	8.8	12.4	…	…	…
470.56	459.77	1202.51	590.72	611.79	1424.20	656.19	768.01	18.4	11.1	25.5	2464.00	1175.00	1289.00
187.39	126.19	328.68	230.54	98.14	…	231.27	…	…	0.3	…	…	172.00	…
55.75	92.24	153.70	58.97	94.73	170.77	68.14	102.63	11.1	15.6	8.3	…	…	…
27.02	32.53	64.93	30.14	34.79	72.00	32.81	39.19	10.9	8.9	12.6	…	…	…
21.56	32.93	51.77	20.31	31.46	56.16	21.49	34.67	8.5	5.8	10.2	…	…	…
16.00	28.25	52.20	20.15	32.05	…	…	…	…	…	…	…	…	…
7.67	29.76	45.03	8.17	36.86	50.02	8.82	41.20	11.1	8.0	11.8	…	…	…
14.20	28.08	43.14	13.82	29.32	44.94	13.81	31.13	4.2	−0.1	6.2	…	…	…
24.56	17.14	46.44	25.00	21.44	55.34	25.43	29.91	19.2	1.7	39.5	…	…	…
14.17	19.04	…	…	…	…	…	…	…	…	…	…	…	…
6.25	25.11	34.03	6.23	27.80	37.25	7.23	30.02	9.5	16.1	8.0	…	…	…
9.98	28.53	36.95	10.24	26.71	43.32	13.59	29.73	17.2	32.7	11.3	…	…	…
21.06	28.67	57.20	23.97	33.23	64.46	27.30	37.16	12.7	13.9	11.8	…	…	…
43.07	41.93	88.35	49.00	39.35	101.59	52.14	49.45	15.0	6.4	25.7	…	…	…
10.61	12.19	31.61	13.21	18.40	34.91	14.43	20.48	10.4	9.2	11.3	…	…	…
23371.64	22374.91	47495.24	24301.36	23193.88	47544.80	24274.42	23270.38	0.1	−0.1	0.3	…	…	…
5083.98	4445.54	9830.38	5242.28	4588.10	9535.23	5117.16	4418.07	−3.0	−2.4	−3.7	10063.00	5397.00	4666.00
2873.34	2769.81	5690.94	2886.58	2804.36	5604.48	2903.81	2700.67	−1.5	0.6	−3.7	5942.00	3070.00	2872.00
2420.36	2653.21	5496.02	2621.30	2874.72	5876.44	2810.80	3065.64	6.9	7.2	6.6	5888.00	2727.00	3161.00
2339.80	2060.25	4585.72	2504.56	2081.16	4466.29	2383.43	2082.86	−2.6	−4.8	0.1	4549.00	2409.00	2140.00
1962.76	1768.73	3780.61	1974.20	1806.41	3752.79	1961.37	1791.42	−0.7	−0.6	−0.8	3823.00	1982.00	1841.00

世界部分国家(地区)商品贸易额(二)

年份 金额 国别(地区)	1990			1992			1993			1994	
	总额	出口	进口	总额	出口	进口	总额	出口	进口	总额	出口
比利时·卢森堡	2386.53	1183.28	1203.25	2487.17	1235.64	1251.53	2317.72	1195.23	1122.49	2629.13	1372.76
西班牙	1430.83	555.28	875.55	1646.14	648.49	997.65	1408.39	610.84	797.55	1651.18	729.29
瑞士	1334.84	637.93	696.91	1231.66	614.03	617.63	1154.16	586.94	567.22	1303.23	662.38
瑞典	1118.08	575.42	542.66	1062.04	561.54	500.50	925.51	498.64	426.87	1130.84	613.52
前苏联	2248.28	1041.77	1206.51	…	…	…	…	…	…	…	…
前苏联欧洲部分	…	…	…	917.69	496.82	420.87	928.54	522.93	405.61	1572.74	853.42
俄罗斯	…	…	…	793.60	423.76	369.84	771.03	442.97	328.06	1181.60	676.42
丹麦	673.65	351.35	322.30	762.52	410.67	351.85	677.18	371.72	305.46	763.04	414.22
挪威	612.64	340.45	272.19	611.09	351.93	259.16	556.70	317.78	238.92	619.88	346.85
奥地利	902.30	411.38	490.92	984.99	443.77	541.22	888.16	402.00	486.16	1003.71	450.31
芬兰	535.75	265.72	270.03	451.39	239.55	211.84	414.80	234.47	180.33	528.72	296.58
爱尔兰	444.29	237.47	206.82	510.15	285.32	224.83	508.16	290.22	217.94	600.65	341.55
葡萄牙	417.77	164.19	253.58	486.65	183.69	302.96	397.06	153.86	243.20	449.48	180.09
波兰	220.40	136.27	84.13	290.25	133.24	157.01	329.77	141.43	188.34	384.25	170.42
前捷克斯洛伐克	249.88	118.82	131.06	241.86	116.56	125.30	…	…	…	…	…
捷克	…	…	…	…	…	…	260.57	132.09	128.48	292.36	142.80
斯洛伐克	…	…	…	…	…	…	118.29	54.69	63.60	130.95	65.92
匈牙利	182.68	95.97	86.71	217.82	106.76	111.06	214.09	88.88	125.21	250.72	106.89
罗马尼亚	156.18	57.75	98.43	105.69	43.63	62.06	114.14	48.92	65.22	132.60	61.51
南斯拉夫	332.02	143.12	188.90	61.10	24.80	36.30	…	…	…	…	…
希腊	278.86	81.06	197.80	330.71	98.39	232.32	307.84	87.77	220.07	308.81	93.92
保加利亚	265.17	134.28	130.89	98.18	45.60	52.58	84.78	37.21	47.57	81.71	39.86
冰岛	32.70	15.91	16.79	32.12	15.28	16.84	27.42	14.00	13.42	30.95	16.23
马尔他	30.91	11.30	19.61	38.92	15.43	23.49	35.29	13.55	21.74	40.13	15.72
非洲	1971.53	1004.88	966.65	1824.20	918.38	905.82	1756.41	864.63	891.78	1870.48	898.31
南非	404.99	228.34	176.65	411.30	224.16	187.14	424.29	233.39	190.90	468.85	244.15
阿尔及利亚	222.49	126.75	95.74	197.85	111.37	86.48	180.00	102.30	77.70	182.50	88.80
埃及	217.40	49.57	167.83	113.88	30.63	83.25	104.66	22.52	82.14	136.93	34.75
利比亚	194.76	138.77	55.99	…	…	…	…	…	…	…	…
摩洛哥	111.90	42.65	69.25	113.33	39.77	73.56	105.90	34.28	71.62	111.93	40.05
突尼斯	90.40	35.27	55.13	104.50	40.19	64.31	100.16	38.02	62.14	112.38	46.57
喀麦隆	34.02	20.02	14.00	30.03	18.40	11.63	23.31	14.43	8.88	20.91	13.70
加蓬	31.35	22.13	9.22	27.82	20.82	7.00	32.17	23.00	9.17	31.06	23.48
尼日利亚	186.53	129.61	56.92	213.72	126.00	87.72	174.36	99.23	75.13	158.93	93.76
肯尼亚	31.55	10.31	21.24	29.10	10.67	18.43	30.71	12.97	17.74	36.55	15.65

金额单位:亿美元

1995		1996			1997			1997 比 1996 增减%			1998 *		
出口	进口	总额	出口	进口	总额	出口	进口	总额	出口	进口	总额	出口	进口
1696.20	1551.09	3185.70	1657.96	1527.74	3210.87	1655.86	1555.01	0.8	-0.1	1.8	3305.00	1717.00	1588.00
910.43	1133.17	2237.96	1020.02	1217.94	2270.91	1043.69	1227.22	1.5	2.3	0.8	2418.00	1090.00	1328.00
780.61	770.06	1506.76	762.05	744.71	1435.81	725.06	710.75	-4.7	-4.9	-4.6	1587.00	787.00	800.00
798.16	646.52	1517.17	848.60	668.57	1477.17	827.37	649.80	-2.6	-2.5	-2.8	1521.00	845.00	676.00
…	…	…	…	…	…	…	…	…	…	…	…	…	…
1052.02	904.65	2129.43	1156.91	972.52	2218.25	1160.20	1058.05	4.2	0.3	8.8	…	…	…
811.37	609.16	1513.88	891.10	622.78	1549.87	873.68	676.19	2.4	-2.0	8.6	1009.00	562.00	447.00
497.63	450.90	945.36	501.01	444.35	922.40	480.42	442.07	-2.4	-4.1	0.5	928.00	470.00	458.00
419.95	329.73	845.74	489.58	356.16	832.47	477.44	355.03	-1.6	-2.5	-0.3	758.00	396.00	362.00
575.95	663.38	1251.48	578.24	673.24	1234.16	584.94	649.22	-1.4	1.2	-3.6	1300.00	617.00	683.00
395.73	281.14	677.00	384.35	292.65	691.04	393.18	297.86	2.1	2.3	1.8	…	424.00	…
446.38	330.68	845.64	486.21	359.43	922.35	531.05	391.30	9.1	9.2	8.9	1070.00	633.00	437.00
202.29	323.49	579.31	238.23	341.08	572.21	233.99	338.22	-1.2	-1.8	-0.8	…	…	…
228.95	290.50	615.77	244.40	371.37	680.59	257.51	423.08	10.5	5.4	13.9	743.00	263.00	480.00
…	…	…	…	…	…	…	…	…	…	…	…	…	…
216.86	253.04	539.18	257.66	281.52	499.39	227.50	271.89	-7.4	-11.7	-3.4	552.00	264.00	288.00
85.95	87.87	199.25	88.18	111.07	190.62	87.91	102.71	-4.3	-0.3	-7.5	…	…	…
124.35	150.46	285.03	126.47	158.56	390.16	184.79	205.37	36.9	46.1	29.5	487.00	229.00	258.00
79.10	102.78	195.20	80.85	114.35	197.03	84.28	112.75	0.9	4.2	-1.4	…	…	…
…	…	59.44	18.42	41.02	…	…	…	…	…	…	…	…	…
109.70	255.09	368.78	94.80	273.98	363.20	86.03	277.17	-1.5	-9.3	1.2	…	…	…
53.62	56.61	103.35	50.62	52.73	100.14	50.05	50.09	-3.1	-1.1	-5.0	…	…	…
18.03	17.55	36.69	16.38	20.31	38.44	18.52	19.92	4.8	13.1	-1.9	…	…	…
19.13	29.42	45.27	17.31	27.96	41.96	16.40	25.56	-7.3	-5.3	-8.6	…	…	…
013.39	1180.51	2305.45	1151.22	1154.23	2374.12	1183.28	1190.84	3.0	2.8	3.2	…	…	…
269.18	296.08	572.50	281.45	291.05	619.03	299.64	319.39	8.1	6.5	9.7	556.00	263.00	293.00
102.40	102.50	213.11	126.21	86.90	…	…	…	…	…	…	…	…	…
34.50	117.60	165.77	35.59	130.38	171.31	39.21	132.10	3.3	10.8	1.3	…	…	…
…	…	…	…	…	…	…	…	…	…	…	…	…	…
47.21	85.42	165.85	68.81	97.04	164.98	69.87	95.11	-0.5	1.5	-2.0	…	…	…
54.75	79.03	132.17	55.17	77.00	134.73	55.59	79.14	1.9	0.8	2.8	…	…	…
16.54	12.01	29.95	17.69	12.26	32.19	18.60	13.59	7.5	5.1	10.8	…	…	…
27.12	8.81	…	…	…	…	…	…	…	…	…	…	…	…
06.37	93.32	266.11	186.14	79.97	…	…	…	…	…	…	…	…	…
8.90	30.06	50.16	20.67	29.49	53.27	20.54	32.73	6.2	-0.6	11.0	…	…	…

世界部分国家(地区)商品贸易额(三)

国别(地区) \ 金额 \ 年份	1990			1992			1993			1994	
	总额	出口	进口	总额	出口	进口	总额	出口	进口	总额	出口
毛里求斯	28.17	11.96	16.21	29.25	13.01	16.24	30.15	12.99	17.16	32.77	13.47
赞比亚	25.70	13.11	12.59	15.51	7.56	7.95	16.81	8.50	8.31	13.57	8.27
津巴布韦	35.79	17.29	18.50	36.44	14.42	22.02	33.82	15.65	18.17	41.22	18.81
刚果(金)	18.87	9.99	8.88	8.47	4.27	4.20	7.41	3.69	3.72	8.01	4.19
坦桑尼亚	16.95	3.31	13.64	18.65	4.12	14.53	19.48	4.50	14.98	20.23	5.19
马拉维	9.92	4.17	5.75	11.31	3.96	7.35	8.64	3.19	5.45	8.20	3.25
塞拉利昂	2.85	1.37	1.48	2.95	1.49	1.46	2.65	1.18	1.47	2.66	1.15
埃塞俄比亚	13.79	2.98	10.81	10.28	1.69	8.59	9.86	1.99	7.87	14.05	3.72
马达加斯加	9.70	3.19	6.51	7.26	2.78	4.48	7.29	2.61	4.68	8.22	3.75
亚洲	16808.41	8676.39	8132.02	20526.33	10591.49	9934.84	22319.61	11412.76	10906.85	25468.44	13088.84
日本	5230.71	2876.48	2354.23	5731.76	3399.11	2332.65	6039.38	3622.86	2416.52	6723.16	3970.48
中国香港	1646.50	821.60	824.90	2428.94	1194.87	1234.07	2738.94	1352.44	1386.50	3132.40	1513.99
中国	1154.36	620.91	533.45	1655.25	849.40	805.85	1940.58	909.70	1030.88	2367.28	1210.47
新加坡	1135.04	527.30	607.74	1355.67	634.35	721.32	1592.37	740.08	852.29	1994.95	968.25
韩国	1348.60	650.16	698.44	1584.07	766.32	817.75	1660.36	822.36	838.00	1983.61	960.13
中国台湾	1219.30	672.14	547.16	1534.77	814.70	720.07	1621.52	850.91	770.61	1783.98	930.49
马来西亚	587.12	294.53	292.59	806.26	407.72	398.54	927.88	471.31	456.57	1183.36	587.55
印度尼西亚	475.12	256.75	218.37	612.47	339.67	272.80	651.51	368.23	283.28	720.38	400.55
泰国	561.02	230.71	330.31	731.47	324.67	406.80	830.39	369.63	460.76	996.74	452.36
土耳其	352.61	129.59	223.02	375.88	147.16	228.72	445.17	153.43	291.74	413.76	181.06
以色列	283.76	115.73	168.03	333.28	130.75	202.53	374.05	147.81	226.24	421.18	168.81
菲律宾	211.03	80.68	130.41	252.01	97.52	154.49	298.43	110.89	187.54	358.50	133.04
印度	415.53	179.70	235.83	432.35	196.41	235.94	443.62	215.73	227.89	518.65	250.22
科威特	108.79	69.56	39.23	138.18	65.67	72.51	172.86	102.44	70.42	179.08	112.28
巴基斯坦	129.65	55.89	73.76	166.96	73.17	93.79	161.89	66.88	95.01	162.54	73.65
阿曼	81.83	55.08	26.81	91.94	54.25	37.69	94.12	52.98	41.14	94.60	55.45
巴林	74.73	37.61	37.12	77.27	34.64	42.63	75.81	37.23	38.58	73.65	36.17
叙利亚	66.12	42.12	24.00	65.83	30.93	34.90	72.86	31.46	41.40	85.14	30.47
斯里兰卡	46.02	19.13	26.89	59.67	24.62	35.05	68.44	28.51	39.93	79.76	32.09
前苏联亚洲部分	…	…	…	64.51	42.11	22.40	71.77	41.55	30.22	204.66	100.35
孟加拉国	52.89	16.71	36.18	58.23	20.98	37.31	62.72	22.78	39.94	72.63	26.61
文莱	32.14	22.13	10.01	35.46	23.70	11.76	33.99	21.98	12.01	39.91	22.96
澳门	32.28	16.94	15.34	36.97	17.49	19.48	37.62	17.63	19.99	39.24	18.34
缅甸	5.95	3.25	2.70	11.82	5.31	6.51	14.00	5.86	8.14	16.70	7.92
尼伯尔	8.76	2.04	6.72	11.44	3.68	7.76	12.74	3.84	8.90	15.17	3.62

金额单位:亿美元

1995		1996			1997			1997比1996增减%			1998 *		
出口	进口	总额	出口	进口	总额	出口	进口	总额	出口	进口	总额	出口	进口
15.37	19.59	40.29	17.51	22.78	38.70	16.16	22.54	-3.9	-7.7	-1.1	…	…	…
10.55	7.08	18.96	10.52	8.44	17.21	9.08	8.13	-9.2	-13.7	-3.7	…	…	…
21.14	26.61	52.14	23.97	28.17	56.00	25.08	30.92	7.4	4.6	9.8	…	…	…
4.38	3.97	10.16	5.92	4.24	…	…	…	…	…	…	…	…	…
6.85	16.79	21.44	7.58	13.86	20.54	7.18	13.36	-4.2	-5.3	-3.6	…	…	…
4.05	4.75	11.04	4.81	6.23	…	…	…	…	…	…	…	…	…
0.25	1.35	2.59	0.47	2.12	…	…	…	…	…	......	…	…	
4.22	11.42	…	4.17	…	…	…	…	…	…	…	…	…	…
3.70	5.43	8.06	2.99	5.07	7.01	2.23	4.78	-13.0	-25.4	-.57	…	…	…
15418.38	14932.57	31613.47	15602.67	16010.80	32515.92	16365.30	16150.62	2.9	4.9	0.9	…	…	…
4432.65	3359.91	7601.04	4109.28	3491.76	7598.93	4210.53	3388.40	-0.0	2.5	-3.0	6685.00	3880.00	2805.00
1737.50	1927.51	3793.00	1807.50	1985.50	3966.79	1880.63	2086.16	4.6	4.0	5.1	3628.00	1741.00	1887.00
1487.97	1291.13	2901.41	1511.97	1389.44	3250.67	1826.90	1423.77	12.0	20.8	2.5	3240.00	1838.00	1402.00
1182.63	1245.02	2563.56	1250.16	1313.40	2574.68	1250.23	1324.45	0.4	0.0	0.8	2113.00	1098.00	1015.00
1250.58	1351.19	2800.54	1297.15	1503.39	2813.56	1367.41	1446.15	0.5	5.4	-3.8	2265.00	1332.00	933.00
1116.59	1035.50	2183.12	1159.42	1023.70	2365.06	1220.81	1144.25	8.3	5.3	11.8	2141.00	1099.00	1042.00
737.15	776.14	1566.71	782.53	784.18	1579.58	789.08	790.50	0.8	0.8	0.8	1318.00	733.00	585.00
454.17	406.30	927.43	498.14	429.29	951.37	534.44	416.93	2.6	7.3	-2.9	762.00	488.00	274.00
561.91	527.97	1276.94	555.26	721.68	…	…	…	…	…	…	954.00	536.00	418.00
216.39	357.10	660.06	230.75	429.31	…	…	…	…	…	…	725.00	261.00	464.00
190.46	295.79	522.96	206.10	316.86	532.85	225.02	307.83	1.9	9.2	-2.8	524.00	233.00	291.00
175.02	283.37	545.39	204.17	341.22	…	250.88	…	…	22.9	…	613.00	293.00	320.00
306.29	347.10	705.34	330.35	374.99	742.58	339.00	403.58	-5.3	2.6	7.6	761.00	332.00	429.00
127.85	77.92	232.63	148.89	83.74	224.71	142.24	82.47	-3.4	-4.5	-1.5	…	…	…
79.92	114.61	214.52	93.21	121.31	203.12	87.17	115.95	-5.3	-6.5	-4.4	…	…	…
60.68	42.48	119.24	73.46	45.78	126.56	76.30	50.26	6.1	3.9	9.8	…	…	…
41.13	37.16	89.73	47.00	42.73	82.70	43.46	39.24	-7.8	-7.5	-8.2	…	…	…
35.63	47.09	93.79	39.99	53.80	79.44	39.16	40.28	-15.3	-2.1	-25.1	…	…	…
37.98	53.07	95.07	40.95	54.12	105.05	46.66	58.39	10.5	13.9	7.9	…	…	…
121.70	104.00	277.75	148.21	129.54	289.19	152.53	427.66	0.9	2.9	-1.5	…	…	…
31.73	65.01	99.18	32.97	66.21	106.78	37.78	69.00	7.7	14.6	4.2	…	…	…
22.73	19.15	…	…	…	…	…	…	…	…	…	…	…	…
19.83	20.26	39.82	19.89	19.93	42.24	21.45	20.79	6.1	7.8	4.3	…	…	…
8.51	13.35	20.99	7.44	13.55	28.87	8.66	20.21	37.5	16.4	49.2	…	…	…
3.46	13.33	18.27	3.85	14.42	21.23	4.02	17.21	16.2	4.4	19.3	…	…	…

世界部分国家(地区)商品贸易额(四)

国别(地区) \ 年份 金额	1990			1992			1993			1994	
	总额	出口	进口	总额	出口	进口	总额	出口	进口	总额	出口
约旦	36.66	10.63	26.03	44.74	12.19	32.55	47.85	12.46	35.39	48.06	14.24
塞浦路斯	35.17	9.48	25.69	42.85	9.84	33.01	34.01	8.67	25.34	39.86	9.68
卡塔尔	52.24	35.29	16.95	57.51	37.36	20.15	50.72	31.81	18.91	…	…
沙特阿拉伯	684.86	444.17	240.69	835.51	502.80	332.71	705.93	423.95	281.98	659.52	426.14
阿富汗	11.71	2.35	9.36	8.04	1.88	6.16	…	…	…	…	…
大洋洲	1049.66	501.00	548.66	1100.70	538.62	562.08	1130.01	550.59	579.42	1298.32	614.66
澳大利亚	817.84	397.60	420.24	866.47	428.39	438.08	881.82	427.04	454.78	1009.50	475.25
新西兰	188.95	93.94	95.01	190.17	97.99	92.18	201.78	105.42	96.36	240.98	121.85
巴布亚新几内亚	23.69	11.77	11.92	34.12	19.27	14.85	38.83	25.84	12.99	41.51	26.30
斐济	12.52	4.98	7.54	10.74	4.43	6.31	11.70	4.50	7.20	13.79	5.50
新喀里多尼亚	13.32	4.49	8.83	13.26	4.09	9.17	12.17	3.59	8.58	12.42	3.66
美属萨摩亚	6.71	3.11	3.60	7.36	3.18	4.18	…	…	…	…	…
法属波里尼西亚	10.40	1.11	9.29	10.01	1.07	8.94	10.00	1.48	8.52	11.07	2.26
所罗门	1.65	0.70	0.95	2.00	1.03	0.97	2.32	1.31	1.01	2.84	1.42
瓦努阿图	1.15	0.19	0.96	1.06	0.24	0.82	1.02	0.23	0.79	1.12	0.25

注:a.包括前民主德国数字

***资料来源:**“世界贸易组织”

资料来源:联合国《统计月报》中国台湾省《统计月报》

金额单位:亿美元

1995			1996			1997			1997 比 1996 增减%			1998 *		
额	出口	进口	总额	出口	进口	总额	出口	进口	总额	出口	进口	总额	出口	进口
5	17.69	36.96	61.10	18.17	42.93	59.37	18.34	41.03	−2.8	0.9	−4.4	…	…	…
9	12.29	36.90	53.66	13.87	39.79	47.99	11.04	36.95	−10.6	−20.4	−7.1	…	…	…
	…	…	…	…	…	…	…	…	…	…	…	…	…	…
1	500.40	280.91	…	…	277.68	…	…	…	…	…	…	625.00	388.00	237.00
	…	…	…	…	…	…	…	…	…	…	…	…	…	…
29	683.89	770.40	1595.38	761.79	833.59	1612.94	778.40	834.54	1.1	2.2	0.1	…	…	…
14	530.97	603.17	1257.29	603.00	654.29	1288.12	629.02	659.10	2.5	4.3	0.7	1206.00	559.00	647.00
4	136.45	139.59	290.87	143.62	147.25	285.72	140.52	145.20	−1.8	−2.2	−1.4	…	…	…
5	26.54	14.52	42.56	25.15	17.41	38.41	21.45	16.96	−9.8	−14.7	−2.6	…	…	…
	6.19	8.67	17.32	7.48	9.84	15.68	6.03	9.65	−9.5	−19.4	−1.9	…	…	…
	5.15	9.12	15.57	5.46	10.11	…	…	…	…	…	…	…	…	…
	…	…	…	…	…	…	…	…	…	…	…	…	…	…
	1.96	10.19	…	…	…	…	…	…	…	…	…	…	…	…
	1.68	1.54	…	…	…	…	…	…	…	…	…	…	…	…
	0.28	0.95	1.27	0.30	0.97	1.29	0.35	0.94	1.6	16.7	−3.1	…	…	…

(对外贸易经济合作部国际贸易经济合作研究院文献信息中心)

世界部分国家(地区)服务贸易额(一)

年份 / 金额 / 国别(地区)	1985			1990			1993			1994	
	总额	出口	进口	总额	出口	进口	总额	出口	进口	总额	出口
世界	7825.00	3809.00	4016.00	16058.00	7888.00	8170.00	19020.00	9445.00	9575.00	20758.00	10364.00
北美	1468.00	772.00	696.00	2808.00	1551.00	1257.00	3277.00	1868.00	1409.00	3519.00	2004.00
加拿大	210.93	86.97	123.96	458.30	183.51	274.79	530.84	212.11	318.73	552.97	232.10
美国	120.67	634.90	571.80	2349.60	1367.50	982.10	2746.00	1656.00	1090.00	2965.90	1772.00
拉美	400.00	179.00	221.00	634.00	291.00	343.00	817.00	357.00	460.00	913.00	416.00
巴西	54.06	19.93	34.13	104.39	37.06	67.33	130.67	39.11	91.56	146.53	48.17
阿根廷	36.16	15.99	20.17	51.40	22.64	28.76	72.41	22.99	49.42	77.15	24.35
智利	16.55	6.56	9.99	37.68	17.85	19.83	50.69	24.45	26.24	56.33	27.64
哥伦比亚	21.99	8.24	13.75	32.31	15.48	16.83	47.04	24.57	22.47	58.65	32.33
墨西哥	97.80	44.36	53.44	172.85	72.22	100.63	200.67	82.96	117.71	224.66	100.75
委内瑞拉	27.42	7.60	19.82	35.11	11.21	23.90	55.91	12.30	43.61	59.59	14.57
秘鲁	14.77	6.26	8.51	17.85	7.15	10.70	20.68	7.41	13.27	24.35	9.51
哥斯达黎加	5.34	2.59	2.75	11.23	5.83	5.40	18.06	10.05	8.01	20.09	11.63
危地马拉	2.20	0.52	1.68	6.76	3.13	3.63	11.73	6.25	5.48	12.60	6.58
多米尼加共和国	8.49	5.79	2.70	15.21	10.86	4.35	22.02	14.74	7.28	24.63	16.95
牙买加	9.53	5.64	3.89	16.42	9.75	6.67	19.96	12.11	7.85	21.63	12.79
特立尼达和多巴哥	9.57	2.45	7.12	7.82	3.22	4.60	7.98	3.43	4.55	7.41	3.17
荷属安的列斯	11.10	6.63	4.47	16.40	11.30	5.10	19.11	13.23	5.88	20.47	13.82
巴拿马	20.53	11.05	9.48	15.40	8.80	6.60	19.62	10.20	9.42	21.45	11.15
萨尔瓦多	4.67	1.96	2.71	5.97	3.01	2.96	7.27	3.62	3.65	7.62	3.38
乌拉圭	6.97	3.76	3.21	8.23	4.60	3.63	17.31	10.20	7.11	21.45	13.24
厄瓜多尔	9.81	3.70	6.11	11.09	5.08	6.01	13.73	6.13	7.60	15.67	7.02
洪都拉斯	2.81	0.90	1.91	3.34	1.21	2.13	4.79	1.91	2.88	5.11	2.07
西欧	3587.00	1936.00	1651.00	8133.00	4176.00	3957.00	8934.00	4620.00	4314.00	9610.00	4955.00
奥地利	158.20	94.85	63.35	368.58	227.54	141.04	470.73	274.67	196.06	496.47	286.07
比利时-卢森堡	191.81	95.21	96.60	489.88	246.90	242.98	563.68	289.11	274.57	689.42	353.92
克罗地亚	…	…	…	…	…	…	34.49	18.07	16.42	43.71	22.93
丹麦	100.98	53.92	47.06	228.37	127.31	101.06	228.81	124.79	104.02	255.75	135.78
芬兰	52.07	23.77	28.30	119.94	45.62	74.32	107.22	44.09	63.13	126.24	56.79
法国	597.37	347.19	250.18	1167.25	662.74	504.51	1295.26	737.96	557.30	1308.60	746.90
德国 a	558.00	228.10	329.90	1308.10	516.00	792.10	1522.80	565.70	957.10	1631.00	590.10
希腊	38.48	25.67	12.81	92.70	65.14	27.56	113.40	81.53	31.87	125.62	91.42

金额单位:亿美元

1995		1996			1997			1997年比1996年增减%			1998		
出口	进口	总额	出口	进口	总额	出口	进口	总额	出口	进口	总额	出口	进口
11911.00	12023.00	25354.00	12689.00	12665.00	26074.00	13115.00	12959.00	2.8	3.4	2.3	25800.00	12900.00	12900.00
2230.00	1646.00	4181.00	2427.00	1754.00	4453.00	2592.00	1861.00	6.5	6.8	6.1	…	…	…
256.96	334.00	643.43	286.34	357.09	652.34	292.90	359.44	1.4	2.3	0.7	636.00	288.00	348.00
1973.30	1311.60	3537.20	2140.30	1396.90	3800.20	2299.00	1501.20	7.4	7.4	7.5	3951.00	2336.00	1615.00
447.00	520.00	1028.00	470.00	558.00	1170.00	513.00	657.00	13.8	9.1	17.7	…	…	…
60.05	131.61	197.12	57.83	139.29	269.07	79.28	189.79	36.5	37.1	36.3	…	…	189.00
26.95	48.07	84.67	30.59	54.08	91.48	31.05	60.43	8.0	1.5	11.7	…	…	…
31.25	34.29	68.67	32.81	35.86	74.44	35.92	38.52	8.4	9.5	7.4	…	…	…
34.23	32.13	76.41	37.43	38.98	82.96	40.08	42.88	8.6	7.1	10.0	…	…	…
95.85	90.20	206.64	106.94	99.70	227.09	111.92	115.17	9.9	4.7	15.5	244.00	119.00	125.00
15.29	46.72	61.22	14.39	46.83	65.82	15.26	50.56	7.5	6.0	8.0	…	…	…
10.43	18.00	33.14	13.24	19.90	36.37	14.47	21.90	9.7	9.3	10.1	…	…	…
12.71	9.33	…	…	…	…	…	…	…	…	…	…	…	…
6.28	6.72	11.71	5.33	6.38	…	…	…	…	…	…	…	…	…
18.55	8.50	30.27	20.71	9.56	…	…	…	…	…	…	…	…	…
13.83	10.38	24.45	13.72	10.73	25.74	14.28	11.46	5.3	4.1	6.8	…	…	…
3.31	2.23	…	…	…	…	…	…	…	…	…	…	…	…
16.56	7.19	21.69	14.23	7.46	21.11	14.24	6.87	-2.7	0.1	-7.9	…	…	…
12.38	2.08	15.47	13.09	2.38	15.81	13.52	2.29	2.2	3.3	-3.8	…	…	…
3.42	4.67	7.75	3.18	4,57	6.30	2.76	3.54	-18.7	-13.2	-22.5	…	…	…
13.09	8.14	21.83	13.88	7.95	23.68	14.65	9.03	8.5	5.5	13.6	…	…	…
8.05	9.32	17.08	8.07	9.01	17.78	6.89	10.89	4.1	-14.6	20.9	…	…	…
2.21	3.26	…	…	…	…	…	…	…	…	…	…	…	…
5691.00	5422.00	11550.00	5932.00	5618.00	11556.00	5981.00	5575.00	0.1	0.8	-0.8	…	…	…
331.23	285.51	657.26	351.46	305.80	559.46	285.32	274.14	-14.8	-18.8	-10.4	597.00	310.00	287.00
343.47	329.76	675.47	345.39	330.08	660.73	339.98	320.75	-2.2	-1.6	-2.8	683.00	347.00	336.00
25.69	27.08	66.81	34.96	31.85	59.65	39.94	19.71	-10.7	14.2	-38.1	…	…	…
146.64	139.79	312.07	163.41	148.66	…	…	…	…	…	…	306.00	157.00	149.00
74.73	94.89	158.04	72.37	85.67	148.54	68.02	80.52	-6.0	-6.0	-6.0	…	…	…
831.10	645.30	1482.10	825.90	656.20	1423.50	802.70	620.80	-4.0	-2.8	-5.4	1414.00	786.00	628.00
751.90	1254.40	2055.40	787.70	1267.70	1955.00	753.60	1201.40	-4.9	-4.3	-5.2	1975.00	757.00	1218.00
95.28	40.03	130.92	92.62	38.30	…	…	…	…	…	…	…	99.00	…

世界部分国家(地区)服务贸易额(二)

国别(地区) \ 年份 金额	1985			1990			1993			1994	
	总额	出口	进口	总额	出口	进口	总额	出口	进口	总额	出口
冰岛	6.63	3.11	3.52	9.67	4.27	5.40	10.78	4.90	5.88	10.82	5.15
爱尔兰	27.56	12.30	15.26	84.31	32.86	51.45	102.98	35.74	67.24	125.49	41.45
意大利	353.84	193.91	159.93	985.71	487.11	498.60	1087.89	541.81	546.08	115.94	563.30
马尔他	4.72	2.61	2.11	12.20	7.21	4.99	14.80	8.92	5.88	16.43	9.75
荷兰	280.25	134.10	146.15	595.76	301.00	294.76	753.10	379.41	373.69	822.54	418.06
挪威	148.13	73.37	74.76	246.99	124.52	122.47	232.86	119.00	113.86	238.21	119.15
葡萄牙	30.83	18.95	11.88	88.27	50.54	37.73	120.54	67.96	52.58	119.56	67.01
斯洛文尼亚	…	…	…	…	…	…	24.01	13.91	10.10	29.14	18.02
西班牙	168.07	126.37	41.70	428.45	276.49	151.96	488.30	304.82	183.48	522.26	337.55
瑞典	125.74	59.55	66.19	304.11	134.52	169.59	255.53	122.98	132.55	279.77	133.83
瑞士	136.59	88.17	48.42	300.88	188.93	111.95	330.20	214.76	115.44	353.88	226.18
土耳其	40.59	28.35	12.24	106.76	78.82	27.94	141.09	105.18	35.91	141.41	107.23
英国	501.36	294.54	206.49	982.00	535.10	446.90	1032.30	563.50	468.80	1154.00	622.70
前南斯拉夫	66.66	32.36	34.30	213.86	63.74	150.12	…	…	…	…	…
中/东欧、波罗地海国家和独联体											
保加利亚	17.01	10.47	6.54	14.37	8.37	6.00	24.01	11.72	12.29	25.03	12.57
捷克	…	…	…	…	…	…	83.79	46.78	37.01	98.04	51.20
匈牙利	12.95	6.16	6.79	49.40	26.76	22.64	53.04	27.69	25.35	59.21	30.46
波兰	39.50	21.04	18.46	60.47	32.00	28.47	78.32	42.01	36.31	104.01	66.55
罗马尼亚	12.70	7.46	5.24	13.97	6.10	7.87	17.13	7.99	9.14	21.89	10.23
俄罗斯	…	…	…	…	…	…	…	…	…	234.49	83.94
斯洛伐克	…	…	…	…	…	…	36.05	19.39	16.66	37.70	22.21
乌克兰	…	…	…	…	…	…	…	…	…	42.85	27.47
非洲	325.00	114.00	211.00	455.00	186.00	269.00	536.00	219.00	317.00	550.00	225.00
南非	44.34	19.82	24.52	75.38	34.43	40.95	83.38	34.15	49.23	90.78	37.95
阿尔及利亚	29.43	5.10	24.33	16.35	4.79	11.56	…	…	…	…	…
埃及	57.73	29.18	28.53	81.38	48.12	33.26	122.40	70.76	51.64	130.75	76.93
利比亚	15.27	0.63	14.64	10.09	0.83	9.26	…	…	…	…	…
摩洛哥	13.94	9.15	4.79	28.11	18.71	9.40	29.05	18.57	10.48	30.84	18.76
突尼斯	13.32	8.84	4.48	22.56	15.74	6.82	31.47	19.52	11.95	33.74	21.74

金额单位:亿美元

	1995		1996			1997			1997年比1996年增减%			1998		
额	出口	进口	总额	出口	进口	总额	出口	进口	总额	出口	进口	总额	出口	进口
7	5.67	6.30	…	…	…	…	…	…	…	…	…	…	…	…
51	47.99	112.52	189.78	55.62	134.16	210.52	60.19	150.33	10.9	8.2	12.1	…	…	180.00
6	652.76	646.70	1361.15	691.85	669.30	1418.74	717.28	701.46	4.2	3.7	4.8	1394.00	701.00	693.00
0	10.60	7.90	18.47	10.64	7.83	…	…	…	…	…	…	…	…	…
7	469.66	448.41	936.14	488.07	448.07	923.41	485.29	438.12	−1.4	−0.6	−2.2	931.00	483.00	448.00
8	131.32	130.36	272.77	139.38	133.39	287.16	142.56	144.60	5.3	2.3	8.4	287.00	139.00	148.00
2	81.61	63.51	147.17	81.62	65.55	136.70	75.22	61.48	−7.1	−7.8	−6.2	…	…	…
8	20.12	13.76	35.26	21.17	14.09	34.71	20.32	14.39	−1.6	−4.0	2.1	…	…	…
0	397.14	217.26	679.67	439.06	240.61	678.33	435.70	242.63	−0.2	−0.8	0.8	753.00	480.00	273.00
8	153.36	171.12	353.20	100.69	186.51	370.46	175.84	194.62	4.9	5.5	4.3	380.00	174.00	206.00
5	260.25	150.40	416.12	262.25	153.87	397.48	256.15	141.33	−4.5	−2.3	−8.1	413.00	263.00	150.00
9	144.75	46.54	189.27	128.95	60.32	272.81	191.93	80.88	44.1	48.8	34.1	…	224.00	…
0	714.60	587.30	1395.50	765.10	630.40	1540.60	855.00	685.60	10.4	11.8	8.8	1756.00	995.00	761.00
	…	…	…	…	…	…	…	…	…	…	…	…	…	…
9	14.31	12.78	26.12	13.66	12.46	24.61	13.08	11.53	−5.8	−4.2	−7.5	…	…	…
7	66.37	48.60	142.70	80.72	61.98	123.25	70.16	53.09	−13.6	−13.1	−14.3	…	…	…
7	42.11	35.56	83.90	49.44	34.46	84.24	48.10	36.14	0.4	−2.7	4.9	…	…	…
5	106.37	70.08	161.00	97.86	63.14	…	…	…	…	…	…	…	89.00	…
	14.76	18.01	34.76	15.52	19.24	33.46	14.03	19.43	−3.7	−9.6	1.0	…	…	…
2	105.21	200.61	316.05	129.46	186.59	322.35	135.20	187.15	2.0	4.4	0.3	307.00	129.00	178.00
3	23.78	18.00	40.56	20.60	19.96	42.13	21.51	20.62	3.9	4.4	3.3	…	…	…
	27.46	13.34	64.24	47.99	16.25	72.05	49.37	22.68	12.2	2.9	39.6	…	…	…
0	249.00	359.00	628.00	268.00	360.00	665.00	277.00	388.00	5.9	3.4	7.8	…	…	…
1	42.54	62.97	101.89	43.97	57.92	109.32	48.82	60.50	7.3	11.0	4.5	…	…	…
	…	…	…	…	…	…	…	…	…	…	…	…	…	…
3	82.62	45.11	137.88	90.79	47.09	168.05	96.51	71.54	21.9	6.3	51.9	…	…	…
	…	…	…	…	…	…	…	…	…	…	…	…	…	…
2	18.59	15.23	35.69	20.66	15.03	33.45	18.86	14.59	−6.3	−8.7	−2.9	…	…	…
	24.01	12.44	36.73	25.27	11.46	36.08	25.52	10.56	−1.8	1.0	−7.9	…	…	…

世界部分国家(地区)服务贸易额(三)

国别(地区) \ 金额 \ 年份	1985			1990			1993			1994	
	总额	出口	进口	总额	出口	进口	总额	出口	进口	总额	出口
喀麦隆	13.38	4.57	8.81	13.87	3.69	10.18	10.86	3.63	7.23	7.85	3.08
加蓬	11.59	1.19	10.40	11.98	2.14	9.84	12.90	2.86	10.04	10.09	2.00
尼日利亚	19.24	3.16	16.08	28.66	9.65	19.01	38.44	11.63	26.81	33.52	3.71
肯尼亚	7.19	4.11	3.08	13.72	7.74	5.98	12.60	7.61	4.99	14.16	8.15
毛里求斯	2.45	1.17	1.28	8.85	4.78	4.07	10.63	5.61	5.02	11.55	6.29
赞比亚	3.06	0.57	2.49	4.65	0.95	3.70	…	…	…	…	…
津巴布韦	7.17	2.71	4.46	7.13	2.53	4.60	8.62	3.45	5.17	9.99	3.54
坦桑尼亚	3.15	1.06	2.09	4.19	1.31	2.88	9.14	3.11	6.03	8.49	4.10
马拉维	1.69	0.26	1.43	3.05	0.37	2.68	2.90	0.30	2.60	2.56	0.22
塞拉利昂	0.58	0.18	0.40	1.12	0.45	0.67	1.06	0.45	0.61	1.79	0.86
埃塞俄比亚	…	…	…	6.08	2.60	3.48	5.38	2.50	2.88	5.65	2.66
马达加斯加	1.78	0.50	1.28	3.01	1.29	1.72	3.57	1.53	2.04	4.33	1.84
中东											
巴林	13.59	8.75	4.84	15.25	8.74	6.51	20.68	12.43	8.25	21.44	13.21
塞浦路斯	8.99	6.04	2.95	24.23	17.60	6.63	27.97	20.45	7.52	32.45	23.98
伊朗	34.90	3.33	31.57	40.46	3.43	37.03	65.32	10.48	54.84	34.72	4.10
以色列	57.71	31.23	26.48	101.49	45.12	56.37	130.74	59.39	71.35	148.69	65.02
约旦	22.44	11.60	10.84	25.48	14.30	11.18	27.09	15.60	11.49	27.40	15.43
科威特	42.59	9.44	33.15	38.58	10.54	28.04	44.00	10.27	33.73	48.31	11.89
叙利亚	12.04	4.65	7.39	14.42	7.40	7.02	23.58	13.11	10.47	30.66	16.16
沙特阿拉伯	…	…	…	157.25	30.31	126.94	172.10	32.83	139.27	122.75	33.47
亚洲(包括大洋洲)	1430.00	614.00	816.00	3119.00	1324.00	1795.00	4223.00	1880.00	2343.00	4917.00	2210.00
澳大利亚	114.67	40.56	74.11	229.56	97.79	131.77	244.26	115.46	128.80	285.58	136.69
孟加拉国	6.08	2.07	4.01	8.50	2.96	5.54	12.17	4.35	7.82	12.76	4.19
柬埔寨	…	…	…	…	…	…	1.77	0.59	1.18	1.77	0.45
中国	51.86	29.25	22.61	98.61	57.48	41.13	225.55	109.92	115.63	321.35	163.54
中国台湾	78.52	27.29	51.23	208.60	69.37	139.23	336.98	132.29	204.69	335.80	131.15
斐济	3.47	2.31	1.16	6.16	3.77	2.39	7.34	4.38	2.96	8.33	4.89
中国香港	124.25	77.31	46.94	291.46	181.28	110.18	432.84	276.90	155.94	497.84	311.42
印度	70.89	32.74	38.15	105.53	46.10	59.43	113.91	50.34	63.57	140.62	60.31
印度尼西亚	58.54	84.40	50.10	83.86	24.88	58.98	134.73	38.78	95.95	158.16	46.80
日本	552.30	205.20	347.10	1256.60	413.80	842.80	1470.90	516.10	954.80	1622.30	567.80

金额单位:亿美元

1995		1996			1997			1997年比1996年增减%			1998		
出口	进口	总额	出口	进口	总额	出口	进口	总额	出口	进口	总额	出口	进口
2.42	4.85	…	…	…	…	…	…	…	…	…	…	…	…
2.48	9.30	…	…	…	…	…	…	…	…	…	…	…	…
5.34	38.38	46.05	6.40	39.65	…	…	…	…	…	…	…	…	…
8.73	7.55	15.68	8.18	7.50	15.11	7.75	7.36	-3.6	-5.3	-1.9	…	…	…
7.73	6.30	16.21	9.55	6.66	15.92	9.14	6.78	-1.8	-4.3	1.8	…	…	…
…	…	…	…	…	…	…	…	…	…	…	…	…	…
…	…	…	…	…	…	…	…	…	…	…	…	…	…
5.66	7.29	14.85	6.02	8.83	11.76	4.60	7.16	-20.8	-23.6	-18.9	…	…	…
…	…	…	…	…	…	…	…	…	…	…	…	…	…
0.71	0.79	…	…	…	…	…	…	…	…	…	…	…	…
3.10	3.42	6.79	3.21	3.58	…	…	…	…	…	…	…	…	…
2.18	2.78	5.32	2.53	2.79	…	…	…	…	…	…	…	…	…
13.21	8.61	…	…	…	…	…	…	…	…	…	…	…	…
26.84	10.84	37.41	25.87	11.54	35.55	24.61	10.94	-5.0	-4.9	-5.2	…	…	…
5.33	21.92	36.42	7.43	28.99	…	…	…	…	…	…	…	…	…
76.69	96.24	183.24	79.62	103.62	192.05	83.38	108.67	4.8	4.7	4.9	…	8700	…
16.89	13.85	31.78	18.30	13.48	…	…	…	…	…	…	…	…	…
11.43	38.46	54.77	12.59	42.18	58.15	15.13	43.02	6.2	20.2	2.0	…	…	…
17.12	13.58	29.59	15.81	13.78	26.68	13.66	13.02	-9.8	-13.6	-5.5	…	…	…
34.80	86.81	153.64	27.72	125.92	184.10	44.84	139.26	19.8	61.8	10.6	…	…	139.00
2610.00	3268.00	6330.00	2844.00	3486.00	6538.00	2978.00	3560.00	3.3	4.7	2.1	…	…	…
156.56	165.35	362.06	180.78	181.28	363.78	182.21	181.57	0.5	0.8	0.2	325.00	158.00	167.00
4.68	11.92	12.76	2.23	10.53	…	…	…	…	…	…	…	…	…
1.03	1.81	3.61	1.52	2.09	3.31	1.49	1.82	-8.3	-2.0	-12.9	…	…	…
184.30	246.35	429.36	205.67	223.69	545.79	245.16	300.63	27.1	19.2	34.4	516.00	230.00	286.00
149.27	229.82	399.04	161.54	237.50	411.33	170.21	241.12	3.1	5.4	1.5	400.00	166.00	234.00
5.24	3.71	9.64	5.77	3.87	…	…	…	…	…	…	…	…	…
343.38	207.96	588.53	373.09	215.44	600.22	372.89	227.33	2.2	-0.1	5.5	569.00	342.00	227.00
67.64	100.62	181.50	76.56	104.94	…	…	…	…	…	…	242.00	105.00	137.00
53.42	132.30	212.39	64.62	147.77	229.25	67.80	161.45	7.9	4.9	9.3	…	…	119.00
639.60	1215.50	1950.50	663.80	1286.70	1902.10	681.30	1220.80	-2.5	2.6	-5.1	1703.00	608.00	1095.00

世界部分国家(地区)服务贸易额(四)

国别(地区) \ 年份 金额	1985			1990			1993			1994	
	总额	出口	进口	总额	出口	进口	总额	出口	进口	总额	出口
韩国	90.04	50.42	212.95	192.05	91.55	100.50	272.04	124.79	147.25	344.80	162.32
马来西亚	56.49	18.34	38.15	91.64	37.70	53.94	156.66	62.95	93.71	211.18	92.00
马尔代夫	0.84	0.61	0.23	1.56	1.19	0.37	2.31	1.76	0.55	2.57	1.95
蒙古	2.21	0.71	1.50	2.03	0.48	1.55	0.90	0.25	0.65	1.23	0.35
缅甸	1.38	0.63	0.75	1.66	0.94	0.72	…	…	…	…	…
尼泊尔	2.05	0.93	1.12	3.25	1.66	1.59	5.30	2.84	2.64	8.16	5.27
新西兰	31.36	14.24	17.12	56.66	24.15	32.51	62.59	28.04	34.55	76.33	35.99
巴基斯坦	17.47	7.40	10.07	30.67	12.13	18.54	36.89	13.24	23.65	36.08	14.36
巴布亚新几内亚	3.23	0.48	2.75	5.91	1.98	3.93	11.24	3.17	8.07	8.55	2.46
菲律宾	27.07	18.62	8.45	46.48	28.97	17.21	76.89	46.17	30.72	113.88	67.49
新加坡	81.10	45.98	35.12	212.98	127.19	85.79	296.32	184.87	111.45	366.56	229.30
斯里兰卡	6.73	2.34	4.39	10.45	4.25	6.20	14.63	6.19	8.44	17.49	7.29
泰国	36.40	18.97	17.43	124.51	62.91	61.60	231.84	108.77	123.07	266.56	114.25
瓦努阿图	0.56	0.36	0.20	0.80	0.56	0.24	0.94	0.64	0.30	1.03	0.70

注:由于服务贸易数据的频繁修订,一些国家和地区的贸易值序列出现多处中断。

a. 1985－1990 年中期的数字是前联邦德国的数字。

资料来源:国际贸易组织《年度报告》。

金额单位:亿美元

1995		1996			1997			1997年比1996年增减%			1998		
出口	进口	总额	出口	进口	总额	出口	进口	总额	出口	进口	总额	出口	进口
221.33	253.94	518.06	226.48	291.58	544.76	254.39	290.37	5.2	12.3	−0.4	466.00	236.00	230.00
111.42	143.05	306.85	139.84	167.01	312.85	145.15	167.70	2.0	3.8	0.4	228.00	109.00	119.00
2.30	0.74	3.64	2.86	0.78	…	…	…	…	…	…	…	…	…
0.47	0.87	…	…	…	…	…	…	…	…	…	…	…	…
…	…	…	…	…	…	…	…	…	…	…	…	…	…
5.92	3.05	9.14	6.79	2.35	10.11	7.95	2.16	10.6	17.1	−8.1	…	…	…
44.00	46.14	96.07	46.45	49.62	91.64	42.72	48.92	−4.6	−8.0	−1.4	…	…	…
14.25	24.20	…	…	…	…	…	…	…	…	…	…	…	…
3.09	6.13	11.83	4.36	7.47	…	…	…	…	…	…	…	…	…
93.23	69.06	223.21	129.29	93.92	292.03	151.30	140.73	30.8	17.0	49.8	…	…	…
297.20	175.32	490.89	298.38	192.51	498.01	303.79	194.22	1.5	1.8	0.9	362.00	182.00	180.00
8.00	11.69	19.14	7.41	11.73	21.20	8.50	12.70	10.8	14.7	8.3	…	…	…
146.52	186.01	360.18	167.04	193.14	330.01	158.50	171.51	−8.4	−5.1	−11.2	250.00	128.00	122.00
0.75	0.35	…	…	…	…	…	…	…	…	…	…	…	…

（对外贸易经济合作部国际贸易经济合作研究院文献信息中心）

发达国家官方发展援助协议额的财政条件 a(一)

1996 年—1997 年平均　　单位:百分比

国别	全部官方发展援助的赠与成分 标准:86%b		官方发展援助中赠与所占比重		官方发展援助贷款中的赠与成分	对最不发达国家官方发展援助总额中的赠与成分 C	对最不发达国家双边官方发展援助中的赠与成分
	1986－1987	1996－1997	双边援助	全部援助			
德国	88.9	93.3	69.8	80.5	64.1	100.0	100.0
澳大利亚	100.0	100.0	100.0	100.0	－	100.0	100.0
奥地利	78.0	96.4	88.3	92.2	54.2	100.0	100.0
比利时	99.1	99.2	94.0	96.6	76.5	99.9	99.7
加拿大	99.9	100.0	100.0	100.0	－	100.0	100.0
丹　麦	97.5	100.0	100.0	100.0	－	100.0	100.0
西班牙	－	90.7	60.6	74.7	63.4	91.4	79.3
美　国	97.0	99.4	98.4	98.8	51.8	99.9	99.7
芬　兰	98.1	99.9	95.5	97.6	52.7	100.0	100.0
法　国	86.3	91.5	78.2	84.1	52.4	97.8	96.4
爱尔兰	100.0	100.0	100.0	100.0	－	100.0	100.0
意大利	93.6	98.6	81.2	94.3	74.9	99.6	98.5
日　本	78.0	78.6	34.8	39.6	64.2	96.3	95.1
卢森堡	－	100.0	100.0	100.0	－	100.0	100.0
挪　威	99.4	99.4	98.4	98.9	30.6	99.0	98.4
新西兰	100.0	100.0	100.0	100.0	－	100.0	100.0
荷　兰	95.9	100.0	100.0	100.0	－	100.0	100.0
葡萄牙	－	99.2	86.6	98.6	39.3	99.5	99.4
英　国	99.7	100.0	100.0	100.0	－	100.0	100.0
瑞　典	100.0	100.0	100.0	100.0	－	100.0	100.0
瑞　士	99.8	100.0	100.0	100.0	－	100.0	100.0
总　计	91.5	91.9	70.1	77.8	63.0	98.9	98.0

注:a)不包括债务重新安排。

b)官方发展援助占国民生产总值的比重明显低于经合组织发展援助委员会平均水平的国家,不能视为已达到发展援助委员会制订的有关援助条件的指标,1997 年未达到的国家有意大利、葡萄牙和美国。

c)包括多边援助中的赠与成分。

资料来源:经济合作与发展组织《1998 年发展合作评论》。

(外贸易经济合作部国际贸易经济合作研究院发展援助研究部)

发达国家官方发展援助协议额的财政条件(二)

国别	赠与在官方发展援助中所占百分比		双边官方发展援助贷款							
			赠与成分百分比		偿还期(年)		宽缓期(年)		利率百分比	
	1996	1997	1996	1997	1996	1997	1996	1997	1996	1997
德国	77.7	84.3	62.6	67.3	33.5	37.3	6.8	8.0	2.0	1.9
澳大利亚	100.0	100.0	–	–	–	–	–	–	–	–
奥地利	94.3	89.8	55.9	53.0	26.7	22.9	7.9	7.5	2.8	2.7
比利时	95.6	97.7	79.6	69.3	28.7	20.8	9.9	10.5	0.0	0.9
加拿大	100.0	100.0	–	–	–	–	–	–	–	–
丹麦	100.0	100.0	–	–	–	–	–	–	–	–
西班牙	67.5	82.4	64.8	60.5	26.8	21.0	9.0	9.5	1.7	1.7
美国	99.2	98.1	52.0	50.9	26.4	27.6	5.9	5.4	3.0	3.2
芬兰	97.0	98.3	–	51.4	–	7.8	–	2.8	–	8.3
法国	82.9	85.7	51.1	53.9	20.5	21.1	7.1	8.2	2.6	2.5
爱尔兰	100.0	100.0	–	–	–	–	–	–	–	–
意大利	98.2	85.7	71.2	75.9	25.6	27.3	12.1	12.1	1.2	1.0
日本	34.1	45.0	67.0	60.8	28.7	29.0	9.2	9.4	2.4	2.4
卢森堡	100.0	100.0	–	–	–	–	–	–	–	–
挪威	99.1	98.8	29.5	31.6	12.4	9.0	3.1	3.9	3.7	2.5
新西兰	100.0	100.0	–	–	–	–	–	–	–	–
荷兰	100.0	100.0	–	–	–	–	–	–	–	–
葡萄牙	100.0	97.5	–	39.3	–	12.0	–	3.0	–	2.0
英国	100.0	100.0	–	–	–	–	–	–	–	–
瑞典	100.0	100.0	–	–	–	–	–	–	–	–
瑞士	100.0	100.0	–	–	–	–	–	–	–	–
总计	76.8	78.9	64.7	60.9	28.6	28.9	8.7	9.1	2.4	2.4

注:不包括债务重新安排。

资料来源:经济合作与发展组织《1998 年发展合作评论》。

(对外贸易经济合作部国际贸易经济合作研究院发展援助研究部)

世界商品贸易额及增长率＊(一)

年份	贸易额(亿美元)			增减率(%)		
	出口	进口	总额	出口	进口	总额
1950	554.00	580.00	1134.00	--	--	--
1955	843.00	892.00	1735.00	52.2	53.8	53.0
1960	1131.00	1194.00	2325.00	34.2	33.9	34.0
1961	1183.00	1245.00	2428.00	4.6	4.3	4.4
1962	1241.00	1321.00	2562.00	4.9	6.1	5.5
1963	1354.00	1435.00	2789.00	9.1	8.6	8.9
1964	1522.00	1610.00	3132.00	12.4	12.2	12.3
1965	1643.00	1743.00	3386.00	8.0	8.3	8.1
1966	1808.00	1921.00	3729.00	10.0	10.2	10.1
1967	1898.00	2015.00	3913.00	5.0	4.9	4.9
1968	2124.00	2248.00	4372.00	11.9	11.6	11.7
1969	2434.00	2565.00	4999.00	14.6	14.1	14.3
1970	3145.81	3289.21	6435.02	--	--	--
1971	3883.90	3663.84	7547.74	23.5	11.4	17.3
1972	4155.34	4340.21	8495.55	7.0	18.5	12.6
1973	5729.67	5999.35	11729.02	37.9	38.2	38.1
1974	8417.57	8607.16	17024.73	46.9	43.5	45.2
1975	8745.99	9045.12	17791.11	3.9	5.1	4.5
1976	9894.95	10135.73	20030.68	13.1	12.1	12.6
1977	11255.42	11605.20	22860.62	13.7	14.5	14.1
1978	12973.87	13471.30	26445.17	15.3	16.1	15.7
1979	16390.50	16868.07	33258.57	26.3	25.2	25.8
1980	19936.25	20474.25	40410.50	21.6	21.4	21.5
1981	19763.11	20360.88	40123.99	−0.9	−0.6	−0.7
1982	18575.50	19222.31	37797.81	−6.0	−5.6	−5.8
1983	18124.94	18718.42	36843.36	−2.4	−2.6	−2.5
1984	19093.15	19799.69	38892.84	5.4	5.8	5.6
1985	19300.05	20005.50	39305.55	1.1	1.0	1.1

世界商品贸易额及增长率*(二)

年份	贸易额(亿美元)			增减率(%)		
	出口	进口	总额	出口	进口	总额
1986	21280.93	21979.05	43259.98	10.3	9.9	10.1
1987	24908.05	25596.64	50504.69	17.0	16.5	16.7
1988	28253.38	29118.79	57372.17	13.4	13.8	13.6
1989	30213.46	31347.24	61560.70	6.9	7.7	7.3
1990	34250.43	35565.09	69815.52	13.4	13.5	13.4
1991	34180.14	35405.11	69585.25	−0.2	−0.4	−0.3
1992	36610.19	37948.62	74558.81	7.1	7.2	7.1
1993	36513.47	37349.64	73863.11	−0.3	−1.6	−0.9
1994	41688.07	42620.93	84309.00	14.2	14.1	14.1
1995	49698.98	50460.62	100159.60	19.2	18.4	18.8
1996	51708.25	53141.37	104849.62	4.0	5.3	4.7
1997	53403.20	54801.29	108204.49	3.3	3.1	3.2
1998	53750.00	55600.00	109350.00	0.6	1.5	1.1

注: * 1970年以前不包括前中央计划经济国家。

资料来源: 联合国《统计月报》

(对外贸易经济合作部国际贸易经济合作研究院文献信息中心)

世界服务贸易额及增长率

年 份	贸易额(亿美元)			增减率(%)		
	出 口	进 口	总 额	出 口	进 口	总 额
1981	4130.00	4120.00	8250.00	-	-	-
1982	4050.00	4000.00	8050.00	-1.9	-2.9	-2.4
1983	3910.00	3840.00	7750.00	-3.5	-4.0	-3.7
1984	4030.00	3970.00	8000.00	3.1	3.4	3.2
1985	3809.00	4016.00	7825.00	-5.5	1.2	-2.2
1986	4496.00	4527.00	9023.00	18.0	12.7	15.3
1987	5328.00	5365.00	10693.00	18.5	18.5	18.5
1988	6048.00	6201.00	12249.00	13.5	15.6	14.6
1989	6640.00	6820.00	13460.00	9.8	10.0	9.9
1990	7888.00	8170.00	16058.00	18.8	19.8	19.3
1991	8330.00	8477.00	16807.00	5.6	3.8	4.7
1992	9312.00	9407.00	18719.00	11.8	11.0	11.4
1993	9445.00	9575.00	19020.00	1.4	1.8	1.6
1994	10364.00	10394.00	20758.00	9.7	8.6	9.1
1995	11911.00	12023.00	23934.00	14.9	15.7	15.3
1996	12689.00	12665.00	25354.00	6.5	5.3	5.9
1997	13115.00	12959.00	26074.00	3.4	2.3	2.8
1998	12900.00	12900.00	25800.00	-1.6	-0.5	-1.1

资料来源:世界贸易组织《年度报告》。

(对外贸易经济合作部国际贸易经济合作研究院文献信息中心)

1987年—1997年世界初级产品出口价格指数(一)

(1990＝100)

项目 \ 年份	1987	1988	1989	1991	1992	1993	1994	1995	1996	1997
食品、饮料和烟草	91	110	109	99	98	97	111	118	125	122
食品	83	106	110	99	101	100	105	114	128	114
其中										
谷物	77	103	114	98	105	98	105	123	148	114
小麦	83	107	125	95	112	104	111	131	153	118
玉米	69	98	102	98	95	93	99	113	151	107
大米	80	105	112	109	99	88	100	119	125	112
油籽、油及油脂、油籽饼及粉	92	125	113	101	105	106	115	124	137	137
肉类	91	97	98	101	96	102	93	77	76	79
牛肉	93	98	100	104	96	102	91	74	70	72
羊肉	81	90	87	87	95	103	104	94	120	124
糖	77	89	96	89	83	88	99	108	101	95
香蕉	70	88	101	104	88	82	81	81	87	92
饮料	138	138	114	93	81	86	150	151	125	165
咖啡	147	159	126	94	73	83	180	184	139	192
可可豆	157	125	98	94	87	88	110	113	115	128
茶叶	84	88	99	91	98	91	90	81	87	117
烟草	90	93	98	106	101	80	88	78	90	104
农业原料	101	111	106	96	99	117	129	135	130	120
其中										
原木	105	111	107	105	117	155	157	148	151	141
棉花	94	77	92	93	70	70	97	119	98	96
羊毛	97	142	117	71	68	58	83	93	84	84
橡胶	114	137	112	96	100	96	130	183	162	118
皮革及革皮	87	95	98	86	82	87	94	96	95	96

1987 年—1997 年世界初级产品出口价格指数(二)

(1990＝100)

项目 \ 年份	1987	1988	1989	1991	1992	1993	1994	1995	1996	1997
黄麻	79	91	91	90	68	66	72	90	111	74
剑麻	72	77	91	94	71	86	85	99	121	109
矿石及有色金属(不包括原油)	79	118	112	87	84	72	84	100	89	92
其中										
铜	67	98	107	88	86	72	87	110	86	86
铝	95	155	119	80	77	70	90	110	92	98
铁矿砂	74	77	86	108	103	91	83	88	93	93
锡	112	118	141	91	100	85	90	102	101	93
镍	55	155	150	92	79	60	71	93	85	78
锌	53	82	109	74	82	64	66	68	68	87
铅	74	81	83	69	67	50	68	78	96	77
磷酸盐石	89	103	105	103	98	83	90	99	113	114
以上总计	88	109	107	94	94	96	109	118	117	113
原油	79	64	78	84	83	73	69	75	89	84
初级产品总计	85	88	94	90	91	90	98	106	109	105

注:以美元计算的指数

资料来源:世界贸易组织《年度报告》。

(对外贸易经济合作部国际贸易经济合作研究院文献信息中心)

1975 年—1997 年世界部分国家和地区工业制成品出口价格指数 a(一)

(1990=100)

国家(地区)	1975	1988	1990	1991	1992	1993	1994	1995	1996	1997
世界总计 b	**48**	**93**	**100**	**100**	**103**	**99**	**101**	**110**	**106**	…
市场经济发达国家	46	92	100	100	103	97	99	110	106	99
北美洲	47	96	100	102	100	99	99	100	100	100
加拿大	58	96	100	99	91	88	84	80	83	77
美国	45	95	100	102	103	103	104	107	106	108
欧洲	46	88	100	98	102	91	93	107	104	94
欧洲联盟	45	88	100	98	102	92	93	107	104	94
奥地利	52	95	100	95	99	91	90	…	…	…
比利时、卢森堡	50	89	100	97	99	90	93	110	105	96
丹麦	44	88	100	96	102	92	97	112	108	…
芬兰	42	85	100	95	90	74	83	105	99	89
法国	49	88	100	96	100	94	98	111	107	96
德国	47	89	100	98	103	93	94	108	101	87
希腊	58	86	100	95	94	81	82	…	…	…
爱尔兰	…	88	100	95	97	96	89	98	97	81
意大利	42	85	100	99	105	89	86	96	98	90
荷兰	48	88	100	96	102	92	92	109	102	…
葡萄牙	…	88	100	101	106	98	94	111	105	96
西班牙	…	83	100	95	109	85	86	99	99	…
瑞典	47	89	100	100	101	82	85	105	106	94
英国	38	91	100	101	102	98	103	114	113	113
欧洲自由贸易联盟	47	89	100	97	101	87	96	116	113	97
冰岛	38	99	100	88	86	76	80	114	106	101
挪威	51	96	100	95	92	80	82	102	96	88
瑞士	43	88	100	98	103	88	99	120	117	100
其它欧洲国家										
马耳他	…	…	…	…	…	…	…	…	…	…

1975—1997 年世界部分国家和地区工业制成品出口价格指数 a(二)

(1990＝100)

国家(地区)	1975	1988	1990	1991	1992	1993	1994	1995	1996	1997
其它市场经济发达国家	50	101	100	107	113	120	129	138	127	121
澳大利亚	56	97	100	92	86	81	88	96	94	89
以色列	…	86	100	101	101	102	101	105	105	102
日本	48	102	100	108	115	124	134	144	133	126
新西兰	47	107	100	94	89	89	98	112	109	102
南非	…	89	100	96	101	100	101	123	…	…
发展中国家	55	97	100	100	103	104	104	111	105	…
中国香港	…	…	100	102	104	104	105	108	108	104
印度	…	…	100	80	92	89	88	86	…	…
韩国	…	…	100	101	106	109	98	102	86	85
巴基斯坦	…	…	100	98	101	98	107	125	123	129
新加坡	…	…	100	101	103	99	108	112	109	102
土耳其	…	…	100	98	100	95	90	106	97	89

注:a 用美元计价的出口单价指数。

b 不包括东欧国家和前苏联。

资料来源:联合国《统计月报》

(对外贸易经济合作部国际贸易经济合作研究院文献信息中心)

发达国家向发展中国家和国际多边机构提供的官方发展援助(一)

净交付额,现值

国别	亿美元							占国民生产总值百分比						
	81－82	86－87	1993	1994	1995	1996	1997	81－82	86－87	1993	1994	1995	1996	1997
德　国	31.66	41.11	69.54	68.18	75.24	76.01	58.57	0.47	0.41	0.36	0.34	0.31	0.33	0.28
澳大利亚	7.66	6.90	9.53	10.91	11.94	10.74	10.61	0.49	0.40	0.35	0.34	0.36	0.28	0.28
奥地利	2.28	1.99	5.44	6.55	7.67	5.57	5.27	0.34	0.19	0.30	0.33	0.33	0.24	0.26
比利时	5.37	6.17	8.10	7.27	10.34	9.13	7.64	0.58	0.48	0.39	0.32	0.38	0.34	0.31
加拿大	11.93	17.90	24.00	22.50	20.67	17.95	20.45	0.42	0.48	0.45	0.43	0.38	0.32	0.34
丹　麦	4.09	7.77	13.40	14.46	16.23	17.72	16.37	0.75	0.88	1.03	1.03	0.96	1.04	0.97
西班牙	2.37	2.17	13.04	13.05	13.48	12.51	12.34	0.13	0.08	0.28	0.28	0.24	0.22	0.23
美　国	69.92	93.40	101.23	99.27	73.67	93.77	68.78	0.23	0.21	0.15	0.14	0.10	0.12	0.09
芬　兰	1.40	3.73	3.55	2.90	3.88	4.08	3.79	0.28	0.48	0.45	0.31	0.32	0.34	0.33
法　国	30.07	46.45	79.15	84.66	84.43	74.51	63.07	0.54	0.58	0.63	0.64	0.55	0.48	0.45
爱尔兰	0.37	0.57	0.81	1.09	1.53	1.79	1.87	0.21	0.23	0.20	0.25	0.29	0.31	0.31
意大利	7.38	25.09	30.43	27.05	16.23	24.16	12.66	0.18	0.37	0.31	0.27	0.15	0.20	0.11
日　本	30.97	64.88	112.59	132.39	144.89	94.39	93.58	0.28	0.30	0.27	0.29	0.28	0.20	0.22
卢森堡	0.05	0.13	0.50	0.59	0.65	0.82	0.95	0.11	0.17	0.35	0.40	0.36	0.44	0.55
挪　威	5.13	8.44	10.14	11.37	12.44	13.11	13.06	0.94	1.13	1.01	1.05	0.87	0.85	0.86
新西兰	0.66	0.81	0.98	1.10	1.23	1.22	1.54	0.28	0.28	0.25	0.24	0.23	0.21	0.26
荷　兰	14.91	19.17	25.25	25.17	32.26	32.46	29.47	1.07	0.99	0.82	0.76	0.81	0.81	0.81
葡萄牙	0.05	0.31	2.35	3.03	2.58	2.18	2.50	0.02	0.10	0.28	0.34	0.25	0.21	0.25
英　国	19.96	18.04	29.20	31.97	32.02	31.99	34.33	0.40	0.29	0.31	0.31	0.29	0.27	0.26

发达国家向发展中国家和国际多边机构提供的官方发展援助(二)

净交付额,现值

国别	亿美元							占国民生产总值百分比						
	81－82	86－87	1993	1994	1995	1996	1997	81－82	86－87	1993	1994	1995	1996	1997
瑞　典	9.53	12.32	17.69	18.19	17.04	19.99	17.31	0.92	0.87	0.99	0.96	0.77	0.84	0.79
瑞　士	2.45	4.84	7.93	9.82	10.84	10.26	9.11	0.24	0.30	0.33	0.36	0.34	0.34	0.34
总　计	**258.20**	**382.21**	**564.86**	**591.52**	**589.26**	**554.38**	**483.24**	**0.34**	**0.33**	**0.30**	**0.30**	**0.27**	**0.25**	**0.22**
其中：														
欧盟国家	129.48	185.04	298.45	304.16	313.58	312.93	266.12	0.45	0.44	0.44	0.42	0.38	0.37	0.33

资料来源:经济合作与发展组织《1998 年发展合作评论》。

（对外贸易经济合作部国际贸易经济合作研究院发展援助研究部）

发达国家和多边机构援助协议额的部门分布(一)

单位:百分比

国别	社会与管理基础设施		经济基础设施		农业		工业与其他产业		方案援助和物资援助		紧急援助		其他		备注:通过NoGg比重a
	75/76	95/96	75/76	95/96	75/76	95/96	75/76	95/96	75/76	95/96	75/76	95/96	75/76	95/96	95/96
德　国	23.4	34.4	17.7	23.7	7.6	7.4	17.7	3.4	5.7	4.0	0.4	5.0	27.6	22.1	2.6
澳大利亚	17.5	50.6	7.3	16.5	4.3	3.6	1.6	1.4	53.1	14.5	0.1	1.4	16.1	12.0	0.6
奥地利	7.0	31.4	0.7	6.5	3.3	1.8	25.2	7.6	–	0.5	1.4	18.7	62.4	33.4	0.5
比利时	3.8	30.2	0.9	5.7	2.1	13.0	1.3	4.1	3.1	8.6	0.5	3.6	88.4	34.9	0.3
加拿大	19.1	24.2	12.0	11.6	8.1	4.0	13.5	2.7	24.1	8.8	0.3	10.7	23.0	37.9	8.5
丹　麦	14.0	34.1	0.0	14.8	11.4	6.9	24.4	1.7	11.6	2.5	2.6	5.7	36.0	34.3	0.5
西班牙	–	37.8	–	14.9	–	6.7	–	7.0	–	1.3	–	1.8	–	30.5	–
美　国	8.7	31.7	2.3	8.9	8.1	5.9	4.1	8.3	38.3	9.0	1.6	9.6	37.0	26.6	8.6
芬　兰	10.9	22.5	8.8	9.8	3.5	7.5	11.0	1.5	7.3	–	2.7	14.3	55.8	44.4	0.7
法　国	53.7	47.0	13.0	9.5	7.0	6.3	16.6	1.6	6.2	8.5	0.4	0.3	3.2	26.9	0.2
爱尔兰	–	47.4	–	7.0	–	5.0	–	1.1	–	–	–	14.4	100.0	25.2	0.1
意大利	14.0	15.8	2.0	11.9	2.9	4.5	28.4	0.4	–	12.1	–	11.4	52.6	43.9	1.0
日　本	3.3	22.6	36.6	43.1	6.0	11.7	20.3	2.6	1.3	2.3	0.1	0.3	32.4	17.4	2.1
卢森堡	–	40.7	–	5.8	–	5.4	–	0.5	–	1.1	–	16.0	–	30.3	12.5
挪　威	25.4	28.3	16.7	18.8	25.5	5.3	7.3	2.8	–	1.3	6.9	22.9	18.2	20.5	–
新西兰	14.8	41.6	34.0	8.6	23.7	13.2	3.1	1.0	13.5	13.1	0.4	5.5	10.4	17.0	2.0

发达国家和多边机构援助协议额的部门分布(二)

单位:百分比

国别	社会与管理基础设施		经济基础设施		农业		工业与其他产业		方案援助和物资援助		紧急援助		其他		备注:通过NoGg比重a
	75/76	95/96	75/76	95/96	75/76	95/96	75/76	95/96	75/76	95/96	75/76	95/96	75/76	95/96	95/96
荷兰	34.3	25.3	15.9	10.4	19.7	9.3	10.1	1.3	3.4	5.2	1.7	9.5	15.0	39.0	9.2
葡萄牙	–	32.6	–	5.9	–	2.3	–	3.4	–	0.3	–	3.0	–	52.5	0.8
英国	4.8	28.3	3.4	15.4	4.3	9.8	54.4	3.7	6.9	9.1	0.3	12.7	26.0	21.0	2.0
瑞典	99.9	34.5	2.5	12.0	2.0	9.0	14.7	1.0	9.4	4.5	2.5	20.9	39.7	17.3	6.0
瑞士	12.3	14.7	13.4	6.1	15.5	8.6	5.2	3.4	10.6	5.3	12.3	11.6	30.6	50.2	5.6
总计	20.2	30.2	10.5	23.4	8.1	8.4	13.6	3.4	18.9	5.3	1.0	5.1	27.7	24.2	3.4

注:a 按交付额统计。NOGa 为非政府组织,可作为政府援助的执行机构。

资料来源:经济合作与发展组织《1998 年发展合作评论》。

(对外贸易经济合作部国际贸易经济合作研究院发展援助研究部)

非经合组织发展援助委员会成员国的官方发展援助

净交付额　单位:亿美元

国别/(地区)	1993	1994	1995	1996	1997
经合组织非 DAC 成员国					
韩国	1.12	1.40	1.16	1.59	1.86
希腊	0.90a	1.22a	1.52a	1.84a	1.73
冰岛	0.07	0.06	..	..	..
捷克共和国	0.20	0.25	..	..	..
土耳其	0.73	0.58	1.07	0.88	..
阿拉伯国家					
沙特阿拉伯	5.49	3.17	1.92	3.27	2.35
阿拉伯联合酋长国	2.39	1.00	0.65	0.31	..
科威特	3.95	5.55	3.84	4.26	3.73
其他国家和地区					
印度	0.25	0.28	..	..	..
中国台北	0.61	0.79	0.92	0.89	0.65
总　计	15.71	14.30	11.08	13.04	10.32
其中:双边援助					
经合组织非 DAC 成员国					
韩国	0.60	0.60	0.71	1.23	1.11
希腊	0.13a	0.30a	0.27a	0.27	0.36
冰岛	0.03	0.02	..	..	..
捷克共和国	0.15	0.21	..	..	
土耳其	0.58	0.20	0.84	..	..
阿拉伯国家					
沙特阿拉伯	3.43	1.76	1.34	1.77	0.79
阿拉伯联合酋长国	2.32	0.92	0.55	0.29	..
科威特	3.49	4.94	3.57	3.77	3.55
其他国家和地区					
印度	0.14	0.15	..	..	..
中国台北	0.57	0.71	0.78	0.89	0.65
总　计	11.44	9.82	8.07	8.23	6.46

注:中国对外也提供援助,但未提供数据。

a:包括所有发展中国家和前苏联东欧国家的受援国。

资料来源:经济合作与发展组织《1998 年发展合作评论》。

(对外贸易经济合作部国际贸易经济合作研究院发展援助研究部)

国际直接投资流量

年　份	发达国家		发展中国家		中东欧		所有国家	
	流进	流出	流进	流出	流进	流出	流进	流出
金额(单位:亿美元)								
1986－1991(年均)	1295.83	1691.55	290.90	113.31	6.58	0.25	1593.31	1805.10
1992	1202.94	1799.84	511.08	207.14	44.39	1.02	1758.41	2008.00
1993	1388.87	2058.10	725.28	349.29	61.43	1.61	2175.59	2409.00
1994	1415.03	2414.81	955.82	425.12	59.14	2.68	2429.99	2842.61
1995	2114.65	3064.65	1055.11	456.42	142.14	4.08	3311.89	3525.14
1996	1953.93	2834.76	1298.13	491.61	123.44	9.93	3375.50	3336.29
1997	2331.15	3592.36	1489.44	611.38	184.28	32.92	4004.86	4236.66
占世界比重(%)								
1986－1991(年均)	81.3	93.77	18.3	6.3	0.4	0.01	100	100
1992	68.5	89.6	29	10.3	2.5	0.1	100	100
1993	63.8	85.4	33.4	14.5	2.8	0.1	100	100
1994	58.2	85.0	39.3	15.0	2.4	0.1	100	100
1995	63.9	86.9	31.9	12.9	4.3	0.1	100	100
1996	57.9	85.1	38.5	14.8	3.7	0.2	100	100
1997	58.2	84.8	37.2	14.4	4.6	0.8	100	100
增长率(%)								
1986－1991年								
1992	－7.2	6.4	75.7	82.8	574.6	308	10.4	11.2
1993	15.5	14.3	41.9	68.6	38.4	57.8	23.7	20
1994	1.9	17.3	31.8	21.7	－3.7	66.5	11.7	18
1995	49.4	26.9	10.4	7.4	140.3	52.2	36.3	24
1996	－7.6	－7.5	23	7.7	－13.2	143.4	19	－5.4
1997	19.3	26.7	14.7	24.4	49.3	231.5	18.6	27

资料来源:联合国贸易和发展会议《1998年世界投资报告》

(对外贸易经济合作部国际贸易经济合作研究院跨国经营研究部)

1998年中国出口额最大的200家企业(一)

金额单位:万美元

位次	企业名称	出口额	位次	企业名称	出口额
1	中国粮油食品进出口总公司	184,160	39	葆祥河北进出口(集团)公司	26,607
2	中国化工进出口总公司	165,840	40	上海轻工国际(集团)有限公司	26,169
3	东方国际(集团)有限公司	162,846	41	东方国际集团上海市服装进出口有限公司	25,840
4	中国有色金属进出口总公司	129,196	42	中国长城工业总公司	25,501
5	中国工艺品进出口总公司	116,947	43	广东省东莞市对外贸易发展集团公司	25,183
6	中国煤炭工业进出口总公司	103,356	44	中化河北进出口公司	25,146
7	中国包装进出口总公司	92,678	45	浙江中大集团股份有限公司	24,876
8	中国钢铁工贸集团公司	87,983	46	广东东莞轻工业品进出口公司	24,758
9	中国电子进出口总公司	84,212	47	中国化工建设总公司	24,757
10	中国北方工业公司	81,295	48	上海兰生(集团)有限公司	23,850
11	中国石化国际事业公司	67,640	49	浙江省嘉兴市进出口公司	22,791
12	中国通用技术(集团)控股有限责任公司	65,717	50	江苏舜天国际集团服装进出口股份有限公司	22,209
13	中国土产畜产进出口总公司	64,841			
14	上海丝绸集团有限公司	59,248	51	江苏省丝绸进出口集团股份有限公司	22,113
15	中国机械设备进出口总公司	56,999	52	东方国际集团上海市针织品进出口有限公司	21,869
16	中国海洋石油总公司	54,678			
17	中国五金矿产进出口总公司	53,063	53	中国深圳对外贸易(集团)公司	21,810
18	中国联合石油有限责任公司	50,684	54	浙江粮油食品进出口股份有限公司	21,809
19	中国烟草进出口总公司	49,934	55	中国国际信托投资公司	21,344
20	中国航空技术进出口总公司	46,001	56	东方国际集团上海市纺织品进出口有限公司	20,949
21	中国纺织品进出口总公司	44,006			
22	中国出口商品基地建设总公司	43,979	57	上海市工艺品进出口公司	20,478
23	中化辽宁进出口公司	43,734	58	中国丝绸进出口总公司	20,371
24	中联油大连公司	40,424	59	中国(福建)对外贸易中心集团	19,874
25	中国船舶工业贸易公司	39,496	60	浙江省纺织品进出口公司	19,494
26	中国机械进出口(集团)有限公司	36,425	61	东方国际集团上海市家用纺织品进出口有限公司	19,209
27	江苏舜天国际集团有限公司	35,634			
28	上海宝钢集团国际经济贸易总公司	35,177	62	江苏省轻工业品集团股份有限公司	18,950
29	江苏国泰国际集团有限公司	34,314	63	大连造船厂	18,789
30	广东省东莞化工机械进出口公司	32,459	64	广东省轻工业品进出口(集团)公司	18,613
31	江苏汇鸿国际集团有限公司	32,179	65	山东省机械进出口公司	18,509
32	葆祥国际服装中心	31,542	66	中国保利科技有限公司	18,388
33	中设江苏机械设备进出口集团公司	31,391	67	广州轻工业品进出口(集团)公司	18,275
34	广东东莞市东成工业发展总公司	30,290	68	广东东莞市建筑材料进出口公司	17,723
35	广东省纺织品进出口(集团)公司	29,875	69	福建省粮油食品进出口公司	17,703
36	浙江省土畜产进出口公司	29,509	70	大连造船新厂	17,623
37	中国石油技术开发公司	29,462	71	广东省东莞化工进出口公司	17,573
38	浙江省丝绸进出口公司	29,416	72	浙江东方集团股份有限公司	17,520

1998年中国出口额最大的200家企业(二)

金额单位:万美元

位次	企业名称	出口额	位次	企业名称	出口额
73	中国技术进出口总公司	17,464	110	厦门建发股份有限公司	13,185
74	江苏省纺织品进出口集团股份有限公司	17,173	111	广东省东莞五金矿产进出口公司	13,175
75	苏州进出口(集团)有限公司	17,161	112	福建省珠宝首饰进出口公司	12,759
76	中国电子进出口广东公司	17,144	113	浙江省畜产进出口公司	12,730
77	江西省粮油食品进出口公司	17,058	114	中国抽纱汕头进出口公司	12,629
78	山东省纺织品进出口公司	16,909	115	广东省东莞工艺品进出口公司	12,587
79	上海兰生股份有限公司	16,560	116	湖南省粮油食品进出口公司	12,460
80	辽宁鞍钢国际经济贸易公司	16,528	117	中国汽车工业进出口总公司	12,243
81	中国华源集团有限公司	16,513	118	上海新联纺进出口公司	12,238
82	中国轻工业品进出口总公司	16,420	119	云南红塔进出口公司	12,221
83	新疆对外经济贸易(集团)公司	16,308	120	中国工程与农机进出口公司	12,169
84	上海市轻工业品进出口公司	16,300	121	上海申达股份有限公司	12,132
85	江苏省海外企业集团有限公司	16,105	122	上海市畜产(集团)有限公司	11,871
86	南京纺织品进出口股份有限公司	15,960	123	北京市服装进出口股份有限公司	11,774
87	中化江苏进出口公司	15,339	124	南通市对外贸易公司	11,610
88	上海机械进出口(集团)公司	15,269	125	江苏省工艺品进出口集团股份有限公司	11,562
89	广东省丝绸进出口(集团)公司	15,101			
90	中国江苏国际经济技术合作公司	14,979	126	北京富亿通进出口有限责任公司	11,555
91	厦门特贸有限公司	14,893	127	安徽省轻工进出口股份有限公司	11,538
92	广州纺织品进出口集团有限公司	14,716	128	浙江省工艺品进出口公司	11,506
93	镇海炼油化工股份有限公司	14,622	129	中国远大集团公司	11,483
94	福建厦门经贸集团有限公司	14,531	130	江苏舜天国际集团机械进出口股份有限公司	11,455
95	广东省东莞纺织品进出口公司	14,460			
96	株洲冶炼厂	14,454	131	中国石化国际事业公司茂名公司	11,424
97	广西钦州市外经贸公司	14,281	132	扬州市对外贸易公司	11,420
98	中国抽纱上海进出口公司	13,961	133	浙江省绍兴市进出口公司	11,275
99	中国首钢国际贸易工程公司	13,904	134	中国烟草云南进出口公司	11,159
100	厦门建发集团股份公司	13,796	135	中国成套设备进出口集团公司	11,051
101	宁波市慈溪进出口公司	13,780	136	江苏省连云港市对外贸易公司	10,964
102	攀钢集团国际经济贸易总公司	13,718	137	广东中山食品水产进出口集团公司	10,930
103	常熟市对外贸易公司	13,675	138	广东省东莞食品进出口公司	10,856
104	广州工艺品番禺进出口公司	13,615	139	中化宁波进出口公司	10,843
105	常州市对外贸易公司	13,598	140	福建省轻工业品进出口集团公司	10,651
106	厦门国贸集团股份有限公司	13,502	141	杭州西湖电子进出口有限公司	10,563
107	江苏汇鸿国际集团针绵织品进出口有限公司	13,500	142	四川省东方电力设备联合公司	10,531
			143	宁波鄞县进出口公司	10,528
108	广东省东莞丝绸进出口总公司	13,467	144	南通市经济技术开发区总公司	10,449
109	深圳中电投资股份有限公司	13,436	145	福建天成集团有限公司	10,438

1998年中国出口额最大的200家企业(三)

金额单位:万美元

位次	企业名称	出口额	位次	企业名称	出口额
146	辽宁省五金矿产进出口公司	10,366	174	福建省五金矿产进出口公司	9,279
147	河北省纺织品进出口(集团)公司	10,347	175	四川省丝绸进出口公司	9,201
148	江苏省技术进出口公司	10,342	176	广东南海轻工业品进出口公司	9,185
149	河北省圣仑进出口集团	10,333	177	中粮黑龙江粮油食品进出口公司	9,160
150	中国工艺美术总公司	10,296	178	镇江市对外贸易集团公司	9,130
151	山东省服装进出口公司	10,256	179	湖北省机械设备进出口公司	9,066
152	辽宁省服装进出口公司	10,217	180	广东省信宜县进出口贸易公司	9,037
153	中国土产畜产浙江茶叶进出口公司	10,181	181	广东宏远集团公司	9,019
154	辽宁成大股份有限公司	10,130	182	陕西省机械设备进出口公司	9,019
155	广东外贸开发公司顺德市公司	10,116	183	江苏省粮油食品进出口集团股份有限公司	8,970
156	武钢集团国际经济贸易总公司	10,112			
157	安徽省粮油食品进出口公司	10,111	184	深圳奥康德石油贸易集团公司	8,847
158	浙江省湖州市进出口公司	10,079	185	广东省工艺品进出口(集团)公司	8,798
159	浙江省温州市进出口公司	10,022	186	中粮山东粮油进出口公司	8,786
160	上海市五金矿产进出口公司	9,868	187	北京富亿通达经贸有限责任公司	8,713
161	中国医药保健品进出口总公司	9,849	188	中电广东惠州总公司	8,664
162	上海市土产进出口公司	9,784	189	青岛益佳集团公司	8,567
163	上海市食品进出口公司	9,774	190	广东省食品进出口(集团)公司	8,547
164	上海服装(集团)有限公司	9,757	191	山东省对外贸易集团有限公司	8,536
165	安徽省服装进出口公司	9,748	192	上海汉森进出口有限公司	8,535
166	中国烟草上海进出口公司	9,738	193	北京市首饰进出口公司	8,516
167	无锡中润(集团)有限公司	9,720	194	中国土木工程集团公司	8,495
168	中国北方工业广州公司	9,713	195	上海钟表进出口有限公司	8,488
169	广州番禺市对外贸易(集团)公司	9,630	196	东方国际集团上海市对外贸易公司	8,444
170	宁波市工艺品进出口公司	9,565	197	上海市化工进出口公司	8,408
171	广东省东莞粮油进出口公司	9,558	198	宁波宁兴公司	8,402
172	广东省东莞畜产进出口公司	9,480	199	安徽芜湖市进出口公司	8,395
173	浙江省萧山市进出口公司	9,345	200	天津服装进出口公司	8,315

1998年中国进出口额最大的500家企业(一)

金额单位:万美元

位次	企　业　名　称	进出口额	出口额	进口额
1	中国化工进出口总公司	562,161	165,840	396,328
2	中国石化国际事业公司	328,507	67,640	260,869
3	中国粮油食品进出口总公司	295,199	184,160	111,040
4	中国通用技术(集团)控股有限责任公司	287,987	65,717	222,269
5	东方国际(集团)有限公司	215,768	162,846	52,917
6	中国有色金属进出口总公司	173,184	129,196	43,984
7	中国航空技术进出口总公司	148,370	46,001	102,373
8	中国国际石油化工联合公司	140,919	361	140,558
9	中国包装进出口总公司	136,664	92,678	43,983
10	中国技术进出口总公司	131,206	17,464	113,742
11	中国钢铁工贸集团公司	130,754	87,983	42,774
12	中国工艺品进出口总公司	124,642	116,947	7,689
13	中国电子进出口总公司	121,186	84,212	36,978
14	中国五金矿产进出口总公司	119,513	53,063	66,448
15	中国煤炭工业进出口总公司	118,939	103,356	15,585
16	上海宝钢集团国际经济贸易总公司	115,829	35,177	80,652
17	中国北方工业公司	103,210	81,295	21,915
18	中国土产畜产进出口总公司	101,447	64,841	36,602
19	中国航空器材进出口公司	96,788	2,245	94,543
20	中国烟草进出口总公司	94,225	49,934	44,295
21	中国机械设备进出口总公司	82,904	56,999	25,907
22	中国机械进出口(集团)有限公司	80,676	36,425	44,249
23	中国海洋石油总公司	78,767	54,678	24,090
24	中国联合石油有限责任公司	78,704	50,684	28,020
25	上海丝绸集团有限公司	76,450	59,248	17,202
26	中国出口商品基地建设总公司	58,559	43,979	14,577
27	中国仪器进出口总公司	58,509	3,831	54,678
28	中国石油技术开发公司	56,793	29,462	27,331
29	中国船舶工业贸易公司	55,875	39,496	16,380
30	中国纺织品进出口总公司	54,219	44,006	10,213
31	江苏舜天国际集团有限公司	53,007	35,634	17,375
32	广东省东莞化工机械进出口公司	52,806	32,459	20,347
33	上海东方航空进出口公司	52,346	6,912	45,434
34	广东东莞市东成工业发展总公司	50,380	30,290	20,090
35	中设江苏机械设备进出口集团公司	48,412	31,391	17,022
36	中国长城工业总公司	44,669	25,501	19,164
37	中化辽宁进出口公司	44,249	43,734	515

1998 年中国进出口额最大的 500 家企业(二)

金额单位:万美元

位次	企 业 名 称	进出口额	出口额	进口额
38	广东省东莞市对外贸易发展集团公司	44,195	25,183	19,011
39	广东珠海振戎公司	42,698	-	42,698
40	中国邮电器材总公司	42,170	181	41,990
41	中国化工建设总公司	41,217	24,757	16,457
42	中联油大连公司	40,432	40,424	8
43	广东东莞轻工业品进出口公司	40,020	24,758	15,262
44	广东省机械进出口(集团)公司	39,669	6,353	33,316
45	江苏国泰国际集团有限公司	39,443	34,314	5,129
46	中国国际信托投资公司	38,850	21,344	17,507
47	中国保利科技有限公司	38,129	18,388	19,741
48	辽宁鞍钢国际经济贸易公司	36,843	16,528	20,315
49	镇海炼油化工股份有限公司	35,679	14,622	21,058
50	上海轻工国际(集团)有限公司	35,305	26,169	9,139
51	江苏汇鸿国际集团有限公司	33,718	32,179	1,538
52	中国深圳对外贸易(集团)公司	33,684	21,810	11,871
53	东方国际集团上海市服装进出口有限公司	33,340	25,840	7,499
54	广东省纺织品进出口(集团)公司	32,975	29,875	3,100
55	广东省东莞化工进出口公司	32,739	17,573	15,166
56	葆祥国际服装中心	31,732	31,542	190
57	浙江省土畜产进出口公司	31,444	29,509	1,935
58	浙江省丝绸进出口公司	30,373	29,416	957
59	浙江省技术进出口有限责任公司	30,116	4,552	25,563
60	江苏省海外企业集团有限公司	29,987	16,105	13,882
61	广东东莞市建筑材料进出口公司	29,970	17,723	12,246
62	中国(福建)对外贸易中心集团	29,066	19,874	9,190
63	东方国际集团上海市对外贸易公司	28,771	8,444	20,327
64	广东省化工进出口(集团)公司	27,726	4,673	23,053
65	中国石化国际事业公司茂名公司	27,708	11,424	16,283
66	中国汽车工业进出口总公司	27,628	12,243	15,387
67	中谷粮油集团公司	27,387	32	27,355
68	中国轻工业品进出口总公司	26,845	16,420	10,427
69	浙江中大集团股份有限公司	26,704	24,876	1,829
70	江苏舜天国际集团服装进出口股份有限公司	26,676	22,209	4,469
71	葆祥河北进出口(集团)公司	26,663	26,607	56
72	上海兰生(集团)有限公司	26,439	23,850	2,591
73	厦门特贸有限公司	26,281	14,893	11,387
74	厦门国贸集团股份有限公司	25,959	13,502	12,457

1998 年中国进出口额最大的500 家企业(三)

金额单位:万美元

位次	企业名称	进出口额	出口额	进口额
75	中化河北进出口公司	25,893	25,146	749
76	大连造船新厂	25,771	17,623	8,149
77	中国航空器材进出口西南公司	25,629	206	25,423
78	广州工艺品番禺进出口公司	25,418	13,615	11,803
79	中国化工供销集团公司	24,915	1,777	23,138
80	新疆对外经济贸易(集团)公司	24,702	16,308	8,394
81	中国首钢国际贸易工程公司	24,474	13,904	10,570
82	浙江省嘉兴市进出口公司	24,230	22,791	1,438
83	大连造船厂	24,150	18,789	5,361
84	东方国际集团上海市针织品进出口有限公司	24,076	21,869	2,207
85	江苏舜天国际集团机械进出口股份有限公司	24,045	11,455	12,590
86	江苏省丝绸进出口集团股份有限公司	23,523	22,113	1,410
87	东方国际集团上海市纺织品进出口有限公司	23,250	20,949	2,301
88	上海市工艺品进出口公司	23,230	20,478	2,753
89	浙江粮油食品进出口股份有限公司	22,762	21,809	954
90	江苏省轻工业品集团股份有限公司	22,551	18,950	3,600
91	广州轻工业品进出口(集团)公司	22,321	18,275	4,046
92	中国电子进出口广东公司	22,267	17,144	5,123
93	中国丝绸进出口总公司	22,238	20,371	1,863
94	广东省东莞五金矿产进出口公司	21,970	13,175	8,795
95	武钢集团国际经济贸易总公司	21,794	10,112	11,682
96	浙江东方集团股份有限公司	21,600	17,520	4,080
97	中国烟草云南进出口公司	21,531	11,159	10,372
98	广东省东莞工艺品进出口公司	21,364	12,587	8,777
99	上海机械进出口(集团)公司	21,227	15,269	5,959
100	广东省轻工业品进出口(集团)公司	21,204	18,613	2,591
101	山东省机械进出口公司	21,036	18,509	2,527
102	中国华源集团有限公司	20,998	16,513	4,489
103	广东省东莞纺织品进出口公司	20,979	14,460	6,520
104	北京富亿通进出口有限责任公司	20,833	11,555	9,278
105	安徽省技术进出口股份有限公司	20,823	7,689	13,134
106	中国远大集团公司	20,750	11,483	9,266
107	广东省东莞丝绸进出口总公司	20,466	13,467	6,980
108	福建省粮油食品进出口公司	20,226	17,703	2,523
109	厦门建发集团股份公司	20,194	13,796	6,397
110	中国南光进出口总公司	20,121	5,019	15,102
111	东方国际集团上海市家用纺织品进出口有限公司	20,087	19,209	878

1998 年中国进出口额最大的 500 家企业(四)

金额单位:万美元

位次	企业名称	进出口额	出口额	进口额
112	浙江省纺织品进出口公司	20,024	19,494	531
113	中化江苏进出口公司	19,381	15,339	4,043
114	杭州西湖电子进出口有限公司	19,295	10,563	8,733
115	苏州进出口(集团)有限公司	19,270	17,161	2,109
116	厦门建发股份有限公司	19,011	13,185	5,826
117	山东省纺织品进出口公司	18,974	16,909	2,065
118	上海市轻工业品进出口公司	18,770	16,300	2,470
119	江苏省纺织品进出口集团股份有限公司	18,468	17,173	1,295
120	上海兰生股份有限公司	18,285	16,560	1,725
121	联想集团控股公司	18,166	23	18,143
122	江西省粮油食品进出口公司	17,552	17,058	495
123	南京纺织品进出口股份有限公司	17,242	15,960	1,282
124	广东省东莞畜产进出口公司	17,235	9,480	7,755
125	福建厦门经贸集团有限公司	17,100	14,531	2,571
126	上海市土产进出口公司	17,071	9,784	7,287
127	深圳中电投资股份有限公司	16,997	13,436	3,560
128	珠海九丰石油化工发展公司	16,916	2,946	13,970
129	广东省东莞食品进出口公司	16,910	10,856	6,054
130	中国抽纱上海进出口公司	16,741	13,961	2,779
131	江南造船(集团)有限责任公司	16,725	3,999	12,726
132	上海航空进出口公司	16,706	1,196	15,510
133	上海市五金矿产进出口公司	16,535	9,868	6,667
134	广东省丝绸进出口(集团)公司	16,308	15,101	1,207
135	广东宏远集团公司	16,076	9,019	7,057
136	南通市经济技术开发区总公司	16,064	10,449	5,616
137	广州纺织品进出口集团有限公司	15,999	14,716	1,283
138	广东省东莞粮油进出口公司	15,979	9,558	6,421
139	常州市对外贸易公司	15,810	13,598	2,212
140	上海市化工进出口公司	15,478	8,408	7,070
141	中粮上海粮油进出口公司	15,431	2,644	12,787
142	中国南方航空进出口贸易公司	15,411	781	14,630
143	中国江苏国际经济技术合作公司	15,305	14,979	326
144	常熟市对外贸易公司	15,153	13,675	1,478
145	攀钢集团国际经济贸易总公司	15,114	13,718	1,396
146	上海市畜产(集团)有限公司	14,988	11,871	3,115
147	北京市服装进出口股份有限公司	14,967	11,774	3,192
148	云南红塔进出口公司	14,837	12,221	2,616

1998年中国进出口额最大的500家企业(五)

金额单位:万美元

位次	企 业 名 称	进出口额	出口额	进口额
149	中国远东国际贸易总公司	14,799	1,736	13,063
150	广东外贸开发公司东莞市公司	14,781	8,013	6,768
151	株洲冶炼厂	14,692	14,454	239
152	河北省五金矿产进出口公司	14,644	6,057	8,587
153	广西钦州市外经贸公司	14,506	14,281	225
154	宁波市慈溪进出口公司	14,505	13,780	726
155	广州保税区康胜国际贸易公司	14,334	7,211	7,123
156	江苏汇鸿国际集团针棉织品进出口有限公司	14,327	13,500	828
157	江苏省技术进出口公司	14,324	10,342	3,982
158	广州番禺市对外贸易(集团)公司	14,318	9,630	4,688
159	上海申达股份有限公司	14,202	12,132	2,070
160	中国北方工业广州公司	14,179	9,713	4,466
161	海尔集团公司	14,145	5,384	8,762
162	汕头海洋(集团)公司	13,892	5,816	8,075
163	齐鲁石化公司国际事业公司	13,783	1,804	11,980
164	南通市对外贸易公司	13,678	11,610	2,069
165	广州市对外贸易黄埔公司	13,622	5,732	7,891
166	山东省对外贸易集团有限公司	13,610	8,536	5,074
167	中国医药保健品进出口总公司	13,547	9,849	3,697
168	安徽芜湖市进出口公司	13,546	8,395	5,151
169	仪征化纤股份有限公司	13,518	593	12,925
170	辽宁省服装进出口公司	13,399	10,217	3,182
171	上海新联纺进出口公司	13,315	12,238	1,078
172	上海服装(集团)有限公司	13,293	9,757	3,536
173	福建省珠宝首饰进出口公司	13,266	12,759	507
174	浙江省畜产进出口公司	13,178	12,730	448
175	中电广东惠州总公司	13,160	8,664	4,496
176	山东省服装进出口公司	13,059	10,256	2,803
177	上海钟表进出口有限公司	13,979	8,488	4,491
178	浙江省温州市进出口公司	12,879	10,022	2,857
179	中国抽纱汕头进出口公司	12,835	12,629	206
180	中国工程与农机进出口公司	12,786	12,169	616
181	广东省番禺对外经济贸易公司	12,705	6,439	6,266
182	湖南省粮油食品进出口公司	12,575	12,460	116
183	浙江省绍兴市进出口公司	12,465	11,275	1,190
184	东方科学仪器进出口公司	12,455	3,173	9,282
185	安徽马钢国际贸易总公司	12,427	6,108	6,319

1998年中国进出口额最大的500家企业(六)

金额单位:万美元

位次	企业名称	进出口额	出口额	进口额
186	中化宁波进出口公司	12,327	10,843	1,484
187	扬州市对外贸易公司	12,326	11,420	906
188	中国烟草上海进出口公司	12,222	9,738	2,485
189	中国工艺美术总公司	12,196	10,296	1,900
190	安徽省轻工进出口股份有限公司	12,188	11,538	649
191	广东南海轻工业品进出口公司	12,126	9,185	2,942
192	江苏省工艺品进出口集团股份有限公司	12,005	11,562	443
193	中国对外贸易开发总公司	11,971	5,144	6,830
194	广东省五金矿产进出口集团公司	11,920	5,472	6,449
195	福建省轻工业品进出口集团公司	11,899	10,651	1,248
196	广东中山食品水产进出口集团公司	11,879	10,930	949
197	江苏省连云港市对外贸易公司	11,872	10,964	907
198	中国金山联合贸易公司	11,871	2,125	9,746
199	四川省东方电力设备联合公司	11,796	10,531	1,266
200	浙江省工艺品进出口公司	11,758	11,506	252
201	上海市申信进出口公司	11,713	1,171	10,543
202	中国冶金进出口辽宁公司	11,614	7,766	3,848
203	辽宁成大股份有限公司	11,612	10,130	1,481
204	中国成套设备进出口集团公司	11,533	11,051	483
205	广东省土产进出口(集团)公司	11,530	7,525	4,005
206	河北省纺织品进出口(集团)公司	11,448	10,347	1,101
207	河北省圣仑进出口集团	11,446	10,333	1,113
208	中粮山东粮油进出口公司	11,420	8,786	2,634
209	宁波鄞县进出口公司	11,395	10,528	867
210	江苏省粮油食品进出口集团股份有限公司	11,343	8,970	2,373
211	中国石化大连公司	11,336	8,056	3,279
212	河北省进出口贸易公司	11,322	7,388	3,934
213	中国一汽集团进出口公司	11,248	1,822	9,426
214	中国饲料集团公司	11,239	55	11,183
215	广东外贸开发公司顺德市公司	11,205	10,116	1,089
216	云南省进出口公司	11,170	2,478	8,692
217	福建天成集团有限公司	11,155	10,438	718
218	辽宁省五金矿产进出口公司	11,119	10,366	753
219	中国广澳开发集团公司	11,103	4,993	6,110
220	上海市食品进出口公司	11,089	9,774	1,314
221	惠州市工艺品进出口公司	10,917	8,176	2,741
222	广东省东莞医药保健品进出口公司	10,863	6,664	4,198

1998 年中国进出口额最大的 500 家企业(七)

金额单位:万美元

位次	企　业　名　称	进出口额	出口额	进口额
223	中粮黑龙江粮油食品进出口公司	10,859	9,160	1,697
224	济南钢铁总厂	10,840	5,887	4,953
225	山东威海市进出口公司	10,837	7,871	2,966
226	湖北省机械设备进出口公司	10,639	9,066	1,573
227	宁波市工艺品进出口公司	10,627	9,565	1,063
228	天津机械进出口集团有限公司	10,625	8,032	2,593
229	中国土产畜产浙江茶叶进出口公司	10,561	10,181	380
230	安徽省粮油食品进出口公司	10,552	10,111	441
231	珠海经济特区国际商业贸易总公司	10,531	3,472	7,059
232	浙江省湖州市进出口公司	10,519	10,079	441
233	广东省邮电通讯技术进出口公司	10,505	385	10,120
234	浙江省对外贸易公司	10,471	6,619	3,852
235	无锡中润(集团)有限公司	10,468	9,720	747
236	中国机械对外经济技术合作总公司	10,416	7,725	2,691
237	深圳奥康德石油贸易集团公司	10,391	8,847	1,544
238	上海高桥石化国际贸易公司	10,373	5,360	5,013
239	安徽省服装进出口公司	10,318	9,748	570
240	上海市机械设备进出口有限公司	10,226	7,297	2,927
241	天津服装进出口公司	10,177	8,315	1,861
242	镇江市对外贸易集团公司	10,168	9,130	1,039
243	广东南海工艺品进出口公司	10,158	6,480	3,678
244	广州对外经济发展总公司	10,143	5,876	4,267
245	福建省五金矿产进出口公司	10,091	9,279	811
246	宁波经济技术开发区进出口公司	10,027	8,185	1,842
247	上海汉森进出口有限公司	10,025	8,535	1,490
248	中国嵩海实业青岛公司	9,995	5,219	4,776
249	辽宁省国际贸易公司	9,984	587	9,397
250	中国陕西国际经济技术合作公司	9,974	2,518	7,456
251	广东省工艺品进出口(集团)公司	9,907	8,798	1,109
252	中国电子进出口彩虹公司	9,707	6,133	3,574
253	浙江省萧山市进出口公司	9,640	9,345	295
254	深圳经济特区发展(集团)总公司	9,640	5,502	4,138
255	青岛益佳集团公司	9,594	8,567	1,028
256	广东美的集团股份有限公司	9,586	7,329	2,257
257	天津汽车工业进出口公司	9,559	1,431	8,128
258	中国土木工程集团公司	9,553	8,495	1,057
259	湖南省华隆进出口公司	9,528	3,365	6,163

1998年中国进出口额最大的500家企业(八)

金额单位:万美元

位次	企业名称	进出口额	出口额	进口额
260	中国电子进出口北京公司	9,476	5,355	4,122
261	江苏省畜产进出口集团股份有限公司	9,416	8,174	1,242
262	广东省对外经济发展东莞公司	9,383	5,736	3,648
263	陕西省机械设备进出口公司	9,332	9,019	313
264	中国华润总公司	9,291	3,550	5,743
265	四川省丝绸进出口公司	9,234	9,201	33
266	辽宁华曦集团公司	9,215	7,152	2,062
267	宁波宁兴公司	9,202	8,402	800
268	云南冶金集团进出口有限公司	9,196	6,233	2,963
269	天津外总集团有限公司	9,165	5,413	3,752
270	四川省机械设备进出口公司	9,129	276	8,853
271	四川长虹机器厂	9,123	78	9,045
272	山东省工艺品进出口(集团)股份有限公司	9,095	7,634,4	1,46
273	广东省信宜县进出口贸易公司	9,039	9,037	2
274	浙江远大贸易公司	8,968	8,168	799
275	中国包装进出口广东公司	8,965	3,549	5,416
276	广东省东莞土产进出口公司	8,913	6,176	2,737
277	广东省食品进出口(集团)公司	8,796	8,547	249
278	浙江省绍兴县进出口公司	8,755	6,244	2,511
279	苏州精达电子电器公司	8,750	4,328	4,422
280	广西五金矿产进出口公司	8,749	8,157	593
281	北京富亿通达经贸有限责任公司	8,722	8,713	10
282	中国航空技术进出口北京公司	8,720	3,354	5,366
283	贵州省粮油食品进出口公司	8,662	1,503	7,159
284	北京工艺进出口集团公司	8,646	7,978	669
285	浙江省医药保健品进出口公司	8,584	8,107	476
286	广东风华高新科技集团有限公司	8,569	6,913	1,656
287	南京机械五金医药保健品进出口股份有限公司	8,564	7,818	745
288	天津食品进出口股份有限公司	8,530	4,147	4,383
289	北京市首饰进出口公司	8,520	8,516	3
290	浙江温州经济技术开发区经济技术开发公司	8,483	5,548	2,935
291	广东昭信企业集团有限公司	8,435	6,851	1,583
292	广东东莞市商业总公司	8,412	4,620	3,792
293	黑龙江绥芬河市金恒基工业原料有限公司	8,411	–	8,411
294	中国烟草广东进出口公司	8,379	4,289	4,091
295	上海华申国际企业(集团)有限公司	8,363	7,382	982
296	浙江省轻工业品进出口公司	8,347	7,436	911
297	广东东莞市水果出口公司	8,268	4,530	3,738

1998年中国进出口额最大的500家企业(九)

金额单位:万美元

位次	企 业 名 称	进出口额	出口额	进口额
298	上海浦东钢铁(集团)有限公司	8,243	4,602	3,641
299	广东省外贸开发公司	8,164	2,116	6,049
300	广西凭祥市进出口贸易公司	8,154	7,628	525
301	中化山东进出口集团公司	8,083	5,953	2,130
302	北方国际集团天津纺织品进出口集团有限公司	8,062	7,552	510
303	辽宁省轻工业品进出口公司	8,013	6,925	1,088
304	广东佛山电子工业集团总公司	8,000	6,313	1,687
305	广州广船国际集装箱厂	7,994	5,796	2,198
306	厦门象屿集团有限公司	7,979	2,491	5,487
307	山东省五金矿产进出口公司	7,961	7,283	677
308	广西粮油食品进出口公司	7,959	7,558	401
309	中国精密机械进出口哈尔滨公司	7,886	306	7,580
310	中国水产(集团)总公司	7,867	5,203	2,666
311	广州开发区商业进出口贸易公司	7,850	5,725	2,125
312	北方国际集团天津亿利达集团有限公司	7,842	7,373	469
313	上海玩具进出口有限公司	7,820	7,446	372
314	浙江物资产业(集团)总公司	7,808	4,981	2,827
315	浙江省化工进出口公司	7,799	7,388	411
316	上海市医药保健品进出口公司	7,755	7,010	745
317	哈尔滨铁路局对外经济技术合作公司	7,724	366	7,358
318	湖北省粮油食品进出口(集团)公司	7,720	7,564	155
319	中国化工建设江苏公司	7,709	5,885	1,823
320	上海新发展进出口贸易实业有限公司	7,693	513	7,180
321	青岛正进实业公司	7,688	3,876	3,813
322	中粮辽宁粮油进出口公司	7,669	6,070	1,599
323	宁波市五矿机械进出口公司	7,609	5,795	1,814
324	甘肃金川有色金属进出口公司	7,557	7,535	22
325	广东中山市轻工业品进出口公司	7,540	6,209	1,331
326	杭州市轻工工艺纺织品进出口公司	7,516	7,210	307
327	福州市电信技术发展有限公司	7,511	-	7,511
328	广州越秀企业(集团)公司	7,495	5,925	1,571
329	广东省畜产进出口集团公司	7,491	6,302	1,189
330	河南省粮油食品进出口公司	7,490	7,286	204
331	广州市白云区对外贸易基地服务公司	7,435	4,772	2,663
332	厦门开元外贸集团有限公司	7,409	3,503	3,906
333	上海汽车进出口公司	7,408	3,867	3,540
334	无锡中瑞集团有限公司	7,398	6,643	754

1998年中国进出口额最大的500家企业(十)

金额单位:万美元

位次	企业名称	进出口额	出口额	进口额
335	广东湛江纺织企业(集团)公司	7,363	3,660	3,703
336	中土畜产进出口上海市茶叶公司	7,347	6,866	482
337	中国华能国际经济贸易公司	7,330	6,247	1,084
338	宁波市对外经济贸易公司	7,314	5,656	1,659
339	中国新兴进出口总公司	7,300	4,714	2,586
340	北京国际贸易公司	7,278	1,319	5,959
341	上海康健进出口公司	7,234	4,491	2,743
342	江苏常州市对外经济技术贸易(集团)公司	7,210	4,783	2,427
343	河北省食品进出口(集团)公司	7,198	7,048	149
344	广东江门市工业产品进出口公司	7,136	6,846	290
345	青岛纺织品联合进出口公司	7,130	6,139	991
346	中国抽纱广东进出口公司	7,129	6,560	569
347	中化天津进出口公司	7,106	6,717	389
348	江苏盐城市对外贸易公司	7,061	6,932	128
349	中国出口商品基地建设上海公司	7,027	4,843	2,183
350	辽宁省机械设备进出口公司	7,027	5,835	1,192
351	山东莱芜钢铁总厂	7,004	5,072	1,933
352	辽宁纺织品进出口公司	6,984	6,153	831
353	广东汕头高新开发区实业发展总公司	6,974	3,500	3,474
354	山东省食品进出口公司	6,938	5,926	1,013
355	山东省诸城市对外贸易公司	6,865	5,889	975
356	上海申航进出口公司	6,861	4,563	2,298
357	江苏吴县市对外贸易公司	6,853	6.200	654
358	辽宁省对外贸易总公司	6,831	4,205	2,626
359	山东省烟台市进出口公司	6,786	5,999	787
360	中国轻工物资供销(集团)总公司	6,785	798	5,987
361	广东南海外贸开发公司	6,780	4,900	1,880
362	中航技国际工贸公司	6,758	1,112	5,647
363	上海对外经济贸易实业公司	6,757	5,229	1,529
364	山东省物产进出口公司	6,754	6,230	525
365	江苏省吴江市外贸集团公司	6,719	6,588	131
366	上海市畜产进出口公司	6,702	4,442	2,260
367	湖南三力通讯经贸有限公司	6,675	-	6,675
368	安徽省化工进出口公司	6,630	5,888	743
369	福建省九州集团股份有限公司	6,628	3,936	2,692
370	广东清远化工机械医药保健品进出口公司	6,602	6,583	19
371	中国航空技术进出口厦门公司	6,593	4,747	1,847

1998年中国进出口额最大的500家企业(十一)

金额单位:万美元

位次	企业名称	进出口额	出口额	进口额
372	安徽铜陵有色金属(集团)公司	6,577	2,577	4,001
373	浙江海宁市进出口公司	6,556	5,504	1,052
374	辽宁省机械进出口公司	6,509	5,089	1,420
375	江苏锡山市对外贸易(集团)公司	6,495	5,867	628
376	中国航空技术进出口深圳公司	6,487	4,002	2,485
377	中国电子进出口珠海公司	6,458	6,293	165
378	中国上海对外贸易中心股份有限公司	6,438	4,662	1,777
379	天津畜产进出口集团有限公司	6,435	5,483	951
380	山东省机械设备进出口集团公司	6,407	4,729	1,678
381	青岛海丰集团股份有限公司	6,386	4,047	2,338
382	中国石化国际事业广州公司	6,376	3,571	2,805
383	中国浙江国际经济技术合作公司	6,340	2,217	4,123
384	新疆机械化工五矿轻工进出口公司	6,334	1,436	4,898
385	中国抽纱山东进出口公司	6,309	6,212	97
386	广东省机械设备进出口(集团)公司	6,306	5,190	1,116
387	中国乡镇企业总公司	6,247	438	5,808
388	河北常山纺织集团有限责任公司	6,243	5,430	813
389	中国成套设备进出口云南股份有限公司	6,237	6,197	41
390	江苏汇鸿国际集团土产进出口有限公司	6,205	6,018	186
391	辽宁省食品进出口公司	6,181	5,210	971
392	广东中山纺织品进出口(集团)公司	6,164	5,803	361
393	中国石化国际事业扬子公司	6,149	3,184	2,965
394	广东省对外经济发展揭东公司	6,148	5,994	153
395	山东省畜产进出口公司	6,144	5,405	739
396	上海海外公司	6,143	4,940	1,203
397	广州畜产进出口公司	6,126	5,251	875
398	上海华源集团进出口有限公司	6,112	4,959	1,153
399	宁波天地集团股份有限公司	6,105	5,486	619
400	山东省医药保健品进出口(集团)有限公司	6,097	5,411	685
401	广州市纺织工业联合进出口公司	6,097	5,450	647
402	无锡市对外贸易公司	6,080	5,382	698
403	山东省丝绸进出口公司	6,079	5,803	276
404	山西煤炭进出口集团公司	6,072	6,069	2
405	广西广达进出口集团公司	6,065	5,457	608
406	广西玉林地区外经贸公司	6,057	6,016	41
407	莆田市外贸公司	6,055	5,278	777
408	电子进出口公司宁波公司	6,021	5,627	394

1998 年中国进出口额最大的 500 家企业(十二)

金额单位:万美元

位次	企业名称	进出口额	出口额	进口额
409	中国北方工业上海公司	6,020	4,496	1,524
410	中化上海浦东贸易公司	6,019	399	5,620
411	中国神马集团有限责任公司	6,017	1,423	4,594
412	天津钢管公司	5,983	3,818	2,165
413	宁波市纺织品进出口公司	5,973	5,818	155
414	中国宁波国际合作(集团)有限责任公司	5,956	4,047	1,909
415	中国包装进出口广东公司	5,950	588	5,362
416	广州粮油食品进出口公司	5,941	4,962	979
417	上海市机械设备成套(集团)公司	5,934	1,772	4,162
418	赣州创业工业集团公司	5,917	5,917	-
419	青岛纺织服装实业集团公司	5,899	5,060	838
420	河南省服装进出口公司	5,898	5,047	851
421	中国电子进出口内蒙古公司	5,887	4,946	942
422	山西明迈特实业贸易有限公司	5,873	5,594	279
423	中国化建大连公司	5,873	5,087	786
424	中国出国人员服务总公司	5,865	1,387	4,479
425	云南五矿集团有限公司	5,842	5,340	501
426	广州开发区宜进实业有限公司	5,836	3,287	2,548
427	温州市鹿城对外贸易公司	5,816	4,283	1,532
428	淮阴市对外贸易公司	5,812	5,575	237
429	锦西葫芦岛锌厂进出口公司	5,802	3,837	1,965
430	中国土产畜产云南茶叶进出口公司	5,736	5,197	539
431	湖南省进出口集团有限公司	5,730	5,053	677
432	浙江台州市进出口公司	5,713	3,254	2,460
433	广州化工进出口公司	5,711	2,027	3,684
434	深圳市物资集团	5,708	1,846	3,861
435	大连纺织品进出口有限公司	5,707	4,431	1,276
436	福建省鞋帽进出口集团公司	5,694	4,975	719
437	天津五金矿产进出口集团有限公司	5,655	5,167	489
438	揭阳市轻工业品进出口公司	5,635	5,635	-
439	浙江省五金矿产进出口公司	5,619	4,622	997
440	中国汽车工业进出口南京公司	5,576	769	4,807
441	陕西省纺织品进出口公司	5,573	5,217	356
442	广东江门土产品进出口公司	5,565	5,014	551
443	上海浦东新区进出口公司	5,554	2,976	2,578
444	福建省针棉毛织品进出口公司	5,552	5,320	232
445	广东鹤山毛纺织总厂	5,546	4,364	1,182

1998年中国进出口额最大的500家企业(十三)

金额单位:万美元

位次	企业名称	进出口额	出口额	进口额
446	上海斯迈克有限公司	5,454	3,805	1,740
447	浙江南天邮电通讯发展集团股份有限公司	5,541	–	5,541
448	天津市渤海化工联合进出口公司	5,540	3,086	2,454
449	上海八达纺织印染服装公司	5,539	4,561	978
450	江苏省五金矿产进出口(集团)公司	5,522	5,039	483
451	江西省畜产进出口公司	5,521	4,860	660
452	广东韶关韶冶进出口公司	5,496	5,456	40
453	广东鹤山土产进出口公司	5,455	5,141	314
454	珠海经济特区珠光公司	5,452	1,619	3,833
455	浙江省机械设备进出口公司	5,442	4,907	535
456	中国广东国际合作(集团)公司	5,440	2,707	2,733
457	江苏江阴市对外贸易公司	5,413	4,757	656
458	中国冶金进出口山西公司	5,388	5,242	146
459	湖南省工艺品进出口公司	5,387	5,354	33
460	浙江省机械进出口公司	5,382	4,539	843
461	吉林化学工业进出口公司	5,356	1,830	3,526
462	广东省宜华企业(集团)有限公司	5,355	5,355	–
463	广东东莞包装进出口公司	5,333	2,889	2,444
464	东北制药总厂进出口公司	5,319	4,330	989
465	TCL电子集团公司	5,315	320	4,995
466	广东阳江纺织品进出口集团公司	5,273	5,266	7
467	山西安泰集团股份有限公司	5,266	4,878	388
468	广东惠州市轻工业品进出口公司	5,250	3,347	1,902
469	上海申宏公司	5,233	4,432	801
470	中国冶金进出口包钢公司	5,233	2,960	2,273
471	宁波市粮油食品进出口公司	5,230	4,462	768
472	广西河池地区外经贸公司	5,215	5,215	–
473	广东揭阳市进出口贸易公司	5,210	5,121	89
474	四川省纺织品进出口公司	5,202	4,926	276
475	北京市针绵织品进出口集团公司	5,193	4,930	263
476	江苏太仓市对外贸易公司	5,179	4,623	557
477	福建省机械设备进出口公司	5,168	4,168	1,000
478	中国医药对外贸易总公司	5,167	3,337	1,833
479	广东顺德纺织进出口公司	5,157	4,330	827
480	山东省肉食蛋品进出口公司	5,150	5,014	137
481	大连华孚进出口有限公司	5,146	3,739	1,407
482	上海电视电子进出口公司	5,141	3,846	1,295

1998年中国进出口额最大的500家企业(十四)

金额单位:万美元

位次	企 业 名 称	进出口额	出口额	进口额
483	珠海轻工工艺品进出口公司	5,111	3,769	1,343
484	广东省梅州电子技术进出口公司	5,110	5,105	6
485	广东阳江市轻出(集团)公司	5,100	4,683	417
486	广东开平土产进出口公司	5,095	5,044	51
487	浙江省桐乡外贸集团股份有限公司	5,085	4,718	367
488	上海科教技术进出口公司	5,083	1,160	3,923
489	上海第一钢铁厂	5,079	1,868	3,211
490	江西省针绵织品进出口公司	5,075	5,070	5
491	中国包装进出口浙江公司	5,045	1,329	3,716
492	陕西省进出口公司	5,036	3,643	1,393
493	中国建筑材料及设备进出口公司	5,017	1,579	3,437
494	浙江省国兴进出口公司	5,007	4,584	423
495	山东滨州印染集团股份有限公司	4,999	4,162	838
496	中国烟草贵州进出口公司	4,993	1,979	3,015
497	福建省土产畜产进出口公司	4,992	4,801	192
498	中国林业国际合作集团公司	4,955	4,144	809
499	武进市对外贸易(集团)公司	4,919	4,489	430
500	浙江省金华市进出口公司	4,903	4,284	619

1997年世界最大100家工程设计咨询公司名录(一)

单位:亿美元

排名	企业名称	国别	International billings	% of Total
1	克瓦纳集团	英国	925.0	79
2	贝克特尔集团	美国	828.0	69
3	布朗陆特公司	美国	734.0	72
4	荷兰咨询公司	荷兰	646.8	100
5	福斯特惠勒公司	美国	629.6	79
6	SNC拉瓦林国际公司	加拿大	599.0	59
7	ABB鲁姆斯全球公司	美国	526.4	82
8	福格洛N.Y.公司	荷兰	471.0	87
9	加克坡瑞集团	芬兰	413.0	85
10	福路丹尼尔公司	美国	407.0	25
11	阿卡第斯公司	荷兰	320.0	62
12	布莱克韦奇公司	美国	319.0	50
13	达奥汗德萨咨询公司	埃及	292.0	99
14	帕森斯公司	美国	276.4	28
15	菲利普霍兹曼公司	德国	261.6	89
16	路易斯伯格集团	美国	257.3	83
17	莫特麦克多纳德公司	英国	254.2	67
18	东洋工程公司	日本	246.0	88
19	NEDECO	荷兰	240.0	100
20	瑞瑟恩工程承包国际公司	美国	235.0	27
21	EGIS集团	法国	230.0	62
22	欧文阿拉普合伙公司	英国	225.0	61
23	AGRA公司	加拿大	223.1	47
24	斯通韦伯斯特公司	美国	189.0	46
25	麦克德莫特国际公司	美国	180.3	80
26	西斯特拉集团	法国	179.3	89
27	蒙赛尔公司	英国	177.7	77
28	MW凯洛格公司	美国	157.5	51
29	西蒙斯国际公司	加拿大	150.8	61
30	太平洋咨询国际集团	日本	141.0	28
31	蒙特哥摩特公司	美国	134.5	33
32	帕森斯布英克霍夫公司	美国	133.9	22
33	海德咨询公司	英国	121.7	53
34	CH2M Hill公司	美国	120.9	16
35	日本Koei公司	日本	113.9	33

1997年世界最大100家工程设计咨询公司名录(二)

单位:亿美元

排名	企业名称	国别	International billings	% of Total
36	蒙科若集团	英国	113.0	60
37	伊莱克特洛威特工程服务公司	美国	109.9	75
38	高德联合公司	美国	108.0	59
39	斯高特威尔森公司	英国	108.0	60
40	法律工程和环保服务公司	美国	106.4	34
41	三星工程公司	韩国	106.0	35
42	URS公司	美国	101.4	13
43	戴姆斯默瑞集团	美国	100.6	20
44	COWI公司	丹麦	91.7	48
45	萨根特朗第LLC公司	美国	91.4	31
46	特拉克特贝尔工程公司	比利时	85.2	27
47	TECHNIP	法国	83.0	54
48	ERM集团	美国	82.5	34
49	斯奈普罗盖蒂	意大利	76.0	34
50	卡尔博集团	丹麦	75.7	49
51	多奇咨询工程公司	德国	73.8	45
52	皇家HASKONING集团	荷兰	70.3	46
53	LG工程公司	韩国	70.0	59
54	现代工程公司	韩国	66.6	50
55	海耳姆斯公司	美国	66.0	22
56	管道工程公司	德国	62.6	54
57	斯勘第咨询国际公司	瑞典	59.9	36
58	拉米耶国际公司	德国	57.9	30
59	BCEOM联合公司	法国	57.0	77
60	哈奇联合公司	加拿大	56.7	40
61	哈泽工程公司	美国	54.6	53
62	CDM公司	美国	52.0	16
63	大林工程公司	韩国	51.8	68
64	戴兹默曼国际公司	美国	50.3	27
65	ICF凯泽国际公司	美国	47.0	8
66	斯哥德默尔公司	美国	43.0	52
67	桑德韦尔国际公司	加拿大	42.2	61
68	ENSR公司	美国	42.0	27
69	莱斯特B公司	美国	42.0	48
70	奈特皮索公司	英国	41.1	94

1997 年世界最大 100 家工程设计咨询公司名录(三)

单位:亿美元

排名	企业名称	国别	International billings	% of Total
71	洛克伍德绿色工程公司	美国	40.4	15
72	弗莱德瑞克公司	美国	40.0	25
73	索哥勒格公司	法国	37.5	41
74	挪威咨询公司	挪威	37.1	43
75	联合咨询工程师	希腊	36.7	99
76	RAMBOLL 集团	丹麦	36.4	21
77	姆斯坦工程公司	美国	36.0	36
78	菲科耐尔公司	德国	36.0	59
79	霍尔麦斯纳沃公司	美国	35.0	24
80	KA 联合工程公司	黎巴嫩	34.4	86
81	BE & K 公司	美国	33.5	14
82	PCG 公司	葡萄牙	33.4	67
83	高尔夫工程公司	法国	33.3	51
84	SWECO 公司	瑞典	32.3	16
85	贝克卡特控股公司	新西兰	31.0	44
86	新克莱尔公司	澳大利亚	30.0	22
87	泰克尼卡公司	西班牙	30.0	43
88	雪山工程公司	澳大利亚	29.7	77
89	T.Y.L 国际公司	美国	28.9	56
90	WS 爱特科斯公司	英国	28.8	15
91	联合承包商国际公司	希腊	28.7	100
92	RTKL 公司	美国	28.1	37
93	科坡罗公司	美国	27.8	33
94	博恩斯 R 企业公司	美国	27.5	13
95	CTM 集团	法国	27.0	28
96	斯坦利技术集团	加拿大	27.0	30
97	DMJM 公司	美国	26.0	11
98	巴特曼工程公司	美国	26.0	58
99	阿基计划公司	德国	25.5	36
100	高点林德尔公司	英国	25.4	67

资料来源:美国《工程新闻记录》1998 年 7 月 20 日

(外经贸部国际贸易经济合作研究院跨国经营研究部)

1997 年全球最大国际工程设计公司的国外市场分布

设计商国籍	公司数量	国外营业收入		中东		亚洲		非洲		欧洲		美国		加拿大		拉美	
		亿美元	%	亿美元	%	亿美元	%	亿美元	%	亿美元	%	亿美元	%	亿美元	%	亿美元	%
美　国	88	70.13	43.7	6.60	48.7	23.68	44.8	3.11	26.4	26.03	51.7	0.0	0.0	3.58	89.8	6.94	52.1
加拿大	14	12.22	7.6	0.69	5.1	2.97	5.6	2.73	23.3	1.22	2.4	2.82	19.7	0.0	0.0	1.79	13.4
欧　洲	65	63.56	39.6	4.11	30.3	17.47	33.1	4.89	41.6	22.50	44.7	10.31	72.1	0.32	7.9	3.96	29.7
英　国	16	20.88	13.0	1.52	11.2	9.48	17.9	0.83	7.1	5.34	10.6	3.09	21.6	0.14	3.4	0.48	3.6
德　国	12	6.24	3.9	0.41	3.0	0.60	1.1	0.90	7.7	1.29	2.6	2.32	16.2	0.0	0.1	0.72	5.4
法　国	7	6.31	3.9	0.50	3.7	1.79	3.4	0.94	8.0	2.47	4.9	0.37	2.6	0.0	0.1	0.23	1.7
意大利	2	0.95	0.6	0.10	0.7	0.38	0.7	0.19	1.6	0.17	0.3	0.0	0.0	0.0	0.0	0.11	0.8
荷　兰	8	17.85	11.1	0.98	7.2	3.30	6.3	0.79	6.7	7.82	15.5	4.34	30.3	0.0	0.0	0.63	4.7
其　他	20	11.32	7.1	0.60	4.5	1.92	3.6	1.24	10.6	5.40	10.7	0.19	1.3	0.17	4.4	1.79	13.4
日　本	11	5.98	3.7	0.22	1.6	4.99	9.4	0.39	3.4	0.09	0.2	0.06	0.4	0.0	0.0	0.22	1.6
所有其他	22	8.43	5.3	1.95	14.4	3.71	7.0	0.63	5.3	0.51	1.0	1.11	7.8	0.09	2.3	0.42	3.2
全部公司	200	160.31	100.0	13.57	100.0	52.82	100.0	11.75	100.0	50.36	100.0	14.31	100.0	3.99	100.0	13.33	100.0

资料来源：美国《工程新闻记录》1998 年 7 月 20 日

（外经贸部国际贸易经济合作研究院跨国经营研究部）

1997 年全球最大国际建筑承包公司的国外市场分布

承包商国籍	公司数量	国外营业收入		中　东		亚　洲		非　洲		欧　洲		美　国		加拿大		拉　美	
		亿美元	%	亿美元	%	亿美元	%	亿美元	%	亿美元	%	亿美元	%	亿美元	%	亿美元	%
美　国	65	245.54	22.3	34.40	32.9	74.88	21.5	15.41	16.4	63.77	21.6	0.0	0.0	11.93	54.4	45.08	46.7
加拿大	7	8.77	0.8	0.0	0.0	0.59	0.2	0.08	0.1	0.10	0.0	7.82	5.8	0.0	0.0	0.16	0.2
欧　洲	70	562.74	51.1	45.26	43.3	102.81	29.6	52.95	56.2	211.39	71.6	101.47	74.6	9.39	42.8	39.10	40.5
英　国	7	126.74	11.5	7.38	7.1	30.69	8.8	2.37	2.5	37.15	12.6	40.48	29.8	4.08	18.6	4.57	4.7
德　国	2	14.81	1.3	4.07	3.9	0.93	0.3	0.0	0.0	8.31	2.8	0.0	0.0	0.24	1.1	1.24	1.3
法　国	10	165.33	15.0	7.21	6.9	27.39	7.9	27.86	29.6	84.08	28.5	9.67	7.1	3.45	15.7	5.65	5.9
意大利	13	94.32	8.6	3.06	2.9	25.82	7.4	7.52	8.0	28.44	9.6	24.61	18.1	1.60	7.3	3.25	3.4
荷　兰	15	62.99	5.7	11.32	10.8	12.12	3.5	9.18	9.8	14.31	4.8	3.94	2.9	0.0	0.0	12.11	12.6
其　他	23	98.55	8.9	12.22	11.7	5.84	1.7	6.01	6.4	39.08	13.2	22.76	16.7	0.0	0.0	12.27	12.7
日　本	19	128.67	11.7	5.85	5.6	87.27	25.1	6.83	7.3	3.73	1.3	16.63	12.2	0.56	2.6	1.82	1.9
中　国	26	40.79	3.7	4.15	4.0	27.81	8.0	7.07	7.5	0.86	0.3	0.55	0.4	0.0	0.2	0.29	0.3
韩　国	10	49.22	4.5	4.62	4.4	38.10	11.0	2.74	2.9	1.86	0.6	1.35	1.0	0.0	0.0	0.54	0.6
所有其他	28	66.51	6.0	10.25	9.8	16.09	4.6	9.06	9.6	13.48	4.6	8.17	6.0	0.0	0.0	9.45	9.8
全部公司	225	1102.24	100.0	104.54	100.0	347.57	100.0	94.15	100.0	295.21	100.0	136.01	100.0	21.93	100.0	96.45	100.0

资料来源:美国《工程新闻记录》1998 年 8 月 17 日

（外经贸部国际贸易经济合作研究院跨国经营研究部）

1997年世界最大100家国际工程承包公司名录(一)

单位:亿美元

排名	企业名称	国别(地区)	International Revenue	Total Revenue
1	克瓦纳集团	英国	7605.0	9614.0
2	贝克特尔集团公司	美国	6347.0	9662.0
3	福陆丹尼尔公司	美国	4940.0	10798.0
4	布依格公司	法国	4478.0	10971.0
5	斯勘斯卡公司	瑞典	3363.0	5916.0
6	GTM 集团	法国	3191.0	7196.0
7	SGE	法国	3109.0	8917.0
8	菲利普霍兹曼股份公司	德国	3040.0	8043.0
9	贝尔芬格柏格股份公司	德国	2747.0	4980.7
10	鲍维斯建筑集团	英国	2516.0	3481.0
11	塞格莱克	法国	2386.0	3916.0
12	现代工程建筑公司	韩国	1948.0	5896.0
13	福斯特惠勒公司	美国	1850.8	2632.0
14	布朗陆特公司	美国	1840.0	3616.0
15	泰克尼普	法国	1793.0	1842.0
16	JGC 株式会社	日本	1702.8	2267.8
17	东洋工程公司	日本	1644.0	1872.0
18	安萨尔多公司	意大利	1608.5	2856.6
19	依姆普莱格罗公司	意大利	1492.0	2549.0
20	鹿岛建设株式会社	日本	1446.0	12167.0
21	欧德布莱克公司	巴西	1416.0	2880.0
22	NCC 公司	瑞典	1400.0	3712.0
23	联合承包商国际公司	希腊	1317.5	1317.5
24	AMEC	英国	1291.0	4619.0
25	凯洛格公司	美国	1271.3	1581.6
26	大林组株式会社	日本	1250.0	11071.0
27	鲍斯特奈德姆国际公司	美国	1228.1	2134.9
28	ABB 鲁姆斯全球公司	美国	1199.5	1593.6
29	中国建筑工程总公司	中国	1179.0	4396.8
30	西松建设株式会社	日本	1138.2	5216.5
31	斯特拉巴格公司	德国	1086.6	3052.7
32	斯耐姆普罗盖蒂公司	意大利	1009.0	1327.0
33	青木建设株式会社	日本	949.6	2629.6
34	麦克德莫特国际公司	美国	925.8	1620.7
35	大成建设株式会社	日本	920.0	12208.0

1997 年世界最大 100 家国际工程承包公司名录(二)

单位:亿美元

排名	企业名称	国别(地区)	International Revenue	Total Revenue
36	东阿建设产业公司	韩国	919.0	3108.0
37	竹中株式会社	日本	913.6	10312.0
38	五洋建设株式会社	日本	861.0	4359.0
39	德拉格多斯建设公司	西班牙	827.0	3346.0
40	福莱特克尔建设公司	新西兰	811.0	991.0
41	瑞瑟恩工程建设者公司	美国	799.0	2125.0
42	布莱克韦奇公司	美国	796.0	1228.0
43	EIFFAGE	法国	763.7	5324.5
44	乔安诺帕拉斯克维斯公司	塞浦路斯	732.5	732.5
45	泰琴特建设集团	意大利	723.0	1411.0
46	沃尔特公司	德国	702.3	2845.0
47	PCL 建设者公司	加拿大	695.0	1274.0
48	索唐克比奇公司	法国	650.0	840.0
49	大气社公司	日本	583.4	1666.9
50	芝加哥桥梁钢铁公司	美国	568.0	897.0
51	中国港湾工程建设集团公司	中国	541.7	1414.1
52	大林工程公司	韩国	529.9	617.2
53	斯通韦伯斯特公司	美国	497.0	887.0
54	雷顿控股公司	澳大利亚	488.0	2276.0
55	NECSO	西班牙	466.0	2347.0
56	塔马克公司	英国	414.0	2622.0
57	埃德祖宾公司	德国	406.0	2250.0
58	戴克霍夫温德曼公司	德国	404.0	2546.0
59	黑利特沃诺公司	德国	401.0	2165.0
60	三星工程公司	韩国	396.0	1146.0
61	双龙工程建设公司	韩国	356.0	1116.0
62	威斯弗莱特公司	德国	355.5	1566.4
63	帕森斯公司	美国	351.4	971.4
64	阿斯特 SPA	意大利	350.8	726.6
65	泰克尼蒙特 SPA	意大利	347.0	477.0
66	康斯坦集团	英国	339.5	899.3
67	JDC 公司	日本	314.8	2554.3
68	佛曼特建设公司	西班牙	304.2	3230.2
69	泰克尼克斯路尼德斯公司	西班牙	302.0	312.0
70	建设者安德瑞德	巴西	290.0	1010.0

1997年世界最大100家国际工程承包公司名录(三)

单位:亿美元

排名	企业名称	国别(地区)	International Revenue	Total Revenue
71	科勒集团	英国	288.6	395.4
72	STFA 集团	土耳其	288.2	364.7
73	BESIX	比利时	281.1	573.8
74	恩卡建设产业公司	土耳其	276.1	377.1
75	格拉格多斯国际公司	西班牙	271.0	271.0
76	中国土木工程集团公司	中国	270.1	274.0
77	LL 地产服务公司	澳大利亚	269.3	761.3
78	费乐威尔集团公司	西班牙	259.8	2348.0
79	荷利马装配集团公司	荷兰	253.0	330.0
80	约翰西斯克父子控股公司	爱尔兰	251.0	621.0
81	保罗 Y.－ITC 建设控股公司	中国香港	233.0	1133.0
82	麦克科耐尔公司	澳大利亚	233.0	281.0
83	中国公路桥梁建设总公司	中国	229.8	625.2
84	爱利丝顿建设公司	美国	220.5	475.2
85	约翰莱英公司	英国	220.0	1875.0
86	东亚建设株式会社	日本	216.0	2602.0
87	莫瑞罗伯特建设者公司	南非	213.0	1454.0
88	凯威特建设集团公司	美国	212.0	2457.0
89	阿斯特公司	意大利	207.8	249.5
90	霍夫曼公司	美国	203.0	833.0
91	现代工程公司	韩国	194.0	310.8
92	索玻诺国际公司	以色列	193.0	193.0
93	户田建设株式会社	日本	191.0	5109.0
94	莫瑞森克奴森公司	美国	191.0	1481.0
95	维特公司	芬兰	188.0	1033.0
96	金盾株式会社	日本	183.0	4431.0
97	地球技术公司	美国	182.9	312.9
98	POSCO 工程建设公司	韩国	182.0	886.0
99	埃尼尔格工程集团	南斯拉夫	173.0	256.3
100	J.S.奥贝瑞西建设公司	美国	172.7	645.0

资料来源:美国《工程新闻记录》(1998年8月17日)

(外经贸部国际贸易经济合作研究院跨国经营研究部)

1997年世界最大的500家企业(一)

收入位次 1997年	收入位次 1996年	公司名称	国别(地区)	收入 金额:百万美元	收入 比1996年变化(%)	利润 金额:百万美元	利润 位次	利润 比1996年变化(%)	资产 金额:百万美元	资产 位次	股东权益 金额:百万美元	股东权益 位次	雇员 人数	雇员 位次
1	1	通用汽车	美国	178,174.0	5.8	6,698.0	6	35.0	228,888.0	46	17,506.0	42	608,000	3
2	2	福特汽车	美国	153,627.0	4.5	6,920.0	5	55.6	279,097.0	34	30,734.0	12	363,892	5
3	3	三井物产[1]	日本	142,688.3	(1.6)	268.7	336	(16.5)	55,070.5	143	5,272.1	252	40,000	292
4	4	三菱商事[1]	日本	128,922.3	(8.0)	388.1	287	(1.5)	71,407.8	123	7,569.4	177	36,000	314
5	6	荷兰皇家/壳牌	英国/荷兰	128,141.7[E]	(0.0)	7,758.2	3	(12.7)	113,781.4	87	59,981.8	2	105,000	105
6	5	伊藤忠商事[1]	日本	126,631.9	(6.6)	(773.9)	484	(797.9)	56,307.9	136	2,956.6	353	6,675[2]	473
7	8	埃克森	美国	122,379.0[E]	2.5	8,460.0	1	12.6	96,064.0	102	43,660.0	4	80,000	149
8	11	沃尔－马特百货公司[3]	美国	119,299.0	12.4	3,526.0	25	15.4	45,525.0	162	18,502.0	36	825,000	2
9	7	丸红[1]	日本	111,121.2	(10.4)	140.4	388	(21.4)	55,403.4	140	3,563.9	323	64,000	187
10	9	佳友商事[1]	日本	102,395.2	(14.2)	209.8	360	–	42,866.1	171	4,318.6	296	29,500	346
11	10	丰田汽车[1]	日本	95,137.0	(12.5)	3,701.3	21	8.0	103,893.8	93	45,158.2	3	159,035	48
12	12	通用电气	美国	90,840.0	14.7	8,203.0	2	12.7	304,012.0	29	34,438.0	10	276,000	15
13	13	日商岩井[1]	日本	81,893.8	3.8	24.7	443	(81.9)	40,799.3	180	2,019.6	403	18,158	408
14	15	国际商用机器(IBM)	美国	78,508.0	3.4	6,093.0	8	12.2	81,499.0	117	19,816.0	29	269,465	17
15	14	日本电报电话[G1]	日本	76,983.7	(1.7)	2,361.3	56	77.5	113,409.5	88	35,989.7	6	226,000	27
16	78	安盛	法国	76,874.4	94.3	1,357.0	109	82.3	401,206.0	13	13,075.0	69	80,613	146
17	20	戴姆勒－奔驰	德国	71,561.4	1.0	4,639.2*	12	161.2	76,190.7	121	19,510.8	32	300,068	9
18	24	大宇	韩国	71,525.8	9.8	526.9	253	12.5	44,860.6	165	6,325.3	212	265,044	20
19	18	日本生命保险公司[1]	日本	71,388.2	(1.6)	2,118.3	62	(24.3)	316,530.4	24	5,575.3	241	75,851	163
20	21	英国石油	英国	71,193.5[E]	1.9	4,046.2	16	1.5	54,099.1	144	23,221.3	19	56,450	222
21	16	日立[1]	日本	68,567.0	(9.4)	28.3	441	(96.4)	75,837.5	122	24,302.5	17	331,494	7

1997 年世界最大的 500 家企业(二)

收入位次		公司名称	国别(地区)	收入		利润			资产		股东权益		雇员	
1997年	1996年			金额:百万美元	比1996年变化(%)	金额:百万美元	位次	比1996年变化(%)	金额:百万美元	位次	金额:百万美元	位次	人数	位次
22	23	大众	德国	65,328.2	(1.8)	772.4	198	76.4	56,517.0	135	7,793.2	170	279,892	14
23	22	松下电器[1]	日本	64,280.6	(5.7)	762.5	202	(37.7)	64,217.8	130	28,272.1	13	275,962	16
24	25	西门子[4]	德国	63,754.6	0.1	1,427.4	101	(24.0)	55,545.9	139	15,108.5	55	386,000	4
25	26	克莱斯勒	美国	61,147.0	(0.4)	2,805.0	45	(20.5)	60,418.0	132	11,362.0	96	121,000	82
26	19	美孚石油	美国	59,978.0[E]	(17.0)	3,272.0	30	10.4	43,559.0	168	19,461.0	33	42,700	282
27	29	美国邮政总局[G4]	美国	58,216.0	3.2	1,264.0	119	(19.3)	53,138.0	148	(1,360.0)	496	898,384	1
28	28	联邦保险股份公司	德国	56,785.3	0.4	1,171.7	130	6.9	211,442.4	50	9,587.6	124	73,290	168
29	30	菲利普·莫里斯	美国	56,114.0[E]	2.9	6,310.0	7	0.1	55,947.0	138	14,920.0	56	152,000	50
30	33	索尼[1]	日本	55,033.0	9.5	1,809.1	78	46,1	48,016.4	155	13,614.8	66	173,000	45
31	27	日产汽车[1]	日本	53,478.2	(9.5)	(114.1)	464	(116.5)	59,120.5	133	9,617.4	122	137,201	62
32	17	美国电话电报	美国	53,261.0	(28.5)[5]	4,638.0	13	(21.5)	58,635.0	134	22,647.0	21	128,000	71
33	32	菲亚特	意大利	52,568.7	4.1	1,418.6	103	(7.7)	69,028.3	128	14,447.1	57	239,457	24
34	38	本田汽车[1]	日本	48,876.3	4.0	2,123.2	60	8.1	36,109.7	197	12,057.7	88	109,400	98
35	31	联合利华	英国/荷兰	48,760.8	(6.4)	5,463.2	10	118.6	31,670.9	210	12,203.0	87	287,000	11
36	36	雀巢	瑞士	48,253.8	(1.4)	2,760.9	48	0.4	37,487.2	192	16,735.5	47	225,808	28
37	106	CS 控股公司[6]	瑞士	48,242.1	74.5	273.7	334	–	472,768.0	4	16,211.7	49	62,412	197
38	34	第一相互生命保险[1]	日本	47,441.8	(3.5)	1,492.4	95	(23.1)	214,993.8	47	2,246.7	392	64,598	185
39	144	波音公司[1]	美国	45,800.0	101.9	(178.0)	467	(116.3)	38,024.0	188	12,953.0	73	239,000	25
40	44	德士古石油	美国	45,187.0[E]	1.4	2,664.0	50	32.0	29,600.0	220	12,766.0	78	29,313	348
41	37	东芝[1]	日本	44,467.2	(8.2)	59.8	422	(90.0)	45,460.0	163	9,010.9	136	186,000	37
42	49	国家农场集团	美国	43,957.0	2.7	3,833.3	18	49.3	103,626.2	94	37,635.4	5	72,655	170

1997年世界最大的500家企业(三)

收入位次 1997年	收入位次 1996年	公司名称	国别(地区)	收入 金额:百万美元	收入 比1996年变化(%)	利润 金额:百万美元	利润 位次	利润 比1996年变化(%)	资产 金额:百万美元	资产 位次	股东权益 金额:百万美元	股东权益 位次	雇员 人数	雇员 位次
43	42	费巴集团	德国	43,881.2[E]	(3.0)	1,621.0	90	(0.7)	44,813.3	166	12,320.4	85	129,960	70
44	39	埃尔夫－阿奎坦	法国	43,572.0[E]	(6.9)	959.5	162	(29.6)	42,048.6	176	13,944.2	62	83,700	136
45	40	东绵[1]	日本	43,399.7	(6.7)	(179.1)	468	(524.3)	17,671.3	289	639.8	474	10,920	457
46	43	东京电力[1]	日本	42,996.9	(3.9)	1,102.4	142	52.2	107,587.4	91	11,714.3	93	42,672[2]	283
47	60	惠普[8]	美国	42,895.0	11.6	3,119.0	36	20.6	31,749.0	209	16,155.0	50	121,900	80
48	45	住友生命保险公司[1]	日本	42,278.6	(4.1)	1,094.4	144	(41.1)	177,845.4	60	2,408.6	381	64,628	184
49	55	杜邦	美国	41,304.0[E]	4.1	2,405.0	55	(33.9)	42,942.0	169	11,270.0	98	98,396	113
50	61	西尔斯·罗巴克	美国	41,296.0	8.0	1,188.0	127	(6.5)	38,700.0	186	5,862.0	229	296,000	10
51	56	德意志银行[9]	德国	40,792.0	3.5	551.5	245	(61.1)	579,992.2	2	17,843.0	41	76,141	162
52	54	富士通[1]	日本	40,613.0	1.6	45.5	433	(88.9)	38,417.8	187	8,888.2	141	180,000	40
53	57	莱因集团[10]	德国	40,232.6[E]	2.4	814.2	185	(0.5)	46,278.7	159	4,850.9	268	136,115	64
54	47	日本电气[1]	日本	39,926.5	(9.1)	336.5	304	(58.6)	37,298.8	193	8,029.6	161	152,450	49
55	51	飞利浦电子[11]	荷兰	39,188.4	(4.5)	2,938.6	43	–	29,316.3	221	9,596.2	123	264,700	21
56	50	德国电信[G]	德国	38,969.1	(7.0)	1,905.4	72	63.1	90,543.1	109	25,966.5	16	216,006	29
57	64	荷兰国际集团	荷兰	38,673.8	7.9	2,104.1	64	6.8	305,983.7	26	22,745.4	20	64,162	186
58	154	旅行者集团	美国	37,609.0	76.2	3,104.0	38	33.2	386,555.0	18	20,893.0	26	67,250	182
59	96	汇丰银行公司	英国	37,474.0	29.8	5,496.0	9	13.1	471,256.4	5	27,055.3	15	132,969	68
60	53	美国万全人寿保险公司[12]	美国	37,073.0	–[13]	610.0	229	–[13]	259,482.0	40	19,718.0	30	79,000	152
61	58	国家碳化氢[G]	意大利	36,961.7[E]	(4.8)	3,003.9	42	4.1	49,334.7	153	16,764.1	46	80,178	148
62	48	法国电气[G]	法国	36,672.9[E]	(10.5)	264.1	338	(27.8)	113,360.3	89	35,220.1	7	116,462	89
63	59	谢夫隆	美国	36,376.0[E]	(6.0)	3,256.0	32	24.9	35,473.0	200	17,472.0	43	39,362	295

1997 年世界最大的 500 家企业(四)

收入位次 1997年	收入位次 1996年	公司名称	国别(地区)	收入 金额:百万美元	收入 比1996年变化(%)	利润 金额:百万美元	利润 位次	利润 比1996年变化(%)	资产 金额:百万美元	资产 位次	股东权益 金额:百万美元	股东权益 位次	雇员 人数	雇员 位次
64	65	宝洁[10]	美国	35,764.0	1.4	3,415.0	27	12.1	27,544.0	233	12,046.0	89	106,000	103
65	63	雷诺汽车	法国	35,623.8	(1.0)	929.9	170	–	38,750.4	185	7,299.0	188	141,315	58
66	73	委内瑞拉石油公司[G]	委内瑞拉	34,801.0[E]	2.8	4,772.0	11	6.2	47,148.0	156	34,555.0	9	56,592	221
67	41	东京－三菱公司[1]	日本	34,749.8	(25.2)	(4,271.6)	498	(1,281.3)	690,461.7	1	18,174.5	39	18,386[2]	405
68	79	花旗银行	美国	34,697.0	6.4	3,591.0	24	(5.2)	310,897.0	25	21,196.0	25	93,700	122
69	66	宝马汽车(BMW)	德国	34,691.5	(0.1)	718.8	210	33.1	29,629.0	219	5,627.2	239	117,624	88
70	67	农业信贷银行	法国	34,014.9	(1.7)	1,689.4	86	14,8	417,973.9	9	20,414.7	27	84,670	133
71	46	鲜京公司[14]	韩国	33,815.9[E]	(23.2)	125.1	396	(60.0)	17,930.4	287	3,094.9	348	30,595	337
72	77	阿莫科	美国	32,836.0[E]	0.3	2,720.0	49	(4.0)	32,489.0	207	16,319.0	48	43,451	277
73	62	都市控股	德国	32,789.6	(10.3)	319.5	314	(21.2)	14,132.6	331	2,307.6	389	177,470	41
74	70	道达尔石油	法国	32,740.6[E]	(5.1)	1,304.1	115	18.2	25,214.4	245	11,074.2	101	54,391	230
75	182	里昂自来水公司[15]	法国	32,626.7	69.4	687.6	215	160.8	78,653.0	119	8,193.8	157	175,000	42
76	87	凯马特[3]	美国	32,183.0	2.4	249.0	343	–	13,558.0	343	5,434.0	245	258,000	23
77	82	巴斯夫	德国	32,178.1[E]	(0.7)	1,866.6	75	0.7	26,685.9	239	12,807.6	76	104,979	106
78	72	标致	法国	32,003.9	(5.6)	(474.3)	475	(430.6)	31,472.0	211	8,808.4	142	140,200	61
79	85	阿尔卡特－阿尔斯通集团	法国	31,846.8	0.5	799.3	190	50.1	41,844.5	177	7,305.2	187	189,549	36
80	83	拜耳[9]	德国	31,731.0	(1.8)	1,696.6	85	(6.3)	30,123.9	216	13,060.6	71	144,600	55
81	121	美林公司	美国	31,731.0	26.9	1,906.0	71	17.7	292,819.0	32	8,329.0	154	56,600	219
82	69	日绵[1]	日本	31,362.1	(9.2)	41.3	435	(5.4)	15,361.6	317	1,144.4	448	18,435	403
83	68	阿西亚·勃朗·勃威力	瑞士	31,265.0	(9.6)	572.0	239	(53.6)	29,784.0	218	5,283.0	251	213,057	30
84	75	明治相互生命保险公司[1]	日本	31,047.3	(6.4)	1,006.6	152	(36.1)	127,824.7	79	1,884.7	410	40.188	291

1997 年世界最大的 500 家企业(五)

收入位次 1997年	收入位次 1996年	公司名称	国别(地区)	收入 金额:百万美元	收入 比1996年变化(%)	利润 金额:百万美元	利润 位次	利润 比1996年变化(%)	资产 金额:百万美元	资产 位次	股东权益 金额:百万美元	股东权益 位次	雇员 人数	雇员 位次
85	76	三菱电机[1]	日本	30,967.3	(6.4)	(862.9)	486	(1,240.3)	31,780.8	208	4,685.9	276	115,206	91
86	93	通用保险股份公司[16]	意大利	30,816.0	4.0	605.0	232	(35.1)	92,678.2	107	6,350.5	211	41,417	287
87	132	J.C. 佩尼公司[3]	美国	30,546.0	29.2	566.0	240	0.2	23,493.0	251	7,357.0	185	260,000	22
88	100	美国国际集团	美国	30,519.5	8.2	3,332.3	28	15.0	163,970.7	65	24,001.1	18	40,000	292
89	80	三菱汽车工业公司[1]	日本	30,428.7	(6.7)	(829.7)	485	(905.7)	25,275.6	244	2,622.8	366	27,324[2]	359
90	107	化学银行	美国	30,381.0	10.8	3,708.0	20	50.7	365,521.0	21	21,742.0	23	69,033	177
91	328	贝尔大西洋公司[17]	美国	30,193.9	130.8	2,454.9	54	30.5	53,964.1	145	12,789.1	77	141,000	59
92	74	赫司特[9]	德国	30,055.2	(11.2)	774.7	197	(44.8)	33,869.3	205	8,904.3	139	118,212	87
93	101	摩托罗拉	美国	29,794.0	6.5	1,180.0	128	2.3	27,278.0	236	13,272.0	68	150,000	51
94	.	教师年会和人寿保险－学院退休股本基金[18]	美国	29,348.4	18.5	1,226.6	122	31.3	214,295.6	48	5,776.6	231	4,824	481
95	86	百事可乐公司	美国	29,292.0[1]	(7.4)	2,142.0	59	86.4	20.101.0	271	6,936.0	198	136,000	65
96	91	家乐福公司	法国	29,002.7	(4.2)	613.9	227	0.6	14,448.3	325	3,614.2	322	123,437	77
97	105	荷兰银行	荷兰	28,945.5	4.7	1,975.0	68	0.8	412,532.7	11	12,746.8	79	76,749	159
98	84	全国保险业集团[G]	法国	28,936.7	(10.3)	48.7	428	–	151,551.3	69	3,244.6	343	11,844[19]	452
99	114	兴业银行	法国	28,724.9	10.4	1,047.1	148	17.9	409,091.0	12	10,532.9	107	55,465	226
100	81	通用水管公司[20]	法国	28,633.7	(11.7)	924.0	171	142.1	42,916.0	170	7,464.3	180	193,323	35
101	99	工业企业联合股份有限公司	德国	28,581.4	1.3	495.8	260	(6.5)	32,536.0	206	4,484.8	286	95,561	117
102	97	墨西哥石油 G	墨西哥	28,565.5[E]	0.5	1,003.0	153	(53.8)	42,715.5	172	19,610.7	31	121,220	81
103	112	洛克希德·马丁公司	美国	28,069.0	4.4	1,300.0	116	(3.5)	28,361.0	225	5,176.0	258	173,000	45
104	104	普天寿公司	英国	27,905.7	0.3	1,371.1	107	(37.6)	178,081.0	59	4,579.4	281	22,120	386
105	109	现代公司	韩国	27,838.0	2.1	5.5	450	(29.0)	1,794.6	497	109.2	492	1,070	497

1997 年世界最大的 500 家企业(六)

收入位次 1997 年	收入位次 1996 年	公司名称	国别(地区)	收入 金额:百万美元	收入 比1996年变化(%)	利润 金额:百万美元	利润 位次	利润 比1996年变化(%)	资产 金额:百万美元	资产 位次	股东权益 金额:百万美元	股东权益 位次	雇员 人数	雇员 位次
106	120	联邦国家抵押协会公司	美国	27,776.9	10.9	3,055.8	40	12.1	391,672.7	17	13,793.0	64	3,500	487
107	117	代顿·赫德森[3]	美国	27,757.0	9.4	751.0	205	62.2	14,191.0	327	4,375.0	293	149,500	52
108	.	摩根－斯坦利集团[21,22]	美国	27,132.0	200.5	2,586.0	51	171.8	302,287.0	30	13,956.0	61	47,277	257
109	108	罗伯特－布施公司	德国	27,027.2	(1.1)	896.5	175	223,5	19,411.2	276	6,023.7	223	180,639	38
110	150	泰斯科[23]	英国	26,938.2	22.8	826.9	183	0.6	12,247.4	366	6,382.2	210	124,172	76
111	92	日本兴业银行[1]	日本	26,917.8	(10.9)	(1,651.0)	494	(1,559.6)	369,174.2	20	9,898.8	115	4,971[2]	480
112	94	法国电信	法国	26,854.4	(9.2)	2,546.6	52	518.4	46,552.6	158	15,574.8	53	165,042	47
113	122	英美烟草工业公司	英国	26,801.6	7.5	1,629.9	89	(30.7)	84,358.2	113	7,817.8	169	81,823	141
114	119	克罗格	美国	26,567.3	5.5	411.7	282	17.7	6,301.3	451	(784.8)	495	212,000	31
115	88	兼松[1]	日本	26,506.3	(14.1)	(22.5)	454	–	11,976.0	370	326.3	481	8,731	466
116	89	苏黎士保险有限公司[9]	瑞士	26,469.0	(14.0)	1,231.5	121	33.7	117,036.9	83	14,162.2	59	42,871	279
117	.	朗讯科技[4]	美国	26,360.0	–	541.0	248	–	23,811.0	250	3,387.0	336	184,000	67
118	130	英国电信[1]	英国	26,293.5	10.2	2,801.5	46	(15.0)	38,995.4	184	18,061.6	40	124,000	75
119	151	雷马克斯股份公司	荷兰	25,920.5	19.6	478.7	266	27.6	9,291.5	417	1,523.5	425	142,020	57
120	98	大荣[23]	日本	25,882.2	(8.5)	9.9	448	–	17,020.7	295	891.7	466	100,000	111
121	71	三星	韩国	25,803.8	(24.7)	15.7	445	(75.7)	9,019.5	420	744.0	472	12,307	447
122	111	伊藤洋华堂[23]	日本	25,606.7	(5.6)	576.5	237	(13.7)	15,626.5	314	7,427.5	181	102,617	108
123	103	三菱重工业[1]	日本	25,222.2	(9.6)	493.7	261	(55.0)	35,483.9	199	10,265.1	112	66,730	183
124	.	意大利电信	意大利	25,129.9	–	1,531.3	93	–	46,094.4	160	16,899.7	45	126,097	74
125	161	英特尔公司	美国	25,070.0	20.3	6,945.0	4	34.7	28,880.0	223	19,295.0	34	64,000	187
126	110	新日本制铁[1]	日本	25,062.7	(7.8)	48.4	429	58.1	35,025.3	202	6,589.4	207	85,500	132
127	125	AUSTATE 保险公司	美国	24,949.0	2.7	3,105.0	37	49.6	80,918.0	118	15,610.0	51	51,400	241

1997年世界最大的500家企业(七)

收入位次		公司名称	国别(地区)	收入		利润			资产		股东权益		雇员	
1997年	1996年			金额:百万美元	比1996年变化(%)	金额:百万美元	位次	比1996年变化(%)	金额:百万美元	位次	金额:百万美元	位次	人数	位次
128	297	SBC电信公司[24]	美国	24,856.0	78.8	1,474.0	96	(29.8)	42,132.0	175	9,892.0	116	118,340	86
129	116	CNP保险公司	法国	24,813.6	(2.3)	280.5	330	(8.7)	95,291.1	104	2,337.4	386	2,438	494
130	135	联合技术公司	美国	24,713.0	5.1	1,072.0	147	18.3	16,719.0	300	4,073.0	307	180,100	39
131	126	慕尼黑再保险公司[10]	德国	24,609.2	1.7	371.3	293	8.9	93,157.9	106	3,282.2	342	18,021	409
132	200	康柏电脑[25]	美国	24,584.0	35.8	1,855.0	76	41.3	14,631.0	324	9,429.0	127	37,004	310
133	137	大都会人寿保险公司[12]	美国	24,374.0	4.9	1,203.0	125	41.0	201,907.0	55	14,007.0	60	44,979	270
134	127	巴黎国民银行	法国	24,343.8	0.9	1,021.5	150	35.5	338,195.6	22	9,812.4	117	52,420	235
135	113	蒂森公司[4]	德国	24,298.3	(7.1)	1,247.1	120	518.9	17,419.9	292	4,035.1	309	127,873	72
136	179	家庭用具公司	美国	24,155.7	23.7	1,160.0	132	23.7	11,188.9	386	7,097.9	195	130,000	69
137	136	沃尔沃	瑞典	24,035.1	3.3	1,355.9	110	(27.1)	20,575.2	269	7,614.3	176	72,900	169
138	123	康纳格拉[26]	美国	24,002.1	(3.3)	615.0	226	225.6	11,277.1	381	2,471.7	373	82,169	139
139	162	BCE公司	加拿大	23,973.8	16.1	(1,109.5)	487	(231.3)	28,160.2	227	6,854.5	200	122,000	79
140	146	俄罗斯天然气[27]	俄罗斯	23,947.7	6.2	3,938.4	17	115.7	107,555.2	92	73,447.9	1	362,200	6
141	156	J·圣斯伯雷公司[28]	英国	23,810.7	12.0	799.7	189	25.1	15,280.0	321	6,886.4	199	114,042	94
142	124	三星电子	韩国	23,809.9	(3.6)	(640.2)	481	(569.7)	18,868.9	278	2,670.5	364	84,100	135
143	145	福蒂斯公司	比/荷	23,796.5	5.1	1,033.0	149	12.0	166,657.9	64	7,725.0	173	35,229	317
144	175	默克公司	美国	23,636.9	19.2	4,614.1	14	18.9	25,811.9	240	12,613.5	80	53,800	232
145	149	美洲银行	美国	23,585.0	6.9	3,210.0	33	11.7	260,159.0	39	19,837.0	28	77,000	156
146	155	通用电话电子	美国	23,260.0	9.0	2,793.6	47	(0.2)	42,141.7	174	8,037.6	160	114,359	93
147	128	富士银行[1]	日本	22,912.0	(4.8)	(2,813.0)	497	(390.6)	413,296.2	10	11,821.8	92	14,615[29]	434
148	134	佳能公司	日本	22,812.7	(3.0)	981.7	156	13.4	22,011.1	259	8,452.5	151	78,767	153

1997 年世界最大的 500 家企业(八)

收入位次 1997年	收入位次 1996年	公司名称	国别(地区)	收入 金额:百万美元	收入 比1996年变化(%)	利润 金额:百万美元	利润 位次	利润 比1996年变化(%)	资产 金额:百万美元	资产 位次	股东权益 金额:百万美元	股东权益 位次	雇员 人数	雇员 位次
149	102	三和银行[1]	日本	22,805.5	(18.5)	(1,485.6)	492	(747.2)	427,077.4	8	13,723.2	65	19,745	399
150	152	强生公司	美国	22,629.0	4.7	3,303.0	29	14.4	21,453.0	263	12,359.0	84	90.500	127
151	139	曼内斯曼公司	德国	22,553.5	(2.1)	282.1	328	10.8	16,389.9	304	3,850.4	317	120,859	84
152	218	塞夫韦商店	美国	22,483.8	30.2	557.4	244	21.0	8,493.9	423	2,149.0	399	147,000	54
153	192	沃尔特·迪斯尼公司[4]	美国	22,473.0	19.9	1,966.0	69	61.9	37,776.0	189	17,285.0	44	108,000	99
154	147	联合包裹运输公司	美国	22,458.0	0.4	909.0	172	(20.7)	15,912.0	309	6,087.0	218	331,000	8
155	118	里昂信贷银行[G]	法国	22,420.5	(11.0)	181.1	372	358.7	249,083.6	42	5,647.1	236	50,789	244
156	166	劳埃德银行	英国	22,313.1	9.5	3,825.1	19	55.5	260,163.4	38	10,291.0	111	82,580	138
157	35	工业复兴	意大利	22,231.6	(54.7)	2,867.7	44	926.5	65,250.7	129	7,025.8	196	126,933	73
158	129	意大利国家电力公司[G]	意大利	22,180.8	(6.9)	1,952.9	70	136.8	53,769.5	146	18,371.0	38	88,957	129
159	191	L.M. 爱立信	瑞典	21,955.8	17.0	1,563.0	91	47.5	18,577.4	281	6,630.6	206	100,774	109
160	178	价格成本公司[30]	美国	21,874.4	11.8	312.2	318	25.5	5,476.3	462	2,468.1	374	42,750	281
161	163	西德意志州银行[G]	德国	21,859.3	6.8	400.0	284	(11.3)	335,771.8	23	7,401.9	182	29.827	344
162	167	皇家太阳联合保险集团	英国	21,844.6	5.6	950.1	167	31.1	99,546.2	98	11,860.8	91	43,485	276
163	213	国民银行	美国	21,734.0	24.1	3,077.0	39	25.5	264,562.0	35	21,337.0	24	80,360	147
164	115	朝日相互生命保险公司[1]	日本	21,678.2	(14.8)	577.1	236	(36.5)	91,307.9	108	1,009.7	457	33,127	328
165	138	关西电力[1]	日本	21,665.5	(6.5)	629.9	223	28.6	52,022.8	151	9,373.7	129	26,343[2]	364
166	153	德果斯顿银行	德国	21,533.6	0.2	957.8	164	(6.2)	376,415.7	19	10,296.7	110	46,169	265
167	95	山多兹公司[9]	瑞士	21,494.2	(26.7)	3,592.3	23	92.7	35,533.3	198	18,374.8	37	87,239	131
168	143	樱花银行[1]	日本	21,292.3	(6.2)	(719.3)	483	(556.6)	398,649.3	14	12,948.8	74	17,420[2]	411
169	141	国民西敏斯特银行	英国	21,154.9	(7.1)	1,100.8	143	60.6	305,082.3	28	12,994.5	72	70,000	175

1997 年世界最大的 500 家企业(九)

收入位次 1997年	收入位次 1996年	公司名称	国别(地区)	收入 金额:百万美元	收入 比1996年变化(%)	利润 金额:百万美元	利润 位次	利润 比1996年变化(%)	资产 金额:百万美元	资产 位次	股东权益 金额:百万美元	股东权益 位次	雇员 人数	雇员 位次
170	176	巴克莱银行	英国	21,128.7	7.3	1,851.1	77	(27.7)	451,948.1	6	12,538.7	81	84,300	134
171	159	USX 公司	美国	21,057.0[E]	(0.1)	988.0	154	4.8	17,284.0	294	5,400.0	247	40,894	289
172	140	佳友银行[1]	日本	21,007.9	(7.9)	(2,047.2)	496	(777.2)	482,707.2	3	12,535.3	82	15,111[2]	430
173	164	中国银行[G]	中国	20,927.4	2.5	1,126.1	138	5.5	305,446.3	27	22,478.2	22	198,487	32
174	311	麦克埃森公司[1]	美国	20,857.3	32.8	154.9	384	15.7	5,607.5	461	1,406.8	431	13,700	441
175	131	日本邮政服务局[G,31]	日本	20,741.0	(12.4)	837.2	181	(33.7)	78,513.3	120	34,981.8	8	142,355	56
176	187	贝尔南方公司	美国	20,561.0	8.0	3,261.0	31	13.9	36,301.0	196	15,165.0	54	81,000	143
177	148	东日本铁道[1]	日本	20,486.6	(8.2)	539.6	249	(14.0)	55,356.1	141	5,739.9	233	77,653[2]	155
178	256	巴西银行[G]	巴西	20,310.2	29.7	532.4	251	–	97,588.4	99	5,378.7	248	76,387	161
179	320	安龙天然气公司	美国	20,273.0	52.6	105.0	403	(82.0)	23,422.0	252	5,618.0	240	15,555	426
180	212	三星生命保险公司[1]	韩国	20,269.1	15.6	65.3	419	25.1	19,534.2	275	314.0	482	9,714	461
181	346	大都会饭店有限公司[32,33]	英国	20,217.3	–	1,323.8	113	–	28,948.2	222	10,903.0	103	75,000	165
182	169	国际造纸	美国	20,096.0	(0.2)	(151.0)	465	(149.8)	26,754.0	238	8,710.0	146	82,000	140
183	188	西格纳	美国	20,038.0	5.7	1,086.0	146	2.8	108,199.0	90	7,932.0	167	47,700	256
184	172	道氏化学	美国	20,018.0	(0.2)	1,808.0	79	(5.2)	24,040.0	248	7,626.0	175	42,861	280
185	195	塞拉里公司[10]	美国	19,734.0	6.0	1,009.0	151	10.2	12,953.0	352	4,280.0	298	141,000	59
186	165	第一劝业银行[1]	日本	19,712.7	(3.3)	(586.7)	479	–	432,189.5	7	13,798.6	63	16,965[2]	418
187	197	MCI 通讯设备公司	美国	19,6530.	6.3	2.0	452	(99.8)	25,305.0	243	11,164.0	100	59,000	208
188	173	洛斯公司	美国	19,647.8[E]	(1.6)	793.6	193	(42.7)	69,577.1	127	9,655.1	119	29,747	345
189	198	商业联合34	英国	19,590.5	6.7	609.4	230	(1.7)	97,316.5	101	7,381.7	183	26,175	365
190	190	瑞士联合银行35	瑞士	19,445.5	2.9	(88.9)	461	–	395,986.2	15	14,388.7	58	27,611	356

1997 年世界最大的 500 家企业(十)

收入位次		公司名称	国别(地区)	收入		利润			资产		股东权益		雇员	
1997年	1996年			金额:百万美元	比1996年变化(%)	金额:百万美元	位次	比1996年变化(%)	金额:百万美元	位次	金额:百万美元	位次	人数	位次
191	158	三井相互生命保险公司[1]	日本	19,433.4	(8.4)	521.4	255	(34.2)	81,750.5	116	803.5	470	23,776	378
192	185	大西洋富田公司	美国	19,272.0[E]	0.5	1,771.0	81	6.5	25,322.0	242	8,680.0	147	24,000	376
193	177	商业银行	德国	19,253.8	(2.2)	763.2	201	(3.5)	287,468.6	33	8,795.8	144	28,711	351
194	170	吉之岛公司36	日本	19,147.4	(4.8)	58.0	423	(78.7)	12,692.2	360	2,571.0	369	41,177[2]	288
195	193	美国百货公司[3]	美国	19,138.9	2.5	280.6	329	(2.3)	8,536.0	422	2,309.1	388	121,000	82
196	381	东邦相互人寿保险公司[1]	日本	19,107.3	63.7	88.9	410	(18.7)	22,507.7	256	169.5	489	2,177	495
197	168	普罗莫德公司	法国	18,961.6	(6.3)	277.4	332	13.8	8,314.7	427	1,587.0	422	50.781	245
198	232	卡特彼勒公司	美国	18,925.0	14.5	1,665.0	87	22.3	20,756.0	268	4,679.0	277	59,863	205
199	214	纽约人寿保险公司	美国	18,899.3	8.9	650.7	218	12.3	84,067.1	114	4,621.7	280	7,003	472
200	189	安田相互人寿保险公司[1]	日本	18,884.7	(0.1)	826.1	184	(32.9)	71,052.2	125	1,153.5	447	20,903	393
201	196	可口可乐公司	美国	18,868.0	1.7	4,129.0	15	18.2	16,940.0	297	7,311.0	186	29,500	346
202	224	千代田相互人寿保险公司[1]	日本	18,849.8	12.3	129.6	391	(40.9)	37,707.1	190	508.8	477	18,728	402
203	174	哥伦比亚医药卫生	美国	18,819.0	(5.5)	(305.0)	472	(120.3)	22,002.0	260	7,250.0	190	285,000	13
204	208	美洲航空公司	美国	18,570.0	4.6	985.0	155	(3.1)	20,915.0	266	6,216.0	215	110,000	96
205	222	艾特纳人寿和意外事故保险公司	美国	18,540.2	11.0	901.1	174	38.4	96,000.6	103	11,195.4	99	40.300	290
206	205	圣－戈班化学公司	法国	18,346.8	2.7	964.3	160	14.1	22,559.7	255	9,173.2	132	106.782	102
207	181	中部电力公司[1]	日本	18,310.7	(5.0)	327.7	308	(3.8)	46,985.7	157	7,136.8	193	20,371[2]	395
208	199	法国船坞公司集团[37]	法国	18,217.9	–	138.0	389	–	14,135.6	330	3,404.2	334	81,000	143
209	180	施乐	美国	18,166.0	(6.9)	1,452.0	99	20.4	27,732.0	231	5,690.0	235	91,400	126
210	235	帝国化学工业公司	英国	18,121.1[1]	10.3	424.3	280	(1.2)	15,239.0	322	240.2	486	69,500	176
211	202	巴西石油公司[G]	巴西	18,050.5[E]	(0.1)	1,402.0	104	110.8	34,230.8	203	18,865.7	35	44,980	269

1997年世界最大的500家企业(十一)

收入位次 1997年	收入位次 1996年	公司名称	国别(地区)	收入 金额:百万美元	收入 比1996年变化(%)	利润 金额:百万美元	利润 位次	利润 比1996年变化(%)	资产 金额:百万美元	资产 位次	股东权益 金额:百万美元	股东权益 位次	雇员 人数	雇员 位次
212	203	桥石轮胎公司	日本	17,936.0	(0.3)	323.5	312	(50.0)	14,179.3	328	5,263.3	253	96,204	116
213	204	中国化工进出口总公司[G]	中国	17,852.7	(0.6)	63.8	420	(10.5)	5,801.6	458	986.1	461	5,943	475
214	217	美国运通公司	美国	17,760.0	2.8	1,991.0	67	4.7	120,003.0	81	9,574.0	125	74,000	167
215	201	东京海上火灾保险公司[1]	日本	17,747.4	(1.9)	296.9	324	27.3	41,239.5	178	4,922.2	266	15,294	429
216	248	J.P.摩根公司	美国	17,701.0	11.6	1,465.0	97	(6.9)	262,159.0	36	11,404.0	95	16,943	419
217	229	斯塔特石油公司[q]	挪威	17,619.2[E]	6.3	609.0	231	(25.6)	17,709.0	288	5,217.6	256	17,177	414
218	171	德意志巴恩公司[G]	德国	17,575.1	(12.5)	228.4	352	(68.7)	36,862.2	194	9,121.7	133	268,273	18
219	266	布鲁肯希尔公司[26]	澳大利亚	17,539.9	17.5	322.2	313	(59.1)	27,962.7	230	9,543.9	126	61,000	199
220	240	联合航空公司	美国	17,378.0	6.2	949.0	168	78.0	15,803.0	310	2,337.0	387	91,700	125
221	186	法国通用保险公司	法国	17,249.2	(9.5)	329.8	307	9.9	82,331.0	115	5,338.3	249	30.722	336
222	231	瓦卢超级市场批发公司[23]	美国	17,201.4	3.9	230.8	351	31.8	4,093.0	482	1,201.9	446	38.016	303
223	183	日本石油[1]	日本	17,116.5[E]	(10.8)	93.5	408	(16.2)	21,400.5	264	4,917.6	267	10.200	458
224	233	莱普索尔	西班牙	17,074.6[E]	3.4	861.2	179	(8.5)	17,523.4	290	6,066.4	221	21,440	391
225	221	RJR纳贝斯克控股公司	美国	17,057.0[E]	(0.0)	381.0	291	(37.6)	30,678.0	214	9,631.0	121	80,000	149
226	226	弗兰茨·哈尼尔股份有限公司	德国	16,907.1	0.9	177.6	374	(13.6)	6,365.6	449	998.9	459	30,469	338
227	211	巴伐利亚联合银行	德国	16,891.5	(4.0)	487.8	264	(9.5)	249,798.2	41	7,772.0	171	22,001	387
228	286	莱曼兄弟公司21	美国	16,883.0	18.4	647.0	219	55.5	151,705.0	68	4,523.0	285	8,340	467
229	206	普鲁伊萨格股份公司[4]	德国	16,806.3	(5.5)	215.8	356	27.2	8,460.4	424	1,642.9	419	62,601	194
230	264	布里斯托－迈尔斯－施贵宝公司	美国	16,701.2	10.9	3,204.7	34	12.4	14,977.0	323	7,219.1	191	53,600	233
231	258	法国国有铁路公司[G]	法国	16,653.3	7.8	(103.8)	463	–	49,105.6	154	3,900.4	315	175,000	42

1997 年世界最大的 500 家企业(十二)

收入位次		公司名称	国别(地区)	收入		利润			资产		股东权益		雇员	
1997 年	1996 年			金额:百万美元	比 1996 年变化(%)	金额:百万美元	位次	比 1996 年变化(%)	金额:百万美元	位次	金额:百万美元	位次	人数	位次
232	223	马自达汽车[1]	日本	16,630.3	(1.1)	(55.4)	459	–	10,921.3	388	2,539.0	370	31,665	333
233	369	英格拉姆·麦克罗公司	美国	16,581.5	37.9	193.6	366	75.0	4,932.2	469	1,038.2	454	12,000	449
234	254	瑞士银行公司[38]	瑞士	16,431.6	4.6	(171.0)	466	–	300,942.8	31	7,476.5	179	27,565	357
235	285	布依格公司	法国	16,406.0	14.4	129.4	392	1.2	13,555.8	344	1,366.5	435	103,190	107
236	216	LG 国际公司	韩国	16,358.7	(5.5)	57.8	424	114.7	1,197.6	498	130.6	490	4,238	485
237	.	公爵能源公司	美国	16,308.9	242.8	974.4	15.8	33.5	24,028.8	249	8,028.7	162	21,000	392
238	246	丰田通商公司[1]	日本	16,297.3	2.3	54.5	425	(1.0)	5,924.8	457	1,033.7	455	4,683	482
239	250	西班牙电话公司	西班牙	16,138.3	1.9	1,298.0	117	2.6	40,840.7	179	13,065.4	70	92,151	124
240	276	阿洪保险公司	荷兰	16,048.4	10.5	1,131.3	135	21.7	134,513.4	77	8,942.2	137	23,429	380
241	267	亚美达科	美国	15,998.0	7.2	2,296.0	57	7.6	25,339.0	241	8,308.0	155	74,359	166
242	281	科尔斯·梅耶[39]	澳大利亚	15,897.5	10.3	303.3	320	41.5	4,989.6	468	1,874.9	411	148.346	53
243	194	鹿岛建设[1]	日本	15,795.3	(15.3)	(61.9)	460	(195.0)	20,129.8	270	2,748.0	360	13,588[2]	443
244	227	日本钢管[1]	日本	15,758.1	(5.5)	116.3	398	(21.5)	22,226.2	258	3,487.5	329	38,336	299
245	239	三洋电器[1]	日本	15,679.2	(4.3)	100.4	404	(36.0)	19,811.6	273	5,628.5	238	67,887	180
246	262	联邦百货[3]	美国	15,668.3	2.9	536.0	250	101.6	13,738.2	335	5,256.3	254	114,700	92
247	209	德国邮政总局[G]	德国	15,654.1	(11.8)	(221.3)	470	(198.7)	11,870.5	372	3,162.4	345	266,823	19
248	294	拉博银行	荷兰	15,634.8	11.4	977.5	157	1.0	208,18.7	52	12,313.7	8b	38,878	297
249	219	法国邮政总局[G]	法国	15,535.0	(9.1)	9.9	447	–	12,804.5	358	1,101.4	449	286.635	12
250	353	荷兰皇家邮电总局[42]	荷兰	15,514.3	24.8	1,375.8	106	(4.7)	18,498.0	282	8,656.6	148	134,923	66
251	252	菲利浦石油	美国	15,424.0[E]	(2.4)	959.0	163	(26.4)	13,860.0	334	4,814.0	272	17,100	417
252	225	罗纳－普朗克公司[41]	法国	15,413.0	(8.1)	(667.2)	482	(188.2)	27,397.9	235	8,489.0	149	68,377	179
253	477	太平洋天然气和电气	美国	15,399.9	60.2	716.0	211	(5.2)	30,557.0	215	8,897.0	140	23,500	379

1997 年世界最大的 500 家企业(十三)

收入位次		公司名称	国别(地区)	收入		利润			资产		股东权益		雇员	
1997年	1996年			金额:百万美元	比1996年变化(%)	金额:百万美元	位次	比1996年变化(%)	金额:百万美元	位次	金额:百万美元	位次	人数	位次
254	234	弗莱明	美国	15,372.7	(6.8)	25.4	442	(4.8)	3,924.0	483	1,089.7	451	39,700	294
255	339	美国西部	美国	15,352.0	18.9	697.0	213	(40.8)	39.860.0	182	11,324.0	97	67,461	181
256	253	皮诺春天百货公司	法国	15,280.0	(2.8)	488.8	263	21.1	11,247.9	384	2,923.3	355	63,301	193
257	.	电子数据系统公司	美国	15,235.6	5.5	730.6	208	69.3	11,174.1	387	5,309.4	250	110,000	96
258	305	普通事故保险公司[42]	英国	15,231.4	10.4	1,159.8	133	42.6	52,476.6	149	6,221.6	214	25,581	368
259	157	巴黎巴银行	法国	15,223.3	(28.2)	1,126.2	137	32.5	244,016.7	44	8,918.6	138	20,000	396
260	236	达诺纳集团	法国	15,159.5	(7.6)	627.8	224	(5.0)	16,385.3	305	7,099.6	194	80,631	145
261	288	明尼苏达矿业制造公司	美国	15,070.0	5.9	2,121.0	61	39.0	13,238.0	346	5,926.0	225	75,639	164
262	241	日理公司[23]	日本	15,005.8	(7.3)	83.2	411	(39.1)	13,638.0	338	2,152.6	398	38,322	300
263	255	瑞士养老金和人寿保险公司[43]	瑞士	14,933.7	–	105.1	402	–	70,125.1	126	4,731.3	274	7,946	468
264	210	大成[1]	日本	14,912.8	(15.3)	(545.5)	478	(1,162.5)	21,732.3	262	2,214.4	393	21,465	390
265	279	桑坦德集团	西班牙	14,886.0	3.0	755.5	203	11,8	170,288.5	62	4,380.3	292	62,285	198
266	289	斯普林德公司	美国	14,873.9	4.5	952.5	165	(19.5)	18,184.8	284	9,025.2	135	51,000	243
267	291	瑞士再保险	瑞士	14,837.1	5.0	1,458.7	98	23.6	53,311.6	147	9,733.5	118	7,588	469
268	237	丽都有限公司	瑞典	14,790.8	(9.8)	46.1	431	(83.3)	10,034.6	403	2,591.2	368	105,950	104
269	245	伊斯曼柯达	美国	14,713.0	(9.4)	5.0	451	(99.6)	13,145.0	347	3,161.0	346	97,500	114
270	270	LG电子	韩国	14,699.6	(0.4)	(601.3)	480	(1,747.3)	11,575.3	377	1,020.9	456	59,686	206
271	306	艾伯森[3]	美国	14,689.5	6.6	516.8	257	4.7	5,218.6	467	2,419.5	377	94,000	121
272	238	巴西电信	巴西	14,666.1[E]	18.0	3,618.3	22	31.9	42,646.7	173	28,040.1	14	87,282	130
273	220	五十铃汽车公司[1]	日本	14,660.3	(14.1)	49.2	427	(42.2)	12,979.7	351	916.5	463	13,520[2]	444

1997年世界最大的500家企业(十四)

收入位次 1997年	收入位次 1996年	公司名称	国别(地区)	收入 金额:百万美元	收入 比1996年变化(%)	利润 金额:百万美元	利润 位次	利润 比1996年变化(%)	资产 金额:百万美元	资产 位次	股东权益 金额:百万美元	股东权益 位次	雇员 人数	雇员 位次
274	247	夏普[1]	日本	14,586.5	(8.2)	201.9	364	(53.1)	15,629.4	313	7,149.0	192	47,981	255
275	215	农林中央银行[1]	日本	14,582.5	(15.8)	1,092.0	145	297.3	391,726.0	16	11,045.5	102	3,000	492
276	316	标准人寿保险公司[44]	英国	14,519.9	8.7	N.A		-	94,655.7	105	N.A.		9,985	460
277	249	日本通运[1]	日本	14,512.5	(8.4)	220.3	354	(9.8)	8,371.7	426	2,409.2	380	60,516	203
278	244	福雷特·克鲁普	德国	14,477.8	(9.4)	187,5	369	93.3	10,920.7	389	1,694.4	417	57,938	214
279	295	爱理德·西格诺	美国	14,472.0	3.6	1,170.0	131	14,7	13,707.0	336	4,386.0	291	70,500	173
280	310	DELHALIE“LE LION”	比利时	14,466.2	7.0	137.9	390	(2.0)	4,886.3	470	913.7	465	107,208	101
281	315	西斯科[10]	美国	14,454.6	7.9	302.5	321	9.3	3,436.6	485	1,400.5	432	32,000	332
282	230	鲁尔煤矿	德国	14,402.8	(13.1)	170.1	377	86.8	16,648.6	302	1,500.0	426	96,240	115
283	363	联邦住宅贷款抵押	美国	14,399.0	18.8	1,395.0	105	12.2	194,597.0	58	7,521.0	178	3,200	490
284	372	第一联合银行	美国	14,329.0	19.6	1,896.0	74	26.5	157,274.0	67	12,032.0	90	43,933	275
285	261	清水建设[1]	日本	14,312.4	(6.2)	(367.4)	473	(879.4)	17,373.9	293	2,250.1	391	15,319	428
286	408	福陆[8]	美国	14,298.5	29.8	146.2	386	(45.5)	4,697.8	474	1,741.1	414	60.679	201
287	257	印度石油[G1]	印度	14,249.2[E]	(9.0)	461.4	270	15.8	7,595.2	438	2,699.9	362	33,832	326
288	265	巴伐利亚抵押与承兑银行	德国	14,230.3	(5.5)	444.0	274	(0.1)	203,540.6	54	5,242.8	255	18,409	404
289	292	美国家庭用品公司	美国	14,196.0	0.8	2,043.1	66	8.5	20,825.1	267	8,175.3	158	60,523	202
290	321	英国航空公司[1]	英国	14,191.2	7.0	755.4	204	(13.9)	18,924.1	277	5,561.7	242	60,770	200
291	399	阿比国家公司	英国	14,171.5	26.4	1,561.1	92	30.9	248,154.6	43	8,026.7	163	24,052	375
292	242	日本烟草[G1]	日本	14,124.8[E]	(12.0)	472.7	268	(38.4)	15,427.9	316	10,166.1	114	20,384	394
293	259	三菱化工[1]	日本	14,121.8	(8.2)	45.7	432	-	15,469.7	315	3,382.4	337	29,185	349
294	282	韩国电力[G]	韩国	14,064.3	(2.3)	588.9	234	(20.7)	27,607.0	232	10,167.3	113	31,252	334
295	273	贝图斯曼公司[10]	德国	14,006.2	(4.9)	499.3	259	4.0	7,778.4	433	1,987.6	405	57,173	215

1997 年世界最大的 500 家企业(十五)

收入位次		公司名称	国别(地区)	收入		利润			资产		股东权益		雇员	
1997 年	1996 年			金额:百万美元	比 1996 年变化(%)	金额:百万美元	位次	比 1996 年变化(%)	金额:百万美元	位次	金额:百万美元	位次	人数	位次
296	.	蒙特爱迪生	意大利	13,897.2	–	874.5	177	–	17,989.6	285	4,531.9	283	27,135	361
297	318	阿–丹–米公司[10]	美国	13,853.3	4.1	377.3	292	(45.8)	11,354.4	380	6,050.1	222	17,160	415
298	312	比利时石油金融[41]	比利时	13,820.9[E]	2.7	616.8	225	19.0	10,893.6	390	4,208.1	301	14,675	433
299	263	储蓄银行集团	法国	13,765.2	(8.8)	346.3	300	(3.1)	213,832.9	49	10,789.2	104	39,200	296
300	243	卡斯塔特	德国	13,720.4	(14.1)	93.6	407	141.3	6,374.8	448	1,381.1	434	94,463	120
301	356	雷锡昂	美国	13,673.5	10.9	526.8	254	(30.8)	28,100.0	229	10,400.0	108	119,200	85
302	283	米其林	法国	13,654.5	(4.9)	665.3	217	17.7	13,581.5	341	3,995.5	312	123,254	78
303	299	太阳相互人寿保险公司[1]	日本	13,606.7	(2.0)	125.5	395	(1.0)	51,185.8	152	538.7	476	15,868	425
304	351	德尔塔航空公司[10]	美国	13,590.0	9.1	854.0	180	447.4	12,741.0	359	3,007.0	350	63,441	192
305	322	挪威水电[G41]	挪威	13,585.1	3.3	735,3	207	(23.5)	15,639.6	311	6,199.2	216	38,271	301
306	280	日本电装公司[1]	日本	13,582.6	(5.8)	579.7	235	(8.5)	13,088.2	348	7,927.7	168	57,084	216
307	357	阿什兰石油[4]	美国	13,567.0[E]	10.3	279.0	331	32.2	7,777.0	434	2,024.0	402	37,200	309
308	352	马克斯–斯潘塞[1]	英国	13,536.5	8.8	1,361.2	108	13.7	12,808.3	357	8,483.7	150	48,200	254
309	370	中国粮油食品进出口总公司	中国	13,526.0	12.5	110.3	401	18.8	4,452.7	476	1,498.8	427	28,000	354
310	365	维亚康母有限公司	美国	13,504.5	6.3	793.6	193	(36.4)	28,288.7	226	13,383.6	67	45,599	266
311	326	美国铝公司	美国	13,481.7	2.7	805.1	188	56.4	13,070.6	350	4,419.4	290	81,600	142
312	364	西北相互人寿保险公司	美国	13,429.9	10.9	689.1	214	11.1	71,080.6	124	4,100.6	306	3,818	486
313	.	NEC	美国	13,378.4	84.3	(102.5)	462	(190.4)	4,800.0	473	1,000.0	458	2,572	493
314	377	沃尔格林公司[30]	美国	13,363.0	13.5	436.0	277	17,3	4,207.0	479	2,373.0	383	70,500	173
315	302	汉莎集团	德国	13,353.9	(3.7)	478.9	265	30.1	11,860.3	373	3,282.5	340	58,250	213
316	300	曼柴油机有限公司[10]	德国	13,343.9	(3.8)	197.2	365	(4.7)	8,045.6	429	2,182.7	395	62,564	195

1997 年世界最大的 500 家企业(十六)

收入位次		公司名称	国别(地区)	收入		利润			资产		股东权益		雇员	
1997 年	1996 年			金额：百万美元	比 1996 年变化(%)	金额：百万美元	位次	比 1996 年变化(%)	金额：百万美元	位次	金额：百万美元	位次	人数	位次
317	350	哈特福特集团	美国	13,305.0	6.7	1,332.0	112	–	131,743.0	78	6,085.0	219	25,000	369
318	457	时代－华纳	美国	13,294.0	32.1	246.0	345	–	34,163.0	204	9,356.0	130	38,200	302
319	464	托斯科	美国	13,281.6[E]	33.9	212.7	358	45.4	5,945.3	456	1,944.1	409	26,500	363
320	349	艾奥瓦牛肉罐头公司	美国	13,258.8	5.7	117.0	397	(41.1)	2,838.9	492	1,237.1	444	38,000	304
321	268	英国轮胎和橡胶公司	英国	13,254.2	(10.9)	1,444.8	100	114.7	12,637.4	361	3,547.7	326	110,498	95
322	342	巴伐利亚州立银行	德国	13,252.3	4.2	345.9	301	14.7	241,682.0	45	6,081.1	220	7,282	471
323	444	第一银行	美国	13,219.1	28.7	1,305.7	114	(8.5)	115,901.3	84	10,376.0	109	56,600	219
324	335	温－迪克西百货公司[10]	美国	13,218.7	2.0	204.4	362	(20.0)	2,921.4	491	1,337.5	438	95,000	119
325	327	固特异轮胎橡胶公司	美国	13,155.1	0.3	558.7	242	449.4	9,917.4	406	3,395.5	335	95,302	118
326	269	日本能源[1]	日本	13,106.3[E]	(11.3)	155.2	383	–	12,314.0	365	774.7	471	14,835	432
327	333	乔治－太平洋	美国	13,094.0	0.5	69.0	415	(55.8)	12,950.0	353	3,474.0	331	46,500	261
328	.	CVS	美国	13,086.5	56.8	37.7	438	(50.0)	5,637.0	460	2,361.0	384	90,000	128
329	331	葛兰素医药公司	英国	13,072.3	0.4	3,030.6	41	(2.8)	13,883.1	333	3,032.7	349	52,501	234
330	329	卡西诺集团	法国	13,065.9	0.0	190.9	368	16.5	7,092.8	440	1,716.7	415	49,990	249
331	275	数字设备公司[10,45]	美国	13,046.8	(10.4)	140.9	387	–	9,692.9	411	3,545.0	327	54,900	228
332	272	出光兴产石油公司[1]	日本	13,021.5[E]	(11.7)	8.2	449	(73.5)	13,701.2	337	593.4	475	4,578	484
333	314	东北电力公司[1]	日本	13,017.0	(3.0)	386.1	288	59.2	29,867.6	217	4,850.1	269	16,478	422
334	338	罗奇公司[9]	瑞士	12,937.2	0.2	(1,400.1)	491	(144.4)	37,554.4	191	12,512.2	83	51,643	239
335	296	日本航空公司[1]	日本	12,884.0	(7.4)	(512.6)	477	–	15,318.7	319	1,387.0	433	17,863[2]	410
336	.	英国煤气公司[46]	英国	12,846.3	–	(1,295.8)	490	–	6,748.2	445	2,157.3	397	15,423	427
337	366	加拿大皇家银行[8]	加拿大	12,810.2	6.2	1,223.0	123	16.8	173,716.1	61	7,373.8	184	50,719	246

1997 年世界最大的 500 家企业(十七)

收入位次		公司名称	国别(地区)	收入		利润			资产		股东权益		雇员	
1997年	1996年			金额:百万美元	比1996年变化(%)	金额:百万美元	位次	比1996年变化(%)	金额:百万美元	位次	金额:百万美元	位次	人数	位次
338	448	哈利法克斯住宅互助协会[47]	英国	12,803.3	14.3	1,715.3	83	94.1	210.021.8	51	11,559.1	94	32,097	331
339	397	迪尔公司[8]	美国	12,791.4	13.9	960.1	161	17.5	16,319.8	306	4,147.3	303	34,400	320
340	324	电通公司[1]	日本	12,777.9	(2.8)	73.9	414	(38.7)	7,022.5	441	2,197.0	394	5,488[2]	478
341	354	斯密克兰－比彻姆	英国	12,769.3	3.2	1,767.6	82	9.4	13,957.1	332	2,947.1	354	55,400	227
342	293	日本交通会社[1]	日本	12,757.5	(9.3)	22.9	444	21.1	3,182.9	488	410.5	478	9,343[2]	465
343	309	亚琛和慕尼黑保险公司[48]	德国	12,745.1	(7.6)	214.1	357	6.7	52,4731	150	1,339.0	437	18,277	407
344	345	五月百货公司[3]	美国	12,685.0	0.7	775.0	196	2.6	9,930.0	405	3,809.0	318	116,000	90
345	367	布拉德斯科银行	巴西	12,666.4	5.1	770.6	199	(6.1)	55,302.5	142	4,993.2	264	62,450	196
346	290	竹中公司	日本	12,662.5	(10.9)	128.4	393	(27.2)	10,829.6	395	2,438.0	376	13,620	442
347	355	全国保险企业公司[12]	美国	12,644.4	2.3	805.6	187	95.1	87,829.9	111	8,795.4	145	29,051	350
348	439	南方天然气公司	美国	12,611.0	21.8	972.0	159	(13.8)	35,271.0	201	9,647.0	120	30,756	335
349	344	毕尔巴鄂－比斯开银行[G]	西班牙	12,589.2	(0.3)	893.6	176	8.6	138,691.1	75	6,101.4	217	60,282	204
350	400	西格拉姆公司[10,41]	加拿大	12,560.0[E]	–	502.0	258	–	20,936.0	265	9,422.0	128	30,000	342
351	323	金伯利－克拉克	美国	12,546.6	(4.6)	901.5	173	(35.8)	11,266.0	382	4,125.3	304	57,000	218
352	446	共荣人寿保险公司[1]	日本	12,546.2	22.6	205.1	361	(34.4)	39,338.5	183	244.4	485	16,819	421
353	308	神户钢铁公司[1]	日本	12,506.1	(8.1)	(39.9)	457	(125.7)	17,983.6	286	2,739.4	361	30,208	340
354	395	辉瑞有限公司	美国	12,504.0	10.6	2,213.0	58	14.7	15,336.0	318	7,933.0	166	49,200	251
355	336	德意志合作银行	德国	12,453.0	(3.8)	185.2	370	1.5	207,741.1	53	2,379.6	382	11,970	451
356	386	澳大利亚国民银行[4]	澳大利亚	12,443.9	8.1	1,710.6	84	5.6	146,245.7	71	9,108.5	134	46,392	263
357	419	伍尔沃斯公司[10]	澳大利亚	12,443.5	14.6	201.9	363	13.9	2,669.4	494	916.3	464	100,000	111
358	340	柏林银行[G]	德国	12,429.0	(3.3)	161.9	381	876.7	197,338.8	57	4,529.8	284	16,907	420

1997 年世界最大的 500 家企业(十八)

收入位次		公司名称	国别(地区)	收入		利润			资产		股东权益		雇员	
1997年	1996年			金额:百万美元	比1996年变化(%)	金额:百万美元	位次	比1996年变化(%)	金额:百万美元	位次	金额:百万美元	位次	人数	位次
359	278	现代汽车公司	韩国	12,391.6	(14.5)	(30.3)	456	(146.0)	6,539.1	446	858.6	468	46,412	262
360	343	奥托邮购两合公司[49]	德国	12,382.7	(2.5)	252.6	341	4.4	4,858.9	472	992.7	460	41,476	286
361	298	北方炼铁联合公司	法国	12,336.7	(11.2)	352.1	298	21.0	10,868.2	392	4,480.6	287	51,394	242
362	319	阿克苏诺贝尔公司	荷兰	12,328.6	(7.4)	827.8	182	5.9	10,583.6	400	4,456.1	288	68,900	178
363	.	德尔电脑[3]	美国	12,327.0	58.9	944.0	169	82.2	4,268.0	478	1,293.0	441	16,160	424
364	402	埃默森电器[4]	美国	12,298.5	10.3	1,121.9	139	10.2	11,463.3	379	5,420.7	246	100,700	110
365	414	加拿大帝国商业银行[8]	加拿大	12,289.4	12.8	1,129.8	136	12.9	168,900.8	63	7,272.3	189	42,446	284
366	480	纽约银行家信托公司	美国	12,176.0	27.3	866.0	178	41.5	140,102.0	74	5,708.0	234	18,286	406
367	341	皮西尼公司[41]	法国	12,133.5	(4.8)	310.8	319	—	9,894.9	407	2,679.3	363	33,960	325
368	317	铃木汽车公司[1]	日本	12,128.3	(9.1)	245.7	346	(17.6)	7,778.6	432	2,808.9	359	13,820[2]	440
369	307	大林公司	日本	12,117.7	(11.5)	95.5	406	(21.0)	17,006.7	296	2,302.3	390	12,184	448
370	251	东海银行	日本	12,103.8	(23.5)	116.1	399	(22.1)	261,870.5	37	7,992.3	164	11,407	454
371	371	浦项综合制铁公司	韩国	12,090.8	0.8	765.5	200	4.1	11,557.8	378	4,262.5	299	27,418	358
372	287	伊塔乌投资银行	巴西	12,045.7	(15.4)	432.1	278	46.8	43,907.1	167	2,482.3	372	48,680	253
373	447	马里奥特国际公司	美国	12,034.0	18.3	335.0	305	9.5	6,322.0	450	1,463.0	428	195,000	33
374	337	住友金属工业银行[1]	日本	11,970.5	(7.5)	32.7	440	(86.1)	18,697.6	279	4,019.4	311	34,290	321
375	332	积水公司[3]	日本	11,949.9	(8.3)	325.5	309	(16.1)	12,895.2	355	6,429.5	209	17,307	412
376	454	英国航空航天公司	英国	11,904.3	17.9	263.7	339	(45.3)	13,593.5	339	2,412.3	379	43,400	278
377	334	米格罗百货公司	瑞士	11,894.2	(8.7)	191.6	367	(8.3)	9,546.3	415	4,156.8	302	57,051	217
378	.	TELSTRA[G,10]	澳大利亚	11,889.6	(0.3)	1,202.9	126	(33.3)	16,846.5	298	6,440.7	208	76,990	157
379	409	雅培制药公司	美国	11,883.5	7.9	2,094.5	65	11.3	12,061.1	368	4,998.7	263	54,487	229
380	260	托尔尼奥保罗银行	意大利	11,870.9	(22.3)	98.5	405	(74.8)	145,045.6	72	5,502.9	244	22,614	382

1997 年世界最大的 500 家企业(十九)

收入位次 1997年	收入位次 1996年	公司名称	国别(地区)	收入 金额:百万美元	收入 比1996年变化(%)	利润 金额:百万美元	利润 位次	利润 比1996年变化(%)	资产 金额:百万美元	资产 位次	股东权益 金额:百万美元	股东权益 位次	雇员 人数	雇员 位次
381	376	奥雷阿尔公司	法国	11,843.2	0.4	682.9	216	(0.1)	10,771.9	397	5,002.4	262	47,242	258
382	456	联合保健公司	美国	11,794.0	17.1	460.0	272	29.3	7,623.0	437	4,534.0	282	30,000	342
383	347	九州电力公司[1]	日本	11,764.0	(6.3)	274.2	333	(22.1)	31,234.3	212	5,024.2	260	14,581[2]	436
384	284	罗克韦尔国际公司[4]	美国	11,759.0	(18.0)	644.0	220	(11.3)	7,971.0	430	4,811.0	273	45,000	267
385	411	自由相互保险公司	美国	11,670.0	6.4	521.0	256	2.0	44,891.0	164	6,771.7	201	23,000	381
386	360	大同人寿保险公司[1]	日本	11,665.2	(4.4)	391.6	286	(29.7)	40,092.5	181	1,092.4	450	22,464	383
387	461	伯根·伯伦斯维格公司[4]	美国	11,660.5	17.3	81.7	413	11.1	2,707.1	493	644.9	473	5,100	479
388	387	拉格代尔集团	法国	11,654.8	1.3	236.5	350	16.5	11,248.1	383	1,977.6	407	46,230	264
389	330	安田火灾海上保险公司[1]	日本	11,637.3	(10.8)	116.0	400	2.8	28,130.1	228	1,978.4	406	11,971	450
390	421	亨克尔公司[9]	德国	11,575.0	6.9	612.6	228	107.2	9,685.6	412	2,822.8	358	54,247	231
391	384	怡和有限公司	中国香港	11,521.6	(0.7)	324.9	311	8.2	11,949.8	371	3,761.0	319	175,000	42
392	443	联邦快递公司[26,50]	美国	11,519.8	12.1	361.2	295	17.4	7,625.5	436	2,962.5	352	107,827	100
393	478	无线电缆公司[1]	英国	11,496.5	19.8	2,115.0	63	96.9	21,853.2	261	5,188.2	257	46,550	260
394	160	日本长期信用银行[1]	日本	11,486.9	(45.3)	(1,211.0)	489	(800.5)	199,216.1	56	7,685.3	174	3,499[2]	488
395	437	塞夫韦商店[1]	英国	11,459.8	9.6	395.8	285	(15.3)	6,857.2	443	3,361.0	338	50,580	247
396	379	理光公司[1]	日本	11,432.2	(2.2)	245.5	347	(4.4)	12,452.1	363	3,562.1	324	63,600	190
397	426	麦当劳	美国	11,408.8	6.8	1,642.5	88	4.4	18,200.0	283	8,800.0	143	237,000	26
398	389	英国钢铁公司[1]	英国	11,407.8	(0.5)	371.1	294	(24.5)	12,925.3	354	7,740.5	172	50,000	248
399	460	强生控制器公司[4]	美国	11,387.4	13.8	288.5	326	22.9	6,048.6	455	1,687.9	418	72,300	171
400	.	微软公司[10]	美国	11,358.0	31.0	3,454.0	26	57.4	14,387.0	326	10,777.0	105	22,232	385
401	·	可口可乐企业	美国	11,278.0	42.4	171.0	376	50.0	17,487.0	291	1,782.0	412	56,000	223

1997 年世界最大的 500 家企业(二十)

收入位次 1997年	收入位次 1996年	公司名称	国别（地区）	收入 金额：百万美元	收入 比1996年变化（%）	利润 金额：百万美元	利润 位次	利润 比1996年变化（%）	资产 金额：百万美元	资产 位次	股东权益 金额：百万美元	股东权益 位次	雇员 人数	雇员 位次
402	462	澳大利亚新闻公司[10]	澳大利亚	11,262.3	13.4	563.5	241	(27.2)	30,981.3	213	15,606.8	52	28,220	353
403	348	川铁公司[1]	日本	11,240.7	(10.4)	(23.2)	455	(311.1)	5,678.7	459	311.9	483	3,308	489
404	405	富士摄影胶片公司[1]	日本	11,226.2	1.0	723.6	209	(4.5)	15,985.0	308	10,727.3	106	36,580	312
405	432	公众超级市场	美国	11,224.4	6.6	354.6	297	33.7	3,295.0	486	2,019.3	404	76,750	158
406	406	惠好公司	美国	11,210.0	0.9	342.0	303	(26.1)	13,075.0	349	4,649.0	278	35,778	316
407	486	阿斯达集团[51]	英国	11,096.1	17.9	419.8	281	18.0	6,087.0	454	3,345.4	339	76,619	160
408	416	安霍伊塞－布希公司	美国	11,066.2[E]	1.7	1,179.2	129	(0.9)	11,727.1	374	4,041.8	308	24,326	374
409	428	西方石油公司	美国	11,061.0[1,E]	4.8	(390.0)	474	(158.4)	15,282.0	320	4,286.0	297	12,380	446
410	463	美国"R"字玩具公司[3]	美国	11,037.8	11.1	490.1	262	14.7	7,963.1	431	4,427.9	289	93,000	123
411	459	太平洋联合公司	美国	11,014.0	9.6	432.0	279	(52.2)	28,764.0	224	8,225.0	156	52,000	237
412	385	国家石油产品公司[G,1]	马来西亚	10,995.4[E]	(4.8)	3,123.5	35	7.3	22,440.3	257	9,343.3	131	14,463	437
413	458	OJ1 制纸公司[1]	日本	10,987.1	9.2	89.6	409	(21.9)	13,464.8	345	3,421.2	332	14,044[2]	439
414	375	朝日玻璃公司[1]	日本	10,971.0	(7.6)	165.9	379	(22.7)	13,578.0	342	4,727.2	275	34,900	318
415	·	卡迪纳尔保健品公司[10]	美国	10,968.0	23.8	181.1	371	61.9	3,108.5	489	1,332.2	439	11,000	455
416	383	大日本印刷公司[1]	日本	10,888.5	(6.4)	460.6	271	(7.6)	10,878.9	391	6,640.4	205	32,682	330
417	·	日本殷田生命保险公司[1]	日本	10,851.7	30.9	211.5	359	(16.1)	27,434.0	234	54.7	493	11,614	453
418	425	金属股份公司[4]	德国	10,831.4	1.2	127.6	394	(0.7)	3,833.9	484	327.5	480	24,964	371
419	441	汤普森－拉莫－伍尔德里奇公司	美国	10,831.3	5.1	(48.5)	458	(110.1)	6,410.0	447	1,624.0	421	79,700	151
420	358	瑞士邮电总局[G,52]	瑞士	10,830.5	(11.9)	178.5	373	(11.7)	N.A		N.A		58,431	212
421	·	施伦伯格公司	荷属安的列斯	10,754.4	19.2	1,295.7	118	52.2	12,096.7	367	6,694.9	202	63,500	191

1997年世界最大的500家企业(二十一)

收入位次 1997年	收入位次 1996年	公司名称	国别(地区)	收入 金额:百万美元	收入 比1996年变化(%)	利润 金额:百万美元	利润 位次	利润 比1996年变化(%)	资产 金额:百万美元	资产 位次	股东权益 金额:百万美元	股东权益 位次	雇员 人数	雇员 位次
422	470	中国石油公司[G]	中国台湾	10,729.1[E]	9.3	384.6	290	39.0	15,633.3	312	8,354.8	153	19,873	397
423	418	富士重工业公司[1]	日本	10,622.8	(2.2)	250.2	342	(28.8)	6,783.4	444	1,266.1	442	19,113	401
424	430	CSX公司	美国	10,621.0	0.8	799.0	191	(6.5)	19,957.0	272	5,766.0	232	46,911	259
425	481	蒙特利尔银行[8]	加拿大	10,573.2	11.0	950.6	166	11.1	147,502.6	70	6,318.5	213	34,286	322
426	417	川崎重工业公司[1]	日本	10,567.6	(2.8)	151.2	385	(24.6)	9,170.6	418	1,567.6	423	26,102	366
427	398	住友电气工业公司[1]	日本	10,566.6	(5.8)	269.8	335	(5.6)	10,716.3	398	4,020.1	310	59,112	207
428	378	德州仪器公司	美国	10,562.0	(9.8)	1,805.0	80	2,765.1	10,849.0	394	5,914.0	226	44,140	273
429	495	达信公司	美国	10,544.0	13.7	558.0	243	120.6	18,610.0	280	3,228.0	344	64,000	187
430	·	KINGFISHER[3]	英国	10,486.6	14.7	633.0	222	44.9	6,093.8	453	2,894.1	356	49,225	250
431	401	高岛屋百货公司[23]	日本	10,463.9	(8.7)	67.7	417	(19.1)	7,002.0	442	1,699.5	416	17,101	416
432	394	凸片印刷公司[1]	日本	10,461.2	(7.5)	386.0	289	101.1	9,753.5	408	5,005.2	261	34,402	319
433	374	宇宙石油公司[1]	日本	10,453.6[E]	(12.1)	43.5	434	(44.6)	9,576.4	414	1,430.2	430	5,678	477
434	388	旭日化学工业公司[1]	日本	10,441.0	(8.9)	169.5	378	(24.7)	9,050.3	419	3,413.9	333	27,792	355
435	435	伯克什·哈索维公司	美国	10,430.0	(0.7)	1,901.6	73	(23.6)	56,110.9	137	31,455.2	11	38,000	304
436	392	中日本铁路公司[1]	日本	10,414.0	(8.3)	265.8	337	(17.7)	45,654.8	161	3,554.0	325	22,447[2]	384
437	427	法国天然气公司[G]	法国	10,339.2	(10.2)	313.2	317	(42.3)	16,731.7	299	2,419.0	378	30,257	339
438	407	松下电工公司[21]	日本	10,333.0	(6.6)	291.1	325	0.7	10,024.9	404	4,220.1	300	36,363	313
439	434	兴业银行	比利时	10,310.5	(1.9)	477.0	267	(2.2)	159,571.3	65	3,699.8	320	27,200	360
440	·	共和工业公司	美国	10,305.6	335.7	439.7	275	—	10,527.3	401	3,484.4	330	56,000	223
441	472	通用电气公司[1]	英国	10,294.4	(0.1)	1,111.7	140	71.7	9,731.7	409	4,344.2	295	71,963	172
442	·	泛加轮油管道公司	加拿大	10,287.6	30.0	330.1	306	5.9	10,182.6	402	2,987.3	35	3,042	491

1997 年世界最大的 500 家企业(二十二)

收入位次		公司名称	国别(地区)	收入		利润			资产		股东权益		雇员	
1997 年	1996 年			金额:百万美元	比 1996 年变化(%)	金额:百万美元	位次	比 1996 年变化(%)	金额:百万美元	位次	金额:百万美元	位次	人数	位次
443	455	大西洋和太平洋茶叶公司[23]	美国	10,262.2	1.7	53.0	421	(13.7)	2,995.3	490	926.6	462	52,400	236
444	465	西北航空公司	美国	10,225.8	3.5	596.5	233	11.3	9,336.2	416	(311.0)	494	48,984	252
445	390	屈曼纸业公司	芬兰	10,211.2	(10.8)	805.6	186	272.4	12,448.8	364	4,843.4	270	33,814	327
446	·	法国航空集团[G,1]	法国	10,185.7	15.4	314.4	316	—	N.A.		N.A.		N.A.	
447	422	雪印乳业公司[1]	日本	10,159.3	(5.8)	32.8	439	(30.2)	4,163.2	480	1,043.5	452	14,938	431
448	·	LOWE'S[3]	美国	10,136.9	17.9	357.5	296	22.4	5,219.3	466	2,600.6	367	58,504	211
449	·	诺基亚[9]	芬兰	10,134.9	18.4	1,205.7	124	69.8	7,663.1	435	3,951.8	313	36,647	311
450	413	川崎钢铁公司[1]	日本	10,132.4	(7.4)	68.9	416	(2.6)	16,242.8	307	3,615.9	321	25,000	369
451	452	英国邮政兑局[G,31]	英国	10,106.4	—	572.7	238	—	9,011.7	421	N.A.		193.633	34
452	451	芝加哥第一国民银行	美国	10,098.0	(0.2)	1,525.0	94	6.2	114,096.0	86	7,960.0	165	33,962	324
453	380	日本西友公司[23]	日本	10,074.6	(13.7)	(468.6)	476	—	11,211.7	385	122.1	491	19,752[2]	398
454	476	吉列公司	美国	10,062.1	3.8	1,427.2	102	50.4	10,864.0	393	4,841.0	271	44,000	274
455	491	乔治·威斯顿公司	加拿大	10,055.1	7.9	176.2	375	0.5	4,107.5	481	1,227.1	445	83,000	137
456	424	西日本铁路公司[1]	日本	10,013.1	(6.7)	162.4	380	(48.7)	19,739.8	274	2,488.4	371	44,581	272
457	467	斯堪的亚集团	瑞典	10,011.5	1.5	445.3	273	162.0	36,626.1	195	1,770.4	413	9,709	462
458	382	卡里普罗公司	意大利	9,993.6	(14.3)	316.4	315	296.8	120,639.9	80	5,931.9	224	24,572	373
459	393	昭和壳牌石油公司	日本	9,984.0[E]	(12.0)	52.8	426	(5.2)	8,075.0	428	1,549.6	424	4,618	483
460	·	GASUNIE	荷兰	9,946.9	(11.3)	41.0	437	(13.6)	3,206.0	487	197.3	488	1,639	496
461	403	三菱信托银行[1]	日本	9,934.8	(10.7)	532.3	252	434.2	142,221.1	73	5,899.4	227	5,797[2]	476

1997年世界最大的500家企业(二十三)

收入位次 1997年	收入位次 1996年	公司名称	国别(地区)	收入 金额:百万美元	收入 比1996年变化(%)	利润 金额:百万美元	利润 位次	利润 比1996年变化(%)	资产 金额:百万美元	资产 位次	股东权益 金额:百万美元	股东权益 位次	雇员 人数	雇员 位次
462	433	意大利商业银行	意大利	9,921.5	(5.6)	243.7	348	(0.5)	115,088.3	85	4,947.7	265	28,383	352
463	184	SEPI[G]	西班牙	9,916.4	—	2,533.7	53	—	16,599.3	303	5,629.3	237	78,000	154
464	361	罗马银行	意大利	9,913.7	(18.7)	(212.1)	469	(369.4)	117,286.9	82	5,896.1	228	30,124	341
465	423	埃德卡中心有限	德国	9,887.3	(8.3)	46.8	430	19.3	2,350.9	496	351.6	479	754	498
466	449	教宝人寿保险公司[1]	韩国	9,821.5	(3.4)	41.2	436	—	14,135.8	329	251.0	484	9,457	464
467	468	美中美食品公司[53]	美国	9,818.4[1]	(0.3)	344.1	302	(40.7)	6,100.0	452	1,042.0	453	45,000	267
468	453	法国宇航[G]	法国	9,767.5	(3.3)	243.0	349	53.1	12,016.6	369	876.0	467	37,673	308
469	431	三菱物业公司[1]	日本	9,743.2	(7.5)	82.0	412	(37.3)	12,592.4	362	2,342.6	385	34,000	323
470	474	英之杰有限公司	英国	9,716.4	(0.7)	12.8	446	(63.6)	5,307.2	464	1,300.4	440	37,889	306
471	·	国泰生命保险公司	中国台湾	9,695.7	9.5	642.9	221	69.6	22,729.2	254	1,974.2	408	N.A.	
472	412	半岛－东方航运公司	英国	9,693.8	(11.5)	545.5	247	39.4	10,590.6	399	4,637.5	279	58,620	210
473	·	西北银行公司	美国	9,659.7	8.7	1,351.0	111	17.1	88,540.2	110	7,022.2	197	55,729	225
474	487	西屋电气公司[54]	美国	9,632.0'	2.5	549.0	246	1,730.0	16,715.0	301	8,080.0	159	51,444	240
475	·	富国银行	美国	9,608.0	10.1	1,155.0	134	7.8	97,456.0	100	12,889.0	75	33,100	329
476	·	DDI[1]	日本	9,599.3	6.4	67.7	418	—	9,724.3	410	1,637.2	420	6,427	474
477	·	新斯科舍银行[8]	加拿大	9,594.2	5.6	1,102.8	141	40.9	138,500.1	76	6,669.8	204	38,648	298
478	·	ENTERGY	美国	9,561.7	33.5	247.7	344	(41.0)	27,000.7	237	6,693.5	203	17,198	413
479	498	麻省相互人寿保险公司	美国	9,551.2	3.5	351.8	299	22.2	63,088.0	131	2,873.4	357	7,360	470
480	496	孟山都公司	美国	9,457.0[1]	2.1	470.0	269	22.1	10,774.0	396	4,104.0	305	21,900	388
481	396	三井不动产公司[1]	日本	9,439.4	(16.3)	(256.8)	471	—	23,297.8	253	3,875.1	316	19,488	400
482	373	海岸公司	美国	9,398.6[E]	(21.2)	301.5	323	(25.1)	11,625.2	376	3,282.4	341	13,200	445
483	·	H.J.亨氏公司[51]	美国	9,357.0	2.7	301.9	322	(54.2)	8,437.8	425	2,440.4	375	44,700	271

1997年世界最大的500家企业(二十四)

收入位次		公司名称	国别(地区)	收入		利润			资产		股东权益		雇员	
1997年	1996年			金额：百万美元	比1996年变化(%)	金额：百万美元	位次	比1996年变化(%)	金额：百万美元	位次	金额：百万美元	位次	人数	位次
484	·	诺威奇联合公司[55]	英国	9,285.0	—	439.0	276	—	86,137.0	112	8,388.8	152	16,325	423
485	440	废物管理公司	美国	9,273.4	(10.2)	(1,176.1)	488	(712.3)	13,589.1	340	1,345.7	436	58,900	209
486	488	熊谷组[1]	日本	9,240.6	(1.7)	(1,872.0)	495	—	12,862.7	356	213.5	487	10,000	459
487	·	爱迪生国际公司	美国	9,235.1	8.1	700.0	212	(2.4)	25,101.0	246	5,527.0	243	14,085	438
488	420	国民劳动银行	意大利	9,198.4	(15.2)	(1,644.9)	493	(1,775.4)	102,682.7	95	5,834.3	230	24,719	372
489	·	LIMITED[3]	美国	9,188.8	6.3	217.4	355	(49.9)	4,268.2	477	2,045.0	401	137,100	63
490	·	耐克公司[26]	美国	9,186.5	42.0	795.8	192	43.9	5,361.2	463	3,155.8	347	21,800	389
491	438	CEA工业公司[G]	法国	9,184.6	(11.6)	325.2	310	(0.0)	24,521.0	247	3,525.8	328	42,106	285
492	·	诺思罗普·格鲁曼公司	美国	9,153.0	13.4	407.0	283	73.9	9,677.0	413	2,623.0	365	52,000	237
493	490	德高沙公司[4]	德国	9,148.2	(1.9)	226.7	353	15.2	5,271.4	465	1,251.1	443	25,736	367
494	471	农场产业[30,56]	美国	9,147.5	(6.5)	N.A.		—	2,645.3	495	822.0	469	14,600	435
495	442	意大利信贷银行	意大利	9,130.6	(11.4)	282.2	327	54.4	99,986.1	97	4,374.8	294	23,903	377
496	·	澳大利亚－新西兰银行[4]	澳大利亚	9,115.7	3.9	788.0	195	(8.4)	100,100.3	96	5,027.4	259	35,926	315
497	·	高露洁	美国	9,056.7	3.5	740.4	206	16.6	7,538.7	439	2,178.6	396	37,800	307
498	473	小松公司[1]	日本	8,994.3	(7.8)	156.7	382	(2.8)	11,710.9	375	3,931.0	314	26,871	362
499	·	太平洋健康系统公司	美国	8,982.7	—	(21.7)	453	—	4,868.0	471	2,062.2	400	9,700	463
500	466	太阳公司	美国	8,968.0[E]	(9.2)	263.0	340	—	4,667.0	475	1,462.0	429	10,937	456
		总计		11,453,516.5		452,032.6			34,187,773.2		3,724,138.3		36,770,153	

定义及解释

收入额及利润额

本表中各公司均应公布其财务数字并向政府部门报告部分或全部数字。本表包括了填报10K表格的美国私营公司和合伙公司，收入额包括至统计之日止中断了的业务收入。商业银行和储蓄机构的收入额含利息收入和无自收入。保险公司的收入额含保险费及年金收入、投资收入和资本损益，但不包含保证金。收入额包括合并的子公司的数字，但营业额除外。

本表中的利润额均为税后利润，已经除去非常贷款或应付款，并减去因财务统计方法变化而引起的重复计算。括号中的数字为亏损数字。利润下降幅度超过100%，反映了从1996年盈利转为1997年亏损。

统计中的财政年度，除特别指明外，均截至到1998年3月31日。外国公司的收入额和利润额均按公司财政年度内的官方平均汇率折算为美元（截止到1997年12月31日，除特别指明外）。

资产和股东权益

表中资产额为公司财政年度末的数字。股东权益为同一天的股本、实收资本和存留收益之和。未包括少数股权益。

外国公司的数字均按各公司的财政年度末的官方汇率折算为美元。

雇员人数

人数均按公司公布的年底实际人数或者全年平均人数统计。

脚注

E　已扣除营业税。

G　国有公司。

·　包括10%以上的中断了的业务的收入。

★　反映了至少10%的特别信贷。

1. 财政年度截至到1998年3月31日的数字。
2. 仅含母公司。
3. 财政年度截至到1998年1月31日的数字。
4. 财政年度截至到1997年9月30日的数字。
5. 包含1996年朗讯科技公司（1997年排名：第117位）终断经营时的收　入额。
6. 1997年9月5日兼并温特图尔集团（1996年排名：第133位）。
7. 1997年8月1日兼并麦道公司（1996年排名：第303位）。
8. 财政年度截止到1997年10月31日的数字。
9. 根据国际会议标准编制的数字。
10. 财政年度截止到1997年6月30日的数字。
11. 于1998年3月16日由菲利普电器公司改为现名。
12. 相互保险公司，此数字根据美国通用会计原则编制。
13. 1997年的数字无法与1996年比较，因为该公司由法定报告转为按通用会计原则报告。
14. 于1998年1月1日由SUNKYONG改为现名。
15. 在1997年6月19日兼并Cie de Suez公司（1996年排名：第227位）之后，由Lyonnais des Eaux该为现名。
16. 于1998年5月29日兼并Aachener & Munchener公司（1997年排名：第343位）。
17. 于1997年8月4日兼并NYNEX公司（1996年排名：第313位）。
18. 由教师年会和人寿保险公司（1996年排名：第304位）及学院退休股本基金（1996年排名：第301位）的法定财务报表数据合并购成。在上年度，这些公司的数据是分别报告的。
19. 不包括CIC集团，该集团与1998年第二季度已被出售。
20. 于1998年5月18日由Cie General des Eaux该为现名。
21. 财政年度截止到1997年11月30日的数字。
22. 于1997年5月31日在兼并Mogan Staniey Group（1996年排名：第325位）之后，由Dean Winter Discover改名为Mogan Staniey Winter Discover，并于1998年3月24日改为现名。

23. 财政年度截止到 1998 年 3 月 24 日的数字。
24. 于 1997 年 4 月 1 日兼并太平洋电讯集团（1996 年排名：第 479 位）。
25. 于 1998 年 6 月 11 日兼并数字设备公司（1997 年排名：第 331 位）。
26. 财政年度截止到 1997 年 5 月 31 日的数字。
27. 按俄罗斯会计标准编制的数字。
28. 财政年度截止到 1998 年 3 月 7 日的数字。
29. 不包括境外雇　员人数。
30. 财政年度截止到 1997 年 8 月 31 日的数字。
31. 财政年度截止到 1997 年 3 月 31 日的数字。
32. 财政年度截止日期由 9 月 30 日改为 12 月 31 日。
33. 于 1997 年 12 月 12 日由 Grand Metropolitan 改为现名。
34. 于 1998 年 6 月 1 日与 General Accident 公司（1977 年排名：第 258 位）合并组成 CGU 公司。
35. 于 1998 年 6 月 29 日被瑞士银行（1997 年排名：第 234 位）兼并。
36. 财政年度截止到 1998 年 2 月 20 日的数字。
37. 财政年度截止到 1996 年 12 月 31 日的数字。
38. 于 1998 年 6 月 29 日兼并瑞士联合银行（1997 年排名：第 190 位）。
39. 财政年度截止到 1997 年 6 月 31 的数字。
40. 于 1998 年 6 月 29 日由 Royal PTT Nederland 改为现名。
41. 根据美国通用会计原则编制的数字。
42. 于 1998 年 6 月 1 日与商业联合公司（1997 年排名：第 189 位）合并组成 CGU 公司。
43. 于 1997 年由合作公司转变为证券公司，因此无法与上一年度的数字相比较。
44. 财政年度截止到 1997 年 11 月 15 的数字。
45. 于 1998 年 6 月 11 日被康柏电脑公司（1997 年排名：第 132 位）兼并。
46. 于 1997 年 2 月 12 日与母公司英国煤气公司（1996 年排名：第 271 位）脱离。
47. 于 1997 年 2 月 6 日由 Halifax Building Society 改为现名。
48. 于 1998 年 5 月 29 日被 Assicurazioni Generali（1997 年排名：第 85 位）兼并。
49. 财政年度截止到 1997 年 2 月 28 日的数字。
50. 于 1998 年 1 月 27 日由联邦快递公司改为现名。
51. 财政年度截止到 1997 年 4 月 30 日的数字。
52. 于 1998 年 1 月 1 日由 PTT Suisse 公司改为现名。
53. 于 1998 年 1 月 1 日由 CPC International 公司改为现名。
54. 于 1997 年 12 月 1 日由 Westinghouse Electric Gorp 改为现名。
55. 于 1997 年由互助公司转变为证券公司，因此无法与上一年度的数字相比较。
56. 合作方仅提供了净边际利　润数据，因此无法与表中的利润数据相比较。

资料来源：美国《财富》杂志

（对外贸易经济合作部国际贸易经济合作研究院文献信息中心）

广 告 索 引

中国煤炭工业进出口集团公司

CNCIEC China National Coal Industry Import and Export (Group) Corp.

中国煤炭工业进出口集团公司(以下简称中煤进出口集团公司)原为中国煤炭工业进出口总公司，成立于1982年7月，是经国务院批准的中国煤炭行业从事对外贸易的经济合作和全国性公司。

中煤进出口集团公司实行工贸结合，经营煤炭生产、销售、运输和进出口贸易；经营煤矿设备、矿产品进出口及工程、技术咨询；承办中外合资、合作经营、生产、加工、工程项目，并开展委托代理、易货、补偿和转口贸易、对外承包工程和劳务输出等业务。

1998年底，国家规定，党政机关与所办经济实体和管理的直属企业脱钩。据此，国家煤炭局提出了重组中煤进出口集团公司并交由国家管理的方案。国家主管部门于1999年4月上旬批复同意，并于5月下旬任命了中煤进出口集团公司领导成员，新的集团公司随即正式运营。

至此，重组的中煤进出口集团公司共有二级单位86个，其中全资子公司33个，分公司7个，办事处2个，控股、参股企业12个、境外办事处6个，境外独资公司3个，境外参股公司2个，另有管理部室、业务部室21个；集团公司共有员工55611人，离退休人员12382人。公司资产总额184亿元，净资产53亿元，资产负债率为71%。目前，集团公司年销售收入150多亿元，进出口总额超过10亿美元，煤炭年贸易量4500万吨(其中出口约3100万吨)，进口约100万吨，国内贸易约1300万吨)。重组后，集团公司的实力得到进一步增强，初步形成了产运销结合、内外贸相统一的格局。目前中煤进出口集团公司已与世界上50多个国家和地区建立了经济贸易合作关系，形成了比较完善的国内国际供销渠道和信息服务网络，在国内外享有良好的信誉。

今后，中煤进出口集团公司将一如既往地奉行“用户第一、服务第一、信誉第一“的宗旨，谒诚欢迎国内外各界人士、新老朋友与我们广泛合作，共展鸿图。

China National Coal Industry Import and Export (Group) Corp.("CNCIEC") was established in July 1982 as a national company. Approved by the State Council,its business is international trade and economic cooperation within the coal sector.

CNCIEC trades coal nationally and is a major force in global markes. It is responsible for the import and export of coal mining equipment and minerals. Moreoverm,it is responsible for project engineering,technological consultation,joint ventures,production trade, and transshipment,international contraction and labor export.

CNCIEC was reorganized in 1999, and a new team of leadership being formed. Up to now,there are total 86 dired subsidiaries(among which,33 fully owned companies,7 branches,2 representative offices,12 partially owned companies 6 overseas branches,3 fully owned overseas companies and 2 partially owned companies in the group corp,and it also has several business departments in the head office.

The total and net assets of the corp.are RMB 18.4 billion and 5.3 billion respectively,forming the liability ratio of 71%.

With its established economic and trade cooperation with over 50 countries in the world,CNCIEC is among China's leading foreign trade companies measured either by volume of export or volume of import and export,and has undertaken a strategic initiative to strengthen its postion in global trading markets while diversifying its operations on a national basis.Whether at home or abroad.CNCIEC will continue to enhanec its reputation as a responsible member of the commercial community.

地址：北京市安定门外大街乙88号　　邮编：100011
Add:CNCIEC BULDING,B-88,ANDINGMENWAI AVE.,DONGCHENG DISTRICT,BEIJING,CHINA
电话(Tel): 010-64287365　　传真(Fax): 010-64287166

业绩突出　享誉世界 **Significant achievements　Worldwide reputation**

国家建材局蚌埠玻璃工业设计研究院
暨中国玻璃发展中心

Bengbu Design & Research Institute for Glass Industry of the State Administration of Building Materials Industry
China Glass Development Center

院长：戴志良
President: Dai Zhi Liang

该院系国家建材局直属的综合甲级设计研究院，拥有各类专业技术人员约550多人，仅高级工程师就有165人。具有13项包括工程设计、总承包、监理等业务范围的甲级资格，更由于该院在建材工业设计院中率先成功地将中国浮法技术推向国际市场，被中国政府授予技术和成套设备、材料出口权。

几十年来，该院先后完成数百项大中型项目和非标设备设计，完成科研开发项目近300项，并有多项设计、科研成果获国家和省部级奖励。截止1998年底，该院完成出口技术、成套设备等合同25项，累计完成出口创汇额达6000万美元。

由中国政府和联合国计划开发署合建的“中国玻璃发展中心”设在该院，现与30多个国家的客商建立了广泛的联系，并形成信息网络，使该院在国际玻璃行业具有较高的知名度。

目前，该院正进一步加大出口经营力度，充分利用设计单位改企建制、重组联合的契机为努力把该院建成跨国经营的国际工程咨询集团公司而奋斗。

Bengbu Design & Research Institute for Glass Industry is a first-class comprehensive design & research Institute under the State Administration of Building Materials Industry.And now it has approximately 550 technical staff in different specialties,among which, 165 are senior engineers. The Institute has gained thirteen first-class qualifications,including engineering design, turn-key projects and construction supervision, etc.Since the Institute has taken the lead among the design institutes for building materials industry to successfully export China Float Glass Technology to the international market, it was authorized by the Chinese govermment the right to export the technology and complete set of equipment & materials.

For decades of Years,the Institute has accomplished hundreds of engineering designs for large and medium scale projects and non-standard equipment,nearly three hundred scientific research items and has won many national and provincial level awards for designs and scientific research achievements.By the end of 1998, the Institute had implemented 25 contracts concerning the export of the technology and complete set of equipment with accumulated export earnings totaling USD60 millions.

China Glass Development Center(CGDC), subsidiary to the Institute, is jointly set up by the Chinese government and United Nations Development Program(UNDP) and has maintained broad and close relationship with the customers in over thirty countries, forming its own information network and making the Institute well-known in world glass community.

Now the Institute is intensifying its export & overseas operation and taking the opportunity of restructuring and making great efforts to become an international engineering consulting group company engaging in mulit-national businesses.

院总部办公大楼
Head Quarters Building

地址：安徽省蚌埠市涂山路1032号
电话：0552-4081011
传真：4081941
邮编：233018
电子信箱：bgdr@mail.ahbbptt.net.cn

Address: 1032 Tu Shan Road, Bengbu, Anhui, PR
Tel: 0552-4081011
Fax: 4081941
Post Code: 233018
E-mail: bgdr @ mail.ahbbptt.net.cn

我院设计并进行工程总承包的印尼TS—3浮法玻璃生产线
The turn-key project of TS-3 float glass production line in Indohesia

中国仪器进出口总公司

China National Instruments Import and Export Corporation (Instrimpex)

中国仪器进出口总公司成立于1955年，是我国最早从事进出口业务的国有大型专业外贸总公司之一。

通过长期不懈的努力，中仪总公司已从一个单纯的进口贸易公司发展成为一个以进出口业务为核心、集国际招投标及采购业务、技术服务和维修、内贸、房地产、物业管理和实业等多种经营为一体的实力雄厚的综合型企业，15家子公司及5家独资、合资制造厂分布在全国不同的省份，在美国、欧洲、非洲、中东、日本、香港等国家和地区设立了10多个海外事处、子公司。1996-1998年，在全国外经贸行业500强企业评比中，中仪总司一直保持在第26位以上的水平。

四十多年来，公司为中国的交通运输、有线无线通讯、广播电视、环保、航、科研、电力、工业制造业等领域引进了大量先进的大型和成套设备、生产和关键 技术 ，从全国第一条海底电缆，第一条微波干线到第一座卫星地面，从第一套大型计算机到全国各大银行、海关、机场的计算机网络系统，从一套空中交通管制系统到各类大型成套设备和工业生产线进口，无不凝聚着仪人的智慧和劳。

中仪总公司自1987年恢复出口以来，一直重视扩大出口，注重效益。通过力，出口产品从一般轻工机电产品发展到成套设备生产线，向国际通讯卫星织出口中标的卫星网遥测、遥控、跟踪服务项目，性能良好，受到国际卫星织的好评，目前正在积极开展大宗产品出口，焦碳、羊绒的出口已有一定规；大力开展各种大型成套设备出口，电站项目、整套广播通讯发射设备、电输变电设备、通信设施、建筑工程承包等已初见成效，同时正与海外公司洽在当地建厂，搞散件装配业务。

中仪总公司在专业外贸公司中是最早与外商合作开展进口产品售后服务业的，目前在全国各省、市与外商合作设立了120多个技术服务维修站、零配寄售库，拥有一支由近千名专业技术人员构成的技术精湛、服务优秀的队伍，以技术服务业在外经贸行业中独树一帜。售后服务业初具网络。

中仪总公司以独资、合资形式设立的制造业，其产主要面向海外出口。位于北京高新技术开发区的京英斯泰克视频技术公司1999年开发、生产和销出中国第一部6信道卫星电视转播车。中仪总公司天津、上海的制造厂生产的各种不锈钢炊具、餐刀具全部出口，在美国进入大型连锁店和超市。

中仪总公司企经营宗旨是：团服务、开拓、高

在市场经济来越成熟的今中仪总公司在营上确立以进出口和技术、实业为主，展内贸和其它服务的产业结构。到2003年中仪总公司将有一个更趋完善的进出口市场体系、售和技术服务网络体系，有一个更具规模的在海内外以合资参股形式设立的企业，有一个具备一定规模的海外市场占有率，有一只更能适应市场经济的优秀经营管理干部队伍，使中仪公司有持续发展的能力。

Established in 1955,China National Instruments Import and Export Corporation (Instrimpex) is a specialized national foreign trade corporation.With its business operations started from 1955,it is one of the first specialized foreign trade corporations engaged in the impotr and export business.During the past four decades,Instrimpex has imported large quantities of advanced equipment,production lines and technologies for China in the fields of transportation,post and telecommunications,machine-building and electronics,petroleum exploitation,geololgical prospecting,environmental protection,aviation,scientific research and power industry.Many of China's first sets of machinery,electronic devices and instruments were imported by Instrimpex,including the first satellite earth station,the first air traffic control system,the first submarine cable,the first 1 million volt super high-voltage elecric power transmission and transformation equipment,the largest color television center equipment,the largest seismic data processing system and the largest computer system for customs administration in China.

Through the unremitting efforts by several generations of Instrimpex people,the corporation has grown from an import-oriented company to a comprehensive enterprise with strong financial strength which focuses on import and export as its core business and conducts diversified operations in international tendering and procurement,pre-and after-sales services for imported and exported produxts,real estate,manufacturing, exhibition, videol manufacturing products and information service,etc.

Recent years have witnessed a constant increase in Instrimpex's import and export volume and turnover,and its operation scale has always been among the top ones in China's 500 large foreign trade enterprises.After several decades of development,Instrimpex has basically formed a pattern of regionalized and network operation and owns fixed assets worth hundreds of millions of US dollars including Instrimpex Building and Beijing Instec Video Technology Company. The corporation has 15 subsidiaries located in different provinces of China and more than 10 overseas offices and subsidiaries in countries and regions like the United State, Germany, Commonwealth of Independent State, Ghana, Japan and Hong Kong. In addition, it also owns several joint ventures in Tianjin, Shanghai,Ningbo and Guangzhou.

Since the resumption of export trade in 1987, Instrimpex has always attached importance to the expansion of export scale and economic efficiency. Through its own efforts, export products have been upgraded from general light industrial goods, machinery and electronic products to complete plants and production lines. Among these products, Beijing Instec Video Technology Company has produced the Chinese first satellite TV broadcasting equipment, which has been exported abroad; and the project of remote metering and control and trace services for satellite network which has won the bid of International Communication Satellite Organization has been well received by the International Satellite Organization due to its good performance. At present, Instrimpex is actively conducting the export business of staple products such as coke and cashmere, which are now taking shape, and Instrimpex is developing vigorously the export of the large complete plants and equipments. The projects being negotiated include power station project, complete sets of broadcasting and communication launching equipments, electric prwer transmission equipments, constructing projects contracting etc. Instrimpex is now negotiating with foreign companies on components and parts assembling in their countries.

Instrimpex is the very first specialized national foreign trade corporation to have cooperated with foreign companies in providing after-sale services for imported products. At present, Instrimpex has set up over 120 technical service stations and spare parts and components consignment depots in various provinces and cities in cooperation with foreign companies, staffed with a contingent of nearly1000 highly skilled professional technicians who are able to provide excellent services. In order to promote the development of export business, the corporation will also establish overseas maintenance stations and consignment depots. At present, the corporation has formed a service system combining maintenance, training, technical exchanges. Product exhibition, spare parts and components consignment and system integration. The technical service provided by Instrimpex is unique in China's foreign economic and trade sector.

Instrimpex has set up manufacturing facilities in Beijing, Shanghai and Tianjin,some wholly-owned by Instrimpex, others with controlling or non-controlling equity participation. Beijing Instec video Technology Company located in Beijing Shangdi High-tech Industrial Development Zone can produce dozen product lines, such as television relay trucks, with qualities reaching world advanced levels for like products. This type of large television relay trucks have been ordered by China Central Television Station (CCTV) and many provincial and municipal television stations. This product demonstrated a good performance when used in the relay station set up by CCTV in Shenzhen during the celebrations for HongKong's return to the motherland. Beijing Instec Video Technology Company has become a highly-reputed enterprise in China's radio and television technology industry.

In the corporate spirit of unity, service, exploration and high efficiency, Instrimpex is looking forward to conducting more extensive cooperation and exchanges with enterprises both at home and abroad on the basis of abiding by the contract and honoring one's commitment

地址：北京西直门外大街6号中仪大厦 邮编：100044
Add: N0.27 Shang Di Eest Road, Haidian District
Beijing 100044
电话(Tel): 86-10-68330301, 68317393
传真(Fax): 010-68318380, 68330528
电子邮件(E-mail):zcb@instrimpex.com.cn

中国国际贸易中心　中国与世界相会之地

China World Trade Center Where One Billion People Meet the World

中国国际贸易中心是目前国内规模巨大的综合性高档商务体，也是仅次于纽约世贸中心的世界第二大世贸中心。地处北京建国门外大街与东三环的交汇处，北京中央商务区的核心地段，占地面积12公顷，一、二期工程总投资6.2亿美元，总建筑面积56万平方米。

国贸中心始建于1985年，1990年8月30日全面开业，主要从事旅游、商务服务设施的建设、经营与管理。

国贸中心主要设施包括：两座38层的顶级写字楼；五星级的中国大饭店和四星级的国贸饭店；两幢30层的国贸南北公寓；国贸商城；展览中心，以及会议中心、娱乐健身设施、国贸花园、多层停车场和各种风味餐厅等，集办公、住宿、餐饮、展览、会议、宴会，购物、娱乐等多种功能于一体，被誉为“城中之城”。

国贸中心的管理机构中国国际贸易中心有限公司于1999年年初成功地在上海证券交易所挂牌上市，发行了“中国国贸”A种股票，开始了企业资本经营与实业经营相结

地址：中国北京建国门外大街一号　邮编：100004

China World Trade Center is the largest A Grade integrated commercial development in China. It is also the second largest trade center in the world,after the World Trad Center in New York.Located at the intersection of Jian Guo Men Wai Avenue and Eastern Third Ring Road,the center boasts a total floor space of 12 hectares ideally placed in Beijing's busiest central business district.The total construction area of 560 thousand square meters represents an overall investment in phases 1 and 2 of 62 million US dollars.

Construction of China World Trade Center began in 1985, the project officially opened for business on August 30, 1990.Core business of the center encompasses development and management of hotel, commercial and residential property services.

The main facilities at the China World Trade Center include: two 38-foor grade A office towers:the 5-star China World Hotel and 4-star Traders Hotel two 30-floored apartment blocks, the China World Shopping Mall, an exhibition and conference center, recreation & fitness facilities, the China World garden, multi level car parks and a wide variety of restaurants catering to a multitude of d different tastes. The Center offers a complete host of functions from offices, hotels,apartments,exhibitions and conferences,to restaurants, banqueting entertainment and shopping. It really is "a city within a city".

The China World Trade Center Co.Ltd., owner of China World Trade Center,was successfully listed on the Shanghai Stock Exchange in early 1999,with A shares issued in the name"CWTC".The floatation marked the drawing of a new ear for the company, signifying its venture into the capital markets and paving way for future

重庆国际贸易中心、重庆外商服务公司

CHONGQING INTERNATIONAL TRADE CENTRE(CQITC)
CHONGQING FOREIGN MAERCHANTS SERVICE COMPANY(CQFMSCO)

重庆国际贸易中心、重庆外商服务公司是两块牌子、一套班子，隶属重庆市外经贸委的综合国有进出口企业，是中国对外服务行业协会常务理事单位。

重庆国际贸易中心：自营和代理除国家统一联合经营的出口商品和国家实行核定公司经营的进出口商品以外的其他商品和技术的进出口业务；经营进出口加工和“三来一补”业务；经营对销贸易和转口贸易。

重庆外商服务公司：重庆市人民政府(1991)20号令指定为外国商社在渝设立常驻代表机构办理审批手续和提供综合服务及管理的外事单位。

COITC, CQFMSCO directly under the command of Chongqing Foreign Economic Relations and Trade Commission is a comprehensive state-owned foreign trade enterprise which operates in two names under one organization,and also a member of council of China Association of Foreign Service Trades.

CQITC:Dealing in and accepting agency of import and export of commodity and technology except those which are unified by state organization and companies assigned; Dealing in processing with given materials,assembling with provided parts, production according to samples and compensation trade;Dealing in counter trade and transit trade.

CQFMSCO is authorized by Chongqing Municipal Government to provide approval procedures for foreign enterprises which intend to set up representative offices in Chongqing and to provide comprehensive and qualified services for foreign enterprises.

地址：中国·重庆市江北区建新北路41-1号　邮编：400020
电话：023-67504232　传真：023-67513402
E-mail: Guomao@ec.com.cn
进出口部电话：023-67513597　023-67515467
外商服务公司电话：023-67514768　023-67514908

ADD: 41-1 JianXin North Road,JiangBei District,Chongqing, China P.C.400020
TEL: 023-67853232　FAX: 023-67850402
E-mail: Guomao@ec.com.cn
Business Department: 023-67726597　023-67854467
CQFMSCO: 023-67744768　023-67744908

佛山普立华照相机有限公司
Premier Camera (China) Ltd.

佛山普立华照相机有限公司是于1990年5月批准创办的中外合资企业。经过九年的矢志努力，目前公司已拥有生产场地2万多平方米，员工3000多人，主要生产普及型系列和APS系列等自动照相机，月产能力达80—90万台，为当今世界产量较大的自动照相机制造企业之一。产品主要销往欧共体、美国、日本、东南亚等150个国家及地区。

公司自创办以来，不断致力于员工队伍的素质建设，特别是工程技术人才的充实、培养和提高。同时，每年都不断增添自动检测和实验仪器与设备，配套和完善工程、生产、品保等体系，并于1997年通过了ISO9002质量体系国际认证。公司全面实行电脑化科学管理。建立全面严格的品质保证系统，坚持“正确地满足所有顾客的要求”的品质政策。

Premier Camera(China)Ltd. Foshan (hereinafter referred to as "PCCL") is a joint-venture corporation, which was approved to be established in May, 1990.With the efforts of 9 years, the corporation has become a certain scale. At present,PCCL occupies over 20,000 square metres plant with more than 3,000 employees. Producing 800,000 to 900,000 pieces of APS and popular series auto-cameras monthly,PCCL becomes one of the largest auto-camera manufacturers. Most of the cameras are been sold in over 150 countries and areas, such as EU,U.S.A., Japan and South-east Asia etc.

Since it was established,the corporation has been endeavoring to cultivate the professional knowledge to its engineers and technicians with continuous improvement and training. At the same time, PCCL increases its testing and experimental equipments every year to strengthen the engineering, manufacturing and quality assurance system. In 1997,the International Quality System Appraisal Organization entitled the ISO 9002 Quality System Certificate to PCCL. An administrational computer network has come into being within the corporation.PCCL strictly takes the series standards of ISO as the quality assurance system and to execute its slogan:"To delight and satisfy all the customers correctly".

法人代表：林德济
地址：广东省佛山市广佛公路乐安开发区乐城一路54号　邮编：528227　电话：(0757)2818753，6489407,6488341　传真：(0757)2818775
LEGAL REPRESENTATIVE: MR. LIN DE JI
ADD: NO.54,1 LEAN ROAD,GUANG FO EXPRESSWAY,FOSHAN,GUANGDONG,CHINA　P.C: 528227　TEL: (0757)2818753,6489407,6488341　FAX: (0757)2818775

天津天航海员技术服务公司

总经理：姜增国

天津天航海员技术服务公司成立于1993年3月，隶属原交通部天津航道局，是一个独立核算、自主经营、具有法人资格的全民所有制经济实体。

该公司作为现中港集团天津航道局与国外客户建立业务联系的一个窗口，有较强的经济技术实力和竞争力。

天津航道局已有100余年的历史。拥有耙吸式挖泥船、绞吸式挖泥船、货船、拖轮、油轮等工程船舶、辅助船舶102艘；各类技术人员1600余名，船员2900余人。

天津天航海员技术服务公司自成立以来，其海员劳务外派事业在业务合作、劳务管理等方面得到迅速、健康的发展。据不完全统计仅1997、1998两年就派出劳务及境外工程人员350余人次，完成劳务营业额近3600万美元。另外，公司在大连海事大学等院校培养了几十名船员干部，充实劳务后备队伍。这些人大都来自河南、辽宁等省区的贫困地区，他们以好学、肯吃苦且钻研业务，为天津航海员技术服务公司赢得了信誉。

现在，天津天航海员技术服务公司的干部职工们正以高昂的斗志和严谨的工作态度为进一步扩大对外经济技术合作而奋力拼搏。

地址：天津市和平区
湖北路31号
通达园C座101室
邮编：300042
电话：Tel:022 23117788
传真：Fax:022 23308396

我公司本着信誉第一的宗旨，
竭诚欢迎新老客户前来洽谈业务。

欧姆龙(大连)有限公司

欧姆龙(大连)有限公司成立于1991年12月19日，注册资本12.2亿日元，占地3.3万平方米，职工1400余名，公司本着"为健康的生活作贡献"的宗旨，致力于家用简便保健仪器的研制和生产并推出了一系列优秀的家用健康仪器。例如，能够简便地测量血压的"自动数字血压计"；可以简单准确地测量体温的"电子体温计"；适合儿童使用的红外线"耳式体温计"；能够治疗肩酸腰痛的"低频治疗仪"以及能够精确指导您的健身活动的"计步器"等。这些产品都在全世界受到了广泛的欢迎。公司现已通过了ISO9002、ISO14001、EN4600等认证，优秀的品质和完善的设计必将使欧姆龙的健康产品成为您高质量生活的最佳伴侣。

OMRON DALIAN CO, LTD was set up on December 19, 1991 with 1,220,000,000 Japanese Yen registered capital and a floor area of 33,000 m^2.Aiming at "making contributions to healthy life", OMRON DALIAN is dedicated to the development and production of convenient healthcare devices for home use and has promoted a series of fine household healthcare devices,such as "automatic digital blood pressure monitor"which can measure blood pressure convenienty;"electronic digital thermometer"which can measure body temperature easily and accurately;infrared "ear thermometer" which is suitable for children; "Pulse massager "which can cure lumbago and "pedometer"which can precisely guide your exercising activities.All these are worldwidely popular items.By now the company has acquired ISO9002, ISO14001, EN4600 certificates.The fine quality and prefect design can surely make OMRON's products the best partner of your high-level life.

地址：大连经济技术开发区松江路3号
电话：0411-7614222
传真：0411-7628494

Address:No.3, Songjiang Road, Dalian Economic and Technical Development Zone
Phone: 0411-7614222
Fax: 0411-7628494

迈向二十一世纪的 中国天津国际经济技术合作公司

China Tianjin International Economic and Technical Cooperative Corporation TOWARDS 21ST CENTURY

西萨摩亚政府办公大楼
Western Samoa Government Building

中国天津国际经济技术合作公司创立于1982年6月1日。经过十多年的创建发展，公司已形成了以国际工程承包、劳务合作、进出口贸易、境内外房地产开发和海内外投资为主体的多元化经营格局，被国家统计局评为"中国行业一百强"，业已成为天津市对外经济合作的骨干企业和重要窗口。

公司遵照国际惯例，一如既往地奉行薄利、保质、重信、守约的经营方针，恪守"至诚、至信、开拓、超越"的司训，愿竭诚与海内外各界通力合作，共同发展，以崭新姿态迈向二十一世纪。

China Tianjin International Economic and Technical Cooperative Corporation (CTIETCC) was established on June 1, 1982. After more than ten years of development,CTIETCC has evolved diversified structure which is composed mainly of contracting overseas projects, labour cooperation, import and export, real estate development and investment at home and abroad. Rated by the state statistics Bureall as "100 enterprises of the trade in China", CTIETCC has become an important "showcase" of Tianjin's foreign economic cooperation.

CTIETCC shall adhere to the international conventions, pursue,as always, the policies of low profits, high quality, good faith, and honouring contracts and commitments, and abide by the corporation's admonition which is "be sincere and faithful, open and aggressive, and aiming high", and cooperate fully with people of all circles around the world to promote joint development.

Legal Representative,President: Mr.Zhao Shu Hua
地址：中国天津市和平区睦南道103号
Add: No.103 Munan Dao,Heping District,Tianjin, China Post Code: 300050
邮编：300050
电话(Tel)：0086-22-23316851
传真(Fax)：0086-22-23316213
公司网址(Corpweb)：http://www.ctietcc.com
信息网站(Infoweb)：http://ctiinet.online.tj.cn
电子信箱(E-mail)：ctietcc@public.tpt.tj.cn,head@ctietcc.com

老挝13号公路
Laos No.13 Highway

改革开放的二十年，发展壮大的二十年
——福建省轮船总公司

刘启闽

没有改革开放，就没有不断发展的省轮。党的十一届三中全会确定改革开放的第二年，即1979年，为搞活、搞好国有企业，省政府就赋予省轮“以船养船、自借自还、税前还贷、滚动发展”的优惠政策，对于这一优惠政策，历届省轮领导人都紧紧把握，并用好用活用足，在没有伸手向国家要一分财政投入的情况下，依靠广大员工的奋发努力，锐意开拓进取，使企业坚定从容地走向市场，并在市场经济的磨练中一步步发展壮大。可以说，改革开放至今的二十年，是省轮许许多多干部员工艰苦奋斗的二十年，也是企业规模不断壮大、企业实力不断增强、企业素质不断提高的二十年。在这二十年间：

总公司共完成货物运输量5000万吨，周转量800亿吨公里，年均分别递增123.76%和127.42%；经营区域由近海为主转向近洋为主；运输航线由国内沿海各港延伸至港澳台地区、日本、东南亚、欧洲等20多个国家和地区的100多个港口。

船舶运力，经历了一个马鞍型的发展与调整过程。到目前止，已拥有自营运输船舶34艘31万载重吨。20年中增加运力58.64万载重吨，报废让售运力27.64万载重吨，净增运力31万载重吨；合资合营船舶也增加8艘5.12万载重吨。同时，经过不断的调整，总公司船舶的技术等级有了很大的提高，运力结构也日趋合理，日益朝着大型化、专业化的趋势发展，适应了运输市场不断变化的需要。

国有资产成倍增值。至1997年底帐面资产总额达8.9亿元，比1978年末增长了8倍；资产净值达3.9亿元，比1978年末增长了9倍，年均分别递增29.65%和11.69%。二十年共实现利润5.8亿元，归还贷款本金6.28亿元，支付利息2.15亿元。这是省轮在没有国家财政拨款的情况下，依靠自贷自还为国家和社会做出的重要贡献。

职工队伍素质不断提高。二十年中企业共投入约2000多万元用于职工的教育培训。目前总公司拥有专业技术管理人员390人，其中中级以上专业技术管理人员117人；船员2300多人，其中职务船员1000多人，全部是高中以上学历。十几年来公司已向境外船公司派出船员2100多人次。高素质、高质量的管理人员和船员队伍，是企业二十年中迅速发展的主要依靠，也是企业今后进一步发展的前提条件。

经过这二十年的建设和发展，公司的经济实力和抵御市场风险能力大为增强，员工队伍的整体素质大有提高，运力结构趋于合理，经营范围及覆盖面显著扩大，企业声誉及其无形资产迅速增值，集团化规模经营的格局已经形成。多年来省轮一直保持着全国大型省级海运企业的地位，并一直被列为全省20家重点骨干企业和省政府紧密联系的20家工交企业之一，1994年跨入了全国5大服务企业500强企业行列，1995年又被国家交通部指定为跟踪的全国10家海运企业之一；1997年10月公司通过了国际安全管理体系认证，取得了航行国际航线的“通行证”。1998年被福建省企业评价中心授予福建省“利税300大”、“300家最大第三产业企业”、“300家最佳形象企业”的称号。

旺旺集团

湖南旺旺食品有限公司
长沙旺旺食品有限公司

Want Want Holdings, Ltd
Hunan Want Want Foods, Ltd.
Changsha Want Want Foods, Ltd.

湖南旺旺食品有限公司于1992年由旺旺集团与湖南华湘进出口集团合作创办高新科技企业，1995年10月又独资成立长沙旺旺食品有限公司，并于1996年初成立配套之工厂——长沙旺旺包装厂。至1998年，在湖南投资额增至7400万美元，注册资本为3300万美元，已经发展成为“全国高新科技百强企业”和“中国500家大型外商企业”中一员，并获卫生部命名“96年执行食品卫生法先进企业”，在湖南也获得了“市场公认名牌产品”和“优秀外资企业”的称号，并于1997年11月通过ISO9002质量认证。

企业的优胜在于产品的优胜，旺旺集团（湖南）现有旺旺、旺仔、浪味、珍旺系列，生产包括米果、饮料、小食品在内共计二十余种产品及配套纸箱，销售遍及全国，部分产品销往东南亚地区，深得消费者好评。

Hunan Want Want Foods Ltd., a high-tech enterprise, was ventured into Hunan under an agreement between Want Want holdings, Ltd., (Taiwan) and Hunan Province Wall Shine Imp. & Exp. Group in 1992. In order to procure further development, Changsha Want Want Foods Ltd. and Changsha Want Want Carton Box Factory, both individual proprietorship of the Group, were incorporated in October, 1995, and began production in October, 1996 and November, 1997 separately. Up to date, the total investment of both Hunan Want Want and Changsha Want Want amounts to 75 million USD, in which the listed capital reaches 33 million USD.

Hunan Want Want happily finds itself listed in "Top 100 High Tech Enterprises in China ". and " Top 500 Foreign Companies in China ". It was nominated by the Department of Public Health and honorably received the Award as the "Leading Company Enforcing the Public Heath Food Law in 1996 ". Locally, Hunan Want Want enjoys the status as the "Trustworthy Product in Hunan" and the esteemed membership of the "Excellent Enterprise in Hunan ". In November 1997, the company received the Certificate of Registration for ISO-9002 Quality System issued by the CCIB Quality Certification Center.

The high quality of the products is the decisive factor of Want Want's prosperity. Want Want Holdings (Hunan) now Produces 20 odd products in its Rice Cracker,Beverage and Snack Plants.In terms of product lines,this company has One-One, Hot Kid, Long Wave and Jim Want series.The products are popular domestically and abroad,and some of them are exported to the South East Asia.

地址：中国湖南省长沙市高新技术开发区望城县旺旺路
电话:(0731) 8063111
邮编：410200
E-mail:wantwant@pubilc.cs.hn.cn

Add:Hunan Want Want Foods Ltd., Want Want Road, Wang Cheng County, Changsha City, Hunan Province, China
Telephone: (0731)8063111
Post Code:410200
E-Mail: wantwant@public.cs.hn.cn

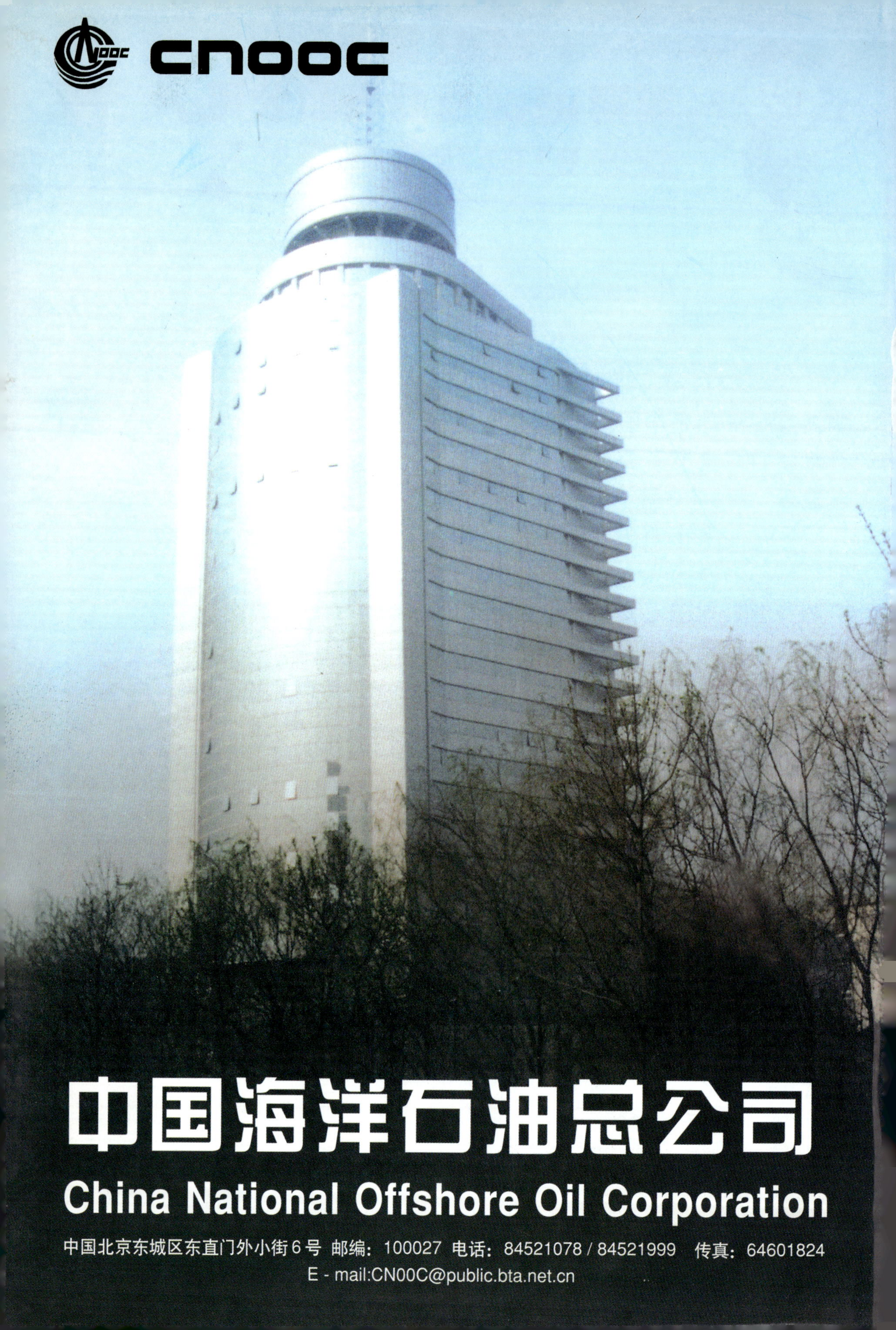
CNOOC
中国海洋石油总公司
China National Offshore Oil Corporation
中国北京东城区东直门外小街6号 邮编：100027 电话：84521078 / 84521999 传真：64601824
E - mail:CN00C@public.bta.net.cn

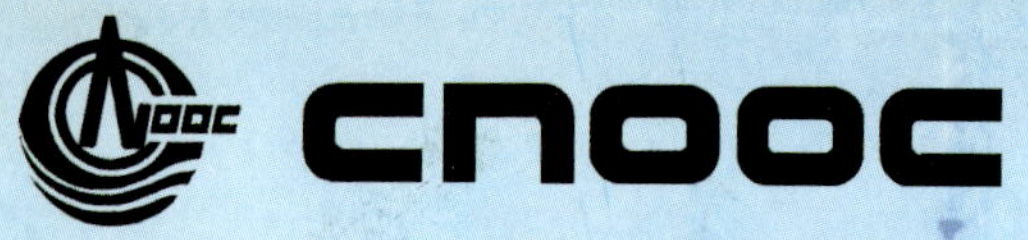

中国海洋石油总公司

中国海洋石油总公司(CNOOC)是经国务院批准于1982年2月成立的国家公司。国务院颁布的《中华人民共和国对外合作开采海洋石油资源条例》规定中国海洋石油总公司享有在对外合作海区内进行石油勘探、开发、生产和销售的专营权，全面负责我国对外合作开采海洋石油天然气资源业务。

总公司注册资本为200亿元人民币。主要从事海上油气勘探、开发、生产；炼油、石油化工和天然气的加工利用；产品销售以及提供有关服务。总公司总部设在北京，国内有25个地区和专业公司(单位)，并在10多家中外合资公司和国内联营公司中拥有股份，海外有4个代表处和3个公司。

海洋石油是我国五十年代起步，八十年代迅速崛起，九十年代呈现高速高效发展态势的资金、技术密集型新兴能源工业。截止1998年底，总公司经过四轮国际招标和多次双边谈判，累计与18个国家和地区的68家公司签订了137个石油合同和协议，外商累计直接投资达60亿美元。累计获石油地质储量18.3亿吨，天然气地质储量4200亿立方米。已建成投产油气田22个；有6个正在开发建设；另有19个正在评价。自"八五"以来，总公司海上原油年产量迅速增长，从1990年的127万吨增加到1995年的841万吨。1996年总公司原油年产量首次突破1,000万吨，达到年产原油1,500万吨、天然气近27亿立方米。1998年生产原油1631万吨、天然气38,6亿立方米、海外生产原油34万吨。油当量达到2037万吨，占全国油当量的11%。

总公司自1982年成立以来，坚持合作与自营并举。坚持以效益为中心的经营原则，取得了高速高效发展的成绩。通过多年对外合作与自营，总公司形成了海洋石油勘探开发十大配套技术，拥有了一支懂得国际惯例、门类齐全配套的技术队伍和在国际上较为先进的装备，具备了海洋石油勘探开发四大能力。海洋石油基地系统正在构建自己的支柱产业，通过生产、生活和社会服务支持油气主业的发展。1998年总公司有职工2.6万人。资产总值已从成立初期的28亿增加到320亿元，净资产达205亿元。按人均年创增加值计算的全员劳动生产率为30.08万元。1998年总公司系统向国家纳税7.7亿元，截至1998年底总公司系统已累计向国家纳税42.4亿元。1998年国际油价大幅下跌，油气销售收入大幅减少。在这种情况下，总公司通过采取有力措施，全年降低成本9.2亿元，实现利润5.9亿元，保持了良好的发展势头。

1998年11月，总公司领导班子顺利完成了正常的换届，新一届领导班子面对石油工业的新形势，在深入分析的基础上，提出了新的六大发展战略。目前，有关油气资产整体在境外上市的工作正在研究之中，这将从根本性促进公司体制和经营机制的转变。

迎着新世纪的曙光，伴随全球经济一体化的进程，中国海洋石油总公司将继续深化改革，建设具有国际竞争力的跨国石油公司。

COVEC 中国海外工程总公司

中国海外工程总公司(英文简称COVEC)是中央大型企业工委所属的以国际工程承包和劳务合作为主业的国有大型综合性企业。公司业务范围包括境内外各类工程承包、工程咨询和施工，成套设备的出口、安装及技术培训，经营进出口业务，对外劳务派遣，提供技术服务和在国内外兴办各类独资和合资合营企业，实施中国政府对外经济技术援助项目等。

公司成立迄今，已与世界上一百多个国家和地区建立了经济贸易合作关系，目前拥有二十六个海内外分支机构，八个国内外合资企业，业务遍及非洲、亚洲、大洋洲、欧洲等三十多个国家和地区。87年至98年底，公司承揽各类项目一千多个，累计完成合同额16亿多美元，营业额11亿多美元。在国内同行业公司中，以每年的经营业绩排序，中国海外工程总公司一直居于前列。1992年以来，连年被列入"中国500家最大服务企业及行业企业评价"排序，1995年以来连续被世界权威的美国《工程新闻记录》列入全球最大225家工程承包商，1997年位于第115位。

中国海外工程总公司弘扬"团结、奋进、优质、高效"的企业精神，经多年的艰苦创业，奋力拼搏，在国际市场的激烈竞争中占有了比较稳定的阵地，树立了良好的企业信誉，培育起四大国际承包工程市场，即以马里、科特迪瓦为主的西非市场，以博茨瓦那、肯尼亚为主的东南非市场，以巴布亚新几内亚为主的南太市场和以越南、新加坡为主的东南亚市场。作为最早进入非洲市场的中国公司之一，以1989年的马里巴马科第二大桥项目为契机，COVEC在非洲的业务得到了迅速发展，形成了以马里、科特迪瓦为中心的群体市场，在西非已成为知名度较高、影响较大的工程承包商品牌。

1996年中国海外工程总公司的业务开始进入发展期，合同额和营业额呈现出较大幅度的增长，并实现了规模与效益并举的良好发展局面。此后公司业务保持持续稳定发展，经济效益连年提高，1998年营业额再创公司历史最好水平。近三年来，公司的国有资产保值增值率均达到110%以上，整体无形资产以1998年6月30日为基准日，价值为6亿5千万元人民币。

中国海外工程总公司坚持以经济效益为中心，以改革为动力，业务上规模，公司集团化，两个文明建设并举的发展方针，坚持一业为主、多种经营。1996年中标承包的巴布亚新几内亚柏一马公路合同额八千万美元，该项目施工条件艰苦，施工难度大，经精心施工，于1998年9月全线贯通。与马里政府合资经营的马里纺织股份有限公司连续四年取得较好的经济效益和社会效益，被马里政府誉为明星企业。所承揽的越南南广义、广平糖厂成套设备出口项目均一次投产成功，被越南有关部门认为是在越执行成套设备项目的优秀中国公司，并给予嘉奖。公司还注重抓好援外工程项目，所承揽的援外项目均被评为优良工程，得到受援国的好评。

中国海外工程总公司不断加强企业内部管理，推行ISO9002国际质量标准认证，规范企业管理和经营行为。公司领导团结务实、廉洁自律，在业务上台阶的同时对精神文明建设常抓不懈，公司连续三年被外贸部评为精神文明建设先进单位，连续三年被国家机关工委评为"中央国家机关文明单位"。

目前，中国海外工程总公司正积极探索经贸结合，内外结合，多种产业并举的发展道路，向经营国际化、组织集团化、管理现代化的大型现代化企业集团迈进。

地址：中国·北京朝阳区东三环北路甲2号（京信大厦）　邮编：100027

电话：(010)64661610

传真：(010)64661630£¨64662812